The SAGE Handbook of
Online Research
Methods

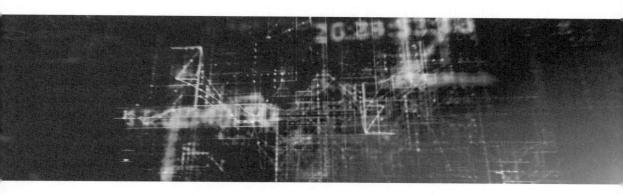

Online research methods are popular, dynamic and fast-changing. Following on from the great success of the first edition, published in 2008, *The SAGE Handbook of Online Research Methods*, second edition, offers updates of existing subject areas and new chapters covering more recent developments, such as social media, big data, data visualization and CAQDAS.

Bringing together the leading names in both qualitative and quantitative online research, this new edition is organised into nine parts:

I	ONLINE RESEARCH METHODS
II	DESIGNING ONLINE RESEARCH
III	ONLINE DATA CAPTURE AND DATA COLLECTION
IV	THE ONLINE SURVEY
V	DIGITAL QUANTITATIVE ANALYSIS
VI	DIGITAL TEXT ANALYSIS
VII	VIRTUAL ETHNOGRAPHY
VIII	ONLINE SECONDARY ANALYSIS: RESOURCES AND METHODS
IX	THE FUTURE OF ONLINE SOCIAL RESEARCH

The SAGE Handbook of Online Research Methods, second edition is an essential resource for all social science students and researchers interested in the contemporary practice of computer-mediated research and scholarship.

Online research methods are exploding in variety and importance. This new SAGE Handbook *provides a much-needed comprehensive treatment of this dynamic and exciting field. From big data, semantic mining, AI, simulations, and visualizations to online focus groups, interviewing, ethnography, video-based research, and much more besides, this volume has everything you need for a broad and deep exploration of the new world of research online.*
Robert Kozinets, Jayne and Hans Hufschmid Chair of Strategic Public Relations, USC Annenberg

In 2008 with the first and very successful edition of the Handbook, *online research was characterized by its 'newness' and by 'caution'. Today's researchers are now 'familiar' with online methods and 'adept at their use', so the second edition of the* Handbook *has updated 27 chapters of the first edition and added nine chapters and two sections: 'Digital Quantitative Analysis' and 'Digital Text Analysis'. Big data, gaming and participatory research are now also present. With a pragmatic focus on the current state-of-the-art, the new* Handbook *remains very attuned to the issues and challenges of online research and its methods.*
Karl van Meter, Lecturer in Social Sciences, Ecole Normale Supérieure

Internet-based research methods is a diffuse and rapidly evolving area and this new edition of the SAGE Handbook of Online Research Methods *provides a much needed overview and assessment of where it currently stands. As well as comprising some updated chapters, this new edition now includes chapters on many new areas, some of which were barely on the horizon when its predecessor was published. As such, this new edition provides much needed advice on the implementation of these methods and an appraisal of the state of the field. It will be invaluable to students and practitioners.*
Alan Bryman, Emeritus Professor, School of Management, University of Leicester

The SAGE Handbook of Online Research Methods, Second Edition, *edited by Nigel Fielding, Raymond Lee and Grant Blank, brings together several of the most noted scholars in the area of web and online survey methodology, along with the contributions of many younger researchers. The result is a compendium of information about online survey design, survey ethics, sampling and data capture, analysis of social network data, content analysis of digital text, online ethnography, and secondary analysis of online data, as well as essays relating online data to artificial intelligences, cartography, and diverse other topics. The authors are to be commended for an excellent update to their first edition, producing volume of significant value to those interested in online research methods, social science, and social theory.*
Dave Garson, Professor, North Carolina State University

The SAGE Handbook of
Online Research
Methods

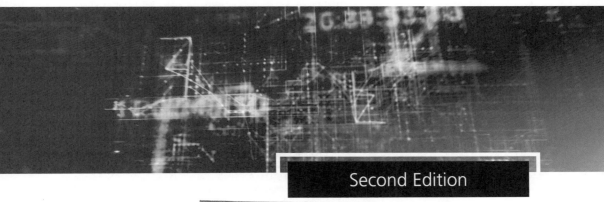

Second Edition

Edited by

Nigel G. Fielding,
Raymond M. Lee
and Grant Blank

SAGE reference

Los Angeles | London | New Delhi | Singapore | Washington DC | Melbourne

Los Angeles | London | New Delhi
Singapore | Washington DC | Melbourne

SAGE Publications Ltd
1 Oliver's Yard
55 City Road
London EC1Y 1SP

SAGE Publications Inc.
2455 Teller Road
Thousand Oaks, California 91320

SAGE Publications India Pvt Ltd
B1/I1 Mohan Cooperative Industrial Area
Mathura Road
New Delhi 110044

SAGE Publications Asia-Pacific Pte Ltd
3 Church Street
#10-04 Samsung Hub
Singapore 049483

Editor: Judi Burger
Editorial assistant: Matthew Oldfield
Production editor: Sushant Nailwal
Copyeditor: Sunrise Setting Limited
Proofreader: Sue Cleave
Indexer: Editors
Marketing manager: Sally Ransom
Cover design: Wendy Scott
Typeset by Cenveo Publisher Services
Printed and bound by
CPI Group (UK) Ltd, Croydon, CR0 4YY

Introduction & editorial arrangement © Nigel G. Fielding,
Raymond M. Lee and Grant Blank, 2017

Chapter 1 © Raymond M. Lee, Nigel G. Fielding and Grant Black, 2017
Chapter 2 © Rebecca Eynon, Jenny Fry and Ralph Schroeder, 2017
Chapter 3 © Karsten Boye Rasmussen, 2017
Chapter 4 © Claire Hewson, 2017
Chapter 5 © Dietmar Janetzko, 2017
Chapter 6 © Ayelet Baram-Tsabari, Elad Segev and Aviv J. Sharon, 2017
Chapter 7 © Martin Innes, Colin Roberts, Alun Preece and David Rogers, 2017
Chapter 8 © Jonathan Bright, 2017
Chapter 9 © Vasja Vehovar and Katja Lozar Manfreda, 2017
Chapter 10 © Ronald D. Fricker Jr, 2017
Chapter 11 © Vera Toepoel, 2017
Chapter 12 © Lars Kaczmirek, 2017
Chapter 13 © Don A. Dillman, Feng Hao and Morgan M. Millar, 2017
Chapter 14 © Bernie Hogan, 2017
Chapter 15 © Javier Borge-Holthoefer and Sandra González-Bailón, 2017
Chapter 16 © Corinna Elsenbroich, 2017
Chapter 17 © Harko Verhagen, Magnus Johansson and Wander Jager, 2017
Chapter 18 © Helen Kennedy and William Allen, 2017

Chapter 19 © Roel Popping, 2017
Chapter 20 © Mike Thelwall, 2017
Chapter 21 © Edward Brent, 2017
Chapter 22 © Nicholas Hookway and Helene Snee, 2017
Chapter 23 © Christine Hine, 2017
Chapter 24 © Henrietta O'Connor and Clare Madge, 2017
Chapter 25 © Katie M. Abrams and Ted J. Gaiser, 2017
Chapter 26 © Jon Hindmarsh, 2017
Chapter 27 © Christina Silver and Sarah L. Bulloch, 2017
Chapter 28 © Louise Corti and Jo Wathan, 2017
Chapter 29 © Patrick Carmichael, 2017
Chapter 30 © David Martin, Samantha Cockings and Samuel Leung, 2017
Chapter 31 © Matthew Zook, Ate Poorthuis and Rich Donohue, 2017
Chapter 32 © Brian Beaton, David Perley, Chris George, Susan O'Donnell, 2017
Chapter 33 © William Revelle, David M. Condon, Joshua Wilt, Jason A. French, Ashley Brown and Lorien G. Elleman, 2017
Chapter 34 © Harrison Smith, Michael Hardey†, Mariann Hardey and Roger Burrows, 2017
Chapter 35 © Michael Fischer, Stephen Lyon and David Zeitlyn, 2017
Chapter 36 © Grant Blank, 2017

First edition published 2008

Library of Congress Control Number: 2016937391

British Library Cataloguing in Publication data

A catalogue record for this book is available from the British Library

ISBN 978-1-4739-1878-8

Contents

List of Figures

List of Tables

Notes on the Editors
and Contributors

THE EDITORS

Nigel G. Fielding is Professor of Sociology at the University of Surrey and a Fellow of the Academy of Social Sciences. He co-directs the CAQDAS Networking Project, which provides training and support in the use of computer software in qualitative data analysis. His research interests are in new technologies for social research, qualitative research methods, and mixed method research design. He has authored or edited 20 books, over 65 journal articles and over 200 other publications. In research methodology his books include a study of the integration of qualitative and quantitative data (*Linking Data*, 1986 and 2014, Sage, with Jane Fielding), an influential book on qualitative software (*Using Computers in Qualitative Research*, 1991, Sage; editor, with Ray Lee), a study of the role of computer technology in qualitative research (Computer Analysis and Qualitative Research, 1998, Sage, with Ray Lee), two four-volume edited sets on Interviewing in the Sage 'Masterworks' series, and the *Handbook of Online Research Methods* (ed., with Ray Lee and Grant Blank; Sage, 2008, second edition 2016). He presently serves on the President's Task Force on the Future of Mixed Methods.

Raymond M. Lee is Emeritus Professor of Social Research Methods at Royal Holloway University of London. He has written extensively on a range of methodological topics. These include the problems and issues involved in research on 'sensitive' topics, research in physically dangerous environments, the use of unobtrusive measures, and the role of new technologies in the research process. His current research focuses on the historical development of interviewing techniques.

Grant Blank is the Survey Research Fellow at the Oxford Internet Institute, University of Oxford, United Kingdom. He is a sociologist specializing in the political and social impact of computers and the Internet, the digital divide, statistical and qualitative methods, and cultural sociology. He is currently working on a project asking how are cultural hierarchies constructed in online reviews of cultural attractions. His other project links sample survey data with census data to generate small area estimates of Internet use in Great Britain. He holds a PhD from the University of Chicago.

THE CONTRIBUTORS

Katie M. Abrams' expertise is at the intersection of strategic communication and food system issues. She uses qualitative and quantitative approaches in her research and has conducted numerous focus groups. She studied agricultural communication at Purdue University (BS) and University of Florida (MS, PhD). Currently, she is an assistant professor in the Department of Journalism and Media Communication at Colorado State University.

William Allen is a Research Officer at the Migration Observatory, in the Centre on Migration, Policy and Society (COMPAS) at the University of Oxford. His research and published work examines the links among media, policy-making and public perceptions about migration issues. He is also interested in how non-academic groups, particularly those in civil society, engage with migration data, research and statistics.

Ayelet Baram-Tsabari (PhD, Weizmann Institute of Science) heads the Science Communication research group at the Faculty of Education in Science and Technology at the Technion – Israel Institute of Technology. Prof. Baram-Tsabari is a member of the Learning in a Networked Society (LINKS) of the Israeli Center for Research Excellence (I-CORE). She is a member of the PCST Network's scientific committee and of the Israel Young Academy, and chairs the research committee at the national council of the Second Authority for Television and Radio. Her research interests include online public engagement with science, and science communication training for scientists.

Brian Beaton is a doctoral candidate in the Faculty of Education at the University of New Brunswick and a researcher with the First Nations Innovation project. He is a Research Associate of the Keewaytinook Okimakanak (KO) Research Institute and the former Coordinator of KO's Kuhkenah Network. He worked with KO from 1994 to 2013 building and supporting a variety of community-owned telecommunications infrastructures and social enterprises that are operational in remote and rural First Nations across Ontario and other parts of Canada.

Javier Borge-Holthoefer received a PhD in Computer Science from the Universitat Rovira i Virgili (URV) in Tarragona (Catalonia, Spain) in 2011. He currently leads the Complex Systems group at the Internet Interdisciplinary Institute (IN3) of the Universitat Oberta de Catalunya (CoSIN3). His research stems from Interdisciplinary Physics and it deals with complex social systems and urban science. Among other appointments, he has taught at the Department of Computer Science and Mathematics and at the Department of Psychology (both in URV). Before joining the IN3, he was a member of the COSNET Lab and held a position as a post-doctoral fellow at the Institute for Biocomputation and Physics of Complex Systems (BIFI), University of Zaragoza (2011–2013). He then moved to Qatar to work as a Scientist at the Qatar Computing Research Institute (QCRI), Hamad bin Khalifa University (2014–2016). With more than 30 peer-reviewed articles, his work has been published (among others) in *Science Advances*, *Social Networks*, *Scientific Reports*, *EPJ Data Science*, *Physical Review E*, *PLoS One* and *Europhysics Letters*. Dr Borge-Holthoefer has also contributed a book and several chapters around the problem of disease and information spreading on complex networks.

Karsten Boye Rasmussen is associate professor in the areas of organization and information technology at Department of Marketing & Management at University of Southern Denmark. He is a sociologist and data scientist and has continued using his experience from data archiving in data warehousing, business intelligence, organisation, methods and metadata in teaching, development and research. Current research is focused on small and medium sized companies and their use of IT comprising websites and the research often includes an angle on data use and methods like nonresponse and unobtrusive measuring in content analysis.

Edward Brent is Professor and Chair of the Department of Sociology at the University of Missouri, Columbia, Missouri. He is also founder and President of Idea Works, Inc., a software technology company applying expert systems and artificial intelligence to categorizing and coding qualitative data. Applications include automating grading and feedback for student essays. He has written extensively in computers and the social sciences, with emphasis on expert systems and artificial intelligence.

Jonathan Bright is a Research Fellow at the Oxford Internet Institute who specialises in computational approaches to the social and political sciences. He has two major research interests: exploring the ways in which new digital technologies are changing political participation; and investigating how new forms of data can enable local and national governments to make better decisions.

Ashley Brown is a doctoral candidate in personality and health psychology at Northwestern University. Her research focuses on computational models of personality, with an emphasis on individual differences in affective experience. She is currently designing a simulation that blends elements of Gray's Reinforcement Sensitivity Theory and Revelle's Cues-Tendencies-Actions model.

Sarah L. Bulloch has experience working with multiple methods and in multiple contexts. She has analysed large UK and international datasets, applying advanced quantitative analysis, including structural equation modelling and multilevel analysis. She has also worked to apply qualitative analysis approaches to video, textual and image data, often using a range of computer assisted qualitative data analysis software (CAQDAS). Sarah has worked at various UK universities, as well as at a large disability charity. At the time of publication she teaches at the CAQDAS Networking Project, University of Surrey as well as providing consultancy in research methods training.

Roger Burrows is currently Professor of Cities in the School of Architecture, Planning & Landscape at Newcastle University. Prior to this he was a Pro-Warden and Professor of Sociology at Goldsmiths, University of London, UK. He has also worked at the Universities of York, Teesside, Surrey, East London and Kingston. A sociologist by background he has published over 130 articles, chapters, books and reports on digital sociology, methods, urban sociology, housing, health and other topics. Between 2005–2007 he was the national coordinator of the ESRC e-Society programme. His current research is on the neighbourhood consequences of the super-rich in London.

Patrick Carmichael is Professor of Education and Director of Research Development at the University of Bedfordshire in the United Kingdom. He has conducted research and written widely on themes in education and social research more generally, including technology-enhanced learning and research; research ethics; and interdisciplinary and inter-professional working. From 2008–2012 he was director of the ESRC-EPSRC research project: 'Ensemble: Semantic Technologies for the Enhancement of Case Based Learning'.

Samantha Cockings is Associate Professor in Geography at the University of Southampton. Her research interests are focused around the geographical representation of population, including automated zone design, spatio-temporal population modelling and analysis of population health. She developed the methods employed by the Office for National Statistics to produce Output Areas and Workplace Zones for the 2011 Census and is part of the team which develops and provides advice on using AZTool, an automated zone design software tool employed by researchers from various academic and non-academic sectors worldwide. She teaches geographical information systems, health geography and general geographical representation concepts and practices to a broad range of undergraduate, postgraduate and applied audiences.

David M. Condon is an Assistant Professor in the Department of Medical Social Sciences at Northwestern University's Feinberg School of Medicine. His research focuses on the development of individual differences assessment models and the application of these models to predict a wide range of important life outcomes.

Louise Corti is an Associate Director at the UK Data Archive based at the University of Essex in Colchester, UK and currently leads the UK Data Service functional areas of Collections Development and Producer Relations. She works closely with data producers from all sectors to ensure that high quality data are created, acquired and shared for research and teaching. Louise's research activities are focused around methods for sharing and reusing social research data and she has directed a number of research awards relating to data support, management and sharing. She was instrumental in helping operationalise the ESRC's Research Data Policy from 1995 and extending this to fully accommodate qualitative data. Louise publishes and edits regularly in books and journals on many aspects of data management, data sharing and reuse of social science data.

Don A. Dillman is Regents Professor of Sociology and Deputy Director for Research in the Social and Economic Sciences Research Center at Washington State University in Pullman. He is author of a well-known book on survey design, *Internet, Phone, Mail and Mixed-Mode Surveys: The Tailored Design Method* (Dillman, Smyth and Christian) now in its fourth edition (Wiley, 2014) and many articles on survey design. A former President of the American Association for Public Opinion Research, his current research emphasizes the development of design principles for conducting high quality mixed-mode surveys of the general public and other survey populations.

Rich Donohue is a postdoctoral scholar at the University of Kentucky and the principle curriculum designer of New Maps Plus, an online graduate education program focused on web mapping. His scholarship bridges the technical implementation of emerging geospatial technologies with GIScience and Web Cartography research. His teaching focuses on web map interface design in support of cartographic interaction and Geovisualization.

Lorien G. Elleman is a PhD psychology student at Northwestern University. His research interests include: exploring personality at the facet and item levels to increase the magnitude of correlations between personality and life outcomes, geographical clustering of personality and sociodemographic correlates, and constructing new behavioral measures of personality using big data.

Corinna Elsenbroich is a computational social scientist with a background in philosophy, computer science and policy research. Her main research interests are agent-based modelling, social ontology and epistemology and collective intentionality and reasoning. She has published several articles on methodological aspects and on models of opinion dynamics, extortion racketeering and a book *Modelling Norms* (with Nigel Gilbert, Springer, 2014). She currently works on modelling collective reasoning and decision making, on methodological innovation in the social sciences and policy research.

Rebecca Eynon is as Associate Professor and Senior Research Fellow at the University of Oxford where she holds a joint academic post between the Oxford Internet Institute (OII) and the Department of Education. Her research examines the connections between digital education and inequalities in a range of settings and life stages. Her work has been supported by the British Academy, the Economic and Social Research Council, the European Commission, Google and the NominetTrust. Prior to joining Oxford in 2005, she was an ESRC Postdoctoral Fellow at the Department of Sociology, City University, London.

Michael Fischer is the Professor of Anthropological Sciences (Kent, UK), Director of the Centre for Social Anthropology and Computing and Vice President of the Human Relations Area Files (Yale), and Director of HRAF Advanced Research Centres (Kent and Yale). Fischer was a pioneer in the 1970s microcomputer revolution, agent based modelling in the 1980s, WWW technology in the 1990s, and complexity and big data in the 2000s. Recent work includes 'The Cultural Grounding of Kinship: A Paradigm Shift', *L'Homme* n. 210 (2014, with D. Read and F.K. Lehman), and 'Applied Agency: Resolving Multiplexed Communication in (and between) Automobiles', *IEEE Technology and Society Magazine*, (2015 with S. Applin), and author of *Applications in Computing for Social Anthropologists*, Routledge (1994).

Jason A. French is a doctoral candidate in personality and cognitive psychology at Northwestern University. His research examines how to measure interests in the broader context of ability and temperament. He has focused on the development of scientific interests.

Ronald D. Fricker Jr is a Professor and Head of the Virginia Tech Department of Statistics. He holds a PhD and an MA in Statistics from Yale University, an MS in Operations Research from The George Washington University and a bachelor's degree from the United States Naval Academy. A Fellow of the American Statistical Association and Elected Member of the International Statistical Institute, Dr Fricker is the author of *Introduction to Statistical Methods for Biosurveillance* (CUP, 2013) and more than 80 other publications.

Jenny Fry is a senior lecturer in publishing at Loughborough University. Her research is focused on digital scholarship and disciplinary cultures. She has been an investigator on a number of externally funded projects – most recently on an AHRC funded project investigating open access mega-journals and the future of scholarly communication. Her teaching focuses on the social shaping of technology, digital cultures and research methods. Prior to joining Loughborough University in 2007 she was a research fellow at the Oxford Internet Institute.

Ted J. Gaiser is an entrepreneur and adjunct faculty member in the Sociology Department at Boston College, where he received his PhD. His experience includes consulting, technology management, and leading and supporting academic online research endeavours. His research has been on online social forms and online research methods. He was one of the first to present and publish on online focus groups, earning him the Founder's Award of Merit from The Social Science Computing Association.

Chris George is a graduate student in the Interdisciplinary Studies program at the University of New Brunswick. Chris, whose home community is Eel River Bar First Nation in New Brunswick, is currently conducting research on 'Nikmájtut Apoqnmatultinej: Reclaiming Indigeneity via ancestral wisdom and new ways of thinking' that is exploring how indigenous methodologies can be conducted within western educational institutions.

Sandra González-Bailón is an assistant professor at the Annenberg School, University of Pennsylvania, where she leads the DiMeNet research group (Digital Media, Networks, and Political Communication). She received a PhD in Sociology from Oxford University (Nuffield College) and spent five years as a Research Fellow at the Oxford Internet Institute. Her research areas include network science, data mining, computational tools, and political communication. She has authored more than thirty journal articles and book chapters, and written op-eds and commentaries for several international outlets on the role that social media plays in collective action and political mobilization. She is the author of the book *Decoding the Social World: When Data Science meets Communication* (forthcoming with MIT Press) and the editor of *The Oxford Handbook of Networked Communication* (forthcoming with Oxford University Press, co-edited with Brooke Foucault-Welles).

Michael Hardey[†] was a Reader in Medical Sociology at the Hull-York Medical School (HYMS) until his untimely death in March 2012. Prior to this he worked at the Universities of Newcastle, Southampton, Surrey and Essex. He made huge contributions to the early literature on e-health and digital sociology more generally. He also worked on the sociology of lone parenthood. He was the co-author (with Roger Burrows) of 'Cartographies of Knowing Capitalism and the Changing Jurisdiction of Empirical Sociology', a chapter published in the first edition of this Handbook, important elements of which remain in the chapter updated for this second edition.

Claire Hewson is Senior Lecturer in Psychology at The Open University. She has a long standing interest in using the Internet in primary research, and has collected data online using a range of methods, including experiments, surveys and psychometrics. She regularly delivers workshops and training sessions on the topic, acted as workshop convenor and editor for the recent British Psychological Society (BPS) guidelines on ethics in Internet-mediated research (2013), and has just published the fully revised 2nd edition of her co-authored book *Internet Research Methods* (Sage, 2016).

Christine Hine is Reader in Sociology in the Department of Sociology at the University of Surrey. Her main research centres on the sociology of science and technology with a particular interest in the role played by new technologies in the knowledge production process. She also has a major interest in the development of ethnography in technical settings, and in 'virtual methods' (the use of the Internet for social research). In particular, she has developed mobile and connective approaches to ethnography which combine online and offline social contexts. She is author of *Virtual Ethnography* (Sage, 2000), *Systematics as Cyberscience* (MIT, 2008), *Understanding Qualitative Research: The Internet* (Oxford, 2012) and *Ethnography for the Internet* (Bloomsbury, 2015) and editor of *Virtual Methods* (Berg, 2005), *New Infrastructures for Knowledge Production* (Information Science Publishing, 2006) and *Virtual Research Methods* (Sage, 2012).

Feng Hao received his PhD from Washington State University and is Assistant Professor of Sociology at the University of South Florida Sarasota-Manatee. His research interests include the interactions between human society and natural environment, employing multiple methodologies to analyze the anthropogenic ecological impact, public opinion about the environment, and the environmental movement. His publications have appeared in *Social Science Quarterly*, *Perspectives on Global Development and Technology*, and *Rural Sociology*. Cross-national projects include comparing environmental concern of the general public in China and the United States.

Mariann Hardey is a lecturer and member of the Marketing Group at Durham University Business School, UK. She is a social media professional and academic and the BBC North East commentator for social media and digital networks. She read literature at the University of Sussex and later undertook a research MA followed by a PhD at the University of York. She has published articles in journals such as *Information, Communication & Society*, the *International Journal of Market Research* and *The Open Medical Informatics Journal* and has also published numerous book chapters.

Jon Hindmarsh is Professor of Work and Interaction in the School of Management & Business at King's College London, UK. He analyses work practice and social interaction using video-based approaches drawn from ethnomethodology and conversation analysis. He has undertaken studies in settings including control rooms, operating theatres, research labs, dental clinics and museums and galleries. Furthermore, he engages in interdisciplinary research to explore the potential for these studies to inform the design and deployment of new technologies. He co-authored *Video in Qualitative Research* (Sage, 2010) with Christian Heath and Paul Luff; co-edited *Organisation, Interaction and Practice: Studies of Ethnomethodology and Conversation Analysis* (CUP, 2010) with Nick Llewellyn; and co-edited *Communication in Healthcare Settings: Policy, Participation and New Technologies* (Wiley-Blackwell, 2010) with Alison Pilnick and Virginia Teas Gill.

Nicholas Hookway is Lecturer in Sociology in the School of Social Sciences at the University of Tasmania, Australia. Nick's principle research interests are morality and social change, social theory and online research methods. He has published recently in *Sociology* and *British Journal of Sociology* and his book *Everyday Moralities: Doing it Ourselves in an Age of Uncertainty* (Ashgate) is forthcoming in 2017. Nick is current co-convenor of the The Australian Sociological Association Cultural Sociology group and is an Associate Editorial Board member of the journal *Sociology*.

Bernie Hogan (PhD Toronto, 2009) is a Research Fellow at the Oxford Internet Institute at the University of Oxford. His methodological work focuses on various forms of online data capture, particularly in terms of social networks. His theoretical work focuses on theories of online identity and their consequence for social cohesion and privacy. He has published widely in peer-reviewed journals, book chapters and peer-reviewed conference proceedings. His latest work, in collaboration with the IMPACT group at Northwestern University focuses on the reliable capture of social, sexual and drug use data. He has received numerous awards including Best Dissertation from the Communication and Technology section of the International Communication Association.

Martin Innes is Director of the Crime and Security Research Institute, and Universities' Police Science Institute at Cardiff University. His research has been highly influential across policy, practitioner and academic communities, both nationally and internationally. He is the author of three books and numerous scholarly articles on aspects of policing, reactions to crime and counter-terrorism. He has acted in an advisory capacity to policing and security agencies, and governments in the USA, Canada, Australia and Holland. He serves on the Professional Committee of the College of Policing.

Wander Jager is working at the University College Groningen and is the managing director of the Groningen Center for Social Complexity Studies. He is working on social complex issues like diffusion of green technology and practices, littering behaviour, crowd behaviour, man–environment interactions, societal polarisation, migration, dynamics of depopulation and dealing with flooding risks. He has published widely in the field of social complexity, and has been guest editor for special issues such as 'The human actor in ecological-economic models' (*Ecological Economics*), 'Complexities in markets' (*Journal of Business Research*), 'Agent-Based Modeling of Innovation Diffusion' (*Journal of Product Innovation and Management*) and Social Simulation in Environmental Psychology (*Journal of Environmental Psychology*).

Dietmar Janetzko studied psychology, philosophy and computer science and holds a PhD both in psychology and education. He is a professor of business computing and business process management at Cologne Business School in Germany. His research interests focus on statistics, data mining, and quantitative analysis of data sourced from the Internet and social media.

Magnus Johansson is a researcher and lecturer at the Department of Game Design, Uppsala University, Campus Gotland. His research interest is often focused on the player and groups of players from a qualitative perspective, often observing the activity of play and how players interact when playing. Previous publications deal with the social aspects of online games such as norms, social rules, harassment, anonymity and toxic gaming. Other perspectives that Johansson have studied include how to create socially believable non-player characters and how to design and evaluate games from a usability perspective.

Lars Kaczmirek is vice scientific director and heads a team which develops and conducts population studies at the department Monitoring Society and Social Change at GESIS – Leibniz Institute for the Social Sciences in Germany. He is also adjunct assistant research scientist at the Center for Political Studies (CPS), Institute for Social Research (ISR), University of Michigan. Lars studied psychology with minors in neurology and computer science and holds a PhD in psychology from the University of Mannheim. He is co-founder and co-editor of the journal 'Survey Methods: Insights from the Field' and has served on the board of the German Society for Online Research (DGOF) both as executive, treasurer and program chair for many years. He is passionate about reducing survey error and has published on various topics in survey research such as questionnaire design, mixed-mode, eyetracking, survey software tools, human–survey interaction, and social media research.

Helen Kennedy is Professor of Digital Society at the University of Sheffield. She recently published a monograph entitled *Post, Mine, Repeat: Social Media Data Mining Becomes Ordinary* (Palgrave Macmillan, 2016). Other recent research includes Seeing Data (www.seeingdata.org), which explored how non-experts relate to data visualisations. She is interested in critical approaches to big data and data visualisations, how to make data more accessible to ordinary citizens, and how people live with data. Over the years, her research has traversed digital media landscapes, covering topics from web homepages to data visualisation, from race, class, gender inequality to learning disability and web accessibility, and from web design to social media data mining and data visualisation.

Samuel Leung is Senior Teaching Fellow in Civil Engineering and Surveying at the University of Portsmouth. His research interests are geomatics and spatial analysis and he has been involved in the development of online geographical referencing resources for social scientists and Pop247 spatio-temporal population modelling methods. Previous to his current position, he has worked as an instructional designer on the Population Analysis for Policies and Programmes project at the London School of Hygiene and Tropical Medicine and immediately before that as a Research Fellow on a range of e-learning and geography research programmes funded by JISC and ESRC at the University of Southampton.

Stephen Lyon is Senior Lecturer at Durham University, UK. His primary research is on cultural models, kinship systems and politics in Pakistan. He has worked with development organisations and Pakistan government departments on agricultural resource management to develop robust predictive models of farmer behaviours using computational tools. He was an early adopter of the internet in the field and may have produced the world's first anthropology field blog (called Weekly and Monthly Updates from the Field). He has authored and edited numerous publications in which he outlines how he has used computers and software in the field and for data analysis.

Clare Madge is a Reader in Human Geography at the University of Leicester. She has written extensively about a range of methodological topics, including feminist methodologies, creative methods, ethics and geographical fieldwork and internet mediated research. She developed a training resource in online research methods with a team based at the University of Leicester (see http://www.restore.ac.uk/orm/).

Katja Lozar Manfreda is an associated professor of statistics at the Faculty of Social Sciences, University of Ljubljana, Slovenia. Her doctoral thesis (2001) was globally the first one in the area of web survey methodology. She was also among the founders of the WebSM site in 1998. She publishes in the area of web surveys and her most cited work (Lozar Manfreda *et al.* 2008) has become a citation classic.

David Martin is Professor of Geography at the University of Southampton. His research interests include all aspects of the geographical representation of population and have included establishment of methods for automated zone design used for publication of small area statistics from the 2001 and 2011 censuses in England and Wales, methods for the gridded modelling of population data, spatio-temporal modelling of small area populations and linkage of administrative population data sources. He is a co-director of the Economic and Social Research Council's (ESRC) National Centre for Research Methods, UK Data Service and Administrative Data Research Centre for England and was Coordinator of the ESRC Census Programme from 2002–2012.

Morgan M. Millar received her PhD in Sociology from Washington State University and is Research Instructor at the University of Utah, Salt Lake City, in the Medical School Division of Epidemiology. Her primary interest is in survey methodology. Her publications have appeared in *Public Opinion Quarterly* and *Survey Practice*. Her current research is examining linkages between social status and the development of cancer.

Henrietta O'Connor is Professor of Sociology in the School of Media, Communication and Sociology at the University of Leicester. Her research interests focus on the sociology of work, youth employment and gender. She also has an active interest in research methods ranging in scope from her work on online research methods to more recent research based around the secondary analysis of qualitative data, qualitative longitudinal research and community restudies.

Susan O'Donnell is an adjunct professor in the Department of Sociology at the University of New Brunswick and a senior researcher at the National Research Council of Canada where she is Vice-Chair of the Research Ethics Board. She has published extensively with her First Nation partners on technology use in remote and rural First Nation communities, including work on research methodologies. O'Donnell is currently the principal investigator of the First Nations Innovation project (http://fn-innovation-pn.com) and the First Mile project (http://firstmile.ca) in partnership with First Nation organizations in Atlantic Canada, Quebec and Ontario.

David Perley is the Director of the Mĩkmaq-Wolastoqey Centre at the University of New Brunswick and an instructor at UNB and St. Thomas University. He is a co-founder of the Wolastoq Language and Culture Centers in Tobique and St. Mary's First Nations in New Brunswick. David is the former Chief and Councillor of the Maliseet Nation at Tobique and has been employed as consultant for federal and provincial departments over the years specializing in Aboriginal Education. His research work supports indigenizing the curriculum with Maliseet and Mĩkmaq language and resources.

Ate Poorthuis is an Assistant Professor in the Humanities, Arts and Social Sciences at Singapore University of Technology and Design. His research is focused on the possibilities and limitations of the analysis and visualization of big data to better understand how our cities work. He is the technical lead on The DOLLY Project, a repository of billions of geolocated social media, that strives to address the difficulties of using big data within the social sciences.

Roel Popping is at the Department of Sociology, University of Groningen. His research interests include methodology, with a specialty in text analysis and interrater reliability. He has applied the text analysis methods in particular on historical shifts in public opinion, values, and scientific knowledge, primarily within the context of post-1989 Central and Eastern Europe.

Alun Preece is Co-Director of the Cardiff University Crime & Security Research Institute and Head of the Knowledge and Data Engineering Group in the School of Computer Science and Informatics. His research interests focus on techniques for information provisioning and decision support in complex environments. He was UK Academic Technical Area Lead (2011–2016) for the 10-year joint US/UK International Technology Alliance in Network and Information Sciences, involving a consortium of 26 US and UK academic, industry and government partners, led by IBM and funded by the US Army Research Laboratory and the UK Ministry of Defence.

William Revelle is a professor of psychology at Northwestern University. As a personality psychologist, his interests range from the biological bases to computational models of personality as means to understand the sources and consequences of individual differences in temperament, cognitive ability and interests. He is particularly interested in applying quantitative methods to studying psychological phenomena.

Colin Roberts is Operations Manager for the Universities' Police Science Institute, Cardiff University, and leads the Institute's research programme on counter-terrorism policing. He holds a PhD from the University of Surrey and an MA in social justice from the University of London. With Professor Martin Innes he worked on the National Reassurance Policing Programme and invented a community intelligence technology for the capture and analysis of signal crimes and disorders. In recent years Colin's main interests have focused on counter-terrorism policing, the time dynamics of conflict, social media analytics and computational methods.

David Rogers is currently employed as a Research Assistant in the Cardiff University School of Computer Science and Informatics. He is applying his interest in Big Data and the Semantic Web to his current work within the OSCAR team developing real-time web collection and analysis tools to provide situational awareness through social media. He is also studying for his PhD titled 'Text Mining of Extremist Narratives on the Web' in which he is looking to evaluate to what degree Web data can be converted into actionable intelligence related to extremism in terms of reliability, usability and timeliness.

Ralph Schroeder is Professor and director of the Master's degree in Social Science of the Internet at the Oxford Internet Institute. Before coming to Oxford University, he was Professor in the School of Technology Management and Economics at Chalmers University in Gothenburg (Sweden). His recent books are *Rethinking Science, Technology and Social Change* (Stanford University Press, 2007) and, co-authored with Eric T. Meyer, *Knowledge Machines: Digital Transformations of the Sciences and Humanities* (MIT Press, 2015). He is currently working on a book about digital media and globalization.

Elad Segev (PhD, Keele University) is a Senior Lecturer in Digital Media and Communications at the Department of Communication, Tel Aviv University. He is the author of *Google and the Digital Divide* (Chandos, 2010), and *International News Flow Online* (Peter Lang, 2016). His research interests include web mining, network analysis, international news, Americanization and globalization, cultural diversity, digital divide, information search, and new applications and methodologies in social science and communication. His studies are published among others in the *Journal of Computer-Mediated Communication*, *Public Understanding of Science*, *Journalism*, *Political Communication*, and the *Journal of the Association for Information Science and Technology*.

Aviv J. Sharon is a PhD student at the Faculty of Education in Technology and Science at the Technion – Israel Institute of Technology. Aviv completed his MSc in Life Sciences at the Weizmann Institute of Science and his undergraduate studies in Biology and Science Education (with distinction) at the Technion. He has also taught biology and biotechnology at a public high school in Haifa, Israel. His research interests lie in the interface between science education and science communication. More specifically, his work examines expressions of science literacy in authentic online environments, especially in the context of controversial personal health decisions. His work has appeared in *Public Understanding of Science* and *PLOS ONE*.

Christina Silver manages the CAQDAS Networking Project, based in the Department of Sociology at the University of Surrey, UK, which provides information, advice, training and on-going support in the use of software designed to facilitate qualitative and mixed methods research. She has trained thousands of researchers to harness CAQDAS tools powerfully and undertaken her own research using qualitative technologies. Christine has published widely in the field, including co-authoring *Using Software in Qualitative Research: A Step-by-Step Guide* with Ann Lewins (Sage Publications) and has developed Five-Level QDA with Nicholas Woolf, a CAQDAS pedagogy that transcends software products and methodologies (www.fivelevelqda.com).

Harrison Smith is a PhD Candidate at the University of Toronto's Faculty of Information. His research focuses on the political economies of geospatial media, surveillance, and mobile digital culture. His thesis explores the economic and cultural implications of location data to inform new methods of audience targeting and clustering for mobile and location based marketing. Harrison is also a research assistant for geothink.ca, a Canadian geospatial and open data research partnership between Canadian universities, municipalities, and the private sector. There, his research focuses on the economic potential of the geospatial web and the sharing economy.

Helene Snee is Senior Lecturer in Sociology at Manchester Metropolitan University, UK. Her research explores stratification with a particular focus on youth and class. Helene is the author of *A Cosmopolitan Journey? Difference, Distinction and Identity Work in Gap Year Travel* (Ashgate, 2014), which was short-listed for the BSA's Philip Abrahams Memorial Prize for the best first and sole-authored book within the discipline of Sociology. She was also a contributor to *Social Class in the 21st Century* (Pelican, 2015). Helene has published journal articles on youth transitions and educational choice; narratives and representations of difference and inequality; and digital methods.

Mike Thelwall is Professor of Information Science and leader of the Statistical Cybermetrics Research Group at the University of Wolverhampton, which he joined in 1989. He is also Docent at the Department of Information Studies at Åbo Akademi University, and a research associate at the Oxford Internet Institute. His PhD was in Pure Mathematics from the University of Lancaster but he is now a social scientist focusing on quantitative methods. His research involves identifying and analysing social and general web phenomena using quantitative-led research methods, including text analysis, link analysis and sentiment analysis, and he pioneered an information science approach to link analysis. Mike has developed a wide range of tools for gathering and analysing web data for Twitter, YouTube, MySpace, blogs and the web in general. His 500+ publications include 278 refereed journal articles, 28 book chapters and three books, including *Introduction to Webometrics*. He is an associate editor of the *Journal of the Association for Information Science and Technology* and sits on three other editorial boards. He led the Wolverhampton contribution to the EU funded projects Acumen, CyberEmotions RESCAR, CREEN, NetReAct, Rindicate and Wiser, and has been funded for research by JISC and non-profit organisations in the UK and Italy. He has also conducted evaluation contracts for the EC (several times), the UNDP (several times), the UNFAO and a UN university. He was a member of the UK's independent review of the role of metrics in research assessment (2014–2015).

Vera Toepoel is professor at the Department of Methods and Statistics at Utrecht University, the Netherlands. She did her PhD on the Design of Web Questionnaires and is the author of many papers about online survey methodology and the book *Doing Surveys Online* published by Sage in 2016. In addition, she is the Chairwoman of the Dutch Platform for Survey Research and President's delegate of RC33 Methods and Logistics of the International Sociological Association.

Vasja Vehovar, PhD is a professor of statistics at the Faculty of Social Sciences, University of Ljubljana, Slovenia, and the head of Centre for Social Informatics (cdi.si). In recent years his main research interest has been web survey methodology. Within this context, he led methodological experiments with web surveys in 1996, co-established the WebSM.org site in 1998, published series of papers and chapters with leading publishers, launched open-source software for web surveys (1KA), and in 2015 co-authored the monograph *Web Survey Methodology* (Sage).

Harko Verhagen is an associate professor at the Department of Computer and Systems Sciences, Stockholm University. His research has focused on agent-based simulation of social interaction, social interaction in and around computer game play, social ontology and agent models, use of social media in online education, and issues of design for hybrid social spaces. He has published over 100 peer-reviewed papers, book chapters etc. and guest edited special issues of journals such as *Computational and Mathematical Organization Theory*, *Journal of Gaming and Virtual Worlds*, and *Logic Journal of the IGPL*. His publication list is available via http://harko.blogs.dsv.su.se/.

Jo Wathan is a Research Fellow in the Cathie Marsh Institute for Social Research, University of Manchester. She has worked on a number of projects relating to data use, data enhancement and teaching with data particularly in relation to major UK surveys and census microdata since completing her PhD based on the Labour Force Survey. Since 2012 she has spent most of her time in two user focused roles within the UK Data Service; as lead for microdata in the census team and as training coordinator. However, she also undertakes some teaching. She spends her spare time working with and enhancing historical census microdata.

Joshua Wilt is a postdoctoral fellow in the department of psychological sciences at Case Western Reserve University, Cleveland, Ohio. His research investigates the affective, behavioral, cognitive, and desire (ABCD) components that are relevant to personality structure and function. His current work examines ABCDs within the context of personality traits and narrative identity.

David Zeitlyn has been doing research in Cameroon for more than 30 years on many topics including divination, sociolinguistics, endangered languages and history. In this work he has explored many ways in which computer assisted research can be undertaken, most recently using computer games and agent based models as elicitation tools. Among other topics he has published on photography and on archives (Annual Reviews 2012) and recently (Oct. 2015) edited a special issue of *History and Anthropology*. David Zeitlyn has been a research Professor of Social Anthropology at the University of Oxford since 2010. Previously he taught at the University of Kent for many years.

Matthew Zook is a Professor of Economic and Information Geography at the University of Kentucky in Lexington, KY. His interest centers on how the geoweb (particularly the practices surrounding user-generated data) and understanding where, when and by whom geo-coded content is being created. He studies the interaction of code, space and place interact as people increasingly use of mobile, digital technologies to navigate through their everyday, lived geographies. Of special interest is the complex and often duplicitous manner that code and content can congeal and individualize our experiences in the hybrid, digitally augmented places that cities are becoming.

Companion Website

Welcome to the companion website for *The SAGE Handbook of Online Research Methods*, Second Edition, edited by Nigel G. Fielding, Ramond M. Lee and Grant Blank.

The resources on the site have been specifically designed to support your study. Visit https://study.sagepub.com/onlineresearchmethods2e to find:

- Editor and Contributor Biographies
- Abstracts
- Colour Illustrations
- Glossary

## PART I

Online Research Methods

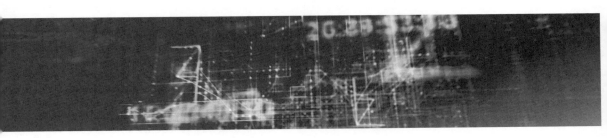

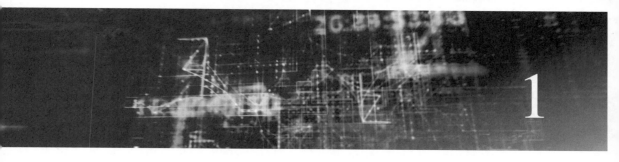

Online Research Methods in the Social Sciences: An Editorial Introduction

Raymond M. Lee,
Nigel G. Fielding and Grant Blank

Online research methods have come of age as the permeation of everyday life by information and communication technologies has grown ever more ubiquitous. Although substantial digital divides remain by country, and within countries by age, gender and socioeconomic status, the number of Internet users worldwide quadrupled between 2000 and 2014, and the current proportion of the world's population using the Internet is now said to be in excess of 40 per cent (International Telecommunications Union, 2015). Information and communication technologies have had socially transformative effects. They increasingly affect how people make and maintain social relationships, the structure of their social networks, how they go about their work, meet their partners, educate their children, how they shop, take their leisure, present themselves to the world and store their memories. Such things are, of course, of interest to social scientists in and of themselves. However, to study them also requires methods of communication, ways of

harvesting and capturing information, observational strategies and tools for collaboration, not to mention analytic techniques adapted to what are often novel forms and volumes of data, all of which themselves have the capacity to be transformed by new technologies.

Introducing the first edition of *The SAGE Handbook of Online Research Methods*, we emphasised the newness of online methods, and the need for a cautious and critical appraisal of their use and potential. Less than a decade onwards, the terrain occupied by online research methods has changed rapidly, social researchers across a wide range of social science disciplines have become much more familiar with such methods, more adept at their use, and more attuned to the issues and challenges that they pose. As before, our primary purpose in this Handbook is to explore this terrain by highlighting across a wide range of areas the key facets of online research methods and their implications for practice. Given our focus, as was true of the first edition, we pay relatively little attention to theoretical discourses on the wider social or cultural significance of online environments. While we recognise the historically contingent and socially constructed nature of the changes wrought by development of Internet-based technologies, we leave investigation of such issues to others. So too, we take largely as a given the infrastructural 'substrate' (Star, 1999) that underpins online practices; the standards, protocols, mechanisms, tools and resources without which activity online would be impossible. Neither do we address in any systematic way the drivers of methodological innovation in the social sciences and the social processes that have allowed new online methodologies to be adopted, diffused and used. The Handbook, in other words, retains a pragmatic focus on the current state of the art and on the further potential of online research methods in the social sciences.

DESIGNING ONLINE RESEARCH

Readers will find in the Handbook comprehensive and detailed coverage of a wide range of online research methods, some possibly more familiar than others. Clearly, though, there are wider issues that crosscut the investigation of particular research problems or the use of particular research methods. For example, in designing a particular study it is necessary to assess how far one's methods and procedures meet the aims and objectives set out for the research, and researchers must attend to the ethical issues surrounding their research.

One debate that emerged early on in relation to online methods was the question of whether the ethical issues they posed were distinct and unique compared to those associated with offline methods. In their chapter on the ethics of online research, Rebecca Eynon, Jenny Fry and Ralph Schroeder argue for the essential continuity between online and offline methods in relation to research ethics, and although they recognise the importance of ethical governance frameworks they emphasise the importance of the need to make ethical judgements in a context-dependent way. They usefully address the issues that arise in a number of different research situations that include the risks and benefits involved in using online methods to gather data directly from individuals and the challenges involved in obtaining informed consent in such situations, the sometimes novel ethical questions that arise when researchers directly study social interactions in virtual environments, and the increasingly important area of how data generated by social media might be analysed in an ethically responsible way. They bring their chapter to a close by pointing to the challenges posed for online researchers by issues relating to the fluid boundaries between public and private, the potential that arises in some cases for third party reuse of data, the complexities that come with a growing interdisciplinary focus in online research and the implications for ethical practice posed by the existence of digital divides.

Although ethical and legal frameworks provide a largely inescapable context within which a given research project must be conducted, the specific methods used in the study need, of course, to be carefully weighed and considered in relation to its aims. This has, perhaps, not always been the case as far as online methods are concerned. Their relative newness has in the past prompted both unthinking enthusiasm on the one hand, or unreasoned resistance, on the other. There is merit, therefore, in taking a careful, balanced and nuanced approach to the strengths and weaknesses of online approaches.

A putative advantage of researching online is that data can be acquired quickly and often in considerable volumes. The temptation exists, thinks Karsten Boye Rasmussen, to accept the benefits this brings without a parallel commitment to scrutinise the quality of the data so produced. In his chapter Rasmussen argues the need for a systematic theoretical model of data quality as a basis for assessing the ability of online methods to generate reliable and valid data. Emphasising within this framework the importance of 'fitness for use', Rasmussen points to opportunities for assessing data quality that arise as traditional research methods such as the survey move online. In addition, online methods provide novel sources of data with a built-in capacity for quality assessment. In both cases the potential to assess and ensure data quality is enhanced by the 'documentality' of online data – in other words its ability to be described via 'metadata', as well as the ability to associate it with 'paradata' – the data produced as part of the process by which data are collected.

ONLINE DATA CAPTURE AND DATA COLLECTION

One can argue with probably only a little exaggeration that for much of the twentieth century direct elicitation was the method of choice for many social scientists. In other words, it was thought that the way to discover what people thought and did was to ask them directly, usually by means of an interview of one sort or another. A relatively unnoticed aspect of this was that the popularity of the interview as a method depended on a variety of technological developments including in the case of qualitative research the miniaturisation of audio recorders (Lee, 2004) and the advent of long-distance telephone lines that, in the United States at least, fostered the development of telephone survey interviewing. In the twenty-first century, there has been a decisive move away from elicitative methods. This shift has largely been fuelled by a massive extension in the availability of online communication technologies, and by a growing ability to measure more and more aspects of everyday life as and when they occur through the use of data harvested from social media sites. Where even

a few years ago names like Twitter, Facebook, Instagram and the like might only have produced quizzical bemusement if not puzzlement, particularly among older social scientists, social media data available in large volumes now form an increasingly large part of the landscape of social science research.

As this Handbook indicates online research methods are very diverse. They are used across the social science disciplines and produce data, whether directly elicited and not, that manifests itself in numeric, graphical, textual and audio-visual formats. The contexts within which online data are produced range from tightly designed experiments through to looser more naturalistic approaches, the gathering of various forms of non-reactive data, not to mention simulations and games or research in virtual environments. Claire Hewson traverses this terrain in her chapter on designing online research. Emphasising the importance of maximising the trustworthiness, reliability and validity of data produced online, Hewson systematically examines the possibilities, trade-offs, constraints and opportunities researchers need to consider when generating obtrusive and unobtrusive research data online.

The machine-readable traces that our increasingly self-documenting and self-archiving world leaves behind can be thought of as 'unobtrusive' or 'nonreactive' measures, to use a term popularised by Webb et al. (1966) half a century ago. Their now classic monograph was partly meant as a rebuke to the often uncritical use of interviews and questionnaires common at the time they were writing, but it also emphasised the creative appropriation of often quite fleeting behavioural manifestations as sources of data. In his chapter, Dietmar Janetzko attempts in particular to extend the conceptual understanding of nonreactive data by examining ways in which the rather 'thin', i.e. non-contextualised, nature of such data can be extended either through triangulating multiple sources of data or the use of newer techniques such as text mining. Janetzko also enumerates the many different sources of nonreactive data to be found online and provides a detailed guide to the complexities of using such material.

As Ayelet Baram-Tsabari, Elad Segev and Aviv J. Sharon point out in their chapter, the term 'data mining' is relatively new in the social sciences but has become increasingly used in the last decade, fuelled it would seem by the growing popularity of online user-generated content. Data mining involves the automated processes associated with the extraction of knowledge from large-scale databases or online repositories. Baram-Tsabari and her colleagues usefully set out how data mining approaches differ from traditional quantitative methods. They examine the characteristics that make datasets suitable for mining as well as the resources needed to analyse them. In the main part of their chapter they give state-of-the-art examples of data mining techniques in relation to studies of mainstream media, data generated by users of social media and metadata.

As do other contributors to this Handbook, Martin Innes, Colin Roberts, Alun Preece and David Rogers see the need for a discerning approach that cautiously welcomes the opportunities created by the abundance of social media data now available while at the same time critically evaluating the social and technical processes implicated in their production, consumption and use. Innes and colleagues guide readers to an understanding of social media instrumentation, providing in the process an overview of how the data available on various social media platforms might be accessed. They also provide a detailed case study of how they combined to mutually implicative effect analysis of the social media data surrounding a particular event with on-the-spot ethnographic observation taking place at the same time.

In his chapter, Jonathan Bright investigates the issues surrounding the use of 'big data' in the social sciences, the large volumes of data about diverse aspects of social life that have become available as the ability to store and process such volumes becomes computationally possible. Bright provides an introduction to methods for capturing big data, as well as the processes involved in rendering the material more useful for analytic purposes through proxy variables and data coding. He then goes on to point to some of the complexities surrounding the analysis of big data, taking a somewhat sceptical view of some elements of current practice. Arguing that the methods training currently available to social scientists is seldom sufficiently oriented to the skills needed to work with big data sources, Bright describes some of the specific elements that make up the toolkit that social scientists increasingly need in order to be able to deal adequately with large datasets.

THE ONLINE SURVEY

Survey researchers have rarely shied away from the latest technological developments available to them and, true to form, were not slow to explore the possibilities for survey deployment opened up by the Internet. In both market and academic research, the use of online surveys is now well established. Nor has development been in any sense static. Researchers have begun to adapt to newer circumstances such as the growth in the use of mobile phones, while looking forward to possibilities that currently remain on the horizon such as the use of smart televisions as survey delivery systems.

Vasja Vehovar and Katja Lozar Manfreda give an overview of the current state of the art in their chapter on online surveys. Conceptually they locate online surveys within a wider set of technologically mediated data collection methods collectively referred to as 'computer-assisted survey information collection' (CASIC). As Vehovar and Manfreda observe, online surveys provide some of the traditional benefits of self-completion methodologies, but with advantages over conventional paper and pencil methods that include cost and error reduction, the possibility to increase respondents' motivation and understanding, as well the ability to use advanced design features not available within non-digital contexts. On the other hand, if researchers are to make effective use of online survey methods, they need to confront a range of issues and challenges. Among the considerations outlined by Vehovar and Manfreda are issues to do with recruitment, sampling and non-response, how design elements are used within a survey instrument and the use of post-survey adjustments. They then extend their discussion to the use of single and mixed-mode surveys as well as mixed-method approaches. Many of these topics are subsequently taken up in detail in the other chapters making up this section of the Handbook.

In his chapter on sampling methods for web and email surveys Ron Fricker swiftly but carefully rehearses the fundamentals of sampling before going on to review the applicability of a range of probability and non-probability sampling methods to online surveys. He profiles the various methods of sampling – including the use of pre-recruited panels – that might be used and looks at the issues and challenges associated with their use. As do other writers in this section, Fricker recognises that the difficulties involved in generating probability samples online encourages the use of mixed-mode surveys. Fricker concludes with a look to the future, suggesting that in the shorter term online survey sampling is likely to remain problematic, but noting that with online technologies still in their infancy it is unclear what the future might bring.

It is difficult to spend any time online without receiving a request to participate in an online survey. Low cost, ease of administration and apparent reach all combine to make survey delivery online attractive to marketeers, bureaucratic administrators and academic researchers alike. As Vera Toepoel points out in her chapter on online survey design, intriguing possibilities emerge from the move to online surveys, particularly in relation to mobile data collection, and the extension of survey materials beyond the merely textual. At every stage, however, researchers need to take on board the concomitant challenges to conventional survey practice thrown up by online surveys. Toepoel identifies these challenges and takes readers through the various stages of designing, collecting and administering an online survey.

Nowadays anyone wanting to mount a survey online can choose from a wide range of survey software products. Lars Kaczmirek makes the point that the market for such software is now very diverse indeed. Settling on a suitable product can be daunting. Kaczmirek's chapter clears a path through the complexities involved. In it he provides a conceptual schema that helps potential users of survey software to identify uses, needs and priorities in a systematic way, allowing them to focus on that which is likely to be best suited to their needs.

Email on its own is a rather imperfect mechanism for online survey recruitment. Researchers often need to combine it with other methods, such as mail or telephone, to obtain an adequate sample of survey participants. Mixing survey modes is not a simple matter, as Don Dillman, Feng Hao and Morgan Millar point out in their chapter on the topic. Dillman will be well-known to many survey researchers as the originator of the 'total design method' (1978) and later the 'tailored designed method' (2000). Rather in the spirit of that work, he and his colleagues offer a holistic, comprehensive and practical account of mixed-mode work, setting out a series of detailed recommendations dealing with the timing and staging of contacts, the use of incentives and the possible ramifications of using different question formats across modes. As do other writers in this section, Dillman and his colleagues draw attention to the possibly problematic implications of the 'smartphone revolution' for survey practice.

DIGITAL QUANTITATIVE ANALYSIS

Much material available online lends itself to quantitative analysis. The cost of ready availability, however, has often been analytic complexity. While for some this might constitute a barrier, the opportunity afforded by online methods to study dynamic and interlinked aspects of social life in ways that are often absent from more traditional approaches has also brought newer tools and approaches to the fore.

It might be a truism to say not one of us is an island, but that social life is inherently relational – with each one of us linked to others through a web of strong and weak ties – is one of the fundamental insights of the social sciences. As its very name doubly implies the Internet is inherently relational. It is not surprising, therefore, that researchers quickly turned to the study of online phenomena such as email, web linkages and social networking sites. Often, as Bernie Hogan points out in his chapter, such studies utilise network analysis, a thriving area of research that emerged from the convergence of work on the mathematics of graphs with empirical studies of social relations by anthropologists and others. Hogan provides a useful primer on network analysis. He looks at the analytic choices one might make in studying an online network. Should one decide, for example, to focus on the relationships within a particular bounded population, the networks associated with particular individuals or the relational paths one can follow from a particular starting point? He points to the practicalities involved in extracting and managing data from online sites and gives a useful outline of techniques involved.

Javier Borge-Holthoefer and Sandra González-Bailón take up and extend the discussion of network methods by focusing on advanced analytic techniques. Noting the importance that now attaches to social media data in studies of social interaction and the potential thus created to revitalise long-standing debates in areas related to interpersonal communication, they argue that analytic techniques suitable to data generated by traditional methods such as surveys need to be revamped. Specifically, they point to the need to define rules for aggregating and filtering data available from online social networks. In their chapter, Borge-Holthoefer and González-Bailón describe a range of newer methods, including approaches borrowed from studies of physical or biological systems that have recently come to the fore.

Introducing her chapter on simulation methods Corinna Elsenbroich observes that the social world is inherently dynamic. There is also a duality to it that social scientists have often encapsulated in distinctions between the micro and the macro, agency and structure and the like, and yet our methods seem best fitted to capture the static elements of social life and only one side or other of its polarity. For Elsenbroich, simulation overcomes these deficiencies. Although there are a number of different kinds of simulation, Elsenbroich focuses on agent-based modelling, a computer-based method in which interactions between micro-units called agents are used to generate macro-level patterns. For example, from simple assumptions about preferences for neighbourhood composition it is possible to examine how patterns of residential segregation might emerge. Heretofore, social simulators have had to rely on sources of data not necessarily well-suited to their purpose. Elsenbroich sees considerable potential for synergy between simulation methods and online research. The availability and dynamic character of much online data makes it amenable to analysis using agent-based modelling, which in turn allows often hard-to-study processes such as diffusion to be analysed.

Gaming was early on an important aspect of online culture. Harko Verhagen, Magnus Johansson and Wander Jager address the issues involved in researching games. One can study how games are played online or look at the social worlds that surround gaming and how they manifest themselves online. Since gaming is typically an immersive activity, the study of games poses a number of methodological challenges, as well as a range of ethical issues. Games shade over into simulations, making them a research method in their own right. Thus, playing a game in which the participants must engage with a difficult problem through processes of interaction and negotiation allows one to gain insight into how such a problem might be dealt with in the real world.

Hans Rosling, doctor, statistician and anti-poverty campaigner, once reputedly said 'Most of us need to listen to the music to understand how beautiful it is. But often that's how we present statistics; we just show the notes we don't play the music'. In their chapter Helen Kennedy and William Allen aim to help online researchers go beyond simply showing the notes by using visualisation techniques to represent data in clear and, more often than not, beautiful ways. Of course, form can sometimes overwhelm content and after defining data visualisation and discussing both the possibilities and the limits of what visualisation can achieve, Kennedy and Allen emphasise the need for a strongly reflexive approach to the use of visualisation. Beyond this, they characterise the state of the art through an examination of the tools and techniques available for creating visualisations and give examples from their own work.

DIGITAL TEXT ANALYSIS

The metaphor of the 'field' comes fairly readily to social scientists, a comfortingly agricultural metaphor for a place where one goes to 'gather' data. For online researchers though, the notion has begun to seem like an anachronism. Rather it is as if one is standing in a river with data flowing, cascading even, from a variety of data providers – individuals, social media sites, companies and so on – and in need of capture. The necessity to deal with volume and flow has encouraged social

scientists to think about ways of automating the analytic process.

Roel Popping looks at the use of content analysis as an analytic strategy. Content analysis is understood here as a systematic, quantitative approach that provides a basis for an understanding of a text or set of texts of interest to a researcher. Popping provides a clear overview to the field. He identifies the major theoretical approaches involved, discussing in each case both manual and machine coding methods. In particular, Popping explores the use of 'modality' analysis, an approach useful for the analysis of opinion statements of the kind often found in newspaper editorials that proclaim the need for some action or promote the desirability of a particular state of affairs. He concludes by providing information about appropriate software and emphasises the need to train coders and to ensure intercoder-reliablity.

One approach that has come to the fore especially with the advent of social media is 'opinion mining' or more broadly 'sentiment analysis', terms used to refer to the automated identification and extraction of opinions and information about affective states from (often voluminous) online texts. Observing that such methods have become increasingly effective, Mike Thelwall discusses the main features of sentiment analysis and the various forms it takes, which might include the detection of subjective statements, the strength of a sentiment, its polarity, emotional tone and so on. The possible applications of sentiment analysis, which include both academic and commercial uses, are now quite extensive and, as Thelwall shows, hold considerable potential for studying patterns of affective communication hitherto not always well-studied by traditional methods.

Edward Brent suggests that the need to deal with large-scale digitised data flows might best be met by means of automated processes, specifically the use of 'intelligent agents' that leverage natural language processing and other artificial intelligence techniques to develop ways of coding data as it flows towards capture by the researcher. Brent sees the vision he sets out as one that will become increasingly important in the future. Inevitably, he observes, concerns arise about privacy, intellectual property, and about the possible deskilling of researchers. Nevertheless, the possibilities are intriguing.

Around the turn of the millennium, the weblog or blog, a relatively new form of online communication, began to become popular. Through the medium of a blog one could produce online content relatively easily and link readily to the work of others similarly engaged. For Nicholas Hookway and Helene Snee part of the interest in blogs lies in the ways in which they make the personal public. In their chapter Hookway and Snee see blogs as 'documents of life' (Plummer, 2001), narratives produced spontaneously that give us insight into how people live their lives, more like traditional forms such as diaries or journals. Using case studies from their research, Hookway and Snee give a clear and detailed account of the processes involved in researching blogs. They look at the practical and technical aspects of doing blog research, as well as issues to do with selecting blogs for analysis and extracting data from them. Analytic issues are also addressed, for example the important issue of authenticity, and Hookway and Snee conclude with discussion of ethical and legal matters.

VIRTUAL ETHNOGRAPHY

Peter Steiner's celebrated 1993 *New Yorker* cartoon in which one dog tells another 'On the Internet, nobody knows you're a dog' hints at some of the attraction online worlds had early on for ethnographers. The online was a space that was novel and exciting and – because or in spite of its technological carapace – perhaps even a bit mysterious. Within that space it might be possible to learn interesting things about identity, culture and the presentation of self. Thus, the online became grist to the ethnographer's mill.

Today, Christine Hine argues in her article on virtual ethnography that there exists 'an internally diverse array of approaches oriented to ethnography in and of online space' rather than a single dominant approach. Hine draws some of the strands together by identifying key methodological issues that surround participation and observation within online research settings and by addressing complexities in the definition of field sites. She offers a typology of ethnographic approaches depending on the degree to which the activities studied are interconnected and how these relate to the goals the researcher brings to the study. Looking forward, Hine addresses the potential for autoethnographic approaches while seeing challenges ahead related to the growing commercialisation of the Internet and the difficulties involved in studying the consumption of online material.

Henrietta O'Connor and Clare Madge point out that despite the proliferation of online methods, online synchronous interviewing where interviewer and interviewee interact remotely but in real time remains, for the present at least, relatively underused. In their detailed chapter, O'Connor and Madge look at the advantages and disadvantages of interviewing online and contrast online interviewing with interviewing face-to-face. As well as discussing the ethical issues involved, they address the practicalities of interviewing online and give advice on available software. In their conclusion, O'Connor and Madge emphasise the need to weigh carefully the strengths and weaknesses of online interviews and look forward to the ways in which newer technological developments might expand the scope for online interviewing.

The opportunities offered by online focus groups, as well as the issues involved in their use, are discussed in the chapter by Katie M. Abrams with Ted J. Gaiser. In this chapter readers will find a discussion of the methodological and technical considerations they will need to bear in mind when selecting a medium for conducting an online focus group. Various approaches and tools are discussed, the medium to be used, whether communication is synchronous or asynchronous, recruitment and the demanding task of moderating an online group. The factors that need to be considered in choosing a particular technology to be used in data collection are also outlined. As with the online interview, ongoing technological developments are likely to open up a space for greater and probably more innovative focus group practice online. The chapter closes with a look at some of the possibilities.

Drawing on the work of a research project devoted to developing tools to support remote working with video data, Jon Hindmarsh's chapter looks to the needs of qualitative researchers who analyse digital video, an area of growing importance in the social sciences. Although software tools for qualitative analysis have become increasingly sophisticated, Hindmarsh notes that they do not always meet the needs of video analysts working in a research tradition associated with ethnomethodology and conversation analysis who focus on small slices of locally situated and occasioned interaction and who prefer to use video data because it allows recurrent viewing and inspection of the data with a high degree of granularity. The analytic needs of such users intersect with an institutional form within the field, the 'data session' in which researchers collectively and collaboratively view video materials for the purpose of analysis. Such sessions require both the physical co-presence of participants and a means of interacting with the video in immediate and complex ways. Hindmarsh describes recent technological developments that provide tools for allowing colleagues who are physically remote from each other to collaborate in a highly interactive and responsive manner in the analysis of visual data.

Beginning in the late 1980s, researchers began to use software tools for the analysis of data from qualitative research studies. Originally somewhat controversial, such tools eventually moved to the mainstream and became what some would regard as an essential feature of contemporary qualitative research practice. Now, as Christina Silver and Sarah L. Bulloch discuss in their chapter, the field of Computer Assisted Qualitative Data AnalysiS (CAQDAS) is being shaped by its relationship to online research methods. As they point out, a number of key trends have become apparent in the past few years. CAQDAS packages are now capable of handling a wider range of data formats, moving beyond textual data to incorporate material from visual, audio, bibliographic and online sources. There is a trend to technologically mediated collaborative working and a move to make software available on a wider range of platforms and in mobile versions, all of which have interesting implications for ethnographic styles of work. Citizen research, collaborative work, as well as use in commercial environments are all facilitated in various ways by recent developments. Silver and Bulloch chart these trends and their ramifications based on a detailed familiarity with available software and the changing nature of the field.

ONLINE SECONDARY ANALYSIS: RESOURCES AND METHODS

Probably most of us today make a fairly serious attempt to reuse and recycle what we produce and consume; however, 'waste not, want not' makes not just environmental sense. The benefits to researchers of using previously collected data as a resource for further study are now well understood and well documented. In addition, many of the tools and resources for doing so are now available online.

Some of the uses to which secondary data can be put are rehearsed by Louise Corti and Jo Wathan in their chapter on online access to quantitative data resources. These include the contextualisation of existing studies, comparative research, replicating existing studies, the asking of new questions of old data, methodological research and so on. Focusing on the United Kingdom's Data Archive at the University of Essex and the Interuniversity Consortium for Political and Social Research (ICPSR) in the United States, Corti and Wathan point to the role of data services in ensuring the availability for reuse of high quality research data. Most users interact with data services via online portals that make it relatively easy to find and access data, but the availability of data in this way depends on a great deal of background work to produce data files and documentation in serviceable and durable form. Now data archives have to deal with new and emerging forms of online data available, for example as the result of open government initiatives, data from online transactions, social media and crowd-sourced data. Corti and Wathan explore how data services assess the provenance and quality of these newer forms of data, look at some existing examples and point to future developments.

The issue of how far qualitative data might lend themselves to secondary analysis has been a somewhat contentious one in the field. Although he recognises the sensibilities some qualitative researchers have in relation to the issue of secondary analysis, Patrick Carmichael underlines the diversity of form, purpose and content that can be found in existing collections of qualitative data and makes a pragmatic case for reuse, not least in relation to research training. Using as a case study a project designed to develop a digital archive of the data emerging from a series of educational evaluation studies, Carmichael addresses issues of various kinds that arise from the secondary analysis of qualitative data. He discusses in a relatively non-technical way strategies for data description and their relationship to existing and emerging network technologies, all of which opens up, in his view, a range of interesting possibilities for the provision of data that can be utilised in highly complex and novel ways. Carmichael concludes by discussing a range of new developments such as 'linked'

and 'open' data, the possibilities that exist for methodological innovation and the ways in which the role of researchers might change in terms of research impact, for example.

Taking a bus to work used to involve turning up at the bus stop and hoping that the service was running to schedule. Now, a smartphone app tells you where the bus is and when it is going to arrive. This is just one example of the role geographical data now plays in everyday life. As David Martin, Samantha Cockings and Samuel Leung point out in their chapter on finding and investigating geographical data online, although much social science data is analysed without reference to its spatial location, almost all the objects of study that social scientists are interested in have a spatial location. In their chapter they examine a range of online sources of geographical data before going on to identify online tools for data linkage, various forms of mapping and spatial analysis. Martin and colleagues are enthusiastic about the potential for greater use of geo-referenced data by social scientists, although they draw attention to the rapid pace of change in the field and caution that there are issues to do with scale, projection, accuracy and precision that might not be apparent to non-geographers.

As Matthew Zook, Ate Poorthuis and Rich Donohue point out, for most of us a map describes locations; it shows us where things are. Social scientists, however, are generally interested in thematic maps that show how social attributes or variables are spatially distributed. Zook and colleagues walk non-specialists through the various stages involved in producing such maps, paying attention to issues of measurement, generalisation and graphic design and detailing some of the software tools available. They then illustrate the issues involved using as the basis for a case study a sample of geotagged tweets using the term 'pizza' sent in the United States between 2012 and 2015. Spatially mapped, these tweets give insight into regional and cultural variations in food consumption, the analysis of which allows

Zook and colleagues to describe the methodological complexities associated with spatial analysis.

THE FUTURE OF ONLINE SOCIAL RESEARCH

New methods throw up unexpected challenges and opportunities and place old problems in a new light. Technological change often makes previously intractable problems and bottlenecks resolvable. The prospect is to know the world in ways not previously possible with tools still to be envisaged. That prospect is an exciting and compelling one, and one that will have widespread methodological implications for social research. At the same time, it should not be forgotten that new technologies also shift the social relations of intellectual production. A case in point is the extent to which access to online data is increasingly constrained and controlled by commercial entities and proprietary interests. The balance of power between researcher and researched has also shifted. Interesting possibilities for citizen research, action research and the use of participatory approaches have opened up as a result. The wider implications of all of this are not entirely clear at present but require careful attention nevertheless.

A critique emerging in recent years associates dominant research traditions in the social sciences with Western colonialism and imperialism and emphasises by contrast the importance of using research to advance the needs, aspirations and cultural integrity of colonised peoples, as defined and articulated by those peoples themselves. Using as a case study their work with First Nations communities in Northern Canada, Brian Beaton, David Perley, Chris George and Susan O'Donnell point to ways in which new technologies coupled to participatory research styles can aid the empowerment of marginalised groups. They describe how

the availability of broadband networks and the use of video-conferencing tools enabled collaborative and participative working with small, widely scattered, remote First Nations communities with some history of suspicion towards research conducted by metropolitan academics.

The advent of mobile communication technologies opens up many possibilities for continuous and mobile data collection; however, as William Revelle, David M. Condon, Joshua Wilt, Jason A. French, Ashley Brown and Lorien G. Elleman suggest, the ability thus provided to collect data online from a large and diverse pool of participants is somewhat constrained by design considerations that limit their ability or willingness to respond to large numbers of items. Using an approach for dealing with the problem, described as 'Synthetic Aperture Personality Assessment', Revelle and colleagues suggest a strategy in which participants are given a small set of items of interest which are then analysed through the use of synthetic covariance matrices using software tools that are freely available.

What Harrison Smith, Michael Hardey, Mariann Hardey and Roger Burrows refer to as the 'Geoweb' or 'geo-spatial web 2.0' is based on what they call a 'new social cartography' that harnesses new technologies to allow ordinary citizens to create and use maps through practices such as crowdsourcing. The contrast here is with 'cartographies of knowing capitalism' in which the power of Geographic Information Systems is harnessed to produce knowledge that aids processes of capital accumulation. Smith and colleagues explore the epistemological dynamics of the Geoweb and the implications that developments such as knowledge production by non-experts and wider use of open data sources have for the social relations of data production. They examine a number of Geoweb tools applications that have potential for future research and praxis.

Michael Fischer, Stephen Lyon and David Zeitlyn look to the future of social science research under the impact of what they call 'Internet and related communications technologies' (IRCT). Fischer and colleagues suggest that short-term trends at least are probably foreseeable from an inspection of what is happening now at the cutting edge (much of which is represented in this Handbook). Extrapolation into the medium term and long term, however, remains problematic. Certainly, online research will become more important as time goes on, although as they argue, current distinctions between online and offline might largely disappear as the two worlds increasingly interpenetrate. Continuing developments in IRCT will have implications right across the research process from the collection of data, through its handling, manipulation and analysis to the means by which findings are disseminated. Moreover, beyond the execution of research, new possibilities will open up for the design, conceptualisation and theorisation of research, while the emergence of formidable ethical challenges is also a possibility. Social scientists will need to respond to developments such as the advent of 'smart' technological assistants and come to terms with the research implications of the Internet of Things. At the very least, the possibilities and options open to coming generations of social scientists will be very different from those faced today.

In the concluding chapter of the Handbook, Grant Blank reminds us that the complex relationship between theory, method and the technologies for recording and analysing data has stood at the heart of disciplined inquiry since the dawn of the Scientific Age. Now, the advent of online methods casts that relationship anew. The promise of new information and communication technologies seems to be that we will have so much data available so readily, in such volumes and in such detail that there will be little need for theory. Usefully revisiting many of the topics discussed in individual chapters of the Handbook, Blank argues by contrast that theory is deeply and continually embedded in the choices we make to deploy online research methods.

CONCLUSION

Information and communication technologies have affected research capacities in all fields of scientific endeavour but, arguably, they are of particular importance to the social sciences, offering means to address some hitherto intractable methodological problems of social science methods while providing a view onto the overall terrain of contemporary human knowledge, albeit one that is very large, very unruly and constantly changing. It is clear that online technologies have had, are having and will have transformative effects on what it is that social researchers do. In the meantime, the emergence of even newer technologies, some of which we can only now imagine, will engage the attention of social researchers. It is with this in mind that we have brought together a range of contributions relating to online research methods. Drawing on authors well known in their field from the United Kingdom, North America, Continental Europe and Australasia, we deliberately sought broad topic coverage in compiling the Handbook. Although all committed to the importance of empirical research, the authors of the preceding articles come from a range of epistemological traditions and embody a variety of methodological styles, substantive commitments and disciplinary affiliations. Many are early adopters who have contributed to the substantive literature in their own particular field and have demonstrated how the often previously unrecognised affordances associated with online methods were capable of extending and enhancing the doing of social science research. Authors who contributed to the first edition of the Handbook have brought their contributions up to date to ensure that readers have the clearest sense of the current state of the art. (Regrettably, we were unable to include updated versions of two chapters from the first edition because authors had competing claims on their time.) In addition, we have added or expanded coverage of some areas – for example big data, gaming and participatory research – where there appears to be new and promising developments. Although some of the areas covered in the Handbook are technically complex, we have encouraged authors to address issues in a clear accessible way so that newcomers have a clear introduction to a particular field while those already familiar with it can be appraised of the newest developments.

New methods throw up unexpected challenges and opportunities and place old problems in a new light. Technological change often makes resolvable previously intractable problems and bottlenecks. In thinking about technological innovation in social research, it seems important to steer a path between a number of different positions. Quite obviously one of these is the kind of naive enthusiasm that is largely a matter of being in thrall to the latest fads and foibles. The newness of a method can lead to unthinking application and a distancing of users from the craft aspects of a particular methodological approach. For any given innovation someone has to be an early adopter. However, just as in artistic experimentation, where what seems outrageous to established taste might be, from the artist's point of view, a subtle exploration of where the boundaries of possibilities lie, so too it is important methodologically to assess what we gain and what we lose with any new way of doing things. This suggests that any assessment of online research methods needs to be sober enough to undermine exaggerated claims but open-minded enough to spot potentiality where it exists. Self-evidently the contributors to this Handbook are enthusiasts for the methods they describe. What they share in addition, however, is a commitment to the critical understanding of those methods. That is, they recognise that the very considerable opportunities opened up by online methods must also be assessed and evaluated. The implications of those methods need to be teased out and the contexts and consequences of their use analysed and theorised. Neither unthinking advocacy of the new or its curmudgeonly rejection serve well the cause of methodological innovation.

There are indications in the early decades of the twenty-first century that the boundaries of social research itself face possible reconfiguration. Although individuals, organisations and governments have always controlled access to data, the extent to which data sources and the methods for extracting data are now controlled by commercial entities represents a new challenge to social scientists. Indeed, it is the political economy of online methods, not always apparent at the level of day-to-day practice, that remains perhaps the most opaque and complex aspect of future methodological development. The ongoing dance of competition and cooperation, accommodation and antagonism between corporations and governments that has been shaped differentially by culture, history and self-interest in North America, Europe and elsewhere will no doubt continue to affect the balance of power between knowledge producers and consumers, including social researchers. Against this, the increasing availability and tractability of online tools and sources makes for a more research-literate and research-inclined orientation amongst non-academic users (Savage and Burrows, 2007). Indeed, it can be argued that the availability of online tools has facilitated a trend to research by 'ordinary' citizens. Citizen research looks like a trend that it would be futile to try to brake, which can presumably be seen as desirable at a time when disengagement from established political institutions is widely remarked. It could also lead to some improvement in the accessibility and design of online information resources on the grounds that lay people will not put up with the more forbidding kinds of information resource that the technically proficient may presently tolerate. This development, however, might also conceivably lead to a degree of competition between amateur and professional researchers, a circumstance that has implications for resources, such as this Handbook, which might have a role in educating or even regulating an expanded user base.

No longer a large rather foreboding machine, its console full of blinking lights, humming away in an air-conditioned room, the computer is now in your pocket. It is used to make calls, send messages, take pictures, check the time of the next train and what is showing at the local multiplex. The quotidian character of computing nowadays as well its massive interconnectedness draws researchers to online environments, just as their traditional tools are themselves being transformed by technology. Soon, everything will be 'smarter', more embedded and more interconnected. Interesting times ahead!

REFERENCES

Dillman, D. A. (1978). *Mail and telephone surveys: The total design method.* New York, NY: Wiley.

Dillman, D. A. (2000). *Mail and internet surveys: The tailored design method (Vol. 2).* New York, NY: Wiley.

International Telecommunication Union. (2015). *Measuring the Information Society Report 2015.* Geneva: International Telecommunication Union.

Lee, R. M. (2004). Recording technologies and the interview in sociology, 1920–2000. *Sociology: Journal of the British Sociological Association*, 38(5), 869–89.

Plummer, K. (2001). *Documents of life 2: An invitation to a critical humanism.* London: Sage Publications.

Savage, M. and Burrows, R. (2007). The coming crisis of empirical sociology. *Sociology*, 41(5), 885–99.

Star, S. L. (1999). The ethnography of infrastructure. *American Behavioral Scientist*, 43(3), 377–91.

Webb, E. J., Campbell, D. T., Schwartz, R. D. and Sechrest, L. (1966). *Unobtrusive measures: Nonreactive research in the social sciences.* Chicago, IL: Rand McNally.

## PART II

Designing Online Research

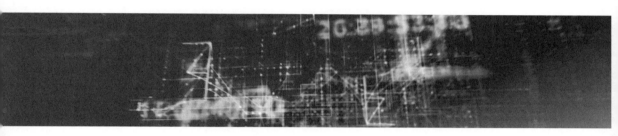

The Ethics of Online Research

Rebecca Eynon, Jenny Fry and Ralph Schroeder

This chapter considers some of the main ethical issues that researchers are likely to encounter in Internet-related research. These issues have been discussed for some time and some guidelines for researchers are established (Markham and Buchanan, 2012); however, there is still considerable debate about the ethics of Internet research – not least because the Internet is still in a formative phase and new phenomena continue to emerge. In this chapter, we will discuss some of the major issues that have been debated and give some indication of how to go about addressing them.

One of the challenges to developing a coherent ethical approach to Internet research is that as the Internet evolves as a space for social interaction and information dissemination, the methods necessary to capture and document such activities are also emergent. Consequently, consideration of ethical issues in a context-independent manner, divorced from matters of methodology and conceptual frameworks, would be limited in scope

and usefulness. In this chapter, we therefore discuss novel ethical dilemmas for Internet researchers in the context of three predominant approaches to gathering Internet-based data: use of online methods to gather data directly from individuals, analysing online interaction within virtual environments, and social media as a research laboratory. Prior to this discussion, we reflect on how ethical issues relating to Internet research might differ from research in traditional settings.

NEW TECHNOLOGY, OLD AND NEW ETHICS

Ethical Governance in Traditional Research Settings

Thus far, the governance of Internet research has been heavily influenced by the well established guidelines in (offline) social research (Basset and O'Riordan, 2002).

These guidelines are typically at the national level (e.g. research councils such as the Australian Research Council (ARC) and the Economic and Social Research Council (ESRC) in the UK) or committees set up at an institutional level (e.g. ethical review committees/ethics committees (UK), Institutional Review Boards (US) or Human Subjects Review Boards (AU)).

Both these mechanisms for external research governance (i.e. beyond that of the individual researcher or research group) have historical roots in the 'human subjects research model'. Three ethical concepts are at the core of institutional and professional research governance based on the 'human subjects model': confidentiality, anonymity and informed consent. These are derived from the basic human right to privacy, although these rights are interpreted differently in different jurisdictions (e.g. the EU and the US; see Reidenberg, 2000; Rule, 2007). However, these regulations originate from the medical sciences and are not always applicable to the social sciences. The human subjects research model is widely used in discussions of online research ethics, although the suitability of applying this model in some online contexts has been questioned (Basset and O'Riordan, 2002).

Institutional governance of research (the interrelationship between legal and ethical interventions) not only varies between institutions, but also from country to country (Buchanan and Ess, 2009). These range from close intervention, which in extreme cases can hinder the progress of research, to minimal guidance that relies on the self-policing of researchers. Differentiation in institutional/professional ethical rules and guidelines illustrates a tension between external (structural) governance and the freedom of self-regulation among individual researchers. Such institutional provisions do not necessarily exempt researchers from further ethical obligations and responsibilities.

Researchers have different relations with research participants and data provided by them, depending on the method and approaches used. For example, it is not uncommon for ethnographers to develop a trust relationship with the people from the communities they observe, and they often come to perceive themselves as custodians of the data they gather. Ethical practices are also shaped by personal ethical frameworks, as well as researchers' cultural and professional ones. As Ess (2006) argues, any emphases on the rights of research participants must be considered further alongside other important rights and values – including (deontological) emphases on the importance of knowledge developed through research and (more utilitarian) emphases on research knowledge as contributing to public policy and debate, along with researchers' rights and interests in pursuing knowledge. This is a recurring issue in relation to the ethics of Internet research and closely related to considerations of 'harm' to research participants (see Ess, 2006, 2013).

There is a blurring of the boundary between ethical and legal considerations and provisions. Ess makes a useful distinction between institutional or legal requirements as against the ethical requirements that can go beyond these (Ess, 2002). In addition to the requirements set by Research Ethics Committees and professional bodies, there are also laws regarding privacy and data protection that govern research in different countries. In Internet research, however, the institutional and legal context may be uncertain because research participants may be online in any geographical context. The global reach of the Internet may thus, as Ess (2006) suggests, entail that researchers take heed of contexts which go beyond their own jurisdictions. This also applies to considerations over and above these institutional and legal requirements, such as what we might do as individual researchers out of a sense of fairness. Here, as well, it is necessary to think 'globally' because values such as privacy may be culturally specific and what is considered an appropriate balance between privacy and freedom of expression will vary between cultures (Fry, 2006; Nakada and Tamura, 2005).

New Ethics for New Settings?

Why should online research require separate or additional treatment? This 'meta-issue' has itself been a major debate that runs through the various individual topics in Internet research (Buchanan and Ess, 2009). Walther (2002), for example, has argued that many of the features of Internet research are similar to those found in other media or in existing offline research. Walther's (2002) arguments are directed against those (particularly Frankel and Siang, 1999) who argue the opposite; namely, that new rules are required for this novel setting because, to give just one example, people may misrepresent their identity online (to which Walther replies that they can also do this offline).

Despite continuing disagreements in this debate, Ess (2002) argues that there has been a convergence on the view that research ethics for online settings are not special and can be derived from the ethics for offline settings. We shall encounter a number of instances later. At the same time, we shall also argue that in some cases there are special considerations that are needed for online research, such as the changed nature of disclosure and informed consent. This arises from the increased domestication (Silverstone *et al.*, 1992) of the Internet in everyday life and the possibilities for technical and methodological innovation.

As noted earlier, Internet research is regulated in a similar way to other areas of academic research, with institutional review boards and ethical committees, alongside professional associations providing guidance. Regardless of the specifics of online ethics, it is important to note that such review boards are not without their critics, and a number of researchers have highlighted concerns about the extent to which ethical review boards can apply a set of largely context-free guidelines in unproblematic ways, the extent to which such processes account for the messiness of

real-life research, and to which such protocols pay sufficient attention to all aspects of the research process, including exiting the field site (Miller, 2013). Ultimately, researchers should not be put off engaging with the review review board or assuming certain kinds of research cannot be done; however, given the innovation in this area it is likely that researchers should not rely solely on the judgements of ethical review boards or take on significant responsibility themselves (Lunnay *et al.*, 2015). Indeed, the Association of Internet Researchers (AoIR) provided an updated set of guidelines for researchers in 2012, and part of this provides a useful framework of questions researchers should ask themselves as they consider the ethics of their research project (Markham and Buchanan, 2012: 8–10).

Sensitivity to Context

Sensitivity to context is important. The AoIR guidelines place an emphasis on this context-dependence, which entails respecting people's values or expectations in different settings. A few examples (in addition to those provided in the AoIR guidelines) will suffice:

Bloggers: the aim in this case is to disseminate the blogger's views, but should everything, including sensitive personal information contained in a blog, be disseminated via research?

Search: from a legal point of view, the release of information by a search provider in anonymized form may not pose a problem, but clearly those who search don't expect to be potentially identified in relation to their search behaviour.

Online games: the context here may be play, but even though these environments are public, is it appropriate to reveal players' names in research publications?

Chatrooms: though a chatroom space may be public, the participants may feel they are part of a trusted community and use the space to communicate intimate details of their lives. Should consideration be given to reproducing the content verbatim in research communications and to what extent should social structures be protected from being disclosed or 'invaded' by researchers?

Internet research ethics thus need to be tailored to different contexts (Sveningsson-Elm, 2009). It may not be sufficient, for example, to stay within the strictures of copyright law (the institutional and legal requirements mentioned in the previous section) or to simply adopt the rule of 'fair use' as with offline publications (Walther, 2002; but see Ess, 2002: 3) in order to be ethically fair to research participants.

APPROACHES TO INTERNET RESEARCH

The following sections deal with the particular ethical issues that arise in using online methods to gather data directly from individuals, analysing online interaction within virtual environments and social media as a research laboratory. The online methods used to gather data directly from individuals that are discussed include surveys, interviews and focus groups. In these cases, researchers use online tools to ask participants for responses to particular questions or issues. The study of online interaction in virtual environments includes participant observation and logging and visualizing the interaction between participants. The analysis of social media as a research laboratory involves capture and analysis of digital traces that people leave online, such as representation of self-identity and social interaction, alongside the use of large-scale experiments to nudge behaviour.

Use of Online Methods to Gather Data Directly from Individuals

For a detailed discussion of how to conduct interviews and surveys see Chapter 24 on interviews by O'Connor and Madge and the

Internet survey section in Part IV of this Handbook. Here, we address the key ethical considerations of these online methods, which raise slightly different ethical challenges to the face-to-face context (Mann, 2003).

Benefits and Risks of Online Research

It is the investigators' responsibility to ensure, as far as they are able, that participants will not come to harm by taking part in any study. In the social sciences, psychological and physical harm to participants may be caused, for example, by research that evokes bad memories or reduces a person's sense of pride or dignity, or by cases where the anonymity of the participant is not maintained as originally agreed (Bier *et al.*, 1996). Trying to ensure harm is not caused by the study is particularly challenging as there may well be unintended consequences of research unforeseen by the researcher (Rees, 1991: 147).

Online research is not intrinsically more likely to be harmful than face-to-face methods, yet it does pose different challenges (Kraut *et al.*, 2004). In online research it is more difficult to assess the risk of participants coming to harm because fewer studies have been conducted from which researchers can learn, and it is harder to judge individuals' reactions to the research (e.g. if a person is getting distressed by an interview question or if a participant feels insulted or harassed by other group members in an online discussion) (Bier *et al.*, 1996; Mann and Stewart, 2000). Strategies to try to address these issues include building a good rapport with participants, establishing 'netiquette' in group discussions (Mann and Stewart, 2000) and providing participants with an easy way to leave the study (Hewson *et al.*, 2003; Nosek *et al.*, 2002).

A second issue is the potential of harm to the researchers. Given the anonymity of the Internet, researchers can come across or receive distressing information of numerous kinds. Examples include people who are contemplating suicide (Lehavot *et al.*, 2012), people who are considering/have committed a crime, people who are bullying others or people who are grieving (Carmack and Degroot, 2014). What a researcher does with such information has ethical, and in some cases legal, implications. It is important for researchers to anticipate and assess these risks prior to beginning the study as far as is possible in order to reduce the potential of harm to themselves and their participants (for detailed advice see Stern, 2003).

Ensuring Confidentiality

Harm can also occur due to breaches of confidentiality and anonymity caused by the misuse of storing or using the data (Fox et al., 2003). Researchers have a responsibility to ensure the confidentiality of data and the privacy of participants at all stages of the process, during all interactions with the participants and when the data is transmitted and stored (Nosek et al., 2002). Given that the perceived anonymity of the Internet may encourage people to discuss topics or disclose more details than they would be willing to in face-to-face situations (Meho, 2006), researchers need to ensure that participants' perceptions of anonymity are met, or if not, made explicit to the participant (see section on informed consent later).

In terms of securely transmitting data, potential solutions include the use of encryption, use of data labels that are meaningless to anyone but the researcher, and the separate transmission of personal data and experimental data (Nosek et al., 2002). In terms of data storage, the data needs to be protected from other people accessing it or tampering with it; this can be an issue in the networked systems commonly in place in universities (Fox et al., 2003). Password-protecting computer directories, saving personal data and experimental data separately (Kraut et al., 2004), encrypting the files so no one else can read them, or coding the data in a way that reduces the likelihood of people being able to trace the data to a specific individual (Pittenger, 2003) are all possible strategies.

The issue of ensuring confidentiality whilst interacting with the participants may arise at various points throughout the research. Participants may wish to contact the researchers up to and including the debriefing stage at the end of the study, yet directly emailing the researchers may compromise anonymity in a number of ways. First, email addresses are often identifiable as they can contain names, geographical location and organizational affiliation. Although people can make use of anonymous email services to cover their identity, these are not 100 per cent effective and tend to promise 'best efforts' as opposed to true anonymity. Second, a copy of all emails is retained on the server of the sending account, any transmitting server and on the destination server and these copies are frequently retained on back up recordings for a number of years (Fox et al., 2003). These issues can be particularly problematic when certain activities are carried out online, for example if verifiable names and addresses or signed agreements are required to fulfil informed consent procedures and/or institutions require personal details when participants are rewarded for the research in the form of prizes or payment. Email should be reduced to a minimum with offline methods or alternative web-based methods utilized where appropriate, for example setting up a forum on the research website for participants to ask questions (Fox et al., 2003) and when offering prizes for participating in the research (a technique that in itself raises ethical questions), maintaining anonymity by purchasing online gift certificates and then providing the certificate number to the participant (Kraut et al., 2004).

Informed Consent

Individuals who choose to participate in any research project must do so on the basis of informed consent, where the individual understands what the goal of the research is and what they are agreeing to do, the potential risks and benefits of taking part, and have details of alternative options that may benefit them.

Participants must have the option to ask any-thing they wish and understand that partici-pation is voluntary and that they can withdraw at any time (Anderson, 1998). In practice, gaining truly informed consent is not straight-forward in any context. The nature of informed consent changes throughout the research process and thus needs to be con-stantly renegotiated (Bier *et al.*, 1996; Sin, 2005). Further, it is difficult to ascertain if informed consent is truly given by the par-ticipant, for example problems and misun-derstandings arise when potential participants do not read documents carefully or fail to ask for clarification from the researcher (see Varnhagen *et al.*, 2005). In face-to-face con-texts it is potentially easier to evaluate if the participant is fully informed about the study compared to online environments. Owing to the distance between the researcher and the participant in online settings, this is some-times more difficult. It is harder to determine whether the participant truly understands what they are consenting to and it may take more time to gain consent because it may require more online discussions to ensure the participants fully understand the implications of participating. This additional online inter-action may put participants off clarifying or asking all the questions they wish about the research (Mann and Stewart, 2000). To try to ensure participants are truly informed in online settings, techniques of increasing the readabil-ity of the document can be used (e.g. reducing the amount of text, use of subheadings and use of colour). Using quizzes to check understand-ing can be another means, although this extra burden on the participants increases the risk of dropout (Varnhagen *et al.*, 2005). Despite these challenges the advantage of online con-sent when compared to face-to-face consent is that participants are likely to feel less pressure to enter into and remain in the study and are therefore more likely to enter and participate in the research freely.

A second important issue is verifying the participant's ability to give informed consent (Kraut *et al.*, 2004). Verifying the ability of an individual to give informed consent is harder in online environments because it is more difficult to know whether or not the online sample includes 'vulnerable groups' (e.g. young people,[1] the elderly or people with mental health issues) and because the extent to which individuals are able or competent to give informed consent varies widely and this is more difficult to judge online. Reducing the chances of a vulnerable group (e.g. young people) being part of a research project can partly be addressed by the recruitment strat-egy utilized. For example, sending specific invitations to known adult participants to access a password-controlled site (Pittenger, 2003) or designing advertising materials that are unlikely to attract or interest young peo-ple when employing a more 'broad brush' strategy (Nosek *et al.*, 2002) may help. Other options include asking for information that only adults would have, such as credit card information, although such activities can increase dropout (Kraut *et al.*, 2004). In prac-tice, verifying identity is really an issue only in research involving controversial topics and/or where the study presents higher risks to potential participants (Pittenger, 2003). Indeed, whether one should try and obtain online consent for high-risk studies at all is open to question (Kraut *et al.*, 2004).

The issues considered in this section have included protecting participants from harm, ensuring confidentiality and informed con-sent. Indeed, these questions are perhaps becoming increasingly challenging to address where the distinction between researcher and researched is becoming more blurred in some settings, such as crowd-sourcing and sites that offer a complex mix of support in return for data (e.g. patientslikeme.com) (Janssens and Kraft, 2012; O'Connor, 2013).

It is a balancing act for researchers to ensure that participants are protected, but at the same time not placing unnecessary and excessive burdens on participants in terms of completing informed consent procedures, ensuring security, etc. (Kraut *et al.*, 2004). Although it is impossible to predict all eventualities in online research, it is useful to always pilot test instruments and consent forms because what works in one context with one group may not work and/or may well produce different ethical questions in another situation (Meho, 2006).

Analysing Interactions in Virtual Environments

To address the questions raised by online environments, we take online virtual worlds as an example. These include social spaces where people, in the form of avatar representations of themselves, interact with each other in the virtual setting for various purposes including gaming, socialising and collaborating (see Bailenson and Schroeder, 2008).

Online Social Settings

Virtual spaces in which people interact online as avatars can be treated as social worlds. These social settings are perhaps most often akin to 'third places' (public parks, coffee shops, street corners) – places that are neither public nor private but in between (Oldenburg, 1989).

Online social spaces exemplify the imperative discussed earlier: to be sensitive to the values and aims of people in different online settings. This sensitivity to context will involve treating different virtual worlds in different ways. There may be events or whole worlds in which people interacting online are behaving in a public way, as in a public meeting or in a virtual world that is open to all for commercial or educational purposes. It may also be, however, that certain spaces within a virtual world, such as an online church (Schroeder *et al.*, 1998), although formally public, include interactions that should be treated as private – such as when personal details are revealed or if a whole online world is expressly designed to provide a private forum for interaction among a group that would be difficult in an offline setting (or in another virtual setting).

For offline participant observation or fieldwork there have been extensive debates in anthropology about the role of the observer and the degree to which researchers should engage in covert or overt observation and these will provide some guidance (see, for example, Angrosino and Rosenberg, 2011; Horst and Miller, 2012; Levy and Hollan, 1998), but virtual spaces present some unique challenges, which are discussed later.

The Role of The Observer

A real difference in online versus offline settings is the researcher's ability to hide completely – or lurk – in the online world. There may be a trade-off in this case between the advantages of covert observation which does not disturb the environment, and revealing one's identity as a researcher, which ensures transparency and participation, but may also lead to changed behaviour on the part of the subjects (for a particularly striking example, where the researcher became 'stalked', see Hudson-Smith, 2002). Anecdotally there have been a number of cases when many researchers descended on an online environment and there was resentment against their presence. Although ultimately the decision to disclose the presence of a researcher is down to the individual project, care needs to be taken to treat each research site with respect. The well-established rule in anthropology – to leave the field so that future researchers are not disadvantaged – must be an important consideration. There are a number of strategies that can be used to approach online communities, gain informed consent and make it clear to all participants what the researcher's role is: approaching key stakeholders for permission to research the community, using a name in the community that highlights your research status and providing a link in your online interactions in the group that communicates more information about your research for anyone to access (see also Roberts, 2015).

Studies of Online Populations

In the physical world people can be covertly recorded (as with closed-circuit television cameras), but in online worlds the possibilities of recording, reproducing and analysing interactions, especially covertly, are more powerful. This raises ethical issues because people using these environments do not necessarily expect to have all their behaviour recorded – even when theoretically giving their consent to this through the end-user license agreement when downloading the software (Chee *et al.*, 2012).

For example, Penumarthy and Börner (2006) analysed where people moved and when they focused their attention in an online virtual world for education. This kind of recording of behaviour is unlikely to be objectionable. If, however, they had counted the number of times that avatars had engaged in particularly unsavoury behaviour, even in a public place, users might reasonably object to this kind of surveillance. There is a fine line between when data about a large online game is aggregated to reveal patterns about behaviour without violating participants' sense that they are under surveillance – and the opposite. The same applies to the analysis of small-scale groups, which can be analysed down to the granularity of the finest details of interaction (Schroeder and Axelsson, 2006).

Thus researchers will need to adapt ethical considerations to the novel technological possibilities and constraints of online virtual worlds. They will continue to face the choice between Kantian duty-based or 'deontological' ethics, with their absolute respect for the individual's aims, as against the calculation of consequentialist or utilitarian ethics, which weighs the balance of harms and benefits. Final choices are likely to be based on the ethical dispositions of the researcher, the nature of the group being researched, what research questions are being asked and how the data will be used (see, for example, Boellstorff *et al.*, 2012; McKee and Porter, 2009; Horst and Miller, 2012).

In terms of the uses and limits of virtual environments for experimental research, see Eynon *et al.*, (2008) for a detailed discussion of the benefits versus the harms and, in particular, discussion of Slater *et al.*'s (2006) virtual reconstruction of the Milgram experiment.

Social Media as a Research Laboratory

The particular characteristics of social media and the way in which they are used provide new challenges for research ethics. Social media has the potential to be ubiquitous and large populations of users are constantly connected from multiple devices. The very 'publicness' of the sites, such as Facebook, YouTube, Twitter and Instagram, imbue interactions with a performative quality, with some individuals using multiple sites to promote themselves in the same way that a company might promote a brand. Individuals are defined by various characteristics from their friendship circles to their consumption patterns. In these spaces we observe the blurring of the distinction between private and public/the public sphere and commerce. The inhabitants of these spaces are akin to a melting pot with teenagers, university students, professionals, celebrities, grandparents, the healthy, the vulnerable, the benevolent and malevolent intermingling in the spaces that comprise the social web.

Determining potential harm in this melting pot is complex, added to which imperatives to share data, advanced data processing capacities and interest in big data by commerce and governments raise a number of new challenges for Internet researchers.

Privacy in Public Online

What unites a whole range of research in this area is the question of what constitutes a private act and how researchers might deal with the issue of 'privacy in public' (Nissenbaum, 1998). A particularly perplexing question is the extent to which researchers should take measures to protect an individual's privacy when the sources of data are publicly accessible. In this regard institutional review boards and ethics committees have proven limited (Zimmer, 2010) and in any case, as Henderson *et al.* (2013) argue, the moral responsibility of researchers to conduct research in an ethically robust way goes beyond the sphere of formal institutional guidelines.

In physical public environments individuals can adapt their behaviours in certain ways in order to create 'partial privacy' when an 'audience' is present – in a restaurant a couple can request a table in an out-of-the-way corner, on a train people having a conversation about a private matter can lower their voices, at a public event an individual may choose to avoid being photographed. Furthermore, members of the 'audience' can avert their 'gaze' in response to subtle social cues that indicate that 'partial privacy' is desired. In other words, privacy is managed in physical spaces through an awareness of mutual attention. To some extent the privacy settings offered by social media platforms afford the management of 'privacy in public', but compared to the subtle and complex ways in which individuals negotiate their privacy in physical public spaces they are crude and limited in their functionality. Individuals are not necessarily aware of privacy settings or think they have been evoked when in actuality they have not (Henderson *et al.*, 2013). The implication of treating publicly accessible social media profiles and other objects as 'public' is that potential ethical dilemmas are likely to be overlooked. This is one of the reasons why there have been a number of initiatives encouraging Internet researchers to share the ethical dilemmas that they have experienced (Markham and Buchanan, 2012) and why 'rules' can be limited given the contextual nature of the ethical issues that emerge.

In law, privacy is a qualified right protected in major legislation such as the 4th Amendment to the US Constitution 1791 and the European Convention on Human Rights 1950. Data privacy laws are gaining ground and have been adopted in more than a hundred countries around the world,

even if implementation in practice is lagging behind (Greenleaf, 2013). Protecting privacy is important from the perspective of a number of ideals: human dignity, individual autonomy, freedom to behave and to associate with others without the continual threat of being observed, freedom to innovate and freedom to think. These ideals reflect the strong relationship between privacy and identity. In constructing their social media profiles individuals are also constructing, or 'performing', multiple aspects of their identity. In contrast to anonymous environments such as chat rooms, virtual worlds and Massively Multi-player Online Games, many social media sites afford targeted identity performance and as a result have been termed by some researchers as 'Nonymous' environments (Grasmuck *et al.*, 2009). Different social media platforms afford different types of performance depending on technical and social affordances of their design. According to Grasmuck *et al.* (2009), for example, Facebook affords three types of targeted performance: 'Self as social actor' (implicit visual claims through photographs and wall posts); 'self as consumer' (listing cultural preferences that define a user, lists of consumption preferences and tastes, such as books, movies, music and appreciated quotes); and 'first-person self' ('about-me' entries, explicit self-description).

In conceptualizing identity performance in such environments several authors have drawn on Goffman's (1959) dramaturgical concept of 'front stage/back stage' (Grasmuck *et al.*, 2009; Hookway, 2008; Rosenberg, 2010; Schultze, 2014). 'Front stage' is where an individual can project their 'possible hoped for selves' (Grasmuck *et al.*, 2009: 165) and 'back stage' serves as a private space where individuals can be free from the 'scrutinizing gaze of others' (Rosenberg, 2010: 27). Photographs of 'self' and 'others', for example, are often selected 'back stage' in private somewhat unguarded moments, without a specific audience in mind and are presented front stage and viewed widely.

Grasmuck *et al.* (2009) argue that the casual selection of photographs with close friends in mind may reveal more to a broad audience than a Facebook user would divulge in a face-to-face interaction where a sense of audience is more acute.

Privacy also plays a role in the management and maintenance of relationships, for example what an individual is willing to share with close friends or a 'neutral' professional (such as a family doctor or a counsellor) might be different to family members. In a study of YouTube, Lange (2008) observed varied levels of 'privately public' behaviour in video making and sharing. An example of this is the 'coming out' video, a recognized genre on YouTube (Thelwall *et al.*, 2012) whereby an individual may choose to come out online, using various mechanisms to target the performance to a specific social group, for example by using a pseudonym that only close friends will recognize and partially hiding the location of a video by using limited/cryptic tags (Lange, 2008). In today's society with pervasive uses of technology, it is not feasible for an individual to expect total privacy and this is reflected in data protection legislation, which rather than being about protecting privacy per se is about giving individuals some control about the information that flows outwards from them.

The traceability of both text and non-text based data[2] via Internet search engines and the use of data mining tools raises the question of how to represent the data when it comes to dissemination and publication, for example should verbatim quotes be used and how should images be represented? Anonymization typically involves the removal of personally identifiable information[3] such as full name, residential address and date of birth. Whereas this level of anonymization might be sufficient to protect the privacy of an individual in a standalone dataset, Internet search and data mining tools enable the re-identification of an individual via triangulation. Users of social media platforms typically have profiles across multiple

platforms and it is this unique overlapping feature that makes the ease of re-identification particularly problematic (Narayanan and Shmatikov, 2009).

Researchers are exploring innovative ways to anonymize data. Markham (2012) has been developing techniques related to 'fabrication' in representing qualitative data, which involves developing typical examples or scenarios that are comprised of composite objects that collectively mask individuals. This approach is controversial, however, and Markham (2012) describes the difficulty experienced by colleagues in getting a manuscript accepted for publication where they had created composite blogs, rather than using verbatim quotes from actual blogs. Some researchers report experiencing the opposite issue of how to acknowledge those individuals who wish to be disclosed and have their data attributed to them (Tilley and Woodthorpe, 2011).

Social media environments are also unique in that they afford the collective construction of identity through sharing, tagging, commenting and automatic feeds from 'friends'. Individuals may work tirelessly on 'front stage' management, but family and friends might reveal glimpses of 'back stage'. This collective element of identity construction further complicates distinguishing between private/public and is just one example of why private/public should be treated as a continuum rather than a straightforward dichotomy (Rosenberg, 2010). As Schultze and Mason (2012: 303) argue, individuals may be performing their identities according to 'situated assumptions of privacy'. Consequently, researchers cannot assume that an entire website is 'public' as a consequence of the intentions of platform developers, Terms of Service agreements or the technical capabilities of privacy settings.

The extent to which an individual may consider lack of mutual attention a breach of privacy will depend on a number of factors, such as cultural attitudes to privacy, individual privacy attitudes (Westin, 1967) and gender.

It is possible that there may be gender differences in the extent to which individuals consider a lack of awareness of 'mutual attention' problematic because it is known that there is a gender dimension to privacy in the context of social media (Thelwall, 2011). Heightened social media privacy concerns amongst women are related to the increased likelihood that they will be victims of malevolent online behaviours such as cyberbullying, cyberstalking (Thelwall, 2011) and revenge porn. It is arguable that 'mutual attention' is at the heart of the ethical dilemma faced by researchers when using publicly available social media data. Of course, informed consent signals 'mutual attention' to research participants, but whether or not a social media profile actually represents a human participant, and thus evokes the human subjects model, has been the topic of much debate in the related literature.

Schultze and Mason (2012) propose the introduction of three new principles to the human subjects model: 'degree of entanglement', 'extent of interaction/intervention' and 'expectation of privacy', each of which could be measured on a sliding scale. The more private the activity and the space within which it occurs, the more the source of the data is seen as a human subject, and the more public, the more the source of the data is seen as the author of a text. Where there is a combination of a high-degree of 'entanglement' and a high expectation of privacy, then this would be indicative that seeking informed consent would be good practice. Consideration of the use of 'big data' for academic versus commercial research purposes can further highlight the complexity of some of the issues raised earlier regarding the use of data gathered from social media platforms, particularly with regard to anonymization, re-identification and recontextualization of data.

Analysing Big Data

Analysis of big data using data collected from social networking sites (and other digital traces) has been among the fastest growing areas of research in recent years. Here, we review two important studies, both using Facebook. The first was a study of the social networks on Facebook (Lewis et al., 2008). The study identified a number of patterns among the 'tastes' from the 'ties among Facebook friends from among students at a "private college in the Northeast U.S."' (Lewis et al., 2008: 331), thus ensuring the anonymity and privacy of those concerned. However, it took Zimmer (2010) little effort to figure out that the study had in fact been done at Harvard University, thus potentially being able to re-identify the subjects and creating a number of ethical issues that would be deemed unacceptable. Among the lessons from this episode is that there needs to be strict ways of ensuring anonymity and thus privacy. The study also raised a number of other issues, including whether consent is needed with a study using data from a private company and also whether it would be possible to make the data available to other researchers for re-use (which was intended in this case, but did not happen because of the concerns raised).

This issue of access to data was also raised in the second study, the 'social contagion' study (Kramer et al., 2014). This research took the form of a 'naturalistic' experiment, dividing almost 700,000 randomly selected Facebook users into two groups and filtering the content of their 'timelines' (their personalized news feeds) such that one group had more positive words and others were unchanged. This type of research, which analysed 3 million posts and 122 million words, certainly fits the definition of big data (Schroeder, 2014a). The finding was that users with more positive words in their feeds subsequently produced more positive words of their own, an important and large-scale confirmation of the 'social contagion' effect whereby what others do affects our own behaviour.

As already mentioned, one set of issues raised by this study is whether the privileged access to research data is afforded to some researchers by this type of study – one of the authors worked at Facebook – which creates unequal access to research materials. The added question here concerns the replicability of the study, which is an essential feature of scientific research and which is made impossible with this kind of proprietary data. The second set of issues revolves around whether carrying out this type of research violates Facebook users' privacy. Here the reply from Facebook was that the study did not breach the 'terms and conditions' that users had signed and so the study did not break laws, even though Facebook has also said that it should have handled 'communicating the study' better (*Guardian*, 2014a). A related question was whether the study should have been subject to the scrutiny of a university 'institutional review board' and thus a different kind of 'consent' apart from the legal terms and conditions required by using the site. In this respect the response was that the academic researchers only carried out the analysis whereas the data collection issues were handled by Facebook. Another response came from research ethicists in an article in *Nature* (Meyer, 2014) who took a stance against the idea that this kind of experiment carried out with a commercial company was ethically unacceptable; instead, these ethicists argued that imposing strictures on this type of commercial research would only drive it underground to the detriment of advancing publicly available knowledge.

There is a third set of issues, which relates to big data and the very idea of undertaking large-scale research which essentially manipulates people (where 'manipulate' simply means doing something to them). These have been discussed by one of the authors of this chapter elsewhere (Schroeder, 2014b), but they are also broader than questions of research ethics and of law and, in this single study, which concern big data research generally. Although the ethical and legal questions around individual cases will likely be dealt with, this larger question will require a

wider debate in society. The larger question concerns the fact that big data methods, often based on social media or other online behaviours, are becoming more widespread. If scientific knowledge about human behaviour based on these methods becomes more powerful, then it will also be able to manipulate people more powerfully. Academic researchers are typically not interested in this type of manipulation (but see the Lewis *et al.*, 2008 study), but perhaps with this knowledge they are becoming the handmaidens of those who are (such as digital media companies, in this case Facebook).

These are difficult questions that relate to the role of science and technology in society as a whole and what the value of large-scale experiments and other 'manipulations' should be. Moreover, such studies should not be ruled out altogether. In some cases, if a greater good can be achieved – for example, if we could find out people's attitudes towards climate change and conserving energy by means of this type of big data study – surely the benefits could outweigh the costs of analysing how behaviour might be manipulated as long as there is minimal or no direct risk involved. It should also be remembered that this type of big data research does not always require a private sector platform – Wikipedia has also been used for big data research (Schroeder and Taylor, 2015) and the data are open to all for replication. Governments are also engaging in big data methods to influence people.

In any event, the spectre of using large-scale online platforms to potentially sway peoples' beliefs hovers uneasily above this type of study. And while academics may largely be disinterestedly concerned with greater knowledge about life online, their research may support non-academic uses which can now, more powerfully, alter peoples' hearts and minds. In the years to come, more people will be online more often and produce vastly greater amounts of digital traces. Academic researchers will need to think hard, beyond ticking boxes on research ethics forms and beyond collaborating with non-academic sources of these data, about the extent to which this type of research improves the world, while at the same time avoiding societal concerns not just about 'big brother' but also of a 'brave new world'. It can be remembered that this novel warned not so much of surveillance, about which there has recently been much discussion, but of a future in which manipulating minds was embraced by the public and seen as benefitting society, much as Facebook argued that the social contagion experiment served to improve the users' experience (*Guardian*, 2014b).

Triangulation of Datasets and Third-Party Reuse

Advancements in the development of resources and tools available on the Internet make the triangulation and third-party reuse of data much more likely. While a standalone dataset may preserve anonymity and privacy, new capabilities for aggregating and combining data could jeopardize such ethical integrity by enabling profiles of individuals to be constructed through triangulation (Oboler *et al.*, 2012). As Kitchin (2013: 264) notes, big data is 'highly resolute, providing fine-grained detail on people's everyday lives', which is why Narayanan and Shmatikov (2009) were able to de-anonymize an anonymous Twitter graph by using a generic re-identification algorithm and triangulating the Twitter data with data available from Flickr. In doing so, Narayanan and Shmatikov (2009) illustrated that in the context of big data anonymization alone is not sufficient to protect privacy. Indeed, social media users have very little control over their data despite the different levels of privacy settings offered by social media sites (Puschmann and Burgess, 2014).

The tracking capabilities built into the very infrastructure of the Internet itself and the tools being developed to exploit the gathering and aggregation of fine-grained data on a large scale mean that the role of researcher as custodian and gatekeeper of personal data becomes radically altered. Tools that enable data to be easily reused by third parties and recontextualized in novel ways undermine the notion of 'context', for example the norms, values and beliefs of groups within online social settings (see earlier section), as a heuristic for developing ethical practices that are socially and culturally appropriate. Gleibs (2014: 359) argues that in the context of big data researchers move away from a legal contract that demarcates private/public space and instead the right to use data becomes a complex psychological contract that needs to take into account perceptions and expectations about individuals' control over the flow of information that relates to them. Reuse and the emergent practice of data profiling by third parties reduces choice for both researcher and research participant in terms of how data is represented and how it travels through media and across actors. The researcher, therefore, may no longer be able to foresee all of the consequences and potential harm of their research, which has implications for 'informed consent' where it is deemed appropriate in large-scale studies. Gleibs (2014) discusses various mechanisms for technically implementing informed consent in the context of social media data and argues that through such technical mechanisms social media users should be 'reminded of the use of data for research and that data created on SNS can be mixed with other sources for new discoveries' (p. 366).

Furthermore, as noted earlier, the vast quantities of social science data being generated by the Internet are of significant commercial value (Schroeder, 2014b), with social media data being an important area of economic growth based on privileged access to data that provides insight into consumer behaviour (Puschmann and Burgess, 2014). Consequently, social science data generated and used by academic researchers may travel beyond the professional boundaries of the social science disciplines and into the private sector, whose practices in relation to ethical considerations may be governed by legal juris-diction, rather than ethical codes of practice. Indeed, the business models and development goals of social media providers and commercial third parties differ, with commercial third parties wanting access to vast quantities of real-time data that enable them to model and predict user behaviour on an unprecedented scale (Puschmann and Burgess, 2014).

There is a school of thought in the application of novel technologies to social science that is on the side of pushing the boundaries until there is a legal intervention. For example, placing responsibility for privacy onto end-users to be aware of and understand the Terms of Service for the social media site. This can be problematic given that in many cases the technology and its capability for triangulating and reprocessing data is so novel that often legal intervention is lagging behind. Therefore, practice is often pushing the boundaries of ethical frameworks and legal interventions, and the analysis of social media data on a real-time or 'near real-time' basis, in particular, is likely to push these boundaries. As Thelwall and Stuart (2006) point out, some techniques are inherently illegal in their mechanisms. For example, web crawling is illegal because crawlers make permanent copies of copyrighted material without the owner's permission.

The rise in the use of big data for academic research thus raises the question of the extent to which Internet researchers should be concerned with the collection and use of potentially harmful data, given that we cannot anticipate all the ways in which it might be reused and by whom. In terms of research excellence, social scientists have always been encouraged to consider only collecting sufficient data to satisfy the immediate objectives of their research, but with the Internet the capabilities for collecting and storing data are so vast that the practicality or desirability of maintaining such practices in the context of new technologies, methods and techniques are brought into question. As illustrated in the earlier case study of Facebook, the opposite

can also happen whereby data generated in the private sector can become available in the public domain and be used as a resource for academic research. Earlier high-profile examples of this were the public release of the Enron and AOL email databases on the Internet. The Enron database was released in the interests of transparency and accountability as part of a legal investigation, but it was not sufficiently anonymized and was retracted after two weeks (see Eynon *et al.* 2008).

CONCLUSION

One of the key challenges in guiding ethical decision making in Internet-based research is in its global reach and the necessity to respect and incorporate diverse cultural practices, ethical governance and legal frameworks. What is different about Internet-based research in contrast to research in the offline world is that the research object is no longer clearly delineated by national boundaries and protected by national research governance. The emergence of novel methods across disciplines also brings an interdisciplinary focus to bear on the Internet as an object of study and challenges existing instruments of research governance that have traditionally been focused along disciplinary dimensions.

At the same time, the online world affords new modes of human interaction and related ethical practices are shaped by the researchers' objectification of those being researched, for example whether individuals participating in an online chatroom are perceived as research subject, research participant, artist (Bruckman, 2002) or author (Bassett and O'Riordan, 2002). There is also a potential convergence between research and commercial data on the Internet and a blurring of boundaries in crowdsourcing and wider public engagement initiatives that lead to questions over who is the researcher and who is researched. Development of aggregator tools and services have led to the informatization of data, whereby data acquires additional value beyond the immediate research context. Consequently, the potential for third-party reuse is much greater than in the offline world. Data sharing and reuse are institutional imperatives with many funding bodies now mandating the submission of datasets to data archives and repositories upon the completion of funding. This entails the development of practices and techniques to anonymize highly sensitive data, with some data being easier to anonymize than others (Markham, 2012; Saunders *et al.*, 2015).

The context of social interactions in online worlds is also important to bear in mind. If we take the position that traces of interaction on the Internet are public and should be treated as such, for example participants have no rights to privacy considerations, how do we address the issue that online bodies and forms of expression have offline instantiations? To what extent do we need to protect these from harm? As tools for tracing social structures become more sophisticated, so too do our capabilities for triangulating data and getting a more holistic view of participants lives. Whereas participants may choose to draw a boundary between their online and offline worlds, and may in fact be online in order to escape the strictures of the offline world, the technologies currently being developed do not necessarily respect such boundaries. The question for us as social scientists is to what lengths we should go to discover people's intentions. This, of course, means that we must disclose ourselves as researchers, which could alter the kind of results we were hoping to obtain. In the context of digital research, participants may be, but are not necessarily, already in the Internet domain. We cannot therefore simply assume that they have *chosen* to be online or what their intentions are in being there. Again this raises the question of whether 'public in everyday life' is equivalent to 'public on the Internet'. All the while, the 'human subjects' research model remains in place and, as Bassett and O'Riordan (2002) have argued,

what is required now is the trying and testing of different models of research governance.

The issues that we have raised in this chapter go beyond responsibilities towards a particular set of research participants and have implications for social, political and ethical aspects of social science research. A significant proportion of the world will not be represented in online research and researchers need to ask whether this is ethical. Certain groups are likely to be under-represented and are therefore less likely to gain benefits from participating. Such an emphasis on the interests of the information-rich may reinforce existing societal divisions (Mann, 2003; Eynon *et al.*, 2009). Researchers have an ethical responsibility to ensure that the research they carry out is of high quality and that conclusions drawn from it can be inferred from the data collected (Pittenger, 2003). Finally, one obvious strategy to adopt under conditions with yet-to-emerge norms that have been sketched here is to be explicit about the ethical decisions that are made in order that others can learn from and debate the issues that arise when reporting findings.

NOTES

1. Acquiring informed consent for participation in research by children is subject to legal frameworks and regulations that differ from country to country. See, for example, Wiles *et al.* (2005) for a discussion of the UK context.
2. An interesting example of how images can be searched using the service Google Images is provided by Henderson *et al.* (2013).
3. Definition of personally identifiable information according to EU/US data protection legislation.

REFERENCES

Anderson, G. (1998) *Fundamentals of Educational Research*. 2nd edn. London: Falmer Press.

Angrosino, M. and Rosenberg, J. (2011) 'Observations on observation: continuities and challenges'. In N.K. Denzin and Y.S. Lincoln (eds.), *The SAGE Handbook of Qualitative Research*. 4th edn. London: Sage Publications. pp. 467–78.

Bailenson, J. and Schroeder, R. (2008) 'Research uses of multi-user virtual environments'. In R. Lee, N. Fielding and G. Blank (eds.), *The SAGE Handbook of Online Research*. London: Sage Publications, pp. 327–42.

Basset, E. and O'Riordan, K. (2002) 'Ethics of Internet research: contesting the human subjects research model', *Ethics and Information Technology*, 4 (3): 233–47.

Bier, M., Sherblom, S. and Gallo, M. (1996) 'Ethical issues in a study of Internet use: uncertainty, responsibility, and the spirit of research relationships', *Ethics and Behavior*, 6 (2): 141–51.

Boellstorff, T., Nardi, B., Pearce, C. and Taylor, T.L. (2012) *Ethnography and Virtual Worlds: A Handbook of Method*. Princeton, NJ: Princeton University Press.

Bruckman, A. (2002) 'Studying the amateur artist: a perspective on disguising data collected in human subjects research on the Internet', *Ethics and Information Technology*, 4 (3): 217–31.

Buchanan, E. and Ess, C. (2009) 'Internet research ethics and the Institutional Review Board: current practices and issues', *Computers and Society*, 39 (3): 43–9.

Carmack, H. J. and Degroot, J. M. (2014) 'Exploiting loss? Ethical considerations, boundaries, and opportunities for the study of death and grief online', *OMEGA – Journal of Death and Dying*, 68 (4): 315–35.

Chee, F. M., Taylor, N. T. and de Castell, S. (2012) 'Re-mediating research ethics: end-user license agreements in online games', *Bulletin of Science, Technology & Society*, 32 (6): 497–506.

Ess, C. (2002) 'Introduction to Special Issue on Internet research ethics', *Ethics and Information Technology*, 4 (3): 177–88.

Ess, C. (2006) 'Ethics and the use of the Internet in social science research'. In A. Joinson, K. McKenna, T. Postmes and U.-D. Reips (eds.), *Oxford Handbook of Internet Psychology*. New York, NY: Oxford University Press. pp. 487–503.

Ess, C. (2013) *Digital Media Ethics*. Cambridge: Polity Press.

Eynon, R., Fry, J. and Schroeder, R. (2008) 'The ethics of internet research'. In R. Lee, N. Fielding and G. Blank (eds.), *The SAGE Handbook of Online Research*. London: Sage Publications, pp. 23–41.

Eynon, R., Schroeder, R. and Fry, J. (2009) 'New techniques in online research: challenges for research ethics', *Twenty-First Century Society*, 4 (2): 187–99.

Fox, J., Murray, C. and Warm, A. (2003) 'Conducting research using Web-based questionnaires: practical, methodological, and ethical considerations', *International Journal of Social Research Methodology*, 6 (2): 167–80.

Frankel, M. and Siang, S. (1999) 'Ethical and legal aspects of human subjects research on the Internet'. Available at: http://www.aaas.org/sites/default/files/migrate/uploads/report2.pdf (accessed 1 June 2016).

Fry, J. (2006) 'Google's privacy responsibilities at home and abroad', *Journal of Librarianship and Information Science*, 38 (3): 135–9.

Gleibs, I. H. (2014) 'Turning virtual public spaces into laboratories: thoughts on conducting online field studies using social network sites', *Analyses of Social Issues and Public Policy*, 14 (1): 352–70.

Goffman, E. (1959) *The Presentation of Self in Everyday Life*. New York, NY: Doubleday.

Grasmuck, S., Martin, J. and Zhao, S. (2009) 'Ethno-racial identity displays on Facebook', *Journal of Computer-Mediated Communication*, 15: 158–88.

Greenleaf, G. (2013) 'Data protection in a globalised network'. In I. Brown (ed.), *Research Handbook on Governance of the Internet*. Cheltenham, UK: Edward Elgar, pp. 221–59.

Guardian (2014a) 'Facebook apologises for psychological experiments on users'. 2 July. Available at: http://www.theguardian.com/technology/2014/jul/02/facebook-apologises-psychological-experiments-on-users (accessed 15 June 2016).

Guardian (2014b) 'Facebook reveals news feed experiment to control emotions'. 29 June. Available at: http://www.theguardian.com/technology/2014/jun/29/facebook-users-emotions-news-feeds (accessed 15 June 2016).

Henderson, M., Johnson, N., and Auld, G. (2013) 'Silences of ethical practice: dilemmas for researchers using social media', *Educational Research and Evaluation: An International*

Journal on Theory and Practice, 19 (6): 546–60.

Hewson, C., Yule, P., Laurent, D. and Vogel, C. (2003) *Internet Research Methods: A Practical Guide for the Social and Behavioural Sciences*. London: Sage Publications.

Hookway, N. (2008) 'Entering the blogosphere: some strategies for using blogs in social research', *Qualitative Research*, 8 (1): 91–113.

Horst, H. and Miller, D. (2012) *Digital Anthropology*. London: Berg.

Hudson-Smith, A. (2002) '30 days in active-worlds – community, design and terrorism in a virtual world'. In R. Schroeder (ed.), *The Social Life of Avatars: Presence and Interaction in Shared Virtual Environments*. London: Springer. pp. 77–89.

Janssens, A. C. J. and Kraft, P. (2012) 'Research conducted using data obtained through online communities: ethical implications of methodological limitations', *PLoS Medicine*, 9 (10): e1001328.

Kitchin, R. (2013) 'Big data and human geography', *Dialogues in Human Geography*, 3 (3): 262–7.

Kramer A., Guillory J. and Hancock J. (2014) 'Experimental evidence of massive-scale emotional contagion through social networks', *Proceedings of the National Academy of Sciences*, 111 (24): 8788–90.

Kraut, R., Olson, J., Banaji, M., Bruckman, A., Cohen, J. and Couper, M. (2004) 'Psychological research online: report of the Board of Scientific Affairs' Advisory Group on the Conduct of Research on the Internet', *American Psychologist*, (59) 2: 105–17.

Lange, P. (2008) 'Publicly private and privately public: social networking on YouTube', *Journal of Computer-Mediate Communication*, 13: 361–80.

Lehavot, K., Ben-Zeev, D. and Neville, R. E. (2012) 'Ethical considerations and social media: a case of suicidal postings on Facebook', *Journal of Dual Diagnosis*, 8 (4): 341–6.

Levy, R. I. and Hollan, D. W. (1998) 'Person-centered interviewing and observation'. In H. R. Bernard (ed.), *Handbook of Methods in Cultural Anthropology*. Walnut Creek, CA: AltaMira, pp. 333–64.

Lewis, K., Kaufman, J., Gonzalez, M., Wimmer, A. and Christakis, N. (2008) 'Tastes, ties, and time: A new social network dataset using Facebook.com', *Social Networks*, 30(4): 330–42.

Lunnay, B., Borlagdan, J., McNaughton, D. and Ward, P. (2015) 'Ethical use of social media to facilitate qualitative research', *Qualitative Health Research*, 25 (1): 99–109.

Mann, C. (2003) 'Generating data online: ethical concerns and challenges for the C21 researcher'. In M. Thorseth (ed.), *Applied Ethics in Internet Research*. Trondheim, Norway: NTNU Publications Series No. 1, pp. 31–49.

Mann, C. and Stewart, F. (2000) *Internet Communication and Qualitative Research: A Handbook for Researching Online*. London: Sage Publications.

Markham, A. (2012) 'Fabrication as ethical practice: qualitative inquiry in ambiguous internet contexts', *Information, Communication and Society*, 5 (3): 334–53.

Markham, A. and Buchanan, E. (2012) 'Ethical decision-making and internet research. Recommendations from the AoIR Ethics Working Committee (Version 2.0)'. Available at: http://aoir.org/reports/ethics2.pdf (accessed 15 June 2016).

McKee, H. A. and Porter, J. E. (2009) *The Ethics of Internet Research: A Historical, Case-Based Process*. New York, NY: Peter Lang.

Meho, L. (2006) 'E-mail interviewing in qualitative research: a methodological discussion', *Journal of the American Society for Information Science and Technology*, 57 (10): 1284–95.

Meyer, M. (2014) 'Misjudgements will drive social trials underground', *Nature*, 511 (7509): 265.

Miller, T. (2013) 'Messy ethics: negotiating the terrain between ethics approval and ethical practice'. In J. McClancy and A. Fuentes (eds.), *Ethics in the Field: Contemporary Challenges*. Oxford: Berghahn.

Nakada, M. and Tamura, T. (2005) 'Japanese conceptions of privacy: an intercultural perspective', *Ethics and Information Technology*, 7 (1): 27–36.

Narayanan, A. and Shmatikov, V. (2009) 'De-anonymizing social networks', *IEEE Symposium on Security & Privacy*. Oakland, CA. Available at: http://www.cs.utexas.edu/~shmat/shmat_oak09.pdf (accessed 15 June 2016).

Nissenbaum, H. (1998) 'Protecting privacy in an information age: the problem of privacy in public', *Law and Philosophy*, 17: 559–96.

Nosek, B., Banaji, M. and Greenwald, A. (2002) 'E-research: ethics, security, design and control in psychological research on the Internet', *Journal of Social Issues*, 58 (1): 161–76.

Oboler, A., Welsh, K. and Cruz, L. (2012) 'The danger of big data: social media as computational social science', *First Monday*, 17 (7).

O'Connor, D. (2013) 'The apomediated world: regulating research when social media has changed research', *The Journal of Law, Medicine & Ethics*, 41 (2): 470–83.

Oldenburg, R. (1989) *The Great Good Place*. New York, NY: Marlowe and Co.

Penumarthy, S. and Börner, K. (2006) 'Analysis and visualization of social diffusion patterns in three-dimensional virtual worlds'. In R. Schroeder and A.-S. Axelsson (eds.), *Avatars at Work and Play: Collaboration and Interaction in Shared Virtual Environments*. Netherlands: Springer, pp. 39–61.

Pittenger, D. (2003) 'Internet research: an opportunity to revisit classic ethical problems in behavioural research', *Ethics and Behavior*, 13 (1): 45–60.

Puschmann, C. and Burgess, J. (2014) 'The politics of Twitter data'. In K. Weller, A. Bruns, J. Burgess, M. Mahrt and C. Puschmann (eds.), *Twitter and Society*. New York, NY: Peter Lang, pp. 43–54.

Rees, T. (1991) 'Ethical issues'. In G. Allan and C. Skinner (eds.), *Handbook for Research Students in the Social Sciences*. New York, NY: Falmer Press, pp. 140–52.

Reidenberg, J. R. (2000) 'Resolving conflicting international data privacy rules in cyberspace', *Stanford Law Review*, 52 (5): 1315–71.

Roberts, L. D. (2015) 'Ethical issues in conducting qualitative research in online communities', *Qualitative Research in Psychology*, 12 (3): 314–25.

Rosenberg, A. (2010) 'Virtual world research ethics and the private/public distinction', *International Journal of Internet Research Ethics*, 3 (12): 23–37.

Rule, J. (2007) *Privacy in Peril: How We Are Sacrificing a Fundamental Right in Exchange for Security and Convenience*. New York, NY: Oxford University Press.

Saunders, B., Kitzinger, J. and Kitzinger, C. (2015) 'Participant anonymity in the Internet age: from theory to practice', *Qualitative Research in Psychology*, 12 (2): 125–37.

Schroeder, R. (2014a) 'Big data: towards a more scientific social science and humanities?'. In M. Graham and W. H. Dutton (eds.), *Society and the Internet*. Oxford: Oxford University Press, pp. 164–76.

Schroeder, R. (2014b) 'Big data and the brave new world of social media research', *Big Data and Society*, July–December: 1–11.

Schroeder, R. and Axelsson, A.S. (eds.) (2006) *Avatars at Work and Play: Collaboration and Interaction in Shared Virtual Environments*. Netherland: Springer Science & Business Media.

Schroeder, R. and Taylor, L. (2015) 'Big data and Wikipedia research: social science knowledge across disciplinary divides', *Information, Communication and Society*, http://dx.doi.org/10.1080/1369118X.2015.1008538

Schroeder, R., Lee, R. M. and Heather, N. (1998) 'The sacred and the virtual: religion in multi-user virtual reality', *Journal of Computer-Mediated Communication*, 4 (2).

Schultze, U. (2014) 'Performing embodied identity in virtual worlds', *European Journal of Information Systems*, 23(1): 84–95.

Schultze, S. and Mason R. O. (2012) 'Studying cyborgs: re-examining Internet studies as human subjects research', *Journal of Information Technology*, 27: 301–12. doi:10.1057/jit.2012.30.

Silverstone, R., Hirsch, E. and Morley, D. (1992) 'Information and communication technologies and the moral economy of the household'. In R. Silverstone and E. Hirsch (eds.), *Consuming Technologies: Media and Information in Domestic Spaces*. London: Routledge, pp. 15–31.

Sin, C. (2005) 'Seeking informed consent: reflections on research practice', *Sociology*, 39 (2): 277–94.

Slater, M., Antley, A., Davison, A., Swapp, D., Guger, C., Barker, C., Pistrang, N. and Sanchez-Vives, M.V. (2006) 'A virtual reprise of the Stanley Milgram obedience experiments', *PLoS ONE*, 1 (1): e39. doi:10.1371/journal.pone.0000039.

Stern, S. (2003) 'Encountering distressing information in online research: a consideration of legal and ethical responsibilities', *New Media and Society*, 5 (2): 249–66.

Sveningsson-Elm, M. (2009) 'How do various notions of privacy influence decision making in qualitative internet research'. In A. Markham and N. Baym (eds.), *Internet Inquiry: Conversation about Method*. Thousand Oaks, CA: Sage Publications, pp. 69–87.

Thelwall, M. (2011) 'Privacy and gender in the social web'. In S. Trepte and L. Reinecke (eds.), *Privacy Online*. Berlin: Springer-Verlag, pp. 251–65.

Thelwall, M. and Stuart, D. (2006) 'Web crawling ethics revisited: cost, privacy and denial of service', *Journal of the American Society for Information Science and Technology*, 57 (13): 1771–9.

Thelwall, T., Sud, P. and Vis, F. (2012) 'Commenting on YouTube videos: from Guatemalan Rock to El Big Bang', *Journal of the American Society for Information Science and Technology*, 63 (3): 616–29.

Tilley, L. and Woodthorpe, K. (2011) 'Is it the end for anonymity as we know it? A critical examination of the ethical principle of anonymity in the context of 21st century demands on the qualitative researcher', *Qualitative Research*, 11(2): 197–212.

Varnhagen, C., Gushta, M., Daniels, J., Peters, T., Parmar, N., Law, D., Hirsch, R., Takach, B. and Johnson, T. (2005) 'How informed is online consent?', *Ethics and Behavior*, (15) 1: 37–48.

Walther, J. (2002) 'Research ethics in Internet-enabled research: human subjects issues and methodological myopia', *Ethics and Information Technology*, 4 (3): 205–16.

Westin, A. (1967) *Privacy and Freedom*. New York, NY: Atheneum.

Wiles, R., Heath, S., Crow, G. and Charles, V. (2005) 'Informed consent in social research: a literature review. NCRM Methods Review Papers NCRM/001'. Available at: http://eprints.ncrm.ac.uk/85/1/MethodsReviewPaperNCRM-001.pdf (accessed 15 June 2016).

Zimmer, M. (2010) '"But the data is already public": on the ethics of research in Facebook', *Ethics and Information Technology*, 12 (4): 313–25.

Data Quality in Online Environments

Karsten Boye Rasmussen

INTRODUCTION

Huge amounts of data are generated on the Internet or online. Furthermore, the term 'to collect data' has become much more appropriate in online environments as a plenitude of data are now available for collection without the traditional research sequence of stimulus–response through use of nonreactive sources including websites, emails, blogs, Internet web logs, commercial transaction data and behaviour on social media. Use of applications on the Internet directly generates data, the Internet acts as the preferred medium for research data collection including new experimental data, and finally all kinds of data have become searchable and then findable and accessible online. This chapter demonstrates how the online environment has improved the data quality – especially the dimension of documentality (metadata) – and also how the researcher must act with caution and not be overconfident simply because data are available and created online.

DATA AND COLLECTIONS OF DATA

Attention to the area of data quality propagated in the 1990s. A business fashion statement was: 'If you cannot measure it, you cannot manage it'. Considerable work on quality of measurement and quality of data arose from the MIT Total Data Quality Management Program (http://web.mit.edu/tdqm/) and further research in the area of data quality is generally based on that work.

The singular datum obtains meaning in its connection to other data. The attribute value of '42' becomes consequential when related to the attribute description (documentation, data on data, metadata) containing data in the form of the word 'age'. With metadata the '42' value becomes a description of a specific entity (a person). In connection with other attributes describing the person, such as data on housing, education or opinions, a record or row of data is constituted in a data table where records with a similar structure describe other persons. We can obtain knowledge because the collection of records (rows) with attributes as columns constitutes a 'flat file' that offers us the potential to analyse, compare and conclude, for example through comparison of whether people in their forties have characteristics among the recorded attributes that differ from other age-groups. When data on entities on different levels are needed (e.g. person, family, neighbourhood) the simple structure of the flat file is suboptimal for storage and maintenance and a more complex database structure including the relationships between entities is required.

This illustrates common definitions of the terms 'data', 'information' and 'knowledge'. Data are thought of as 'facts' and information as 'meaningful facts', as in Drucker's (1988: 46) definition of information as 'data endowed with relevance and purpose'. In spite of the hierarchical concepts where knowledge is defined as information that through accumulation and structuring becomes 'larger, longer living structures of meaningful facts' (Checkland and Holwell, 1997: 90) we often use the terms interchangeably (Huang et al., 1999: 13; Pipino et al., 2002: 212; Wang, 1998: 58; Ge and Helfert, 2013: 77). Maintaining rigorous distinctions between the terms is an unnatural restraint of common use and data quality is therefore considered an all-embracing term for obtaining information quality and quality in our knowledge.

Analysis, Research and Data-Driven Action

Commercial organizations ultimately act on data when they store huge and complex data collections in a 'data warehouse', described as 'a subject-oriented, integrated, non-volatile, and time variant collection of data in support of management's decisions' (Inmon, 1996: 33). Scientific research builds upon earlier research, but scientific research is also considered to be for the public good through dissemination to society. A parallel dissemination of knowledge takes place in the organization,

but commercialization leads to more instrumental 'truths' answering questions like: 'What are the characteristics of our most profitable customers?' Decisions following the answer can be so fully modelled in algorithms that machines are 'data-driven'. Data has then become 'machine-actionable'. Obtaining the highest quality of the data becomes crucial.

APPROACHES TO DATA QUALITY

Approaches to data quality (Wang and Strong, 1996: 20) can be categorized into: (1) the intuitive approach based on exemplifying data problems; (2) the empirical and inductive survey approach; and (3) the theoretical or ontological and deductive approach. These approaches will now be examined.

The Intuitive Approach to Data Quality

Intuitive approaches to data quality are often focused on showing the prevalence of the problem. PricewaterhouseCoopers (PwC) concluded 'that 75 percent of 599 companies surveyed experienced financial pain from defective data' (Computerworld.com, December 17, 2001, accessed: July 27, 2016). Time is money and more than 80 per cent of employees at companies have experienced lack of data quality that cost them more time consumption, while 50 per cent mentioned lower reputation as a consequence (Rasmussen, 2010: 65). Books on the subject exemplify this with listings of corporate disasters due to low data quality (English, 1999: 7–10; Huang et al., 1999: 2) as well as governmental disasters like *Challenger* and USS *Vincennes* (Ge and Helfert, 2013: 76). Second, error rates in data fields are published as 'about 1–5 percent' (Redman, 1998), which demonstrates data quality figures far from the Six Sigma goal of '3.4 defects per million' (http://www.isixsigma.com/dictionary/sigma-level/, accessed: July 27, 2016). Third, often a metric of the financial loss is presented and Redman (1998) estimated relative loss at 8–12 per cent of revenue. Case studies also bear evidence like 'about 14 percent of the potential taxes due are not collected' (Watson *et al.*, 2002: 496). A survey among employees of larger Danish companies identified such reasons for poor data quality as 'external data' and 'data migration', the top-scoring reason being 'data entry in the company' (Rasmussen, 2010: 60).

Although definitively understandable, the intuitive approach lacks theoretical rigor and methodological information explaining how the dimensions and their definitions of data quality (as illustrated in Table 3.1) emerge from the somewhat unsystematic and sporadic description of single data cases (English, 1999: 141–54; Fox *et al.*, 1994: 13–17).

The dimensions certainly make sense 'intuitively' and even more when negated: a less correct value cannot be considered an improvement, data out-of-date cannot be preferred to more current data, having more missing data and missing observations and thus greater uncertainty cannot enhance our analysis. In business, consistency is what managers desire, with a 'single version of the truth' (Dyché and Levy, 2006), but on the other hand, some degree of redundancy is desirable to perform comparisons of values that were thought to be identical and thus to evaluate and improve the data quality.

Prescriptive Data Quality – Best Practice

Often GIGO – 'garbage in, garbage out' – is cited as if it was a truism (Levitin and

Redman, 1998; Berg and Heagele, 1997). The idea dates back to Babbage (Lidwell *et al.*, 2010: 112) and implies the focus should be on input improvement. However, acquiring higher data quality has costs. Developments towards a formula for optimal allocation of resources have been presented (Ballou and Tayi, 1989, 1999) and approaches to cost and value (cost/benefit) of data quality are summarized and structurally presented in a framework by Ge and Helfert (2013). Costs might be too high: 'there may be no commercial market for this level of performance' (D'Angelo and Troy, 2000: 43) and 'the data acquisition costs exceeded the total decision reward' (Trull, 1966: 276). High data quality is not an ultimate and fixed goal but a result of a balance between the costs and the resulting rewards. In social science research, optimal data quality is an even more difficult concept because on the one hand the data of scientific endeavours are prescribed to accomplish the highest possible quality and on the other hand inadequate financing forces researchers to be very creative to obtain a data quality that presents a satisficing 'good enough'.

The Empirical Approach to Data Quality

The empirical approach moves the focus from the data to the users' experience of data. Wang and Strong (1996) performed a user study of data quality in replication of a much-cited study by DeLone and McLean (1992) on information systems success with the subtitle 'The Quest for the Dependent Variable'. Wang and Strong surveyed users'

Table 3.1 Data quality dimensions and measurement definitions

Accuracy	The fraction of data close to the considered correct value
Currentness	The fraction of data not out-of-date
Completeness	The fraction of data that has values for all attributes of all entities supposed to have values
Consistency	The fraction of data that satisfies all constraints

Source: Adapted from Fox *et al.* (1994).

Table 3.2 Data quality dimensions in the hierarchical conceptual framework

Data quality			
Intrinsic data quality – Accuracy of data	Contextual data quality – Relevancy of data	Representational data quality – Representation of data	Accessibility data quality – Accessibility of data
Believability Accuracy Objectivity Reputation	Value-added Relevancy Timeliness Completeness Appropriate amount of data	Interpretability Ease of understanding Representational consistency Concise representation	Accessibility Access security

Source: Adapted from Wang and Strong (1996: 20).

assessment of the importance of a multitude of data quality attributes discovered in a first-stage survey. Reduction of the numerous quality descriptors from twenty to fifteen dimensions, which were placed within the central categories shown in Table 3.2.

Accessibility has now joined the collection of dimensions. Users need access to the data. The quote 'If only HP knew what HP knows' is often used as an example of the huge amounts of important tacit knowledge buried in the individuals of a large organization like Hewlett-Packard. But even externalized information and great accumulations of data can exist without being of any use if users are unable to access them.

The Theoretical Foundation of Data Quality

The intuitive approach suffers from unsystematic methods and the perils of subjective bias through the investigators' personal idiosyncrasies. However, the empirical approach runs a similar risk by aggregating extracted subjectivities of generally found misconceptions, biases and prejudices among data users. A systematic theoretical approach where distinctions within data quality are derived from theoretical assumptions improves the coverage of the problem area of data quality. Such an ontological approach is demonstrated in an article on design of information systems in order to deliver high quality data (Wand and Wang, 1996).

Wand and Wang view the information system (IS) as a representation of the real-world system (RW). The approach has parallels: 'quality of data representation and recording' (Fox *et al.*, 1994: 13), 'conceptual view' (Levitin and Redman, 1995), 'system' approach (Huang *et al.*, 1999: 34) and in the semantic part of the semiotic approach by Price and Shanks (2004). The basic understanding in these approaches is that 'the world is made of things that possess properties' (Wand and Wang, 1996: 89). It is fair to add that many of these 'things', like humans and their relations, are not 'things'. The information system is a representation of the real world: 'observing the state of the information system … enables the inference of a state of the real world system'(Wand and Wang, 1996: 90). Mistakes happen, and the mapping between information systems states and the states of the real world reveals three categories of data quality deficiencies – incompleteness, ambiguity and meaninglessness – as shown in Table 3.3.

In principle, all information systems must be 'incomplete' because not all states in the real world can have a representation in the information system. The missing n:n multiplicity can be regarded as a special case of 'ambiguity'. The 'meaningless' category can also be viewed as arising when data exists, but the metadata linking it to the real world has been lost. Without appropriate metadata the data become worthless.

My critique of the ontological approach is concerned with the absolute nature of the categories. The practical requirement of data

Table 3.3   Representational mapping of the states of the Real World (RW) and the Information System (IS)

Representation outcome	Multiplicity RW:IS	Explanation
Proper	1:1 1:n	Proper representation exists when a state from the information system can be mapped to a single state in the real world. If 1:n is accepted then redundancy (superfluous states) is allowed in the information system.
Incomplete	1:0	Incomplete representation occurs when a state in the real world does not have a representation in the information system. The mapping is not exhaustive, the information is missing.
Ambiguous	n:1	Ambiguous representation occurs when a single state in the information system is covering more than one state in the real world. This situation precludes the proper inverse mapping from the system to the real world.
Meaningless	0:1	Meaningless representation occurs when a state in the information system cannot be mapped to any state in the real world system. The data exists without connection to the real world.

Source: Adapted from Wand and Wang (1996: 90).

quality calls for a measurement with more nuances than the abrupt distinction between 'perfect' and 'not perfect' because less than perfect might be an acceptable data quality. Likewise, 'incompleteness' will normally be regarded as being measured by degree, and accuracy or precision are also usually a question of percentage or number of decimals rather than a dichotomy. I find that the theoretical approach that was supposed to counteract the pragmatic view ends up ignoring pragmatism and becomes of little practical use.

A more comprehensive theoretical approach to the categorization of data quality is the application of semiotics found in Price and Shanks (2004). The authors stringently start with definitions of key concepts, which in semiotics include 'sign', but here also include 'data' and 'metadata'. The three levels of semiotics are used to form similar relationships in assignment of quality: (1) syntactic quality is how well data corresponds to stored metadata, which can be exemplified by data conformance to contingencies of the database; (2) semantic quality is how the stored data corresponds to the represented external phenomena – the data carries meaning; (3) pragmatic quality is how data are suitable and worthwhile for a given use. The semiotic

approach thus demonstrates how a theoretical approach can include pragmatics.

Data Quality as 'Fitness for use'

The pragmatic 'proof of the pudding' for data quality is the use of the data, referred to as 'fitness for use' (Bruckner and Schiefer, 2000; Wang and Strong, 1996) for the 'data consumer' (Strong *et al.*, 1997: 104). 'Fitness for use' is a rephrasing of the concept of pragmatic information quality (English, 1999: 151). However, even though the concept of 'fitness for use' has strengths as a departure point for further investigation, it does not present any directions for how to measure the fitness or how to decide that some data are unfit. 'Fitness for use' is a truism like 'All the news that's fit to print' from the byline of the *New York Times*. If the news was printed, the news was fit – otherwise not!

The concept of 'fitness for use' implies subjectivity. In the semiotic framework of Price and Shanks (2004), the authors investigate the degree of objectivity ranging from the syntactic 'completely objective' to the pragmatic 'completely subjective'. The semiotic framework thus points out the subjectivity embedded in the pragmatism of data quality. This subjectivity leads to relativity as demonstrated in the quote: 'The single most significant source of error in data analysis is misapplication of data that would be reasonably accurate in the right context' (Loebl, 1990, cited in Levitin and Redman, 1998: 94). The citations draw attention to the context of data use and the relativity moves our attention from the data to the importance of the capabilities of users of the data in evaluating data quality.

Comparison of values forms the basis of measuring the quality of data. The compared values do not have to have an equal existence. Fürber and Hepp (2013: 144) therefore declare the quality of data to be 'determined by the comparison of data's current state (status quo) to its desired state'. They furthermore develop the data requirements in RDF (Resource Description Framework) and foresee the Semantic Web's potential to form a basis of evaluation of data quality. The 'desired state' combined with strong subjectivity is also found in Redman's (2005: 32) procedure for measurement of accuracy where experts are relied upon to inspect data and mark 'each attribute that is obviously erred'.

Taking data 'fitness for use' to the extreme we might ask: do data not possess any quality if not used? In the commercial surroundings the process of building the data warehouse will often have an inclination toward urgency and immediate use, but the developers also build a platform for unforeseen creative uses of the data because an inflexible system would present extreme maintenance costs when satisfying new demands. The 'for use' could be 'for future use'. Many applications draw upon the same data and these applications are utilized by many different users (Tayi and Ballou, 1998). A key design question is the concept and realization of granularity. Data collected on a weekly level on the time-dimension can be aggregated to month and year, but the change to a smaller granularity is impossible. A parallel argument applies to data archives. Research and the

safekeeping of human history, however, has a timescale for possible use stretching towards infinity. We simply cannot know what will be valuable research data in the future.

Although 'fitness for use' can be experienced as being too compliant, subjective, practical and pragmatic for use in science, we have to accept that it is difficult to gain acceptance and to deduct practical implications to data quality concepts from other more rigid foundational approaches. Fundamentally, this is illustrated by the ISO 9000 standards for quality management and quality assurance that define quality as fitness in the form of 'degree to which a set of inherent characteristics of an object fulfils requirements' (ISO 9000, 2015: section 3.6.2).

ONLINE CREATION, METADATA AND DOCUMENTALITY, AND THE NOVEL ONLINE DATA

The following sections will move through three significant impacts of the Internet on data quality. First, it examines how traditional types of data have evolved in the new online environment. Second, it demonstrates that the availability of data online has propelled the evolution of metadata to exciting promises for the future. Finally, new special types of data are created in the online environment. New types of data can be analysed in their own right but they can also be a welcome enhancement when mixed with traditional types of data for a more comprehensive production of knowledge.

TRADITIONAL PRIMARY DATA CREATED ONLINE

With the Internet, a new medium for data collection has transformed social science research concerning traditional data. Besides the self-administered postal paper questionnaire or the interviewer-based survey carried out face-to-face or by telephone, we now also have Internet surveys in the form of web and email questionnaires (Dillman *et al.*, 2014; see also Part IV, this volume).

Web Surveys

It took many years before the diffusion of telephone ownership reached saturation, which finally made the telephone medium suitable for random selection of respondents. Likewise, earlier web surveys faced sampling problems because of the populations' uneven access to the Internet, as well as unevenness in regard to the technical abilities of the respondents' bandwidth, computing power and software (updated web browsers). Internet accessibility has in some countries quickly reached maturity making the medium attractive; however, telephone ownership in some places has now become an unreliable medium for selection because some people might have several phones, non-registered mobile phones, landlines are becoming sparse and national area codes have become relocatable.

Web surveys have additional attractive features. The online questionnaire can rely on extensive software for support to allow more complicated answering structures where software will enforce consistency because skip patterns are simply invisible to the respondents when they are exclusively prompted for answers to the individually relevant questions. Experiments using different sequencing of questions are also more easily carried out in web surveys as well as online paradata enhancing data of the web survey.

Email Surveys: Coverage, Sampling and the Right Respondent

Surveys previously distributed as postal mail can now be distributed by email. Compared to ordinary mail, some similar items such as

introduction, instructions and link to the web questionnaires are more easily contained in the email. Email surveys exist in several forms (see Dillman *et al.*, this volume).

When use and access to the Internet is unevenly distributed, coverage problems are entailed when the sample is reduced to email owners while the researcher had the full population in mind. History repeats itself. Again coverage problems cannot be overcome by securing a large number of respondents because the Internet has not made sampling theory redundant. Self-selection is a general problem in Internet-based research (Ruths and Pfeffer, 2014). Non-compliance must be expected to create a systematic bias. The insistence that respondents are selected with a known and often equal probability is the cornerstone of generalization in statistical inference from the sample to the population. Furthermore, without controls an email questionnaire or a link to a web questionnaire can be forwarded to others, creating sampling errors and the novel problem of exceeding the 100 per cent answer rate! Ensuring that only selected email respondents respond – and only respond once – can be secured by links including identification of the recipient or a log-in procedure.

The Success and Hazards of Internet Surveys

Among the advantages of Internet and email surveys is the quicker turnaround than the traditional postal or face-to-face questionnaire. Large amounts of questionnaires can be completed in a single day (Dillman *et al.*, 2014: 303) thus raising data quality by securing timely data. It is also important that web surveys have a lower cost.

With the Internet and supportive software for web surveys, conducting surveys has become easier and many more surveys are taking place. The survey method can, to some extent, be seen as a victim of its own success. By being approached too often, many respondents become more reluctant to participate.

Online data collection includes the perils of research being judged by the respondents as individual surveillance and this is accentuated when including new types of online data. It must be expected that individuals most sensitive to possible identification will refrain from participation in online research and thus create data quality imperfection by lack of completeness. A web questionnaire with open access implies some anonymity; however, this generates data quality shortcomings in completeness because the researcher cannot control the sample selection.

DATA ACCUMULATIONS AND DOCUMENTALITY

Primary data are collected for a specific investigation while secondary data are reused by other than the primary investigators. Data are being shared and this also requires sharing the knowledge of the creation of the dataset. Experience from data archives all over the world shows that primary investigators have human memories (Carmichael, this volume; Corti and Wathan, this volume). Thus a documentation process including the externalization of tacit knowledge becomes necessary for the successful reuse of data.

The use of data is possible only with the metadata description of the data. As earlier exemplified the stored data value '42' is in itself meaningless. Only by applying the description does it achieve meaning as an age value belonging to a record containing attributes describing an individual. The metadata, including a complete description of the investigation, selection, survey plan and data collection process is necessary for evaluating validity, reliability, accuracy, precision, bias, representativeness, etc. Honesty goes a long way and the primary investigator's reflections about, and problems with, the data are part of the documentation. No exact metric is

available, but nevertheless documentality is thought of as being measurable. In the Wang and Strong model (Table 3.2) this is the area of 'Representational data quality'. However, I find metadata so significant a contributor to the quality of data that a special name for the dimension – 'documentality' – is appropriate. As 'documentum' in Latin stands for 'pattern' and 'model', a dataset having a high documentality is not only useful, but it also incorporates a design that other studies can build upon. My argumentation for documentality as the primary dimension of data quality does not degrade other dimensions. They are truly all dimensions because, for example, high documentality cannot compensate for low completeness or low accuracy.

Naturally, just as with earlier types of data, data collected online can be turned from primary data into secondary data when made available to other users. Suitable data might exist in repositories, but without documentation they will remain hidden to the potential user. Readily available data without the high-level documentation will stay useless. The Internet raises the possibility of identification of data through searching of metadata, as well as the possibility of having much more expedient use and direct data access through unassisted and swift download or online analysis of data.

Huge collections of secondary research data are available online from data archives all over the world. Especially for science data it is important that the complete documentation is what makes critique of the scientific procedures and methods possible, and critique adds value to the dataset (Blank and Rasmussen, 2004). High documentality was recognized as crucial by research data archives early on; with good metadata primary data collections could and would be reused by other researchers, agencies and students. As research data collection is expensive it also makes economic sense to exploit the primary effort further. The recognition was systematically set into action in the Data Documentation Initiative for developing a common metadata standard (Blank and Rasmussen, 2004; Rasmussen and Blank, 2007). The continuing development of the Initiative has reached substantial heights and is now readying data for the Semantic Web (Wackerow and Vardigan, 2015). High documentality will indeed make possible the meaningful retrieval of research results from a vast number of datasets situated at many different physical locations.

NEW TYPES OF DATA COLLECTED ONLINE

The Internet has made possible some completely new types of direct recording of actual behaviour. These new types of data and their potential for research will be discussed in the following sections. The online world is a powerful creator of data types as well as a creator of tremendous amounts of data (see Baram-Tsabari *et al.*, this volume). The bigger data require more powerful computers and more storage capacity (Varian, 2014) and software packages compete in fast access and processing.

Nonreactive Data

One of the most intriguing features of the online world is the existence of complete and timely non-sampled data in the form of electronic traces of human online behaviour. This brings us a richness of data that can be accessed and acquired at little cost. As respondents' reflections upon behaviour, attitudes and beliefs are not directly observable, we normally attempt to gain insight through a stimulus–response sequence; however, with behaviour leaving electronic traces, these data are nonreactive and unobtrusive (see Janetzko, this volume).

Although the concept of research use of unobtrusive data is not new (Webb et al., 1966) the online world now creates a wealth

of data as humans are performing deliberate statements, choices, and design. This chapter's sections present the data quality issues of nonreactive data available in online phenomena like email, web logs, blogs, social media and websites.

Investigation of emails

Instead of sending out a questionnaire to the membership of an Internet mailing list, a non-reactive approach is analysis of the actual communicative behaviour taking place on the mailing list (Rasmussen and de Vries, 2005). The structural fields of emails, such as sender, date and subject (see Social Network Analysis (SNA) section, Hogan, this volume) carry a high accuracy. A 'thread' is formed by the starting mail and the following responses. Completeness might seem high because all communication can be analysed; however, completeness is low if the researchers' intention is to infer the results to the complete membership of the mailing list because passive members are excluded from the sample.

Web Log Analysis

The similar dilemma of data quality is faced when analysing website 'hits'. The accuracy is high concerning the webpage and the exact time the user browsed the website, but the knowledge of the user is limited because additional user information is only available for registered users and seldom extends beyond name and address. Additional user information can be obtained through website pop-up questionnaires but these data must be expected to be highly biased because of self-selection.

Separate sessions from the same user cannot be interlinked on the basis of the IP address, as these often are dynamically assigned (varying between sessions). In order to analyse returning users, more technology has to be applied, typically in the form of accepted cookies or through user log-in to the website.

Business decisions are to a large extent evidence-based and data-driven. On a commercial website the 'click-stream analysis' can determine whether non-buyers move in other patterns than those of buyers, and it is easy for the website constructors to carry out experiments like a random assignment of one of two pictures to a webpage and then quickly – data will have high currentness – conclude which picture triggers the most sales. Experimentation in commercial surroundings might look like research but the data are not necessarily sufficient to explain why users chose a picture as more preferred.

Commercial use of tracking can also be obtained by logging specific embedded elements in the webpage code. Logging can also involve running JavaScript in the user's browser as in Google Analytics. Furthermore, the user's browser can run special applications tracking the user across the various websites visited. Legally this can be applied where individuals have joined an opinion panel accepting tracking of their behaviour (e.g. installation of the Alexa toolbar by Amazon.com).

Paradata

Couper (2005: 493) introduced the concept of paradata in 1998 as an extension of metadata, where paradata are defined as data about the process (of data collection), and an edited book on paradata was published in 2013 (Kreuter, 2013). Attempts to contact, refusal conversion and time spent by the interviewer will, in a non-web questionnaire, belong to paradata.

In research the process of answering a web survey can be monitored in a web log at the server side. It is also possible to carry out data collection at the client side (Heerwegh, 2003). With local running JavaScript on the client machine, additional local data on the process of answering the web questionnaire

can be obtained. The level can move from the questionnaire to the page to the single question – it is even possible to track the doing and undoing of choices in different types of answering mechanisms (drop-down lists, radio-buttons, click-items, give value, etc.) (Heerwegh and Loosveldt, 2002). Paradata including 'click-through-behaviour' have been used to identify data quality problems (Stieger and Reips, 2010: 1492).

Blog Analysis

A 'blog' – an abbreviation of 'weblog' – is not to be confused with the 'web log' of server actions. The phenomenon started as a single author's statements presented on a dedicated website but has developed to multi-authored blogs. The most recent blog entry is shown at the top and the activity of entering a new one is covered by the verb 'to blog'. There is a strong connection to mailing lists because connected blog entries and collections of emails on a mailing list concerning a subject can be analysed for both structural information and content; another similarity is to synchronize communication in chatroom facilities (see Abrams with Gaiser, this volume). The research quality of blogs must be considered as anecdotal for public opinion measurement because blogs are highly incomplete due to a skewed population of bloggers (see Hookway and Snee, this volume).

Twitter and the Network of the Social Network

Twitter is micro-blogging, using up to 140 characters and having further structural components in the form of subject identification by #hashtag, user addressing by the @-prefix and retweet features. Twitter has been used for network analysis with colourful network graphics (Bruns, 2012). Retweets and content have also been researched, for example Denef *et al.* (2013) identified different

Twitter practices comparing two police forces during the UK riots in 2011. It is interesting that Twitter data on the same riots form the basis of an evaluation of Twitter as a breaking news tool for journalists (Vis, 2013).

Data from social networks like Twitter, Facebook, Snapchat, etc. can be expected to continue to form the basis of much analysis as virtual space is now an essential part of human life. However, researchers have to contemplate that a large portion of people – including people who have quite adequate capabilities concerning information technology – choose not to display their opinions and behaviour on social media. Incompleteness becomes a data quality problem if researchers carelessly define their target population.

The public tweets of Twitter are considered worth archiving parallel to depositing newspapers in pre-digital age. It was announced that all Twitter data would become available through the Library of Congress in the US; however, the archive is not yet available despite a 2010 announcement (Zimmer, 2015). Researchers are pushing but the magnitude (170 billion historical tweets) and the continuous growth was perhaps not considered.

New Online Experiment Data: Amazon Mechanical Turk

Social science experiments have often been based on college students, a fact which in itself presents a bias. Furthermore, many practicalities and logistics are involved in having persons physically attending experiment labs on the university campus, thus attending certain places at certain times. When Amazon introduced the crowdsourcing website named Mechanical Turk (mturc. com) this presented a new method for research experiments. The Mechanical Turk is essentially a panel survey mechanism where participants receive compensation for carrying out human intelligence tasks (HIT) defined by the employer (researcher). The chess

automaton called Mechanical Turk had a hidden human inside the machine; similarly, humans are necessary for the Amazon Mechanical Turk. The tasks as well as the compensations can be quite small. It is the easy access and the accumulation that makes sense to both the worker and the researcher. When investigating whether Mechanical Turk could provide high-quality data a group of researchers concluded that data were 'at least as reliable as those obtained via traditional methods' (Buhrmester *et al.*, 2011). Furthermore, the samples were more diverse than the typical American college samples and obtaining data was less expensive and speedier. Mechanical Turk workers must agree that their employers can attach ratings to their performance, thus building the worker's reputation. Later research has concluded that selection of Mechanical Turk workers with high reputation can ensure high-quality data (Peer *et al.*, 2014). Symmetrically, workers can rate employers. If a worker attempts to optimize earnings by very quickly clicking through a questionnaire – or perhaps having this task being performed by some automaton – the employer might have included check questions to control for attention and human intelligence involvement. An example of this is the attention check question: 'While watching the television, have you ever had a fatal heart attack?' (Paolacci *et al.*, 2010). Selecting only the workers giving the correct answer 'never' will raise the data quality. The high data quality, the improved economy and the possibility of obtaining fast results lead to the conclusion that better experiment research data can be obtained through the use of Amazon Mechanical Turk.

Improvements of Qualitative Data

Increasing amounts of new text data imply that not only quantitative methods should be applied. Exhaustive research on text in emails, blogs, chats, tweets, etc. can add in-depth analysis to quantifications. For example, traditionally it has demanded months of painstaking work to tag text for research, but powerful and intelligent software tools and text mining in commercial packages (Chakraborty *et al.*, 2013) can improve the quality of the unstructured data through more complete and consistent tagging.

Following the Electronic Traces

The customer-oriented company analyses the relationships with its customers by noticing, remembering, learning and finally acting towards the customers (Berry and Linoff, 2004: 3). The customer leaves electronic traces of their behaviour and the company performs aggregation and categorization handling large data volumes. When a customer 'churns' to another company, attention is required. If data patterns show that current customers display similar shifting behaviour (e.g. emptying their bank account), the company in time can react towards these customers (provided they are profitable). The company can also direct the collected information on customers towards other customers, as in 'collaborative filtering'. The Internet (book)shop Amazon perfected this by profiling customers and finding 'nearest neighbours' in basing recommendations upon the chosen item, as in 'customers who shopped for this item also shopped for these items:…'.

These commercial examples have research parallels with suitable adaptation of the commercial methods. In a public social science research project, the 'churn' can be an individual movement from a status of 'welfare recipient' to a status of 'job ready'. Registration in information systems means that all types of behaviour activities leave electronic traces, including consultations with social workers and pursuing relevant job courses. Likewise, the health sector can be viewed as interactions, treatments, and moves to another individual status (e.g. the movements between 'born', 'hospitalized','out-of-hospital', 'dead'). Because of the eagerness to improve and the great costs involved in the health sector, treatments are meticulously registered and ought to be accessible for research.

Open Data

Open data is a new concept and a public movement. OpenDataFoundation.org describes itself as 'a non-profit organization dedicated to the adoption of global metadata standards and the development of open-source solutions promoting the use of statistical data. We focus on improving data and metadata accessibility and overall quality…'. The approach to liberation of data and making public data freely accessible and useful also exists in national endeavours like the Danish website opendata.dk, where the larger cities of Denmark have established a central repository of governmental and planning data. For example, the data on placement of public pumps for bicycles in Odense is available. Such a small dataset of a very narrow subject matter can be regarded as unimportant but these example data can be combined with many other data sources that could be brought together into a bicycle app driven by the public data. The government is required to keep track of many endeavours and opening the data for use will benefit by making the government more transparent (Janssen *et al.*, 2012). Furthermore, as app builders and app users demand current and accurate data, they will report breaches of data quality, thus leading to a further improvement of public data quality that will also benefit research.

Collections of Websites and Website Data

Research on Internet websites is often considered as being as free as a walk in the park. However, research might violate 'terms of service' of websites by performing high-scale automated and repeated access that can drain a website of resources (Allen *et al.*, 2006), as exemplified through research meticulously collecting data on the bids for all items on eBay.

Limitation of access to data has also seriously damaged the possibility of performing webometric research that earlier was supported through APIs (application programming interface) of the most popular search engines of Google and Yahoo! (Thelwall and Sud, 2012). The data on how websites refer users to other websites through links, such as data on prior searches, are very valuable to a search company and therefore protected against use by competitors – and researchers. It is equally natural that researchers desire to include these data to grasp contemporary social life.

Incessant updating of websites and digital applications in general makes data ephemeral and challenges data quality relating to accuracy and consistency. The currentness might simply prove to be too high as research will have difficulty in accessing anything but the present. The Internet Archive seeks to prevent our fall into 'the digital dark ages' and supports open and free access under the slogan 'Universal Access to Knowledge'. The Internet Archive houses among its collections The Wayback Machine that stores the enormous amount of 498 billion web pages (mid-2016). The Wayback Machine makes 'web time travel' and web history possible as websites are continuously harvested. The Wayback Machine is a supplier for research and a positive literature review of The Wayback Machine research (Arora *et al.*, 2015) was itself based upon an Internet resource, namely Google Scholar.

The Danish 'netarkivet.dk' recently celebrated its tenth anniversary while another Nordic archive, the Swedish 'Kulturarw3', is nearly as old as the Internet Archive (1997 and 1996, respectively). Brügger (2011) showed that the Danish archive performs three different strategies of archiving: (1) snapshot approach (web crawling harvesting with a defined frequency); (2) event-based

(a collection of websites related to a specific election) and (3) selective (often including very frequent harvesting of central websites). The strategies are pursued in the hope of being able to deliver data fulfilling future demands.

Nonreactive research using collections of emails, blogs, social media, etc. has an ethics dimension. When access to information is gained through administrators' approval, there is no direct informed consent from the individuals. Consequently, researchers need to take great care as breaches to reveal information at the individual level can prove disastrous to future research.

Mixed Modes and Mixed Methods

Multimethod research covers the use in the same investigation of more than one method (Witte, 2004). Each of the different modes of doing surveys with questionnaires (postal, with interviewer, face-to-face, telephone, web-mode) have their pros and cons. Sometimes a mode-specific design taking full advantage of the mode (Dillman *et al.*, this volume) might be recommended.

Mixing with data collection methods other than the questionnaire is often desirable. Questionnaire data can be combined with information available from the nonreactive data available on the Internet. As an example, the low response rate obtained through a company questionnaire was investigated through micro-archiving and evaluation of the websites of these companies. The responding and nonresponding companies were found not to show any significant difference in regards to their functional website quality (Rasmussen and Thimm, 2015).

CONCLUSION

This chapter has demonstrated that data quality is not a straightforward, one-dimensional concept. The Internet is a medium available for conducting higher-quality data research through data from web surveys, emails, blogs, social media and online experimentation. The online medium results in an overall high syntactic quality (consistency) as errors are more easily caught 'on the fly' – in real time (also high currentness) – by systematic software involved in the process of data collection. The high documentality of online data also improves our possibilities of getting the right data and getting the data right through searches on metadata and identifying relevant data materials. Furthermore, we benefit from the Internet in the ability to obtain nonreactive data relating directly to the actual behaviour of research subjects, thus improving accuracy.

The online world is an overwhelming resource of data of higher quality. We can now envision how more comprehensive research is to be obtained by combining traces on the Internet of actual behaviour and mixing these data with qualitative, in-depth investigations to reveal connections between behaviour, attitudes and beliefs.

REFERENCES

Allen, Gove N., Burk, Dan L. and Davis, Gordon B. (2006) 'Academic data collection in electronic environments: defining acceptable use of internet resources', *MIS Quarterly*, 30 (3): 599–610.

Arora, Sanjay K., Li, Yin, Youtie, Jan and Shapira, Philip (2015) 'Using the Wayback Machine to mine websites in the social sciences: a methodological resource', *Journal of the Association for Information Science and Technology* (online 5 May 2015).

Ballou, Donald P. and Tayi, Giri Kumar (1989) 'Methodology for allocating resources for data quality enhancement', *Communications of the ACM*, 32 (3): 320–329.

Ballou, Donald P. and Tayi, Giri Kumar (1999) 'Enhancing data quality in data warehouse environments', *Communications of the ACM*, 42 (1): 73–78.

Berg, Dennis and Heagele, Christopher (1997) 'Improving data quality: a management perspective and model'. In Barquin, Ramon C. and Edelstein, Herbert, A. (eds.), *Building, Using, and Managing the Data Warehouse*. Upper Saddle River, NJ: Prentice Hall, pp. 85–99.

Berry, Michael J.A. and Linoff, Gordon S. (2004) *Data Mining Techniques: For Marketing, Sales, and Customer Relationship Management*. 2nd edn. Hoboken, NJ: John Wiley & Sons.

Blank, Grant and Rasmussen, Karsten B. (2004) 'The data documentation initiative. The value and significance of a worldwide standard', *Social Science Computer Review*, 22 (3): 307–318.

Bruckner, Robert M. and Schiefer, Josef (2000) 'Using portfolio theory for automatically processing information about data quality in data warehouse environments', *Advances in Information Systems, Proceedings,* 1909: 34–43.

Brügger, Niels (2011) 'Web archiving – between past, present, and future'. In Consalvo, Mia and Ess, Charles (eds.), *The Handbook of Internet Studies*. New York, NY: Wiley, chapter 2.

Bruns, Axel (2012) 'How long is a Tweet? Mapping dynamic conversation networks on Twitter using Gawk and Gephi', *Information, Communication & Society*, January 2012: 1–29.

Buhrmester, Michael, Kwang, Tracy and Gosling, Samuel D. (2011) 'Amazon's Mechanical Turk: a new source of inexpensive yet high-quality data?', *Perspectives on Psychological Science*, 6 (1): 3–5 (+ 5 p. online supplement).

Chakraborty, Goutam, Pagolu, Murali and Garla, Satish (2013) *Text Mining and Analysis: Practical Methods, Examples, and Case Studies Using SAS*. Cary, NC: SAS Institute.

Checkland, Peter and Holwell, Sue (1997) *Information, Systems and Information Systems – Making Sense of the Field*. Chichester, UK: John Wiley & Sons.

Couper, Mick P. (2005) 'Technology trends in survey data collection', *Social Science Computer Review*, 23 (4): 486–501.

D'Angelo, John and Troy, Bob (2000) 'Integrated data management improves return on investment', *Oil and Gas Journal*, July 31: 40–44.

DeLone, William H. and McLean, Ephraim R. (1992) 'Information systems success: the quest for the dependent variable', *Information Systems Research*, 3 (1): 60–95.

Denef, Sebastian, Bayerl, Petra S. and Kaptein, Nico (2013) 'Social Media and the Police: Tweeting Practices of British Police Forces during the August 2011 Riots', *Proceedings of the SIGCHI Conference on Human Factors in Computing Systems*, ACM, New York.

Dillman, Don A., Smyth, Jolene D. and Christian, Leah Melani (2014) *Internet, Phone, Mail, and Mixed-Mode Surveys. The Tailored Design Method*. 4th edn. Hoboken, NJ: John Wiley & Sons.

Drucker, Peter F. (1988) 'The coming of the new organization', *Harvard Business Review*, January-February 1988: 45–53.

Dyché, Jill and Levy, Evan (2006) *Customer Data Integration: Reaching a Single Version of the Truth*. Wiley and SAS Business Series. Hoboken, NJ: John Wiley & Sons.

English, Larry P. (1999) *Improving Data Warehouse and Business Information Quality: Methods for Reducing Costs and Increasing Profits*. Hoboken, NJ: John Wiley and Sons.

Fox, Christoper, Levitin, Anany V. and Redman, Thomas C. (1994) 'The notion of data and its quality dimension', *Information Processing and Management*, 30 (1): 9–19.

Fürber, Christian and Hepp, Martin (2013) 'Using semantic web technologies for data quality management'. In Sadiq, Shazia (ed.), *Handbook of Data Quality*. Berlin: Springer-Verlag, pp. 141–161.

Ge, Mouzhi and Helfert, Markus (2013) 'Cost and value management for data quality'. In Sadiq, Shazia (ed.), *Handbook of Data Quality*. Berlin: Springer-Verlag, pp. 75–92.

Heerwegh, Dirk (2003) 'Explaining response latencies and changing answers using client-side paradata from a web survey', *Social Science Computer Review*, 21 (3): 360–373.

Heerwegh, Dirk and Loosveldt, Geert (2002) 'An evaluation of the effect of response formats on data quality in web surveys', *Social Science Computer Review*, 20 (4): 471–484.

Huang, Kuan-Tsae, Lee, Yang W. and Wang, Richard Y. (1999) *Quality Information and Knowledge*. Upper Saddle River, NJ: Prentice Hall.

Inmon, William H. (1996) *Building the Data Warehouse*. 2nd edn. New York, NY: John Wiley & Sons.

ISO 9000 (2015) https://www.iso.org/obp/ui/#iso:std:iso:9000:ed-4:v1:en (accessed: July 27, 2016).

Janssen, Marijn, Charalabidis, Yannis and Zuiderwijk, Anneke (2012) 'Benefits, adoption barriers and myths of open data and open government', *Information Systems Management*, 29 (4): 258–268.

Kreuter, Frauke (ed.) (2013) *Improving Surveys with Paradata: Analytic Uses of Process Information*. Hoboken, NJ: John Wiley & Sons.

Levitin, Anany V. and Redman, Thomas C. (1995) 'Quality dimensions of a conceptual view', *Information Processing and Management*, 31 (1): 81–88.

Levitin, Anany V. and Redman, Thomas C. (1998) 'Data as a resource: properties, implications, and prescriptions', *Sloan Management Review*, 40 (1) Fall: 89–101.

Lidwell, William, Holden, Kristina and Butler, Jill (2010) *Universal Principles of Design, Revised and Updated: 125 Ways to Enhance Usability, Influence Perception, Increase Appeal, Make Better Design Decisions, and Teach through Design*. 2nd edn. Beverly, MA: Rockport Publishers.

Loebl, Andrew S. (1990) 'Accuracy and relevance and the quality of data'. In Lippins, Gunar E. and Uppuluri, V.R.R. (eds) *Data Quality Control: Theory and Pragmatics*. New York, NY: Marcel Dekker, pp.105–144.

Paolacci, Gabriele, Chandler, Jesse and Ipeirotis, Panagiotis G. (2010) 'Running experiments on Amazon Mechanical Turk', *Judgment and Decision Making*, 5 (5), 411–419.

Peer, Eyal, Vosgerau, Joachim and Acquisti, Alessandro (2014) 'Reputation as a sufficient condition for data quality on Amazon Mechanical Turk', *Behavior Research Methods*, 46 (4): 1023–1031.

Pipino, Leo L., Lee, Yang W. and Wang, Richard Y. (2002) 'Data quality assessment', *Communications of the ACM*, 45 (4): 211–218.

Price, Rosanne J. and Shanks, Graeme G. (2004) 'A semiotic information quality framework'. 'Decision support in an uncertain and complex world', Prato, Italy, 1–3 July 2004, IFIP

TC8/WG8.3 International Conference, pp. 658–672.

Rasmussen, Karsten B. (2010) 'Datakvalitet i virksomheden' (Data quality in the company), *Ledelse & Erhvervsøkonomi*, 2010 (1): 55–68.

Rasmussen, Karsten B. and Blank, Grant (2007) 'The data documentation initiative: a preservation standard for research', *Archival Science*, 7 (1): 55–71.

Rasmussen, Karsten B. and de Vries, Repke (2005) 'Growing virtuality in a professional association: a data-driven approach'. HCI conference 2005, Las Vegas, Nevada, 22–27 July, 5 p.

Rasmussen, Karsten B. and Thimm, Heiko (2015) 'Circumventing nonresponse – upgrading traditional company survey data with unobtrusive data from company websites', *Bulletin of Sociological Methodology/ Bulletin de Methodologie Sociologique*, 127 (1): 85–96.

Redman, Thomas C. (1998) 'The impact of poor data quality on the typical enterprise', *Communications of the ACM*, 41 (2): 79–82.

Redman, Thomas C. (2005) 'Measuring data accuracy: a framework and review'. In Wang, Richard Y., Pierce, Elizabeth M., Madnick, Stuart E. and Fisher, Craig W. (eds.), *Information Quality*. New York, NY: Routledge, pp. 21–36.

Ruths, Derek and Pfeffer, Jürgen (2014) 'Social media for large studies of behaviour', *Science*, 346 (6213): 1063–1064.

Stieger, Stefan and Reips, Ulf-Dietrich (2010) 'What are participants doing while filling in an online questionnaire: a paradata collection tool and an empirical study', *Computers in Human Behaviour*, 26 (6): 1488–1495.

Strong, Diane M., Lee, Yang W. and Wang, Richard Y. (1997) 'Data quality in context', *Communications of the ACM*, 40 (5): 103–110.

Tayi, Giri K. and Ballou, Donald P. (1998) 'Examining data quality', *Communications of the ACM*, 41 (2): 54–57.

Thelwall, Mike and Sud, Pardeep (2012) 'Webometric research with the Bing Search API 2.0', *Journal of Informetrics*, 6 (1): 44–52.

Trull, Samuel G. (1966) 'Some factors involved in determining total decision success', *Management Science Series B, Managerial*, 12 (6): B270–80.

Varian, Hal R. (2014) 'Big Data: new tricks for econometrics', *Journal of Economic Perspectives*, 28 (2): 3–27.

Vis, Farida (2013) 'Twitter as a reporting tool for breaking news. Journalists tweeting the 2011 riots', *Digital Journalism*, 1 (1): 27–47.

Wackerow, Joachim and Vardigan, Mary (guest eds.) (2015) 'DDI and Semantic Web', *IASSIST Quarterly (special issue)*, 38 (4)–39 (1).

Wand, Yair and Wang, Richard Y. (1996) 'Anchoring data quality dimensions in ontological foundations', *Communications of the ACM*, 39 (11): 86–95.

Wang, Richard Y. (1998) 'A product perspective on total data quality management', *Communications of the ACM*, 41 (2): 58–65.

Wang, Richard Y. and Strong, Diane M. (1996) 'Beyond accuracy: what data quality means to data consumers', *Journal of Management Information Systems*, 12 (4): 5–24.

Watson, Hugh J., Goodhue, Dale L. and Wixom, Barbara H. (2002) 'The benefits of data warehousing: why some organizations realize exceptional payoffs', *Information and Management*, 39 (6): 491–502.

Webb, Eugene J., Campbell, Donald T., Schwartz, Richard D. and Sechrest, L. (1966) *Unobtrusive Measures. Nonreactive Research in the Social Sciences*. Chicago, IL: Rand McNally & Co.

Witte, James (2004) 'The case for multimethod research: large sample design and the study of life online'. In Howard Philip N. and Jones Steve (eds.), *Society Online*. Thousand Oaks, CA: Sage Publications, pp. xv–xxxiv.

Zimmer, Michael (2015) 'The Twitter archive at the Library of Congress: challenges for information practice and information policy', *First Monday* 20 (7): 10.

## PART III

Online Data Capture and Data Collection

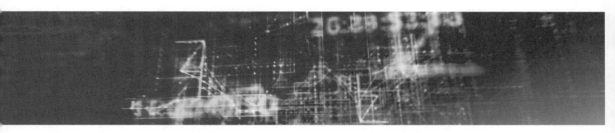

## 4

Research Design and Tools for Online Research

Claire Hewson

INTRODUCTION

This chapter provides an overview of tools and techniques for conducting Internet-based research within a framework that considers the design issues and choices which emerge. Focus is on *primary* Internet research procedures, referred to as Internet-mediated research (IMR) (Hewson *et al.*, 2003). Internet-mediated research involves the gathering of novel, original data to be subjected to analysis in order to provide new evidence in relation to a particular research question (Hewson *et al.*, 2003). From around the mid-1990s when pioneers started piloting online data-collection methods, the field of IMR has grown considerably, expanding across a diverse range of academic disciplines as more and more researchers, students and professionals have started to make use of these techniques. Certain methods have now become relatively well-established, such as the web-based survey, whilst others are

emerging and under development (such as 'data scraping' and 'big data' approaches). The emergence of software tools for assisting in the design and deployment of IMR studies has facilitated developments over the last decade or so, for example there now exists a large selection of software packages for creating and disseminating web-based surveys. Such tools, as well as ongoing developments in relevant Internet technologies, have now rendered many of the earlier programming guides (e.g. Göritz and Birnbaum, 2005; Hewson *et al.*, 2003) redundant in many IMR contexts. The current popularity of IMR methods is attested by the range of recent texts on the topic (see Further Reading), as well as the range of journal articles reporting studies that have used Internet-based data collection methods (as cited throughout this chapter). Methodological reflections and evaluations, and design and implementation guides (e.g. Reips, 2010; Hewson *et al.*, 2016) are now prevalent across a range of

Table 4.1   IMR-dedicated resources, information and meetings

Association of Internet Researchers (AoIR: aoir.org)

GESIS (www.gesis.org/en/services/study-planning/online-surveys)

General Online Research (GoR: www.gor.de)

Online Research Methods (ORM: www.restore.ac.uk/orm)

WebDataNet (http://webdatanet.cbs.dk/)

WebSurveyMethodology (WebSM: www.websm.org)

IMR methods and research contexts. There now also exists various resources and organisations which offer dedicated information on IMR methods, often available online (and, also, in a consultancy capacity), as well as regular conferences and workshops on IMR methods. See Table 4.1 for a selection of these.

Thus, there is now a wealth of information for researchers to draw upon in informing and directing IMR research design. Present focus is on design issues and solutions which emerge specifically within an IMR context (best practice guidelines for traditional offline methods are assumed here; useful guides include Bryman, 2012; Creswell, 2014).[1] Surveys and questionnaires, experiments, interviews and focus groups, observation (including recently emerging data scraping techniques) and document analysis are considered. The discussion is organised around the 'obtrusive–unobtrusive' dimension, which has been proposed as a useful way of classifying different IMR methods (Hewson *et al.*, 2016), and key ethics considerations are highlighted where relevant (a more detailed consideration of ethics issues in IMR is provided in Chapter 2, this volume).

DESIGN ISSUES AND TOOLS FOR INTERNET-MEDIATED RESEARCH

A key principle to keep in mind is that IMR studies, like any other study, require careful planning, design and piloting. However, given the widespread perception of Internet-based procedures as being able to quickly and cost-effectively generate large pools of data, and their particular appeal when time and cost constraints are high, there is a danger that researchers may be tempted to implement poorly designed studies. It is crucial for trustworthiness, reliability and validity that researchers avoid this approach, take time to properly explore the existing available guidelines and to pilot procedures as extensively as possible before gathering data within the main phase of a research study (Reips and Krantz, 2010). Of course, given the relative novelty of many IMR procedures, problems will emerge, and lessons will need to be learned. However, as already noted, some methods have now become fairly well-established and lessons learned from the earlier attempts have led to the development of more effective and well-tested solutions, techniques and procedures. This chapter considers what has been learned to date, outlining key design choices, caveats and principles of best practice. First, some advantages and disadvantages of IMR approaches are highlighted (particularly compared with offline methods), with a focus on relating these to research aims and goals, in order that the reader can gain an impression of how IMR approaches might facilitate and enhance their own research. Then, design issues relating to specific obtrusive and unobtrusive IMR methods are considered, including an overview of the most common tools and resources to draw upon to implement the most common types of IMR study.

Advantages and Disadvantages of IMR Designs

Advantages

A number of advantages of IMR have now been well-established, many early speculations about potential benefits having been confirmed, across a broad range of studies reporting these outcomes. Key advantages include cost- and time-efficiency; ready access to a potentially vast, geographically diverse participant pool; and easier access to select, specialist populations. The latter may be especially helpful for qualitative approaches, whilst large samples sizes can be especially beneficial for quantitative research designs, conferring benefits such as enhanced statistical power (Musch and Reips, 2000). Cross-cultural research may be facilitated in IMR due to the broad geographical reach. Cost and time savings may be especially beneficial in situations where resources (funding, researcher time, research assistance) are sparse (e.g. Carter-Pokras et al., 2006).

Other potential benefits of online approaches relate to the nature of the online interactional medium – in particular, that interactions can emerge which are fairly elaborate in the richness of communication exchange, but where perceived (and actual) anonymity levels, and levels of perceived privacy, can be high. This feature is not easily achieved in offline contexts. This could benefit both quantitative and qualitative designs in a variety of ways, such as reducing social desirability effects, and promoting greater candour and higher levels of self-disclosure (Joinson and Payne, 2007), reducing biases resulting from the perception of biosocial attributes (Hewson et al., 1996) and balancing out power relationships between participants in online conversational contexts (Madge and O'Connor, 2002). Research on sensitive topics may particularly benefit from reduced social desirability and enhanced candour effects (e.g. Hessler et al., 2003), although it should also be noted that there is evidence that these effects may pertain only to visually anonymous contexts (Joinson, 2001).

Finally, IMR methods expand and enhance the scope for carrying out unobtrusive observational research, compared with offline methods, due to the readily accessible traces of online activity and interaction that users leave behind (e.g. Tonkin et al., 2012). This confers benefits, including easier access to topic-specific naturalistic communication data, such as that retrieved from searchable online discussion group archives, and enhanced access to other forms of behavioural trace data, such as web page navigations, Google searches and social media friendship links.

Disadvantages

Several potential disadvantages in IMR have raised concerns amongst social and behavioural researchers, particularly in terms of how these may impact upon the reliability and validity (or 'trustworthiness') of IMR data. Key concerns have included the biased nature of the Internet User Population (IUP) and the implications of this for the generalisability of data derived from IMR studies (Schmidt, 1997); reduced levels of researcher control in IMR contexts compared with offline methods, and implications for the reliability and validity of IMR studies (Hewson et al., 2003); possible negative effects emerging from the nature of the online communication medium, such as the introduction of ambiguities, misunderstandings and superficiality into conversational exchanges (Davis et al., 2004). The latter issue is perhaps most relevant for qualitative research designs, such as in-depth interviews, whilst issues of sample bias and reduced control are likely to be more problematic for quantitative approaches. However, issues of reduced levels of researcher control may also be relevant to qualitative methods, such as online focus group interviews, which could suffer unexpected effects due to software and hardware failures, potentially causing problems for the running of a study. Despite the aforementioned concerns, a range of studies across different disciplines and research areas has now demonstrated that IMR procedures can generate valid, reliable data, comparable to that which can be achieved in offline research settings (as discussed later). This has led some researchers to argue that issues relating to sample representativeness and levels of control are not overly prohibitive for IMR (Hewson *et al.*, 2016). Reports from qualitative researchers of having obtained high quality data, for example in online interview contexts (see later examples), suggest that neither is the nature of the online communication medium overly prohibitive for IMR.

Finally, demands on the levels of technical expertise required of researchers (or IT support teams) and equipment required in order to implement IMR studies has been noted as a possible disadvantage (Hewson *et al.*, 2003). However, recent developments have alleviated this concern to some extent because there now exists a range of tools to assist in implementing IMR studies, such as online survey software packages.

Design Issues in Obtrusive Internet-Mediated Research

The main methods associated with obtrusive approaches in IMR are surveys (including questionnaires and psychometric test instruments), experiments, interviews and focus groups. In this section, tools and design considerations are outlined for these key methods. Researchers have also undertaken participant observation approaches online, particularly in the context of ethnographic research, which can be considered examples of obtrusive IMR; some examples are mentioned in the later section on observational IMR methods, alongside unobtrusive observational approaches.

Tools, Procedures and Design Considerations in Implementing Online Surveys, Experiments, Interviews and Focus Groups

Surveys

Surveys and questionnaires have been the most commonly implemented IMR methods to date. Their recent ubiquity has been

facilitated by the emergence of a range of software solutions for implementation (see Table 4.2). These solutions allow researchers to construct *web-based surveys* (which involve placing an HTML web *form* on the World Wide Web) without requiring high levels of technical computing expertise. Consequently, web-based surveys have been used across a broad range of social and behavioural research disciplines, including psychology, sociology, marketing research, political science, geography and economics. Numerous guides, resources and tools now exist to help researchers design and implement web-based surveys (see Further Reading; and resources in Tables 4.1 and 4.2).

Web-based surveys have a number of advantages over traditional pen and paper methods and alternative online survey methods, such as sending questions in the body of an email message, which nevertheless may be useful in some contexts (e.g. see Bigelsen and Schupak, 2011). First, they allow a far greater range of functions to be employed, which can serve to enhance reliability. These include features such as response completeness and format checking, answer piping, skip logic and randomisation. They can also enhance reliability by allowing tighter control over presentation parameters, compared with simple text-based email approaches (the latter may lead to questions arriving misaligned, or in an undesired presentation format). This is an important consideration in designing an IMR survey or questionnaire, given that it has long been recognised by survey researchers that a range of presentation parameters, as well as different

Table 4.2   Software tools for IMR surveys and experiments

SurveyMonkey (www.surveymonkey.com)

Qualtrics (www.qualtrics.com)

Limesurvey (limesurvey.com)

WEBEXP (www.webexp.info)

WEXTOR (http://wextor.org/wextor/en)

response formats, can affect participants' responses and lead to potential biases (and, in web-based survey approaches, it has been demonstrated that even minor variations in presentation format can influence participants' responses, e.g. Couper *et al.*, 2004). Data security is also enhanced compared with email methods, which is an important ethical consideration in most research contexts. Responding to a web-based survey is also relatively straightforward for the participant, as long as they have a web browser and an active Internet connection. Email approaches can require more effort and also allow participants to edit the content in undesirable ways (such as delete or edit questions), and this may cause unanticipated problems (see Hewson, 2003).

Deciding which of the many available software packages will be most suitable for implementing a web-based survey requires some effort and research. Reviews of these packages exist (e.g. Carter-Pokras, *et al.*, 2006; Hewson, 2012), but these can become quickly dated (new packages are emerging all the time and the features of existing ones are in a state of flux). Some websites (e.g. WebSM) offer regularly updated lists of what is currently available along with a summary of key features, which can be useful for browsing the available options initially, before narrowing down possible choices. However, researchers should also carefully check the home pages of the relevant software packages they are interested in for completely up-to-date information. Different packages will serve different goals and design requirements, as well as budget and technical expertise constraints. Two very popular packages for social science researchers are SurveyMonkey (discussed by Hewson *et al.*, 2016) and Qualtrics, both of which require a subscription fee (although SurveyMonkey also offers a limited-function free version). A freely available 'open source' option is Limesurvey. Open source software benefits from continual development via input from a community of active users (in addition to being free), but generally

demands greater levels of technical expertise to manage and use (e.g. typically requiring software to be installed and managed on the user's own server). Flexibility and robustness are both important desirable features when selecting web-based survey software (Crawford, 2002) and rigid, inflexible systems are likely to be problematic (some packages allow HTML code to be directly edited, for example, which can be particularly useful in expanding the range of presentation format options available).

The various guides on good practice in web-based survey design are invaluable, but researchers should keep in mind that trade-offs can emerge. For example, the use of cookies (small pieces of information stored on a local computer by a web server via a web browser) has been recommended for tracking participants in order to detect multiple submissions and thus enhance validity, but this practice has also been identified as problematic in relation to privacy issues in IMR (Hewson *et al.*, 2016). Such conflicts will sometimes emerge and decisions need to be made taking into account the demands, requirements and features of the particular research study, including key methodological and ethical considerations. For many survey designs, one of the available software packages will likely prove suitable for implementation. However, in some cases, bespoke systems may be necessary, for example where audio or video are incorporated, or very precise display configurations are necessary (Castro and Hyslop, 2013, offer a general programming guide). Bespoke options are more likely to be required for experimental designs, however, which are now discussed.

Experiments

Experiments on the Internet, like surveys, have typically been administered via the web and the process is very similar in that participants access a web page where the experimental materials reside and undertake the experimental procedure by remote interaction with a web server via their web browser. The key difference is that experimental designs are typically more complex and thus require the use of more sophisticated technical implementations, involving advanced programming techniques. In the early days of IMR, this meant that these methods were prohibitive for researchers who were not either accomplished programmers or had access to dedicated technical support because, unlike web-based surveys, the necessary programming skills often required to implement a web experiment design are not easy to acquire quickly. For example, features such as precise timings in stimulus displays, incorporating graphics and animations, randomly assigning participants to conditions, etc., may need to be incorporated in experimental designs and require more sophisticated programming techniques and systems to implement (see Hewson *et al.*, 2003; Schmidt, 2002). More recently, however, as with web-based surveys, a number of packages to assist in creating and disseminating web experiments have become available (see Table 4.2; Rademacher and Lippke, 2007).

As with web-based surveys, there are many reasons why web-based approaches for IMR experiments are to be preferred, mainly relating to issues of enhanced control, validity and reliability, as highlighted earlier. However, alternative approaches are possible and may, in some contexts, still be useful. Hewson (1994), for example, reports implementing an IMR experiment using email (Hewson, 2003, provides a case-study summary), by sending different experimental text-based materials to participants via their email account, after first having posted participation requests to a selection of Usenet newsgroups. However, various unanticipated problems emerged relating primarily to lack of researcher control and unanticipated participant behaviours. Although these did not crucially undermine the findings in this particular case, such factors could prove detrimental. Web experiments are to be preferred in most situations where this option is feasible. Advantages of

web-based approaches compared with traditional face to face (ftf) laboratory experiments include some of the general advantages of IMR methods, including cost- and time-efficiency, facilitation of cross-cultural research and potentially reduced social desirability effects.

The issue of reduced levels of control in IMR and the potential problems this may give rise to (compared with offline ftf approaches, in particular) is especially pertinent for experimental designs, where tight control over variables (such as display parameters, participant behaviours and so on) is crucial to ensure the validity of an experimental study. In IMR, technical issues such as different hardware and software configurations and network traffic performance can lead to unintended variations in stimulus displays. These issues, along with unanticipated and unwanted participant behaviours (e.g. multi-tasking, collaborating with others, hacking into alternative experimental conditions, etc.) could imaginably lead to an entire study being invalidated. Software packages for web-based experiments which carefully adhere to good design principles and practices for IMR can be helpful in alleviating such concerns (e.g. Reips and Krantz, 2010). It is also encouraging that a number of researchers have now demonstrated that IMR experiments can lead to high quality, valid data, comparable with that achievable offline, including designs using audio and video (e.g. Knoll *et al.*, 2011) and precise reaction time measures (e.g. Corley and Scheepers, 2002), both previously thought to be problematic for IMR studies. Experiments involving interaction between two or more users have now also been successfully carried out (e.g. Horton *et al.*, 2011), although these may often require bespoke programming solutions due to their greater technological complexity. For useful discussions of issues to consider in IMR experiment design and suggested solutions, see Reips and Krantz (2010); Reips (2010) and Hewson *et al.* (2016). A key issue concerns how to maximise levels of control, which is crucial for the internal validity of experimental designs.[2]

Finally, and similarly to web-based surveys, trade-offs can emerge in web experiment design. For example, simple low-tech implementations may be more accessible (for both participants and researcher) but are likely to suffer reliability and validity issues, whilst high-tech solutions can allow greater levels of control and functionality but place greater demands on both the researcher's levels of expertise (or available technical support) and the resources and equipment required (by both researcher and participant). This can lead to necessary trade-offs, which must be assessed, and decisions made that take into account the goals and requirements of the particular research study. A recommended strategy is to use the lowest-tech solution possible that serves the study design requirements and, where more advanced systems are required, to alert participants in advance of any less common, necessary software and hardware requirements needed to participate (Hewson *et al.*, 2016).

Interviews and Focus Groups

IMR interviews and focus groups may be carried out using either *synchronous* or *asynchronous* communication technologies. The former includes Instant Messaging (IM) and Chat software, and the latter includes email, mailing lists and discussion forums. Whilst most online interviewers have used text-based approaches (e.g. email, discussion forums), multimedia applications can also be supported (e.g. using Skype). Table 4.3 lists some useful tools and resources for supporting IMR interviews and focus groups. For a more detailed discussion of the various tools available, see Hewson *et al.* (2016). The issues involved in deciding which approach (synchronous or asynchronous, text-based or multimedia) to adopt concern the impact that these different approaches can have on the nature of the communication process and the data obtained, and how this may interact with the research study goals and aims.

Possible drawbacks of IMR interview methods, compared with traditional offline approaches, include potential ambiguities and misunderstandings which may arise in communicative exchanges due to the lack of extralinguistic cues normally available in offline interactions. This has possible implications for the quality of data derived from online interviews. Online interviewers, however, have often reported obtaining rich, detailed, reflective, high quality data (e.g. Bowker and Tuffin, 2004; McDermott and Roen, 2012). Less successful reports tend to have used synchronous approaches, which have been known to lead to playful, less elaborate and less sincere responses (e.g. Davis *et al.*, 2004). The latter could perhaps be due to the expectations of online chat-based interactions, for example as more playful (Gaiser, 1997) or the requirement that participants type in real time, allowing less time

Table 4.3   Useful resources and tools for IMR interviews, observation and document analysis

Mailing list software
LISTSERV® (www.lsoft.com/products/listserv.asp)
PhpList (www.phplist.com)
Discussion forum software
Google groups (www.groups.google.com)
Yuku (www.yuku.com)
Instant messaging software
Apple's iMessage for iPhone and iPad
WhatsApp for smart phones (www.whatsapp.com/)
ICQ ('I Seek You': www.icq.com/en)
Chat software
'mIRC' for Windows (www.mirc.com/)
Google Talk (www.google.com/talk)
Skype (www.skype.com/en/)
Blogs, social networking sites, virtual reality environments
Blogger (blogger.com)
Twitter (twitter.com)
Facebook (facebook.com)
YouTube (youtube.com)
Second Life (secondlife.com)

for reflection and relying more on familiarity and proficiency with this conversational medium (with similar demands placed on the researcher). The more relaxed timescale of asynchronous approaches can allow greater scope for reflection and checking external sources, which could help produce more reflective, reflexive, detailed and perhaps accurate responses. Nevertheless, some researchers have also reported obtaining rich, high quality data using synchronous methods (e.g. Madge and O'Connor, 2002). In these cases, careful rapport-building strategies tend to have been used (e.g. initial researcher self-disclosure), which may well be an important factor in producing high quality data. Good rapport has traditionally been considered important for obtaining rich, candid qualitative interview data (Barratt, 2012). Less successful reports often do not report such strategies and they also report poor rapport with participants (e.g. Strickland *et al.*, 2003). Adopting careful rapport-building techniques in IMR interview research is recommended to overcome potential barriers associated with the lack of proximal contact with participants (Jowett *et al.*, 2011). Another possible strategy for overcoming the possible negative effects arising from a lack of extralinguistic cues in IMR interviews is to use multimedia approaches. Hanna (2012) reports about conducting interviews using Skype but notes that technical problems interfered with the smooth running of the interviews. Whilst this approach still suffers from technical issues related to limited bandwidths, network traffic, lost connections, etc., ongoing developments in supporting technologies may well make multimedia interview approaches in IMR more viable in the future.

A possible disadvantage of asynchronous interview approaches in IMR (compared with synchronous online approaches and offline ftf approaches) is reduced continuity and flow of the communication (e.g. Bowker and Tuffin, 2004). Gaiser (2008) has pointed out the difficulty for the researcher in monitoring asynchronous focus group discussions which would require them to be available 24 hours a day because participants (perhaps broadly geographically dispersed) may be logging on and contributing at any time. This may reduce the control the researcher has over the continuity and flow of topics. In cases where ongoing close monitoring of a discussion is beneficial, synchronous approaches may thus be preferred. Synchronous approaches may also benefit from the use of emoticons (e.g. :-)) and acronyms (e.g. ROTFL, rolling on the floor laughing) which can serve as substitutes for extra-linguistic information and which tend to be more prevalent in synchronous than asynchronous communications. This might add richness to a conversation, which could be particularly useful for some research goals perhaps where the types of well-considered, reflective responses more likely to be generated by asynchronous approaches are not required. It should be noted that the level of proficiency and experience of an online conversant will affect the extent to which such 'extralinguistic' devices can be usefully employed to provide more expressive communications.

One possible advantage of both synchronous and asynchronous (text-based) IMR interviews over offline (particularly ftf) methods is the potential reduction of social desirability effects due to heightened levels of anonymity and perceived privacy, possibly leading to enhanced candour and disclosure. This could especially benefit research on sensitive and personal topics. Some researchers have reported these effects (e.g. Madge and O'Connor, 2002). As well as enhancing candour, heightened anonymity may also balance out power relationships (e.g. due to a lack of perception of biosocial characteristics). Further, empowerment may emerge from the enhanced control that participants have over how, when and where to participate, which may particularly benefit certain groups, such as the pregnant women on home bed-rest studied by Adler and Zarchin (2002) who were able to participate from home. Thus, ease of access and participation (not having to visit a physical research site) may offer benefits over traditional offline methods by enhancing participation opportunities. Asynchronous approaches may be especially beneficial in this way because they generally impose lower demands on levels of typing proficiency, dexterity and stamina.

In summary, there are clear reasons why online interviews may be preferred to offline methods; however, studies which rely crucially on the analysis of extralinguistic cues may be less suited to an IMR approach that relies on text-based communication. Cross-cultural research may particularly benefit from an IMR approach due to the facilitation of participation by geographically dispersed participants – asynchronous approaches offer most scope here because presence all together at one particular time is not required. As with other IMR methods, trade-offs will emerge. For example, features that lead to higher levels of anonymity may produce more candid responses but may also hinder relational development and establishing good rapport. It has been suggested that the features of synchronous and asynchronous online interview approaches may complement each other, and thus the two approaches may usefully be combined within the same study (Hewson, 2007). For further discussion of online interviews and the relative merits of synchronous and asynchronous approaches, see Chapter 24 of the present volume.

Sampling Procedures and Issues of Access in Obtrusive IMR Designs

IMR methods for obtrusive research typically involve sampling from the IUP. This approach offers researchers access to a broad, diverse population of potential participants with scope to acquire very large sample sizes more cost- and time-efficiently than is possible using offline methods (e.g. Reece et al., 2010) and to recruit select, hard-to-access populations, e.g. via specialist

discussion groups in ways not achievable offline (e.g. Bigelsen and Schupak, 2011). Researchers have also reported generating very large sample sizes from specialist populations (e.g. Hirshfield et al., 2010). However, concerns remain about the representativeness of data generated from Internet-accessed samples due to potential biases inherent within the IUP and the limited scope for implementing probability sampling methods online. Essentially, probability sampling from the entire IUP is not possible due to the lack of a central register of all Internet users. This issue of *representativeness* of IMR samples is most relevant to quantitative survey-based research approaches, which often require probability samples in order to make valid generalisations from sample data to a broader population (e.g. as in some marketing and social survey research). For other IMR methods, as discussed here, representative samples are arguably less crucial. For example, experimental designs make sacrifices to external validity in the service of achieving internal validity, which allows inferences regarding cause–effect relationships (Mook, 1983). Furthermore, in some areas (e.g. cognitive psychology), the processes being studied are often assumed to be relatively universal and probability sampling is therefore less necessary.[3] Qualitative approaches are typically less concerned with generalising from samples to populations than generating sample data that allows rich insights into individuals' perspectives, interpretations and constructions of meaning, and are therefore also less affected by issues relating to sample representativeness. Disciplinary differences and differing research traditions and goals will clearly influence the extent to which sampling from the IUP might be seen to pose particular problems beyond those which are already present in offline approaches.

Particularly useful in relation to the issue of the quality of data that can be generated by Internet-accessed samples are studies that have compared different online and offline sampling strategies. Such studies have reported online samples to be more diverse in various ways than traditional offline convenience samples, such as undergraduate students who are commonly used in much psychological research[4] (e.g. Gosling et al., 2004). Most importantly, a number of studies across a range of research areas and disciplines have shown that IMR studies using Internet-recruited samples, including non-probability volunteer samples, can generate high-quality, valid data comparable to that achieved offline, even in cases where broader generalisability is required (e.g. Brock et al., 2012; Stephenson and Crete, 2010). The use of probability samples in IMR has been explored (e.g. using large-scale online probability panels) with reports that these can produce data of at least equivalent quality to that achieved using offline probability samples (e.g. Heeren, 2008; Yeager et al., 2011), perhaps even conferring benefits over offline samples due to reduced social desirability effects (Chang and Krosnick, 2009). Despite these encouraging findings, for some research areas and goals ongoing problems in obtaining broadly representative probability samples online remains problematic (see Chapter 10, this volume). Still, shifting patterns of Internet access, usage and structures may change the scope for obtaining probability samples from the IUP in the future. It is also worth noting that existing offline sampling methods may themselves be impacted by socio-technological developments (e.g. random digit dialing (RDD) methods may be impacted by the shift from use of landline telephones to mobile telephones). Some strategies which can be used to obtain samples in IMR are now considered.

A common sampling approach for obtrusive IMR methods is to obtain 'true volunteer' samples by placing adverts in public spaces for potential participants to view and respond to if they wish (Hewson et al., 2016). Adverts may be placed on any of the online study clearing houses available (e.g. Online Psychology Research UK:

www.onlinepsychresearch.co.uk) or posted in newsgroups, online discussion forums and social media spaces (ethical protocols permitting, see Chapter 2, this volume). This approach can lead to very large sample sizes, cost- and time-efficiently. In contexts where obtaining broadly representative samples is not crucial, this method may be useful and has been shown to be able to lead to high quality data (see aforementioned examples). When posting to online public spaces, certain procedures are to be recommended. First, in accord with the rules of 'netiquette', permission from discussion-group moderators should always be sought prior to posting participation requests (Hewson, 2007). Selection of which discussion groups to post requests to will depend on the research question and goals. For example, some researchers (e.g. Bigelsen and Schupak, 2011) have reported successfully targeting particular discussion groups in order to obtain samples with certain characteristics. Posting to newsgroups with a large volume of 'traffic' may not be the best approach in order to generate large sample sizes because participation requests may go unnoticed amongst other postings (Buckley and Vogel, 2003). There is evidence that posting follow-up requests (Coomber, 1997) and high issue salience (Birnbaum, 2001) can be important for generating larger sample sizes in IMR.

One problem with the method just described is that it precludes measurement of the sampling frame. This is especially so when placing an advert on a web page, but also applies when posting requests to newsgroups where the readership is not known. Further, it is difficult to determine the number of potential participants who saw the participation request and thus had the opportunity to take part. This means that factors such as response rate and response bias, for example, cannot be measured. For research contexts where this information is important, such methods will therefore not be suitable. Contacting individuals directly by email (or other similar channels, such as social networking site (SNS) private messaging) may allow the closest approximation of the sampling frame and thus who had the opportunity to participate, but this practice has been more controversial in terms of whether the approach should be considered an invasion of privacy which goes against the rules of netiquette and research ethics protocols (e.g. British Psychological Society, 2013). Also, issues such as dormant email addresses make measurement of the sampling frame less than fully reliable using this approach. However, such direct contact strategies do open up possibilities for obtaining probability samples in IMR, for example using list-based approaches (see Chapter 10, this volume). Another option for obtaining probability samples in IMR is to use online probability panels, mentioned earlier. Access to such panels can be expensive, however, and the issue of 'time in sample' bias must also be considered. These panels may be useful in contexts where samples approximating those achievable using offline probability methods (e.g. RDD) are required and that the research budget allows.

Finally, another option in IMR is to sample offline and ask participants to access and complete a study online. However, this approach may undermine many of the benefits of IMR, such as easy, quick, cheap access to a geographically diverse and very large population of potential participants. The approach also still relies on participants having Internet access (which cannot be assumed) and this may impose similar restrictions on who can take part as when using Internet-based sampling procedures. Sampling offline for an IMR study may thus not confer many (if any) additional benefits to sampling online. In summary, there is no doubt that IMR researchers today have access to a massive, expansive diverse population of potential participants (Hewson *et al.*, 2016). Different sampling approaches have been outlined here, along with consideration of when they might be most useful for the various obtrusive IMR methods discussed.

Design Issues in Unobtrusive Internet-Mediated Research

Unobtrusive approaches in IMR involve observation (which can also be carried out obtrusively, see later) and document analysis. This section considers design issues related to these approaches and the tools and resources that can support them. The distinction between observation and document analysis techniques in IMR can become blurred, but a useful working definition classifies observational approaches as those which study online behaviours and interactions, either as traces or in real time, whilst document analysis involves accessing and analysing static published documents and media placed on the Internet, often as a final authored product (Hewson *et al.*, 2016). Blurred boundaries can emerge due to the idiosyncratic nature of the technologies and services supported by the Internet. For example, blogs may appear as relatively static published documents (which may receive regular, or less regular, updates), as more interactive, fluid, discussion and comment spaces, or as something in between (see Herring *et al.*, 2005, for further discussion). Some IMR studies using blogs are considered here as examples of document analysis.

Tools, Procedures and Design Considerations in Implementing Unobtrusive Observation and Document Analysis

Observation

The scope for carrying out observational IMR is expansive given the wealth of traces of interactions and behaviours online (facilitated by developments including 'Web 2.0' and the 'Internet of Things'). Such approaches can be divided into those that make use of contentful information, such as text-based conversational exchanges (e.g. harvested from discussion group archives), and those that gather information about the structures and processes of online interactions and behaviours (e.g. friendship networks on SNS). Here, examples are offered that represent some of the main approaches possible in observational IMR and some key design choices are highlighted.

Observation of linguistic content online is possible using some of the same tools and technologies discussed in relation to interview approaches, including mailing lists, discussion forums and online chat software. Stored archives of online (in most cases, asynchronous) discussions are abundant and easily accessible and searchable (see Hewson *et al.*, 2016 for some guidance on how to do this). This can enable non-participant, non-disclosed (for one thing, contacting all contributors to disclose research intentions is likely to be impracticable), cost- and time-effective unobtrusive observation of topic-specific content. Such logs of naturalistic conversational exchanges are not readily available in offline settings, conferring an advantage of IMR approaches (Hewson *et al.*, 2016). Alternatively, researchers may access and follow discussions as they unfold in real time (in asynchronous and synchronous contexts), which opens up possibilities for participant observation approaches. The same considerations raised in relation to online interview approaches regarding the types of communications that can emerge from asynchronous versus synchronous discussions are also relevant here.

As well as deciding whether to use participant or non-participant observation approaches, researchers need to decide whether to disclose (or not) their research intentions and how these choices will interact (e.g. non-disclosure in synchronous chatroom settings may be more difficult, although it has been reported to be successful in some cases, e.g. Al-Sa'Di and Hamdan, 2005). As with offline research, issues related to ecological validity are relevant in deciding whether to disclose the research and/or participate when carrying out an observational study. For a discussion of 'virtual ethnography' methods in IMR, which generally use

disclosed participant approaches in which the researcher becomes immersed in an online community, see Chapter 23, this volume. Researchers have also used non-disclosed, non-participant (e.g. Tackett-Gibson, 2008) and participant (e.g. Brotsky and Giles, 2007) approaches, but these remain highly controversial due to issues and debates about individuals' privacy rights online (and the blurred nature of the public–private domain distinction online; see Hewson, 2015). This issue is compounded in non-disclosed participant approaches because these will also involve an element of deception. Factors to take into account in making appropriate design choices include likely individual privacy expectations; the sensitivity of the topic and material; and the potential for causing harm either by confidentiality breaches or disrupting existing social structures (British Psychological Society, 2013). In relation to the latter, a noteworthy example is reported by Tackett-Gibson (2008) who intended to disclose intentions to observe an online group but was blocked from doing so (being allowed, rather, to lurk and observe unobtrusively) by moderators who felt disclosure may harm the group. Contacting moderators is generally good practice and can be useful in helping inform design decisions. Other researchers have felt that disclosure was appropriate in participant observation contexts due to respecting the privacy rights of group members (e.g. Fox *et al.*, 2005).

Observations which move beyond purely linguistic interactions are also possible in IMR using resources such as SNSs and Virtual Reality Environments (VREs; see Bainbridge, 2007; and also Table 4.3). Such approaches offer scope for obtaining richer data than is possible with linguistic observation approaches (e.g. incorporating extra-linguistic information, such as multimedia sources and spatial navigations within a virtual environment) and, for example, allow more controlled observations to be carried out (e.g. using experimental designs). IMR researchers implementing observational research methods (unobtrusively) have made use of media sharing sites, such as YouTube (e.g. Yoo and Kim, 2012), and SNSs, such as Facebook (e.g. Moreno *et al.*, 2011). If using synchronous multimedia technologies, such as VREs, conducting an observational study unobtrusively may be more difficult (as with linguistic synchronous technologies). As well as using existing sites, it is possible to set up a bespoke environment created specifically for the purposes of a research study and this strategy may be especially useful in implementing experimental designs (obtrusively, e.g. Givaty *et al.*, 1998). The latter strategy may also be beneficial where high levels of confidentiality and security over research data are required, such as in highly sensitive research contexts.

Observational approaches that harvest data about the *structures* and *processes* of online interactions and behaviours (as opposed to accessing online content, as in the examples discussed earlier) have expanded dramatically over the last decade or so, facilitated by developments such as Web 2.0 and the wide range of commercial and leisure services now available on the Internet (and 'Apps' for mobile devices, such as smartphones and tablets). Online Social Network Analysis (SNA) has emerged as an established approach with demonstrated benefits, such as enabling more accurate behavioural data to be obtained, for example, which do not rely on memory reports (see Chapter 14, this volume). The wealth of traces of online activity that are automatically logged daily by a vast population of users provides enormous scope for harvesting 'big data' sets across a range of domains and potential research topics (e.g. as in capturing all Google searches over a certain period). Such approaches have received increasing attention over recent years. For a relevant project and discussion of big data approaches (including a list of related publications), see Oxford Internet Institute (n.d), Ackland (2013) and the discussion of sampling tools and techniques later.

In summary, observational IMR approaches can confer a number of benefits over offline methods as outlined earlier, including cost- and time-savings, which can enable access to larger sample sizes than is possible offline (e.g. Givaty *et al.*, 1998), and enhanced scope for unobtrusive observation of highly topic-specific sources (e.g. Tonkin *et al.*, 2012). These benefits also apply to document analysis approaches in IMR, which although there are fewer examples available to date, have also been successfully applied in an IMR context, as shall now be discussed.

Document Analysis

The wealth of potential online documentary data available on the Internet, including web pages, scientific articles, news articles, poems, diaries, bibliographies, artists' portfolios and so on, provides plenty of scope for document analysis in IMR. In searching the Internet to locate documentary sources for primary research, some of the principles and issues raised in the next section are relevant (see also Hewson *et al.*, 2016). Some researchers have used web pages as documentary sources, for example Thoreau (2006) carried out a qualitative analysis of text and images from an online magazine (*Ouch!*, which is produced largely by and for disabled people), pointing out that the IMR methods allowed data to be gathered which are not easily obtainable using offline methods. Similarly, Heinz *et al.* (2002) carried out an analysis of gay, lesbian, bisexual and transgender websites, noting how this allowed the collapsing of geographical boundaries in ways not easily achievable offline, leading them to conclude that IMR methods can help facilitate cross-cultural research. A number of researchers have also used blogs in IMR, which could be seen as a form of document analysis (although note the earlier point regarding the status of blogs and the various forms they can take). Blogs are now abundant and often freely available for access from online public spaces, and they are also often easily searchable for specific content. This can confer advantages in being able to locate and access highly specific content for a particular research study. For example, Marcus *et al.* (2012) report acquiring rich, informative data from blogs of young people with mental health concerns, noting that the IMR method allowed this traditionally under-researched, under-treated population to be reached. Ethics issues will emerge and need to be carefully considered when accessing existing online sources, as with observational research approaches. These include considerations relating to what can reasonably be considered to be 'public' and 'private' online, as well as issues related to copyright law and ownership of online published content (British Psychological Society, 2013).

As well as locating existing documents, document analysts may also choose to solicit documents online. Hessler *et al.* (2003) adopted this approach in a study examining adolescent risk behaviour that involved asking adolescents to keep and submit (by email) personal diaries. These authors report that the online method had benefits in establishing better levels of rapport and disclosure than is often the case in offline ftf (interview) methods with adolescents. However, ethics issues must be very carefully considered when carrying out online research with vulnerable (in this case young) participants, as well as when using non-secure (here, email) methods in sensitive research contexts (see Hessler *et al.*, 2003, for a discussion of the safeguards implemented to address these issues in this case). In summary, the ready access to large volumes of data and the cost-effectiveness of obtaining this in a form ready for analysis are key benefits of document analysis techniques in IMR. Studies carried out to date have shown that enhanced access to hard-to-reach populations and broader geographical reach can also be benefits of an IMR approach.

Sampling Techniques in Unobtrusive IMR Designs

Sampling for unobtrusive IMR methods involves locating and accessing online data sources rather than people. Researchers carrying out unobtrusive IMR studies have sampled from a range of sources, including newsgroup posts (Bordia, 1996), Tweets (Tonkin *et al.*, 2012), web pages (Horvath *et al.*, 2012) and blogs (Herring *et al.*, 2005). Apart from negotiating the public/private domain distinction issue and whether informed consent from the individuals who have produced the data is required (as well as the issue of copyright and ownership, as noted earlier), similar considerations apply for unobtrusive IMR sampling approaches as those that emerge in thinking about obtrusive methods. If using quantitative approaches, where broadly representative data are required, techniques that generate large representative samples of, for example, blogs will be preferred (e.g. see Herring *et al.*, 2005, who discuss procedures for randomly sampling from blogs; also Hinduja and Patchin, 2008, who randomly sampled MySpace profile pages). In qualitative research, on the other hand, it may often be appropriate to locate more select, specialist discussions (or multimedia sources) that can be traced and analysed using some of the tools available (see Hewson *et al.*, 2016). As noted earlier, documents can also be solicited and in such contexts copyright restrictions and privacy concerns will not be an issue, but careful informed consent procedures will be required. For research contexts requiring 'naturalistic' data, archives of naturally occurring, non-reactive, online interactions will be more suitable. As always, the research goals and context will determine which techniques are most appropriate. For further discussion of the various techniques and tools (e.g. web crawler programs) available for accessing existing web-based content for use as data in unobtrusive IMR, see Ackland (2013).

SUMMARY AND CONCLUSIONS

This chapter has reviewed the use of the Internet as a tool for conducting primary research in the social and behavioural sciences and considered some key design choices and issues that emerge. Examples were presented that serve to illustrate the widespread successful implementation of IMR procedures across a range of disciplines, research traditions and domains of investigation. Advantages and novel opportunities afforded by an IMR approach were highlighted and potential drawbacks, problems and caveats considered. Explication of the relative strengths and weaknesses of a range of IMR procedures, compared with each other and with traditional offline approaches, indicated that trade-offs often emerge. Design decisions should always be made within the context of the aims and goals of an individual research study, and this is especially pertinent in IMR where many competing design choices and procedures still remain to be fully explored and developed.

In summary, two key conclusions can be derived from the present discussion. First, IMR presents a promising, now well-established method that has been clearly demonstrated to have the potential to provide valid, reliable data and research findings across a broad range of disciplines and methodological approaches. Second, although significant progress has been made over the last decade or so, many issues and procedures in IMR remain to be further explored and developed, particularly relating to more recently emerging data scraping approaches. Future attempts by researchers working across a diverse range of disciplines and fields will no doubt contribute to the further elucidation and explication of sound design principles, which can lead to valid, reliable, trustworthy data generated by IMR studies.

NOTES

1   Many good design principles for offline research will naturally generalise to an IMR context (e.g. how to word survey questions), but this may not always be the case. For example, as Reips (2010) has pointed out, reading screen-based materials is more demanding than flicking through printed pages (which may impact upon factors such as recommended maximum survey length). Such instances will be highlighted here where relevant.

2   Note also, however, that the greater variability in IMR experiments, compared with laboratory-based offline settings, may serve as a test of the external validity of an effect, where an IMR experiment is able to replicate an effect previously established offline (Reips, 2002).

3   However, see Henrich et al. (2010) for a challenge to this assumption.

4   For evidence, see Arnett (2008) and Hewson et al. (2016).

REFERENCES

Ackland, R. (2013). *Web Social Science: Concepts, Data and Tools for Social Scientists in the Digital Age*. London: Sage Publications.

Adler, C. L. and Zarchin, Y. R. (2002). 'The "Virtual Focus Group": using the Internet to reach pregnant women on home bed rest', *Journal of Obstetric, Gynecologic, & Neonatal Nursing*, 31(4), 418–27.

Al-Sa'Di, R. and Hamdan, J.M. (2005). '"Synchronous online chat" English: Computer-mediated communication', *World Englishes*, 24(4), 409–24.

Arnett, J. (2008). 'The neglected 95%: Why American psychology needs to become less American', *American Psychologist*, 63(7), 602–14.

Bainbridge, W. S. (2007). 'The scientific research potential of virtual worlds', *Science*, 317(5837), 472–76.

Barratt, M. J. (2012). 'The efficacy of interviewing young drug users through online chat', *Drug and Alcohol Review*, 31(4), 566–72.

Bigelsen, J. and Schupak, C. (2011). 'Compulsive fantasy: proposed evidence of an under-reported syndrome through a systematic study of 90 self-identified non-normative fantasizers', *Consciousness and Cognition*, 20, 1634–48.

Birnbaum, M. H. (2001). 'A web-based program of research and decision making'. In U.-D. Reips and M. Bosnjak (eds.), *Dimensions of Internet Science*. Lengerich, Germany: Pabst Science Publishers, pp. 23–55.

Bordia, P. (1996). 'Studying verbal interaction on the Internet: the case of rumour transmission research', *Behavior Research Methods, Instruments, and Computers*, 28, 149–51.

Bowker, N. and Tuffin, K. (2004). 'Using the online medium for discursive research about people with disabilities', *Social Science Computer Review*, 22(2), 228–41.

British Psychological Society (2013). Ethics guidelines for Internet-mediated research. Report of the Working Party on Conducting Research on the Internet. *British Psychological Society*. INF206/1.2013. Available at: http://www.bps.org.uk/system/files/Public%20files/inf206-guidelines-for-internet-mediated-research.pdf (accessed 25 July 2016).

Brock, R. L., Barry, R. A., Lawrence, E., Dey, J. and Rolffs, J. (2012). 'Internet administration of paper-and-pencil questionnaires used in couple research: assessing psychometric equivalence', *Assessment*, 19(2), 226–42.

Brotsky, S. R. and Giles, D. (2007). 'Inside the "pro-ana" community: a covert online participant observation', *Eating Disorders*, 15(2), 93–109.

Bryman, A. (2012). *Social Research Methods*. 4th edn. Oxford: Oxford University Press.

Buckley, M. and Vogel, C. (2003). 'Improving Internet research methods: a web laboratory'. Paper presented at IADIS International Conference WWW/Internet, Algarve, Portugal.

Carter-Pokras, O., McClellan, L. and Zambrana, E. (2006). 'Surveying free and low-cost survey software', *Journal of the National Medical Association*, 98(6), 881–6.

Castro, E. and Hyslop, B. (2013). *HTML and CSS: Visual Quickstart Guide*. 8th edn. Berkeley, CA: Peachpit Press.

Chang, L. and Krosnick, J. A. (2009). 'National surveys via RDD telephone interviewing versus the Internet: comparing sample representativeness and response quality', *Public Opinion Quarterly*, 73(4), 641–78.

Coomber, R. (1997). 'Using the Internet for survey research', *Sociological Research Online*, 2(2). Available at: http://www.socresonline.org.uk/2/2/coomber.htm (accessed 25 July 2016).

Corley, M. and Scheepers, C. (2002). 'Syntactic priming in English sentence production:

categorical and latency evidence from an Internet-based study', *Psychonomic Bulletin Review*, 9(1), 126–31.

Couper, M. P., Tourangeau, R., Conrad, F. G. and Crawford, S. (2004). 'What they see is what we get: response options for web surveys', *Social Science Computer Review*, 24(2), 227–45.

Crawford, S. (2002). 'Evaluation of web survey data collection systems', *Field Methods*, 14(3), 307–21.

Creswell, J. W. (2014). *Research Design: Qualitative, Quantitative and Mixed Methods Approaches*. 4th edn. Thousand Oaks, CA: Sage Publications.

Davis, M., Bolding, G., Hart, G., Sherr, L. and Elford, J. (2004). 'Reflecting on the experience of interviewing online: perspectives from the Internet and HIV study in London', *AIDS CARE*, 16(8), 944–52.

Fox, N., Ward, K. and O'Rourke, A. (2005). 'Pro-anorexia, weight-loss drugs and the internet: an "anti-recovery" explanatory model of anorexia', *Sociology of Health & Illness*, 27(7), 944–71.

Gaiser, T. (1997). 'Conducting online focus groups: a methodological discussion', *Social Science Computer Review*, 15(2), 135–44.

Gaiser, T. (2008). 'Online focus groups'. In N. Fielding, R. M. Lee, and G. Blank (eds.), *The SAGE Handbook of Online Research Methods*. London: Sage Publications, pp. 290–306.

Givaty, G., van Veen, H. A. H. C., Christou, C. and Bülthoff, H. H. (1998). 'Tele-experiments – experiments on spatial cognition using VRML-based multimedia'. Available at: http://www.ece.uwaterloo.ca/vrml98/cdrom/papers/givaty/givaty.pdf (accessed 10 June 2006).

Göritz, A. S. and Birnbaum, M. H. (2005). 'Generic HTML form processor: a versatile PHP script to save web-collected data into a MySQL database', *Behavior Research Methods, Instruments and Computers*, 37(4), 703–10.

Gosling, S. D., Vazire, S., Srivastava, S. and John, O. P. (2004). 'Should we trust web-based studies? A comparative analysis of six preconceptions about Internet questionnaires', *American Psychologist*, 59(2), 93–104.

Hanna, P. (2012). 'Using internet technologies (such as Skype) as a research medium: a research note', *Qualitative Research*, *12*(2), 239–42.

Heeren, T., Edwards, E. M., Dennis, J. M., Rodkin, S., Hingson, R. W. and Rosenbloom, D. L. (2008). 'A comparison of results from an alcohol survey of a prerecruited Internet panel and the National Epidemiologic Survey on Alcohol and Related Conditions', *Alcoholism: Clinical and Experimental Research*, *32*(2), 222–9.

Heinz, B., Gu, L., Inuzuka, A. and Zender, R. (2002). 'Under the rainbow flag: webbing global gay identities', *International Journal of Sexuality and Gender Studies*, *7*(2–3), 107–24.

Henrich, J., Heine, S. J. and Norenzayan, A. (2010). 'The weirdest people in the world?', *Behavioral and Brain Sciences*, *33*, 61–135.

Herring, S.C., Scheidt, L.A., Bonus, S. and Wright, E. (2005). 'Weblogs as a bridging genre', *Information, Technology & People*, *18*(2), 142–71.

Hessler, R. M., Downing, J., Beltz, C., Pelliccio, A., Powell, M. and Vale, W. (2003). 'Qualitative research on adolescent risk using e-mail: a methodological assessment', *Qualitative Sociology*, *26*(1), 111–24.

Hewson, C. (1994). 'Empirical evidence regarding the folk psychological concept of belief'. In A. Ram and K. Eiselt (eds.), *Proceedings of the Sixteenth Annual Conference of the Cognitive Science Society*, Atlanta, GA.

Hewson, C. (2003). 'Case study 1: empirical evidence regarding the folk psychological concept of belief'. In C. M. Hewson, P. Yule, D. Laurent and C. M. Vogel (eds.), *Internet Research Methods: A Practical Guide for the Social and Behavioural Sciences*. London: Sage Publications, pp. 125–9.

Hewson, C. (2007). 'Gathering data on the Internet: qualitative approaches and possibilities for mixed methods research'. In A. Joinson, K. McKenna, U. Reips and T. Postmes (eds.), *Oxford Handbook of Internet Psychology*. Oxford: Oxford University Press, pp. 405–28.

Hewson, C. (2012). 'Recommendations for implementing online surveys and simple experiments in social and behavioural research: a review and evaluation of existing online survey software packages'. Poster presented at the General Online Research Conference, March 2012, Mannheim, Germany. Available at: http://conftool.gor. de/conftool12/index.php?page=browseSessi ons&presentations=show

Hewson, C. (2015). 'Ethics issues in digital methods research'. In H. Snee, C. Hine, Y. Morey, S. Roberts and H. Watson (eds.). *Digital Methods for Social Science: An Interdisciplinary Guide to Research Innovation*. Basingstoke, UK: Palgrave Macmillan, pp. 206–21.

Hewson, C., Laurent, D. and Vogel, C. M. (1996). 'Proper methodologies for psychological and sociological studies conducted via the Internet', *Behavior Research Methods, Instruments, and Computers*, *32*, 186–91.

Hewson, C., Vogel, C. and Laurent, D. (2016). *Internet Research Methods*. 2nd edn. London: Sage Publications.

Hewson, C., Yule, P., Laurent, D. and Vogel, C. M. (2003). *Internet Research Methods: A Practical Guide for the Social and Behavioural Sciences*. London: Sage Publications.

Hinduja, S. and Patchin, J. W. (2008). 'Personal information of adolescents on the Internet: a quantitative content analysis of MySpace', *Journal of Adolescence*, *31*(1), 125–46.

Hirshfield, S., Chiasson, M. A., Wagmiller, R. L., Remien, R. H., Humberstone, M., Scheinmann, R. and Grov, C. (2010). 'Sexual dysfunction in an Internet sample of US men who have sex with men', *Journal of Sexual Medicine*, *7*, 3104–14.

Horton, J. J., Rand, D. G. and Zeckhause, R. J. (2011). 'The online laboratory: conducting experiments in a real labor market', *Experimental Economics*, *14*, 399–425.

Horvath, K. J., Iantaffi, A., Grey, J. A. and Waiter, B. (2012). 'Hackers: militants or merry pranksters? A content analysis of defaced web pages', *Health Communication*, *27*(5), 457–66.

Joinson, A. N. (2001). 'Self-disclosure in computer-mediated communication: the role of self awareness and visual anonymity', *European Journal of Social Psychology 31*, 177–92.

Joinson, A. and Paine, C. B. (2007). 'Self-disclosure, privacy and the Internet'. In A. Joinson, K. McKenna, T. Postmes and U.-D. Reips (eds.), *Oxford Handbook of Internet Psychology*. Oxford: Oxford University Press, pp. 235–250.

Jowett, A., Peel, E. and Shaw, R. (2011). 'Online interviewing in psychology: reflections on the process', *Qualitative Research in Psychology*, *8*, 354–69.

Knoll, M. A., Uther, M. and Costall, A. (2011). 'Using the Internet for speech research: an evaluative study examining affect in speech', *Behaviour & Information Technology*, *30*(6), 845–51.

Madge, C. and O'Connor, H. (2002). 'On-line with e-mums: exploring the Internet as a medium for research', *Area*, *34*(1), 92–102.

Marcus, M.A., Westra, H.A., Eastwood, J.D. and Barnes, K.L. (2012). What are young adults saying about mental health? An analysis of Internet blogs. *Journal of Medical Internet Research*, *14*(1). http://www.ncbi.nlm.nih.gov/pmc/articles/PMC3374526/ (accessed 25 July 2016).

McDermott, E. and Roen, K. (2012). 'Youth on the virtual edge', *Qualitative Health Research*, *22*(4), 560–70.

Mook, D. G. (1983). 'In defense of external invalidity', *American Psychologist*, *38*, 379–87.

Moreno, M. A., Jelenchick, L. A., Egan, K. G., Cox, E., Young, H., Gannon, K. E. and Becker, T. (2011). 'Feeling bad on Facebook: depression disclosures by college students on a social networking site', *Depression and Anxiety*, *28*(6), 447–55.

Musch, J. and Reips, U.-D. (2000). 'A brief history of web experimenting'. In M. H. Birnbaum (ed.), *Psychological Experiments on the Internet*. San Diego, CA: Academic Press.

Oxford Internet Institute (n.d.). Accessing and Using Big Data to Advance Social Science Knowledge. Available at: http://www.oii.ox.ac.uk/research/projects/?id=98 (accessed 25 July 2016).

Rademacher, J. D. M. and Lippke, S. (2007). 'Dynamic online surveys and experiments with the free open-source software dynQuest', *Behavior Research Methods*, *39*(3), 415–26.

Reece, M., Rosenberger, J. G., Schick, V., Herbenick, D., Dodge, B. and Novak, D. S. (2010). 'Characteristics of vibrator use by gay and bisexually identified men in the United States', *Journal of Sexual Medicine*, *7*, 3467–76.

Reips, U.-D. (2002). 'Standards for Internet-based experimenting', *Experimental Psychology*, *49*(4), 243–56.

Reips, U.-D. (2010). 'Designing and formatting Internet-based research'. In S. D. Gosling and J. A. Johnson (eds.), *Advanced Methods for Conducting Online Behavioral Research*. Washington DC: American Psychological Association, pp. 29–43.

Reips, U.-D. and Krantz, J. H. (2010). 'Conducting true experiments on the web', In S. D. Gosling and J. A. Johnson (eds.), *Advanced Methods for Conducting Online Behavioral Research*. Washington DC: American Psychological Association, pp. 193–216.

Schmidt, W. C. (1997). 'World-Wide Web survey research: benefits, potential, problems, and solutions', *Behavior Research Methods, Instruments, and Computers*, *29*, 274–9.

Schmidt, W. C. (2002). 'A server-side program for delivering experiments with animations', *Behavior Research Methods Instruments, and Computers*, *34*(2), 208–17.

Stephenson, L. B. and Crete, J. (2010). 'Studying political behavior: a comparison of Internet and telephone surveys', *International Journal of Public Opinion Research*, *23*(1), 24–55.

Strickland, O. L., Moloney, M. F., Dietrich, A. S., Myerburg, J. D., Cotsonis, G. A. and Johnson, R. (2003). 'Measurement issues related to data collection on the World Wide Web', *Advances in Nursing Science*, *26*(4), 246–56.

Tackett-Gibson, M. (2008). 'Constructions of risk and harm in online discussions of ketamine use', *Addiction Research & Theory*, *16*(3), 245–57.

Thoreau, E. (2006). 'Ouch! An examination of the self-representation of disabled people on the Internet', *Journal of Computer-Mediated Communication*, *11*(2), 442–68.

Tonkin, E., Pfeiffer, H. D. and Tourte, G. (2012). 'Twitter, information sharing and the London riots?', *Bulletin of the American Society for Information Science and Technology*, *38*(2), 49–57.

Yeager, D. S., Krosnick, J. A., Chang, L., Javitz, H. S., Levendusky, M. S., Simpser, A. and Wang, R. (2011). 'Comparing the accuracy of RDD telephone surveys and Internet surveys conducted with probability and non-probability samples', *Public Opinion Quarterly*, *75*(4), 709–47.

Yoo, J. H. and Kim, J.-H. (2012). 'Obesity in the new media: a content analysis of obesity videos on YouTube', *Health Communication*, *27*(1), 86–97.

FURTHER READING

Callegaro, M., Lozar Manfreda, K. and Vehovar, V. (2015). *Web Survey Methodology*. London: Sage Publications.

Couper, M. P. (2008). *Designing Effective Web Surveys*. New York, NY: Cambridge University Press.

Gosling, S. D. and Johnson, J. A. (eds.) (2010). *Advanced Methods for Conducting Online Behavioral Research*. Washington DC: American Psychological Association.

Hewson, C. M., Laurent, D. and Vogel, C. M. (2016). *Internet Research Methods: A Practical Guide for the Social and Behavioural Sciences*. 2nd edn. London: Sage Publications.

Snee, H., Hine, C., Morey, Y., Roberts, S. and Watson, H. (2015). *Digital Methods for Social Science: An Interdisciplinary Guide to Research Innovation*. Basingstoke, UK: Palgrave Macmillan.

## 5

Nonreactive Data Collection Online

Dietmar Janetzko

INTRODUCTION

In nonreactive data collection, people under investigation are usually not aware that they are being studied so that their behaviour is not affected by the data collection procedure (Lee, 2000; Webb *et al.,* 2000; Fritsche and Linneweber, 2006). Nonreactive data collection is often called unobtrusive, indirect, hidden, naturalistic, noninvasive or nondisruptive because it does not introduce a high-profile data collection procedure into a naturalistic setting. The defining criterion for nonreactive data collection is not a feature of the method per se, but nonawareness of the data-recording process[1] on the side of the person(s) under study. In their classic work on nonreactive research in the social sciences, Webb and his colleagues (1966), distinguished three kinds of nonreactive data: physical traces, simple observations and archival records provided they have been collected in a nonreactive way.

Gathering data in a nonreactive manner is not confined to more traditional research settings (e.g. laboratory, field). In fact, major strands of social science research conducted online are concerned with nonreactive data collection. In addition to features of more traditional types of nonreactive data collection, e.g. being noninvasive, its online equivalent allows researchers to investigate large numbers of people. Combining nonreactive data collection with other kinds of data gathering in order to study the same phenomenon, i.e. using methodological triangulation (Denzin, 1970; Jick, 1979; Mathison, 1988; Webb *et al.,* 2000), ideally enhances confidence in the research findings. The versatility and thus the scope of nonreactive data collection conducted online is very large. This contrasts with other research methods that are often specifically associated with particular disciplines, e.g. experiments in psychology or analyses of document corpora in linguistics. Nonreactive data collection even stretches the boundaries of academic studies because it has become an important addition to the arsenal of methods in areas like marketing and e-commerce (Manjoo, 2003) and the work of the secret services (Zetter, 2006; Greenwald and MacAskill, 2013; Lyon, 2014). Each of those areas has a particular affinity to particular nonreactive data collection methods. For instance, while techniques for acquiring a data profile of website visitors (e.g. via cookies) are of interest to marketing and e-commerce, they are less important in social science studies.

EPISTEMOLOGICAL PERSPECTIVE ON NONREACTIVE DATA COLLECTION

Nonreactive Data Collection on the Web and Elsewhere

How does nonreactive data collection on the Internet differ from other approaches to unobtrusive data gathering? First, simple observations, i.e. observation without any intervention of the researcher and analysis of archival records are the major types of nonreactive data collection on the Internet. Second, nonreactive data collection is carried out in an automated and objective way such that large volumes of data can be acquired with high precision. Third, while traditional nonreactive data collection may or may not cover visual and aural cues, this kind of information is generally missing in data collection on the Internet. As a consequence, characteristics of the person being studied such as appearance, height and weight, attire, gender, age, ethnic group, facial expressions, eye contact, body language, gestures and emotional responses are not generally available (Dholakia and Zhang, 2004). But on the other side, when data is gathered in a nonreactive way on the Internet, some types of 'sub-symbolic information' (Hofmann et al., 2006), like hesitations to make a decision or time spent reading, can be collected very precisely and in large quantities. Finally, it should be mentioned that nonreactive data is

often gathered for administrative purposes in order to organize a study or to improve the overall data quality (e.g. by identifying people that appear to participate repeatedly in a study).

Are the people studied on the Internet in a nonreactive way really unaware of possible data-recording procedures? Speaking either of awareness or of nonawareness is of course an oversimplification because people may suspect that they are or will be studied without being fully aware of it. Given that data collection on the Internet is often covered in the news or in popular media (e.g. Arthur, 2006), it cannot be ruled out that many people might actually suspect or know that their behaviour and communication can easily be recorded. Online behaviour changes provoked by awareness of data recording can be expected on two levels. First, there is increased motivation to use anonymizing services or to resort to *data poisoning*, i.e. providing wrong or misleading information (Anonymous, 2007a). Second, there may be some form of self-censored communication caused by privacy concerns (Eynon et al., this volume; Joinson et al., 2010). Both reactions (leaving out information and providing false information) can be different strategies of identity management on the Internet. It is still an open research question about which strategy is chosen if concern regarding hidden data collection is high.

THIN DESCRIPTIONS – THICK DESCRIPTIONS

Nonreactive data collection on the Internet provides the researcher with information that may come in large quantities (e.g. log file data). Usually, however, the information from data gathered in a nonreactive way is limited. Email logs reveal networks of communicating people and the intensity of the relationships involved. But in itself an email log offers only limited insight into the content of the messages exchanged. Likewise, measuring the time a person stays on a website does not tell why that website has been visited in the first place, or what the person studied is actually doing or thinking. In the terms of the philosopher Gilbert Ryle (1971) and the ethnologist Clifford J. Geertz (1973), data gathered in a nonreactive way on the Internet usually constitutes a *thin description*. A description is called 'thin' if it lacks contextual cues that could make it meaningful to an external observer. That nonreactive data gathered on the Internet often leads to thin descriptions is a consequence of the narrow coding schemas implemented by most data-recording devices used on the Internet. This should not be surprising. Many of the recording procedures used for social science research on the Internet (e.g. server logging, email logging)[2] have been created for quite different purposes, for example, technical maintenance. As a consequence, only some aspects of the behavioural spectrum of people are selected and recorded, which do not necessarily match the phenomena a social science investigation strives to address. A richer picture of the phenomenon under study would emerge if data collection were not narrowed down to one or to a few measures. This could be achieved, for instance, by studying a person's communication patterns over a long period of time or by backing up these observations with other forms of data collection. In the terms of Ryle and Geertz, this procedure would ideally lead to a *thick description*. By providing a richer account of the phenomena studied, thick descriptions are usually less prone to erroneous conclusions.

In fact, a considerable part of the research that pivots around nonreactive data gathered on the Internet strives to go beyond what is given by thin descriptions and to obtain thick descriptions instead. Thick descriptions cannot be accomplished just by quantitatively increasing the data in the sense of adding more data records while sticking to the data-encoding schema that has been

used in the first place. There are basically two kinds of approaches for arriving at a richer description: data combination and data exploitation. To illustrate data combination and data exploitation, as opposed to a simple quantitative increase of data, it is useful to conceive of a dataset in terms of the rectangular data format used by most statistical software packages, for example, SPSS or R. A given rectangular data matrix (Figure 5.1, top) can be extended in two ways. *Vertical enlargement* (Figure 5.1, bottom left) means that an existing dataset is quantitatively extended by additional data records or rows in a data table. Seen from the viewpoint of inference statistics this may prove important (e.g. to improve the statistical power of an analysis). However, a narrow data-encoding schema that has led to thin descriptions cannot be fixed in this way. *Horizontal enlargement* of a data matrix (Figure 5.1, bottom right) may address limitations caused by either a narrow data-encoding schema or simply by a lack of relevant data. Horizontal enlargement can be achieved by way of data enrichment, i.e. by considering data from different sources or independent measurement processes (triangulation, Webb *et al.*, 2000) or by data exploitation, i.e. analytically inferring data (e.g. via text or data mining). For instance, it is possible to extract the title of the page accessed by the user before visiting the current page (Anonymous, 2007b). This means that not only technical information (e.g. a URL), but also textual information is available that can then be deployed to enrich the information on a visitor.

Horizontal enlargement of data sets is a data usage pattern that describes a large number of activities in online research. The data that is added via horizontal enlargement may be used for a number of purposes (Figure 5.2). If the number of variables is too large, variable/feature selection is imperative. If among a large set of candidate predicators the suitable variables have been identified, then a number of statistical options are available. These include options to validate

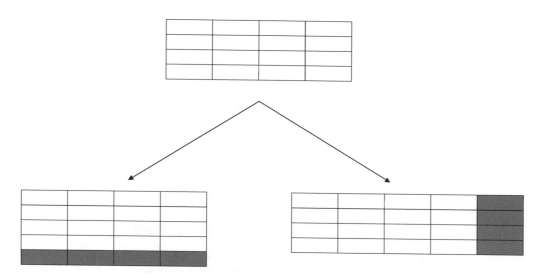

Figure 5.1   Vertical (bottom left) and horizontal enlargement (bottom right) of a data matrix (top)

existing variables, to infer new variables, to de-anonymize data or to introduce metadata. The choice among these options depends of course on the research question.

For instance, Mark Claypool and his colleagues (2001) analysed the degree of interest of website visitors on the basis of a combination of different kinds of nonreactive data (mouse clicks and movements, scrolling, time elapsed) and reactive data (explicit ratings of websites). This data usage pattern can be described as a horizontal enlargement of the set of reactive data with the goal of validating them. Likewise, Barjak (2006) relied on a combination of archive data to show that increased usage of Internet communication,

i.e. email and online information sources, is indicative of a high research productivity (measured by articles published). An example of a study that combined nonreactive data with data from other sources is the work of Dubois and Bothorel (2006). The authors used server log data on document access and indicators of similarity between documents to relate social network analysis (see Hogan, this volume) to the semantics of the documents accessed. Kossinets and Watts (2006) made use of a combination of email logs and other data (gender, age, friendship links, joint activities) to identify factors that contribute to the development of social networks. Using appropriate algorithms allows the researcher to infer information that *prima facie* is not provided by the data gathered (data exploitation). An example of data exploitation is work to infer the reputation of email sending domains on the basis of user judgements and data mining techniques (Taylor, 2006). Bradley Taylor, an employee of Google Inc., describes how Gmail – Google's free email service – estimates the sender reputation of emails (spammy, not spammy), or more specifically, the sending domain. 'Spamminess'

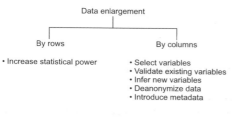

Figure 5.2   Analytical options resulting from vertical and horizontal enlargement

is not a variable in email logs and its estimation is another example of a horizontal extension of a dataset. Taylor (2006) elaborates on the idea that email reputation is estimated on the basis of the sender, instead of analysing the email message. Although the sending domain is recorded in a nonreactive way, other kinds of information are recorded in reactive ways (e.g. how many times a user marked an email as spam). This inferred information about the spam risk of a sending domain is taken to augment the data recorded in a nonreactive way.

TECHNICAL PERSPECTIVE ON NONREACTIVE DATA COLLECTION CONDUCTED ONLINE

Archival Sources

Social science data can be obtained from a large number of data archives run by public institutions and accessible over the Internet. Likewise, most of the datasets of those freely accessible archives owe their existence to institutional support. Usually, the datasets maintained by public archives have been collected in a reactive way.[3] For example, the University of California, San Diego, runs a website that presents Internet data archives, of which many allow a user to download data. One of the largest social science data archives listed there is that of the Cornell Institute of Social and Economic Research (CISER), which maintains an archive of Internet data for social scientists (Cornell University, 2006). Among the large collection of datasets that are accessible via the website of the CISER are data on public opinion; on demographic, economic and social indicators for India; on how Americans use personal, work and leisure time; and many more. Data can be accessed either via searching or browsing by subject area. Usually, entry to the site is possible by way of a guest login; however, a number of files can be reached only by users affiliated with Cornell University.

At present, by contrast, researchers interested in nonreactive data can rarely bank on institutionally maintained archives. Still, there are some freely accessible datasets gathered in a nonreactive way. Most were made accessible by error, chance, data leaks, or as a consequence of legal investigations (e.g. Klimt and Yang, 2004). Cases in point are the Enron dataset and the AOL (America Online) data, both of which attracted a lot of media attention.

The Enron Dataset

In December 2001 the Enron Corporation, an American energy company based in Houston, Texas, collapsed and had to declare bankruptcy. Since issues like planned accounting fraud were involved, the Federal Energy Regulator of the United States investigated the case. For legal reasons, some of the documents inspected had to be made public. Among those was a dataset of about 200,000 email messages exchanged between 151 people (most of which were senior managers of Enron) collected between mid-1998 and mid-2002 (Klimt and Yang, 2004). This data is nonreactive because none of the Enron employees could possibly anticipate that their communication pattern was not only logged, but would eventually be made public. In fact, the Enron dataset has become a kind of *Drosophila*, i.e. the preferred data source, for many scientific studies, a case in point being social network analyses (Culotta *et al.*, 2004). To the extent that data of this kind is increasingly available online, examining the inner world of institutions might well become much easier than it has been in the past.

The AOL Dataset

Search engines log the search requests (keywords) entered by users. Clearly, this data reveals a lot about the interests of people. On the basis of the assumption that people deploying a search engine are not aware their search requests are recorded and archived, this data can be classified as nonreactive. In August 2006 AOL published a huge dataset of search requests of 650,000 subscribers. Making this dataset public was motivated partly in compliance with requests by US state authorities, partly due to errors by employees (Wray, 2006). The data had been sorted by anonymous user IDs. Nevertheless, it soon became obvious that it was possible to trace back search requests to the people that entered them (Barbaro and Zeller, 2006). AOL quickly closed down the website where the data had been published, but in the meantime, the dataset had been downloaded several hundred times. A number of mirror sites have been set up such that the data is in fact available (e.g. America Online Data Set, 2006).

Technical Procedures for Nonreactive Data Collection Online

Data recording works like a filter on a complex phenomenon to be studied: some aspects will usually be filtered away, while others pass through. Only aspects of the phenomenon that pass the filter will be recorded and start a career as data. For instance, when an interview is recorded and transcribed, words will pass the filter and become data. However, many nonverbal aspects e.g. the facial expressions or the body language of the interviewee along with most paraverbal aspects, e.g. the particular sound of the voice, will usually be filtered away. Nonreactive data collection is not exempted from this rule. Procedures for nonreactive data collection differ with regard to their filter profiles. Filtering carried out by a data collection procedure does not just relate to the subject-matter side, i.e. the content of the phenomenon under study. It also defines the format of the data obtained. For instance, some nonreactive data collection procedures will generate *relational data* (e.g. email logs) that are, for example, amenable to social network analyses, while others will provide *attribute data* (e.g. environment variables), which are usually quantitative. Data from access log files (attribute data) may be transformed into relational data with two people being related by having accessed the same document (e.g. Schwartz and Wood, 1993; Sha and Aalst, 2003). A methodologically sound application of nonreactive data collection methods has to account for the filter profile of the method used. In what follows, some of the most common techniques for nonreactive data collection are presented. Note, however, that nonreactive data collection methods are a rapidly developing field. Introduction of new methods or extensions or innovative applications of old methods are quite common. A case in point is the more recent development of nonreactive data collection in social media via *application programming interfaces* (APIs) and mobile phones.

Server Log File Data: A number of computer applications generate text-based log files that report on the technical operations carried out. These reporting or logging facilities may be configured and will then work in an automated way, thereby gathering data in a nonreactive manner. Technical devices used to enable communication on the World Wide Web make extensive use of logging, which can be carried out on the side of the HTTP (HyperText Transfer Protocol) server (web server) or on the side of the client (web browser). Serverside logging reports on page requests of many users on one HTTP server. By contrast, clientside logging covers the page requests of one user on many servers (Etgen and Cantor, 1999). Serverside logging is more often used than clientside logging. While serverside logs are standardized, clientside logs are not. Usually, installation of special software and agreement of the user to install this software is required to carry out nonreactive logging on the client side (Hong and Landay, 2001). Clientside logs may provide a more precise account of user activities because they can be geared towards the data required. A discussion of server log files follows, as this kind of logging is in widespread use.

Server log files keep track of the server interaction with other computers, which is achieved by a logging procedure that generates different types of log file. Important types of log file are documents that refer to page requests by clients (access log) and documents that report on errors, which may or may not occur when the page requests are processed (error log). Access log files stick to log file formats that are either widely accepted as standards (e.g. common log format, extended log file format, or the W3C Extended Log Format) or vendor-specific (e.g. IAS Format Log Files by Microsoft). In addition, a number of servers support a user-defined format (custom log file format). The filter profile of access log file data is determined by the log formats, more precisely by the field information they cover. Typical examples of fields in an access log file are time and date of the request, bytes sent, identifier of the client or IP address of the requesting computer. The common log file format, for instance, makes use of the following fields:

host identifier username date:time request status-code bytes

Next is an example that shows an instantiation of this format with specific data:

125.125.125.125   dsmith   [10/Oct/ 1999:21:15:05 +0500] "GET/index.html HTTP/1.0" 200 1043

Usually a single request for one HTML (HyperText Markup Language) document will generate several entries (lines) in the access log file, similar to the one shown previously. This is due to the fact that retrieval of each embedded document (e.g. graphics, scripting or audio files) will lead to a separate entry (line) in the log file.

Server log files provide an automatic and fast way to collect huge amounts of data, the assessment of which requires software support. Log file analyzers use log file data to generate summary statistics on the number of page requests, the domains, the time spent on a website or on particular documents, etc. The field of log file analyzer software is in constant flux. The rapid pace of development has been facilitated by standard formats used to generate server logs. Some log file analyzers provide more advanced features, like statistics on site-response times, or individual web-browsing patterns (i.e. the paths a user takes when visiting a website), which are usually not available in summary statistics. Prominent examples of log file analyzers are AWStats, Analog, and Deep Log Analyzer, all of which are free. Some log file analyzers (e.g. AWStats) identify not only the country, but also the region or the city of website visitors. Reports on visitors with high geographical resolution are facilitated by augmenting log file data with geotargeting databases that represent associations between IP and geographical data (country, region or city). Geotargeting databases are commercially provided by vendors like MaxMind and IP2Country. Apart from its commercial products, MaxMinds also offers free (Open Source) versions of their geotargeting databases (GeoLite). In general, server log files are easily available. Sometimes, however, access to a server is difficult or impossible. Most of the information provided by server log files can still be gathered by using hosted services, which collect and analyze the traffic on a website of interest. This is achieved by adding a code snippet to the website intended to be analysed.

Access log files provide quantitative attribute data. This data is often used to identify web-browsing patterns which in turn may be taken to study information-seeking on the web (Choo et al., 2002) or to evaluate a website (e.g. its usability or attractiveness). Huntington and colleagues (2007) used log file data gathered on the website of a major publishing house (Elsevier) in conjunction with questionnaire data (horizontal enlargement) to study searches for information on a website. The results obtained lend support to a classification of users according to their site navigation style. Users who employ the menu tend to focus on a particular type of publication (e.g. articles in press). Users who make use of the search facility of the site are more likely to study more diverse materials. Associated issues are further discussed in Hogan (this volume).

Email Server Logs: Email is the dominant type of communication on the Internet and email archives provide a valuable source of information for understanding the individuals and communities (Perer *et al.*, 2006). Email archives are created and updated whenever emails are sent or received, which is recorded by sending email servers such as Sendmail or Qmail. These systems generate and keep log files that cover information on the email addresses of senders and receivers, the time/date of sending and receiving the email and a checksum (e.g. md5sum) that verifies the integrity of the message. Table 5.1 shows email logs used by Bhattacharyya *et al.* (2002) in a study of malicious email tracking (simulated data). Email logs are of prime importance to combat spam or to detect whether an email server has been hijacked in order to send spam. Since they are a serious threat to online privacy, many organizations delete email logs every few days.

Similar to other kinds of nonreactive data collection method, the filtering profile of email logs is determined by its technical underpinnings. Usually, the content of the message is not part of email logs.[4] Instead, email logs report on interaction patterns in terms of sender, receiver and time. They reveal frequency and directionality of communication, both of which can be used to estimate the intensity of a relationship. This filtering profile makes email logs a valuable resource for analysing social relations. Email logs are often harnessed to identify and analyse communities in factual or virtual groups (e.g. Tyler *et al.*, 2003) and to study the information flow in such groups (Wu *et al.*, 2004). Kossinets and Watts (2006) used a combination of email logs and other data (gender, age, friendship links, joint activities) to identify factors that drive the development of social networks.

Instant Messaging Log Files: Instant Messaging (IM) is a type of written communication via the Internet or smartphones that has become increasingly popular in the last few years. The main difference between email and IM is that the latter is a faster form of interaction. Instant messenger clients usually indicate whether other users are online, which may encourage communication among participants. While the procedure of writing an email still has much in common with traditional letter writing, IM is more similar to a conversation in that the exchanges are usually immediate. There are a large number of instant messenger clients (e.g. ICQ, Google Talk, AOL Instant Messenger, Messenger Plus or Adium) that implement instant messaging protocols like Jabber or Internet Relay Chat (IRC). The filtering profile of IM is usually characterized by recordings of timestamped text messages. However, whether and which kinds of log file are recorded by an instant messenger client depends on the protocol used. Some client systems do not generate log files; others offer the option for log file recording, and still others record the communications by default. It is therefore

Table 5.1 Email logs (simulated data)

md5sum	Sender address	Recipient address	Time	Date
Zi5XtPiykp …	toohot@pb.com	monica@columbia.edu	11:34:00	1/17/02
EpC0Gwnyii …	bob@ccny.edu	helana@gls.com	11:34:00	1/17/02
9Qiqw7xyg0 …	elvis@columbia.edu	allen@microsoft.com	11:34:00	1/17/02

debatable whether data collection via IM is nonreactive.

Scott (2003) found that communication skills were more developed among those participants who made extensive use of IM. This finding contrasts partially with the results of an investigation carried out by Quan-Haase et al. (2005). When analysing the usage of IM for workplace collaboration they found that the overall connectivity was improved, and new forms of collaboration emerged. However, IM was also used as a shield to avoid face-to-face communication with superiors.

In recent years, instant messaging apps for mobile phones like WhatsApp, Viber and WeChat have become increasingly popular. Apart from text messages these applications also facilitate the exchange of audio messages, videos and images. Phone messaging apps leverage several means for data gathering like log files and the recording and export of chat history. In addition, there is additional software available that allows recording of even more features of the communication. Almost inevitably, however, this software leads to infringement of privacy.

The use of messaging apps for scientific studies is only in its infancy. A study by Johnston et al. (2015) explored the use of WhatsApp by using reactive data collection. The goal of the study was to examine the deployment of WhatsApp messaging in a healthcare setting. It combined qualitative and quantitative methods to analyse communication patterns in surgical teams in the UK that involve interns and more senior team members. The study revealed which messages are responded to faster than others, and it indicated that using messaging apps contributes to flattening the hierarchy in surgical teams.

Environment Variables

Whenever an HTML document is requested via the Internet by a client (browser) the web server allocates values to so-called environment variables, for example the date and time of a document request, the type of browser used and a status code that specifies the success or failure of the request. Environment variables have much in common with access log data. For instance, the values of environment variables also cover information that is technical in nature. In contrast to access log files, the information provided by environment variables is usually only kept temporarily. However, programming languages like Perl may be used to transfer this information to permanent storage. Likewise, environment variables can be logged in the access log file. Data collection can easily be accomplished via environment variables. Since this procedure is carried out on the serverside it is not affected by user decisions on the clientside, like switching off JavaScript.

Cookies

Cookies capture information on a visitor to a website (e.g. the date and time of a person's visit, the parts of the website being requested or the actions performed). There are different types of cookies. In what follows, the focus is on the most basic type of cookie, viz., the first party cookie or HTTP cookie. Without mechanisms like cookies a website could not 'remember' the most recent actions of a particular visitor, let alone activities performed weeks before. It is not the kind of information gathered that makes cookies special but the way the information is represented. Although generated and set by a server, cookies are saved on the client computer. This information can be used when a user revisits a website at a later point in time. Cookies are often employed in areas like marketing and e-commerce to recognize previous visitors to a website. In social science studies conducted online, cookies are not employed very often. Similar to nonreactive data methods like environment variables, the usage of cookies is often related to the technical administration of an online study (e.g. assessing the sample of participants, the preferred time of participation, detecting visitors who participate repeatedly in a study).

Time Measurement

Every activity has a duration. While measuring an activity is quite complex or even impossible, measuring the time required to perform it is comparatively simple. The same is true for latencies, i.e. the time before an activity is actually carried out. Thus, time measurement is an indirect approach to examining activities. A study by Tyler and Tang (2003) shows that timing in online email communication works as a nonverbal cue. The authors conducted face-to-face interviews, which revealed that latencies between receiving an email and replying to it are often used to communicate a message. While the majority of emails are answered within 24 hours, a reply may be delayed intentionally to create a particular impression (e.g. being busy). Analysing the response times in 16,000 emails selected from the Enron dataset, Kalman and Rafaeli (2005) found supporting evidence for many of the results reported by Tyler and Tang (2003). For instance, the majority of email replies (84 percent) had in fact been generated within 24 hours. The work of Perer *et al.* (2006) extends the findings of Tyler and Tang (2003) by delineating that the temporal patterns of email exchanges reflect not only situational information, but also the intensity of relationships over longer periods of time. Using an email archive of an individual that spans 15 years and a longitudinal study design, the authors identified long-term relationships as evidenced by email exchange patterns. Moreover, they developed methods to visualize these 'rhythms' of relationships.

APIs (Application Programming Interfaces)

In social media like Facebook, Twitter or YouTube, data can be collected in a nonreactive way simply by copying available data manually from the website of interest. But manual data collection of this kind has obvious limits. For instance, a continuous monitoring or a broad coverage of social media is hardly feasible. A more systematic approach to collecting nonreactive data is possible by way of application programming interfaces or APIs (Janetzko, 2016). APIs make different computer systems interoperable. A researcher can use their computer-based data collection device to source data via an API from a social network. With regard to nonreactive data collection this means that data can be collected from external sources that provide an API. Under the roof of one API there are usually different 'endpoints', each of which allows targeted operations. For instance, the Facebook API provides an endpoint for collecting the information about 'likes', one to glean comments and many other endpoints. There are restricted APIs and endpoints and public ones. Access to the former is subject to conditions, e.g. fees, while the latter type of API can be accessed freely. Public APIs of social media like Facebook or Twitter facilitate nonreactive data collection in social media in a systematic and computationally controlled manner. Although public APIs are freely accessible, they are subject to limitations that concern the volume and/or the kind of information made available. The public APIs offered by Twitter are the streaming API and REST API. In a nutshell, the streaming API facilitates access to Tweets on an ongoing basis. It provides two public endpoints, the filter and the sample endpoint. The former returns a stream of Tweets that match one or several keywords. The latter returns 1 per cent of the overall stream of all Tweets made accessible by the 'firehose', i.e. a restricted endpoint of the streaming API. The REST API is similar to a search engine in that it returns Tweets that match keywords. Facebook organizes access to its data via one API, the graph API in connection with a large number of endpoints.

Public APIs are subject to a number of rate limits that put a cap on the volume of data that can be collected. In addition, privacy policies restrict data access. This applies in particular to Facebook and it often limits its attractiveness for researchers who consider working with the graph API of Facebook. In general, data that cannot be accessed via the public GUI (graphical user interface) of social media cannot be accessed via an API either. Facebook researchers, however, obviously make intensive use of nonreactive data collection as evidenced by a work on social contagion via Facebook (Kramer *et al.*, 2014). The study suggests that emotions expressed by somebody on Facebook influence others within their friend network.

In the early days, collection and deployment of data from social media was often methodologically naïve. This has changed over the years. For instance, more recently many researchers ask what the data from Twitter actually represent. Although there is common agreement that data from Twitter are not representative of a society or country, a study by Morstatter, Pfeffer and Liu (2014) raised the question whether Twitter's public APIs are representative of the overall stream of data. This is the so-called firehose, which is available only via a commercial endpoint of the streaming API. Morstatter and his colleagues found that Tweets accessed via the sample API are representative of the overall activity on Twitter that manifests itself via the firehose. But clearly, not every study needs to be representative in order to be of scientific value. Nonreactive data collection in social networks using APIs may pave the way for innovative studies which, however, may be debatable from an ethical point of view. A case in point are studies of social honeypots that work with fake profiles to attract and then study social spammers (e.g. Lee *et al.*, 2010).

Mobile phone data

Although mobile phone networks are different from the Internet, the convergence between both types of networks is increasing. This is true on a technological level, but even more so on the level of its daily use via a single device, i.e. a smartphone. This is the reason why the burgeoning research area of mobile phone data analysis is addressed in this chapter.

When using a mobile phone, a variety of different kinds of data is generated. Among these are data that a user produces voluntarily and thus reactively, e.g. data collected by fitness apps, but also data generated involuntarily or nonreactively, e.g. *call detail records* (CDRs). CDRs are data that telephone companies gather mainly for billing purposes. It includes metadata about a telephone call like the numbers of the calling party and the called party, duration of the call, call type and the location where a call or text message has been initiated.

More recently, CDRs of mobile phones have attracted a lot of attention from scholars of computational social science (Blondel, 2015; Dong *et al.*, 2015). Interest in this data has been sparked by the socio-spatial analytical options of CDRs and by the ubiquitous use of mobile phones and thus the sheer amount of this type of nonreactive data. Mobile phone data have been used, e.g., to analyse population movement patterns. Among the applications of CDRs are traffic management and monitoring (Steenbruggen *et al.*, 2013) and the analysis of population movement patterns, in connection with large crises like the outbreak of Ebola in West Africa (Wesolowski *et al.*, 2014). Acquiring CDRs for analysis is challenging. Its access and use is strictly regulated by privacy policies and laws; the data files are huge and the process of data anonymization is costly. There are, however, several initiatives that make this data available for research purposes. Orange, the French telecommunication firm, and Sonatel, the major telecommunication company of Senegal, have jointly launched an initiative called *data 4 development* (d4d). With the intention to foster the development in Senegal in areas like health, agriculture, transport and energy, d4d grants scientists working in this area access to anonymized data from the mobile phone network in Senegal. Another example of freely accessible mobile phone data is the Nodobo dataset (McDiarmid *et al.*, 2013). Nodobo is a study set up at the University of Strathclyde, UK, to examine communication patterns on the mobile phone use of 27 students from September 2010 to February 2011.

DISCUSSION AND CONCLUSION

Research methods like nonreactive online data collection are conceptual tools that help to accomplish scientific objectives. They are relatively new in the repertoire of social science research methods. Still, methods to gather nonreactive data online in a controlled way possess the characteristics of more traditional research methods in social science: they make phenomena of interest visible, tangible, comparable and debatable. In doing so, nonreactive data collection facilitates interfacing phenomena under study and theories about them. Moreover, nonreactive data may help in specifying whether and to what degree scientific standards (e.g. objectivity, reliability, validity) of a discipline are met. Methods of nonreactive data collection allow the researcher to study both social phenomena via the Internet, which could likewise be investigated by using other, more traditional methods, and social phenomena peculiar to the Internet (e.g. online dating). With regard to the latter they provide the researcher with a lens to investigate phenomena that are usually not accessible with other methods. However, the relative exclusiveness of nonreactive research methods comes at a price. This is partly due to intrinsic shortcomings of nonreactive data. In fact, limitations of nonreactive data usage have already been outlined by Webb *et al.* (2000) and in the discussion inspired by this work (e.g. Rathje, 1979; Babbie, 1998). Partly, however, other shortcomings like the lack of appropriate social science theories are made visible in the light of nonreactive data.

Nonreactive data by their very nature raise serious ethical questions. Nonreactive data collection means hidden data collection. This in itself may be considered a breach of privacy. Privacy issues become even more pressing if a horizontal enlargement of data gathered in a nonreactive way is carried out. This type of 'data pooling' may become a serious threat to online privacy if it links nonreactive data to reactive data (e.g. names) such that data becomes personally identifiable.

Establishing the validity of nonreactive data is urgently needed if nonreactive data are not self-explanatory and the data collected provide only a thin description. In fact, it is not objectivity or reliability that is difficult to achieve by using nonreactive methods, but validity. Validation in turn should not be reduced to finding yet another data source that can be taken to confirm or negate findings.

The usage of nonreactive data often reveals a theory/method mismatch. For instance, nonreactive, Internet-based data collation methods operate at a level of precision not matched by most social science theories that underlie the majority of studies carried out online (e.g. with respect to temporal resolution). Vice versa, most traditional social science concepts need to be better specified in order to make them amenable to nonreactive data collection conducted online. Quite often, theories are not only underspecified, but simply missing entirely. Often in such cases, work centring around nonreactive techniques more or less exclusively addresses visualization of phenomena that are perhaps not properly understood. A fruitful development of research can be expected when nonreactive data collection is dovetailed with existing work in the area studied. This applies to mobile phone data analysis, which more recently has become a prolific area of scholarly activity, e.g. on topics like migration (Williams *et al.*, 2015)

Although spam, phishing or other kinds of Internet fraud have not been reported as a problem for nonreactive data collection conducted online, checks and balances should be put in place early on in order to identify problems caused by fraud or malicious attacks. Spam is usually a one-way email communication that will not affect analysis of email logs that are turned into relation data. Access log files can be distorted by web crawlers that visit websites in order to collect information (e.g. for search engines). Appropriate server configuration may help to weed out access log entries produced by web crawlers (Taylor, 2002). To use nonreactive data properly is to address these issues.

NOTES

1 Recordings of nonreactive online data (e.g. log files) are done on a physical level. Strictly speaking, data like log files are not physical traces left by people under study, but the physical aspects of the recording process.
2 Server or mail logs are data about other data (server transactions or emails). Thus, they are metadata.
3 Why do archives run by public institutions seem to be hesitant about including data collected in a nonreactive manner? Clearly, any institution that maintains a nonreactive dataset archive would put itself at legal risk by making datasets accessible that have been collected without the consent of the people studied (see, Flicker *et al.*, 2004).
4 For an example of an analysis of email content, see White *et al.* (2004).

REFERENCES

America Online Data Set. (2006) 'Mirror site of data of search requested, provided by AOL on August 6, 2006'. Retrieved 15 August 2016 from https://archive.org/details/AOL_search_data_leak_2006

Anonymous. (2007a) 'How to lie to people: achieving anonymity through disinformation and data poisoning'. Retrieved 15 August 2016 from http://www.textfiles.com/uploads/howtolie.txt

Anonymous. (2007b) 'GSNR – PHP class can be used to retrieve the title of the page visited by the user before accessing the current page'. Retrieved 15 August 2016 from http://www.phpclasses.org/browse/package/4034.html

Arthur, C. (2006) 'Is it possible to be identified by your "clickprint"?'. *Guardian*, 28 September, p. 2.

Babbie, E. (1998) *The Practice of Social Research*. 8th edn. Belmont, CA: Wadsworth.

Barbaro, M. and Zeller Jr, T. (2006) 'The face behind AOL user 4417749'. *New York Times*, 9 August.

Barjak, F. (2006) 'Research productivity in the Internet era'. *Scientometrics*, 68 (3), 343–60.

Best, S.J. and Krueger, B.S. (2004) *Internet Data Collection*. Thousand Oaks, CA: Sage Publications.

Bhattacharyyaa, M., Schultz, M.G., Eskin, E., Hershkop, S. and Stolfo, S.J. (2002) 'MET: An Experimental System for Malicious Email Tracking'. Proceedings of the 2002 New Security Paradigms Workshop (NSPW2002), Virginia Beach, VA: 23–26 September. Retrieved 15 October 2015 from http://ids.cs.columbia.edu/sites/default/files/met-nspw02.pdf

Blaikie, N. (1991) 'A critique of the use of triangulation in social research', *Quality and Quantity*, 25, 115–36.

Blondel, V. D., Decuyper, A. and Krings, G. (2015) 'A survey of results on mobile phone datasets analysis'. *EPJ Data Science*, 4(1),1. doi:10.1140/epjds/s13688-015-0046-0.

Choo, C.W., Detlor, B. and Turnbull, D. (2002) 'Information seeking on the web: an integrated model of browsing and searching', *First Monday*, 5 (2). Retrieved 15 August 2016 from http://www.firstmonday.org/ojs/index.php/fm/article/view/729

Claypool, M., Le, P., Waseda, M. and Brown, D. (2001) 'Implicit Interest Indicators'. In C. Sidner & J. Moore (eds.), Proceedings of the 6th International Conference on Intelligent User Interfaces, ACM, Santa Fe, NM, pp. 33–40.

Cornell University, Cornell Institute of Social and Economic Research. (2006) 'Internet data for social scientists'. Retrieved 22 August 2006 from http://www.ciser.cornell.edu/ASPs/datasource.asp

Culotta, A., Bekkerman, R. and McCallum, A. (2004) 'Extracting social networks and contact information from email'. Proceedings of the First Conference on Email and AntiSpam (CEAS), 30–31 July, Mountain View, CA.

Retrieved 12 October 2015 from http://scholarworks.umass.edu/cgi/viewcontent.cgi?article=1035&context=cs_faculty_pubs

Denzin, N. (1970) *The Research Act in Sociology: A Theoretical Introduction to Sociological Methods*. Chicago, IL: Aldine.

Dholakia, N. and Zhang, D. (2004) 'Online qualitative research in the age of e-commerce: data sources and approaches', *Forum Qualitative Sozialforschung/Forum: Qualitative Social Research*, 5 (2). Retrieved 15 August 2016 from http://www.qualitative-research.net/index.php/fqs/article/viewArticle/594/1289

Dong, Y., Pinelli, F., Gkoufas, Y., Nabi, Z., Calabrese, F. and Chawla, N. V. (2015). 'Inferring unusual crowd events from mobile phone call detail records', *Joint European Conference on Machine Learning and Knowledge Discovery in Databases*. Springer International Publishing.

Dubois, V. and Bothorel, C. (2006) 'From semantic to social: an integrated approach for content and usage analysis'. Proceedings of the 2nd Workshop on Semantic Network Analysis, Collocated with the 3rd European Semantic Web Conference, Budva, Montenegro, 12 June.

Etgen, M. and Cantor, J. (1999) 'What does getting WET (web event-logging tool) mean for web usability'. Proceedings of Fifth Human Factors and the Web Conference, Gaithersburg, MD, June.

Flicker, S., Haans, D. and Skinner, H. (2004) 'Ethical dilemmas in research on Internet communities', *Quality Health Research*, 14 (1).

Fritsche, I. and Linneweber, V. (2006) 'Nonreactive methods in psychological research'. In M. Eid and E.D. Diener (eds.), *Handbook of Multimethod Measurement in Psychology*. Washington, DC: American Psychological Association, pp. 189–203.

Geertz, C. (1973) 'Thick description'. In C. Geertz (ed.), *The Interpretation of Cultures: Selected Essays*. New York, NY: Basic Books, pp. 3–30.

Greenwald, G. and MacAskill, E. (2013) 'NSA Prism program taps in to user data of Apple, Google and others'. *Guardian*, 7 June.

Hesse-Biber, S.N. and Johnson, R.B. (eds.). (2015) *The Oxford Handbook of Multimethod and Mixed Methods Research Inquiry*. Oxford: Oxford University Press.

Hofmann, K., Reed, C. and Holz, H. (2006) 'Unobtrusive data collection for web-based social navigation'. Workshop on the Social Navigation and Community Based Adaptation Technologies in Conjunction with Adaptive Hypermedia and Adaptive Web-Based Systems (AH '06) Dublin, Ireland, 20 June. Retrieved 12 October 2015 from http://www.sis.pitt.edu/~paws/SNC_BAT06/crc/hofmann.pdf

Hong, J.I. and Landay, J.A. (2001) 'WebQuilt: a framework for capturing and visualizing the web experience'. The Tenth International World Wide Web Conference, Hong Kong, 15 May. Retrieved 12 October 2015 from http://repository.cmu.edu/cgi/viewcontent.cgi?article=1060&context=hcii

Huntington, P.D.N., Jamali, H. and Watkinson, W. (2007) 'Site navigation and its impact on content viewed by the virtual scholar: a deep log analysis', *Journal of Information Science*, 33, 598–610. Retrieved 12 October 2015 from http://jis.sagepub.com/content/33/5/598.full.pdf

Janetzko, D. (1999) *Statistische Anwendungen im Internet. In Netzumgebungen Daten erheben, auswerten und praesentieren*. [Statistical Data Collection on the Internet]. Muenchen, Germany: Addison-Wesley.

Janetzko, D. (2016) 'The role of APIs in data sampling from social media'. In A. Quan-Haase and L. Sloan (eds.), *SAGE Handbook of Social Media Methods*. London: Sage Publications.

Jick, T. (1979) 'Mixing qualitative and quantitative methods: triangulation in action', *Administrative Science Quarterly*, 24, 602–11.

Johnston, M.J., King, D., Arora, S., Behar, N., Athanasiou, T., Sevdalis, N. and Darzi, A. (2015) 'Smartphones let surgeons know WhatsApp: an analysis of communication in emergency surgical teams', *The American Journal of Surgery*, 209 (1), 45–51.

Joinson, A. N., Reips, U.-D., Buchanan, T. and Schofield, C.B.P. (2010) 'Privacy, trust, and self-disclosure online', *Human–Computer Interaction*, 25(1), 1–24.

Kalman, Y.M. and Rafaeli, S. (2005) 'Email chronemics: unobtrusive profiling of response times'. In R.H. Sprague (ed.), Proceedings of the 38th Hawaii International Conference on System Sciences, Big Island, Hawaii, 3–6 January. Los Alamitos, CA: IEEE Computer Society Press. pp. 108–18.

Klimt, B. and Yang, Y. (2004) 'Introducing the Enron Corpus'. Proceedings of the First Conference on Email and AntiSpam (CEAS), 30–31 July, Mountain View, CA. Retrieved 15 August 2016 from http://nl.ijs.si/janes/wp-content/uploads/2014/09/klimtyang04a.pdf

Kossinets, G. and Watts, D.J. (2006) 'Empirical analysis of an evolving social network', *Science*, 311 (5757), 88–90.

Kramer, A.D.I., Guillory, J.E. and Hancock, J.T. (2014) 'Experimental evidence of massive-scale emotional contagion through social networks', *Proceedings of the National Academy of Sciences* 111.24, 8788–90.

Lee, K., Caverlee, J. and Webb, S. (2010) 'Uncovering social spammers: social honeypots + machine learning'. In Fabio Crestani and Stephane Marchand-Maillet and Hsin-Hsi Chen, Efthimis N. Efthimiadis and Jacques Savoy (eds.), Proceedings of the 33rd International ACM SIGIR Conference on Research and Development in Information. Geneva, Switzerland, July 19–23.

Lee, R.M. (2000) *Unobtrusive Methods in Social Research*. Buckingham, UK: Open University Press.

Lyon, D. (2014) 'Surveillance, Snowden, and big data: capacities, consequences, critique', *Big Data & Society*, doi:10.1177/2053951714541861.

Manjoo, F. (2003) 'Your TV is watching you'. *Salon*. Retrieved 15 August 2016 from http://www.salon.com/2003/05/08/future_tv/

Mathison, S. (1988) 'Why triangulate?', *Educational Researcher*, 17 (2), 13–17.

McDiarmid, A., Bell, S., Irvine, J. and Banford, J. (2013) Nodobo: detailed mobile phone usage dataset. Unpublished paper. Retrieved 15 August 2016 from http://nodobo.com/papers/iet-el.pdf

Morstatter, F., Pfeffer, J. and Liu, H. (2014) 'When is it biased? Assessing the representativeness of Twitter's streaming API'. Proceedings of the Companion Publication of the 23rd International Conference on World Wide Web Companion. International World Wide Web Conferences Steering Committee, April 7–11, Seoul, Korea.

Perer, A., Shneiderman, B. and Oard, D.W. (2006) 'Using rhythms of relationships to understand email archives', *Journal of the American Society for Information Science and Technology*, 57 (14), 1936–48. Retrieved 15 August 2015 from http://perer.org/papers/adamPerer-EmailVis-JASIST2006.pdf

Quan-Haase, A., Cothrel, J. and Wellman, B. (2005) 'Instant messaging for collaboration: a case study of a high-tech firm', *Journal of Computer-Mediated Communication*, 10 (4). Retrieved 15 August 2015 from http://onlinelibrary.wiley.com/doi/10.1111/j.1083-6101.2005.tb00276.x/full

Rathje, W.L. (1979) 'Trace measures', In L. Sechrest (ed.), *Unobtrusive Measurement Today*. San Francisco, CA: JosseyBass, pp. 75–91.

Ryle, G. (1971) *Collected Papers* (Vol. 2). London: Hutchinson.

Schwartz, M.F. and Wood, D.C.M. (1993) 'Discovering shared interests using graph analysis', *Communications of the ACM*, 36 (8), 78–89.

Scott, N. (2003) 'Socialization in the "virtual hallway": instant messaging in the asynchronous web-based distance education classroom', *The Internet and Higher Education*, 5 (4), 363–72. Retrieved 4 September 2006 from http://dlist.sir.arizona.edu/735/

Sha, L. and Aalst, J. van (2003) 'An application of social network analysis to knowledge building'. Poster session presented at the IKIT Summer Institute 2003, Toronto, ON, Canada. Retrieved 4 September 2006 from http://www.educ.sfu.ca/kb/Papers/Sha.pdf

Steenbruggen, J., Borzacchiello, M.T., Nijkamp, P. and Scholten, H. (2013) 'Mobile phone data from GSM networks for traffic parameter and urban spatial pattern assessment: a review of applications and opportunities', *GeoJournal*, 78 (2), 223–43.

Taylor, B. (2006) 'Sender reputation in a large webmail service'. Proceedings of the Third Conference on Email and AntiSpam (CEAS) 27–28 July, Mountain View, CA. Retrieved 1 September 2006 from http://www.ceas.cc/

Taylor, D. (2002) 'How can I filter robot crawler hits out of my Apache access log file?'. Ask Dave Taylor. Retrieved 3 July 2007 from http://www.askdavetaylor.com/how_can_i_filter_robot_crawler_hits_out_of_my_apache_access_log_file.html

Tyler, J.R. and Tang, J.C. (2003) 'When can I expect an email response? A study of rhythms in email usage'. Proceedings of the Eighth European Conference on Computer

Supported Cooperative Work (ECSCW) 2003, Helsinki, September. Deventer, The Netherlands: Kluwer. Retrieved 22 August 2006 from http://www1.cs.columbia.edu/ids/publications/metnspw02.pdf

Tyler, J.R., Wilkinson, D.M. and Huberman, B.A. (2003) *Email as Spectroscopy: Automated Discovery of Community Structure within Organizations*. Deventer, The Netherlands: Kluwer.

Webb, E.J., Campbell, D., Schwartz, R.D.D. and Sechrest, L. (1966) *Unobtrusive Methods: Nonreactive Research in the Social Sciences*. Chicago, IL: Rand McNally.

Webb, E.J., Campbell, D.T., Schwartz, R.D.D. and Sechrest, L. (2000) *Unobtrusive Measures*. Thousand Oaks, CA: Sage Publications.

Wesolowski, A., Buckee, C.O., Bengtsson, L., Wetter, E., Lu, X. and Tatem, A.J. (2014) 'Commentary: containing the Ebola outbreak – the potential and challenge of mobile network data', *PLoS Currents*, 6.

White, C., Moyer, C., Stern, D. and Katz, S. (2004) 'A content analysis of email communication between patients and their providers: patients get the message', *Journal of the American Medical Informatics Association*, 11, 260–7.

Williams, N. E., Thomas, T. A., Dunbar, M., Eagle, N. and Dobra, A. (2015) 'Measures of human mobility using mobile phone records enhanced with GIS data', *PLoS ONE*. Retrieved 14 October 2015 from http://journals.plos.org/plosone/article?id=10.1371/journal.pone.0133630

Wray, R. (2006) 'AOL sacks three workers for releasing customers' data', *Guardian*, 22 August.

Wu, F., Huberman, B.A., Adamic, L.A. and Tyler, J.R. (2004) 'Information flow in social groups', *Physica A*, 337, 327–35. Retrieved 5 September 2006 from www.hpl.hp.com/shl/papers/flow/flow.pdf

Zetter, K. (2006) 'Is the NSA spying on U.S. Internet traffic?' *Salon*. Retrieved 28 August 2006 from http://dir.salon.com/story/tech/feature/2003/05/08/future_tv/index2.html? pn=1

FURTHER READING

Whether you apply for a job, make use of a search engine or chat in social networks – unobtrusive data collection will take place. Employers will check the profile of an application online and Internet companies will record all online activities. But despite the rise of online social networks with their unprecedented possibilities for nonreactive data collection, the discussion on nonreactive data collection is still in its infancy. This is true both with regard to the technical side and the methodological side of this new group of research methods.

We lack a good technical introduction that covers the full spectrum of technical procedures for nonreactive data collection on the Internet. More general introductions to online data collection are provided by Janetzko (1999) (in German), Best and Krueger (2004) and Hesse-Biber and Johnson (2015). Many of the ideas that Eugene Webb and his colleagues have outlined in their pioneering work on unobtrusive data are still valid, which is why the revised edition of their book titled *Unobtrusive Measures* published in 2000 is a rewarding read. One of the most salient aspects of using data gathered in a nonreactive way is the combination of different data sources or recording processes. This theme was already present in the work of Webb *et al.* (1966) and among authors of the 1970s who strongly advocated multimethod research, in particular triangulation. The methodological literature of subsequent years is more sceptical about these concepts (Blaikie, 1991; Mathison, 1988) and should also be considered in order to learn more about the benefits and pitfalls of using nonreactive data and combining it with other kinds of data.

6

What's New? The Applications of Data Mining and Big Data in the Social Sciences

Ayelet Baram-Tsabari, Elad Segev
and Aviv J. Sharon

INTRODUCTION

This chapter discusses how data mining techniques differ from traditional quantitative methods and illustrates their current applications in the social sciences. It begins with a definition of data mining followed by a critical assessment of data mining techniques. These include the conscious and unconscious epistemological premises of scholars using data mining and traditional quantitative methods for data collection, the different resources available, the typical procedures, and their potential outcomes.

The second part of this chapter surveys state-of-the-art social science research that uses data mining techniques and classifies these studies into three groups: (1) studies of the mainstream media, (2) studies of user-generated data, and (3) studies of meta-data. The first group uses data mining to dramatically increase the volume of the corpus (making the sample closer to the population itself). The second group of studies considers both content and structural patterns of communication in social media channels (for example, the network analyses of Wikipedia discussions among editors or the Twitter communication flow). The last group of studies uses 'second-hand' data or meta-data aggregated by other automatic means. One example is studies that employ Google Trends data to analyze searches in Google. These studies can provide something of the bigger picture, although they depart from the original sources.

Finally, the last section discusses the advantages and disadvantages of data mining compared to traditional quantitative methods of data collection. It also presents future directions for data mining research.

USE OF DATA MINING IN SOCIAL SCIENCE PUBLICATIONS

The term 'data mining' was rarely used in social science publications before the mid-1990s. Since then, however, the number of publications that mention this term has grown rapidly. Of all publications indexed in *Scopus*, one of the largest bibliographic databases available, 2,135 social science publications used the term 'data mining' between 1995 and 2004. By comparison, a decade later, between 2005 and 2014, it was found in 29,970 publications.

In most disciplines, including life sciences, health, and physical sciences, the use of 'data mining' has grown in the last 15 years with the rise in social media and the popularization of Web 2.0.

Figure 6.1 summarizes the annual number of publications that mentioned the term 'data mining' in different disciplines based on the *Scopus* database. It shows that since 2008 there have been more publications each year in the social sciences than in health and life sciences that made use of this term. However, the number of indexed titles in *Scopus* from each discipline differs, ranging from 4,300 in the life sciences to 6,800 in the health sciences. After standardizing the results based on the number of indexed titles, the number of publications mentioning 'data mining' per title in 2014 was highest in the life sciences (one publication per title on average), but still higher in the social sciences than in the health sciences (0.84 compared to 0.56 publications per title).

More specifically, most publications mentioning the term 'data mining' fell under business and management, which includes the subfield of information systems and technology. In fact, about 60 percent of all social science publications using the term 'data mining' between 1994 and 2014 were related to business and management. By comparison, only about 4 percent of all social science publications were related to psychology. It is worth noting, however, that although *Scopus* displays a wide range of social science disciplines, its index is limited and certainly does not equally represent all social science disciplines (Harzing, 2010).

Another measure of centrality is the existence of dedicated journals. Although the first journal devoted primarily to analytics in the biological sciences, *Computers in Biology and Medicine*, began publication in 1970, the first journal targeted towards learning analytics and educational data mining in the learning sciences, the *Journal of Educational Data Mining*, began publication in 2009 (Baker and Siemens, 2014).

DEFINITIONS

'Data mining' is a research approach that draws heavily on computer science and

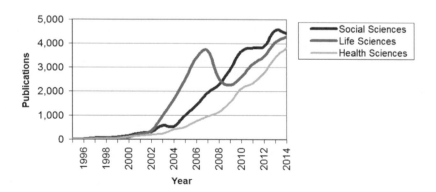

Figure 6.1 The annual number of publications that mentioned the term 'data mining' in different disciplines

Note: Physical sciences were not included because they had a much higher volume of publications.

emerged in response to the huge amounts of data being created, collected and aggregated in recent years (Smyth, 2000). For example, in the Human Microbiome Project, 5 terabytes of DNA data were collected from the microbial communities inhabiting the bodies of 300 participants, allowing researchers to deduce their effects on human health (Einkauf, 2013). In astronomy, researchers have recently created a large 3D map of part of the universe, weighing hundreds of terabytes, containing data about nearly half a billion stars and galaxies (Sloan Digital Sky Survey, 2015). The social sciences also experience a deluge of data. Social media platforms such as Facebook record behaviors from hundreds of millions of active daily users ('Company Info,' 2015). Data from increasingly popular online applications allow social scientists to study individual behavior in real time in a way that is both fine-grained and massively global in scale, making it possible to obtain precise real-time measurements across large and diverse populations (Golder and Macy, 2011). Because the volumes of data in question are so large, much of the data collected and generated in the world are never examined in depth. Traditional quantitative methods struggle to cope with these large datasets or 'big data', which explains the shift towards novel approaches such as data mining.

A word of explanation about the terminology: 'data mining' is the action usually undertaken to study 'big data'; however, one can mine data that are not 'big' or study big data other than by mining it. Depending on the definition, visualizing big data, for example, can be seen as part of the data mining process, or independent of it.

'Data mining' is defined in at least two different ways. In many cases, it is said to be one step in a process referred to as *knowledge discovery from data* (or from *databases*; KDD) (e.g.Dunham, 2003). Specifically, data mining has been defined as 'the automated or convenient extraction of patterns representing knowledge implicitly stored or captured

in large databases, data warehouses, the Web, other massive information repositories, or data streams' (Han *et al.*, 2012, p. xxiii).

Some examples of patterns include linear equations (e.g. a model predicting student achievement based on measures of student interest in the subject), rules (e.g. if a Facebook user identifies as conservative, most of his/her friends are likely to identify as conservative as well), clusters (e.g. types of galaxies grouped by a collection of several measured properties), graphs (e.g. networks of interacting Twitter accounts), tree structures (e.g. decision trees or family trees), and recurrent patterns in time series (e.g. recurring peaks of Internet searches for different types of keywords).

Alternatively, 'data mining' has been used to refer not only to a particular step of KDD but to the *entire process*, including preliminary steps such as data gathering, cleaning and preprocessing, and concluding steps, such as presentation (Grossman, Kamath, Kegelmeyer, Kumar, & Namburu, 2001; Han *et al.*, 2012). This broader definition considers, for example, the integration of multiple data sources as part of the data mining process. For instance, integrating Google Trends data for certain keywords with Wikipedia traffic data for corresponding articles can be considered part of the data mining process (Segev and Sharon, 2016). By contrast, the first narrower definition reserves the term 'data mining' for the subsequent step, in which patterns are automatically discovered and characterized in this dataset.

Here, we use the broader definition of 'data mining', in accordance with certain recent books on the subject, and with common parlance in industry, media, and research circles (Han *et al.*, 2012).

Importantly, data mining is typically applied to existing 'observational datasets', which were often not designed for this purpose. Hence data mining typically does not address preliminary data collection issues, such as experimental design or questionnaire design (Hand, Blunt, Kelly, & Adams,

2000; Hand, Mannila, & Smyth, 2001). This situation raises questions relating to validity. For example, one may use a decade worth of questions sent to the Ask-a-Scientist site in order to characterize students' interest in science (Baram-Tsabari *et al.*, 2009). However, this sample represents users that were motivated to learn more about science, and not necessarily the entire population.

Finally, some authors emphasize the contribution of the data mining process and stress its exploratory nature, as elaborated later. This implies that the outcome of the process is often expected to be 'interesting', 'unusual', or 'unexpected' (Hand *et al.*, 2000, p. 119), 'novel' (Hand *et al.*, 2001: 1), or 'at first unknown' (Giudici, 2003: 2). The data owner is not necessarily the person performing the data mining, and may have specialized knowledge that could help evaluate the emerging patterns and put them into context.

HOW IS DATA MINING DIFFERENT FROM TRADITIONAL QUANTITATIVE METHODS?

Epistemological Premises

Fayyad *et al.* (1996) distinguished between two types of data mining analysis: (1) hypothesis-driven analysis, called 'verification', similar to what is often found in traditional quantitative analysis, and (2) autonomous, automated pattern-finding, called 'discovery'. The latter type is more common in data mining and is subdivided into 'description', in which the system detects patterns in the data for the user, and 'prediction', in which the system makes a claim about the future behavior of an entity. When structures are found in the dataset, some or all of them are evaluated for their meaning or value by a domain expert (Hand *et al.*, 2000).

Thus, to some extent, the epistemological premises of most discovery-type data mining studies may be similar to the inductive process of qualitative research. In this approach, recurrent patterns are gleaned from the data and continuously revisited and re-interpreted by the researcher. Emerging themes, categories, concepts, or theories are evaluated in light of the research questions (Merriam, 2009).

The flexibility of data mining may provide new ways to operationalize existing concepts in a more comprehensive, generalizable or updated fashion. For example, instead of measuring happiness based on self-reports, it can be measured from spontaneous expressions on Twitter (Dodds *et al.*, 2011). In the example of massive open online courses (MOOCs), researchers found they needed new conceptualizations to make sense of the data. DeBoer and colleagues (2014) consider four basic variables: enrollment, participation, curriculum, and achievement, to demonstrate the inadequacy of conventional interpretations of quantitative analysis and reporting. Drawing from 230 million clicks from over 150,000 participants, they present new educational variables and different interpretations of existing variables at different scales (DeBoer *et al.*, 2014).

An example of a new variable arising from data structure and availability can be found in Backstrom *et al.* (2011) who proposed a new measure for the analysis of personal networks, based on the way in which individuals divide their attention across contacts (e.g. focus a large fraction of their interactions on a small set of close friends). The researchers suggested using these new ideas in any context where detailed interaction data are available (Backstrom *et al.*, 2011).

Resources and Characteristics of the Data

Forms of Datasets

The web offers various forms of data that can be mined, including (hyper)text and multimedia, graphs, actions and interactions, networked data (e.g. social networks), and others.

In some cases, the dataset can be dynamic and continue to evolve during the study. Data mining deals with the storage, retrieval, and updating of such datasets as well as with their analysis (Bramer, 2007; Han *et al.*, 2012).

The choice of platform also crucially influences the theoretical and methodological approaches to research. Veltri (2012) noted that years after the advent of television as the main form of mass media, printed media were used comparatively more frequently because textual data could be analyzed in both quantitative and qualitative approaches through consolidated methodologies. Textual data are still the prime source for data mining. Twitter, for example, has been used widely due to its convenient approach to data mining and structure that enables the study of asymmetrical influence relationships.

Data Availability and Quality

Useful and accessible data sources change over time – from Yahoo! Answers (Bouguessa *et al.*, 2008) to Second Life (Bakshy *et al.*, 2009) to Twitter and beyond. In many cases, the datasets often represent samples not chosen by the researcher, which may be random or not. For example, when researchers use data from Google Trends or a Twitter stream, they are studying a sample made available by the company.

Obtaining large datasets often requires considerable resources, such as those at the disposal of governmental agencies (e.g. the US National Security Agency) or private companies (e.g. Facebook, Coursera, and Google). These datasets are often available to a privileged set of researchers (Lazer *et al.*, 2009). Even when datasets are made available by for-profit corporations, data accuracy, transparency and stability may be an issue. For example, Google Trends does not divulge raw search numbers for Google web searches, but only relative shares of a sample of the total searches, scaled to a range of 0 to 100. Wikipedia traffic statistics, by contrast, are made available in raw form on an article by article basis. Perhaps the fact that

the website is operated by the Wikimedia Foundation, which is a non-profit organization, contributes to the transparency afforded by these datasets.

Historical Data

The nature of data mining and its sources sometimes allows for the development and application of new research methods in the social sciences, such as the ability to follow people in retrospect, akin to a retrospective cohort study. Budak and Watts (2015), who studied social movements in the context of the Gezi uprising in Turkey, could follow the Twitter activity of 30,000 users, both active and non-active participants, before, during, and after the events took place. They suggest that Twitter made it possible to construct 'ex-post panels months or even years after the events of interest have taken place, making it especially attractive for studying events such as political uprisings that are hard-to-impossible for researchers to anticipate and so do not lend themselves to traditional panel designs' (Budak and Watts, 2015: 27).

Research Population

Some datasets make entire populations available for analysis, rather than a sample. In these cases, the statistical notion of inference is irrelevant, and yet even in such cases, the representativeness of the entire populations should be addressed. Consider, for example, administrative data. Millions of national health service patients may be available for analysis. This could provide a great opportunity to study patients, but a poor way to study the health of the entire population because healthy people will not be included. Similarly, Facebook users or Google Search users are not representative of the entire population. They may be a much more heterogeneous research population than undergraduate psychology students participating in studies for credit, but still represent a certain group of people, which may not always be useful to study general questions in the social sciences.

Sizes of Datasets

Datasets may easily reach sizes on the order of 10^5–10^6 datapoints or more. Traditional quantitative methods were originally developed for use with small samples of data, and may 'break down' when analyzing such large sample sizes (Little & Schucking, 2008: 420). Testing hypotheses at stringent significance levels is not likely to help because the likelihood of making a Type I error grows with very large datasets. This may lead to a case of 'just about anything will be significant with this sample size'.

In addition, traditional studies and data mining studies often differ in terms of the format in which the data are stored. While a small dataset can be saved in a simple 'flat' file, large datasets must be stored in databases with efficient scalable designs in order to obtain timely results. The algorithms used for analyzing the datasets must also be designed for speed. The development and assessment of such databases and algorithms is a key concern among data miners (Dunham, 2003; Hand *et al.*, 2000; Little & Schucking, 2008).

Limitations of Datasets

The randomized, controlled samples typically analyzed in quantitative studies are traditionally considered the gold standard for statistical inference, but are often expensive or difficult to obtain. By contrast, convenience samples collected by a non-researcher may represent particular subpopulations more authentically, and may contain valuable meta-data about how the data were collected and for what purpose. Such data may therefore have high ecological validity, which might not otherwise be obtainable in a random sample collected by a researcher.

Resources Needed

Since traditional quantitative research is typically not computationally intensive, it can often be calculated on a personal computer by a user with an understanding of descriptive and inferential statistics and familiarity with statistical software packages. Some of these have standard, point-and-click user interfaces, such as IBM SPSS Statistics or Rstudio.

Data mining large datasets, by contrast, requires either working with databases or knowing how to access them through application programming interfaces (API). Although user-friendly data mining software packages are now available, such as Weka (www.cs.waikato.ac.nz/ml/weka/), programming knowledge is still a huge advantage for the data miner. Furthermore, computationally intensive data mining tasks may require powerful computers with large memory resources, etc. For example, in Veltri's (2012) study of nanotechnology discourse on Twitter, computing power was an important factor in determining the sampling strategy and sample size.

Procedure

The entire process of KDD is iterative and typically includes the following steps, where data miners can go back and forth between any step until they are ready to move on (modified from Dunham, 2003; Fayyad *et al.*, 1996; Han *et al.*, 2012):

1 *Data cleaning, integration and selection* – Removing poor quality data, errors and random noise, handling missing data, mapping data to a single naming convention, combining several sources of data, as needed, and retrieving data from the database. For example, a study on exposure to ideologically diverse news and opinion on Facebook only considered users who were at least 18 years old, logged in at least 4 days a week and self-reported their ideological affiliation (Bakshy *et al.*, 2015). In a study on portrayal of physical activity on Twitter, relevant keywords from a governmental health website were selected to gather appropriate Tweets from the Twitter API (Yoon, Elhadad, & Bakken, 2013).

2 *Data transformation* – Traditional quantitative methods are typically applied for just a few dependent or independent variables, such as the combined effects of age and gender on attitudes toward genetically modified foods and

childhood vaccines. By contrast, mining business transaction data may yield dozens of values per transaction, such as (1) the date and time, (2) the location, (3) the total cost, (4) the items sold, (5) discounts given, etc., giving many possible independent variables for analysis. Hence, data must be converted or encoded into common formats, summarized or aggregated into forms appropriate for mining, and reduced in dimensionality. For example, the users might be automatically binned according to the number of Facebook friends they have, or how often they log in. Alternatively, this challenge is addressed by applying dimensionality reduction methods common in data mining, such as wavelet transforms, principal components analysis, and attribute subset selection (Han *et al.*, 2012).

3   *Data mining* – Applying algorithms to extract data patterns. Some of these patterns may be *descriptive*, e.g.:

- Exploring and summarizing the dataset using interactive and visual representations, e.g. scatterplots, boxplots, histograms, or principal components analysis. These include extracting measures such as averages, medians and interquartile ranges of Facebook activity rates of the population constructed, or, representing the changes in search volumes for Nobel Prize discoveries after they were announced in public (Baram-Tsabari & Segev, 2015).
- *Clustering* – Partitioning the data into groups, e.g. dividing Internet users into groups based on similar usage habits of a particular website (Giudici, 2003), or clustering search volume time series based on the strength of their correlations with (1) related news coverage and (2) the academic calendar (Segev & Baram-Tsabari, 2012).
- *Association rules* – Describing relationships between variables, e.g. market basket analysis, yielding rules such as '60% of the time that bread is sold, so are pretzels, and [...] 70% of the time jelly is also sold' (Dunham, 2003: 9) or 'among the 30% of students who entered a wrong answer to this question, 70% entered the answer "100 meters"' (Ben-Naim, Bain, & Marcus, 2009).
- *Sequence discovery* – Determining sequential patterns in data, e.g. detecting frequent sequences of pages accessed and buttons clicked on a website, such as whether users typically click the 'Subscribe

to Our Newsletter' button after viewing the 'Products' and 'About Us' pages, in that order (Dunham, 2003), or determining that scientific terms appearing in the news, e.g. 'tsunami', often see bursts of Google searches and, in the same week or in following weeks, increased visits to corresponding Wikipedia articles (Segev and Sharon, 2016).

In addition to descriptive patterns, certain patterns mined from data can be *predictive*. Prediction comes in two classes, classification and regression. In both cases, the goal is to infer the value of a *predicted* variable using some combination of *predictor* variables:

- *Classification* – Sorting data items into one of several predefined classes, e.g. automatically sorting newly found stars and galaxies into categories, based on the features of a set of known stars and galaxies (Hand *et al.*, 2001), or determining which college students are at risk of dropout based on data from student information systems and course management systems (Arnold, 2010). In this case, the predicted variable can only be attributed to one of a discrete set of values.
- *Regression* – Predicting the value of a continuous variable, e.g. predicting a person's spending based on his or her monthly income (Hand *et al.*, 2001), or predicting the severity of influenza outbreaks using search engine query data (Ginsberg *et al.*, 2009). In this case, the predicted variable is continuous.

4   *Pattern evaluation* – Identifying patterns representing knowledge based on measures of 'unusualness', 'unexpectedness', or 'interestingness' (Hand *et al.*, 2000); some of these may be objective and others subjective. The patterns can be considered interesting if (1) they are easy to understand, (2) they are valid on new or test datasets with at least a certain degree of certainty, (3) they are unexpected, (4) they confirm a hypothesis, (5) they are potentially useful or actionable (Han *et al.*, 2012).

For example, let us consider a pattern found in transactions from a pharmacy, where a certain homeopathic remedy X was found to be likely bought along with dietary supplement Y. The associations can be evaluated by several objective quantitative measures including (1) support (i.e. what percent of transactions contain either X, or Y, or both?), (2) confidence (i.e. if a transaction contains X, what is the probability that it contains Y?) and (3) correlation (i.e. to what extent does the occurrence of X imply the occurrence of Y, or vice versa?). These measures could be used to filter the list of patterns before submitting them for subjective review by a domain expert (Han *et al.*, 2012).

5 *Knowledge presentation* – Visualizing and representing mined knowledge to the user, for example by using scatter plots or decision trees to represent predictions made by the model for oncologists and other decision-makers. For example, cartography and Geographic Information Science (GIS) use visualizations of social media (Twitter) and search engines (Yahoo, Bing) to map social activity (Tsou *et al.*, 2013) and to take advantage of spatio-temporal footprints from Flickr (Li *et al.*, 2013).

CURRENT STATE OF THE ART AND POTENTIAL OUTCOMES

We divide the data mining research presented here into three groups based on the different corpora employed: (1) studies that look at mainstream media (such as popular news sites), (2) studies that examine user-generated content (social media, online forums, reader comments, Wikipedia, blogs, etc.), and (3) studies that look at user activity (such as queries to search engines and log files). These categories not only differ in terms of research focus but also in terms of their data mining strategies and potential to understand the content as well as the structure and flow of communication.

The first group uses data mining to dramatically increase the volume of the corpus (making the sample closer to the population itself). The second group of studies can consider the structural patterns of communication using network analysis (for example, the network analyses of the Wikipedia discussions among editors, or network analysis of Twitter communication flow). The last group does not look directly at the content but

rather at the behavior of users. It departs from the original sources, but has the advantage of looking at the macro picture better than others. We now provide examples of studies in each group and discuss their potential and limitations compared to equivalent studies using traditional methods.

Data Mining in Mainstream Media

One of the significant advantages of studies employing data mining of mainstream content such as news portals is that they dramatically increase the sample size. When studying news portals, Segev (2015) examined more than a million news items from 35 popular news sites in 10 different languages. This can be compared to a very similar large-scale study conducted by Wu (2000) that examined about 34,000 news items generated from a multinational research project in 38 countries. Very often, studies employing data mining techniques, such as the one conducted by Segev (2015), do not use a sample but rather collect and analyze the entire population; that is, all the news items that were published in a particular period.

Another advantage is the ability to dramatically increase the time span of investigation. When online news archives are available, they allow mining of much more content over much longer periods. Jones, Van Aelst and Vliegenthart (2013), for example, employed online archives of two American newspapers to study changes over a period of 57 years. Similarly, Segev, Sheafer and Shenhav (2013) used the online archives of American and German newspapers to study and compare trends of news content over a period of 50 years. Before the availability of online news archives, scholars wanting to study temporal changes in the news tended to sample a very short period of a week or less in each year (Larson and Hardy, 1977; Wilke, 1987).

After collecting the data, researchers need to choose whether to employ qualitative or quantitative analysis. As noted earlier, data mining is not only about data collection, but also about the ability to automatically filter out irrelevant information and find reoccurring patterns in the corpus. For example, when studying positive and negative sentiments of countries in the news, Segev and Miesch (2011) collected only relevant sentences, and further defined the positive and negative terms associated with the country under investigation.

As a result, data mining studies provide analyses of much larger datasets at a much longer time span than was previously possible. This methodological advantage can help identify patterns more accurately on the macro-level. For example, in Segev (2015) the ability to identify over- and under-represented countries in the news called for a modification of the theory of news flow. Since the sample in this case was closer to the entire population, there were many more patterns available in the data. Naturally, not everything is digitized and data mining research is therefore still limited in scope.

Data Mining of User-Generated Content[1]

Data mining social media has a great methodological advantage: it can take what was once invisible and private and make it reachable and researchable (Boyd et al., 2010). These properties make this type of research extremely attractive to social scientists.

In some cases, the written text itself is the subject of investigation. For example, a statistical analysis of 107 million Twitter messages was used to study changes in the nature of written language. Eisenstein et al. (2014: 1) identified high-level patterns in the diffusion of linguistic change over the United States. They concluded that 'rather than moving towards a single unified "netspeak" dialect, language evolution in computer-mediated communication reproduces existing fault lines in spoken American English'.

Pavalanathan and Eisenstein (2015) found that Tweets with hashtags are more formal, while reply Tweets use more slang.

In other cases, user-generated content becomes an indicator of another general social phenomenon, such as emotions and happiness. Dodds et al. (2011) used nearly 4.6 billion Tweets posted by over 63 million unique users to create a 'text-based hedonometer' following the use of over 10,000 individual words. Similarly, using data from 500 million Tweets from 84 countries, in which 1,000 words are used as indicators of positive and negative emotions, Golder and Macy (2011) have identified individual-level mood rhythms in cultures across the globe. They found, for example, that individuals awaken in a good mood that deteriorates as the day progresses, and that people are happier on weekends. Previous studies exploring the same questions have relied heavily on retrospective self-reports of small homogeneous samples of American undergraduates.

Social media data that were generated in one context are often anonymized and employed in entirely different contexts. A fascinating case of the private-becoming-researchable is a study aiming at explaining the relative persistence of same-race romantic relationships, based on evidence from an online dating community involving more than 250,000 people in the United States. Researchers studied the frequency with which individuals both express a preference for same-race romantic partners and act to choose same-race partners. Findings indicate that the ideologically conservative are much more likely than liberals to state a preference for same-race partners. At the same time, both men and women of all political persuasions generally act as if they prefer same-race relationships even when they claim not to (Anderson et al., 2014).

In some cases, studies use social media to explore general sociological phenomena, while other studies look at social media as a subject of investigation. How do social media affect the composition of news consumption?

Do these media promote exposure to news from politically heterogeneous individuals (Messing and Westwood, 2012)? Bakshy et al. (2015) examined how 10.1 million US Facebook users interact with socially shared news. They tested the extent to which ideologically heterogeneous friends could potentially expose individuals to cross-cutting content, the effect of the platform's algorithm and users' choices to click through to ideologically discordant content. Compared to algorithmic ranking, they found that individuals' choices about what to consume had a stronger effect limiting exposure to content that could challenge their worldview (Bakshy et al., 2015).

In a study of social media platforms, Kahle et al., (2016) compare patterns of engagement on the five different social media platforms used by European Organization for Nuclear Research (CERN) communication. They found that audience interactions with the posts were more common on platforms with smaller audiences. Facebook researchers used survey and audience logs of 222,000 Facebook users' posts to estimate the size of the passive audience – those who do not interact with the content they see. They found that publicly visible signals, such as friend count, likes, and comments, varied widely and did not strongly indicate the audience of a single post (Bernstein et al., 2013).

Aral and Walker (2012) used randomized experimentation to identify influence and susceptibility in networks using a representative sample of 1.3 million Facebook users. In the context of the decision to adopt a product offered, they found that influential individuals are less susceptible to influence than noninfluential individuals, and that they cluster in the network, while susceptible individuals do not.

Many projects passively monitor Twitter communication about different diseases ('infodemiology'): public health studies (Chew and Eysenbach, 2010), health issues (e.g. insomnia: Jamison-Powell et al, 2012), and environmental issues (e.g. nuclear risk:

Binder, 2012; Li et al., submitted). Most of this research has focused on English-language social media. An exception is work by Wang et al. (2015) who investigated the value of Chinese social media for monitoring air quality trends and related public perceptions. Their analysis was based on 93 million messages from Sina Weibo, China's largest microblogging service. Such works depend to a large extent on the choice of keywords and hashtags, which are required to be comprehensive and relevant to the topic. Wang et al.'s study is also interesting in that the reliability of the data filters was evaluated by comparing message volume per city to air particle pollution rates obtained from the Chinese government for 74 cities. They found that the volume of pollution-related messages was highly correlated with particle pollution levels, and concluded that messages in Sina Weibo were quantitatively indicative of true particle pollution levels (Wang et al., 2015).

Mining User Activity

Unlike the previous groups of studies, studies looking at user activities usually employ databases that were already gathered and structured by other parties. Log files of website visits are an example of such a database gathered by the server, registering details about the users and the content they viewed. The access to such databases is usually restricted to the website operators, but some websites allow viewing certain activities in their sites for different reasons. Google Trends is an example of a publicly available database that allows researchers to study and compare the queries entered to Google in different topics and regions.

Scheitle (2011) found a significant correlation between Google's searches and survey data for several social measurements in the US. This includes the Gallup survey for the most important social issues and the Religious Congregations and Membership Study of church membership and attendance.

His study shows that search data provides a very good proxy for studying social phenomena or general interests. Similarly, search data was used by Segev and Baram-Tsabari (2012) to reflect public interest in science. They compared the trends of searches of scientific terms with the trends of mentions in mainstream news media and the academic calendar. Their study distinguished between well-established scientific terms (such as 'genetics') that were searched during the academic year, and ad hoc scientific terms (such as 'Mars Rover') that corresponded with media coverage. Google Trends was used in this case not only to learn about people's interests in science but also to identify 'teachable moments', where people are more open and likely to learn about the surrounding world (see also Baram-Tsabari and Segev, 2011, 2015).

Search query data are not only useful for studying actual user interests, but also for predicting future outcomes and behaviors. In the field of economics and marketing, Choi and Varian (2012) found Google Trends data to be very useful and accurate in predicting automobile sales, home sales, retail sales, and travel behavior. Ginsberg *et al.* (2009) analyzed Google search queries to track influenza-like illnesses in a population. They assumed that a sharp increase in searches related to influenza could indicate the actual outbreak of the epidemic due to the high correlation between these searches and physician visits. Their findings revealed that data mining of search queries could predict the geographical centers and spread patterns of epidemics immediately and accurately. More recent studies, however, have questioned these findings (Butler, 2013; Lazer *et al.*, 2014), showing that Google search queries drastically overestimate the peak flu levels. Thus, the use of search query data in such cases may complement but still not replace traditional epidemiological surveillance networks.

The analysis of search queries can be further obtained through log files, a technique also known as 'web log mining'. Web servers store not only visitor-specific information on their log files, but also the website redirecting to them as well as the search queries used. Ravid *et al.* (2007) used the log files of the citizen advice bureau website to analyze more than 260,000 search queries. This method can help with mapping the main interests and concerns of online users and further cater to their information needs.

The advantages and potential of mining user activity are enormous. Compared to surveys that are limited to a small portion of the population, log files make it possible to look at the information uses of all visitors in a specific domain. Additionally, although surveys and interviews are prone to social desirability bias, mining the actual activity of users is much more reliable and accurate in revealing general social interests and needs, particularly when it comes to sensitive issues, such as in Anderson *et al.*'s (2014) study of online dating preferences or the studies of health-related search queries (Butler, 2013; Ginsberg *et al.*, 2009; Lazer *et al.*, 2014) mentioned earlier.

On the other hand, user activity data, unless obtained as part of a laboratory experiment, does not enable the high resolution that is often achieved in qualitative analyses. In most cases data is anonymized and researchers are unable to trace back to the users for more in-depth investigations. The Segev and Baram-Tsabari (2012) study on Google Trends could not trace back to specific users to examine the reasons for their search, and the use or knowledge they acquired. Compared to interviews and surveys, mining user activities is limited to the specific instances allowed by and directed through the interfaces. For example, log files may only show the specific webpages visited by users or the information they enter within specific input fields. Similarly, due to the space constraints and technical limitations, searches in Google are very often phrased as a few keywords rather than long and full questions. Finally, not all information and activities are online.

These characteristics significantly limit the scope of study possible by data mining techniques.

Studies that Combine Components of the Three Groups

Some studies combine different corpora as well as traditional and data mining techniques to study a phenomenon from various angles. This was the case in a study conducted by Wolfsfeld et al., (2013) to examine the role of social media during the Arab Spring. They examined whether social media activity could predict or explain the intensity of the uprising compared to traditional political variables, and whether it preceded or followed the uprising events.

For this purpose, apart from gathering traditional political and economic measurements, they operationalized social media variables for each of the 22 Arab countries, using three different methods: (1) analyzing periodical surveys of social media use, (2) examining Google search trends for social media terms, and (3) comparing the most popular searches in Google in different periods. To determine the extent of the uprising in each country, they used data from several mainstream newspapers and online sources. Thus, the methodological approaches in this study were mixed, ranging from traditional collection of macro-political, economic, and technological variables (such as GDP, democratic level, or Internet penetration), survey data (the use of social media), and the analysis of user activity meta-data (using Google Trends).

The findings all pointed to a common conclusion in which political and economic variables were much better predictors of the social uprising than social media variables, and increases in the use of the social media were more likely to follow the protest activity than to precede it. In other words, there was empirical validation of their theoretical premises regarding the limited role of social media in social uprising, particularly due to the triangulation of different approaches.

CONCLUSION

Data mining clearly holds vast potential and merit for social science applications. At its best it allows for real-time, remote-sensing, in vivo and non-invasive research, involving a diversity of participants and a massive amount of data. But it also can be misused and misinterpreted, or alternatively used only by privileged scholars with access to the data, making replication almost impossible.

This chapter could have included a list of 'obstacles and pitfalls' for using data mining, but these are not really obstacles. Rather they are considerations that should be acknowledged when choosing a research approach, interpreting findings, and drawing operative conclusions. For example, even when using probability sampling from an online population data mining may represent a convenient sample in at least three ways: it is almost always a self-selecting sample of users, it is mostly based on found data that were not collected with the needs of social research in mind, and it is almost always a platform selected for the availability of the data and not its representativeness. This partly explains why Twitter has been the focus of so many studies in the last decade.

Similar to the way that controlled experiments in medicine test a new drug against the best available treatment,[2] we should not ask whether data mining is a good approach for the social sciences, but rather compare its affordances with the best alternative method in a given context. An example is content analysis, which increasingly involves big data, and computational linguistic methods, such as word co-occurrence, topic detection, and sentiment analysis. These methods allow for very different volumes of data to be analyzed. Laslo et al. (2011) analyzed manually about 600 reader comments using content analysis to identify and characterize scientific and ethical content, compared to Veltri (2012) who automatically analyzed 24,000 Tweets to identify positive and negative sentiment regarding nanotechnology.

Nevertheless, adding natural language processing and unsupervised machine learning to social scientists' toolbox does not replace manual content analysis. It allows researchers to ask very interesting questions using vast amounts of data, but at the same time is very limited in terms of deriving meaning from content. This is, naturally, a generalization. Advances in extracting meaning from text are being used, for example, in the field of learning science (McNamara, 2011). Still, social scientists should take the promises for automatic detection of nearly everything with a grain of salt. These promises are sometimes based on highly optimistic views of state of the art technologies, a perception that anyone can write or adapt code in-house, and a basic assumption that whatever counts can be counted. Furthermore, these techniques are currently far less powerful in languages used by relatively small populations. For these reasons, we join Shah *et al.* (2015) in their call for a hybrid approach – manual and computational – to content analysis.

In their survey of educational data mining and learning analytics, Baker and Siemens (2014) concluded that these methods have been applied to an ever-widening range of data sources and to answering an expanding range of research questions. They have the potential to substantially increase the sophistication of how the field understands learning, thus contributing both to theory and practice. We believe these trends of widening data sources and expanding research questions are true of many more fields within the social sciences.

NOTES

1   In this section we refer to content, in its traditional sense, but also to user behaviors such as liking and sharing content published by others on social media.

2   Helsinki Declaration, Paragraph 33. 'The benefits, risks, burdens and effectiveness of a new intervention must be tested against those of the best proven intervention(s)…' http://www.wma.net/en/30publications/10policies/b3/ (accessed January 2015).

REFERENCES

Anderson, A., Goel, S., Huber, G., Malhotra, N., and Watts, D. J. (2014). 'Political ideology and racial preferences in online dating', *Sociological Science, 1*, 28–40.

Aral, S., and Walker, D. (2012). 'Identifying influential and susceptible members of social networks', *Science, 337*(6092), 337–341.

Arnold, K. (2010). 'Signals: Applying Academic Analytics', *EDUCAUSE Quarterly, 33*(1). Retrieved from www.educause.edu/library/EQM10110

Backstrom, L., Bakshy, E., Kleinberg, J. M., Lento, T. M., and Rosenn, I. (2011). 'Center of attention: How Facebook users allocate attention across friends', *International AAAI Conference on Web and Social Media (ICWSM,), 11*, 23.

Baker, R., and Siemens, G. (2014). 'Educational Data Mining and Learning Analytics'. In R. K. Sawyer (Ed.), *The Cambridge Handbook of the Learning Sciences. 2nd Edition* (pp. 253–274). Cambridge: Cambridge University Press.

Bakshy, E., Karrer, B., and Adamic, L. A. (2009). 'Social influence and the diffusion of user-created content'. Paper presented at the Proceedings of the 10th ACM conference on Electronic Commerce. July 9–10, 2009. Stanford, CA.

Bakshy, E., Messing, S., and Adamic, L. (2015). 'Exposure to ideologically diverse news and opinion on Facebook', *Science, 348*(6239), 1130–2. doi: 10.1126/science.aaa1160.

Baram-Tsabari, A., and Segev, E. (2015). 'The half-life of a "teachable moment": The case of Nobel laureates', *Public Understanding of Science, 24*(3), 326–37. doi: 10.1177/0963662513491369.

Baram-Tsabari, A., and Segev, E. (2011). 'Exploring new web-based tools to identify public interest in science', *Public Understanding of Science, 20*(1), 130–143.

Baram-Tsabari, A., Sethi, R. J., Bry, L., and Yarden, A. (2009). 'Asking scientists: A decade of questions analyzed by age, gender and country', *Science Education*, *93*(1), 131–160.

Ben-Naim, D., Bain, M., and Marcus, N. (2009). A User-Driven and Data-Driven Approach for Supporting Teachers in Reflection and Adaptation of Adaptive Tutorials. In *Educational Data Mining 2009* (pp. 21–30). Retrieved from http://www.educationaldatamining. org/conferences/index.php/EDM/2009/ paper/view/1465/1431

Bernstein, M. S., Bakshy, E., Burke, M., and Karrer, B. (2013). 'Quantifying the invisible audience in social networks'. Paper presented at the Proceedings of the SIGCHI Conference on Human Factors in Computing Systems. 27 April–2 May, 2013. Paris, France.

Binder, A. R. (2012). 'Figuring out #Fukushima: An initial look at functions and content of US Twitter commentary about nuclear risk', *Environmental Communication: A Journal of Nature and Culture*, *6*(2), 268–277.

Bouguessa, M., Dumoulin, B., and Wang, S. (2008). 'Identifying authoritative actors in question-answering forums: The case of *Yahoo! answers*'. Paper presented at the Proceedings of the 14th ACM SIGKDD international conference on Knowledge Discovery and Data Mining. August 24–27, 2008. Las Vegas, NV.

Boyd, D., Golder, S., and Lotan, G. (2010). 'Tweet, tweet, retweet: Conversational aspects of retweeting on Twitter'. Paper presented at the HICSS 43rd Hawaii International Conference on System Sciences. January 5–8, 2010. Honolulu, HI.

Bramer, M. (2007). *Principles of Data Mining*. London: Springer-Verlag.

Budak, C., and Watts, D. J. (2015). 'Dissecting the spirit of Gezi: Influence vs. selection in the Occupy Gezi movement', *Sociological Science*, July 22, 2015. doi: 10.15195/v2.a18.

Butler, D. (2013). 'When Google got flu wrong', *Nature*, *494*(7436), 155.

Chew, C, and Eysenbach, G. (2010). 'Pandemics in the age of Twitter: Content analysis of Tweets during the 2009 H1N1 outbreak', *PloS ONE*, *5*(11), e14118. doi:10.1371/ journal.pone.0014118.

Choi, H., and Varian, H. (2012). 'Predicting the present with Google Trends', *Economic Record*, *88*(s1), 2–9. doi:10.1111/j.1475-4932.2012.00809.x. Available from: http:// www.google.com/googleblogs/pdfs/google_ predicting_the_present.pdf (accessed January 2013).

Company Info. (2015). *Facebook Newsroom*. Retrieved from http://newsroom.fb.com/ company-info/

DeBoer, J., Ho, A. D., Stump, G. S., and Breslow, L. (2014). 'Changing "course": Reconceptualizing educational variables for massive open online courses', *Educational Researcher*, *43*(2), 74–84. doi: 10.3102/ 0013189x14523038.

Dodds, P. S., Harris, K. D., Kloumann, I. M., Bliss, C. A., and Danforth, C. M. (2011). 'Temporal patterns of happiness and information in a global social network: Hedonometrics and Twitter', *PLoS ONE* *6*(12), e26752. doi:10.1371/journal.pone.0026752.

Dunham, M. H. (2003). *Data Mining: Introductory and Advanced Topics*. Upper Saddle River, New Jersey: Pearson Education.

Einkauf, J. (2013). Human Microbiome Project Data Set. *Amazon Web Services*. Retrieved from http://aws.amazon.com/datasets/ 1903160021374413

Eisenstein, J., O'Connor, B., Smith, N. A., and Xing, E. P. (2014). 'Diffusion of lexical change in social media', *PLoS ONE*, *9*(11), e113114. doi:10.1371/journal.pone.0113114

Fayyad, U., Piatetsky-Shapiro, G., and Smyth, P. (1996). 'From data mining to knowledge discovery in databases', *AI Magazine*, 17(3), 37–54. doi: 10.1609/aimag.v17i3.1230.

Ginsberg, J., Mohebbi, M. H., Patel, R. S., Brammer, L., Smolinski, M. S., and Brilliant, L. (2009). 'Detecting influenza epidemics using search engine query data', *Nature*, 457, 1012–1014.

Giudici, P. (2003). *Applied Data Mining: Statistical Methods for Business and Industry*. West Sussex, England: John Wiley & Sons.

Golder, S. A., and Macy, M. W. (2011). 'Diurnal and seasonal mood vary with work, sleep, and daylength across diverse cultures', *Science*, 333, 1878–1881.

Grossman, R. L., Kamath, C., Kegelmeyer, P., Kumar, V., and Namburu, R. R. (2001). *Data Mining for Scientific and Engineering*

Applications. Dordrecht, The Netherlands: Kluwer Academic Publishers.

Han, J., Kamber, M., and Pei, J. (2012). *Data Mining: Concepts and Techniques* (3rd edn). Waltham, Massachusetts: Morgan Kaufmann Publishers.

Hand, D. J., Blunt, G., Kelly, M. G., and Adams, N. M. (2000). 'Data mining for fun and profit', *Statistical Science*, *15*(2), 111–126.

Hand, D. J., Mannila, H., and Smyth, P. (2001). *Principles of Data Mining*. Cambridge, MA: MIT.

Harzing, A. W. (2010). 'Citation analysis across disciplines: The impact of different data sources and citation metrics'. Harzing.com. Available at: http://www.harzing.com/data_metrics_comparison.htm

Jamison-Powell, S., Linehan, C., Daley, L., Garbett, A., and Lawson, S. (2012). 'I can't get no sleep: Discussing #insomnia on twitter'. Paper presented at the Proceedings of the SIGCHI Conference on Human Factors in Computing Systems, New York, NY: ACM, pp. 1501–1510.

Jones, T. M., Van Aelst, P., and Vliegenthart, R. (2013). 'Foreign nation visibility in U.S. news coverage: A longitudinal analysis (1950–2006)', *Communication Research*, *40*(3), 417–436. doi:10.1177/0093650211415845.

Kahle, K., Sharon, A. J., and Baram-Tsabari, A. (2016). 'Footprints of fascination: Digital traces of public engagement with particle physics on CERN's social media platforms', *PLoS ONE 11*(5): e0156409. doi:10.1371/journal.pone.0156409.

Larson, J., and Hardy, A. (1977). 'International affairs coverage on network television news: A study of news flow', *International Communication Gazette*, *23*(4), 241–256. doi:10.1177/001654927702300404.

Laslo, E., Baram-Tsabari, A., and Lewenstein, B. V. (2011). 'A growth medium for the message: Online science journalism affordances for exploring public discourse of science and ethics', *Journalism: Theory, Practice and Criticism*, *12*(7), 847–870.

Lazer, D., Kennedy, R., King, G., and Vespignani, A. (2014). 'The parable of Google Flu: traps in big data analysis', *Science*, *343*(14 March)., 1203–1205.

Lazer, D., Pentland, A. S., Adamic, L., Aral, S., Barabasi, A. L., Brewer, D., Christakis, N., Contractor, N., Fowler, J., and Gutmann, M. (2009). 'Life in the network: The coming age of computational social science', *Science* (New York, NY), *323*(5915), 721.

Li, L., Goodchild, M. F., and Xu, B. (2013). 'Spatial, temporal, and socioeconomic patterns in the use of Twitter and Flickr.', *Cartography and Geographic Information Science*, *40*(2), 61–77. doi: 10.1080/15230406.2013.777139.

Li, N., Akin, H., Su, L. Y-F., Brossard, D., Xenos, M. A., and Scheufele, D. A. (forthcoming). 'Tweeting disaster: A content analysis of online discourse about nuclear power in the wake of the Fukushima Daiichi nuclear accident', *Journal of Science Communication*.

Little, B., and Schucking, M. (2008). 'Data Mining, Statistical Data Analysis, or Advanced Analytics: Methodology, Implementation, and Applied Techniques'. In N. Fielding, R. M. Lee, and G. Blank (Eds.), *The SAGE Handbook of Online Research Methods* (pp. 419–442). London: Sage Publications.

McNamara, D. S. (2011). 'Computational methods to extract meaning from text and advance theories of human cognition', *Topics in Cognitive Science*, *3*(1), 3–17.

Merriam, S. B. (2009). *Qualitative Research: A Guide to Design and Implementation*. San Francisco: Jossey-Bass.

Messing, S., and Westwood, S. J. (2012). 'Selective exposure in the age of social media: Endorsements trump partisan source affiliation when selecting news online', *Communication Research*. doi:10.1177/0093650212466406.

Pavalanathan, U., and Eisenstein, J. (2015). 'Audience-modulated variation in online social media', *American Speech*, *90*(2), 187–213.

Ravid, G., Bar-Ilan, J., Baruchson-Arbib, S., and Rafaeli, S. (2007). 'Popularity and findability through log analysis of search terms and queries: The case of a multilingual public service website', *Journal of Information Science*, *33*(5), 567–583. doi:10.1177/0165551506076326.

Scheitle, C. P. (2011). 'Google's Insights for Search: A note evaluating the use of search engine data in social research', *Social Science Quarterly*, *92*(1), 285–295. doi: 10.1111/j.1540-6237.2011.00768.x.

Segev, E. (2015). 'Visible and invisible countries: News-flow theory revised',

Journalism, 16(3), 412–428. doi:10.1177/1464884914521579.

Segev, E., and Baram-Tsabari, A. (2012). 'Seeking science information online: Data mining Google to better understand the roles of the media and the education system', *Public Understanding of Science, 21*(7), 813–29. http://doi.org/10.1177/0963662510387560

Segev, E. and Miesch, R. (2011). 'A systematic procedure for detecting news biases: The case of Israel in European news sites', *International Journal of Communication, 5*, 1947–66. doi:1932-8036/20111947.

Segev, E. and Sharon, A. (2016). 'Temporal patterns of scientific information-seeking on *Google* and *Wikipedia*', *Public Understanding of Science*. doi:10.1177/0963662516648565.

Segev, E., Sheafer, T., and Shenhav, S. (2013). 'Is the world getting flatter? A new method for examining structural trends in the news', *Journal of the American Society for Information Science and Technology, 64*(12), 2537–2547. doi:10.1002/asi.22932.

Shah, D. V., Cappella, J. N., and Neuman, W. R. (2015). 'Big data, digital media, and computational social science: Possibilities and perils', *Annals of the American Academy of Political and Social Science, 659*(1), 6–13.

Sloan Digital Sky Survey. (2015). The Sloan Digital Sky Survey Opens a New Public View of the Sky. *SDSS*. Retrieved from http://www.sdss.org/releases/the-sloan-digital-sky-survey-opens-a-new-public-view-of-the-sky/

Smyth, P. (2000). 'Data mining: Data analysis on a grand scale?', *Statistical Methods in Medical Research, 9*(4), 309–327. http://doi.org/10.1177/096228020000900402

Tsou, M.-H., Yang, J.-A., Lusher, D., Han, S., Spitzberg, B., Gawron, J. M., Gupta, D., and An, L. (2013). 'Mapping social activities and concepts with social media (Twitter) and web search engines (Yahoo and Bing): a case study in 2012 US Presidential Election', *Cartography and Geographic Information Science, 40*(4), 337–348. doi: 10.1080/15230406.2013.799738.

Veltri, G. A. (2012). 'Microblogging and nanotweets: Nanotechnology on Twitter', *Public Understanding of Science, 22*(7), 832–49. doi: 10.1177/0963662512463510.

Wang, S., Paul, M., and Dredze, M. (2015). 'Social media as a sensor of air quality and public response in China', *Journal of Medical Internet Research, 17*(3), e22.

Wilke, J. (1987). 'Foreign news coverage and international news flow over three centuries', *International Communication Gazette, 39*(3), 147–180. doi:10.1177/001654928703900301.

Wolfsfeld, G., Segev, E., and Sheafer, T. (2013). 'The social media and the Arab Spring: Politics comes first', *The International Journal of Press/Politics, 18*(2), 115–137. doi:10.1177/1940161212471716.

Wu, D. H. (2000). 'Systematic determinants of international news coverage', *Journal of Communication, 50*(2), 113–130. doi:10.1111/j.1460-2466.2000.tb02844.x.

Yoon, S., Elhadad, N., and Bakken, S. (2013). A 'Practical Approach for Content Mining of Tweets', *American Journal of Preventive Medicine, 45*(1), 122–129. http://doi.org/10.1016/j.amepre.2013.02.025

## 7

Of Instruments and Data: Social Media Uses, Abuses and Analysis

Martin Innes, Colin Roberts,
Alun Preece and David Rogers

Sociological research and measurement require
something like a 'theory of instrumentation' and a
'theory of data'...the fundamental events of social
action should be clarified before imposing measurement postulates with which they may not be in
correspondence. (Cicourel, 1964: 1–2)

In his influential deliberation upon the interactions between theory and method in sociological research, Aaron Cicourel was
concerned to elaborate how empirical data is
an artefact of the research instruments
deployed in its elicitation. Writing during a
moment when social research was evolving
rapidly in terms of both quantitative and
qualitative methods, he cautioned of a need to
attend far more carefully to such matters.

In recent years, associated with theories
of the information age and the wider implications of the arrival of 'big data', there has
been a rush of innovation in social research
as a range of disciplines have manoeuvred
to understand and interrogate the implications of a profoundly different information
environment. Individual disciplines have

responded to these developments with particular inflections, but there is broad agreement
that the situation has shifted from 'information scarcity' to 'information abundance'.
The implication being that studies no longer
have to be designed on the basis of a pre-
sumption of going out and collecting 'rare'
data, but must engage with the rather different demands associated with marshalling and
making sense of massive amounts of potentially research relevant materials.

Cast as socially disruptive developments,
these socio-technological processes are being
ascribed both positive and negative potential
consequences. For social research, they have
the potential to enable us to study previously imperceptible dimensions of social life
and its interactional and institutional orders.
Others caution though, that this trajectory of
development may actually induce a crisis for
social research. Such concerns pivot around
Savage and Burrows's (2007) suggestion that
these technologies place powerful tools and
methods for analysing social data into the

hands of corporations and think tanks who can use them without the conceptual and methodological rigour that trained academic researchers invoke.

These more critical interrogations of big social data have been summarised recently by Pasquale (2015) in his inquisition of an increasingly 'black box' society. He contends that social life is increasingly ordered by and dependent upon processes and algorithmic formulae that are not disclosed or publicly visible. As a consequence of which, fateful decisions are taken without either the decision-takers or those subject to these decisions really understanding how or why particular courses of action have been arrived at (see also Schneier, 2015). Similar concerns apply to these new frontiers of social research, where, as will be discussed, claims are mounted upon the basis of analyses of social media data that are difficult to validate or evaluate.

Accordingly, this chapter covers both the opportunities and challenges attending the increasing role and influence of social media in social research, including platforms such as Facebook, Twitter and Instagram. In framing this approach, we are conscious that 'pure' academic studies are not necessarily the primary or even main forum where research using social media data is being used. Commercial research applications, often motivated by an intent to improve the effectiveness and efficiency of marketing goods and services to public audiences have been the vanguard of these developments. More recently, government departments and agencies have demonstrated increasing interest in harnessing social media analytics for public service delivery and development. To understand how and why such applications have been developed and implemented, it is necessary to understand three key components of social media analysis: the structure, processes and regulation of the communication platforms themselves (in both one-to-one and one-to-many configurations); the data collection processes and algorithms; and

the interpretative and sense-making actions that frame the outputs of analysis and data visualisations.

Cutting across the academic, commercial and governmental policy sectors, a key pattern of development has involved a number of free or purchasable products that effectively 'lower the barriers to entry' for those wishing to engage analysis of social media data in their research. These tools are placing increasingly powerful capacities and capabilities for processing and visualising social media data into the hands of people who previously would not have been positioned to undertake analyses of large volumes of material. Whilst this self-evidently possesses positive potential, it equally carries some epistemological risks. 'Researchers' not fully trained in the 'dark arts' of social research may not be sufficiently appreciative of how their tools and their analytic decisions may influence the validity and reliability of any findings.

Set against this backdrop where social media is being engaged across a range of 'basic' and 'applied' forms by a diversity of actors, it is our intent that the chapter should speak to two principal audiences and their respective concerns:

- First, we want to distil some 'how to' principles for social researchers seeking to embed social media analysis within their research designs;
- Second, and equally important, we are looking to increase the literacy of a wider audience, in order that they can meaningfully and critically engage with these new currents in the conduct of social research. This is about the criterion with which to validate and evaluate research informed by these techniques.

In seeking to understand how social researchers can analyse, utilise and evaluate social media data and the claims it is used to develop, we draw upon Cicourel's instruction that any such attempt needs to be scaffolded by a 'theory of instrumentation' and a 'theory of data'. The former is especially important because the label 'social media' tends to obscure how specific facets of the individual technological platforms establish different affordances for social research and their uses for research purposes. Similarly, developing a 'theory' of social media data is a vital task because they are not neutral reflections of events and actions in the 'real world', but are instead involved in propelling how these actions and events are performed and interpreted.

Having framed the discussions in these terms, the next section examines how social media analysis has been conducted to inform studies of a variety of social problems and issues. This is followed by a more critical appraisal of what the developing evidence base suggests in terms of where social media analytics can legitimately and appropriately be deployed, and where it cannot. In the penultimate section, we provide a case study account to develop a number of the key themes from the preceding sections and to suggest how these may evolve into the future. The conclusion reflects upon how social media affords new opportunities and insights for conducting innovative social research, but which have equally been 'over-sold'. An attempt is made to delineate the boundaries between what social media based research methods can and cannot do.

UNDERSTANDING SOCIAL MEDIA INSTRUMENTATION

A theory of instrumentation is concerned with the ways social knowledge and action are formatted and framed by the methods used to attend to them. In developing an understanding of how and why such matters are important to our current concerns, insightful analogies can be drawn with Donald Mackenzie's (2006, 2014) ongoing work on financial markets and the ways big data and trading algorithms are transforming the social worlds of high finance. In an early output from this work, Mackenzie (2006)

sought to distinguish between financial instruments that were functioning as 'engines' or 'cameras'. The former referring to where they were directly 'driving' processes of social change. The counter-point to which, he suggested, were their functioning as a 'camera' – taking snapshot representations of social reality.

These are concepts that can be usefully imported into a discussion of how social media can enable new instruments for social research. But rather than an 'either/or' distinction, it is more appropriate to conceive of social media as performing simultaneously as both an engine and camera. That is, these naturally occurring data are frequently part of the events and processes that they comment upon, shaping and steering public narratives and understandings.

These inter-locking features are especially well illuminated in Brym et al.'s (2014) analysis of the role of social media in the political uprisings in Egypt in 2011. In a number of popular narratives of how and why the overthrow of the Mubarak regime occurred, social media were ascribed a significant social impact upon the organisational dynamics of the protest movement. However, their analysis suggests the presence and functions of social media were less a causal 'engine' of revolt, than were far more orthodox sentiments of grievance and malcontent. But what social media did supply was a channel of communication outside of state-owned broadcast media, via which those who felt aggrieved could rapidly disseminate and share representations of their concerns. In sum, they suggest that the impacts and consequences of social media in Egypt may have been mythologised and over-claimed. This is a cautionary note about the potential for overstating the causal influence of social media that we will return to several times in this chapter.

The extent to which particular communications are integrated within and achieve influence in these ways depends, at least in part, upon the affordances and technological features associated with individual social media platforms. This was noted by Procter *et al.* (2013) in their analysis of the 2011 London Riots. They identified that the Blackberry Messenger (BBM) application allowed those engaged in propagating disorder to communicate on a private network that the police could not monitor, thereby giving them an informational advantage through which to organise and coordinate their collective actions. More generally, however, the salience of this socio-technical interaction in understanding the heterogeneous properties of social media has been underplayed. Too many studies focus upon presenting empirical data derived from social media without disentangling who the different social media are used by, why, how, when and for what purposes.

In terms of general patterns in users and use, the trend is upwards. The Global Web Index reports that time spent on social networks like Facebook has risen from 1.61 hours to 1.72, and time on micro-blogs such as Twitter has risen to 0.81 hours daily for the average user (Mander, 2014). Social networking now accounts for almost 30 per cent of daily Internet activities, with micro-blogging approaching the 15 per cent mark (Mander, 2014). Facebook has, for some time, been the leading platform in terms of active usage with over 40 per cent of Internet users actively engaging at least monthly. Twitter, YouTube and Google+ (the latter two both owned by Google) form the 'second tier' of social media, each with just over 20 per cent of Internet users active on their platforms, whilst the 5th ranked social media platform, Instagram (owned by Facebook), sees just over 15 per cent of all Internet users holding an active account (Mander, 2015).

As noted previously, social media platforms are far from homogeneous. Each possesses a particular set of features and regulatory principles that define the nature of content and behaviour of its users. Kietzmann *et al.* (2011) formalised seven functional building blocks of social media and micro-blogging platforms: presence, sharing, relationships, identity, conversations, reputation and groups.

These building blocks relate to how user availability is broadcast to others, how content is propagated across the platform's network, the depth of relationship between users, the level of privacy that users maintain, their level of communication, the importance given to social status with regards to users and content, and the extent to which users form communities. These components can be used to construct useful comparative summary profiles of major social media sites in terms of their primary and secondary features. For example, as outlined in Figure 7.1, using these seven components, Haefner (2014) demonstrates how Facebook has evolved into a megalithic service, supporting to some degree all seven of the building blocks. YouTube on the other hand has remained focused on only four of the seven blocks, with a stronger emphasis on sharing than it had before.

Facebook and Google+ are the megaliths of social media platforms, geared towards being the social hubs for users with article sharing, instant messaging and group pages amongst their core features. The remaining three have more streamlined functionality, with an emphasis on content sharing and discussion through specific mediums (YouTube: video; Instagram: images/video; Twitter: images/video/text). Cross-compatibility of social media platforms is also becoming more prevalent, with both Facebook and Google+ allowing for the inclusion of external social media content (through the article sharing features), thereby positioning themselves as gateways to other platforms.

In terms of user demographics, all are dominated by younger users, with 50 per cent of active users aged 35 or below. Instagram's users tend to be younger, whilst in comparison, Facebook's user base

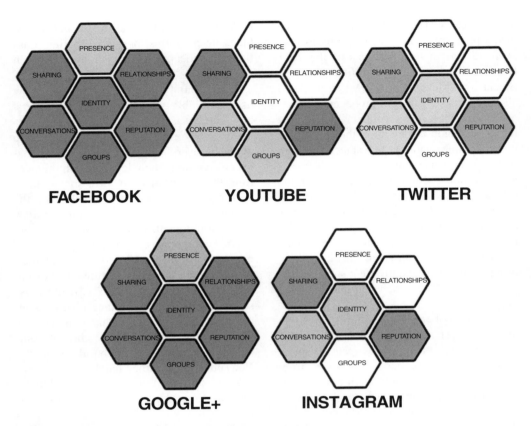

Figure 7.1   Social media honeycombs of top 5 platforms

Source: Adapted from Haefner (2014).

is more mature. The 'second tier' platforms have fairly similar demographics (see Figure 7.2 below).

Duggan *et al.* (2015) highlight a significant overlap between Twitter and Instagram users, with over 50 per cent of users on each site present on the other. In terms of multiple platform use, Facebook is used by over 8 out of 10 users of the other social media platforms listed in the study.

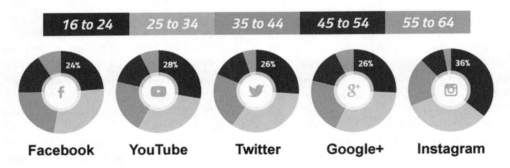

Figure 7.2   Platform usage by age

Source: Adapted from Mander (2015).

Access to Researchable Data on Social Media

Social media platforms provide application programming interfaces (API) that allow programmatic access (access by computational programs) to their social data, often as a limited free service, with more open access available at a cost. The sheer volume of data that can be produced from a social media platform is vast, with 31.24 per cent of all web traffic being attributed to social media platforms in the final quarter of 2014 (up 8.53 per cent from the previous year).[1] These APIs enable users to build systems and tools that can autonomously collect, submit and process social media content.

For instance, access to the Facebook Platform is via the Graph API, which provides programmatic read and write functions for third-party applications. The Graph API provides a means of accessing the Facebook social graph – a semantic representation of all the users, pages, groups, events and media present on the site, describing the relationships between these objects. Each object is uniquely identified with a numerical ID, with some core objects (users and pages) having unique names associated with them as well. The relationships between objects can be used to identify other objects connected via that relationship.

Access to these kinds of data is reliant on individual users granting permission for their information to be viewed in the form of an access token. To obtain access tokens from users, a Facebook app must be registered to the Facebook Developers site. Users are then required to log in to the app via one of a number of 'login flows' provided by Facebook,[2] where they explicitly grant permission for the app to access the user's information and their relationships to other Facebook objects.

Instagram offers its own API and supporting site,[3] holding the same broad principles in terms of access rights as Facebook. Instagram is centred on the sharing of multiple types of media and so most discourse on the site is attached to media posts. A standard query returns the latest 150 comments linked to a media item, but researchers using this functionality need to log repeated calls in order to catch new comments as they have been added. Instagram also offers a subscription streaming service,[4] which can notify a client of new media posts meeting specific search criteria, registered users, tags, named locations or geographic areas. Finally, Instagram provides a list of enterprise partners whom they deem experts in the management of data surrounding the Instagram platform.[5]

Google provides API services for both YouTube and Google+ data, with supporting functionality and documentation via the Google Developers website.[6] These services allow researchers and business analysts to locate and retrieve public comments posted on both platforms. The YouTube Data API allows for many standard operations available on the YouTube website to be performed, with query options allowing for keyword, locational, regional or topical searches.

Google+ is supported by its own API, which is similar to YouTube's, focusing upon Activities, Comments and People. Like the services made available by Facebook and Instagram, these APIs require authorisation credentials to be passed to the endpoints when any request is made. Access through these two APIs is limited by daily access quotas (defaulted to 50,000 quota units), where each action is costed in quota units. An example being that each part of a 'read request' costs approximately 2 units of the daily quota. The intent being to encourage intelligent querying.

Of all the available social media platforms, of most interest to academic social research in the last few years has been Twitter. As a micro-blogging tool access to Twitter is provided through the Twitter REST API,[7] with data collection achieved through the Search API, Streaming API and Firehose.

The Search API facilitates historical paginated searching of Tweets, retrieving those meeting search criteria defined by a combination of keywords, geographic constraints and user IDs. The search criteria are compared against recently published Tweets, with the service holding 7 days' worth of cached Tweets available to search against, limited to 180 queries per 15-minute window.

The Streaming API allows for real-time collection of public data through a persistent connection. Access to this is limited by the fact that, if the search criteria associated with the streaming connection begins to match more than 1 per cent of all Tweets currently being published, Twitter enforces a sampling limitation to the amount of data returned. To circumvent this 1 per cent limitation being applied to the Streaming API, researchers may subscribe to the Twitter Firehose, which provides full streamed access to the Twitter dataset. This is the only way to guarantee that you are collecting 100 per cent of the Tweets that match your search criteria at all times. The drawbacks to using the Firehose relative to the Streaming API are cost-based, with Twitter charging around US$500 to US$3000 per month for its usage, with access provided by a small number of resellers.[8]

Importantly, it has been shown that the Streaming API is not uniformly sampled when the 1 per cent limitation is being applied, to the point where sometimes the Streaming API can show negative correlation against the Firehose in top hashtag counts (Morstatter *et al.* 2013). This can be alleviated through using multiple Streaming API connections with more focused query sets, reducing the chance of hitting the 1 per cent limit in a connection.

Across these platforms, additional services and analytic tools have been developed to support businesses and researchers in understanding how trends, topics, brands and events are propagated and received within a social media community and platform. The majority of these seem to be geared towards providing business insights into advertising campaigns and public perception. Some of these tools and services are fully integrated into the platforms such as Facebook Insights, whereas some are popular third party services that may or may not have some form of affiliation with the platform.

Attending to the pragmatic details of these platforms and how they work is important for understanding how data derived from individual instruments are subtly configured and structured in ways that render them more suitable and amenable for engaging with certain forms of questions rather than others. As Kitchin (2014) identifies, amongst social scientists, engagement with these epistemological issues has lagged behind more prosaic considerations. There are rather different issues associated with making sense of data that is naturally occurring at scale, when compared with the more bounded and limited datasets that have been the standard fare of social research. Following boyd and Crawford (2012), the operationalisation of these social media platforms typically blends elements of technology, analysis and mythology.

Of these elements, it is the mythic quality that is arguably the most neglected. Taking a catholic view of social research spanning both scholarly and policy applications and conducted by a range of actors including scholars, think tanks and private companies, the possibilities of what social media analysis can actually deliver have frequently been over-sold and misunderstood. Returning to the arguments made by Pasquale (2015) rehearsed at the beginning of this chapter, this is because the instruments tend to be treated as a black box. The concept of 'social media' and label of 'social media data' imply a degree of homogeneity that is probably inappropriate. As our understandings of social media mature and develop, the notion that different platforms are more and less effective for different modes of analysis and generating different forms of data will likely become more accepted.

UNDERSTANDING SOCIAL MEDIA DATA

Digging into the mythology that swirls around social media to critique its uses and applications is not intended to wholly usurp its status or use, but instead to be far more clear-eyed about how it can be used effectively in research.

Shifting focus from the instrumentation to the data that it generates, one common issue is how the 'bigness' of the data frequently elides its representativeness. This often takes the form that authors, whilst acknowledging the issues with their data, forego any such concerns on the grounds that 'there is just so much of it, it must tell us something'. This discourse has a sheen of attractiveness because the data themselves are naturally occurring, and do not rely upon the kinds of formal sampling frames required for many more orthodox research designs. Concerns have been articulated, however, with the 'messiness' of the data derived from social media. Edwards *et al.* (2013), for instance, discuss the numerous flaws associated with 'low fidelity', unrepresentativeness and the absence of key demographic variables.

A second order of concern relates to how, just because data are derived from novel sources does not mean that the ways they are processed and analysed is equally innovative. For example, trenchantly critiquing Procter *et al.*'s (2013) interpretation of 2.6 million Tweets collected around the 2011 riots in England, Chan and Bennett Moses (2015: 6) point out that the analysis conducted was essentially 'traditional media content analysis'. Their concern being that the formers' claim to significant innovation is restricted to data collection techniques, rather than analysis and interpretation. The point is that it is the latter that are necessary conditions for generating the more profound insights that will speak to genuinely novel theory and understanding.

For many years now the principal epistemological fault-line in social research has been drawn between whether one is a proponent of 'qualitative' or 'quantitative' research designs (Fielding and Schreier, 2001), where the former is understood as affording increased 'depth' of insight and understanding, and the latter more oriented to providing a 'breadth' of vision. More recently, however, and inflected by increasing interest in and appreciation of multi-method research designs, these divisions have been less accentuated (Creswell and Plano Clark, 2011). Instead, they have been replaced, at least in some quarters, by a divide between advocacy of naturalistic and experimental approaches.

Advocates of social media research frequently assert that part of its value derives from how it is 'naturally' occurring from within online digital interactions. This is not to say that experimental research cannot, or indeed has not, been conducted using social media data, for example Facebook manipulating peoples' news feed to test the consequences upon their affective states (see Smith *et al.*, this volume). The point is that the preponderance of social research using social media has been based upon data derived naturally from online social transactions. In this sense, it has been coherent with the lessening of the epistemological divide between quantitative and qualitative method, noted previously. Indeed, one of the principal values of social media data is that it occasions simultaneous application of quantitative, qualitative and visual methods to process and interpret it comprehensively.

SOME USES AND ABUSES OF SOCIAL MEDIA

Having outlined some key issues and debates surrounding research using social media at quite an abstract and conceptual level, we now shift to a more grounded register, focused upon dissecting several examples of how researchers have folded the kinds of data and instruments described earlier into their research designs. Rather than organising this discussion in terms of quantitative and qualitative methodologies, we focus upon several substantive themes where clusters of studies based upon and informed by social media data can be detected. This foregrounds, with more precision, how social media analytics is being harnessed to speak to some of the foundational conceptual concerns of social research, and how extracting meaning and insight from such materials is understood as being predicated upon a blend of statistics and more 'high resolution' interpretative methods.

Researching Social Identity

Alice Marwick (2013) discusses how increasingly pervasive social media platforms have been re-shaping our conceptions and practices of self- and social-identity. Her particular interest is with how peoples' digital public personas and reputations are increasingly 'brand-like' – being actively projected and protected. In the process, she contends, our conceptions of privacy and selfhood are being profoundly reconfigured. Although she does not invoke such an analogy, her analysis could be seen as being in a tradition initiated by Erving Goffman (1959) in attending to the presentation of self in everyday life. In focusing upon digital social identities, however, she picks up a theme traceable back to Meyrowitz (1985) that media communications technologies are collapsing the boundaries between the front-stage and back-stage dimensions of sociality that were so pivotal in Goffman's analysis.

Given the interests of this chapter, what is important about this approach is its use of fairly traditional qualitative analyses and reporting. They stand in contra-distinction to the avowed tendency to quantification that is apparent across the social media research landscape, as analysts work with large volumes of material. Rather than be seduced by the allure of such methods, Marwick focuses instead upon a more detailed qualitative accounting. This enables her to showcase how people actively edit their digital identities to publicise aspects they perceive as especially appealing to their social network.

Researching Social Problems: Google Flu Trends

One of the highest profile applications of social media research has been in the area of health epidemiology and using people's online health tracking behaviours to construct inferences about the spread of viruses. Google Flu Trends (GFT) is an approach that takes users' search queries about flu-like symptoms as an indicator of the spread of these across space and time. By comparing these to baseline data for a particular region derived from more standard forms of population health surveillance, an estimate can be made about whether levels of online search activity are in excess of that which would normally be anticipated. During its initial implementation significant claims were made for the accuracy of GFT, in particular that as a method it could provide an anticipatory warning indicator for regional flu outbreaks by picking up increases in symptomology ten days prior to existing methods. However, subsequent analyses have queried and questioned such claims.

Writing in the journal *Nature*, Butler (2013) suggested GFT's significant overestimation of US flu occurrence in January 2013 resulted from failing to correct for an increase in flu-related searches by people who were not ill due to widespread publicity for GFT.[9] This exemplifies a more general pattern of behaviour that Hacking (1995) labels 'the looping effects of humankind'. He reminds us that social agency means there are not linear causal relationships between how people act and changes to their social environment. Applied to processes of social adoption of new technologies, the technologies, human actions and subjectivities all adapt.

Picking up on the interactive nature of socio-technical innovations, Lazer *et al.*'s (2014) analysis of GFT in '*Science*' accented the influence of routine technical changes introduced by Google to its search algorithms.[10] He made several additional important points, including:

- The high sensitivity of social media algorithms to the search terms chosen to collect data (Google has never documented the 45 terms it used);
- The difficulty in replicating results of such algorithms when the major social media providers' systems are always changing for commercial reasons (what Lazer labels 'blue team' dynamics);
- The danger that analytics algorithms are prone to manipulation/gamification by users ('red team' dynamics in Lazer's terms – though he does not believe this played a part in the GFT January 2013 failure); and
- A general lack of transparency in the mainstream social media platforms, which undermines replicability of results over time.

Layered on top of which are additional concerns about the representativeness of the sample population, particularly in terms of the digital divide and downplaying of offline effects.

Coda

This necessarily selective discussion of how social media methods have been applied by researchers is intended to impart a feel for the principal currents and issues. Collectively, the varied examples sketch some of the possibilities and potential of social media to propel and reinvigorate research agendas in respect of some fundamental concerns of the social sciences. They provide new opportunities for studying social structures and processes from alternative vantage points with comparatively high resolution data, thereby illuminating hitherto imperceptible features.

Equally, however, the preceding discussion has foregrounded some more problematic aspects of these applications. These include a tendency for 'overclaiming', both in terms of the overall influence of social media, but also in terms of the validity and reliability of findings premised upon data derived from such sources. Oftentimes this can be traced back to the mistaken belief that the comparative vastness of the dataset must endow any analysis based upon it with some explanatory power. However, as has already been noted, in social

media environments volume does not equate with representativeness.

This is exemplified by the interest in sentiment analysis. Because of how different 'user communities' form around different social media platforms, analyses of data from these can provide broad indicators of public emotion, but should not be seen as providing measures of this. Indeed, more generally, social media appears to get more interesting when it is understood as providing digital traces of social action, rather than when it is employed to monitor sentiments.

A third issue concerns the limited nature of the analysis conducted. For example, many empirical studies orient themselves through a discussion of big data and accent the volume of the dataset available for their study, sometimes claiming millions of datapoints available to be processed. However, more careful reading ascertains that, in actuality, coding and analytic procedures were applied to far more limited samples of the material. This is frequently a pragmatic response to the issues and represents where the state of the art of social media analysis *actually* is, rather than where some would like it to be. Such issues are compounded by a need for more sophisticated and nuanced analytic tools that engage more thoroughly with theory. Many existing tools rely on fairly basic content analysis techniques. Whilst such approaches are not without value, they are limited in the insights they afford. Especially given the diversity and complexity of the social institutions and interactions they are being directed towards.

It is for these reasons that thinking of social media as constituting both an engine and a camera is important because this recognises that these communications are not neutral representations of events in the world, but frequently propel social dynamics in terms of how they unfold and are socially constructed. It is here, once again, that establishing a theory of instrumentation and of data is so important in understanding how these components interact in shaping the story of an event and the ways people react to it. Extending this line of argument, it is also the case that a number of research applications of social media would benefit from a more thorough and meaningful engagement with substantive middle-range theories pertaining to the particular study's area of interest. For whilst patterns in data can be interesting, as Wright Mills (1959) identified five decades ago, pure 'abstracted empiricism' cannot inform us of these patterns' significance, nor whether they should be invested with meaning.

One final point relevant to this section, likely to be of increasing salience in the near future, concerns public permission and ethics. In an environment where normative conceptions of privacy and 'the public' are being challenged and reconfigured, especially in light of a stream of revelations about how governments and multinational corporations are using these methods to surveil citizens and consumers, such issues will be rendered increasingly important for the research community.

Engaging with these issues requires us to understand, in far more depth, the boundaries of public permission for different uses. How does it matter, in terms of establishing generalisable ethical principles for instance, that different technological platforms and thus the research instruments plugged into these, conceive of their raw data and its owners in different ways? On the one hand, social media offers the potential for studying aspects of social life in ways that are relatively less demanding of research subjects, especially when compared with some more orthodox research instruments that require them to answer questions, or permit access and entry to a social setting. After all social media are naturally occurring data that researchers can scoop up and harvest, often without any direct intervention in respect of the social phenomena they are seeking to study, and with far less inconvenience to their subjects/participants.

But at the same time, these data gathering and processing techniques also possess an inherent potential for a curious blend of remoteness and intrusion. Studies of commercial and governmental data-mining and surveillance have documented a quite startling plethora of uses to which such data can be put (see Pasquale, 2015; Schneier, 2015). This can routinely include detailing peoples' private relationships, identities and behavioural routines. As general public awareness of these increases, it will raise vital questions about where public permission sits for similar kinds of research. Equally profoundly, such developments are challenging some of our accepted conventions about the very nature of privacy and the 'public realm'.

CASE STUDY: BLENDING FAST AND DEEP DATA

The preceding sections have sketched some key aspects of what research methodologies integrating social media data and instrumentation can and cannot do. Our intent in formulating this account has been to review how social media is being utilised by researchers; teasing out the new affordances of such approaches; avoiding the more hyperbolic claims that have a tendency to become attached to some of this work. To elaborate some of these themes, the next section switches register to develop a more in-depth and detailed case study account of a particular piece of research. In so doing, we focus upon how such instruments and data could be integrated within mixed method research designs and for the purposes of multiple source data triangulation (Fielding, 2009).

The case study pivoted around the NATO Summit held in South Wales on the 3 and 4 September 2014. The Summit was on such a scale that its key activities were split between the cities of Cardiff and Newport, with other areas across South Wales impacted also. With several geopolitical crises emerging in the lead up to the meeting, it was cast as requiring a security operation that was 'unprecedented' in the United Kingdom – a claim

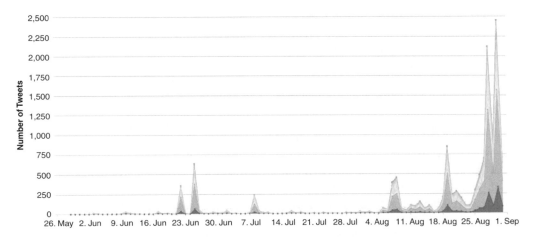

Figure 7.3   Social media volumetric timeline for the Wales NATO Summit

manifested on land, at sea and in the air. Over 9,300 police officers drawn from all 43 forces in England and Wales, plus security details from all participating countries, were on the ground in South Wales. A 'no-fly' exclusion zone was imposed across the whole of South Wales and South West England for the period of the meeting, and for the week preceding the event 'Nighthawk' military helicopters and police helicopters became a regular site over Cardiff and Newport. In addition to which, seven international warships were stationed in Cardiff Bay.

Given the uniqueness of the event, the authors decided to extend their existing research programme exploring the application of social media analytics to policing and security issues, to encompass the NATO Summit. A small team of experienced social researchers and computer scientists started planning for the event approximately 5 months prior to the Summit itself. Data collection commenced by monitoring key hashtags and terms, which were progressively refined and expanded by the research team as more details about the Summit itself were publicly revealed. As the actual date of the Summit got closer, so the intensity of the effort increased and the precision of the collection enhanced.

Figure 7.3 depicts the basic volume of Twitter traffic detected in the run-up to the Summit. It shows an association between social media traffic and key events, with peaks in the volume of communications tracking key announcements and developments.

Moving from left to right across the graph, the peaks are associated with the following sequence of events:

- June 22: Summit on national news
- June 25: Logo revealed
- July 8: School closures announced
- August 7: Road closures announced
- August 8: No-fly zone announced
- August 19: 'Ring of steel' traffic delays
- August 28: 'Ring of steel' on national news
- August 30: First protest in Newport

Three key findings emerged from this analysis. First, general public attitudes towards the NATO Summit were broadly negative. Of particular interest was a pronounced 'shock' effect detectable in the data, when on the Sunday prior to the Summit, large numbers of highly visible armed police appeared on the streets of Cardiff and Newport, with little prior warning to the general public. This generated a lot of negative sentiment and emotion being communicated on Twitter. Second, there then followed a softening of public attitudes, which seemed to reflect a deliberate police strategy to engage positively with the public when out on patrol. The data collection picked up a lot of visual images of members of the public posing with armed police for 'selfies'. However, this effect shouldn't be over-stated – there was a softening in negative attitudes, but it did not tip into a majority viewing the Summit overall as positive. Third, by analysing the relatively small proportion of geo-coded Tweets in South Wales it was observed that there were micro-geographies of public sentiment present in different localities. In Cardiff Bay where the warships were berthed, the mood on social media was far more positive because families took the opportunity to see the Navy ships up close, than in the City Centre where disruption was more evident.

Of particular interest, the research team were not the only ones tracking online public sentiment associated with the NATO Summit, the police were using their own platform to perform the same task. This was part of a more general effort on their part to use social media for community engagement and 'open source' intelligence purposes. Post-event they used these data to project a public relations story in the broadcast media about the positive public reaction to a high visibility policing operation. It is certainly true that public attitudes to the police did improve as a result of a direct instruction to the officers to engage positively with the public. However, what the police didn't do was baseline their data properly, so whilst public sentiment did move towards a more pro-police position, the majority of the Twitter community remained negative about the Summit.

A Multi-Method, Multi-Site Design

Tracking and tracing public sentiments in reaction to significant social events has rapidly become a standard application of social media analytics. However, the research effort mobilised for the NATO Summit was intended to test a more innovative, flexible and agile form of ethnographic practice. This sought to implement social media analysis as a solution to some challenges associated with conducting qualitative observational research of intense social events occurring across a large geographical space, but lasting a short period of time, where the precise manifestation of interesting moments is difficult to anticipate. We were especially interested in aspects of the policing operation and how it was responding to the risks and threats posed by multiple protest groups who were assembling around the Summit. Some protests were planned and choreographed, but others were far more spontaneous and 'pop up' in design. Such issues were compounded by the fact that potentially interesting developments were frequently occurring simultaneously.

The principal NATO Summit sites were the Celtic Manor Hotel in Newport where the main meeting of world leaders was held; the 'peace camp' in Tredegar Park Newport, home to a couple of hundred protestors; Cardiff City Centre where several demonstrations and key civic receptions were held and where physical security apparatus caused significant disruption; and Cardiff Bay where the warships were stationed. The distances involved and the fluid nature of activities of interest and how these two qualities interacted posed obvious challenges in terms of positioning field researchers for them to stand the best chance of observing the kinds of action that was the focus of the study. To respond to these circumstances a decision was taken to establish an 'Open Source Communications Analysis Room' (OSCAR) housing the SENTINEL platform to engage in 'real-time' analysis of social media communications associated with the Summit. The idea being that the team in the room would use this stream of data to direct 'field teams' of researchers to where potentially interesting events were emerging according to reports on social media.

One way of thinking about this effort is that it was seeking to blend 'fast data' and 'deep data'. Data scientists define 'big data' and assign it three principal qualities of volume, velocity and variety. The label of big data explicitly privileges the volume attribute of this triptych. However, equally significant we would contend, especially in the sorts of situations described here, is the velocity with which information, news and rumours can travel across social space. In relation to events gravitating around the Summit itself, social media afforded an 'open source' situational awareness in that the communications provided digital traces of breaking events across a wide area, far more quickly than is possible by other methods. However, what these data provided is a very surface impression of what was actually happening. To get a deeper understanding of developments 'on the ground' it was vital to engage in direct observation by researchers co-present with the events *in situ*.

Adopting this approach wherein the direction of the ethnographic gaze is steered by exogenous sources obviously has implications for some of the established precepts of intensive fieldwork. The value of ethnography as a methodology is premised upon its capacity to deliver 'deep' insights into situated social action. To accomplish this, it routinely requires researchers to embed themselves in a particular setting and situation and, through relatively long-term exposure to the rhythms and routines in front of them, to detect patterns. When it works, it is an approach that is uniquely positioned to illuminate the contingent complexities of many social processes. However, the well rehearsed limitation of such an approach is that the researcher's attention and awareness is necessarily framed by what happens in front of them. This is fine if one has located 'where the action is' but manifestly less productive 'where the action isn't'. Such pressures are compounded when, as with a high profile summit, the key action is time bounded. Leading to a recognition that, if for whatever reason an observer is not in the right place at the right time, they will miss the scene altogether.[11]

As the OSCAR methodology was operationalised, however, it became apparent that it afforded additional unanticipated benefits and opportunities. First, there was the ability to use the observers on the ground to 'tune' the attention of the data collection tool to collect digital information to enrich understanding of the social processes in play across South Wales. Second, it provided a mechanism to 'ground truth' the events being 'detected' on social media.

For the purposes of the field testing of the performance of the social media analytics functions in this tasking role, a team of eight researchers was deployed over the three main days of the Summit. Having this number available enabled the researchers to deploy to different sites simultaneously and to rotate team members in terms of rest breaks. On day one the focus was upon testing communication methods between staff in the room and out in the field. Activity on day two was more focused upon field researchers observing interesting incidents, and then calling on the social media analysis team to establish the correspondence between the direct and digital observations. Day three saw a more concerted effort to use social media analysis to direct the activities of the field teams. One particular aspect of the OSCAR methodology that was explored was whether layering social media data onto materials collected via direct observation could facilitate an enhanced understanding of the social processes involved by extending the awareness of the researchers.

In his critique of big data, Schneier (2015) notes that in policy and commercial applications an especially valued quality of social media data is its application as a 'time machine' – enabling one to temporally track back in order to understand the sequence of events preceding an interesting occurrence. One of the challenges for ethnographers is to be able to know what happened prior to and after they finished their 'eyes on' observation. The orthodox solution to which is long-term embedding of the researcher. However, the materials collected by SENTINEL definitely afforded a capacity to track an object or individual across space, far beyond what even a small team could realistically hope to achieve on their own.

It transpired that for the field teams using non-public Twitter accounts to receive directions from and feedback to the OSCAR team, typing field notes on their mobile phones felt less incongruous given today's norms of public behaviour than trying to hand write them. These Tweets provided useful contemporaneous notes and sequences that could be written up more fully subsequent to the events. As the fieldwork evolved, it also became apparent that the research teams were augmenting their written Tweets with pictures taken using the camera functions on their mobile devices. These visual records captured a lot of important information that could be used to validate and supplement the written field records produced at a later point. An especially helpful aspect of this was that the geotagging function of the phones meant that it was possible to establish the precise location of where the picture was taken and the metadata of the Tweet also 'timestamped' these. The latter proved helpful in disentangling complex sequences of action and counterreaction that were sometimes observed.

By way of example, on 2 September a protest march was held in Cardiff City Centre, resulting in several altercations between a small number of marchers and police. Several arrests were made that were directly observed by the field teams as a result of the monitoring being conducted in the OSCAR which ensured that 'the boots on the ground' were directed to these events as they were unfolding. In particular, later that same afternoon the OSCAR team identified a Tweet using the 'NotoNATO' account calling for a protest against the arrests the following morning outside Cardiff Magistrate's Court. Based upon this information identified online, a decision was taken for a field team to attend the court to see what if anything happened. They established that despite this call to mobilise, no-one attended, illuminating how social media

rhetoric does not necessarily translate into offline action. The wider implication being that we cannot equate social media data with what has or will actually happen. It is a refraction rather than a reflection.

The purpose of discussing this field experiment has been to try and think creatively about how research integrating the collection and analysis of social media materials might open up new vistas and ways of seeing for social researchers. The most obvious way to approach this is to treat social media analysis in a 'pure' form as a distinctive methodological frame. Indeed, it is precisely this approach that scaffolds the vast majority of the accounts currently circulating in the research methods literature. An alternative proposition, however, is to think about what new perspectives and concepts might be opened up by integrating such methods with other forms of methodological practice. Herein, we have focused upon blending the deep and rich insights gleaned from direct observations, with the speed of situational awareness facilitated by real-time analysis of social media flows.

In studying a large-scale event, like the NATO Summit taking place over a wide geographic area for a short temporal duration and involving synchronous events of interest, several strategies could frame the research design. Herein, we have started to outline a form of 'crowd-sourced ethnography'. Other blends between social media instruments and data, and other established research methods, can be imagined.

CONCLUSIONS

A key axiom of science and technology studies has been the tendency to over-estimate the near-term effects, and underestimate the breadth and depth of the transformative longer term changes to social orders that will be wrought by new technologies. Based upon our review of the current state of the art in respect of the use of social media instruments and data within social research, it appears at least plausible that a similar pattern of development is and will pertain.

There has been a notable tendency in some quarters to over-claim the insights that can be gleaned from collecting and analysing social media. It is for this reason that we have been keen to frame the discussion in relation to the kinds of epistemological standards and evaluative mechanisms that would be used to test the robustness and rigour of other methods because we need to be cautious about distinguishing the promissory potential of research that pivots around analyses of social media, and where higher degrees of confidence can be maintained.

Social media function as both an engine and a camera. They input into the definition of the situation and the ways in which events, individuals and institutions are collectively and collaboratively configured. At the same time, they provide representations and digital traces that enable us to see and thus study aspects of social life that were hitherto largely imperceptible. But maintaining an awareness that such representations are being deliberately and artfully constructed and reconstructed via social media communications is vital if the social research community is to utilise them appropriately. This is consistent with Amoore and Piotukh's (2015) recent insightful contribution where they contend that data collection and processing algorithms are functioning as increasingly significant 'instruments of perception'. Similar to processes of human perceptual apparatus and cognition, they frame collective attention by steering our gaze towards some things and away from others.

It is for this reason that in the case study we chose to highlight social media usage in both 'pure' and 'blended' forms. The kinds of fast data derivable from real-time analysis of naturally occurring social media can augment and re-orient how social scientists seek 'deep' ethnographic data. But for both the 'do-ers' and 'users' of such research there are important issues to resolve about how to validate and evaluate research based upon social media. It is because of this that articulating a theory of social media instrumentation and the data it generates is so important.

NOTES

1 https://blog.shareaholic.com/social-media-traffic-trends-01-2015/ (accessed 29 October 2015).
2 https://developers.facebook.com/docs/facebook-login/v2.2 (accessed 2 June 2015).
3 https://instagram.com/developer (accessed 2 June 2015).
4 https://instagram.com/developer/realtime (accessed 2 June 2015).
5 https://instagram.com/developer/business (accessed 2 June 2015).
6 https://developers.google.com (accessed 30 June 2015).
7 https://dev.twitter.com/rest/public (accessed 30 June 2015).
8 https://datasciencebusiness.wordpress.com/2014/12/14/accessing-twitter-data-the-firehose/ (accessed 12 September 2015).
9 http://www.nature.com/news/when-google-got-flu-wrong-1.12413 (accessed 15 March 2016).
10 http://gking.harvard.edu/files/gking/files/0314policyforumff.pdf (accessed 15 March 2016).
11 There is a useful literature on 'team ethnography' relevant to this aspect of the research (see Erickson, 1998), albeit this does not attend to the utility of online/offline coordination that we are seeking to bring to the fore here.

REFERENCES

Amoore, L. and Piotukh, V. (2015) 'Life beyond big data governing with little analytics', *Economy and Society*, 44: 341–66.

boyd, D. and Crawford, K. (2012) 'Critical questions for Big Data: provocations for a cultural, technological and scholarly phenomenon', *Information, Communication and Society*, 15(5): 662–79.

Brym, R., Godbout, M., Hoffbauer, A., Menard, G. and Zhang, T. H. (2014) 'Social media in the 2011 Egyptian uprising', *British Journal of Sociology*, 65(2): 266–92.

Butler, D. (2013) 'When Google got flu wrong'. *Nature,* 494: 155–156.

Chan, J. and Bennett Moses, L. (2015) 'Is Big Data challenging criminology', *Theoretical Criminology*, 20(1): 21–39.

Cicourel, A. (1964) *Method and Meausurement in Sociology*. New York, NY: The Free Press.

Creswell, J. and Plano Clark, V. (2011) *Designing and Conducting Mixed Methods Research*. 2nd edn. Thousand Oaks: Sage Publications.

Duggan, M., Ellison, N. B., Lampe, C., Lenhart, A. and Madden, M. (2015) 'Demographics of key social networking platforms'. Pew Research Center. Available at: http://www.pewinternet.org/2015/01/09/demographics-of-key-social-networking-platforms-2/ (accessed 15 March 2016).

Edwards, A., Housley, W., Williams, M., Sloan, L. and Williams, M. (2013) 'Digital social research, social media and the sociological imagination: surrogacy, augmentation and re-orientation', *International Journal of Social Research Methodology,* 16(3): 245–60.

Erickson, K. (1998) *Doing Team Ethnography: Warnings and Advice*. Thousand Oaks, CA: Sage Publications.

Fielding, N. (2009) 'Going out on a limb: post-modernism and multiple method research', *Current Sociology*, 57/3; 427–47.

Fielding, N. and Schreier, M. (2001) 'Introduction: on the compatibility between qualitative and quantitative research methods', *Forum Qualitative Social Research*, 2(1): Art. 4.

Goffman, E. (1959) *The Presentation of Self in Everyday Life*. London: Penguin Books.

Hacking, I. (1995) 'The looping effects of human kind'. In D. Sperber, D. Premack and A. Premack (eds.), *Causal Cognition: A Multidisciplinary Debate*. Oxford: Oxford University Press, pp. 351–83.

Haefner, N. (2014) Selling & the Social Media Honeycomb. NIBL blog. Available at: http://blog.nibl.com/selling-the-social-media-honeycomb/ (accessed 15 March 2016).

Kietzmann, J. H., Hermkens, K., McCarthy, I. P. and Silvestre, B. S. (2011) 'Social media? Get serious! Understanding the functional building blocks of social media', *Business Horizons*, 54: 241–51.

Kitchin, R. (2014) 'Big Data, new epistemologies and paradigm shifts', *Big Data and Society*, April–June: 1–12.

Lazer, D., Kennedy, R., King, G. and Vespignani, A. (2014) 'The parable of Google Flu: Traps in big data analysis'. *Science* [Online]. Available at: http://science.sciencemag.org/content/343/6176/1203 (accessed 15 January 2016).

Mackenzie, D. (2006) *An Engine not a Camera: How Financial Models Make Markets*. Cambridge, MA: MIT Press.

Mackenzie, D. (2014) 'A sociology of algorithms: high-frequency trading and the shaping of markets',(working paper) Available at: http://www.sps.ed.ac.uk/__data/assets/pdf_file/0004/156298/Algorithms25.pdf (accessed 20 July 2016)

Mander, J. (2014) Global Web Index Social Summary Q4–2014. Global Web Index. http://insight.globalwebindex.net/hs-fs/hub/304927/file-2377691590-pdf/Reports/GWI_Social_Summary_Q4_2014.pdf?submissionGuid=ea2e5afa-9faa-4b92-a1be-93e4518e8b78 (accessed 1 June 2015)

Mander, J. (2015) Global Web Index Social Q1–2015. Global Web Index. http://www.thewebmate.com/wp-content/uploads/2015/05/GWI-Social-Report-Q1-2015.pdf (accessed 2 June 2015).

Marwick, A. (2013) *Status Update: Celebrity, Publicity and Branding in the Social Media Age*. New Haven, CT: Yale University Press.

Meyrowitz, J. (1985) *No Sense of Place*. New York, NY: Oxford University Press.

Morstatter, F., Pfeffer, J., Liu, H. and Carley, K. M. (2013) 'Is the sample good enough? Comparing data from Twitter's streaming API with Twitter's Firehose', arXiv preprint, arXiv:1306.5204.

Pasquale, F. (2015) *The Black Box Society*. Cambridge, MA: Harvard University Press.

Procter, R., Vis, F. and Voss, A. (2013) 'Reading the riots on Twitter: methodological innovation for the analysis of Big Data', *International Journal of Social Research Methodology,* 16(3): 197–214.

Savage, M. and Burrows, R. (2007) 'The coming crisis of empirical sociology', *Sociology,* 41(5): 885–99.

Schneier, B. (2015) *Data and Goliath: The Hidden Battles to Collect Your Data and Control Your World*. New York, NY: W.W. Norton & Co.

Wright Mills, C. (1959) *The Sociological Imagination*. Oxford: Oxford University Press.

'Big Social Science': Doing Big Data in the Social Sciences[1]

Jonathan Bright

The term 'big data' first emerged in the field of computer science (Cox and Ellsworth 1997), employed to describe not just a large amount of information, but one that was so large that it required a change of processing strategy because it could not fit in the memory of the computer which needed to process it (around 100 gigabytes at the time). The field of study of big data as originally conceived revolved around solving the processing challenges thrown up by these very large datasets. As computers have increased in power and capacity, the amount of data needed to be 'big' has increased correspondingly, but big data bottlenecks nevertheless continue to be confronted in a variety of disciplines (see Howe *et al.* 2008; Marx 2013). The focus of this chapter is however on the social sciences, and here big data has taken on a different and arguably much looser meaning. One of the features of human life over the last few decades has been its digitisation. This digitisation has made human life inexorably more 'quantifiable' (boyd and Crawford 2012:

667) because digital devices leave traces that can be captured. This has led to the creation of large new sources of data on all sorts of aspects of social life. The big data approach to the social sciences involves the exploitation of these data sources to answer questions about society. Although many of these datasets are large in absolute terms, the scale of big data is not what distinguishes it in the social sciences because the field of research is not about looking at ways to deal with this scale.

The adoption of these data sources into the social sciences is not straightforward, with some arguing they threaten a crisis in the social scientist's place in the world (Savage and Burrows 2007). Nevertheless, such data also implies considerable opportunities for social researchers to understand more about society (Lazer *et al.* 2009), and the big data opportunity has hence been highlighted in a wide variety of different sub-disciplines of the social sciences (see Eynon 2013; González-Bailón 2013; Schöch 2013; Taylor *et al.* 2014). Broadly speaking, these opportunities can be grouped under three headings. First, and most obviously, big data has quantified certain social activities that previously have been very difficult to study systematically. For example, one recent study (Bakshy *et al.* 2012) examined the information diffusion activities of 250 million users of the social network Facebook, observing the types of information they shared with others on the same network. Second, and related to this, big data provides the opportunity to conduct large-scale studies of rare events, which conventional random sampling techniques would be unlikely to discover (or discover in sufficient numbers). Take, for example, Goel *et al.*'s (2013) study of 'viral diffusion'. This study harvested data from social media platforms such as Twitter in order to explore the dynamics of unusual 'viral' bits of internet content. A final advantage is that big data are often cheap and rapid for social scientists to employ, hence PhD students and junior researchers can work with large, novel datasets that previously would have required grants to create. This implies that theory and hypotheses can be tested more rapidly and more widely than was previously the case, in more social contexts and with fewer resources.

METHODOLOGICAL ISSUES IN BIG DATA RESEARCH: DATA CAPTURE, CODING AND ANALYSIS

The major focus of this chapter, however, is not on the challenges and opportunities of big data research in general, but the practicalities of actually doing it. Big data in the social sciences is a general term: an umbrella concept to describe social science performed on datasets produced by digital trace data. Big data 'methods' is therefore an equally broad concept: a family of techniques that are frequently but by no means universally applied to big data studies. In this chapter,

I separate these methods into three subheadings, each broadly corresponding to a stage of research: data capture, data interpretation and data analysis. Some of the methods described will be familiar to most social scientists, but require some modification or changes to deal with the scale of the data; others are more novel and emerge from recent work in computer science. A settled consensus has not emerged in any area: most big data studies contain within them a significant element of novelty and experimentation. I have therefore given as much focus on describing the problems (which will undoubtedly persist) as describing current solutions (which may well soon be superseded). I should highlight, however, that I do not address the ethics of big data research, which is tackled in full in Eynon *et al.*, this volume.

Data Capture

Big social data can come from a wide variety of sources, which I will refer to here as 'data institutions'. Utility providers, mobile phone companies, web servers, banks, government departments, global positioning system (GPS) trackers, social media platforms; all are potentially incorporable for social research (and the list is only likely to grow). Despite this heterogeneity of sources, in practice data capture occurs through one of three major techniques, which can be distinguished by the extent to which the organisation that generates the data cooperates actively with the researcher. First, some data institutions have been willing to make agreements with either individual researchers or the research community at large to share data held on their servers. For example, friendship structures have been investigated with mobile phone data (Eagle *et al.* 2009). These institutions may furthermore make their data systematically available for free download. For example, Wikipedia makes statistics on the amount of people visiting its website openly accessible, facilitating their use for research (see Yasseri and Bright 2014, 2016). Some institutions have even worked with researchers to conduct very large-scale field experiments (see Bakshy *et al.* 2015). In these cases, data capture is simple because the transfer of data is facilitated by the organisation in question (although the organisation itself is likely to be selective in what data they do share, taking into account its own objectives and priorities).

Second, and especially common in the case of social media studies, data may be made available through an Application Programming Interface (API). Such interfaces, it is worth highlighting, are typically designed to allow developers to build applications that make use of a limited subset of the data in real time, for example a development company might build an application that allows people to find local supermarkets, based on data from the Google Places API. Nevertheless, the API can also be used to collect data for research purposes (a good introduction to this can be found in Russell 2013). Several considerations are important when capturing data through an API. On a technical level, researchers require sufficient familiarity with a programming language to instruct their own computer to download the data they are interested in (further remarks on the specifics of programming for big data research are given in the next section). Furthermore, researchers need to be aware of the limitations applied to the data within the API. Institutions that make their data available in this fashion are under no obligation to make it complete and, indeed, will often only provide partial data in order to prevent competitors from harvesting all of it. Hence, for example, researchers have worried that data coming from the Twitter API may exhibit systematic biases or offer an incomplete picture for certain research questions (González-Bailón 2014). Capturing historical data may also be difficult.

A final method of big data capture is what has come to be called 'web scraping' (for an in-depth introduction, see Schrenk 2007).

Many sources of potential big data are directly visible and freely available on the web, but are not accessible in a format that facilitates their analysis. For example, records of bills passed through the UK legislature are freely available online, but not in the form of a dataset that would allow factors relating to their passage to be studied. However, the fact that the data is visible to anyone with a web browser means that a dataset could be created by laboriously visiting every page on which it is contained and recording the relevant information. Web scraping involves writing a computer program that takes care of this task automatically (as was conducted in Bright 2014). Web scraping is typically more complicated than accessing data over an API because it involves exploring the underlying structure of a web page as it is delivered to your computer in HyperText Markup Language (HTML). HTML pages can be labyrinthine and, again, are not designed to facilitate research, meaning that the effort involved in doing this can be high. For example, in one recent project with Tom Nicholls, we looked at factors affecting the persistence of news articles on the front pages of seven different online news outlets in the UK. Each one of these outlets required the creation of a separate bespoke web scraper, which was able to recognise (for example) the title of each news article or where it appeared on the front page (Bright and Nicholls 2014). A further complicating factor is that many websites currently implement software that prevents automatic scrapers from obtaining too much information, again largely because they are worried that competitors might steal their data.

A final area worth highlighting, which affects data capture through both APIs and web scraping, is the legal aspect. Most major data institutions are aware of the interest of the research community in their data and are typically tolerant of studies that collect data for not-for-profit research. However, publishing the (raw) data collected might be problematic – as I have highlighted, these institutions may also have a business model to protect. Web scraping also needs to be done with care in order to not overwhelm the web server in question with a large number of requests. In both cases, researchers should take heed of the terms of service, which are almost always a part of API use and are also often found on websites.

Data Interpretation: Proxy Variables and Coding

As highlighted earlier, big data is not data that was typically created for the purposes of research. From the perspective of researchers, it is, as Harford (2014) puts it, 'found data' – serendipitously discovered data that can be put to use answering research questions. This characteristic means that big datasets, whilst often being large in the sense of the number of observations, are frequently quite narrow in terms of the amount of information held on each observation.

The 'narrowness' of big data makes two practices particularly common in this type of analysis. First, there is the use of proxy variables: creative interpretations of data to indicate underlying variables of interest. Consider, for example, data taken from an online discussion forum (see Gillani et al. 2014). Researchers may be interested to examine the social network structure within that forum; however, the social network itself is not visible. Hence a common practice would be to look instead at the structure of discussion, which is visible: if two people contribute to the same conversation thread, this could indicate a link between them. But within this practice, multiple options exist. If someone leaves a reply on a discussion thread, does that connect them to the person who responded most recently, the person who started the thread or everyone else on the thread? Furthermore, over what time period should the network be considered? Conversation networks are inherently ephemeral, which means looking, for example, at

one week's conversations which may produce a different picture to one month's. All of these options are potentially valid, but each one may lead to a different interpretation of the network. In such cases, the best strategy is usually to test hypotheses on all possible operationalisations of the proxy variable and report results for all tests.

Second, it is also quite common for further variables to be added to each observation through data coding. Coding, of course, refers to the practice of classifying collected data into certain categories or along certain scales in order to make it more amenable for analysis. For example, statements might be classified as positive or negative, while news articles or policy initiatives might be classified by topic. Big data coding is often performed on 'unstructured' text, which is contained within many types of big dataset. Big data is sometimes characterised as messy and unstructured in and of itself. This is a little misleading because it implies it is full of error and noise, which is not necessarily true. Data obtained over an API is highly structured almost by definition because without this structure the applications cannot be programmed. Figure 8.1, for example, shows some of the information contained in a Tweet that can be obtained from the Twitter API, which is highly structured. Nevertheless many types of data contain an unstructured 'field', where some free text has been entered by a user.[2] For example, medical records may contain structured observations, such as the date and time of a patient's visit, together with more unstructured doctor's notes about the subject of that visit (Murdoch and Detsky 2013). Or as in the Tweet shown below (Figure 8.1), the text of the Tweet itself, and the user's description on their profile, can be considered unstructured text.

Coding big data has an obvious practical problem: the scale of the data. Of course, even within a big data context, coding can still be performed manually by simply selecting a more limited subset of data. For example, in a recent study with Monica Bulger and

```
 1  {u'contributors': None,
 2   u'coordinates': {u'coordinates': [32.5695, 15.54234], u'type': u'Point'},
 3   u'created_at': u'Thu May 14 23:05:08 +0000 2015',
 4   u'entities': {u'hashtags': [{u'indices': [51, 72],
 5                                u'text': u'PrincessOfNorthSudan'}],
 6                 u'symbols': [],
 7                 u'trends': [],
 8                 u'urls': [],
 9                 u'user_mentions': []},
10   u'favorite_count': 0,
11   u'favorited': False,
12   u'filter_level': u'low',
13   u'geo': {u'coordinates': [15.54234, 32.5695], u'type': u'Point'},
14   u'id': 598987438824886273L,
15   u'id_str': u'598987438824886273',
16   u'in_reply_to_screen_name': None,
17   u'in_reply_to_status_id': None,
18   u'in_reply_to_status_id_str': None,
19   u'in_reply_to_user_id': None,
20   u'in_reply_to_user_id_str': None,
21   u'lang': u'ar',
22   u'place': {u'attributes': {},
23              u'bounding_box': {u'coordinates': [[[21.8094486900002,
24                                                   8.68164174400006],
25                                                  [21.8094486900002,
26                                                   22.2269648230001],
27                                                  [38.6038517590001,
28                                                   22.2269648230001],
29                                                  [38.6038517590001,
30                                                   8.68164174400006]]],
31                                u'type': u'Polygon'},
32              u'country': u'Sudan',
33              u'country_code': u'SD',
34              u'full_name': u'Sudan',
35              u'id': u'c55f354cd83b910d',
36              u'name': u'Sudan',
37              u'place_type': u'country',
38              u'url': u'https://api.twitter.com/1.1/geo/id/c55f354cd83b910d.json'},
39   u'possibly_sensitive': False,
40   u'retweet_count': 0,
41   u'retweeted': False,
42   u'source': u'<a href="http://twitter.com/download/android" rel="nofollow">Twitter for Android</a>',
```

Figure 8.1   The structure of a Tweet

Source: The Twitter API

Cristobal Cobo, we analysed a large dataset of people creating offline study groups to support online learning (Bulger *et al.* 2015). Our analysis was simply based on taking a random sample from within this large dataset and then coding this sample by hand using standard qualitative techniques. In this instance, the 'big data' aspect of our study allowed us to perform a large-scale general analysis, and also acted as a sampling frame for our smaller, more in-depth work. Arguably, this type of manual coding is a strong approach in many situations because standard statistical techniques are of course well adapted to making inferences from the smaller random sample to the full big dataset.

However, such limited samples also sacrifice some of the potential advantages of big data highlighted earlier, and therefore the majority of coding of big data is achieved through what is now being called 'automatic content analysis' (ACA) (see Popping, this volume; Grimmer and Stewart 2013), in other words training a computer program to classify text for the researcher. ACA, and the closely related fields of natural language processing and machine learning, are large sub-fields within computer science and linguistics, and I will not attempt to offer an overview of the state of the art in these areas; rather, I will point to the two most commonly used techniques in the field.

The first is what is known as a 'dictionary approach'. The researcher develops a list of keywords that they believe relates to the categories of interest, and then the computer counts appearances of these keywords in the text of interest. For example, when analysing a large set of news articles over the last 100 years, Chadefaux (2014) used this method to detect articles referring to an imminent outbreak of war. The dictionary approach has considerable advantages in terms of simplicity of implementation (and also communication of the results). However, it will only ever be as strong as the list of keywords developed, and some topics will naturally lend themselves to this type of classification better than others. For example, automatic gender recognition is frequently based on a dictionary approach, matching a name given in a free text field to a list of names classified by gender. But many names are gender neutral (e.g. Chris) or can by typically male in one language and typically female in another (e.g. Andrea, which is typically male in Italian and female in English). Importantly, in cases where the approach works poorly, dictionary techniques can be difficult to fix and the researcher has little choice but to keep experimenting with different permutations of keywords, hoping to find the right result.

The second is what is described as a 'machine learning' approach. Rather than relying on the researcher to select the keywords of interest, the computer itself is used to select the most informative and relevant words for classification. To take a simple example, a 'naïve Bayesian' classifier takes a group of bits of text, each one pre-classified as belonging, or not, to a given category of interest (for example, whether the text is about politics or not). The classifier then looks at all the words in both groups of text, evaluating the relative prevalence of each word in each.[3] Words that appear frequently in the category of interest and infrequently outside it become the basis for classification (for example, 'government' might appear frequently in text relating to politics and infrequently outside it). Machine learning approaches to automatic content analysis typically perform better than dictionary approaches; they also have the advantage of being more systematic than their dictionary equivalents. However, they also require the hand classification of a large corpus of articles for training, meaning that the actual benefits of classification in terms of time saved for the researcher are smaller (for a more in-depth description of this type of classifier, see Harrington 2012: 61–82).[4]

Automatic content analysis needs to be evaluated for accuracy. This can be achieved by taking a random sample of pieces of text for classification and exploring how many classifications were performed accurately. Two types of mistake are possible, equivalent to Type I and Type II errors in statistics: a false positive, where the computer incorrectly included the text in the category of interest, and a false negative, where the reverse is true. The rate of these two types of errors gives the two most common types of statistics through which ACA approaches are analysed: precision, which is the percentage of all positives that were true positives, and recall, which is given by the number of true positives divided by the sum of true positives and false negatives. Frequently, these two statistics are inversely related, with higher precision being at the expense of lower recall. These measures are sometimes combined into an F1 score, which is the harmonic mean of both precision and recall.

Data Analysis

The analysis of big data is at once the most straightforward and potentially most troubling aspect of big social science. It is straightforward because if data collection

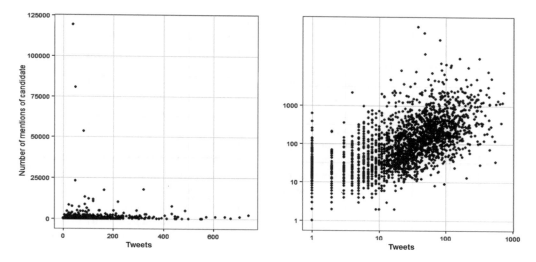

Figure 8.2   Twitter activity during the UK's 2015 general election: normal axes and log axes compared

Source: The Twitter API

and coding are complete, the data itself should come in the form of a matrix to which statistical analyses from the standard quantitative toolbox can be applied. Statistical tests found in many of the standout pieces of big data analysis are themselves nothing out of the ordinary. For example, in a now famous experiment on social influence on voting carried out on Facebook (Bond *et al.* 2012), a dataset that was millions of lines long was analysed with the 100-year-old t-test, which had been created primarily to deal with a problem of small sample size (Box 1987). The description of the types of test available that could be used is well beyond the scope of this chapter (readers unfamiliar with the options in this area should consult Agresti and Finlay 2009). In this section, I will simply make some points about their application in the context of very large datasets.

A first basic point is that many variables observed in big data analysis have highly skewed or heavy-tailed distributions (Barabási and Réka 1999). This type of distribution is seen often enough to make it a feature of big data methods in general. A logarithmic transform will typically improve

both the graphical display of this data and the validity of statistical tests performed on it. Such transforms are simple to execute in statistics packages, even if they do make subsequent interpretation of the results a little more complex. For example, Figure 8.2 shows activity on Twitter for candidates in the UK's 2015 general election on a normal scale (left panel) and log scale (right panel). On the normal scale, the need to display the few candidates who were mentioned tens of thousands of times or who authored hundreds of Tweets means that variation within the majority of candidates is not visible. The logarithmic transformation of the axes resolves this problem.

Second, it is worth considering the extent to which the big data 'sample' that is taken actually approaches the size of the population of interest. Although a large dataset is typically preferable to a small one, the return in terms of precision diminishes as well – going from 10 observations to 1,000 makes a major difference in terms of the width of confidence intervals, *ceteris paribus*, whereas going from 1,000,010 to 1,001,000 makes hardly any at all. The rationale behind the effort involved in collecting and coding very large datasets therefore becomes less clear if the analysis technique involved is designed to deal with small samples. In many cases, it may be possible to collect the entire 'population' of data, rendering the use of statistical significance testing theoretically somewhat meaningless.

Third, and more importantly perhaps, even if they are performed it is worth adopting a sceptical approach to tests of statistical significance because most well-used ones in the social sciences are very sensitive to sample size. When samples are in the millions, discovery of statistically significant results is almost inevitable (although I should highlight again that big data in the social sciences does not necessarily imply millions of observations). Critiques of significance testing predate the rise of big data itself (Cohen 1994), although the emergence of very large sample sizes gives them a particular importance (Lin *et al.* 2013). Two major recommendations have been made to ameliorate this problem. One is the importance of discussing the actual size of *effects* observed, rather than just their statistical significance and direction (Sullivan and Feinn 2012). The 'effect' in the context of a regression model refers to the change in the dependent variable typically observed after a one-unit increase in an independent variable (for a good summary of how to report effect sizes for different types of regression models, see Vittinghoff *et al.* 2005). For example, we might produce a regression model showing that people who earn more are also more likely to sign electronic petitions, which would support the 'resource' model of political participation that suggests that those who are better off in time, money and skills are more politically active (Brady *et al.* 1995). However, it would also be useful to know how big the difference is: does earning £1,000 more a year make you twice as likely to sign a petition, or do you have to earn £100,000 more a year before doubling the chance of signing? It is also worth considering the distribution of the independent variable of interest: if most

people earn between £20,000 and £30,000, for instance, then the 'impact' of having a salary of £100,000 is unlikely to be experienced by many people. Effect sizes can also be standardised and benchmarks are available for interpreting the importance of standardised effect sizes in abstract (see Cohen 1988; Rosenthal 1996), although this practice is less common.

Furthermore, statistics relating to the goodness of fit of the model (such as R^2) and associated measures that also take into account the complexity of the model (such as the Akaike or Bayesian Information Criteria) are also worth discussing alongside any consideration of the statistical significance of a model itself, especially when comparisons are being drawn between multiple models. These statistics are not sensitive to sample size in the same way (although they do take it into account). For example, it is perfectly possible to generate a regression model with lots of statistically significant coefficients that has a very low overall explanatory power (measured as R^2). Whether this is important or not depends on whether the aim is to seek an overall explanation for the dependent variable (in which case a low R^2 indicates that much remains unexplained) or whether it is the independent variable itself which is of interest (in which case low R^2 is less important).

Graphical methods for exploratory data analysis have also been proposed as an alternative (or complement) to *p*-values (Cohen 1994: 1001). Comparisons of boxplots and histograms are as valuable in big data analysis as they are in more traditional settings. In terms of graphical methods, however, it is worth highlighting that not all of them can be straightforwardly translated into the big data arena. For example, standard scatter plots may be difficult to interpret if the amount of points is very large. In these cases, two-dimensional histograms may be more appropriate (see Figure 8.3). These graphics divide the area of the plot into two-dimensional 'bins', with the strength of shading in each bin indicating the amount of observations that fall within it

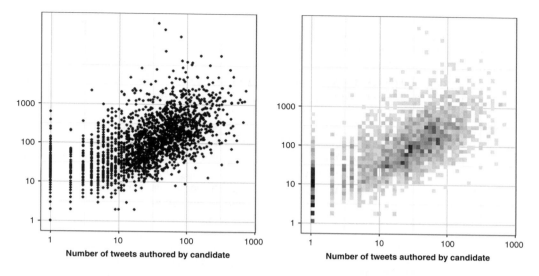

Figure 8.3   Scatter plot compared with 2D histogram. The 2D histogram shows a large quantity of data at the very left of the x-axis, something not visible in the scatter plot.

Source: The Twitter API

(in the figure we can see, for instance, a large amount of observations fall on the far left of the x-axis). Another example in this context is standard network diagrams, which show relationships between different actors in a network: as the amount of actors increase the connections between them will increasingly overlap and make the overall network harder and harder to interpret. Again, visualisation methods that group actors in some way (such as grouping different subsections of the network) may be helpful.

A final point worth mentioning in this section is the growing possibility for 'data mining' techniques to be applied to the social sciences (Baram-Tsabari *et al.* this volume). These techniques, broadly speaking, involve testing hypotheses en masse in datasets in the search for any statistically significant relationships. Any social scientist with a basic grasp of statistics would react with horror to such a technique: an unknowable amount of Type I errors will of course be mixed in with all the actually statistically significant results (a Type I error is when the null hypothesis is incorrectly rejected and hence a statistically

significant relationship is erroneously reported). However, data mining is widely applied in the business world with considerable success (although the scope of business analytics may be much narrower than the social sciences). The key to validating results discovered through data mining is to continually test and refine on new sources of data, and with each successive round of testing, Type I errors should be eliminated and only 'true' relationships remain. Such an approach would be a significant departure from normal social science practice and challenge fundamental assumptions that structure grant making and journal publications (relationships discovered in such a way would have to be continually re-tested, rather than being 'accepted' once published). Nevertheless, the potential is also considerable.

DOING BIG DATA RESEARCH

In this section, building on the previous remarks, I want to go into more specific detail about how to do the type of big data research described earlier. I will do so by describing the toolkit that I believe is necessary for researchers to tackle this kind of research (although I would note as well that, increasingly, research teams with multiple abilities and skills are being applied to big data research). The discussion is divided into two sections: ability to write scripts and the need for infrastructural support. These tools are not necessarily tied to one particular programming language or environment, although in each section I highlight the most commonly use packages in the field.

Tool 1: Ability to Script

A fundamental aspect of big data research is the ability to write 'scripts' – small pieces of computer code that can be rapidly brought together to solve bespoke problems. Big data research requires automation that includes instructing the computer to download millions of lines of data, to extract relevant parts of a JSON object into a dataset, to perform automatic content analysis on downloaded text, and more. The standard approach to automation in the social sciences is through the use of pre-existing computer programs with (relatively) easy-to-use graphical user interfaces, for example Atlas.ti for manual coding, statistical software packages such as SPSS and Stata for analysis, etc. However, equivalents of these packages have yet to emerge for big data research (especially in terms of data collection). Furthermore, it seems unlikely that they will emerge in the near future. Big data research is incredibly heterogeneous in terms of input. New sources of data and new applications emerge all the time, whilst existing data sources update their access requirements and change their websites. Any software package released would therefore quickly become out of date. For this reason, I promote a scripting ability as a fundamental part of the big data research toolkit. Of course, scripting, which is done in

a computer programming language, also relies on technology that others have built to be kept up to date. However, the community of developers which does the updating is much larger than in a social science context because programming languages have wide applications across a host of business and research domains.

An obvious first question for the novice scripter is which language to learn. Programming languages evolve constantly, and in purely functional terms there is not much to choose between them – any language could achieve all of the tasks described in the first section. Nevertheless, the social science research community has, by and large, gravitated towards a single language, Python, as the de facto standard (Döring 2008). Python is a 'high-level' language. Broadly speaking, this means that the grammar and structure of the language itself resemble human language more than they do the language that machines process in (without delving into too much detail, Python programs are translated automatically into other code that can actually be run by a computer processor). This, in theory at least, makes the language easier to learn and program in than other lower level languages such as C. The trade-off is programs written in higher level languages are typically slower to execute. Software developers, who wish to sell the programs they develop, place a lot of emphasis on writing fast, efficient code; however, for a social science scripter this is less of an issue (although I will return to this a little later when discussing Hadoop). Furthermore, Python is a language with a very active developer community, many of whom are developing packages specifically for social science applications. Python has readily available packages for natural language processing, for accessing data through APIs, for social network analysis and a whole host of other functions. Choosing the language that fits in with this community of developers is an obvious advantage for the novice programmer. The only major competitor to Python in big data-driven social sciences is R. Most readers will be familiar with

R as a statistics package; however, it is also a fully fledged programming language and, for example, has been used for streaming Tweets from the Twitter API[5] or running machine learning algorithms. The difference between the two is largely a matter of taste.

An introduction to the actual specifics of coding in Python is beyond the scope of this chapter. *Mining the Social Web* is probably the standout textbook in the field specifically for big data access in Python (Russell 2013) and a variety of other good introductory materials are available online.[6] A simple example (see Figure 8.4) might serve to give an overall impression of what Python looks like and how it works in a big data context. In this example, the aim of the script is to find out how many news stories on the front page of the *Guardian* news website have been shared on Facebook, and write the results to a file, which could be used in further analysis.

I will briefly describe what happens in this code. Following an import statement on line 1, which adds in certain extra functionalities and commands to Python, and the creation of a new output file called 'facebook-shares.txt' on line 2, which is ready to receive output as it is produced, the main part of the script begins on line 4, where Python is instructed to read in the RSS feed of the *Guardian*'s front page. Line 5 creates a 'for loop', which tells Python to execute the subsequent lines of code on each of the entries in the RSS list (each entry is a news article on the front page). For each entry, Python queries the Facebook API to find out how many times it has been shared (lines 6 and 7), data which is returned in a JSON format. Not all articles have been shared – on lines 9 and 10 we address this problem by setting the number of shares for this type of article to 0 using an 'if' statement. Lines 12–15 then write out the results for this article to the output file. The 'for loop' is defined by the indented code from lines 6–15. Once this code has been executed for each article in the list, the script is finished and the output file is shut on line 17.

This simple example serves to illustrate two basic points. First, although readers new to programming may not have understood everything, it will hopefully be apparent that overall the script is quite simple and short. Used over a number of weeks, it could create an impression of the social reaction generated on the world's largest social network by one of the most read news websites in the world.

```
1   import feedparser, urllib2, json
2   output = open("facebook-shares.txt", "w")
3
4   d = feedparser.parse("http://www.theguardian.com/uk/rss")
5   for entry in d["entries"]:
6       response = urllib2.urlopen("http://graph.facebook.com/?id=" + entry["link"])
7       sharecount = json.loads(response.read())
8
9       if not "shares" in sharecount:
10          sharecount["shares"] = 0
11
12      output.write(entry["title"].encode("ascii", "ignore"))
13      output.write(";")
14      output.write(str(sharecount["shares"]))
15      output.write("\n")
16
17  output.close()
```

Figure 8.4   A simple Python script displayed in Notepad++ (a popular free source code editor)

Source: Author

We can easily imagine how small further extensions to this code could be used to answer a whole host of research questions. Second, the language Python is expressed in is very similar to human language: the 'for loop' and 'if' statement, which are two fundamental parts of any programming language, are written in an almost human readable way. In other words, this shows both the relative accessibility of Python as a language and the huge potential it has for those who know how to use it.

Tool 2: Infrastructural Support

A further area worth discussing is the infrastructural support potentially required for doing big data research. The majority of contemporary social science work is done on the personal computers of the researchers involved, either desktop machines provided by universities or commonly a laptop. In many cases, these machines will be sufficient for a large portion of the tasks highlighted previously. In some areas, however, this might be more problematic. In this section, I want to highlight where these problems might arise and also the potential solutions, sensitive to the fact that social science itself is often done with relatively constrained resources and that well-staffed, high-performance computing centres are not a realistic expectation for most faculties in the near future.

A first and obvious area where the personal computing approach to big data may fall short is in the need to maintain an 'always on' network connection to collect data over an extended period of time. This would be implied, for example, in the news article sharing example highlighted in Figure 8.1, where the researcher would need to continually access the RSS feed over a period of weeks or months. For example, in one recent project (Bright 2016) I tracked social sharing of news articles over a period of several weeks, which involved accessing the front page of the BBC news website once every 15 minutes. The best response to this problem is to set up a

server. A server is a computer that is designed to be always on and, at least in theory, technical support staff should be available 24/7 if something causes it to fail. Persuading an IT services manager to create a server account is, from the researcher's perspective, an ideal solution. If no such account can be created, cloud server providers such as Heroku[7] may fill a gap, and they also typically offer a limited trial account for free.

A second area is in the technical capacity to process and analyse the data. When presented with a new dataset to analyse, the standard approach to memory management of common statistical packages, such as Stata and R, is to try and load the entire dataset into what is known as the 'conventional memory' or RAM of the computer, which is likely to be several gigabytes in size. However, there will be many big datasets that comfortably exceed this limit. The solution to this problem depends on the scale of the data. If it can fit onto the hard drive of a personal computer, statistics languages such as Stata and R can make use of packages that have been developed to process the data in chunks. For example, the 'biglm' package in R facilitates the production of linear models in a big data context. If the dataset cannot fit on the researcher's computer (10s of terabytes or more), the solution will require the creation of space on a dedicated departmental server (and here cloud services are unlikely to be much use because the time taken and cost required to transfer the data via the Internet onto the cloud would be prohibitive). Processing speeds are also an issue with data on this scale. Here, some departments have started to look towards the creation of 'Hadoop'[8] clusters – essentially a software framework that facilitates the division and distribution of tasks onto multiple computers. Such clusters can considerably decrease the time required to process very large datasets; however, they do also require considerable investment. In general, I perceive such clusters as being a future aspiration for departments interested in big data research, rather than a prerequisite for getting started.

CONCLUSIONS

This chapter has aimed to present some of the opportunities opened up by the potential incorporation of big data into the social sciences, but it has also highlighted some of the challenges that big data research throws up, with practical advice on how to overcome them. It has also attempted to elaborate the toolkit which researchers need to tackle big data work.

I want to conclude by offering reflections on two major challenges for the integration of big data into the social sciences in general. The first has already been highlighted earlier: big data is largely created by private institutions whose primary goal is not to facilitate social research. This has two consequences. First, the way in which they create their data may change over time, invalidating past results. For example, as the service Google offers to customers has evolved, the possibility of using Google search data to predict flu outcomes has apparently decreased (Lazer *et al.* 2014). More broadly, as the Internet itself continues to evolve rapidly, research results that were valid at a certain point in time might start to get out of date only a few years later (the latest big shift is the emergence of mobile phones as the primary means of Internet access). Second, when data is made available by private companies to researchers, some have started to wonder how results can be replicated or they have worried about a divide creeping into social sciences between the data haves and have-nots (Huberman 2012). In some senses, this critique misses a larger point, which is that the general availability of data to junior researchers is now much greater than it was, say, twenty years ago, and even those without access to Facebook still have huge volumes of data with which they can work. This is exciting and promises an era of innovation in both methods and substantive topics. Nevertheless, the point about replication is valid. How to resolve this problem is unclear. I would suggest that in terms of Twitter data,

for example, we are moving in the direction of replication being based on new data (in the same way that, for example, studies of disease might seek to replicate results based on a new set of patients). If I wanted to replicate Goel *et al.*'s (2013) study on virality, I would do so with my own data captured through the Twitter API.

The second more pernicious challenge is the big data skills gap. At the time of writing, the discipline most interested in big data – computational social science – consists by and large of computer scientists, physicists and mathematicians interested in studying complex systems in general, who find in the social world the most complex system of all. Although the quality of work and insight coming out of this field is fascinating, I think the existence of this field poses a major danger to social science research because it takes place largely in isolation from mainstream social science conferences and publication routes, and often pays little attention to existing large volumes of empirical and theoretical work (in some ways, it is the realisation of the fear of Savage and Burrows (2007) that social scientists would be marginalised in their own discipline). The reason few social scientists work in these fields is that the type of skills described in the second section of this chapter are not commonly found in the training component of most undergraduate and graduate social science degrees. Those social scientists who do work with big data are therefore either self-taught enthusiasts or have migrated from other disciplines, such as computer science. Incorporating programming into the methods component of a social science degree will not be easy – it would require both a change in hiring practices and a refocusing of undergraduate programmes onto methods-related subjects. However, it would, I believe, be a great shame if social science cannot train big data researchers who can contribute in the same way as computer scientists and physicists, perhaps with less advanced technical ability but compensating with theoretical and substantive knowledge. Hopefully this situation will improve with time.

NOTES

1   This work was supported by a grant from the Wiener-Anspach foundation. I would like to thank Scott Hale for providing some of the data used in the chapter, and an anonymous reviewer for insightful comments and critiques.
2   It is also slightly misleading to classify text as unstructured because it is full of grammatical structure, which computational linguists make use of in order to understand it.
3   Such classifiers do not have to rely solely on text – any type of input can be accepted.
4   There is also an approach to machine learning that does not have this requirement, so-called 'unsupervised' machine learning. For a more in-depth introduction to all sorts of automatic content analysis techniques for social scientists, see Grimmer and Stewart (2013).
5   See http://cran.r-project.org/web/packages/twitteR/twitteR.pdf (accessed 16 August 2016).
6   See, for example, http://www.codecademy.com/ (accessed 16 August 2016).
7   https://www.heroku.com/ (accessed 16 August 2016).
8   See https://hadoop.apache.org/ (accessed 16 August 2016).

REFERENCES

Agresti, Alan, and Barbara Finlay. 2009. *Statistical Methods for the Social Sciences*. Harlow, UK: Pearson Education.

Bakshy, Eytan, Itamar Rosenn, Cameron Marlow and Lada Adamic. 2012. 'The Role of Social Networks in Information Diffusion', *Proceedings of the 21st International Conference on World Wide Web*, 519–28.

Bakshy, Eytan, Solomon Messing and Lada Adamic. 2015. 'Exposure to Ideologically Diverse News and Opinion on Facebook', *Science* 348(6239): 1130–32.

Barabási, Albert-László, and Réka Albert. 1999. 'Emergence of Scaling in Random Networks', *Science* 286(5439): 509–12.

Bond, Robert M., Christopher J. Fariss, Jason J. Jones, Adam D. I. Kramer, Cameron Marlow, Jaime E. Settle and James H. Fowler. 2012. 'A 61-Million-Person Experiment in Social Influence and Political Mobilization', *Nature* 489(7415): 295–98.

Box, Joan Fisher. 1987. 'Guinness, Gosset, Fisher, and Small Samples', *Statistical Science* 2(1): 45–52.

boyd, Danah, and Kate Crawford. 2012. 'Critical Questions for Big Data', *Information, Communication & Society* 15(5): 662–79.

Brady, Henry E., Sidney Verba and Kay Lehman Schlozman. 1995. 'Beyond SES: A Resource Model of Political Participation', *American Political Science Review* 89(2): 271–94.

Bright, Jonathan. 2014. 'In Search of the Politics of Security', *The British Journal of Politics & International Relations* 17(4): 585–603.

Bright, Jonathan. 2016. 'The Social News Gap: How News Reading and News Sharing Diverge', *Journal of Communication* 66(3): 343–65.

Bright, Jonathan, and Tom Nicholls. 2014. 'The Life and Death of Political News: Measuring the Impact of the Audience Agenda Using Online Data', *Social Science Computer Review* 32(2): 170–81.

Bulger, Monica, Jonathan Bright and Cristobal Cobo. 2015. 'The Real Component of Virtual Learning: Motivations for Face-To-Face MOOC Meetings in Developing and Industrialised Countries', *Information, Communication & Society* 18(10): 1200–16.

Chadefaux, Thomas. 2014. 'Early Warning Signals for War in the News', *Journal of Peace Research* 51(1): 5–18.

Cohen, Jacob. 1988. *Statistical Power Analysis for the Behavioral Sciences*. Mahwah, NJ: Lawrence Erlbaum.

Cohen, Jacob. 1994. 'The Earth Is Round (p <.05)', *American Psychologist* 49(12): 997–1003.

Cox, Michael, and David Ellsworth. 1997. 'Application-Controlled Demand Paging for out-of-Core Visualization'. In *VIS '97 Proceedings of the 8th Conference on Visualization '97*, Los Alamitos, CA: IEEE Computer Society Press, 235–ff.

Döring, Holger. 2008. 'Evaluating Scripting Languages : How Python Can Help Political Methodologists', *The Political Methodologist* 16(1): 8–12

Eagle, Nathan, Alex Sandy Pentland and David Lazer. 2009. 'Inferring Friendship Network Structure by Using Mobile Phone Data', *Proceedings of the National Academy of*

Sciences of the United States of America 106(36): 15274–78.

Eynon, Rebecca. 2013. 'The Rise of Big Data: What Does It Mean for Education, Technology, and Media Research?', *Learning, Media and Technology* 38(3): 237–40.

Gillani, Nabeel, Taha Yasseri, Rebecca Eynon and Isis Hjorth. 2014. 'Structural Limitations of Learning in a Crowd: Communication Vulnerability and Information Diffusion in MOOCs', *Scientific Reports* 4: 6447.

Goel, Sharad, Ashton Anderson, Jake Hofman and Duncan Watts. 2013. 'The Structural Virality of Online Diffusion', *Preprint* (2013).

González-Bailón, Sandra. 2013. 'Social Science in the Era of Big Data', *Policy & Internet* 5(2): 147–60.

González-Bailón, Sandra. 2014. 'Assessing the Bias in Samples of Large Online Networks', *Social Networks* 38: 16–27.

Grimmer, Justin, and Brandon M. Stewart. 2013. 'Text as Data: The Promise and Pitfalls of Automatic Content Analysis Methods for Political Texts', *Political Analysis* 21(3): 267–97.

Harford, Tim. 2014. 'Big Data: Are We Making a Big Mistake?', *Financial Times*. https://www.ft.com/content/21a6e7d8-b479-11e3-a09a-00144feabdc0 (accessed 16 August 2016).

Harrington, Peter. 2012. *Machine Learning in Action*. Shelter Island, NY: Manning.

Howe, Doug, Maria Costanzo, Petra Fey, Takashi Gojobori, Linda Hannick, Winston Hide, David P. Hill, Renate Kania, Mary Schaeffer, Susan St Pierre, Simon Twigger, Owen White and Seung Yon Rhee. 2008. 'Big Data: The Future of Biocuration', *Nature* 455(7209): 47–50.

Huberman, Bernardo A. 2012. 'Sociology of Science: Big Data Deserve a Bigger Audience', *Nature* 482(7385): 308.

Lazer, David, Pentland, Alex (Sandy), Adamic, Lada, Aral, Sinan, Barabasi, Albert Laszlo, … and Van Alstyne, Marshall. 2009. 'Life in the Network: The Coming Age of Computational Social Science', *Science,* 323(5915): 721–23.

Lazer, David, Ryan Kennedy, Gary King and Alessandro Vespignani. 2014. 'The Parable of Google Flu: Traps in Big Data Analysis', *Science* 343(6167): 1203–5.

Lin, Mingfeng, Henry C. Lucas and Galit Shmueli. 2013. 'Too Big to Fail: Large Samples and the *p*-Value Problem', *Information Systems Research* 24(4): 906–17.

Marx, Vivien. 2013. 'Biology: The Big Challenges of Big Data', *Nature* 498(7453): 255–60.

Murdoch, Travis B, and Allan S. Detsky. 2013. 'The Inevitable Application of Big Data to Health Care', *JAMA* 309(13): 1351–52.

Rosenthal, James A. 1996. 'Qualitative Descriptors of Strength of Association and Effect Size', *Journal of Social Service Research* 21(4): 37–59.

Russell, Matthew A. 2013. *Mining the Social Web: Data Mining Facebook, Twitter, LinkedIn, Google+, GitHub, and More*. Sebastopol, CA: O'Reilly Media.

Savage, Mike, and Roger Burrows. 2007. 'The Coming Crisis of Empirical Sociology', *Sociology* 41(5): 885–99.

Schöch, Christof. 2013. 'Big? Smart? Clean? Messy? Data in the Humanities', *Journal of Digital Humanities* 2(3).

Schrenk, Michael. 2007. *Screen Webbots, Spiders, and Screen Scrapers: a Guide to Developing Internet Agents with PHP/CURL*. San Francisco, CA: No Starch Press.

Sullivan, Gail M., and Richard Feinn. 2012. 'Using Effect Size – or Why the *P* Value Is Not Enough', *Journal of Graduate Medical Education* 4(3): 279–82.

Taylor, Linnet, Ralph Schroeder, and Eric Meyer. 2014. 'Emerging Practices and Perspectives on Big Data Analysis in Economics: Bigger and Better or More of the Same?', *Big Data & Society* 1(2): 2053951714536877.

Vittinghoff, Eric, D. Glidden, S.C. Shiboski, and C.E. McCulloch. 2005. *Regression Methods in Biostatistics: Linear, Logistic, Survival and Repeated Measures Models*. New York, NY: Springer-Verlag.

Yasseri, Taha, and Jonathan Bright. 2014. 'Can Electoral Popularity Be Predicted Using Socially Generated Big Data?', *it – Information Technology* 56(5): 246–53.

Yasseri, Taha, and Jonathan Bright. 2016. 'Wikipedia Traffic Data and Electoral Prediction: Towards Theoretically Informed Models' *EPJ Data Science* 5(22) [Online].

## PART IV

The Online Survey

## 9

Overview: Online Surveys

Vasja Vehovar and Katja Lozar Manfreda

INTRODUCTION

Survey data collection – based on standardized questionnaires delivered to a sample (or the whole of the target population) – is an important data collection tool in a variety of contemporary research fields. Its beginnings stretch far into the past (de Leeuw, 2005; Groves *et al.*, 2009), while the modern breakthrough occurred only in the 1930s with the application of probability sampling.

Survey research has always been open to new technological advancements, starting with expansion of telephone surveys in the 1960s, computer-assisted face-to-face surveys in the 1980s, Internet surveys in the 1990s and related mobile surveys in 2010s. According to ESOMAR (2014), spending for online surveys already has a dominant – and still increasing – share among all market research quantitative methods. Similarly, we can observe an increase in the corresponding usage in official and academic surveys (e.g. Ainsaar, *et al.*, 2013), while online surveys

over mobile phones are the most exposed technology (Greenbook, 2015). Due to rapid expansion, online surveys also raise many new methodological issues.

COMPUTER-ASSISTED SURVEY INFORMATION COLLECTION

General Context

The introduction of computer technology enabled a variety of survey modes, which are covered under the term 'computer-assisted survey information collection' (CASIC). CASIC can be further nested in computer-assisted data collection (CADAC), which in addition encompasses other types of computer-related data collection (e.g. electronic recordings). Initial CASIC modes were interviewer-administered, with an interviewer reading and completing the survey questionnaire remotely (through the telephone, CATI) and then also in a face-to-face situation

(CAPI, CASI) (see Table 9.1). Information communication technology (ICT) enables significant improvements over traditional paper-and-pencil modes. Answers collected from the respondents are immediately stored in a computer database and ready for further processing. This reduces time, costs and errors arising from the transcription of paper questionnaires. Furthermore, computers enable various features, such as question skips and filters, randomization of response options, control of answer validity, inclusion of multimedia elements, and many others.

Later on, computerized self-administered questionnaires (CSAQ) – where respondents themselves complete the survey questionnaire – also appeared. Various options emerged here, some of the most typical being described in Table 9.1. Self-administration is beneficial for both researchers and respondents. Respondents can complete a

questionnaire at the time, place and pace of their own preference and with an increased sense of privacy, while absence of interviewers greatly reduces costs of research. In addition, increased sense of privacy and absence of interviewer-related biases can importantly contribute to higher data quality.

Internet surveys were enabled by various technological advancements: speed of transmission procedures, evolution of standardized web browsers, development of email clients and various other technologies (Lozar Manfreda, 2001). At the beginning, Internet surveys were often performed via email (Bachmann et al., 1996; Sheehan and Hoy, 1999), where respondents mark their answers into the reply email text. This evolved further and modern email surveys can use HyperText Markup Language (HTML) elements (e.g. radio buttons, checkboxes) so they are attractive and convenient for

Table 9.1   CASIC modes according to interviewer involvement

CASIC mode	Interviewer involvement	Brief description
CAPI (Computer-assisted personal interviewing)	Physically present	An interviewer brings a portable computer with the questionnaire to respondents, asks questions and enters answers into it.
CASI (Computer-assisted self-interviewing, Audio-CASI, Video-CASI)	Physically present	Similar to CAPI, but respondents answer the questionnaire on an interviewer's computer by themselves. In audio/video-CASI questions are presented using audio/video clips.
CATI (Computer-assisted telephone interviewing)	Remotely present	An interviewer calls respondents by phone (fixed or mobile) and enters answers into the computerized questionnaire.
CAVI (Computer-assisted video interviewing)	Remotely present	An interviewer calls respondents and conducts the interview via video-conferencing system.
Disk-by-mail	Not present (CSAQ – computerized self-administered questionnaires)	Respondents answer – using their own computer – the questionnaire on a floppy disk sent by researcher and returned by respondent via mail.
TDE (Touch-tone data entry)	Not present (CSAQ)	Respondents listen to pre-recorded questions and respond by pressing appropriate numeric keys on a telephone handset.
IVR (Interactive voice response)	Not present (CSAQ)	Voice communication with a computer system using the telephone. Respondents provide answers orally.
Internet surveys	Not present (CSAQ)	Questionnaires are communicated using Internet technology (e.g. email or web).
Virtual interviewer surveys	Not present (CSAQ)	Questions are presented to respondents using some kind of animated virtual interviewer, usually through the Internet.

short questionnaires where interaction is not required (e.g. no skips). However, the majority of Internet surveys today do involve some type of interaction. In such a case we typically talk about web surveys (the first study was published by Pitkow and Recker, 1994), where respondents access and answer the survey questionnaire using a standard web browser on their personal computer or some other device. The responses are subsequently transmitted to a web server, which also provides interactivity (e.g. question depends on a previous answer). Questionnaires based on modern web technologies encompass all advanced and interactive features of computerized questionnaires. Web surveys can use different options with respect to input and output interfaces. For example, video questionnaires can be used to convey survey questions to respondents and the answers can also be video recorded and decoded with speech recognition. However, here we predominantly limit our discussion to the currently prevailing web survey option based on written questions presented on the screen of a respondent's device, which are answered manually by respondents using

mouse, keyboard or touch screen. Graphical and multimedia elements can be used here to enhance the content of the questionnaire.

Internet surveys can also be regarded as part of the larger online survey family, which is a subset of CASIC. Figure 9.1 summarizes the hierarchy of CASIC types down to web and email surveys as prevailing options of Internet surveys. We follow here the conceptualization from Callegaro *et al.*, (2015: 12) and define online surveys as computerized questionnaires (i.e. digital format instead of paper), which rely on some ICT network to mediate the survey process. Besides the Internet this can also include, for example, local area computer networks within an organization or mobile communication network (e.g. SMS surveys over mobile phones). It is also essential for online surveys that responses are transmitted from respondent (i.e. from client device, such as personal computer or mobile phone) to researchers (i.e. to server computer) automatically. Formally, the DBM survey is thus not online, because the respondents need to mail the disc with the responses to researcher. Similarly, the responses filled into the questionnaire

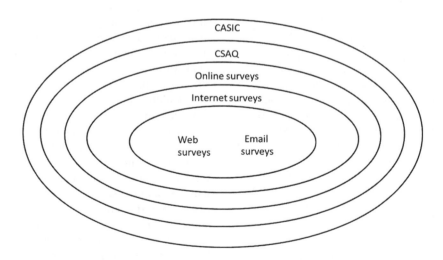

Figure 9.1   A simplified hierarchy of computer-assisted survey information collection (CASIC), computerized self-administered questionnaire (CSAQ), online surveys, Internet surveys and web and email surveys

created in some text processor format (e.g. MS Word), which then need to be attached to an email and sent to the researcher, are not online surveys, because transmission of responses is not automatic simply by pressing one button (e.g. SUBMIT, SEND etc.) as in online web or email surveys.

The web and email surveys are thus the two main types of Internet surveys. While in web surveys the questionnaire is accessed and answered by respondents using a web browser, email surveys require an email application (either stand-alone or in a web browser) and can run entirely without web and web browsers. Still, web and email surveys belong to Internet surveys, because the Internet mediates the communication process.

If not explicitly denoted differently, we treat online surveys, Internet surveys, web surveys and email surveys as being without interviewer's involvement, so they all belong to the CSAQ family. As CSAQ by definition means no interviewer is involved, we also reject the term CAWI (computer assisted web interviewing) for web surveys.

In the remainder of this chapter, we mainly relate to web surveys as the prevailing option when talking about CASIC, CSAQ, online surveys and also when talking about Internet surveys. We also speak mostly about web surveys completed by respondents using desktops/notebooks as the prevailing device, while mobile web surveys with respondents using smartphones or tablets are – although rapidly increasing – still a less used option. Due to technical, usability and methodological turbulences, which accompany the expansion of mobile surveys, we reflect on them here very briefly – compared to web surveys run on personal computer or notebook. The state of the art in mobile surveys in the mid-2010s is fully explored in Callegaro *et al.* (2015: 192).

Technological Aspects

Early web surveys were presented in plain HTML forms and did not offer much interactivity. Today, technologically, interaction can be provided at server-side or at client-side. The former is usually based on HTML forms, while the latter enables execution of the entire questionnaire features on the respondent's computer using technologies like Java. Client-side surveys are in principle more powerful and flexible because they can perform advanced features (like skips and answer validity checks) in real-time and without interaction with the web server. However, there are also serious disadvantages connected to this option (i.e. costs, standardization, lack of control from the server during the answering process), so they almost disappeared in web surveys. Still, we can observe a certain revival in recent years with mobile web surveys – more precisely with CSAQ on mobile devices (e.g. smartphone, tablet) – and related applications (apps) that run the questionnaire on a client device (e.g. a smartphone).

In web surveys, multimedia elements present very beneficial additions to questionnaire text, increase respondents' motivation and foster the understanding of questions (Emde and Fuchs, 2012; Lozar Manfreda *et al.*, 2002; Toepoel and Couper, 2011; Tourangeau *et al.*, 2013). However, web surveys with a larger number of advanced features and multimedia elements can be demanding in bandwidth requirements, which is nevertheless a rapidly diminishing restriction.

One of the benefits of Internet surveys – which relate to web surveys and also to email surveys – is the possibility of their distribution across various devices. As noted, mobile phones (especially smartphones) are becoming particularly important for survey research. However, at their introduction in the early 2000s, problems with small screens, delays in introduction of faster (and cheaper) communication and lack of standardization (Tjøstheim *et al.*, 2005) limited their use for surveying. This has changed dramatically in the late 2000s with the introduction of new generations of mobile communication networks, advanced mobile devices (i.e. smartphones, tablets) and touch-screen technologies. Another device with promising potential is interactive TV (or other variants, such as WebTV, ITV), which integrates traditional TV technology and access to Internet services. This technology could bring surveys closer to respondents' daily activities (e.g. TV watching). However, it still awaits final elaboration and optimization of the technology and its usability.

Technologically, in the early years of Internet surveys, preparing and conducting surveys required programming knowledge and understanding of computer networks. Nowadays, this task is manageable by virtually anyone with general computer literacy. This is enabled by specialized software tools with friendly interfaces, which offer various features of questionnaire design, respondent recruiting, survey project administration and data analysis. According to the WebSM (2015) online database there are currently around 300 of these products in the English language on the market.

KEY METHODOLOGICAL ISSUES

Sampling

One of the initial steps in conducting survey research is the decision about target population from which we choose a sample. Here, the differences between probability samples (where we know the positive inclusion probabilities for all units of the target population in advance) and non-probability ones are crucial.

Probability samples applied in Internet surveys are highly affected by the problems of non-coverage and sampling frames, particularly in the case of surveying the general population. The first problem arises from the fact that not all members (of the general population) have access to the Internet. Data for 2014 show that few EU member states have more than 90 per cent of their households with Internet access, with an average of

81 per cent (Eurostat, 2015), while in the US in 2013, 74 per cent of households had access to the Internet (US Census Bureau, 2013). On the other hand, the non-coverage problem is not that severe in the case of some specific populations (e.g. employees, members, customers). In establishment surveys in particular, it is almost a non-existent problem, as the coverage of organizations (e.g. schools, companies) is already close to complete, at least in developed countries. Of course, when we observe the Internet globally, there are numerous developing countries where the penetration among households or organizations is dramatically lower.

Invitations to Internet surveys are most conveniently distributed using email, but that causes severe problems. There are no email directories of the general population of Internet users that might be used as a sampling frame. This further limits the use of this type of probability Internet survey to specific populations for which such directories exist, for example, members of an organization. Both coverage and frame problems can significantly impact data quality and should be adequately reported when disseminating the results of the research (American Association for Public Opinion Research (AAPOR), 2015).

The problems of probability samples largely contribute to the overall image of Internet surveys, which are often perceived as inherently related to non-probability samples (Terhanian and Bremer, 2005). This is of course not true because probability Internet surveys do exist, as well as non-probability traditional surveys. But it is true that the majority of web survey questionnaires completed today are of non-probability type, either done by do-it-yourself (DIY) non-professional researchers or by wide utilization of non-probability online panels of Internet users (sometimes also called access panels). As these panels become the major recruitment channel for contemporary survey research, professional standards are rapidly developing to cover the problems of panel recruitment, management, monitoring and

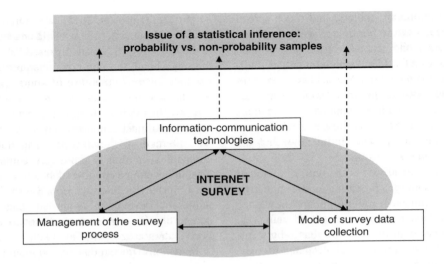

Figure 9.2   Spurious links between statistical inference and the components of Internet surveys: survey management, survey mode and ICTs

maintenance (ESOMAR, 2015). In addition, a corresponding ISO standard for access panels has been developed – ISO 26362:2009 (ISO, 2009).

When discussing sampling issues, it should be stressed that mode of survey data collection and related sampling design are completely separate issues and are not a priori related. As is evident from Figure 9.2, survey management, survey mode and ICTs are closely interrelated, but none of these components is inherently linked to the issue of non-probability samples. There are only spurious links arising from the practice of many (inexpensive) Internet surveys using non-probability sampling. The problem of inference from non-probability samples should thus be considered as a purely statistical issue, which equally applies to other survey modes.

Invitations to Internet Surveys

Depending on the availability of a sampling frame, we can speak about list-based and non-list-based Internet surveys, which can both be probability or non-probability, depending on

the (quality) of the sampling frame (Callegaro *et al.*, 2015: 8). The non-list-based Internet surveys where no list of units from the target population is available in advance, are usually based on general invitations where a URL link to a survey is published on some websites or (less commonly) in other media. This clearly leads to self-selection bias, which is out of researchers' control, and consequently to non-probability samples. Still, an advanced recruitment into non-probability samples – from quota selection to stratification and matching approaches (for detailed treatments, see Callegaro *et al.*, 2015: 48) – can provide important improvements. A careful invitation strategy can build non-probability samples, which provide effective cost–benefit ratios, i.e. relatively high levels of data quality can be obtained given the costs.

An approach to probability sample selection in the case of non-list-based Internet surveys is inviting randomly selected visitors to a specific website (i.e. intercept recruiting). This is usually implemented using pop-up windows containing a general invitation to the Internet survey, which appears only to randomly selected visitors.

On the other hand, in list-based surveys where a sample frame exists in advance, individual invitations can be sent to eligible participants, either by email or some other way, depending on the contact information from the sample frame. If the sample frame is of good quality and covers the target population, probability sampling is possible. Of course, in list-based Internet surveys using individual invitations we can also end up with non-probability samples, as in cases of incomplete lists or self-selected lists of target population or non-probability online panels. It should be noted, however, that unsolicited email invitations and intercept surveys that interrupt users' tasks might breach professional standards (e.g. ESOMAR, 2015; MRA, 2000; Market Research Society (MRS), 2014).

Traditional solicitation modes (like face-to-face, telephone or mail invitations) to Internet surveys may help overcome the issues of probability samples in Internet surveys, but impose significantly higher costs and their effectiveness as regards response rate is questionable. Telephone recruiting seldom provides an overall response rate above 10 per cent among Internet users (e.g. Pratesi *et al.*, 2004) and much the same is often true for mail recruiting. Nevertheless, exceptions exist for very salient topics, such as the general cancer preservation study (Bälter, 2005), where mail invitation to an Internet survey achieved around 50 per cent overall response rate. Similarly, the use of appealing incentives can significantly improve the participation (Göritz, 2006), which is often the case in probability-based online panels.

Nonresponse Problem

Several forms of nonresponse may occur in Internet surveys (Bosnjak, 2001; Vehovar *et al.*, 2002; Callegaro *et al.*, 2015). In surveys in general, invited participants can refuse participation altogether (unit nonresponse), terminate participation during the process (break-off or partial response) or answer questions selectively (item nonresponse). In Internet surveys, several other nonresponse patterns can be observed, thanks to paradata information (e.g. lurking respondents, combination of partial and item nonresponse, etc.).

Nonresponse may result in nonresponse error which basically arises because measurement is not performed for all questions on all units included in the sample (Groves *et al.*, 2009). This is especially prominent if nonrespondents and respondents significantly differ in characteristics that are in the scope of a specific project.

Response rates in Internet surveys are generally lower than with other survey modes (Lozar Manfreda *et al.*, 2008) and they also vary considerably – from less than one per cent for non-list-based surveys with general invitations (measured as number of clicks to the survey among those exposed to the invitation) to almost 100 per cent in surveys of specific populations, such as members of an association. This also depends on complexity of the Internet survey response process, which is especially apparent when email invitations are used (Vehovar *et al.*, 2002).

In order to increase response rates, respondents can be offered monetary or some other form of award (e.g. lottery ticket) as an incentive (Göritz, 2006). Additionally, multiple contacts (pre-notice and follow-up) (Cook *et al.*, 2000, Callegaro *et al.*, 2015: 152) and using Internet surveys in mixed-mode systems may help. The issues arising from nonresponse in Internet surveys and the strategies of increasing response rates are further addressed by Callegaro *et al.*, (2015: 130) and also by Fricker and by Dillman *et al.* (both this volume).

Questionnaire Design

Wording, visual design and other elements of a survey questionnaire present the main communication channel between researcher and respondents. Web questionnaires differ importantly from paper-and-pencil CSAQ. They are navigated using a mouse and a keyboard, which may cause the loss of eye–hand centralization (Bowker and Dillman, 2000). Human–computer interaction research (as summarized by Callegaro et al., 2015: 65) also shows that compared to paper-and-pencil modes, individuals behave somewhat differently when reading the text on the Internet.

Modern web questionnaires and email questionnaires with HTML elements offer a range of design features, like different question types, advanced questionnaire features, images and multimedia, and thus offer possibilities for many innovative approaches. Bälter (2005), for example, suggested using computer games design to increase response rates to Internet surveys; however, such elements can cause a variety of potentially unpredicted effects resulting in lower validity and reliability of data. All designing features therefore need to be subjected to prior methodological evaluation (e.g. using experiments) in order to minimize the possibilities of the unpredicted effects. When this is not possible, a conservative approach is recommended, i.e. advanced features are to be used only when there is clear evidence of their overall benefits (e.g. when helping respondents to understand questions or motivate response), also taking into account all potential deficiencies.

It should be mentioned that measurement error in Internet surveys can arise not only because of the questionnaire design, but also due to the respondent or the survey mode itself (Groves et al., 2009). Respondents' motivation, computer literacy, abilities, privacy concerns and many other factors influence their answers. Proper questionnaire design can help lower the measurement error by offering a user-friendly survey experience, raising the motivation of respondents and providing for precise responses (Peytchev and Petrova, 2002).

Post-Survey Adjustments and Statistical Inference

We have to be clearly aware that standard statistical inference procedures (e.g. computing estimates and confidence intervals) typically assume probability samples. Real-world survey practice, particularly in marketing research and in public opinion polling, which massively neglects the principles of probability sampling, increasingly requires statisticians to elaborate this problem and specify the conditions when standard statistical inference (developed for probability samples) can be applied on non-probability samples as an approximation. Alternatively, users expect that statisticians will also develop new approaches for dealing with non-probability samples. Issues of statistical inference from non-probability samples are thus amongst the most challenging in contemporary survey methodology and statistics. We should recall that the profession not long ago (e.g. AAPOR, 2006) still required that confidence intervals could only be calculated with probability sample surveys. However, this strict attitude is slowly softening as can be seen from the AAPOR report on non-probability sampling (Baker et al., 2013) and the recent AAPOR Code (2015, paragraph 10).

Besides substantial (commercial) pressures to validate non-probability Internet samples, there seems to be nothing methodologically new compared to similar problems with non-probability sampling in traditional survey modes (mail, telephone and face-to-face). One specific exception is the development of advanced statistical modelling which, amongst other input, also incorporates results from non-probability Internet surveys; however, as this usually requires considerable statistical resources, it appears only in very specific situations, such as voting predictions. The voting predictions based on non-probability samples actually perform increasingly well (e.g. Drexler, 2015), although problems do occur occasionally, as with the 2015 British general election (Mellon and Prosser, 2015). Besides rare situations of specific modelling, the non-probability Internet samples can also be partially helped with approximations related to certain probability sampling design principles (e.g. applying quotas or matching to obtain 'representativity') in the sampling design stage and with various elaborated post-survey adjustments in the estimation stage. Of course, these measures cannot fully compensate for the essential problem (i.e. unknown inclusion probabilities), and so the precision of the estimates (e.g. confidence intervals) cannot be properly estimated in (Internet) non-probability samples, as is the case with probability samples.

An exhaustive overview of studies, which evaluated non-probability Internet surveys against probability surveys and other external benchmarks (Callegaro et al., 2014) showed considerable discrepancies in survey estimates; however, for many variables these discrepancies would still be acceptably small, especially when the differences in costs are taken into account – the cost of a minute of respondent's time in non-probability online panels is typically in the range of a few tens of cents. On the other hand, with probability online panels the minute usually costs at least 1–2 dollars/euros, while with face-to-face surveys this can surpass 10 dollars/euros per minute. As a consequence, the reality is that non-probability Internet surveys (particularly non-probability online panels) actually do satisfy the majority of the contemporary requests for surveys, particularly when surveying the general population, at least in commercial and DIY sector. However, there exist many variables and topics, especially in official statistics and academic research (e.g. unemployment), which do require probability sampling, either online or with traditional survey modes.

In any case, practitioners in different fields developed their own tailored procedures – in sample design, post-survey adjustment and estimation stage – based on experience and trial–error approaches, in order to guarantee sufficient survey data quality for specific practical purposes. Various post-survey procedures were thus developed in Internet survey practice for situations where sampling deviates from probability selection, or when we face non-coverage and nonresponse problems.

Within this context we predominantly talk about editing, imputation and weighting approaches. The latter is particularly popular and is used in many different ways, including the adjustment of the sample to known population socio-demographic controls. Still, we should not expect too much from weighting, because very often these corrections do not remove the bulk of the biases (Vehovar et al., 1999). At best, they may remove up to one half of the corresponding bias (Tourangeau et al., 2013), while differences between various weighting procedures are usually very small (Baker et al., 2013).

RELATED ISSUES

Errors, Costs and Management

The process of survey implementation is essentially a managerial issue, which is especially apparent in large projects. Numerous quality standards for general and ICT-supported survey data collection are aimed at providing the managerial principles for successful survey research (Biemer and Lyberg, 2003). In addition to data quality, the survey management should also scrutinize and optimize the costs of research.

Costs and errors (data quality) are very closely related. Lower costs are often regarded as one of the key advantages of Internet surveys in comparison to other survey modes. In practice it turns out that this advantage is not that straightforward and is often questionable. For example, costs might substantially increase when traditional solicitation methods (e.g. telephone, mail) are employed to achieve a higher response rate. The same applies to incentives or probability panels of the general population, which are very demanding in terms of maintenance costs. Cost-effectiveness of Internet surveys should thus be evaluated with respect to errors. Few such evaluations are available to date. One of them (Vehovar et al., 2001) discussed the mean square error (MSE) approach (Groves, 1989), which integrated sampling error and nonresponse bias. The study found that Internet surveys with mail invitations perform better than telephone surveys in the case of longer questionnaires because in Internet surveys the gain from large sample size outweighs the nonresponse bias. It is therefore crucial that quality standards, together with managerial practices, take into account costs and errors of survey research. A more general approach to the problem is presented in Vehovar *et al.* (2010) and Vannieuwenhuyze (2014).

Survey Modes

Internet surveys – and particularly web surveys – are still relatively new and pose certain validity and reliability issues in comparison to traditional survey modes to which they are often compared. Two aspects of Internet surveys are particularly prominent in such comparisons: response rate and quality of survey answers.

We already mentioned that response rate comparisons are usually not favourable for Internet surveys. Meta-analyses showed that on average web and email surveys gain lower response rates than other survey modes when comparable implementation procedures are used (Lozar Manfreda *et al.*, 2008). However, the issue that is still awaiting exploration is the corresponding comparison with mode-related costs taken into account. Namely, as Internet surveys usually require less resources, the savings could be invested in other measures to increase response rates (e.g. incentives), and therefore when comparing two designs within the same budget, the Internet surveys might outperform the traditional one.

Quality of survey responses is typically measured with indicators such as item non-response, acquiescence, non-differentiation, length of answers to open-ended responses, etc. Several studies found Internet surveys performing better on these indicators in comparison to telephone and mail surveys (Fricker *et al.*, 2005; Kwak and Radler, 2002). Chang and Krosnick (2002) also confirmed generally lower measurement errors in Internet surveys. Particularly with sensitive topics (e.g. gambling, adultery and other social undesired behaviours), differences between the modes can increase. However, we may also add that the Internet surveys (as well as other CSAQ) usually perform better – in terms of measurement errors – than traditional modes (Tourangeau *et al.*, 2013).

Mixed-Mode Systems

Due to the problems of non-coverage and nonresponse, Internet surveys are often used in mixed-mode survey systems, offering opportunities for compensating the weaknesses of individual modes (de Leeuw, 2005). Here, different modes for contacting respondents and different modes in the measurement stage (questionnaire completion) are combined (Biemer and Lyberg, 2003). For example, in order to increase response rates, the first contact attempt is made by email and the nonrespondents are later contacted by telephone. Telephone respondents might also be screened and asked for their email addresses, to which the invitation to do an Internet survey is later sent. Similarly, the data collection (measurement) can be performed using different modes for different population segments (e.g. Internet survey for Internet users and mail survey for non-users) or at diverse stages of the process (e.g. Internet survey in the first stage and telephone survey for nonrespondents in the second stage). In some cases, the decision on the mode of questionnaire completion might even be left to respondents. Several other more or less common options of mixed-mode systems involving Internet surveys also exist (de Leeuw and Hox, 2011; Dillman *et al.*, 2014).

Although combining different modes for contacting respondents is usually beneficial as regards response rates and the non-coverage problem, employing mixed-modes in the measurement stage (i.e. questionnaire completion) of the survey process may result in specific mode-effect problems. Even when only the web is used for questionnaire completion, the differences in question presentation can cause unforeseen effects on respondents' answers, and the problem is much more severe when several modes are combined. For example, check-all-that-apply (commonly used in web and paper surveys) and forced-choice format (common in telephone surveys) perform differently when utilized for the same question (Smyth *et al.*, 2006; Callegaro *et al.*, 2015): respondents endorse more answers, but need longer to provide answers in the latter format. There might also be a conflict because of questionnaire-designing possibilities offered by Internet surveys, but not by traditional modes, such as use of advanced graphical elements or multimedia (Dillman *et al.*, 2014). It is therefore necessary to take appropriate measures for reducing such effects.

There is no uniform answer to how to successfully address mode–effects issues. In so-called unimode or unified design (Dillman *et al.*, 2014), differences in how questions are posed are minimized across different modes. On the other hand, the mode-specific design suggests using different designing approaches for different modes, in line with their specifics and capabilities. According to this approach, unique features of Internet surveys (e.g. possibility of using images or multimedia) should be deployed if they can contribute to higher data quality. This might be done even if other modes in the research design do not offer such possibilities.

We should add that when more modes are involved in the solicitation and/or measurement stage of the survey process, effective survey project management is of extreme importance because it enables the control and optimization of complex iterative processes (see Figure 9.3). Introducing another mode in any stage of an initial Internet survey is very

likely to substantially increase the administration and the costs of research; however, as we stressed earlier, costs and errors should be regarded as strongly interconnected. The mixed-mode systems are effective only when the selected modes for solicitation and measurement offer a higher overall data quality so that this outweighs the increased costs. Needless to say, both factors (data quality and costs) are difficult to measure very precisely and it is even more difficult to combine them. As we already mentioned in discussing costs, one potential direction is to minimize the product of means squared error and the cost (Vehovar *et al.*, 2010; Vannieuwenhuyze, 2014).

Mixing Research Methods

We have to sharply separate mixing of the survey modes from mixing surveys with qualitative data collection approaches, i.e. mixing methods. The latter is strongly related to historical discussion about quantitative and qualitative methods in social science methodology (Morgan, 2014).

With quantitative research we usually employ standardized questionnaires or an observational form of data collection on larger samples of the target population. Another key characteristic is that in quantitative research we basically deal – after coding – with numbers. Qualitative methods, on the other hand, are characterized by exploring concepts and by the absence of standardization; typical examples include in-depth interviews, focus groups and ethnography, but new specific analytic approaches are continuously expanding. While quantitative and qualitative approaches are historically separated and even in confrontation, they increasingly cohabit in so-called mixed methods or combined-method approaches. Today, most substantive research fields draw on both approaches. The combinations of qualitative and quantitative methods can be qualitative preliminary, quantitative preliminary,

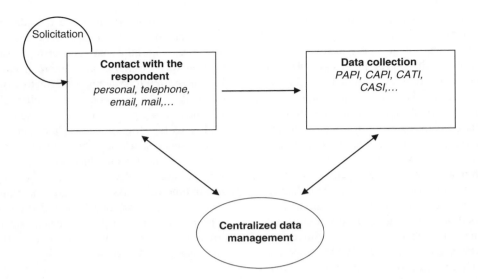

Figure 9.3   Solicitation and data collection modes through centralized data management

qualitative follow-up and quantitative follow-up (Morgan, 2014). For example, qualitative methods are used to formulate and test a survey questionnaire (qualitative preliminary), or focus groups are employed to pursue findings from a survey (qualitative follow-up).

With the Internet, these combinations fruitfully expand because the mixing of methods can be performed easily and inexpensively (Lobe and Vehovar, 2009). Flexible combinations of quantitative and qualitative approaches, like combinations of Internet surveys and in-depth interviews, can be very effective in providing higher validity and explanatory power of collected data. When we have permanently at our disposal a large database of potential respondents (either from online panels or from some online community), we can, for example, start with qualitative research (e.g. online in-depth interviews), which is followed with one week (or less) of Internet surveying. After analysing results, we can simply continue with the same survey, modify it or we may perform more qualitative research (e.g. online focus groups). Of course, many methodological issues arise here, from the allocation of resources to these methods and the attention

given to results from each method to the problem of combining (sometimes contradictory) findings. Nevertheless, the Internet enables us to integrate surveys into a very powerful circle of mixed research methods. This can be further extended by the emerging concepts of e-Social Science, where the entire process of research is conducted on the Internet, from conceptualization and questionnaire design to data collection, analysis, dissemination and archiving (Vehovar *et al.,* 2014).

Ethics, Guides and Standards

Survey research professionals in general have developed a variety of standards and best practice guides to ensure that research is conducted in line with ethical and quality principles (like AAPOR, ESOMAR, WAPOR). General survey standards, which are already widely available, can also largely be applied to Internet surveys.

However, with the introduction of Internet surveys new ethical issues emerge. In addition, because of easy implementation, many Internet surveys are conducted by non-professionals lacking methodological skills, which puts special importance on standards and ethics. Such specifics of Internet surveys need to be addressed by an extension of the current standards or development of completely new ones.

Several specialized standards and codes for Internet surveys are already available (e.g. ESOMAR, 2015; Association of Internet Researchers (AoIR), 2012; BVM, 2007; MRA, 2000; MRS, 2014). In general, they cover the basic principles of Internet survey data collection, including the main issues stated earlier. Some organizations have also incorporated their guidelines and codes for Internet-based research into their existing documents (Council of American Survey Research Organizations (CASRO), 2011). Some specific documents relate to a special type or usage of Internet surveys, such as online access panels, which are addressed by the *Quality Standards for Access Panels* (EFAMRO, 2006) and by ESOMAR (2015), or psychological research addressed by the American Psychological Association (Kraut *et al.*, 2004).

The most common ethical issues include the problem of unsolicited email invitations, privacy and security threats, obtaining of informed consent online, combining data from different sources, and surveying children and minorities, among others. For further discussion of these and other general aspects of Internet research ethics, see the chapter by Eynon *et al.* (this volume).

THE CURRENT AND FUTURE APPLICATIONS

Application Areas

Internet surveys provide a vast application potential for a variety of research topics. On the one hand, we can observe this most visibly with the expansion of entertainment Internet surveys and online voting (e.g. quick daily polls posted on various websites or participation in interactive shows or events). On the other hand, Internet surveys are increasingly replacing other survey modes. This replacement process is very complex and its speed is determined by numerous interrelated factors from technology, economy, culture and legislation to politics. The most visible areas where this change was fully implemented are commercial surveys. In marketing research, ESOMAR (2014) global trends clearly show that online surveys have become the dominant quantitative research method. The factors that impact this replacement process are discussed in detail by Vonk *et al.* (2006), with specific reference to the Netherlands.

Academic, public and government (particularly statistical offices) bodies are much slower in this replacement process. This is partly because they are bound by strict regulations with respect to quality standards, particularly sampling and response rates. This is also due to more rigid management structures and decision processes. Some early adopters (e.g. Statistics Norway), which made the Internet survey option compulsory for all establishment surveys, have faced numerous practical difficulties. In addition, publicly funded surveys are often very complex and involve long-term integrated data collection where change of the survey mode can cause serious problems for time-series data. Nevertheless, the experiences with decennial censuses were generally very positive in all countries that offered web options (e.g. Conrad and Couper, 2004).

Of course, when we talk about application areas, we should be aware that some are more suitable for Internet surveys, such as employee surveys, customer satisfaction surveys, membership surveys (including faculty and student surveys) and establishment surveys. General population surveys are more problematic, however, where online panels rapidly take the leading role. We should also add that the revolutionizing potential of Internet surveys is not limited to survey research in a narrow sense. Administrative forms, Internet psychological testing and online experiments are typical examples of such applications. Further, there are increasing numbers of areas where Internet surveys are becoming a component in a larger integrated process, such as public administration (i.e. e-government), customer relationship marketing (CRM) or e-learning. In addition, particularly the mobile Internet surveys can be integrated in numerous business (e.g. satisfaction with location services), administration (e.g. feedback in application forms) and research processes (e.g. continues reporting, diaries, ethnographic studies). A systematic overview on contemporary usage of Internet surveys is provided in Callegaro *et al.* (2015: 25).

Technological Trends

The Internet and related communication technologies are dramatically changing modern survey research. In the near future we can expect nothing but further expansion and turbulence. New technologies are likely to foster the extension of the current CASIC modes. For example, text-to-speech (TTS) technologies will make the implementation of Interactive Voice Response (IVR) surveys more efficient. New CASIC modes will expand related to virtual interviewers and to the integration of other technologies (e.g. GIS) into the data collection process. Fast development can also be expected in the expansion of CASIC modes to interactive TV, mobile phones and other wearable technologies. Mobile phones particularly raise numerous technological issues, especially with respect to speed of access, costs, interfaces and to the relation between browser-based surveys and mobile application surveys (apps).

A specific stream of technological trends relates to additional data, apart from the respondents' answers, which can be collected easily during surveying. We speak about paradata – data about the process of data collection (Couper, 2005), such as contact-info paradata (outcomes to an (email)

invitation, access to the questionnaire, last question answered), device-type paradata (user agent string, detection of JavaScript and Flash, cookie and IP recording) and questionnaire navigation paradata (time spent per screen, keystrokes and mouse-clicks, change of answers, real-time validation messages) (Callegaro *et al.*, 2015: 121). These data can present a valuable source of information for preparation and monitoring of a survey project. They can be also treated as a component of the growing body of so-called big data.

Another trend is the move toward continuous measurement (Couper, 2005). Self-administered surveys distributed through mobile devices will enable surveying of individuals virtually anywhere at any time. Such continuous measurement, however, is not limited to surveys. It can be expected that research will be based increasingly on observation. For example, collecting information on TV watching, credit card transactions and phone call patterns can tell a lot about an individual's life. While technical implementation might be easy, it is much harder to overcome methodological, ethical and legal issues arising from such measurement.

We can also expect further advances in related software support. This includes integration of mixed-mode systems, mixed methods, as well as support for multiple devices, further inclusion of audio, video, TTS and other features, including multilanguage support. We may add that this will also stimulate the democratization of survey research and DIY surveys. The classic survey industry may thus suffer a considerable shift of clients to the DIY segment, but also directly to software vendors.

Research Challenges

The hottest research question is perhaps whether the probability-based online panels can provide results that meet academic and governmental standards for data quality. Can such a panel replace the General Social

Survey, Labour Force Survey or European Social Survey? Large research projects have recently been launched in various developed countries to address these issues (e.g. the Netherlands, the US, UK and Germany), however, the results are still ambiguous (e.g. Ainsaar *et al.*, 2013).

Important research challenges are also currently related to specific methodological aspects of mobile surveys. We can expect that in a few years the share of Internet surveys answered on mobile devices will move from the 2015 level of 10–20 per cent to become a majority. However, numerous turbulences related to technological issues – which in the 2010s are still rapidly changing the methodological aspects (for details, see Callegaro *et al.*, 2015: 192) – need to settle down first before more stable methodological solutions can be developed. As mentioned, this is also the main reason for not further elaborating these surveys in this chapter. We had in fact a similar situation in the first decade of Internet surveys, where temporary technological obstacles (e.g. dial-up access, which soon became an obsolete problem) strongly interfered with methodological issues.

Other important streams of future research can be targeted towards the development of the virtual interviewer and, in particular, towards costs and data quality optimization.

CONCLUSION

Technological advancements opened new possibilities for survey research, and Internet surveys are probably the most revolutionizing contemporary innovation in this field. They have already become an important tool for a variety of survey research practices, including marketing and social research, as well as official statistics. Convenience of self-administration, computerization and Internet-based data transfer substantially broadens the potentials of survey research. This is especially highlighted within the possibilities of advanced

questionnaire features, inclusion of multimedia elements, remote survey management, multiple devices and lowering of the research costs. Benefits and logic of Internet surveys are also increasingly being adopted in other research areas, including psychological research, e-learning, e-government, and other developing and emerging fields.

Nevertheless, further expansion and development of technologies is needed to enable the utilization of the full range of Internet survey potentials. As Internet and related communication technologies become available across the general population as a whole, problems of coverage will be easier to overcome, particularly because future development of mobile devices will allow a much higher degree of their use for survey research. Technological progress will also continuously foster the globalization of suppliers (software, services), the integration with other approaches (qualitative, off-line measurement, observations), and combining data from different sources and devices.

As for now, serious methodological issues of Internet surveys still persist. In addition to coverage, sampling and nonresponse problems, these also arise from the lack of comprehensive knowledge on the most appropriate design and implementation, particularly in relation to multiple devices (e.g. mobile phones, tablets, interactive TV). As methodological research on these topics continues, it is likely that new standards for Internet surveying will emerge, which will in particular address various privacy and ethical dilemmas.

REFERENCES

Ainsaar, M., Lilleoja, L., Lumiste, K. and Roots, A. (2013). *ESS Mixed Mode Experiment Results in Estonia (CAWI and CAPI Mode Sequential Design)*. Estonia: University of Tartu.

American Association for Public Opinion Research (AAPOR). (2006). 'Reporting of margin of error or sampling error in online and other surveys of self-selected individuals'. Retrieved 11 December 2006 from http://www.aapor.org/pdfs/2006/samp_err_stmt.pdf

American Association for Public Opinion Research (AAPOR). (2015). 'Best practices for research'. Retrieved 25 June 2015 from http://www.aapor.org/AAPORKentico/Standards-Ethics/Best-Practices.aspx

Association of Internet Researchers (AoIR). (2012). 'Ethical decision-making and internet research'. Retrieved 6 July 2015 from http://aoir.org/

Bachmann, D. P., Elfrink, J. and Vazzana, G. (1996). 'Tracking the progress of email versus snail-mail', *Marketing Research*, *8*(2), 31–5.

Baker, R. P., Brick, M. J., Bates, N., Battaglia, M. P., Couper, M. P., Dever, J. A., Gile, K. J. and Tourangeau, R. (2013). 'Report of the AAPOR task-force on non-probability sampling'. Retrieved 30 June 2015 from http://www.aapor.org/

Bälter, O. (2005). 'Using computer games design to increase response rates'. Paper presented at the ESF SCSS Exploratory Workshop: Internet Survey Methodology: Toward Concerted European Research Efforts, Dubrovnik, Croatia.

Biemer, P. P. and Lyberg, L.E. (2003). *Introduction to Survey Quality*. Hoboken, NJ: John Wiley.

Bosnjak, M. (2001). 'Participation in non-restricted web surveys: a typology and explanatory model for item-nonresponse'. In U.-D. Reips and M. Bosnjak (eds.), *Dimensions of Internet Science*. Lengerich, Germany: Pabst Science Publishers, pp. 193–207.

Bowker, D. and Dillman, D. A. (2000). 'An experimental evaluation of left and right oriented screens for web questionnaires'. Presented at the The American Association for Public Opinion Research (AAPOR) 55th Annual Conference, May 18–20, Portland, OR.

BVM. (2007). *Rat der Deutschen Markt- und Sozialforschung*. Berlin: BVM. Retrieved 6 July 2015 from http://bvm.org/rat-der-dt-marktforschung/

Callegaro, M., Baker, R., Bethlehem, J., Göritz, A., Krosnick, J. and Lavrakas, P. (eds.). (2014). *Online Panel Research: A Data Quality Perspective*. Series in Survey Methodology. New York, NY: Wiley.

Callegaro, M., Lozar Manfreda, K. and Vehovar, V. (2015). *Web Survey Methodology*. London: Sage Publications.

Chang, L. and Krosnick, J. A. (2002). 'The accuracy of self-reports: comparisons of an RDD telephone with Internet surveys by Harris Interactive and Knowledge Networks'. Presented at the The American Association for Public Opinion Research (AAPOR) 57th Annual Conference, May 16–19, St. Pete Beach, FL.

Conrad, F. G. and Couper, M. P. (2004). 'Usability, comparability and data quality across modes and technologies in census data collection'. Technical report prepared for the US Census Bureau through the Gunnison Consulting Group and the University of Michigan. Washington, DC: Gunnison Consulting Group.

Cook, C., Heath, F. and Thompson, R. L. (2000). 'A meta-analysis of response rates in Web or Internet-based surveys', *Educational and Psychological Measurement*, *60*(6), 821–36.

Council of American Survey Research Organizations (CASRO). (2011). *Code of Standards and Ethics for Survey Research*. Port Jefferson, NY: Council of American Survey Research Organizations.

Couper, M. P. (2005). 'Technology trends in survey data collection', *Social Science Computer Review*, *23*(4), 486–501.

de Leeuw, E. D. (2005). 'To mix or not to mix data collection modes in surveys', *Journal of Official Statistics*, *21*(2), 233–55.

de Leeuw, E. D. and Hox, J. (2011). 'Internet surveys as a part of a mixed-mode design'. In M. Das, P. Ester and L. Kaczmirek (eds.), *Social and Behavioral Research and the Internet. Advances in Applied Methods and Research Strategies*. New York, NY: Routledge, pp. 45–76.

Dillman, D. A., Smyth, J. D. and Christian, L. M. (2014). *Internet, Phone, Mail, and Mixed-Mode Surveys. The Tailored Design Method*. 4th edn. Hoboken, NJ: Wiley.

Drexler, K. (2015, April 2). 'US election statistics: a resource guide'. Retrieved 30 June 2015 from http://www.loc.gov/rr/program/bib/elections/statistics.html#online

EFAMRO. (European Federation of Associations of Marketing Research Organizations). (2006). 'Quality standards for access panels'.

Retrieved 14 October 2006 from: http://www.efamro.com/

Emde, M. and Fuchs, M. (2012). 'Exploring animated faces scales in web surveys: drawbacks and prospects', *Survey Practice*, 5(1).

ESOMAR. (European Society to Opinion and Marketing Research). (2014). *Global Market Research 2014*. Amsterdam: ESOMAR.

ESOMAR. (2015). 'ESOMAR/GRBN guideline for online research'. Retrieved 25 June 2015 from: https://www.esomar.org/knowledge-and-standards/codes-and-guidelines/esomar-grbn-online-research-guideline-draft.php

Eurostat. (2015). 'Information Society Statistics'. Retrieved 25 June 2015 from http://ec.europa.eu/eurostat/data/database

Fricker, S., Galesic, M., Tourangeau, R. and Yan, T. (2005). 'An experimental comparison of web and telephone surveys', *Public Opinion Quarterly*, 69(3), 370–92.

Göritz, A. S. (2006). 'Cash lotteries as incentives in online panels', *Social Science Computer Review*, 24(4), 445–59.

Greenbook. (2015). 'Greenbook research industry trends report'. Retrieved 30 June 2015, from http://www.greenbook.org/grit

Groves, R. M. (1989). *Survey Errors and Survey Costs*. New York, NY: Wiley.

Groves, R. M., Fowler Jr, F. J., Couper, M. P., Lepkowski, J. M., Singer, E. and Tourangeau, R. (2009). *Survey Methodology*. 2nd edn. Hoboken, NJ: Wiley.

ISO. (2009). *ISO 26362: Access Panels in Market, Opinion, and Social Research – Vocabulary and Service Requirements*. Geneva: International Organization for Standardization.

Kraut, R., Olson, J., Banaji, M., Bruckman, A., Cohen, J. and Couper, M. P. (2004). 'Psychological research online', *American Psychologist*, 59(2), 105–17.

Kwak, N. and Radler, B. T. (2002). 'A comparison between mail and web surveys: response pattern, respondent profile, and data quality', *Journal of Official Statistics*, 18(2), 257–73.

Lobe, B. and Vehovar, V. (2009). 'Towards a flexible online mixed method design with a feedback loop', *Quality and Quantity*, 43(4), 585–97.

Lozar Manfreda, K. (2001). *Web survey errors*. PhD Thesis. Ljubljana, Slovenia: University of Ljubljana, Faculty of Social Sciences.

Lozar Manfreda, K., Batagelj, Z. and Vehovar, V. (2002). 'Design of web survey questionnaires: three basic experiments', *Journal of Computer-Mediated Communication*, 7(3).

Lozar Manfreda, K., Bosnjak, M., Berzelak, J., Haas, I. and Vehovar, V. (2008). 'Web surveys versus other survey modes – a meta-analysis comparing response rates', *International Journal of Market Research*, 50(1), 79–104.

Mellon, J. and Prosser C. (2015). 'Investigating the Great British polling miss: evidence from the British Election Study (15 July 2015)'. Retrieved 20 August 2015 from SSRN http://ssrn.com/abstract=2631165 or http://dx.doi.org/10.2139/ssrn.2631165

Morgan, D. L. (2014). *Integrating Qualitative and Quantitative Methods: A Pragmatic Approach*. Los Angeles, CA: Sage Publications.

MRA. (2000). 'Use of the Internet for conducting opinion and marketing research: ethical guidelines'. Retrieved 30 June 2015 from http://www.mra-net.org/pdf/Internet_ethics_guidelines.pdf

MRS. (Market Research Society). (2014). *MRS Guidelines for Online Research*. Retrieved 26 June 2015 from https://www.mrs.org.uk/pdf/2014–09–01%20Online%20Research%20Guidelines.pdf

Peytchev, A. and Petrova, E. (2002). 'Statistical data validation in web instruments – an empirical study'. Presented at the The American Association for Public Opinion Research (AAPOR) 57th Annual Conference, May 16–19, St. Pete Beach, FL.

Pitkow, J. E. and Recker, M. M. (1994). 'Results from the first World-Wide Web user survey', *Journal of Computer Networks and ISDN Systems*, 27(2), 243–54.

Pratesi, M., Lozar Manfreda, K., Biffignandi, S. and Vehovar, V. (2004). 'List-based web surveys: quality, timeliness, and nonresponse in the steps of the participation flow', *Journal of Official Statistics*, 20(3), 451–65.

Schonlau, M., Fricker Jr, R. D. and Elliott, M. N. (2002). *Conducting Research Surveys via Email and the Web*. Santa Monica, CA: RAND.

Sheehan, K. B. and Hoy, M. G. (1999). 'Using email to survey Internet users in the United States: methodology and assessment', *Journal of Computer-Mediated Communication*, 4(3).

Smyth, J. D., Dillman, D. A., Christian, L. M. and Stern, M. J. (2006). 'Comparing check-all and forced-choice question formats in web surveys', *Public Opinion Quarterly*, 70(1), 66–77.

Terhanian, G. and Bremer, J. (2005). 'Creative applications of selection bias modelling in market research'. Paper presented at the International Statistical Institute, 55th Session, April 5–12, Sydney, Australia.

Tjøstheim, I., Thalberg, S., Nordlund, B. and Vestgården, J. I. (2005). 'Are mobile phone users ready for MCASI?' In ESOMAR (ed.), *Excellence in International Research*. Amsterdam: ESOMAR, pp. 465–88.

Toepoel, V. and Couper, M. P. (2011). 'Can verbal instructions counteract visual context effects in web surveys?', *Public Opinion Quarterly*, 75(1), 1–18.

Tourangeau, R., Conrad, F. C. and Couper, M. P. (2013). *The Science of Web Surveys*. Oxford: Oxford University Press.

US Census Bureau. (2013). 'Computer and Internet access in the United States: 2013'. Retrieved 23 December 2014 from http://www.census.gov/hhes/computer/publications/2013.html

Vannieuwenhuyze, J. (2014). 'On the relative advantage of mixed-mode versus single-mode surveys', *Survey Research Methods*, 8(1), 31–42.

Vehovar, V., Berzelak, N. and Lozar Manfreda, K. (2010). 'Mobile phones in an environment of competing survey modes: applying metric for evaluation of costs and errors', *Social Science Computer Review*, 28(3), 303–18.

Vehovar, V., Lozar Manfreda, K. and Batagelj, Z. (1999). 'Web surveys: can the weighting solve the problem?', Proceedings of the Survey Research Methods Section, American Statistical Association, Alexandria, VA: AMSTAT, pp. 962–7.

Vehovar, V., Lozar Manfreda, K. and Batagelj, Z. (2001). 'Sensitivity of e-commerce measurement to the survey instrument', *International Journal of Electronic Commerce*, 6(1), 31–52.

Vehovar, V., Lozar Manfreda, K. and Zaletel, M. (2002). 'Nonresponse in web surveys'. In R. M. Groves, D. A. Dillman, J. L. Eltinge and R. J. A. Little (eds.), *Survey Nonresponse*. New York, NY: John Wiley, pp. 229–42.

Vehovar, V., Petrovcic,, A. and Slavec, A. (2014). 'e-Social science perspective on survey process: towards an integrated web questionnaire development platform'. In U. Engel, B. Jann, P. Lynn, A. Scherpenzeel and P. Sturgis (eds.), *Improving Survey Methods*. New York; London: Routledge, pp. 170–83.

Vonk, T., van Ossenbruggen, R. and Willems, P. (2006). 'The effects of panel recruitment and management on research results: a study across 19 online panels'. Presented at the Panel Research Conference 2006. Amsterdam: ESOMAR.

WebSM. (2015). 'Web survey methodology portal'. Retrieved 30 June 2015 from www.websm.org.

FURTHER READING

Web Survey Methodology by Callegaro *et al.* (2015) provides an overview of two decades of research in web survey methodology. The book discusses the latest techniques for collecting valid and reliable data and offers a comprehensive overview of research issues. It covers key concepts and key findings in the literature, including measurement, nonresponse, adjustments, paradata and cost issues, as well as some latest topics in survey research such as Internet panels, mobile surveys, e-social sciences and mixed modes.

Internet, Phone, Mail, and Mixed-Mode Surveys. The Tailored Design Method by Dillman *et al.* (2014) provides an overview of many aspects of modern survey research. The book elaborates strategies and tactics to increase response rate and the quality of survey data. It also provides a suggestion on how and when it is appropriate to choose certain survey method (e.g. mail, telephone, Internet).

Online Panel Research: A Data Quality Perspective by Callegaro *et al.* (2014) provides a careful examination of the quality of data being generated by online panels. The book addresses a wide range of topics, such as coverage bias, nonresponse, measurement error, adjustment techniques, the relationship between nonresponse and measurement error, impact of smartphone adoption on data collection, Internet rating panels and operational issues.

Survey Methodology by Robert M. Groves *et al.* (2009) covers the most important aspects of general survey methodology. It focuses on basic and advanced principles of survey design, implementation and management. As such, it presents a valuable reference for successful survey research.

The Web Survey Methodology Website (WebSM, 2015) is a comprehensive online portal dedicated to the methodology of web surveys and related fields. Its extensive bibliographical database offers information on almost 3,000 references covering topics related to Internet surveys.

## 10

Sampling Methods for Online Surveys

Ronald D. Fricker Jr

INTRODUCTION

In the context of conducting surveys or collecting data, sampling is the selection of a subset of a larger population to survey. This chapter focuses on sampling methods for web and email surveys, which taken together we call 'online' surveys. In our discussion we will frequently compare sampling methods for online surveys to various types of non-online surveys, such as those conducted by postal mail and telephone, which in the aggregate we refer to as 'traditional' surveys (see also Dillman *et al.*, this volume).

The chapter begins with a general overview of sampling. Since there are many fine textbooks on the mechanics and mathematics of sampling, we restrict our discussion to the main ideas that are necessary to ground our discussion on sampling for online surveys. Readers already well versed in the fundamentals of survey sampling may wish to proceed directly to the section on Sampling Methods for Internet-based Surveys.

WHY SAMPLE?

Surveys are conducted to gather information about a population. Sometimes the survey is conducted as a *census*, where the goal is to survey every unit in the population. However, it is frequently impractical or impossible to survey an entire population, perhaps owing to either cost constraints or some other practical constraint, such as that it may not be possible to identify all the members of the population.

An alternative to conducting a census is to select a sample from the population and survey only those sampled units. As shown in Figure 10.1, the idea is to draw a sample from the population and use data collected from the sample to infer information about the entire population. To conduct *statistical inference* (i.e. to be able to make quantitative statements about the unobserved population statistic), the sample must be drawn in such a fashion that one can be confident that the sample is representative of the population

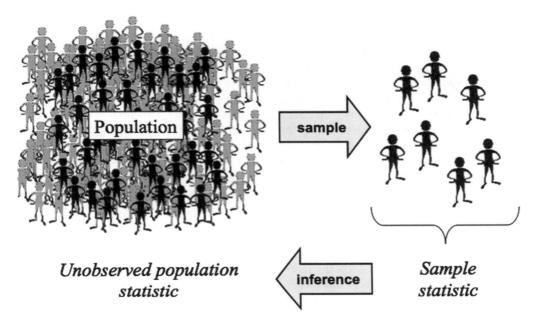

Population

sample

Unobserved population statistic

inference

Sample statistic

Figure 10.1   An illustration of sampling. When it is impossible or infeasible to observe a population statistic directly, data from a sample appropriately drawn from the population can be used to infer information about the population.

Source: Author.

and that one can both calculate appropriate sample statistics and estimate their standard errors. To achieve these goals, as will be discussed in this chapter, one must use a probability-based sampling methodology.

A survey administered to a sample can have a number of advantages over a census, including:

- lower cost
- less effort to administer
- better response rates
- greater accuracy

The advantages of lower cost and less effort are obvious: keeping all else constant, reducing the number of surveys should cost less and take less effort to field and analyse. However, that a survey based on a sample rather than a census can give better response rates and greater accuracy is less obvious, and yet greater survey accuracy *can* result

when the sampling error is more than offset by a decrease in nonresponse and other biases, perhaps due to increased response rates. That is, for a fixed level of effort (or funding), a sample allows the surveying organization to put more effort into maximizing responses from those surveyed, perhaps via more effort invested in survey design and pre-testing, or perhaps via more detailed non-response follow-up.

What does all of this have to do with online surveys? Before the Internet, large surveys were generally expensive to administer and hence survey professionals gave careful thought to how to best conduct a survey in order to maximize information accuracy while minimizing costs. However, as illustrated in Figure 10.2, the Internet now provides easy access to a plethora of inexpensive survey software, as well as to millions of potential survey respondents, and it has lowered other costs and barriers to surveying. While this is good news for survey researchers, these same factors have also facilitated a proliferation of bad survey research practice.

For example, in an online survey the marginal cost of collecting additional data can be virtually zero. At first blush, this seems to be an attractive argument in favour of attempting to conduct censuses, or for simply surveying large numbers of individuals without regard to how the individuals are recruited into the sample. In fact, these approaches are being used more frequently with online surveys, without much thought being given to alternative sampling strategies or to the potential impact such choices have on the accuracy of the survey results. The result is a proliferation of poorly conducted 'censuses' and surveys based on large convenience samples that are likely to yield less accurate information than a well-conducted survey of a smaller sample.

Conducting surveys, as in all forms of data collection, requires making compromises. Specifically, there are almost always trade-offs to be made between the amount of data that can be collected and the accuracy of the data collected. Hence, it is critical for researchers to have a firm grasp of the trade-offs they implicitly or explicitly make when choosing a sampling method for collecting their data.

AN OVERVIEW OF SAMPLING

There are many ways to draw samples from a population – and there are also many ways that sampling can go awry. We intuitively think of a good sample as one that is representative of the population from which the sample has been drawn. By 'representative' we do not necessarily mean the sample matches the population in terms of observable characteristics, but rather that the results from the data we collect from the sample are consistent with the results we would have obtained if we had collected data on the entire population.

Of course, the phrase 'consistent with' is vague and, if this was an exposition of the mathematics of sampling, would require a precise definition. However, we will not cover the details of survey sampling here.[1] Rather, in this section we will describe the various sampling methods and discuss the main issues in characterizing the accuracy of a survey, with a particular focus on terminology and definitions, in order that we can put the subsequent discussion about online surveys in an appropriate context.

Sources of Error in Surveys

The primary purpose of a survey is to gather information about a population. However, even when a survey is conducted as a census, the results can be affected by several sources of error. A good survey design seeks to reduce all types of error – not only the sampling error arising from surveying a sample of the population. Table 10.1 lists the four general categories of survey error as presented and defined in Groves (2004) as part of his 'Total Survey Error' approach.

Errors of coverage occur when some part of the population cannot be included in the sample. To be precise, Groves specifies three different populations:

1 The population of inference is the population that the researcher ultimately intends to draw conclusions about.
2 The target population is the population of inference less various groups that the researcher has chosen to disregard.
3 The frame population is that portion of the target population which the survey materials or devices delimit, identify and subsequently allow access to (Wright and Tsao, 1983).

The *survey sample* consists of those members of the sampling frame who are chosen to be surveyed, and *coverage error* is the difference between the frame population and the population of inference.

Figure 10.2 Logos for various Internet survey software companies (accessed November 2015)

Sampling error arises when a sample of the target population is surveyed. It results from the fact that different samples will generate different survey data. Roughly speaking, assuming a random sample, sampling error is reduced by increasing the sample size.

Nonresponse errors occur when data is not collected on either entire respondents (*unit nonresponse*) or individual survey questions (*item nonresponse*). Groves (2004) calls nonresponse 'an error of nonobservation'. The response rate, which is the ratio of the number of survey respondents to the number sampled, is often taken as a measure of how well the survey results can be generalized. Higher response rates are taken to imply a lower likelihood of *nonresponse bias*.

Measurement error arises when the survey response differs from the 'true' response. For example, respondents may not answer sensitive questions honestly for a variety of reasons, or respondents may misinterpret or make errors in answering questions. Measurement error is reduced in a variety of ways, including careful testing and revision of the survey instrument and questions, choice of survey mode or modes, etc.

Sampling Methods

Survey sampling can be grouped into two broad categories: *probability-based sampling* (also loosely called 'random sampling') and

Table 10.1 Sources of survey error according to Groves (2004)

Type of error	Definition
Coverage	'…the failure to give any chance of sample selection to some persons in the population'.
Sampling	'…heterogeneity on the survey measure among persons in the population'.
Nonresponse	'…the failure to collect data on all persons in the sample'.
Measurement	'…inaccuracies in responses recorded on the survey instruments'.

non-probability sampling. A probability-based sample is one in which the respondents are selected using some sort of probabilistic mechanism, and where the probability with which every member of the frame population could have been selected into the sample is known. The sampling probabilities do not necessarily have to be equal for each member of the sampling frame.

Types of probability sample include simple random sampling (SRS), stratified random sampling, cluster sampling and systematic sampling. There are important analytical and practical considerations associated with how one draws and subsequently analyses the results from each of these types of probability-based sampling schemes, but space limitations preclude covering them here. Readers interested in such details should consult texts such as Kish (1965), Cochran (1977), Fink (2003) or Fowler Jr (2002).

Non-probability samples, sometimes called *convenience samples*, occur when either the probability that every unit or respondent included in the sample cannot be determined or it is left up to each individual to choose to participate in the survey. For probability samples, the surveyor selects the sample using some probabilistic mechanism and the individuals in the population have no control over this process. In contrast, for example, a web survey may simply be posted on a website where it is left up to those browsing through the site to decide to participate in the survey ('opt in') or not. As the name implies, such non-probability samples are often used because it is somehow convenient to do so.

Although in a probability-based survey the participants can choose not to participate in the survey ('opt out'), rigorous surveys seek to minimize the number who decide not to participate (i.e. nonresponse). In both cases it is possible to have bias, but in non-probability surveys the bias has the potential to be much greater because it is likely that those who opt in are not representative of the general population. Furthermore, in non-probability surveys there is often no way to assess the potential magnitude

of the bias because there is generally no information on those who chose *not* to opt in.

Non-probability-based samples often require much less time and effort, and thus are usually less costly to generate, but generally they do not support formal statistical inference. However, non-probability-based samples can be useful for research in other ways. For example, early in the course of research, responses from a convenience sample might be useful in developing hypotheses. Responses from convenience samples might also be useful for identifying issues, defining ranges of alternatives or collecting other sorts of non-inferential data. For a detailed discussion on the application of various types of non-probability-based sampling method to qualitative research, see Patton (2002). Specific types of non-probability samples include quota sampling, snowball sampling and judgment sampling.

Bias versus Variance

If a sample is systematically not representative of the population of inference in some way, then the resulting analysis is likely to be biased. For example, results from a survey of Internet users about personal computer usage are unlikely to accurately quantify computer usage in the general population simply because the sample is comprised only of those who use computers. Furthermore, it is important to recognize that taking larger samples will not correct for bias, nor is a large sample evidence of a lack of bias. For example, an estimate of average computer usage based on a sample of Internet users will likely overestimate the average usage in the general population *regardless of how many Internet users are surveyed*.

Randomization, meaning randomly selecting respondents from the population of interest, is used to minimize the chance of bias. The idea is that by randomly choosing potential survey respondents *from the entire population* the sample is likely to 'look like' the population, even in terms of those characteristics that cannot be observed or known. This latter point is worth emphasizing. Probability samples mitigate the chance of sampling bias in both observable *and unobservable* characteristics.

Variance, on the other hand, is simply a measure of variation in the observed data. It is used to calculate the *standard error* of a statistic, which is a measure of the variability of the statistic. The precision of statistical estimates drawn via probabilistic sampling mechanisms is improved by larger sample sizes because (all else held constant) larger samples sizes result in smaller standard errors.

Bias can creep into survey results in many different ways. In the absence of significant nonresponse, probability-based sampling is the best way to minimize the possibility of bias. Convenience sampling, on the other hand, is generally assumed to have a higher likelihood of generating a biased sample. However, even with randomization, surveys of and about people may be subject to other kinds of bias. For example, sensitivity bias can result in respondents overstating or understating certain things, particularly with socially delicate questions such as questions about income or sexual orientation.

SAMPLING METHODS FOR INTERNET-BASED SURVEYS

This section describes specific online survey approaches and the sampling methods that are applicable to each. We concentrate on differentiating whether particular sampling methods and their associated surveys allow for generalization of survey results to populations of inference or not, providing examples of some surveys that were done appropriately and well, and others that were less so. Examples that fall into the latter category should not be taken as a condemnation of a particular survey or sampling method, but rather as illustrations of inappropriate application, execution, analysis, etc. Couper (2000: 465–6) perhaps said it best,

> Any critique of a particular web survey approach must be done in the context of its intended purpose and the claims it makes. Glorifying or condemning an entire approach to survey data collection should not be done on the basis of a single implementation, nor should all Web surveys be treated as equal.

Furthermore, as we previously discussed, simply because a particular method does not allow for generalizing beyond the sample does not imply that the methods and resulting data are not useful in other research contexts.

Similar to Couper (2000), Table 10.2 lists the most common probability and non-probability sampling methods, and indicates which online survey mode or modes may be used with each method. For example, it is possible to conduct both web and email surveys using a list-based sampling frame methodology. Conversely, while it is feasible to conduct

Table 10.2 Types of online survey and associated sampling methods

Sampling method	Web	Email
Probability-based		
Surveys using a list-based sampling frame	✓	✓
Surveys using non-list-based random sampling	✓	✓
Intercept (pop-up) surveys	✓	
Mixed-mode surveys with online option	✓	✓
Pre-recruited panel surveys	✓	✓
Non-probability		
Entertainment polls	✓	
Unrestricted self-selected surveys	✓	
Surveys using 'harvested' email lists (and data)	✓	✓
Opt-in panels (volunteer or paid)	✓	

an entertainment poll by email, virtually all such polls are conducted via web surveys.

Surveys using a List-Based Sampling Frame

Sampling for online surveys using a list-based sampling frame can be conducted just as one would for a traditional survey using a sampling frame. Simple random sampling in this situation is straightforward to implement and requires nothing more than contact information (generally an email address for an online survey) on each unit in the sampling frame. Of course, although only contact information is required to field the survey, having additional information about each unit in the sampling frame is desirable to assess (and perhaps adjust for) nonresponse effects.

While online surveys using list-based sampling frames can be conducted either via the web or by email, if an all-electronic approach is preferred the invitation to take the survey will almost always be made via email. And, because email lists of general populations are generally not available, this survey approach is most applicable to large homogeneous groups for which a sampling frame with email addresses can be assembled (for example, universities, government organizations, large corporations, etc.). Couper (2000) calls these 'list-based samples of high-coverage populations'.

In more complicated sampling schemes, such as a stratified sampling, auxiliary information about each unit, such as membership in the relevant strata, must be available and linked to the unit's contact information. More complicated multi-stage and cluster sampling schemes can be difficult or even impossible to implement for online surveys. First, to implement without having to directly contact respondents will likely require significant auxiliary data, which is unlikely to be available except in the case of specialized populations. Second, if offline contact is required,

then the researchers are likely to have to resort to the telephone or mail in order to ensure that sufficient coverage and response rates are achieved.

An example of a multi-stage sampling procedure, used for an online survey of real estate journalists for which no sampling frame existed, is reported by Jackob *et al.* (2005). For this study, the researchers first assembled a list of publications that would include journalists who were relevant to the study. From this list a stratified random sample of publications was drawn, separately for each of five European countries. They then contacted the managing editor at each sampled publication and obtained the necessary contact information for all the journalists who were 'occupied with real-estate issues'. All the journalists identified by the managing editors were then solicited to participate in a web survey. Jackob *et al.* (2005) concluded that it 'takes a lot of effort especially during the phase of preparation and planning' to assemble the necessary data and then to conduct an online survey using a multi-stage sampling methodology.

Surveys using Non-List-Based Random Sampling

Non-list-based random sampling methods allow for the selection of a probability-based sample without the need to actually enumerate a sampling frame. With traditional surveys, random digit dialing (RDD) is a non-list-based random sampling method that is used mainly for telephone surveys.

There is no equivalent of RDD for online surveys. For example, it is not possible (practically speaking) to generate random email addresses (see the Issues and Challenges in Internet-based Survey Sampling section). Hence, with the exception of intercept surveys, online surveys requiring non-list-based random sampling depend on contacting potential respondents via some traditional means such as RDD, which introduces other complications and costs. For example, surveyors must either screen potential respondents to ensure they have Internet access or field a survey with multiple response modes. Surveys with multiple response modes introduce further complications, both in terms of fielding complexity and possible mode effects (again, see the Issues and Challenges in Internet-based Survey Sampling section).

Intercept Surveys

Intercept surveys on the web are pop-up surveys that frequently use systematic sampling for every k^{th} visitor to a website or web page. These surveys seem to be most useful as customer satisfaction surveys or marketing surveys. This type of systematic sampling can provide information that is generalizable to particular populations, such as those that visit a particular website/page. The surveys can be restricted to only those with certain IP (Internet Protocol) addresses, allowing one to target more specific subsets of visitors, and 'cookies' can be used to restrict the submission of multiple surveys from the same computer.

A potential issue with this type of survey is nonresponse. Comley (2000) reports typical response rates in the 15 to 30 per cent range, with the lowest response rates occurring for poorly targeted and/or poorly designed surveys. The highest response rates were obtained for surveys that were relevant to the individual, either in terms of the particular survey questions or, in the case of marketing surveys, the commercial brand being surveyed.

As discussed in Couper (2000), an important issue with intercept surveys is that there is no way to assess nonresponse bias, simply because no information is available on those that choose not to complete a survey. Comley (2000) hypothesizes that responses may be biased towards those who are more satisfied with a particular product, brand or website; towards those potential respondents who are

more computer and Internet savvy; and away from heavy Internet users who are conditioned to ignore pop-ups. Another source of nonresponse bias for intercept surveys implemented as pop-up browser windows is pop-up blocker software, at least to the extent that pop-up blocker software is used differentially by various portions of the web-browsing community.

Pre-recruited Panel Surveys

Pre-recruited panel surveys are, generally speaking, groups of individuals who have agreed in advance to participate in a series of surveys. For online surveys requiring probability samples, these individuals are generally recruited via some means other than the web or email – most often by telephone or postal mail (see Toepoel, 2012, for guidance on how to build an online panel of respondents).

For a longitudinal effort consisting of a series of surveys, researchers may recruit panel members specifically for that effort. For smaller efforts or for single surveys, a number of companies maintain panels of individuals, pre-recruited via a probability-based sampling methodology, from which sub-samples can be drawn according to a researcher's specification. Knowledge Networks, for example, recruits all of its panel members via telephone using RDD, and it provides equipment and Internet access to those that do not have it in an attempt to maintain a panel that is a statistically valid cross section of the population (see Pineau and Dennis, 2004, for additional detail). Other companies such as Qualtrics provide panel management software so that companies and researchers can assemble and manage their own panel or panels.[2]

Pre-recruited, Internet-enabled panels can provide the speed of online surveys while simultaneously eliminating the often-lengthy recruitment process normally required. As such, they can be an attractive option to researchers who desire to field an online survey, but who require a sample that can be generalized to populations outside of the Internet-user community.

However, pre-recruited panels are not without their potential drawbacks. In particular, researchers should be aware that long-term panel participants may respond differently to surveys and survey questions than first-time participants (called 'panel conditioning' or 'time-in-sample bias'). Nonresponse can also be an issue if the combined loss of potential respondents throughout all the recruitment and participation stages is significant. However, as Couper (2000) concludes, '… in theory at least, this approach begins with a probability sample of the full (telephone) population, and assuming no nonresponse error permits inference to the population…'.

Unrestricted Self-Selected Surveys

As with entertainment polls, unrestricted, self-selected surveys are surveys that are open to the public for anyone to participate in. They may simply be posted on a website so that anyone browsing through may choose to take the survey, or they may be promoted via website banners or other online advertisements, or they may be publicized in traditional print and broadcast media. Regardless of how they are promoted (or not), the key characteristics of these types of surveys are that there are no restrictions on who can participate, and it is up to the individual to choose to participate (opt in). Unrestricted, self-selected surveys are a form of convenience sampling and, as such, the results cannot be generalized to a larger population.

The web can also facilitate access to individuals who are difficult to reach either because they are hard to identify or locate, or perhaps exist in such small numbers that probability-based sampling would be unlikely to reach them in sufficient numbers. Coomber (1997) describes such a use of the web for fielding a survey to collect information from drug dealers about drug adulteration/dilution. By posting invitations to participate in a survey on various drug-related discussion groups, Coomber collected data from 80 survey respondents (that he deemed reliable) located in 14 countries on four different continents. The sample was certainly not generalizable, but it also provided data that was unlikely to be collected in any other way, and which Coomber found consistent with other research.

In addition, Alvarez et al. (2002) proposed that these types of non-probability sample can be useful and appropriate for conducting experiments (say, in the design of web pages or web surveys) by randomly assigning members of the sample to control and experimental groups. In terms of psychology experiments, Siah (2005) states, 'For experimental research on the Internet, the advantage of yielding a heterogeneous sample seems persuasive considering that the most common criticism of psychological research is its over-reliance on college student samples'.

Opt-in Panels (volunteer or paid)

Opt-in panels are similar in concept to the pre-recruited panels, except the volunteers are not recruited using a probability-based method; rather, participants choose to participate, perhaps after coming across a solicitation on a website. In this regard, volunteer panels are similar to unrestricted, self-selected surveys except that those who opt in do so to take a continuing series of surveys. Harris Interactive manages such an opt-in panel. Its website (www.harrispollonline.com) banner says, 'Take Surveys. Earn Stuff. It's That Simple'. Often these panels are focused on market research, soliciting consumer opinions about commercial products, and participants sometimes do it for monetary incentives.

Researchers are also paying respondents to take surveys on sites like Mechanical Turk (www.mturk.com/mturk/welcome). On these sites, surveys (and other tasks) are posted and people complete the tasks for a price. As reported on NPR's All Tech Considered (NPR, 2014):

> You can buy just about anything on Amazon.com – clothes, books, electronics. You can buy answers, too. College students and professors are doing all sorts of research on an Amazon site called Mechanical Turk.
>
> Need 200 smokers for your survey on lung cancer? Have a moral dilemma to pose for your paper on Kierkegaard? Now researchers can log in, offer a few pennies in payment and watch the data roll in.

The article goes on to say,

> Berinsky, over at MIT, says researchers save not just weeks of effort, but great amounts of money as well. He pays a couple cents per participant, compared to the $10 or $15 he used to pay. OK, so MTurk is fast and cheap. Is it good? How reliable are the data? The research shows that the population of Turkers is pretty representative, more so than signing up college students.

However, as 'Steven O' says in the comments section of the website,

> Selection bias is still an issue – sample size doesn't help if you have a non-random sample. For alpha testing, fine, but I would be very interested to see a study showing how Mechanical Turk respondents (those online and motivated to take a survey by at most $2.50/hour) represent most target populations. 'Better than college students' is a low bar to beat.

The issue, as with all non-probability samples, is that those taking the survey are unlikely to be representative of the population of inference. For example, those working on the Mechanical Turk site are likely to be younger, more computer literate and of a lower socio-economic stratum than the general population. Furthermore, on sites like this, it is difficult to limit the respondents to a specific geographic location or nationality. Whether this is a problem depends on the objectives of the specific research effort.

ISSUES AND CHALLENGES IN INTERNET-BASED SURVEY SAMPLING

All survey modes have their strengths and weaknesses; online surveys are no different in this regard. The various strengths and weaknesses are more or less important, depending on the survey's purpose. Drawing an appropriate sample that will provide the data necessary to appropriately address the research objective is critical. Hence, in this section we focus on the issues and challenges related to sampling for online surveys.

Sampling Frame and Coverage Challenges

A frequent impediment for conducting large-scale, online surveys is the lack of a sampling frame. Simply put, no single registry or list of email addresses exists and thus list-based sampling frames are generally available only for specific populations (government organizations, corporations, etc.).

Compounding this difficulty, and leaving aside the issue of population coverage to be discussed shortly, it is impossible to employ a frameless sampling strategy because for all practical purposes one cannot assemble random email addresses. Of course, it is theoretically possible to 'construct' email addresses by repeatedly randomly concatenating letters, numbers and symbols, but the sheer variety of email addresses means most of the constructed addresses will not work. More importantly, the unstructured nature of the Internet means that even if one could tolerate the multitude of undeliverable email messages that would result, they would not be useful as the basis for a probability sample.

In terms of coverage, it is widely recognized that online surveys using only samples of Internet users do not generalize to the general public. Although Internet penetration into households continues at a rapid pace (Figure 10.3 shows the top 20 countries with the highest Internet penetration as of the end of 2013),

#	Country or Region	Population, 2014 Est	Internet Users Year 2000	Internet Users Dec 2013	Penetration (% Population)	% Growth 2000 - 2013
	TOP 20 COUNTRIES WITH HIGHEST NUMBER OF INTERNET USERS - December 31, 2013					
1	China	1,355,692,576	22,500,000	620,907,200	45.8 %	2,659.6 %
2	United States	318,892,103	95,354,000	268,507,150	84.2 %	181.6 %
3	India	1,236,344,631	5,000,000	195,248,950	15.8 %	3,805.0 %
4	Brazil	202,656,788	5,000,000	109,773,650	54.2 %	2,095.5 %
5	Japan	127,103,388	47,080,000	109,626,672	86.2 %	132.9 %
6	Russia	142,470,272	3,100,000	87,476,747	61.4 %	2,721.8 %
7	Germany	80,996,685	24,000,000	69,779,160	86.2 %	190.7 %
8	Nigeria	177,155,754	200,000	67,319,186	38.0 %	33,559.6 %
9	United Kingdom	63,742,977	15,400,000	57,266,690	89.8 %	271.9 %
10	France	66,259,012	8,500,000	55,221,000	83.3 %	549.7 %
11	Indonesia	253,609,643	2,000,000	55,000,000	21.7 %	2,650.0 %
12	Mexico	120,286,655	2,712,400	52,276,580	43.5 %	1,827.3 %
13	Iran	80,840,713	250,000	45,000,000	55.7 %	17,900.0 %
14	Philippines	107,668,231	2,000,000	44,200,540	41.1 %	2,110.0 %
15	Egypt	86,895,099	450,000	43,065,211	49.6 %	9,470.0 %
16	Korea	49,039,986	19,040,000	41,571,196	84.8 %	118.3 %
17	Vietnam	93,421,835	200,000	41,012,186	43.9 %	20,406.1 %
18	Turkey	81,619,392	2,000,000	37,748,969	46.3 %	1,787.4 %
19	Italy	61,680,122	13,200,000	36,058,199	58.5 %	173.2 %
20	Spain	47,737,941	5,387,800	35,705,960	74.8 %	562.7 %
	TOP 20 Countries	4,754,113,803	273,374,200	2,072,765,246	43.6 %	658.2 %
	Rest of the World	2,427,744,816	87,611,292	729,713,688	30.1 %	732.9 %
	Total World Users	7,181,858,619	360,985,492	2,802,478,934	39.0 %	676.3 %

Figure 10.3   Top 20 countries with the highest Internet penetration as of 31 December 2013

Source: Internet World Stats, 2015.

the penetration is far from complete (compared to, say, the telephone) and varies widely by country and region of the world.[3] The point is, if the target of inference is the general public, considerable coverage error remains for any sample drawn strictly from Internet users. Furthermore, it is worth emphasizing that even with 100 per cent Internet penetration, the difficulty of obtaining a true probability sample from the general population remains.

Now, even if there is minimal coverage error for a particular online survey effort, when using only an online survey mode the target population must also be sufficiently computer literate and have both regular and easy access to the Internet to facilitate responding to the survey. Simply put, just because an organization maintains a list of email addresses for everyone in the organization, it does not necessarily follow that every individual on the list has equal access. Lack of equal access could result in significant selection and nonresponse biases.

Mixed-Mode Surveys using Online and Traditional Media

For some surveys it may be fiscally and operationally possible to contact respondents by some mode other than email, such as mail or telephone. In these cases, the survey target population can be broader than that for which an email sampling frame is available, up to and including the general population. But at present such a survey must also use multiple survey modes to allow respondents without Internet access the ability to participate. Mixed-mode surveys may also be useful for alleviating selection bias for populations with uneven or unequal Internet access, and the sequential use of survey modes can increase response rates.

For example, Dillman (2007: 456) describes a study in which surveys that were fielded using one mode were then followed up with an alternate mode three weeks later. As shown in Table 10.3, in all cases the response rate increased after the follow-up. Now, of course, some of this increase can be attributed simply to the fact that a follow-up effort was conducted. However, the magnitude of the increases also suggests that offering a different response mode in the follow-up can be beneficial.

However, mixed-mode surveys are subject to other issues. Two of the most important are mode effects and respondent mode preferences. Mode effects arise when the type of survey affects how respondents answer questions. Comparisons between online surveys and traditional surveys have found conflicting results, with some researchers reporting mode effects and others not (see, for example, the discussion and results in Schonlau *et al.*, 2004: 130). Although not strictly a sampling issue, the point is that researchers should be prepared for the existence of mode effects in a mixed-mode survey. Vehovar and Lozar

Manfreda's overview chapter (this volume) explores in greater detail the issues of combining data from online and traditional surveys.

In addition, when online surveys are part of a mixed-mode approach, it is important to be aware that the literature currently seems to show that respondents will tend to favour the traditional survey mode over an online mode (see, for example, the discussions in Schonlau *et al.*, 2002; Couper, 2000: 486–7). Fricker Jr and Schonlau (2002: 351), in a study of the literature on web-based surveys, found 'that for most of the studies respondents currently tend to choose mail when given a choice between web and mail. In fact, even when respondents are contacted electronically it is not axiomatic that they will prefer to respond electronically'.

The tendency to favour non-online survey modes leads Schonlau *et al.* (2002: 75) to recommend for mixed-mode mail and web surveys that:

> … the most effective use of the Web at the moment seems to involve a sequential fielding scheme in which respondents are first encouraged to complete the survey via the Web and then non-respondents are subsequently sent a paper survey in the mail. This approach has the advantage of maximizing the potential for cost savings from using Internet while maintaining the population coverage and response rates of a mail survey.

Web-Based Recruitment Issues and Effects

Whether email addresses are constructed, assembled from third-party sources or

Table 10.3 As reported in Dillman (2007), using an alternate survey mode as a follow-up to an initial survey mode can result in higher overall response rates

Initial survey mode and response rate	Follow-up survey mode and combined response rate	Response rate increase
Mail (75%)	Telephone (83%)	8%
Telephone (43%)	Mail (80%)	37%
IVR[1] (28%)	Telephone (50%)	22%
Web (13%)	Telephone (48%)	35%

Note: [1] IVR stands for Interactive Voice Response. These are automated telephone surveys in which pre-recorded questions are used and respondents' answers are collected using voice-recognition technology.

harvested directly from the web, there is the issue of unsolicited survey email as spam. For example, Sheehan (1999) conducted a survey with email addresses harvested from www.Four11.com and stated, 'Several individuals receiving the solicitation email censured the researchers for sending out unsolicited emails, and accused the researchers of "spamming"'. They further recounted that 'One [ISP] system operator [who observed a large number of email messages originating from a single address] then contacted his counterpart at our university'.

In addition, distributing an unsolicited online survey is also not without its perils, for example Andrews *et al.*'s (2002: 203) report on a study of 'hard-to-involve Internet users' – those who lurk in, but do not participate publicly in online discussion forums. In their study, an invitation to participate in a web survey was posted as a message to 375 online community discussion boards. Although they collected 1,188 valid responses (out of 77,582 discussion board members), they also 'received unsolicited email offers, some of which were pornographic in content or aggressive in tone' and they had their web server hacked twice, once with the infection of a virus.

In spite of the challenges and possible perils, it is possible to recruit survey participants from the web. For example, Alvarez *et al.* (2002) conducted two online recruitment efforts – one using banner advertisements on web pages and another using a subscription check box. In brief, their results were as follows.

In the first recruitment effort, Alvarez and colleagues ran four 'banner' campaigns in 2000 with the intention of recruiting survey participants using webpage banner advertisements. In the first campaign, which is representative of the other three, an animated banner advertisement resulted in more than 3.5 million 'impressions' (the number of times the banner was displayed), which resulted in the banner being clicked 10,652 times, or a rate of 3 clicks per 1,000 displays.

From these 10,652 clicks, 599 survey participants were recruited.

In the second recruitment effort, the authors ran a 'subscription' campaign in 2001 in which they arranged with a commercial organization to have a check box added to subscription forms on various websites. Essentially, Internet users who were registering for some service were given an opportunity to check a box on the service's subscription form indicating their willingness to participate in a survey. As part of this effort, the authors conducted two recruitment drives, each of which was intended to net 10,000 subscriptions. Across the two campaigns, 6,789 new survey participants were obtained from 21,378 subscribers.

The good news from the Alvarez *et al.* (2002) study is that even though the banner approach yielded fewer new survey participants, both methods resulted in a significant number of potential survey respondents over a relatively short period of time: 3,431 new subjects over the course of six or seven weeks from the banner campaigns, and 6,789 new subjects over the course of three weeks from the subscription campaigns. Each banner subject cost about $7.29 to recruit, while the subscription subjects cost only $1.27 per subject. (Unfortunately, the authors did not present any data on survey completion rates, so we do not know whether there were differences between the two samples that might have favoured one over the other).

The bad news is that the two groups differed significantly in all the demographic categories collected (gender, age, race and education) and they differed in how they answered questions on exactly the same survey. In addition, both groups differed significantly from the demographics of the Internet population as measured by the August 2000 Current Population Survey. The problem, of course, is that there are clear effects associated with how subjects are recruited, such that the resulting samples are different even from the general Internet population. Shillewaert *et al.* (1998) found similar recruitment method biases; therefore, although it is possible to ethically recruit survey participants from the web, it seems that the recruitment methodology affects the types of individual that self-select into the sample.

Improving Response Rates for Online Surveys

Response rates have a direct effect on sampling: the higher the response rate, the fewer people need to be sampled to achieve a desired number of survey completions. In addition, higher response rates are associated with lower nonresponse bias.

Unfortunately, in a summary of the academic survey-related literature up through 2001, Fricker Jr and Schonlau (2002: 350) concluded that 'Web-only research surveys have currently only achieved fairly modest response rates, at least as documented in the literature'. Fricker *et al.* (2005: 373) similarly summarized the state of affairs as 'Web surveys generally report fairly low response rates'.

A good illustration of this is the Couper *et al.* (1999) study in which employees of five US federal government statistical agencies were randomly given a mail or email survey. Comparable procedures were used for both modes, and yet higher response rates were obtained for mail (68–76 per cent) than for email (37–63 per cent) across all the agencies.

Incentives are a common and effective means for increasing response rates in traditional surveys. Göritz (2006) is an excellent review of the use of incentives in survey research in which she distinguishes their use in traditional surveys from online surveys and provides a nice discussion of the issues associated with using incentives in online surveys. Open issues include:

- how best to deliver an incentive electronically;
- whether it is better to provide the incentive prior to a respondent taking the survey or after;

- whether incentives have different effects for individuals taking a survey one time versus pre-recruited panel members who take a series of surveys.

Individual studies of online surveys have generally found incentives to have little or no effect. For example, Comley (2000) found that incentives had little effect on response rates for pop-up surveys, and Kypri and Gallagher (2003) found no effect in a web-based survey. However, Göritz (2006) conducted a meta-analysis of 32 experiments evaluating the impact of incentives on survey 'response' (the fraction of those solicited to take the survey that actually called up the first page of the survey) and 26 experiments evaluating the effect of incentives on survey 'retention' (the fraction of those who viewed the first page that actually completed the survey). From the meta-analysis, Göritz concluded that 'material incentives promote response and retention in Web surveys' (p. 63) where 'material incentives increase the odds of a person responding by 19% over the odds without incentives' and 'an incentive increased retention by 4.2% on average' (p. 65).

In addition to incentives, Dillman *et al.* (2014) and Dillman *et al.* (1999) have put forward a number of survey procedural recommendations to increase survey response rates, based on equivalent methods for traditional surveys, which we will not re-cover here because they are mainly related to survey design and fielding procedures. Although we do note that the recommendations seem sensible, Couper (2000) cautions that 'there is at present little experimental literature on what works and what does not'.

Bigger Samples are not Always Better

With online surveys using a list-based sampling frame, rather than sending the survey out to a sample, researchers often simply send the survey out to the entire sampling frame. That is, researchers naively conducting (all electronic) online surveys – where the marginal costs for additional surveys can be virtually nil – often fail to recognize that a large number of participants does not necessarily mean that the sample is representative of the population of interest. As we previously discussed, for both probability and non-probability-based samples, larger sample sizes do not necessarily mean the sample is more representative of any greater population – a sample can be biased whether it is large or small.

One might argue that in these situations the researchers are attempting to conduct a census, but in practice they are forgoing a probability sample in favour of a convenience sample by allowing members of the sampling frame to opt into the survey. Dillman *et al.* (1999) summarized this practice as follows: '... the ease of collecting hundreds, thousands, or even tens of thousands of responses to web questionnaires at virtually no cost, except for constructing and posting, appears to be encouraging a singular emphasis on the reduction of sampling error'. By this Dillman *et al.* (1999) mean that researchers who focus only on reducing sampling error by trying to collect as large a sample as possible miss the point that it is equally important to reduce coverage, measurement and nonresponse error in order to be able to accurately generalize from the sample data.

A myopic focus on large sample sizes – and the idea that large samples equate to sample representativeness which equates to generalizability – occurs with convenience sample-based web and email surveys as well. 'Survey2000' is an excellent example of this type of focus. A large-scale, unrestricted, self-selected survey conducted as a collaborative effort between the National Geographic Society (NGS) and some academic researchers, Survey2000 was fielded in 1998. The survey was posted on the NGS's website and participants were solicited both with a link on the NGS homepage and via advertisements in NGS periodicals, other magazines and newspapers.

Upon completion of the effort, Witte *et al.* (2000) reported that more than 80,000 surveys were initiated and slightly more than 50,000 were completed. Although this is an impressively large number of survey completions, the unrestricted, self-selected sampling strategy clearly results in a convenience sample that is not generalizable to any larger population. However, Witte *et al.* (2000) go to extraordinary lengths to rationalize that their results are somehow generalizable, while simultaneously demonstrating that the results of the survey generally do not correspond to known population quantities.

Misrepresenting Convenience Samples

A related and significant concern with non-probability-based sampling methods, both for online and traditional surveys, is that survey accuracy is characterized only in terms of sampling error and without regard to the potential biases that may be present in the results. Although this has always been a concern with all types of surveys, the ease and spread of online surveys seems to have exacerbated the practice. For example, the results of an 'E-Poll' were explained as follows:

THE OTHER HALF/E-Poll® Survey of 1,007 respondents was conducted January 16–20, 2003. A representative group of adults 18+ were randomly selected from the E-Poll online panel. At a 95 per cent confidence level, a sample error of +/– 3 per cent is assumed for statistics based on the total sample of 1,007 respondents. Statistics based on sub-samples of the respondents are more sensitive to sampling error. (From a press release posted on the E-Poll website.)

No mention was made in the press release that the 'E-Poll online panel' consisted of individuals who had chosen to participate in online polls, nor that they were unlikely to be representative of the general population. Rather, it leaves readers with an incorrect impression that the results apply to the general population when, in fact, the margin of error for this particular survey is valid only for adult members of the E-Poll online panel.

In response to the proliferation of such misleading statements, the American Association for Public Opinion Research (AAPOR) has publicly stated that 'The reporting of a margin of sampling error associated with an opt-in or self-identified sample (that is, in a survey or poll where respondents are self-selecting) is misleading.' They go on to say, 'AAPOR considers it harmful to include statements about the theoretical calculation of sampling error in descriptions of such studies, especially when those statements mislead the reader into thinking that the survey is based on a probability sample of the full target population. The harm comes from the inferences that the margin of sampling error estimates can be interpreted like those of probability sample surveys' (AAPOR, 2016).

CONCLUSION

Every survey effort can be classified according to how the respondents are contacted (the contact mode), how they are asked to complete the survey (the response mode) and then how subsequent communication is conducted (the follow-up mode). Each of these can be executed in different media where the media are telephone, mail, web, email and so forth. For example, respondents may be contacted by telephone to participate in a web survey with follow-up done by mail.

Explicitly specifying contact, response and follow-up modes is often irrelevant for traditional surveys because respondents that have been asked to take, say, a telephone survey have generally been contacted via the same mode. Although not a strict rule – for example, a telephone survey may be preceded by mailed invitations to each survey respondent – it is often the case. In comparison, given the challenges that we have discussed in this chapter,

the contact, response and follow-up modes are much more likely to differ with online surveys.

In terms of sampling for online surveys, what is relevant is that the sampling methodology is generally driven by the contact mode, *not* the response mode. Hence, as shown in Table 10.4, we can organize sampling strategies by contact mode where the check marks indicate which sampling strategies are mainly associated with the various contact methods.

For example, although systematic sampling can be applied to phone or mail surveys, the telephone is not likely to be used as a contact medium for an online survey using systematic sampling, and hence those cells in the table are not checked. Similarly, although there is a plethora of phone-in entertainment polls, neither the telephone nor postal mail is used to contact respondents to take online entertainment polls.

From Table 10.4 we can broadly summarize the current state of the art for the various online survey methods and their limitations as follows.

- Entirely web-based surveys, meaning surveys in which the potential respondents are contacted on the web and take a web survey, are chiefly limited to collecting data from non-probability-based samples. The exception is systematic sampling for pop-up/intercept surveys, which are predominantly used for customer-satisfaction types of survey associated with specific websites or web pages.
- Respondent contact for online surveys using non-probability samples can also be conducted via traditional (non-online) media and advertising.
- Research surveys that require probability sampling are very limited when using an online contact mode (web and email).
- Email is useful as a contact mode only if a list of email addresses is available. Such a list is an actual or de facto sampling frame from which a sample may be drawn or a census attempted.
- The population of inference is usually quite limited when using an email address sampling frame. It is generally the sampling frame itself.
- A poorly conducted census of an entire email list may limit the survey results even further because

Table 10.4 Sampling strategies for online surveys by contact mode

Contact method		Sampling strategy								
		Probability-based					Non-probability-based			
		List-based sampling frames	Non-list-based random sampling	Systematic sampling	Mixed-mode survey with online option	Pre-recruited survey panel	Entertainment polls	Unrestricted self-selected surveys	Harvested email lists	Volunteer (opt-in) panels
Online	Web			✓			✓	✓		✓
	Email	✓							✓	
Offline	Telephone	✓	✓		✓	✓				
	Postal mail	✓			✓					
	In-person				✓					
	Other: TV, print advertising, etc.						✓	✓		✓

nonresponse and other biases may preclude generalizing even to the sample frame.

- If the research objectives require inferring from the survey results to some general population, then respondents will most likely have to be contacted by a non-online medium.
- If the population of inference is a population in which some of the members do not have email/web access, then the contact mode will have to be a non-online medium.

Under such conditions, the survey will have to be conducted using a mixed mode, so that those without Internet access can participate. Conversely, lack of a non-online survey mode will result in coverage error with the likely consequence of systematic bias.

Pre-recruited panels can provide ready access to pools of online survey respondents, but to allow generalization to some larger, general population such panels need to be recruited using probability sampling methods from the general population (usually via RDD). Even under such conditions, researchers need to carefully consider whether the panel is likely to be subject to other types of bias.

AAPOR Online Panel Recommendations

In 2008, the AAPOR Executive Council established an Opt-in Online Panel Task Force with the charge of 'reviewing the current empirical findings related to opt-in online panels utilized for data collection and developing recommendations for AAPOR members' (Baker *et al.*, 2010: 3). Among others, the report made the following recommendations:

- Researchers should avoid nonprobability online panels when one of the research objectives is to accurately estimate population values.
- Although mode effects may account for some of the differences observed in comparative studies, the use of nonprobability sampling in surveys with online panels is likely the more significant factor in the overall accuracy of surveys using this method.

- There are times when a nonprobability online panel is an appropriate choice.
- Research aimed at evaluating and testing techniques used in other disciplines to make population inferences from nonprobability samples is interesting but inconclusive (Baker *et al.*, 2010: 758–9).

Looking to the Future

What does the future hold for online survey sampling? At this point in the Internet's development, with its rapid expansion and continued evolution, it's truly impossible to say. But we can hazard a few guesses.

First, if the Internet continues to expand, but largely maintains its current structure, then advances in sampling methods that will allow random sampling of and inference to general populations will be at best slow and difficult to develop. This follows from the fact that Internet-wide sampling frames are simply unavailable under the current Internet structure/organization, and general frameless sampling strategies does not yet exist. Unless the way the Internet is organized and operated changes, it seems this will continue to be the case into the foreseeable future.

That said, survey methodologists should endeavour to develop new sampling paradigms for online surveys. The fundamental requirement for a probability-based sampling scheme is that every member of the target population has a known, non-zero probability of being sampled. Although in traditional surveys this can be achieved via various frame and frameless sampling strategies, it does not necessarily follow that online surveys must use those same sampling strategies. Rather, new sampling methods that take advantage of the unique characteristics of the Internet, such as the near-zero marginal cost for contacting potential respondents, should be explored and developed.

In addition, researchers considering conducting an online survey should consider whether the capabilities of the web can be leveraged to collect the desired data in some other innovative fashion. For example, Lockett and Blackman (2004) present a case study of Xenon Laboratories, an Internet-based financial services firm that employed a novel approach to market research. Xenon Laboratories wanted to collect data on foreign exchange charges by credit card companies on business travellers. They recognized that neither the travellers nor the credit card companies were likely to respond to a survey on this topic, whether fielded over the web or otherwise. Instead, Xenon Laboratories developed the Travel Expenses Calculator (www.xe.com/tec) and the Credit Card Charges Calculator (www.xe.com/ccc) and posted them on the web for anyone to use for free. These tools help foreign business travellers to accurately calculate the cost of a business expense receipt in terms of their own currency. Lockett and Blackman (2004) say,

> On the basis of this information [input by those using the calculators] it is possible to conduct basic market research by aggregating the inputted calculations. Xenon is now in the unique position to analyse whether or not the different card providers employ the same charging levels and whether or not these companies' charge structures vary according to geographical region.

They go on to conclude, 'This value-added approach, which is mutually beneficial to both parties, is an important and novel approach to market research'.

Second, it is also possible that technological innovation will facilitate other means of sampling for online surveys (and for conducting the surveys themselves, for that matter). For example, current trends seem to point towards a merging of the Internet with traditional technologies such as television and telephone. Indeed, all of these services are merging into one common household device through which a consumer can simultaneously watch television, surf the web, send email and place telephone calls – otherwise known as the smartphone. Depending on how smartphone and related technology evolves, various types of random sampling methodologies, as well as new survey modes,

may become possible. For example, it may become feasible, and perhaps even desirable, to sample respondents via RDD and then send the potential respondent a text message with an embedded URL to a web survey. Or, perhaps via RDD a survey interviewer calls the potential respondent and then in real time the respondent completes an interviewer-assisted, web-based survey. Or, sometime in the future, it may also be possible to use smartphone companies' subscriber listings as sampling frames (much as telephone directories were used pre-RDD in the mid-1900s). Or it may be that some other state emerges that lends itself to some form of sampling that is not possible today. The point is that the Internet is still very much in its infancy, and the current difficulties surrounding sampling for online surveys described in this chapter may or may not continue into the future.

To put this in a historical context, note that although the telephone was invented in the late 1800s and telephone systems developed and expanded rapidly through the early 1900s, it was not until the mid-1900s that telephone coverage was sufficiently large and standards for telephone numbers adopted that made RDD possible. In fact, the foundational ideas for an efficient RDD sampling methodology were not proposed until the early 1960s (Cooper, 1964), after which it took roughly another decade of discussion and development before RDD as we know it today became commonplace.[4] In total, it was roughly a *century* after the invention of the telephone before RDD became an accepted sampling methodology.

In comparison, the web has been in existence, in a commercial sense, for only a little more than a decade or two. As with the telephone in the late 1800s and early 1900s, we are in a period of technological innovation and expansion with the Internet. However, unlike the telephone, given today's pace of innovation, the Internet and how we use it is likely to be quite different even just a few years from now. How this affects sampling for online surveys remains to be seen.

NOTES

1 Readers interested in the mathematics should consult one of the classic texts such as Kish (1965) or Cochran (1977); readers interested in a summary treatment of the mathematics and/or a more detailed discussion of the sampling process may consult a number of other texts, such as Fink (2003) or Fowler Jr (2002). For those specifically interested in sampling methods for qualitative research, see Patton (2002).

2 See, for example, www.qualtrics.com/online-sample/

3 For example, as of 31 December 2013, Internet World Stats (2015) reported that the top 50 countries and regions of the world had a combined Internet penetration of 84.4 per cent, ranging from a high of 96.9 per cent for the Falkland Islands to 73.9 per cent for Puerto Rico. In comparison, Internet penetration for the rest of the world was estimated to be 31.6 per cent.

4 See, for example, 'Random Digit Dialing as a method of telephone sampling' (Glasser and Metzger, 1972); 'An empirical assessment of two telephone sampling designs' (Groves, 1978); and 'Random Digit Dialing: a sampling technique for telephone surveys' (Cummings, 1979).

REFERENCES

Alvarez, R.M., Sherman, R.P. and Van Beselaere, C. (2002) 'Subject acquisition for web-based surveys', 12 September. Accessed at survey.caltech.edu/alvarez.pdf on 29 September 2006.

American Association for Public Opinion Research (AAPOR). (2016) 'Opt-In Surveys and Margin of Error'. Accessed at http://www.aapor.org/Education-Resources/For-Researchers/Poll-Survey-FAQ/Opt-In-Surveys-and-Margin-of-Error.aspx on 2 August 2016.

Andrews, D., Nonnecke, B. and Preece, J. (2002) 'Electronic survey methodology: a case study in reaching hard-to-involve Internet users', *International Journal of Human-Computer Interaction*, 12 (2): 185–210.

Baker, R., Blumberg, S.J., Brick, J.M., Couper, M.P., Courtright, M., Dennis, J.M., Dillman, D., Frankel, M.R., Garland, P., Groves, R.M., Kennedy, C., Krosnick, J., Lavrakas, P.J., Lee, S., Link, M., Piekarski, L., Rao, K., Thomas,

R.K., and D. Zahs (2010). 'Research Synthesis: AAPOR Report on Online Panels', *Public Opinion Quarterly*, 74 (4): 711–81.

Callegaro, M., Baker, R., Bethlehem, J., Göritz, A.S., Krosnick, J.A., and Lavrakas, P.J. (2014) *Online Panel Research: A Data Quality Perspective*. Wiley Series in Survey Methodology. New York, NY: John Wiley & Sons.

Cochran, W.G. (1977) *Sampling Techniques*. New York, NY: John Wiley.

Comley, P. (2000) 'Pop-up surveys: what works, what doesn't work and what will work in the future'. Proceedings of the ESOMAR Worldwide Internet Conference Net Effects 3, Vol. 237. Amsterdam: ESOMAR. Accessed at www.virtualsurveys.com/news/papers/paper_4.asp on 21 September 2006.

Coomber, R. (1997) 'Using the Internet for survey research', *Sociological Research Online*, 2: 14–23.

Cooper, S.L. (1964) 'Random sampling by telephone: an improved method', *Journal of Marketing Research*, 1 (4): 45–8.

Couper, M.P. (2000) 'Review: web surveys: a review of issues and approaches', *Public Opinion Quarterly*, 64 (4): 464–94.

Couper, M.P., Blair, J. and Triplett, T. (1999) 'A comparison of mail and email for a survey of employees in federal statistical agencies', *Journal of Official Statistics*, 15 (1): 39–56.

Cummings, K.M. (1979) 'Random digit dialing: a sampling technique for telephone surveys', *Public Opinion Quarterly*, 43 (2): 233–44.

Dillman, D.A. (2007) *Mail and Internet Surveys: The Tailored Design Method*. 2nd edn. New York, NY: John Wiley.

Dillman, D.A., Smyth, J.D. and Christian, L.M. (2014) *Internet, Phone, Mail, and Mixed-Mode Surveys: The Tailored Design Method*. 4th edn. New York, NY: John Wiley.

Dillman, D.A., Tortora, R.D. and Bowker, D. (1999) 'Principles for constructing web surveys', Accessed at www.sesrc.wsu.edu/dillman/papers/websurveyppr.pdf on 27 January 2005.

Fink, A. (2003) *How to Sample in Surveys. The Survey Kit*. 2nd edn. Vol 7. Thousand Oaks, CA: Sage Publications.

Fowler Jr, F.J. (2002) *Survey Research Methods. Applied Social Research Methods Series*. 3rd edn. Vol. 1. Thousand Oaks, CA: Sage Publications.

Fricker Jr, R.D. and Schonlau, M. (2002) 'Advantages and disadvantages of Internet research surveys: evidence from the literature', *Field Methods*, 14: 347–67.

Fricker, S., Galesic, M., Tourangeau, R. and Yan, T. (2005) 'An experimental comparison of web and telephone surveys', *Public Opinion Quarterly*, 69 (3): 370–92.

Glasser, G.J. and Metzger, G.D. (1972) 'Random-digit dialing as a method of telephone sampling', *Journal of Marketing Research*, 9 (1): 59–64.

Göritz, A.S. (2006) 'Incentives in web studies: methodological issues and a review', *International Journal of Internet Science*, 1 (1): 58–70.

Groves, R.M. (1978) 'An empirical comparison of two telephone sample designs', *Journal of Marketing Research*, 15 (4): 622–31.

Groves, R.M. (2004) *Survey Errors and Survey Costs*. New York, NY: John Wiley.

Internet World Stats (2015) 'Top 20 Internet countries versus World'. Accessed at www.Internetworldstats.com/top20.htm on 10 May 2015.

Jackob, N., Arens, J. and Zerback, T. (2005) 'Sampling procedure, questionnaire design, online implementation, and survey response in a multinational online journalist survey'. Paper presented at the Joint WAPOR/ISSC Conference: Conducting International Social Surveys. Accessed at ciss.ris.org/uploadi/editor/1132070316WAPORPaper.pdf on 30 September 2006.

Kish, L. (1965) *Survey Sampling*. New York, NY: Wiley-Interscience. (New edition February 1995).

Kypri, K. and Gallagher, S.J. (2003) 'Incentives to increase participation in an Internet survey of alcohol use: a controlled experiment', *Alcohol and Alcoholism*, 38 (5): 437–41.

Lockett, A. and Blackman, I. (2004) 'Conducting market research using the Internet: the case of Xenon Laboratories', *Journal of Business and Industrial Marketing*, 19 (3): 178–87.

Midwest Book Review (2003) 'Book review: take advantage of the Internet and preserve data integrity'. Accessed at www.amazon.com/Conducting-Research-Surveys-Email-Web/dp/0833031104/sr=1–3/qid=1160191573/ref=sr_1_3/102–5971652–1424906?ie=UTF8&s=books on 6 October 2006.

NPR (2014) 'Post a Survey on Mechanical Turk and Watch the Results Roll In'. Accessed at www.npr.org/blogs/alltechconsidered/2014/03/05/279669610/post-a-survey-on-mechanical-turk-and-watch-the-results-roll-in on 2 August 2016.

Patton, M.Q. (2002) *Qualitative Evaluation and Research Methods*. London: Sage Publications.

Pineau, V. and Dennis, J.M. (2004) 'Methodology for probability-based recruitment for a web-enabled panel', 21 November. Accessed at www.knowledgenetworks.com/ganp/reviewer-info.html on 21 July 2006.

Schonlau, M., Fricker Jr, R.D. and Elliott, M.N. (2002) *Conducting Research Surveys via Email and the Web*. MR-1480-RC. Santa Monica, CA: RAND.

Schonlau, M., Zapert, K., Simon, L.P., Sanstad, K.H., Marcus, S.M., Adams, J., Spranca, M., Kan, H., Turner, R. and Berry, S.H. (2004) 'A comparison between responses from a propensity-weighted web survey and an identical RDD survey', *Social Science Computer Review*, 22 (1): 128–38.

Sheehan, K.B. (1999) 'Using email to survey Internet users in the United States: methodology and assessment', *Journal of Computer-Mediated Communication*, (4) 3. Accessed at http://jcmc.indiana.edu/vol14/issue3/sheehan.html on 6 July 2006.

Shillewaert, N., Langerak, F. and Duhamel, T. (1998) 'Non-probability sampling for WWW surveys: a comparison of methods', *Journal of the Market Research Society*, 40 (4): 307–22.

Siah, C.Y. (2005) 'All that glitters is not gold: examining the perils and obstacles in collecting data on the Internet', *International Negotiation*, 10: 115–30.

Toepoel, V. (2012). 'Building your own online panel via email and other digital media'. In L. Gideon (ed.), *Handbook of Survey Methodology for the Social Sciences*. New York, NY: Springer, pp. 345–60.

Witte, J.C., Amoroso, L.M. and Howard, P.E.N. (2000) 'Research methodology: method and representation in Internet-based survey tools – mobility, community, and cultural identity in Survey2000', *Social Sciences Computer Review*, 18 (2): 179–95.

Wright, T. and Tsao, H.J. (1983) 'A frame on frames: an annotated bibliography'. In T. Wright (ed.), *Statistical Methods and the Improvement of Data Quality*. New York, NY: Academic Press, pp. 25–72.

FURTHER READING

Mail and Internet Surveys: The Tailored Design Method by Dillman (2007) and *Survey Errors and Survey Costs* by Groves (2004) both focus on the entire process of designing and fielding surveys, not just sampling.

Conducting Research Surveys via Email and the Web by Schonlau *et al.* (2002) 'is a practical and accessible guide to applying the pervasiveness of the Internet to the gathering of survey data in a much faster and significantly less expensive manner than traditional means of phone or mail communications' (Midwest Book Review, 2003).

'Review: web surveys: a review of issues and approaches' by Couper (2000), published in the *Public Opinion Quarterly*, is an excellent and highly cited article that emphasizes many of the points and ideas discussed in this chapter. It also provides additional examples to those presented in this chapter.

Sampling Techniques by Cochran (1977) is one of the classic texts on the mathematical details of survey sampling, covering a wide range of sampling methods applicable to all types of survey effort.

Online Panel Research: A Data Quality Perspective by Callegaro *et al.* (2014) is a detailed examination of and exposition about the current state of online panel research methodology. The text nicely summarizes what is currently known about the quality of data obtained via online panels, and it discusses the various sorts of errors and biases that can affect online panel results.

Research Synthesis: AAPOR Report on Online Panels by Baker *et al.* (2010) summarizes the results of a report commissioned by the American Association of Public Opinion Research (AAPOR) Executive Council with the charge of 'reviewing the current empirical findings related to opt-in online panels utilized for data collection and developing recommendations for AAPOR members' (Baker *et al.*, 2010: 712). The authors are recognized survey experts from a variety of fields and disciplines and the resulting report is an authoritative treatment of the current state of the art in using online panels for surveying.

## 11

Online Survey Design

Vera Toepoel

INTRODUCTION TO ONLINE SURVEYS

Online surveys are the dominant survey mode for most countries. In an era with high costs for other modes of administration, declining response rates, concerns about registered telephone numbers and increased Internet penetration rates, everyone is doing an online survey. Online surveys are cheap and fast. Software is available for free and surveys can be conducted at virtually no cost. Every action or transaction seems to be followed by a follow-up survey. However, online surveys are not without downfalls and obtaining proper survey data requires effort and knowledge on the part of the researcher. Online surveys are unique in the fact that a researcher never knows how exactly the questionnaire is going to appear on a respondent's screen. In addition, respondents use a range of different devices to complete surveys. In this chapter we discuss the design of the survey instrument, the actual fieldwork, and Internet-related issues related to processing of the data.

Devices

New technologies affecting online survey design pose radical challenges to established survey design conventions but also make available new affordances that can aid the survey researcher and respondents. Online devices offer new possibilities for online surveys (American Association for Public Opinion Research (AAPOR) Taskforce, 2014). Global positioning systems (GPS) make it possible to track the physical location of a respondent. Automatically recording travel behavior can reduce the burden of travel survey diary completion and is more objective than retrospective self-reports. Scanning Quick Response (QR) codes can be used to collect information on consumer goods or other items containing a barcode or QR code. They can also be used to direct respondents to a URL for additional information or a survey link. Capturing photos, sound or video can also enhance survey findings. In modern society, people are used to sharing visual information online, and this visual information can enrich the data obtained via surveys. Bluetooth-enabled devices can wirelessly connect to external devices and can collect bio health information (e.g. blood pressure, glucose, weight, heartbeat, pulse pressure) from portable medical devices and mobile sensors (e.g accelerometers). Lastly, apps can typically take greater advantage of smartphone capabilities, such as push notifications, camera, GPS, etc., than traditional browser-based surveys.

As well as the increasing Internet penetration rate on computers, there is also a considerable growth in the number of people using smartphones and other mobile devices with a high-speed connection to the web. This means that researchers should take the size and other features of devices into account in the design of their surveys (Callegaro, 2010). Online survey software increasingly uses a responsive design, in which the software optimizes the questionnaire according to user agent strings that detect the type of device used. In addition, more app-like surveys are being deployed (Buskirk and Andres, 2012). Although the varying screen sizes of different devices are a challenge for designing an online survey, the use of mobile phones for survey completion comes with advantages. Mobile surveys offer the possibility of using Random Digit Dialing (RDD), a probability-approach that is typically lacking for online surveys because they don't have a suitable sampling frame. There is no administrative list of email addresses for the general population. In addition, mobile devices give the opportunity to complete a survey on the go, possibly reducing nonresponse rates. Toepoel and Lugtig (2014) report 11 percent of respondents in a general population survey in the Netherlands answering a survey on the road, while 6 percent reported being outside.

Online surveys can nowadays be seen as mixed-device surveys (Toepoel, 2016). Devices differ strongly in screen sizes and method of navigation (keyboard and mouse versus touchscreen). The question arises if data obtained via mobile phones is equivalent to data obtained via regular desktop PCs. Most studies comparing mobile and PC answers found no clear differences between them with regards to survey measurement error (de Bruijne and Wijnant, 2013; Lynn and Kaminska, 2013; Mavletova, 2013; Toepoel and Lugtig, 2014; Wells *et al.*, 2013). It is important to separate selection effects from measurement error. Lugtig and Toepoel (2015), for example, show that mobile phones tend to produce more measurement error, but this is related to selection effects (young people using mobile phones and producing more measurement error) and not to the device use itself. Toepoel and Lugtig (2014) demonstrate that mobile surveys seem to work just as other Internet devices once the questionnaire is optimized for mobile phone completion.

Research on the evaluation of mobile surveys shows mixed results. Either there are no significant differences in respondents' evaluation of the questionnaire or people who have completed the survey on a smartphone are less positive about the survey than their PC counterparts. This could be related to issues bearing on the design of the survey instrument (e.g. how comfortable it is to complete on small screen sizes with touchscreen) and the population. Respondents with experience in completing surveys on a mobile phone are more positive in their evaluation of a mobile survey (Toepoel and Funke, 2015). For online surveys on mobile phones to work, it is important to use a responsive design so that the survey layout is automatically adapted to the device used. Important to note is that each browser has a different way of dealing with questionnaire formats. For example, some browsers turn dropdown menus into scrolling wheels on mobile devices. Updates in mobile survey software can also change the appearance of the survey. Pre-testing on different devices and in different browsers might not only be important before the fieldwork starts, but is also recommended during the fieldwork to avoid any changes in visual appearance. Another issue associated with mobile phone completion is the length of the questionnaire. A ten-minute questionnaire might have been acceptable a couple of years ago, but for mobile phone completion it is already considered long (see Dillman *et al.*, this volume).

Ethical Aspects of Survey Design

Surveys that are conducted online introduce new ethical issues (Groves *et al.*, 2009). Internet tracking tools can be used to improve the design of a website or to target a specific population (Singer and Couper, 2010). Cookies can collect information about the users' behavior across Internet sessions. They are small amounts of data that are stored on the computer of the web server. Cookies collect information about the user, such as preferences, profile information and searches, and retrieve this information upon the next visit. Turow (2003) showed that only 23 percent of Internet users would agree to give information to websites to get personal offers if asked. Participants are often unaware of the amount of information researchers can obtain with online surveys.

Paradata is data obtained during a respondent's completion of the survey. Server-side paradata collects data from the server logs when respondents visit the online survey. They typically memorize every visit a respondent makes to each Internet page of the online questionnaire and connect this information to an identifying code and time stamp. Because server-side paradata only enables researchers to track progress across visits to pages, placing fewer questions on a single screen increases the informational value of this sort of paradata. Client-side paradata actually observes respondent actions at the level of specific questions. The order of responding, mouse movements, response latencies, the changing of answers and other respondent behaviors are typically monitored by survey researchers (Toepoel, 2016). Researchers often collect these client-side paradata

using JavaScript. Respondents are often not informed about the use and the existence of this kind of information, which goes against the principle of informed consent.

Informed consent serves to make sure that respondents comprehend what they agree to so they can make an informed and voluntary decision as to whether they want to participate or not (Keller and Lee, 2003). Obtaining informed consent can be problematic in online surveys because a legally binding signature is difficult to obtain (Kraut *et al.*, 2004). Online studies therefore often document consent by giving respondents a question where they ask if they agree to the conditions provided in an information statement. Since there is often no real-life contact between the researcher and the respondent, it is difficult to determine to what extent respondents fully understand the information provided in the informed consent. Singer and Couper (2010) argue that online surveys should add hyperlinks to explain certain concepts or ask potential respondents questions, which can help determine whether the respondent actually understood the informed consent statement provided.

In addition to informed consent, debriefing can be problematic in online surveys. When respondents drop out during the survey, they jeopardize an adequate debriefing. Nosek *et al.* (2002) suggest to either ask respondents for their email addresses at the start of the study to be able to email the debriefing afterwards or automatically present the debriefing when a respondent leaves the study before completing it.

Although the researcher is responsible for protecting respondents' privacy and ensuring confidentiality, there are ways confidentiality in online surveys typically could be jeopardized. Hackers can get access to personal information, and so-called 'sniffing programs' can keep their eyes on data that are being transmitted (Kraut *et al.*, 2004). To prevent these things happening, researchers can either refrain from collecting personal identifying information or separate these data from research data obtained in the study. A key or code known to the survey administrator but not to anyone else can then be used to link the personal information to the substantive data.

Another problem that can present itself is that it can be difficult to identify multiple submissions from the same individual or whether the right person is answering the survey. Duplicate and fraudulent responses can be the result of innocent behavior, but can also be deliberately done to receive incentives or influence the results of a study. The latter can be referred to as 'ballot stuffing'. Cookies and the recording of IP addresses can be used as detection methods, but neither is foolproof (Singer and Couper, 2010).

THE DESIGN OF THE SURVEY

Access Control

Personal identification codes can be used in order to allow people to complete the survey only once and to (try to) make sure that the right people are answering the survey. Potential respondents can get a personal link in an email message (automatic login procedure) or can be provided with a general link with a username and password (manual login procedure). The URL should be short, understandable and easy to retype. Long URLs may wrap over two or more lines causing the link not to work or to be difficult to copy and paste. This can prevent potential respondents from completing the survey.

Survey Layout

Designing a survey is not as easy as it may seem because a researcher has many tools available in online surveys. Researchers have to make all kinds of design choices, such as using a scrolling or paging design, answer options, routing, error messages, etc. Surveys should follow the logic of a conversation and

visual heuristics play an important role in the question-answering process in online surveys. Many researchers spend a considerable amount of time in designing the look and feel of their survey. Research shows little evidence of the (positive) effect of the layout of the survey in terms of the use of color, font, placement of logos, etc. (Couper, 2008; Toepoel, 2016). Decisions about particular questions, answer categories, ordering, etc., can have a more profound effect on the data obtained.

It is important to note that the intentions of the researcher or programmer for the online survey are mediated through the hardware, software, and user preferences of the respondent. The questionnaire seen by the respondent will not be exactly same as intended by the researcher because of different operating systems, browsers, and screen configurations. In addition, the fact that one respondent might see something different from another respondent forms a significant methodological challenge. Therefore, it is of critical importance to test the online survey using different devices, browsers, and screen resolutions.

Paging versus Scrolling

One of the first decisions to make while programming an online survey is the use of either a paging or a scrolling design. In scrolling designs, the entire survey is placed on a single screen whereas in paging designs each question is presented on a single screen (Figures 11.1 and 11.2). There are also alternatives along this continuum, where multiple items are placed on a screen, i.e. in matrix (Figure 11.3) or grid questions.

An advantage of the scrolling design is the fact that the respondent has a complete overview of the entire questionnaires. In this design, the respondent can estimate directly the length of the overview, as well as other questions that will be proposed. A disadvantage is when a respondent closes the browser before pressing a submit button, no information is transmitted to the server and all answers are lost. Another disadvantage is that checks and routing are more difficult to implement and, if they are implemented, may confuse respondents because they pop up only once the entire survey is submitted to the server. The answers in a paging design are transmitted and saved for each question because after completing a question on each page a submit button must be pressed in order to proceed in the survey. Data is immediately stored, so respondents could also stop and finish the survey in another time and place without any information being lost. A disadvantage of the paging design is the lack of context for the respondent, who is unable to see the entire survey or see the progress in a survey. Presenting several items on a single screen in a matrix reduces the number of screens. However, inter-item correlations tend to be higher in matrix questions because items that are grouped on one screen are seen as also belonging together conceptually (Couper *et al.*, 2001; Toepoel *et al.*, 2009).

Welcome Screen and Thank you Message

The survey always starts with some kind of welcome screen (Figure 11.4). This is the first page the respondent sees when he or she opens the survey. The majority of the break-offs drop out on this initial page. Unfortunately, existing research shows little evidence of text or layout that increases response rates or reduces drop out. In general, the welcome screen should assure the respondents that they have arrived at the right place and should encourage them to proceed to fill out the questionnaire. The welcome screen should contain some identifying information (where the survey is from and what the survey is about), some lines about privacy and confidentiality, and the estimated time to complete the survey. Some additional information can be given, but it is best to keep the text on the welcome screen as brief as possible to prevent respondents from breaking off before they actually start answering a question (Toepoel, 2016).

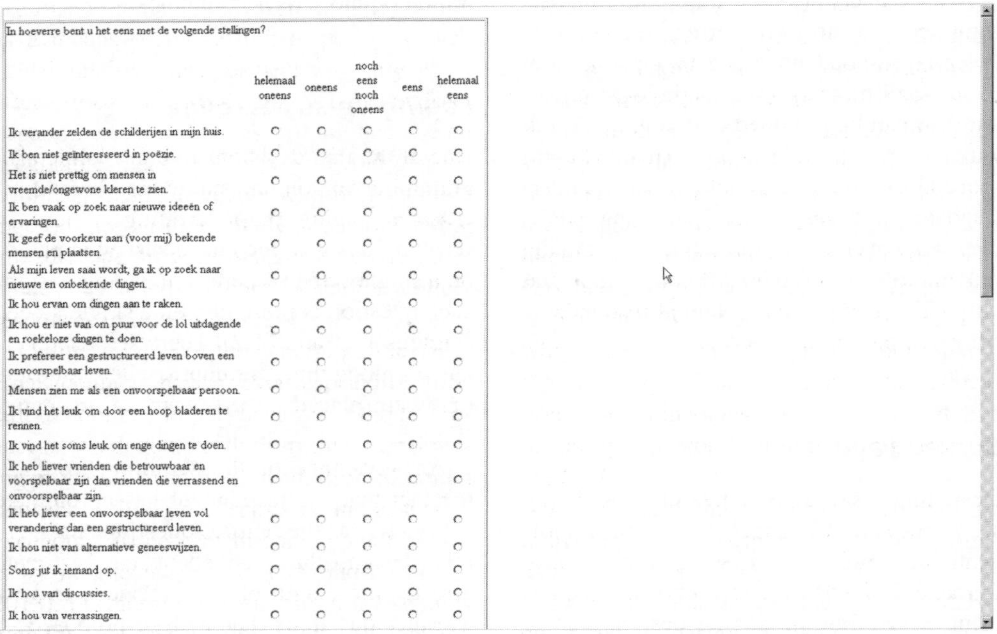

Figure 11.1   Scrolling design (scroll bar at right hand side; text in Dutch)

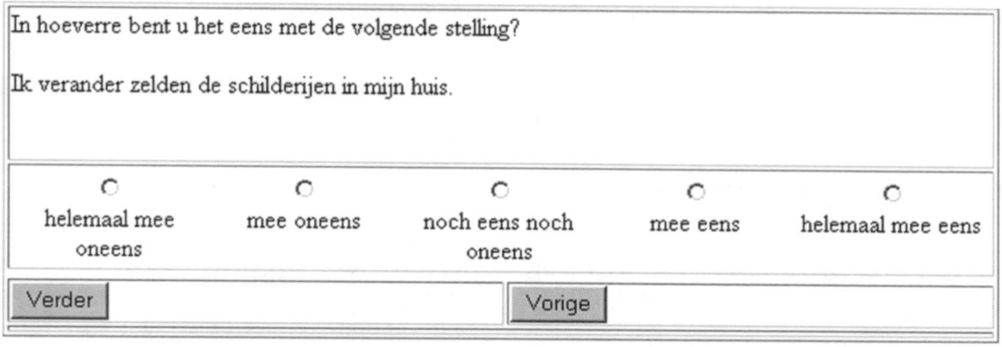

In hoeverre bent u het eens met de volgende stelling?

Ik verander zelden de schilderijen in mijn huis.

○	○	○	○	○
helemaal mee oneens	mee oneens	noch eens noch oneens	mee eens	helemaal mee eens

Verder   Vorige

Figure 11.2   Paging design (one question per screen; text in Dutch)

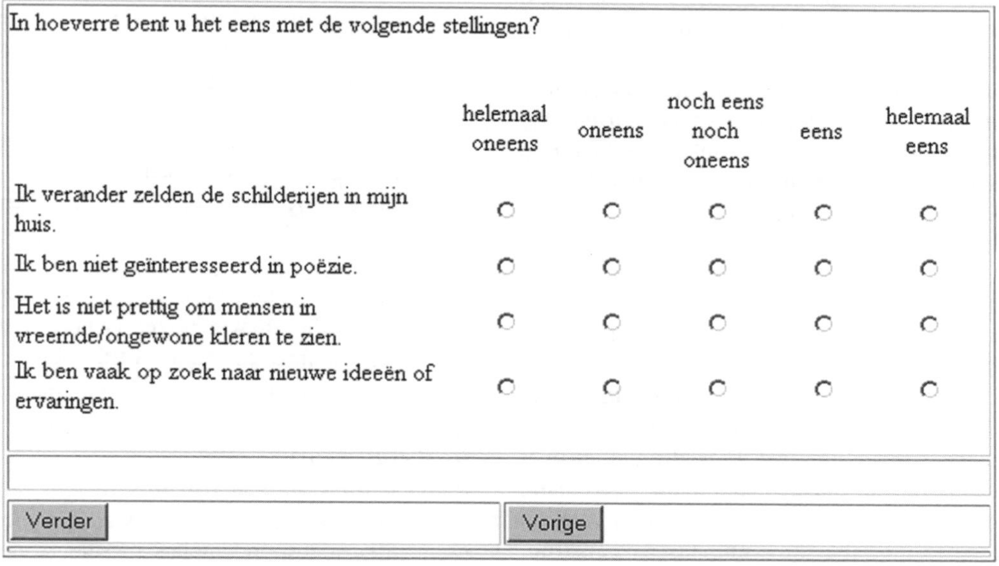

In hoeverre bent u het eens met de volgende stellingen?

	helemaal oneens	oneens	noch eens noch oneens	eens	helemaal eens
Ik verander zelden de schilderijen in mijn huis.	○	○	○	○	○
Ik ben niet geïnteresseerd in poëzie.	○	○	○	○	○
Het is niet prettig om mensen in vreemde/ongewone kleren te zien.	○	○	○	○	○
Ik ben vaak op zoek naar nieuwe ideeën of ervaringen.	○	○	○	○	○

Verder   Vorige

Figure 11.3   Matrix question (text in Dutch)

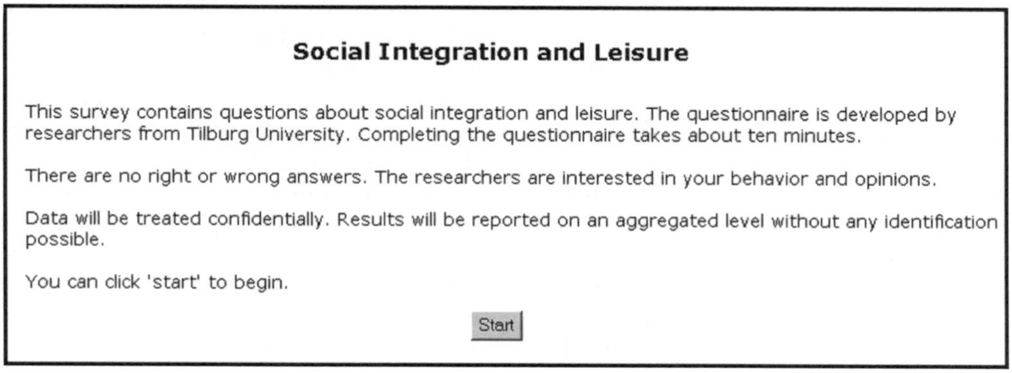

Social Integration and Leisure

This survey contains questions about social integration and leisure. The questionnaire is developed by researchers from Tilburg University. Completing the questionnaire takes about ten minutes.

There are no right or wrong answers. The researchers are interested in your behavior and opinions.

Data will be treated confidentially. Results will be reported on an aggregated level without any identification possible.

You can click 'start' to begin.

Start

Figure 11.4   Welcome screen

Thank you for filling out our survey. If you want to get updates about the results, please send an email to V.Toepoel@uu.nl

Figure 11.5 Thank you message

The survey should always end with some kind of thank you message (Figure 11.5).

Question and Instruction Text

Question text should be clear and unambiguous. Sometimes it can be helpful to put some emphasis on certain words. For example, by using **bold** or *italics*. Never underline because respondents might think it is a hyperlink that is not working. A hyperlink with a pop-up screen can be used to explain a concept; however, not every respondent will click on the hyperlink and therefore not every respondent will treat the concept in the same manner. In addition, the usability of pop-up screens depends on personal settings and on the devices being used.

Place instruction text between the question text and the answer categories. Do not place instruction text beneath the answer categories because respondents need them before reporting an answer. It is a good idea to give the same emphasis on instruction text throughout the survey. For example, always use a blank line between the question text and the instruction text and place the instruction text in *italics* (and not between brackets).

Answer Formats

There are several elements available to form question and answer formats in web surveys. The most important ones are radio buttons, checkboxes, dropdown menus, bars, and text fields. Decisions about which element to use are often based on random decision making on the part of the researcher or programmer. For example, standard questions such as gender, date of birth, and education can be offered in different ways: radio buttons (either horizontally or vertically aligned), text fields, and drop boxes. Answer spaces, appropriate labels on answer categories, and the use of visual signals can help respondents to understand what the researchers want. For example, Christian *et al.* (2007) found that a successive series of visual language manipulations improved respondents' use of the desired format (two digits for the month and four digits for the year) for reporting dates from 45 percent to 96 percent. Fewer digits for the month than the year, the use of symbols (MM/YYYY) instead of words (month year) and the placement of instructions right before the answer boxes (where they are needed) improved the use of the desired format by respondents.

Radio Buttons

Radio buttons are round button images that can be clicked to provide an answer. They are used when a respondent has to select only one response in a range of answer categories. Answer categories should be mutually exclusive. Radio buttons can be vertically aligned (as in the example in Figure 11.6) or horizontally aligned (see Figure 11.2).

In questions where a 'don't know' option is added, make sure that the 'don't know' option is visually different from the substantive options. By not separating substantive response options from non-substantive response options, respondents might mistake the visual midpoint for the conceptual midpoint. Visual separation can be done by adding extra space between the substantive and non-substantive options (see Figure 11.6) or by using a separate 'don't know' button.

On a scale of 1 to 5, where 1 means very dissatisfied and 5 means very satisfied, how satisfied are you with the Dutch education system?

○ 1 very dissatisfied

○ 2 somewhat dissatisfied

○ 3 neutral

○ 4 somewhat satisfied

○ 5 very satisfied

○ don't know

Next

Figure 11.6 Example of radio buttons (vertically aligned). Note that the non-substantive 'don't know' option is visually separated from the substantive options.

Software that uses a responsive design often operates by making the entire cell clickable (including the answer text), not only the circle at the left. This makes it easier on mobile phones with small screen sizes to select the desired answer.

Checkboxes

Checkboxes (Figure 11.7) are squares that can be ticked to provide an answer. They are used when more than one answer is possible ('check all that apply' questions). Good software allows users to program soft or hard checks in a checkbox item, for example that the option 'none of the above' should not be selected in case of other selections, or to restrict the number of options selected (e.g. maximum three).

Dropdown Menus

In dropdown menus (Figure 11.8), answer options are presented in a list that only becomes visible when the respondent presses the arrow on the right hand side (and the list drops down).

Couper *et al.* (2004) find evidence that visible response options in a dropdown menu are endorsed more frequently and therefore the initial display should show no substantive answer option. Figure 11.8 is therefore an example of a badly designed dropdown menu. Dropdown menus should be used sparingly because they require a lot of hand–eye movement from respondents in a long list. In addition, every browser uses dropdown menus differently, which can cause measurement effects.

Please tell me which of the following foods you use on a daily basis?

☐ Milk products
☑ Meat
☐ Vegetables
☑ Bread
☐ Fruit
☐ Butter or oil

Figure 11.7 Example of checkboxes

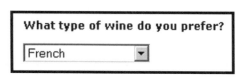

What type of wine do you prefer?

French ▼

Figure 11.8 Dropdown menu with one item initially displayed

Bars

Visual analogue scales (Figure 11.9) or slider bars (Figure 11.10) are often used for scalar questions.

Slider bars make use of the 'drag and drop' principle. The initial position of the handle influences answer distributions and their usability is questionable. A better way to work with bars is to use visual analogue scales, in which the respondent has to point and click to provide an answer. The main advantage of visual analogue scales is their extensive range and limited use of space, making them especially suited for survey completion on mobile phones. Toepoel and Funke (2015) experimented with different answer formats, and evaluation questions showed that respondents evaluate bars in mobile surveys more positively compared to radio buttons.

Text Fields

Text fields can be divided into text boxes and text areas. Text boxes are small and should be used for relatively short input, such as one word or a few numbers. Text areas allow lengthy responses and should be used for open-ended questions. In both cases, text and numeric input are allowed. Good software allows you to build soft checks (e.g. an

'@' is necessary for an email address). The size of the box or area should match the desired length of the answer. Longer text fields produce longer responses (Christian and Dillman, 2004; Couper et al., 2001; Smith, 1995). Research has shown that respondents can provide misleading answers if the text field is too long, for example instead of simply providing a number, respondents would enter 'about 3' or 'between 4 and 5' in a text field that was too long for the desired numerical input (Couper et al., 2001: 248).

Grids or Matrixes

Grids or matrixes are a widely used tool in web surveys. They are a series of items where the rows are a set of items and the columns the response options. Figure 11.3 shows an example of a grid or matrix question.

The major advantage of grid or matrix questions is the efficient use of space: many questions can be presented on a single screen, speeding up the response process. On the other hand, these types of questions are relatively difficult for respondents because so much text is presented on a single screen and response quality tends to be lower compared to single questions (higher item nonresponse, higher inter-item correlations).

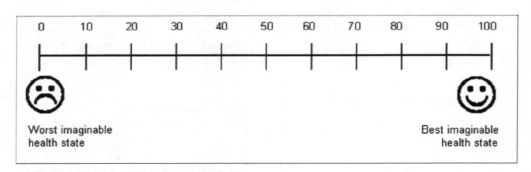

Figure 11.9   Example of a visual analogue scale

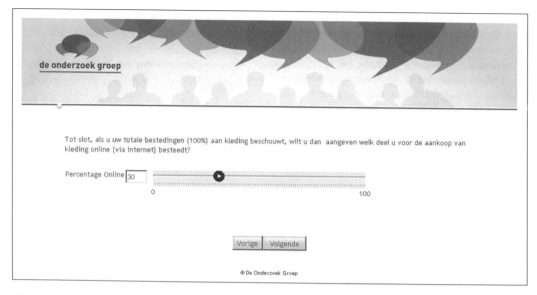

Figure 11.10   Example of a slider bar

In addition, they are not suited for mobile phone completion.

Scalar Questions and Labeling

One of the most commonly used types of question is a scalar question. A frequently used example is a Likert-scale, where respondents report on a continuum (agree–disagree) where they fit. There are many ways to design these rating scales. One decision is about the number of scale points. Between five and eleven is common practice. When traditional radio buttons are used, an 11-point scale takes quite some space on a screen. An eleven-point scale might therefore not be the best option for mobile phone completion (Toepoel and Funke, 2015). Eleven-point scales allow a higher level of precision, but they also require more cognitive effort from respondents. This could lead to satisficing behavior and other measurement effects. De Beuckelaer *et al.* (2013) demonstrate that an 11-point scale has advantages for analyses with regards to reliability. However, they also demonstrate that a 7-point scale is an acceptable alternative. A further reduction to a 5-point scale is not recommendable due to less differentiation and a higher level of inconsistent answering behavior.

Another choice to make is to use a fully labeled scale or only verbally label the endpoints (polar point scale). Response quality tends to be better in fully labeled scales; however, in case of many response options, it can be difficult to develop labels for all points. In such cases, labeling only the endpoints and providing numbers for every option is the best alternative. Only labeling the endpoints without any numbering results in higher levels of measurement error, as does adding negative numbers (e.g. −2 to 2) or color (Toepoel and Dillman, 2012). In matrix questions, adding headers per item helps to improve the clarity of the answer options but, on the other hand, makes the layout a little crowded due to the increase of text on a single screen. Toepoel *et al.* (2009) show no effect of headers on response quality.

Box 11.1 Guidelines for designing Internet surveys

Toepoel and Dillman (2012) have written an extensive review on how visual design affects respondents' answers. The following guidelines for designing Internet surveys are proposed:

1. The size of the answer box should match the size of the answer desired.
2. Make sure every (substantive) answer option gets the same visual emphasis.
3. Place ordinal scales consistently in a decremental or incremental order.
4. Make sure that the visual midpoint of a scale coincides with the conceptual midpoint.
5. If you present multiple items per screen, be aware that correlations might be higher between items, especially in polar point scales.
6. Use fully labeled scales. If this is not desirable, add numbers starting with 1 to the polar point scale.
7. Use a logical order of response options (e.g. a progression) and be aware that respondents extract meaning from that order.
8. Preferably, present answer options randomly, to avoid order effects.
9. Use instructions right in front of the answer options and make sure respondents do not have to put effort into reading them.
10. Avoid using gratuitous visual language like pictures, numbers, and colors unnecessary for the correct interpretation of questions.
11. When comparing results from different studies, make sure respondents get the same (visual) stimulus.

In addition, take into account that some respondents will complete the Internet survey on a mobile device with small screen size.

Routing

The rules that control the flow of the survey are variously called skips, branching, filters, pipes, routing, etc. One of the major advantages of online surveys is that they can lead the respondent through the questionnaire. Decisions on what question should be answered (often based on prior responses) can be made by the researcher or programmer, and can be taken out of the hands of the respondent. There are different ways to program routing, which is often dependent on the software used. The more complex (and often expensive) survey software allows you to program the most complex algorithms, for example based on a series of prior responses. There are basically two approaches to routing. The first approach is linear programming ('go to'): the selection of a response option triggers the system to display the next applicable question. The second approach is more object-related (if answer A to Q1 and A to Q2, go to Q3.1, else go to Q3.2; Couper, 2008). The latter approach offers more flexibility in programming.

Routing can be implemented in scrolling surveys, but routing needs to be very simple in order not to confuse respondents. Where respondents are not aware of routing in page-by-page designs (this being done in the 'back office' and not visible to respondents), in scrolling designs new questions can pop-up or disappear due to a previous response, and this might confuse respondents. Note that in both designs, routing affects elements such as question numbering and progress indicators, and researchers should think carefully on how to present these elements to respondents if there are major skips in the questionnaire.

Interactive Features

One of the main advantages of online surveys over other modes of administration is the use of interactive features, visual communication, and multimedia. One could easily add animation, a video, sound, etc. Due to personal settings, interactive features will not work for every respondent, nor will they be seen by every respondent in the same manner.

With the adding of interactive elements, the meaning of survey questions may change. For example, Toepoel and Couper (2011) have demonstrated that the use of pictures can severely change the meaning of a question. The placement of a picture with a high frequency behavior (e.g. grocery shopping) showed higher frequencies than the same question in a version with the showing of no picture or a low frequency picture (e.g. department store shopping). The effect was also apparent in follow-up questions. Interactive features should only be used when they add value to the survey.

Numbering and Progress Indicator

Numbering helps to distinguish one question from the next and in determining the length of the survey; however, in case of many skip questions (routing), numbering can confuse respondents because they could skip from 5 to 8 without knowing why. A way to help respondents determine how far along they are in a survey is by using progress indicators. The use of progress indicators may sometimes increase the number of break-offs because people want to abandon the survey if they think the remainder of the survey is too long. In addition, due to routing it is difficult to show the right progress in the survey. Sometimes people can skip from 5 percent to 40 percent after one single question because the answer to that question means they do not have to answer some follow-up questions. That means that people are actually further in the survey than the progress bar can indicate. Some people might therefore unnecessarily abandon the survey. Research on progress indicators shows mixed results. Indicating survey length at the beginning of the survey is a good alternative.

Other Issues in Designing Surveys

An attribute of web surveys (for example, relative to paper surveys) is the ability to make it necessary to provide an answer before going forward in the survey (mandatory fields). This is commonly done, although it is questionable what answers mean when respondents do not have an option to skip an item and are forced to reply within the response categories provided.

Another feature of online surveys is the possibility to add checks. Error messages can be divided into hard and soft checks. Hard checks make it impossible for the respondent to proceed without submitting or changing a response. Soft checks can be ignored by the respondent. In case of edit checks it can be helpful to program a hard check, otherwise soft checks are more respondent-friendly.

Randomization is another major advantage of online surveys. One important reason to randomize questions is to control for measurement error, for example context or order effects. Answer options can be randomized, but also questions and entire sections can be randomly offered to respondents when using high-end software. In addition, separate modules can be randomly assigned to different respondents to reduce the burden of the response task.

'Fills' are variable question texts that are often based on prior responses. For example, if the answer to Q1 (What is the name of your youngest child) is 'Isis', then Q2 can be adapted to 'How old is Isis?'. Fills are a way to personalize and customize the survey. However, it is very important to test all the fills to see that they work (e.g. do not result in 'How old is?' or 'How old is ^child1?'). Online surveys allow us to use the answer of a previous question or wave in a fill. This can be done to improve the accuracy and reduce respondent burden.

FIELDWORK

Recruitment of Respondents

Unfortunately, there is no complete list of email addresses for the general population.

In general, only institutions that provide email addresses to their clients (students, employees) have the opportunity to survey the complete population via the web. Mostly, it is impossible to draw a probability sample from the entire population because not every member of the population is registered or has access to the web. In order to recruit respondents, a researcher either has to rely on offline methods (such as Address Based Sampling or RDD and maybe even provide equipment to non-Internet users) or go into the realms of convenience sampling. With the increase in mobile phone penetration rates, it is possible to use RDD for recruitment and then switch over to the online survey within the device.

Offline recruitment methods, such as face-to-face visits or telephone interviews, often result in higher cooperation rates compared to online methods because of the personal contact with the interviewer. Paper invitations cannot profit from interviewers; however, responses to paper-and-pencil surveys have been relatively stable over time. A URL could be added to a paper invitation in order to make it possible to complete the survey online. For further discussion, see Dillman *et al.* and Fricker, in this volume.

Online methods cannot profit from personal contact and response rates tend to be low. On the other hand, responses usually return within a couple of days and online surveys have virtually no costs. Online recruitment can be done via email, websites and social network sites.

Mass mailings with email invitations are cost effective and fast. The downside of using email addresses lies in the frequent change of email addresses, the fact that an email cannot be delivered when there is something misspelled, and spam filters may block the delivery of the email. In addition, many people get an enormous amount of email in their inbox and the invitation might be easily overlooked. When recruiting via email, it is important that the salutation is personal, the content of the invitation is short and to the point, and the authority of the email signature and the profile of the officeholder making the request is high (Couper, 2008).

'River sampling' refers to recruiting potential respondents visiting one or more websites where survey invitations have been placed. A larger number of websites might alleviate the need to take account of the nature of the websites and still obtain a rather heterogeneous sample (AAPOR, 2013). The successfulness of this approach depends on which websites are used, how many places it appears, and when the invitation is posted (Lozar Manfreda and Vehovar, 2008).

Another way of recruiting respondents online is via social network sites. The reach of each network site differs per country. A combination of new (digital) methods and traditional methods (a so-called mixed-mode approach) probably works best, especially when making multiple contacts (see also the *Tailored Design Method* by Dillman, 2007).

The Survey Invitation

The survey invitation should be intriguing, simple, friendly, trustworthy, motivating, interesting, informative, and above all else short. Especially when using online methods for recruitment, for example banners or text, it is important to give all the relevant information while being brief. Subject lines for survey invitations mainly use one of the following texts (Toepoel, 2012):

1 They identify the survey request (keywords: survey, research, opinion);
2 They identify incentives for participating (keywords: win, dollar, prize, lottery);
3 They include a plea (e.g. we need your help);
4 They reinforce the nature of an existing relationship (keywords depend on the relationship, e.g. our client, member, identification of the purchase of a particular product, etc.).

Some research has experimented with the information in the subject line, but results are inconclusive. Zhang (2011) found that framing the request 'to win' resulted in a five-percentage point higher response rate in relation to 'to help'. The effect died out after multiple contacts. Kent and Brandal (2003) found that a prize subject line produced lower response rates compared to a subject line that stated that the request was about a survey. Dillman (2013) has shown that regional information can be a trigger for responding. Toepoel (2016) and Scherpenzeel and Toepoel (2012) found no effects of the content of the survey invitation. The effect of the content of the survey invitation is probably related to the nature of the survey (such as topic, length, incentives) and the population. A pre-test can help to determine what the optimal text of the survey invitation would be.

Incentives

Incentives are commonly used in online surveys as a reward for participation. Literature shows that prepaid cash incentives work best (for meta-analyses, see Church, 1993; Singer et al., 1999; Göritz, 2006). These prepaid cash incentives are often provided in an envelope via regular mail. Bank transfers are also used, although they are not the same as money in the hand. Vouchers for commercial parties are an alternative, although many respondents do not redeem them. Lotteries are probably the most commonly used incentives in online surveys; however, there is little to no evidence that they work as incentives in improving response rates (Church, 1993; Harris et al., 2008; Singer et al., 2000). The amount to be spent on incentives depends on the variable survey costs and the response rate (without incentive), although the first is the biggest driver. When survey costs are high, a large incentive becomes preferable as it accounts for a smaller percentage of total costs (Saunders et al., 2006). In online surveys, these variable survey costs are very low. Göritz (2004) concludes that incentives seem to be less effective in online surveys than in other modes of administration. She also concludes that promised incentives

(conditional on participation) seem to work better in online surveys than in other modes of administration. In longitudinal surveys, conditional incentives over several waves might be beneficial to keep respondents motivated over time.

Fieldwork Period

The turnaround of online surveys is very fast. On average, most surveys are completed within a couple of days; however, considerable time is needed to plan the fieldwork. Developing the questionnaire, careful programming of the online instrument, and pre-testing need to make sure that the online survey produces data of high quality. In addition, the recruitment of respondents can be time consuming because response rates for online surveys tend to be low.

Figure 11.11 shows the return rate from three surveys in a Dutch panel. Most surveys come in at the first day. After a couple of days, responses tend to die out. This would be the perfect timing for a reminder. Good survey software allows us to track respondents and identify nonrespondents for the reminder email. Otherwise, a reminder can be sent to the entire distribution list, distinguishing between people who have already responded (a small 'thank you' note) and nonrespondents (another plea). Reminders can be repeatedly sent, although their effect will be less pronounced the more often they are used. The effect of a reminder is apparent in Figure 11.11. Again, after only a couple of days, responses decline. The average fieldwork period is a little more than one week.

The length of the fieldwork often depends on the response rates. Without any prior information, it is difficult to predict response rates. Response rates are likely to increase when:

1 You use multiple contact attempts;
2 You use different modes;
3 You use a sender who is an authority or a highly trustworthy source;

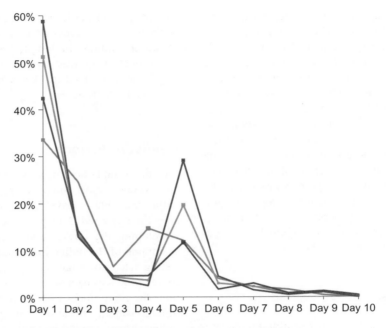

Figure 11.11   Typical response process. A reminder was sent at day 4.

4   The invitation is personalized;
5   Incentives are used (unconditional, cash);
6   The survey is salient to respondents (Toepoel, 2016).

Note that a solid sampling frame and sampling procedures are better predictors of survey quality than mere response rates. Low response rates with equal response probabilities of demographic subgroups should be preferred to high response rates of non-representative (volunteering) survey respondents (Toepoel, 2016). The number of survey invitations, completes and incompletes (dropouts/break-offs) should always be reported in the survey documentation as an indicator of response quality.

It can be helpful to add an open-ended question at the end of the survey that allows the respondent to give any remarks or comments that were raised while completing the survey. This gives insight into difficult questions, routing errors, and misunderstandings. See the website of the LISS Panel (www.lissdata.nl) for examples of evaluation questions.

PROCESSING OF DATA

Data cleaning after the fieldwork has ended is not a unique requirement of online surveys. The advantage of online surveys is that they should be free of range and routing errors because good survey software should be able to detect them. However, test cases (entries made by the researcher while testing the questionnaire) will need to be deleted from the file, and variable and value labels should be checked. A codebook should accompany any dataset and it should be written in a way that another person could replicate and understand what has been done. Codebooks should include how the respondents were recruited (including response rates and the number of incompletes) as well as (possible) randomization variables, instruction text, variables, question text, value and variable labels, and routing. Online surveys should also include screenshots to demonstrate how the questionnaire appeared. This could help in determining any measurement effects related to visual design.

Weighting, Imputation, and Reference Surveys

Weighting is not unique to online surveys, but is commonly used to give an opportunity at correcting for self-selection and undercoverage effects typical for online surveys. Propensity score adjustments are often used to indicate online survey participation. Propensity scores are obtained by modeling a variable that indicates whether or not someone participates in the online survey (Scherpenzeel and Bethlehem, 2010: 116). Logistic regression models are used where the dependent variable is an indicator for online survey participation and the independent variables are predictors for online survey participation. These auxiliary variables range from socio-demographics to webographics (indicating web behavior and other lifestyle variables). Based on these variables, a prediction is made of how likely it is that given the data observed for a person, this person would participate in the online survey (Scherpenzeel and Bethlehem, 2010). Based on these likelihoods, data can be stratified based on categories of participation. Weights are assigned to inflate (weight > 1) data obtained from people who are very likely to participate or deflate (weight < 1) data obtained from those who are unlikely to participate in an online survey.

Apart from weighting techniques, imputation can be used. Where weighting variables correct for unit nonresponse, item imputation (replacing missing values with substituted values) is used to correct for item nonresponse (e.g. at the individual question level). Since the true score is not known and single predictions do not portray this uncertainty, a commonly implemented strategy is to use multiple imputations. Instead of imputing one value, the same missing value is imputed several times. Most software packages have a function to do multiple imputations.

Sometimes a reference survey is used to compare data obtained via a volunteer online sample with those obtained via a probability-based survey. Based on the probability sample a population distribution can be estimated. The assumption in estimating the population distribution is that there is no or negligible nonresponse (Scherpenzeel and Bethlehem, 2010). Based on this estimation, the responses from the volunteer survey can be compared and tested to see how they differ or resemble the population. The reference survey is essentially a tool to obtain lacking population distribution information.

The best way to compare a sample to the population distribution is via official statistics. National statistical offices may register variables such as gender, age, education, and income that can be used for inferences. Some behavioral variables may be registered as well. It is important to use the same question text and answer categories as used in official statistics to be able to compare results. Attitudinal questions are not measured via official statistics and in cases of attitudinal questions a reference survey can be helpful.

CONCLUSION

This chapter discussed issues associated with designing online survey instruments. Measurement effects can affect data quality when the questionnaire is not optimally programmed. Online surveys are typically completed on a range of different devices, such as mobile phone, tablet, and regular desktop PC. This results in design challenges because mobile phone screen sizes are typically small. In addition, this places a greater emphasis on testing surveys on a wide variety of devices, screens, and browsers. The researcher has no control over the device on which a user chooses to access the questionnaire, and so it has to work equally well on a 23-inch screen and a 5-inch screen. Mobile surveys might be seen as a synthesis of all previous survey modes, combining the positive attributes of both interviewer and self-administered surveys and also using RDD to randomly recruit respondents, offering the possibility of adding new elements for data administration. In addition, mobile surveys can change mode within device (e.g. telephone and online survey).

The rise of online surveys is accompanied with the rise of big data. Administrative data, transaction data, social media data, and sensor data can be used alongside information obtained via surveys to get an optimal amount and quality of data. It is of critical importance to design the online survey instrument optimally to enable survey data to be related to these other kinds of data.

REFERENCES

American Association for Public Opinion Research (AAPOR). (2013). Report of the AAPOR Task Force on Non-Probability Sampling. Retrieved from https://www.aapor.org/AAPOR_Main/media/MainSiteFiles/NPS_TF_Report_Final_7_revised_FNL_6_22_13.pdf (accessed on 11 August 2016).

American Association for Public Opinion Research (AAPOR) Taskforce. (2014). Mobile Technologies for Conducting, Augmenting and Potentially Replacing Surveys: Report of the AAPOR Taskforce on Emerging Technologies in Public Opinion Research. Retrieved from https://www.aapor.org/AAPOR_Main/media/MainSiteFiles/REVISED_Mobile_Technology_Report_Final_revised10June14.pdf (accessed on 11 August 2016).

Buskirk, T.D. and Andrus, C. (2012). Smart Surveys for Smart Phones: Exploring Various Approaches for Conducting Online Mobile Surveys via Smartphones. *Survey Practice*. Retrieved from http://surveypractice.wordpress.com/2012/02/21/smart-surveys-for-smart-phones/ (accessed on 11 August 2016).

Callegaro, M. (2010). Do You Know Which Device Your Respondent Has Used to Take Your Online Survey? *Survey Practice*, 3 (6).

Christian, L.M. and Dillman, D.A. (2004). The Influence of Graphical and Symbolic Language Manipulations to Self-Administered Questions. *Public Opinion Quarterly*, 68, 57–80.

Christian, L.M., Dillman, D.A. and Smyth, J.D. (2007). Helping Respondents Get It Right the First Time: The Influence of Words, Symbols, and Graphics in Web Surveys. *Public Opinion Quarterly Advance Access*, 113–25.

Church, A.H. (1993). Estimating the Effect of Incentives on Mail Survey Response Rates: A Meta-Analysis. *Public Opinion Quarterly*, 57, 62–79.

Couper, M.P. (2008). *Designing Effective Web Surveys.* Cambridge: Cambridge University Press.

Couper, M.P., Tourangeau, R. and Conrad, F.G. (2004). What They See Is What We Get. Response Options for Web Surveys. *Public Opinion Quarterly*, 22, 111–27.

Couper, M.P., Traugott, M.W. and Lamias, M.J. (2001). Web Survey Design and Administration. *Public Opinion Quarterly,* 65, 230–53.

Dillman, D.A. (2007). *Mail and Internet Surveys. The Tailored Design Method.* Hoboken, NJ: John Wiley & Sons.

Dillman, D.A. (2013). Pushing the US General Public to the Web in Household Surveys: Is it worth the effort? Paper presented at the Congress of the European Survey Research Association, 15–19 July, Ljubljana, Slovenia.

De Beuckelaer, A.L., Toonen, S. and Davidov, E. (2013). On the Optimal Number of Scale Points in Graded Pair Comparisons. *Quality & Quantity*, 47, 2869–82.

de Bruijne, M. and Wijnant, A. (2013). Comparing Survey Results Obtained via Mobile Devices and Computers: An Experiment with a Mobile Web Survey on a Heterogeneous Group of Mobile Devices Versus a Computer-Assisted Web Survey. *Social Science Computer Review*, 31, 482–504. doi:10.1177/0894439313483976.

Göritz, A.S. (2004). The Impact of Material Incentives on Response Quantity, Response Quality, Sample Composition, Survey Outcome, and Cost in Online Access Panels. *International Journal of Market Research,* 46, 327–45.

Göritz, A.S. (2006). Incentives in Web Surveys: Methodological Issues and a Review. *International Journal of Internet Science*, 1, 58–70.

Groves, R.M., Fowler Jr, F.J., Couper, M.P., Lepkowski, J.M., Singer, E. and Tourangeau, R. (2009). *Survey Methodology*. Hoboken, NJ: John Wiley & Sons.

Harris, I.A., Khoo, O.K., Young, J.M., Solomon, M.J. and Rae, H. (2008). Lottery Incentives Did Not Improve Response Rate to a Mailed Survey: A Randomized Controlled Trial. *Journal of Clinical Epidemiology*, 61, 609–10.

Keller, H.E. and Lee, S. (2003). Ethical Issues Surrounding Human Participants Research Using the Internet. *Ethics & Behavior*, 13 (3), 211–219.

Kent, R. and Brandal, H. (2003). Improving Email Response in a Permission Marketing Context. *International Journal of Market Research*, 45, 489–506.

Kraut, R., Olson, J., Babaji, M., Bruckman, A., Cohen, J. and Couper, M. (2004). Psychological Research Online: Report of Board of Scientific Affairs Advisory Group on the Conduct of Research on the Internet. *American Psychologist*, 59 (2), 105–17.

Lozar Manfreda, K. and Vehovar, V. (2008). Internet Surveys. In: E. de Leeuw, J.J. Hox, D. Dillman (eds.), *International Handbook of Survey Methodology*. New York, NY: European Association of Methodology, pp. 264–84.

Lugtig, P. and Toepoel, V. (2015). The Use of PCs, Smartphones, and Tablets in a Probability-Based Panel Survey – Effects on Survey Measurement Error. *Social Science Computer Review*, doi: 10.1177/0894439315574248.

Lynn, P. and Kaminska, O. (2013). The Impact of Mobile Phones on Survey Measurement Error. *Public Opinion Quarterly*, 77, 586–605.

Mavletova, A. (2013). Data Quality in PC and Mobile Web Surveys. *Social Science Computer Review*, 31, 725–43.

Nosek, B.A., Banaji, M.R. and Greenwald, A.G. (2002). E-Research: Ethics, Security, Design, and Control in Psychological Research on the Internet. *Journal of Social Issues*, 58 (1), 161–76.

Saunders, J., Jobber, D. and Mitchell, V. (2006). The Optimum Prepaid Monetary Incentives for Mail Surveys. *Journal of the Operational Research Society*, 57, 1224–30.

Scherpenzeel, A.C. and Bethlehem, J.G. (2010). How Representative Are Online Panels? Problems of Coverage and Selection and Possible Solutions. In: M. Das, P. Ester and L. Kaczmirek (eds.), *Social and Behavioral Research and the Internet. Advances in Applied Methods and Research Strategies*. London: Routledge, pp. 105–32.

Scherpenzeel, A.C. and Toepoel, V. (2012). Recruiting a Probability Sample for an Online Panel: Effects of Contact Mode, Incentives and Information. *Public Opinion Quarterly*, 76, 470–90.

Singer, E. and Couper, M.P. (2010). Ethical Considerations in Internet Surveys. In: M. Das, P. Ester and L. Kaczmirek (eds.), *Social and Behavioral Research and the Internet. Advances in Applied Methods and Research Strategies*. London: Routledge, pp. 133–64.

Singer, E., Van Hoewyk, J. and Maher, M.P. (2000). 'Experiments with Incentives in Telephone Surveys', *Public Opinion Quarterly*, 64, 171–88.

Singer, E., Van Hoewyk, J., Gebler, N., Raghunathan, T. and McGonagle, K. (1999). The Effect of Incentives in Interviewer-Mediated Surveys. *Journal of Official Statistics*, 15, 217–30.

Smith, T.W. (1995). Little Things Matter: A Sampler of How Differences in Questionnaire Format Can Affect Survey Responses. *Proceedings of the American Statistical Association, Survey Research Methods Section*, 1046–51.

Toepoel, V. (2012). Effects of Incentives in Surveys. In: L. Gideon (ed.), *The Handbook of Survey Methodology in Social Sciences*. Springer, pp. 209–26.

Toepoel, V. (2016). *Doing Surveys Online*. London: Sage Publications.

Toepoel, V. and Couper, M.P. (2011). Can Verbal Instructions Counteract Visual Context Effects in Web Surveys? *Public Opinion Quarterly*, 75, 1–18.

Toepoel, V. and Dillman, D.A. (2012). How Visual Design Affects the Interpretability of Survey Questions. In: M. Das, P. Ester and L. Kaczmirek (eds.), *Social and Behavioral Research and the Internet. Advances in Applied Methods and Research Strategies*. London: Routledge, pp. 165–90.

Toepoel, V. and Funke, F. (2015). Bars or Buttons: An Investigation of the Interaction between Response Formats and Number of Scale Points in Mobile and Desktop Settings from a Data Quality and Respondent's Evaluation Perspective. Paper presented at the European Survey Research Conference, Reykjavik, 14 July 2015.

Toepoel, V. and Lugtig, P. (2014). What Happens If You Offer a Mobile Option to Your Web Panel? Evidence from a Probability-Based Panel of Internet-Users. *Social Science Computer Review*. doi:10.1177/0894439313510482.

Toepoel, V., Das, M. and van Soest, A. (2009). Design of Web Questionnaires: The Effect of Number of Items Per Screen. *Field Methods*, 21(2).

Turow, J. (2003). *Americans and Online Privacy: The System Is Broken*. Philadelphia, PA: Annenberg Public Policy Center of the University of Pennsylvania. Retrieved from http://repository.upenn.edu/cgi/viewcontent. cgi?article=1411&context=asc_papers (accessed on 11 August 2016).

Wells, T., Bailey, J. and Link, M. (2013). Filling the Void: Gaining a Better Understanding of Tablet-based Surveys. *Survey Practice*, 6 (1).

Zhang, C. (2011). Impact on Data Quality of Making Incentives Salient in Web Survey Invitations. Presented at the Annual American Public Opinion Research Congress, Phoenix, 12 May 2011.

12

Online Survey Software

Lars Kaczmirek

INTRODUCTION

In 2008 when the first version of this chapter was published, many online survey software tools were already available which differed largely in terms of costs and capabilities. This work was among the first publications to organize the many feature lists that were available at that time into a coherent framework. Since then several new professional products have entered the arena and innovations in web technology and cheaper hardware have led to both new fascinating possibilities for researchers and challenges for software companies alike. Researchers can choose between several hundred companies who compete in the market offering online survey software services.

Considering the vast amount of resources that specialized online survey software companies or the open-source community have invested to build their products, there are only a few very specific circumstances where a cost–benefit analysis would suggest

developing your own software solution from scratch. Large companies who need total control of the developing roadmap and have special needs in terms of security may be among those few cases. Such conditions seldom apply to social research except possibly in the case of the largest government surveys. The majority will benefit from using software as a service (SaaS) or by buying such a solution for in-house usage on company servers. Although much more expensive, an in-house solution can be feasible if business integration (for example, with marketing or sales-force) or special demands on data security (beyond the ambit of European and national laws, such as trade secrets or unwillingness to deposit data with other companies) requires adaptations to a software package.

The days when it was reasonable to hire a student assistant to put together a couple of HTML (HyperText Markup Language) pages and pipe the answers into a database are long gone. Even for a one-time, fire-and-forget, quick-and-dirty survey, free software would be a better choice. Software can speed up the implementation process of a survey while allowing for various configurations, features and designs at the same time. Software helps to avoid typical errors and flaws with state-of-the-art presets and solutions. Standards developed in the field of online survey methodology are already implemented in advanced software solutions. Some software products provide solutions for problems that possibly become prominent in a later stage of the survey process (for example data validation and cleaning). Further important advantages of software solutions include scalability, data integrity, availability and stability of the survey, and security of data.

Modern software packages do not require programming knowledge to quickly set up a small survey. They use point-and-click graphical user interfaces (GUI) for administration. Nevertheless, for complex surveys, programming and scripting is supported by advanced software packages.

The market is highly diversified, potentially satisfying nearly every need. There are low cost solutions (some free of charge) and professional products ranging from a few hundred US dollars to some tens of thousands of dollars. These cost-intensive solutions afford high-scaled, worldwide, multiple-language, multi-mode survey designs. Cheap solutions sound promising; however, they usually lack important features and can be more expensive when comparing the total costs of ownership. Hidden costs that could add substantially to the overall costs are in-house implementation work and additional adaptation work which are common when choosing an open-source solution.

This chapter is neither about quantitative analysis software such as SAS, SPSS, Stata or R, nor is it about companies who provide (market) research as a full service, including the whole process from programming the questionnaire, through data collection, to reporting. Such an overview focusing on the US is given by Evans and Mathur (2005). Rather, this chapter focuses on online survey

software tools and services which help to master some or most of the phases in online survey research. In this chapter, 'software' refers to 'online survey software'. The term online survey as used in this chapter is synonymous with web survey and Internet survey and encompasses mobile technology and hybrid solutions like software that supports smartphones, tablets, PCs and other devices that are able to process webpages. Often the technical terms used by programmers or computer scientists differ from the terms established in survey methodology. To ease communication similar terms are noted in brackets to help the reader identify the same features in different software packages (e.g. grid questions and matrix questions usually refer to the same concept).

RESOURCES AND APPROACHES

Searching for Online Survey Software Solutions

Several websites list software comparisons of different products on a per feature basis. Among those are the software companies themselves which aim to distinguish their products from the competitors. Fortunately, public funds were invested to build up independent resources for survey researchers. Two non-profit organizations are especially noteworthy and have taken on the task to collect and disseminate information in the area of online surveys, including online survey software.

WebSM Site (Web Survey Methodology Site, http://websm.org/), located in Slovenia at the University of Ljubljana, collects and disseminates information about methodological issues of web surveys and fosters collaboration among researchers in the field. From 2003 to 2005 it was funded by the European Union, and the American Association for Public Opinion Research (AAPOR) has granted the Warren J. Mitofsky innovators award 2009 to Vasja Vehovar and Katja Lozar Manfreda for the WebSM site. WebSM categorizes software according to language, pricing, code availability (open/viewable or closed/non-viewable source) and type of hosting. It also publishes the WebSM report series with annual survey software reports and reports on survey apps, interaction speed of software, pricing and feature lists (all available from http://www.websm. org/c/1283/Software/).

Exploring Online Research Methods (ORM), located in the UK at the University of Southampton, is 'an online research methods training programme for the social sciences' (www.restore.ac.uk/orm/). The training modules are useful for both beginners and experienced users and contain reading material and substantial learning courses. It was funded by the Economic and Social Research Council (ESRC) from May 2004 to July 2006. The module 'Technical guide' (http://www. restore.ac.uk/orm/technical/techcontents_c. htm) introduces the distinction between 'software plus hosting' and 'software only'. It explains differences between open-source and commercial options as well as cost aspects. The training package is completed by an opportunity to create one's own checklist of survey features.

In combination both resources provide substantial guidance towards choosing and categorizing survey software. While the goal of WebSM is to be exhaustive and to list all available products and information sources, ORM provides know-how for evaluating and prioritizing the different categories and features.

Literature Overview on Online Survey Software

The early years of online survey software reviewing were dominated by reviews which compared specific products (e.g. Crawford, 2002), reviewed single products (computer magazines and online blogs), presented and discussed lists of features in working papers (NEON, 2003) or at conferences (Vehovar et al., 2005; Crawford, 2006; Berzelak et al., 2006; Zukerberg, 2006). A noteworthy report which documents the selection process among 74 products was issued by the United States Army Research Institute for the Behavioral and Social Sciences (Heinen et al., 2009). Others inspected research companies and their involvement with online surveys (Evans and Mathur, 2005).

The research group around Vehovar and Lozar Manfreda has continued to assess survey software on the WebSM Site and published a couple of reports in the WebSM report series. Together with Callegaro they synthesized their knowledge to provide an overview of 'integrated ICT support for the web survey process' (Callegaro et al., 2015: 215–30). Here, they show that the online survey industry is still heavily focused on features that support programming the questionnaire and data collection. As they point out, this is the key business and thus not surprising and yet they find it remarkable that many steps which are part of every survey are only weakly supported, such as sampling, quality testing, calculation of response rates, fieldwork monitoring, or data preparation, among others. Users have to be careful in their choices if they need such features. Comprehensively, Callegaro and colleagues identify and describe 19 features which define advanced web survey software (well-developed and versatile software packages are also called 'enterprise solutions'). Their overview adds substantially to the discussion of the importance of interface speed and GUI efficiency, and they present results from their own work, including a useful prescription for a process to narrow down the many choices during a purchase decision for an advanced tool.

Pointer (2010: 16–30) provides a rich overview in the main areas of online survey software. He explains when to buy a whole system, develop one of your own, or use software as a service; he also gives advice on cost considerations and then runs the reader through a series of features. He briefly touches upon capacity issues, data protection and security, data reporting/monitoring, integration with other tools, engaging surveys, and how to assess one's own organization and its potential.

Online survey software is only one part of a heterogeneous market, though. For research projects involving panel designs, whether longitudinal or online access panel designs, Macer (2014) offers a comprehensive assessment of online panel software. He focuses on the capabilities that are unique to panel-based research: the administration of the database with its panel members and the tasks that link online survey software to panel management. Descriptions of features are combined with results from a survey he conducted among online panel software companies. (Both the questionnaire and data are available for download from www.wiley.com/go/online_panel and http://dx.doi.org/10.4232/1.11885, respectively.)

Most of the presented approaches have in common that they first categorize the available features and then sort or discuss each feature as being part of one of the following categories:

1 A basic feature is a 'must have' in the sense that it is a commodity even in the low-budget sector. If such a feature is missing, the product is not mature enough for the market. Examples for 'must haves' are open-answer questions ('open-ended questions', 'free-response questions'), a way to send emails to respondents, possible exclusion of multiple responses and data export.
2 A best practice or intermediate feature is a 'should have', a good standard practice in every reasonable product, for example skip logic and branching, real-time data validation and a way to deal with the special demands of 'don't know' answer categories.
3 An advanced feature might be a useful addition. Probably every survey project will benefit from a couple of advanced features, although the requirements differ between projects. Some advanced features are part of all major enterprise survey software; others are not (e.g. special

pretesting capabilities, special survey designs like 360-degree feedback, accessibility compliance, automatic processing of bounced emails). They are required for some projects or expected to become a standard in the next generation of survey software. This includes, for example, support for mobile surveys, multi-language support, availability of application programming interfaces (API) and business integration, for example as part of customer satisfaction surveys or user experience surveys.
4 Future features have either been implemented in a use case, are on the wish-list of survey methodologists and other users, or can reasonably be expected based on current technical developments and how new technology could be harnessed for survey research.

It is helpful to recall these four baskets when discussing features because it helps to understand what might increase a price quote from a vendor of advanced software and what to expect in the low-end of the market.

Different User Types and Prioritizing Features

Online survey software can be categorized in various ways. Dozens of features may be compared with each other while different pricing strategies add to the complexity. This makes it difficult for potential buyers to compare products with each other. Furthermore, software companies differ in their business strategy (Crawford, 2002). To help users prioritize the features, several simplified user types are outlined in Table 12.1.

CENTRAL DECISIONS IN SURVEY SOFTWARE

Before going into the details of single features that your software should include there are three decisions which help to quickly reduce the number of eligible products for a given project. I refer to these decisions as the

Table 12.1 Typical user types, their main needs and likely priorities

User type	Important aspects are...	Is likely to gain from concentrating on...
University member	Frequent changes in students and staff	Fast to learn point-and-click interfaces, web interface
Student, teacher	Few respondents, simple questionnaire	Low cost, web interface, on-the-fly simple reporting modules
Research scientist	Data collection, scholarly publishing	Documentation, export functionality
Experimenter	Randomization of treatments / design / pages / items, paradata	Specific (advanced) support for randomization with good documentation and proper data export, customizable question types
Market researcher	Managing several survey projects at once, tight schedules, standardized steps of analysis	Quick survey set-up, reusable templates, question types tailored to the market researcher's product, reporting modules
Big project or large organization	Has several experienced survey researchers with access to additional labour	Flexibility, availability of scripting languages, code access or an API

core design decisions in survey software. Researchers need to decide whether they want

1 a web-based interface for survey administration, a local installation or a mix of both;
2 a web-based interface for respondents or a client-side solution like an app;
3 hosted software or an in-house set-up.

The next sections provide background information on these core decisions.

Interface for Administration

The product interface for the administration can either be a desktop application (client-side), or it can be a web interface (server-side). The first includes the need to install a program on a local computer (similar to a word processor) from which the survey is then administered. After the set-up, the survey is then uploaded to a server to start data collection. The advantages of client-side applications are fast interaction response times of the system during set-up and in-house control of the survey before the collection phase. Nevertheless, the drawbacks of such an approach are likely to predominate. First, a local installation leaves maintenance and updates to the end-user. If the survey is to be administered from several locations, project members need to share the actual survey versions and maintain some sort of version control. Contrastingly, web interfaces have the advantage that all data is stored in a central location and only the servers need maintenance. The administration of surveys is easily achieved through browsers. This usually means that it is possible to provide appropriate access to every person involved in the survey project. As servers usually implement some sort of backup and security plan, the data is safer than on a local machine where a hard disk drive breakdown or theft can be a severe threat. With the emerging trend towards interactive Internet technology, web interfaces can be as responsive, fast and usable as desktop installations (such as cloud-based software – well-known examples include online spreadsheets and documents which look, run and feel similar to the well-established desktop software applications). However, there are considerable differences in interface speed among web-based software (Čehovin and Vehovar, 2012). In addition, it should be noted that some software packages which require local installation for set-up and analysis provide a web interface for the purpose of field control and data export. Nevertheless, web interfaces are the most common approach and a reasonable choice in general.

Interface for Respondents

The interface for respondents can be based on server-side or client-side technology. The server-side approach is the most common. Here, the server delivers question pages to respondents who participate via standard browsers. Download times are kept short because only necessary questions need to be downloaded (the server deals with branching and filter issues). Furthermore, respondents do not have access to the program running on the server, which is a security advantage.

In special cases, client-side technologies can be favourable, especially if no continuous Internet connection is available (e.g. with mobile devices or personal interviewers) or a stronger control over the client computer is needed (e.g. for ability tests with very precise reaction time measures). However, it should be noted that as the costs for online connections have become increasingly low, connection costs are no longer a major reason to employ client-side technology. There are considerable drawbacks of client-side approaches: (a) the initial download time can be substantial, which is likely to increase dropout; (b) the program needs to be executed by respondents, which is a task often warned against due to the massive circulation of malware and spyware; (c) the program might not run at all, owing to the high variety in software and hardware environments on local computers. Speaking from a survey methodology perspective, client-side solutions are likely to introduce a higher coverage error than server-side solutions.

Server Set-up

If a survey is hosted this means that a service provider maintains a server on which the survey project is able to run. Many survey software companies combine the service of providing both the software and the server functionality (SaaS, software as a service). This is a very common and established set-up.

In some cases, an in-house installation may be preferred. These are, for example, special adaptation or extension needs for the product (if they cannot be provided by the software vendor), or the requirement that confidential data should not leave the organization.

Summarizing, a hosted solution with a web interface combines convenience (centralized configuration, performance) and security with a good cost–performance ratio. This makes in-house server installations profitable only for large-scale projects with special implementation needs or requirements for control. Table 12.2 summarizes the three core decisions and adds six additional aspects to consider when choosing survey software.

ASSESSING WEB SURVEY SOFTWARE

A Framework for Survey Software: the Survey Data Life Cycle

The many possible approaches to sorting and categorizing survey software described in the previous sections make it useful to discuss the many features in a general framework of the online survey process. Such a framework makes it easier to see which methodological concepts are covered by software, which aspects are not supported so far and what users need at which stage in the survey process. The framework is also applicable to surveys in general, allowing the researcher to match his or her project to the framework and see whether an online approach is feasible. A framework that conforms to these ideas is the survey data life cycle (Table 12.3). The life cycle covers all possible phases during a survey project, from the first ideas and preparations to the deposit of the data for secondary analyses and archiving. The phases of empirical research (Diekmann, 1998) and the research process (Schnell et al., 1995) both fit into such a view. The survey data life cycle model in this chapter refers to the phases described and continuously updated by the

Table 12.2 Core design decisions in survey software and additional considerations

1. Type of product interface for administration (server-side versus client-side). Widely used: server-side.	How is the survey project administered? Is it a desktop application to be installed on a local computer (client-side)? Or does the product use a web-based interface that can be administered through a server (server-side)?
2. Type of product interface for respondents (server-side versus client-side). Widely used: server-side.	How is the survey delivered to respondents? Is it a server-side solution where the questionnaire is mainly processed on a server? Or is it a client-side solution (e.g. Java) which requires the download of some sort of program for the respondents?
3. Type of server set-up (hosted versus in-house). Widely used: hosted.	Where is the server located? Is the survey hosted by a company which also provides the Internet connection (hosted)? Or can the surveys be maintained on a local server allowing full control and responsibility for the research group (in-house)?
4. Platform and system architecture. Widely used: Apache or Microsoft's ISS.	What programming language and database are employed? What type of server architecture does the product support?
5. Language support. Recommendation: native language and English.	In what languages is the software interface available (both administration and respondent interface)? Are all required characters supported and maybe right-to-left languages?
6. Location and responsibility. Recommendation: contact address in own country.	Is there a company or organization responsible for the product? In which country is the company providing the product or service located? What laws apply?
7. Type of license. Recommendable depending on budget: free or non-free software.	Is it free software (e.g. GNU General public license, open-source) or non-free software (proprietary)? This involves considerations of viewable source code and the possibility to extend the product with own modules. With the availability of APIs in proprietary software this is becoming less of an issue.
8. Pricing strategy. Note: liability often requires a charge.	What aspects are considered in calculating a price quote, or is the product freeware? Consider the total amount of questions in a survey, how many invitations/survey completes are needed per month, the duration the software should be available to respondents, and which modes need to be supported.
9. Demos, tutorials, examples. Recommendation: should be available.	Are demonstrations, tutorials, the handbook, or free trials available to allow for an assessment of the product?

Inter-University Consortium for Political and Social Research (ICPSR, 2012). In the following description I have added and adapted the various steps of a prototypical process in online survey research (e.g. technical set-up and reporting) to match this framework and extended it to include the survey software perspective.

Steps one to five describe activities in preparation of the actual data collection. They are usually controlled by the researcher. Steps six to nine contain activities during data collection in the field and the creation of a suitable dataset. These data collection and file creation steps are often outsourced to another company, especially in the case of personal

and telephone interviews. Steps ten to thirteen are scholarly activities of analysing the data, writing a report and preparing the dataset for later reference. The last steps include activities like archiving and disseminating the dataset to the scientific community. These steps are analytic categories.

Real survey projects, especially those with a tight schedule, often make it necessary to pursue several steps simultaneously. Similarly, work may be arranged in a different order, or previous steps can be repeated where the outcome was unsatisfactory. The next sections take a close look at various features in survey software and explain what users can reasonably expect from survey

Table 12.3 Model of survey data life cycle and corresponding steps of conducting an online survey

Phase 1: Proposal development and data management plans
1. Preparing and clarifying the survey design
Phase 2: Project start-up
2. Determining the main method of investigation
3. Creating and designing the questionnaire
4. Technical set-up, programming the questionnaire
5. Pretest, testing and revising the questionnaire and set-up
Phase 3: Data collection and file creation
6. Sampling, recruiting participants
7. Data collection, fielding the survey
8. Data processing
9. Data cleaning and editing
Phase 4: Data analysis
10. Data analysis
11. Reporting
12. Distributing results
Phase 5: Preparing data for sharing
13. Exhaustive documentation
14. Data preparation for archive (e.g. translation)
Phase 6: Depositing data
15. Compliance with dissemination standards and formats
16. Metadata preparation
17. Online analysis-ready files
18. Evaluation, usage statistics
19. Secondary analysis, meta-analysis

Source: Adapted from Inter-University Consortium for Political and Social Research (ICPSR), 2012.

software in the field and what can be gained by using advanced survey software.

Preparing and Clarifying the Survey Design

The first step in any research project is to specify the research question and review previous research about the topic. Fundamental concepts should be defined. Usually, survey software is first considered at a later stage in the data life cycle. It is therefore not surprising that an elaborate record system to file information about these important preliminaries is missing in most survey systems.

Important aspects in this early stage are: principal investigators, funding sources, data collector/producer, project description (ICPSR, 2012). Inexpensive products may offer only a project title, but for larger-scale projects more descriptors might be necessary. As long as more sophisticated implementations for social scientists do not exist, the open text fields or comment fields may be used to store this information. Although still rare, existing and ready-to-use item libraries within the survey software system should be browsable in this stage of research. Nevertheless, researchers may check other comprehensive resources as well, for example the question bank at the UK Data Service (http://discover.ukdataservice.ac.uk/variables) or question libraries in various other surveys (see also NCRM for new resources, http://www.ncrm.ac.uk/).

Determining the Main Method of Investigation

After the research question is clarified, the appropriate method of investigation needs to be determined. With the growth of survey software comes the extension to other survey modes. Similar to computer-assisted telephone interviewing (CATI) software, which extended its capabilities to online surveys, online survey software companies develop extensions to incorporate other modes into one package (see Dillman *et al.*, this volume). Where mobile access is available or if the software has an offline mode, online surveys can be utilized in interviewer-administered surveys as well. This might require only a few changes to the survey software if the questionnaire designers and programmers are able to implement the control needed by interviewers. Paper questionnaires require an extra module, owing to the lack of interactivity in a paper version. Dropdown boxes need an appropriate representation, which might be a full list in the case of only five items, or an open text field in the case of a complete list of country names. More important, paper has size restrictions that need to be matched to question formats and page breaks. Automatic filtering might also lead to additional instructions in a paper questionnaire. A panel module is helpful in maintaining a group of respondents during a longer period of time for repeated (longitudinal) surveys. It helps in keeping the individual-related participant's data up to date, and informs them about the project status or their incentives. Support for CATI is still rare in genuine online survey software as telephone labs bring a complete new set of requirements with them. Although interviewers could type the answers into web forms, interviewers need adjustments like auto-forwarding and special instructions in the questionnaire. Telephone calling management needs to be addressed as well. As devices other than computers are connected to the Internet they are also supported by survey software, such as smartphones and tablets. These devices differ in screen sizes and multimedia capabilities from those used on computers. Advanced software therefore automatically detects a respondent's device and delivers a suitable question format.

Creating and Designing the Questionnaire

It is useful to consider three aspects of questionnaire design: the available question types, the flow of the questionnaire and the overall look and feel. This subsection summarizes the features available in questionnaire design. For a complete discussion, the reader is referred to the chapter by Toepoel (this volume). Others provide extensive coverage of questionnaire design issues as well (Couper, 2008; Foddy, 1993; Dillman et al., 2014; Tourangeau et al., 2013).

Question types are available in many different forms. Basic, predefined question formats include check one answer, check all that apply, grid questions (sometimes also referred to as matrix questions), bipolar scales with labels at both ends and open text answers. Software packages tend to list dozens of possible variations, thereby increasing the overall number of explicitly available question types in the product. The answer labels can be positioned at the top, at the bottom, or at both ends in the case of rating questions. An option to add 'Something else. Please specify …' with an open answer field should be available. More advanced question types are constant sum, graphical ranking, biographical landscapes and questions with lookup tables. Pictures as answer options are an advanced option as well as video, not to be confused with common background or logo graphics. It is common practice among companies to show a list of available question types, so the researcher is able to check whether his or her requirements are met. If a necessary question type is missing, advanced software packages allow users to program their own customized question type.

Controlling the flow of the questionnaire is implemented in software in many ways. Page breaks can be set as necessary (one or more questions per page). Adaptive filter techniques help to skip questions that do not apply. More advanced but still reasonable branching and filtering techniques help to implement concepts like randomization of items or pages, looping to ask the same question for a list of items, and probing for additional details for selected answers. Software can also draw from data collected in previous surveys or earlier questions and present this information to a respondent or it can use calculated variables. With the integration of panel software, a survey may, for example, ask questions about a respondent's children by referring to their names without having to collect these data again.

Overall look and feel relates to the ways that the general survey appearance can be customized. A logo, header, footer and the possible inclusion of a progress indicator (for cautionary use, see Villar et al., 2013) are among the basic features. With low-budget solutions some of the following customizations might not be available: free formatting of text font, layout of single question types, colour variations, variation in the appearance of navigation buttons. A good practice in survey software is the use of templates to define the style of the questionnaire (in technical terms, this is done using CSS, cascading style sheets). Separating the content from the design is generally good programming practice to allow the template to be re-used in other surveys as well.

Technical Set-up, Programming the Questionnaire

This step describes the features that help programmers during questionnaire implementation. The administrative interface of a survey software program allows researchers to set up a survey ready to go into the field. Most survey solutions have a GUI to enter the questionnaire. Although a GUI is generally perceived as an interface that speeds up and makes implementing a questionnaire easier than programming, Callegaro *et al.* (2015: 223) point out: 'Within the general usability aspects of the web survey software the speed, in terms of page loading time when creating and editing a web questionnaire, may be a serious problem for a researcher during the process of creating the questionnaire'. Only the immature and the most advanced survey solutions need programming skills for implementation. The first can easily be identified by lack of features (e.g. no built-in filter functionality), while the latter support large-scale projects, have high initial costs and use their own proprietary scripting language. Still missing in many software packages, which otherwise support more than one mode, is the possibility to include mode-specific text in order that an interviewer-administered version of the questionnaire, for example, could show additional information which would be lacking or reworded in a self-administered questionnaire.

Programmers may be supported by the following features: mass import of a list of questions and answers, automatic fallback procedures to achieve higher accessibility (e.g. in case of disabled JavaScript), easy changes of item and page sequence, templates for questions and answers, graphical libraries, standard texts for privacy, data protection, welcome page and final page, syntax checker and programmable system messages. It should be possible to visually separate extra answer categories such as 'Don't Know' (DK) and 'No Opinion' (NO) from the main answers. In addition, a survey package may have built-in support for some technical challenges: loops, placeholders to be automatically filled with previous answers or preloaded data (also referred to as prefills and piping), calculation within placeholders, insertion of external pages or code and probing. The latter allows asking an additional set of questions on a set of items that have been chosen by a respondent, for example a selected set of known brands among a larger list of brands.

Many technical problems can cause havoc with data if not anticipated. Security measures need to be taken by the software provider and researcher alike (see the section on ethical and data protection issues in this chapter).

The following example illustrates a basic methodological requirement that can become a challenge for programmers if it is neglected by the software product. It is common and good practice in paper-based surveys to use identical spaces between the answer points in a scale ('equidistance'). This triviality is a challenge for browsers because they tend to use dynamic column widths which adjust to the text and the width of the screen. It is thus important that the software either includes measures to solve this problem or that it provides possible solutions for the programmer.

Pretest, Testing and Revising the Questionnaire and Set-up

Before the real launch every questionnaire should undergo at least one thorough pretest

(Converse and Presser, 1986). Generally, features supporting pretesting can be categorized as intermediate or advanced. The definition and handling of user roles as testers in a survey system is simple and straightforward. Respondents that are marked as testers will then not be counted as eligible respondents when they visit the survey. A tester should be able to override forced answer controls. The survey system should allow testers to comment on each page separately. Although version control is a standard in software development, it is still missing in most survey software packages for the construction of a survey. A nice feature is the possibility to manage attributes such as 'assigned to' or 'solved' that are similar to a bug-control system (e.g. the bug tracker Bugzilla). Researchers should be able to quickly switch between viewing a comment and the corresponding page. Necessary for thorough pretesting is the ability to arbitrarily choose the survey path as a tester, especially in the case of randomized branches. Summarizing, the complex functionality needed for pretesting is equal to adding an extra module to survey packages.

Sampling, Recruiting Participants

All survey packages support various sampling methods. Regardless of whether it is an intercept or pop-up survey, a link on a website, a link in an email, a link in a mobile message (SMS), or a Quick Response (QR) code, a participant always starts the survey by visiting the survey's web page. Fricker's chapter (this volume) provides an in-depth overview of the various sampling methods and problems associated with them. Methodologically and technically, personalized surveys and anonymous surveys can be distinguished. Personalized surveys allow for some kind of identification. This can be a code in the link (very respondent-friendly) or a login name with a password. An anonymous survey uses the same link for all participants,

leaving it to the software to distinguish and identify individuals (e.g. by placing a cookie). Basic list management of email addresses and personalized invitation emails is provided by most packages. A quota management module is an intermediate feature.

Other aspects of sample management are concerned with response identification. In accordance with AAPOR's Standard Definitions (2015), survey software should distinguish between respondents (returned questionnaires: complete and partial with sufficient information) and eligible 'non-interviews'. Non-interviews need to be further refined into no response, break-offs, visits to only the first page and lurkers. Further distinctions into 'unknown eligibility' (email returned due to wrong address – in technical terms: a 'bounced email') and 'not eligible' (e.g. quota filled) are add-ons, but nevertheless necessary to calculate response rates. Two major challenges that are mostly not supported in survey software are (1) to decide when a break-off has sufficient information to be relabelled as a partially returned questionnaire and (2) to identify seemingly complete responders as lurkers – a lurker being someone who has visited the last page of a questionnaire but not provided any (or random) answers. Whereas the first problem could easily be solved by providing an adjustable definition of how many answers are needed, the second problem of random answers is not solved yet. Some software packages calculate a quality index that takes into account the number of answers and the speed of participation compared to all other respondents to aid researchers in the step of data cleaning.

Data Collection, Fielding the Survey

The step of actual data collection contains the aspects of (a) the respondents' user experience while the survey is in the field and (b) the researcher's ability to monitor the field.

A great advantage of online surveys is their timeliness and immediate feedback capabilities. As such, the researcher is able to monitor in real time how many respondents are taking the survey at this very moment as well as all other disposition codes. This also includes information about the break-offs for every page, item non-response and information about date and time of responses.

Concerning the user experience, various aspects can be adjusted. A few examples are the way real-time validations should be administered (for a thorough overview, see Peytchev and Crawford, 2005) and whether respondents should be able to go back to previous questions. An important aspect might be the possibility to encrypt the connection from and to respondents (in technical terms: secure socket layer (SSL) technology). A save-and-continue feature ensures that respondents can resume where they left off. In addition, a software package should strive for device independency, so that participation without specific hardware like a mouse is possible.

Data Processing

Data processing is sometimes simultaneously done while data is still being collected. A survey researcher should always be able to download the actual dataset from the server (in technical terms: a data dump). It should be possible to download the data in various formats. An advantage of genuine statistical package formats is that the data is already fully labelled, correctly formatted and missing data codes are defined. A non-standard but highly recommendable feature is the implementation of encryption for the transmission of the data, which should be enabled if available (in technical terms: SSL-encryption). Survey packages should also ensure compliance with local data protection laws. At least, survey data and personal data should be separated and not mixed within a standard data export. In the case of email addresses being collected to pay incentives

via a voucher, it is advisable to achieve a complete separation from data (which should include randomization of the sequence to prevent matching by guessing). In a later stage of the survey project, the individual-related data should be deleted from the servers (this includes erasing existing backups).

Advanced survey software can provide an integrated data processing unit, which allows researchers to collect and/or merge data from various sources, seamlessly integrating the data flow into one dataset. This is necessarily the case with additional modules providing CATI, CAPI (computer-assisted personal interviewing), paper-and-pencil or mobile support. The challenge in integrating external sources lies in the automatic recoding and formatting of the data to fit into the final dataset.

Data Cleaning and Editing

After the field stage is closed, the dataset can be finalized. The next steps are often done outside the software packages with an exception: some software packages offer to delete single cases on the server, which makes it possible to start the cleaning during field time. The drawback is that researchers usually have to keep track of their activities on their own. Programs may offer automatic cleaning of wrong entries in cases where respondents provided answers for questions which, according to the branching, should not have been delivered to them (e.g. when a respondent goes back and follows a different filter path). Finally, the dataset is downloaded from the server and the cases are examined for remaining inconsistencies.

Data Analysis, Reporting and Distributing Results

Packages offering support for data analysis range from simple frequency distributions to professional-looking diagrams and graphics. Furthermore, report templates can be generated to automatically generate ready-for-delivery reports. Powerful reporting modules are able to meet market researchers' requirements for professionally designed reports. A view onto individual cases may be provided but can obviously collide with data protection requirements. Some programs can offer automatic feedback to a respondent, together with a comparison with other respondents' answers.

Exhaustive Documentation

Thorough documentation practices are rare in survey packages. Although most are able to provide a view of the whole questionnaire on the screen, difficulties arise when it comes to printing. An exhaustive documentation would include: (1) screenshots or an overview from a respondent's point of view; (2) complete information on system messages, alerts and validity checks; (3) full branching information; (4) a codebook with answer options and resulting code; (5) process documentation; (6) information about the project as described in the section on preparing and clarifying the survey design. Further activities as listed in the data life cycle (Table 12.3) are not within the focus of today's online survey software packages.

ETHICAL AND DATA PROTECTION ISSUES IN SURVEY SOFTWARE

Ethics, legislation, codes of conduct and good practice have several implications for survey software packages. Ethical aspects of Internet research are illustrated and discussed by Eynon *et al.* (this volume) and Hewson *et al.* (2016). The European Parliament and Council (1995) have published a data protection directive, which is enacted in the legislation of European states, for example the 1998 Data Protection Act in Great Britain (UK Government, 1998). The

ISO 20252:2006–04 standard on market, opinion and social research has set the worldwide benchmark for good survey practice, covering all stages of survey research. Thiele and Kaczmirek (2010) cover the different aspects of security and data protection in terms of collection, storage and feedback to participants in online surveys. Summarizing these sources, the most important topics are informed consent, disclosure, confidentiality, anonymity, data protection, accuracy of data and security.

The following selected examples show that some aspects may seem unproblematic although they can turn out to be major violations of laws and/or regulations. In some countries storing IP addresses together with answers might be a breach of anonymity requirements because IP addresses are considered to be personal information similar to names or email addresses. Furthermore, a growing problem is the collection of additional behavioural data (paradata) during participation. Owing to technical developments, it is easy to collect paradata such as time stamps and mouse clicks (Couper, 2005). In analogy, the respondents of a telephone interview would be asked in the beginning whether they allow the recording of the interview, which makes the generation of paradata possible. In accordance with the rule that data collection should be appropriate to the research question, additional or hidden behavioural data should be collected only when it is vital for the research question. Respondents then need to be informed beforehand. In conflict with this, most survey software packages automatically collect time stamps. Mouse clicks are more complicated but can be collected as well. Software should enable the researcher to turn off automatic data collection when it is unnecessary, thus avoiding unnecessary burden in the process of achieving informed consent.

The requirements of confidentiality and anonymity make it necessary that personal data and survey data are, and remain, separated in the software design. It must be impossible for a researcher to match these datasets. Nevertheless, a data protection officer must be able to identify single datasets to be able to comply with enquiries concerning the right of information access and removal from the dataset. This can be achieved by granting different access rights to different people in the research team: whereas the researcher would be able to export the whole but anonymous dataset, the data protection officer would be able to view only a single entry at a time.

CONCLUSION AND FUTURE DEVELOPMENTS

The number of available survey software products is too large for a single survey researcher to thoroughly compare them. Furthermore, software packages differ greatly in terms of quality and features. This chapter presented an organization scheme to sort survey software according to major differences and to support the reader in his or her assessment of features with regard to the survey data life cycle or online survey process.

The main focus of survey software development in the past could be seen in reducing the overall project time, including the resources needed to program a survey, gather the data and produce a quick report. New features make questionnaire programming faster by providing new question types, presets, a fast-responding user interface, question imports and scripting capabilities. They speed up the steps after data collection by providing ready-to-use reporting tools. In scholarly publications, one often reads that such enhancements have made it easy for nearly everyone to conduct surveys over the Internet, while making it hard to separate the wheat from the chaff: many small 'quick-and-dirty' surveys do not conform to the simplest rules of survey methodology (e.g. sampling procedures) and survey

craftsmanship (e.g. unambiguous question wording). The data quality of such undertakings is questionable and may have a negative effect on the perceived value of surveys to the public. Ethical issues such as fully informed consent also happen to be neglected or forgotten in such quick undertakings. Survey software companies could guide researchers by providing links to ethical guidelines and by including standard privacy statements and informed consent agreements as templates. Responsible survey software companies already provide standard presets, which result in a working survey that is based on methodological knowledge. For reasons of quality assurance, future developments should broaden pretesting and documentation capabilities of survey software. Several standards are available and await implementation, such as the already mentioned AAPOR standard definitions, but others are also promising. For example, the Data Documentation Initiative (DDI, see http://www.ddialliance.org/) has gained momentum in project documentation and archives worldwide.

An often-used critique against online surveys is the need for an Internet connection and the ability to use this technology. In a broader sense, this also applies to the accessibility of online surveys. Many survey software products do not conform even slightly to accessibility guidelines or the corresponding laws. During tests with visually impaired people who used screen readers, it became apparent that some surveys are equivalent to a blank sheet of paper. Here, a major challenge is that these implementations made heavy use of tables for layout purposes instead of using techniques that are compliant with accessibility standards. In the past, it was necessary to use table layouts to reach a similar visual appearance in different browsers. As a negative side effect, table layouts impose a barrier to visually impaired users. Adding to this problem, most products do not produce HTML code that conforms to the code specifications given by the W3C consortium, which means that the survey web pages do not validate. Although every reasonable vendor will claim that the survey pages are thoroughly tested in several browsers and with different versions, the lack of conformity to the formal standard makes this hard to check (see http://validator.w3.org/docs/why.html for the importance of validation). Fortunately, it is possible to program an accessible questionnaire with several of the advanced software packages, and some off-the-shelf products have made it part of their standard feature set as well.

A large development is the integration of other technologies and the convergence of different modes into one survey suite. Clearly, mixed-mode, multi-language approaches have gained ground and are expanding. Regardless of how a response is collected – whether it is a paper questionnaire, speech via a landline number or a mobile phone, a web survey via a computer or TV – all responses will be directed into one processing line. The integration of other technologies not only covers new ways of communication but also accommodates new data sources. With GPS (global positioning system) or IP resolution to street level, geographic information could automatically be added to survey data and respondents could be tracked over a period of time. Medical appliances built into clothes or wearables (e.g. fitness trackers) may be used to detect biomarkers (e.g. environmental cues such as smoke) and collect various health-related data such as heart rate, respiration rate, insulin deficiency, etc. This data could be transmitted to the researcher in real time as mobile connections become cheaper. With smartphones widely available, studies are conducted that ask respondents several questions every hour (referred to as experience sampling and event sampling). Overall, a vast new amount of possible data collection opportunities towards the 'transparent human being' arise, and with them new challenges for an ethical code of conduct.

ACKNOWLEDGEMENTS

Preparations for this work reach back into 2003 when I examined survey software solutions in order to offer consultation services to organizations on their online survey projects. During the WebSM project (2003–2005) and beyond, discussions about having the best software features continued (e.g. Kaczmirek, 2006). I would like to acknowledge the help and professional support of the following people: Wolfgang Bandilla, Michael Bosnjak, Gina-Qian Cheung, Christoph Constien, Mick P. Couper, Sarah Heinz, Sandra Ludwig, Katja Lozar Manfreda, Wolfgang Neubarth, Olaf Thiele, Nicole Schulze and Vasja Vehovar.

REFERENCES

American Association for Public Opinion Research (AAPOR). (2015) *Standard Definitions: Final Dispositions of Case Codes and Outcome Rates for Surveys*. 8th edn. AAPOR.

Berzelak, J., Lozar Manfreda, K. and Vehovar, V. (2006) 'Software Tools for Web Surveys: The More You Pay, The More You Get'. Paper presented at the Applied Statistics International Conference, Ribno (Bled), Slovenia.

Callegaro, M., Lozar Manfreda, K. and Vehovar, V. (2015) *Web Survey Methodology*. London: Sage Publications.

Čehovin, G. and Vehovar, V. (2012) *WebSM Study: Speed and Efficiency of Online Survey Tools* (technical report). Ljubljana, Slovenia: WebSM.

Converse, J.M. and Presser, S. (1986) *Survey Questions: Handcrafting the Standardized Questionnaire*. Newbury Park, CA: Sage University Paper.

Couper, M.P. (2005) 'Technology Trends in Survey Data Collection', *Social Science Computer Review*, 23: 486–501.

Couper, M.P. (2008) *Designing Effective Web Surveys*. Cambridge: Cambridge University Press.

Crawford, S. (2002) 'Evaluation of Web Survey Data Collection Systems', *Field Methods*, 14: 349–63.

Crawford, S. (2006) 'The Social Science Web Survey System: Moving from 2.0 to 3.0'. Paper presented at the International Field Directors and Technologies Conference (IFD&TC), May 21–24, Montréal, Canada.

Diekmann, A. (1998) *Empirische Sozialforschung [Empirical Social Research]*. Hamburg: Rowohlt.

Dillman, D.A., Smyth, J.D. and Christian, L.M. (2014). *Internet, Phone, Mail, and Mixed-Mode Surveys: The Tailored Design Method*. New York, NY: John Wiley & Sons.

European Parliament and Council (1995) *Directive 95/46/EC on the Protection of Individuals with Regard to the Processing of Personal Data and on the Free Movement of Such Data*. Retrieved 3 June 2007 from http://eur-lex.europa.eu/LexUriServ/LexUriServ.do?uri=CELEX:31995L0046:EN:HTML

Evans, J.R. and Mathur, A. (2005) 'The Value of Online Surveys', *Internet Research*, 15(2): 195–219.

Foddy, W. (1993) *Constructing Questions for Interviews and Questionnaires: Theory and Practice in Social Research*. Cambridge: Cambridge University Press.

Heinen, B.A., Meiman, E., Fien-Helfman, D.A. Ayine, S.K. and Khan, A.A. (2009). *Survey Software Evaluation*. (ARI Contractor Report 2009–01). United States Army Research Institute for the Behavioral and Social Sciences. Retrieved 8 August 2016 from www.dtic.mil/cgi-bin/GetTRDoc?AD=ADA495855

Hewson, C., Vogel, C. and Laurent, D. (2016). *Internet Research Methods*. London: Sage Publications.

Inter-University Consortium for Political and Social Research (ICPSR). (2012). *Guide to Social Science Data Preparation and Archiving: Best Practice Throughout the Data Life Cycle*. 5th edn. Ann Arbor, MI: ICPSR.

ISO 20252:2006–04 *Market, Opinion and Social Research: Vocabulary and Service Requirements*. Berlin: Beuth.

Kaczmirek, L. (2006) 'What software should I use? What are the right questions to be asked?' International Field Directors and Technologies Conference (IFD&TC), May 21–24, Montréal, Canada.

Macer, T. (2014). 'Online Panel Software'. In M. Callegaro, R. Baker, J. Bethlehem, A.S. Göritz, J.A. Krosnick and P.L. Lavrakas (eds.), *Online Panel Research. A Data Quality Perspective*. Chichester, UK: John Wiley & Sons, pp. 413–40.

NEON, Arbeitsgruppe im BVM Berufsverband Deutscher Marktund Sozialforscher e.V. (2003) *Anforderungen an Online-Umfrage-Software [Demands on Online Survey Software]*. Berlin: BVM. Retrieved 8 August 2016 from http://bvm.org/fileadmin/pdf/Recht_Berufskodizes/Checklisten/CL_2003_Online_Umfrage_Software.pdf

Peytchev, A. and Crawford, S. (2005) 'A Typology of Real-Time Validations in Web-Based Surveys', *Social Science Computer Review*, 23: 235–49.

Pointer, R. (2010). *The Handbook of Online and Social Media Research. Tools and Techniques for Market Researchers*. Chichester, UK: John Wiley & Sons.

Schnell, R., Hill, P.B. and Esser, E. (1995) *Methoden der empirischen Sozialforschung [Methods of the Empirical Social Research]*. Munich: Oldenburg Verlag.

Thiele, O. and Kaczmirek, L. (2010) 'Security and Data Protection: Collection, Storage, and Feedback in Internet Research'. In S.D. Gosling and J.A. Johnson (eds.), *Advanced Methods for Behavioral Research on the Internet*. Washington, DC: American Psychological Association., pp. 235–53.

Tourangeau, R., Conrad, G.C. and Couper, M.P. (2013). *The Science of Web Surveys*. Oxford: Oxford University Press.

UK Government (1998) *Data Protection Act 1998*. Retrieved 8 August 2016 from http://www.legislation.gov.uk/ukpga/1998/29/contents

Vehovar, V., Koren, G., Lozar Manfreda, K. and Berzelak, J. (2005) 'What Is Important When Choosing Web Survey Software'. Paper presented at the ESF Workshop on Web Surveys, Dubrovnik, Croatia.

Villar, A., Callegaro, M. and Yang, Y. (2013) 'Where Am I? A Meta-Analysis of Experiments on the Effects of Progress Indicators for Web Surveys', *Social Science Computer Review*, 31: 744–62.

Zukerberg, A. (2006) 'Evaluating Off The Shelf Internet Survey Tools'. Paper presented at the International Field Director's and Technologies Conference (IFD & TC), May 21–24, Montréal, Canada.

FURTHER READING

Few publications focus on online survey software as such and they are covered in the literature overview in this chapter. Interested readers should broaden their search to the design of online surveys in general (see elsewhere in this volume; Dillman *et al.*, 2014; Tourangeau *et al.*, 2013; Couper, 2008; ISO 20252:2006–04). All major design aspects can be reflected in software and should be considered before choosing a product.

INTERNET RESOURCES

AAPOR Standards and Best Practices (http://www.aapor.org/Standards-Ethics. aspx). Useful documents on topics including ethical guidelines, codes of conduct, disclosure FAQ, and standard definitions for response rates and disposition codes, among others.

Exploring Online Research Methods (http://www.restore.ac.uk/orm/). 'An online [free] research methods training programme for the social science community'.

Variable and question bank at the UK Data Service (http://discover.ukdataservice.ac.uk/variables). Examples of specific research questions within their administered context, information on surveys and questionnaire development.

WebSM, Web Survey Methodology Site (http://websm.org/). An information portal covering all aspects of online survey methodology. It includes a comprehensive bibliography search, software search, news, events and guides.

## 13

Improving the Effectiveness of Online Data Collection by Mixing Survey Modes

Don A. Dillman, Feng Hao and Morgan M. Millar

Survey research is trending toward greater use of online data collection, utilizing email as a means of requesting response to web questionnaires, and yet nearly twenty years after efforts to collect data over the Internet began in earnest, this has still not become an acceptable means for surveying the general public. Instead, surveyors who prefer online methods are far more likely to be conducting mixed-mode surveys, whereby two or more modes are used to contact and/or collect responses to questionnaires.

Online surveys of the general public using email contacts have proved especially difficult to conduct, in part because of the lack of access to adequate sample frames for drawing probability samples. In addition, although household Internet access is increasing – exceeding 80 percent in some countries – it is by no means universal (Mohorko *et al.*, 2013). Furthermore, even within households with Internet access, some adults still lack the skills and/or willingness to respond to questionnaires online (Robinson *et al.*, 2015).

Additionally, the practice of using emails to contact individuals with whom the surveyor has no prior relationship is actively discouraged by survey standards organizations in some countries, such as the United States.

Yet another barrier to conducting such surveys is that email messages requesting Internet survey responses are likely to elicit low response rates along with a considerable likelihood of nonresponse error, i.e. respondents being significantly different from nonrespondents (Dillman *et al.*, 2014). Those who answer such surveys are more likely than nonrespondents to have higher education, higher incomes, be younger, and live in multiple-person households (e.g. Rookey *et al.*, 2008).

Additionally, the greater reliance of some individuals on smartphones as their dominant, or even sole, means of being electronically connected, is producing formidable questionnaire design challenges. Many question formats traditionally used in other survey modes have structures that cannot easily be displayed on pocket-sized devices. However, changing those question formats without also revising them for other survey modes raises the likelihood of measurement differences.

A substantial amount of research now exists to provide guidance for mixing web with other modes of surveying. The purpose in this chapter is to utilize this research to offer design recommendations aimed at achieving higher quality survey results than those typically obtained by using a purely email contact approach to Internet data collection.

CONCEPTUAL BACKGROUND

The quality of sample survey results is affected by four sources of error – coverage error, sampling error, nonresponse error, and measurement error (Dillman *et al.*, 2014). Mixing multiple modes aims to improve survey quality by effectively reducing error from each of these sources.

In the mid-1990s, Internet surveys were envisioned as the likely solution for error concerns that were developing for random digit dialing (RDD) telephone interviews. Once the dominant mode for surveying the general public, RDD telephone interviewing began to encounter several problems. For one, the switch from landlines (the traditional sampling frame) to mobile (or cell) phones was beginning in earnest, creating formidable coverage problems. That trend has now progressed to the point that a majority of U.S. households (53 percent) are now cell phone only (Blumberg and Luke, 2015). Cell phone replacements also tend to be an individual, rather than household possession, making sampling more complex. Furthermore, phone numbers are now transportable, meaning that area codes are no longer reliable for pinpointing geographic location (Dillman *et al.*, 2014).

In addition to these logistical challenges associated with telephone interviewing, perhaps of greater concern is the dramatic cultural shift in how phones are used. Cell phones are now more often used for asynchronous email and text messages than two-way voice conversations. People rarely answer ringing phones, instead relying on voicemail to screen unwanted calls. Being asked to share personal information and opinions over a telephone call is no longer part of modern culture, unless previous communications have established that expectation. In short, the cold call to conduct a survey no longer fits well with societal norms, and therefore response rates to telephone interviews have declined greatly.

Faced with these challenges, surveyors initially viewed Internet surveys as a quick, less costly and more effective replacement to telephone interviewing. If people could be contacted by email and respond over the Internet, survey costs could be dramatically reduced. Now, 20 years later, the challenges of telephone interviewing have increased further, with response rates often falling into the single digits, but despite initial optimism, email-administered web surveys are not yet an adequate replacement.

The most fundamental error challenge for online-only surveys of the general public is coverage. There is no email sample frame for giving all households or individuals a known nonzero probability of being selected for data collection. Without this, results cannot be generalized to a defined survey population (Dillman *et al.*, 2014). Additionally, 15–20 percent of households do not have adequate Internet access for responding to web surveys.

Furthermore, response rates to web surveys using only email contacts are typically quite low (Dillman *et al.*, 2014). But, more importantly, the degree of nonresponse error, i.e. the extent to which survey respondents are different from nonrespondents, is considerable when responses are obtained only over the Internet (Smyth *et al.*, 2010; Messer and Dillman, 2011). This is partly the result of people lacking Internet access. It is also the case because this access and people's familiarity with using a computer are closely associated with their education, income, family status, and age.

However, when using multiple response modes – combining data collected from paper questionnaires, web questionnaires completed on a variety of devices, and/or telephone interviews – the possibility of measurement differences across modes is considerable. Thus, when combining multiple response modes, careful steps are needed to minimize measurement differences.

In this chapter, we provide recommendations for preparing, designing and implementing mixed-mode surveys with an online component. These recommendations aim to simultaneously reduce these sources of error while 'pushing' respondents toward online responding, in hopes of reducing survey costs while also maintaining survey quality.

Recommendation 1: Whenever possible, obtain multiple modes of contact information to provide additional means for improving survey coverage

In the past, when contact with individuals and households was only by landline telephone or postal addresses, organizations often assigned staff to keep that contact information current. The technology-dependent nature of modern society has changed this situation dramatically. There are considerably more ways to contact people these days. Many people now have individual rather than household addresses and phone numbers. In addition, individuals may have multiple phone numbers and telephones (e.g. personal and business, landline and cell), multiple email addresses, and in some cases multiple residences. Providing contact information to organizations is increasingly left up to the individuals themselves, who are allowed to choose their preferred form of contact.

When single-mode surveying dominated the landscape, survey sponsors often obtained

only a single form of contact information. This is no longer adequate for most surveys. When the updating of contact information – whether postal addresses, phone numbers, or email addresses – is left up to individuals, as it now tends to be, such changes often do not get made. This means information is commonly outdated. Additionally, individuals may make a deliberate effort to keep certain ways of contacting them available only to their closest friends and select acquaintances. Furthermore, as a result of various societal trends, contact information of all types change more frequently now than it did in previous decades (Dillman *et al.*, 2014), so having multiple forms of contact information increases the likelihood that surveyors will have at least one accurate method of getting in touch with sample members. The ability to contact more people in the sample reduces the potential for coverage error. Collecting multiple forms of contact information also has implications for improving response, as discussed further in the following recommendations.

Recommendation 2: Use Postal Mail for the first contact to help legitimize web surveys and provide an unconditional token cash incentive with the request for response

Administering web surveys of the general public is especially challenging because of the aforementioned lack of a sampling frame of email addresses. Those interested in surveying representative samples of U.S. households are increasingly considering the use of postal contacts because sampling frames of residential addresses now offer the best coverage of all contact methods, with more than 95 percent of household addresses included. Integrating an initial postal contact into a web survey therefore provides a means of utilizing an acceptable random sample of U.S. households. Similar procedures can also be used in certain European countries whose governments maintain comprehensive household registration lists.

Another common problem for many online surveys is that utilizing email messages as the sole means of contacting sample members has been rather ineffective as a means of obtaining acceptable levels of response. Response rates to email-only surveys are seldom more than 20 percent, even for specialized populations such as students, clients, or university faculty (Dillman *et al.*, 2014). Utilizing an initial postal invitation helps to overcome these low response rates in two important ways.

One way postal letters increase web response is by providing legitimacy to the survey. Trust has emerged as one of the most significant barriers to obtaining responses to online surveys (Dillman *et al.*, 2014). Sample members often know little or nothing about the organization sponsoring the survey, or whether that organization can be trusted. The high prevalence of spam and phishing scams sent via email has made many people wary of opening unsolicited messages from unknown sources. A postal letter printed on official stationery can provide an opportunity to demonstrate legitimacy through a more formal-looking, less-suspicious mode of contact. Its message can explain who is sponsoring a survey and its purpose. It should include the sponsor's mailing address, a telephone number for contacting the sponsor for additional information, as well as a website to encourage sample members to learn more about the organization and the survey.

The second reason why a postal contact can improve web survey response is that it provides a way for including an incentive for responding to the survey. The research literature is quite clear that a modest cash incentive of a few dollars or other local currency sent in advance is more effective for increasing response rates than payments promised to all who respond. In addition, cash incentives are much more effective than material incentives or contributions to charity. The likely reason for the considerable effectiveness

of pre-incentives for increasing web survey response in particular is that a significant barrier to responding to the postal request for an online response is the effort it takes to go from the letter to a computer and enter the required URL and password information, as explained in Dillman *et al.* (2014). Thus, an initial postal contact combines two important features that can contribute to obtaining improved response rates.

Recommendation 3: Where culturally appropriate, use a telephone contact to 'push' respondents to the web

Despite the difficulties now associated with RDD telephone interviewing, there are situations in which a phone call can be quite effective in encouraging individuals to respond to a survey over the Internet. A recent paper presented at an international conference on web data collection discussed the use of a telephone call to ask people to respond a survey conducted over the Internet in Iceland (Zajc *et al.*, 2015). The phone call was followed by a mail request, and this approach exhibited considerable success; 49 percent of the contacted households responded over the web and an additional 8 percent by a follow-up mail questionnaire (Zajc *et al.*, 2015). About 95 percent of Icelandic households have Internet access, which is one of the highest coverage rates in the world. The authors also noted that Iceland is a relatively small and homogenous country, and telephone calls are not ignored nor are they as alienating as they now appear to be in larger, more heterogeneous countries. This approach of utilizing a telephone call at the outset of a survey may also work in other locations that do not have the same barriers present in the U.S.

An initial phone call may also be advantageous in surveys conducted internationally. When telephone interviewing first developed in the U.S., 'long-distance' calls were rare and expensive. Consequently, survey requests made by telephone demanded attention. Now that many Internet surveys are international, and the cost of international telephone calls is decreasing, incorporating an overseas telephone call may offer a similar advantage as a long-distance call once did by signaling importance and thus the legitimacy of an Internet survey.

This concept was evaluated in a survey of Chinese Environmental Movement Organizations for which telephone numbers and email addresses were available (Hao, 2014). The initial contact with the test organizations was made from the U.S. by the researcher, who was raised in China. After identifying himself, he explained the purpose of his call and asked to speak with a responsible person who could complete the survey. He confirmed the email addresses of these requested individuals, and then later that day he sent an email request with the URL and password needed for completing the survey. Follow-up contacts were then made by email, and if a response was not received, then by another telephone call. The follow-up telephone call was important because it

reminded people that there was a survey in their inbox waiting to be completed and legitimized its presence. The average middle-aged Chinese person, which probably describes individuals in charge of such organizations, seems more likely to complete daily communications via phone rather than email. A total of 35 percent of the 46 organizations responded after the initial telephone call and email follow-up, and response climbed to 70 percent after two more emails and the additional telephone reminder. The increase in response rate that occurred as a result of the telephone contacts is presented in Figure 13.1.

In this case, the use of the telephone made it possible to know that a real person was involved in conducting the survey, and that it was possible for the respondent to ask questions, both of which conveyed an overall sense that the survey was legitimate. One feature of combining telephone with email that makes it particularly useful is that these two modes of communication can be used in a timely way, something that would not have been feasible with postal mail.

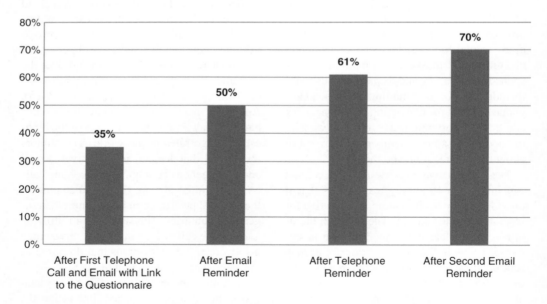

Figure 13.1   Cumulative response rate over time to survey of Chinese environmental movement organizations

Source: Hao, 2014.

Recommendation 4: When possible, use multiple modes of follow-up contacts to increase the likelihood that communications to sample units will be acknowledged and acted upon

Several decades of research have shown that one of the most powerful ways to increase survey response is to make multiple contacts with sample members. This practice has been routinely implemented for quite some time in all single-mode surveys; however, multiple contacts via the same mode may not always be as beneficial as they once were. Over the years, follow-up phone calls in RDD surveys have lost much of their effectiveness. The development of caller-identification, call-blocking, and the ability to use voicemail to screen calls have made it very difficult for surveyors to reach people over the phone. Similarly, emails are increasingly filtered, with many subject to deletion without the body of the message even being read, and now that fewer essential communications are sent by postal mail, letters are also more likely to be discarded without being opened.

However, depending on the household, some forms of communication are probably more likely to be attended to than others. Having multiple ways of contacting people provides more opportunities to get a survey request heard and acted upon. When one has no choice but to just send emails, follow-up emails are prone to being deleted without being read, just as the same letters in the same envelopes or repeated telephone calls are ignored when each is the only means of reaching people. A new and different form of contact than what has already been used will likely garner more attention, and may also help convey the legitimacy of the surveys in a way that email-only contacts cannot. Thus, obtaining multiple means of contact provides a basis for developing an effective implementation strategy.

Mail as a contact mode offers the potential for considerable variation in each contact; options include regular business stationery of various sizes and colors, postcards, larger envelopes (especially when paper questionnaires are being

sent), and even delivery by couriers like UPS or FedEx. Utilizing several variations seems more likely to get letters opened and attended to. A survey of PhD students conducted under considerable time pressure illustrates connecting this recommendation with other recommendations presented in this chapter (Millar, 2013).

In this study, an initial request to respond by web was sent by postal mail, along with a US$2 pre-incentive (Recommendation 2). No paper response alternative was mentioned at this time (Recommendation 6). An email follow-up to the initial postal letter was sent three days after the postal letter was sent to provide an electronic link for responding, followed by another email four days later. Eight days following that, a postal follow-up request was sent, which now offered the opportunity to respond by mail using an enclosed paper questionnaire. Then, a few days later, one additional email request was sent. Thus, three emails were intermingled with two postal contacts in support of trying to push as many respondents as possible to reply via the Internet, but also eventually providing a paper alternative for those who had not completed the web questionnaire. Two aspects of the results, shown in Figure 13.2, are particularly striking. One is the quick increase in response resulting from the first email message that followed the initial postal request. After that email, the response rate increased by 21 percentage points in only 10 hours, and 40 percentage points in five days. The second dramatic effect is that 32 percent of those who received the paper questionnaire and additional email actually responded, bringing the final survey response rate to 77 percent, which is extraordinarily high for a population of this nature. About half of the responses following the paper questionnaire mailing came by mail and the other half by web. These results demonstrate the great potential of intermingling multiple survey modes.

Supplementing mail or email contacts with telephone calls, or even text messages, introduces another way of varying contacts so that they are less repetitive, and as a consequence, less likely to be ignored. When telephone numbers are available, a phone call can be

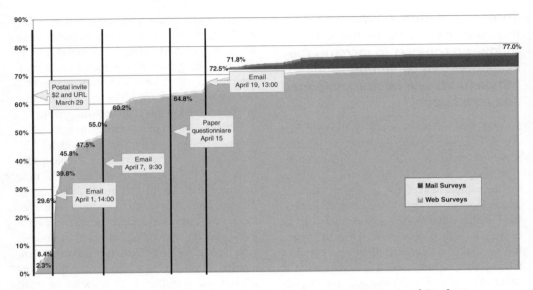

Figure 13.2   Cumulative response rate over time to the 2013 WSU Doctoral Student Experience Survey

Source: Adapted from Millar, 2013.

used later in a mail contact sequence to reach people in a different way. Much of the difficulty with telephone-only data collection in the U.S. stems from people's reluctance to talk with unannounced callers. So, while starting out with a phone call in the U.S. and most European countries is not as effective as in the past, sending either mail or email contacts, or both, before calling provides information that will legitimize a later voice call. Together, postal, email, and/or telephone contacts offer the potential to connect with individuals and households in a better and more thoughtful way than typically happened in the past with single-mode surveys.

Recommendation 5: Provide mail or telephone as an alternative mode of responding in order to improve representation of demographic groups that are unable and/or less likely to respond online

Although Internet access is becoming increasingly common, it has yet to become

universally available to all households; therefore, when conducting surveys of the general public, it is necessary to provide an alternative mode of responding for those unable to reply by web. Considerable research has made it clear that people who respond to Internet surveys tend to have different characteristics than those who respond to mail questionnaires or telephone interviews. As illustrated in Table 13.1, web respondents tend to be younger, have higher educational attainment, are more likely to be married, more likely to be employed, and have higher incomes (Rookey *et al.*, 2008; Smyth *et al.*, 2010; Messer and Dillman, 2011).

When utilizing postal contacts, a paper questionnaire can be sent to all households that have not responded to requests to answer an online questionnaire. In addition, telephone numbers can be matched with some addresses, and those households called with a request to be interviewed over the phone. Part of the effectiveness of offering an alternative response mode is to obtain answers to survey questions from those who do not have Internet access. Research has also shown that it

Table 13.1   Demographic differences between web and mail respondents in three studies

	Rookey et al., 2008		Smyth et al., 2010		Messer and Dillman, 2011	
	Web	Mail	Web	Mail	Web	Mail
Age (mean (x̄) or % ≤50)	x̄ = 52	x̄ =61	x̄ = 51	x̄ = 62	63%	49%
Education (% with college degree)	65%	40%	31%	14%	41%	35%
Marital status (% married)	73%	67%	74%	43%	63%	55%
Employment (% employed)	58%	38%	51%	35%	68%	59%
Income (% ≥ $50,000)	*	*	61%	31%	65%	56%

Note: * Income data not available for Rookey et al. 2008 study.

is effective in obtaining responses from households that do have Internet access (Smyth *et al.*, 2010), but for whatever reason – perhaps lack of computer skills or discomfort with sharing personal information online – do not want to participate in a web survey. These additional contacts are also likely to be effective, partly because they are simply an additional request that tries to accommodate the needs or proclivities of individual sample members.

Recommendation 6: Encourage online responses to the initial mail request by withholding alternative modes of responding until later in the data collection process

To obtain response rates to general public web surveys that are significantly higher than can now be obtained by RDD telephone interviewing or requesting web responses via email contacts, surveyors can implement Recommendation 2 while also *withholding* the opportunity to respond by mail or another mode, as discussed in Recommendation 5. This approach involves contacting sample members via postal mail and first asking that they complete an online questionnaire, without mentioning a paper questionnaire option as an alternative means of responding (Dillman *et al.*, 2014).

This strategy was tested multiple times between 2007 and 2012 in five general public studies conducted using postal addresses within a total of five U.S. states: Washington,

Idaho, Nebraska, Pennsylvania, and Alabama (Smyth *et al.*, 2010; Messer and Dillman, 2011; Messer, 2012; Edwards *et al.*, 2014). These studies were on a wide variety of topics, including community quality of life issues, impacts of the economic recession, water management issues, and preferences regarding energy production. Each questionnaire entailed responding to 90–140 individual items, which was estimated to take at least 20–25 minutes to complete.

All five surveys used random samples of residential addresses (without names) obtained from the U.S. Postal Service. Each of these studies relied solely on postal contacts throughout the research process. All included a US$4 or US$5 cash incentive with the first response request, and some employed a second cash incentive later in the implementation process.

Each study was comprised of multiple experimental treatment groups that varied in terms of mode(s) of response requested and other details. However, all had at least one treatment in which the postal contacts initially asked for responses to an online questionnaire, and then in later contacts also provided an opportunity to respond via a paper questionnaire if the household was unable or unwilling to complete a web questionnaire. This 'web-push' strategy, in which web response is first offered, followed by a later option of responding by mail, produced response rates that ranged from 31 percent to 55 percent, with a mean of 43 percent. These web-push response rates are much higher than what is

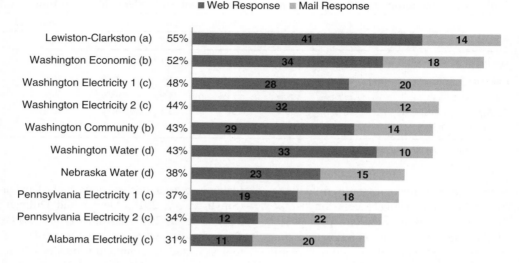

Figure 13.3   Response rates by mode, for ten treatments across five studies using the 'web-push' approach (overall combined response rates in parentheses)

Sources: (a) Smyth *et al.,* 2010; (b) Messer *et al.,* 2011; (c) Messer, 2012; (d) Edwards *et al.,* 2014.

possible using only email contacts requesting online responses or via telephone interviews. The web-push design also resulted on average in about 60 percent of the responses being submitted over the Internet, with the remainder coming by mail after later postal contacts. Figure 13.3 illustrates the overall response rates, plus the response percentage obtained by each mode, within each of the web-push treatments used within all five studies.

One of these studies included an experimental test of a US$5 cash incentive. Results demonstrated that this incentive is quite effective not only for increasing overall response, but also for increasing the proportion of responses provided by web. On the other hand, no incentive produced only 13 percent online response, and inclusion of US$5 produced a 31 percent web response. The treatment group that received the incentive attained a total response rate of 46 percent, based on an additional 15 percent of the household sample responding by mail. This total was much higher than the combined web plus mail total of 26 percent that responded to the non-incentive group (Messer and Dillman,

2011). Thus, cash incentives not only benefit overall response rates, but also ease the burden of online responses specifically, as mentioned under Recommendation 2.

When interpreting these results and considering their implications, it is important to recognize that the response rates obtained by the web-push method were lower than those obtained by comparable treatment groups that only requested responses to a paper questionnaire ('mail-only'). On average, the mail-only approach obtained response rates about ten percentage points higher (53 percent versus 43 percent) than the web-push method, which included a late mail response option. It is reasonable, therefore, to ask why one does not simply use mail alone and not withhold the sending of a paper questionnaire.

Surveyors may have a variety of reasons for preferring online data collection. One justification for the web-push approach is that responses start coming in more quickly than mail responses. Online responses are submitted instantaneously after respondents complete them, whereas paper questionnaires take a few days to be returned through postal mail. Similarly, web data collection allows researchers to begin analyzing data almost instantly after responses are submitted, whereas paper responses must be converted into an analyzable format through the data entry process, which can take considerable time and substantial resources, depending upon the staff available for such tasks.

A second commonly used reason for pushing responses to the web is the expectation that there will be less item nonresponse than occurs with paper questionnaires. Indeed, an analysis of the first three studies referenced earlier showed that the rate of item nonresponse for web questionnaires ranged from 2.7 to 6.1 percent, while mail item nonresponse ranged from 6.2 to 11.6 percent. However, when the combination of all web-push group responses (web plus mail) was compared to the mail-only total for these studies, the overall item nonresponse rates were virtually the same: 3.6 percent to 8.0 percent for push-to-web and 4.2 to 8.1 percent for mail-only treatment groups (Messer *et al.*, 2012). The likely explanation for the lack of overall difference in item nonresponse rates between the web-push treatments and the mail-only treatments is that early respondents, regardless of mode, are more conscientious or capable of responding than those who wait until late in the data collection process to respond. Since paper questionnaires were used in both treatment groups for picking up late respondents, the overall quality of responses did not differ significantly across the web-push versus mail-only data collection treatments in these particular studies.

Another reason many surveyors prefer web over mail is the expectation that it might decrease costs of data collection. Certainly costs will be lower when surveyors are only using emails to contact sample members, but, as noted earlier, this strategy will probably not produce high response rates. In the studies examining the web-push approach, both web and then later paper responses were elicited using postal mailings, which has different implications for overall cost differences across modes. A meticulous analysis of all costs for two studies conducted in Washington showed that the cost per respondent was actually significantly higher for the web-push method than for mail-only (Messer and Dillman, 2011). The reason for this finding is simply the lower number of responses across which costs were distributed; the mailing costs for the different treatments were about the same. Although gathering web responses saved in terms of the costs of return postage, printing of paper questionnaires, and performing data entry from paper questionnaires, these savings were partially negated by the organizational costs of setting up and staffing the web data collection process.

Overall, evidence comparing web-push versus postal mail data collection within the general public suggest that at this point in time, the combination of web followed by mail data collection may not necessarily be more cost effective than mail-only surveys. However, we anticipate that the costs for the web-push method will likely decrease if, as we expect, it becomes more effective in future years. One indication of the future cost effectiveness of pushing online responses comes from the National Science Foundation's National Survey of College Graduates, a nationwide sample of individuals with four-year college degrees (Finamore and Dillman, 2013). An experiment was designed to push respondents in one of three different directions at the outset of the study. One group of sampled individuals was first offered web response, followed by mail, and then telephone. A second group received a request to respond by mail first, followed by web, and then telephone. The third group was first called by telephone, and then later given the offer of web, and finally mail. The final response rates to these three groups were quite similar, ranging from 75 to 77 percent, with each mode contributing significantly to these final response rates. Within all three treatments, the first-offered mode obtained the highest response rate: 42 percent for the telephone-first group, 43 percent for the web-first group, and 47 percent for the mail-first group. However, the cost per respondent varied dramatically from only US$48 for the web-first treatment to US$66 for mail-first, and US$75 for telephone-first. This study seems particularly useful for highlighting the potential that a web-push strategy has for eventually becoming more cost-effective than mail-only surveys. The target population of this study, the college educated, is a group that is very likely to use the Internet. Within this sub-population, there is relatively little hesitation about responding to web surveys. Although the public at large may not have yet reached this level of comfort with the Internet, we consider the results of this study an indicator of what may happen to survey costs as the use of the Internet continues to spread into nearly everyone's life and as responding to web surveys becomes increasingly established and accepted.

Recommendation 7: Avoid providing a choice of mail or web responses in the initial mail contact unless a quick email follow-up is made to support an online response

Offering a choice of survey response modes when contacting sample units with a request to respond to a survey might seem like a reasonable way of increasing response rates; however, it is not effective if one's interest is in increasing the proportion of online responses.

In a survey of a sample of household addresses, Smyth *et al.* (2010) found that offering a simultaneous choice of responding to an enclosed paper questionnaire or online resulted in a response rate of 63 percent of households; however, 80 percent of those responses came by mail. The likely reason that the vast majority responded by paper was the convenience of not having to switch to a computer and transfer access and password information to the web. Giving a choice, therefore, does not seem to favor receiving online returns. This study also

found that simply asking people to respond to an enclosed paper questionnaire (with no web option) obtained a response rate of 71 percent, significantly higher than when a choice of modes was offered, suggesting that offering a choice can have a negative response effect.

A later meta-analysis of multiple studies examining the effect of simultaneously offering a choice of responding by web or mail showed that in only one of 19 cases did the choice option obtain a higher response rate than only offering mail response (Medway and Fulton, 2012). Even among a population of college students, a technologically savvy group whose members all had Internet access, offering a choice of either mode did not fare better than simply offering mail response (Millar and Dillman, 2011). The reason why offering a choice seems to have a negative impact on response, as explained in Millar and Dillman (2011), may be that offering a choice makes the response task more complex, as shown in decision-making research by Schwartz (2004). A lower response may also happen because providing a choice could encourage a delay in decision-making that ultimately leads to not following through with responding.

A second study discussed by Millar and Dillman (2011) was developed from the perspective that a timely contact by the other mode in which people have the option of responding might overcome the negative effects of choice. Mail contacts were sent to samples of undergraduate students in which they were given the choice of responding online or by an enclosed paper questionnaire. One treatment received a total of five mail contacts requesting a response. The other treatment group received the same number of contacts. However, two of the postal contacts were replaced with email messages, one of which was sent three days after the original mailing. The email message explained that it was sent as an effort to make it 'easier to respond' by providing an electronic link to the survey web page. This treatment group obtained a significantly higher response rate than the group using only postal contacts (47 percent versus 41 percent, respectively). In addition, it received a significantly higher percentage of responses via the online questionnaire (54 percent versus 41 percent). The 47 percent response rate was also higher than that of a treatment group using only mail for both contacts and response (44 percent), as well as a web-only response group (42 percent), which substituted email messages for two of the mail contacts. It is clear from this experiment that being able to make contacts by both mail and email pays off for improving overall response as well as the proportion of online responses received.

Recommendation 8: Use unified mode construction for writing and presenting survey questions to respondents

Recommendations 1–7 are focused on improving coverage and response by mixing contact modes and providing alternative modes for asking and answering questions. Recommendation 8 focuses on a potential downside of using more than one response mode: the possibility of differences in measurement being obtained across multiple response modes.

Traditionally, when surveying was dominated by asking questions in only one survey mode (typically in-person or telephone interviews) questions were written to fit the mode, regardless of how that format would work in other modes (Dillman and Christian, 2005). Thus, show-cards were given to in-person respondents to help them understand long questions with many response choices. Over the telephone, an emphasis was placed on shortening questions to use fewer words and categories because show-cards could not be used to assist the respondent. For both types of interviews, answer categories were spoken as part of the question, and certain categories such as 'no opinion' or 'refusal' were hidden from the respondent. Mail questionnaires

could not hide categories, and so they were either presented to respondents or not, and the available response choices were not typically included in the question itself, but simply listed after the question. Web surveying has presented new alternatives, including radio buttons for 'choose one' answers and HTML boxes for questions that allow more than one choice to be selected, a format seldom used in interviews. Other web survey options, such as dropdown menus, graphical displays, fill-ins from previous answers, and other changes have been facilitated by technological developments that could not be done in any other mode.

It should not be surprising that different answers are often obtained as a result of questions being optimized for a particular mode. In the early 2000s, it became apparent at the U.S. Census Bureau that questions asked in the Decennial Census were being fitted to the mode, regardless of consequences for other modes. A 120-page report was produced showing that these question format variations result in measurement differences across modes, and it therefore proposed 21 guidelines for creating the same stimuli across survey modes in order to minimize measurement differences (Martin *et al.*, 2007).

There are two distinct issues involved in being able to achieve unified question construction (using the same question format) across survey modes. One is question structure and the other is the specific wording of questions. One example, mentioned earlier, is to either include non-substantive responses such as 'don't know' or 'prefer not to answer' as visible choices to all respondents, rather than doing that differently by mode.

Another example, and one that is considerably more problematic to address, is illustrated by comparing 'check-all-that-apply' questions to 'forced-choice' formats. An example of a check-all question (a format commonly used in web surveys) is, 'Which of the following is a reason that you bought the home in which you now live? Please check all that apply'. The question might be followed by 5–10 possible answers. To use that same structure in a telephone interview would be awkward and difficult to answer. Consequently, that sort of question is asked in a forced-choice format, i.e. individually reading each category and asking, 'Is <insert> a reason or not a reason that you bought your current home?'. The web version of the question is strongly encouraged by the availability of the HTML answer box format, while the telephone version is strongly encouraged by being able to structure the question in an easier-to-answer way. However, allowing such differences across two modes will undoubtedly result in different patterns of responses, and research illustrates that fewer choices will be marked on the web check-all format than in the telephone forced-choice format (Smyth *et al.*, 2008). Alternatively, using unified mode construction, i.e. using the same format in both telephone and web, has been shown to result in respondents providing equivalent answers.

Another source of measurement differences across modes is variation in the visual layouts of questions. Responses (and the lack of responses) are affected by the use of graphics, numbers, and symbols. These features are often more powerful than words in getting people to navigate correctly through web and mail surveys, and may also affect respondents' choice of answer categories. For example, research shows that the use of arrows, bold type, how answer categories are labeled, the size of answer spaces, the amount of space between scalar categories, the choice of linear versus multi-column layout of scale categories, and many other display issues influence answers (Christian and Dillman, 2004).

One of the most important findings from this research is that when wording and visual layouts are kept about the same, as can be done for mail and web surveys, measurement differences can be kept to a minimum. Thus, from a practical standpoint, combining mail and web responses does not raise major measurement concerns unless different question structures are used for the same items.

Consequently, when web-push methods that rely on mail response follow-up are used, the gains in coverage and response will not be mitigated by differences in measurement, although surveyors may need to carefully consider how the increasing use of smartphones may change the visual display of web surveys (see later).

It may not be possible to adequately reduce mode differences in measurement when telephone interviewing is used as a follow-up to web. For example, telephone responses tend to exhibit greater social desirability and acquiescence (e.g. Dillman *et al.*, 2014) than is the case for the web. In addition, it has been shown that telephone respondents tend to give more positive and extreme responses on opinion scales than web respondents, including on items that are likely to exhibit little or no social desirability (Christian *et al.*, 2008).

Recommendation 9: Make it possible to respond online via a smartphone, but avoid 'pushing' respondents to do so

Nearly two-thirds of U.S. adults now own smartphones (Pew Research Center, 2015a), and that number will undoubtedly continue to grow. For some, smartphones are only one of multiple devices they possess (Barlas *et al.*, 2015), but for others, they are the only device used for sending and receiving messages, whether by text or email, and accessing the web. The rapid adoption of smartphones is perhaps the newest major issue that survey research must contend with because they are changing the ways in which people connect with and communicate through the Internet. This has several implications for survey research.

First is the manner in which people utilize their smartphones for emailing and Internet access. For those whose smartphone is their only source of web access, they are likely to perform a wide range of tasks on their phones. For those with multiple devices, their use of each can be situational. For example, when on-the-go, many people use their phones to quickly check email and make decisions on whether to delete or hold messages for further use when they get to a desktop or laptop computer. In addition, smartphones are often used in multi-tasking environments, such as when individuals are also attending meetings with other people, and even physically moving from one place to another. Surveyors would probably prefer that people not respond to their questions, which can be time consuming and require concentration, while their attention is focused elsewhere. We must also recognize, however, that these days many online tasks are commencing when people are on-the-go or multi-tasking.

The second major issue that smartphones present to surveyors has to do with the visual display of web questionnaires on these small devices. Smartphones are not, for the most part, questionnaire friendly. The manner in which websites are constructed is not always compatible with viewing on these small screens. Although screen size has crept upwards, it must remain small enough to allow for devices to fit into pockets or bags. This limits the visual features that can be incorporated into a web questionnaire. Providing answers to open-ended questions can also be quite difficult on a phone's small keyboard. Furthermore, each generation of mobile devices has a learning curve associated with its use, and some people stick with older models, or even feature phones, to avoid the cost and discomfort of adapting to new ways of receiving, accessing, and handling messages. This makes for a very diverse set of device platforms, as well as a wide range of skill and comfort levels among users, that surveyors must consider. Williams *et al.* (2015) reported in excess of 200 different screen designs of varying dimensions and with different viewable spaces, and Barlas *et al.* (2015) reported 221 unique screen resolutions in their web panel experimentation.

Survey researchers have noted numerous problems when respondents attempt to complete traditional question formats on mobile devices. For example, Sarraf *et al.* (2015) found that the common question format of the item-on-the left with answer categories horizontally displayed to the right and the four-point scale placed below it, resulted in early abandonment of the response process and a dramatic increase in missing responses. Other researchers have shown similar results when grid questions and other items placed in traditional web formats prevented effective completion of surveys on smartphones, unless a format optimized for smartphones was employed (Stern *et al.*, 2015; Williams *et al.*, 2015; Barlas *et al.*, 2015). A recent summary of differences between how people respond to smartphones versus other web formats has been presented by Couper, Antoun and Mavletova (in press). It is also apparent that evidence on some issues, for example the quality of answers to open-ended questions, is as yet inconclusive. Much research remains to be done on these topics as individuals work to integrate smartphones with their work and leisure patterns.

Given the difficulties of responding on phones, it seems unlikely that many people would *choose* to respond to a survey via a smartphone if a desktop, laptop, or tablet was also available to them. Indeed, a few years ago this appeared to be the case. In 2011, we attempted to encourage college students to respond to a web survey using their smartphones. Despite explicit encouragement to use mobile devices, we were only able to convince about 7 percent of respondents to use their phones, while the remainder opted to use a more traditional computer (Millar and Dillman, 2012).

However, there is reason to believe that circumstances are quickly changing. Among segments of the population we would expect to be heavily relying on smartphones, such as college students, the percentage who are responding to online surveys on mobile devices is growing. For example, Sarraf *et al.* (2015) reported that although in 2011 only 4 percent of respondents to the National

Survey of Student Engagement answered over smartphones, this percentage had increased to 13 percent by 2013, and was up to 27 percent in 2015. But this trend is not isolated to just the younger generation. Pew Research Center's American Trends Panel, a nationally representative, probability-based panel that is primarily web-based, reported that 26 percent of respondents completed Pew's most recent survey on a smartphone, and another 8 percent did so on a tablet (Pew Research Center, 2015b). Additionally, Barlas *et al.* (2015) reported that among respondents of the Gfk computer national probability panel, approximately 15 percent now use smartphones and 10 percent use tablets. Greater use of mobile phones for responding to surveys has also been noted in the Netherlands, Germany and other European countries (de Bruijne, 2015; Couper, Antoun and Mavletova, in press). At the same time, it has been consistently shown by many researchers that survey break-off rates are significantly higher for smartphones than for other types of web surveys.

Clearly, these pieces of evidence confirm what many web surveyors have recently recognized: at least some, if not a sizable portion, of respondents to web surveys will attempt to access and complete the questionnaire from their smartphone (Link *et al.*, 2014) – and we only expect this percentage to continue climbing as web content becomes increasingly compatible with mobile devices. It seems necessary, therefore, that surveyors design their web questionnaires in ways that are conducive to responding via mobile devices.

Many have begun proposing ways in which surveys should be designed differently for smartphones than for computers. To address the way in which many people use their phones on-the-go, researchers wanting to make surveys conducive to mobile responding are beginning to consider making questions and questionnaires simpler and shorter. To address visual display problems, survey websites need to be constructed in ways that ensure they will adequately display on multiple small screens. Some suggestions offered

by researchers to address these issues include simplification by removing graphics, logos, and certain response methods; asking more than one question per screen; using a unique URL in the invitation to avoid passwords; and texting invitations to respond, provided permission has been obtained (McGeeney, 2015). If questions are designed specifically for smartphones in these ways, this means that question structures, wordings, and visual layouts will be different than what is currently used in many established surveys, a challenge pointed out by Mistichelli *et al.* (2015) of the U.S. Census Bureau. Revising existing question formats involves changing the ways questions have been asked – in some cases for decades. If such changes are made, we must also consider the effects they may have on mixed-mode surveys because creating a common question stimulus across modes may become more challenging. It is clear, therefore, that optimizing surveys for smartphones will not be simple.

Given these challenges, at this point in time it seems advisable *not* to push individuals to smartphones as a preferred way of responding, especially if questions have to be presented differently than in the other modes in mixed-mode (and device) surveys. Indeed, it may be desirable to diplomatically discourage people from responding on smartphones if a survey is long or has complex questions. Over time, though, it seems necessary to create question structures that will work on smartphones and consider mirroring these in other survey modes, just as initial designs needed for desktops and laptops, e.g. explicitly presenting 'don't know' and 'prefer not to answer' categories, were built into telephone interviews in order to keep the question stimulus the same. As mobile technology continues to advance and become more embedded in everyday life, trends in how surveys are done will continue to change, and researchers need to keep thinking ahead about ways in which surveys can be compatible with increasingly fast-paced, technologically reliant, and multi-tasking lifestyles that now exist in most industrialized countries, while recognizing that differences in smartphone usage across such countries continues to vary widely (Metzler and Fuchs, 2014).

CONCLUSION

Online surveys with responses being provided from multiple devices – desktops, laptops, tablets, and smartphones – have become a permanent part of our survey environment, and yet obtaining responses from representative samples of the general public remains difficult, especially when surveyors want to make the survey data collection process entirely electronic. Such attempts face formidable barriers, ranging from Internet coverage limitations and an inability to obtain adequate email samples to low response rates that are not representative of the survey population.

We have lost RDD telephone surveys as the accepted workhorse for household surveys. They are no longer effective for reasons of coverage as well as response. A majority of households no longer have landlines, but are dependent upon cell phones, possessed mostly by individuals rather than the household unit. Some households have no Internet access; others have Internet access, but some members of the household lack Internet skills or simply prefer not to use it. In some households, people who use computers have moved from desktops and laptops to mostly relying upon tablets and smartphones. These devices are used nearly everywhere that the individual goes, and some of the things the individual does are more conducive to completing surveys than others.

A mixed-mode approach to obtaining and perhaps pushing or nudging people to respond online to survey requests is a necessary response to the heterogeneity of the general public. The nine recommendations expressed in this chapter are aimed at increasing the likelihood of response by using multiple options to communicate response requests and providing multiple options for how answers to survey questions are offered.

The mixed-mode designs discussed here deal simultaneously with providing means of improving survey coverage and increasing the likelihood of people being contacted. The combinations of contact modes and response modes are aimed at achieving synergy that will increase the likelihood of individuals from all demographic groups responding to survey requests.

The fundamental survey design challenge we face is that we can be neither too far ahead, nor too far behind, of the people we wish to survey. Finding the optimal spot to be in is extraordinarily difficult because of the enormous heterogeneity that exists with regard to households and the ways available for communicating with them. Mixed-mode designs significantly increase our options for being able to find, contact, and obtain survey responses that are critical for understanding the attitudes and behaviors that now characterize our society.

REFERENCES

Barlas, Frances, Randall K. Thomas, and Patricia Graham. 2015. 'Mobility Enabled: Effects of Mobile Devices on Survey Response and Substantive measures'. Gfk Custom Research Presentation to the Federal Economic Statistics Advisory Committee, June 12.

Blumberg, Stephen J. and Julian V. Luke. 2015. 'Wireless Substitution: Early Release of Estimates from the National Health Interview Survey, July–December 2014'. Center for Disease Control. Available at http://www.cdc.gov/nchs/nhis/releases.htm (Accessed December 12, 2015).

Christian, Leah Melani and Don A. Dillman. 2004. 'The Influence of Graphical and Symbolic Language Manipulations on Responses to Self-Administered Questions', *Public Opinion Quarterly* 68(1): 58–81.

Christian, Leah Melani, Don A. Dillman, and Jolene D. Smyth. 2008. 'The Effects of Mode and Format on Answers to Scalar Questions in Telephone and Web Surveys'. In James Lepkowski, Clyde Tucker, J. Michael Brick, Edith de Leeuw, Lilli Japec, Paul J. Lavrakas, Michael W. Link, and Roberta L. Sangster (eds.), *Advances in Telephone Survey Methodology*. New York, NY: Wiley-Interscience. pp. 250–75.

Couper, Mick P., Christopher Antoun and Aigul Mavletova. In Press. 'Mobile Web Surveys: A Total Survey Error Perspective'. In Paul P. Biemer, Brad Edwards, Frauke Kreuter, Lars E. Lyberg, Clyde Tucker, Brady T. West, and Stephanie Eckman (eds.), *Total Survey Error in Practice*. Hoboken, NJ: John Wiley & Sons.

de Bruijne, Marika. 2015. *Designing Web Surveys for the Multi-Device Internet*. No.456 Center Dissertation Series, Center for Economic Research, Tilburg University, The Netherlands.

Dillman, Don A. and Leah Melani Christian. 2005. 'Survey Mode as a Source of Instability across Surveys', *Field Methods* 17(1): 30–52.

Dillman, Don A., Jolene D. Smyth, and Leah Melani Christian. 2014. *Internet, Phone, Mail and Mixed-Mode Surveys: The Tailored Design Method*. 4th edn. Hoboken, NJ: John Wiley & Sons.

Edwards, Michelle L., Don A. Dillman and Jolene D. Smyth. 2014. 'An Experimental Test of the Effects of Survey Sponsorship on Internet and Mail Survey Response', *Public Opinion Quarterly* 78(3): 734–50.

Finamore, John and Don A. Dillman. 2013. 'How Mode Sequence Affects Responses by Internet, Mail and Telephone in the National Survey of College Graduates'. Presentation to European Survey Research Association, Ljubljana, Slovenia, July 18.

Hao, Feng. 2014. 'A survey of Environmental Movement Organizations in China'. Unpublished data. Social and Economic Sciences Research Center, Washington State University, Pullman, WA.

Link, Michael W., Joe Murphy, Michael F. Schober, Trent D. Buskirk, Jennifer Hunter Childs, and Casey Langer Tesfaye. 2014. 'Mobile Technologies for Conducting, Augmenting and Potentially Replacing Surveys: Report of the AAPOR Task Force on Emerging Technologies in Public Opinion Research.' American Association for Public Opinion Research (AAPOR). Available at: http://www.aapor.org/AAPOR_Main/media/MainSiteFiles/REVISED_Mobile_Technology_Report_Final_revised10June14.pdf (Accessed July 21, 2016)

Martin, Elizabeth, Jennifer Hunter Childs, Theresa DeMaio, Joan Hill, Courtney Reiser, Eleanor Gerber, Kathleen Styles, and Don Dillman. 2007. 'Guidelines for Designing Questionnaires for Administration in Different Modes'. U.S. Census Bureau, Washington DC.

McGeeney, Kyley, 2015. 'Tips for Creating Web Surveys for Completion on a Mobile Device'. Pew Research Center, June 11.

Medway, Rebecca and Jenna Fulton. 2012. 'When More Gets You Less: A Meta-Analysis of the Effect of Concurrent Web Options on Mail Survey Response Rates'. *Public Opinion Quarterly* 76(4): 733–46.

Messer, Benjamin L. 2012. 'Pushing Households to the Web: Results from Web+mail Experiments Using Address Based Samples of the General Public and Mail Contact Procedures'. PhD Dissertation. Washington State University, Pullman, WA.

Messer, Benjamin L. and Don A. Dillman. 2011. 'Surveying the General Public Over the Internet Using Address-Based Sampling and Mail Contact Procedures.' *Public Opinion Quarterly* 75(3): 429–57.

Messer, Benjamin L., Michelle L. Edwards, and Don A. Dillman. (2012). 'Determinants of Web & Mail Item Nonresponse in Address-Based Samples of the General Public', *Survey Practice*, April. Available at http://www.surveypractice.org/index.php/SurveyPractice/issue/view/17 (Accessed July 21, 2016)

Metzler, Anke and Fuchs, Marek. 2014. 'Coverage Error in Mobile Web Surveys across European Countries'. Paper presented at the Internet Survey Methodology Workshop, Bozen-Bolzano, Italy, December 1–3.

Millar, Morgan. M. 2013. 'Determining whether Research is Interdisciplinary: An Analysis of New Indicators' (Technical Report 13–049). Social and Economic Sciences Research Center, Washington State University, Pullman, WA.

Millar, Morgan M. and Don A. Dillman. 2011. 'Improving Response to Web and Mixed-Mode Surveys'. *Public Opinion Quarterly* 75 (2): 249–69.

Millar, Morgan M. and Don A. Dillman. 2012. 'Encouraging Survey Response via Smartphones: Effects on Respondents' Use of Mobile Devices and Survey Response Rates'. *Survey Practice* 5(4). http://www.surveypractice.org/index.php/SurveyPractice/issue/view/17 (Accessed July 21, 2016)

Mistichelli, Joe, Glenn Eanes and Rachel Horwitz. 2015. Centurion: Internet Data Collection and Responsive Design. Presentation to Federal Economic Statistics Advisory Committee, June 12.

Mohorko, Anja, Edith de Leeuw, and Joop Hox. 2013. 'Internet Coverage and Coverage Bias in Europe: Developments across Countries and Over Time'. *Journal of Official Statistics* 29 (4): 609–22.

Pew Research Center. 2015a. 'The Smartphone Difference.' Available at http://www.pewInternet.org/2015/04/01/us-smartphone-use-in-2015/ (Accessed November 16, 2015)

Pew Research Center. 2015b. 'Building Pew Research Center's American Trends Panel'. Available at http://www.pewresearch.org/2015/04/08/building-pew-research-centers-american-trends-panel/ (Accessed November 15, 2015)

Robinson, Laura, Shelia R. Cotten, Hiroshi Ono, Anabel Quan-Haase, Gustavo Mesch, Wenhong Chen, Jeremy Schulz, Timothy M. Hale, and Michael J. Stern. 2015. 'Digital Inequalities and Why They Matter', *Information, Communication & Society* 18(5): 569–82.

Rookey, Bryan D., Steve Hanway, and Don A. Dillman, 2008. 'Does a Probability-Based Household Panel Benefit from Assignment to Postal Response as an Alternative to Internet-only?', *Public Opinion Quarterly.* 72(5): 962–84.

Sarraf, Shimon, Jennifer Brooks, and James S. Cole. 2015. 'What is the Impact of Smartphone Optimization on Long Surveys?' Presentation to American Association for Public Opinion Research Annual Conference, Hollywood, FL, May 16.

Schwartz, Barry. 2004. *The Paradox of Choice: Why More is Less.* New York, NY: Harper-Collins.

Smyth, Jolene D., Leah Melani Christian, and Don A. Dillman. 2008. 'Does "Yes or No" on the Telephone Mean the Same as Check-All-That-Apply on the Web?' *Public Opinion Quarterly* 72(1): 103–11.

Smyth, Jolene D., Don A. Dillman, Leah Melani Christian, and Allison C. O'Neill. 2010. 'Using the Internet to Survey Small Towns and Communities: Limitations and Possibilities in the Early 21st Century'. *American Behavioral Scientist* 53: 1423–48.

Stern, Michael J., David Sterrett, Ipek Bilgen, Ethan Rajker, Gwendolyn Rugg, and Jiwon Baek. 2015. 'The Effects of Grids on Web Surveys Completed with Mobile Devices'. Presentation to American Association for Public Opinion Research Annual Conference, Hollywood, FL, May 15.

Williams, Douglas, Aaron Maitland, Andrew Mercer, and Roger Tourangeau. 2015. 'The Impact of Screen Size on Data Quality'. Presentation to American Association for Public Opinion Research Annual Conference, Hollywood, FL, May 16.

Zajc, Nono, Gudbjorg Andrea Jonsdottir, Ana Slavec, and Katja Lozar Manfreda. 2015. 'Surveying the General Population in Countries with High Internet Penetration: Is Combining Web and Mail Survey Mode Still Needed?' Presentation to WEBDATANET Conference in Salamanca, Spain, May 26.

## PART V

Digital Quantitative Analysis

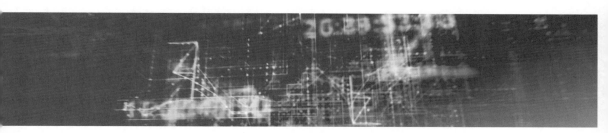

## 14

Online Social Networks: Concepts for Data Collection and Analysis

Bernie Hogan

INTRODUCTION

Even by its name, the Internet pre-supposes the metaphor of a network. Pictures of networks adorn many of the now proliferating books on the Internet and some of the most popular platforms online now call themselves social network sites. In the decade since the previous version of this chapter, the idea that one can study the Internet as a network has become a foregone conclusion. Yet, not all networks are equivalent and not all networks are accessible. The following work is an updated version of the original chapter that similarly moves through many of the fundamentals of social networks and the Internet.

Other than the name, why would the Internet and the notion of a social network be so closely intertwined? By its design, the Internet seeks to minimize concerns for spatial distance in favour of other forms of closeness. This is not to say space is no longer relevant. From the stark digital divides

between countries to the popularity of location-based social networking and dating, space is an extremely important factor conditioning who is likely to interact with whom. We might say that space *conditions* these interactions, but these interactions themselves are structured as networks and often best analysed as such.

Networks are based on a simple mathematical concept – the graph. The notion of a graph is centuries old. As legend goes, it was originally conceived by Euler as a way to solve a folk puzzle about whether it was possible to cross seven bridges connecting an island without retracing steps (it is not; Euler, 1752). The simple idea of a graph is that we have two sets, a set of roughly comparable objects, typically called 'nodes', and a set of pairs of such objects, typically called 'edges'.[1] These edges are also roughly comparable within a given data set, such as flows between countries, friendships, email messages or some other way of denoting an association between two people. Social network analysis might look at all the followers on Twitter, an entire store of email messages, the algorithms behind 'people you might know' on Facebook, the links between webpages or the friendship structure of a set of people that is only partially observed on any given social media platform.

Other techniques such as Actor Network Theory will articulate all sorts of associations. For example, one might link a person to an office, a computer, one's boss and one's ideologies (Latour *et al.*, 2012). For social network analysis such loose linkages between differing types of objects dilute the power of networks by hampering our ability to look at comparable structures. The purpose of social network analysis is not simply to code any association into something more abstract, but to identify *social structures* that can limit or enable nodes in the network based on how the network is connected. These social structures reveal both enduring abstract truths about our universe (such as the ubiquity of extremely skewed or 'power-law' networks) as well as more particular facts about how technology steers social life in historically patterned ways.

HOW NETWORK STRUCTURE MAKES A DIFFERENCE

The key issue with networks is that we can learn about the world through the way in which people are connected, rather than merely through the attributes of the people themselves. Being connected in one way might lead to everyone learning about a fad (or getting a virus) quickly, whereas being connected in another might help people contain the virus or miss out on the fad.

Consider the following stylized graphic of three different network structures (Figure 14.1). The first is one we would call a 'star graph'. This structure has a key focal node and every other node must go through this star in order to reach each other. This is like

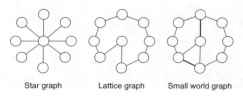

Star graph   Lattice graph   Small world graph

Figure 14.1   Three prototypical graph structures. From left: a star graph, a lattice graph and a hybrid of the two, a small world graph.

an old telephone switchboard. We would say this graph is *maximally centralized*. This centralization means that the paths between any two nodes are efficient and obvious. These paths are efficient because they take only two hops and obvious because we would always know which hops to take, first we hop to the central node and then to the target node. The second network structure is a ring lattice. This network is very inefficient. If two nodes are adjacent (meaning they are directly connected by an edge) then the path is obvious, but what if 'A' wants to reach 'D'? Either route takes three hops.

If the paths on a ring lattice are so much slower, why would anyone ever use one? The ring lattice is more durable. If you only remove one node in the star graph you either do not disrupt the network at all or you completely disrupt it. In the ring lattice, if you remove one node, everyone can still reach everyone (but just barely).

The third network is very much like a ring lattice with one exception – there are a few randomly rewired connections added. This third network has some really remarkable properties. First, it is more robust than either of the two networks and second it is almost as efficient as the star graph. Yet, it is clustered. This third network is called a 'small world' network. Most human networks are some variation on such small worlds (Watts, 2003). That means that most people make connections with the same local people, but yet the global network structure is still connected, robust and efficient.

The difference between Social Networks and other Networks

Depending on the field you are in, you are likely to hear about how social networks are different from other kinds of networks, such as gene expression networks or information networks. This distinction undermines the many commonalities between these networks. For example, we can see evidence of power laws and small worlds in traffic patterns, gene expression and neurons, in addition to Twitter and Facebook networks (Watts, 2003). A further distinction proffered about networks is that most social networks come from vague, self-reported proxies, unlike digital data, which is precise and objective.

Granted, there are differences between social networks and biological networks, as well as advantages to trace data over self-reported data. However, these particular distinctions are as much about preserving specific epistemologies as they are about effectively answering the question at hand.

The next section introduces several of the key techniques for analysing social networks as well as some of the common strategies for transforming and cleaning networks. If the last decade is any indication, however, we must be mindful to consider that this is still a field in flux. The dominant software 10 years from now is likely to change, as is our ability to access network data. Although I offer signposts to specific pieces of software, no particular tool will by itself be sufficient to perform an end-to-end analysis of networks that includes the key stages of capture, cleaning, analysis and representation.

THREE LEVELS OF 'SIMPLE' NETWORKS

We can define a simple network as one that merely considers nodes as discrete entities and edges as some sort of association between these nodes. This might be friends on Facebook, links between webpages, retweets on Twitter or replies on a message board.

Level 1: The Personal Network

A personal network is one that is immediately recognizable to most people: it is the *set of personal connections linked to a focal individual*. We might talk about a certain network as 'my network'. For example, we can consider all the people who follow or friend someone on Twitter. Using the language of that platform, if I follow someone on Twitter they are my friend. If they follow me, they are my follower. The intersection of these two groups represents 'reciprocal ties' or accounts that I follow and who follow me. If we consider all of these people together (i.e. we take the 'union' of the friend list and follower list) as of this writing, this includes 2,441 accounts. Of these, 70.4 percent only follow me, 13.2 percent are only followed by me ('friends') and 16.4 percent are reciprocal.

If we think of only the relationship between the focal individual in a personal network (who we conventionally call 'ego') and all the others (who we conventionally call 'alters'), then we have a 1.0-degree network. If we consider all these people and their friends we have a 2.0-degree network. But if we consider the friendships between people I know as some sort of halfway point, this is colloquially called a 1.5-degree network. This 1.5-degree network is often the one that is the most interesting because friends who know each other end up clustered together. Figure 14.2 is a representation of my Facebook network where the connections between friends are shown, and the network is clustered according to the underlying friendship structure. I will return to this network in the section on analysis.

Sociologists have regularly looked at personal networks prior to and since the inception of the Internet. In both cases, researchers typically want to know whether the size and composition of a personal network make a

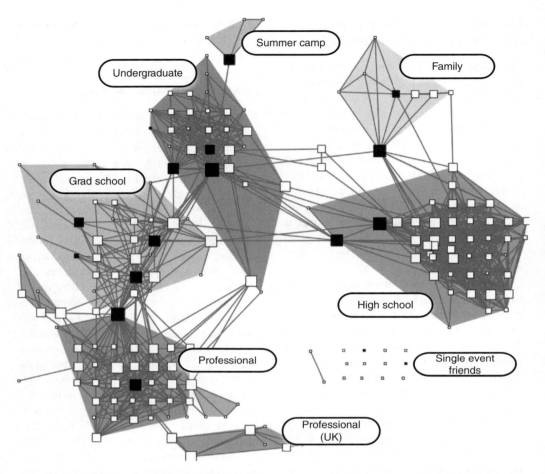

Figure 14.2   A sociogram representation of the author's Facebook friendships in 2008. Nodes are arranged using a variant of a standard force-directed layout. The convex hulls were produced using the Girvan–Newman algorithm.

difference in some manner. For example, do larger Facebook networks correlate with personality? Indeed, they seem to be correlated not only with extraversion (Quercia *et al.*, 2012; Golbeck and Robles, 2011) but also with differences in capacity for name–face recognition (Kanai *et al.*, 2011). Do alters in these networks share more in common with ego than one might expect by chance? Indeed, networks appear to be more homogenous by race, age and gender than a random sample of the population. This notion of like-attracting-like is known as 'homophily' in the social

network literature (McPherson *et al.*, 2001) and is closely related to the notion of 'assortativity' in network science (Newman, 2003).

Level 2: Partial Networks

For some research questions we want to look beyond the connections around ego. We might be interested in the diffusion of a hashtag, the structure of links between university web-pages or the spread of some computer virus. In this case, for practical reasons we cannot consider the entire network structure. We do not need to download all of Twitter to look at a hashtag, nor look at every computer to look at the spread of a computer virus. In these cases, we are doing partial network analysis. In this case, we typically start with a specific *term or set of nodes* and then use an *algorithm* in order to extend the number of nodes. For example, consider the spread of the term 'Frankenfood' (a term used by activists to indicate concerns with genetically modified organisms). Starting with a seed set of *n* pages returned from Google, one can then follow the links found on each page. If those linked pages contain the word Frankenfood, one continues. If those linked pages do not contain the word, the program ignores them (see Ackland, 2013).

Partial networks are commonly used in the collection and analysis of terms, for the diffusion of ideas and the articulation of different groups in a specific domain. We might look at the diffusion of a meme on Twitter, or look to political blogs for evidence of polarization.

A now classic example of polarization is demonstrated in the Adamic and Glance paper 'Divided they Blog' (2005), which demonstrated how the field of political bloggers in the 2004 U.S. election would primarily link within their own ideological camp with notably few links across the camps. To do this work, Adamic and Glance used a spidering strategy to capture what was a reasonably thorough, if not complete, set of American political blogs.

To capture partial online networks, researchers would typically crawl the web using a 'web spider'. These can either be built from scratch using a programming language (such as Python) or captured using off-the-shelf web crawling solutions such as SocSciBot (Thelwall, 2009) or VOSON (Ackland, 2013).

Level 3: Whole Networks

We can describe a set of nodes and the connections between them as a whole network

when we can articulate a meaningful reason why these nodes and not others should be included. That is to say, a whole network implies a *meaningful boundary*. All children in a school class or everyone on Snapchat could be considered whole networks. The school class is probably a practically obtainable whole network, whereas only a very privileged few would ever be able to analyse the entirety of the Snapchat network.

To note, not every boundary is meaningful. For example, the set of people who respond to my online questionnaire is not a particularly meaningful boundary because we should not expect that responding to my questionnaire is going to be a reason for the observable network qualities. On the other hand, a network derived from a questionnaire given to *every member* of an online forum, or better *the complete set of posts and replies* from that forum would be an example of a whole network.

For the very intrepid researcher, networks as large as all of Facebook can be analysed as a whole network. In doing so, past researchers have learned that it takes on average 3.5 hops to get from one person to another on the social network site.[2] Five years ago it was 3.75 hops on average (Backstrom *et al.*, 2012). This indicates first, that Facebook is indeed a small world network and second, that once the network is a small world (as was the case 5 years ago) it is very hard to make it much smaller.

LEVELS OF 'COMPLEX' NETWORKS

The analysis of simple networks tends to be considerably more straightforward than the analysis of more complex networks. What then is a complex network? In this case, I use the word complex loosely to mean networks of multiple type, rather than the more formal physics definition of the network as a 'complex system'. Three kinds of complex networks that often show up in analysis are discussed next.

Type 1: Multiplex Networks

Networks do not have to merely signify one type of relation between nodes. For example, if we consider every student in a school as a whole network, we could look at the nominations of friends, but also look at study groups, shared sports teams, bully–victim relationships, sexual contact networks or the friendship graph on any given social media platform. In this sense, the network is not merely a 'Facebook network' or a 'Twitter network'; instead, it is a multiplex network because it includes edges of multiple types.

The analysis of multiplex networks is more common in offline network studies, where one might look at the commonalities between a network of sexual contacts and a network of drug users, or between a network of those who give advice in an office alongside the network of those who socialize after work. Often such multiplex networks are reduced to a single network if either tie exists or both ties exist.

Type 2: Temporal Networks

All empirical networks imply some sort of time dimension insofar as the network was not created in its current form nor will it remain in that form forever. Nodes and links are added to the Internet as web pages are created and people join.

Temporal networks online tend to operate differently than offline. Whereas offline networks are typically captured at intervals (such as nominating friendships within school at the beginning of every term), online networks are typically built from interactions that take place continuously. For example, an email network is really the flattening of a long series of discrete messages from one person to *n* other people.

We can think about the analysis of temporal networks in several ways. The first is to flatten the entire network so that we lose all the temporal information – any links that were created persist in this flattened network.

The second way is to create slices, such that we can compare the network from one time slice to a network at another time slice (Mucha *et al.*, 2010; Snijders, 2001). The advantage here is that we can analyse each slice independently and compare. The disadvantage is that the slices are often done at arbitrary cut-points. The third way is to think of the network as a long stream of 'relational events', and one might thus run a relational events model (Butts, 2008), which is a formidable social network version of an event history model. The fourth is to think of the network as moving through a window, wherein we calculate our metrics for all interactions within, say, the last 30 days, and then plot the network across these sliding windows (Kossinets and Watts, 2006).

Type 3: Modal Networks

Up to now we have referred to networks where all the nodes were of one type, such as members on a message board, friends on Facebook, etc. We can also think of networks as being comprised of 'joint membership', for example we might have a set of individuals who all attend concerts in London, or those who star in the same movies. If a network contains 'members and memberships' or 'people and events', then we can think of such a network as a two-mode network. The people are not linked directly, but linked by their shared association.

Some of the most commonly used networks are two-mode networks. For example, many people have heard of a common cocktail party game called 'the Kevin Bacon game'. This is where you try to link an actor to Kevin Bacon through movies that starred both actors. For example, Jon Hamm of *Madmen* was in the movie *The Town* with Jeff Martineau. Martineau was in the movie *R.I.P.D.* with Kevin Bacon. This is a two-mode network because it links actors through co-starring. Other examples of popular two-mode networks include author co-citation networks and collaborative filtering networks (e.g. 'people who bought that book also bought these books').

One word of caution about modal networks is that sometimes these networks are a little too easy to construct. We might make a network of shared likes on Facebook, for example. Is this network meaningful? In some respects, it can help us appreciate which products are most likely to be 'liked' by two people, but those two people do not really know each other at all. If two people are in a movie, we can say there is a plausible link between these two people, but two people who both like Taylor Swift might not have much else in common.

There are some clever algorithms for the analysis of two-mode networks, but often these networks are reduced to a one-mode network. For example, we would not have a network of actor→movie←actor, but merely an actor↔actor network where the edge means 'co-star'. In the latter network, we would give the 'co-star' link a weight of three if the actors co-starred in three movies together. This process of taking a two-mode network and creating a one-mode network is called 'bipartite projection'.

SOURCES OF ONLINE SOCIAL NETWORKS

As stated in the introduction, the Internet is often considered a network. More accurately, it is a 'network of networks'. The Internet itself is a physical system of wires and switches that coordinate traffic coming through a number of protocols by routing digital packets. Perhaps the most familiar protocol is the HTTP (or HyperText Transfer Protocol). There are numerous other protocols such as FTP (File Transfer Protocol) and RTSP (Real Time Streaming Protocol).

Humans made the Internet. As such, we could assert that virtually all networks derived from the Internet are social networks in some

respect. For example, Hu (2015) notes how the network of Internet infrastructure that powers 'the cloud' started as fibre optic cables laid along railway lines. For the purposes of this chapter, however, we are more specifically interested in networks where we can characterize the nodes of the networks as being people, or strictly speaking, 'accounts' or pages created by people. This is a reasonably important distinction because:

- Accounts can belong to multiple people (such as a brand page on Facebook);
- People can have multiple accounts (such as pseudonyms and novelty accounts on Twitter);
- Some accounts are run by 'bots' or algorithms that interact on a platform (such as vandalism clean-up bots on Wikipedia, or spam email accounts).

We shall now cover several sources of social network data online:

- Weblogs and other linked pages
- Threaded conversations on the web
- Email traffic
- Twitter networks
- Social network sites more broadly

Weblogs and other Linked Pages

The World Wide Web (WWW) made its introduction in 1992. Prior to this, the Internet primarily linked documents using a hodgepodge of competing systems such as gopher, USEnet and email. With the joint introduction of the WWW and HTTP, online documents had a common standard that allowed for specialized documents called 'web pages' and other documents to be referred to using the same standard protocol. Each document that was served was initially a static web page. The web was a roaring success and received exponential growth during the 'dotcom boom' of the nineties.

During the early explosive growth of the web a few major advances were made. For example, Barabasi and Albert (1999) discovered that the distribution of links on the web followed a noteworthy statistical distribution

called a 'power law'. A power law distribution happens when we have extremely
skewed distributions. For example, most
websites have very few links in or out. A
handful of websites such as Amazon have
many links in and others such as Google have
many links out. As such, it is not meaningful
to talk about the average number of links on a
web page because this number includes pages
with such vastly different numbers of links.

Even in Barabasi and Albert's huge analysis of the web, they conceded that this is still
only a partial analysis. Thus, as mentioned
earlier, virtually all URL-based analysis will
be of a partial network.

As the web matured, the value of a link
analysis has receded considerably. Rarely do
we think of the Internet as comprising a series
of static webpages with links to each other.
A great deal of content is instead embedded
within a single platform, such as Facebook,
rather than across a series of weblogs on
WordPress. The idea that an individual would
create a standalone page for themselves or
their interests is very anachronistic at this
point. However, one enduring set of pages
would be weblogs. Most blogs consist of a
home page with periodically updated stories
by the site maintainer(s). Blogs commonly
link to news stories as well as other blogs.

To capture links on the web, one can use a
web crawler that will download a page, look
for the URLs on that page and follow each in
turn. These networks are like the partial networks discussed earlier.

Threaded Conversations on the Web

Interactions on the Internet often take place
on forums, lists, or in the comment sections
of newspapers and blogs. In all cases, we
have an instance where there are parent comments and children comments. The parents
come first and the children represent the
replies to these previous comments. In this
way, comments typically represent a 'tree'

structure. That is, each post can be seen as a
root and each reply the start of a shoot. Some
trees are wide and shallow, where everyone
replies to the root comment. Some trees are
narrow and deep, such as when two people
argue back and forth but the thread has few
participants overall.

There have been numerous approaches to
threaded conversations on the web. The most
prolific is probably the work of Smith and
his former Microsoft Research colleagues on
USEnet threads (Smith, 1999; Welser et al.,
2007). One of the key characteristics of this
work is the way in which it focuses primarily on the accounts rather than the messages.
That is, one account initiates and replies
many times over. Viewed over time, one can
get a sense of the individual and their specific
communication style or 'social role' (Welser
et al., 2007). Another approach is to look at
the thread itself as the subject of inquiry. This
is the approach of González-Bailón *et al.*
(2010). They focused more on the different
types of emergent threads on a message board
than on the actors. Smith and colleagues were
able to identify types of users by their social
network signature. González-Bailón and colleagues were able to identify types of threads
by their social network signature.

Email Traffic

Email traffic shares many properties with
threaded conversations. Each email thread is
started by one account and others can reply
to the message. However, one difference
between emails and threaded lists is that an
email message is typically 'addressed'. In a
forum thread, everyone in a group can read
the message and choose whether to reply. For
an email message, one needs to be sent that
message directly. As such, one now has an
issue that emerges with threads, but to a
greater extent – how does one deal with a
message sent to multiple people? Is there
a link to the initial recipient or to all the
recipients? Within email, one also has spam

messages and threaded distribution lists as well as messages sent or cc'd to the inbox owner.

For dealing with email, there are some strategies that appear to be more plausible than others. It depends, however, on the source of the email. For example, if one is using an email mail store from a server, one has access to the headers for all email on that domain, such as all @oii.ox.ac.uk email. However, strict policies about deleting email have the potential to drive individuals away from their corporate accounts for anything other than official correspondence. That said, one can still gather a massive database and derive interesting results. For example, Kossinets and Watts (2006) analysed millions of messages in a year-long email spool from an unnamed university in the US. Using this they were able to note both the stability of the network over time as well as some of the demographic characteristics that seem to be correlated with increased email (in network terms, the term 'homophily' is used to refer to such patterns of dyadic similarity).

One of the key ways to trim messages is to trim the network based on features of the network structure. Figure 14.3 suggests an approach to trimming email based on key thresholds.

Zone 1: all messages in a mail store – this includes spam, distribution lists, broadcast announcements, etc. This is the white region in Figure 14.3.

Zone 2: ego's asymmetric neighbourhood – authors who have sent messages directly to ego, or received messages directly from ego. This eliminates messages to distribution lists that are forwarded to ego (because ego is not a direct recipient, for example 'C' in Figure 14.3 has never sent a message to ego so C is excluded). It also eliminates messages bcc'd to ego and any distribution lists to which ego has never sent a message. In the case of distribution lists and bcc'd message, ego's address does not show up in the 'to' or 'cc' line of a message header. In Figure 14.3, ego has sent a message to 'DL' so it is included.

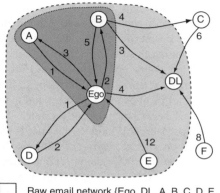

Raw email network {Ego, DL, A, B, C, D, E, F}

Ego's neighbourhood {Ego, DL, A, B, D, E}

Ego's neighbourhood trimmed to symmetric ties with in + out > 4 messages {Ego, A, B}

Figure 14.3 An example schema for filtering emails in a mail store. The outer zones imply all mail in the inbox and the inner zones refer to mail that fits certain qualities, such as mail that has been reciprocated.

Zone 3: ego's symmetric neighbourhood – there has to be a message from ego to alter and from alter to ego. This will eliminate all remaining distribution lists because they do not send to ego. It will also eliminate spam/junk mail/receipts and all other senders to which ego never replies. This would include both 'A' and 'B'.

Zone 4: ego's thresholded neighbourhood – there has to be at least n messages from ego and (or) n messages from alter. The figure does not visually differentiate zones 3 and 4, but if someone only sent a single message to ego and received a single reply they would be in zone 3 but not zone 4. This differentiates 'significant contacts' from fleeting/isolated correspondence. As an example, Adamic and Adar (2005) use six messages from and to ego. The actual amount to use varies by project, but should be justified substantively because there are few heuristics for an appropriate threshold.

Although it is not always easy to gain access to email mail stores, there are a number of email data sets available for practicing social network analysis. The most utilized set is the Enron email data set. After members of the Enron Corporation were convicted of fraud and collusion over email, the judge ordered the entire email corpus of Enron's servers to be released. This includes professional email from external partners and many individuals never convicted of a crime.[3] The second approach is Windows-specific. If one has email on a local version of Outlook, the Excel add-on NodeXL can import one's email (see Hansen *et al.*, 2011: Ch. 8). This importation can be done on slices, such as email featuring a certain word, author or time range. As is the case with all these methods, if one can parse email and wrangle data in a programming language, there are numerous methods for gaining access to and cleaning email.

Twitter Networks

Twitter is the reigning champion of Internet-based social network analysis. Although Twitter does not have the sort of market share or audience of Facebook or Sina Weibo, it does have a very convenient Application Programming Interface (API) for accessing a substantial portion of Twitter's functionality. Furthermore, those who post on Twitter often speak about current political events, protests and social issues, making the analysis of Twitter data particularly ripe. APIs are the protocols that enable platforms, such as Facebook, Twitter, Weibo and Google, to give a modest and carefully controlled set of data to the third party that requests it. Twitter's API permits anyone with a Twitter account limited access to the recent tweets and followers of any public account. It also permits a user to track data from the 'stream'.

By default, one can access up to 10 percent of all tweets at any point by opening a stream listener. Twitter does not guarantee which 10 percent is available. As such, people often use 'track terms' to filter the stream down to, for example, Justin Bieber tweets. That way, unless more than 10 percent of Twitter is talking about the pop sensation, then the user is going to get most, if not all tweets. There are a few exceptions to this, some of which have been publicly discovered (Morstatter *et al.*, 2013).

There are a number of collectors available to capture data from Twitter. As mentioned earlier, NodeXL is a relatively user-friendly Twitter collector that automatically downloads data in a format amenable to analysis. However, one must be mindful of the ways in which such data are collected in the first place. For many, it is straightforward enough to merely download the data using a programming language. The following code snippet is a relatively complete and simple example in Python that can download tweets and create a network. For a more involved series of examples, see Russell (2013).

```
# Comments in Python are lines that start with a hash
import tweepy

# The keys can be found by going to http://apps.twitter.com/
# From there, create a new application.
# It will subsequently give you the following tokens
CONSUMER_KEY = "XXXXXXXXXXXXXXXXXXXXXXXXXX"
CONSUMER_SECRET = "XXXXXXXXXXXXXXXXXXXXXXXXXXXXXXXXXXXXXXXXXXXXXXXXXXXX"
ACCESS_TOKEN = "XXXXXXXXXXXXXXXXXXXXXXXXXXXXXXXXXXXXXXXXXXXXXXXXXX"
ACCESS_TOKEN_SECRET = "XXXXXXXXXXXXXXXXXXXXXXXXXXXXXXXXXXXXXXXXXXXXX"

# This creates the worker that will communicate with twitter
auth = tweepy.OAuthHandler(CONSUMER_KEY,CONSUMER_SECRET)
auth.set_access_token(ACCESS_TOKEN, ACCESS_TOKEN_SECRET)
api = tweepy.API(auth)
```

```
# This creates a 'set' and adds all the friends to the set
# Replace my twitter name with any public account
friend_set = set([])
for friend_id in api.friends_ids('blurky'):
    friend_set.add(friend_id)

# Let's create a set and add all the followers
follower_set = set([])
for follower_id in api.followers_ids('blurky'):
    follower_set.add(follower_id)

# We can now report on some statistics about the
# degree 1.0 personal network on twitter.
num_total = len(follower_set.union(friend_set))
num_reciprocal = len(follower_set.intersection(friend_set))
num_only_followers = len(follower_set - friend_set)
num_only_friends = len(friend_set - follower_set)

print("This account interacts with %s accounts in total." % num_total)
print("Total friends: \t\t%s" % len(friend_set))
print("Total followers: \t%s" % len(follower_set))
print("Reciprocal: \t\t%s" % num_reciprocal)
print("Only followers: \t%s" % num_only_followers)
print("Only friends: \t\t%s" % num_only_friends)
```

This particular snippet will report on the number of friends and followers for a particular user (the author in this case). This snippet is instructive in many ways about Twitter and also about networks on the Internet in general. Notice that this is a 'degree 1.0' personal network. That is to say that this code will retrieve the in-links and out-links for a particular account. It will not collect the links between the friends and followers of a single account. Thus, if one were to visualize this as a network it would look like a star graph with some arrows pointing in either direction.

At the top of the code is a place where a user can insert four different keys. These keys are all generated by Twitter using the Twitter Application interface. This is because Twitter's data is restricted using a system called 'OAuth'. The OAuth system is a way for third parties (such as this program) to work on behalf of a user without having to know the user's login credentials. In this case, one merely enters these keys and requests an API worker using these credentials. OAuth has now become one of the standards for accessing data from social media platforms.

One of the things that OAuth regulates is the number of queries that can be done. Most platforms, including the aforementioned ones as well as Google, will restrict the number of queries done in a time window. This is especially critical for work on social networks. For example, on Twitter, because one can only make 180 calls every 15 minutes, this limits the sort of networks that one can collect through Twitter. Although 180 calls might seem like a lot, one must query the user IDs in batches of 100. If one person has 18,001 followers, the first 18,000 will be returned within the 15-minute window and the user will have to wait up to 00:14:59 for the next follower. This is particularly acute when dealing with networks. Normally one would want to get a list of followers, and then for each of them get their list of followers. Capturing such a long follower list for everyone in the personal network would take more time than the rate limiting would feasibly allow (Hogan, 2013).

As getting the Degree 1.5 network (or the Degree 2.0 network) appears to be prohibitive on Twitter, many people have instead focused on conversational networks rather than friend/follower networks. For these networks, the links are between people who tweet and those who @mention or retweet the original poster. Although Twitter has been particularly tight with friend or follower API requests, their recent API changes have made it more generous when downloading tweets. Creating a network based on @mentions is now the default behaviour for the tweet collector within NodeXL.

Social Network Sites More Broadly

From the perspective of social network analysis, we can classify social network sites along a number of dimensions. Each of these makes a difference to the type of network we can create as well as the plausibility of getting such networks. I cannot provide an extensive overview of the following list of platforms, although I will spend significant time on Facebook. Instead, I encourage the reader to consider these as potential sites for different purposes.[4]

- Link type
  - Undirected (Facebook friends, LinkedIn Contacts)
  - Directed (Twitter follows and mentions, YouTube subscribers, Tumblr followers)
- Has an API
  - Yes, for content only (Facebook)
  - Yes, for friends and content but very rate limited (e.g. Twitter, Instagram, Pinterest)
  - Yes, and can get friendship data (e.g. Google+, Weibo)
  - No, but spidering is possible (e.g. Resident Advisor)
  - No and spidering is difficult or impossible (e.g. Snapchat, Whatsapp)

Social network sites are, by definition, sites that allow users to link to distinct profiles. Most social media sites have a means for signifying links between two people. These links are often to place the user in a feed, allow access to photos or messaging or simply to signify friendship. Most sites can be understood as permutations of Twitter. That is, the links are available either through conversations or through direct friend links.

Sometimes these links are accessible through an API, but typically they are slow to access or not accessible at all. A handful of sites provide no access through their API or, like Snapchat, have no public facing API at all.[5]

FACEBOOK AND THE CASE OF CHANGING APIs

Shortly after the publication of the first version of this chapter, Facebook opened up their APIs to developers. Initially, the API was very simple, allowing only very simple queries such as asking whether two people know each other. With 500 friends, this would amount to roughly 125,000 possible friendship pairs. As the API evolved, along with knowledge of what was possible, complex inner join SQL queries made it possible to capture even very large personal networks efficiently. As concerns about privacy and the ethics of social network research has intensified (more on this later), Facebook have reacted by restricting queries so that an application can only learn about friendships between those who use the app. Getting everyone in a Facebook group or friendship network to add an app just so that they can be measured is typically unrealistic. As such, virtually all external work on Facebook networks has ceased. Working with the company on their secure servers is still possible, however, and it is by working with the company that numerous scholars have arrived at significant revelations about the size and structure of the total Facebook network, as well as how influential Facebook is about voting (Bond et al., 2012) and other practices sensitive to social influence (Aral and Walker, 2012).

ETHICS AND ALTERNATIVE APPROACHES

With the demise of the Facebook API for friendships and the general increasing concerns about links between people, most companies are now a little more reluctant to share their data so freely through APIs. Many companies do provide data dumps, while anonymous data dumps are still hosted by a number of third parties. That said, if one is analysing data that has been previously collected, it is wise to consult one's local ethics review board. Sometimes this data was collected in less than virtuous ways (such as hacking into a company and copying the entire database). Other times, however, this data is simply made available to the public.

One of the reasons that the Facebook API was limited was due to the concerns about the ethics of capturing links between people other than the respondent. This is a legitimate concern and one that has been a part of social network analysis for some time. There are several issues at play here. The first is consent. If one is capturing social networks, they are capturing links between people. One party might have given consent but the other did not. For this reason, network analysts tend to not report or distribute the network outside of the study. The authors of the 'Tastes, Ties and Time' study (Lewis *et al.*, 2008) were sorely criticized for attempting to release an anonymized version of their data. It was evident that this data could not be anonymized and was far more sensitive than the authors anticipated (Zimmer, 2010). As a rule of thumb, it is not appropriate to collect private networks without the consent of the users. Public networks are fair, but when one creates new links or associations this can be potentially harmful. For example, this might involve inferring networks by triangulating Facebook and Twitter when in fact the users consider these as separate. Ultimately, due to the complex nature of networks and the difficulty in anonymization, researchers should take care not to publicly present networks that can be 'reverse engineered' to expose people. Or said otherwise, in the absence of the possibility of anonymity, researchers must be absolutely cognizant of the importance of confidentiality.

STATISTICAL TECHNIQUES FOR NETWORK ANALYSIS

It might come as a surprise that so little of a paper on analysing social networks via the Internet focuses on the actual metrics used for analysis. This is because much of the analysis that is done on networks in general is relatively standard. There is now a profusion of excellent textbooks on networks, from the intensely mathematical physics-oriented text by Newman (2010) to the social science-oriented text by Borgatti *et al.* (2013). For many starting out in networks, the key is to determine what sort of network is to be analysed. Thereafter, it is a matter of exploring the network at various scales. I shall now discuss analysis at a number of scales: monadic (one node), dyadic (two nodes), triadic (three nodes), meso (clusters of nodes), and the level of the whole network. These are merely entry level analyses, although the field of network analysis continues to evolve at a rapid pace. The chapter by Borge-Holthoefer and González-Bailón in this volume will further introduce the reader to more advanced topics.

Monadic Analysis: The Position of a Specific Node

Research questions in network analysis often focus on specific nodes and their relationship to the entire network. For example, if we think of a Twitter account, we might ask how many followers does the account have? Does this account link two or more distinct clusters in the wider network? Is it easy for tweets from this account to reach other accounts? How many of one's followers follow each other? These are questions related to the general network concept called 'centrality'. Defining a node as more or less central is often a critical question in networks. Here is a brief summary of key centrality measures:

- *Degree centrality.* The total number of nodes adjacent to a given node. This can be a count, or it can be normalized by dividing by the total number of nodes (thereby giving a score between 0 and 1). Degree centrality is useful to get a broad sense of which nodes are most well connected (Freeman, 1979).

- *In- (Out-) degree centrality.* This is the same as degree but only counts edges going into a node or out from a node.
- *Eigenvector centrality.* Eigenvector centrality is like degree, but it takes into account the centrality of the adjacent nodes. It is better to have five links to very well connected nodes than 10 links to poorly connected nodes.
- *Closeness centrality.* This measure reports how easy it is for a node to reach all the other nodes in a network (Freeman, 1979).
- *Betweenness centrality.* This measure indicates how much a node is 'between' others. Conventionally we would explore how many shortest paths in the network include a node (Freeman, 1979). A variant that uses random walks (Newman, 2005) also gives very strong results.
- *Local clustering coefficient.* How many of one's peers are connected to each other? This measure helps to evaluate the small-world cohesion in the network (Watts and Strogatz, 1998).

Dyadic Analysis: How Do Two Nodes Relate

One of the most enduring facets of social networks is the persistence of reciprocity. In many examples of real world networks, we should expect to find reciprocal connections. In the case of friendship networks, it is highly probable that if I nominate someone as a friend they will nominate me. However, it is not inevitable. Unreciprocated nominations show evidence of hierarchy i.e., popular people are often nominated as friends by those who they would not nominate.

Many social network sites embed notions of reciprocity into their platforms in specific ways. Twitter allows for directed links that may or may not be reciprocal (as seen in the earlier example), whereas all friendships on Facebook are reciprocal but links are not. For example, Lewis *et al.* (2008) show how photo tagging on Facebook is very

asymmetric, even if friendship nominations are symmetric.

Further to a dyadic analysis is the previously stated notion of homophily. This is where we might ask whether individuals of like type are particularly prone to link to each other. For example, are bloggers of high status likely to link to other high-status bloggers or to low-degree blogs of their friends? McPherson *et al.* (2001) offer an excellent overview of homophily and explain many of its subtleties. As they note, homophily is so pervasive in social networks that it is not enough to ask if homophily exists in a network, but to ponder what sort of homophily provides the logic for organizing the network.

Assortative mixing is a slightly different variant on homophily. This measure looks at whether individuals are likely to link to others who are similar, dissimilar or both. Newman (2003) gives a clear overview of the use of assortative mixing online. Interestingly, he shows that social networks are highly assorted in terms of degree. This means that people of high degree frequently link to people of high degree and low degree to those of low degree. This can be contrasted with networks such as the Internet infrastructure where servers of high degree link to computers of low degree.

Triadic Analysis: The Basics of Social Structure

In many respects, triads are the building blocks of social structure rather than dyads. This is partly because the myriad combinations of possible triads are significantly larger than the combinations of dyads. However, some triads are particularly important. For example, the now-foundational paper by Granovetter (1973) theorizes that two friends who are close to a third tend to become friends and then share redundant information. We can also look to the presence of cycles (A talks to B, B to C, and C to A) versus hierarchy (A reports to B, B reports to C, and

A also reports to C) within the network. There are now ways to estimate the statistically significant presence of certain kinds of triads (called configurations in the social statistics literature and motifs in the computer science literature). We refer to these as exponential random graph models (Holland and Leinhardt, 1981).

Meso Level Details: Networks as Clustered

Networks cluster at scales above the triad. Entire groups of bloggers link to each other, and Facebook friends tend to indicate social clusters (Brooks *et al.*, 2014). In the past 15 years, there have been tremendous strides in the detection of these clusters (or 'communities' in physics parlance). Porter *et al.* (2009) provide a relatively gentle introduction to this technique.

Two key points are relevant. First is the notion of 'modularity'. This metric compares the number of edges within a community to the number of edges between communities. If most of the edges are within communities, the graph is said to be very modular. The maximum score is +1 and we tend to consider networks with a modularity above 0.3 as good. If most connections go between groups (e.g. most, but not all, connections in a sex network go between genders), then the modularity is negative. A modularity score around zero indicates that the communities are no more distinct than a random distribution of edges. Modularity is not the only benchmark for community structure, but it is a relatively common one. The second point is that most community detection algorithms typically pick up on the same thing, but do so with different levels of granularity and efficiency. Two methods in particular, the 'Louvain' method (featured in the program Gephi) and the 'Infomap' algorithm, appear to be particularly good at finding solutions with high modularity scores (i.e. very distinct communities) very efficiently.

Considering the Network as a Whole: Density and Clustering

Density is a measure of the number of edges within a graph divided by the maximum number of edges possible. It is a common measure and a useful first measure when comparing graphs of similar size or the same graph over time. That said, it can be misleading when comparing graphs of substantially different sizes. This leads to the perennial problem of how to say if a graph is sparse or dense. One solution is to only discuss a network's density in relation to the density of similar networks. However, in many other cases, researchers are not interested in density per se, but in how clustered the graph is.

Clustering coefficient is a measure that scales much more efficiently than density. The local clustering coefficient (discussed earlier) is a measure of how well connected the nodes are around a given node. The clustering coefficient is the arithmetic mean of the local clustering coefficient for all nodes in the graph. When the clustering coefficient is large it implies that a graph is highly clustered around a few nodes, when it is low it implies that the links in the graph are relatively evenly spread among all the nodes. Applying the clustering coefficient, Kossinets and Watts (2006) showed that the email network at a large American university did not get more clustered as the school year progressed. Individual networks got more or less clustered as people added new individuals or deleted old ties, but the overall clustering of the graph remained very consistent.

SOFTWARE PACKAGES FOR ANALYSIS

No network analysis package is complete, and a review of any set of packages is likely to be out of date quickly. However, it is still possible to offer some guidance. First, there are a host of different formats for network data. The program NodeXL is perhaps the most versatile insofar as one can paste data directly into Excel and then export it to a variety of formats. However, NodeXL is severely limited in advanced statistical routines. For this, one might turn to UCInet or Pajek for standard social network analysis routines (featured in Borgatti *et al.*, 2013). If one knows Python, the Networkx and iGraph packages are both available for network analysis and can handle extremely large graphs. The application Gephi has many online tutorials and produces very attractive graphs. Like NodeXL, Gephi also includes rudimentary statistics and excellent data conversion options. For advanced modeling, the R statistical language is now the dominant entry point, although a small number of routines still run primarily in Matlab. Each of these programs has a small but committed series of practitioners and a host of online resources and tutorials available. By being able to convert data and patiently walk through tutorials, all of these programs can be accessible to the motivated researcher.

CONCLUSION

Social network analysis offers a powerful framework for detecting and interpreting social relationships online. Within social network analysis are a host of analytic techniques ranging from simple centrality scores to sophisticated multilevel modeling; however, gathering these networks is a time-intensive and challenging task. Online networks make this task somewhat easier through the use of passive networks (such as email stores and web pages), but the increase in efficiency leads to additional challenges about when to stop collecting and what sorts of relations are substantively meaningful. Overcoming these challenges takes patience, a good dose of technical skills with scripting languages or custom software and some trial and error. Analysing networks is therefore as much about understanding what sort

of structure is worth considering as simply finding that structure in the networks. The tasks of selecting which data and what level of analysis are essential. This chapter barely scratches the surface, but at least it points to many of the now key substantive readings and textbooks in the field for more advanced analysis.

NOTES

1 The pedantic network scholar might say 'but nodes can also be called vertices and edges could also be arcs, ties, or relations'. Indeed, the multidisciplinary field of networks is overloaded with too many terms owing to the independent use of networks in many fields in the twentieth century (Freeman, 2004). Thus, for more experienced readers, I ask for some latitude in the interest of narrative clarity.
2 https://research.facebook.com/blog/three-and-a-half-degrees-of-separation/ (Accessed: August 18, 2016)
3 The canonical version of this data is available from https://www.cs.cmu.edu/~enron/ (Accessed: August 18, 2016)
4 The relationship between social media platform and link type is further explained in Hogan and Wellman (2014).
5 The website http://programmableweb.com/ has an extensive and up-to-date list of online APIs and how to access them.

REFERENCES

Ackland, R. (2013). *Web social science: Concepts, data and tools for social scientists in the digital age*. Thousand Oaks, CA: Sage Publications.
Adamic, L. A. and Adar, E. (2005). How to search a social network. *Social Networks*, 27(3), 187–203.
Adamic, L. A. and Glance, N. (2005). The political blogosphere and the 2004 US election: divided they blog. In *Proceedings of the 3rd International Workshop on Link Discovery*, New York, NY: ACM, pp. 36–43.
Aral, S. and Walker, D. (2012). Identifying influential and susceptible members of social

networks. *Science*, *337*(6092), 337–41. doi:10.1126/science.1215842.

Backstrom, L., Boldi, P., Rosa, M., Ugander, J. and Vigna, S. (2012). Four degrees of separation. *Proceedings of the 3rd Annual ACM Web Science Conference on WebSci*, *12*, 33–42. doi:10.1145/2380718.2380723.

Barabasi, A.-L. and Albert, R. (1999). Emergence of scaling in random networks. *Science*, *286*(5439), 509–12.

Bond, R. M., Fariss, C. J., Jones, J. J., Kramer, A. D. I., Marlow, C., Settle, J. E. and Fowler, J. H. (2012). A 61-million-person experiment in social influence and political mobilization. *Nature*, *489*(7415), 295–8.

Borgatti, S. P., Everett, M. G. and Johnson, J. C. (2013). *Analyzing social networks*. Thousand Oaks, CA: Sage Publications.

Brooks, B., Hogan, B., Ellison, N., Lampe, C. and Vitak, J. (2014). Assessing structural correlates to social capital in Facebook ego networks. *Social Networks*, *38*(1), 1–15. doi:10.1016/j.socnet.2014.01.002.

Butts, C. T. (2008). A relational event framework for social action. *Sociological Methodology*, *38*(1), 155–200.

Euler, L. (1752 [1741]) Solutio problematis ad geometriam situs pertinentis (1736). *Commentarii Academiae Scientiarum Imperialis Petropolitanae 8*: 128–40.

Freeman, L. C. (1979). Centrality in social networks conceptual clarification. *Social Networks*, *1*(3), 215–39.

Freeman, L. C. (2004). *The development of social network analysis: a study in the sociology of science*. Vancouver, BC: Empirical Press.

Golbeck, J. and Robles, C. (2011). Predicting personality with social media. *CHI '11 Extended Abstracts on Human Factors in Computing Systems*, 253–62.

González-Bailón, S., Kaltenbrunner, A. and Banchs, R. E. (2010). The structure of political discussion networks: a model for the analysis of online deliberation. *Journal of Information Technology*, 1–14. doi:10.1057/jit.2010.2.

Granovetter, M. (1973). The strength of weak ties. *American Journal of Sociology*, *78*, 1360–80.

Hansen, D., Shneiderman, B. and Smith, M. A. (2010). *Analyzing social media with NodeXL*. Burlington, MA: Morgan Kaufmann.

Hogan, B. (2013). Comment on elena pavan/1 considering platforms as actors. *Sociologica*, *7*(3), 1–14. doi:10.2383/75767.

Hogan, B. and Wellman, B. (2014). The relational self-portrait: selfies meet social networks. In M. Graham and W. H. Dutton (eds.), *Society and the Internet: how networks of information and communication are changing our lives*. Oxford: Oxford University Press, pp. 53–66.

Holland, P. and Leinhardt, S. (1981). An exponential family of probability distributions for directed graphs. *Journal of the American Statistical Association*, *76*, 33–65.

Hu, T.-H. (2015). *A Prehistory of the Cloud*. Cambridge, MA: MIT Press.

Kanai, R., Bahrami, B., Roylance, R. and Rees, G. (2011). Online social network size is reflected in human brain structure. *Proceedings of the Royal Society B: Biological Sciences*, (October). doi:10.1098/rspb.2011.1959.

Kossinets, G. and Watts, D. J. (2006). Empirical analysis of an evolving social network. *Science*, *311*(5757), 88–90.

Latour, B., Jensen, P., Venturini, T., Grauwin, S. and Boullier, D. (2012). 'The whole is always smaller than its parts' – a digital test of Gabriel Tardes' monads. *British Journal of Sociology*, *63*(4), 590–615. doi:10.1111/j.1468-4446.2012.01428.x.

Lewis, K., Kaufman, J., Gonzalez, M., Wimmer, A. and Christakis, N. (2008). Tastes, ties, and time: a new social network dataset using Facebook.com. *Social Networks*, *30*(4), 330–42.

McPherson, J. M., Smith-Lovin, L. and Cook, J. M. (2001). Birds of a Feather: homophily in social networks. *Annual Review of Sociology*, *27*, 415–44.

Morstatter, F., Pfeffer, J., Liu, H. and Carley, K. (2013). Is the sample good enough? Comparing data from Twitter's streaming API with Twitter's Firehose. *Proceedings of ICWSM*, 400–8. doi:10.1007/978-3-319-05579-4_10.

Mucha, P. J., Richardson, T., Macon, K., Porter, M. A. and Onnela, J.-P. (2010). Community structure in time-dependent, multiscale, and multiplex networks. *Science*, *328*(5980), 876–8. doi:10.1126/science.1184819.

Newman, M. E. J. (2003). Mixing patterns in networks. *Physical Review E*, *67*, 026126, 1–13.

Newman, M. E. J. (2005). A measure of betweenness centrality based on random walks. *Social Networks*, *27*, 39–54.

Newman, M. E. J. (2010). *Networks: an introduction*. Oxford: Oxford University Press.

Porter, M. A. P., Onnela, J.-P. and Mucha, P. J. (2009). Communities in networks. *Notices of the AMS*, *56*(9), 1082–166.

Quercia, D., Lambiotte, R., Stillwell, D., Kosinski, M. and Crowcroft, J. (2012). The personality of popular Facebook users. In *Proceedings of the ACM 2012 Conference on Computer Supported Cooperative Work*. New York, NY: ACM, pp. 955–64. doi:10.1145/2145204.2145346.

Russell, M. A. (2013). *Mining the social web*. 2nd edn. Sebastopol, CA: O'Reilly Media.

Smith, M. A. (1999). Invisible crowds in cyberspace: mapping the social structure of Usenet. In M. A. Smith and P. Kollock (eds.), *Communities in cyberspace*. London: Routledge, pp. 195–219.

Snijders, T. A. B. (2001). The statistical evaluation of social network dynamics. *Sociological Methodology*, *31*(1), 361–95.

Thelwall, M. (2009). Introduction to webometrics: quantitative web research for the social sciences. *Synthesis Lectures on Information Concepts, Retrieval, and Services*, *1*(1).

Watts, D. (2003). *Six degrees*. New York, NY: W. W. Norton & Co.

Watts, D. and Strogatz, S. (1998). Collective dynamics of 'small-world' networks. *Nature*, *393*, 440–2.

Welser, H. T., Gleave, E., Fisher, D. and Smith, M. (2007). Visualizing the signatures of social roles in online discussion groups. *Journal of Social Structure*, *8*(2).

Zimmer, M. (2010). 'But the data is already public': on the ethics of research in Facebook. *Ethics and Information Technology*, *12*(4), 313–25. doi:10.1007/s10676-010-9227-5.

## 15

Scale, Time, and Activity Patterns: Advanced Methods for the Analysis of Online Networks

Javier Borge-Holthoefer
and Sandra González-Bailón

NETWORK RESEARCH AND DIGITAL DATA

Social media and web technologies have become a prominent source of data for researchers interested in the analysis of social interactions and communication dynamics. Online data help us revisit old theoretical accounts of interpersonal influence, diffusion processes, or group formation. In other words, they offer an empirical domain in which to test and develop social theory. The analysis of online networks, however, also creates methodological challenges that are new to researchers used to employing more traditional measurement instruments like surveys or name generators, which are tailored to yield smaller and more static data. One difference, for instance, is that the higher temporal resolution of online data demands defining some rules to aggregate activity in the form of network ties. Large network data also requires applying methods that can offer a simplified map of the structure, or that

allow filtering irrelevant, noisy information and retain only the significant connections. This chapter offers an overview of some of those methods, illustrating how advanced techniques help us manage and analyze online networks and develop our theoretical understanding of social interactions and communication in the digital age.

Our discussion centers on three types of methods. First, we offer an overview of techniques that are advanced in their approach to data in the sense that they go beyond mere description: they operate on the basis of null models that help determine departure from randomness. These techniques, which include community detection methods and backbone extraction, have entered the category of mainstream to the extent that they are available in public software libraries and standard statistical packages (appropriate references are given in the pages that follow). Second, we discuss what we call second-order methods, like role identification and core-periphery analysis, which often rely on the results of prior analysis of the network – for instance, the use of community detection to find the most informative partition of nodes or the most relevant bridging connections. The findings of these methods are contingent on the appropriateness of prior analyses, hence their second-order nature. Finally, we introduce unconventional approaches to online data, where 'unconventional' refers to their lack of prevalence in social science research. These include modeling evolving networks and the time series of network metrics, and methodologies borrowed from the analysis of biological or physical systems. Our focus is on the analysis of large, fast-evolving networks, and therefore we do not consider statistical approaches applicable to smaller networks like Exponential Random Graph Models (ERGM) and their temporal version (TERGM), which are excellently introduced and discussed elsewhere (Lusher *et al.* 2012; Snijders 2011; Carrington *et al.* 2005). We end the chapter with a discussion of open areas that require further research, for instance the analysis and modeling of multilayered networks. First, though, we start by briefly outlining the characteristics of online data and some of the limitations to take into account when analyzing digital trails.

THE NATURE OF ONLINE DATA

Digital technologies allow mapping the structure of social interactions in ways that are precluded by more traditional measurement tools (e.g. name generators in surveys; see, for instance, Burt, 1984). Online data are more granular and help researchers depict the social world with higher resolution, allowing us to consider questions that span several levels of analysis, from individuals to groups and to aggregate dynamics (Watts 2007; Lazer *et al.* 2009; Golder and Macy 2014). Data, however, are never perfect. The quality of the data collected from online sources can be affected by three factors: the representativeness of the sample with respect to the population of interest; the ability to relate online activity with offline behavior; and the policies that constrain data collection (most likely, in the form of the application programming interfaces, or APIs, made available by online platforms to grant access to their data). The relative importance of each of these limitations depends on the research question at hand: if the goal is to analyze how social media is being used to, say, organize political protests (one of the areas that has attracted much attention in recent years, see González-Bailón and Wang (2016) for a summary), then the population of interest does not need to be representative of the whole population if only a non-representative segment participates in political protests. Likewise, if the goal of the research is to understand how digital technologies are being used to discuss politics, the relation with offline behavior might not necessarily be within the scope of the project (although it probably still is the next natural question to ask).

In the last few years, research has started to illuminate in a systematic manner how these factors affect the quality of online data and the analyses that follow. For instance, researchers have looked at the impact that different APIs have on Twitter samples and identified the nature of the bias that results from that filtering (González-Bailón *et al.* 2014a; Morstatter *et al.* 2013). The way in which APIs filter access to data is outside the control of researchers; however, prior work shows that other parameters defined during the data collection (for instance, the selection of keywords to identify relevant streams of communication) are more relevant in shaping the structure of the data collected. In other words, careful consideration should be given to the substantive context to be analyzed, and sensitivity analyses should be conducted to ensure that results are not affected by a specific selection of keywords. Similarly, researchers interested in social media data as a substitute to more traditional sources of information like surveys, are advancing in our understanding of the representativeness of those data (Barberá and Rivero 2014) and their ability to cast light on traditional measures like ideology position or the degree of self-selection (Barberá et al. 2015a; Barberá 2015). Researchers are also illuminating the extent to which online behavior is related to offline actions (Bond et al. 2012), but determining the existence of that link is still one of the challenges associated with the analysis of online data (Golder and Macy 2014).

On the background of these methodological challenges, the analysis of digital data is also stirring new ethical questions. Prominent amongst them is the issue of informed consent. Even if a great deal of social media data are publicly available, this does not mean there is implied consent on the part of the users to have their activity and behavior analyzed (boyd and Crawford 2012). However, informed consent is not a feasible option for the analysis of most online data, which is usually too large in scale and retroactive – so locating the users involved would prove logistically impossible for most researchers. Anonymizing and aggregating the data in a way that protects the identity of individual users is one of the ways in which researchers deal with these ethical considerations. Most of the methods in this chapter focus on analyzing the structure and dynamics of communication networks, that is, they disregard the meaning of the actual content exchanged and pay instead attention to the building blocks that form those networks, which aggregate individual nodes into larger units of analysis (i.e. the identity of those users is irrelevant, what matters is their network position relative to other users). Before conducting research with online data, however, researchers should consider the goals of their work through the lens of ethical standards and address the concerns raised by their institutional review boards.

REDUCTION TECHNIQUES

Online interactions tend to generate large networks that are difficult to grasp without a statistical summary of their structure. Networks can be described from different levels of analysis. At the micro level, the focus lies on single nodes and their specific positions within the overall structure; this level can be described in terms of node degree, clustering coefficient or betweenness, amongst other metrics. At the macro level, the focus shifts to the aggregation of those metrics and the properties of their distribution. At this level, relevant statistics are the average degree (k), the range of the degree distribution $P(k)$, the average path length L, or the average clustering coefficient C. Between these two extremes, we have a third level of analysis, the mesoscale, which aims to account for the complexity of networks between the position of individual nodes and the relational properties of the collectives they form. It is at this level where reduction techniques like community detection or backbone extraction operate.

Both community detection and backbone extraction aim to simplify the complexity of network data by building a simpler version that retains the relevant features of the original structure but makes it more tractable computationally. In the case of community detection, 'simpler' means a network with less nodes but that still reproduces the organizational logic of the original network. In the case of backbone extraction, 'simpler' means a network with less links but that preserves only those that are statistically significant. Figure 15.1 illustrates how an undirected, weighted network can be transformed by these two techniques. The original network is, for the purposes of this example, a random realization of a small world network (Watts 1999; Watts and Strogatz 1998) with 100 nodes and 500 edges (Figure 15.1A); the width of the edges is proportional to their strength, which could account for, say, the number of times two people communicate through social media. A version of this network reduced through community detection contains five nodes and ten edges (Figure 15.1B); another version reduced through

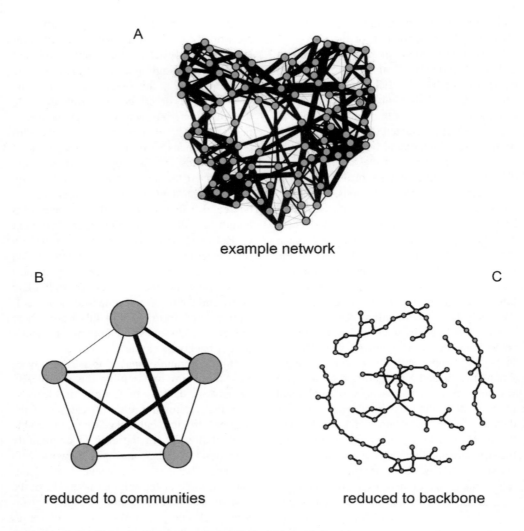

Figure 15.1   Schematic representation of reduction techniques

backbone extraction contains 94 nodes and 97 edges (Figure 15.1C). In both instances, the reduced networks offer a simpler representation of the original structure. The value of these simplifications, of course, depends on the research question. Reducing networks is also more relevant when they are orders of magnitude larger than the example network used here – the sort of network that would not be possible to visualize in a meaningful way. The following two sections explain in

more detail the logic of network reduction techniques and why they uncover important insights in the analysis of online interactions.

Techniques to Group Nodes

The problem of community detection has been the subject of discussion in various disciplines. In machine learning, the problem is stated in terms of classification and clustering: the first relates to assigning entities to a predefined set of categories; the second (and this is the problem that interests us here) attempts to discover coherent groups in a given dataset and to assign entities to those groups. In real complex networks there is often no way to find out, a priori, how many communities can be discovered, but in general we can assume that there are more than two, which makes the clustering process quite costly. Algorithmic challenges aside, identifying communities is important because they affect the dynamics of the network. Research has shown that the existence of clustered groups influences the performance of dynamics like epidemic spreading, synchronization phenomena or information diffusion (Lancichinetti and Fortunato 2009; Girvan and Newman 2002; Newman *et al.* 2006; Newman 2012). Therefore, paying attention to the network structure at the meso level can help us retrieve important information that would be missed if we only analyzed the structure at the individual or macro level.

A community is a subset of nodes in a network that displays denser connectivity internally than externally. In 2002, Girvan and Newman came up with a formalization of this intuition under the form of the following equation

$$Q = \frac{1}{2m} \sum_{i,j} \left(a_{ij} - p_{ij} \right) \delta_{(c_i, c_j)} \qquad 1$$

where the sum runs over all pairs of nodes, $A = \{a_{ij}\}$ in the adjacency matrix representing the observed network, $P = \{p_{ij}\}$ represents the probability of an edge existing between nodes i and j in the null model (more on this later), m is the total number of edges in the graph, and $\delta_{(c_i, c_j)}$ is the Kronecker delta, valued 1 if nodes i and j belong to the same community (Ci = Cj), and 0 otherwise. The term $(a_{ij} - p_{ij})$ can be interpreted as a measure of distance, i.e. how far the actual network is from its random counterpart. Therefore, the larger the $(a_{ij} - p_{ij})$ difference, the more modular the network is considered to be

because its random counterpart lacks, by construction, any systematic community organization. The term $(a_{ij} - p_{ij})$ is a normalizing factor (m stands for the total number of links in the network); this term guarantees that the score Q (known as *modularity* score) will lie in the range [0,1].

Any network with N nodes can be encoded as an $N \times N$ matrix. In the simplest case (unweighted, undirected), such a matrix is symmetric and can contain only 0s (link absence) or 1s (link presence). The term 'adjacency' simply refers to the fact that non-zero values express node–node adjacency (connection). The mathematical expression (Equation 1) merely implies that, for a given classification of nodes in groups, one can measure the quality of the partition with the modularity coefficient Q. For instance, we could start by randomly classifying the nodes in a network in a number of categories and calculating the modularity score. We could then move one node from its original category to a different one and calculate again the modularity score. If it improves, we keep the reclassification of nodes; if it does not work, we revert it. The process continues until no nodes are left untouched. The community partition that is selected at the end of the process is that amongst all possible classifications that maximizes the modularity coefficient Q. Given that the solution is sub-optimal (maximizing Q is an NP-hard problem[1]), the challenge of the community detection approach is to come up with an algorithm (i.e. an automated way to iterate the steps just described) that yields a computationally feasible and efficient optimization of the modularity score. This challenge has been approached from a number of different angles developed to deal with the computational costs of clustering nodes in very large networks, i.e. networks in the order of millions of nodes (Arenas *et al.* 2007). A useful review of the different methods available can be found in Fortunato (2010).

The key of the modularity score is that it assesses the significance of a node classification against the benchmark of a null model, which in Equation (1) is captured by the term p_{ij}. The expression is incomplete unless we specify which type of structure i and j belong to in the random, null model (that is, in the randomly generated network). If our random baseline is a network where each node has equal probability to link with any other node (a so-called Bernoulli random graph, see Boccaletti *et al.* 2006) and N is the number of nodes in the network, then $p_{ij} = 2m/N(N–1) \ \forall i,j$; in other words, ties in this random benchmark are formed in a flip-of-the-coin fashion. Of course, online networks do not typically display these patterns of connectivity (which translate into a Poissonian degree distribution, i.e. a distribution of node centrality that is approximately normal); instead, online networks tend to display patterns that are substantially more heterogeneous (i.e. the degree distribution is skewed). Because the null model term (p_{ij}) in Equation (1) should be able to render a faithful random counterpart of the original topology, the equation finally reads:

$$Q = \frac{1}{2m} \sum_{i,j} \left(a_{ij} - \frac{k_i k_j}{2m} \right) \delta_{(c_i,c_j)} \qquad 2$$

in which the probabilistic term mimics the so-called *configuration model* (Newman 2003; Catanzaro *et al.* 2005), which is a random network that reproduces both the probability of ties $P(k)$ and the degree sequence (i.e. the degree distribution in the original network, which captures the centrality of nodes, that is, how many connections they have). In the network literature, 'k' typically expresses 'degree' (i.e. number of connections or centrality). When we want to express the degree of a particular node, we just add a subscript: k_i refers to the degree of some node i; k_j refers to the degree of some node j.

The configuration model provides a more stringent and valid random benchmark with which to compare the structure of the observed network. Widely used software packages for the analysis of communities

in networks offer ready-made algorithms which efficiently optimize the modularity coefficient under the constraints of the configuration model (for instance, C++, Python and R^2). Such software also offers tools to generalize the analysis of communities to scenarios where networks are directed, weighted, signed, or bipartite (Arenas *et al.* 2008; Gómez *et al.* 2009). Some approaches, however, have their own version of modularity or do not aim to maximize it, and before applying a community detection method, researchers should therefore first familiarize themselves with the underlying logic.

Algorithmic developments aside, community detection has opened a fruitful research avenue to investigate the determinants and effects of modularity in networks. In what is already a classic study on ideological polarization in online networks, Adamic and Glance used community detection to identify conservative and liberal communities in the blogosphere (Adamic and Glance 2005). A later study replicated the analysis with social media, finding only partial evidence of polarization in political discussions (Conover *et al.* 2011). The analysis of communities has also been used to illuminate the characteristics of online collegiate social networks (Traud *et al.* 2011) and the structure of protest campaigns in social media (González-Bailón and Wang 2016). In addition, modularity detection has been used to analyze digitized offline records, including the study of party polarization (Moody and Mucha 2013) and fragmentation in the House of Representatives of the U.S. Congress (Porter *et al.* 2005). In all these studies, community detection helps identify structural holes in networks (areas where connections are less dense) and open fault lines in the overall structure – in other words, areas where information is less likely to travel because there are relatively fewer channels for its dissemination.

To sum up, community detection techniques have been predominantly developed to discover high-quality node partitions in the form of disjoint sets of categories, i.e.

a node can only belong to a single module. However, the discovery of fuzzy, overlapping communities is also an important aspect of the problem, inasmuch as entities (i.e. users in social media discussing politics) rarely belong to one and only one category. The discussion of these techniques is beyond the scope of this chapter, but readers should be aware that it is also possible to identify overlapping communities.

Techniques to Filter Links

A second approach to reducing the complexity of large networks consists of eliminating edges so that only those relevant are retained. This approach is especially meaningful for weighted networks, that is, networks where links have a value or bandwidth. For instance, if a network is mapping online interactions in the form of mentions in Twitter, then a link connecting user i with user j will have a value equal to the number of times that user i mentioned user j; the minimum value will be 1 (otherwise, the link would not exist), and the maximum will depend on how often those two users interact (also on how the data are aggregated: a network mapping interactions over a year will have links with more bandwidth than a network mapping activity over a day). Likewise, if a network is mapping the number of common likes that two Facebook users share, the more affinities they have (i.e. they both like the same movie, author, and city) the stronger their connection will be. In brief, online data usually allow us to reconstruct not only interactions and relationships, but also the strength of those ties. Techniques to filter links use the edge strength as the criterion to simplify network structure.

The simplest approach is to use a global threshold to determine which ties need to be removed. If a network maps email communication in an organization, and our goal is to identify the co-workers that exchange information more often, then we could prune irrelevant exchange by eliminating the ties with lower weight, i.e. ties signaling occasional communication. The way in which we determine that threshold depends on the empirical context, but usually it involves examining the distribution of weights and normalizing its range so that we can progressively remove the weakest links (by, say, percentile increments). This type of thresholding helps identify the core of a network in terms of volume of communication but also in terms of connectivity: a progressive removal of edges will likely result in an increasing number of disconnected components (as, for instance, in the network represented in Figure 15.1C). Research has shown that the choice of a threshold condition affects the resulting network structure dramatically (de Choudhury et al. 2010); this means that a strong rationale should guide the application of this method if online networks are to be used as proxies for interpersonal communication.

A limitation of the global threshold approach is that it does not take into account the fact that some nodes are more active than others and so they have more and stronger connections; for a more peripheral node, a globally weak tie might still be strong, i.e. obtaining a fraction of the number of Retweets (RTs) that a celebrity usually receives might still be big for a common Twitter user. Acknowledging and controlling for this local disparity requires, again, defining a null model to determine what counts as an exceptional connection, i.e. a significant departure from randomness, considering that connectivity in networks varies significantly from node to node. Depending on the nature of the network, there are two strategies available: conventional t-tests to identify significant links and a comparison of observed weights with a random weight allocation, a criterion known as the 'disparity filter'. They both respond to similar ideas of significance testing, but they are made operational following a different logic.

The first option, using a t-test to identify significant links, is particularly appropriate when links measure a fraction or percentage of activity. For instance, in a study on language networks, researchers measured the number of Twitter users that published messages in more than one language; according to their data, two languages (the nodes in the network) are connected when users tweeting in a language are also tweeting in another language (Ronen *et al.* 2014). The more users are tweeting in two languages, the higher the weight of the edge connecting those two languages; of course, that weight depends on how many speakers a language has overall (i.e. there are more English-speaking Twitter users than, say, Catalan-speaking users). A good way to control for that variation, and identify connections that are statistically significant with respect to the population of speakers in a given language, is to use standard methods of correlation between binary variables (the *phi* coefficient) and the *t*-statistic to assess the significance of the association. The goal of this exercise is to eliminate ties that might result from a random distribution rather than a genuine association between nodes – in this case, languages.

The second option, called the *disparity filter* (Serrano *et al.* 2009), relies on first normalizing the weights of edges linking node *i* with its neighbors. This normalization accounts for local disparity and allows each node to assess the importance of its connections. Then, the filter proceeds by identifying the links that should be preserved. The null model, which defines the links that one should expect by chance, is built by randomly assigning the normalized weights from a uniform distribution; the filter algorithm then calculates the probability that the observed weight would have occurred under that null model. When that probability is small enough (following usual *p*-value thresholds), the link is preserved as revealing a significant organizing principle in the network. This approach has been used, among other applications, to map user interests in social media (Olson and Neal 2015). Overall, it offers a useful method to reduce the amount of information contained in large networks while preserving the

heterogeneous distribution of centrality usually exhibited by such networks.

CORE-PERIPHERY ANALYSIS

The previous section introduced techniques to reduce the amount of information contained in a network without disregarding the important components that define its structure. This section is about identifying types of nodes in line with what the structure reveals about their positions and, more specifically, about their similarities. The analysis of social networks has long paid attention to notions of structural equivalence, that is, to how similar nodes are in how they connect to other nodes (Lorrain and White 1971; Burt 1976). Identifying structurally similar nodes is important because it can provide the conceptual basis on which to explain similar behavior. In the context of digital networks, and social media in particular, measures of structural similarity can help find nodes that behave similarly in the production and exchange of information; in large networks, this is a useful way to group nodes in manageable categories that account for observed dynamics in, say, information exchange. Here, we focus on strategies that aim to find similar nodes in terms of their position in core-periphery structures (Borgatti and Everett 1999; Rombach *et al.* 2014).

A network has a core-periphery structure when there is a subset of nodes that are very well connected to each other and to peripheral nodes (this would be the core); and another set of nodes that are well connected to the core, but not well connected to each other (these would be the periphery). This core-periphery structure is illustrated in Figure 15.2A. One way to separate core and peripheral nodes is by using the *k*-core decomposition of the network, illustrated in Figure 15.2B; another way is by employing community detection to differentiate nodes that are central locally, globally or both, as illustrated in Figure 15.2C. The following two sections explore these two strategies in more detail.

K-Core Decomposition

A *k*-core is a maximal subgraph in which each vertex has at least degree *k* (Seidman 1983; Alvarez-Hamelin *et al.* 2005). The *k*-core decomposition is a recursive approach that progressively trims the least connected nodes in a network (i.e. those with lower degree) in order to identify the most central ones. Figure 15.2B illustrates the *k*-core decomposition of a random graph. Node degree is in the range of 1 to 5, but there are only four cores: because the method is recursive, some of the nodes with degree 5 end up being classified in lower *k*-shells. Nodes classified in higher *k*-shells not only have higher degree: they are also connected to nodes that are central as well. At the base of the decomposition procedure lies the

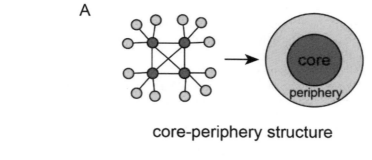

core-periphery structure

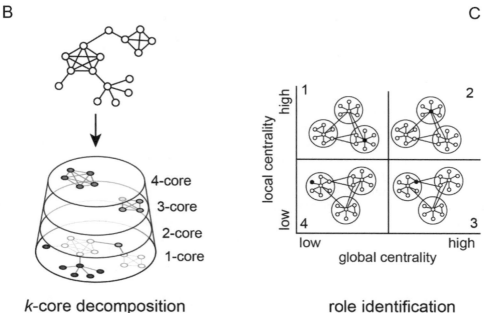

k-core decomposition

role identification

Figure 15.2   Core-periphery structures and role identification

most peripheral nodes; at the highest level, those that are most central are more cohesively linked. The classification of nodes according to their k-core reveals information that is not contained by other centrality measures like degree centrality, betweenness, or eigenvector centrality. The reason is that the k-core reveals characteristics of the network at the meso scale that remain hidden under the lens of those other metrics; it focuses on the structural footprints that cohesion leaves in the network between the levels of the individual node and the overall structure.

The k-core decomposition technique is a computationally efficient way to separate groups of nodes that are highly embedded in a network from those that are more loosely connected. In the context of political protests and social media use, the k-core of users was shown to correlate with their ability to trigger information cascades; that is, core users were more likely to initiate chain reactions in the diffusion of protest-related messages (González-Bailón et al. 2011). Degree centrality, which only captures information about the position of individual nodes, regardless of how their neighbors in the network are connected, did not show that level of association with the ability to diffuse information. A more recent study also used the k-core decomposition of social media networks to analyze the production of information and the overall reach of protest-related messages (Barberá et al. 2015b). The study showed that there is an important division of labor between core and peripheral users: core users generate most of the information, but peripheral participants provide the amplifier that makes those messages resonate more widely in the network.

Role Identification

A more nuanced way to differentiate types of nodes in large-scale networks involves using its structural properties at the local and meso levels: the idea is to identify nodes that are similar in how they connect locally and globally. Figure 15.2C illustrates one such approach, first formulated as a tool to analyze metabolic networks (Guimera and Nunes Amaral 2005) but more recently adapted to summarize the structure of large-scale networks of communication (González-Bailón et al. 2014b). The method requires a partition of nodes in groups where connections are denser internally than externally – a partition that can be obtained using one of the community detection methods introduced earlier (with all the caveats discussed). Once nodes are assigned to groups, it is possible to calculate two metrics summarizing their position in the network: a measure of local centrality (summarizing their position within the community to which they belong) and a network of global centrality (summarizing their position with respect to the nodes classified in other communities). This provides a space that expands on the notion of core-periphery by identifying a core and a periphery simultaneously at the local and global levels.

Four types of nodes emerge as a result of these analyses: nodes that are central locally (within their communities) but not globally (i.e. they do not connect to nodes in other communities); nodes that are central both at the local and global levels; nodes that are central globally, but not locally (they are peripheral in their communities); and nodes that are peripheral on both levels of analysis. The relevance of this classification derives from the fact that nodes that are similar in their connections might behave similarly in the dynamics being channeled by the network. From a topological point of view, the nodes that are central globally are those keeping the network together, i.e. they create the bridges that allow different communities to be connected in a single component. Research suggests that these structural positions are associated to similar behavior; in the context of social media, nodes in central positions at the local and global levels (quadrant 2 in

Figure 15.2C) have been shown to be those that engage more actively in the diffusion of information (González-Bailón *et al.* 2014b). Nodes that are locally central, however, might play other functions that are also relevant for the cohesiveness of the network, like helping to forge group identity.

TEMPORAL DYNAMICS

Digital networks and the prevalence of online communication has also spurred methodological developments in the analysis of temporal networks. Researchers have always been aware that networks are not stationary objects: their composition and structure change over time. However, the rate of those changes was, in the past, slow enough to justify not paying too much attention to them, and assume that networks remained more or less constant. For instance, on the web the hyperlinks that connect any two pages change over the period of weeks, months and years; this is much slower than the rate at which users navigate those links, better characterized in terms of seconds, minutes, and hours. What this means is that it is highly unlikely that topological changes on the structure of the web have a significant impact on the

short-term dynamics of information-seeking behavior. However, social media and new web technologies are accelerating the rate of change in network topology, with consequences that we are still trying to understand. This is the main reason why we need a theory of temporal networks so that we can explain what happens when the dynamics of a network (i.e. changes in its topology) and the dynamics taking place through the network (i.e. information flow) occur at a similar timescale (Vespignani 2012).

Temporal Networks

As seen earlier, networks can encode information about the strength of a relationship in the form of edge weights. Weights, however, are just one type of edge attribute; many other attributes can be assigned to characterize the ties connecting nodes. In this section, we are interested in one such alternative, namely an edge attribute that indicates *time* (also a sequence of times) or *time intervals.* Figure 15.3 illustrates how edge weights can be used to encode temporal information. In Figure 15.3A, the weights account for the time of activation, say the days when two people communicated; in Figure 15.3B, weights account for the intervals during

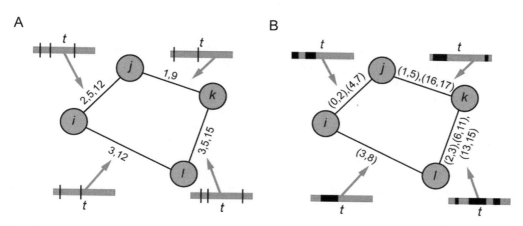

Figure 15.3 Networks encoding temporal information

which the link was active, for instance, the length of their different conversations. A network that contains temporal information for the edges is known as a *contact* network, where ties indicate the state (active/inactive) of an interaction channel.

Accounting for temporal information has important consequences for how we characterize networks. The definition of topological features like shortest paths, degree, clustering, etc. require only a few (but simple and intuitive) adaptations to generalize from unweighted to weighted networks. This is not the case for contact networks. For example, the edges between nodes of temporal networks need not be transitive. In static networks, if i is directly connected to j and j is directly connected to k, then i is indirectly connected to k via the path over j, as in the unweighted version of the networks depicted in Figure 15.3. However, in temporal networks, if the edge (i,j) is active only at a later point in time than the edge (j,k), then i and k are disconnected because nothing can propagate from i to k through j (Holme 2005). The same logic applies with the degree of a node, the definition of which demands some theory: should the degree be a simple aggregation of all observed degrees over time? Should it be an average? The definition of structural features (path, degree and other metrics) changes non-trivially when applied to temporal networks, a change that propagates to the many other measures that rely on those basic concepts (Holme and Saramäki 2012).

Properties like reachability, distance, or connectivity now heavily depend on the restrictions imposed by temporal dynamics. The consequences are not, of course, limited to the structural characterization: if the topology of a contact network encodes such novelties, any new theory considering the dynamics taking place through the network is necessarily affected as well. This means that brand new algorithms are needed to provide suitable synthetic and null models (Kovanen et al. 2011; Kovanen et al. 2013; Perra et al. 2012) as well as new characterizations of

the dynamics unfolding on these topologies, including epidemics (Liu et al. 2013), random walks (Perra et al. 2012; Ribeiro 2013), or threshold cascade models (Backlund 2014). It also means that classic theories in the analysis of social networks, like the strength of weak ties argument, need to be revisited through the lens of digital data and how their higher resolution allow us to redefine the notion of tie strength (Karsai et al. 2014).

Temporal Bipartite Networks: Information Ecosystems

An alternative way to inspect time-evolving networks is using a multi-slice representation. Under this representation, a system is viewed as a sequence of snapshots, each of which encodes the aggregation of activity over a certain time step Δt. This perspective has not been widely used in the analysis of social networks, despite the fact that digital traces are usually time-stamped.

We discuss here a particular example taken from Borge-Holthoefer et al. (2015). The object under study is a *bipartite* multi-slice network, in which Twitter users (*agents*) interact with hashtags (*memes*), and inter-agent or inter-hashtag connections are not allowed ('bipartite' is the name given to networks that have two types of nodes). The advantage of a bipartite perspective is that it overcomes the inherent limitations of research that focuses only on agents (Cattuto et al. 2007) or on memes (Leskovec et al. 2009), but not on their mutual interactions. In addition, the object under study is not a single network but a series of them, which represent different stages in the evolution of a certain topic, and each stage is represented by the aggregation of activity given a certain period of time with range Δt. A link is laid in the nth slice between agent u and meme h if u used h in the period $(n-1)\Delta t < t \leq n\Delta t$. Each snapshot can be analyzed to observe the (co-)evolution of interaction patterns in order to understand the mechanisms behind topic build-up and decay (in this instance, as assessed by hashtag use). In our example, the patterns analyzed are community structure (see earlier) and the *nestedness* of the network, a concept that is illustrated by the schematic adjacency matrices in Figure 15.4.

Like modularity, the nestedness of a network refers to a certain topological arrangement of nodes at the mesoscale. In a perfectly nested network, there are specialists (i.e. nodes that use few hashtags) and generalists (i.e. nodes that use many hashtags). In Figure 15.4 B, user 1 would be a generalist because she is using many different hashtags, and user 6 is a specialist because she only uses a specific keyword. The amount of nestedness for a given topology can be estimated with different methods, but Non-Overlapping Decreasing Fill (NODF) is the simplest and the most widely used (Almeida-Neto *et al.* 2008). The decreasing fill condition imposes that a pair of rows (columns) can only contribute to the nestedness if the number of interactions of row (column) i, is greater or equal to the marginal total of row (column) j. In this case, the paired nestedness N_{ij} is equal to the paired overlap (PO_{ij}), i.e. the number of shared interactions between rows (columns) i, j. The metric can be formulated as:

$$NODF = \frac{\sum_{ij} N_{ij}}{\frac{m(m-1)}{2} + \frac{n(n-1)}{2}}$$

where m is the number of nodes of type A (i.e. hashtags) and n is the number of nodes of type B (i.e. users) and

$$N_{ij} = 0 \text{ if } k_i < k_j$$

$$N_{ij} = PO \text{ if } k_i \geq k_j$$

This measure is irrelevant if it is not compared with an appropriate null model (which, in bipartite networks, typically follows the spirit of the configuration model introduced earlier, but adapted to the characteristics of bipartite structures). This assessment consists of calculating the NODF metric on a large number of random networks; the significance of the observed NODF is expressed as a z-score, i.e. the number of standard deviations between the observed value and the random average.

The choice of modularity and nestedness to characterize a network is not casual. There is evidence that modularity dominates a topology in which nodes are engaged in

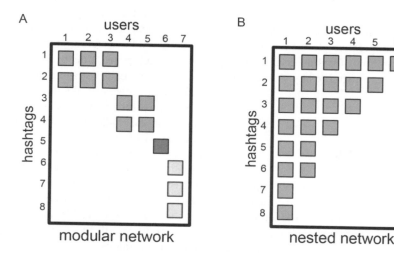

Figure 15.4 Illustration of modular and nested structures

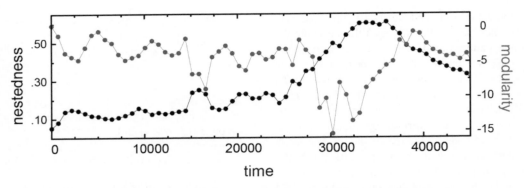

Figure 15.5   Temporal evolution of modularity and nestedness in a social network

competitive interaction, whereas nestedness is typically observed in systems in which mutualism is a major driving factor (Kamilar and Atkinson 2014; Saavedra *et al.* 2009; Thébault and Fontaine 2010). A similar logic of competition versus cooperation is also present in online networks, where agents and memes strive for scarce resources – visibility and attention. Screening the temporal evolution of these two patterns, as illustrated in Figure 15.5, sheds light on the stages at which competitive interactions prevail (when the topic is yet not well-defined) and those at which mutualism dominates (that is, when the coordination of attention is maximized). This approach to online networks as *information ecosystems* (understood as evolving interaction structures driven by competitive cooperative forces) offers a novel understanding of online communication and how it is constrained by scarce cognitive resources.

FUTURE DIRECTIONS

Digital technologies are providing unprecedented data to map social interactions and analyze the effects of interdependence. However, the nature of large-scale data sets is also encouraging the use of methods that can make the most out of that information, which

is richer in the details provided at different temporal and measurement scales. This chapter has offered an overview of some of the methods that are being applied to the analysis of online communication and large-scale networks, but there are many other lines of research that will need to be developed in future work. One of the most promising avenues for future work involves the analysis of multiple networks formalized as multi-layered structures (Kivelä *et al.* 2014). These networks, known as multiplex, aim to capture the ever more prevalent fact that we are not embedded in single structures but in multiple networks at once, and that whatever dynamics take place in one of those layers (i.e. Twitter) is relevant to understanding what happens in other layers (i.e. Facebook, Instagram, Foursquare, face-to-face networks). Achieving a deep understanding of such systems calls for the generalization of 'traditional' network theory, developing a more powerful mathematical framework to cope with the challenges posed by multilayer systems (De Domenico *et al.* 2013). For instance, an adjacency matrix (which is the usual way to represent networks) can no longer encode the subtleties of multiplexed systems for which adjacency tensors are instead being used (Kolda and Bader 2009). This modifies all the underlying algebra implicit in mainstream network research, which means that new software and tools will need to be developed in conjunction with theoretical intuitions that help develop those tools.

Another line for future research involves combining online data with offline behavior, which is still the pending issue in much research analyzing digital networks (Golder and Macy 2014). Although obtaining offline data that can be linked to online activity is always difficult for good and legitimate privacy reasons, some recent studies on time-constrained social mobilization have shed important light on how communication through online networks leads to offline action (Pickard *et al.* 2011; Rutherford *et al.* 2013). This research is based on search contests in which participants need to find objects that are spatially distributed. Based on recruitment dynamics triggered by participant themselves, these studies illuminate the spillover effects that online communication has on social mobilization and they combine an experimental setting (the mobilization task) with observational data (participants' networks and how they mobilize their contacts through social media or other means of communication). The analysis of the recruitment dynamics that result from these experiments sheds important light on the consequences of information diffusion through online networks. As human communication comes to rely more and more on online networks, having the tools to analyze their properties and dynamics will be of increasing importance for the advancement of social theory and research.

NOTES

1 What this means is that the number of possible partitions grows exponentially with the size of the network, and so an exhaustive search of the optimal partition becomes computationally unfeasible.
2 See igraph http://igraph.org (C++, Python, R) or NetworkX https://networkx.github.io/ (Python). Both accessed in November 2015.

REFERENCES

Adamic, Lada, and Natalie S. Glance. 2005. 'The Political Blogosphere and the 2004 U.S. Election: Divided They Blog'. 2nd Annual Workshop on the Weblogging Ecosystem: Aggregation, Analysis and Dynamics, WWW 2005, Japan.

Almeida-Neto, Mário, Paulo Guimarães, Paulo R. Guimarães, Rafael D. Loyola, and Werner Ulrich. 2008. 'A consistent metric for nestedness analysis in ecological systems: reconciling concept and measurement'. *Oikos* 117 (8):1227–39. doi:10.1111/j.0030-1299.2008.16644.x.

Alvarez-Hamelin, J. Ignacio, Luca Dall'Asta, Alain Barrat, and Alessandro Vespignani. 2005. 'Large scale networks fingerprinting and visualization using the k-core decomposition'. *Advances in Neural Information Processing Systems* 18: 41–50.

Arenas, Alex, Angel Fernández, and Sergi Gómez. 2008. 'Analysis of the structure of complex networks at different resolution levels'. *New Journal of Physics* 10 (5): 053039.

Arenas, Alex, Jordi Duch, Angel Fernández, and Sergi Gómez. 2007. 'Size reduction of complex networks preserving modularity'. *New Journal of Physics* 9 (6):176.

Backlund, Ville-Pekka, Jari Saramäki, and Raj Kumar Pan. 2014. 'Effects of temporal correlations on cascades: threshold models on temporal networks'. *Physical Review E* 89 (6): 062815.

Barberá, Pablo. 2015. 'Birds of the same feather Tweet together: Bayesian ideal point estimation using Twitter data'. *Political Analysis* 23 (1): 76–91. doi:10.1093/pan/mpu011.

Barberá, Pablo, and Gonzalo Rivero. 2014. 'Understanding the political representativeness of Twitter users'. *Social Science Computer Review*. doi:10.1177/0894439314558836.

Barberá, Pablo, John T. Jost, Jonathan Nagler, Joshua A. Tucker, and Richard Bonneau. 2015a. 'Tweeting from left to right: is online political communication more than an echo chamber?' *Psychological Science* 26 (10): 1531–42. doi:10.1177/0956797615594620.

Barberá, Pablo, Ning Wang, Richard Bonneau, John Jost, Jonathan Nagler, Joshua Tucker, and Sandra González-Bailón. 2015b. 'The critical periphery in the growth of social protests'. *PloS ONE* 10 (11).

Boccaletti, Stefano, Vito, Latora, Yamir, Moreno, Martin, Chavez, and Dong-Uk, Hwang. 2006. 'Complex networks: structure and dynamics'. *Physics Reports* 424 (4–5): 175–308.

Bond, Robert M., Christopher J. Fariss, Jason J. Jones, Adam D. I. Kramer, Cameron A. Marlow, Jaime E. Settle, and James H. Fowler. 2012. 'A 61-million-person experiment in social influence and political mobilization'. *Nature* 489: 295–8. doi:10.1038/nature11421.

Borgatti, Stephen P., and Martin G. Everett. 1999. 'Models of core/periphery structures'. *Social Networks* 21 (4): 375–95.

Borge-Holthoefer, Javier, Raquel Baños, Carlos Gracia-Lázaro, and Yamir Moreno. 2015. 'The nested assembly of collective attention in online social systems'. *arXiv*: 1501.06809.

boyd, danah, and Kate Crawford. 2012. 'Critical questions for big data. Provocations for a cultural, technological, and scholarly phenomenon'. *Information, Communication & Society* 15 (5): 662–79.

Burt, Ronald S. 1976. 'Positions in networks'. *Social Forces* 55 (1): 93–122. doi:10.2307/2577097.

Burt, Ronald S. 1984. 'Network items and the general social survey'. *Social Networks* 6: 293–339.

Carrington, Peter J., John Scott, and Stanley Wasserman. 2005. *Models and Methods in Social Network Analysis*. Cambridge: Cambridge University Press.

Catanzaro, Michele, Marián Boguñá, and Romualdo Pastor-Satorras. 2005. 'Generation of uncorrelated random scale-free networks'. *Physical Review E* 71 (2): 027103.

Cattuto, Ciro, Vittorio Loreto, and Luciano Pietronero. 2007. 'Semiotic dynamics and collaborative tagging'. *Proceedings of the National Academy of Sciences* 104 (5): 1461–4. doi:10.1073/pnas.0610487104.

Conover, Michael, D., Jacob Ratkiewicz, Matthew, Francisco, Bruno, Gonçalves, Alessandro Flammini, and Filippo Menczer. 2011. 'Political Polarization on Twitter'. AAAI International Conference on Weblogs and Social Media (ICWSM), July 17–21, Barcelona, Spain.

De Choudhury, Munmun, Winter A. Mason, Jake M. Hofman, and Duncan J. Watts. 2010. 'Inferring relevant social networks from interpersonal communication'. Proceedings of the 19th International Conference on World Wide Web, April 26–30, Raleigh, NC.

De Domenico, Manlio, Albert Solé-Ribalta, Emanuele Cozzo, Mikko Kivelä, Yamir Moreno, Mason A. Porter, Sergio Gómez, and Alex Arenas. 2013. 'Mathematical formulation of multilayer networks'. *Physical Review X* 3 (4): 041022.

Fortunato, Santo. 2010. 'Community detection in graphs'. *Physics Reports* 486 (3–5): 75–174.

Girvan, M., and M.E.J. Newman. 2002. 'Community structure in social and biological networks'. *Proceedings of the National Academy of Sciences* 99 (12): 7821–6. doi:10.1073/pnas.122653799.

Golder, Scott A., and Michael W. Macy. 2014. 'Digital footprints: opportunities and challenges for online social research'. *Annual Review of Sociology* 40 (1): 129–52. doi:10.1146/annurev-soc-071913-043145.

Gómez, Sergio, Pablo Jensen, and Alex Arenas. 2009. 'Analysis of community structure in networks of correlated data'. *Physical Review E* 80 (1): 016114.

González-Bailón, Sandra, and Ning Wang. 2016. 'Networked discontent: the anatomy of protest campaigns in social media'. *Social Networks* 44: 95–104.

González-Bailón, Sandra, Javier Borge-Holthoefer, Alejandro Rivero, and Yamir Moreno. 2011. 'The dynamics of protest recruitment through an online network'. *Scientific Reports* 1: 197.

González-Bailón, Sandra, Ning Wang, Alejandro Rivero, Javier Borge-Holthoefer, and Yamir Moreno. 2014a. 'Assessing the bias in samples of large online networks'. *Social Networks* 38 (1): 16–27. doi:10.1016/j.socnet.2014.01.004.

González-Bailón, Sandra, Ning Wang, and Javier Borge-Holthoefer. 2014b. 'The emergence of roles in large-scale networks of communication'. *EPJ Data Science* 3 (1): 1–16. doi:10.1140/epjds/s13688-014-0032-y.

Guimerà, Roger, and Luís A. Nunes Amaral. 2005. 'Functional cartography of complex metabolic networks'. *Nature* 433 (7028): 895–900.

Holme, Petter. 2005. 'Network reachability of real-world contact sequences'. *Physical Review E* 71 (4): 046119.

Holme, Petter, and Jari Saramäki. 2012. 'Temporal networks'. *Physics Reports* 519 (3): 97–125.

Kamilar, Jason M., and Quentin D. Atkinson. 2014. 'Cultural assemblages show nested structure in humans and chimpanzees but not orangutans'. *Proceedings of the National Academy of Sciences* 111 (1): 111–15. doi:10.1073/pnas.1313318110.

Karsai, Márton, Nicola Perra, and Alessandro Vespignani. 2014. 'Time varying networks and the weakness of strong ties'. *Scientific Reports* 4: 4001.

Kivelä, Mikko, Alex Arenas, Marc Barthelemy, James P. Gleeson, Yamir Moreno, and Mason A. Porter. 2014. 'Multilayer networks'. *Journal of Complex Networks* 2 (3): 203–71. doi:10.1093/comnet/cnu016.

Kolda, Tamara G., and Brett W. Bader. 2009. 'Tensor decompositions and applications'. *SIAM Review* 51 (3) : 455–500. doi:10.1137/07070111X.

Kovanen, Lauri, Kimmo Kaski, János Kertész, and Jari Saramäki. 2013. 'Temporal motifs reveal homophily, gender-specific patterns, and group talk in call sequences'. *Proceedings of the National Academy of Sciences* 110 (45): 18070–5. doi:10.1073/pnas.1307941110.

Kovanen, Lauri, Márton Karsai, Kimmo Kaski, János Kertész, and Jari Saramäki. 2011. 'Temporal motifs in time-dependent networks'. *Journal of Statistical Mechanics: Theory and Experiment* 2011 (11): P11005.

Lancichinetti, Andrea, and Santo Fortunato. 2009. 'Community detection algorithms: a comparative analysis'. *Physical Review E* 80 (5): 056117.

Lazer, David, Alex Pentland, Lada Adamic, Sinan Aral, Albert-László Barabási, Devon Brewer, Nicholas A. Christakis, Noshir S. Contractor, James H. Fowler, Myron Gutmann, Tony Jebara, Gary King, Michael W. Macy, Deb Roy, and Marshall Van Alstyne. 2009. 'Computational social science'. *Science* 323: 721–3.

Leskovec, Jure, Lars Backstrom, and Jon Kleinberg. 2009. 'Meme-tracking and the dynamics of the news cycle'. *Proceedings of International Conference of the Association for Computing Machinery's Special Interest Group on Knowledge Discovery and Data Mining*, 28 June–1 July, Paris, France.

Liu, Su-Yu, Andrea Baronchelli, and Nicola Perra. 2013. 'Contagion dynamics in time-varying metapopulation networks'. *Physical Review E* 87 (3): 032805.

Lorrain, François, and Harrison C. White. 1971. 'Structural equivalence of individuals in social networks'. *Journal of Mathematical Sociology* 1 (1): 49–80. doi:10.1080/0022250X.1971.9989788.

Lusher, Dean, Johan Koskinen, and Garry Robins. 2012. *Exponential Random Graph Models for Social Networks: Theory, Methods, and Applications*. Cambridge: Cambridge University Press.

Moody, James, and Peter J. Mucha. 2013. 'Portrait of political party polarization'. *Network Science* 1 (01): 119–21. doi:10.1017/nws.2012.3.

Morstatter, Fred, Jurgen Pfeffer, Huan Liu, and Kathleen M. Carley. 2013. 'Is the sample good enough? Comparing data from Twitter's streaming API with Twitter's Firehose'. AAAI International Conference on Weblogs and Social Media (ICWSM), 8–10 July, Boston, MA.

Newman, Mark, E. J. 2003. 'The structure and function of complex networks'. *SIAM Review* 45 (2): 167–256. doi:10.1137/S003614450342480.

Newman, Mark, E. J. 2012. 'Communities, modules and large-scale structure in networks'. *Nature Physics* 8. doi:10.1038/nphys2162.

Newman, Mark, E. J., Albert-László Barabási, and Duncan J. Watts (eds.). 2006. *The Structure and Dynamics of Networks*. Princeton, NJ: Princeton University Press.

Olson, Randal S., and Zachary P. Neal. 2015. 'Navigating the massive world of reddit: using backbone networks to map user interests in social media'. *PeerJ Computer Science* 1: e4. doi:10.7717/peerj-cs.4.

Perra, Nicola, Bruno Gonçalves, Romualdo Pastor-Satorras, and Alessandro Vespignani. 2012. 'Activity driven modeling of time varying networks'. *Scientific Reports* 2: 469.

Perra, Nicola, Andrea Baronchelli, Delia Mocanu, Bruno Gonçalves, Romualdo Pastor-Satorras, and Alessandro Vespignani. 2012. 'Random walks and search in time-varying networks'. *Physical Review Letters* 109 (23): 238701.

Pickard, Galen, Wei Pan, Iyad Rahwan, Manuel Cebrian, Riley Crane, Anmol Madan, and Alex Pentland. 2011. 'Time-critical social mobilization'. *Science* 334 (6055): 509–12. doi:10.1126/science.1205869.

Porter, Mason A., Peter J. Mucha, Mark E. J. Newman, and Casey M. Warmbrand. 2005. 'A network analysis of committees in the US House of Representatives'. *Proceedings of the National Academy of Sciences* 102 (20): 7057–62.

Ribeiro, Bruno, Nicola Perra, and Andrea Baronchelli. 2013. 'Quantifying the effect of temporal resolution on time-varying networks'. *Scientific Reports* 3: 3006.

Rombach, M. Puck, Mason A. Porter, James H. Fowler, and Peter J. Mucha. 2014. 'Core-periphery structure in networks'. *SIAM Journal on Applied Mathematics* 74 (1): 167–90. doi:10.1137/120881683.

Ronen, Shahar, Bruno Gonçalves, Kevin Z. Hu, Alessandro Vespignani, Steven Pinker, and César A. Hidalgo. 2014. 'Links that speak: the global language network and its association with global fame'. *Proceedings of the National Academy of Sciences* 111 (52): E5616–22. doi:10.1073/pnas.1410931111.

Rutherford, Alex, Manuel Cebrian, Iyad Rahwan, Sohan Dsouza, James McInerney, Victor Naroditskiy, Matteo Venanzi, Nicholas R. Jennings, J. R. deLara, Eero Wahlstedt, and Steven U. Miller. 2013. 'Targeted social mobilization in a global manhunt'. *PLoS ONE* 8 (9): e74628. doi:10.1371/journal.pone.0074628.

Saavedra, Serguei, Felix Reed-Tsochas, and Brian Uzzi. 2009. 'A simple model of bipartite cooperation for ecological and organizational networks'. *Nature* 457 (7228): 463–6.

Seidman, Stephen B. 1983. 'Network structure and minimum degree'. *Social Networks* 5: 269–87.

Serrano, M. Ángeles, Marián Boguñá, and Alessandro Vespignani. 2009. 'Extracting the multiscale backbone of complex weighted networks'. *Proceedings of the National Academy of Sciences* 106 (16): 6483–8. doi:10.1073/pnas.0808904106.

Snijders, Tom A.B. 2011. 'Statistical models for social networks'. *Annual Review of Sociology* 37: 129–51.

Thébault, Elisa, and Colin Fontaine. 2010. 'Stability of ecological communities and the architecture of mutualistic and trophic networks'. *Science* 329 (5993): 853–6. doi:10.1126/science.1188321.

Traud, Amanda, Eric Kelsic, Peter Mucha, and Mason Porter. 2011. 'Comparing community structure to characteristics in online collegiate social networks'. *SIAM Review* 53 (3): 526–43. doi:10.1137/080734315.

Vespignani, Alessandro. 2012. 'Modelling dynamical processes in complex socio-technical systems'. *Nature Physisc* 8 (1): 32–9.

Watts, Duncan J. 1999. 'Networks, dynamics and the small world phenomenon'. *American Journal of Sociology* 105 (2): 493–527. doi:10.1086/210318.

Watts, Duncan J. 2007. 'A twenty-first century science'. *Nature* 445: 489.

Watts, Duncan J., and Steven H. Strogatz. 1998. 'Collective dynamics of "small world" networks'. *Nature* 393 (4): 440–2.

## 16

Social Simulation and Online Research Methods

Corinna Elsenbroich

INTRODUCTION

Social science is the endeavour to understand social phenomena, phenomena such as social order, norms, stratification, inequality, group formation, etc. Most social phenomena are dynamic – inequality can get better or worse, groups form and change, order is broken up and re-established, norms change over time. Dynamics are at the heart of societies and must be at the heart of the undertaking to understand them. By replicating processes underlying social macro-phenomena, social simulation is a methodology for understanding societies which takes the dynamic element of the social world as a starting point.

Social simulation is a relatively novel method in the social sciences, using computer models that recreate essential dynamics of human actions and interactions. The focus of this chapter is on agent-based modelling (ABM), a simulation method that generates macro patterns from the interactions of micro-units called *agents*. Two other

simulation methods, System Dynamics and micro-simulation, are also briefly discussed. The great advantage of simulation modelling in general is the possibility to recreate processes; the great advantage of ABM, over and above this, is the ability to model micro–macro dependencies.

The micro–macro link, or the structure–agency problem, is one of the oldest questions in the social sciences. Theories transcending the dichotomy are, for example, Giddens' *Structuration Theory* which bridges the individual and social by stressing the feedback between agency and structure, emphasising in particular how structure results from individual actions but in turn provides motivations for future actions (Giddens, 1986). Structuration Theory describes a feedback dynamic between the micro and the macro level, extending over time. On a more empirical level, fine-grained ethnographic approaches recognise process and could be described as in themselves a dynamic analysis of phenomena (see, for example, Agar, 1996). Often the data remain fairly small scale and too contextual to allow for society-level generalisations. Simulations are inherently dynamic because they are models of processes (Hartmann,1996).

This chapter introduces social simulation, including a discussion on how to build a model. Three kinds of simulations that reproduce social processes in different ways are discussed – the third kind of simulation, ABM, is the focus of this chapter. The chapter also discusses data-driven applications of ABM in the social sciences, how to use ABM as a research method and ABM in relation to online data.

WHAT IS SOCIAL SIMULATION

Modelling is an essential part of the endeavour to understand the world. Models represent essential features of a phenomenon of interest, leaving out unnecessary aspects. In the social sciences there are several such abstractions used to understand the social world (e.g. models of individual choice and social exchange) leaning on models in economics. These are models abstracting from a person's structural circumstances, focusing solely on the individual aspects (e.g. Coleman, 1990; Homans, 1958).

Statistical and probability models have been used in the social sciences since the nineteenth century and form the basis of quantitative social science. These models are the foundation of making generalisations about the social world, either in the description of statistical facts, i.e. frequency distributions in a population or in relating variables to elicit causal relationships for explanation or even prediction. The latter is riddled with problems, starting from simple mistaking of correlations as causal relationships, to problems of aggregation (see Blalock, 1985). Statistical methods have become more refined, integrating more structure into the analysis to deal with spurious associations (e.g. structural equation modelling) as well as data resulting

from different levels of analysis (e.g. multi-level modelling).

The last 20 years saw the rise of a new kind of modelling of social phenomena in the form of computer simulations, replicating the dynamics found in society. Developments in computer technology, both in hardware and software, mean that models incorporating huge amounts of data can be run with relative ease. Developments of object-oriented computer languages allow the programming of single, 'independent objects' to interact with each other. In this section we discuss three kinds of simulation used in the social sciences: System Dynamics, micro-simulation and ABM. They all replicate dynamics over time, but they deviate in some basic assumptions as well as the kinds of understanding they provide (Gilbert and Troitzsch, 2005).

System Dynamics

System Dynamics is a kind of macro-simulation in which a system is described via a set of system variables and dynamic equations, for example differential or integral equations. A System Dynamics model replicates a closed system, showing how changes to one part of the system affect other parts.

One reason for simulating systems of equations, rather than solving them analytically, is that often the equations are non-linear. The systems modelled using System Dynamics are usually characterised by having interacting, interdependent variables and feedback loops. System Dynamics models are based on 'stocks' and 'flows' where quantities change step-by-step over time.

An interesting social science example is the 'flow' of (re)offenders through a justice system (Ormerod *et al.*, 2001). A person can be a *non-offender*, an *offender* or a *re-offender* and they can be *free* or *in prison* for a certain amount of time. This model is useful to ascertain what happens if prison sentences are prolonged or shortened or rates of re-offending changed.

A downside of System Dynamics models is that in order to build one, at least a good one, one needs to have very detailed understanding *in advance* of how the system works. One needs to understand what rate of non-offenders turn to offending in each time-step, and how many are reoffending. Any system can be modelled using System Dynamics, *as long as the relevant causal connections and dynamic equations are known.* This is both the advantage and disadvantage of Systems Dynamics. If the system is rather well understood, for example the thermodynamic equations of the weather system, a System Dynamics model is a useful tool and the simulation will be elegant and instructive. In social science, these causal connections are rarely well understood, posing a challenge for the application of System Dynamics; nonetheless, for social subsystems where stocks and flows are relatively well understood System Dynamics models have been widely used, in particular for policy modelling. For more details on System Dynamics modelling, see Forrester (1971) or Sterman (2000).

Micro-simulation

A second prominent simulation method in the social sciences is micro-simulation. A micro-simulation does not take a systems perspective, but it individually models the units that make up the system, for example people. The dynamics in a micro-simulation are also based on change equations, but this time the equations describe an individual's transition from one state to the next, for example becoming unemployed or dying. The initialisation of a micro-simulation model is a set of individuals with a set of attributes and a set of transition probabilities of how attributes might change from one time-step to the next. For example, micro-simulation is used to estimate population demands by taking a current population with relevant attributes such as age, wealth and education levels and advancing each

individual time-step to its next set of values. Adding a birth rate to add individuals to the simulation, and age-specific death rates, a micro-simulation can be a useful tool to estimate long-term demands on, for example, schools or pensions. Taken together these separate transitions produce an aggregate system-level analysis. Micro-simulation is used, for example, for population dynamics estimates and tax revenue estimations. It needs a lot of input data to specify the individuals and the likely dynamics, and these are estimated from knowledge about the aggregate level, for example birth and death rates, income distributions, etc. No causal interconnections between the constituent parts of the system are assumed. Because the specifications are made on the constituent parts – the individuals in the system – no causal connections need to be known, but there being no interaction between the individuals means that interdependencies and feedback loops cannot be modelled. This lack of interaction between the individuals makes micro-simulation of limited use for explaining social phenomena, most of which result from just such interactions. However, micro-simulation is a very useful data-driven and predictive simulation method, and has been widely used as a tool for policy analysis (Bourguignon and Spadaro, 2006). For more details on micro-simulation, see Troitzsch *et al.* (1996), Spielauer (2011) and Li (2013).

ABM

Although it seems obvious that societies are made up of individuals and their interactions, taking this view on board methodologically is a rather recent phenomenon, one which is conceptually underpinned by developments in complexity theory and made practically possible by the developments in computers which allow the fast computation of many entities and many steps.

An agent-based model is an individual-based computer program similar to a micro-simulation model, but whereas in a micro-simulation the dynamic is brought about by transition probabilities, agent-based models are driven by the interactions between agents and between agents and their environment. An agent-based model is also somewhat similar to a System Dynamics model because the motivation of building an ABM is to understand a social system and its dynamics. But whereas a System Dynamics model inputs the mechanisms of how a system works and then looks at the impact of certain changes, an ABM generates the system from the interactions of the individuals that make up the system. Although all simulation methods replicate dynamics over time, there are some specific benefits of ABM for the social sciences.

Structure and Agency

ABM is a simulation method that not only models the system over time but also models the interrelationships of different system levels, that is, modelling macro and micro level and their interaction.

ABMs allow for the modelling of structure without eradicating individuals' agency. In fact, agency is the fundamental ingredient of agent-based models, and the constituent parts are agents, which make autonomous decisions about their actions. How agents make decisions, which aspects they take into account and the complexity of the decision procedure can vary substantially between models (for a review, see Balke and Gilbert, 2014). The complexity of the agents and their decision making is dependent on the purpose of the model and the specific research question(s) it is designed to answer and it is an important decision of the model design.

Heterogeneity

That people are different is a defining feature of the social world. Differences are sometimes fairly well defined, such as gender, ethnicity, wealth and class, but there are also less tangible ones such as preferences, motivations and goals, which can be even more

important for the explanation of social phenomena. Micro-simulation already tackles heterogeneity, but mainly for the tangible, quantifiable aspects. In an ABM, the ethereal heterogeneous aspects of individuals can also be modelled in any way relevant for the understanding of the target system, for example their attitudes, individual memories and decisions.

Spatiality

In an ABM, agents interact in some sort of 'space'. Spatiality can be highly relevant for social phenomena because population density, distribution of resources or the structure of a network influence individuals' behaviours. Space here does not necessarily mean a physical environment. Space could be anything which relates agents to each other, for example friendship network, group membership, knowledge, information, opinions, etc.

We discuss two well-known ABMs – segregation and opinion dynamics – to illustrate the ideas of agency-structure dynamics, heterogeneity and spatiality.

Segregation   The first example is a model of segregation (Schelling, 1971). Agents are of two colours, red and green in the original but replicated in black and white in Figure 16.1. Agents are randomly scattered on a two-dimensional grid of patches. Agents have a preference regarding their neighbourhood composition, expressed as a *tolerance threshold*. If an agent is unhappy with its neighbourhood, i.e. if there are too many agents of the other colour, it has the possibility to move to another patch. The interesting result from this model is how high levels of segregation consistently come about from very mild neighbourhood preferences. Figure 16.1 shows three tolerance thresholds – 25, 30 and 50 per cent similar wanted in a), b) and c) respectively. The resulting segregation levels can be seen in the patterns on the grid, which show no segregation for a 25 per cent threshold but clearly show areas of black only and white only occupation for 30 per cent and

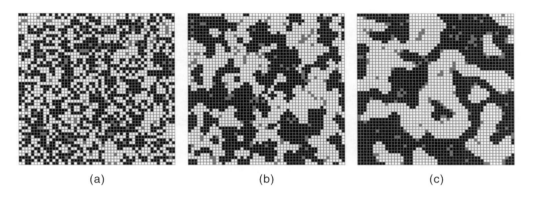

(a)   (b)   (c)

Figure 16.1   Segregation model: a) showing a tolerance threshold of 25%, b) of 30% and c) of 50%

Source: Figure produced with Wilensky, U. (1997).

50 per cent similar wanted. Numerically, segregation levels lie at 75 per cent for thresholds of 30 per cent and 80 per cent for a threshold of 50 per cent. Segregation levels are thus much higher than might be anticipated from the relatively low individual requirements of having a third of one's neighbours similar.

An interesting aspect of the segregation model is that there are a number of *phase transition*s. Below a tolerance threshold of about 27 per cent, segregation does not occur. Thresholds in the interval of 27–55 per cent result in high levels of segregation (>70 per cent). Between the thresholds of 55–75% per cent, segregation increases to nearly 100 per cent, but the system does not stabilise with 'unhappy', and is thus constantly moving agents in the border regions. Above 75 per cent, segregation levels drop to 50 per cent, but only because the system does not settle at all, with almost all agents constantly on the move.

Opinion dynamics   The second example is concerned with the dynamics of opinions, i.e. how opinions might change due to social influence. The model is called the Bounded Confidence (BC) model of opinion dynamics (Hegselmann and Krause, 2002). The BC model consists of a set of individuals, each of which has a certain *opinion*, given by a *real number* from the interval [0,1]. An opinion *profile* is the set of all opinions at time *t*. An

opinion profile can be thought of as a line between 0 and 1 with individuals located on that line, depending on the real number value of their opinion (see Figure 16.2a). At each time-step, an individual takes into account other agents' opinions, but only of those individuals whose opinions are not too dissimilar from its own opinion. The similarity relationship is expressed by a *confidence interval* ε. Imagine the agents on the opinion profile line. The opinions within a confidence interval are those within a certain distance on the opinion profile line (see Figure 16.2a). The opinion of an individual at time *t+1* is the average of the opinions of those agents within its confidence interval.

The starting point for this model is a set of simple assumptions about social influence on an agent's opinion:

Opinion averaging: people's opinion changes depending on who they interact with.
Confidence interval: only those people with opinions not too different have an influence.

The BC model implements heterogeneity of agents by assigning them different initial opinions. The space in this model is a line, representing a set of possible opinions. Agents are positioned on this line and move up or down the line according to the new opinion they adopt in *t+1*.

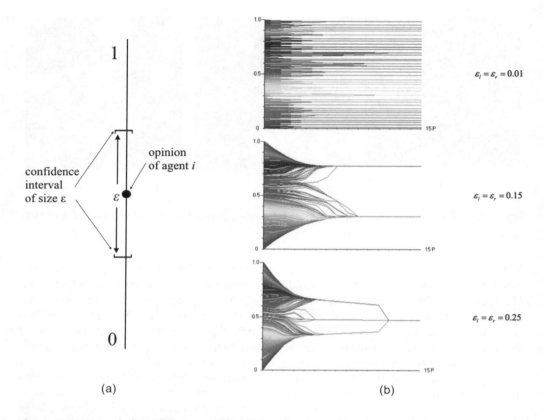

Figure 16.2   Bounded Confidence model; (a) showing a graphic representation of a confidence interval ε, (b) showing runs of the model with confidence intervals ε = 0.01, ε = 0.15, ε = 0.25

Source: Reproduced from Hegselmann and Krause (2002), part (b).

The model is used to investigate the building of consensus or disagreement. The level of opinion alignment reached is dependent on the size of the confidence interval ε. There are three general resulting opinion profiles: (1) plurality, a range of surviving opinions, (2) polarization, two opinions survive at a relatively large distance from each other and (3) consensus, only one opinion survives (see Figure 16.2b). For very low levels of ε, a plurality of opinions persists. For a random uniform initial distribution of opinions, a homogenous, symmetric confidence interval and simultaneous updating, three phase transitions can be identified for values of $\varepsilon = 0.15$ leading to polarization and $\varepsilon = 0.25$ leading to consensus.

Summary

Both System Dynamics and micro-simulation are heavily data-driven simulations. For System Dynamics this is because a system, in particular its causal relationships, has to be well understood to build such a model. Micro-simulation is a stochastic simulation in which demographic developments are modelled over time, using detailed initialisation data as well as well-calibrated transition probabilities. Their advantages and shortcomings for use in the social sciences were discussed in the beginning of this section. The third method, ABM, is able to model the interactions of individuals resulting in the emergence of social phenomena.

One common allegation levelled against ABM is that models are over-simplified, developing 'toy models' rather than anything useful for the understanding of the social world. Of course, the segregation model does not explain segregation levels in New York or Boston, but it shows that segregation levels can escalate from rather mild preferences about individual neighbourhoods and the ability to move. Similarly, the BC model does not explain the shift from centre left governments back to conservatism in Europe in the early 2000s. What it does, however, is to allow for an exploration of the influence of larger and smaller confidence intervals on the development of opinions in a society, e.g. the conditions under which consensus is built or where extreme opinions pull the middle ground. The inputs that inform these simulations are a 'puzzle', for example high levels of segregation or shifts in opinions over time and some hypotheses of relevant aspects, such as neighbourhood preferences and confidence intervals. In addition, these models can inspire empirical research and further empirical models. For segregation models, Bruch (2014) and Benenson *et al.* (2009) discuss data-driven and calibrated models of neighbourhood dynamics and residential segregation. For opinion dynamics, an empirical example is Van Eck *et al.* (2011), who present an empirically grounded ABM on the role of opinion leaders on the diffusion of innovation.

For general overviews of social simulation, see Gilbert and Troitzsch (2005); for ABM, see Gilbert (2008); for an analysis of the contribution of ABM to modelling in the social sciences, see Elsenbroich and Gilbert (2014) and Bianchi and Squazzoni (2015).

In the next section, we discuss two examples of ABM based on 'real data' to illustrate more recent developments in ABM.

DATA-DRIVEN ABM

In the beginning, ABM was dominated by rather abstract simulations, like the segregation and the BC model mentioned earlier. Although abstract simulations heavily simplify the target system, they are useful to understand basic dynamics of interaction and allow for a deep understanding of the isolated dynamics modelled. Nonetheless, they should never be thought of as replicating a target system. The segregation model does not replicate segregation in North American cities, it does not even *explain* segregation in North American cities. What it does, however, is to show that even mild preferences about the composition of neighbourhoods can lead to high levels of segregation. Abstract ABM are often used to understand very basic dynamics, such as segregation, diffusion, markets or opinion dynamics. Isolating a particular dynamic allows for a very deep understanding of this particular dynamic but also means that models largely stay aloof from real world applications. Although ABM has a history of creating abstract models, in the past two decades more empirically based ABM have become widespread, leading to increasing acceptance of ABM as a method in the social sciences as well as in policy analysis and evaluation. This section focuses on data-driven ABM, highlighting some general problems of ABM and data, and discussing in more depth two data-driven models.

Data Problems for Simulations

ABM has developed since the early days of 'toy models'. Some see it as maturing but that underrates the enduring prominence, as well as the usefulness of so called toy models. However, since the turn of the century ABM has also become an empirically informed social science with well calibrated and validated models, used for exploring and understanding social phenomena such as land-use (Valbuena *et al.*, 2010), urban regeneration (Picascia, 2014), markets (Macal and North, 2005) or burglary (Groff, 2007). For an overview of empirically driven ABM, see the special issue of *Journal for*

Artificial Societies and Social Simulation (2015: 18/1) on grounded simulation.

Despite the increasing use of data in ABM, it is worth discussing some endemic problems of existing data.

1 Static data: social science data are largely cross sectional, showing the state of the world at a specific point in time. Given the dynamic nature of ABM, static data are of limited use, although they might be used for calibration or validation (see, for example, the section 'A model of ethnic segregation at the workplace'). Longitudinal datasets are much more useful but because of the cost of maintaining those datasets, they are few and far between. Panel data are more promising but are often marred by the problem of inadequacy (see point 2).

2 Discontinuous/expedient questions: existing longitudinal or panel datasets are often discontinuous, changing questions slightly from one collection to the next, making the data more difficult to use overall and also for ABM, which relies on continuity for validation purposes. Another problem is that the questions being asked in longitudinal and panel data are often not detailed enough or are simply the wrong kinds of questions (see point 3) for application in ABM. One reason for this is that the data collections are expensive and cumbersome and thus do not allow for more detailed data.

3 Wrong questions: when discussing heterogeneity in ABM we discussed the differences in motivations, desires and goals between agents. Although data can be found describing a range of different motivations, etc., it is almost impossible to find data on the *distributions* of these attributes in society. But not knowing these distributions makes the calibration of an ABM with data very difficult indeed.

Despite these problems, data-driven ABM are on the rise and there is increasing use of ABM in policy modelling.

Empirical Simulation

In this section we discuss two mid-range ABM, using empirical data for model building and validation. The two models represent very different uses of empirical data. The first model we discuss is a model of the English housing market, which implements qualitative data on buyer, seller and estate agent behaviours together with a 'real world' background economy.

A Model of the UK Housing Market

Gilbert *et al.* (2008) describes an ABM of the English housing market. The housing market-specific dynamics are implemented using behaviour rules for stylised buyer, seller and realtor agents. Buyers are looking for a suitable house. Sellers want to achieve the maximum price. Realtors judge the value of a house by looking at the prices of similar, recently sold houses in the neighbourhood and put on a certain mark-up, for example 10 per cent. The price of houses that stay on the market for too long is incrementally reduced after a certain number of time-steps. These dynamics are implemented on a basic background economy, including household income, saving rates, interest rates, unemployment, etc.

The model is set up with a random distribution of houses of varying prices. The realtors are initialised with a certain neighbourhood in which they operate. House owners sell either when a property becomes empty (e.g. death or they have to leave the area due to job relocation), when their mortgages become too expensive for their income (e.g. due to unemployment) or when they want to trade up (e.g. have a significant income increase). Buyers choose the maximally affordable house, given their personal finances.

The first interesting outcome is the emergence of expensive and cheaper areas (Figure 16.3). This is the visual feature of ABM mentioned earlier where clustering effects can be seen directly from the visual simulation output.

Further interesting outcomes from the simulation are:

The importance of first time buyers: newcomers to the market are important to maintain prices because otherwise demand for lower

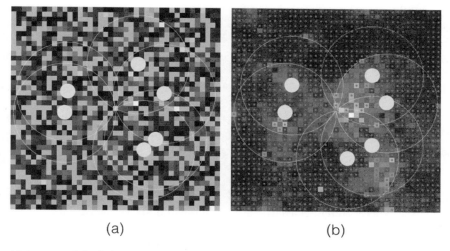

(a)   (b)

Figure 16.3   A model of the English housing market; (a) shows a random initialisation where darker shade represents a higher price. The round dots represent estate agents and the circles their area, (b) shows the model after 1000 ticks, showing a clear emergence of more expensive (darker) and cheaper (lighter) areas

Source: Figure produced with Gilbert et al. (2001).

price properties dries up, meaning people cannot trade up.

Sensitivity of prices to interest rates: if general affordability is kept constant, a rise in interest rates will lead to a drop in house prices as the price potential owners can afford falls.

Demand and supply: sharp increases in demand lead to an immediate sharp increase in house prices as supply is slow to increase. Sharp decreases in demand lead to immediate sharp falls in house prices.

This simulation uses both qualitative and quantitative data. The background economy is calibrated to actual levels, i.e. interest rates at about 3 per cent, mean income at around £30,000, affordability (the proportion of income spent on housing) is set at 25 per cent, etc. In addition to these quantitative measures implemented in the model, the agents' behaviours are informed by qualitative data, asking realtors how they value houses and observing behaviours of the housing market, such as the price reduction of a property that does not sell.

The outputs are patterns of long-term housing market trends, like bubbles and crashes, the house price distribution, median time a house is on the market and the median house price. The model allows the investigation of the influence of interest rates, deposits, stamp duty, etc. on the housing market. The model output can be compared to historical housing market crashes, such as the hike in interest rates in the mid-1990s and the reduction of first-time buyers due to high deposits demanded for the issuing of a mortgage following the 2008 financial crisis.

A Model of Ethnic Segregation at the Workplace

Abdou and Gilbert (2009) describe a model of a labour market, situated in society, to investigate ethnic segregation at the workplace. Rather than having tolerance thresholds as in the segregation model (see earlier), this model looks at the effects of social networks and societal segregation together with different hiring procedures on the segregation levels of workplaces. The agents in this model have a unified level of labour market qualifications and belong to two different social groups, red or green. Red is a minority group in society with a proportion of $0<P<0.5$ (P is the input parameter of level of minority). Agents are linked in social networks, made up of directed links and a maximum number S of nodes (S is the input parameter for the size of the egocentric network).

In the simulation the agents are fired with a certain probability. Agents are hired either randomly or by referral from current workers in the firm. Workers refer agents who are in their social networks and the networks, in turn, are formed by adding or deleting workmates, friends or random acquaintances. This formation is dependent on homophily levels in an agent's workplace and society at large. Segregation statistics for workplaces and overall society are calculated and plotted.

Results from the simulation show that referral hiring leads to increased levels of workplace and social segregation; however, workplace and social segregation can co-evolve even when hiring is random and society is initially integrated. In the model, this is mainly due

to firing being informed by the homophily levels of a firm. Figure 16.4 shows the coevolution of workplace and social segregation and of homophily levels for the majority and minority.

In addition, referral hiring is beneficial for minority groups if the population is highly segregated, but harmful for higher levels of integration.

What is particularly interesting about this model is that it is empirically calibrated and validated using a variety of datasets: the Worker's Status in Industrial Enterprise Survey (WSIES), the Social Contact Survey (SCS) and other empirical data gathered by the modellers. The model parameters are calibrated against the datasets and the resulting levels of social and workplace segregation, majority and minority unemployment are very close to those found in the empirical data.

The main results from the simulation are that even random hiring can lead to segregated workplaces, that majority groups are more homophilous than minority groups and that referral hiring can be beneficial for minority groups. Given the relative simplicity of the dynamics together with the ability to calibrate and validate the modelling input

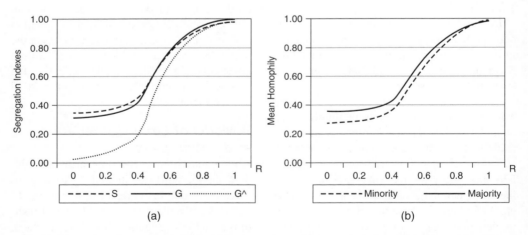

(a)   (b)

Figure 16.4 Work place segregation; (a) shows the co-evolution of workplace segregation (G and G^) and social segregation (S), (b) shows the mean homophily of minority and majority groups for different levels of referral hiring *R*

Source: Reproduced from Fig. 2 and Fig. 3 from Abdou and Gilbert (2009).

and output, this model shows how quantitative data can play a detailed role in ABM.

Summary

We have seen two data-driven ABM, which use different kinds of data in different ways. The housing model uses general economic input data together with empirically informed stylised agent behaviour rules to recreate the English housing market. The results are validated comparing the patterns of house price development and exploring the dependencies of economic factors such as interest rates and deposits on house prices. The segregation model also uses abstracted agent behaviours, but the parameters such as segregation levels in work places and society in general are calibrated from data, and the simulation model is validated specifically against the particular case of Coptic Christians versus Muslims in Egyptian society.

These are just two examples of a plethora of empirical ABM. Some other models using data for ABM in different ways are discussed in Agar (2005), which integrates ethnographic data, and Manzo (2013) using large national survey data from the INSEE, the French national bureau of statistics.

BUILDING AN ABM

In some ways building an ABM is exactly the same as any other piece of research. There will be a general topic area of interest and a particular research question that the ABM is supposed to tackle. It should be clear from the previous section that ABM is a methodology that is particularly useful for answering research questions about temporal and structural dynamics. When starting to think about an ABM, one should also keep in mind who the users of the model will be. Is it only oneself that will use the model to explore a social phenomenon, are other researchers going to use the model, or is

it targeted at stakeholders such as policy makers? The model design and implementation will be markedly influenced by the envisaged users of the model. The following summarises the main points to think about when designing an ABM. For more detail on how to specify a model, see Gilbert (2008: ch. 4).

Literature Research

After defining the research questions, the next step is to scope the literature background in the topic area. Two things are particularly important here for the development of an ABM. First, what is the literature relevant for the model? This might be theoretical literature as well as empirical research into the phenomenon of interest. Theory might provide a background theory for the design of the agents,[1] whilst empirical research will provide ideas about general macro-level aspects of the domain, such as patterns, as well as data for the validation of the ABM. Second, what are the existing simulation models relevant for the model? This might be models that tackle a similar subject area (e.g. energy consumption) or that use particular settings such as networks or models that are structurally similar to the envisaged model (e.g. social influence dynamics, segregation).[2]

Level of Generality

After this the thoughts can turn to the model itself. The first decision that needs to be made is what level of generality or abstraction the model is targeted at. Earlier, we discussed abstract and mid-range models. Abstract models focus on the general patterns of a system, such as segregation clustering and opinion radicalisation. Mid-range models, in addition to replicating general patterns, want to replicate some pattern in more detail and want to at least have some foundation for the agent behaviours implemented and some of the values of the background variables. A third kind of ABM is a facsimile model, which is highly specific to a particular case and replicates the world as closely as possible (e.g. Dean *et al.* 1999). The decision of which level the model should sit at is a very important decision because it informs all further decisions regarding model specification, data requirements, validation and interpretation.

Static Model

Having made the decision of which level of abstraction a model should sit at, the objects in the model have to be specified. A model consists of agents, an environment in which they are situated and other objects such as resources. What type of agents does the model have (e.g. buyers and seller)? Is the environment spatial (e.g. grassland) or non-spatial (e.g. friendship networks)? Is there a resource like food or energy that the environment or agents store and consume? Agents, the environment and other objects need to be specified by attributes relevant for the modelling. For example, if the model is of the housing market, agents might need an income and wealth, a mortgage; the environment needs houses; and houses need prices and owners. These attributes need to have values for their initialisation. The income of agents in the model could be normally distributed or could be informed by actual income distribution data. Whether the initial values are calibrated against data or not depends partly on the level of abstraction the model is pitched at, partly on data availability and partly on the research question. Once all these questions are answered, a *static* model can be specified.

Model Dynamics

As discussed earlier, the unique feature of ABM is the modelling of temporal and structural dynamics. After specifying the static model, the next task is to specify how the system changes. Remember how a System

Dynamics model transitioned from one state to the next by specifying the 'stocks' and 'flows' through the system (e.g. money in an economy), and micro-simulation transitioned by executing probability distributions over a set of initialised agents (e.g. probability of death by age group). In an ABM, the dynamics result from the interactions of agents with each other and the environment. There are varying kinds of interactions. Agents can, for example, consume or exchange resources, communicate with each other, move about in the environment, etc. The questions to be answered are (a) what are the relevant actions that agents may execute in the model and (b) under what conditions do agents make which decisions. In the housing model, for example, agents buy and sell houses to each other. The condition for buying a particular house is to have enough money to do so, but also to have gathered the information that this particular house is for sale. Actions and their conditions can quickly become rather complicated and it is advisable to draw a diagram to summarise the model (for an introduction to UML for ABM[3], see Bersini, 2012).

Implementation

Now that the model design has been produced, the model can be implemented. There are many programming languages suitable for ABM, and ABM have been implemented in a range of specialist software products. General software packages for ABM include Swarm, Repast, Repast Symphony and AnyLogic. Some packages are specifically for cognitively complex agents, such as MASON, MAS-SOC and Soar. Some are targeted at very large systems with thousands or millions of agents, e.g. FLAME. Another set is developed to integrate ABM and GIS.[4] The package that is most often used in the social sciences is NetLogo (Wilensky, 1999). NetLogo is a programming language specifically developed for ABM. It is very easy to learn and has excellent documentation, including tutorials and models published online.[5] It is also developed in such a way that it has a highly usable interface and inbuilt tools for model debugging and analysis. The decision of language is again informed by the kind of model that is going to be built, but NetLogo is a good choice for most models in the social sciences (see Gilbert, 2008; for NetLogo limitations, see Railsback and Grimm, 2011: ch. 24; Wilensky and Rand, 2015).

Verification

After implementation, a model needs to be *verified*. Verification means to check that the model does what it is supposed to do. This is an important aspect of programming because it is easy to introduce bugs into a program. It helps to build models in a modular way and test procedures as they are added to isolate and eradicate problems with the code immediately. More on verification in ABM can be found in Gilbert and Troitzsch (2005: ch. 9); Railsback and Grimm (2011: ch. 6) and Wilensky and Rand (2015: ch. 7).

Outputs and Validation

Whereas verification checks whether the code is correct, validation is the check whether the model in fact represents the phenomenon it sets out to represent. Already in the design stage of the model the validation of the model should be kept in mind when deciding the model outputs. The outputs are important for answering the research question but consideration has to be given to what can be measured in the model and what kind of data is available for comparison. The kind of validation possible and necessary for a model depends on its level of abstraction. For abstract models the replication of rough patterns might be sufficient (see Railsback and Grimm, 2011); the more data-driven and concrete a model, the more data-driven and

detailed the validation needs to be. For the segregation model, it is sufficient that it replicates segregated neighbourhoods. The housing model set out to recreate some persisting features of the UK housing market, such as sensitivity of house prices to interest rates, the effects of demand shocks and the importance of first-time buyers, and it also managed to replicate the known dynamics. For more on validation, see Gilbert (2008: ch. 3) and Wilensky and Rand (2015: ch. 7).

Summary

Using ABM as a research method in the social sciences is very similar to any other method, including careful research design, learning specialist tools (here a programming language) and checking one's findings against the real world and existing knowledge. ABM are the appropriate method when the research is focused on temporal or structural dynamics, when heterogeneity is relevant, when spatial aspects might play a role and when interactions between people drive change.

ONLINE RESEARCH METHODS AND ABM

We have seen that ABM has the ability to integrate different kinds of social science data, for example by informing behaviour rules with qualitative data and calibrating and validating models with quantitative data. But we have also seen that there are some problems of current social science data in relation to ABM (see earlier). Behaviour rules extrapolated from qualitative data are difficult to operationalise, and data collected for statistical analysis often measure aspects irrelevant to the simulation, are patchy and not connected to agent-specific data for the calibration of models. The biggest data problem for ABM, however, is related to its capacity to model dynamics or processes – there is very little data on processes. Despite the existence of excellent longitudinal datasets (e.g. the UK Census and cohort studies), data are few and far between and often still have the problem of not capturing the relevant aspects, in particular in linking micro and macro aspects of phenomena.

In the previous section, we discussed two data-driven models, which rely on different kinds of data and use data in different ways. A new kind of data that has appeared is *online data*, big datasets of people's networks, communications, shopping behaviour and information gathering. Given this rise of online data which is almost parallel with the development of data driven ABM, it is surprising that there is relatively little cross-fertilisation despite an explosion in computational social science approaches to online data, mainly in the form of data mining. This is particularly surprising because the two fields have great potential for cross-fertilisation. The integration of the two fields could enrich both, with aspects of online data being particularly useful for ABM validation and ABM having the potential to test the viability of online data for the explanation of social phenomena and elicit underlying processes (e.g. Wierzbicki *et al.*, 2014). In this section, we briefly summarise some existing research and point to future possibilities on how these areas could work together (see Schatten *et al.*, 2015).

There are two main areas where integration has happened. ABM has been used to study individual behaviour and network structures, either by analysing individuals' data from network dynamics (Fontana and Terna, 2014) or modelling aspects of the networks directly, such as hierarchies emerging from communication (Gabbriellini, 2014). The models use the possibility of extracting structural network data from online social networks. This is a great advantage because the networks are very large and do not contain problems associated with self-report methods (see Chattoe and Hamill, 2005).

The second application is to analyse online behaviour such as app installation (Gleeson *et al.*, 2014) or information diffusion (Rand *et al.*, 2015). The above models investigate competing hypotheses about the micro behaviour rules, i.e. recency versus cumulative and Bass versus Cascade, testing which result in the more realistic patterns (see Goldenberg et al., 2001 for the former and Bass, 1969 for the latter). Diffusion models are interested in the communication and information transmitted through networks rather than the networks themselves.

The existence and collection of online data provides a new resource that might help with some of the problems of ABM and traditional data. Four aspects are particularly important:

a)　*Ubiquitous availability*

The amount of online data available is extraordinary and encompasses all sorts of aspects from sentiment analysis to networks. This amount of data allows ABM to be informed in much more detailed ways over a much larger population than many traditional data sources would.

b)　*Dynamics*

Online data can be collected over time, continuously or in short time intervals, leading to detailed time series datasets. Although the data do not capture the underlying processes, these datasets are much more appropriate for validation of simulation models than widely separated snapshots in longitudinal studies. Rand *et al.* (2015) discuss the importance of relatively small time intervals for use in validation because replicating outcomes becomes easier the further apart the comparison points are. This points to the problem of under-determination of models by normal longitudinal data, which usually only has measurements at relatively far apart points.

c) Concurrency

Collecting online data is cheap and not time bound. Whereas traditional data collection conducts a set of interviews or surveys with the analysis following the completed collection, for online data the collection can be done repeatedly to collect more or different aspects or to extend datasets to elicit dynamics further into the future.

d) Ontologies

Web ontologies are a major research field in computer science. Polhill (2015) introduces a NetLogo extension to extract OWL[6] ontologies from an ABM, and Troitzsch (2015) presents an application of the extension to an existing model, detailing how it helps in developing ABM further.

The combination of ABM with big data in general (and online data in particular) has started and, given the possibilities discussed in this paper, fast acceleration of this integration is to be expected.

CONCLUSIONS

Social simulation is an exciting addition to the social science research methods portfolio. It is able to assist the understanding of temporal and structural dynamics, heterogeneity and spatiality by modelling relevant aspects of the target system to be explained. The ability to model individuals and have macro phenomena emerge from their interactions is a particularly social science-friendly feature of ABM.

We discussed abstract and data-driven ABM, emphasising how all of them can play a role in social science research and the understanding of social phenomena. We went through the process of designing,

implementing and validating a model. We also discussed data problems of ABM, problems of having the right kind of micro data for initialising models, statistical and longitudinal data for calibration and validation, etc. We described three ways in which online data might be useful for social simulation. Ubiquitous availability of online data allows for the easy combination of several social aspects, like networks or sentiments. Dynamics of online data, i.e. the ability to get detailed time sequence data, allows for much more informed model building.

Online data has great potential to inform and enhance ABM. In return, ABM can help to make sense of online data, which is too often analysed without remembering the social nature of its origin. By using models stipulating decision mechanisms of network formation, hierarchy construction, app installation or replicating the behaviours of posting on Twitter, the social aspects of Big Data are highlighted and explored and their adequacy in explaining the social tested.

NOTES

1 A variety of bounded rationality approaches and theories of individual decision making from cognitive and social psychology have been popular in ABM. For a review, see Elsenbroich and Gilbert (2014).
2 Many ABM are openly available in places like https://www.openabm.org and http://modelingcommons.org (accessed 25 July 2016).
3 UML is a Unified Modeling Language, cf. Fowler (2003).
4 For a comprehensive list of software products, see for example Allan (2010). For a comparison and discussion, see Railsback et al. (2006) or Nikolai and Madey (2009).
5 All models discussed are available as NetLogo versions.
6 OWL is a Web Ontology Language which is used to represent things and their relationships on the web (Becherhofer et al., 2003).

REFERENCES

Abdou, M. and Gilbert, N. (2009) 'Modelling the emergence and dynamics of social and workplace segregation', *Mind & Society*, 8: 173–91.

Agar, M. H. (1996) *The Professional Stranger: An Informal Introduction to Ethnography.* Vol. 2. San Diego, CA: Academic Press.

Agar, M. H. (2005) 'Agents in living color: towards emic agent-based models', *Journal of Artificial Societies and Social Simulation,* 8(1):4.

Allan, R.J. (2010) Survey of Agent Based Modelling and Simulation Tools. Technical Report DL-TR-2010-007, Science and Technology Facilities Council (STFC), Warrington WA4 4AD, 48.

Balke, T. and Gilbert, N. (2014) 'How do agents make decisions? A survey', *Journal of Artificial Societies and Social Simulation*, 17(3): 13.

Bass, F. M. (1969) 'A new product growth for model consumer durables', *Management Science*, 15(5): 215–27.

Becherhofer, S., Volz, R. & Lord, P. (2003) 'Cooking the semantic web with the OWL API'. In Fensel, D., Sycara, K. & Mylopoulos, J. (eds.) *Second International Semantic Web Conference*, ISWC 2003, Sanibel Island, Florida, 20–23 October 2003. *Lecture Notes in Computer Science,* 2870, 659–675.

Benenson, I., Hatna, E. and Or, E. (2009) 'From Schelling to spatially explicit modeling of urban ethnic and economic residential dynamics', *Sociological Methods Research*, 37: 463–97.

Bersini, H. (2012) 'UML for ABM', *Journal of Artificial Societies and Social Simulation* 15(1): 9.

Bianchi, F. and Squazzoni, F. (2015) 'Agent-based models in sociology', *WIREs Comput Stat*, 7: 284–306. doi:10.1002/wics.1356.

Blalock, H. M. (1985) *Causal Models in the Social Sciences*. New Brunswick, NJ: Aldine Transaction.

Bourguignon, F. and Spadaro, A. (2006) 'Microsimulation as a tool for evaluating redistribution policies', Technical Report, Society of the Study of Economic Inequality – Working Paper Series.

Bruch, E. E. (2014) 'How population structure shapes neighborhood segregation', *American Journal of Sociology*, 119: 1221–78.

Chattoe, E. and Hamill, H. 2005. 'It's not who you know – it's what you know about people you don't know that counts', *British Journal of Criminology*, 45(6): 1–17.

Coleman, J. S. (1990) *Foundations of Social Theory*. Cambridge, MA: Harvard University Press.

Dean, J. S., Gumerman, G. J., Epstein, J. M., Axtell, R., Swedlund, A. C., Parker, Miles T., McCarroll, S. (1999) 'Understanding Anasazi culture change through agent-based modeling'. In T. Kohler and G. Gumermann (eds.), *Dynamics in Human and Primate Societies.* Oxford: Oxford University Press, pp. 179–206.

Elsenbroich, C. and Gilbert, N. 2014. *Modelling Norms*. Berlin: Springer.

Fontana, M. and Terna, P. (2014) 'From agent-based models to network analysis (and return): the policy-making perspective', SwarmFest 2014, University of Notre Dame.

Forrester, J. W. (1971) 'Counterintuitive behavior of social systems', *Technology Review*, 73(3): 52–68.

Fowler, M. (2003) *UML Distilled: A Brief Guide to the Standard Object Modeling Language* (3rd ed.). Addison-Wesley.

Gabbriellini, S. (2014) 'Status and participation in online task groups: an agent-based model'. In G. Manzo (ed.), *Analytical Sociology: Actions and Networks*. Chichester, UK: John Wiley & Sons, pp. 317–38.

Giddens, A. (1986) *The Constitution of Society: Outline of the Theory of Structuration.* Berkeley, CA: University of California Press.

Gilbert, N. (2008) *Agent-Based Models*. Number 153 in Quantitative Applications in the Social Sciences. London: Sage Publications.

Gilbert, N. and Troitzsch, K. G. (2005) *Simulation for the Social Scientist*. 2nd ed. Maidenhead, UK: Open University Press.

Gilbert, N., Hawksworth, J. C. and Swinney, P. A. (2008) 'An agent-based model of the UK housing market'. Technical Report, CRESS University of Surrey. Available from http://cress.soc.surrey.ac.uk/housingmarket/ukhm. html (accessed 25 July 2016).

Gleeson, J. P., Cellai, D., Onnela, J.-P., Porter, M. A. and Reed-Tsochas, F. (2014) 'A simple generative model of collective online behavior'. *Proceedings of the National Academy of*

Sciences of the United States of America, 111(29): 10411–15.

Goldenberg, J., Libai, B. and Muller, E. (2001) 'Talk of the network: a complex systems look at the underlying process of word-of-mouth', *Marketing Letters*, 12(3): 211–23.

Groff, E. R. (2007) '"Situating" simulation to model human spatio-temporal interactions: an example using crime events', *Transactions in GIS*, 11(4): 507–30.

Hartmann, S. (1996) 'The world as a process: simulations in the natural and social sciences'. In R. Hegselmann, (ed.), *Modelling and Simulation in the Social Sciences from a Philosophy of Science Point of View*, Theory and Decision Library. Dordrecht: Kluwer, pp. 77–100.

Hegselmann, R. and Krause, U. (2002) 'Opinion dynamics and bounded confidence: models, analysis and simulation', *Journal of Artificial Societies and Social Simulation*, 5(3).

Homans, G. C. (1958) 'Social behaviour as exchange', *American Journal of Sociology*, 63: 597–606.

Li, J. (2013) 'A survey of dynamic microsimulation models: uses, model structure and methodology', *International Journal of Microsimulation*, 6(2): 3–55.

Macal, C. M. and North, M. J. (2005) 'Validation of an agent-based model of deregulated electric power markets'. In Proceedings of North American Computational Social and Organization Science (NAACSOS), Notre Dame, IN USA (June 2005).

Manzo, G. (2013) 'Educational choices and social interactions: a formal model and a computational test'. In G. E. Birkelund (ed.), *Class and Stratification Analysis*. Comparative Social Research, Vol. 30. Bingley, UK: Emerald Group Publishing, pp. 47–100.

Nikolai, C. and Madey, G. (2009) 'Tools of the trade: a survey of various agent based modeling platforms', *Journal of Artificial Societies and Social Simulation*, 12(2): 2. Available from http://jasss.soc.surrey.ac.uk/12/2/2.html (accessed 25 July 2016)

Ormerod, P., Mounfield, C. and Smith, L. (2001) 'Non-linear modelling of burglary and violent crime in the UK'. Technical Report, Volterra Consulting Ltd for the Home Office UK.

Picascia, S. (2014) 'A theory driven, spatially explicit agent-based simulation to model the economic and social implications of urban regeneration', Proceedings of *European Social Simulation Association Conference*, Barcelona, 2014. http://ddd.uab.cat/record/125597 (accessed 25 July 2016).

Polhill, J. G. (2015) 'Extracting OWL ontologies from agent-based models: a NetLogo extension', *Journal of Artificial Societies and Social Simulation*, 18(2): 15.

Railsback, S. F. and Grimm, V. (2011) *Agent-Based and Individual-Based Modelling: A Practical Introduction*. Princeton, NJ: Princeton University Press.

Railsback, S. F. and Lytinen, S. L. and Jackson S. K. (2006) 'Agent-based simulation platforms: review and development recommendations', *Simulation*, 82: 609–23.

Rand, W., Herrmann, J., Schein, B. and Vodopivec, N. (2015) 'An agent-based model of urgent diffusion in social media', *Journal of Artificial Societies and Social Simulation*, 18 (2): 1.

Schatten, M., Seva, J. and Duric, B. O. (2015) 'An introduction to social semantic web mining & big data analytics for political attitudes and mentalities research', *European Quarterly of Political Attitudes and Mentalities*, 4(1): 40–62.

Schelling, T. (1971) 'Dynamic models of segregation', *Journal of Mathematical Sociology*, 1: 143–86.

Spielauer, M. (2011) 'What is social science microsimulation?', *Social Science Computer Review*, 29(1): 9–20.

Sterman, J. D. (2000) *Business Dynamics: Systems Thinking and Modeling for a Complex World*. Boston, MA: Irwin/McGraw-Hill.

Troitzsch, K. G. (2015) 'What one can learn from extracting OWL ontologies from a NetLogo model that was not designed for such an exercise', *Journal of Artificial Societies and Social Simulation*, 18(2): 14.

Troitzsch, K. G., Mueller, U., Gilbert, G. N. and Doran, J. E. (1996) *Social Science Microsimulation*. Berlin: Springer.

Valbuena, D., Verburg, P., Veldkamp, A., Bregt, A. K. and Ligtenberg, A. (2010) 'Effects of farmers' decisions on the landscape structure of a Dutch rural region: an agent-based approach', *Landscape and Urban Planning*, 97(2): 98–110.

Van Eck, P. S., Jager, W., Leeflang, P. S. H. (2011) 'Opinion leaders' role in innovation diffusion: a simulation study', *Journal of Product Innovation Management*, 28: 187–203.

Wierzbicki, A., Adamska, P., Abramczuk, K., Papaioannou, T., Aberer, K. and Rejmund, E. (2014) 'Studying web content credibility by social simulation', *Journal of Artificial Societies and Social Simulation* 17(3): 6.

Wilensky, U. (1997) NetLogo Segregation model. http://ccl.northwestern.edu/netlogo/models/Segregation. Center for Connected Learning and Computer-Based Modeling, Northwestern University, Evanston, IL.

Wilensky, U. (1999) NetLogo. http://ccl.northwestern.edu/netlogo/ (accessed 25 July 2016).

Wilensky, U. and Rand, W. (2015) *An Introduction to Agent-Based Modeling: Modeling Natural, Social, and Engineered Complex Systems with NetLogo.* Cambridge, MA: MIT Press.

## 17

Games and Online Research Methods

Harko Verhagen, Magnus Johansson
and Wander Jager

INTRODUCTION

Computer games are an increasingly ubiquitous aspect of life for large parts of the population. This not only includes games on desktop or laptop computers, tablets, and special game consoles but also mobile phones and smartphones. Ranging from long-lasting sessions to short interactions, from stand-alone games to games intertwined with social networking sites such as Facebook, and based on different types of gaming challenges, many game genres can be defined. Online games are widespread, 41 per cent of 2013 Oxford Internet Survey respondents state they play online games (Dutton *et al.* 2013). For the purpose of this chapter we will confine ourselves to games played online or out-of-game interaction expressed online.

Research on in-game behavior can have different purposes. We will address the study of in-game interaction and communication of games developed solely for the sake of playing (and selling) games as well as games developed for other purposes, such as learning or to replace lab experiments. In the former case, ethical issues of interfering with game-play while studying in-game behavior need to be addressed. The latter – games developed for research – is a promising method particularly for gathering data to initialize settings in agent-based simulation models of human social interaction. This requires a formalization and implementation of behavioral theories to create believable and reliable artificial social entities for games, such as game entities developed using the Consumat approach (Jager, 2000) in the Energy Transition Game (ETG; see later). More specifically, it encourages implementing models of behavioral theories, which generally describe parts of the processes driving human behavior, usually by showing the correlations (beta values) between concepts. Some theories focus on norms, whereas other theories address habitual behavior. To combine these theoretical insights in a formal (i.e. causal) model, a connecting conceptual framework is helpful.

The Consumat approach is an example of such a framework, aiming at connecting a number of theoretical perspectives (see the section on the Energy Transition Game approach for more details). This contributes to the development of formal rules describing *when* (mechanism selection) and *how* (causal modeling) a certain process is being executed and enables the closing of a 'causal loop' where the behavior of many individual agents also serves as the input for their behavior in a next time-step. Building these formal models may in itself create possibilities of interaction between researchers in the different social sciences and even other sciences connected to the content of the game. Developing and playing agent-based games allows for real-time interaction with virtual populations and can contribute to gamification of policy making, in that the virtual populations can be used as a probing device for the effects of policies under consideration.

Online data connected to gameplay can be used for analysis of, for example, inter-action patterns discussions on gameplay and in-game events including social behavior, and discussions of games in general. We describe aspects of these different types of out-of-game data available online and what questions research using these has addressed. We also discuss the use of collaborative environments in organizational settings which shares some of the characteristics of online gaming research. Finally, we will give some examples of each of the types of research and future research possibilities.

GAME STUDIES

The study of computer games is a relatively new research area, which is hardly a surprise given that computer games as such first appeared in the early 1950s. Games in which players interact in large numbers rather than as two competing individuals (e.g. playing a game of tennis, which was first realized in 1958 on an oscilloscope) are even newer, starting from 1974 when Mazewar became the first game in which multiple players using different computers could interact in a shared graphical space. This was the start of one of the more popular forms of computer gaming, and perhaps the one usually thought of when discussing gameplay or gamers, namely Massive Multiplayer Online Games (MMOG).

Many different research disciplines can be and have been applied to game research. Computer games are technological media artifacts that are popular in large parts of the population and which in many cases contain a storyline, interact with the different senses, and allow for human-to-human and human-to-non-human interaction (where the computer plays the non-human or non-player characters (NPC)). Gameplay is also fluid in the sense that no two sessions of gameplay are exactly alike, thus differing from other media and getting closer to a performance. Social and behavioral sciences, as well as humanities and technology, therefore have an interest in the study of computer games. For this chapter we will focus on the interest in the social and behavioral sciences.

The way games are approached as a domain of research may start from three possible foci:

- The player
- The game
- The world

These three areas constitute a breakdown of the most common and important properties found in definitions of games (Juul, 2003). They pay attention to the activities of playing games, how the players perceive their activities and what possible consequences of playing games influence the world outside such activities. However, we may note that the world can mean the in-game world or the world outside the game, the latter being the more usual meaning. Leaving aside philo-sophical debates on how to define a game, we visit the foci describing ways each of them are studied (in particular online) and what ethical issues are specific to online game studies.

We also distinguish between studying the behavior of players in natural games versus games that have been specifically developed for studying player behavior. For example, collaborative behavior in *World of Warcraft* is not as specific as studying players in a laboratory game (e.g. managing an energy transition). Given that in social sciences or societal challenges experiments in the laboratory or the real world are hard or even impossible to perform, games can be a new way to study how people interact, learn and collaborate in managing complex situations and problems. The final section of this chapter will give an example of the latter.

STUDYING PLAYERS IN AND OF ONLINE GAMES

The study of players by necessity is intertwined with the study of playing the game itself, since no observation of player behaviors in-game would be possible or relevant without participation. The activity as such is highly related to who might be interested. Each game genre and delivery method (be it computer, smartphone or special console, standalone (sandbox) or via Internet (online)) has its own population. Studying the players in games thus starts with understanding who the players of the game are and deciding if that population is the one suited for the research issue at hand. For example, if the research question is on teenage boys and violence, a game such as *Wordfeud* (a computerized version of Scrabble) may be of less interest to recruit participants or to use as a probe into social reality, nor is the game itself suitable for the research question.

Secondary data can be found online as well. Most games have discussion fora on the Internet that are attached to the game publisher or on more general websites. Games in which groups of players cooperate in a stable group, such as guilds in *World of Warcraft* for example, usually have discussion online for their guild alone as well. Not all forums will be open to the general audience but those that are can be of use in research on the social part of gaming out of game. Examples of the use of such data can be found in Johansson *et al.* (2015) and Johansson (2013), where data from both closed and open player forums were used in order to describe certain aspects of different online games. When using data from closed forums, access was granted by the goodwill of the players and, in the process, consent to the use of the data was granted. In the case of using openly available data from forums, however, the data is freely accessible in online chat forums, and in such cases extra caution is necessary in order not to trespass on the players' integrity and goodwill. Other sources include video recordings of gameplay available online or even live streaming of gameplay such as at http://www.twitch.tv/

Primary data – empirical data on the players – can be obtained in several ways as well. Studying the gameplay during actual gameplay at a 'mechanical' level can be done by collecting data from the interaction with the computer (use of commands to move around, chat logs, etc.) either by logging these directly or recording them via a camera (see, for example, Eklund and Johansson 2013). The same goes for what is presented to the player on the screen, logs of in-game communication via chat channels or voice channels, etc. Timestamping will allow the use of these to recreate gameplay and probe the player after a game session, using stimulated recall as a data collection technique. An alternative to this would be thinking-aloud for data collection, but this may be perceived as cognitively challenging and influence gameplay, especially in fast-paced games. In the case of single player sandbox games, however, there are few alternatives, apart from introspection, that gather data by playing the game while doing research. Collecting data out of game-play can be done using the normal set of methods such as interviews, focus groups, etc. This also applies to playing by proxy, i.e. a group playing a game via one player interacting with the game world.

Once multiple players are playing simultaneously as in an MMOG setting, other options become possible. Usually researchers take an ethnographic approach, becoming part of the group of players active in the game. This of course brings an extra element to the table. To make a meaningful analysis of the primary data, extensive knowledge of the game at hand helps and enables deep embedding. In the ethnographic case, a relevant understanding of, and skill in, gameplay is essential. To be part of the group, one has to melt in, as in all ethnographic study. The more one stands out from the environment, the more problematic acceptance is. The use of ethnographic methods and the specific demands that studying games make have been discussed in (Taylor 2006) and Boellstorff *et al.* (2012), where the most important aspects of ethnography in virtual worlds have been summarized. Digital ethnography is more than the ethnographic study of the virtual world – it also extends to the use of digital data (in the form of diverse media recordings and digital devices used in daily life) for ethnography of human interaction in general. Digital ethnography may therefore inform many of the practices of ethnography in virtual worlds because it considers many different sources of data going beyond taking field notes and observation (Uimonen, 2012). This strategy can be summed up as: 'get what you can, when you can get it!' The result of digital ethnography is often vast amounts of data collected from various sources, and also includes possibilities of sensitive data being collected. Due to the nature of studying players and their interactions, we should discuss the nature of the research environment we are dealing with and how we can close in on this activity without neglecting ethical considerations.

STUDYING THE WORLD OF AND AROUND ONLINE GAMES

The world inside the game – the game world – can be sheltered from outside inputs apart from the player, as in a sandbox game. Here, the interaction is with the NPCs and the storyline or idea behind the game. Sharing the game world with other players – either as direct and sole opponents when playing a game of *Pong*; as part of a world containing both human and non-human players; as part of a world that is seemingly alive; or anything in between – brings a new dynamic to the table. How the world is perceived and interacted with is the issue in the previous section. What is of interest in this section is how gameplay and real-world interaction feed into each other. For example, when studying gaming in a game cafe using participatory observation, observation and interviews, Jonsson (2012) discovered that although game cafes are public spaces, it is rarely the case that new ties are created between visitors. Gaming is done in a group of familiar friends, sometimes playing online with or against each other via the Internet while in the same room. Eklund (2012) comes to the same conclusion based on focus-group sessions – gaming in groups is more often than not based on previous ties, be it friends or family. Both these studies show that gaming is very much a social activity.

This social activity is extended outside of direct gameplay, as can be seen from the many forums on games, gaming and game groups found on the Internet. Indeed, gaming can be seen as a phenomenon and perhaps even a subculture consisting of 'gamers'. Gamers are not all players of computer games, but are prototypical hard-core game players usually seen as connected to a few genres. Internet poker may be big but its players are not seen as gamers. Instead, it is mostly first-person shooter games or long-lasting adventure games (typically involving roleplaying) in Tolkien-inspired worlds that qualify. As a subculture, there are high overlaps in the latter group with visiting game or comic book conventions, in (mostly female) activities, such as cosplay (short for costume play, where costumes or fashion inspired by fictional characters from movies or comic strips are worn). A special subcategory is gamers that modify (mod for short) existing games, creating variants of a game (which sometimes become more popular than the original game).

Finally, as a subgenre of computer games, we wish to name pervasive gaming. Here gameplay is staged in the real world, blending the game world and the real world. This encompasses the use of the real world as a physical setting and a social setting, including players and non-players sharing the game location. The non-players are usually not aware of gameplay going on, which may give rise to ethical issues. Using global positioning systems (GPS) coordinates to drive the game in geographical space, the activity may be interruptive of everyday life for the non-participants, while the interruption of the life of the players is intentional (thus the term 'pervasive'). Like the ethical conflicts in participatory observation, this activity poses ethical questions to the game designers. For example, when given the assignment of following a person in a certain location, if that person is not part of the game it can induce an uncomfortable feeling of being pursued by a stranger. An example of such games is the so-called Assassination games, of which *Killer* is one popular version. Players hunt down and kill other players in geographically limited areas, e.g. a university campus where the weapons are common objects such as bananas or carrots. Each player can be both a target and a hunter; however, players are unaware of who the other players are except their targeted victim. Thus, any human in the area can be considered a potential hunter, creating possible involuntary involvement of non-player bystanders.

A special mention should be made here of economics. In many games, internal economic systems exist that can be used to study human behavior from an economical perspective. Since most game currencies can be exchanged to non-digital money, using either official exchange rates as defined by the game developers, or exchange rates that spontaneously arise, even in the economic sense, game worlds and non-game worlds are interconnected.

ETHICAL CONSIDERATIONS WHEN STUDYING GAMES AND GAMERS

Sandbox types of games, such as *Minecraft*, are less problematic when concerning primary data because there usually are ways to 'pause' the interaction between the player and the game. Only recently have online modes been added to this type of game, opening up player-versus-player settings. Ethical issues in the sandbox game case are only related to the reporting of the results, making sure we do not disclose the identity of the respondents. If respondents are minors, the legal status and definition of which is different in different countries, consent from the caretakers is usually needed.

In online games, the situation is more complicated. Since online games are usually open to many simultaneously participating players, the effects of the research are shared by a large set of players impossible to define and approach beforehand. These effects are most noticeable when the participant observation path is chosen. When participant observation is used in games, we often rely on different sources of data being collected at the same time. It is, for instance, not uncommon to both do in-game video recordings, capture chat logs, record in-game sound, and capture screen shots (Boellstorff *et al.*, 2012), in addition to regular field notes, but the researcher has still to balance observing and playing. If performance as a player is hindered by performance as a researcher, this will result in diminished play quality for all players in the game world. Even if a few of them have given their consent for being part of a research project and being researched upon, 'innocent bystanders' are hit as well. Obtaining informed consent from all possible players may in reality be impossible. From a methodological perspective, it is unclear if and how the announcement of a player as a researcher affects the other players. In high-paced games, with little time for reflection, the effect is probably minimal. This is not a reason to totally neglect the privacy of our respondents; on the contrary, what we can do is to make sure that we always leave our research site (in this case a game world) intact, for other researchers to have access in the future. But changes in the game world due to gameplay can be irreversible. One example that highlights the responsibility we have as researchers to leave a research site intact and fulfil our ethical responsibilities is Meyers's (2008) study of the MMOG 'City of Heroes/Villains'. This raised some controversy because the researcher played the game while griefing[1] to measure players' reactions to what could be considered unwanted behavior. The study upset players of the Heroes/Villains community but it also raised the question of what is permissible behavior as a researcher.

Using secondary data is more problematic, especially if it is data collected online in discussion forums, for example. Players often discuss their favorite games online in different forums. Some players are part of guilds and clans, formalized groups to play together in a specific game, and these groups usually have discussion forums as well. All these forums may be used as a source for data collection. However, we have the same difficulties asking for permission (informed consent) because we tap into ongoing (and thus past) discussion. Players may even already have left the forum, and thus be impossible to reach. Since the information may be located using a search engine, anonymizing of data when using quotes is problematic. Concealing identity may thus involve changing the data using paraphrasing, a problematic practice.

Strategies for always protecting the respondents include:

- **Be careful**

Always protect your informants and the research site, not only to protect the player community, but also to protect the access to these communities for forthcoming researchers.

- **Try to get informed consent when possible** (and do not interfere with the object of the study)

Some groups of players like the focus of research being their favorite pastime activities and will help researchers gain access to their group.

- **Treat data with care**

Recorded data may be sensitive so we should make sure that it does not fall into the wrong hands. This may imply encryption of the data or minimizing the physical risk of the data falling into the wrong hands.

- **Anonymize the data**

Make sure that player names are replaced and that the identity of your respondents is kept safe.

- **Consider all aspects of anonymity in relation to the collected material.**

There are numerous ways for players to identify other players, and not only through their nickname or character name in a game. Sometimes, and in MMOGs in particular, players may have come across gear and equipment that is not easily accessible for other players. This means that players can be identified through the equipment they are carrying. As mentioned earlier, when using out-of-game data, make sure readers cannot find out who said what by searching for literal quotes. What can be done to protect the respondents in this case is to not quote directly if controversial topics are discussed.

We can always choose to portray the discussions indirectly, or perhaps through paraphrasing to hide the origins of the discussion. Always think twice about the consequences and always use common sense.

GAMES AS A RESEARCH METHODOLOGY

Apart from studying games and gaming as an activity, either in a natural setting or a lab setting, games can also be used as a research strategy to study human interaction via a game rather than in real life. With the possibilities of data collection described earlier, this can result in very rich data. When the game is perceived as 'real' or at least when players are absorbed by the gaming activity (in a state of flow), the behavior will be close to real-life behavior. Most research now sees the line between 'real life' and 'virtual life' or 'flesh world' versus 'digital world' not as the clear border it once was but rather as a blurry permeated fine line in a large grey zone. We will now describe a game that is used to offer students an insight into complex systems but that also can be used to study the behavior of the students in the game to test theoretical models of choice behavior.

ENERGY TRANSITION GAME: AN EXAMPLE

Many problems on our planet are characterized by complex and sometimes unpredictable behavior. Studying how these problems evolve and finding promising strategies to mitigate them becomes a matter of multidisciplinary research focused around interacting multilevel models. An example is the energy system on earth, which is a complex system dealing with technology development, scarcity, political influence, geo-politics, consumer behavior, environmental developments, and

climate change to name a few. To gain insight into the different processes driving such a complex system, ranging from micro (human) level to macro (interstate and global level) and encompassing natural science, social science, and even the humanities, is not an easy task. Constructing theoretically realistic artificial populations that can be parameterized using field data is a critical task in developing policy games that address current societal challenges. Playing such games in teams of people may generate data that help understanding, recognizing, and adapting to the sometimes fast developments in society. Games are therefore expected to become an increasingly important tool to study the multi-stakeholder management of complicated issues involving the behavior of large populations.

We recently developed a simulation game called the Energy Transition Game (ETG) when we were teaching students the complexities of managing systemic transitions and multidisciplinary collaboration at the University College Groningen. The unique feature of this game is the inclusion of an artificial population of simulated people. As such, this game is an 'agent-based game' (Jager and Van der Vegt, 2015) where the players have to interact with an autonomous heterogeneous population that also interacts with itself. The artificial population used is based on the Consumat approach (Jager, 2000), which has been developed as a generic framework to guide the development of social simulation models. The basic drivers of behavior in the Consumat framework are *needs*, and the fulfillment of those needs results in *satisfaction*. To perform a particular behavior, an agent possesses *abilities* (e.g. income), which relate to its capacity to actually use particular behavioral options. In the Consumat approach four basic decisional strategies are implemented: repetition, imitation, deliberation, and inquiring. In case of low uncertainty and high satisfaction, agents engage in *repetition*, which is the mechanism behind habitual behavior. A high uncertainty combined with high satisfaction results in *imitation*. When satisfaction is low, the agents are more motivated to invest effort in improving their situation. When they are certain but dissatisfied, therefore, they will engage in *deliberation*, which is a form of optimizing or homo-economicus behavior. Dissatisfaction combined with uncertainty results in *inquiring*, where the behavior of comparable others is evaluated and copied when expected satisfaction increases. Social decision making is usually directed at similar others, where similarity is related to abilities. Agents have a memory for behavioral opportunities and other agents' behavior and abilities, which is only updated if cognitively demanding strategies are being used. The four quadrants of the Consumat approach are thus based on the following collection of theories:

1   Automated behavior, habits, reflexes (*repetition* models)
2   Reasoned behavior, attitude theory, theory of reasoned behavior, homo-economicus (*deliberation* models)
3   Social learning, communication (*inquiring* models)
4   Imitation, norms, mirroring (*imitation* models)

Student groups take the player role of energy companies or political parties, competing for market share and votes of the artificial population. Players have individual goals, but can also be held collectively responsible for achieving a transition to sustainability. Development of energy prices and technologies, consumers choosing energy providers, energy companies deciding upon their portfolio and marketing, politics influencing the energy market with taxation, and subsidies, all come together in this transition.

The ETG model currently runs in NetLogo (Wilensky, 1999) and is composed of the following parts:

The Simulated Population

The simulated population consists of 400 agents connected in a randomly generated network (Toivonen *et al.*, 2006). The agents are heterogeneous concerning their preferences, and may choose between different energy providers (company players) and regularly vote for one of the two political parties (political players).

At the start of the game, each agent is assigned starting values for the following variables:

- Ambition level
- Certainty of an agent
- The importance of greenness of energy
- The importance of energy price
- The importance of energy safety

Each agent makes choices based on their current satisfaction and level of certainty, as explained in the Consumat approach description. If the satisfaction of an agent with an energy provider is lower than the ambition of an agent, the agent becomes unsatisfied. If the percentage of friends (links in the network) using the same energy provider is lower than the certainty variable, the agent becomes uncertain.

The Companies

The companies, which are the players' role, make an offering to the consumers by composing a mixture of energy sources. This mixture can be composed of solar, wind, gas, oil, nuclear, coal, or recycling. The raw prices of these energy sources can change over time as a function of underlying scenarios addressing scarcity and technology development. Also, the emissions (greenness) and safety of the different sources will be captured. Company players further decide upon their profit margin and the proportion of their profit devoted to marketing (informing the consumers). The company players can obtain information about the other companies concerning their market share. In making decisions, the company players have the possibility of polling the artificial consumer population to find out about their levels of satisfaction.

The Political Parties

Two political parties, also players' roles, have been implemented – one in the government and the other in the opposition. The government has the possibility of changing the raw prices of the different energy sources by taxing and subsidizing. The opposition party also sets taxation and subsidies. The artificial population evaluates which of the subsidy/taxation regimes is most favorable for them, and they vote accordingly for the party providing them the highest satisfaction level. Political parties have information on their popularity (percentage of voters), and see the elections approaching.

The Game Dilemma

The game confronts the different players with a complicated dilemma. The company players compete for the customers, trying to get as many customers as they can and setting a profit margin such that they make a profit. But they also are responsible for a reduction in CO_2 emissions, which is a collective outcome. Individual (company) and collective (CO_2) outcomes may therefore conflict. The company players have to base their strategy on the (expected) developments concerning the energy scenarios (technology and scarcity), the expectations concerning the subsidies and taxation the policy players impose, and the preferences, happiness, and behavior of the artificial population. The policy players can be instructed with a mission, for example stimulating the transition towards a sustainable energy system, thereby reducing the CO_2 emissions drastically. However, they can only influence the system when they are in power, which implies they compete for the votes of the artificial population. They are also responsible for the financial balance because subsidizing may be appreciated more by the voters than taxation, but this may result in a negative financial balance of

the country. This competition between political parties implies that they are confronted with the sometimes conflicting interests between obtaining (or keeping) power and reaching their political goals. The overall game setting is thus rather complicated for both companies and politics because the energy sources change (scenarios), elections take place with possible regime changes, and energy companies constantly explore possibilities for improving their performance. Surprises can also be included in the scenarios, such as a nuclear disaster, which will cause a sudden change in the population's evaluation of different energy sources.

Often a catch-22 situation emerges because despite being aware of the need for a transition in the energy system, an exclusive focus on company and political party interests often results in very limited CO_2 reductions. This signifies the importance of communication between the different players about their goals and strategies, and sometimes negotiations and agreements are made concerning the minimal efforts of the different players. Authorities can also be charged to control if the different players indeed comply with the agreements.

RUNNING THE ENERGY TRANSITION GAME ON THE INTERNET AND COLLECTING DATA

The advantage of running the game on the Internet is that we can bring together different players from different backgrounds and cultures in a single game. For example, it is possible to have a team playing from a Graduate School of Business Sciences from Japan with a team of U.S. students from a school of sustainability, a team of social science students from the Netherlands, and a team from a political science department from Sweden. Including negotiations in the game offers a platform allowing for a rich learning environment for intercultural negotiations. What is critically important is that it is possible to form different types of teams on the basis of expertise. It is therefore possible to compose interdisciplinary teams versus mono-disciplinary teams and explore their performance.

As a data collection tool, such an Internet game offers new possibilities to study how the players collect information, what actions they take, and how they communicate/collaborate in a dynamic environment.

In relation to the collection of data on how the groups collect information, it is possible to track the information search behavior of the groups. For example, the company players can ask for information on both the actions and performance of their competitors, as well as on the motivations and satisfaction of the population. Collecting this information in a dynamic environment may sometimes be costly in time, especially when changes are happening fast.

In relation to the actions they take, it is possible to track the settings they choose for their company or political party over time. This can obviously be linked with the developments in the underlying scenarios and the timing of elections.

Although direct face-to-face interaction is possible in a local implementation of the game, running the game on the Internet offers interesting possibilities to collect data on the interaction/negotiation process. This also requires the development of clear interaction possibilities (group and individual chat function), which can be monitored. A simple chat function may provide the first possibility to implement communication in the game, offering the players a platform to exchange ideas and make agreements, either on a group level or between individual players making alliances. Because it is possible to cheat, the players can control if all players comply with the agreements. It is also possible to administer a (financial) punishment to cheating players.

Having such a data-collection system running allows for monitoring in detail how multiple groups of players respond to dynamical changes, such as sudden price falls or raises. For example, using data on information searches, a distinction can be made between players following a proactive strategy who make decisions on the basis of information search versus players following a more reactive strategy who respond to actions of other players and external events. It also becomes possible to explore if the likeliness of employing either more proactive versus reactive strategies is related to turbulences in the system (political changes, strong changes in the scenarios). Coupling this information with data on the team-composition (i.e. mono- versus multi-disciplinary), it becomes possible to observe how different teams respond to different developments in a complex system and how well they perform (on an individual and a collective level). Experiments can be conducted where teams are being confronted with different types of shocks in the system. This will open the possibility of studying the decision-making process of different types of groups, and the adequacy of their decisions concerning performing in a complex system. Using specifically designed tools to measure group learning (see Scholz *et al.*, 2014) makes it possible to identify the learning processes that take place and to identify processes such as group-think that may hamper the distribution of relevant information under certain (e.g. crisis) conditions. It is also possible to identify the concepts that individuals use in describing the context, and follow to what extent these concepts will be shared in the group decision making.

Obviously, to maximize the analytical power it is necessary to have a good insight into the composition of the teams playing the game. An online intake questionnaire can be developed to identify disciplinary background (key concepts being used), experience, as well as the role played in a group (e.g. Belbin, 2010). This would allow for a detailed description of the different teams interacting in the game.

Using traditional experimental designs in laboratory settings would make it extremely difficult to study the relation between within- and between-group variables concerning their performance in complex dynamical situations because of the large number of possible set-ups and dynamical developments. However, playing such games in a serious game context on the Internet makes it possible to develop a growing dataset of group interactions. Such big data will allow exploration of what conditions favor the management of a complex system such as the energy transition. Considering that many societal challenges are structured in the same way as the energy transition system, collecting data from Internet-based agent-based games may provide valuable insights into the identification of effective management strategies.

CONCLUSIONS

In this chapter we have introduced research in, on, and using games to non-game researchers. Gaming is very much a social activity, or as Huizinga (1938/1955) would call it, the essence of being human. Computer gaming is part of that. It is part of social life and may form or reinforce existing ties. It also can be used to study social life – interaction patterns, economic behavior, the forming of organizational structures, the origin of systems of norms, etc. The availability of data on many of these processes is higher in the digital world than in the non-digital world, and in the case of gaming we can even build games to produce data on the processes we are interested in, replacing lab studies. The ubiquity of games and their social side effects also means that research on non-digital social life needs to pose the question of whether gaming interaction is to be considered part of the explanans or explanandum of what is being studied.

NOTE

1 'Griefing' is the act of irritating and angering people in video games through the use of destruction, construction or social engineering. Popularized in *Minecraft* by teams, griefing has become a serious problem for server administrators who wish to foster building and protect builders.

REFERENCES

Belbin, R. M., (2010). *Team Roles at Work*. 2nd ed. Oxford: Butterworth Heinemann.

Boellstorff, T., Nardi, B. A., Pearce, C. and Taylor. T. L. (2012). *Ethnography and Virtual Worlds: A Handbook of Method*. Princeton, NJ: Princeton University Press.

Dutton, W. H., Blank, G. and Groseli, D. (2013). 'OxIS 2013 Report: Cultures of the Internet'. Oxford Internet Institute, University of Oxford.

Eklund, L. (2012). 'The sociality of gaming – a mixed methods approach to understanding digital gaming as a social leisure activity'. PhD thesis, Stockholm University.

Eklund, L. and Johansson, M. (2013). 'Played and designed sociality in a massive multiplayer online game', *Eludamos - Journal for Computer Game Culture*, 7(1): 35–54.

Huizinga, J. (1938). 'Homo ludens: Proeve eener bepaling van het spelelement der cultuur'. Groningen, Wolters-Noordhoff. (Original Dutch edition). English translation: Huizinga, J. (1955). 'Homo ludens; a study of the play-element in culture'. Boston: Beacon Press.

Jager, W. (2000). 'Modelling Consumer Behavior'. Doctoral thesis, University of Groningen, Centre for Environmental and Traffic Psychology.

Jager, W. and Van der Vegt, G. (2015). 'Management of complex systems: towards agent based gaming for policy'. In: M. Janssen, M. A. Wimmer and A. Deljoo (eds.), *Policy Practice and Digital Science – Integrating Complex Systems, Social Simulation and Public Administration in Policy Research* (Series: Public Administration and Information Technology). Berlin: Springer Verlag, pp. 291–303.

Johansson, M. (2013). '"If you obey all the rules, you miss all the fun": a study on the rules of guilds and clans in online games', *Journal of Gaming & Virtual Worlds*, 5(1): 77–95.

Johansson, M., Verhagen, H. and Kou, Y. (2015). I am being watched by the Tribunal: trust and control in Multiplayer Online Battle Arena games. In Foundations of Digital Games 2015. Foundations of Digital Games. Available via: http://www.fdg2015.org/papers/fdg2015_paper_37.pdf Last accessed 29 July 2016.

Jonsson, F. (2012). 'Hanging out in the game café: contextualising co-located computer game play practices and experiences'. PhD thesis, Stockholm University.

Juul, J. (2003). 'The game, the player, the world: looking for a heart of gameness'. In: M. Copier and J. Raessens (eds.), *Level Up: Digital Games Research Conference Proceedings*. Utrecht: Utrecht University, pp. 30–45.

Meyers, D. (2008). Play and punishment: the sad and curious case of Twixt. Unpublished manuscript. Available from https://docs.google.com/viewer?url=https://web.archive.org/web/20090611225940/http://www.masscomm.loyno.edu/%7Edmyers/F99%20classes/Myers_PlayPunishment_031508.doc. Last accessed 29 July 2016.

Scholz, G., Dewulf, A. and Pahl-Wostl, C. (2014). 'An analytical framework of social learning facilitated by participatory methods', *Systemic Practice and Action Research*, 27(6): 575–91.

Taylor, T. L. (2006). *Play Between Worlds – Exploring Online Game Culture*. Cambridge, MA: MIT Press.

Toivonen, R., Onnela, J. P., Saramäki, J., Hyvönen, J. and Kaski, K. (2006). 'A model for social networks', *Physica A: Statistical Mechanics and its Applications*, 371(2): 851–60.

Uimonen, P. (2012). *Digital Drama: Teaching and Learning Art and Media in Tanzania*. London: Routledge.

Wilensky, U. (1999). NetLogo. Available from http://ccl.northwestern.edu/netlogo/ Last accessed 29 July 2016.

## 18

Data Visualisation as an Emerging Tool for Online Research

Helen Kennedy and William Allen

INTRODUCTION

This chapter focuses on data visualisation, an increasingly important method in the online research toolset and a means of communicating research results to peers and the wider public. This is not a 'how-to' chapter; it does not guide the reader through the process of making data visualisations. That project would require more words than are available here and, anyway, is best undertaken by professional data visualisers. There are several good, how-to books written by visualisation practitioners, such as Cairo (2013), Few (2012), Kirk (2016), Tufte (1983) and Yau (2013), which readers can turn to for guidance on the visualisation process, and we draw on some of them here. We describe ourselves as academics who are researchers *of* and researchers *with* data visualisation who, in the process of doing our research, have witnessed and reflected on a growth in academic visualisation. Responding to this phenomenon and other issues relating to the spread of data and visualisations, this chapter focuses on how online researchers might think critically about them, something which, we suggest, is a pre-requisite to producing good visualisations.

The chapter starts with a brief note about what data visualisation is, before moving to a longer discussion of claims about what data visualisations can and cannot do. We consider it vital to foreground these questions before moving on to a discussion of the processes of creating and engaging with data visualisations. The subsequent section on visualisation tools, techniques and processes aims to point readers in the direction of resources and highlight key principles and approaches, rather than cover this subject matter comprehensively. The chapter then moves to focus on examples of using data visualisation within social science research, drawing on our own experiences. It concludes by summarising what we consider to be the key issues for online researchers seeking to use data visualisation in their research, noting the importance of attending to audiences, their needs and the contexts of their visualisation use.

We have been researching (and researching with) data and their visualisation for several years. Together with Rosemary Lucy Hill and Andy Kirk, in 2014 and 2015 we worked on Seeing Data (http://seeing-data.org/), a research project that explored the factors in visualisation consumption and production processes that affect user engagement. Before that, Will worked with data visualisation through his work for the Migration Observatory (http://www.migrationobservatory.ox.ac.uk/) at the University of Oxford and Helen researched the spread of data mining (Kennedy, 2016), and we both continue doing these things. We draw on our research in this chapter and on some of the publications that have resulted from it, which we have authored in collaboration with Hill, Kirk and others.

A NOTE ON WHAT DATA VISUALISATION IS (AND IS NOT)

A data visualisation is a visual representation of data, often in charts and graphs. It shows statistical, numerical data in visual ways in order to help people make sense of data. Experts believe representing data visually makes it possible to communicate data effectively and gives people the opportunity to analyse and examine large datasets which would otherwise be difficult to understand (for example, Few, 2008). In *Data Visualisation: A Handbook for Data Driven Design*, a publication aimed at social science researchers unfamiliar with the area, Andy Kirk defines data visualisation as 'the representation and presentation of data to facilitate understanding' (2016: 19). He then breaks down this definition with reference to each of its core elements. *Representation* refers to the choices made about the visual form in which the data will be portrayed, such as

decisions about which chart types to use, whereas *presentation* refers to decisions about the visualisation design, such as colour choice, composition, level of interactivity and annotation. For Kirk, and in the view of other visualisers, there are two main ways in which visualisations 'facilitate understanding': the first is to communicate data and the second is to enable their exploration or analysis (Kennedy, 2014). Both modes are relevant to online researchers: we may use visualisation to communicate our research data to expert peers or non-expert publics, or we may visualise our data in order to explore and analyse them. For example, a powerful tool like Tableau makes it possible to 'see' data (and identify patterns within them) in ways that are simply not possible with large datasets presented in tabular form. We may also produce visualisations which enable our audiences to do this, as seen in the case study examples discussed later.

Of course, a defining feature of a data visualisation is that it has data at its heart. This differentiates it from an infographic, which is traditionally static, made for print-based consumption and explains phenomena graphically but may contain no data, or data in charts which exist alongside other illustrations like photographs. A data visualisation is also different from an information visualisation: in the latter, information is the output; whereas in the former, data are the input, although these terms are often used interchangeably. There is, of course, much more to data visualisation than these simple definitions suggest, as we demonstrate in the next section.

WHAT DATA VISUALISATION CAN (AND CANNOT) DO

What are data visualisations used for, what can they do and how might online researchers integrate them into their practice? A number of visualisation professionals assert that visualisations can promote greater understanding of data by making them accessible and transparent (Few, 2008; Zambrano and Engelhardt, 2008). Experts and practitioners often express a belief that, through visualisation, they can 'do good with data', the trademarked tagline of US-based visualisation agency Periscopic (Periscopic, 2014). This view that visualisation is a way of 'doing good with data' was widespread amongst visualisation designers who we interviewed for our Seeing Data research (Kennedy, 2014; Kennedy *et al.*, 2016a).

The idea that visualisation can promote awareness can be traced back to the work of Otto and Marie Neurath in the mid-nineteenth century and their development of the graphical language Isotype, a visual way of representing quantitative information via icons (Zambrano and Engelhardt, 2008). The Neuraths believed that 'visual education is related to the extension of intellectual democracy within single communities and within mankind' (Neurath *et al.*, 1973: 247). They put their ideas into practice in museums they directed, where they used charts to enable the general public to develop understanding of 'the problems the community of Vienna had to tackle' (Neurath, quoted in Zambrano and Engelhardt, 2008: 283).

Zambrano and Engelhardt link the ideas of the Neuraths to contemporary projects like GapMinder (http://www.gapminder.org/world), which describes itself as 'a modern "museum" that helps making the world understandable, using the Internet' and aims to promote global sustainable development by visualising related statistics (Stiftelsen Gapminder, n.d.). The efforts of other contemporary visualisers can also be seen in this vein, such as Stefanie Posavec's 'Open Data Playground' (http://www.stefanieposavec.co.uk/data/#/open-data-playground/), a set of floor-based games that provide people with the opportunity to play with materialisations of open datasets and make sense of the data for themselves. These projects, in different ways, reflect the belief that

visualisations make data transparent, summed up in the words of Stephen Few (2008): 'infovis can make the world a better place'.

However, as we note in an article co-authored with Hill and Aiello (Kennedy *et al.*, 2016a), critical commentators argue that data visualisations can privilege certain viewpoints, perpetuate existing power relations and or create new ones, and they often draw on examples of visualisations in the media as evidence of this view. These include the US Republican party's visualisation of the Democrats' proposed reforms to healthcare, described by Valarakis (2014) as an over-complicated visualisation which serves to make the proposed reforms seem over-complicated too, and the UK newspaper *Daily Express*'s use of visualisations to communicate an anti-trade union ideology, studied by Dick (2015).

These and other commentators observe that data visualisations are not neutral windows onto data; rather, visualisations are the result of numerous choices: as Ambrosio points out, 'visual manifestations [of data] are themselves informed by judgement, discernment and choice' (2015: 137). Yet although there are many subjective processes involved in visualising data, some critics argue that the resulting visualisation often 'pretends to be coherent and tidy' (Ruppert, 2014). Visualisations and the data within them seem objective, even though they are not. This appearance has a number of origins. First, they report numbers, historically trusted because they appear universal, impersonal and neutral, as Porter (1995) and others have argued. Second, data and visualisation are often associated with science, also seen to be objective and therefore trustworthy. Third, as we argue with Hill and Aiello (Kennedy *et al.*, 2016a), the conventions that have been established over time also work to imbue visualisations with the quality of objectivity, producing the impression that visualisations are 'showing the facts, telling it like it is, offering windows onto data' (Kennedy *et al.*, 2016a: 716).

The shape that visualised data take is the result not only of the decisions and priorities of the data visualiser and the data gatherer, but also of the makers of the visualisation and data gathering software used. Human decisions influence and shape the design, development, arrangement and implementation of data and their visualisation in many ways. Consequently, data are never 'raw' – the very concept of 'raw data', as Bowker (2005) puts it, is an oxymoron. Data, like their visualisation, are generated through processes which necessarily involve interpretation. These interpretations are in turn biased by the subjective filters that individual humans apply as they make them (Bollier, 2010). To understand how visualisations turn out the way that they do, it is necessary to acknowledge the roles of the people, software packages and processes that produce them.

Most good data visualisers recognise that both of the perspectives discussed in this section (that visualisation can make data accessible and that visualisation involves manipulating data) are valid. Kirk's book (2016) includes extensive discussion of the ways in which visualisation involves decision making, about what to prioritise, what to leave out, how to present and represent data, all of which influence how visualisations – and data – look. He argues that for a visualisation to be trustworthy, all data treatments and transformations – including smoothing, cleaning, converting and adjusting – must be noted and shared with users. Doing this means making transparent the perspective that has influenced the visualisation design. A good example of how different perspectives on the same data can lead to different design decisions and therefore different messages can be seen in 'Iraq's Bloody Toll' and responses to it. This visualisation, produced in 2011 by Simon Scarr for the *South China Morning Post* and reproduced in Figure 18.1, is deliberately evocative. The use of an upside-down bar chart with rounded rather than square ends, the colour red (visible at the original URL) and the visualisation's title all communicate a clear message: 'too many deaths in Iraq' (Hill,

2014). In 2014, Andy Cotgreave of Tableau drew on this visualisation to respond to an article in *The Guardian* newspaper's datablog entitled 'Why you should never trust a data visualisation' (Burn-Murdoch, 2013)[1] in which the author expressed concern about the credibility that is often attached to data visualisations. In Cotgreave's (2014) response, shown in Figure 18.2, he shows how the same data can have a very different effect with three simple changes to 'Iraq's Bloody Toll': he flips the bar chart up, changes the title to 'Iraq: Deaths on the Decline' and makes the visualisation blue, not red (Figure 18.2, colour change visible at original URL). In so doing, he points to the impossibility of neutrality in data visualisation. The same data can be represented in different ways to create different messages, all of which are ostensibly trustworthy.

These points are relevant to online researchers because considering how data visualisation can be used in different contexts is an important component of good, reflective visualisation practice. Researchers using and producing data visualisations need to understand them sociologically in order to do so well. As we note with Hill and Aiello, almost 30 years ago Fyfe and Law (1988) urged sociologists to take the visual seriously in the study of social life, because '[d]epiction, picturing and seeing are ubiquitous features in the process by which most human beings come to know the world as it really *is* for them' (Fyfe and Law, 1988: 2, cited in Kennedy *et al.*, 2016a: 732). This need remains, especially for researchers working with data visualisation.

DOING DATA VISUALISATION I: TOOLS, TECHNIQUES, PROCESS

In this section, we provide some brief commentary on the tools, techniques and process of data visualisation. In doing so, we draw heavily on Kirk's book and website.

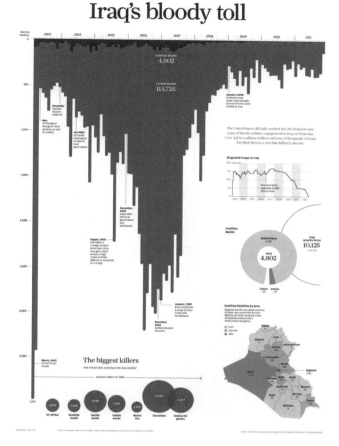

Figure 18.1   'Iraq's Bloody Toll' by Scarr (2011)

Tools: Software

There is a huge and wide range of software for data visualisation. The resources page of Kirk's Visualising Data website (http://www.visualisingdata.com/resources/) lists 298 tools, applications and platforms that can be used in the data visualisation process. These range from software which is specifically for visualisation (such as Big Picture, Chart Builder, D3, Graphviz and others which specialise in particular chart types, such as e-Sankey), to tools to help with the aesthetic aspects of visualisation (such as 0 To 255 and other colour-selection tools) and programming languages like Python. Kirk categorises

these resources into tools for data handling; charting tools; programming-based tools; multivariate, mapping and web-based tools; specialist tools; and resources for working with colour. We comment on four tools below, because they are widely used (Tableau and NVivo), important (D3) or freely available and not complex to use (Raw). These are just a few examples of available tools, and this brief discussion is far from comprehensive. Interested readers are encouraged to visit Kirk's site for more detail.

One particularly popular visualisation tool is Tableau, available in both Desktop (paid) and Public (free) versions. Featuring many different chart types, as well as

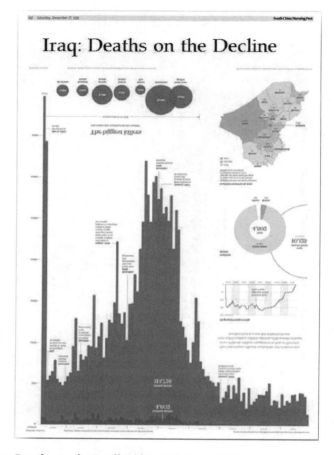

Figure 18.2 'Iraq: Deaths on the Decline' by Cotgreave (2014)

drag-and-drop interfaces, this tool offers a range of options for visualising data and publishing the results. (Some of the case study visualisations within this chapter were created using Tableau Public). A large user-community provides answers to common questions as well as guidance for combining datasets in the Tableau format. Users should note that using the Public, free version of Tableau means making data publically available, hence the name.

D3 is an important programming library for creating dynamic and interactive data visualisations. It is a JavaScript library for manipulating documents based on data using HTML (HyperText Markup Language),

SVG (Scalable Vector Graphics) and CSS (Cascading Style Sheets). In using these web-based languages, it produces visualisations which adhere to web standards, meaning that they can be embedded in webpages which will function across browsers and devices, now and into the future.

Raw is an open web application to create custom visualisations on top of the D3.js library through a simple interface. Primarily conceived as a tool for designers and visualisation experts, Raw enables visualisations to be exported and embedded in webpages. Even though it is a web application, Raw does not store data. Therefore, data are only available to the person who originally uploads them. Raw is open, customisable and free to download.

Many qualitative researchers will already use NVivo, an application for collecting, organising and analysing data gathered through interviews, focus groups and other methods. Like other software for handling qualitative and quantitative data, NVivo also offers the option of visualising data in a range of chart types, such as bar charts, hierarchical clusters, word trees, cluster diagrams and geographical maps. These can be used by researchers both to explore their own data and to communicate them to their audiences. Other available software for qualitative data include QDA Miner and MaxQDA. QDA Miner provides options to visualise where codes generated by the researcher appear in textual data, which can reveal patterns of co-occurrence. MaxQDA contains similar features, including the ability to create word clouds of most frequently occurring words, but it is, not it is worth specifically highlighting one particular tool called the 'Document Portrait'. After dividing selected texts into equal segments that are represented by a square or circle as the user wishes, this portrait function assigns a colour to each symbol that corresponds with its given code. The researcher can sort and display these coloured symbols to get a sense of the proportions of different codes in a set of texts, or to identify which codes are used most frequently. Newer versions of MaxQDA allow users to click through the resulting 'portrait' of symbols to access the underlying textual data, too.

Techniques: Graph and Chart Types

On our Seeing Data project website, we include a section entitled 'Understanding Data Visualisations', which aims to help people who are interested in data visualisations but not experts to make sense of them. One subsection, Inside The Chart (http://seeingdata.org/sections/inside-the-chart/), introduces what we see as 14 of the most commonly used graph and chart types, explaining what they show, how they should be read, their limitations and alternative charts which can be used to show similar data. Amongst these are familiar charts such as the ubiquitous bar chart, stacked bar chart, pie chart and line chart; fairly common and easy-to-read visualisations such as the choropleth map and the symbol map; and more complex forms including the radar chart, tree map, Sankey diagram, scatter plot, heat map, slope graph, stacked area chart and stream graph. All of these are shown in Figure 18.3 below.

Kirk's book (2016) identifies 50 common chart types. There, he provides this useful categorisation to assist readers in understanding the types of data and relationships between data that they commonly represent:

- **Categorical chart types:** used for comparing categories and distributions of quantitative values (for example, bar charts)
- **Hierarchical chart types:** used for comparing part-to-whole relationships and hierarchies (for example, pie charts and tree maps)
- **Relationship chart types:** used for graphing relationships through correlations and connections (for example, a scatter plot or a Sankey diagram)
- **Temporal chart types:** used for showing trends and activities over time (for example, a line chart or a stream graph)
- **Spatial data chart types:** used for mapping spatial data (for example, in a symbol or chloropleth map) (Kirk, 2016: 158)

Process: Principles, Purpose and other Professional Practices

In addition to discussing tools and chart types, Kirk proposes three guiding principles for visualisation design. Visualisations should be seen to be trustworthy, accessible and elegant, argues Kirk, and designers need to consider how to produce visualisations that comply with these principles. Kirk presents 'the purpose map', reproduced in Figure 18.4, as a way of ensuring that all thinking and decision making is aligned to these principles,

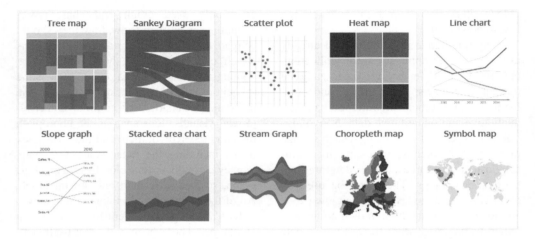

Figure 18.3   Screenshot of the Seeing Data website showing 14 common chart types
Source: http://seeingdata.org/sections/inside-the-chart/

as well as adhering to the desired outcomes of the visualisation.

The purpose map brings together what Kirk defines as the experience and the tone of a visualisation. As the map shows, Kirk argues that

there are three types of intentions with regard to user experience, which he defines as follows:

- **Explanatory:** in which visualisers 'will provide the viewer with a visual portrayal of the subject's

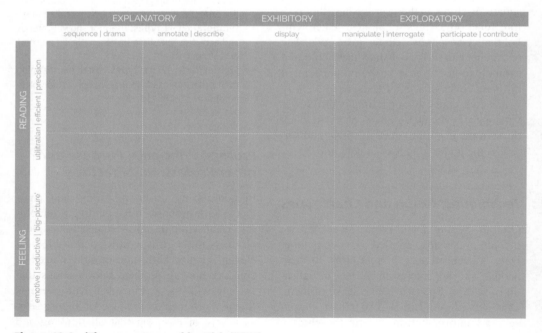

Figure 18.4   'The purpose map' by Kirk (2016)

data *and* will also take some responsibility to bring key insights to the surface, rather than leave the prospect of interpreting the meaning of the information entirely to the viewer' (Kirk, 2016: 77).

- **Exploratory:** in which visualisers help users find their own insights, usually through digital, interactive and participatory experiences which allow them to interrogate and manipulate data. Users are free to interact and explore, but might ask themselves: what do you want me to do with this?
- **Exhibitory:** neither explanatory nor exploratory. Kirk describes visualisations which fall into this category as 'simply visual displays of data'. Viewers have to do the work of interpreting meaning (unlike in explanatory visualisations) – like artworks, they depend on 'the interpretative capacity of the viewer' and so are suited to audiences with subject knowledge who can do their own interpreting. They may support explanation given elsewhere, for example in accompanying text or in a presentation.

Although these three intention types are neither mutually exclusive nor exhaustive, the purpose map provides a useful rule-of-thumb guide to visualisation design. Also, particular intentions do not always equate to the use of particular chart types, although simple charts like bar charts and stacked bar charts are more explanatory, and interactive visualisations using a range of chart types are likely to be more exploratory. Researchers using data visualisation to communicate with expert peers and non-expert publics will often have more explanatory than exhibitory or exploratory purposes. However, we are likely to move towards exploratory approaches as we increasingly share datasets with our audiences and invite them to explore and analyse data for themselves.

The vertical axis of the purpose map relates to the intended tone of the visualisation, which for Kirk exists on a spectrum from reading to feeling. A visualisation which is intended to be *read* prioritises perceptual accuracy, is utilitarian and pragmatic – 'no-frills', Kirk calls it – for example, a simple bar chart. Readable visualisations like bar charts facilitate trustworthiness and accessibility, he

argues. In contrast, visualisations that are intended to be *felt* (like a tree map, for example) are used when visualisers 'place more importance on extracting a *gist* of the big, medium and small values and a general *sense* of the relationships that exist. Sometimes an "at-a-glance" sense of scale is simply the most suitable way to portray a subject's values' (Kirk, 2016: 84). It was this sense that visualisations are *felt* as much as they are *read* that motivated us to explore the factors that affect visualisation engagement on Seeing Data, including feelings and emotions. The tone adopted in a visualisation depends on its purpose, but the choices made need to be compatible with attributes of the data.

Two other important decisions in the visualisation production process relate to the extent to which annotation and interactivity will be included. Alan Smith, data visualisation editor at the *Financial Times* newspaper, claims that people are afraid of writing on graphs (Smith, 2016). However, as Smith shows through his own examples, annotations can be extremely useful in helping users navigate. But there are many kinds of annotation available. Kirk distinguishes project annotation, such as titles and subtitles, introductions, user guides and footnotes (which can include links to data sources and credits) from chart annotations, which include labels (axis labels and value labels), legends, reading guides and captions. The challenge, writes Kirk, is to know how much annotation is the right amount: too much might result in a cluttered chart and a patronised audience, whereas too little might leave users struggling to find their own way around a visualisation. In our research, we found that annotation was hugely valued by users unfamiliar with visualisation as a communication form.

The amount of interactivity in a visualisation is another important consideration in the design process. Interactive features usually allow users to adjust the data they are shown or how it is presented, and so support the accessibility principle, according to Kirk. At the time of writing, there is much enthusiasm about the personalisation and gamification of visualisation that interactivity enables, but it is worth noting that in our research, we found that without a clear purpose, these features were not always appreciated by visualisation users. For online researchers using visualisation to communicate data in a journal article or conference presentation, questions about how much and what kind of interactivity are likely to be redundant, but once we start to communicate our research online to non-expert as well as expert audiences, the question gains relevance.

Of course, there are many more considerations than these when producing a data visualisation, such as decisions about axes, scales and which graphical symbols to use. These presentation choices relate to the 'how-to' of data visualisation, addressed comprehensively in the guidebooks we referenced at the start of this chapter. Colour is a particularly important dimension of visualisation because it is a powerful sensory cue and therefore an influential visual property which can have an immediate impact on users and audiences: the different emotional impacts of Figures 18.1 and 18.2 are tied directly to colour. As Kirk notes, every feature of a visualisation has colour properties, and designers should primarily use colour to establish meaning, not to provide decoration. In a similar way, decisions about axes, scales and graphical symbols (and their related forms and areas) should be driven by an understanding of the meaning that is to be conveyed and should emerge from the data in order that the most appropriate combination for presenting data is chosen (see Kirk (2016) for extensive discussion of these considerations).

There is clearly a lot to think about in order to produce a good data visualisation: which tools to use, which chart type is appropriate, whether to include annotation and interactivity. These are in addition to expertise in doing statistical analysis, handling large datasets and comprehending the ideological work that visualisations do to make and shape the data. As Helen argues elsewhere

with Hill (Kennedy and Hill, 2016), the growing availability of data and concomitant expectation that researchers will gather, mine, analyse and visualise could be seen as what Gill describes as 'the hidden injuries of neo-liberal academia' (Gill, 2009). In other words, enthusiasm about big data translates into pressure on researchers to engage with them and visualise them, despite sometimes having neither the requisite skills nor the time to acquire them. Neoliberal regimes mean that academic researchers individually shoulder the responsibility of struggling to adapt to ever-changing pressures, of which learning how to make good data visualisations is the most recent example. We consider this to be a serious issue for online researchers wishing to keep their skills current, so we acknowledge it here, if only to break the silence around these hidden injuries, as Gill suggests we should.

DOING DATA VISUALISATION II: EXAMPLES FROM MIGRATION STUDIES

This section demonstrates how the process of visualisation unfolds in a research setting by drawing on examples from The Migration Observatory where Will works. The Observatory is an independent organisation based at the University of Oxford that aims to inform public debate about immigration through original and secondary research. In an article written by Will about how British civil society organisations perceive data and research, he uses a critical realist orientation (Bhaskar, 1975) to highlight how factors such as the presence of diverse audiences, organisational objectives and available skills contribute to how these groups think about what 'useful' evidence looks like (Allen, 2016). In a similar way here, we attend to the ways in which such contextual factors shaped the representation and presentation of data in the visualisations we discuss. Because of the importance of such factors, we start with a discussion of the context, values and objectives of the Migration Observatory.

The Migration Observatory: Context, Values, Objectives

The Migration Observatory was founded as a politically independent body that brings data and research evidence about immigration and its impacts into public discussions. These discussions happen in the media, policy and government, and civil society, which includes charities and voluntary groups working with migrants, asylum seekers or refugees. The Observatory tries to work in ways that match its stated values of authoritativeness, independence, clarity, comprehensiveness and engagement. Most people encounter its materials, many of which are text-based, through its website (www.migrationobserva-tory.ox.ac.uk). Migration Observatory materials aim to put potentially complicated statistics into clear, simple summaries, sometimes turning textual insights into visual forms such as charts and maps. These outputs are important in the UK context for several reasons: immigration is a significant issue for the British public (Ipsos MORI, 2016); policy activity which aims to deal with the issue has real impacts on immigrants and also on UK citizens; and media and civil society groups, who are increasingly vocal players in the debate about immigration, increasingly turn to data to build their stories and cases. In this context, there is a pressing need to communicate information about migration and its socioeconomic impacts – and visualisations are a crucial way of meeting this need.

These details about the Migration Observatory and its work matter because visualisations exist in particular informational and political contexts. The Observatory makes visualisations for users in journalism, policy, civil society and for interested members of the public. These audiences have different kinds of skills, available time and end goals in accessing data – factors that we, along with Hill and Kirk, argue influence how visualisations are received (Kennedy et al., under revision). These circumstances and audiences inform our broader arguments about what visualisations can do and why critical thinking about visualisation matters.

Case Study One: Migration in the Census

'Migration in the Census' aimed to analyse portions of the 2011 UK Census data (http://www.ons.gov.uk/census/2011census), released by the ONS, that related to the foreign-born population in the UK, and make key points within them accessible and available to audiences at national, regional and local levels.[2] To achieve this, the Observatory produced a series of briefings that provided summaries of results for each of the 12 regions across the UK, as well as summaries for England and Great Britain as wholes. These summaries include interactive maps, generated with Tableau Public, that allow users to filter and customise the visualisations according to their needs and interests. Figure 18.5, depicting the proportion of all foreign-born people who are EU-born in each English and Welsh local authority illustrates the style of these maps. In the online version, when users hover over a particular local authority, they see precise details including the number of EU-born people recorded in that area, drawn directly from the Census. As the proportion of EU-born people (among all foreign-born people) increases in a given local authority, the darker blue that area becomes.

These features are illustrative of the Observatory's visualisation practice: given the potentially wide-ranging audiences noted earlier and the Observatory's value of independence, the goal is to give users a means to engage with the visualisation without suggesting a particular endpoint or conclusion.

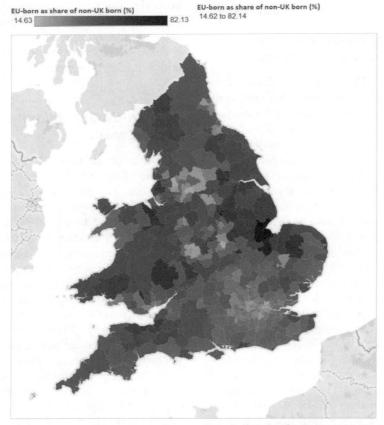

EU-born (excl. UK-born) residents as share of local non-UK born: England & Wales 2011
Map provided by www.migrationobservatory.ox.ac.uk

EU-born as share of non-UK born (%)
14.63   82.13

EU-born as share of non-UK born (%)
14.62 to 82.14

Source: England & Wales Census 2011, ONS.
Note: 'Old' EU refers to member countries of the EU in 2001. EU Accession countries refers to countries that joined the EU between 2001 and 2011, namely Bulgaria, Czech Republic, Cyprus (EU part), Estonia, Hungary, Latvia, Lithuania, Malta, Poland, Romania, Slovakia and Slovenia.

Figure 18.5   EU-born residents as share of local non-UK born, England and Wales
Source: http://public.tableau.com/views/MAPEU-bornresidents2011/EU-bornasshareoflocalnon-UKborn?:embed=y&&:load OrderID=1&:display_count=yes

In Kirk's (2016) terms, this kind of map facilitates *exploration* rather than *explanation*: viewers can metaphorically fly around the country as their curiosities dictate. The maps enable users to *read* specific values by hovering over certain areas; they do not attempt to get viewers to *feel* the issue in charged or emotive ways. That the image is rendered in blue (visible in the online version) is in

keeping with the Observatory's branding colour palette. As we found on Seeing Data, these colours evoke authority and objectivity. Furthermore, as we argue elsewhere (Kennedy *et al.,* 2016a), the convention of viewing a country from above appears to remove one kind of perspective and offers the user an 'unemotional' or 'objective' viewpoint. This advances the Observatory's mission of evidence-based, 'neutral' interventions within a politicised arena.

By dividing the data by region and highlighting patterns specific to particular areas, the Observatory also aimed for a high degree of personalisation in the visualisation, which also fits with its context and values. First, enabling audiences to locate information relevant to the places with which they are familiar is one way of engaging with them and making large datasets accessible. Second, instead of imposing an arbitrary cut-off point based on population sizes, all English and Welsh local authorities are included, and this adheres to the value of comprehensiveness. Third, the interactive maps are standalone items, with little editorial or annotation that supports a single interpretation or perspective, which adheres to the value of independence. Thus the Observatory handles a politicised issue as transparently as possible (even though data are never really neutral, as we noted previously).

In collaboration with visualisation agency Clever Franke and as part of Seeing Data research, the Observatory subsequently expanded on these qualities of exploration and personalisation to produce a more comprehensive visualisation of the same data. This second visualisation added features such as searching by local authority name and comparing two areas side-by-side. It also represented other aspects of foreign-born people that the Census asked about, such as region of origin, sex, time period of arrival and employment status. Figure 18.6 illustrates how the visualisation displays key data about the size of the foreign-born population in each authority. Users can also choose to compare other demographic dimensions, or click around the circles that represent different local authorities and explore their curiosities. These extended exploratory and customizable features also fit with the Observatory's values and aims of providing comprehensive and independent information: the visualisation provides users with an opportunity to engage with the data in a self-directed manner and to access precise values relating to whichever local authority they wished.[3] 'Migration in the Census' shows how the process of visualising a large and complicated dataset is governed

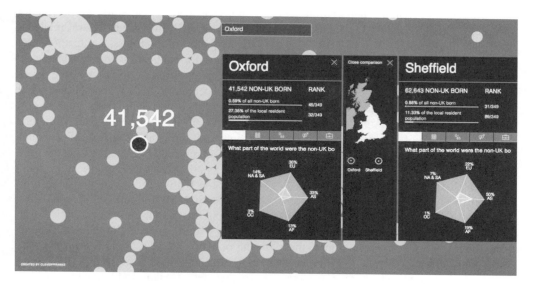

Figure 18.6   Screenshot of 'Migration in the Census' (comparative view)
Source: www.compas.ox.ac.uk/migrationinthecensus

by motivating factors that influence the appearance of the final visualisation.

Case Study Two: Migration in the News

The second case study relates to Observatory research into the ways in which the British press describes migrant groups, including asylum seekers and refugees. Based on a landmark project in linguistics that examined a similar question over the 1996–2005 period (Gabrielatos and Baker, 2008), 'Migration in the News' extended this research to look first at the 2010–2012 period, and then later at 2006–2013. This section describes how visualisations were developed on this project, the kinds of decisions made along the way and their impacts on eventual outputs.[4]

The rationale for the 'Migration in the Media' project relates to the Observatory value of comprehensiveness: that is, a belief in the importance of understanding how the press as a whole describes migrant groups (Allen, 2014). In its first stage, the project aimed to collect, as far as possible, all news coverage mentioning key migration terms like 'immigrant', 'asylum', 'deportation' and 'refugees'. This totalled 58,351 items, comprising nearly 44 million words. Then, using statistical tests, it identified which words consistently described the terms 'immigrant(s)', 'migrant(s)', 'asylum seeker(s)' and 'refugee(s)'. These descriptors are known as 'modifiers'. The two main findings were that immigrants were most consistently described as 'illegal' during this period, while asylum seekers were described as 'failed' (Blinder and Allen, 2016).

Visualising these results presented some challenges. Qualitative data about modifiers needed to be linked with quantitative data about their frequencies. Furthermore, these results were different across three types of publication: tabloids, which tend to focus on entertainment or celebrity news; broadsheets which tend to represent 'traditional'

news reporting or journalism; and mid-markets which typically have a mix of both. For example, how could a visualisation show that 'illegal' was far and away the most frequent, consistent modifier for 'immigrants' in the tabloid press? Figure 18.7 shows an early attempt to visualise this finding, using the 'bubble chart' feature in Tableau Public.

On the one hand, this visualisation clearly makes its point, a point so large as to be unmissable. The word 'illegal' visibly modifies 'immigrants' much more than 'Eastern European' or 'EU'. But on the other hand, there are some problems with it. The size of the 'illegal' bubble suggests that this term is remarkably frequent, but comparison is limited to two other terms. What's more, the visualisation did not allow simultaneous comparison across publication types. In addition, the human brain has difficulty in determining the area of circles compared to the features of other shapes like the lengths of bars (Spence and Lewandowsky, 1991). So, although this cluster of circles had some appeal, the visualisation could potentially introduce some confusion, which goes against the Observatory's value of clarity.

In a subsequent iteration, squares replaced circles, a legend gave users information about how differently sized squares related to the frequency of modifiers, and features such as toggles for publication types enabled users to compare different subsets of the press. The Observatory added annotation, which it believed would help users make sense of some of its representational decisions. Figure 18.8 shows a screenshot of the visualisation as it currently exists, showing the prevalence of 'illegal' as a descriptor of migrants across the British press.[5] At the same time, as in the first 'Migration in the Census' visualisation, this output also aimed to give users control over its presentational form, depending on their interests. And, as with the local authority-level data, it also reports the precise frequencies of each modifier when the user hovers over the relevant square, allowing users to read values efficiently.

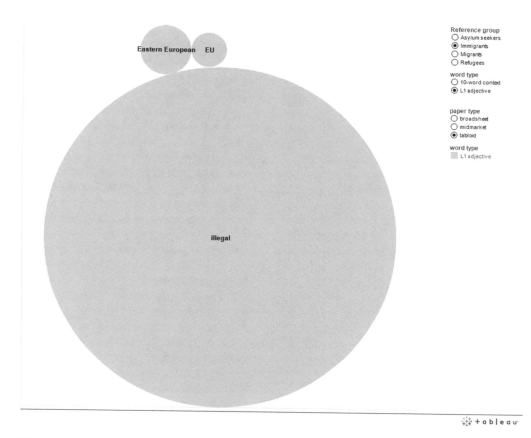

Figure 18.7 Modifiers of 'immigrants' in the tabloid press, 2010–2012

After completing this study of the 2010–2012 period, the Observatory expanded its perspective longitudinally to include all available national UK newspaper coverage mentioning the same set of key terms from 2006 to 2013 – totalling about 90 million words. Again in collaboration with Clever Franke, this stage aimed to show how the frequency of mentions of each migrant group changed in the press over time, as well as how the kinds of modifiers used to describe each group differed among subsets of the press. Unlike the original visualisation in Figure 18.8 that mainly emphasised *reading* data, this newer visualisation attended to *feeling* data by communicating overall impressions about the nature of press coverage. The goal was to show how press coverage had changed

over time, rather than show static, aggregated results, and so seeing the direction and general scale of these changes was more important than reading precise figures.

Figure 18.9 shows a portion of the visualisation. It depicts the changing frequencies of each key term – 'immigrants', 'migrants', 'asylum seekers' and 'refugees' – over the seven-year period. As the user moves along the timeline, the relative size of each key word increases and decreases according to its frequency in the dataset. These key words are differentiated by colour using the same palette from the Observatory's other publications: the colouration of each word signals which line in the underlying chart it corresponds with, allowing the viewer, at a glance, to get a sense of which terms were used

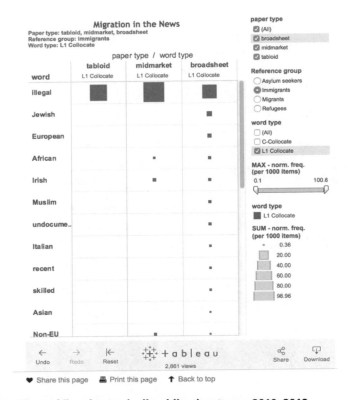

Figure 18.8   Modifiers of 'immigrants', all publication types, 2010–2012
Source: http://public.tableau.com/views/MigrationintheNews/MigrationintheNewsinteractive?:embed=y&:loadOrderID=0&:
display_count=yes

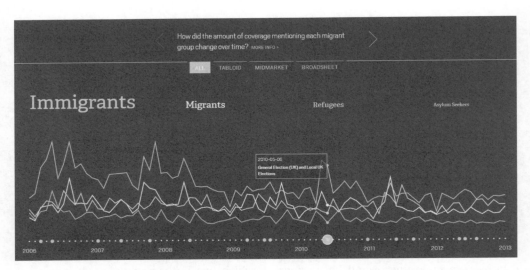

Figure 18.9   Screenshot of frequency analysis with annotation, all publications (a work-in-progress version of the interactive 'Migration in the News' visualisation can be found at www.compas.ox.ac.uk/migrationinthenews)

more frequently without reading specific data points. Users can also choose different subsets of the press, or get more information about the methods by which the data were generated by clicking 'more info'. Additional contextual information is available through annotations connected to nodes on the timeline. These signal, for example, when elections occurred or when particularly important policies involving immigration became law. Some of these project and chart annotations aim to be explanatory, but they also aim to make the visualisation trustworthy and engaging, given that explaining data handling processes is an essential component of good, professional and honest visualisation practice (Kirk, 2016).

Another section of the visualisation attempts to give a sense of how different modifiers are associated with each key term. In the earlier visualisation, frequency was indicated through the size of squares and users could pick out specific values by hovering over them. This visualisation, in contrast, depicts frequency through the saturation of colour, as seen in Figure 18.10 (and more clearly online www.compas.ox.ac.uk/migrationinthenews). Throughout the visualisation, the same colours express findings about the same key terms, to guide the user through the different parts. Also, because the

project focused on differences over time, the top 100 modifiers were included in the analysis where possible. The intended effect was a 'wall of words', where frequent modifiers would stand out by glowing more brightly. Here again the difference between feeling and reading numbers is important: although the visualisation does not show precisely how much more frequently 'failed' modifies 'asylum seekers' compared to, say, 'child' or 'genuine', users can immediately sense which words are most frequent without referring to precise figures.

These two case study projects illustrate how the Observatory uses visualisations to achieve its aims, and how decisions and thinking about some of the issues discussed earlier in this chapter align with the Observatory's values. Enabling exploration of extended datasets aligns with comprehensiveness, and presenting region-specific snapshots is a way of engaging with audiences who might have more local rather than national interests. Highlighting how these datasets are limited – what the data can and cannot say – aligns with authoritativeness, and project annotations that make complex statistics understandable aim to achieve clarity. The overall project of including lots of different kinds of data, in ways that are customisable yet clearly marked, aims to present an

Figure 18.10   Screenshot of modifiers of 'asylum seekers', all publications

independent view of this complicated issue. These examples illustrate how key questions about visualisation such as 'what works', 'for whom' and 'under what circumstances' are addressed in practice. Thinking critically about its own visualisation practice, iterating and revising visualisations accordingly (and if feasible) are integral to the ways in which the Observatory makes and shares its visualisations.

TOWARDS GOOD DATA VISUALISATION PRACTICE FOR ONLINE RESEARCHERS

One aspect of data visualisation that we have not discussed in any length in this chapter is users and audiences. This is somewhat ironic given that our main research interest in this field relates to the views of users, who we consider to be either overlooked or decontextualised in studies of information and data visualisation. By this we mean that visualisation research which *does* involve users provides little information about them and ignores socio-cultural and contextual factors of the kinds discussed in the previous section, which play a significant role in visualisation consumption and engagement. Our research was therefore informed by our critique of psychology-influenced studies of visualisation reception which aim to separate out perceptual processes from the messy contexts in which they take place. The research that we undertook confirmed that a range of socio-cultural factors affect engagement, including the subject matter of the visualisation, its original location or media source, users' beliefs and opinions, the time that users have at their disposal to explore visualised data, users' confidence in the skills that they think they need to make sense of a visualisation (such as statistical and visual literacy, language skills and critical thinking skills) and the emotional dimensions of engaging with diverse elements of a visualisation

(aesthetics, the data themselves, the subject matter and the source). We report extensively on these findings elsewhere (Kennedy, 2015; Kennedy *et al.*, under revision).

For online researchers, the primary audience for our data visualisations will often be peers who encounter them in conference presentations, journal articles or other scholarly publications. But visualisation is also a method for communicating our research to broader, non-specialist audiences, something that is increasingly significant in the UK context because having an impact beyond our scholarly communities is an ever more important measure of research excellence. Researchers producing data visualisations for both expert peers and non-expert wider publics need to be attentive to who their audiences are and what needs they have. They also need to navigate the ways in which the factors discussed in the previous paragraph might impact on the user groups' engagement with visualisations.

Data visualisation promises to make data accessible and transparent to broad audiences, and it certainly has the potential to do that. But it is not a simple window onto data: online researchers need to be alert to what might be called the politics of data visualisation – that is, the work that visualisations do to communicate data in certain ways – and in so doing, to produce visualisations reflectively, in ways that are aware of contexts and audiences, as well as more pragmatic questions of what tools to use and what chart types to include. Being aware of all of these things and so producing good visualisations does not come easily, and the provision of resources to enable researchers to develop these skills is also a political issue. We have suggested some solutions to some of these problems, such as abiding by professional principles or engaging in practices which help users become aware of the choices made in producing a visualisation (for example, including annotations such as a link to a data source or an explanation of the ways in which data have been treated). If we have one message for readers of this chapter, it is to be attentive to what it is that we are doing when we visualise our data, for whom, in what contexts and with what effects.

NOTES

1 This article was itself a response to a blogpost called, 'Why you should never trust a data scientist' (Warden 2013).
2 Full details of the project and the whole suite of materials are available at http://www.migrationobservatory.ox.ac.uk/projects/census
3 As long as that local authority was English or Welsh: a key limitation of this visualisation was its exclusion of Scotland and Northern Ireland.
4 For more details about the 2010–2012 dataset, methods and results, see Allen (2014) and Blinder and Allen (2016).
5 Full details of the initial project (covering 2010–2012) and the accompanying visualisation itself can be found at http://migrationobservatory.ox.ac.uk/projects/media

REFERENCES

Allen, W. (2014) 'Does comprehensiveness matter? Reflections on analysing and visualising UK press portrayals of migrant groups'. Paper presented at the Computation Journalism Symposium, 24–25 October, Columbia University, New York.

Allen, W. (2016) 'Factors that impact how civil society intermediaries perceive evidence', *Evidence & Policy: A Journal of Research, Debate and Practice*. DOI: http://dx.doi.org/10.1332/174426416X14538259555968

Ambrosio, C. (2015) 'Objectivity and representative practices across artistic and scientific visualization'. In A. Carusi, A. S. Hoel, T. Webmoor and S. Woolgar (eds.), *Visualization in the Age of Computerization* (pp. 118–44). London: Routledge.

Bhaskar, R. (1975) *A Realist Theory of Science*. London: Verso.

Blinder, S. and Allen, W. (2016) 'Constructing immigrants: portrayals of migrant groups in British national newspapers, 2010–2012', *International Migration Review*, 50: 3–40.

Bollier, D. (2010) *The Promise and Peril of Big Data*. Available at http://www.aspeninstitute.org/publications/promise-peril-big-data

Bowker, G. (2005) *Memory Practices in the Sciences*. Cambridge, MA: MIT Press.

Burn-Murdoch, J. (2013) 'Why you should never trust a data visualisation', *Guardian*. Available at http://www.theguardian.com/news/datablog/2013/jul/24/why-you-should-never-trust-a-data-visualisation

Cairo, A. (2012) *The Functional Art: An Introduction to Information Graphics and Visualization*. San Francisco, CA: New Riders.

Cotgreave, A. (2014) 'Controlling your message with title, colour and orientation', Gravy Anecdote, 16 October. http://gravyanecdote.com/uncategorized/should-you-trust-a-data-visualisation

Crawford, K. (2013) 'Algorithmic illusions: hidden biases of big data'. Presentation at the Strata Conference, February 26–28, 2013. Available at https://www.youtube.com/watch?v=irP5RCdpilc

Dick, M. (2015) 'Just fancy that: an analysis of infographic propaganda in *The Daily Express*, 1956–1959', *Journalism Studies*, 16(2), 152–74.

Few, S. (2008) 'What ordinary people need most from information visualization today', *Perceptual Edge: Visual Business Intelligence Newsletter*. Available at: http://www.perceptualedge.com/articles/visual_business_intelligence/what_people_need_from_infovis.pdf

Few, S. (2012) *Show Me The Numbers: Designing Tables and Graphs to Enlighten*. Burlingame, CA: Analytics Press.

Fyfe, G. and Law, J. (eds.) (1988) *Picturing Power: Visual Depiction and Social Relations*. London: Routledge.

Gabrielatos, C. and Baker, P. (2008) 'Fleeing, sneaking, flooding: A corpus analysis of discursive constructions of refugees and asylum seekers in the UK press, 1996–2005', *Journal of English Linguistics*, 36(1), 5–38.

Gill, R. (2009) 'Breaking the silence: the hidden injuries of neo-liberal academia'. In R. Ryan-Flood and R. Gill (eds.), *Secrecy and Silence in the Research Process: Feminist Reflections*. London: Routledge, pp. 228–44.

Hill, R. L. (2014) 'How social semiotics can help us understand big data visualisations'.

Seeing Data. Available at http://seeingdata.org/how-social-semiotics-can-help-us-understand-big-data-visualisations/

Ipsos MORI. (2016) 'Economist/Ipsos MORI January 2016 Issues Index: concern about immigration returns to prominence'. Available at: https://www.ipsos-mori.com/researchpublications/researcharchive/3691/Economist-Ipsos-MORI-January-2016-Issues-index.aspx

Kennedy, H. (2014) 'How do visualization professionals think about users?'. Seeing Data. Available at http://seeingdata.org/visualization-professionals-think-users/

Kennedy, H. (2015) 'Seeing data: visualisation design should consider how we respond to data emotionally as well as rationally'. LSE Impact Blog. Available at http://blogs.lse.ac.uk/impactofsocialsciences/2015/07/22/seeing-data-how-people-engage-with-data-visualisations

Kennedy, H. (2016) *Post, Mine, Repeat: Social Media Data Mining Becomes Ordinary*. Basingstoke, UK: Palgrave Macmillan.

Kennedy, H. and Hill, R.L. (2016) 'The pleasure and pain of visualising data in times of data power', *Television and New Media*. Available at: http://tvn.sagepub.com/content/early/2016/09/07/1527476416667823.abstract.

Kennedy, H., Hill, R. L., Aiello, G. and Allen, W. (2016a) 'The work that visualisation conventions do', *Information, Communication and Society*, 19(6): 715–735.

Kennedy, H., Hill, R. L., Allen, W. and Kirk, A. (under revision) '(Big) data visualisations and their users: how socio-cultural factors challenge existing definitions of effectiveness', *First Monday*.

Kirk, A. (2016) *Data Visualisation: A Handbook for Data Driven Design*. London: Sage Publications.

Korzybski, A. (1931) 'A non-Aristotelian system and its necessity for rigour in mathematics and physics'. Presentation at the American Mathematical Society/American Association for the Advancement of Science, New Orleans, Louisiana, 28 December 1931. Reprinted in *Science and Sanity*, 1933: 747–61.

Neurath, O., Neurath, M. and Cohen, R. S. (1973) *Empiricism and Sociology*. Vol. 1. Dordrecht: Reidel.

Periscopic. (2014) Homepage. Available at http://www.periscopic.com/

Porter, T. M. (1995) *Trust in Numbers: The Pursuit of Objectivity in Science and Public Life*. Princeton, NJ: Princeton University Press.

Ruppert, E. (2014) 'Visualising a journal: big data and society'. Paper presented at the ICS Visual & Digital Cultures Research Seminar, Leeds. 13th May 2014.

Scarr, S. (2011) Iraq's Bloody Toll'. *South China Morning Post*, 17 December. Available at www.scmp.com/infographics/article/1284683/iraqs-bloody-toll

Smith, A. (2016) 'Crafting charts that can withstand the data deluge', *Financial Times*. Available at http://www.ft.com/cms/s/0/3f195d40-b851-11e5-b151-8e15c9a029fb.html#axzz3yFKKUQ7M

Spence, I. and Lewandowsky, S. (1991) 'Displaying proportions and percentages', *Applied Cognitive Psychology*, 5(1): 61–77.

Stiftelsen Gapminder (n.d.) Gapminder. Available at http://www.gapminder.org/

Tufte, E. R. (1983) *The Visual Display of Quantitative Information*. Cheshire, CT: Graphics Press.

Valarakis, A. (2014) *On Data Visualization: Rhetoric and the Revival of the Body Politic*. (MA), University of Amsterdam.

Warden, P. (2013) 'Why you should never trust a data scientist', Pete Warden's blog. Available at http://petewarden.com/2013/07/18/why-you-should-never-trust-a-data-scientist

Yau, N. (2013) *Data Points: Visualization That Means Something*. New York, NY: John Wiley & Sons.

Zambrano, R. N. and Engelhardt, Y. (2008). 'Diagrams for the masses'. In G. Stapleton, J. Howse and J. Lee (eds.), *Diagrams 2008*. Berlin: Springer Verlag, pp. 282–92.

## PART VI

Digital Text Analysis

## 19

Online Tools for Content Analysis

Roel Popping

INTRODUCTION

Content analysis is a systematic reduction of a flow of text to a standard set of statistically manipulable symbols representing the presence, the intensity, or the frequency of some characteristics, which allows making replicable and valid inferences from text to their context. In most situations the source of the text is investigated, but this should not exclude the text itself, the audience or the receivers of the text. It involves measurement. Qualitative data are quantified for the purpose of affording statistical inference. In the past it was performed by human coders. Based on a so-called codebook these coders noted whether what was mentioned in the variables involved was found in the texts under study or not.

This changed very much when the computer came in in the 1960s. The software, the General Inquirer, was an aide for the quantification of texts and transcripts, it could code faster and more consistently than humans

(Stone *et al.*, 1966). Now the emphasis came to be on the occurrence of particular themes. A list of search entries per theme was to be developed. These search entries are words or phrases that are understood as indicating the occurrence of the corresponding theme. The themes and their search entries are kept in a so-called dictionary. Texts and dictionary are input for the software to be used, output is a data matrix with the themes in the columns and the texts in the rows. In a cell, one finds how many times the theme was mentioned in the corresponding piece of text.

At first, content analysis was used primarily to draw conclusions regarding the source of the message. Communication is broader, however; it also involves the message, the channel, and the audience. The four aspects of communication represent the most common contextual variables used in content analysis. A fundamental characteristic of content analysis is that it is concerned with the communicative act post hoc.

Researchers investigating the message usually look at the occurrence of specific themes in the texts. Today this approach is known as the thematic approach. A dictionary is often used, which informs how search entries, words or word phrases refer to themes one is interested in as they occur in a text. The frequency of occurrences or co-occurrences of themes is the basis for the analyses that should give an answer to the research question. This is the approach that is followed in most research and it can be performed automatically.

Language can be very ambiguous – to start with, a word can have different meanings. The meaning of a word can even change over time; however, the correct meaning usually becomes clear when the context is taken into account. Software only recognizes search entries; therefore, the dictionary should contain guidelines to overcome potential problems. The word 'bank' for example is often rephrased as bank#1 to indicate the place where one brings his or her money, as bank#2 to refer to the edge of a river, and eventually as bank#3 to refer to that one can sit on (as in 'banks of seats'). There are more possibilities as will be shown later.

Two other approaches also receive increasing attention: the semantic and the network approach. These approaches involve not only the identification of alternative themes, but also the encoding of relations among themes in texts. These relational methods for encoding texts are strikingly similar. In each case, a Subject–Verb–Object (S–V–O) syntax is applied during the encoding process, or even a Subject–Valence–Verb–Object (S–V–V–O) syntax, in which the valence can reflect negation, evaluation, intensity, etc. These 'clause-based content analyses' afford inferences about how texts' sources use words in their speech or writings. The methods associated with the new approaches differ primarily according to the research purposes to which each one's relationally encoded texts can be applied. In the semantic approach, variables indicate interrelations that themes may have in texts. The network approach methodologies

afford variables that characterize entire networks of semantically related themes.

In all three approaches texts are coded, and in all three the researcher might understand the texts instrumentally; they might be interpreted in terms of the researcher's theory. This is called the *instrumental* approach (Shapiro, 1997). This approach is generally followed. It is differentiated from the *representational* approach, where the source's perspective is used to interpret the texts under study. Here the intended meaning of the source must be identified. This usually demands an interpretation by a human coder. Regardless of whether the source's or researcher's perspectives are used in interpreting texts, these perspectives must be made explicit for the reader to evaluate the validity of conclusions that are made.

Many researchers who prefer machine coding based on a dictionary follow the instrumental approach. This method of coding is very fast and it is therefore no problem to analyse all available texts. But one needs to be cautious because it often looks as if the texts used are an ad hoc population of texts. The population should at least be indicated and motivated. This concern is especially relevant to analyses of blogs or Tweets that become available (see also Hookway and Snee, this volume). On the other hand, the volume of texts can never be an argument against manual coding. Sampling is the solution to this 'problem'.

This approach, which focuses on generating a data matrix to be used in statistical analysis, differs from qualitative analysis, which is a collective noun for various approaches. Software for this type of research focuses on theory building, text base management, coding and retrieving for descriptive and interpretative analysis. It is not directed to quantification for statistical inferences. Berelson (1952: 116ff) makes the following two remarks with regard to qualitative analysis:

(1) Much 'qualitative' analysis is quasi-quantitative... Just as quantitative analysis assigns relative frequencies to different qualities (or categories), so qualitative analysis usually contains quantitative

statements in rough form. They may be less explicit but they are nonetheless frequency statements about the incidence of general categories… (2) 'Qualitative' analysis is often based upon presence–absence of particular content (rather than relative frequencies).

Content analysis is also used in the fields of linguistics and information retrieval. This will not be considered here.

My goal is to describe more recent developments within the three approaches mentioned. Here we will see that coding can be performed from the two perspectives just mentioned; we will also see that the computer plays an important role in the process each time. The three approaches – thematic, semantic and network – will subsequently be discussed, each initially regarding manual coding, and then machine coding. Extra attention will be given to the so-called modality analysis, which is seen as a very challenging development. Finally, some issues that might affect the use of content analysis will be outlined.

THEMATIC APPROACH TO CONTENT ANALYSIS

Thematic content analysis is the term for any content analysis in which variables indicate the occurrence (or frequency of occurrence) of particular themes or concepts. In this section we specify what themes and concepts are, followed by how these can be recognized in a text, but we also cover difficulties with the approach. In the sub-sections, machine coding and manual coding are discussed, as well as the problem of ambiguity in texts. Machine learning is dealt with as part of machine coding.

A concept is 'a single idea, or ideational kernel, regardless [of whether] it is represented by a single word or a phrase' (Carley, 1993: 81). Practitioners of thematic content analysis usually reserve the term 'theme' for broader classes of concepts. The theme is usually concentrated on a specific referent (e.g. the president, the U.S., British foreign policy, communism). Thematic content analysis allows the researcher to determine what, and how frequently, themes (co-) occur in texts. The method is particularly useful when the researcher is interested in the prominence of various themes in texts, possibly reflecting broad cultural shifts. With respect to a certain research question, therefore, one also needs context variables between which perspectives can be compared, for example the (type of) newspaper in which the text has been published. The first software for content analysis was designed for thematic content analysis based on a dictionary. The analysis is based on a deductive rule-based approach to operationalization. The approach can only be used effectively if a complete theory is available of how the theoretical themes of interest manifest themselves in natural language. This theory, which is the researcher's theory, becomes visible in the dictionary. For this reason, the instrumental approach to coding is followed.

The dictionary-based methods have hardly changed since the development of the first software. For these methods to work well, the scores attached to words must closely align with how the words are used in a particular context. If a dictionary is developed for a specific application, then this assumption should be easily justified. But when dictionaries are created in one substantive area and then applied to another, problems can occur. Dictionaries, therefore, should be used with substantial caution. Scholars must either explicitly establish that word lists created in other contexts are applicable to a particular domain, or create a problem-specific dictionary. In either instance, scholars must validate their results. However, measures from dictionaries are rarely validated, and instead standard practice in using dictionaries is to assume the measures created from a dictionary are correct and then apply them to the problem.

In thematic content analysis one can report occurrences and co-occurrences of themes.

Occurrences indicate the prominence of themes. When compared across contexts they can afford inferences about culture's changing themes, ideas, issues and dilemmas or differences between media in representing news content about the same issue. Looking at co-occurrences means looking at associations among themes. This analysis is known as contingency analysis. In this type of analysis, the goal is to calculate associations among occurrence measures and to infer what the resulting pattern of association means. Problems occur if these inferences are about how themes are related. Assume the following text block is investigated: 'The man likes detective stories, but his wife prefers love themes'. The themes MAN (represented by 'the man') and LOVE THEME (represented by 'love themes') co-occur in this block, but no relation between the two is specified. For such inferences relations should have been encoded a priori, not via ad hoc post hoc looks at the texts. Texts should therefore be divided into distinct blocks, for example chapters, paragraphs, sentences, clauses (sentences or part-of-a-sentence that explicitly or implicitly contain an inflected verb, an optional subject and/or object, plus all modifiers related to this verb, subject, and object). Now the co-occurrences can be investigated on the level of the clause. If not, this would lead to ecological fallacy in the interpretation of the data because inferences about the nature of clauses would be deduced from inference from the text to which the clause belongs.

An example of a thematic text analysis is found in Namenwirth (1969) who studied differences between British prestige and mass newspapers with respect to some orientational dimensions. The orientations are considered as marks of distinction with respect to the newspapers, but also with respect to cognitive styles of elites and masses in general. Lots of themes have been investigated. To reduce their number in the analysis, principal component analysis has been applied.

Machine Coding

Looking at publications in which text analysis is used, it turns out that most investigators use the machine to do the coding based on a dictionary. Researchers using full automated software are imposing the software developer's theoretical perspective on the speaker's/author's words. If that is what they intend, then its developers need to have reduced this theory to concrete algorithms in their content analysis software and to have made their theory–algorithm relations clear to users (otherwise users might end up naively believing that the software has somehow 'revealed' a perspective-free [i.e. incontestably true] rendering of the texts).

Today, some software offers the possibility to enter one's own dictionary, others use dictionaries provided by the developer or by a team around this developer. Constructing a dictionary is a challenging task. The dictionary should be valid; this implies among others that maintenance deserves a lot of attention. Dictionaries usually cover specific fields.

An example of a dictionary that is well maintained by the researcher is the one that is part of the LIWC software (Linguistic Inquiry and Word Count) for measuring people's physical and mental health (Pennebaker et al., 2003). The software allows users to determine the degree to which any text uses positive or negative emotions, self-references, causal words and 70 other language dimensions.

In recent years, there have been two innovations that receive serious attention: supervised learning and analysis of co-occurrence of words. Both are extensions of the thematic instrumental approach.

Machine Learning

Researchers using dictionaries follow a deductive approach. Today, however, inductive approaches are also becoming available. This happens when machine learning is used.

A machine learning algorithm is trained with known data and derives rules by which the given decisions can be reproduced. An algorithm takes texts and their correct coding assignments as inputs, derives a 'probabilistic dictionary' (Pennings and Keman, 2002) from this data, and uses this information for the coding of new texts.

The method is a purely statistical approach, which can be used in any language and with any topic category. No assumptions are made about syntax; any text is treated as a simple bag of words. The approach is solely based on superficial, i.e. lexical, features of a text and the assumption that single words or word combinations provide enough information for thematic coding. The training process resembles conventional coder training; it is heavily based on example documents. The computer classifier is treated like any human coder, but with limited language skills and no contextual knowledge. The method is seen by its users as an ideal complement and extension to classic thematic content analysis. Compared to traditional methods of automated content analysis, supervised learning does not require different operationalization strategies; however, one has to remember that any automatic classification is only as good as its training material. Making a correct decision often depends on a lot of context knowledge.

For more details on the methods used in machine learning, see Grimmer and Stewart (2013). Schrodt (2012) reports on actual software developments. The Comparative Party Manifesto Project, in which different aspects of party performance as well as the structure and development of party systems is studied, is an example of where this method is used. The project is based on quantitative content analyses of parties' election programmes from many countries. Laver *et al.*, (2003) contains an extended introduction into this project, including a mathematical model of the way the learning process works. A kind of state-of-the-art of the project is presented in Geminas (2013).

Analysis based on Co-occurrence

One way to reduce the amount of information in texts has been to apply principal component analysis or multidimensional scaling based on co-occurring words or co-occurring themes. In this way, Miller (1997) could demonstrate stakeholder influence on news and patterns of change in frames across time.

Today natural language processing is becoming used to analyse texts. One method is Latent Dirichlet Allocation (LDA), a hierarchical Bayesian technique that automatically discovers topics that these texts contain. It is based on the idea that each document is a mixture of a small number of topics and that each word is attributable to one of these topics (Blei *et al.*, 2003). Following an iterative process, a descending hierarchical classification method decomposes classes until a predetermined number of iterations fails to result in further divisions. The result is a hierarchy of classes, which can then be schematized as a tree diagram.

An example of a study using such a technique is Schonhardt-Bailey (2005), who analysed speeches on National and Homeland Security by presidency candidates Bush and Kerry in 2004. The software found seven classes of groups of words that could be labelled. The groups could further be reduced to two groups, one containing speeches that were especially US-specific, the other containing speeches dealing with the global order. The first group contained nearly all the speeches by Kelly, the other group speeches by Bush.

Manual Coding

Most machine coding is based on a dictionary. A dictionary usually does not catch the latent meaning of text, and usually there will also be problems with ambiguous texts. These problems might be solved when manual coding is applied, at least as a supplement to machine coding. This way of coding became possible from the moment operating

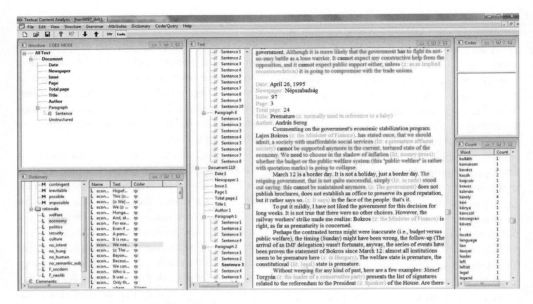

Figure 19.1   Example Textual Content Analysis window

systems and programs made it possible that complete texts could be made visible on the screen of the computer or terminal and allowed users to indicate which search entry or which sentence had been coded. At first, this software was developed for performing qualitative research, but later software for quantitative research also appeared. Figure 19.1 shows what appears on the screen when the software Textual Content Analysis (TCA) for manual coding is used (Roberts, 2008).

Here, several windows are opened. At the top left, we see how the data are structured. At the bottom, the themes used are listed. As can be seen, these themes might refer to words or phrases that are literally present in the text (manifest), but also to interpretations by the coder (latent). The window to the right of this window shows all sentences that have been coded. Further to the right is an overview of how the texts are structured (in this case: document, paragraph, sentences and attributes to indicate characteristics of the text, like sequence number, date, title, etc.). The texts follow, here coded parts are indicated by shading. Finally, at the very right

is a word count. When the mouse is moved over a coded text (either word or sentence) the window right at the top shows how it has been coded. Specific words in the text can be looked for in a 'key word in context' (KWIC) window, here search entries can be indicated and coded at once. When coding has finished a data matrix is generated that can be entered into software for statistical analysis. Today, software for qualitative research also produces a data matrix (see Silver and Bulloch, this volume). The main difference to software for qualitative research is that the goal is different: a data matrix is generated using known themes. Qualitative researchers look for themes and relations between these themes in the context of theory development or a detailed description in a case study. Themes, but also units, can therefore be defined on several levels (e.g. referential versus factual code) and there are often facilities for memoing and transcribing texts.

Coding in this way allows exploration of textual representation. A lot of ambiguity can be overcome and it is easier to code the latent meaning of what is expressed. This is possible because the context is taken into account; however, it is necessary that the motivation for choices is explained (Popping and Roberts, 2009). This does not mean that human coding is flawless. Mikhaylov *et al.* (2012) reported dramatic figures for the reliability of the human coding in the Comparative Manifestos Project. Leites *et al.* (1951) investigate speeches on the occasion of Stalin's seventieth birthday with different Soviet Politburo members. Here choices for assigning specific codes are motivated in great detail. This helps very much in understanding the coding process. Therefore it is good for the validity of the study and probably would have had a positive effect on the reliability if it were computed.

Ambiguity

A big problem with the use of sentences is that they contain ambiguity, i.e. there is doubt or uncertainty about meaning or intention. Several types of ambiguity can be distinguished. A good solution is currently unavailable and the types can be recognised when manual coding is performed. Lexical ambiguity refers to the situation in which a word or a phrase is a homonym; it has more than one meaning in the language to which it belongs. For example, 'bank', as was mentioned before, can refer to a bench, but also to a financial institution and to the edge of a river. The context in which an ambiguous word is used often makes it evident which meaning is intended. Sometimes the correct reading can be found automatically. Word sense disambiguation is an algorithmic method that automatically associates the appropriate meaning with a word in context (Navigli, 2009). The method is instrumental and based on probabilities, and the information that is used comes from an explicit lexicon or knowledge base or it is gained by training on some corpus. Today, lexical ambiguity in text can be resolved with a reasonable degree of accuracy when this method

is used. Schrodt (2012) reports the implementation of these algorithms in software. Where the correct meaning is to be indicated in the text and one does not want to rephrase the word, it is often possible to replace the word with a synonym that has only one meaning. Another solution is to look for homonyms in the texts and to replace them by synonyms that are not ambiguous or by alternative words, for example 'bank#1' to indicate the financial institution.

Syntactic ambiguity arises when a complex phrase or a sentence can be parsed in more than one way. The phrase 'The Dutch sociology teacher' leaves open whether the sociology teacher is a Dutchman or whether the teacher teaches Dutch sociology.

Semantic ambiguity arises when a word or theme has an inherently diffuse meaning based on widespread or informal usage. Here one might distinguish idiomatic ambiguity, which characterizes expressions that lack clear meaning for those who are 'outsiders' to a particular social group, for example 'You'll eat your words!'. Such expressions are found when data from blogs or Tweets are used which contain a very informal content setting and slang.

Illocutionary ambiguity characterizes statements with meanings that vary as a function of statements made prior to them in context, for example 'Stop!' (What I am doing, or how I am doing it?) and 'Pete bought that software' (an awful purchase, or just a purchase?).

Besides ambiguity, typographical errors also occur in texts. For the greater part, such errors are corrected by applying a grammar checker. Search engines that identify textual attributes through exact matching of queries and character strings cannot identify expressions with typographical errors or misspellings; this can cause omissions of potentially relevant texts. The problem is addressed by fuzzy search options that take a variety of similarities into account: typographical, phonetic and stemming similarities. A stem is the root of a word (a form which is not further analysable), together with any derivational affixes, to which inflectional affixes are added.

At this moment, no standard methods (coding rules) are available to overcome these problems. Word sense disambiguation is still under development. In my view, the other problems are usually ignored or even not recognized. An exception is Popping and Roberts (2009) who explain in detail how they made their choices with regard to types of modal auxiliary verbs and rationales as used in studies they performed, among which is Roberts, Popping and Pan (2009).

SEMANTIC APPROACH TO CONTENT ANALYSIS

Semantic content analyses yield information on how themes are related according to an a priori specified semantic grammar. This type of analysis expands the types of questions that a researcher can answer. Referring to propaganda techniques in making this point, Roberts (1989: 169) notes that in a thematic analysis a possible research question would be: 'What themes are mentioned in propaganda that are not mentioned in other communications?'. Using the semantic approach, the question can be extended to: 'What syntactic strategies are used by political leaders when their policies fail (or succeed)?'. Unlike the former question, the latter asks about concrete relations among themes used within different social contexts.

This section introduces the semantic approach and attention is given to the way in which coding of semantic relations is performed automatically and manually. A new source of ambiguity is also introduced later.

Semantically encoding data requires that one fits themes that occur in a clause into a semantic grammar. Usually valence information (regarding negation, evaluation, etc.) is subsumed under the verb component. For this reason, one sometimes refers to a semantic grammar as having an S–V–V–O form.

By taking relational characteristics of the text into account, semantic content analysis improves upon thematic content analysis methods and overcomes many of its problems. Based on a thematic content analysis, co-occurrence of subject and object can be identified. In semantic content analysis, the relation is specified and can be investigated.

Sometimes thematic text analysts will wrongly interpret co-occurrences of themes (i.e. correlations between word frequencies) as indicative of specific semantic relations among these themes. In the thematic approach, themes are counted and nothing is specified with respect to any co-occurrence. In the semantic approach, relations among themes are also encoded. This overcomes the limitations of the contingency analysis for inferences about theme occurrences.

A second point is that practitioners of contingency analysis assume that their thematic categories can be used to capture what words mean at their face value, as it were. In parallel fashion, one might be tempted to map thematic relations according to their surface grammatical relations (e.g. S–V–O). This approach can work if one's texts are highly descriptive. More generally, however, one should take into account that the intended meanings of most natural language expressions are inherently ambiguous.

The information contained in a verb can refer to four formal properties (Carley, 1993: 94 ff): directionality (one- or two-way), strength (defined as intensity, certainty, frequency, and so on), sign (positive, negative) and meaning (the content). Classes of meaning can be generated, for example:

- Similarity: indicates that one theme is identical with or looks like (a part of) another, for example 'The boy resembles his brother'.
- Causal: indicates a cause-effect relation, for example 'Car driving causes pollution'.
- Relation: indicates an association, an ordering, an evaluation, or a realization, for example 'The number of students has increased'.
- Classification: indicates a genus–species relation, for example 'A bike is a vehicle'.

- Structure: indicates a part–whole relation, for example 'The roof is a part of the house'.
- Affective: indicates a judgment of the subject about the object, for example 'Bill has a bad relationship with his boss'.

Machine Coding

Software that automatically codes clauses in text uses a parser, a tool that analyses text according to the rules of a formal grammar. It is a method of understanding the exact meaning of a sentence. It usually emphasizes the importance of grammatical divisions such as subject and predicate. The parser allows coding of simple S–V–O statements. For each of the three parts dictionaries are available, and therefore the texts will be coded instrumentally.

In this way, Gottschalk was able to measure psychological states such as hostility, depression and hope, according to his perspective on states that are reflected in how people relate words (Gottschalk and Bechtel, 1989).

Schrodt (2012), using highly descriptive simple texts (lead sentences in news service articles on international conflict), was able by using his KEDS (now Tabari) software to automatically analyse event data. His data are on the level of the clause. He found that the theme relations follow sufficiently fixed, descriptive formulae and their surface relations are nearly always unambiguous. Note, this unambiguity holds for this research project.

The development of advanced parsers is still going on. A difficulty is that the general framework of semantic analysis is language- and topic-agnostic; the actual computerized text processing is not. The parsing and coding is tailored for a domain-specific research question. Van Atteveldt, Kleinnijenhuis and Ruigrok (2008) contains a good overview of the state of the art with regard to developments in parsing as it is today. Parsers are able now to recognize semantic roles.

Manual Coding

The coder, when applying a generic semantic grammar to relatively unstructured texts, is not supposed to identify surface grammatical relations of themes, but rather to identify each theme's role within the functional form(s) appropriate to its clause of origin. Such identifications can only be made after selecting the appropriate functional form. This requires the coder to look beyond the clause. The coder has to understand both the source's intentions and the social context within which the clause appeared. Coding in a semantic text analysis based on this grammar takes a representative approach to texts. Coding clauses might become very complex. This becomes visible when the distinction between main and subordinate clauses is made. Subordinate clauses are ordinarily those related to a main clause by conjunctions ('because', 'since', 'when'), relative pronouns ('which', 'who', 'that') or proxies. Proxy clauses replace either the subject or the object of a clause.

The TCA software mentioned earlier contains a template for graphical mapping. Here it is possible to define an S–V–O structure and to code the parts separately. A window at the right-upper corner and below the window containing the actual codes shows the coding according to the structure defined when the cursor is moved over the coded text. Depending on the research question the source of the text and the audience might also be mentioned.

Other software that allows the coding of S–V–O tuples is PC-ACE (Franzosi *et al.*, 2013), which allows users to code the data in such a way that they can be entered into a relational database package. The database consists of a set of relations, each of which contains one or more attributes. The coding task to be performed in this software is too complex to have it performed automatically – software for qualitative analysis cannot handle this complexity.

Most programs for qualitative analysis only use hierarchical relations (themes are split into subthemes), but Atlas.ti uses horizontal relations that can be compared to a verb.

Ambiguity

A generic semantic grammar to facilitate coders' disambiguation of illocutionary ambiguities in natural language was developed by Roberts (1989), who distinguished a four-fold semantic grammar that enables the unambiguous encoding of clauses. The four forms are:

- The description of a state of the art
- The description of a process
- The evaluation of a state of the art
- The evaluation of a process

As soon as a clause is translated into one of these forms, coding can be performed in a correct way. When machine coding is applied the possible ambiguity due to the structure of the sentence is not detected. This problem has not yet been solved, although today artificial intelligence and parsers are being used to assist in performing a correct text analysis.

A form of ambiguity that occurs very often is found in sentences that are in passive voice. Passive voice is used when the focus is on the action. It is not important or not known, however, who or what is performing the action. An example is: 'My bike was stolen', which can be rewritten as 'Someone stole my bike'. The sentence must be formulated in active form. Now one must note that the subject of the passive voice becomes the object of the active sentence and that the form of the verb is changed from *to be* + past particle to finite form. The types of ambiguity as mentioned before will continue to exist. A detailed example is found in Roberts (1997).

MODALITY ANALYSIS

Opinion statements appearing in newspaper editorials or in speeches are very interesting because they are about the need or desirability of some action. This need or desirability becomes visible in the use of modal auxiliary verbs. These are verbs that are usually used with the infinitive form of another verb to express possibility, inevitability, impossibility or contingency. In each modal usage there are two verbs associated with the subject, namely a modal auxiliary verb (e.g. want, hope, ought, refuse) and a main verb in infinitive form (an action). These usages are not intended to convey facts or to describe events; they are used to communicate something about the likelihood of the S–V–O relation. A semantic content analysis that investigates such uses of modal auxiliary verbs is called a 'modality analysis' (Roberts *et al.*, 2010). The semantic grammar has the Subject–Modal-auxiliary-verb–Verb–Object (or S–M–V–O) form. This can be presented by using a different terminology: Agency–Position–Action–Object:

Subject	Agency	the initiator of an activity;
Modal-auxiliary verb	Position	the position regarding the agency's activity;
Verb	Action	the activity under consideration;
Object	Object	the target of this activity.

Positions are only taken by intentional agents; the agent cannot be any arbitrary subject. It can only be a person (or institution represented by persons) and not a 'thing'. The position commonly involves the use of a modal auxiliary verb. For example, an editorial that states 'Our politicians ought to cooperate more' would be encoded as politicians (agent) ought (position) to cooperate (action) with politicians (object).

A modal clause is recognizable whenever it conveys intentionality in a way that can be transformed (in a manner agreeable to a native speaker) to a form that includes a modal auxiliary verb. The coder's challenge now is to capture how a text's author understands others' motivations (thereby getting into the mind of someone who is getting into someone else's mind, as it were). Because modal auxiliary verbs convey intentionality, they can be used to learn about people's motivations, their ideas about a future society and thus about their ideological shifts as individuals or groups, e.g. political parties. They can also be used to learn about motivations that exist with respect to certain specific persons or groups.

The semantic grammar used in a modality analysis always has two parts at its core. There is a modal form, indicating possibility, impossibility, inevitability or contingency, and an associated rationale. These modal forms can be used to understand human motives during interactions and to distinguish subtle nuances in discourse. Many examples are presented in Popping and Roberts (2009).

Through modal usage, a text's source (i.e. its author or speaker) socially constructs what constitutes the possible, the impossible, the inevitable and the contingent regarding the agent–action–object relation. Moreover, it is always reasonable for the source of a modal clause to be queried as to the rationale or explanation of 'why' the agent is able, required, permitted, etc. regarding the clause's predicate. For example, a politician might follow his statement 'We had to impose austere economic measures' with the rationale 'otherwise our economy would have stagnated'.

The TCA software has a window that shows the graphical mapping: 'There is a [political, economic, cultural, security] reason why something is [possible, impossible, inevitable, contingent] for a Hungarian.' This mapping is used in Roberts, Popping and Pan (2009: 512). Their study on Hungarian society is based on the premise that social systems are justified via the discursive use of modal statements and their associated rationales. Within authoritarian states such modal discourse usually reflects a relatively coherent 'modality of permission'; however, when the citizens unite to overthrow the totalitarian leaders, their activities are typically justified in terms of a 'modality of achievement' (based on market justice among competitors) versus a 'modality of necessity' (based on

social justice for the masses). These three discursive modalities can be differentiated using content analysis. An analysis of editorials during Hungary's first years of post-Soviet democratization suggests that as late as 1997 Hungarian political discourse was heading toward a modality of necessity, more like the predominant political modality in Western Europe than the achievement modality that characterizes political discourse in the U.S.

NETWORK APPROACH TO CONTENT ANALYSIS

Network content analysis originated with the observation that after one has encoded semantic relations among themes, one can proceed to construct networks of semantically related themes. When a theme represents a person, for example, one can now investigate the position of that person in the network by applying statistical indices for networks. More generally, when themes are depicted as networks, one is afforded more information than the frequency at which specific themes are related in each block of text, and can characterize themes and/or linkages according to their position within the network. A relation between themes might refer to various properties, as was indicated before. By using scores on these properties the information in networks can be represented. This constitutes the representation of the model. The data can be analysed statistically. Attention is first given to machine coding, and then to manual coding.

Machine Coding

A type of study that is currently receiving more and more attention is the one in which detailed sociocultural ethnographies are conducted based on characteristic descriptions from texts and fusing the results from varied sources. Tambayong and Carley (2013) focus on changes in political networks in Sudan. They were interested in themes that were aliases of political agents. By allowing their software, the AutoMap program, to filter out these agents and the relations between them, they were able to construct a network based on these agents and by using network statistics, they could indicate the relevance of each agent, even from different perspectives. This type of study is increasing, especially based on data from Tweets and blogs. The impression is that themes that can be related are sufficient for the investigators who perform these studies. Questions about the research problem and the design of the study as addressed earlier are often ignored. The same holds for the sample or even population that is investigated.

Manual Coding

For many years, two network methods that allow statistical inferences received most attention: network evaluation approaches and cognitive mapping. These methods start from different positions. In both methods the representational approach is followed. The network evaluation approach has its roots in evaluative assertion analysis (Osgood *et al.*, 1956), which starts from the position that every language has three kinds of words:

- Common meaning terms: words that have a common evaluation among 'reasonably sophisticated users of the language'. The common meaning of words such as 'peace' is always positive; whereas that of words like 'enemy' is always negative in connotation.
- Attitude objects: these have no fixed evaluative meaning. A word like 'car' is likely to be evaluated differently by different people.
- Verbal connectors: words that indicate the association ('it is...') or dissociation ('it is not...') of attitude objects with common meaning terms or with other attitude objects.

By investigating how attitude objects are associated or dissociated, one can investigate how

these attitude objects are valued in a text. For this it is necessary to parse texts into clauses, in which the three word-types can be found.

The network evaluation approach has been used in particular to investigate how newspapers report on issues in which governments are involved (Kleinnijenhuis *et al.*, 1997). In order to do so, two specific themes are needed. The user can encode a statement as a positive (is good) or negative (is bad) evaluation of a theme by relating it to the abstract theme 'Ideal'. The statement 'the man is friendly' is reformulated into 'the man has a good relationship with the Ideal (of the statement's source)'. By connecting a theme to the theme 'Real', the user can encode a statement as an affirmation that a theme's referent exists (is) or does not exist (is not). The statement 'unrest is rampant' is changed to 'Reality shows a high level of unrest'.

Cognitive mapping involves extracting relations from texts and then representing the 'mental models' or 'cognitive maps' that individual sources had in their memory at the time the relations were expressed. Within a cognitive map, the meaning of a theme is the aggregate set of relations it has to all other themes that make up a conceptual network. Mental models are dynamic structures that are constructed and expanded as individuals make inferences and gather information. They contain specific information about particular items and also general (or social) knowledge. A transcript of an individual's speech is a reflection of the individual's mental model at a particular point in time. Accordingly, such texts may be thought of as a sampling of information from the individual's memory.

The map comparison method (Carley, 1993) affords not only graphic descriptions of individuals' mental models, but also comparisons among models maintained by various social groups. Carley (1994) showed how the method is used in four different fields that are related to culture and how it differs from thematic content analysis. In one of the studies she portrays the development over time of the theme 'Robot', as used in science fiction.

A new field of research in which mapping is used is presented in Popping and Wittek (2015). They look at negotiations. The position that parties take in negotiations can be represented as a cognitive map of a game theoretic model. The authors explained the voting behaviour in the Dutch parliament over a certain time with respect to motions. They could explain 60 per cent of this behaviour; one third of this amount was due to the positions taken by parliament and government during negotiations.

MANUAL VERSUS MACHINE CODING

Trade-offs between manual and machine coding are often presented in methods literature. A number of attributes are nearly always mentioned: manual coding is slow, and therefore only used for small data sets and it does not use dictionaries; native coders can code complex sentence structures and can interpret all kinds of ambiguous texts; the coding is not replicable and is expensive as coders and trainers have to be paid; machine coding is fast and suited for large data sets; it is possible to modify dictionaries; simple sentence structures are to be coded, containing literal (manifest), present-time text; and as soon as the dictionary has been developed, there are hardly any costs.

The question of what is necessary for the purpose of your study is hardly posed. In other words, sometimes new technological affordances threaten accepted methodological standards.

SOME OTHER REMARKS

A lot of software for quantitative text analysis has been developed by researchers themselves and is usually written in the context of a specific study. This generally implies the software is not for general use, but if others want to use it, this is fine. Documentation is usually poor and the software is as it comes. This implies there has not always been a complete control for imaginable bugs, and errors are not captured. In software for qualitative research, this is generally taken good care of because private companies are responsible for the software. Popping (2015) formulated a number of questions a user should ask before choosing the software that will be used. He also referred to an often suggested disadvantage of manual coding – that code assignments are not reliable. Every researcher has to learn that coders need training, at least part of the data should be coded twice, and intercoder reliability has to be computed. The quality of manually coded data is often higher than that of machine coded data, certainly when complex texts are used.

Texts on which a study will be based are found more and more on the Internet (direct or via organizations like LexisNexis), and eventually as a blog or Tweet. These texts will be downloaded and formatted in such a way that they can be entered into software for text analysis. This all is a question of text mining (Lee *et al.*, 2010).

Prospective users should question whether the software used has a facility to weed out false positives – i.e. it must be possible to do away with texts that are selected (based on the keywords) but do not fulfil the requirements for inclusion in the dataset to be used. An estimation of possible false negatives is also needed – i.e. texts that are not selected but that should have been selected. The data should actually constitute the population of texts that can be used. From this population a representative sample can be drawn.

COMPUTER PROGRAMS

Table 19.1 shows an overview of a number of computer programs that are available today. Most programs to be used when instrumental

Table 19.1 Some computer programs for content analysis and their URL

Type of analysis	Way of coding	Program name	URL
Thematic	Instrumental	Diction	www.dictionsoftware.com
		LIWC	www.liwc.net
		TextQuest	www.textquest.de
		WordStat	provalisresearch.com
		YoshiCoder	sourceforge.net
	Representational	TCA	www.stat.iastate.edu/tca
Semantic	Instrumental	Tabari	eventdata.parusanalytics.com
	Representational	TCA	www.stat.iastate.edu/tca
		PC-ACE	sociology.emory.edu/faculty/rfranzosi/pc-ace
Network	Instrumental		
	Representational	Automap	http://www.casos.cs.cmu.edu/projects/automap

coding applies demand a dictionary. In the table, programs for machine learning are not listed. This overview is not exhaustive.

Well-known programs for qualitative research include Atlas.ti, NVivo, MaxQDA, QDA Miner.

CONCLUSION

Recent developments in the field of quantitative content analysis have been sketched in broad terms. A lot of attention has been given to problems that seem to be overlooked. On the one hand, language is very complex and ambiguous; this should be taken into account. Coder training and explanation of choices is a must, as is the software for managing the coding process. On the other hand, a good research question makes demands. Software can perform analyses on enormous amounts of texts in a very short time. This might be helpful, but it is not the criterion for good research.

REFERENCES

Berelson, B. (1952). *Content Analysis in Communication Research*. New York, NY: Free Press.

Blei, D.M., Ng, A.Y., Jordan, M.I. and Lafferty, J. (2003). 'Latent Dirichlet allocation', *Journal of Machine Learning Research*, 3 (4–5): 993–1022.

Carley, K. (1993). 'Coding choices for textual analysis: a comparison of content analysis and map analysis'. In: P.V. Marsden (ed.), *Sociological Methodology*. Cambridge, MA: Basil Blackwell, pp. 75–126.

Carley, K. (1994). 'Extracting culture through textual analysis', *Poetics*, 22 (4): 291–312.

Franzosi, R., Doyle, S., McClelland, L.E., Putnam Rankin, C. and Vicari, S. (2013). 'Quantitative narrative analysis software options compared: PC-ACE and CAQDAS (ATLAS.ti, MAXqda, and NVivo)', *Quality & Quantity*, 47 (6): 3219–47.

Geminas, K. (2013). 'What to do (and not to do) with the Comparative Manifestos Project data', *Political Studies*, 61 (1): 3–23.

Gottschalk, L.A. and Bechtel, R. (1989). 'Artificial intelligence and the computerization of the content analysis of natural language', *Artificial Intelligence in Medicine*, 1 (1): 131–7.

Grimmer, J. and Stewart, B.M. (2013). 'Text as data: the promise and pitfalls of automatic content analysis methods for political texts', *Political Analysis*, 21 (3): 267–97.

Kleinnijenhuis, J., De Ridder, J.A. and Rietberg, E.M. (1997). 'Reasoning in economic discourse: an application of the network approach to the Dutch press'. In C.W. Roberts (ed.), *Text Analysis for the Social Sciences: Methods for Drawing Statistical Inferences from Texts and Transcripts*. Mahwah, NJ: Lawrence Erlbaum Associates, pp. 191–207.

Laver, M., Benoit, K. and Garry, J. (2003). 'Extracting policy positions from political texts using words as data', *American Political Science Review*, 97 (2): 311–31.

Lee, S., Song, J. and Kim, Y. (2010). 'An empirical comparison of four text mining methods', *Journal of Computer Information Systems*, 51 (1): 1–10.

Leites, N., Bernaut, E. and Garthoff, R.L. (1951). 'Politburo images of Stalin', *World Politics*, 3 (3): 317–39.

Mikhaylov, S., Laver, M. and Benoit. K. (2012). 'Coder reliability and misclassification in the human coding of party manifestos', *Political Analysis*, 20 (1): 78–91.

Miller, M.M. (1997). 'Frame mapping and analysis of news coverage of contentious issues', *Social Science Computer Review*, 15 (4): 367–78.

Namenwirth, J.Z. (1969). 'Marks of distinction: an analysis of British mass and prestige newspaper editorials', *American Journal of Sociology*, 74 (4): 343–60.

Navigli, R. (2009). 'Word sense disambiguation: a survey', ACM *Computing Surveys*, 41 (2): 1–69.

Osgood, C.E., Saporta, S. and Nunnally, J.C. (1956). 'Evaluative assertion analysis', *Litera,* 3: 47–102.

Pennebaker, J.W., Mehl, M.R. and Niederhoffer, K.G. (2003). 'Psychological aspects of natural language use: our words, our selves', *Annual Review of Psychology*, 54: 547–77.

Pennings, P. and Keman, H. (2002). 'Towards a new methodology of estimating party policy positions', *Quality & Quantity*, 36 (1): 55–79.

Popping, R. (2015). 'Analyzing open-ended questions by means of text analysis procedures', *Bulletin de Méthodologie Sociologique*, 128: 23–39.

Popping, R. and Roberts, C.W. (2009). 'Coding issues in semantic text analysis', *Field Methods*, 21 (3): 244–64.

Popping, R. and Wittek, R. (2015). 'Success and failure of parliamentary motions. A social dilemma approach', *PLoS ONE*, 10 (8): e0133510.

Roberts, C.W. (1989). 'Other than counting words: a linguistic approach to content analysis', *Social Forces*, 68 (1): 147–77.

Roberts, C.W. (1997). 'A generic semantic grammar for quantitative text analysis: applications to East and West Berlin radio news content from 1979', *Sociological Methodology*, 27: 89–129.

Roberts, C.W. (2008). *'The' Fifth Modality: On Languages that Shape our Motivations and Cultures*. Leiden, the Netherlands: Brill.

Roberts, C.W., Popping, R. and Pan, Y. (2009). 'Modalities of democratic transformation: forms of public discourse within Hungary's largest newspaper, 1990–1997', *International Sociology*, 24 (4): 498–525.

Roberts, C.W., Zuell, C., Landmann, J. and Wang, Y. (2010). 'Modality analysis: a semantic grammar for imputations of intentionality in texts', *Quality & Quantity,* 44 (2): 239–57.

Schonhardt-Bailey, C. (2005). 'Measuring ideas more effectively: an analysis of Bush and Kerry's national security speeches', *PS: Political Science and Politics*, 38 (4): 701–11.

Schrodt, P.A. (2012). 'Precedents, progress and prospects in political event data', *International Interactions*, 38 (4): 546–69.

Shapiro, G. (1997). 'The future of coders: human judgments in a world of sophisticated software'. In C.W. Roberts (ed.), *Text Analysis for the Social Sciences: Methods for Drawing Statistical Inferences from Texts and Transcripts*. Mahwah, NJ: Lawrence Erlbaum, pp. 225–38.

Stone, P.J., Dunphy, D.C., Smith, M.S. and Ogilvie, D.M. (1966). *The General Inquirer: A Computer Approach to Content Analysis*. Cambridge, MA: MIT Press.

Tambayong, L. and Carley, K.M. (2013). 'Network text analysis in computer-intensive rapid ethnography retrieval: an example from political networks of Sudan', *Journal of Social Structure*, 13 (2): 1–24.

Van Atteveldt, W., Kleinnijenhuis, J. and Ruigrok, N.S. (2008). 'Parsing semantic networks, and political authority using syntactic analysis to extract semantic relations from Dutch newspaper articles', *Political Analysis*, 16 (4): 428–46.

## 20

Sentiment Analysis for Small and Big Data

Mike Thelwall

INTRODUCTION

There are now effective methods to automatically detect sentiment in text and these are capable of human-like levels of performance in some contexts. These programs have been used primarily to analyse online texts, both for research and commercial applications, and are valuable to help gain insights into public opinions about the topics, products and issues discussed online. Automated sentiment analysis naturally has Big Data applications because it allows huge amounts of text to be processed rapidly, enabling sentiment-related insights to be gained about issues that might not otherwise be detectable with small amounts of data.

Opinion mining is concerned with developing software to automatically extract user opinions about products or other entities from text, typically from online sources (Cambria *et al.*, 2013; Feldman, 2013; Liu, 2012; Liu and Zhang, 2012; Pang and Lee, 2008). This is also sometimes called sentiment analysis

but the latter term also encompasses programs that extract sentiments from text for other purposes, such as to estimate the affective state of the text author. The remainder of this chapter uses the latter term. There are several different core tasks for sentiment analysis and they are sometimes carried out by separate systems and sometimes by a single system, with the user selecting the desired type of output. In the following, a text could be an entire document, a sentence or a part of a sentence, with or without embedded metadata.

- *Subjectivity detection*: texts are classified as containing expressions of sentiment (subjective) or not (objective).
- *Polarity detection*: texts are classified as positive or negative overall.
- *Sentiment strength detection*: texts are classified for the overall strength of positive and/or negative sentiment, or for the overall strength of sentiment and its polarity.
- *Emotion detection*: texts are classified for the predominant emotion (e.g. unhappy, angry), perhaps in addition to its strength, or the degree to

which a fixed number of different emotions are evident.

- *Aspect-based sentiment analysis*: texts are dissected to identify the aspects of a product that are discussed and the sentiments expressed about these aspects.

Another variant is concept-based sentiment analysis (e.g. Poria *et al.*, 2014), which is similar to aspect-based sentiment analysis except that there is an explicit focus on using semantic resources to identify sentiment about concepts rather than about individual nouns, although the end result may be similar if similar nouns are clustered rather than analysed semantically.

Applications of sentiment analysis vary from direct, such as detecting whether sentiments towards unhealthy food vary by geographic area (Widener and Li, 2014), to indirect applications that enhance software designed for other tasks. For example, it seems reasonable to believe that a sentiment analysis capability would enhance the ability for autonomous agents and robots to interact effectively with humans (Mavridis, 2015), and sentiment analysis has already been embedded into web crawlers (Vural *et al.*, 2014) and automatic chat systems (Skowron *et al.*, 2011), but the most widespread application is to aid social media monitoring by companies and large organisations.

Sentiment analysis algorithms are typically evaluated by comparing their outputs (e.g. a decision about whether a text is positive, negative or neutral) with the judgements of human coders for the same set of at least 1,000 texts. These judgements must be made by people following precise and consistent instructions (e.g. Wiebe *et al.*, 2005) or in some cases the texts may have opinions registered by their authors, such as for reviews that are accompanied by an overall score (Turney, 2002). Depending on the precise outputs of the sentiment analysis system (e.g. sentiment polarities or strengths) a system's score might be the percentage of texts given the same ratings as those of the human

coders or a metric for the correlation between the human and computer scores. If more than one sentiment analysis method is compared, then the one with the highest score compared with the human coders would be assumed to be the best. The assumption here is that the human judges' scores are essentially correct and hence can form the gold standard against which all algorithms should be compared.

This chapter reviews the main different sentiment analysis methods, including both lexical and machine learning approaches, as well as the main tasks, such as polarity detection, sentiment strength detection and fine-grained emotion detection. It also covers important related tasks, such as the need to customise software designed for one type of text before it can be applied efficiently to another and to detect the target of any sentiment expression. The chapter also reviews sentiment analyses research applications involving either Big Data or small scale samples of online texts, showing the range of current applications as well as the potential to deploy the methods to investigate a wide range of issues. Most of this research focuses on the social sciences, and on issues for which public opinion data is relevant. Some of the research also analyses the affective component of online communication within the social web in contexts such as political debates and communication between friends, when sentiment forms an important component of the interactions.

LEXICAL APPROACHES

Lexical sentiment analysis algorithms centre on a pre-defined lexical resource, such as a list or network of sentiment words. Whereas some methods exploit this resource through simple matching in text, other algorithms exploit a range of natural language processing techniques in an attempt to leverage more information from the text.

Simple Lexical Methods

A simple lexical sentiment analysis method might start with a list of positive and negative words and then either count how often they occur in a given text or apply a formula, such as a weighted sum, in order to categorise the text as positive, negative or neutral. Most algorithms go further than this, however, and include additional processing steps, such as to detect negation or to recognise emoticons. Unlike other strategies, lexical methods tend to be flexible and do not need a set of human-coded training texts for each topic area in order to work but need a human-coded lexicon instead (e.g. Tong, 2001). Such human-coded lexicons are readily available for some languages, such as ANEW for English (Nielsen, 2011).

SentiStrength (http://sentistrength.wlv.ac.uk) is a lexical sentiment strength detection program (Thelwall *et al.*, 2010). It has a manually curated list of 2,489 sentiment words and word stems. These derive from a combination of the psychology text analysis program LIWC (Tausczik and Pennebaker, 2010), the General Inquirer lexicon (Stone *et al.*, 1962) and manually identified additional terms, including neologisms and slang. The core action of SentiStrength is to process a sentence to identify all terms that are in its sentiment lexicon, looking up their polarity and strength. Each sentence is then assigned the strengths of its most positive and most negative term. For example, the text 'tired but good day' would score 3 out of 5 for positivity because good is in the lexicon with score 3 (1 indicates no positivity and 5 indicates very strong positivity). It would also score −2 on a scale of −1 (no negativity) to −5 (very strong negativity) for negative sentiment, so the system output would be (−2, 3). A sentence without any recognised sentiment terms would be assigned (−1, 1), indicating no positive sentiment and no negative sentiment. This method fails when typical term sentiments are modified by surrounding words and so there are additional rules for dealing with negation, questions and booster words (e.g. very). There are also rules for other ways of expressing sentiment, such as idioms, emoticons, emphatic spelling (e.g. Maaaaarieeee) and punctuation (e.g. hello!!!).

Despite the use of simple non-linguistic methods, SentiStrength has human-like accuracy on the short informal texts found in a wide range of different types of social web sites, including Twitter (Thelwall *et al.*, 2011). In other words, for some types of social web texts, its sentiment scores agree with human coder scores about as much as the human coder scores agree with each other. SentiStrength's simple approach also allows it to be fast (14,000 Tweets per second) and flexible – its lexicon can be manually customised and there are versions in many different languages.

Sentiment analysis algorithms can also exploit linguistic information by identifying the relationships between different segments of text within a sentence. For example, the word *but* in the middle of a sentence suggests that one of the two halves of the sentence is positive and the other is negative. If an algorithm can identify the polarity of one of the two segments with some certainty then it can infer that the other one has the opposite polarity, and with enough examples can also deduce new sentiment-bearing terms for a lexicon in this way (Zhang and Singh, 2014).

Natural Language Processing

Linguistic methods extend the basic lexical approach by incorporating linguistic knowledge and resources. For example, instead of using a list of affective terms, resources such as WordNetAffect (Strapparava and Valitutti, 2004) or SentiWordNet (Esuli and Sebastiani, 2006) allow terms in text to be matched to their root word form (e.g. *go, going, went* all map to the verb *go*) and reveal semantic relationships between words (e.g. *better* is weaker than *best*). This extra information can be harnessed to make a more powerful algorithm, but may make the resulting algorithm less flexible and substantially slower.

Adjectives can be given special treatment in sentiment analysis if they can be identified through linguistic methods. This is useful because they express sentiment more frequently than other types of word. This can be achieved with the natural language processing technique of Part Of Speech (POS) tagging. For this, a POS tagger application uses a set of learned heuristics to tag each word in a text with its part of speech. For example, this might convert 'beautiful shoes' to 'beautiful_JJ shoes_NNS' where JJ is the POS tag for adjective and NNS is for plural nouns. An algorithm could use this information to extract all adjectives or, if context is needed for the adjectives, specific POS patterns involving adjectives, such as all consecutive words where the first is an adjective and the second is a type of noun.

SO-CAL is a linguistic lexical algorithm for sentiment strength detection in English and Spanish (Taboada *et al.*, 2011; Taboada and Grieve, 2004). It uses dictionaries of adjectives, lemmatised (i.e. converted to a standard form) nouns, adverbs and lemmatised verbs compiled from a variety of sources, each with a human-assigned single sentiment polarity and strength integer score between −5 and +5. Some multi-word expressions are also included. SO-CAL includes rules for dealing with negation, intensifiers (e.g. extremely) and irrealis (connoting that a proposition is nonactual or nonfactual, e.g. would). SO-CAL classifies a document with the average of the sentiment expressions of its component parts, in conjunction with its additional rules mentioned earlier.

Automatic Word and Phrase Sentiment Association

Although some lexical methods exploit human constructed sentiment resources, knowledge-poor methods instead detect the sentiment associations of words and phrases automatically. This has the advantage that it can adapt to cope with domain-specific terms that are common in a set of texts from one source but are otherwise too rare to be incorporated into a general sentiment analysis program. It can also work for phrases rather than individual words. For example, a program processing a set of TV reviews might identify that the phrase 'large screen' occurred frequently and seemed to express sentiment, triggering a method to detect whether it is usually positive or negative.

Pointwise Mutual Information (PMI) is a commonly used metric for assessing whether a term or set of terms is likely to have a positive or negative connotation (Turney, 2002). It is useful when they have been automatically extracted by a heuristic that does not include polarity information. For example, a simple rule might extract all instances of adjectives followed by nouns, hoping that many will indicate sentiment (e.g. large screen, beautiful colour). The PMI formula used to assess polarity is

$$PMI(s,t) = P(s \land t)/P(s)P(t)$$

where $P(s)$ and $P(t)$ are the probabilities of s and t occurring in a text in a given corpus, respectively, and $P(s \land t)$ is the probability that they both occur in the same text. If s and t occur independently of each other, then $P(s \land t) = P(s)P(t)$ but if they tend to co-occur then $P(s \land t) > P(s)P(t)$ and so $PMI(s,t) > 1$. This can be useful to estimate the polarity of a new term or set of terms if s has a known polarity. For example, if PMI('good', 'large screen') >1 then this suggests that 'large screen' tends to occur in the texts that contain 'good' and is perhaps more likely to be positive. More generally when comparing PMI('good','large screen') with PMI('bad','large screen'), if one is much larger than the other then 'large screen' is likely to be a reliable indicator of polarity. Although this is a simple example, PMI is simple, fast and flexible, with many uses in sentiment analysis.

The Turney (2002) algorithm exploits PMI by first processing a set of reviews to extract all phrases that obey any of a set of linguistic patterns (e.g. adjective followed by noun). For each phrase, PMI values are calculated for both 'poor' and 'excellent', using a commercial search engine query to estimate the number of web pages matching the appropriate query. This effectively uses the web itself as a corpus and the estimated polarity of the phrase is generated by a formula based on the two PMI values. The estimated polarity of a document is the average of the polarities of all of the detected phrases.

A weakness of the Turney algorithm is that the use of the web as a corpus can cause problems with context-dependant words and phrases, such as *scary*, which is positive for horror movies.

MACHINE LEARNING

Sentiment detection can be treated as a text classification problem and tackled with generic machine learning methods. This works by converting each text into numerical vectors of features, which typically record the frequency of a list of words and short phrases (with or without linguistic classifications) in each document within a corpus. About 1,000 of these documents must have been pre-classified by human coders (i.e. the training set) and then the machine learning stage produces an algorithm that has learned how to predict the sentiment of the classified texts. There are many techniques that can be used for the machine learning stage, such as naïve Bayes, support vector machines and decision tree learning, many of which produce different types of prediction algorithms (e.g. a mathematical formula or a set of rules). The trained algorithm is then a sentiment analysis classifier that can be applied to unclassified texts to predict their sentiment (Pang *et al.*, 2002). Machine learning seems to work well for texts that are focused around a specific topic (e.g. movie reviews) but classifiers trained for one topic can perform poorly on others (Aue and Gamon, 2005).

A key stage in machine learning is the conversion of texts into feature vectors, which are sets of relevant terms or properties. Without an appropriate choice of features, no machine learning algorithm will work well. These features need to capture the essence of the way in which sentiment is expressed in a text whilst ignoring all extraneous information. This latter part is important because unnecessary information can confuse the machine learning training stage and substantially weaken the final algorithm. Most systems extract either individual words for features or all phrases with 1–3 words in conjunction with a frequency threshold to exclude rare ones. The basic approach of making a simple frequency vector for the words or phrases can be improved by giving higher weightings to those that are relatively rare in the corpus and by taking into account the length of each document (Paltoglou and Thelwall, 2010).

For social science applications, an important limitation of machine learning is that it can introduce systematic sources of bias. For example, if specific issues within a news corpus tend to attract strong negative views (e.g. Israel–Palestine conflicts), then phrases associated with the issue can be picked as effective indicators of negativity. The result would be a trained algorithm that tended to classify texts about controversial issues as negative, rather than detecting negative sentiment about them (Thelwall *et al.*, 2012).

SARCASM DETECTION

The accuracy of sentiment analysis algorithms can be reduced by the presence of significant amounts of sarcasm (Thelwall *et al*, 2012). This is because sarcastic texts often contain an expression of sentiment that is intended to be interpreted with the opposite polarity (e.g. 'I am extremely happy to be injured'), and also because sarcasm is associated with negative reviews (Filatova, 2012). In theory, the impact of sarcasm could be reduced if it is detected in text, but detection is difficult and dependent on both the topic and the language of a text (e.g. Burgers *et al.*, 2012). For example, political sarcasm in Portuguese is often accompanied by the diminutive form of the name of a politician (Carvalho *et al.*, 2009), but this linguistic style seems to occur in few other languages.

Successful sarcasm detection relies upon the sarcasm containing standard phrases or phrase patterns that are common in sarcastic texts but rare otherwise (e.g. Justo *et al.*, 2014). Such phrases are topic-dependent, which makes the construction of a general purpose sarcasm detector difficult. For example, a common type of book review sarcasm is praise for the cover rather than the content of a volume (Davidov *et al.*, 2010). However, a promising new approach has successfully detected explicit sarcasm in the sense of Tweets containing the #sarcasm hashtag. It exploits linguistic styles associated with figurative language, such as the use of rare words or unusual synonyms (Barbieri *et al.*, 2014).

LANGUAGE ISSUES

Most of the studies reviewed in this chapter have analysed English texts. Whilst the principles are similar for most languages, it is not straightforward to start with a method that has been shown to work in one language and apply it to a different language. The first problem is that there are many more resources for English, such as lists of sentiment terms and part of speech taggers, than for any other language and some languages have very few language resources of any type. In addition, the way in which sentiment is expressed varies substantially between languages. In Chinese the phrase *not good* is equivalent to *bad* in English but in English the negating term weakens the sentiment as well as inverting it, but not in Chinese.

Perhaps the most fundamental difference between languages is that sentences in some languages, such as Chinese, do not have markers between words. There are two main solutions to this issue: either apply a word segmenting algorithm to artificially add spaces between inferred words (Huang *et al.*, 2014) or use an n-gram method that looks for patterns of characters, irrespective of whether they are part of the same word or not (Zagibalov & Carroll, 2008). A more minor problem is that some languages glue words together to change their meaning. For example, a Turkish word can be negated by adding a negating ending to it and so a sentiment analysis algorithm may need to first separate such words and then process the sentiment negating parts of them separately (Vural *et al.*, 2013).

ADDITIONAL SENTIMENT ANALYSIS TASKS

Domain Transfer

Although some sentiment analysis programs are general purpose, most are designed for one type of product review. The domain transfer problem is the task of efficiently generating a sentiment analysis system for a new domain, such as reviews of a new product by re-using existing systems rather than building a completely new system (Blitzer *et al.*, 2006; Melville *et al.*, 2009). Here the term 'domain' is used to refer to the theme of the documents analysed. The most time-consuming part of making a new system is often the generation of a large and reliable corpus of human-coded texts for the new domain. Existing systems are likely not to perform optimally on a new domain because different features will be discussed and different ways of expressing sentiment may be used. As a result, they need to be adapted for the new (target) domain. When developing a system for a new domain, it can be important to choose the most similar domain with a classified system to start from because a classifier built from a highly dissimilar domain will not work well on the new domain (Ponomareva and Thelwall, 2012). Domain transfer approaches include training only on classified texts from the source domain that are reasonably similar to texts in the target domain, including a small amount of classified texts from the target domain in the training set, attempting to identify features (e.g. words) in the source domain that correspond to features in the target domain, and generating an ensemble of classifiers that are each trained on a different domain and combining their results (Aue and Gamon, 2005; Blitzer *et al.*, 2006).

An alternative strategy is to train a system on multiple different domains, but detect if each feature is domain-independent (Ida *et al.*, 2013). Presumably, general terms like *good* would be detected as domain-independent and more specific terms like *heavy* would be classified as domain-dependent. This approach enables a system to take advantage of additional data from other domains when training for each specific domain.

Although these strategies are all designed to deal with creating a system for a new specific domain based upon existing systems for different specific domains, a variant of the problem is to tailor a generic sentiment analysis system to be more effective on a specific domain. The general program SentiStrength can exploit a corpus of human coded texts for a specific topic to learn improved domain-specific sentiment polarities and strengths for words in its existing sentiment term lexicon. It can also learn new words to add to its lexicon by recognising those that often occur in texts that would otherwise be misclassified (Thelwall and Buckley, 2013).

Aspect-based Sentiment Analysis

Aspect-based (or feature-based) sentiment analysis is concerned with tying expressions of sentiment to specific aspects of an entity (typically a product) that are being discussed, even if multiple aspects are discussed within a single sentence. For example, if a comment reports 'The décor was lovely but the portions were too small' then it would be useful to pair décor with lovely and portions with too small. Here, both décor and portions are aspects of the restaurant entity that is being reviewed. An aspect-based sentiment analysis application might process a collection of reviews and then report the number of positive and negative comments about a list of aspects of the reviewed entity (Liu *et al.*, 2005). This challenging task typically includes automatically deciding which aspects are mentioned in a review and the sentiment orientation of the mention of the aspect, as well as resolving indirect references and synonyms so that different ways of mentioning the same aspect can be grouped together. As an example of an indirect reference, a review might state that a phone went for a long time before needing charging, and this could be recorded as a positive comment about the battery life aspect. Aspect-based sentiment analysis software typically involves natural language processing of the text in conjunction with pattern learning heuristics and linguistic resources in order to solve these problems. For example, association rule learning may be used to identify common connections between aspects and describing terms (Liu *et al*, 2005; Liu & Zhang, 2012).

Aspect-based sentiment analysis is most relevant for product reviews, where dense combinations of aspects and sentiments can be expected. It is less useful for microblogs, where there may not be enough space to discuss multiple aspects of a product.

Customisation for Specific Tasks

Although the texts in some sentiment analysis tasks are clearly self-contained units, such as product or movie reviews, in other cases, the texts may form a natural part of a set. In the latter case, information about the sentiment in other parts of the set may help to generate a better classification of each individual text. For example, in a dialog, it would be strange to see a sudden and isolated expression of positive or negative sentiment in an otherwise calm discussion. In response, some systems have attempted to use information about the classifications of sentiment in texts adjacent to the one being classified. The simplest approach is damping: reducing large deviations in sentiment strength on the basis that they are more likely to have been caused by classification errors than by a sudden sentiment change. This has been shown to work to some extent but the effectiveness of damping rules depends on the relationship between the posts (e.g. dialogs, monologs, multi-user interactions) and the nature of the damping to an extent that it is prohibitively time-consuming to implement in practice (Thelwall et al., 2013).

A similar logical enhancement to sentiment analysis is to analyse all the comments made by a particular reviewer in order to help classify their reviews, and this is effective in many contexts in which the evidence is available (Basiri et al., 2014).

Emotion Detection

Although most systems attempt to detect positive and negative sentiment, some go further by attempting to detect expressions of different types of emotion (Canales and Martínez-Barco, 2014). This is more difficult than polarity detection because it is harder to infer a fine-grained emotion unless it is explicitly described in a text. One study, for example, compared lexical and machine learning approaches for detecting the strength of anger, disgust, fear, joy, sadness and surprise (Strapparava and Mihalcea, 2008). The results suggested that the best method varies by overall objective but a linguistic lexical approach with both WordNet Affect and SentiWordNet

performed well. A more detailed method can detect not just the emotion expressed but also the person that is apparently experiencing the emotion (Mohammad et al., 2014).

APPLICATIONS

Mining Product Reviews for Customer Opinion Information

Automatically extracting customer opinions is the main commercial application of sentiment analysis. An example of a simple but apparently useful system for product reviews is Opinion Observer, which automatically produces graphs of the main features in a set of products reviewed and the number of positive and negative comments about each feature. The potential purchaser of the products can quickly compare the graphs for the products that they are interested in and gain insights into what others believe to be their good and bad points (Liu et al., 2005). This is similar to the Microsoft Pulse system that reads a collection of product reviews and creates an interactive tree map visualisation illustrating the main product-related clusters of terms, each within a rectangle proportional in size to the volume of related comments and colour-coded for sentiment. A large green rectangle containing the word 'drive' in a car tree map, for example, would indicate that many reviews discussed drive-related aspects of the car and they were typically negative about it. Clicking on the rectangle in the system would reveal individual drive-related reviews (Gamon et al., 2005). An alternative (Google) approach is to cluster aspects of the reviews and to list the reviews in clusters (e.g. food, service, value), giving overall sentiment scores for the clusters as well as a polarity estimate for each individual review aspect (Blair-Goldensohn et al., 2008).

Although there seems to be little concrete evidence of the value of consumer opinion information to organisations, it seems likely that it has wide value to large companies and for companies with products and services that people Tweet about. For example, one case study of the airline industry has shown that useful information can be extracted from social web sentiment analyses (Misopoulos et al., 2014).

These 'products' can include services or anything else that people review or critically analyse online, such as healthcare problems in patient forums (Greaves et al., 2013). Products can also be analysed by third parties with a vested interest, such as health workers analysing online discussions of tobacco-related projects with an agenda to reduce their use (Myslín et al., 2013).

Other Commercial Intelligence Applications

In principle, the applications described earlier for product reviews could also be applied to any type of text containing evaluations, perhaps even if evaluation is not the primary purpose of the set of texts. One such application processes text within an organisation's internal social network in order to identify the themes discussed and their sentiments, as a management information tool (Subramanian et al., 2013).

Organisations may also wish to track the flow of opinions over time for individual users or groups of users and there are some applications that can do this. OpinionFinder uses complex visualisations to illustrate changes in topics, sentiments and volume of discussions over time in order to give an understanding of how an opinion developed or changed (Wu et al., 2012). This could help organisations to assess how a bad opinion about them emerged in the social web.

A Big Data style sentiment analysis application is to predict changes in prices or values of commodities, currencies or shares based upon relevant changes in sentiment extracted from the news or the social web. The belief

behind this is that automatic methods may pick up small changes in market sentiment, perhaps even when they are not evident to experts. Thus, embedding sentiment analysis capabilities within online trading systems might improve their performance. There have been several attempts to build such systems, with some apparent success (Bollen et al., 2011; Nassirtoussi et al., 2015), but these are difficult to convincingly evaluate because a practical system would incorporate sentiment as a single component within a large range of indicators (e.g. Nassirtoussi et al., 2014). The value of sentiment as an indicator is also likely to vary by market segment.

News and Blogs

News is a natural discussion topic for the social web and there have been several attempts to design sentiment analysis software for online news sites and blogs. One program detected the people that were discussed most positively and negatively in news stories and blog posts, finding substantial differences between the two (Godbole et al., 2007).

Politics

Politics is a natural online discussion topic and this has been recognised by news media by monitoring sentiment in social media during elections (Wang et al., 2012) or during key events, such as televised leaders' debates (e.g. Diakopoulos and Shamma, 2010). There are also some sentiment analysis programs designed specifically for political discussions (Van Atteveldt et al., 2008; Young and Soroka, 2012) or with political adaptations (Vilares Calvo et al., 2015). Several studies have attempted to assess political opinions or predict election outcomes using sentiment analysis in social media (Chung and Mustafaraj, 2011; O'Connor et al., 2010; Tumasjan et al., 2010), but this is difficult because the proportion of those online varies by political affiliation, including due to factors such as age and education level. In addition, more outspoken people are likely to be overrepresented online, and these may tend to associate with particular parties, such as those that are new or particularly radical. As a result, any serious attempt to predict election outcomes from Twitter would need to correct for a range of biases in order to be credible (Metaxas *et al.*, 2011). This is in addition to the problem of sarcasm, which makes texts that are part of political discussions particularly difficult to classify for sentiment (Bakliwal *et al.*, 2013; Thelwall *et al.*, 2012). Moreover, one study has shown that sentiment in Twitter can have little relationship with sentiment in the print news (Murthy and Petto, 2015), which casts further doubt on the value of Twitter as a reflector of public opinion. Nevertheless, the sentiment of political Tweets can give insights into the role of Twitter within political discussions (Vilares Calvo *et al.,* 2015).

A potential application of sentiment analysis would be to automatically discover the political affiliations of social media users, but this is difficult (Malouf and Mullen, 2008) and can be done by analysing the topics that they discuss without the need to harness sentiment as well (Conover *et al.*, 2011).

An interesting type of analysis for media is a minute-by-minute sentiment analysis of important political events, such as televised debates. Analysing sentiment in Twitter during the debates, for example, can point to topics within the debate that provoked the strongest reactions and the strongest positive or negative responses. Tying these results to the times when the different leaders were talking can also give insights into their performances (Diakopoulos and Shamma, 2010).

Big Data Social Web Investigations

Classic Big Data sentiment analysis applications process large volumes of text in order to identify sentiment-related patterns, even if too slight to be evident in lower volumes of data. One study analysed four million texts from blogs, Digg.com and online BBC discussion forums, looking for evidence that sentiments expressed by participants could be contagious in the sense of triggering similar sentiments from others. Partial evidence was found for this by analysing chains of consecutive texts with similar sentiments and showing mathematically that these chains were longer than if sentiment was expressed randomly (Chmiel *et al.*, 2011). This empirical evidence supports the common sense understanding that sentiments expressed in communication affect the tone of subsequent contributions. One reason why sentiment may spread in the social web is the influence of a small number of popular individuals (Bae and Lee, 2012; Zhao *et al.*, 2014).

There have been many attempts to harness sentiment in social media in order to predict changes in stock market or commodity prices on the basis that automatic methods might pick up slight changes in sentiment about a company or product before many human experts detect it. Some of these approaches appear to have had success but it seems that an effective system would incorporate sentiment as one component within a system that is reading multiple signals (Kazemian *et al.*, 2014).

Other studies have focused on the expressive style of individuals in the social web rather than on communication segments (i.e. consecutive texts) and have found that people tend to use similar levels of positivity and negativity in their social network comments to that of their friends (Bollen *et al.*, 2011; Thelwall, 2010). It is not clear whether this reflects happy people befriending each other and unhappy people befriending, happiness and sadness spreading between friends, or just friends having similar expressive styles within the social web (e.g. routinely sending cheerful messages or discussing a common interest in gothic rock).

On a huge scale, one study has used Tweets gathered from across the globe to analyse cultural and other factors that affect the relationship between sentiments expressed in Tweets and the time of day. They found, for example, that people seem to wake later at weekends and seem to express more happiness than during the week (Golder and Macy, 2011). An analysis of Facebook posts, in contrast, demonstrated a link between sentiments expressed and rainfall (Coviello *et al.*, 2014). Whilst these results are unsurprising, they show that is it now possible to conduct international studies of sentiment with millions of participants – without the need for extensive funding if the free Twitter API is used.

TOOLS FOR SENTIMENT ANALYSIS

There are a number of options available for those wishing to apply sentiment analysis to their data. Most business users probably access sentiment analysis as a component within an online social media gathering and analytics service, such as Pulsar (pulsarplatform.com) or Topsy (topsy.com). These are not ideal for research because the algorithms used are typically not described by the service provider and hence operate as black box solutions, although some companies give broad information (www.lexalytics.com/technical-info/sentiment-analysis, accessed 13 July 2016). Some algorithms are also built into commercial analytics software, such as SPSS Text Analytics for Surveys and SAS Sentiment Analysis. To evaluate one of these systems, it would be useful to find out as much information as possible about how the system works and how it has been tested. A good system would presumably be kept up to date and backed by academic research, but in any case it is worth testing with at least 100 relevant texts (irrelevant texts could give misleading results) in order to discover how often the system gives reasonable answers.

Researchers wishing to know more about the sentiment analysis algorithm used, or even to create their own or modify an existing algorithm, have a number of options

available. Some of the published sentiment analysis programs are available from their authors (online or via email) without charge for research, including SentiStrength (sentistrength.wlv.ac.uk: Windows and Java versions). Few seem to be open source, however, although they have an associated published article describing how they work.

Some resources are also available free online to help with building or testing sentiment analysis systems, such as the sentiment lexicons and human coded corpora of Maite Taboada (https://www.sfu.ca/~mtaboada/research/SFU_Review_Corpus.html, accessed 13 July 2016) and Bing Liu (http://www.cs.uic.edu/~liub/FBS/sentiment-analysis.html, accessed 13 July 2016) and the linguistic resources of SentiWordNet (sentiwordnet.isti.cnr.it) and SenticNet (Cambria *et al.*, 2014). It is also possible to create sentiment analysis programs using machine learning methods with general purpose machine learning environments, such as Weka, and natural language processing toolkits, such as GATE (gate.ac.uk/sentiment). Natural language processing toolkits are available for Python (nltk.org), Java (nlp.stanford.edu/software), C++ (nlp.lsi.upc.edu/freeling), R (e.g. with the qdap package) and other languages.

Finally, it would also be reasonable to use content analysis software, such as NVivo, to help with human coding of sentiment in text, if an automatic method was not possible or desirable. Also worth a mention is QDA Miner by Provalis. It includes sentiment analysis and ships with several dictionaries that can be modified to suit the research purpose. These programs would be appropriate if there were relatively few texts to analyse or if the texts were difficult to automatically analyse due to the topic or the presence of sarcasm or figurative language.

SUMMARY

Sentiment analysis, the automatic detection affective content in text, is a mature research area with a range of tools that can detect sentiment in different ways and for different purposes. Whilst lexical approaches tend to be generic in the sense of being designed to work across different topics and types of text, machine learning tends to need recalibrating on each different topic or text type, although they may perform better as a result. Depending on the system, the output may be an overall polarity judgement for each text, an indication of the strength of positivity and/or negativity, an indication of the strengths of various kinds of emotions, or a collection of information about the aspects discussed and their sentiments. Existing software often performs with a level of accuracy that is similar to that of humans classifying discrete texts, but is much faster and cheaper for large volumes of text.

The availability of effective sentiment analysis software has given rise to many commercial and research applications. In the commercial domain, it is now routine for companies to monitor the sentiment of important product and brand names in social media, perhaps as part of their wider social media monitoring activities. This is made possible by web intelligence companies that provide an easy web interface to access the data and data processing techniques. Nevertheless, there may be sinister overtones to some applications of sentiment analysis. It is now relatively easy for commercial and political organisations to monitor the sentiments of relevant groups of people that post text online and this may give the monitoring organisations the enhanced ability to get their message across – they may even attempt to manipulate groups more directly (Andrejevic, 2011). Moreover, this is also problematic if people are being directly or indirectly manipulated through information gained by sentiment analysis applied without their knowledge to text that they may have believed was private, and which was in any case written for another purpose (Kennedy, 2012).

Researchers have also found ways to combine social web data collection with sentiment analysis to gain insights into public opinions or reactions to news, health and financial market issues, either developing and assessing software for this or generating new understandings for the research. Despite the studies reviewed, it seems that there is still enormous potential to widen this basic approach to investigate issues of public concern that have not yet been investigated. For those opening up new research areas in this way, there are some important lessons from the research reviewed here to bear in mind. First, sentiment analysis software estimates sentiment but makes mistakes, even if it achieves human-level accuracy overall. It is likely to be particularly inaccurate for sets of texts where sarcasm is prevalent, probably including most online political discussions. Second, its performance varies by topic and text type, and so results should not be taken at face value and, where possible, evaluated and customised. Third, there may be systematic sources of bias in the results, especially if machine learning algorithms are used, and these should be checked whenever any trends are observed.

REFERENCES

Andrejevic, M. (2011). 'The work that affective economics does', *Cultural Studies*, 25(4–5), 604–20.

Aue, A. and Gamon, M. (2005). 'Customizing sentiment classifiers to new domains: a case study'. In Proceedings of Recent Advances in Natural Language Processing (RANLP2005). http://research.microsoft.com/pubs/65430/new_domain_sentiment.pdf (accessed 13 July, 2016).

Bae, Y. and Lee, H. (2012). 'Sentiment analysis of Twitter audiences: measuring the positive or negative influence of popular Twitterers'. *Journal of the American Society for Information Science and Technology*, 63(12), 2521–35.

Bakliwal, A., Foster, J., van der Puil, J., O'Brien, R., Tounsi, L. and Hughes, M. (2013). 'Sentiment analysis of political tweets: towards an accurate classifier'. In Proceedings of the Workshop on Language in Social Media (LASM 2013), Atlanta, GA, June 13. Stroudsburg, PA: Association for Computational Linguistics. pp. 49–58.

Barbieri, F., Saggion, H. and Ronzano, F. (2014). 'Modelling sarcasm in Twitter, a novel approach'. 5th Workshop on Computational Approaches to Subjectivity, Sentiment and Social Media Analysis (WASSA 2014), Baltimore, MA: ACL, pp. 50–8.

Basiri, M. E., Ghasem-Aghaee, N. and Naghsh-Nilchi, A. R. (2014). 'Exploiting reviewers comment histories for sentiment analysis'. *Journal of Information Science*, 40(3), 313–28.

Blair-Goldensohn, S., Hannan, K., McDonald, R., Neylon, T., Reis, G. A. and Reynar, J. (2008). 'Building a sentiment summarizer for local service reviews'. In WWW Workshop on NLP in the Information Explosion Era. Vol. 14. https://static.googleusercontent.com/media/research.google.com/en//pubs/archive/34368.pdf (accessed 13 July, 2016).

Blitzer, J., McDonald, R. and Pereira, F. (2006). 'Domain adaptation with structural correspondence learning'. In Proceedings of the 2006 Conference on Empirical Methods in Natural Language Processing. Stroudsburg, PA: Association for Computational Linguistics, pp. 120–8.

Bollen, J., Gonçalves, B., Ruan, G. and Mao, H. (2011). 'Happiness is assortative in online social networks'. *Artificial Life*, 17(3), 237–51.

Bollen, J., Mao, H. and Zeng, X. (2011). Twitter mood predicts the stock market. *Journal of Computational Science*, 2(1), 1–8.

Burgers, C., Van Mulken, M. and Schellens, P. J. (2012). 'Verbal irony differences in usage across written genres'. *Journal of Language and Social Psychology*, 31(3), 290–310.

Cambria, E., Olsher, D. and Rajagopal, D. (2014). 'SenticNet 3: a common and common-sense knowledge base for cognition-driven sentiment analysis'. In Twenty-eighth AAAI Conference on Artificial Intelligence, July 27–31, Québec, Canada. http://sentic.net/senticnet-3.pdf (accessed 13 July, 2016).

Cambria, E., Schuller, B., Xia, Y. and Havasi, C. (2013). 'New avenues in opinion mining and sentiment analysis'. *IEEE Intelligent Systems*, 28(2), 15–21.

Canales, L. and Martínez-Barco, P. (2014). 'Emotion detection from text: a survey'. In Proceedings of the Workshop on Natural Language Processing in the 5th Information Systems Research Working Days (JISIC 2014), pp. 1–8.

Carvalho, P., Sarmento, L., Silva, M. J. and De Oliveira, E. (2009). 'Clues for detecting irony in user-generated contents: oh...!! It's so easy;-)'. In Proceedings of the 1st international CIKM Workshop on Topic-Sentiment Analysis for Mass Opinion. New York, NY: ACM Press. pp. 53–6.

Chmiel, A., Sienkiewicz, J., Thelwall, M., Paltoglou, G., Buckley, K., Kappas, A. and Hołyst, J.A. (2011). 'Collective emotions online and their influence on community life'. *PLoS ONE*, 6(7): e22207.

Chung, J.E. and Mustafaraj, E. (2011). 'Can collective sentiment expressed on Twitter predict political elections?' In W. Burgard and D. Roth (eds.), Proceedings of the Twenty-Fifth AAAI Conference on Artificial Intelligence, August 7–11. Menlo Park, CA: AAAI Press, pp. 1770–1.

Conover, M. D., Gonçalves, B., Ratkiewicz, J., Flammini, A. and Menczer, F. (2011). 'Predicting the political alignment of Twitter users'. In Privacy, Security, Risk and Trust (PASSAT) and 2011 IEEE Third International Conference on Social Computing (SocialCom). Los Alamitos, CA: IEEE Press, pp. 192–9.

Coviello, L., Sohn, Y., Kramer, A.D.I., Marlow, C., Franceschetti, M., Christakis, N.A. and Fowler, J.H. (2014). 'Detecting emotional contagion in massive social networks'. *PLoS ONE*, 9(3), e90315. doi:10.1371/journal.pone.0090315.

Davidov, D., Tsur, O. and Rappoport, A. (2010). 'Semi-supervised recognition of sarcastic sentences in Twitter and Amazon'. In Proceedings of the Fourteenth Conference on Computational Natural Language Learning. Stroudsburg, PA: Association for Computational Linguistics, pp. 107–16.

Diakopoulos, N. A. and Shamma, D. A. (2010). 'Characterizing debate performance via aggregated Twitter sentiment'. In Proceedings of the SIGCHI Conference on Human Factors in Computing Systems. New York, NY: ACM Press, pp. 1195–8.

Esuli, A. and Sebastiani, F. (2006). 'SentiWordNet: a publicly available lexical resource for opinion mining'. In Proceedings of fifth International Conference on Language Resources and Evaluation (LREC-2006), Genoa, Italy, Vol. 6, pp. 417–22.

Feldman, R. (2013). 'Techniques and applications for sentiment analysis'. *Communications of the ACM*, 56(4), 82–9.

Filatova, E. (2012). 'Irony and sarcasm: corpus generation and analysis using crowdsourcing'. In Eighth International Conference on Language Resources and Evaluation (LREC2012). Istanbul: European Language Resources Association, pp. 392–8.

Gamon, M., Aue, A., Corston-Oliver, S. and Ringger, E. (2005). 'Pulse: mining customer opinions from free text'. In A. Famili (ed.) *Advances in Intelligent Data Analysis VI.* Berlin: Springer, pp. 21–32.

Godbole, N., Srinivasaiah, M. and Skiena, S. (2007). 'Large-scale sentiment analysis for news and blogs'. In Proceedings of the International Conference on Weblogs and Social Media (ICWSM2007). Boulder, CO: AAAI Press. http://www.icwsm.org/papers/3–Godbole-Srinivasaiah-Skiena.pdf (accessed 13 July, 2016).

Golder, S. A. and Macy, M. W. (2011). 'Diurnal and seasonal mood vary with work, sleep, and daylength across diverse cultures'. *Science*, 333(6051), 1878–81.

Greaves, F., Ramirez-Cano, D., Millett, C., Darzi, A. and Donaldson, L. (2013). 'Harnessing the cloud of patient experience: using social media to detect poor quality healthcare'. *BMJ Quality & Safety*, 22(3), 251–5.

Huang, M., Ye, B., Wang, Y., Chen, H., Cheng, J. and Zhu, X. (2014). 'New word detection for sentiment analysis'. In Proceedings of the 52nd Annual Meeting of the Association for Computational Linguistics, Baltimore, MA: ACL Press, pp. 531–41.

Ida, Y., Nakamura, T. and Matsumoto, T. (2013). 'Domain-dependent/independent topic switching model for online reviews with numerical ratings'. In Proceedings of the 22nd ACM International Conference on Conference on Information & Knowledge Management. New York, NY: ACM Press, pp. 229–38.

Justo, R., Corcoran, T., Lukin, S. M., Walker, M. and Torres, M. I. (2014). 'Extracting relevant knowledge for the detection of sarcasm and nastiness in the social web'. *Knowledge-Based Systems,* 69(1), 124–33.

Kazemian, S., Zhao, S. and Penn, G. (2014). 'Evaluating sentiment analysis evaluation: A case study in securities trading'. 5th Workshop on Computational Approaches to Subjectivity, Sentiment and Social Media Analysis (WASSA 2014), Baltimore, MA: ACL, pp. 119–27.

Kennedy, H. (2012). 'Perspectives on sentiment analysis'. *Journal of Broadcasting & Electronic Media*, 56(4), 435–50.

Liu, B. (2012). *Sentiment Analysis and Opinion Mining*. New York, NY: Morgan Claypool.

Liu, B. and Zhang, L. (2012). 'A survey of opinion mining and sentiment analysis'. In C.C. Aggarwal, C. Zhai (eds.), *Mining Text Data.* Berlin: Springer, pp. 415–63.

Liu, B., Hu, M. and Cheng, J. (2005). 'Opinion observer: analyzing and comparing opinions on the web'. In Proceedings of the 14th International Conference on World Wide Web. New York, NY: ACM Press, pp. 342–51.

Malouf, R. and Mullen, T. (2008). 'Taking sides: user classification for informal online political discourse'. *Internet Research*, 18(2), 177–90.

Mavridis, N. (2015). 'A review of verbal and non-verbal human–robot interactive communication'. *Robotics and Autonomous Systems*, 63(1), 22–35.

Melville, P., Gryc, W. and Lawrence, R. D. (2009). 'Sentiment analysis of blogs by combining lexical knowledge with text classification'. In Proceedings of the 15th ACM SIGKDD International Conference on Knowledge Discovery and Data Mining. New York, NY: ACM Press, pp. 1275–84.

Metaxas, P. T., Mustafaraj, E. and Gayo-Avello, D. (2011). 'How (not) to predict elections'. In Privacy, Security, Risk and Trust (PASSAT). Los Alamitos, CA: IEEE Press, pp. 165–71.

Misopoulos, F., Mitic, M., Kapoulas, A. and Karapiperis, C. (2014). 'Uncovering customer service experiences with Twitter: the case of airline industry'. *Management Decision*, 52(4), 705–23.

Mohammad, S. M., Zhu, X. and Martin, J. (2014). 'Semantic role labeling of emotions in Tweets'. 5th Workshop on Computational

Approaches to Subjectivity, Sentiment and Social Media Analysis (WASSA 2014), Baltimore, MA: ACL, pp. 32–41.

Murthy, D. and Petto, L. R. (2015). 'Comparing print coverage and tweets in elections. A case study of the 2011–2012 US Republican primaries'. *Social Science Computer Review*, 0894439314541925.

Myslín, M., Zhu, S. H., Chapman, W. and Conway, M. (2013). 'Using Twitter to examine smoking behavior and perceptions of emerging tobacco products'. *Journal of Medical Internet Research*, 15(8), e174.

Nassirtoussi, A., Aghabozorgi, S., Teh, Y. and Ngo, D. (2014). 'Text mining for market prediction: a systematic review'. *Expert Systems with Applications*, 41(16), 7653–70.

Nassirtoussi, A. Aghabozorgi, S., Wah, T. and Ngo, D. (2015). 'Text mining of news-headlines for FOREX market prediction: a multi-layer dimension reduction algorithm with semantics and sentiment'. *Expert Systems with Applications*, 42(1), 306–24.

Nielsen, F. Å. (2011). 'A new ANEW: evaluation of a word list for sentiment analysis in microblogs'. In Workshop on Making Sense of Microposts: big things come in small packages. pp. 93–8. CEUR Workshop Proceedings, no. 718. http://ceur-ws.org/Vol-718/paper_16.pdf (accessed 13 July 2016).

O'Connor, B., Balasubramanyan, R., Routledge, B. R. and Smith, N. A. (2010). 'From Tweets to polls: linking text sentiment to public opinion time series'. *International Conference on Web and Social Media*, 11, 122–9.

Paltoglou, G. and Thelwall, M. (2010). 'A study of information retrieval weighting schemes for sentiment analysis'. In Proceedings of the 48th Annual Meeting of the Association for Computational Linguistics. Stroudsburg, PA: Association for Computational Linguistics, pp. 1386–95.

Pang, B. and Lee, L. (2008). 'Opinion mining and sentiment analysis'. *Foundations and Trends in Information Retrieval*, 2(1–2), 1–135.

Pang, B., Lee, L. and Vaithyanathan, S. (2002). 'Thumbs up?: Sentiment classification using machine learning techniques'. In Proceedings of the ACL-02 conference on Empirical Methods in Natural Language Processing, Vol. 10. Stroudsburg, PA: Association for Computational Linguistics, pp. 79–86.

Ponomareva, N. and Thelwall, M. (2012). 'Biographies or blenders: which resource is best for cross-domain sentiment analysis?'. In A. Gelbukh (ed.), *Computational Linguistics and Intelligent Text Processing*. Berlin: Springer, pp. 488–99.

Poria, S., Cambria, E., Winterstein, G. and Huang, G. B. (2014). 'Sentic patterns: dependency-based rules for concept-level sentiment analysis'. *Knowledge-Based Systems*, 69(1), 45–63.

Skowron, M., Theunis, M., Rank, S. and Borowiec, A. (2011). 'Effect of affective profile on communication patterns and affective expressions in interactions with a dialog system'. In S. D'Mello, A. Graesser, B. Schuller, J. Martin (eds.), *Affective Computing and Intelligent Interaction*. Berlin: Springer, pp. 347–56.

Stone, P. J., Bales, R. F., Namenwirth, J. Z. and Ogilvie, D. M. (1962). 'The General Inquirer: a computer system for content analysis and retrieval based on the sentence as a unit of information'. *Behavioral Science*, 7(4), 484–98.

Strapparava, C. and Mihalcea, R. (2008). 'Learning to identify emotions in text'. In Proceedings of the 2008 ACM Symposium on Applied Computing. New York, NY: ACM Press, pp. 1556–60.

Strapparava, C. and Valitutti, A. (2004). 'WordNet Affect: an affective extension of WordNet'. In N. Calzolari (ed.) Proceedings of the 4th International Conference on Language Resources and Evaluation (LREC-2004), Lisbon, Portugal, Vol. 4, pp. 1083–86.

Subramanian, S., Bear, M. E., Setayesh, M. and Horton, N. (2013). US Patent Application 14/021,798.

Taboada, M. and Grieve, J. (2004). 'Analyzing appraisal automatically'. In Proceedings of AAAI Spring Symposium on Exploring Attitude and Affect in Text (AAAI Technical Report), Stanford University, CA. Menlo Park, CA: AAAI Press, pp. 158–61.

Taboada, M., Brooke, J., Tofiloski, M., Voll, K. and Stede, M. (2011). 'Lexicon-based methods for sentiment analysis'. *Computational Linguistics*, 37(2), 267–307.

Tausczik, Y. R. and Pennebaker, J. W. (2010). 'The psychological meaning of words: LIWC and computerized text analysis methods'.

Journal of Language and Social Psychology, 29(1), 24–54.

Thelwall, M. (2010). 'Emotion homophily in social network site messages'. First Monday, 15(4). http://firstmonday.org/ojs/index.php/fm/article/view/2897/2483 (accessed 13 July 2016).

Thelwall, M. and Buckley, K. (2013). 'Topic-based sentiment analysis for the Social Web: the role of mood and issue-related words'. *Journal of the American Society for Information Science and Technology*, 64(8), 1608–17.

Thelwall, M., Buckley, K. and Paltoglou, G. (2011). 'Sentiment in Twitter events'. *Journal of the American Society for Information Science and Technology*, 62(2), 406–18.

Thelwall, M., Buckley, K. and Paltoglou, G. (2012). 'Sentiment strength detection for the social Web'. *Journal of the American Society for Information Science and Technology*, 63(1), 163–73.

Thelwall, M., Buckley, K., Paltoglou, G., Cai, D. and Kappas, A. (2010). 'Sentiment strength detection in short informal text'. *Journal of the American Society for Information Science and Technology*, 61(12), 2544–58.

Thelwall, M., Buckley, K., Paltoglou, G., Skowron, M., Garcia, D., Gobron, S., Ahn, J., Kappas, A., Küster, D. and Holyst, J.A. (2013). 'Damping sentiment analysis in online communication: discussions, monologs and dialogs'. In A. Gelbukh (ed.), *CICLing 2013*, Part II, LNCS 7817. Heidelberg: Springer, pp. 1–12.

Tong, R. (2001). 'An operational system for detecting and tracking opinions in on-line discussions'. Working Notes of the ACM SIGIR 2001 Workshop on Operational Text Classification. New York, NY: ACM, pp. 1–6.

Tumasjan, A., Sprenger, T. O., Sandner, P. G. and Welpe, I. M. (2010). 'Predicting elections with Twitter: what 140 characters reveal about political sentiment'. In International AAAI Conference on Weblogs and Social Media (ICWSM2010), pp. 178–85. https://www.aaai.org/ocs/index.php/ICWSM/ICWSM10/paper/view/1441 (accessed 13 July 2016).

Turney, P.D. (2002). 'Thumbs up or thumbs down?: Semantic orientation applied to unsupervised classification of reviews'. In Proceedings of the 40th Annual Meeting on Association for Computational Linguistics (ACL2002). Stroudsburg, PA: Association for Computational Linguistics, pp. 417–24.

van Atteveldt, W., Kleinnijenhuis, J., Ruigrok, N. and Schlobach, S. (2008). 'Good news or bad news? Conducting sentiment analysis on Dutch text to distinguish between positive and negative relations'. *Journal of Information Technology & Politics*, 5(1), 73–94.

Vilares Calvo, D., Thelwall, M. and Alonso, M.A. (2015). 'The megaphone of the people? Spanish SentiStrength for real-time analysis of political tweets'. *Journal of Information Science*, 41(6), 799–813.

Vural, A.G., Cambazoglu, B.B. and Karagoz, P. (2014). 'Sentiment-focused web crawling'. *ACM Transactions on the Web*, 8(4), article 22.

Vural, A.G., Cambazoglu, B.B., Senkul, P. & Tokgoz, O. (2013). 'A framework for sentiment analysis in Turkish: application to polarity detection of movie reviews in Turkish'. In *Computer and Information Sciences III*, London: Springer, pp. 437–45.

Wang, H., Can, D., Kazemzadeh, A., Bar, F. and Narayanan, S. (2012). 'A system for real-time Twitter sentiment analysis of 2012 US presidential election cycle'. In Proceedings of the ACL 2012 System Demonstrations. Stroudsburg, PA: Association for Computational Linguistics, pp. 115–20.

Widener, M. J. and Li, W. (2014). 'Using geolocated Twitter data to monitor the prevalence of healthy and unhealthy food references across the US'. *Applied Geography*, 54(1), 189–97.

Wiebe, J., Wilson, T. and Cardie, C. (2005). 'Annotating expressions of opinions and emotions in language'. *Language Resources and Evaluation*, 39(2–3), 165–210.

Wu, Y., Liu, S., Yan, K., Liu, M. and Wu, F. (2012). 'OpinionFlow: visual analysis of opinion diffusion on social media'. *IEEE Transactions on Visualization and Computer Graphics*, 20(12), 1763–72.

Young, L. and Soroka, S. (2012). 'Affective news: the automated coding of sentiment in political texts'. *Political Communication*, 29(2), 205–31.

Zagibalov, T. and Carroll, J. (2008). 'Unsupervised classification of sentiment and objectivity in Chinese text'. In Proceedings of the 22nd International Conference on Computational Linguistics (Coling 2008), Manchester, UK: ICCL, pp. 1073–80.

Zhang, Z. and Singh, M. P. (2014). 'ReNew: a semi-supervised framework for generating domain-specific lexicons and sentiment analysis'. In Proceedings of the 52nd Annual Meeting of the Association for Computational Linguistics, Baltimore, MA: ACL Press, pp. 542–51.

Zhao, K., Yen, J., Greer, G., Qiu, B., Mitra, P. and Portier, K. (2014). 'Finding influential users of online health communities: A new metric based on sentiment influence'. *Journal of the American Medical Informatics Association*, 21(e2), e212–18.

## 21

Artificial Intelligence/Expert Systems and Online Research

Edward Brent

The size and rapid growth of the Internet demands new strategies for handling the deluge of available data. Social researchers can no longer think just in terms of *data sets* – fixed collections of information gathered as part of a single study that together represent the information available relevant to some topic at some point in time. Today, we are inundated with digitized data flows. A *digitized data flow* is an ongoing influx of new information available in digitized format, often from multiple sources, typically large in volume, and likely to continue at least for the foreseeable future. Examples of such data flows include news articles, data input in an ongoing web survey, essay tests, published articles, term papers, personnel records, medical records, research proposals, manuscripts submitted for publication, arrest records, birth and death records, requests for assistance received by help desks, email, and ... well you get the idea. There are LOTS of data flows.

Researchers in many areas find themselves in a position similar to that of assessment researchers in which new technologies and the Internet have led to a sea change where the issue is now less how to collect data and more how to analyze it.

> This technology has completely solved the problem of data collection; it is now possible to collect vast quantities of performance data, in excruciating detail with complete accuracy ... The challenge now rests more squarely on the need to make sense of this mountain of data.
>
> Williamson *et al.*, 2006: 6

Data flows require rethinking social research. Because new data are continually appearing, it would be very valuable to us to have a way to automate the monitoring as much as possible. For example, social science researchers need to have a way to monitor changing literature in their areas of research interest, funding agencies need ways to assess new research proposals submitted each year, instructors need ways to grade essays submitted in response to assignments, and politicians need to monitor public opinion preceding elections.

Although traditional mathematical and statistical approaches can address many of these problems, artificial intelligence and expert systems approaches are not restricted to formal provable algorithms, are compatible with qualitative as well as quantitative views, and can be used for problems intractable to other analyses. These techniques include text analysis which can be used in a wide range of applications to find structured patterns in unstructured text, expert systems permit automation of reasoning modeled after that of human experts, intelligent agents permit modeling interactions of multiple actors in diverse networks, and a wide range of automated learning algorithms permit systems that can learn and adapt to incoming data. We will see how these strengths have been brought to bear in network analysis, event data analysis, and essay grading.

TRADITIONAL SOCIAL RESEARCH ONLINE

To better understand how social research on the web might be automated, let us first examine how such research has long been conducted. We consider an example project that illustrates common strengths and weaknesses.

McCully (2005) studied public service anti-drug television commercials. Fortunately for him, as in many areas of social life, various agencies and research groups had already created web pages containing over 100 such announcements. He considered the literature and the available data and formulated a research problem in which he planned to perform a thematic analysis of such messages. He then conducted an exhaustive search using various indexing and search services for the Internet until he obtained a final sample of 108 announcements meeting his criteria. He saved the digitized videos for each announcement along with any text information in a local file folder on his own computer. Based

on his review of the announcements he came up with a system of codes that he then systematically applied to each announcement. Finally, in his analysis he used examples to illustrate the various themes and reported on the relative frequencies of the themes in the data. Similar methods are used to analyze a wide range of media on the Internet, including newspaper articles, web pages, blogs, and so on. McCully used Qualrus™, a qualitative analysis program. Most contemporary research of media on the web uses qualitative analysis programs such as Qualrus, Dedoose, Atlas.ti, or NVivo, and/or statistical packages for quantitative analysis such as SPSS® or SAS®.

This traditional approach has a number of strengths: it is flexible and gives the researcher great control over the entire process. It also makes it possible to conduct both theory-based studies and grounded theory studies with concepts emerging out of the data collected.

However, the traditional research approach also has a number of weaknesses. Different researchers often develop coding schemes independently. If they are shared, it is usually only in print form and considerable effort would be required by other researchers to code additional data with those codes. The coded data themselves are often privately held by the researcher and unavailable to others, with the exception of graduate students and collaborating colleagues. This style of research must struggle to be cumulative and objective.

Even using analysis software, research on the Internet using traditional strategies remains expensive and time-consuming. This largely manual research process is unlikely to be able to keep up with the size and rapid growth of the Internet (or other massive data flows) except for projects of very restricted scope that sample only a small fraction of eligible web pages. Unfortunately, for some important research projects, and for many common day-to-day tasks in which data are monitored for assessment or quality control purposes, sampling may not be possible and the entire population should be examined. For such projects an automated form of analysis may be essential. An automated research process would be able to handle huge volumes of data and rapid changes in data, would increase objectivity, and would reduce response time. Clearly, it is worthwhile to examine strategies for automating social research on the web. The most promising of those strategies are based on artificial intelligence and expert systems.

ARTIFICIAL INTELLIGENCE AND EXPERT SYSTEMS

The American Association for Artificial Intelligence (www.aai.org) on their homepage defines *artificial intelligence* (AI) as 'the scientific understanding of the mechanisms underlying thought and intelligent behavior and their embodiment in machines'. AI has many subfields including robotics, expert systems, natural language processing, machine learning, and intelligent agents.

The term 'artificial intelligence' was first used in 1955 in a proposal for the Dartmouth Summer Research Project on Artificial Intelligence by McCarthy *et al.* AI has become so deeply entrenched in modern computing and commerce that we often don't even realize it is there.

'Artificial intelligence has accomplished more than people realize', said futurist Ray Kurzweil. 'It permeates our economic infrastructure ... AI technology is used by banks to police transactions for fraud, by cell phone companies for voice recognition, and by search engines to scour the web and organize data'.

Cohn, 2006: n.p.

A few short years later, we have usable if imperfect tools and services to translate from one language to another (Luckerson, 2015), autonomously driving cars being test driven on highways in some jurisdictions, and automated sentiment analysis programs that mine

social media such as Tweets to predict election results (Reed, 2010).

The subfield of AI most closely related to online research seeks to mirror human reasoning for complex tasks. Earliest attempts, epitomized by the General Problem Solver approach of Newell *et al.* (1959), were based on the flawed premise that reasoning by itself would be sufficient to solve virtually any problem. By the 1980s, it was clear to most that specific substantive knowledge was required to solve problems (Hayes-Roth *et al.*, 1983). Such programs are often called either *knowledge-based systems* (KBS) because they are based on domain knowledge, or *expert systems* (ES) because they are meant to perform tasks once thought possible only for human experts (for an overview of expert systems, see Giarratano and Riley, 2005).

ESs have a number of advantages. They are easy to use, can solve problems that cannot be solved using other approaches, and can make rapid progress through rapid prototyping. Rule-based expert systems are created in a process that Feigenbaum called '*knowledge engineering*' (cited in Hayes-Roth, 1983: 45) in which expert knowledge is represented as a body of related facts and rules using an *expert system shell*, a general program for representing a wide range of expert knowledge. These rules often resemble how substantive experts solve problems and are much more accessible than programming languages. Further assistance is provided by a *knowledge engineer*, someone familiar with expert systems, who works with a substantive expert to translate their knowledge into facts and rules. Many important problems have no formal algorithmic or mathematical solution, and yet human experts solve those problems routinely and usually achieve success. Expert systems can use '*heuristics*', rules of thumb or other shortcuts that work most of the time but which do not provide provably true solutions. Those systems were often good enough to match human expert performance and could be applied to a wide range of problems for which there was no formal solution. Finally, because they were so simple and straightforward to create, expert systems could also be used for rapid prototyping, in which a 'quick and dirty' solution is created for testing that can be modified and improved, often dramatically speeding development when compared to other approaches. These advantages led to widespread adoption of ESs in the 1980s and 1990s and numerous successes. Successful applications of ESs in wide ranging applications have continued in ensuing decades and can be found in journals like *Expert Systems with Applications*. These include many intelligent learning applications (Uday *et al.*, 2011), applied social sciences (Drigs *et al.*, 2004), and geography (Filis *et al.*, 2003).

Gaines (2013: 150) suggests 'The semantic web framework has replaced expert systems shells as the target representation and inference framework for knowledge acquisition'. Certainly the semantic web employs many of the same technologies used in the AI/ES approach and makes them available online; however, the semantic web takes a very different approach than the AI/ES approach to research. The semantic web is based on the notion that the substantive content of web pages can be marked up based on a shared framework in a manner permitting content to be accessed with autonomous computer programs (agents) for selective retrieval and analysis, permitting computers to become capable of analyzing all the data on the Web (Berners-Lee *et al.*, 2001). This approach may be adequate for tasks like web commerce where users generally view the data through the same lens. However, a single ontology or classification system is inadequate for social research when researchers having different ontological views approach the data very differently (O'Hara, 2004; Gruber, 2007). Shirky (2005) argues centrally controlled taxonomic categorization schemes are inherently limited. Instead of top–down ontologies, he advocates 'bottom–up, community-based tagging methods' (Motta, 2006). Edelman (2004), for example,

discusses contested terms that have one meaning for some people and quite a different meaning for others. We need look no further than the contrasting definitions of social class of Marx and Weber or the different ways in which the term 'jihad' is used by different people to understand this point (El-Nawawy, 2004). 'It's likely that future semantic annotations will also reflect such radically different viewpoints on the same events' (Motta, 2006). Instead of a singular view imposed by a semantic web, there will need to be diverse views developed by competing researchers using the AI/ES perspective.

Problems with Expert Systems

Expert systems also had to overcome important limitations, the most important of which were a knowledge acquisition bottleneck, narrow specialization, and limitations of logic as implemented in particular ES shells. The most commonly cited problem with ES is the 'knowledge acquisition bottleneck' (Hayes-Roth *et al.*, 1983: 129) because so much time and effort are required by highly trained and expensive experts and knowledge engineers to create them. A second problem is extreme specialization. You can't have a 'General Expert' system any more than you can have a human who is expert at everything. ES form narrow silos of expertise excellent for a narrow domain of tasks but of little benefit outside that domain. They often lack 'common sense' and do not know what they don't know, and so applying an ES for understanding groups of adolescents to groups of businesswomen is likely to produce poor results and have no warnings or understanding that it might be poor. A third problem is the expert system shells sometimes relied on a narrow range of logic that were in some cases inadequate for solving complex problems (Gaines, 2013: 1148).

As ES have evolved these problems have been largely resolved (Gaines, 2013). Because ES are defined by their application more than their methodologies, ES have been implemented with diverse methodologies avoiding limitations of the rule-based approach. For example, Liao (2005: 94) surveys ES methodologies from 1995 to 2004 and classifies them into eleven categories: 'rule-based systems, knowledge-based systems, neural networks, fuzzy ESs, object oriented methodology, case-based reasoning, system architecture, intelligent agent systems, database methodology, modeling, and ontology'. Machine learning strategies in ES help reduce the knowledge acquisition bottleneck. ES are often integrated with other programs in systems providing comprehensive solutions for a wide range of issues beyond the narrow expertise of a single ES, and more powerful 'description logics' have been developed (Baader *et al.*, 2003) that are capable of more advanced reasoning.

THE AI/ES APPROACH TO ONLINE RESEARCH

Although there are a number of expert systems available on the Internet addressing a wide range of topics (Grove, 2000), the issue of how expert systems can be used for online research has not been addressed elsewhere. The AI/ES approach to online research has to address the same fundamental issues faced by traditional social research on the web. It is a hybrid in which researchers develop their own knowledge framework and then use natural language processing (NLP) and a range of other AI strategies to code and analyze web pages based on that framework. In many cases these procedures must be learned and refined using machine learning strategies.

We begin with three examples of active research areas that, while not perfectly epitomizing everything about the AI/ES approach, illustrate key features. Next we consider the research tasks faced and show how the AI/ES approach differs from more traditional research, such as that of McCully (2005), using

examples from these different lines of inquiry to illustrate the points. The examples are international event data analysis, social network analysis, and automated essay grading.

International Event Data Analysis

Several different research teams use automated coding programs to analyze international news events. The basic approach is illustrated by Gerner *et al.* (2002) who used the TABARI automated coding program to code headlines of more than 200,000 international news events over a period from 1979 to 2002 from news feeds provided by Reuters and Agence France Presse. Today those news feeds are routinely available to subscribers over the Internet. This is one of many studies of this type that use automated coding to generate very large data sets for detailed analysis. Those programs use different variants of natural language understanding strategies to perform the coding and a variety of coding schemes to analyze those data. This particular study compared one coding scheme (CAMEO) with another earlier coding scheme (WEIS).

Most political event analysis work initially involved relatively small samples of event data in specific domains and required a long time to code. However, by 2011, with funding from the National Science Foundation and Defense Advanced Research Projects Agency in the U.S., Schrodt (2011) and his team were able to generate high-volume, near real-time coding of 'about 26-million sentences generated from 8-million stories condensed from around 30 gigabytes of text', all coded in six minutes. These automated analyses have all but supplanted traditional analysis so that 'by the mid-2000s, virtually all refereed articles in political science journal used machine-coded, rather than human-coded, event data' (Schrodt, 2011:1). King and Lowe (2004) found that machine coding is comparable in accuracy to human coding. However, Schrodt (2011) argues that validation of coding of political events by comparing machine coding to human coding is irrelevant because human coding of events in real time is not possible, and coding accuracy for human coders is unlikely to exceed 70 percent at best.

Social Network Analysis

There are a wide range of approaches to network analysis. For decades, researchers have used published citation indices to examine changing networks of researchers in particular disciplines (Garfield, 1979). More recently, a number of researchers have conducted full-text analyses of published works using automated procedures to extract citations and natural language understanding strategies to categorize citations (Teufel and Moens, 2002; Kas *et al.*, 2012), including categories such as 'contrastive', 'supportive', or 'neutral' (Teufel and Moens, 2002: Fig. 5). Work by Carley and her colleagues often applies AI/ES strategies to examine networks. In Carley's earlier 'map analysis', she constructed semantic maps for teams based on interviews and other texts (Carley, 1993) to understand how teams and their ideas evolve over time. More recent work often uses full-text analysis of scientific papers automatically extracting citations as a basis for network analysis of trends and patterns in scientific communities (Kas *et al.*, 2012). Moon and Carley (2007) employed several AI/ES strategies using text analysis to extract network information from open source texts and then examined multi-agent models to simulate behavior. Mooney *et al.* (2004) used relational data mining and inductive logic programming to discover links in networks.

AI/ES approaches to network analysis are scalable and permit application to complex network problems, which is essential because most interesting networks are complex. Researchers have made efforts to insure that these efforts rise above naïve curve-fitting to suggest hypotheses and theories that can be tested empirically (Schreiber and

Carley, 2004). The complexity of these computational models makes common validation practices in social sciences and engineering inadequate (Carley, 2009) and requires combining data from disparate sources, building models, running virtual experiments and then comparing those with historic events while avoiding overfitting to specific situations (Carley, 2009), a validation process further refined into a calibrated grounding strategy (Schreiber and Carley, 2013) in which empirical data provide the initial grounding followed by varying specific representations and processes of the model, and then correlating various model results with real-world data to see which agent interactions are validated.

Automated Essay Grading

Automated essay grading provides other examples of the AI/ES approach. This author and his colleagues (Brent *et al.*, 2006; Brent and Townsend, 2007) use the SAGrader™ program to automatically code and grade student essays submitted over the web. Other automated essay grading programs are now in use for high-stakes tests such as the SAT (Scholastic Aptitude Test). Different automated essay grading programs often use very different criteria for assessing essays. In fact, they differ so fundamentally that it is, in at least some respects, unfortunate that they are called 'essay grading' programs. Some focus on grammar and form, while others focus on content (Deane, 2006).

SAGrader uses an ES approach based on specific learning objectives, making it able to provide clear personalized feedback and a formative learning experience (Atkisson *et al.*, 2010). Most other essay grading programs use some form of machine learning such as latent semantic analysis (Landauer *et al.*, 2003) and have been widely criticized for providing poor feedback which is 'long, generic, and redundant' (Dikli, 2010) and fixed, repetitive, too-general, and inaccurate (Grimes and Warschauer, 2010). All of these programs must be developed and tested using human-scored essays. Machine learning requires large samples of human-scored essays, while SAGrader's expert system approach requires smaller training samples of human-scored essays but requires a trained expert to implement the system (Atkisson *et al.*, 2010). Once developed and validated, all of these programs provide scalable solutions that can automatically grade essays.

Each of these three research examples illustrate the AI/ES approach. Different research teams take very different views and must create their own knowledge frameworks and then impose that structure upon the data for analysis. The Internet is the source of data for the analyses. Heavy use is made of a variety of AI and ES techniques to code and analyze the data.

Table 21.1 provides a list of common research tasks used in online research. Following that, each task, and how these two approaches address it, is described in greater detail.

Research Infrastructure

The Internet replaces a pre-Internet infrastructure of audiotapes, transcribed interviews, file cabinets of paper field notes, and photographs with a digital infrastructure serving those same functions. World Wide Web (WWW) protocols permit communication, Universal Resource Locators (URL) identify addresses of important data, the Resource Description Framework (RDF) is a standard

model for interchange and syntax, text from many world languages is converted to Unicode, and audio, graphics, video, and other data are displayed in standard formats such as wav, pdf, or avi files.

Digitized Sources

Most online research relies on data providers to digitize information by scanning pictures, recording audio or video, and capturing or scanning digital text as part of everyday transactions, social media, student work, or organizational records. Massive digital data flows have shifted the bottleneck in social research from digitizing to making sense of the mass of digital data available.

Each example of the AI/ES approach to online research requires that ongoing processes be set up to digitize the data. Citation analyses are conducted on full-text publications made available from standard bibliographic databases. International event analysis usually monitors an existing digitized Internet newsfeed, such as Reuters (www.reuters.com/news/world (accessed 17 July 2016)). Essay grading typically requires that students submit their papers electronically.

Data Retrieval and Sampling

For traditional online social research, the researcher typically uses search engines such

Table 21.1   Research tasks in online research

Research task	Description
Research infrastructure	A means to record, store, and share data
Digitized sources	Data must be digitized for online access
Data retrieval and sampling	A subset of data is selected for analysis
Data conversion	Further conversion or pre-processing is often required
Structured data	Data may be organized and formatted to facilitate analysis
Knowledge	A theory is used to make sense of the results
Coding data	Concepts from the theory are tagged in the database
Analysis	Data are reexamined for different purposes

as Google® to find a sample of web pages of interest. Those are then combined into a fixed dataset for the study. That was the case for McCully's (2005) media study. In contrast, the AI/ES approach often focuses on ongoing data flows. In the AI/ES approach, student essays can be graded as they are submitted over the web, and incoming headlines in an RSS (Really Simple Syndication) news feed for international events can be continuously monitored. (An RSS feed is a format for displaying a summary or complete text of frequently updated content from a web site such as blogs, news headlines, or changing stock market prices.) The greatest effort for data flows is often the data management effort required to set up a system to collect digitized data from that flow, and sampling from the flow becomes nearly trivial. For example, automated grading of essays requires that a system be set up in which students can submit their essays digitally to a central site. Digital libraries provide the up-to-date bibliographic sources used in citation analyses of social networks. Particular records can then be accessed by user programs using extensible markup language (XML) queries or database queries.

Online research using automated procedures is often conducted on all sources available for analysis. That is, the entire population of data is examined, not just a sample. McCully's (2005) traditional analysis, of course, examined a modest sample of cases. However, Carley's network analyses based on citations often examine all texts available for a particular domain, and essay grading programs are used to grade and provide feedback for all student submissions to a particular assignment.

Some researchers analyze the entire population of a data flow because of distrust for samples. For example, Morstatter *et al.* (2013) examined Tweets for a given time period and found the sample provided by Twitter's Streaming API was less likely to match the full population from all tweets during a period (the 'Twitter Firehose'). In addition,

full populations of Internet data flows can be truly massive, requiring expensive automated systems usually implemented on the Cloud (servers leased from large providers like Amazon that can be dynamically scaled to respond to demand).

Data Conversion

Sometimes initial digitization of data is sufficient to make the data readable by humans, but does not make data accessible to automated analysis. For example, documents in Adobe's Portable Document Format (PDF) can be encrypted to prevent conversion to text, and other video, audio, and graphic files may not be compatible with automated procedures. These must be converted for automated analysis with the AI/ES approach.

AI strategies provide considerable help in converting various forms of data into digital form. Speech recognition programs (like Dragon NaturallySpeaking®) have made great strides at converting spoken speech to text, although they are not yet capable of automatically transcribing interviews of multiple subjects. Handwriting recognition programs use AI strategies to translate handwritten or hand-printed text into digitized text. Optical character recognition (OCR) programs (such as ABBYY FineReader® OCR) use AI strategies to translate visual images of printed text into text format. Of the three speech-to-text, handwriting-to-text, and images-to-text programs, OCR programs are the most mature technology, offering surprisingly good results. Although they do introduce some errors, OCR programs can sometimes correctly convert complex formats with multiple columns, embedded figures, tables, and other challenging features. These programs can be used to convert PDF files to HyperText Markup Language (HTML) files, for example, providing far greater access to the meaning of the text. The most effective strategy, however, remains acquiring the initial data in digitized text form and avoiding the need for conversion.

Structured Data

One strategy to make data easier to analyze automatically using the AI/ES approach is to create structured data. Unstructured data in the form of free text requires greater effort for computer programs to detect particular kinds of information. Organizing the data into different segments each tagged to indicate its type makes it easier to retrieve information for analysis. XML is a general-purpose markup language designed to be readable by humans, while at the same time providing metadata tags for various kinds of substantive content that can be easily recognized by computers. XML permits users to create their own tags for containing metadata to indicate the kinds of information located at various places in the document. For example, a tag begins a segment of text specifying the abstract and marks the end of that segment.

In many cases, the data has a known structure that can be encoded systematically in an XML schema. Although XML tags provide a generic technology that can be used to label segments of text, an XML schema (www.w3.org/XML/Schema (accessed 17 July 2016)) is a standardized set of XML tags designed to include important categories for a particular knowledge domain. Many sources of data have a regular structure that can be used to facilitate retrieval and analysis, including personnel records, event transactions, or bibliographic data. Bibliographic data, for example, can be separated into segments based on an XML schema including tags for author, title, source, abstract, and so on. An XML schema for representing statistical metadata (the information about data sets) would include tags for variable name, variable label, level of measurement, and so on. An effort to standardize statistical metadata is found in the Data Documentation Initiative (www.ddialliance.org (accessed 17 July 2016).

Online literature reviews illustrate many ways in which structured data could make social research easier. Digital libraries (https://www.nsf.gov/news/news_summ.jsp?cntn_id=103048 (accessed 7 July 2016)) today make most professional journal articles and many books accessible in digital form over the Internet. A typical literature review involves the researcher logging into multiple digitized databases such as Academic Search Premier, Lexis Nexis Academic, or Sociological Abstracts, PsycINFO, or JSTOR. Then they must conduct several searches in each database using different interfaces in an attempt to locate relevant articles. When the databases include full text they can download the article and store a copy on their local machine or print it. The databases often contain only abstracts, and researchers must then decide whether it is worthwhile to pay for immediate access or visit a library to obtain a full text copy. There have been notable efforts to provide additional structure to bibliographic data to make them even easier to analyze. These include structured abstracts required by the National Library of Medicine (Bayley and Eldredge, 2003), which require the author to provide more detailed initial tagging of the abstract.

Knowledge

In all these research approaches, knowledge both guides the research and is altered by the findings. In traditional research, this knowledge is expressed informally as a verbal theory, giving researchers great flexibility to express their ideas, but providing no way for the computer to manipulate or reason about those ideas. McCully (2005) could choose to express his theory in any manner he wished, but received no help from the computer in reasoning about it or applying it to different web pages.

In the AI/ES approach, the knowledge base used to represent and reason about a substantive domain must be expressed formally in an *ontology* so that computer programs can detect and reason about that knowledge. Ontologies in computer science generally consist of a *semantic network* linking individual objects, classes of objects, attributes or features describing those objects, and relationships among objects (Quillian, 1966). Ontologies can be thought of as a formal representation of a theory. That formality can help expose gaps in reasoning or inconsistencies and may help researchers develop better theories. However, such formal representations may appear too inflexible for some researchers or may be unsuitable for specific problems. Ontologies are crucial for the AI/ES approach, providing an explicit representation of knowledge that can be accessed directly by applications and manipulated and reasoned about to draw inferences. An ontology for U.S. Presidential politics, for example, might include links such as 'Hillary Clinton is a Presidential candidate', 'New Hampshire has a Presidential primary', 'New Hampshire's primary is the first', and 'Candidates who do well in early primaries are more likely to win the election'. That semántic network provides a basis for reasoning about why Clinton visited New Hampshire and why we care.

There are *domain-specific ontologies* that express knowledge about a specific substantive domain (such as an ontology describing small group behavior, or an ontology describing social science research strategies) and *upper ontologies* that express knowledge about a common core of objects useful across many specific domains. One upper ontology is OpenCyc (www.opencyc.org), which contains roughly 50,000 terms and 300,000 assertions relating those terms to one another. One well-known ontology language is CycL which is used by the Cyc Project (www.cyc.com/) and is based on first-order predicate calculus. Another is OWL, the Web Ontology Language (www.w3.org/TR/owl-features/ (accessed 17 July 2016)). OWL is an ontology language often used on the World Wide Web.

The AI/ES approach permits multiple and competing theories. The same web page may be viewed very differently from those different perspectives. Web page developers need not express nor even understand all of those views. Researchers who share the paradigm must develop the ontology for that paradigm. How this can work is made clear for both the essay grading and international event data analysis examples. Different essay grading programs often employ very different feature sets for assessing essays. Some, such as SAGrader, emphasize semantic content while others emphasize statistical models. International event data analysis illustrates the problem of multiple paradigms. Several distinct coding typologies are commonly used (Schrodt and Gerner, 2001; Leng, 1987; McClelland, 1976; Azar, 1982; see, for example, http://vranet.com/IDEA.aspx (accessed 17 July 2016)). Gerner *et al.* (2002), for example, point to problems in older event codes, arguing for the need to broaden the focus beyond state actors and to deal with important issues of ethnic conflict and third-party mediation. More recently, DARPA funded the Integrated Conflict Early Warning Systems (ICEWS) leading to advances in event coding software such as TABARI and the application of this approach on a much larger scale (Schrodt, 2011). In addition to the multiple perspectives of different research teams, people and groups being studied often have their own world views with what some call a 'folksonomy' – a taxonomy or ontology of concepts and categories used by that group to express how they view the world (Gruber, 2007).

The research tasks faced by the AI/ES approach mirror those tasks faced by any research, and so they need to reflect the diversity of research. One important distinction is between top–down theory-driven research and bottom–up data-driven research. Rule-based expert systems express social theory as a set of rules and can be implemented in the AI/ES perspective using the Rule Interchange Format (RIF). An example of this approach is provided by the SAGrader™ program. Human experts (instructors or educational designers) specify the educational objectives of assignments as a rubric, which is then elaborated by knowledge engineers who specify the parameters of the system for detecting whether particular objectives have been met in the text of student submissions to the assignment. Similar top–down approaches are employed in the event history and network analyses based on citations.

The alternative data-driven approach to theory development characterizes traditional research using grounded theory (Glaser and Strauss, 1967). Here, instead of testing an existing theory, one goal of the research is to develop new theory. In the AI/ES approach, this data-driven process is often automated through the use of statistical models or machine learning algorithms. *Machine learning* is a sub-field of AI using one or more strategies to learn to recognize underlying patterns in data. It is often applied to find structure in text, but it can also be used for visual pattern recognition, such as facial recognition routines used by Google and others (Harris, 2015)

One form of machine learning is *data mining* (Hand *et al.*, 2001), which encompasses various procedures such as clustering and pattern recognition algorithms that search large data sets for patterns. Data mining is usually a-theoretical, identifying patterns in data and summarizing those without regard for developing a theory or a conceptual framework. One risk is that such models will 'over-fit' the data, finding patterns which on the surface appear useful but which do not hold up in further research. Data mining often uses *unsupervised learning*, procedures which look for a pattern among cases based on the inherent characteristics of the cases themselves. For example, clustering algorithms collect cases into groups of similar cases. Unsupervised learning algorithms, such as cluster analysis or mixture models, will always find some patterns in the data. It remains for the researcher to examine those patterns and determine whether they add theoretically meaningful insight. Such procedures might find clusters of academics working in a discipline in Carley's network analysis based on citations. But it remains

for Carley or other researchers to explain the theoretical importance of those clusters.

Coding Data

In traditional social research the investigator codes content using a coding scheme of her choosing. Coded data marks the theoretically meaningful categorizations in the data. The process of coding data links the data to theory based on operational definitions identifying characteristics of the data, which can be used as measures of the occurrence of specific concepts. The technology used for doing this can be the same as that used to structure the data pre-theoretically using XML tags in an XML schema. The difference is, in this XML schema the categories are based on the theory or ontology.

In traditional research, the research team has complete control over coding but must do all the work themselves in a complex, expensive, and time-consuming process that often limits the scope of research. In the AI/ES approach, just as in traditional research, the encoding of data must be consistent with the particular theoretical perspective. Hence, encoding data must be done independently for different perspectives. The burden of coding rests on the researchers who share that perspective. For online research examining massive data flows, it would be impractical to code all the data manually. A key aspect of the AI/ES approach, therefore, is to develop an effective way to automate encoding of data for analysis, often through some form of natural language processing.

Natural language processing is a subfield of artificial intelligence in which computer software is used to automatically generate and understand natural human language. Natural language generation systems convert information from databases into normal sounding language, while natural language understanding systems convert normal language into more formal representations of knowledge that the computer can manipulate. Natural language processing is particularly important as a method for converting unstructured data (such as free text writing with no obvious pattern) into a form permitting analysis because a large proportion of the information encountered in everyday life is unstructured. There are many different strategies for implementing natural language processing (Cole *et al.*, 1997). Two fundamentally different strategies are (1) statistical strategies that essentially treat text as a bag of words and then look for patterns in those words, and (2) linguistic strategies based on some combination of semantics and syntax to assess meaning. A number of open source tools for text analysis and natural language processing can be found on the web (e.g. Cunningham *et al.*, 2011).

Natural language processing strategies are a part of each of the sample AI/ES strategies. Essay grading programs employ a wide array of strategies for recognizing important features in essays. Intelligent Essay Assessor (IEA) by Landauer *et al.* (2003) employs a purely statistical approach called latent semantic analysis (LSA). This approach treats essays like a 'bag of words' using a matrix of word frequencies by essays and factor analysis to find an underlying semantic space. It then locates each essay in that space and assesses how closely it matches essays with known scores. E-rater uses a combination of statistical and linguistic approaches. It uses syntactic, discourse structure, and content features to predict scores for essays after the program has been trained to match human coders. SAGrader uses a strategy that blends linguistic, statistical, and AI approaches. It uses *fuzzy logic* to detect key concepts in student papers and a *semantic network* to represent the semantic information that should be present in good essays. All these programs *require learning* before they can be used to grade essays in a specific domain. Statistical models such as LSA, for example, typically require hundreds of essays for training.

Event coding programs for the analysis of international event data use computational linguistic approaches to code headlines from news feeds. The Kansas Event Data System (KEDS; see Schrodt *et al.*, 1994) uses simple linguistic parsing of the news reports to identify the political actors and actions that are reported. This system can recognize compound nouns and compound verb phrases and determine the references of pronouns. Finally, network analysis by Carley and others based on citations uses natural language strategies to identify citations and categorize them (Kas *et al.*, 2012).

None of these programs is a general natural language program that can be used right out of the box for coding a web page or data source. Each of them provides an algorithm that can be used to code texts in specific domains. For each of them, the researcher has to configure the program for a domain, giving the program some idea of the kinds of text it will be assessing and in some cases specifying the ontology. The program then has to be trained to recognize important patterns in the data until it reaches an acceptable level of performance. In some cases, researchers must train the program explicitly by specifying particular parameters such as the important concepts and text phrases which indicate that a concept is present in a web page. For analyzing a massive data flow, this process of training needs to be automated as much as possible to handle the high volume of data and the possibility of new changes. This automation typically requires some form of supervised machine learning to train the program.

In *supervised learning*, human judges set the standard against which the program is assessed. Supervised learning is often employed to train a computer program to make distinctions made by humans and to validate the program against that human standard. The need for human judgments in supervised learning makes it impossible to fully automate this form of learning. Supervised learning is both more expensive and more time-consuming than fully automated procedures, but it is often more useful.

AI offers several supervised learning algorithms. *Artificial neural networks* (Anderson, 1995) attempt to mimic the reasoning of the human brain by linking a series of artificial neurons to one another which are exposed to inputs and generating outputs. Those neurons respond to stimuli by altering their connections to other neurons and changing their outputs, creating an adaptive system capable of learning to solve problems. A *genetic algorithm* (Holland, 1975; Mitchell, 1996) is a learning algorithm modeled on evolutionary biology. A randomly selected population of candidate solutions is assessed for fitness on some index, and then fit candidates are selected at random and recombined to generate additional solution candidates. This process is repeated and successive generations should provide improved fit to the data as they inherit properties of good solutions.

Analysis

In traditional social research on the web, the researcher conducts analysis manually but they may use a qualitative analysis program such as Qualrus, NVivo, or Atlas.ti; or statistical programs, such as SAS or SPSS. In McCully's (2005) media study, for example, he was free to select the mode of analysis of his own choosing with little constraint other than trying to learn from similar past research.

In the AI/ES approach, analyses are automated and can vary dramatically from one program to another. For example, all essay grading programs produce scores, although the precision and complexity of the scores varies. Some produce explanations. Most of these essay grading programs simply perform a *one-time analysis* (grading) of papers. However, some of them, such as SAGrader, provide for *ongoing monitoring* of student performance as students revise and resubmit their papers. Studies of international event data analysis also employ a variety of analysis strategies, depending on their particular emphases. Many monitor events over time and use some form of time series or forecasting analysis (see, for example, http://eventdata.parusanalytics.com/index.html (accessed 17 July 2016)).

In the AI/ES approach, analysis of data flows is often accomplished at least in part with the use of intelligent agents. An *intelligent agent* is a software program possessing some form of AI, sufficient to sense changes in a complex environment and act upon those changes to achieve certain goals on behalf of users. Intelligent agents often incorporate built-in rules for rule-based reasoning modeled after expert systems. In SAGrader, for example, thousands of small autonomous expert systems act as intelligent agents to examine passages of text, with each determining whether a particular code should be applied or whether a particular combination of codes has occurred in a pattern indicating a learning objective has been met.

Another use of agents is in a *multi-agent system* (MAS) for modeling social interaction and aspects of social life (Weiss, 1999). The Center for Research in Social Simulation (CRESS) is one of the leading centers in agent-based modeling and also the location for the leading journal in this area (*Journal of Artificial Societies and Social Simulation*, JASS). Very large multi-agent models usually rely on parallel distributed processing taking place on the Cloud. Multi-agent models are easily distributed because essentially each agent operates autonomously and many agents can be modeled on separate computers with little loss of efficiency.

DISCUSSION AND CONCLUSION

The use of AI techniques to conduct social research on the web in the AI/ES approach is transforming social research. They have already transformed the study of international event data.

> This change in the ability of machines to handle NLP problems was reflected in event data research: in 1990 almost all event data projects used human coders, whereas in 2000 almost all projects used automated coding. This transformation meant that projects that once would have required tens of

thousands of dollars, a flock of student coders with a complex supervisory infrastructure and months of painstaking effort could be done by a single researcher in a few days or weeks, provided appropriate pre-existing dictionaries were available.

Schrodt and Gerner, 2001: 2–3

The AI/ES approach is one that is likely to be increasingly important in the future (Baumgartner and McCarthy, 2007). Social scientists and computer scientists are using similar approaches to automate coding for a number of other important applications, including automated classification of congressional legislation (Purpura and Hillard, 2006), legislative speeches (Quinn *et al.*, 2006), the classification of scientific abstracts (Blei and Lafferty, 2006), the classification of newspaper articles (Newman *et al.*, 2006), coding of job candidate surveys (Giorgetti *et al.*, 2002), and coding the content of public comments submitted to federal agencies (Shulman, et al., 2006).

Admittedly, the use of AI strategies to automate social research on the web raises a number of legitimate concerns. The availability of automated research on the web makes it easier to extract information from the web about individuals in ways that will further erode their privacy. However, such data are already available on the web and national intelligence agencies are already using automated software to mine it.

Another concern is whether such programs will deskill social research, perhaps threatening some research jobs. However, these programs treat technology, not as a machine to replace human labor, but as a tool to help make our work more efficient and permitting us to study new issues we could not address before (Hage and Powers, 1992). It seems far more likely these programs will enable researchers rather than deskill them.

Intellectual property issues are another concern. Content providers on the web often provide metadata needed to find relevant materials freely for unrestricted analysis by researchers, while for the primary content they often limit access through legal (such as patents or copyrights), financial (such as royalties or user access fees), and technological means (such as encrypted pdf files) to make it harder for others to copy, analyze, and redistribute their work. How these issues will be worked out remains to be seen.

The AI/ES approach has potentially far-reaching consequences. The work invested in developing formal ontologies within paradigms is likely to force researchers to be more precise in their thinking and to clarify ambiguities. Making that explicit representation of knowledge widely available will encourage greater scrutiny both from within the paradigm and from outside, and may enhance scientific progress. Being able to state competing theoretical perspectives precisely enough for automation opens up the possibility of applying those competing perspectives to the same data to test their relative merits in an objective manner. The transparency afforded by these automated methods provides a level of accountability and replicability for research that cannot be matched when human researchers are making judgments. Other researchers can examine the processes and the results, and if problems are found it is economically viable to redo the research.

The ability of the AI/ES approach to process massive amounts of data quickly and inexpensively means that for the first time in a very long time, researchers might actually be able to keep up with the deluge of data and information being produced all around them. Imagine not just scanning articles in literature reviews and hoping you caught the most important publications, but being able to systematically scan the literature and even have fresh daily updates. If successful and widely used, the AI/ES approach could help researchers manage and make sense of far more information than ever before. This makes it possible to study problems that would have been intractable using traditional research procedures. Being able to do this on an ongoing basis offers possible benefits for managing real-world processes that are at the heart of many of these data flows. This has already been seen in the areas of essay grading and international event data analysis. Today, such programs permit the use of more writing in large classes where student essays can be graded economically, and international events to be analyzed more often and more quickly. One day it may be possible to use these procedures for real-time analysis to shape foreign policy, review proposals, grade student papers, track the literature, study organizational processes, and so on.

The programs required for the AI/ES approach capable of using NLU and machine learning strategies to automatically code massive amounts of data, the knowledge structures developed for specific substantive domains, and the huge sets of processed data they generate provide a valuable research infrastructure that should be cumulative within paradigms and can be widely shared among researchers. KEDS provides an example of such an infrastructure whose programs and datasets have provided a valuable resource for a large number of political scientists. These resources can be shared among researchers and can be re-purposed for still other applications, many of which we cannot yet anticipate. They should make excellent teaching tools to help students learn about the substantive topic, the theoretical perspective, and the process of research. They should also be useful for real-world applications such as policy making and management. The development of new programs using NLU strategies to automatically code a wide range of data, the generation of very large datasets for shared use by researchers, the establishment of ongoing real-time monitoring and analysis for social research in specific domains, and studies of the impact of these tools on research are all important areas begging for further research.

SUGGESTED WEBSITES AND RELEVANT SOFTWARE

Websites

CAMEO Coding Scheme: www.eventdata. parusanalytics.com/data.dir/cameo.html (accessed 21 October 2015)

XML: www.w3.org/XML/Schema (accessed 21 October 2015)

Data Documentation Inititative: www. ddialliance.org/dtd/index.html (accessed 21 October 2015)

Upper level semantic network (Cycorp): www. cyc.com/ (accessed 21 October 2015)

OWL, Web Ontology Language: www.w3.org/ TR/owl-features (accessed 21 October 2015)

Kansas Event Data System project (KEDS): http://web.ku.edu/keds (accessed 21 October 2015)

Reuters news feed: www.reuters.com/news/ international (accessed 21 October 2015)

ICEWS: www.lockheedmartin.com/us/products/ W-ICEWS.html (accessed 21 October 2015)

TABARI: www.eventdata.parusanalytics.com/ software.dir/tabari.html (accessed 21 October 2015)

WEIS Coding Scheme: www.eventdata. parusanalytics.com/data.dir/weis.html (accessed 21 October 2015)

Inter-University Consortium for Political and Social Research (ICPSR): www.icpsr.umich. edu (accessed 21 October 2015)

ESDS Qualidata: www.esds.ac.uk/qualidata/ about/advisory.asp (accessed 21 October 2015)

NSF Digital Library Initiative: www.dli2.nsf.gov/ glossary.html#D (accessed 21 October 2015)

Journal of Artificial Societies and Social Simulation (JASS): http://jasss.soc.surrey. ac.uk/7/4/1.html (accessed 21 October 2015)

American Association for Artificial Intelligence: www.aai.org (accessed 21 October 2015)

OpenCyc: www.opencyc.org (accessed 21 October 2015)

CRESS, Center for Research in Social Simulation: www.cress.soc.surrey.ac.uk/ (accessed 21 October 2015)

Software

Qualitative Analysis programs

Qualrus: www.qualrus.com (accessed 21 October 2015)

Atlas.ti: www.atlasti.com/ (accessed 21 October 2015)

Dedoose: www.dedoose.com/ (accessed 21 October 2015)

NVivo: www.qsrinternational.com/products_ nvivo.aspx (accessed 21 October 2015)

Essay grading programs
SAGrader: www.sagrader.com (accessed 21
October 2015)
E-rater and C-rater: www.ets.org/research/
erater.html (accessed 21 October 2015)
Intelligent Essay Assessor: www.pearsonkt.
com/prodIEA.shtml (accessed 21 October
2015)
Speech recognition software: Dragon
NaturallySpeaking®
Optical character recognition (OCR) software:
ABBYY FineReader®

REFERENCES

Anderson, James A. (1995) *An Introduction to Neural Networks.* Boston, MA: MIT Press.

Atkisson, Curtis, Monaghan, Colin, and Brent, Edward (2010) 'Using computational techniques to fill the gap between qualitative data analysis and text analytics', KWALON, 45: 6–19.

Azar, Edward E. (1982) *The Codebook of the Conflict and Peace Data Bank (COPDAB).* College Park, MD: Center for International Development, University of Maryland.

Baader, Franz, Calvanese, Deborah, McGuinness, Daniele, Nardi, D., and Patel-Schneider, Peter F. (eds.) (2003) *The Description Logic Handbook.* Cambridge: Cambridge University Press.

Baumgartner, Frank R. and McCarthy, John (2007) 'New computer science applications in automated text identification and classification for the social sciences'. A Workshop at Penn State University, August 15–17.

Bayley, Liz and Eldredge, Jonathan (2003) 'The structured abstract: an essential tool for researchers', *Hypothesis,* 17 (1): 1, 11–13.

Berners-Lee, Tim, Hendler, James, and Lassila, Ora (2001) 'The semantic web', *Scientific American*, May.

Blei, David M. and Lafferty, John D. (2006) 'Dynamic topic models'. Proceedings of the 23rd International Conference on Machine Learning, Pittsburgh. pp. 113–20.

Brent, Edward and Townsend, Martha (2007) 'Automated essay grading in the sociology classroom: finding common ground'.

In Patricia Frietag Ericsson and Richard Haswell (eds.), *Machine Scoring of Student Essays: Truth or Consequences?* Boulder, CO: Utah State University Press, chapter 10.

Brent, Edward, Carnahan, Theodore, and McCully, Jeff (2006) 'Students improve learning by 20 percentage points with essay grading program'. Available at www.ideaworks.com/sagrader/whitepapers/improves_learning.html (accessed 17 July 2016).

Carley, Kathleen (1993) 'Coding choices for textual analysis: a comparison of content analysis and map analysis', *Sociological Methodology*, 23: 75–126.

Carley, Kathleen (2009) 'Computational modeling for reasoning about the social behavior of humans', *Computational and Mathematical Organization Theory,* 15: 47–59.

Cohn, David (2006) 'AI reaches the golden years,' *Wired News*, July 17. Available at http://archive.wired.com/science/discoveries/news/2006/07/71389 (accessed 17 July 2016).

Cole, Robert, Mariani, Joseph, Uszkoreit, Hans, Battista Varile, Giovanni, Zanen, Annie, Zampolli, Antonio, and Zue, Victor (eds.) (1997) *Survey of the State of the Art in Human Language Technology.* Cambridge, UK: Cambridge University Press.

Cunningham, Hamish, Maynard, Diana, and Bontcheva, Kalina (2011) *Text processing with GATE (Version 6).* University of Sheffield Department of Computer Science. 15 April 2011. ISBN 0956599311. Available from Amazon. BibTex. https://www.amazon.com/Text-Processing-GATE-Version-6/dp/0956599311/ref=sr_1_fkmr2_3?s=books&ie=UTF8&qid=1468850158&sr=1-3-fkmr2&keywords=Cunningham%2C+et+al.+%282011%29+Text+processing+with+GATE+ISBN+0956599311 (accessed 17 July 2016).

Deane, Paul (2006) 'Strategies for evidence identification through linguistic assessment of textual responses'. In David M. Williamson, Robert J. Mislevy and Isaac I. Bejar (eds.), *Automated Scoring of Complex Tasks in Computer-Based Testing.* Mahwah, NJ: Lawrence Erlbaum Associates, chapter 9.

Dikli, Semire (2010) 'The nature of automated essay scoring feedback', *CALICO Journal*, 28 (1): 99–134.

ARTIFICIAL INTELLIGENCE/EXPERT SYSTEMS AND ONLINE RESEARCH

377

Drigs, A., Kouremenos, S., Vrettos, S., and Kouremenos, D. (2004) 'An expert system for job matching of the unemployed', Expert Systems with Applications, 26: 217–24.

Edelman, Marc (2004) 'When networks don't work: the rise and fall of civil society initiatives in Central America'. In June Nash (ed.) Social Movements: An Anthropological Reader. Oxford, UK: Blackwell, pp. 29–45.

El-Nawawy, Mohammed (2004) 'Terrorist or freedom fighter? The Arab media coverage of "terrorism" or "so-called terrorism"', Global Media Journal, 3 (5).

Filis, Ioannis, V., Sabrakos, M., Yialouris, Constantine, P., Sideridis, A. B., and Mahaman, Bader Dioula (2003) GEDAS: an integrated geographical expert database system', Expert Systems with Applications, 24: 25–34.

Gaines, Brian R. (2013) 'Knowledge acquisition: past, present and future', International Journal of Human–Computer Studies, 71: 135–56.

Garfield, Eugene (1979) Citation Indexing: Its Theory and Application in Science, Technology and Humanities. New York, NY: John Wiley & Sons.

Gerner, Deborah J., Schrodt, Philip A., Yilmaz, Omur, and Abu-Jabr, Rajaa (2002) 'Conflict and Mediation Event Observations (CAMEO): a new event data framework for a post Cold War world'. Presented at the 2002 Annual Meeting of the American Political Science Association, New Orleans, March, 2002.

Giarratano, Joseph C. and Riley, Gary (2005) Expert Systems, Principles and Programming. Boston, MA: Brooks/Cole.

Giorgetti, Daniela, Prodanof, Irina, and Sebastiani, Fabrizio (2002) 'Mapping an automated survey coding task into a probabilistic text categorization framework'. In Elisabete Ranchod and Nuno J. Mamede (eds.), Advances in Natural Language Processing. Heidelberg: Springer Verlag, pp. 115–124.

Glaser, Barney and Strauss, Anselm (1967) The Discovery of Grounded Theory. Chicago, IL: AldineTransaction..

Grimes, Douglas and Warschauer, Mark (2010) 'Utility in a fallible tool. A multi-site case study of automated writing evaluation', Journal of Technology, Learning, and Assessment, 8 (6).

Grove, Ralph (2000) 'Internet-based expert systems', Expert Systems, 17 (3): 129–35.

Gruber, Tom (2007) 'Ontology of folksonomy: a mash-up of apples and oranges', International Journal on Semantic Web & Information Systems, 3(2). Available at http://tomgruber.org/writing/ontology-of-folksonomy.htm (accessed 17 July 2016).

Hage, Jerald and Powers, Charles H. (1992) Post-Industrial Lives: Roles and Relationships in the 21st Century. Newbury Park, CA: Sage Publications.

Hand, David, Mannila, Heikki, and Smyth, Padhraic (2001) Principles of Data Mining. Cambridge, MA: MIT Press.

Harris, Derrick (2015) 'Google: our new system for recognizing faces is the best one ever', Fortune, March 17. Available at http://fortune.com/2015/03/17/google-facenet-artificial-intelligence/ (accessed 19 July 2016).

Hayes-Roth, Frederick, Waterman, Donald, and Lenat, Douglas (1983) Building Expert Systems. Boston, MA: Addison-Wesley.

Holland, John H. (1975) Adaptation in Natural and Artificial Systems. Ann Arbor, MI: University of Michigan Press.

Kas, Miray, Carley, Kathleen M., and Carley, L. Richard (2012) 'Trends in science networks: understanding structures and statistics of scientific networks', Social Network Analysis and Mining, 2 (2): 169–87.

King, Gary and Lowe, Will (2004) 'An automated information extraction tool for international conflict data with performance as good as human coders: a rare events evaluation design', International Organization, 57 (3): 617–42.

Landauer, Thomas K., Laham, Darrell, and Foltz, Peter W. (2003) 'Automated scoring and annotation of essays with the Intelligent Essay Assessor'. In Mark D. Shermis and Jill C. Burstein (eds.), Automated Essay Scoring: A Cross-Disciplinary Perspective. Mahwah, NJ: Lawrence Erlbaum Associates, pp. 87–112.

Leng, Russell J. (1987) Behavioral Correlates of War, 1816–1975. Ann Arbor, MI: ICPSR Inter-University Consortium for Political and Social Research.

Liao, Shu-Hsien (2005) 'Expert system methodologies and applications – a decade review from 1995 to 2004', Expert Systems with Applications, 28: 93–103.

Luckerson, Victor (2015) 'This Google app will soon automatically translate foreign languages', *Time*, January 12. Available at http://time.com/3663628/google-instant-translation-skype/ (accessed 19 July 2016).

McCarthy, John, Minsky, Marvin L., Rochester, Nathaniel, and Shannon, Claude E. (1955) 'Proposal for Dartmouth Summer Research Project on Artificial Intelligence'. Available at: http://www-formal.stanford.edu/jmc/history/dartmouth.html (California).

McClelland, Charles A. (1976) *World Event/Interaction Survey Codebook* (ICPSR 5211). Ann Arbor, MI: Inter-University Consortium for Political and Social Research.

McCully, Jeffrey (2005) 'An analysis of public service anti-drug advertisements'. Masters thesis. University of Missouri, Columbia, MO.

Mitchell, Melanie (1996) *An Introduction to Genetic Algorithms.* Cambridge, MA: MIT Press.

Moon, Il-Chul and Carley, Kathleen (2007) 'Modeling and simulating terrorist networks in social and geospatial dimensions'. *IEEE Intelligent Systems,* 22(5): 40–49.

Mooney, Raymond J., Melville, Prem, Tang, Lappoon R., Shavlik, Jude, de Castro Dutra, Inês, Page, David, and Costa, Vítor S. (2004) 'Relational data mining with inductive logic programming for link discovery.' In *Data Mining: Next Generation Challenges and Future Directions*. California: AAI Press. pp. 1–14.

Morstatter, Fred, Pfeffer, Jürgen, Liu, Huan, and Carley, Kathleen M. (2013) 'Is the sample good enough? Comparing data from Twitter's streaming API with Twitter's Firehose'. Scheduled in the 2013 proceedings of International AAAI Conference on Weblogs and Social Media (ICWSM), Boston, MA, July 8–11.

Motta, Enrico (2006) 'Knowledge publishing and access on the semantic web: a sociotechnological analysis', *IEEE Intelligent Systems*, 88–90.

Newell, Allen., Shaw, J.C. and Simon, Herbert A. (1959) 'Report on a general problem-solving program'. Proceedings of the International Conference on Information Processing, RAND Corporation, Santa Monica, CA, pp. 256–264.

Newman, David, Chemudugunta, Caitanya, and Smyth, Padhraic (2006) 'Statistical entity-topic models'. Proceedings of the 12th ACM SIGKDD International Conference on Knowledge Discovery and Data Mining, Philadelphia, August 20–23, pp. 680–686.

O'Hara, Kieron (2004) 'Ontologies and technologies: knowledge representation or misrepresentation', *SIGIR Forum*, 38 (2). Available at http://sigir.org/files/forum/2004D/ohara_sigirforum_2004d.pdf (accessed 17 July 2016).

Purpura, Stephen and Hillard, Dustin (2006) 'Automated classification of congressional legislation'. Proceedings of the National Conference on Digital Government (dg.o.2006). May 21–24, San Diego, CA., pp. 219–225.

Quillian, M. Ross. (1966) *Semantic Memory.* Cambridge: Bolt, Beranek & Newman.

Quinn, Kevin M., Monroe, Burt L., Colaresi, Michael, Crespin, Michael H., and Radev, Dragomir R. (2006) 'An automated method of topic-coding legislative speech over time with application to the 105th–108th US Senate'. Paper presented to the Society for Political Methodology, University of California, Davis, CA, July 20–22.

Reed, David (2010) 'Making sense of online chatter', *Columbia Business Times*, July 23. Available at http://columbiabusinesstimes.com/8490/2010/07/23/making-sense-of-online-chatter/ (accessed 19 July 2016).

Schreiber, Craig and Carley, Kathleen (2004) 'Going beyond the data: empirical validation leading to grounded theory'. Research Showcase @ CMU. Carnegie Mellon University, Pittsburgh, PA, Institute for Software Research School of Computer Science.

Schreiber, Craig and Carley, Kathleen N. (2013) 'Validating agent interactions in construct against empirical communication networks using the calibrated grounding technique', *IEEE Transactions on Systems, Man, and Cybernetics: Systems*, 43 (1).

Schrodt, Philip A. (2011) 'Automated production of high-volume, near-real-time political event data'. Paper presented at the New Methodologies and Their Applications in Comparative Politics and International Relations Workshop, Princeton University, NJ, February 4–5.

Schrodt, Philip A. and Gerner, Deborah J. (2001) *Analyzing International Event Data.* Available at http://web.ku.edu/keds/papers.

dir/automated.html (accessed 21 October 2015).

Schrodt, Philip A., Davis, Shannon G., and Weddle, Judith L. (1994) 'Political science: KEDS – a program for the machine coding of event data', *Social Science Computer Review*, 12 (4): 561–87.

Shirky, Clay (2005) 'Ontology is overrated: categories, links and tags'. Available at www.shirky.com/writings/ontology_overrated.html (accessed 17 July 2016).

Shulman, Stuart, Hovy, Eduard, Callan, Jamie, and Zavestoski, Stephen (2006) 'Progress in language processing technology for electronic rulemaking (research highlight)'. Proceedings of the Sixth National Conference on Digital Government Research, May 16–18, San Diego, CA, pp. 249–50.

Teufel, Simone and Moens, Marc (2002) 'Summarizing scientific articles: experiments with relevance and rhetorical status', *Computational Linguistics*, 28 (4): 409–45.

Uday, Kumar M., Mamatha, J., Jain, Sandesh, Jain, and Dhanander K. (2011) 'Intelligent Online Assessment Methodology'. 2011 7th International Conference on Next Generation Web Services Practices, Salamanca, Spain, October 19–21.

Weiss, Gerhard (ed.) (1999) *Multiagent Systems, A Modern Approach to Distributed Artificial Intelligence*. Cambridge, MA: MIT Press.

Williamson, David M., Mislevy, Robert J., and Bejar, Isaac I. (2006). *Automated Scoring of Complex Tasks in Computer-Based Testing*. Mahway, NJ: Lawrence Erlbaum Associates.

## 22

The Blogosphere

Nicholas Hookway and Helene Snee

INTRODUCTION

Since the late-2000s blog analysis has developed from a novel to increasingly adopted research method. Blogs are a user-generated form of web content, where Internet users both produce and consume content at the same time as communicating and interacting with each other. Evan Williams, co-creator of popular blogging program Blogger, argues that the defining features of blogs are 'frequency, brevity and personality' (Turnbull, 2002). Like other Web 2.0 applications, blogs reflect a wider shift in late-modern 'confessional society' where people curate and reflect upon their personal lives in the public realm (Beer, 2008). For Bauman, the confessional society is defined as one which is 'notorious for effacing the boundary which once separated the private from the public' (Bauman, 2007: 2). Personal blogs are the quintessential early twenty-first century new media, generating data with this confessional quality that is simultaneously private and public.

In the chapter, we consider blogs as contemporary 'documents of life'. We should state at this point that there is a range of other methods that use blogs as data. Blog analysis may take a quantitative approach, for example content analysis (Chapter 19) and network analysis (Chapters 14, 15); also see Thelwall (2014). Within qualitative traditions, researchers may want to take an approach aligned with virtual ethnography (Chapters 23–27; Hine, 2015). Moreover, blogs offer researchers reflexive opportunities as a research diary (Wakeford and Cohen, 2008) as well as the possibility to engage with wider audiences within and beyond the academy as part of a trend towards public social science (Lupton, 2014; Wade and Sharp, 2013). Here, we reflect on our own experiences of the blogosphere and projects based on qualitative thematic analysis of these new forms of personal documents.

Drawing on our own research on gap years (Snee) and everyday moralities (Hookway), we argue that blogs offer rich first-person textual accounts of everyday life. Blogs offer spontaneous narratives produced in the course of everyday life unprovoked by a researcher. Although blogs are spontaneous – not produced in interaction with a researcher – they are, like other public texts, shaped and tailored to an imagined audience. Accordingly, we treat blogs as representations of experience rather than objective or 'truthful' accounts. We consider the practical, methodological and ethical issues involved in doing blog research, including sampling, collecting and analysing blog data; issues of representation and authenticity; whether blogs should be considered private or public, and if the people who create them are subjects or authors. We also critically reflect on the methodological and ethical implications of the different decisions we made in our own research projects. We conclude that embracing new confessional technologies like blogs can provide a powerful way to capture everyday life and can make a modest contribution to developing new empirical repertoires in sociology (Savage and Burrows, 2007: 895).

BLOGS AS CONTEMPORARY 'DOCUMENTS OF LIFE'

Blogs are a contemporary 'document of life' (Plummer, 2001). Such artefacts are 'expressions of personal life' (Plummer, 2001: 17), and include diaries, letters, biographies, self-observation, personal notes, photographs and films. The use of personal documents in social science research has an established history and can be traced to the pioneering work of Chicago School sociologists Thomas and Znaniecki (1918/1958), who claimed they were 'the perfect type of sociological material' (Thomas and Znaniecki 1918/1958: 1832–3). More recently, Ferrarotti (2003: 25) argues that 'read[ing] a society through a biography' enables researchers to unpack the 'explosive subjectivity' of the social world as it is experienced from the position of the

individual within the concrete category of the everyday. For both of our projects, blogs promised a new type of 'document of life' that enabled access to first person and spontaneous narratives of experience and action.

In the years since the advent of Web 2.0, researchers have gained increased access to these insights into biographical experience and subjective understandings of the world through vast 'archives of everyday life' (Beer and Burrows, 2007) generated through social media. In this context, blogs share similarities with diaries, and blog analysis is an analogous method to diary research. Like diaries, blogs are personal documents produced in real time, with no precise addressee (Ariosio, 2010). As such, blog researchers may take inspiration from 'offline' diary research. Plummer (2001: 49) suggests that 'diaries may be one of the better tools for getting at the day-to-day experiences of a personal life'. Through diary research, social actors can be understood as both observers and informants (Toms and Duff, 2002: 1233).

These personal documents may be either unsolicited or solicited by a researcher; however, both forms of diaries present challenges. In the case of unsolicited diaries (those spontaneously maintained without the researcher's involvement), it can be difficult to both identify suitable participants and ensure content meets the aims of the research. Solicited diaries, which are written for purposes of a research project, may overcome these issues but then pose additional problems in finding participants willing to create and maintain a diary over a period of time.

Blogs, on the other hand, have the spontaneity of naturally occurring diaries, while being easier to find and access than unsolicited personal documents. The narratives found in personal blogs are spontaneous in the sense that they are documents produced by people 'carrying out their activities … without any link with research goals or aims' (Arosio, 2010: 25). There are also important differences between blogs and diaries, with often implicit, if not explicit audiences for blogs (Hookway, 2008: 96). In this way, blogs are similar to other types of public text, shaped by imagined audiences as bloggers choose, select and even inflate what they believe to be important to record and communicate. Moreover, if these are public blogs, they are visible to anyone with Internet access, and are interactive (Arosio, 2010: 31). These differences pose particular practical, methodological and ethical issues for blog researchers, which we consider in later sections; however, blogs also offer a number of advantages compared to diary research and other types of qualitative data.

Uses of Blogs: Why do Blog Analysis?

It is difficult to outline the 'typical' blog. Even in the gap year study, which sampled a relatively homogeneous group of bloggers in terms of age and background, there was considerable variety in length of post, frequency of posting, range of multimedia elements, if they blogged before and after the period of the gap year itself – and even whether they wrote a full account of their time overseas. What they did offer, and which was the main focus of the study, was the use of the blog medium to provide a record and narrative of a particular experience. Blogs are a practically and methodological attractive research method for social researchers wanting to capture first-person accounts of everyday life. They offer an unobtrusive method that provides unsolicited narratives unadulterated by the scrutiny of a researcher. One of the key advantages of blog analysis is that the narratives found in personal blogs are spontaneous, and offer something different to those that would be available through interaction with a researcher. Blogs give access to intensely personal and candid accounts of everyday life that reflect what is important to the blogger without the prompting of a researcher. Further, blogs capture situated understandings and experiences, converging

traditional self-reflective forms of data like diaries, letters, biography, self-observation, personal notes, images, photographs and video, into a multimedia and interactive archive of everyday life.

Blogs can help avoid some problems associated with collecting sensitive information via interview or focus-group methods (Elliot, 1997). Like 'offline' diaries, blogs capture an 'ever-changing present' (Elliot, 1997: 3), where there is a tight union between everyday experience and the record of that experience (Toms and Duff, 2002). This proximity between event and record means that blogs are less susceptible to problems of retrospective recall and reconstruction than interviews and focus groups, which might be important if the goal of the research is to capture external 'truth' (Verbrugge, 1980).

As we noted in the introduction, blogs can have a 'confessional' quality, making them particularly appealing to qualitative researchers interested in providing rich and detailed first-person accounts of everyday practices and experiences. If blogs are anonymous or relatively unidentifiable, blogging can have a revelatory or confessional feel, where a less polished and even 'uglier' self can be expressed. Blogs can take a researcher 'back-stage' (Goffman, 1959) in a way that traditional qualitative techniques like interviews or focus-groups may not, giving access to a less-perfect, less managed and potentially more honest account of self and experience. One can express one's faults, one's mishaps – whatever might be difficult to tell as we 'enter the presence of others' (Goffman, 1959:1). As one blogger reflected in Hookway's study: 'the point of my blog is to have a space in my life where I can be anonymous and express the "real" me, however confronting or ugly that might be' (28-year-old male, *LiveJournal*, 2009).

Blogs are also pre-existing text which bypasses the resource intensiveness of tape recorders and transcription (Liamputtong and Ezzy, 2005: 232). They can also give researchers access to populations geographically or socially removed from the researcher (Hessler *et al.*, Mann and Stewart, 2000; 2003). Their global nature means they are well positioned for conducting comparative research, and may have empirical applications for contemporary discussions of globalisation (Hookway, 2008). For example, researchers could conduct global comparisons of an infinite range of behaviours from approaches to weight loss to understandings of celebrity culture. Blogs can also be a useful tool to analyse everyday responses to global events from wars and terrorism to mega sporting events. Moreover, the archived nature of blogs makes them amenable to examining social processes over time, meaning they can be useful for conducting longitudinal forms of research. These qualities of practicality and capacity to shed light on social and psychological processes across space and time, together with their insight into everyday life, combine to make blogs a valid addition to the qualitative researcher's toolkit.

There are two broad types of research questions that blog data are appropriate for:

1 Projects focused on analysing blogs and blogging as a phenomenon and how the medium itself is implicated in a range of communication practices and behaviours; and
2 Projects focused on using blogs to examine representations of wider social practices and everyday life.

The first type of research question typically involves projects that investigate the qualities and characteristics of blogging and their uses and implications across broad areas of social life from identity and community building, education, health and travel, to commerce, business and marketing. For example, Hodkinson (2007) investigated the symbolic and practical significance of online journals for young people; Sanford (2010) explored weight-loss blogs as a support tool for people diagnosed as 'morbidly obese'; and Sharman (2014) analysed blogs as a source of contestation to mainstream climate science.

The second type of research question is more interested in using blogs to elicit data on social phenomena beyond blogging itself, approaching bloggers as both observers and informants of everyday life (Toms and Duff, 2002). Our use of blogs to investigate everyday moralities and gap-year travel are examples of this type of blog analysis. Other examples are blogs being used to analyse health and illness (Clarke and van Amerom, 2008), weight loss (Leggatt-Cook and Chamberlain, 2012), global sporting events (Dart, 2009), cosmopolitanism, travel and tourism (Enoch and Grossman, 2010) and bereavement and religion (Bakker and Paris, 2013). In both our projects, accessing experiences through blogs made it possible to examine participants' own frameworks of understanding and their own language, reflections and stories that predated the interests of a researcher. The following section provides some more detail on our respective blog projects.

The Everyday Morality and Gap-Year Case Studies

Hookway's research explored everyday Australian moralities: the sources, strategies and experiences of modern moral decision-making. The study focused on everyday moral worlds, something that is difficult to explore using traditional qualitative methods such as interviews that ask people *directly* about their moral beliefs (Phillips and Harding, 1985). Hookway felt it was hard to contextualise such a topic so that it was meaningful for the participant, and he was concerned that it could also result in people attempting to present themselves in a specific moral light, abstracted from the way that morality is grounded in their day-to-day lives. Consequently, in addition to the general advantages outlined earlier, blogs offered Hookway an alternative way to 'get at' spontaneous accounts of everyday morality. The study was based upon 44 Australian blogs sampled from the hosting website Livejournal, along with 25 online interviews. Hookway found that morality was depicted by the bloggers as an actively created and autonomous do-it-yourself project and suggested that self, body, emotions and authenticity may play an important role in contemporary moralities.

Snee's study into overseas 'gap years' by British youth was driven by a similar concern with how experiences are understood and represented. Gap years – a period of 'time out' overseas at transitional moments – are now a well-established activity, particularly for young people before starting higher education. Snee's interest was in representations of cultural difference, the drawing of distinctions of taste, and the implications for identity work for this potentially cosmopolitan activity. The study drew on the concept of 'frames' (Goffman, 1974) to consider how bloggers understand their gap years and make them meaningful for audiences. Blog analysis allowed Snee to consider what young people themselves considered important to share about their gap years. Thirty-nine blogs written by 'gappers' to document their journeys were sampled, which were supplemented with nine interviews. Her findings suggest that gap years tend to follow fairly standard 'scripts' and reproduce ideas about value and worth that question the status of the gap year as a progressive, cosmopolitan enterprise.

THE PROCESS OF BLOG RESEARCH

There are four basic steps to doing blog research. Here we outline these steps and illustrate the process, drawing on the previous case studies and highlighting the pros and cons of different strategies. First, however, we provide a brief overview of the technical and practical aspects of blogs.

Technical and Practical Aspects

There is a range of blog platforms available. The blog landscape is dynamic, with new platforms and technologies constantly entering and evolving. Popular platforms are Blogger, WordPress, Tumblr, LiveJournal, Medium and Weebly. Blogger and LiveJournal are 'blogging veterans', having existed since 1999 while Tumblr and Medium are examples of newer offerings. Blog search engines are also subject to flux. For example, two of the search engines – Google Blog Search[1] and Technorati – used on the Gap Year project are now defunct. There are two main ways to search for blogs: using an Internet-wide search engine such as BlogSearchEngine.org or Ice Rocket Blog Search or a specific blog platform search engine such as those provided by LiveJournal and WordPress.

Different blog platforms are orientated toward different purposes. For example, Tumblr is geared toward short-form blogging, typically around re-posting web content, while Blogger and WordPress are orientated toward long-format blogging. Most blog platforms require sign-up through an email or social media account (e.g. Facebook or Twitter) and establishment of one's own blog profile. Blog platforms are typically free to sign-up to, but have paid options that enhance functionality, such as customisation and advanced search functions. Most of the search tools on blog platforms are limited to keyword searches. A paid LiveJournal account provides access to LiveJournal's advanced search options, which enables searching by age and location. Some blog platforms do not have search engines (e.g. Blogger) but you can search through interests established on a blog profile page or doing a Google search within a blog website.[2] Most blog content is publicly available and searchable through search engines, but platforms such as Blogger, Wordpress and LiveJournal have features that allow bloggers to keep their posts private or to restrict visibility.

Selection Criteria

The first stage of the process is to *develop selection criteria*. As with other forms of qualitative research, this can be understood using the principle of a theoretical sampling frame: 'which is meaningful theoretically, because it builds in certain characteristics or criteria which help to develop and test [the] theory or explanation' (Mason, 2002: 94). In the gap year study, for example, the subjects of interest were blogs written by young people who framed their period of time out overseas between school and university as a 'gap year', and to also explore different types of gap years to consider issues of status and value in gap year experiences. The search parameters to be used and guidelines for data collection thus need to be established at this stage. Snee developed her theoretical sampling frame alongside the following criteria for inclusion: if it was clear that the author was from the UK and took their year out overseas; if it was clear that they had taken their gap year between school and university; and if they were of sufficient length to provide enough data (e.g. they did not consist of a solitary post). Similarly, Hookway's selection criteria were 'diary-style' blogs that contained *at least* two posts which reflected on issues of everyday morality and were written by urban Australian bloggers. Hookway sampled blogs written by those over the age of 18 that were socially and culturally diverse. Establishing these selection criteria meant that the blogs collected using the methods detailed next could be scanned and then included or discarded from the sample.

Collecting Data

Second, the blog researcher needs to collect blog data by *'searching'*, *'trawling'* or *'solicitation'*. *Searching* employs the use of search engines (including those provided by specific blog platforms like Livejournal) to find posts containing a particular word or phrase. For example, the gap year study employed two (now defunct) Internet-wide blog search engines (Google Blog Search and Technorati), alongside the search facilities on three specific blog platforms (Myspace, LiveJournal and Globenotes) to search for blogs containing the phrase 'gap year'. *Trawling* also utilises platform search facilities but in a slightly different way. This method involves searching for a group of bloggers who meet particular characteristics and then using the selection criteria to identify suitable posts to include within the sample. Hookway employed this technique in the everyday morality project to first search for bloggers within specific age ranges and locations, and then read the blogs returned in the search results for posts that reflected on everyday moral decision-making. *Solicitation* seeks to recruit bloggers to become involved in the research and consequently is a more active/interactive form of collection. This method was also used in the everyday morality project by advertising on LiveJournal community pages.

Deciding which of these three data collection methods is appropriate should be considered in relation to the theoretical sampling frame, along with the limitations of each technique. The gap year study focused on the framing of experiences (and the meanings attached), and so identifying blogs that used the specific phrase 'gap year' was key. However, searching in this way generated a considerable number of results, the vast majority of which were not relevant. This was because they were blogs that discussed gap years, but were not written by a gapper; they were spam blogs[3] (Li and Walejko, 2008); or they did not meet the selection criteria. A total of 700 blogs were inspected and recorded during this phase of the research, and it is vital for blog researchers to stay organised if they take this approach. The searching process continued until a final sample of 39 was constructed. Blog searches are most suitable if there is a specific topic or focus for the data required, but this can be a laborious process that involves sifting through unsuitable results.

Hookway employed a mixture of blog trawling and blog solicitation in the everyday moralities project. This was focused on the LiveJournal blogging platform, singled out for its interface, search capabilities, Australian market share and predominantly diary-style blogs. The trawling phases used the advanced search functions of LiveJournal to find blogs by age and location (which required becoming a paid member) and then manually examining the results for references to morality or incidences of moral decision-making. However, trawling results in similar issues to searching, returning a considerable number of blogs which might meet the profile required, but which then have to be read to check they fit the topic of study. Moreover, these searches can still be limited because even the advanced features of LiveJournal do not search by gender or ethnicity, and so Hookway's sampling had to be done manually. A more productive strategy was to actively recruit by posting a research invite in 55 LiveJournal communities, with the consent of the community moderators. This blog solicitation resulted in more relevant data being collected because those who were interested in taking part in the research could then contact Hookway and direct him to specific posts on moral issues. This approach has the benefits of identification and relevance associated with solicited 'offline' diary research, but avoids many of the problems because these blogs are not created and maintained at the request of a researcher. The downside of this approach, however, is that it results in a self-selecting sample, potentially compounding the limitations of researching blog populations, which is explored later.

Online Presence

The third stage is an optional one, but recommended. Both Hookway and Snee interviewed a subsample of their bloggers. After constructing the sample, Snee contacted all of the bloggers via contact details on their blogs, or their blog comments if no details

were available. She successfully completed just nine face-to-face interviews, with no responses from many. Hookway, on the other hand, was able to do 25 online interviews with bloggers. Part of this is down to the data collection method employed because utilising blog solicitation and flagging a potential interview in the research invite meant that those who sent links to their blogs were already interested in participating in the study. A key element in this successful recruitment was establishing an *online presence*: a research website and Hookway's own LiveJournal research blog. As well as some practical benefits such as communicating with the bloggers, providing information sheets and consent forms, and disseminating the research, having an online presence helps to reassure potential participants that both the study and the researcher are legitimate. Moreover, by setting up a blog on the same platform, Hookway entered into a more interactive 'give and take' relationship with the bloggers.

Preparing Data for Analysis

Once the sample is finalised, the next stage in the process is to determine how to manage the data for analysis. Snee manually saved each blog post as a text file and then created a single file for each individual blog that could be imported into the Computer Aided Qualitative Analysis Software (CAQDAS) Atlas.ti. It is worth pointing out that this was primarily a pragmatic decision based on the researcher's technical skills and knowledge. At the time of the study, CAQDAS was limited in how it could deal with online data, and so this part of the analysis focused on written text only. More recent versions of NVivo, for example, allow for whole webpages and multimedia elements to be imported and coded (see Chapter 27).

However, the use of CAQDAS has been subject to some debate in qualitative research. Hookway's view was that CAQDAS was unsuitable for his data in the everyday moralities project due to the fractured and unstructured nature of the research topic and concerns that it would have lost the contextual richness of the blog narratives and 'thinned' the data as fragmented codes (Ezzy, 2000: 118). This was also a concern for the gap year project, and more generally for any studies concerned with exploring narratives in these 'documents of life'. However, the research was based on an 'analysis of narratives', which aims to identify general themes and concepts in narrative accounts (Polkinghorne, 1995), rather than narrative analysis (see the following section). Not all studies will be suited to CAQDAS, but to mitigate some of the potential limitations it is advisable for blog researchers to maintain a sensitivity to the overall story by reading each blog *in situ* and writing summaries. Whether CAQDAS is appropriate depends on the methods of analysis and the methodological grounding of the research.

BLOG ANALYSIS

Although most blog analysis is focused on text, some researchers have investigated the visual aspects. For example, Scheidt and Wright (2004) explored visual trends in blogs, and Badger (2004) investigated how images and illustration shape the construction and reception of blogs. The visual aspects of blogs – photos, videos, images – provide researchers with a wider 'bandwidth' in which to capture identity and experience outside of text. Visual content also works to connect the researcher to the blogger. However, researchers need to consider whether non-textual elements such as image, video and music are integral to the goals of the project and how these dimensions are to be best incorporated into the analysis. There is a need to balance the potential of blog data and what is methodologically interesting with pragmatic concerns (Snee, 2012: 183). It is easy to get excited about the visual

elements of blogs but in practice analysing non-textual content can be difficult and time-consuming.

In terms of analysing text, conventional qualitative methods of text-analysis like narrative analysis, discourse analysis, content analysis and thematic analysis are all suitable for analysing blog data. The focus of narrative inquiry, for example, is how participants use stories to interpret their biographical experience, create meaning and construct identity (Riessman, 1993). The chronological sequencing of biographical experience that defines blogging – each blog post adds to a sequential account of self and experience – makes blogging practices amenable to different modes of narrative inquiry. An example of the application of narrative analysis to blogs is Tussyadiah and Fesenmaier (2008: 303) who analysed blog travel stories according to story characterisation (e.g. hero or heroine), temporal dimension (morning, afternoon and evening), relational organisation (why and how of character action) and space categorisation (spatial plotting of attractions and places).

Other blogs researchers have employed pattern based approaches such as qualitative content analysis and thematic analysis. Huffaker and Calvert (2005), for example, used content analysis to examine the broad characteristics of teen blogs, paying attention to gender differences in personal information disclosure, how intimate topics like sexual identity are presented and how language is used to express self and emotion. This was a quantitative type of content analysis where a set of hypotheses was tested using a randomly-selected sample of teenage blogs and analysed using a content analysis software package. The package allowed the researchers to create 'language scores for tone and semantic features' (Huffaker and Calvert, 2005: np). Qualitative content analysis (very similar to thematic analysis) is popular in the qualitative analysis of travel blogs and is used to decipher the subjective meanings bloggers attach to their travel experiences and how these might differ from official accounts (see Enoch and Grossman, 2010). For example, Enoch and Grossman (2010) used what they called 'interpretive content analysis' to investigate ideas of cosmopolitanism using the blogs of Israeli and Danish backpackers to India.

Our respective projects on gap years and everyday moralities are examples of thematic analysis. For the everyday morality study, narrative analysis was considered but the segmented nature of the blogs did not seem to lend itself to a form of analysis premised on analysing how the parts of a biographical past are 'storied' into a meaningful and coherent whole (Chase, 2003: 656; Riessman, 1993: 2). For Hookway, the blogs sampled exemplified narratives of self but they tended to develop as a 'database narrative' (Lopez, 2009: 738) where posted fragments of self are disconnected from each other.

Narrative analysis may prove more worthwhile for particular blog types organised around a specific phenomenon or experience (e.g. travel blogs, weight-loss blogs, etc.) where posts are less sequentially and thematically fractured. Although in practice there can be little difference between researchers claiming to use content or thematic analysis (e.g. Enoch and Grossman's content analysis looks rather like the thematic analyses we both conducted). Content analysis usually involves some form of counting or numerical description based around a set of developed codes, whereas thematic analysis is more attuned to the qualitative features of a text, and is more about capturing meaning and rich descriptions of people's life-world (Joffe and Yardley, 2004: 56).

Hookway analysed the blogs – combined with follow-up interviews – using thematic analysis. Here the empirical materials were combined, read, re-read and organised according to developed themes, categories and concepts in order to draw a picture of the ways in which morality was formulated and practiced. Largely inductive in nature, thematic analysis provided room for theory to be built according to new patterns and themes

that were developed from the data itself (Liamputtong and Ezzy, 2005: 265). Our experiences of conducting blog analysis ran into a number of practical issues, however.

PRACTICAL ISSUES IN BLOG RESEARCH

So far, we have outlined the benefits of blog research, but we now turn to a range of potential difficulties, which researchers need to consider when evaluating blogs as a data source. First, we consider the practical matters associated with the nature of blog data: finding suitable blogs during the data collection phase, and then handling data during analysis.

As blog data is not elicited by the researcher, but is spontaneous and naturally occurring, researchers have to seek out blogs that match the aims of the research. The volume of data in the blogosphere means that this can take some time. We discussed the different strategies for data collection earlier, noting that both searching and trawling can be time-consuming. A considerable amount of 'blog weeding' is required because the results may be irrelevant. For example, Snee gathered over 700 blogs to produce her sample of 39 gap year blogs using the searching method. Initially, the sample size was 40, however one blog was discarded when it transpired during contact with the blogger that she had taken her year out half-way through her university course, and consequently did not meet the selection criteria. Even with careful inspection, such quality issues are a risk in blog research, which we explore in more detail later.

Hookway encountered similar problems during the trawling phase of the everyday morality data collection. Reading 200 blogs over four months generated a sample of only 11 that were relevant. It is harder to search for appropriate content in studies that have a broad research topic such as 'everyday morality', rather than a specific phrase like 'gap years'. Moreover, some searches/trawls returned blogs or posts set to private in both studies. Finally, the sheer volume of text in each blog can make it a laborious task to check whether the blogs are relevant or not. These practical issues highlight the importance of carefully planning the selection criteria and collection strategy at the start of the blog research process. As we recounted earlier, it was necessary for Hookway to change the data collection strategy to blog solicitation in order to be more efficient in matching the content of the LiveJournal blogs to the project's aims.

The second practical matter is the textual features of blogs in terms of the volume of data and their multimedia elements. Both case studies required grappling with masses of data. One practical solution to this is to have defined parameters around what to include in the sample. For example, Snee concentrated on blog posts that described planning the gap year, covered the period of time out itself, and any posts in which the blogger reflected upon their experiences on their return. Similarly, Hookway concentrated on the past year of posts in the every day morality study. This still resulted in a considerable sample that contained hundreds of instances of everyday moral encounters, moments, descriptions and reflections: over 100,000 words on topics ranging from the ethics of breaking up a relationship, veganism, loyalty and friendship, to being able to live a moral life as an atheist. In order to deal with this fragmented and voluminous data set, Hookway developed overarching themes of analysis from the dominant topics in the blogs sampled, such as love and morality and moral individualism, and then conducted a concentrated thematic analysis within these spheres. While fragmentation was less of an issue for Snee, who had more defined stories of gap years to explore, the sheer amount of data she had to deal with was staggering. The 39 blogs sampled yielded over a *million* words when converted into text files (although this did include absolutely all the text on a page, including menus and headings).

Undoubtedly, blogs are meant to be read, and the words that were contained within were the foundation of both case studies; however, it is important to remember that these are also interactive and multimedia forms of text (Scheidt and Wright, 2004). One blog page can contain not only the text of the post itself (which can be edited and reworded by the author) but also pictures, video clips, text or visual comments from readers and responses from the author, hyperlinks to other websites, advertisements from the host website and audio files. They also offer expression via design and style customisation. Moreover, blogs are live documents compared to their offline counterparts, such as diaries, because they can be edited and updated indefinitely. As we noted earlier, there is certainly scope for researchers to take better advantage of the multimedia qualities of blogs, say for example, through visual methods of analysis (Snee, 2012: 183). We suggest that researchers need to consider this potential but also the pragmatic and methodological decisions that need to be made regarding time, cost and how to best meet the aims of the project. In the everyday morality project, Hookway decided to focus only on written text captured on a specific data and time, and to only include interactive comments where they complemented or added to the moral position developed in the original post. Snee took a similar approach in the gap year study, although the blogs were read online to be able to view any photographs or videos that were specifically discussed in the posts.

THE QUALITY OF BLOG DATA

In addition to practical issues concerning matching research aims to blog content and analysing large volumes of multimedia blog content, there are also methodological issues concerning the quality of blog data. Interpreting documentary sources, according to Scott (1990), relies on assessing authenticity, credibility, representativeness and meaning (Scott, 1990: 6). Meaning, which refers to whether the reader can comprehend the source, was not an issue for either of the case studies discussed here, but may pose a problem for researchers interested in foreign language blogs or which use an unfamiliar vocabulary. In this section, we focus first on concerns over the 'representativeness' of populations captured through blog analysis, and second the authenticity of authorship and the credibility of blog accounts.

Homogeneity of Blog Population

Blog populations can be relatively homogeneous. This is important to consider in light of the representativeness of the sample and the conclusions that can be drawn about the wider population. Although Internet usage has dramatically expanded in recent years a number of 'digital divides' remain. The latest Oxford Internet Institute Survey (Dutton *et al.*, 2013) found that writing a blog is undertaken by one in five people in the UK, but certain populations were more or less likely to undertake this activity. Household income was one factor, with low incomes associated with lower levels of blogging. Lifecourse is also important: 41 per cent of UK students blogged compared to 22 per cent of employed people and just 5 per cent of the retired. Moreover, research shows that bloggers tend to be young (54 per cent are under the age of 30) and female (Lenhart and Fox, 2006).

The characteristics of blogging mean that they may be a good source of data for examining certain groups. This is clearly the case for Snee's gap year study. However, this was a problem for Hookway who wanted to capture a wider and more diverse range of moral experiences than those articulated by young women. The work-around for Hookway was to use LiveJournal's search engine to sample older bloggers and to manually select male bloggers (LiveJournal's advanced search engine does not allow searches by gender).

Although the concentration of blogging among young people was advantageous for Snee, there were still issues of representativeness that needed to be considered. Clearly not all young gappers blogged about their experiences, and if those that do are largely from privileged backgrounds, this means only a quite selective and particular classed experience of gap-year travel is being represented. This was also an issue for Hookway, who although making attempts to capture a diversity of experience, was left with a sample that did not in any way capture the range and diversity of the broader Australian population. The sample generated was highly homogeneous comprised of predominantly white, urban, mainly tertiary educated, middle-class and young service professionals. Non-bloggers, particularly those from less privileged social backgrounds, might articulate morality and selfhood in very different ways. Researchers thus need to consider the limitations of blogger populations when thinking about employing blog methodologies and what implications this has for achieving the aims and objectives of the research. Again this is not necessarily a barrier to blog research but it does shape the sorts of conclusions that can be made. A further consideration for some blog researchers is the 'truth' of blog accounts.

Blogs, Authenticity and Trustworthiness

The veracity of blog data is important to consider in relation to verifying the identity of bloggers. Scott (1990) asks researchers to consider if documentary sources are 'authentic' – that is, that they are genuine and that authorship can be verified. Most blog authors explicitly state their age and gender. This information can usually be found on the profile home page or can be found through reading the first couple of posts. However, there is no guarantee that this background information is truthful or accurate. For example, in the gap year study it was not always easy to establish whether the blogs met the selection criteria or to establish demographic details for the sample. Depending on the platform, blogs might explicitly provide the blogger's age, location and gender, but this is not always explicit and there is no guarantee that this information is accurate. As noted earlier, it only emerged that one blogger did not meet these criteria when Snee made contact with her.

The issue of identifying blog participants may pose problems for researchers who are looking to make conclusions, for example, about the social position of participants in relation to the chosen area of study. The importance of the 'truth' of blog data therefore depends on whether a researcher is looking at how blogs work to produce particular effects or whether they are looking at how blogs correspond with an 'offline' reality.

Scott's (1990) criteria for evaluating documentary sources also ask the researcher to consider if the data is credible, i.e. it does not contain distortions. Both authors were routinely questioned on the truthfulness of blog data when presenting their research. The online anonymity of blogging raised issues about potential identity play and deception. How do you know the bloggers are 'telling the truth' was a typical question. These concerns are rooted in the mediated nature of online representations, where '[a] nonymity in text-based environments gives one more choice and control in the presentation of self, whether or not the presentation is perceived as intended' (Markham, 2005: 809). The desire to 'create a better story' is also something researchers need to be wary of. For example, new bloggers may want to increase their profile by fabricating incidents, or employees may write ingratiating accounts about an organisation to improve career prospects.

The question of the importance of 'truthfulness' again depends on the aims and objectives of the research. Although it seemed unlikely that our blog data was 'faked', this was not of crucial methodological concern. We approached the blog data as providing insight into the stories told about gap years or moral life rather than 'transparent representations' of actual experience (Germann Molz, 2007: 79). Like other forms of qualitative research, this approach to blog analysis recognises that there may be more than one equally credible account (Heath *et al.*, 2009: 89). Even if bloggers do not tell the 'truth', these 'fabrications' would still tell us something about the manner in which specific social and cultural ideas about travel or morality are constructed. Consequently, qualitative blog analysis has much in common with wider quality concerns such as Lincoln and Guba's (1986) concept of 'trustworthiness'. Moreover, concerns regarding the 'authenticity' of blog accounts in terms of genuine authorship could be replaced with attempts to ensure that the bloggers are fairly represented by the researcher – an alternative interpretation of authenticity suggested by Lincoln and Guba (1986).

However, the issue of truthfulness may be an important consideration for a researcher wanting to read off external 'truths' from the textual data – for example, the researcher seeking trustworthy accounts of weight loss or becoming a parent. Using the multimedia elements of blogs, such as images and video, and the links a blogger may post to other online content or social media can help to build up a 'picture' of the events in question. Another strategy to alleviate concerns is to supplement blog data with interviews. As discussed, both the gap-year and everyday morality project combined blog data with blogger interviews. As the blogs were limited to whatever the author had chosen to record, interviews provided a means to seek clarification, to explore absences and implicit meanings and to contextualise online representations in terms of articulations of offline experience. This form of triangulation can also provide a technique to reinforce the 'trustworthiness' of the blog analysis (Lincoln and Guba, 1986).

Both Snee and Hookway found no fundamental differences between the blog and interview narratives, although the bloggers mentioned that their online diaries were filtered somewhat for particular audiences. For example, one gap year interviewee kept his blog fairly formal and reserved some of the more hedonistic and playful discussions for his friends on Facebook. Another interviewee was conscious that her vicar and other members of her community would be reading her blog, and wrote her account accordingly. These blogs can therefore be seen as 'public' accounts of experience. Concerns about 'authenticity' should not prevent social researchers utilising blog data but they are part of deciding whether blogs are an appropriate methodological choice for meeting the aims of the research (Snee, 2012: 186). Additional questions arise when we consider how the blurring of boundaries online may present particular ethical challenges.

ETHICAL ISSUES

New online data sources such as blogs present new and challenging ethical dilemmas and controversies (Chapter 2). This is because there is a range of questions over how conventional notions of private and public apply in online research venues (British Psychological Society, 2013; Markham *et al.*, 2012). As we noted in the introduction, one of the defining features of the 'confessional society' (Bauman, 2007) is that what is public and what is private is not clearly demarcated. Contemporary documentary sources such as blogs mean that researchers can access a range of personal data online which is freely offered. We could argue that if this is put into the public domain then there cannot be any reasonable expectation that this data will be protected. However, it is precisely because the boundaries between public and private have blurred that these issues are not quite straightforward to resolve.

Although the boundary between public and private has changed, not all online material

is necessarily 'fair game'. It is crucial that blog researchers evaluate the privacy of the sources of their data. A classic perspective on this from Frankel and Siang (1999) notes two main factors. The first is technological privacy, for example blogs that are protected by a password. Blog platforms often enable users to restrict postings to particular audiences. This means that bloggers often take part in what Ford (2011) calls the 'active management of privacy'. The second factor considers the psychological perspective of the bloggers. Frankel and Siang (1999) advocate a combined approach.

Assessing bloggers' perceptions of privacy can be difficult. The blogosphere is a mediated environment characterised by 'feelings of anonymity online ... or the (in)visibility of audience in blogs' (Hudson and Bruckman, 2005: 299). Wilkinson and Thelwall (2011) suggest that Moor's (2004) definitions of natural and normative privacy can help with the ethics of using personal information. Situations where we would expect to be hidden are naturally private, whereas normative privacy refers to situations where we would expect others to protect us. Bloggers cannot reasonably expect anything they post in a public web page to be private because they are neither technically nor normatively private. This does not mean that researchers do not have a responsibility towards the bloggers in this context, as research suggests blogs may be viewed as part of a person's identity (Markham *et al.*, 2012: 10). Blog researchers need to decide if they are treating personal blogs as representations of human subjects or as texts produced by authors (Lomborg, 2013: 21–2). This has implications for two crucial decisions: whether informed consent is required to use blogs as data and how to report the data when writing up.

First, informed consent is required when researching human subjects, but this does not apply to public, published material. Second, ethical guidelines usually prescribe that researchers employ measures such as anonymisation to protect the identity of human subjects. The complication with online data such as blogs is its 'traceability' (Beaulieu and Estalella, 2012: 34). Directly quoting a blog post in a publication means that even if the identity of the blogger is hidden, their blog can be found. Some researchers consequently advocate paraphrasing rather than direct quotations in qualitative personal research (Wilkinson and Thelwall, 2011). On the other hand, we may view bloggers as authors and recognise this authorship through appropriate citation (Bassett and O'Riordan, 2002: 244).

Ethical Strategies in the Case Studies

The AoIR guidelines suggest that assessing the principles related to human subjects may oversimplify the issues at hand: 'the question of whether one is dealing with a human subject is different from the question about whether information is linked to individuals' (Markham *et al.*, 2012: 7). In addition, the guidelines also highlight the importance of a contextual approach to research ethics and establishing what is appropriate for the specific online space, rather than prescribed rules. Here, we conclude our discussion of ethics in blog research by considering the strategies from the gap year and everyday morality case studies. Although these are always open to re-evaluation and critical examination (see Snee, 2013), we suggest these as ways through some of the complexity regarding privacy and the protection of human subjects outlined earlier.

In both case studies, the blogs were neither technically nor normatively private. In the everyday morality research, the blogs sampled were located in the public domain, with little expectation of privacy, with the bloggers all over 18 and with little potential for harm, and so consent could be waived. Further, LiveJournal blogs are public not only in the sense of being publicly accessible – and heeding the advice of Waskul and Douglass

(1996) and the AoIR (Markham *et al.*, 2012) – but also in how they are defined by users. The exception proves the rule: LiveJournal blogs that are interpreted by bloggers as 'private' are made 'friends only'. Thus, accessible blogs may be personal but they are not private. A similar approach was taken in the gap year study. Moreover, the gap year bloggers did seem to reference a potentially unknown reader (e.g. biographical notes introduced with 'for those of you who don't know me'). In the case of the bloggers who were interviewed, consent was sought to use both the interview and blog data, given that they were more directly involved in the research.

Both Snee and Hookway found the guidelines from Bruckman helpful in presenting their qualitative data for publication. Bruckman (2002: 229) suggests a 'continuum of possibilities' of disguise for levels of protection for the producers of online data. Although the gap year blogs were in the public domain, a decision was made to adopt 'moderate disguise' in the gap year study (Bruckman, 2002) because the data were linked to individuals. This meant that personal or identifiable details were changed, and both names and pseudonyms were anonymised. Verbatim quotations were used, however, although without a direct link to the blog. Of course, the use of verbatim quotations means that these are traceable, yet this was deemed, at the time, to offer an appropriate minimisation of harm while still retaining the meaning of the blog data.

Copyright

Alongside privacy issues, blog researchers need to be aware of copyright law (Jacobson, 2009: 137; Walther, 2002; British Psychological Society, 2013: 8). In Australia, the UK and the US, Internet content is automatically copyrighted (Australian Copyright Council, 2005; UK Intellectual Property Office, 2013; US Copyright Office, 2000). The moment a blog entry is uploaded onto a blog hosting application it is protected by copyright, and bloggers

therefore have exclusive rights over the reproduction of their work. Although this would
appear to be significantly limiting for researchers, there are special provisions built into the
copyright act(s) which allow for 'fair dealing'
of copyrighted material for the purposes of
study or research. Fair use needs to be determined on a case-by-case basis, but it would
seem that blog researchers are relatively unimpeded by 'fair-dealing' restrictions. However,
such use usually requires 'sufficient acknowl-
edgement' (UK Intellectual Property Office,
2013), reflecting ethical concerns over the
authorship of blogs.

CONCLUSION

This chapter set out to provide an overview
of the practice of blog research based on our
own experience of using blogs to do qualitative analysis. Blogs are an attractive method
for researchers interested in gathering rich
personal accounts of everyday life unprovoked by a researcher. We approach blogs as
contemporary 'documents of life' that provide a number of practical and methodological benefits for developing qualitative insight
into a range of experiences, processes and
practices and how they are storied and understood. Blogs share the benefits of diaries as
'expressions of personal life' but are easier to
access than unsolicited diaries and are spontaneous in ways that research-driven diaries are
not. Not only do blogs offer situated accounts
of everyday life based on what is important to
the blogger, they also offer considerable practical benefits, including being instantaneous
and publicly available, extending population
access and offering the potential for comparative and longitudinal research.

We showed that there are two main types
of blog research questions: (1) research about
the medium of blogging; and (2) research
that uses blogs to examine representations
of wider social practices and experiences.
The everyday morality and gap year studies

were examples of the latter, using blogs to
analyse how experiences of gap year travel
and moral decision making are understood
and represented. We outlined four key steps
to doing blog research: developing selection criteria; collecting data via 'searching',
'trawling' or 'solicitation'; establishing an
online presence; and preparing data for analysis. The multimedia nature of blogs means
they are amenable to a range of visual and
text-based analysis techniques, including
conventional methods of text-analysis such
as thematic analysis, discourse analysis and
content analysis. Both of us analysed our
blog data using thematic analysis; while Snee
made effective use of CAQDAS, Hookway
adopted a 'manual' approach largely due to
the unspecific nature of his research topic.

It can be time consuming finding blog
content that meets the aims of the research,
and dealing with the multimedia elements of
blogs and the large volumes of data they generate can present challenges. Here we urge
the importance of developing clear selection
criteria before data collection begins and
to consider 'solicitation' techniques if the
research topic is relatively undefined, like
in the case of Hookway's study on morality. Methodologically, blogs can pose problems around representativeness of the sample
due to the homogeneity of blog populations,
raise concerns about authenticity, and pose
difficulties with verifying the background
information of participants. Although these
measures of validity were not critical to
the gap year and everyday moralities projects – we were concerned with gaining
insight into participant accounts rather than
'accurate' presentations of experience –
they will be important to other projects and
need to be evaluated as part of considering
blog research. Like other forms of Internet
research, blogs raise complex ethical questions that researchers must face. Are blogs
publicly available data that researchers can
use freely or is informed consent required?
Are researchers dealing with human subjects
who need to be protected or authors whose

work needs to be acknowledged? Although we argue that public blogs are neither technically or normatively private and thus consent is not needed, we also advocate a contextual approach that takes into account bloggers' own perceptions of privacy, the vulnerability of the blogging population and the potential for harm.

Blogs are an exciting and innovative research method for accessing accounts of personal life but need to be carefully considered in terms of the sometimes tricky practical, methodological and ethical issues they present. The novelty of blog methods also means that the medium can take precedence when sharing research findings and that researchers need to be prepared to justify their chosen method. Blog methodologies may play a modest role in responding to claims of a 'coming crisis of empirical sociology' (Savage and Burrows, 2007). This crisis refers to social scientists losing their monopoly on empirical research as new forms of data embedded in multiple information technologies and the routine transactional data of organisations surpass the empirical capacities and resources of researchers. Embracing new 'confessional' technologies like blogs are part of 'rethinking the repertoires of empirical sociology' (Savage and Burrows, 2007: 895) and enables research into the nature of contemporary selves, identities and relationships.

NOTES

1   A work-around for using Google blog search is explained here http://www.netforlawyers.com/content/google-kills-blog-search-engine-109 (accessed June 2016).
2   Where a blog platform does not have a built-in search feature, you can use Google to search the site for your term by using the site: somesime.com modifier. For example, to search for blogs on gap-years on Blogger: site: Blogger.com 'gap-years'.
3   A spam-blog is a fake blog developed to increase web traffic to an affiliated website.

REFERENCES

Arioso, L. (2010) 'Personal documents on the Internet: what's new and what's old', *Journal of Comparative Research in Anthropology and Sociology*, 1(2): 23–38.
Australian Copyright Council (2005) 'Information sheet: an introduction to copyright in Australia'. Available at https://www.copyright.org.au/acc_prod/ACC/Information_Sheets/An_Introduction_to_Copyright_in_Australia.aspx (accessed August 2016).
Badger, M. (2004) 'Visual blogs'. In L.J. Gurak, S. Antonijevic, L. Johnson, C. Ratliff, and J. Reyman (eds.), *Into the Blogosphere: Rhetoric, Community, and Culture of Weblogs*. Available at http://blog.lib.umn.edu/blogosphere/visual_blogs.html (accessed March 2006).
Bakker, J.K. and Paris, J. (2013) 'Bereavement and religion online: stillbirth, neonatal loss and parental religiosity', *Journal for the Scientific Study of Religion,* 52(4): 657–74.
Bassett, E.H. and O'Riordan, K. (2002) 'Ethics of Internet research: contesting the human subjects research model', *Ethics and Information Technology*, 4: 233–47.
Bauman, Z. (2007) *Consuming Life*. Cambridge: Polity Press.
Beaulieu, A. and Estalella, A. (2012) 'Rethinking research ethics for mediated settings', *Information, Communication and Society,* 15(1): 23–42.
Beer, D. (2008) 'Researching a confessional society', *International Journal of Market Research,* 50(5): 619–29.
Beer, D. and Burrows, R. (2007) 'Sociology and, of and in Web 2.0: some initial considerations', *Sociological Research Online*, 12(5). Available at http://www.socresonline.org.uk/12/5/17.html (accessed January 2016).
British Psychological Society (2013) *Ethics Guidelines for Internet-mediated Research*. Leicester: Author. Available at http://www.bps.org.uk/system/files/Public%20files/inf206-guidelines-for-internet-mediated-research.pdf (accessed January 2016).
Bruckman, A. (2002) 'Studying the amateur artist: a perspective on disguising data collected in human subjects research on the Internet', *Ethics and Information Technology*, 4: 217–31.

Chase, S.E. (2003) 'Narrative inquiry: multiple lenses, approaches, voices'. in N.K. Denzin and Y.S. Lincoln (eds.), *The Sage Handbook of Qualitative Research*. 3rd edn. Thousand Oaks, CA: Sage Publications, pp. 651–81.

Clarke, J. and van Amerom, G. (2008) 'A comparison of blogs by depressed men and women', *Issues in Mental Health Nursing*, 29(3): 243–64.

Dart, J.J (2009) 'Blogging the 2006 FIFA World Cup Finals', *Sociology of Sport Journal*, 26(1): 107–126.

Dutton, W.H. and Blank, G., with D. Grosselj (2013) *Cultures of the Internet: the Internet in Britain (Oxford Internet Survey Report 2013)*. Oxford: Oxford Internet Institute.

Elliot, H. (1997) 'The use of diaries in sociological research on health experience', *Sociological Research Online* [Online] 2(2). Available at http://www.socresonline.org.uk/2/2/7.html (accessed August 2016).

Enoch, Y. and Grossman, R. (2010) 'Blogs of Israeli and Danish backpackers to India', *Annals of Tourism Research,* 37(2): 520–36b.

Ezzy, D. (2000) *Qualitative Research Methods: A Health Focus*. Melbourne: Oxford University Press.

Ferrarotti, F. (2003) *On the Science of Uncertainty: The Biographical Method in Social Research*. Lanham, MD: Lexington Books.

Ford, S.M. (2011) 'Reconceptualising the public/private distinction in the age of information technology', *Information, Communication and Society*, 14(4): 550–67.

Frankel, M. and Siang, S. (1999) 'Ethical and legal aspects of human subjects research on the Internet', *American Association for the Advancement of Science Workshop Report*. Available at http://www.aaas.org/spp/dspp/srfl/projects/intres.main.htm (accessed November 2015).

Germann Molz, J. (2007) 'Eating difference: the cosmopolitan mobilities of culinary tourism', *Space and Culture*, 10(1): 77–93.

Goffman, E. (1959) *The Presentation of Self in Everyday Life*. Harmondsworth, UK: Penguin.

Goffman, E. (1974) *Frame Analysis: An Essay on the Organization of Experience*. Boston, MA: Northeastern University Press

Heath, S., Brooks, R., Cleaver, E. and Ireland, E. (2009) *Researching Young People's Lives*. London: Sage Publications.

Hessler, R.M., Downing, J., Beltz, C., Pelliccio, A., Powell, M. and Vale, W. (2003) 'Qualitative research on adolescent risk using e-mail: a methodological assessment', *Qualitative Sociology* 26(1): 111–24.

Hine, C. (2015) *Ethnography for the Internet: Embedded, Embodied and Everyday*. London: Bloomsbury.

Hodkinson, P. (2007) 'Interactive online journals and individualization', *New Media Society*, 9(4): 625–50.

Hookway, N. (2008) '"Entering the blogosphere": some strategies for using blogs in social research' *Qualitative Research*, 8(1): 91–113.

Hudson, J.M. and Bruckman, A. (2005) 'Using empirical data to reason about Internet research ethics'. In H. Gellersen et al. (eds) *ECSCW 2005: Proceedings of the Ninth European Conference on Computer-Supported Cooperative Work*, 18–22 September 2005. Paris, France.

Huffaker, D.A., and Calvert, S. L. (2005) 'Gender, identity, and language use in teenage blogs', *Journal of Computer-Mediated Communication*, 10(2). doi:10.1111/j.1083–6101.2005.tb00238.

Jacobson, M.H. (ed.) (2009) *Encountering the Everyday: An Introduction to the Sociologies of the Unnoticed*. Basingstoke, UK: Palgrave.

Joffe, H. and Yardley, L. (2004) 'Content and thematic analysis'. In D.F Marks and L. Yardley (eds.), *Research Methods for Clinical and Health Psychology*. London: Sage Publications, pp. 56–68.

Leggatt-Cook, C. and Chamberlain, K. (2012) 'Blogging for weight-loss: personal accountability, writing selves and the weight-loss blogosphere', *Sociology of Health and Illness*, 34(7): 963–77.

Lenhart, A. and Fox, S. (2006) Bloggers: A Portrait of the Internet's New Storytellers. Pew Internet and American Life Project. Available at http://www.pewinternet.org/files/old-media/Files/Reports/2006/PIP%20Bloggers%20Report%20July%2019%202006.pdf.pdf (accessed August 2016).

Li, D., and Walejko, G. (2008) 'Splogs and abandoned blogs: the perils of sampling bloggers and their blogs', *Information, Communication and Society*, 11(2): 279–96.

Liamputtong, P. and Ezzy, D. (2005) *Qualitative Research Methods*. Melbourne: Oxford University Press.

Lincoln, Y.S. and Guba, E.G. (1986) 'But is it rigorous? Trustworthiness and authenticity in naturalistic evaluation', *New Directions for Program Evaluation*, 30: 73–84.

Lomborg, S. (2013) 'Personal Internet archives and ethics', *Research Ethics,* 9(1): 20–31.

Lopez, L.K. (2009) 'The radical act of 'mommy blogging': redefining motherhood through the blogosphere', *New Media and Society*, 11: 729–47.

Lupton, D. (2014) *Digital Sociology*. London: Routledge.

Mann, C. and Stewart, F. (2000) *Internet Communication and Qualitative Research: A Handbook for Researching Online*. London: Sage Publications.

Markham, A.N. (2005) 'The Methods, Politics and Ethics of Representation in Online Ethnography'. In N.K. Denzin and Y.S. Lincoln (eds.), *The SAGE Handbook of Qualitative Research*. Thousand Oaks: Sage, pp. 793–820.

Markham, A.N., Buchanan, E.A. and the AoIR Ethics Working Committee (2012) *Ethical Decision-Making and Internet Research: Recommendations from the AoIR Ethics Working Committee*. Available at http://aoir.org/reports/ethics2.pdf (accessed August 2016).

Mason, J. (2002) *Qualitative Researching*. London: Sage Publications.

Moor, J.H. (2004) 'Towards a theory of privacy for the information age'. In R.A. Spinello and H.T. Tvani (eds.), *Readings in CyberEthics*. 2nd ed. Sudbury, MA: Jones and Bartlett, pp. 407–17.

Phillips, D. and Harding, S. (1985) 'The structure of moral values'. In M. Abrams, D. Gerard and N. Timms (eds.), *Values and Social Change in Britain*. London: Macmillan, pp. 93–108.

Plummer, K. (2001) *Documents of Life 2: An Invitation to a Critical Humanism. Vol 2*. London: Sage Publications.

Polkinghorne, D.E. (1995) 'Narrative configuration in qualitative analysis', *International Journal of Qualitative Studies in Education*, 8(1): 5–23.

Riessman, C.K. (1993) *Narrative Analysis*. Newbury Park, CA: Sage Publications.

Sanford, A. (2010) '"I can air my feelings instead of eating them": blogging as social support for the morbidly obese', *Communication Studies*, 61(5): 567–84.

Savage, M. and Burrows, R. (2007) 'The coming crisis of empirical sociology', *Sociology* 41(5): 885–900.

Scheidt, L. and Wright, E. (2004) 'Common visual design elements of Weblos'. In L.J. Gurak, S. Antonijevic, L. Johnson, C. Ratliff, and J. Reyman (eds.), *Into the Blogosphere: Rhetoric, Community, and Culture of Weblogs*. Available at http://blog.lib.umn.edu/blogosphere/common_visual.html (accessed August 2016).

Scott, J. (1990) *A Matter of Record, Documentary Sources in Social Research*. Cambridge: Polity Press.

Sharman, A. (2014) 'Mapping the climate sceptical blogosphere', *Global Environmental Change* 26: 159–70.

Snee, H. (2012) 'Youth research in Web 2.0: a case study in blog analysis'. In S. Health and C. Walker (eds), *Innovations in Youth Research*. Baskingstoke: Palgrave, pp. 178–194

Snee, H. (2013) 'Making ethical decisions in an online context: reflections on using blogs to explore narratives of experience', *Methodological Innovations Online*, 8(2): 52–67.

Thelwall, M. (2014) *Big Data and Social Web Research Methods*. Available at http://www.scit.wlv.ac.uk/~cm1993/papers/IntroductionToWebometricsAndSocialWebAnalysis.pdf (accessed August 2016).

Thomas, W.I. and Znaniecki, F. ([1918] 1958) *The Polish Peasant in Europe and America*. New York, NY: Dover Publications.

Toms, E.G. and Duff, W. (2002) '"I spent 1½ hours sifting through one large box…": diaries as information behaviour of the archives user: lessons learned', *Journal of the American Society for Information Science and Technology,* 53(4): 1232–8.

Turnbull, G. (2002) 'The state of the blog part two: blogger present'. In J. Rodzvilla (ed.), *We've Got Blog: How Weblogs are Changing our Culture*. Cambridge: Perseus Publishing, pp. 81–85

Tussyadiah, I.P. and Fesenmaier, D.R. (2008) 'Marketing place through first-person stories – an analysis of Pennsylvania

Roadtripper Blog', *Journal of Travel and Tourism Marketing*, 25(3): 299–311.

UK Intellectual Property Office (2013) *Copyright*. Available at http://www.ipo.gov.uk/types/copy.htm (accessed January 2016).

US Copyright Office (2000) *Copyright Basics*. Available at http://www.copyright.gov/circs/circ1.html#wci (accessed May 2006).

Verbrugge, L.M. (1980) 'Health Diaries', *Medical Care*, 18(1): 73–95.

Wade, L. and Sharp, G. (2013) 'Sociological images blogging as public sociology', *Social Science Computer Review*, 31(2): 221–8.

Wakeford, N. and Cohen, K. (2008) 'Fieldnotes in public: using blogs for research'. In N. Fielding, R.M. Lee and G. Blank (eds.), *The SAGE Handbook of Online Research Methods*. London: Sage Publications, pp. 307–26.

Walther, J.B. (2002) 'Research ethics in Internet-enabled research: human subjects issues and methodological myopia', *Ethics and Information Technology* 4: 205–16.

Waskul, D. and Douglass, M. (1996) 'Considering the electronic participant: some polemical observations on the ethics of on-line research', *The Information Society*, 12(2): 129–39.

Wilkinson, D. and Thelwall, M. (2011) 'Researching personal information on the public web: methods and ethics', *Social Science Computer Review*, 29(4): 387–401.

## PART VII

Virtual Ethnography

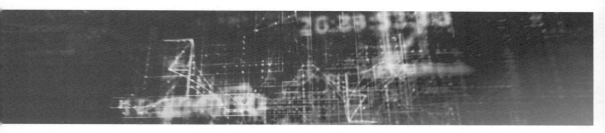

23

Ethnographies of Online Communities and Social Media: Modes, Varieties, Affordances

Christine Hine

INTRODUCTION

Widespread popular recognition of the richness and diversity of social interactions enabled by the Internet has gone hand-in-hand with the development of ethnographic methodologies for documenting those interactions and exploring their implications. The established ethnographic tradition of viewing the researcher as an embodied research instrument has been transferred to the social spaces of the Internet. The ethnographic focus on studying social practices, in depth and detail, as they make sense for those involved in them, has enabled ethnographers to find out what people actually do with the Internet in specific circumstances. Ethnography conducted in online settings has been instrumental in demonstrating the complex social nature of Internet-based interactions and enabling us to explore the new cultural formations that emerge online. This chapter first outlines the development of a range of approaches to online ethnography that have

emerged as the Internet has evolved and then moves to examine in more detail some of the specific methodological challenges that have been encountered as ethnographic principles are applied within online settings.

Beyond the specific details of how to operate within a given field site, ethnographers also make decisions about the most appropriate way to define their field site. In addition to the development of ethnographic approaches for field sites contained wholly online, a variety of more spatially complex ethnographic field sites have emerged, exploring the complex and contingent connections between online and offline social spaces. These concerns form the focus of the third section of the chapter. The fourth section then considers a further set of key methodological issues focused on the contribution an ethnographer's embodied experiences as they navigate the field makes to the ethnographic project. The final section of the chapter then takes a look forward and considers the challenges on the horizon for ethnographers interested in exploring online spaces as new platforms for online interaction are developed and as the Internet becomes ever-more pervasive.

ONLINE ETHNOGRAPHY AND VIRTUAL ETHNOGRAPHY: EVOLVING APPROACHES

A diffuse and disciplinarily diverse set of approaches to ethnography in online domains has emerged, using a variety of terms including online ethnography, virtual ethnography, netnography and cyberethnography. Baym's (1995, 2000) account of a newsgroup discussing soap opera viewing led the way in establishing that online contexts could be sites for ethnographic study. Even at this early stage, ethnographers were pointing out that being online would not mean the same thing to everyone. Markham (1998), for example, argued for a reflexive approach to ethnography in online contexts, open to the varying meanings of online activities and the different emotions attendant on inhabiting online space. Similarly, Hine (2000) described a virtual ethnography which took online spaces seriously as a site for interaction but did not assume that there was a singular virtual domain that would necessarily be distinguishable from 'the real'. As the Internet developed, so too did approaches to ethnography in the various online spaces that emerged. Kendall (2002) completed fieldwork focusing on gender in an online forum and Senft (2008) described, through ethnographic observation and participation, the experience of 'camgirls' streaming their lives across the Internet via webcam. Netnography (Kozinets 2010) was developed to enable efficient study of online domains, often deployed in a marketing context for purposes of understanding consumer motivations and behaviours. Anthropologically oriented ethnographic studies of online spaces have included Boellstorff's (2008) study of Second Life, Nardi's (2010) exploration of *World of Warcraft* and Coleman's (2013) ethnography of a hacker community involving extensive online fieldwork. As the Internet matured, various forms of online ethnography have developed that relate to the underlying principles of the parent methodology, but have adapted to the conditions offered by online interactions and the particular concerns of their parent disciplines.

The nature and role of ethnographic attention to online spaces has developed over time. Robinson and Schulz (2009) identify three different phases of online ethnography: pioneering approaches which saw the Internet as a new domain for identity formation and stressed the distinctiveness of online social formations; legitimising approaches which stressed the transfer of offline methodological concerns into the online domain and took a more sceptical stance on the distinctiveness of online space; and a more recently emergent set of multi-modal approaches which include consideration of video and audio data alongside textual data, and seek to contextualise online interactions within offline spaces. Robinson and Schulz (2009) stress that approaches to online ethnography have changed as the Internet itself has changed and also as the aspirations of researchers have taken different forms over time. Researchers have different notions of the nature of online space and also diverse disciplinary affiliations, theoretical aspirations and methodological influences. There is no single form of online ethnography, but instead an internally diverse array of approaches oriented to ethnography in and of online space.

Internet studies have been a rich field for methodological development, and this development both within and beyond online ethnography continues as the Internet itself has evolved and in particular with the advent of social media. Giglietto *et al.* (2012) note that the methodological traditions which dominate in studies of the Internet vary between different online and social media platforms: their review of social media research methods divides the dominant methodologies into ethnographic, statistical and computational, and suggests that although ethnographic approaches led the way in many online fields, in the case of Twitter the computational methods came first and were only subsequently complemented by qualitative approaches. Social media have, indeed, dramatically transformed the landscape for social research in the access they offer to large-scale data on everyday activities, which has in turn fostered computational approaches. As a result, as well as the adaptation of existing methods to the new conditions, self-consciously novel digital methods for social research have emerged (Marres 2012; Orton-Johnson and Prior 2013; Rogers 2013; Ruppert *et al.* 2013). The advent of 'big data' does not, however, mean laying aside small-scale qualitative approaches like ethnography. The 'big data' transformation has fostered computational analysis, but there have also been calls to continue to pay attention to smaller scale, qualitative approaches that can explore how the large-scale patterns come about and investigate what they mean to participants (boyd and Crawford 2012). Mixed method research designs have emerged in Internet studies, allowing for combinations of large-scale and small-scale focus, through which researchers explore both patterns and meanings (Hesse-Biber and Griffin 2013). As I will argue in later sections of this chapter, ethnographic methods that look outwards to the embedding of Internet activities in diverse contexts and also inwards to autoethnographic accounts of how such forms of connection feel, may be very significant in allowing us to grasp the forms of sociality enabled by the Internet and may form a suitable complement, or even counter, to big data approaches.

Ethnography has therefore been significant for some time in interrogating the social conditions of online space, and it continues to be important despite the advent of big data and large-scale computational analysis prompted by social media. Coleman (2010) argues that ethnography of online spaces is particularly significant because these domains have incontrovertibly emerged as central sites of experience in many aspects of everyday life. Ethnography documents the significance of these spaces and, as Coleman (2010) stresses, also acts against a tendency to universalise the digital by highlighting the heterogeneity and specificity of online spaces. As experience of online ethnography has developed, a rich vein of methodological writing has emerged, analysing the methods of participant-observation in online space and exploring the extent to which the issues faced by online ethnographers are distinctive. The question of what, if anything, is different enough about online ethnographic practice to deserve a separate demarcation, whether as online, virtual, cyber- or digital, has preoccupied a number of reviewers, as the next section will detail.

HOW TO DO ONLINE ETHNOGRAPHY: METHODS AND ETHICS

There has been a lot said about the specifics of doing ethnography online. It has often been found necessary to specify what online ethnographers should do, to a degree not mirrored in accounts of ethnography conducted in more conventional sites. To some extent, this is a matter of adapting to technical issues, as different online platforms offer distinctive qualities in terms of the forms of self-presentation and interaction open to the ethnographer, and as ethnographers explore the potential offered by archives for moving backwards in time, and adapt to the different forms of data to be collected and analysed. These are practical issues, concerned with the classic ethnographic challenges of getting into the field and deciding what to do once one is there, and it is very helpful for ethnographers to be able to learn from the experience of others in similar fields. Addressing these concerns, a very useful handbook discussing techniques and approaches employed by ethnographers in virtual worlds now exists (Boellstorff *et al.* 2012). In practice, however, *this* handbook and indeed much of the discussion around online ethnography has focused on more fundamental methodological issues, concerning not just how to choose to manifest oneself, what roles to adopt, and how to collect data, but also what the status might be of the ethnographic knowledge generated. As Robinson and Schulz (2009) describe, a need has been felt to legitimise online ethnography as ethnography, and this concern has generated considerable amounts of published reflection.

Steinmetz (2012) identifies questions of identity and authenticity as recurring concerns for online ethnographers. Dilemmas about how authenticity is to be judged in the setting, and whether an online-only notion of authenticity and performed identity suffices or online observations supplemented instead with some triangulation from other sources, have been present since the early days of online ethnography (Paccagnella 1997). Within an online setting, there are questions about the role that the ethnographer should take, and the impact this may have on the knowledge of the setting that they can acquire. Most sociological studies terming themselves ethnographic in online settings do involve some form of participation. Some studies, however, push the concept of ethnography a long way from the tradition of immersive, experiential study. Frederick and Perrone (2014), for example, rely upon ethnographic content analysis (Altheide 1987) and a form of 'instant ethnography' (Ferrell *et al.* 2008) in terming their study of online contact advertisements on Craigslist as ethnographic. As Garcia *et al.* (2009) discuss, merely lurking or collecting data without immersion in the setting poses some problems for ethnographic interpretation, and active participation offers considerable epistemic purchase. Acknowledging the benefits of being actively involved, however, still leaves many issues of the exact nature of

participation and the extent to which the ethnographer's role is commensurate with that of participants unresolved. The discussion of the extent to which ethnographers online can be construed as co-present with informants continues (Bengtsson 2014).

Ethical concerns arise repeatedly in reviews of online ethnography: Robinson and Schulz (2009) identify ethical issues such as whether participants can be made aware of the ethnographer's presence in appropriate ways in various online platforms as one of the key concerns of the online ethnographer; Murthy (2008) discusses the troubling tendency for online ethnographies to be conducted covertly; and Garcia *et al.* (2009) identify dilemmas created by the need to define whether online spaces are public, the decisions to be made on whether, and how, the ethnographer should identify themselves to participants, and the need to protect participants' privacy and autonomy. These reviewers identify ethical issues which are arguably not fundamentally different to those faced by offline ethnographers, who also have to navigate complex notions of public and private and their own variable visibility for participants. The ethical issue arguably arises as a topic for discussion because of a tendency on the part of some online ethnographers to treat online spaces as if the usual ethical rules do not apply, rather than because of some essential difference between online and offline space. In a sense, the marked category of online ethnography creates the need to discuss the ethical problem afresh. Markham (2006) makes a case for a situated approach to online research ethics focused on asking questions of each situation rather than expecting there to be a standard set of approaches that may always be deemed ethical. A useful set of resources based on this situational approach to online research ethics is provided by the Association of Internet Researchers (Ess and AoIR Ethics Working Committee 2002; Markham and Buchanan 2012).

Latterly there has been discussion of whether new platforms change any of the methodological issues that online ethnographers encounter. Underberg and Zorn (2013) explore the potential offered by new media technologies for more participatory designs, using digital technologies to build cultural representations of and with participants. Gallagher *et al.* (2013) similarly argue that social media can facilitate collaborative research which actively involves participants in the research process. Baker (2013) demonstrates that social media can be a source of data, a tool for keeping in touch with participants and a form of contextualisation for other kinds of data. In similar vein, Murthy (2013) explores the potential that ethnographies involving social networking sites and smartphones offer for organisational studies. Such developments in participatory technologies have implications for our notion of what the field site is: Postill and Pink (2012) suggest that the shift to Web 2.0 has added new concerns to debates about ethnography online, prompting a shift away from notions of community and network that Postill and Pink (2012) suggest have unhelpfully dominated ethnographic thinking about online activities.

This section has identified some key methodological concerns that online ethnographers face:

- How to judge authenticity and whether to triangulate observations in online space with other forms of observation
- Whether and how actively to participate in the setting
- How to behave ethically and respect participants' privacy and autonomy
- How to respond to developing technologies which do not fit neatly with concepts of online community

Whilst these challenges may recur across many online studies, the answers are very much dependent on the setting and the theoretical interests of the ethnographer concerned. The outcome of much of the ethnographic work focused on the Internet is to argue precisely that we should not be expecting the same methodological strategies to apply regardless of the platform. The issues encountered by ethnographers across listservers, Second Life, WhatsApp and Facebook, for example, will be very different, and yet these ethnographers will also still share dilemmas that are identifiably similar to those that offline ethnographers face. When ethnographers go online, the techniques they use may differ from those that work offline, and novel ethical issues may arise, but there is considerable purchase in reminding ourselves that the ethnographic project and the challenges it faces are, in many ways the same online as offline (Marshall 2010).

Marking out a specific set of issues relating to online ethnography is therefore not always helpful to ethnographers, even though the demarcation of online ethnography does draw attention to potentially useful techniques by signposting a body of methodological literature and conferring a certain legitimacy (Kozinets 2012). The demarcation of online ethnography sometimes indexes a distinctive theoretical aspiration to explore what it is that is characteristic of the emerging digital culture that has become so embedded in contemporary life (Boellstorff 2010; Miller and Horst 2012). For many social scientists, however, this will not be their primary goal, and their theoretical aspirations may well draw them towards a version of ethnography which includes online activities, but does not specifically topicalise the digital as a theoretical concern. In the following section, the emergence of a diverse array of research designs is explored, including, but not confined to online settings. Here the question of how to define a field site becomes particularly prominent.

DEFINING A FIELD SITE: BLENDED, MULTI-SITED, NETWORKED AND CONNECTIVE DESIGNS

All ethnographers need a working sense of the field site that forms the focus of their study and this can be particularly challenging if a study is conducted partly online and partly offline (Hine 2008; Steinmetz 2012; Tunçalp and Patrick 2014), as now arises in many circumstances. The multiple embedding of the Internet in everyday life problematises the notion of a pre-existing, clearly bounded ethnographic field. Mobile telephony and a mobile Internet, which is multiply embedded and taken-for-granted (Ling 2012), further compound the challenges of demarcating fields. Looking for the 'variously dynamic and changing circumstances' of participants' lives (Gold 1997: 395) becomes an ever-more challenging task. The researcher faces constant dilemmas in deciding which of the possible array of dynamic and changing circumstances to pursue. This recognition of the contingent nature of the field is not a problem confined to online ethnographers because the constructed nature of the field is already an acknowledged issue in anthropology (Gupta and Ferguson 1997; Amit 1999), if not so closely examined in sociology. However, the increasing social science interest in activities that span dynamic and fragmented mediatised fields leads us into a new consciousness of these issues.

Garcia et al. (2009) state strongly that although few studies of contemporary society can avoid addressing the Internet in some way, there are also few questions that can be answered by exploring online space alone. Hallett and Barber (2014) similarly argue that studying the way of life of many groups of people now has to involve taking seriously the online dimensions of that way of life as well as offline activities. This conflicts somewhat in tone with Boellstorff's (2010) discussion of different notions of the field, which defends online-only fields as a fruitful approach, but they all share a strong assertion that the definition of the field should be appropriate to the research question. Hine (2014) finds the demarcation of a specifically online ethnography no longer helpful in the face of an Internet that is multiply embedded in diverse frames of meaning-making both online and offline. A blended, mobile or networked research design can have a very direct pay-off in terms of the kind of contribution that the author is able to make because they are able to reflect the complexity of lived experience across different spaces rather than confining their aspirations to a description of online space alone. Theoretical interests within substantive fields of sociology, for example in the nature and significance of social movements, or the construction of identity, rarely confine themselves to interest only in what people do within a specific medium, and hence research designs that span media are required. Policy concerns are also rarely focused solely on activities within the virtual realm, but spill out into an interest in how online activities are experienced and utilised in other domains. Dyke (2013) uses a blended approach, combining ethnography of an online pro-anorexia community and an eating disorder prevention project based in schools and youth centres. The study explores the interaction between the online and offline spaces as young people navigate between them. The policy recommendations made by the researcher as a result of the study highlight the need to understand how online and offline spaces combine in the lives of young people at risk of eating disorders in order to frame successful interventions. Dyke (2013) demonstrates that although it may be challenging for the ethnographer to track issues between online and offline spaces, these very challenges may be theoretically and practically enlightening.

Study of social movements, in particular, appears to benefit from multi-modal and multi-sited designs. Postill and Pink (2012) make a case for the study of social movements in a 'messy' web of interconnections involving social media that acquire distinctive significance in particular places among the groups that use them. Treré (2012) and Farinosi and Treré (2011) similarly make a case for multi-modal study of social movements, which takes social media seriously as a site where events take place, but embeds this social media activity in the real-life contexts that these forms of activism are designed to affect. Beyond the study of social movements, multi-sited or networked ethnographic studies include Farnsworth and Austrin's (2010) study of poker, Burrell's (2009) ethnography of the Internet in Accra, Beneito-Montagut's (2011) study of emotion online, and Orton-Johnson's (2012) multi-sited ethnography of knitting and online spaces. Although netnography is often practiced as an online-only study, Kozinets (2010) identifies the possibility of blending netnography and conventional ethnography. Among studies that do explicitly claim to blend ethnography and netnography are Nichols and Rine (2012) in their study of identity narratives within a de-industrialising community. Hine (2014) argues that the 'e-cubed' Internet (embedded, embodied and everyday) benefits from a connective approach to ethnography. In this connective approach the frames of meaning-making for online activities are acknowledged to be multiple, and the connections which the ethnographer chooses to pursue therefore have to be viewed as strategic choices rather than as dictated by the prior boundaries of the field as an autonomous agent.

Within studies that combine online and offline, a variety of means are available to the ethnographer to define starting points and to decide where to move. Observation may begin online and move offline to conduct interviews which contextualise the online phenomena, as practised by Sade-Beck (2008) in a study of communities focused on bereavement. Blended studies may also start offline, as Miller and Slater (2000) argued. Studies focused on online phenomena may even be conducted from a predominantly offline perspective. Mabweazara (2010) studied journalists' use of information and communication technologies using a conventional ethnographic approach, finding it challenging to grasp this dispersed and fragmented way of working, but valuing the potential that participant observation and in-depth interviews offer to see the uses of ICTs from different positioning, and experiencing it as challenging, but

not impossible, to study the embedding of online activities in the offline ethnographically. The choice of research design, including decisions whether to include both offline and online data collection and whether to focus on synchronous or asynchronous communication depend on the aspirations of the researcher and the qualities of the group in focus (Wilkerson *et al.* 2014).

Field sites including online activities may take a wide variety of forms and the grounds for deciding which form of activities to observe and participate in will differ depending on the goals of the ethnographer. Some of the successful approaches to defining a field site outlined earlier are summarised next, varying according to the nature of the activities concerned or the strategy employed by the ethnographer for moving between them (although different terms are favoured by different authors and there is significant overlap between them):

- *Online:* the ethnographer studies activities within some online space (or connected set of spaces) on their own terms, without seeking to situate those activities within offline spaces.
- *Multi-modal:* different communication modes (potentially including face-to-face communication, documents, telephone, social networking sites, other online spaces) are studied because they are used by an identifiable group of people who form the focus of the study.
- *Multi-sited:* a set of interconnected sites are identified, either in advance of the study or as the study progresses, offering insights into different facets of the experience of interest.
- *Blended:* a study which combines two (or more) approaches – often online and offline observation – in order to explore a given phenomenon. The actual form of the blending varies, possibly involving a structured comparison between the two approaches, or possibly a more dynamic blending involving the ethnographer moving between sites as in a networked, multi-sited or connective approach.
- *Networked:* a set of interconnections are followed by the ethnographer by tracing the flow of communication between a group of people or activity of interest. New sites may emerge in a

dynamic fashion in the course of the study, rather than being identified in advance.

- *Connective:* the ethnographer moves between different modes of communication and locations (online or offline) according to a set of theoretically driven interests focusing on the contingent connections that emerge as people appropriate and make sense of online activities offline and vice versa.

As Postill and Pink (2012) argue, in many cases it may be productive to leave open the question of what the connection between social media activities and face-to-face locales might be because the ethnographer focuses on tracing forms of sociality that span online and offline, within a broader interest in finding out about the socio-political reality of forms of activity that involve, but are not confined within, social media and online spaces. In these fragmented mediatised domains of activity, the researcher actively constructs the field. It can be argued that this wide array of possible ways to define the study places an increased responsibility on the ethnographer to be reflexive about the decisions that they take when deciding what will count as the field site.

AUTOETHNOGRAPHY ONLINE

Reflexivity in relation to the definition of the field site in question is important, but this does not exhaust the importance of reflexivity within ethnographies involving online activities. There is an emergent strand of online ethnography that focuses on the embodied experience of the online researcher as an important source of insight in its own right. These studies build on recent developments in autoethnography as a means to tap into subjectivity and expose hidden structures of feeling not amenable to the more conventional ethnographic accounts which are, to some extent, always limited by what participants can verbalise and recount to the ethnographer (Reed-Danahay 1997; Ellis

2004; Ellis *et al.* 2010). Autoethnographers are often full participants in the situations that they recount. Whilst also embedded within academic disciplines, and hence attuned to what may be interesting or topical from various theoretical perspectives, autoethnographies often tread lightly with theoretical content and literature review and concentrate on evocation. Such writing has been accused of self-indulgence, focusing too much on the author's inner world at the expense of a rigorous attention to the perspective of others (Sparkes 2002). It is, however, some form of solution to the challenges posed for ethnography by the complex, fragmented and messy world that arises from the contingent connections between online and offline spaces. Autoethnography focuses the attention on how it feels to navigate such connections.

The term autoethnography is sometimes applied to participants' ongoing attempts to articulate and portray their own situation, rather than to a specific academic ethnographic project. Autoethnography can be used in this sense in relation to online interactions, in that the portrayals that participants post online can be viewed as reflexive texts which articulate their readings of their own culture (Nemeth and Gropper 2008; Jacobs 2010). This usage, however, is currently in the minority, and a narrower sense of autoethnography as a conscious form of methodological approach from someone within the academic community appears to have come to dominate. This form of autoethnography, as applied to online spaces, seems to have potential to make some significant contributions to our ability to work out what online interactions may mean to the people engaged in them.

The online ethnographer is always, in some sense, a participant, in that in order to be present in online spaces the ethnographer has to use the same technologies that participants are using. In order to be an ethnographer of a gaming site, for example, it may be necessary for the ethnographer to become highly skilled at playing the game just in order to stay alive long enough to experience the setting, quite apart from any aspirations to an epistemological purchase offered by the immersive experience. Along the spectrum between participant as observer and observer as participant (Gold 1958), the online ethnographer is always to some extent a participant as observer, in that they use the same medium to communicate as participants use (although they may, of course, also use other modes of communication, and in fact participants too often combine various modes rather than sticking to just one). Reflecting on the social conditions created by using a particular communication medium can become an important part of the online ethnographer's insights.

Autoethnographic approaches to online ethnography were pioneered by Markham (1998) with a focus on how it felt to navigate online space and communicate in various ways with online others. Markham (1998) used this account to highlight the contingency of the online experience, arguing that she, and those she met online, did not always view computer-mediated communication as a place, but might also experience it as a tool or as a way of being. Other autoethnographic accounts of online experience have followed, fuelled by the increasing acceptance, albeit usually as an alternative or niche approach, of authoethnography as a legitimate methodology. The nuances of online identity practices can effectively be explored through autoethnography: Dumitrica and Gaden (2008) made powerful use of autoethnography to explore the experience of gender in the virtual world Second Life; and Gatson (2011), without explicitly naming her project as 'autoethnographic', conducted a study of the online 'selling project' relying on participation in online and offline activities, systematic survey and reflection on the author's own selling practices.

Autoethnographies have also effectively explored pedagogy in online spaces. Lee (2008) writes an account of the experience of teaching an online course. As with much autoethnographic writing, Lee's focus is on evocation rather than precise theoretical

contribution as she recounts how the activities of moderating the online course are interwoven with the pressures and sensations of her offline life. The theoretical aspiration remains implicit: Lee writes to show us how the experience feels rather than telling us what we should make of her insights within a conventional sociological framework. Kruse's (2006) autoethnography focuses on the experience of being the online student rather than the tutor, recounting the process of learning to play the mandolin via online tuition and reflecting on the various forms of connection and isolation that he experienced. Henning (2012) explores the experience of a teacher-turned student: having taught online courses she then discusses the insights gained from becoming a student on such a course for the first time. Tschida and Sevier (2013) use an autoethnographic approach to explore the experience of teaching an online course, highlighting the challenges to their pedagogic practices and expectations compared to their experiences of face-to-face teaching.

Autonetnography also exists (Kozinets and Kedzior 2009) and is defined as a form of observation through searching and lurking and making reflective fieldnotes. Wilkinson and Patterson (2014) supplement an initial autonetnographic phase exploring consumer-created 'mash-ups' of the Peppa Pig brand posted to YouTube with online interviews including video elicitation. The term autonetnography, here, denotes an observational phase that focuses on the experience of the researcher as an active agent exploring the territory, and also, as with many studies termed netnographic, indicates a specific focus on consumption activities as exhibited online. Similarly, Beer and Penfold-Mounce (2009) explore celebrity gossip online by positioning themselves to search for it as any Internet user might, although without describing their study as ethnographic or netnographic.

In other cases, the ethnographer's use of their own experience extends beyond a reflection on immersion in the same medium as participants to occupation of a specific role.

Baym (1995, 2000) moved from full participant in a soap opera discussion group to ethnographer of the group. Hughey (2008) began as a participant in the forum devoted to African American fraternities and sororities that he later studied, framing his role as that of observant participant and combining an active participant observation that involved starting discussion threads of his own with content analysis and interviews. In fan studies, the researcher is often to some extent an insider in the fan community being studied, and thus it is possibly not surprising that autoethnography of online fan communities should emerge. Monaco (2010) moves around different online manifestations of fandom and sites related to the television programme which is her focus, as well as exploring her changing relations to the text engendered by engagement with these various online sites. Autoethnography offers an opportunity to explore how at least one audience member navigates and finds meanings in diverse manifestations of the fan object both online and offline. These contingent occasions of connection-making can otherwise prove quite methodologically intransigent because an observing ethnographer would find it difficult to follow participants between sites. Parry (2012) includes online sites within an autoethnographic study of football fandom, discussing the online sites as they become part of the flow of experience of being a fan, and reflecting on how this engagement feels and how it impacts on other daily activities. Being an insider to some extent also brings with it some distinctive ethical concerns relating to the nature of any covert observation that the insider role may bring with it. Paechter (2013) conducted a retrospective insider/outsider ethnography, tackling a group in which she had been a long-term full participant, making the study overt retrospectively and analysing archived posts going back through her time as participant.

The autoethnographic perspective turns the researcher's focus inwards to explore how a particular form of experience feels, but the autoethnographer is also tasked with reflecting on the ways in which a wider world, in the form of social structures and constraints, becomes effectively present for the individual in their everyday experience. Autoethnographers think about themselves as social beings. Through autoethnographies of online experience, we are therefore able to find out how standard infrastructures are made into personal experiences, and how online forms of interaction shape who we can be to one another as social beings. The autoethnographer situates Internet experiences and explores the multiple ways in which they make sense. Because autoethnographers start with the subjective experience, they are able to produce a multi-faceted perspective on the Internet, not limited by a prior understanding of what the field site for understanding a particular phenomenon should be. Autoethnographic approaches, like blended, multi-sited, networked and connective approaches, are able to develop ambitious theoretical aspirations because they follow the trails of phenomena wherever they may lead, and do not confine themselves artificially to a medium-based definition of what 'online' means.

A WAY FORWARD...

It can be said that in contemporary society the Internet is disappearing (Parks 2009) because people do not consciously go online, or even use one medium at a time, but combine media in an ad hoc fashion and practice multi-tasking across devices. Having faced up to the crisis of representation (Denzin 1997), ethnographers appear to be encountering a new crisis of agency: we are confronted by too many choices on how to make field sites and are required to take overt responsibility for the way in which we chose to define the field in any specific set of circumstances. It is no longer easy to fall back on the notion that there is a defined field site which pre-exists the ethnographer's arrival. An ethnographer will forge field sites in line with their aspirations for the study, and sometimes these field sites will be wholly based online, but ethnographers will often find themselves travelling beyond purely online sites and may not adopt any a priori sense of what the boundaries of the field site might be.

Even while the ethnographer becomes conscious of and takes responsibility for agency in defining the field, it is also important to take account of some of the less obvious forms of agency which are exerted by the field itself, leading us in some directions and not others and imperceptibly shaping our studies of the Internet. We need to reflect on the various forms of resistance that the field puts in the way of what we can know. Two key forms of resistance that online domains place in the way of the ethnographer are the increasing commercialisation and proprietary ownership of online space and also the relative invisibility of practices of consumption of online material. Commercialisation renders certain parts of the Internet less accessible to ethnographic study (Kozinets 2010) because proprietary concerns turn it into a series of password-protected closed worlds (Lievrouw 2012) where the ethnographer may need to negotiate informed consent, not just with the authors of online texts but with the commercial organisations whom participants may not even realise claim ownership of their words. Ethnographers cannot assume online that informants have the right to grant access, and proprietary ownership may well place some online spaces off limits for study. Where there are concerns over privacy and proprietary ownership, Internet users are often prompted to seek out more secretive or ephemeral forms of online interaction, and here online ethnographers will be faced by many of the problems that have already always been faced offline, in finding out what participants are up to in their fleeting interactions in private spaces (Gehl 2014). The prospect of a social life openly available for ethnographic study in online space may prove to be only a temporary and quite restricted phenomenon. It is important not to over-generalise from the phenomena that are fortuitously openly available for study now.

Linked to the concern with the retreat into more private, ephemeral forms of online interaction is the broader question of how consumption and interpretation practices are to be built into ethnography. Many people read online content without posting messages themselves, and their activity leaves no visible traces for the online ethnographer to see, but it is potentially highly consequential for their lives. Online ethnography is often predominantly focused on the available data from active contributors, and yet these active contributors form the tip of an iceberg in terms of understanding the overall online environment as a social phenomenon. To explore the Internet as an embedded social phenomenon, and as a component of contemporary lived existence, we need to acknowledge diverse forms of engagement with online space, including its role in people's calibration of themselves as social beings and their development of reflexive understandings of their place in the world. Not all socially significant Internet use leaves a lasting trace, nor is it immediately visible to the gaze of online methods. Blended and multi-sited designs and autoethnographies of consumption are a useful contribution to the effort of understanding the embedding of the Internet in everyday life, but there is still considerable work to be done in excavating the repercussions of the invisible nature of the consumption of online content, which so often stymies ethnographic effort focused on what is visible online. Anthropological approaches to ethnography have proved particularly fruitful in exploring these wider dimensions of digitally suffused culture (Horst and Miller 2013).

Online-only ethnography is relatively cheap, and often minimally disruptive to the lifestyle of the ethnographer compared to other ethnographic approaches. Online-only ethnography does have a significant contribution to make, particularly in working out the dynamics of interpersonal relations and exploring contemporary practices of meaning-making and identity formation. Online spaces have provided unprecedented access for ethnographers to experience and explore everyday life in depth and detail, and this should have a significant contribution to make to social science. However, when we study an online space as social scientists it is important to make the broader theoretical aspiration clear, and thus to demarcate the study as 'virtual' or as 'netnography' may sometimes be unhelpful. Whether we study online-only field sites or conduct blended studies that move around differently mediated forms of space, these studies should be contributing to the development of social science, and to use the epithet 'virtual' or to mark our studies netnographies is potentially an unhelpful act of distancing from the broader theoretical territory. In order to cement policy-relevant or theoretically ambitious disciplinary contributions, more complex, more challenging studies that span the online/offline border and deal with less visible aspects of the Internet as a social phenomenon also need to be carried out. It is important not to give the impression that online-only studies are enough. In the heavily politicised and cost-conscious domain of research funding, it is important to point out that the cheapest study is not necessarily the best, and that qualitative research in complex online/offline fields will not be quick, easy or cheap, but offers possibly one of the best ways to capture and interrogate these emergent forms of sociality that defy generalisation.

REFERENCES

Altheide, D. L. (1987) 'Reflections: ethnographic content analysis', *Qualitative Sociology*, 10(1): 65–77.

Amit, V. (ed.) (1999) *Constructing the Field*. London: Routledge.

Baker, S. (2013) 'Conceptualising the use of Facebook in ethnographic research: as tool, as data and as context', *Ethnography and Education*, 8(2): 131–45.

Baym, N. (1995) 'The emergence of community in computer-mediated communication'. In S. Jones (ed.), *Cybersociety*. Thousand Oaks, CA: Sage Publications, pp. 138–63.

Baym, N. K. (2000) *Tune In, Log On: Soaps, Fandom and Online Community*. Thousand Oaks, CA: Sage Publications.

Beer, D. and R. Penfold-Mounce (2009) 'Celebrity gossip and the new melodramatic imagination', *Sociological Research Online*, 14. Available at http://www.socresonline.org.uk/14/2/2.html (accessed 23 July 2016).

Beneito-Montagut, R. (2011) 'Ethnography goes online: towards a user-centred methodology to research interpersonal communication on the Internet', *Qualitative Research*, 11(6): 716–35.

Bengtsson, S. (2014) 'Faraway, so close! Proximity and distance in ethnography online', *Media, Culture and Society*, 11(6): 862–77.

Boellstorff, T. (2008) *Coming of Age in Second Life: an Anthropologist Explores the Virtually Human*. Princeton, NJ: Princeton University Press.

Boellstorff, T. (2010) 'A typology of ethnographic scales for virtual worlds'. In W. S. Bainbridge (ed.), *Online Worlds: Convergence of the Real and the Virtual*. London: Springer, pp. 123–33.

Boellstorff, T., B. Nardi, C. Pearce and T. L. Taylor (2012) *Ethnography and Virtual Worlds: A Handbook of Method*. Princeton, NJ: Princeton University Press.

boyd, D. and K. Crawford (2012) 'Critical questions for big data: provocations for a cultural, technological, and scholarly phenomenon', *Information, Communication and Society*, 15(5): 662–79.

Burrell, J. (2009) 'The field site as a network: a strategy for locating ethnographic research', *Field Methods*, 21(2): 181–99.

Coleman, E. G. (2010) 'Ethnographic approaches to digital media', *Annual Review of Anthropology*, 39(1): 487–505.

Coleman, E. G. (2013) *Coding Freedom: The Ethics and Aesthetics of Hacking*. Princeton, NJ: Princeton University Press.

Denzin, N. K. (1997) *Interpretive Ethnography: Ethnographic Practices for the 21st Century*. Thousand Oaks, CA: Sage Publications.

Dumitrica, D. and G. Gaden (2008) 'Knee-high boots and six-pack abs: autoethnographic reflections on gender and technology in Second Life', *Journal of Virtual Worlds Research,* 1. Available at http://journals.tdl.org/jvwr/article/view/323 (accessed 23 July 2016).

Dyke, S. (2013) 'Utilising a blended ethnographic approach to explore the online and offline lives of pro-ana community members', *Ethnography and Education,* 8(2): 146–61.

Ellis, C. (2004) *The Ethnographic I: A Methodological Novel about Autoethnography.* Walnut Creek, CA: Alta Mira.

Ellis, C., T. E. Adams and A. P. Bochner (2010) 'Autoethnography: an overview', *Forum Qualitative Sozialforschung/Forum: Qualitative Social Research,* 12. Available at http://www.qualitative-research.net/index.php/fqs/article/view/1589/3095 (accessed 23 July 2016).

Ess, C. and AoIR Ethics Working Committee (2002) *Ethical Decision-Making and Internet Research: Recommendations from the AoIR Ethics Working Committee.* Available at http://www.aoir.org/reports/ethics.pdf (accessed 23 July 2016).

Farinosi, M. and E. Treré (2011) 'Inside the "People of the Wheelbarrows": participation between online and offline dimension in the post-quake social movement', *Journal of Community Informatics,* 6. Available at http://ci-journal.net/index.php/ciej/article/viewArticle/761 (accessed 23 July 2016).

Farnsworth, J. and T. Austrin (2010) 'The ethnography of new media worlds? Following the case of global poker', *New Media and Society,* 12(7): 1120–36.

Ferrell, J., K. Hayward and J. Young (2008) *Cultural Criminology: An Invitation.* London: Sage Publications.

Frederick, B. J. and D. Perrone (2014) '"Party N Play" on the Internet: subcultural formation, Craigslist, and escaping from stigma', *Deviant Behavior,* 35(11): 859–84.

Gallagher, K., A. Wessels and B. Y. Ntelioglou (2013) 'Becoming a networked public: digital ethnography, youth and global research collectives', *Ethnography and Education,* 8(2): 177–93.

Garcia, A. C., A. I. Standlee, J. Bechkoff and Y. Cui (2009) 'Ethnographic approaches to the Internet and computer-mediated communication', *Journal of Contemporary Ethnography,* 38(1): 52–84.

Gatson, S. N. (2011) 'Self-naming practices on the Internet: identity, authenticity, and community', *Cultural Studies, Critical Methodologies,* 11(3): 224–35.

Gehl, R. W. (2014) 'Power/freedom on the dark web: a digital ethnography of the Dark Web Social Network'. *New Media and Society.*

Giglietto, F., L. Rossi and D. Bennato (2012) 'The open laboratory: limits and possibilities of using Facebook, Twitter, and YouTube as a research data source', *Journal of Technology in Human Services,* 30(3–4): 145–59.

Gold, R. L. (1958) 'Roles in sociological field observations', *Social Forces,* 36(3): 217–23.

Gold, R. L. (1997) 'The ethnographic method in sociology', *Qualitative Inquiry,* 3(4): 388–402.

Gupta, A. and J. Ferguson (1997) *Anthropological Locations: Boundaries and Grounds of a Field Science.* Berkeley, CA: University of California Press.

Hallett, R. E. and K. Barber (2014) 'Ethnographic research in a cyber era', *Journal of Contemporary Ethnography,* 43(3): 306–30.

Henning, T. B. (2012) 'Writing professor as adult learner: an autoethnography of online professional development', *Journal of Asynchronous Learning Networks,* 16(2): 9–26.

Hesse-Biber, S. and A. J. Griffin (2013) 'Internet-mediated technologies and mixed methods research: problems and prospects', *Journal of Mixed Methods Research,* 7(1): 43–61.

Hine, C. (2000) *Virtual Ethnography.* London: Sage Publications.

Hine, C. (2008) 'How can qualitative Internet researchers define the boundaries of their projects?'. In A. N. Markham and N. Baym (eds.), *Internet Inquiry: Conversations about Method.* Thousand Oaks, CA: Sage Publications, pp. 1–20.

Hine, C. (2014) *Ethnography for the Internet: Embedded, Embodied and Everyday.* Oxford: Berg.

Horst, H. A. and D. Miller (2013) *Digital Anthropology.* London: Bloomsbury Publishing.

Hughey, M. W. (2008) 'Virtual (br)others and (re)sisters: authentic black fraternity and sorority identity on the Internet', *Journal of Contemporary Ethnography,* 37(5): 528–60.

Jacobs, K. (2010) 'Lizzy Kinsey and the Adult Friendfinders: an ethnographic study of Internet sex and pornographic self-display in Hong Kong', *Culture, Health and Sexuality,* 12(6): 691–703.

Kendall, L. (2002) *Hanging Out in the Virtual Pub: Masculinities and Relationships Online.* Berkeley, CA: University of California Press.

Kozinets, R. V. (2010) *Netnography: Doing Ethnographic Research Online.* London: Sage Publications.

Kozinets, R. V. (2012) 'Marketing netnography: prom/ot(ulgat)ing a new research method', *Methodological Innovations Online,* 7(1): 37–45.

Kozinets, R. V. and R. Kedzior (2009) 'I, Avatar: auto-netnographic research in virtual worlds'. In N. T. Wood and M. R. Solomon (eds.), *Virtual Social Identity and Consumer Behavior.* New York, NY: ME Sharpe, pp. 3–19.

Kruse, N. B. (2013) 'Locating "The Road to Lisdoonvarna" via autoethnography: Pathways, barriers and detours in self-directed online music learning', *Journal of Music, Technology & Education,* 5(3): 293–308.

Lee, K. V. (2008) 'A neophyte about online teaching: almost done', *Qualitative Inquiry,* 14(7): 1180–86.

Lievrouw, L. A. (2012) 'The next decade in Internet time: ways ahead for new media studies', *Information, Communication and Society,* 15(5): 616–38.

Ling, R. (2012) *Taken for Grantedness: The Embedding of Mobile Communication into Society.* Cambridge, MA: MIT Press.

Mabweazara, H. M. (2010) 'Researching the use of new technologies (ICTs) in Zimbabwean newsrooms: an ethnographic approach', *Qualitative Research,* 10(6): 659–77.

Markham, A. N. (1998) *Life Online: Researching Real Experience in Virtual space.* Walnut Creek, CA: Altamira Press.

Markham, A. N. (2006) 'Ethic as method, method as ethic: a case for reflexivity in qualitative ICT research', *Journal of Information Ethics,* 15(2): 37–54.

Markham, A. N. and E. Buchanan (2012) *Ethical Decision-Making and Internet Research: Recommendations from the AoIR Ethics Committee (Version 2.0).* Association of Internet Researchers. Available at http://aoir.org/reports/ethics2.pdf (accessed 23 July 2016).

Marres, N. (2012) 'The redistribution of methods: on intervention in digital social research, broadly conceived', *Sociological Review,* 60: 139–65.

Marshall, J. (2010) 'Ambiguity, oscillation and disorder: online ethnography and the making of culture', *Cosmopolitan Civil Societies: An Interdisciplinary Journal,* 2. Available at http://epress.lib.uts.edu.au/ojs/index.php/mcs/article/view/1598/1859 (accessed 23 July 2016).

Miller, D. and H. A. Horst (2012) 'The digital and the human: a prospectus for digital anthropology'. In H. A. Horst and D. Miller (eds.), *Digital Anthropology.* London: Berg, pp. 3–38.

Miller, D. and D. Slater (2000) *The Internet: An Ethnographic Approach.* Oxford: Berg.

Monaco, J. (2010) 'Memory work, autoethnography and the construction of a fan-ethnography', *Participations,* 7. Available at http://www.participations.org/Volume%207/Issue%201/monaco.htm (accessed 23 July 2016).

Murthy, D. (2008) 'Digital ethnography: an examination of the use of new technologies for social research', *Sociology,* 42(5): 837–55.

Murthy, D. (2013) 'Ethnographic Research 2.0: the potentialities of emergent digital technologies for qualitative organizational research', *Journal of Organizational Ethnography,* 2(1): 23–36.

Nardi, B. A. (2010) *My Life as a Night Elf Priest: An Anthropological Account of World of Warcraft.* Ann Arbor, MI: University of Michigan Press.

Nemeth, D. J. and R. C. Gropper (2008) 'A cyber-ethnographic foray into GRandT Internet photo blogs', *Romani Studies,* 18(1): 39–70.

Nichols, L. T. and J. Rine (2012) 'Collective identity narratives: historical and emergent stories of selfhood in a deindustrializing community', *Studies in Symbolic Interaction,* 39: 121–49.

Orton-Johnson, K. (2012) 'Knit, purl and upload: new technologies, digital mediations and the experience of leisure', *Leisure Studies,* 33(3): 305–21.

Orton-Johnson, K. and N. Prior (eds.) (2013) *Digital Sociology: Critical Perspectives.* Basingstoke, UK: Palgrave Macmillan.

Paccagnella, L. (1997) 'Getting the seats of your pants dirty: strategies for ethnographic research on virtual communities', *Journal of Computer-Mediated Communication,* 3(1). Available at http://onlinelibrary.wiley.com/doi/10.1111/j.1083-6101.1997.tb00065.x/abstract (accessed 23 July 2016).

Paechter, C. (2013) 'Researching sensitive issues online: implications of a hybrid insider/outsider position in a retrospective ethnographic study', *Qualitative Research,* 13(1): 71–86.

Parks, M. (2009) 'What will we study when the Internet disappears?', *Journal of Computer-Mediated Communication,* 14(3): 724–9.

Parry, K. D. (2012) 'Game of two passions: a football fan's autoethnography', *Qualitative Research Journal,* 12(2): 238–50.

Postill, J. and S. Pink (2012) 'Social media ethnography: the digital researcher in a messy web', *Media International Australia,* 145: 123–34.

Reed-Danahay, D. (ed.) (1997) *Auto/Ethnography: Rewriting the Self and the Social.* Oxford, Berg.

Robinson, L. and J. Schulz (2009) 'New avenues for sociological inquiry: evolving forms of ethnographic practice', *Sociology,* 43(4): 685–98.

Rogers, R. (2013) *Digital Methods.* Cambridge, MA: MIT Press.

Ruppert, E., J. Law and M. Savage (2013) 'Reassembling social science methods: the challenge of digital devices', *Theory, Culture and Society,* 30(4): 22–46.

Sade-Beck, L. (2008) 'Internet ethnography: online and offline', *International Journal of Qualitative Methods,* 3(2): 45–51.

Senft, T. M. (2008) *Camgirls: Celebrity and Community in the Age of Social Networks.* New York, NY: Peter Lang.

Sparkes, A. C. (2002) 'Autoethnography: self-indulgence or something more?'. In A. P. Bochner and C. Ellis (eds.), *Ethnographically Speaking: Autoethnography, Literature, and Aesthetics.* Walnut Creek, CA: AltaMira, pp. 209–32.

Steinmetz, K. F. (2012) 'Message received: virtual ethnography in online message boards', *International Journal of Qualitative Methods,* 11(1): 26–39.

Treré, E. (2012) 'Social movements as information ecologies: exploring the coevolution of multiple Internet technologies for activism', *International Journal of Communication,* 6: 19.

Tschida, C. M. and B. R. Sevier (2013) 'Teaching social studies online: an exemplar for examining the broader implications of online methods courses in teacher education', *Journal of Online Learning and Teaching,* 9. Available at http://jolt.merlot.org/vol9no4/tschida_1213.pdf (accessed 23 July 2016).

Tunçalp, D. and Patrick L. Lê (2014) '(Re)locating boundaries: a systematic review of online ethnography', *Journal of Organizational Ethnography,* 3(1): 59–79.

Underberg, N. and E. Zorn (2013) *Digital Ethnography: Anthropology, Narrative, and New Media.* Austin, TX: University of Texas Press.

Wilkerson, J. M., A. Iantaffi, J. A. Grey, W. O. Bockting and B. R. S. Rosser (2014) 'Recommendations for Internet-based qualitative health research with hard-to-reach populations',. *Qualitative Health Research,* 24(4): 561–74.

Wilkinson, C. and A. Patterson (2014) 'Peppa Piggy in the middle of marketers and mashup makers'. In S. Brown and S. Ponsonby-McCabe (eds.), *Brand Mascots: And Other Marketing Animals.* Abingdon, UK: Routledge, pp. 123–40.

## 24

Online Interviewing

Henrietta O'Connor and Clare Madge

INTRODUCTION

According to Krotoski (2010: 2), the development of the Internet over the last few decades has resulted in researchers experiencing a 'golden age of research online'. Online research methods have correspondingly proliferated in all fields of social science. Use of these methods mitigates the distance of space, enables research to be easily internationalised without the usual associated travel costs and can be valuable for researchers contacting groups or individuals who may otherwise be difficult to reach (see, for example Barratt, 2012; McDermott and Roen, 2012). Over the last decade online research methods have become firmly established as a legitimate means of data collection for social scientists, removing some of the 'considerable anxiety about just how far existing tried and tested research methods are appropriate for technologically mediated interactions' (Hine, 2005: 1). Indeed, the use of an Internet-mediated methodology is moving from the

realm of the novel and innovative into the mainstream and routine. This is particularly the case with online surveys and email interviews, which have flourished in many subdisciplines of the social sciences. In contrast, online synchronous interviewing (somewhat surprisingly) still remains a relatively uncommon approach to online data collection, although its use is also on the rise based on interfaces such as instant messaging (Hinchcliffe and Gavin, 2009) and video-based technologies such as Skype (Cater, 2011; Hanna, 2012; Deakin and Wakefield, 2014).

This chapter provides an overview of online interviewing. It begins by examining the use of asynchronous and synchronous online interviews. The chapter goes on to debate some of the advantages and limitations of online interviewing, particularly in relation to conventional face-to-face interviewing. Some useful sources to aid consideration of online ethics are then briefly discussed. A more practical technical section follows which advises on appropriate software for the conduct of online interviewing. Finally, we conclude by reflecting on the methodological progress and future of online interviewing.

ONLINE INTERVIEWS

The use of online interviews in social science research has become more widespread over the last decade (Hooley *et al.* 2011; James and Busher, 2009; Salmons, 2015). Wilkerson *et al.* (2014) offer useful guidelines for making decisions about the design and conduct of qualitative online research. These relate to questions about whether an online study is the most appropriate approach for a particular research project and whether to employ synchronous or asynchronous methods (see Table 24.1). To aid decisions surrounding which type of interview strategy to employ, the following section of the chapter examines the use of synchronous and asynchronous online interviews in social research (see Table 24.2). We begin by exploring the asynchronous interview.

Asynchronous Interviews

Online interviews, conducted in non-real time or asynchronously, are now a fairly common data collection strategy used by social scientists. There are now numerous examples of research carried out using asynchronous interviews, most often facilitated via email (see, for example, Mann and Stewart, 2000; Illingworth 2001, 2006; Kivits 2004, 2005; James and Busher, 2006; James, 2007; Ison, 2009; Bjerke, 2010; Burns, 2010). Indeed, interviews conducted through the use of email have been one of the most widely used online methods to date.

There are a number of advantages to using an asynchronous online interview, not least the relative technological simplicity of email. However, it is important to remember that for some individuals, techno-competence may be inhibited by disabilities such as dyslexia or visual impairment (Clark, 2007) or other, more physical limitations which may make computer use difficult. However, Bowker and Tuffin (2004: 230) suggest quite the opposite, arguing that 'the flexibility surrounding online data gathering may aid participation for those with disabilities. Indeed, irrespective of physical coordination, mobility and speech capacity, the textual nature of online interaction affords people with diverse operating techniques the capacity to participate'. Ison (2009) supports this stance, illustrating that email interviews are particularly suited for people with verbal communication impairments, such as cerebral palsy, because the flexible and asynchronous nature of the email interview can increase opportunities for participant involvement and enhance the quality and inclusiveness of research data.

A second distinct advantage of the email interview is that interviewees can answer the interview questions entirely at their own convenience. There are no time restrictions and this can be particularly valuable when participants are located in different time zones. Emails can be answered any time of day or night that suits the respondent. The lack of temporal restrictions also enables both the interviewer and interviewee to spend time considering their questions and answers, and perhaps composing, recomposing and editing responses to questions. James (2007) shows how this can enable the research process to become more reflexive, allowing both researcher and participant to reflect on the interview data and experience. That said, email interviews can also be used to construct an 'almost instantaneous dialogue between researcher and subject … if desired' (Selwyn and Robson 1998: 2), responses can be immediate and a relatively fast-paced exchange of questions and responses can be achieved.

Nevertheless, James and Busher (2006: 417) suggest that an advantage of email interviews is that there is no need for the exchange to be fast-paced. They stress that much of the value of email interviews lies in the opportunity for

Table 24.1 Decision-making checklist for type of online qualitative data collection

Directions: answer the following questions to decide between online or offline study design.   *Yes – online*   *No – offline*
If you respond 'Yes' to most items, consider online data collection.

Administrative considerations

Can staff transfer offline qualitative data collection skills to an online environment with minimal training?

Is there money in the budget to cover the costs of online qualitative data collection software?

Is there money in the budget to cover the costs of online recruitment?

Does the budget limit the ability to pay a transcriptionist to produce written transcripts of audio or video recordings?

Are members of the research team trained to code disjointed text transcripts, audio, video or other visual files collected online from study participants?

Population considerations

Are members of your population able to use the technology required to participate in your online study with minimal training?

Do members of your population have access to the technology required to participate in an online study, including high-speed Internet access?

If members of your population will be dependent on community spaces, e.g. libraries or Internet cafés, to participate in an online study, are you confident the location will not limit the time they can participate or bias their responses?

Do members of your population have the literacy to participate in online text-based data collection, e.g. message boards or chat rooms?

Is it important to have participants from geographically diverse locations?

Data collection considerations

Compared with offline data collection, will online data collection increase the confidentiality of participants?

Is it desirable for your study participants to have greater perceived anonymity?

Is it desirable for your study participants to have greater perceived homogeneity?

If collecting data online, do you have access to strong data security systems, e.g. a dedicated study server and data encryption?

If collecting data online, is there technical support for members of the research team?

If collecting data online, is there technical support for participants?

Are there significant barriers to securing participant transportation or a physical space if data were collected offline?

If collecting data online, are you confident that members of the research team will be able to build rapport with study participants?

If collecting data online, does your qualitative data collection software allow participants to record emotional reactions, e.g. emoticons?

If the viewing of media is critical to your study, will the qualitative data collection software you are using support the media, e.g. hyperlinks, photographs, videos?

Does the study timeline prohibit delayed access to data while it is being transcribed?

Is it important to have every comment date and time stamped and linked to a participant identification number?

Are there significant barriers to securing participant transportation or a physical space if data were collected offline?

Directions: answer the following questions to help you determine whether you should use   *Yes –*   *No –*
synchronous (yes) or asynchronous (no) data collection, or both. If your responses are in both   *synchronous*   *asynchronous*
columns, consider whether it would be beneficial to use both data collection methods.

Are you expecting to have participants who lack experience communicating with other people in an online chat room environment?

Is participants' reflexivity important to you? Are participants more likely to be engaged if they are allowed to participate on their own time?

Are you willing to sacrifice the spontaneity of an interactive conversation to allow for reflexivity or to accommodate participants' schedules?

Does your retention plan allow you to contact participants who do not log into an asynchronous data collection tool within an agreed-on period of time?

Are you confident that if your retention plan is implemented appropriately, participant dropout will be minimal?

Is the use of the constant-comparative method critical to your study design?

Source: Abridged from Wilkerson *et al.* (2014: 569–71).

Table 24.2   A comparison of the characteristics of offline and online interviews

	Asynchronous online interview	Synchronous online interview	Onsite face-to-face interview	Telephone interview	VOI interview
Venue	Email and discussion board	Chatroom or conferencing site	Onsite venue	Telephone provider	VOI provider
Temporal restrictions	Non-real time	Real time	Real time	Real time	Real time
Limitations	No time constraints	Constrained by time	Constrained by time	Constrained by time	Constrained by time
Software requirements	Simple, familiar	More complex	n/a	n/a	More complex
Technical ability	Low	Medium	n/a	n/a	Medium
Speed of response	Time to reflect included	Spontaneous	Spontaneous	Spontaneous	Spontaneous
Format of response	Written	Written	Oral and non-visual clues	Oral	Oral and potential for visual clues
Disadvantages	Easy to ignore or delete	Technical issues	Cost	Technical issues	Technical issues
Transcription	Generated automatically	Generated automatically	Not generated	Not generated	Not generated
Cost	Low cost	Low cost	Higher cost	Higher cost	Low cost

Source: O'Connor et al. (2008).

respondents to think about their responses, 'drafting and redrafting what they wanted to write' (p. 406). Indeed, they conclude by suggesting that email interviews are particularly suitable when 'snappy answers are not required'. Although email interviews do allow respondents considerable time to compose, edit and redraft responses to questions, this could be perceived as a disadvantage. A response that has been so well-considered and carefully thought about is likely to produce a 'socially desirable' answer rather than a more spontaneous response which can be generated through synchronous interviews or by more traditional face-to-face interviews (Joinson, 2005).

Some of the advantages of email interviewing can then also represent disadvantages. For example, although technologically an email interview may be simple to administer, it is also easy for a respondent to ignore or delete emails if s/he is too busy or loses interest in the process. The frequent time lag between an interviewer posting a question and the interviewee emailing a reply may result in a certain level of spontaneity being lost and this may impact on the richness of the data generated. Sanders (2005: 75–6) compared

the data gathered via email interviews to that collected in face-to-face interviews using the same structure and questions and found that the email interviews did not generate the same quality of data. She argues that

the essence of the inquiry was often misunderstood or answers would diverge to other subjects. It was difficult to maintain the flow of dialogue … and because of the asynchronous nature of email contact, the lack of spontaneity meant that it was difficult to probe and threads were easily lost.
Sanders, 2005: 75–6

Additionally, the reliance on a text-based interview process can also lead to the researcher becoming 'a victim of his or her own imagination and preconceptions' (Bjerke, 2010: 1718) when interviewing people via email. In a situation where the participants and the researcher cannot see or hear each other and the researcher has to rely solely on the written text to understand the participant, there are concerns that valuable nonverbal data may be lost in the email interview process. Further issues revolve around the fact that researchers cannot safely ask 'knowledge' questions because respondents can simply check the answers on the Internet. Finally, there may still be age/generation differences in how comfortable respondents are with computer-mediated interaction via email. Despite the increasing prevalence of Internet access amongst the UK population, older people remain less likely to use the Internet and a 'grey digital divide' persists (Morris, 2007).

Despite these complexities involved in email interviews, there are clearly further advantages of this asynchronous online method. First, the time-consuming nature of transcription of interviews is reduced, if not eliminated altogether. As Burns (2010: 11.3) notes 'comments, opinions, interpretations, even humour reflecting on various things' were already transcribed in her email interviews. Second, Burns (2010) also suggests that because email interviews are interactive on an individual basis, in that the researcher responds to the interests and responses of an individual participant, the result is a more 'personal touch' to the interview process. Finally, on the practical front, because online email interviews remove the need to travel to an interview venue, the cost of email interviews is minimal.

Synchronous interviews

In contrast to the growing body of literature that focuses on asynchronous interviews, there has been more limited academic assessment of the advantages and limitations of synchronous online interviews. Indeed, with the exception of an early flurry of research which used synchronous interviews (Gaiser, 1997; Smith, 1997; Chen and Hinton, 1999; Mann and Stewart, 2000; O'Connor and Madge, 2001), there have been relatively few recent empirical studies (Hinchcliffe and Gavin, 2009; Enochsson, 2011; Jowett *et al.*, 2011), although there is a growing body of work examining Skype as a medium for synchronous interviewing, using both audio and video (Cater, 2011; Hanna, 2012; Deakin and Wakefield, 2014).

The reasons for the low take-up of synchronous interviewing are unclear. Certainly online synchronous interviews can be more complicated to set up than a basic email interview and this may, in part, explain the lower levels of usage of this type of interviewing. For example, a researcher planning to generate data in this way must begin by selecting an appropriate software package such as conferencing software (Madge *et al.*, 2009; Sedgwick and Spiers, 2009) or access to a chatroom or instant messaging service (Hinchcliffe and Gavin, 2009; Barratt 2012; McDermott and Roen, 2012) to facilitate the interview. This can be perceived as requiring rather sophisticated technological skills compared to the use of email, which may act as a disincentive for using this approach. Moreover, as Deakin and Wakefield (2014: 605) note, some participants may not have the technological competence, familiarity with online communication, software requirements or regular high-speed Internet provision to enable them to participate in a synchronous online interview, which may act as a further disincentive.

However, this type of interview does also have distinct advantages and, in many respects more closely resembles a conventional face-to-face interview, thereby overcoming some of the limitations of an online asynchronous exchange. As Chen and Hinton (1999) have observed, 'real time' online interviews can provide greater spontaneity than online asynchronous interviews, enabling respondents to answer immediately and, in the case of synchronous focus groups, interact with one another.

Perhaps the most widely used approach to online synchronous interviews has been facilitation through conferencing software (O'Connor and Madge 2001; Madge *et al.*, 2009; Jowett *et al.*, 2011). Relevant software can be downloaded by the participants and the chatroom type environment facilitates the synchronous nature of the interviews. Figure 24.1 illustrates a typical conferencing interface as seen by participants.

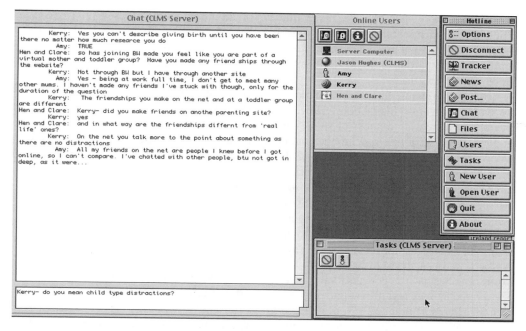

Figure 24.1   Screenshot of the virtual interface during synchronous chat
Source: O'Connor and Madge (2001).

The screen consists of a number of different windows and a tool bar. There is a large 'chat' window in which the dialogue is displayed, beneath this is a smaller window where users type their text, and press return; seconds later the contribution is displayed, prefixed with their name.

Such interfaces are most familiar to those who regularly use 'chatroom' facilities. This may mean that such an approach to interviewing is most suited to individuals who regularly use chatrooms, for example teenagers (Enochsson, 2011), university students (Hinchcliffe and Gavin, 2009) or specific 'marginalized' communities (Barratt, 2012; McDermott and Roen, 2012).

An important advantage of the synchronous interview already alluded to, is that the real time nature of the exchanges has much in common with the conventional onsite interview. Unlike asynchronous interviews, where there is time to edit and redraft responses, synchronous interviews can generate more spontaneous answers. This can result in responses being more 'honest' in nature as there is little time to consider the social desirability of the response in the 'fast and furious environment' (Mann and Stewart, 2000: 153) of the synchronous chat. A downside of this environment is that the fast-paced nature of the discussion generates interview transcripts which can be difficult to interpret. Contributions can be fragmented and rarely follow a sequential form because the interviewer may post a new question before the respondent has fully replied to the previous question. This results in a transcript that resembles a 'written conversation'. On the positive side, however, as with email interviews, there is no need for the researcher to transcribe interviews as transcripts are automatically created. That said, Jowett *et al.* (2011: 358) found that it took at least twice as long to produce a comparable amount of transcript data in online interviews compared to those conduced face-to-face. Although online interviewing may therefore be more time efficient for the researcher (reducing travel times, for example), it may be more time consuming for the participant, and result in the production of less data.

Most synchronous interviews employed are based on textual interactions. However, recently an increasing number of studies are employing Skype, a free synchronous online service that provides the opportunity for audio or video interviewing. On Skype, interviews can be conducted in real time via the instant messaging feature, which allows multiple users to participate simultaneously by typing their comments in a 'common room' (Moylan *et al.*, 2015: 41). All conversations are saved in Skype and can then be searched for keywords or concepts. The conversation can also be exported in plain text format into programs such as Microsoft products (Word or Excel) or a specialised qualitative data analysis program (Moylan *et al.*, 2015: 41). Skype has greater national and international recognition than other online software applications that are available and the video calling facility provides the researcher with an opportunity to not just talk to their respondent but also to see them in real time (Deakin and Wakefield, 2014). Sullivan (2012) therefore suggests that Skype interviews can provide access to verbal and nonverbal cues, which are not available in text-based online interviewing, thus providing an equal authenticity level with face-to-face interviews, although Cater (2011) observes that the 'head shot' provided by the webcam may create obstacles in observing all of the participant's body language. This 'head shot' problem can be overcome by other video-teleconferencing applications, such as Access Grid, which is also advantageous owing to its lack of lag and freeze problems (Fielding, 2011). Hanna (2012) further observes that audio and video data can be easily downloaded onto the researcher's computer work station, although technical hitches, such as webcams not functioning correctly, can also impede the interview process. Table 24.3 summarises some of the benefits and drawbacks

of Skype interviews (based on Deakin and Wakefield, 2014).

There are also a number of key differences between synchronous and asynchronous interviews. These differences relate to the choice of software, the virtual interface and the temporal characteristics of each type of interview. However, many other challenges presented by the virtual venue are remarkably similar regardless of the type of online interview. In the following section, we go on to consider in detail some of these affordances and limitations of online interviewing, particularly in relation to face-to-face interviewing.

POTENTIALS AND LIMITATIONS OF ONLINE INTERVIEWS

Researchers who have used online synchronous or asynchronous interviews report many differences between online interviews and face-to-face interviews. There are now several useful sources which can act as a guide to the practice of online interviewing (see, for example, Hooley *et al.* 2011; James and Busher, 2009; Salmons, 2015; Wilkerson *et al.*, 2014). It is no longer simply the case that 'face-to-face interaction … becomes the gold standard against which the performance of computer-mediated interaction is judged' (Hine, 2005: 4): online interviewing is now increasingly valued in and of itself as a valid and legitimate research method. That said, many challenges still remain, and there is still a divergence of opinions over the suitability and validity of online interviewing. Jowett *et al.* (2011: 366), for example, still consider that there 'is a lack of reflection and reflexivity' surrounding online interviewing and that 'there remains no clear consensus about the suitability of the Internet as medium for conducting qualitative interviews', while Deakin and Wakefield (2014: 604) argue that online interviews are still often presented as a 'second choice' to the 'gold standard' of face-to-face interviews. This notion implies that offline methods are

Table 24.3 Benefits and drawbacks of Skype interviews

Issue	Benefits	Drawbacks
Recruitment	Allows interviewees and interviewer flexibility in terms of organising the interview time	Potential interviewees may be put off participating if they do not know how to use Skype
Logistical and technological considerations	Health and safety concerns reduced when interviewing at night Cost effective Time effective Greater flexibility of researcher and interviewee in terms of interview time In the vast majority of cases, no technological problems were encountered because researchers were appropriately trained in the use of Skype	In some cases, recording material will need to be purchased and interviews conducted in specific locations where Skype is available The distance between researcher and interviewee can make it easier for participants to drop out as they feel less commitment to the process than with face-to-face interviews Technological problems in some cases lead to issues in sound quality making recording difficult Technological or signal problems can make the building of rapport difficult
Ethics	There is no need to obtain phone numbers from participants Interviewees can withdraw with the click of a button Anonymity can be easily ensured	Gaining informed consent verbally can make the beginning of the interview feel very formal and may not set the right tone for an interview Ethical issues may arise in taking video or audio recordings of the interview. Participants need to be made fully aware of this. Participants may feel uncomfortable being filmed in their own home
Rapport	In the majority of cases, building rapport can be established just as well as in face-to-face interviews. Exchanging emails, messages or reports can facilitate this process	When interviewing a reserved interviewee, building rapport can be difficult
Audio or video	Audio and video allow interviewees to choose the level of contact they wish to engage in	Video is not possible in some cases as it can reduce sound quality
Absentees	Time and money have not been spent if the interviewee does not log on to complete the interview	Participants appear to be more likely to 'drop out' of the interview last minute or without notice

Source: Deakin and Wakefield (2014: 613).

'problem-free' and without their own limitations and disadvantages. In the same way that the discussion of the differences between quantitative and qualitative research methods often 'ends up being addressed in terms of what quantitative research is not' (Bryman, 2004: 267), online methods are often debated with a focus on what they lack. This rather ignores the pitfalls that can be associated with offline interviewing as much as online interviewing and the different possibilities offered by each approach.

We shall now consider some of the challenges that remain, including online recruitment, representativeness, interview conduct and design, respondent identity verification, building rapport and online interaction.

Online Recruitment

A key concern for conducting both onsite and online interviews is the recruitment of an appropriate group of respondents. The Internet provides access to groups of users with tightly defined and narrow interests, for example, new parents (O'Connor and Madge, 2001), breast cancer patients (Sharf, 1997; Orgad, 2005), users of health-related websites (Kivits, 2004, 2005), university students (Hinchcliffe and Gavin, 2009) or 'hard to reach' populations (Mann and Stewart, 2000).

However, although participants with narrowly defined interests are potentially easy to locate online, the process of recruitment can be complex. One approach to gaining access to users of specific websites is through contact with website page owners or moderators directly. For O'Connor and Madge (2001), whose interest was in new parents' use of a particular parenting website, contacting the website providers directly was a logical first step in accessing respondents. Similarly, both Murray and Sixsmith (1998) and Kivits (2004) accessed respondents by contacting the 'moderator' of the boards and arranging access and permission to use the site for contacting participants. Such an approach can also result in valuable publicity and support for the research. Increasingly social networking sites such as Twitter and Facebook have proved to be fertile grounds for recruiting respondents with shared or narrowly defined interests (Moore *et al.*, 2015).

Researchers report varying levels of success with different approaches to recruitment. One approach is the posting of a general message to a bulletin board, introducing the research and advertising for volunteers to participate. Care must be taken, however, when posting to discussion groups to request participation. Hewson *et al.* (2003:116) suggest that netiquette demands that postings to a newsgroup or discussion forum should be relevant, but this poses a problem because most researchers' invitations to join a research project will not be directly relevant to the intended discussion. This raises ethical issues for the online researcher. The best practice is to approach the moderator of the list or newsgroup or discussion forum directly to get permission for the invitation posting but to be sensitive to the fact that such an invitation may be considered spamming and therefore unacceptable (Madge, 2012).

Representativeness

Selecting research respondents from the online world also raises issues of representativeness, common to all social science research. However, there are issues associated with the Internet that raise issues of

representativeness specific to the type of research, not least access to the Internet itself. As Mann and Stewart (2000: 31) suggest, 'access to the Internet is a matter not only of economics, but also of one's place in the world in terms of gender, culture, ethnicity and language'.

The digital divide can therefore still be a very real barrier and some individuals and geographical areas are less Internet-connected than others. This raises a serious shortcoming of Internet-based research, often promoted as offering research potential unrestricted by geographical boundaries. Online research methods remain

> very geographically specific, limiting who we can 'speak' to and whose lives we can engage with. The potential to be involved in a study using online research methods is, therefore, partial, so any grand claims of the utility of such methods for internationalizing research must be treated with some caution.
>
> Madge, 2006: n.p.

Orgad's (2005) work is a good example of online research that she acknowledges suffers from biases outlined earlier. Her research, which was focused on users of breast cancer related online spaces, was biased in a number of ways. First, participants were recruited through specialist websites which were located by searching for only 'top-level global domain websites' (defined as those with addresses ending with .com, .org and .net). As a consequence of this rather restricted search process, the research suffered a North American bias as all other 'national domain websites' were excluded from the study. She also restricted her research to English language websites.

Other issues can impact in the representativeness of online research. For example, there is no central register of Internet users and although some websites may have membership lists, these do not include 'lurkers' or individuals who have chosen not to register. Likewise, a sample group drawn in the ways outlined earlier will inevitably exclude from the sample those individuals who chose not to answer calls for respondents.

Finally, Salmons (2015: 127) makes an important distinction between interviewing online and sampling and recruiting online, which depends to a great extent on whether the research is concerned with 'online or technology-mediated behaviours, culture, practices, attitudes or experiences' or whether the Internet is being used simply as a means of recruiting participants for research into offline lives. She, like Comley (1996) and Coomber (1997) almost two decades earlier, suggest that the Internet is particularly suitable as a methodological tool when researching specific groups of Internet users. Gaiser (1997: 136) is in agreement, stating that: '… if the research question involves an online social phenomenon, a potential strength of the method is to be researching in the location of interest'.

Conducting the Interview

Much of the existing research based on data generated through online interviews has to date focused on adapting offline practices, such as techniques for building rapport (O'Connor and Madge, 2001). Researchers have stressed the importance of replicating, as closely as possible, the face-to-face method, with James and Busher (2006: 405) seeking a methodological approach that 'replicated as closely as possible … the normal processes of qualitative, face-to-face interviewing'.

Conventional interview etiquette, as well as procedural research ethics protocol, suggests that in a face-to-face interview, the interviewer begins by providing a brief introduction to the research project, an explanation of the interview procedure and perhaps a general overview of the questions included in the interview. In most cases, the interviewer would have had prior contact with the interviewee, making initial contact and arranging a suitable venue and interview time. During these interactions, the research project would

have been introduced and the research project aims outlined. The virtual interviewer will often lack these early interactions, and opportunities for the building of rapport, gleaning facts concerning profile data and ensuring that the participant feels at ease are possibly missed. It is important, therefore, for the virtual interviewer to develop strategies that compensate for the lack of face-to-face meetings. These strategies are discussed in more detail next.

Designing the Interview Script

Before commencing the interview, there is a need to decide how to inform participants about the interview procedure, for example a brief introduction to the aims of the interview, the estimated length of the interview and the types of question. It is also particularly important that a mutually convenient time to conduct the online interview is arranged, given that interviewees may be in different time zones or have variously timed work commitments (Jowett *et al.* 2011). It may also be necessary to remind participants how to contribute to an online discussion. For example, James and Busher (2006: 408) sent participants detailed 'rubrics' explaining the format of their email interviews and outlining data protection and privacy issues; O'Connor and Madge (2001) also provided participants with general information and an explanation of the process at the outset of their interviews (see Box 24.1).

This introduction was followed with another prepared piece of text that introduced the researchers by describing their gender, age, ethnicity and family and employment status. This was done with two specific aims in mind – in the absence of visual cues O'Connor and Madge (2001) wanted to create a text-based picture of themselves, first to facilitate rapport and second to elicit profile data from the respondents, which would have been visually apparent in a face-to-face interview. This method of establishing respondent

---

Box 24.1   Example

Guidelines

We want the interview to flow as much as possible and for you to feel that you can contribute exactly what you want to the discussion – almost as if we were having a conversation. However, we think it might be worth mentioning a few guidelines prior to starting the discussion.

As this is an 'interview' we do have some topics that we would like to cover and we will probably use these to guide the discussion. However, please feel free to ask questions yourselves and to raise any topics that you think are relevant that we have not mentioned – but do try and stick as much as possible to the theme of the Internet and parenting.

It may take a while for the response you send to appear on screen – a good technique to speed the process up is to press return frequently, i.e. send the text every few words – don't wait till you have a complete sentence. Because of this, the discussion may get a bit 'jumbled'. If this happens we may need to intervene.

This virtual interview is an 'experiment' and we anticipate there may be teething problems – we apologise for this in advance!

Do you have any questions before we start the discussion?

---

identity and building rapport is discussed in more detail next.

Establishing Respondent Identity

In the virtual setting, the interviewer cannot make any assessment of the socio-demographic information which may have an impact on the interview. Indeed, Ward (1999) found that as a consequence of this, interviewees asked her questions about her own socio-demographic profile, which changed the power relations of the interview and gave her less control as an interviewer. It is perhaps necessary, therefore, to find other ways of obtaining socio-demographic information and to adapt conventional techniques accordingly. O'Connor and Madge (2001) made use of carefully designed personal introductions to allow for the loss of face-to-face interaction and in the hope that participants would follow their 'model' and provide similar profile information, such as age, number and age of children and ethnicity. This approach proved successful and respondents mirrored

the contributions of the researchers, providing detailed profile data, which also gave respondents information about the other members of the focus group.

Although such methods can be successful, Thurlow *et al.* (2004: 53) suggest that this mechanism is unnecessary in the virtual world. They argue that questions which would be unacceptably direct in a face-to-face encounter are widely used and accepted in the online environment. For example, abbreviations such as A/S/L or ALSP are often used to request information on the age, sex, location and a picture of those online. Of course, another advantage of the online interview is that there is no need for any participant to divulge personal information and encounters can be anonymous. This can help to minimize interviewer bias and can help when discussing sensitive topics with respondents who do not want to be identifiable in any way. The corollary of this is that participants may not always be what they seem because it is possible in an online environment to hide or invent personas. Hewson *et al.* (2003) argue that researchers cannot ever be certain of respondent identity in an online situation because there is always the possibility of users inventing an online personality or at least not being entirely truthful in describing themselves. The issue of verifying respondent identity in an online setting is discussed in more depth later in the chapter.

The anonymous nature of online research and its lack of visuality may present researchers with new challenges. Visual cues are absent from non-video mediated online interactions and this renders traditional interview techniques such as nods, smiles and silences redundant, although Skovholt *et al.* (2014) do suggest that emoticons may act as 'contextualization cues', providing information about how specific online communication is supposed to be interpreted. Other issues arise, such as online silence, which can represent a number of scenarios – it could be that the respondent has withdrawn from the research or it could be that he/she has been interrupted by someone/something else or it could be due to a hardware or software problem. As O'Connor and Madge (2001: 10.11) found, a silence may occur because the respondent is 'thinking, typing or had declined to answer the question'. The interviewer can interpret silences in any of these ways. It is important, therefore, that the researcher puts strategies in place to cope with such silences. James and Busher (2006) sent chatty reminder emails to non-responders during their email interviews. O'Connor and Madge (2001) dealt with silences by very direct questioning as to the whereabouts of the respondent – in a manner which may have been construed as impolite in face-to-face encounters. In deciding how to handle 'silences', it is imperative that the online researcher acts in an ethical manner, allowing respondents to use silence as a way of withdrawing from the research. Ethical issues relating to withdrawal are discussed in more depth later.

Although a lack of visual indicators means that it can be difficult to make use of conventional interviewing tools, this is more than compensated for by other advantages of the virtual arena. A key advantage of the anonymous nature of online interaction is that there are no nonverbal cues to misread, which can also potentially place respondents on a more level playing field. Moreover, respondents, secure in the knowledge that they are anonymous, have been found to answer with far more candour than those taking part in face-to-face interviews. As Hinchcliffe and Gavin (2009: 331) noted, respondents in their study 'valued perceived anonymity over embodied experience … (and) reflected that they felt they could be more honest as they were not in the presence of another person'. Similarly, Enochsson (2011: 20) found that the young people in his study particularly valued anonymity, enabling them to 'write about difficult matters because there is time to think'. This was particularly the case for girls, who wrote longer answers in the online interviews compared to those conducted face-to-face. As such, online researchers report that the virtual interview is frequently characterised by the candid nature of responses.

Building Rapport

Building rapport online, without the usual visual cues used in a face-to-face interview, can be a challenge for the online interviewer. Research conducted face-to-face relies quite heavily on visual cues and such cues can be helpful in building rapport. In the disembodied online interview, both the interviewer and interviewee are relying on the written word as a means of building rapport. The interviewer cannot use body language (facial expression, body posture) or vocal qualities (tone, speed, volume) to interpret what the interviewee is saying (Jowett *et al.*, 2011: 360). Orgad (2005: 55) has therefore argued that 'there is a real challenge in building rapport online. Trust, a fragile commodity … seems ever more fragile in a disembodied, anonymous and textual setting'.

One technique which online interviewers have used is sharing personal information as a means of creating virtual rapport. Both Kivits (2005) and O'Connor and Madge (2001) shared such information to replicate, online, the kind of rapport they believed would have occurred 'naturally' in a face-to-face meeting. O'Connor and Madge (2001) were influenced by feminist approaches to research, which stress the importance of equal power relationships within interviewer/interviewee exchanges and self-disclosure on the part of the interviewer. Within such approaches it is suggested that shared characteristics between interviewer and respondent will often result in a good level of rapport, with minimum effort. By developing detailed textual exchanges rich with self-disclosure and by posting visual aids, they aimed to create virtually what would exist in a face-to-face environment. They stressed aspects of similarity between themselves and their respondents such as gender, age, ethnicity, limited parenting experience and the challenge of arranging life around young children and newborn babies to create an interview environment which was 'anonymous, safe and non-threatening' (2001: 11.2).

However, it may be that going to such lengths to replicate traditional interview methods in an online setting is a misplaced technique. As suggested earlier in this chapter, the use of online interviews thus far represents little more than a change of 'place'. Aside from interviewing in a virtual rather than a 'real' space, online researchers have done little more than transfer conventional, and in some cases outdated, approaches to a new arena. However, progress made in the offline world has not necessarily been reflected in online research practice. For example, offline researchers have begun to question the value of self-disclosure as a means of stressing similarities in the interview process. Abell et al. (2006: 241) suggest that the success of the self-disclosure strategy depends 'upon acts of "doing similarity" being received as such by the respondents'. They stress that there is a real risk that respondents will not perceive self-disclosure in the way it is intended and,

rather than encouraging rapport, this technique may serve to inhibit the respondent. They go on to argue that 'often through a sharing of experiences, the interviewer paradoxically exemplifies differences between themselves and the interviewee'. In an online environment where 'a stranger wanting to do academic research is seen as an unwelcome, arbitrary intrusion' (Paccagnella, 1997: 3) and where there may therefore already be a risk of the researcher being perceived as an 'outsider', it is important that researchers are aware of current debates, not just online but also offline.

ETHICAL DILEMMAS IN ONLINE INTERVIEWING

Throughout this chapter, we have touched upon the ethical challenges presented by online interviewing. These issues are covered in much greater depth by Ess (2009), Krotoski (2010), Whiteman (2012) and Eynon et al. (this volume). Whilst many of the ethical dilemmas that arise when conducting online interviews may mirror those faced when carrying out face-to-face interviews (Krotoski, 2010: 4), an online researcher will undoubtedly also be faced with ethical challenges specifically pertaining to the online environment. This has resulted in a series of guidelines being produced to help researchers weave their way through the process of online research in an ethical manner. These include a general set of guidelines produced by the Association of Internet Researchers (AoIR) Ethics Working Committee (Markham and Buchanan, 2012) and more subject specific guiding principles, for example in geography (Madge, 2012), education (Convery and Cox, 2012) and psychology (British Psychological Society, 2013). According to Convery and Cox (2012: 50), it is unrealistic to expect that any single set of guidelines can cover all ethical situations of online research for there 'is simply too much diversity across Internet cultures, values and modes of operation'. Rather they argue for a form of 'negotiated ethics', a situated approach grounded in the specifics of the online community, the methodology and the research question(s). This does not mean an 'anything goes' relativist approach, rather an open, pluralistic policy in relation to online ethical issues (Ess, 2009).

Having noted some useful sources to aid consideration of online ethics, the following section of this chapter moves on to introduce more practical advice. A technical guide is provided that includes information on selecting software for online interviewing.

TECHNICAL GUIDE

A wide variety of software and services are available to facilitate online communication and, depending on the context of the research, it is possible for researchers to make use of any of these to carry out online interviews. However, as Salmons (2015: 74) warns: 'The moment you write about (or worse, buy) any kind of software or hardware, a new option is bound to appear that is smaller, lighter and faster'. This warning is worth heeding when planning any kind of online interview. In the following section of this chapter an overview of some of the more common types of software and services available for asynchronous and synchronous online interviews with individuals and groups is provided.

Asynchronous Interviews

Software for asynchronous interviews can be divided into two types: email applications and discussion board software and services. Email is particularly appropriate for individual interviews, although the 'copy-to' function of most email applications may allow their use for small group interviews. The main advantages of using email are that it is more likely to be familiar and available to

researchers and participants, it does not present problems with the compatibility of different software and systems, and it allows responses to be made privately. Discussion board software and services are more likely to be of use for asynchronous group interviews because they allow multiple participants to view and respond to postings from the researcher or other participants when convenient. Like email, discussion boards are unlikely to present compatibility problems and any participant with an Internet-enabled computer is likely to be able to access and contribute to a board.

Researchers planning to carry out interviews via discussion boards may wish to target an existing discussion board on a website or to create and moderate their own board for invited participants. Although there are particular ethical issues that must be considered where an existing board is used, there is likely to be less technical difficulty for the researcher, who simply requires access to a computer with an Internet connection. Creating a discussion board for the interviews, however, involves the use either of a software and hosting service or the installation of software on a server which the researcher has access to. Where a software and hosting service is used, the process is relatively straightforward from a technical perspective. The discussion board can usually be designed and managed through a simple interface on the website of the hosting service and the location of the board can be distributed to participants through sending the URL or adding a link to the board to any webpage. Options such as requiring a password for access and selecting threaded or flat boards are frequently offered, and it is often possible to sample the service through fully functional demonstrations for trial periods. Pricing for these services can vary, and most services charge monthly fees. A number of free services are available, although these frequently include advertising. In all cases, it is necessary to check that the privacy and data security offered is adequate for the research. In cases where the researcher has access to a server, it is possible to obtain and install discussion board software for use in the research. Again, prices vary and there are a number of free open-source examples as well as commercial packages. A listing of both software-only options and software and hosting providers is available from the following website: http://thinkofit.com/webconf/.

Synchronous Interviews

A wide range of software and services are available for synchronous interviews, including online chat facilities, 'instant messaging' and video-based technologies. Many of these services offer facilities for both individual and group interviews and allow for communication via text or via audio and video.

The rise of social media and social network sites (SNS) such as Facebook and Twitter have meant that chatrooms, a previously rich resource for online researchers, have become less important as recruitment sites. Instead, networks of users with shared interests are relatively easy to locate via SNS (Moore et al., 2015). Once participants have been successfully recruited, it is relatively straightforward to access a range of free 'instant messaging' services (WhatsApp, Facebook Messenger and Gmail Chat), which provide a more secure and appropriate platform for synchronous interviews.

The key advantage of these services over the free online chat providers is that instant messaging software can be used to set up chats specifically for interviews that can be limited to invited participants only and in which the researcher has a great deal of control over the discussion. One-to-one and group communication is possible with many of the services and automatic transcription is frequently available. A number of extra facilities such as file transfer and desktop sharing are often also available. All the services allow real-time text-based

messaging and some also offer video conferencing and/or Internet telephony facilities. This makes audio and video communication possible where the researcher and participants have broadband Internet connections and the necessary equipment (webcams and/or microphones and speakers). The growth of these services along with the increase in the number, usage and availability of Internet telephony services such as Skype, which allows one-to-one and multi-user audio communication over the Internet, is making their use for audio interviewing increasingly realistic. In most cases, however, users of one type of instant messaging or Internet telephony software cannot communicate with users of a different type, and the researcher will need to ensure that all participants have the same software installed. It is also likely to be necessary to provide lists of minimum requirements for participants, such as a broadband Internet connection and any required peripherals.

There has also recently been a proliferation of commercial interviewing apps which can be downloaded onto smartphone and tablet technologies (for a review, see http://interviewingsoftware.com). Similarly, Moylan et al. (2015: 45) identify several useful websites that exist to help the online researcher keep abreast of emerging trends in technology. These include the ProfHacker blog on the Chronicle of Higher Education website (www.chronicle.com/blogs/profhacker), Bamboo DiRT (dirt.projectbamboo.org), Mobile and Cloud Qualitative Research Apps (www.nova.edu/ssss/QR/apps.html) and the American Historical Association 'Digital Toolbox for Historians' (pinterest.com/ahahistorians/adigital-tool-box-for-historians). Further technical details can also be found in the 'Exploring online research methods' website (http://www.restore.ac.uk/orm/interviewsinttechnical.htm). A final useful and relatively new application is DragonDictate, which can automatically generate transcripts from audio recordings.

CONCLUSION

To conclude, we first reflected on the methodological progress of online interviewing before considering the future of online interviewing. Regarding methodological progress, although the data collected through synchronous and asynchronous online interviewing can be valuable to the researcher, we still urge that the potential of online research should not be exaggerated. Indeed, Hine's (2004) caution of a decade ago is still relevant today: 'Internet-based research is no different from other forms of research. Just as we craft interviews appropriate for particular settings, so too we must learn to craft appropriate forms of online interview'. That said, it is clear that the data collected through online interviewing can be as rich and valuable as that generated during face-to-face interviewing. Indeed, some argue that the quality of responses gained is much the same as responses produced by more traditional methods (Deakin and Wakefield, 2014: 606). For example, the occurrence of pauses, repetitions and recasts under conditions of face-to-face and online interviews do not differ significantly (Cabaroglu *et al.*, 2010). It must, however, be remembered that many of the issues and problems of conventional research methods still apply because as Kitchin (1998: 395) commented some time ago '…the vast majority of social spaces on the Internet bear a remarkable resemblance to real world locales'.

Online interviews can therefore be a useful additional tool for social researchers, but we would not suggest that this approach is appropriate for all types of research and neither do we suggest that online methods will ever replace face-to-face approaches to research. As Wilkerson *et al.* (2014: 569–70) illustrate, there are a range of decisions to be made in evaluating the respective advantages and disadvantages of online interviewing compared to face-to-face interviewing in relation to the specific topic that is to be investigated. At present, it appears that synchronous

and asynchronous online interviews occupy a growing mainstream position in the world of social research. Increasingly, researchers who use online interviews adapt face-to-face research practices while also developing online specific practices. That said, even amongst those researchers who have successfully used online interviews, there can still remain some lingering scepticism surrounding their use. This is apparent in the continued use of face-to-face research to supplement and 'verify' data collected through online interviews (Orgad, 2005; Sanders, 2005; James and Busher, 2006). This approach weakens the position of online interviews because it suggests that they cannot stand alone as a research method. It also invalidates one of the main advantages of online research, which is the ability for researchers to expand the spatial boundaries of their research agenda without the traditional high costs this entails. However, although online researchers are still sometimes hesitant about the role of online interviews, their use has simultaneously become more mainstream, and a critical and reflexive stance towards these online methods is to be encouraged.

What, then, is the future for online interviews? Ever more rapid developments in the field of computer-medicated communications technology offer new and different media to the social researcher. Some of the issues discussed in this chapter relate to the lack of visibility during online encounters. The increasing use of VOIP (voice over Internet protocol) technologies such as Skype mean that online interviews are not solely restricted to text-based exchanges, but this does not mean that text-based online interviews have become an irrelevance, rather that the range of online interviewing formats have expanded, as have the associated issues with employing a visual online format. Similarly, new mobile technologies such as smart phones and tablets that are facilitated by increasingly available Wi-Fi Internet access enable the location of the interview to become 'much more fluid and temporary' (Deakin and Wakefield,

2014: 609). The advent of a plethora of new applications available on the wireless Internet, and cloud-based computing, will have further implications for online interviewing (Van Doorn, 2013; Moylan *et al.*, 2015). One significant issue is the production of ever more sophisticated Internet technologies and the rapidity of change in this sector that will present challenges to the online researcher, demanding that they become ever more contingent, flexible and innovative in adapting these technologies to produce high quality, nuanced online research methodologies.

REFERENCES

Abell, J., Locke, A., Condor, S., Gibson, S. and Stevenson, C. (2006) Trying similarity, doing difference: the role of interviewer self-disclosure in interview talk with young people. *Qualitative Research*, 6 (2) pp. 221–44.

Barratt, M. J. (2012) The efficacy of interviewing young drug users through online chat. *Drug and Alcohol Review*, 31 (4), pp. 566–72.

Bjerke, T.N. (2010) When my eyes bring pain to my soul, and vice versa: Facing preconceptions in email and face-to-face interviews. *Qualitative Health Research*, 20(12): 1717–24.

Bowker, N. and Tuffin, K. (2004) Using the online medium for discursive research about people with disabilities. *Social Science Computer Review*, 22 (2), pp. 228–41.

British Psychological Society (2013) Ethics Guidelines for Internet-mediated Research. INF206/1.2013. Leicester: Author. Available from: www.bps.org.uk/publications/policy-andguidelines/research-guidelines-policydocuments/research-guidelines-poli (accessed 10 October 2015).

Bryman, A. (2004) *Social Research Methods*. Oxford: Oxford University Press.

Burns, E. (2010) Developing email interview practices in qualitative research. *Sociological Research Online*, 15 (4), pp. 8. http://www.socresonline.org.uk/15/4/8/8.pdf (accessed 6 October 2015).

Cabaroglu, N., Basaran, S. and Roberts, J. (2010) A comparison between the occurrence of pauses, repetitions and recasts under conditions of face-to-face and computer-mediated communication: a preliminary study. *Turkish Online Journal of Educational Technology*, 9 (2): pp. 4–23.

Cater, J. K. (2011) Skype: a cost-effective method for qualitative research. *Rehabilitation Counselors and Educators Journal*, 4, pp. 10–17.

Chen, P. and Hinton, S. M. (1999) Realtime interviewing using the world wide web. *Sociological Research Online*, 4(3) from http://www.socresonline.org.uk/4/3/chen.html

Clark, G. (2007) Going beyond our limits: issues for able and disabled students. *Journal of Geography in Higher Education*, 31 (1), pp. 211–18.

Comley, P. (1996) The use of the Internet as a data collection method. ESOMAR/EMAC Symposium, Edinburgh, November 1996.

Convery, I. and Cox, D. (2012) A review of research ethics in Internet-based research. *Practitioner Research in Higher Education*, 6 (1), pp. 50–7.

Coomber, R. (1997) Using the Internet for survey research. *Sociological Research Online*, 2, p. 2.

Deakin, H. and Wakefield, K. (2014) Skype interviewing: reflections of two PhD researchers. *Qualitative Research*, 14 (5), pp. 603–16.

Enochsson, A. B. (2011) Who benefits from synchronous online communication? A comparison of face-to-face and synchronous online interviews with children. *Procedia – Social and Behavioral Sciences*, 28, pp. 15–22.

Ess, C. (2009) *Digital Media Ethics*. Cambridge: Polity.

Fielding, J. (2011) User satisfaction and user experiences with Access Grid as a medium for social science research. *International Journal of Social Research Methodology*, 14, pp. 1–13.

Gaiser, T. (1997) Conducting online focus groups: A methodological discussion. *Social Science Computer Review*, 15(2): 135–44.

Hanna, P. (2012) Using Internet technologies (such as Skype) as a research medium: a research note. *Qualitative Research*, 12 (2), pp. 239–42.

Hewson, C., Yule, P., Laurent, D. and Vogel, C. (2003) *Internet Research Methods*. London: Sage Publications.

Hinchcliffe, V. and Gavin, H. (2009) Social and virtual networks: evaluating synchronous online interviewing using instant messenger. *The Qualitative Report*, 14 (2), pp. 318–40.

Hine, C. (2004) Social research methods and the Internet: a thematic review. *Sociological Research Online*, 9, p. 2.

Hine, C. (2005) Virtual methods and the sociology of cyber-social-scientific knowledge. In C. Hine (ed.), *Virtual Methods: Issues in Social Research on the Internet*. Oxford: Berg. pp. 1–13.

Hooley, T., Wellens, J. and Marriott, J. (2011) *What is Online Research? Using the Internet for Social Science Research*. Chicago, IL. A&C Black.

Illingworth, N. (2001) The Internet matters: exploring the use of the Internet as a research tool. *Sociological Research Online*, 6, 2. Available from: http://www.socresonline.org.uk/6/2/illingworth.html (accessed 30 September 2015).

Illingworth, N. (2006) Content, context, reflexivity and the qualitative research encounter: telling stories in the virtual realm. Available from: http://www.socresonline.org.uk/11/1/illingworth.html (accessed 10 October 2015).

Ison, N. L. (2009) Having their say: email interviews for research data collection with people who have verbal communication impairment. *International Journal of Social Research Methodology*, 12 (2), pp. 161–72.

James, N. (2007) The use of email interviewing as a qualitative method of inquiry in educational research. *British Educational Research Journal*, 33 (6), pp. 963–76.

James, N. and Busher, H. (2006) Credibility, authenticity and voice: dilemmas in online interviewing. *Qualitative Research*, 6 (3): pp. 403–20.

James, N. and Busher, H. (2009) *Online Interviewing*. Chicago, IL: Sage Publications.

Joinson, A. N. (2005) Internet behaviour and the design of virtual methods. In C. Hine (ed.), *Virtual Methods: Issues in Social Research on the Internet*. Oxford: Berg, pp. 21–34.

Jowett, A., Peel, E. and Shaw, R. (2011) Online interviewing in psychology: reflections on the process. *Qualitative Research in Psychology*, 8 (4), pp. 354–69.

Kitchin, R. (1998) Towards geographies of cyberspace. *Progress in Human Geography*, 22 (3), pp. 385–406.

Kivits, J. (2004) Researching the informed patient: the case of online health information. *Information, Communication and Society*, 7 (4), pp. 510–30.

Kivits, J. (2005) Online interviewing and the research relationship. In C. Hine (ed.), *Virtual Methods: Issues in Social Research on the Internet*. Oxford: Berg, pp. 35–49.

Krotoski, A. (2010) Introduction to the special issue: research ethics in online communities. *International Journal of Internet Research Ethics*, 3 (12), pp. 1–6.

Madge, C. (2012) Developing a geographers' agenda for online research ethics. In J. Hughes (ed.), *SAGE Internet Research Methods*. London: Sage Publications, pp. 251–78.

Madge C. (2006) 'International inequalities, the digital divide and online ethics'. Available frm http://www.restore.ac.uk/orm/ethics/ethinequalities1.htm (accessed 1 October 2015).

Madge, C., Meek, J., Wellens, J. and Hooley, T. (2009) Facebook, social integration and informal learning at university: 'It is more for socialising and talking to friends about work than for actually doing work'. *Learning, Media and Technology*, 34 (2), pp. 141–15.

Mann, C. and Stewart, F. (2000) *Internet Communication and Qualitative Research*. London: Sage Publications.

Markham, A. and Buchanan, E. with contributions from the AoIR Ethics Working Committee (2012) *Ethical Decision-Making and Internet Research: Recommendations from the AOIR Ethics Working Committee (Version 2.0)*. Available from: http://www.aoir.org/reports/ethics2.pdf (accessed 10 October 2015).

McDermott, E. and Roen, K. (2012) Youth on the virtual edge researching marginalized sexualities and genders online. *Qualitative Health Research*, 22 (4), pp. 560–70.

Moore, T., McKee, K. and McLoughlin, P. (2015) Online focus groups and qualitative research in the social sciences: their merits and limitations in a study of housing and youth. *People, Place and Policy*, 9 (1). Available from: http://extra.shu.ac.uk/ppp-online/online-focus-groups-and-qualitative-research-in-the-social-sciences-their-merits-and-limitations-in-a-study-of-housing-and-youth/ (accessed 10 October 2015).

Morris, A. (2007) E-literacy and the grey digital divide: a review with recommendations *Journal of Information Literacy*, 1 (3). Available from: http://jil.lboro.ac.uk/ojs/index.php/JIL/article/view/RA-V1-I3-2007-2 (accessed 18 August 2016).

Moylan, C. A., Derr, A. S. and Lindhorst, T. (2015) Increasingly mobile: how new technologies can enhance qualitative research. *Qualitative Social Work*, 14 (1), pp. 36–47.

Murray, C. and Sixsmith, J. (1998) E-mail: A qualitative research medium for interviewing? *International Journal of Social Research Methodology*, 1(2): 103–21.

O'Connor, H. and Madge, C. (2001) Cyber-mothers: Online synchronous interviewing using conferencing software. *Sociological Research Online*, 5(4) from http://www.socresonline.org.uk/5/4/o%27connor.html

O'Connor, H., Madge, C., Shaw, R. and Wellens, J. (2008) Internet-based interviewing. In Fielding, N., Lee, R. M. and Blank, G. (eds.), *The SAGE Handbook of Online Research Methods*. London: Routledge. pp. 271–289.

Orgad, S. (2005) From online to offline and back: moving from online to offline relationships with research informants. In C. Hine (ed.), *Virtual Methods: Issues in Social Research on the Internet*. Oxford: Berg. pp. 51–65.

Paccagnella, L. (1997) Getting the seat of your pants dirty: Strategies for ethnographic research on virtual communities. *Journal of Computer-Mediated Communication*, 3(1): 267–288.

Salmons, J. (2015) *Qualitative Online Interviews: Strategies, Design, and Skills*. Chicago, IL: Sage Publications.

Sanders, T. (2005) Researching the online sex community, in Hine, C. (ed.) *Virtual Methods: Issues in Social Research on the Internet*. Oxford: Berg. pp. 67–79.

Sedgwick, M. and Spiers, J. (2009) The use of videoconferencing as a medium for the qualitative interview. *International Journal of Qualitative Methods*, 8 (1), pp. 1–11.

Selwyn, N. and Robson, K. (1998) Using email as a research tool. *Social Research Update, Issue 21*. Guildford: University of Surrey.

Sharf, B. (1997) Communicating breast cancer online: support and empowerment on the Internet. *Women and Health,* 26 (1), pp. 65–84.

Skovholt, K., Grønning, A. and Kankaanranta, A. (2014) The communicative functions of emoticons in workplace e-mails: : -). *Journal of Computer-Mediated Communication*, 19, pp. 780–97.

Smith, C. (1997) Casting the net: Surveying an Internet population. *Journal of Computer-Mediated Communication*, 3(1) from http://jcmc.indiana.edu/vol3/issue1/smith.html

Sullivan, J. R. (2012) Skype: an appropriate method of data collection for qualitative interviews? *The Hilltop Review*, 6, pp. 54–60.

Thurlow, C., Lengel, L. and Tomic, A. (2004) *Computer Mediated Communication: Social Interaction and the Internet*. London: Sage Publications.

Van Doorn, N. (2013) Assembling the affective field: how smartphone technology impacts ethnographic research practice. *Qualitative Inquiry,* 19 (5): pp. 385–96.

Ward, K. J. (1999) The cyber-ethnographic (re) construction of two feminist online communities. *Sociological Research Online,* 4 (1).

Whiteman, N. (2012) *Undoing Ethics. Rethinking Practice in Online Research*. New York, NY: Springer.

Wilkerson J.M., Iantaffi, A., Grey, J.A., Bockting, W.O. and Rosser B.R.S. (2014) Recommendations for Internet-based qualitative health research with hard-to-reach populations. *Qualitative Health Research*, 24(4): 561–74.

FURTHER READING

James, N. and Busher, H. (2009) *Online Interviewing*. Chicago, IL: Sage Publications.

Hooley, T., Wellens, J. and Marriott, J. (2011) *What is Online Research? Using the Internet for Social Science Research*. Chicago, IL: A&C Black.

Salmons, J. (2015) *Qualitative Online Interviews: Strategies, Design, and Skills*. Chicago, IL: Sage Publications.

Mann, C. and Stewart, F. (2000) *Internet Communication and Qualitative Research*. London: Sage Publications.

ReStore, National Centre for Research Methods, http://www.restore.ac.uk/orm/ (accessed 2 October 2015).

## 25

Online Focus Groups

Katie M. Abrams with Ted J. Gaiser

INTRODUCTION TO ONLINE FOCUS GROUPS

The purpose of a focus group is to enable a researcher to evaluate ideas in a group setting. The environment of a focus group is often thought of as a more natural setting for gathering data, as opposed to a one-on-one interview, and enables researchers to gain additional insights from the dialog and interaction between participants. Focus groups can be employed for many diverse purposes. Politicians use the technique to assess public opinion and develop policy. Marketers assess many aspects of public opinion, from specific consumer preferences to test marketing new products. For social scientists, a focus group often represents an inexpensive means for gathering qualitative data and exploring social phenomena.

Much of the seminal literature describing the focus group method was developed with face-to-face communication in mind. Focus group methods are designed to create a group environment in which typically six to eight participants who have some commonality feel comfortable sharing a wide variety of ideas on a specific topic or focus with facilitation by a trained moderator. Since many texts offer details on the method in general and its validity, reliability and generalizability (see, for example, Krueger and Casey, 2014), this chapter will focus on the unique aspects of those conducted online. Although many of the same fundamentals of the method apply, the online medium has some nuances.

Online focus groups are distinguished from face-to-face or in-person focus groups in that they take place in a networked computer environment. They can be categorized into asynchronous (participants contribute during different times, e.g. emails, forums) or synchronous (participants contribute during the same time, e.g. chat, conference) group interactions. Online focus groups may seem like the natural choice to study online social groups or topics related to the Internet;

however, they are also useful to study a variety of topics and populations. Given the extent to which people are communicating over the Internet, the medium seems even more suitable to facilitating focus groups than in years past. Specialized applications are also now available to enhance group communication, as will be discussed in a later section.

There are many benefits to conducting focus groups in an online setting: they are relatively inexpensive, provide greater and easier access to a broad range of research participants, and can take less time to collect data. Video communication online via webcams can offer researchers rich data similar to face-to-face focus groups (Abrams *et al.*, 2015). In addition, the technique allows for more specific framing of research topics and issues by participants, limiting researcher bias. These and other benefits, along with the challenges presented by the online environment, will be developed later in the chapter.

CONSIDERATIONS FOR THE ONLINE SETTING

Before choosing to conduct focus groups online, thinking through the topic, questions, and any tasks the researcher seeks to do is important to determining whether offline techniques are more suitable. Poytner (2010) provides a starting point for consideration (Table 25.1). Wilkerson and colleagues (2014: 569–70) provide a more detailed checklist that can also be used to decide whether online or offline focus groups are worthwhile.

Some other broad considerations are useful as well, particularly those relating to participants. Most researchers suggest online focus groups use fewer participants than face-to-face. Recommendations vary depending on whether the focus group will be conducted asynchronously (10 to 30 participants) or synchronously (3 to 8 participants) (Poytner, 2010). Besides size of the focus groups, the possibilities for the heterogeneity or homogeneity of participants are also more expansive when they are facilitated online. Researchers seeking data that would be enhanced with heterogeneous groups can have participants from different geographic locations using online methods, which could also add additional variance of other demographic variables (e.g. rural/urban, ethnicities, occupation, socioeconomic status, and so on). With location removed as a barrier for participation, forming homogeneous groups can also be easier. For example, those who share a unique experience, such as being brought up in a military family, are not bound by geographic area. In fact, the sample may be more limited if location were a factor as it is with face-to-face focus groups. The ability to acquire diverse opinions with relative ease is a considerable strength of the method. Participants can be recruited from various locations globally, from diverse life experiences, etc. Although this is true, it is

Table 25.1 Focus groups tasks' suitability to online medium

Opinion	Description
Better online	Factual lists, e.g. what is in your refrigerator, what products do you use? Polling*
Same online	Word associations Lists of ideas
Needs changes online	Brainstorming Annotating images
Less good online	Picture or product sorts Paired tasks

Source: Poytner (2010: 120); *Addition.

important to bear in mind that online access is not yet universal. As such, a sample will most likely reflect the perspective of a more educated and higher socially located population that has the resources for access either through work or home environments. That said, however, the focus group method still allows for a diversity of participation from within that particular group of people that have access to the technology.

An additional consideration that researchers should make with regard to location is participants' Internet connection speeds (although location is not the only influence on this). The United States Federal Communication Commission (n.d.) states 1 megabit per second (Mbps) is the minimum required for basic video conferencing or interactive web pages (perhaps most similar to a web chat interface) and 5 Mbps for high definition video conferencing, but that is if no other networked devices or applications are simultaneously accessing the participant's Internet connection. Akamai's State of the Internet (Belson, 2016) report shows global broadband adoption at 73 percent. It also reports average connection speed of 116 countries at 4.5 Mbps (4 Mbps constitutes broadband speed). Several countries have so little connectivity (e.g. Iran, Pakistan, Croatia, El Salvador) that they are not registered by Akamai's methods. Notably, some of these countries do show up in their report on mobile connectivity, which only includes 54 countries, showing that connectivity to the Internet in some countries is dominated by mobile connections. Mobile connectivity is slower, especially for countries that do not have much standard connectivity (~0.9–2.5 Mbps). Mobile connections are worth noting because some people may use their cell phone data plans to connect to the Internet with computers or laptops. A more useful reason is that many Internet communication tools suitable for conducting focus groups offer a mobile device interface, as will be discussed later in the chapter. Researchers should consult available data on connectivity speeds

of their potential participants and capacity requirements of the chosen application to facilitate focus groups. Using a screening questionnaire asking potential participants for the type of connection they have (dial-up, satellite, digital subscriber line (DSL), cable, cell phone service data connection, etc.) is helpful. It may be best to choose an online facilitation medium for the lowest common denominator of participants' connection speeds. Otherwise, those in the focus group who have the slower or less reliable network connection may not participate as much due to lag time and/or missing parts of the discussion.

MODERATING

To begin organizing an online focus group, it is important to determine whether or not a mix of individuals across many boundaries of space and time is preferred as well as the depth of data desired. This decision may drive which type of group and which technology will be used. For example, including international participants will probably necessitate an asynchronous focus group scheduled to span several days simply because of time differences. As a result, the discussion will probably be facilitated by the use of some kind of email and/or listserv environment. This type of focus group is relatively easy to coordinate, has limited technology requirements, is easily captured in email file storage or digest form for analysis purposes, and requires little to no technical training and support for participants. In addition, this type of focus group can be started quickly and is likely to be the least expensive option. However, given the time span and fact that the moderator will not always be 'present', it can be a significant challenge to manage the group, limiting the moderator's control of discussion threads and requiring a high level of flexibility.

An introduction exercise is useful for helping the group begin to bond. Face-to-face groups are likely to use a different approach, enabling participants to informally interact prior to the start of a discussion. There might be a beverage and snack, for example, over which participants see each other, engage in small talk, ask questions about each other's participation, etc. This opportunity may be unavailable online, thus requiring some type of replacement.

The intention with an introduction exercise is to enable trust and to set participants at ease so they feel comfortable participating in the focus group. The exercise can also be designed to compensate for the lack of a face-to-face context in which people would see the moderator, the space, and one another, and establish a tone for what will follow. An introduction exercise enables the researcher to establish a spatial tone for the new environment. It also humanizes the members, helping to create a safe space for interacting. In conventional settings this can often be achieved by the environment, the way participants are greeted, and the way researchers present themselves.

One of the keys to successful focus groups is appropriate care in moderating. It is difficult and demands a great deal of reflection. Stewart and Williams (2005) found that for synchronous online focus groups the scripts and conversations are often more complex and interweaving because participants can speak/type simultaneously. They concluded, therefore, that moderators in online focus groups require the skills of not only conventional moderators, but also competence in the technology that is used for the focus group in order to organize chaotic discussions.

It can, however, be problematic at any time during the research effort to limit the moderator's involvement because this could be experienced by participants as a lack of guidance and facilitation. Confusion can ensue, derailing discussion and limiting the overall effectiveness of the focus group. Lacking visual and verbal cues such as nods, smiles, and vocal acknowledgments may leave participants confused about what they are supposed

to do. Online group moderating therefore needs a delicate balance between influence that could increase moderator bias and sustaining the work of the group by providing adequate leadership (Gaiser, 1997).

APPROACHES

Synchronous versus Asynchronous

One unique feature to conducting focus groups online is the ability to do them with participants and moderator at the same time (synchronous) or at different times (asynchronous). Whether asynchronous methods using bulletin boards, email, social media, or online research communities are truly focus groups has been questioned in the literature, especially when interaction among participants becomes more limited or is non-existent (Bloor *et al.*, 2001). A foundation component of focus groups is the interaction and dialogue among participants to elicit fuller dimensions of the discussion topic (Kitzinger, 1994). What makes the asynchronous online focus group different from interviews in these instances of low group interaction is that participants are likely aware of others' contributions; however, empirical research examining the extent to which others' responses are considered by participants in asynchronous techniques is currently absent from the literature. Still, researchers using this approach do describe their procedures as focus group methodology and, as will be elaborated on later, asynchronous communication over the Internet is the norm.

Conducted synchronously, online focus groups more closely approximate the face-to-face medium because everyone is online at the same time in the chosen communication application (e.g. video conference platform, chat room), just as they would be physically for a live focus group. If researchers are conducting some focus groups face-to-face, but must conduct others online due to geographic constraints of participants or researchers, then a synchronous approach can help produce similar data between online and offline collection methods, particularly if webcams or integrated cameras (such as those in cell phones, laptops, and tablets) are used (Abrams *et al.*, 2015). This approach is also desirable for researchers seeking to have the live interaction among participants that may reveal important and unanticipated data on the topic. On the other hand, it can also lead to only a few people or one person dominating the discussion. It can happen as a result of personalities in the group but also because the limited time leads discussion to move quickly (Sweet, 2001). Synchronous online focus groups overcome a major downside of asynchronous modes: they create better focus on questions throughout the discussion because participants generally avoid talking (if using audiovisual) at the same time. It is also suitable for gathering more immediate or top-of-mind responses, which, depending on the topic, are more similar to people's natural thought processing of the issue (Poynter, 2010). Gathering first impressions and reactions to communication and marketing materials or food products, for example, are topics in which researchers may not want participants to think deeply about, reflect upon, and/or conduct their own research before responding. The tools available for conducting synchronous focus groups, especially if video communication is desired, can be more costly. Although free applications are available, they are more prone to technical problems largely due to the network capacity required to facilitate live communication and lack of technical support. Applications will be discussed later in greater detail.

Another consideration for the synchronous approach is the time factor. From the researcher's perspective, conducting it synchronously means he/she will have data in the amount of time the focus group lasts (one to two hours). However, from the participants' perspective, this approach may mean it takes more of their time, even if it is only a perceptual assumption rather than what actually happens. Despite increased synchronous communication over the Internet, the approach may still seem less natural to participants in the online environment. Poynter (2010) highlights how asynchronicity is a cornerstone of modern society, thanks largely to the Internet. 'It underpins 24-hour shopping, disintermediation (for example, the way ATMs have replaced bank tellers, and websites have replaced travel agents), time-shifted TV viewing, and the shift from broadcast to podcast' (Poynter, 2010: 111). Empirical research has shown adults and adolescents perceive participating when most convenient for them as a key advantage of asynchronous focus groups (Zwaanswijk and van Dulmen, 2014). In a synchronous online focus group, participants are essentially confined (but perhaps not as much as with face-to-face groups) to the full length of the focus group. Although they presumably have the right to leave/log out at any time, social pressure makes it unlikely. The time commitment may dissuade some people from participating, but for the researcher, it is not only more efficient, but also means fewer participants drop out. Organizing the synchronous online focus group can be more difficult because everyone has to be available at the same time (Poynter, 2010). Time differences between participants and between participants and researchers can also pose challenges in communicating exactly when it will take place and simply identifying a convenient block of time for all.

Asynchronous online focus groups are much more distinctive, especially compared to face-to-face groups. A key feature of this technique is that it allows participants and the moderator 'time to think about answers, to be reflective and introspective, and for views and reactions to mature' (Poytner, 2010: 133). Moderators can more thoroughly review responses and probe more participants (Turner, 2008). Some of the earliest online focus groups were conducted asynchronously using email or bulletin boards. These discussions take place over time and can range from a few days to a few months. The moderator sends or posts questions to participants and allows them to respond. Responses can happen in sequence or participants can also go back to earlier threads to add comments later as they are perhaps spurred by additional thought and/or discussion. Online tools like email, bulletin boards or discussion forums, and social media, offer features and communication conventions that add special context to the data as well as participation. Participants could share pictures or short videos, given the time and encouragement to do so. In a marketing research context, for example, it might be useful for participants to take photos or a video of a product in use. (Additional features not unique to asynchronicity are discussed in the following section).

An important consideration is the potential for reduced interaction among participants, especially in larger groups. Participants may instead focus on only responding to the moderator's posts (Turner, 2008). When the group is too large, some may feel their contributions are insignificant, demotivating levels of participation and perhaps leading to drop-outs (Poytner, 2010). Having the large group to begin with may leave the researcher with a sufficient number of active participants, but they could be excluding an important segment of their population who simply may not find this method suitable to their communication preferences. The moderator must make additional effort to encourage participants to read and react to one another's contributions and use other collaborative tasks; this is especially important if benefits from the group interactions are helpful to the research.

Text, Video and Virtual Environments Communication Mediums

Much of the literature on online focus groups was centered on those conducted using primarily text-based communication through chat applications, email, or bulletin board/forums. Only since 2011 has the prevalence of online video communication and its usage increased due to integration of cameras into computer monitors, laptops, and other devices (e.g. smartphones, tablets) and the advent of low-cost or free technology to use it (e.g. Google Hangouts, Skype; see also 'Webcam penetration and adoption rates', 2011). Online, multi-user virtual environment applications (e.g. Second Life) in which people are embodied in avatars, meet in a virtual space, and communicate via typing or audio from networked microphones offer an additional avenue for conducting focus groups despite not being used by the mainstream population. This section discusses the three forms of communication mediums for conducting online focus groups.

Text-based facilitation mediums have several advantages: no transcription is required, likelihood of a participant dominating discussion is reduced, participants can remain anonymous to the group, it accommodates multiple languages, and has a lower technological barrier. Some of these advantages also have disadvantages.

Not having to transcribe data is appealing, but researchers will still have to make some decisions about what data to include in analysis or whether to edit. For example, side conversations irrelevant to the topic can occur among participants, and misspellings, grammatical errors, and abbreviations are common. With abbreviations or confusing misspellings, moderators should ask participants to clarify ambiguous meanings, both for other participants and data analysis. Intentional misspellings and punctuation are used to communicate tone of voice or non-verbal information. Examples include 'repeating vowels ('Noooo way'), repeating punctuation (!!!! or ???), and all capital letters (That was GREAT!)' (Liamputtong, 2011: 156). Text-based communication can also be augmented by emoticons, emojis, and hashtags to convey sentiment that might normally be communicated in tone of voice or non-verbal body language. Emoticons are much more established, while emojis (graphical icons) and hashtags have become more commonplace since communication via social media increased. Although hashtags were originally designed to help users identify social media posts as pertaining to a particular topic through hyperlinking the hashtag to a separate feed, people began using them to communicate underlying sentiment or to serve as a form of metacommunication (Daer et al., 2014). This phenomenon has transferred into people's communication in other environments like text messaging, web page and blog commenting, and even face-to-face (Daer et al., 2014). Although methodological research has not yet noted the use of hashtags in text-based online focus groups, researchers should be prepared to see them as a part of their data, especially among adolescent and young adult participants.

In synchronous focus groups, because participants can be typing responses at the same time, dominant participants cannot 'silence' others through the required turn-taking in communication and the moderator having to move discussion forward due to time constraints. Dominant participants still emerge in a different way by being faster typists (contributing more frequently or more text/ information) (Mann and Stewart, 2000). In fact, text-only, synchronous focus groups can be overwhelming for participants who are not accustomed to communicating in this manner (Campbell et al., 2001). After some time, group dynamics do emerge, even in this type of online communication, and traditional dominant personalities may need to be controlled by the moderator if it seems to be inhibiting others' participation.

Participants' ability to remain anonymous is particularly beneficial for discussing certain topics that are associated with social stigma, sensitive in nature, or taboo. Perceptions of anonymity increase participants' self-disclosure (Joinson, 2001; Wilkerson et al., 2014). The asynchronous, online text-only focus group medium produces fewer socially desirable and dishonest responses from participants compared to face-to-face approaches (Tates et al., 2009). Even if the topic is not sensitive in nature, participants also tend to feel more open to disagreeing with others, presumably due to the perceptions of anonymity and also because of the lack of additional communicative factors like tone of voice and non-verbal expression (Reid and Reid, 2005). Participant anonymity may pose other challenges though because it 'allows individuals to conceal all or parts of their identity, or in fact allows them to adopt an alternative identity' (Rodham and Gavin, 2006: 94). There is no way to guarantee participants are truly part of the target population. Arguably, this is not unique to online research methods because all human subjects research relies heavily on people's honesty and integrity.

When researchers require participants whose preferred language is different from their own or participants in a single group with different languages, text-based mediums offer a unique solution to enhance communication. Auto-text-translators can help with this issue. Browser plug-ins like Google Translate and translate features built into specialized, paid applications are not perfect, but they can at least convey important information.

Finally, in some respects, the technological barrier is lower with text-based facilitation mediums because most people are more equipped for and accustomed to communicating online by typing. Slower connection speeds are amenable to text-based communication and participants do not have to have webcams or microphones. Audiovisual communication online often requires some sort of download of additional application(s) or web browser plug-in to work, whereas most text-based communication tools (particularly asynchronous collection tools) do not. With less hardware and software, set-up instructions are not as lengthy. Even though people are more experienced with face-to-face communication, most are not yet used to talking to others through a computer or interfaces designed for video communication online (Abrams et al., 2015). It is still not truly a face-to-face environment. Communicating online via text is simply more established, although audio and visual communication online is catching up.

Many have argued the main limitation to text-based focus groups is the lack of verbal and visual interaction (Liamputtong, 2011), and that is the key advantage to using video-based focus groups. Video focus groups use people's webcams and online video conferencing applications to conduct them synchronously. They can also be done asynchronously by using platforms that allow researchers to create groups and participants to upload videos, but research or mention of this technique in other literature does not yet exist. Besides potentially enhancing communication among participants and between moderator and participants, video techniques are useful to researchers wanting to gain deeper insights than verbal constructs allow. 'As participants use visual images and metaphors to help describe their identities, experiences, and practices, researchers are able to obtain more detailed narratives' (Wilkerson *et al.*, 2014: 567). During the transcription process, researchers can also denote tone of voice, facial expressions, and body language to enhance understanding of the data for the analysis phase.

Literature discussing the potential of video mediums for conducting focus groups is limited to passing mentions of its potential. Seemingly, the first study is one I (Abrams) conducted with colleagues comparing data between face-to-face, online text-only, and online video (Abrams *et al.*, 2015); those findings are presented in the data quality section below. Although not in the 2015 publication, we also reflected on the logistics between the three approaches, and so I will present some of that analysis here in the form of recommendations for preparing for online, video-based focus groups.

- When the online video conferencing/meeting software caps the number of video feeds allowed at one time, turning off the moderator's feed (when not needed) is one solution and can encourage more naturalistic group interaction.

- The moderator requires additional training on the tools being used to facilitate the focus group to ensure he/she can focus on moderating.
- Send participants set-up instructions in advance to ensure they have the required software, browser plug-ins, and hardware working properly. Include these set-up instructions in two reminders about the focus group.
- Account for technical difficulties, especially in the beginning of the focus groups, and schedule about 10–15 minutes of extra time to help participants assimilate to the interface and video-based discussion process.
- The moderator should not jump in at every silence in the discussion. More silences in between participants' contributions may be encountered due to more careful turn-taking in the video-based focus group compared to other mediums. Participants seem to hesitate before speaking more frequently perhaps because they worry they missed a verbal or auditory cue that someone else was or is trying to speak.

Online virtual environments are another avenue for conducting focus groups. Second Life is one of the most popular tools and it has about 41.8 million total users (Voyager, 2015); however, the number of active users may only be around 400,000 to 500,000 based on login statistics (Nino, 2015). Compare that to the social media site of Facebook with 936 million daily active users (Facebook, 2015) and you can see Second Life is not used by the mainstream population. Still, these tools offer some advantages over webcam and text-based mediums. Participants embody themselves through an avatar, which is a graphical version of the user, but it does not have to look anything like them if they desire. Participants could choose to make their avatar appear older or younger, male/female/androgynous, or even have non-human features, among other alterations. This allows participants to remain more anonymous to the group, similar to text-only mediums. Like video tools, virtual reality tools also require participants to download software and have a computer graphics card fast enough to handle the graphical interface. Unlike text and webcam mediums, virtual reality gives participants a space in which they can move about and 'be' in a space together. Although participants can do some non-verbal communication through their avatars, it has to be intentional/purposeful and is more limited than what is conveyed face-to-face (webcam or in-person) (Kamberelis and Dimitriadis, 2014). These tools can be set up to allow participants to communicate through microphones or text. Stewart and Williams (2005) reported that focus groups conducted in an online virtual reality setting produced more engaging discussion and interaction among participants than text-only settings. Nonetheless, the learning curve for virtual reality interfaces poses an issue if the population is not already adept at interacting in such spaces. Other questions relating to how group dynamics and discussion is affected by physical features of participants' avatars are also important to consider especially when the topic relates to such factors as race, gender, age, ethnicity, etc.

TOOLS

The range of tools available to conduct online focus groups is as wide as you can imagine with the number of Internet communication platforms in existence. This section focuses on three types: specialized focus group software, paid online meeting applications, and free applications. The specific tools mentioned are listed in Table 25.2.

As research conducted over the Internet has taken off, so has the marketplace for specialized applications and support for doing so. Researchers will find a number of options depending on their interests, needs, and budget. Finished packages offer dedicated technical support and were designed specifically to meet researchers' and participants' needs. As such, they come with a range of options to aid researchers and most are user-friendly, even for novices. Itracks is one company among many that offers researchers the ability to conduct focus groups using a chat tool (synchronous), bulletin board (asynchronous), and video (synchronous). Another company, 2020, offers QualBoard for conducting asynchronous online focus groups using a bulletin board-type tool with the option of enabling participants to contribute via webcam. Some of these tools even help participants set up their camera and audio for ideal clarity with positioning and lighting. This is very important to achieve the full benefit of the audiovisual data and for recording purposes. Specialized, paid tools also automatically record and save all data transmitted during the discussions. These two companies are among many available – a detailed list can be found in GreenBook (2015). Other unique tools are often built into the interface of these paid packages, like virtual white boards that both researchers and participants can use, multimedia sharing (static documents like PDFs and PowerPoints, websites, audio, images, video), emojis, and polls. An important

Table 25.2   Online focus groups tools

Type	Name
Specialized focus group software[1]	iTracks, QualBoard
Paid, online meeting applications	Adobe Connect, Citrix GoToMeeting, Cisco WebEx, Zoom, Google Hangouts for Work, Microsoft Skype for Business
Online learning platforms	Blackboard, Desire to Learn, Moodle
Free online meeting applications	Google Hangouts, Skype
Free forum tools	ProBoards, Lefora
Multi-user virtual environments	Meshmoon, Second Life
Social media	Facebook Groups

Notes: [1] Many more can be found in GreenBook (2015).

feature to check for is whether their interface adapts well to mobile devices or if they have a separate mobile device application.

Paid, online meeting or conference applications are another option to help facilitate focus groups. Since they are designed to facilitate meetings and group communication online, conducting focus groups with them is also possible. Several have similar features to specialized focus group applications, like white boards and multimedia sharing. Most also typically have mobile device applications making it easy for participants to join from their preferred device. Being paid, they also have dedicated technical support and most people will find them user-friendly. Recording features may need to be activated, but typically, this is an available function. Some may already be familiar with the tool and interface because they are increasingly used in education and workplaces. The technical support may not be as dedicated during your focus group time as with a company providing a specialized focus group application, but it is likely to be better than support from free applications. Adobe Connect, Citrix GoToMeeting, Cisco WebEx, Zoom, Google Hangouts for Work, and Microsoft Skype for Business are a few of the popular online meeting applications. Hangouts and Skype also have free versions. If your company or institution already pays for a license for such a tool, you may be able to use it for your focus groups, avoiding additional cost. I will mention distance education or online learning platforms as another option in this section because they are similar to online meeting applications in that they are often fee-based (except for Moodle, which is open source), have dedicated support, and were designed to facilitate group interaction. The cost of these tools is often greater; however, researchers in education may already have access to them through their institution's license. Online learning platforms offer multiple tools to conduct focus groups asynchronously (discussion boards) or synchronously (chats, audio, and video). These platforms would allow focus groups to continue over time and in multiple modes through a single interface. For example, you could conduct a synchronous focus group and continue it or conduct a second one with the same participants asynchronously. Such an approach could help overcome some issues with group interaction in asynchronous modes. Because online learning platforms include so many tools to facilitate learning, the interface, if not edited or designed properly, may be overwhelming to some novices.

For online multi-user virtual environments, there are paid tools available. One is Meshmoon (http://www.meshmoon.com) in which users can easily create their desired 3D space and invite participants. Participants do not have to pay or even create accounts. Not having to create an account is a benefit over free tools.

There are numerous free tools available to facilitate group communication. The most useful tools are ones that are used by many people and have text, audio, and audiovisual capabilities. In 2013, Skype had about 300 million users worldwide (Steele, 2013). Google Hangouts has not released usage statistics, but anyone with a Google account (2.2 billion people) has access to the tool (Ahmad, 2015). Google Hangouts and Skype support chat, voice, and video with the download of their application or browser plug-in. Google Hangouts includes tools to share visuals (emojis, stickers, and photos) and allows up to nine people on video calls. Skype lets users share their device screens, photos, and files, and includes emojis, and allows up to ten people on video calls. Both of these tools have mobile device applications as well. For asynchronous group communication, forum tools are an option. ProBoards (https://www.proboards.com) and Lefora (http://www.lefora.com) are two of many options available. Features to look for are privacy (to keep non-research participants out), data exportation possibilities, mobile device compatibility, intuitiveness of user interface, and account creation and set-up requirements for participants.

As mentioned in the previous section, Second Life is the most popular online multi-user virtual environment that can be used entirely free of charge. Creating spaces to conduct focus groups, however, requires some skill and expertise. Some universities and institutions have already created virtual space in Second Life that researchers may be able to access.

Probably the biggest disadvantage of the free tools is the lack of built-in recording or saving features. Text-based tools often reserve data export features for their paid versions, and so saving the transcripts will have to be a more tedious job for the researcher. Recording video and audio requires additional software and technical set-up on the researcher's computer. Tech bloggers offer instructions and tips on how to do this if you conduct a Web search for 'how to record [insert name of free tool here]'. It seems the simplest options for recording are not free. For example, Evaer (http://www.evaer.com) is US$19.95. With video-based focus groups, video and audio quality is not that good (pixelated, echoes, static) and lag or dropped signals are also quite possible, even on high-speed Internet connections. By default, Google Hangouts and Skype save group chats, but this does mean the data is also saved on participants' accounts, possibly posing confidentiality problems. Additionally, advertisements may display on free versions and these ads are often customized to match the content shared in the tool. This means if the group is discussing skin conditions, skin care products may be advertised, which could pose concerns to participants over the confidentiality of their information.

Researchers might also consider the possibility of using social media tools to conduct focus groups because many of them are free to use and, depending on the population, participants may already be familiar with using them. Facebook Groups offers the most viable means for conducting an asynchronous focus group. It would even allow participants to share images, videos, and use emojis. A Facebook Group can be set to 'secret'

so that it does not show up in searches and only those who are invited can join. The posts are only viewable by those in the group. The biggest disadvantage is privacy and it poses an ethical dilemma for researchers. Social media companies do not own the content but typically, under the terms of agreement, users grant permission for the company to use, distribute and share the content subject to applicable privacy settings. However, even once content is deleted, companies often retain it (Scherker, 2014). What participants share in a focus group over social media could be used to sell them products as well.

With free tools, support is limited to their help Web pages or databases, community forums, and maybe email. This likely means the researcher will be responsible for helping participants get the application and hardware ready for the focus group. Keep in mind that if a researcher has to write or download instructions for participants to configure an application to operate on a computer, he/she will probably have a difficult time maintaining participants. It is one thing to commit your time to participate in an interesting discussion; it is yet another to have to spend time configuring your computer (which may also be against company policy if a participant is joining the discussion while at work). The other dilemma of needing to instruct participants to configure an application is that the moderator, by default, becomes the technical support staff.

SETTING EFFECTS

Bloor *et al.* (2001) offer a critical point to ponder: a neutral venue for conducting a focus group does not exist so no matter the setting, recognizing the impact of the venue itself on the data is crucial. Online focus group settings have different effects on data, and understanding those effects is paramount to planning studies and ensuring positive outcomes.

Much of the research comparing data between online and face-to-face focus group settings has focused on synchronous, text-based online approaches. Specifically, word count (measured as words per participant and total word count) and the number of ideas generated have been the focus. Although word count is not a direct measure of richness, its strong associations with the other variables that indicate richness (more personal response and response with more specific knowledge) make it a good indicator of data quality and richness. Several studies have concluded that online synchronous text-based focus groups might have their place in research for their ability to capture the same amount of unique ideas as face-to-face focus groups with fewer words, but do not offer the same level of depth. Underhill and Olmsted (2003) found that participants in online text-based synchronous and also face-to-face focus groups produced similar amounts of topic-related comments and unique ideas. Schneider *et al.* (2002) found online text-based synchronous focus groups led to shorter responses (interpreted as less elaboration) than face-to-face focus groups. Finally, Brüggen and Willems (2009) asserted that online text-only focus group data have less depth because participants do not provide comments as lengthy as those in face-to-face focus groups.

Our study comparing online video, online text-only, and face-to-face settings examined (a) the amount of topic-related data, (b) the amount of unrelated data – no theme, socializing, medium-related, (c) researcher ratings of data richness, and (d) word count and linguistic characteristics of data (Abrams *et al.*, 2015). Results showed that face-to-face focus groups yielded the most topic-related data and least distractions (e.g. socializing and technology distractions). Online video focus groups yielded the lowest percentage of topic-related data due to technology distractions and socializing, but the average participant contributions were much longer. In addition, the richness of data generated in online video

focus groups was similar to that produced in face-to-face focus groups. Online text-only focus groups yielded the greatest percentage of unrelated as well as socializing data, the least number of words, and less richness compared with face-to-face and online video focus groups (Abrams *et al.*, 2015). Online text-only focus groups therefore seem better suited to generating ideas rather than depth on a topic, while online video can provide data similar in richness to face-to-face settings resulting from better interaction among participants and richer communication.

RECRUITING AND INFORMED CONSENT

The issues of recruitment and informed consent are intricately linked. The typical rule of thumb for acquiring informed consent is when there is potential for some form of risk in relation to one's participation in a study. However, it should be noted that 'the risks to human subjects in social science research are often vague and difficult to define; they may involve less physical harm than psychological distress, invasion of privacy, or social embarrassment' (Nelkin, 1994: 363).

Online risk is somewhat different from risk in a traditional focus group. In person, identification, for example, is physical and how others perceive an individual's specific contributions to a discussion is much more obvious. In fact, that type of interaction is one of the benefits of a face-to-face focus group. A flinch, a smile or chuckle may impact further participation or alter the revelation of certain personal details. Online, however, the loss of self-presentation – a perceived anonymity – may lead naïve participants to overly reveal potentially embarrassing details, etc. In this way, vulnerability and risk is slightly different online from in person.

There will be few, if any, known risks involved in many online studies; however, informed consent is still warranted. There is a possibility that others could gain access to study data, or that a participant might self-disclose data that could be damaging to him or herself, and in some environments individuals might access traceable information such as an IP address. A good informed consent document offers the opportunity for the researcher to clarify expectations and provides a basis for the researcher's obligation to participants. There should be details included in the informed consent regarding the technology, how it may and may not impact such things as anonymity and expectations.

It is important to remember that the electronic environment lends itself to a unique ethical dilemma: others' access to the data (Williams *et al.*, 1988). As such, this concern should be clearly identified in the informed consent process. In the online environment, researchers cannot control who saves the data or how they use it. Although others' access to the data is frequently not of concern, it needs to be appreciated that by virtue of asking someone to participate in a discussion a researcher is also exposing that participant to potential misrepresentation of their contribution in someone else's research or other context. Recognizing how futile and naïve it would be to think individuals can be prevented from keeping log files of group discussions, and also appreciating that making it a concern with the group might drive those storing the data into the recesses, researchers are encouraged to be direct about the issue in the consent form. It might be helpful, for example, to indicate in the informed consent that participants should not record the focus group for any purpose.

Once there is clarity regarding the specifics of consent, recruitment can commence. Recruitment should be driven by a given study's sampling requirements. As in offline research techniques, if a researcher is considering sampling, he/she has a sense of a sampling need based on intuition and a set of assumptions about what sample will yield the most significant understanding of the subject matter. In this way, the researcher is using purposive sampling (Babbie, 2015).

Researchers are encouraged to recruit in different locations on the Internet. They might review and post on community spaces such as LinkedIn and Facebook, post in newsgroups and listserv discussion lists, and seek out spaces where a particular study sample might frequent online, such as gaming environments, male and female community sites, and forums, as a way of pursuing potential participants. When participants indicate an interest, researchers should create a distribution list, and mail appropriate personal information, details about the study, and expectations of participants. They should also include a more detailed statement about the project and what people are agreeing to when they agree to participate.

Recruiting in this manner is not unlike recruiting offline. Researchers often post notices on bulletin boards, in publications, and so forth, as well as telephoning or emailing past participants, members of organizations, etc., who are in some type of listing.

One of the challenges for most research is the best and most appropriate means by which to recruit. The most significant challenge is being intrusive in online locations, not unlike the telemarketing recruitment call during the family dinner hour. Being respectful of online groups and virtual communities requires researchers to seriously consider the means by which to recruit. For example, is it necessary to secure the approval of the management, most often a group administrator, prior to posting? In most cases, it might be best to request that the administrator or host post the recruitment notice. This may minimize misunderstandings and limit the potential for people to feel as though they have been 'spammed', the Internet term for annoying advertisements and general information messages (Fahey, 1994).

In addition, the researcher has a responsibility to be clear on the nature, or lack thereof, of anonymity online. Participants may be naïve, believing that a simple promise of anonymity means just that: that they are anonymous. However, email addresses,

IP addresses, message content, and chat dialogs may all be traceable and accessible at various times during, and after, the research effort. As such, it's important that participants be dissuaded of their delusion of online anonymity prior to participating in a discussion. Researchers are still obliged to make attempts at enabling anonymity, but need to be clear with participants that best attempts do not directly equate with actual anonymity.

FUTURE POTENTIALS

The Internet has played a foundational part in advances and innovations in all parts of our lives and will continue along this trajectory. It is evidenced by the digitization and networking of so many aspects of our lives, like physical activity, public and private transit, healthcare, energy use, and commerce, to name just a few. Focus group research could be paired with participants' digital data for deeper insight that could drastically improve our understanding of a variety of social phenomena and human behavior.

To conduct focus groups, video and virtual reality will continue to expand as powerful tools. Video conferencing technology has established itself as viable, especially as Internet speed and audiovisual compression improves. The possibility of communicating in real-time with people of different languages is also not far off. Skype is beta testing live translation of voice and text chat with current users (Skype, 2015). As people become more accustomed to communicating with video online, the novelty of it will be less of a distraction.

At the time of the first edition of this chapter, virtual environments were mentioned as simply a space online where people embody an avatar and meet in a constructed world, as in Second Life. Today, virtual reality technology is far more advanced. The possibility of people interacting in virtual environments is not through their home computer and an avatar but through immersing the individual in the environment with a portable headset or something along the lines of Google Glass. The possibility of this technology becoming mainstream is evidenced by Facebook's US$2.3 billion purchase of Oculus Rift for its immersive virtual reality technology. 'The Rift – a pair of goggles with an in-built screen that uses software to create a 3D artificial environment – has become so sophisticated it allows the wearer to suspend belief and accept what they are seeing as real' (Ensor, 2015). In 2015, the Oculus Rift CEO announced the headset will come to market at a price of US$1,500, but that includes the cost of a computer that can give the user the richest experience. A near-term goal for the company is to bring the cost down to US$200–US$400 (Murphy, 2015). Researchers on a tighter budget may find potential in bringing people together in a virtual reality-type experience by using Google Cardboard, which promises to deliver immersive experiences to everyone. It is a folded cardboard apparatus usable with most smartphones. With Cardboard, Google aims to encourage development of virtual reality applications and technology.

Given Facebook's investment in virtual reality technology and continued advancement of group communication features, social media also shows future promise for conducting focus groups online. Although it can be done today, as discussed earlier, it is not ideal. The ubiquitous use of social media already makes it possible for people to use other applications without having to create separate accounts; they just login with their social media account. This takes away one common barrier with free tools. In 2016, most social media tools only offer one-to-one live video chats/calls (e.g. Facebook Messenger) or one-to-many (e.g. Facebook Live, Twitter Periscope). Given these current capabilities, live group video chat features through social media may be here before we know it.

REFERENCES

Abrams, K.M., Wang, Z., Song, Y.J. and Galindo-Gonzalez, S. (2015) 'Data richness trade-offs between face-to-face, online audiovisual, and online text-only focus groups', *Social Science Computer Review*, 33(1): 80–96.

Ahmad, I. (2015) Fascinating #SocialMedia Stats 2015: Facebook, Twitter, Pinterest, Google+. *Digital Information World,* February 1. Available at http://www.digitalinforma-tionworld.com/2015/02/fascinating-social-networking-stats-2015.html (accessed 18 May, 2015).

Babbie, E. (2015) *The Practice of Social Research*. 14th edn. Boston, MA: Cengage Learning.

Belson, D. (ed). (2016) Akamai's State of the Internet Q1 2016 Report. *Akamai*, 9(1). Available at https://www.akamai.com/us/en/multimedia/documents/state-of-the-internet/akamai-state-of-the-internet-report-q1-2016.pdf (accessed 18 June, 2016).

Bloor, M., Frankland, J., Thomas, M. and Robson, K. (eds.) (2001) *Focus Groups in Social Research*. London: Sage Publications.

Brüggen, E. and Willems, P. (2009) 'A critical comparison of offline focus groups, online focus groups and e-Delphi', *International Journal of Market Research,* 51(3): 363–81.

Campbell, M. K., Meier, A., Carr, C., Enga, Z., James, A. S., Reedy, J. and Zheng, B. (2001) 'Health behavior changes after colon cancer: a comparison of findings from face-to-face and on-line focus groups', *Family & Community Health*, 24(3), 88–103.

Daer, A. R., Hoffman, R. and Goodman, S. (2014) 'Rhetorical functions of hashtag forms across social media applications'. In Proceedings of the 32nd ACM International Conference on The Design of Communication, ACM Digital Library, September. Available at http://dl.acm.org/citation.cfm?id=2666231 (accessed 18 May, 2015).

Ensor, J. (2015) 'Oculus Rift's Palmer Luckey: "I brought virtual reality back from the dead"', *The Telegraph*, January 2. Available at http://www.telegraph.co.uk/technology/11309013/Oculus-Rifts-Palmer-Luckey-I-brought-virtual-reality-back-from-the-dead.html (accessed 18 May, 2015).

Facebook (2015) Stats. Available at http://newsroom.fb.com/company-info (accessed 18 May, 2015).

Fahey, T. (1994) *Net.speak: The Internet Dictionary.* Indianapolis, IN: Hayden Press.

Gaiser, T.J. (1997) 'Conducting online focus groups: a methodological discussion', *Social Science Computer Review,* 15(2): 135–44.

GreenBook. (2015) Online focus groups. Available at http://www.greenbook.org/market-research-firms/online-focus-groups (accessed 18 May, 2015).

Joinson, A. (2001) 'Self-disclosure in computer-mediated communication: the role of self-awareness and visual anonymity', *European Journal of Social Psychology,* 31: 177–92.

Kamberelis, G. and Dimitriadis, G. (2014) 'Focus group research: retrospect and prospect'. In P. Leavy, (ed.), *The Oxford Handbook of Qualitative Research*. Oxford, NY: Oxford University Press, pp. 315–40.

Kitzinger, J. (1994) 'The methodology of focus groups: the importance of interaction between research participants', *Sociology of Health & Illness,* 16(1): 103–21.

Krueger, R.A. and Casey, M.A. (2014) *Focus Groups: A Practical Guide for Applied Research*. 5th ed. Thousand Oaks, CA: Sage Publications.

Liamputtong, P. (2011) *Focus Group Methodology: Principle and Practice*. Thousand Oaks, CA: Sage Publications.

Mann, C. and Stewart, F. (2000) *Internet Communication and Qualitative Research. New Technologies and Social Research Series*. London: Sage Publications.

Murphy, D. (2015) '$1,500 for Consumer Oculus Rift and PC?', *PC Magazine,* May 28. Available at http://www.pcmag.com/article2/0,2817,2484805,00.asp (accessed 3 June, 2015).

Nelkin, D. (1994) 'Forbidden research: limits to inquiry in the social sciences'. In E. Erwin, S. Gendin, and L. Kleiman (eds.), *Ethical Issues in Scientific Research: An Anthology.* New York, NY: Garland Press, pp. 355–70.

Nino, T. (2015) 'Second Life statistical charts', *Dwell On It,* May 26. Available at http://dwellonit.taterunino.net/sl-statistical-charts (accessed 3 June, 2015).

Poynter, R. (2010) *The Handbook of Online and Social Media Research: Tools and Techniques for Market Researchers*. West Sussex: John Wiley & Sons.

Reid, D.J. and Reid, F.J.M. (2005) 'Online focus groups: an in-depth comparison of computer-mediated and conventional focus group discussions', *International Journal of Market Research*, 47: 131–62.

Rodham, K. and Gavin, J. (2006) 'The ethics of using the internet to collect qualitative research data', *Research Ethics Review*, 2(3): 92–7.

Scherker, A. (2014) 'Didn't read Facebook's fine print? Here's exactly what it says', *Huffington Post*, July 21. Available at http://www.huffingtonpost.com/2014/07/21/facebook-terms-condition_n_5551965.html (accessed 10 May, 2015).

Schneider, S., Kerwin, J., Frechtling, J., and Vivari, B. (2002) 'Characteristics of the discussion in online and face-to-face focus groups', *Social Science Computer Review*, 20(1): 31–42.

Skype (2015) Welcome to Skype Translator Preview. Available at http://www.skype.com/en/translator-preview (accessed 18 May, 2015).

Steele, E. (2013) 'Skype celebrates a decade of meaningful conversations', *Skype*, August 28. Available at http://blogs.skype.com/2013/08/28/skype-celebrates-a-decade-of-meaningful-conversations (accessed 18 May, 2015).

Stewart, K. and Williams, M. (2005) 'Researching online populations: the use of online focus groups for social research', *Qualitative Research*, 5(4): 395–416.

Sweet, C. (2001) 'Designing and conducting virtual focus groups', *Qualitative Market Research: An International Journal*, 4(3): 130–5.

Tates, K., Zwaanswijk, M., Otten, R., van Dulmen, S., Hoogerbrugge, P., Kamps, W., and Bensing, J. (2009) 'Online focus groups as a tool to collect data in hard-to-include populations: examples from pediatric oncology', *BMC Medical Research Methodology*, 9(1). doi:10.1186/1471–2288-9–15.

Turner, S. (2008) 'Choosing the right approach comes down to serving each project's needs', *Quirk's Marketing Research Review*, July. Available at http://www.quirks.com/articles/2008/20080701.aspx (accessed 3 June, 2015).

Underhill, C. and Olmsted, M. (2003) 'An experimental comparison of computer-mediated and face-to-face focus groups', *Social Science Computer Review*, 21(4): 506–12.

United States Federal Communication Commission (n.d.) Broadband Speed Guide. Available at https://www.fcc.gov/guides/broadband-speed-guide (accessed 3 June, 2015).

Voyager, D. (2015) 'Second Life grid stats', *Daniel Voyager's Blog*, April 30. Available at https://danielvoyager.wordpress.com/sl-metrics (accessed 18 May, 2015).

Webcam penetration rates and adoption. (2011, July 5) Available at http://zugara.com/webcam-penetration-rates-adoption (accessed 18 July, 2016).

Wilkerson, J.M., Iantaffi, A., Grey, J.A., Bockting, W.O., and Rosser, B.R.S. (2014) 'Recommendations for internet-based qualitative health research with hard-to-reach populations', *Qualitative Health Research*, 24(4): 561–74.

Williams, F., Rice, R.E. and Rogers, E.M. (1988) *Research Methods and the New Media*. New York: Free Press.

Zwaanswijk, M. and van Dulmen, S. (2014) 'Advantages of asynchronous online focus groups and face-to-face focus groups as perceived by child, adolescent and adult participants: A survey study', *BMC Research Notes*, 7(1): 756–63.

FURTHER READING

Krueger, R.A. and Casey, M.A. (2014) *Focus Groups: A Practical Guide for Applied Research*. 5th edn. Thousand Oaks, CA: Sage Publications. Helps researchers think through all parts of focus group research, including those conducted online.

Poynter, R. (2010) *The Handbook of Online and Social Media Research: Tools and Techniques for Market Researchers*. Chichester, UK: John Wiley & Sons. Despite being oriented toward market research, it provides a practical guide to planning and conducting research online.

## 26

Tools for Collaboration in Video-based Research

Jon Hindmarsh

INTRODUCTION

The emergence of a range of new communication technologies has opened up numerous opportunities for qualitative research in the social sciences. These opportunities often relate to the very topics, domains and data-sets open to researchers. So, for example, new technologies deliver new sites of sociality, including the innumerable online communities of the web. They also deliver new forms of social scientific data, ranging from electronic blogs and chats through to forms of sensor data relevant to the analysis of social action and activity. However, they also provide new means through which qualitative researchers can share data and collaborate on research projects – thus new communication technologies not only deliver new 'substance' to qualitative social science, but also novel possibilities for the very 'organisation' of research efforts. This chapter explores one case for which technologies are affording new opportunities to engage in

collaborative qualitative data analysis: the case of digital video in social research.

The use of video in the social sciences has grown significantly and now digital video provides new ways of working with, collaborating over and presenting video-based social scientific data. In parallel, there has been an increase in funding support for national and international research projects and networks. Therefore, there are very real opportunities to create 'collaboratories' for video-based research, where the notion of a collaboratory refers to '... a center without walls, in which researchers can perform their research without regard to physical location – interacting with colleagues ... sharing data and computational resources' (Wulf 1989: 19). However, these possibilities demand consideration of a range of practical and organisational problems in the coordination and management of distributed research teams.

This chapter draws on findings from Mixed Media Grid (MiMeG) (see Fraser *et al.* 2006), a research project concerned with the development of tools to support remote working with and around video data in the social sciences, and explores these challenges in some detail. In particular, the chapter considers the development of digital video analysis in the social sciences, the practical problems facing inter-institutional research teams using digital video, and issues raised for emerging technological solutions.

THE EMERGENCE OF DIGITAL VIDEO IN SOCIAL RESEARCH

The use of film in the social sciences has a long and distinguished history (see Heath *et al.* 2010). However, it is mainly to be found in anthropology (and to a lesser extent management studies) rather than sociology. The seminal ethnographic films of A.C. Haddon and others had a distinctive impact on the development of ethnography and they leave a legacy of recordings and scholarship that remains significant to contemporary anthropological endeavours (see Banks, 2001). Meanwhile in management science, Henry Ford, building on the scientific management principles of F.W. Taylor, used film to record, analyse and streamline the organisation of industrial work tasks – research that informed decisions on how to divide tasks between humans and machines on the assembly lines (see Bryan, 2003).

As the twentieth century unfolded, film and later video equipment became increasingly affordable and manageable, and the opportunities of the research instrument became more widely appreciated by social scientists. Now that near-broadcast quality camcorders are available relatively cheaply, we see significant schools of video-based research not only in anthropology, but also in sociology, psychology, education, geography, linguistics and more. These encompass research as wide-ranging as studies of the use of interactive whiteboards in classrooms, through to unpacking the organisation of teamwork in operating theatres.

The fact that video-based research has such a wide range of applications is in part due to its amenability to both quantitative and qualitative approaches to analysis. However, the primary focus for this chapter will be on the qualitative analysis of video materials. Indeed, the affordances of video for qualitative researchers are well documented. As Grimshaw summarises:

> The two principal advantages of SIR [Sound–Image Data Records] are density and permanence. Other records may have one or the other of these attributes; no other has both. (Grimshaw, 1982: 122)

Video captures a version of an event as it happens. It provides opportunities to record aspects of social activities in real time: talk, bodily conduct, material environment, tool use, etc., which give density to the data record. It also resists *in the first instance* reduction to category or code and thus preserves the original record for repeated scrutiny, which delivers the permanence of the data record. Thus, unlike other forms of social scientific data, there is opportunity for 'time-out', to play back in order to reframe, refocus and re-evaluate the analytic gaze. These are very powerful opportunities for the researcher. They allow for multiple reviews of the data – to assess the validity of analytic claims, to explore different issues on different occasions, or to consider the same issue from multiple perspectives.

In some ways, many classical analytic approaches in the social sciences do not need or appreciate the level of granularity that video affords, and therefore much of the qualitative use of video is clustered around approaches that do work at that level of granularity and that therefore can exploit these affordances. For example, one of the most dominant uses of recorded video as data (as opposed to the use of video as illustration or aide-memoire) concerns the study of the real-time production of social order, steered in the main by the approaches of ethnomethodology and conversation analysis. These studies consider the range of resources that participants bring to bear in making sense of, and participating in, the conduct of others (see, for example, Goodwin, 2013; Heath, 2013; Mondada, 2014). Indeed, one of the foundational principles of ethnomethodology is that the sense of any action for participants is inseparable from the immediate context of its production. This notion of 'indexicality' drives the analyst to evidence claims about social action with regard to the local context and to remain sensitive to the emergent character of context.

The notion of context that is invoked in this analytic work does not prioritise 'setting' or 'the identities of participants', but rather the radically local interactional context; that is, what has just been said and done (see Heritage, 1984). Indeed, each action in interaction is seen to be context-shaped (intimately organised with regard to the immediately prior action) and context-renewing (creating the context in which the next action will be seen and understood). It is this approach to context that delivers 'evidence' for analytic claims in such video-based studies because, through each next action, participants display their orientation to, and understanding of, the immediately prior action. In this regard, and like many other qualitative approaches, the participants' perspective is paramount.

To facilitate exploration of this *sequential organisation* of activities, the analytic approach involves the detailed transcription of conduct (for more information, see Heath *et al.*, 2010). The density of the video record also enables the analyst to consider how the local ecology of bodies, objects, texts, tools and technologies feature in the action and activity under scrutiny. This adds to the complexity of the transcription work as it involves not only the detailed transcription of talk, but also the various visual and material forms of conduct that constitute the interaction (for a discussion of alternative approaches to the transcription of audio-visual data, see Bezemer and Mavers, 2011).

As Michael Agar suggests with regard to ethnographic inquiry more generally, the

work of developing a 'critical way of seeing, in my experience at least, comes out of numerous cycles through a little bit of data, massive amounts of thinking about that data' (Agar, 1991: 193). Similarly, qualitative approaches to the analysis of video are driven by consideration of single instances and, in so doing, these approaches exploit the density and permanence of the video data record. This close scrutiny of video data places distinctive demands on technological support for such analytic work.

SHARING VIDEO DATA

The permanence of the video record also allows raw data to be shared in various ways with colleagues and peers. Digital video, over and above its analogue predecessor, provides more flexible ways of manipulating, presenting and sharing social scientific data. Even relatively basic computer software packages allow for fairly complex means of reproducing, enhancing and juxtaposing images. For instance, the free video-editing software for the Apple Mac (iMovie) can be used to digitally 'zoom in' on interesting phenomena, 'spotlight' relevant conduct or create picture-in-picture videos to assist analysis or presentation. Furthermore, Internet-based technologies provide a range of ways of sharing, distributing and disseminating video data, via email, Dropbox or even through electronic journal publications that enable digital video data to be incorporated into scholarly articles (e.g. Sociological Research Online, http://www.socresonline.org.uk/, or Academy of Management Discoveries, http://amd.aom.org/).

The value of showing and sharing raw data with colleagues and peers should not be underestimated. One criticism of ethnography, for example, concerns the lack of 'transparency' in ethnographic inquiry; that is to say, critics highlight the difficulties of recovering what the researcher saw and experienced, and thus the very basis for their analysis. Within video-based research, the core data are potentially available to be examined in relation to presented or published research accounts. Furthermore, video enables colleagues, and indeed students and supervisors, to work together on the same materials. Thus there is support for very closely organised collaborative analytic work. One key institution for this collaborative video analysis comes in the form of the 'data session'.

COLLABORATIVE VIDEO ANALYSIS: THE DATA SESSION

As social scientists began to analyse the organisation of social interaction through the detailed consideration of recorded materials, whether audio or video, they also recognised the value of being able to share data with others, show those data to others and discuss emerging analyses with regard to those data. Indeed, the 'data session' has become a common form for the collaborative analysis of recorded materials in certain sub-disciplines of the social sciences. These data sessions essentially involve a number of researchers viewing, commenting on and analysing video data together. Thus, they facilitate collaborative interrogation of short stretches of recorded data (from a few seconds to a few minutes, depending on approach and concerns) and enable participants to explore tentative formulations and analyses and to receive immediate comment, contribution and feedback from colleagues in relation to those data.

In many situations, researchers in the social sciences receive comments on their work only through informal conversations, more formal presentations or drafts of written work. Sometimes survey researchers will discuss aspects of their data to explore inter-rater reliability or field researchers will share and discuss their field notes on collaborative projects. However, the video data session provides opportunities for colleagues and

peers to co-participate in analytic work on an unprecedented level. They are able to make observations on data of naturally occurring interactions, consider the analytic significance of those observations, interrogate an order to events, suggest avenues for further inquiry, draw parallels with observations from other settings, recommend relevant literature and the like. This can be an invaluable means for kick-starting (or restarting) analytic endeavours.

Whilst the sessions are common features of everyday practice and training within various fields in the social sciences (Tutt and Hindmarsh, 2011; Antaki *et al.*, 2008), it would be misleading to suggest that the practices of running data sessions are consistent across all cases. Participants can range in number from a minimum of two to a quite sizeable small group, of maybe twenty or so. The data session can be highly structured, with a formal introduction to the data, then the viewing of the data, a few minutes for participants to make notes, and subsequently an opportunity for everyone to raise a point or an issue before the session progresses further. Alternatively, someone can just start the video and then anyone can ask questions, raise issues and the session can develop more organically.

For some time, video data were displayed using video players and TVs, but it is of course far more common for digital video to be played directly from computers via screens or projectors (see Figure 26.1). These sessions require participants to be able to see and discuss video-based source materials, but usually participants also have to hand additional forms of mixed media data, including transcripts, images and drawings. For example, participants will routinely share documents to chart, map or transcribe action unfolding on the video. The most common of these is some sort of transcript of the talk and actions of participants featured on screen. Depending on the type of research, this can range from 'soundbites' through to detailed phonetic and gestural transcripts. There may also be 'indigenous materials' relevant to the analysis, such

Figure 26.1 Three video-based data sessions – they can range in number of participants and also in display technologies (e.g. TV, laptop and computer screen are depicted here)

as documents taken from the scene (e.g. log books, record cards, computer printouts) or physical artefacts, such as instruments or tools; photographs of elements of the scene (e.g. signs, whiteboards, technologies); documentary materials that relate to the setting, such as pages from manuals or textbooks that describe standard procedures or rules for settings such as this one; traditional field notes made by the researcher during phases of data collection; or sketches or diagrams produced during the data session to clarify the standard ecology of the setting or the character of the tools and technologies in use.

Participants also often use multiple camera viewpoints, and so two, three or more recordings of a scene may have been taken that provide different angles and perspectives with which to piece together adequate descriptions of the action. Digital video affords skipping

between clips and angles and, as a result, data sessions can be fluid, allowing people to ask for different views, comparative clips and the like.

During a data session, the nature of the equipment used normally demands that one participant takes control of the video playback for the duration of the session. Most frequently, control of the video falls to the owner of the data; that is, the person who brings the data to the session. This individual's first-hand experience of the data – and most likely the research setting – is highly relevant. They deal with questions about the data, how they were collected, who features on screen, the nature of activities in the setting and the like. Thus the ethnographic background remains critical to unpacking action on screen.

Data sessions are used to support a range of different kinds of activities. They can be key regular group activities for stable research collectives, whether they are formal institutionally bound groups (e.g. DARG[1] at Loughborough University, CLIC[2] at UCLA[3] or WIT[4] at King's College London) or informal (and maybe more transient) groups that nevertheless meet regularly for the purposes of data sessions. They can form key meetings for research projects to discuss data or they can be critical events for graduate schools, whether to bring together supervisors with individual students or to form a focus for a number of students working with one or a small number of supervisors. However, the changing nature of research collaborations is now suggesting a need for support for collaborative data analysis at distance and, more specifically, distributed, rather than purely collocated, data sessions.

DISTRIBUTED TEAMS AND VIDEO-BASED RESEARCH

Within the last few decades we have witnessed the emergence of highly networked global research communities. Changes in the funding and organisation of contemporary research have led to increasingly multidisciplinary, multi-organisational and multinational research projects (Cummings and Kiesler, 2005). The demands on these research teams are such that Internet and related communication technologies are increasingly adopted for the purposes of providing the communicational infrastructures to support collaborations between distributed research laboratories or groups, termed 'collaboratories' (Wulf, 1989). In various ways, these represent new forms for organising scientific project work (Finholt, 2002). The early adoption of the Internet and the development of the World Wide Web were stimulated by scientists keen to use them as mechanisms to share data (Berners-Lee, 1999; Hafner and Lyons, 1998). However, research teams and collectives are now drawing on increasingly innovative technologies to share data and expertise and to provide a forum for virtual meetings between groups.

Although these trends are usually discussed with reference to research in the natural sciences, the developments are equally relevant to the social sciences. The US National Science Foundation, the UK Research Councils and the research programmes of the European Union all positively encourage multi-institutional projects across the breadth of research activities. Given the geographical separation between partners within these projects, there are significant time and resource constraints on meeting face-to-face to collaborate on work, which draw Cummings and Kiesler to note that:

> A major challenge for dispersed scientific collaborations is coordinating work so that scientists can effectively use one another's ideas and expertise without frequent face-to-face interaction. (Cummings and Kiesler, 2005: 704)

Within video-based research there are numerous examples of explicitly funded national and international groups that undertake data sessions as a key element of their co-working. These can range from single projects bridging two or more institutions, through to formal networks and consortia involving many institutions. There are even larger numbers of researchers who come together more irregularly and informally to learn from one another's working practices and work in progress. There are numerous examples of research teams and networks across individual nations, across Europe, between the US and Europe, Japan and the US, Japan and Europe and so forth.

It is generally recognised that 'distance matters' (Olson and Olson, 2000) and that collocation is the 'gold standard' for collaboration; however, researchers within these fields are exploring methods and means for undertaking distributed or remote collaborative analysis on video materials. Thus, technologies are sought to enable collaborators to more readily participate in colleagues' research, whether or not they are geographically collocated. Indeed, unlike analogue video, digital video would seem to lend itself to such collaborations. Digital video files 'are simply computer files (albeit large ones) that can be viewed, copied, published on the web or attached to an e-mail for delivery anywhere in the world, any number of times' (Shrum et al., 2005), without degradation in original file quality. They raise greater opportunities for sharing and distribution amongst research teams and the Internet, and related communication technologies are providing novel ways to exploit these opportunities.

COMPUTER AIDED QUALITATIVE ANALYSIS SOFTWARE, COLLABORATION AND VIDEO ANALYSIS

Silver and Pataschnik (2011) have called on video-based researchers to outline more explicitly the software that they use in developing their analyses. In a series of interviews undertaken with leading video analysts in the social scientists, we have explored these matters (see Fraser et al., 2006). Interestingly, many video analysts principally use tools developed for the work of (amateur) video editing, management and production. Software such as Final Cut, Adobe Premiere, iMovie, MovieMaker (to capture and edit video); Adobe Photoshop (to enhance selected images for publication); Audacity, Sound Soap or Soundstudio (to 'clean' and edit digital audio); CatDV (to catalogue large corpora of digital video) and the like are routinely adopted by video analysts in the social sciences.

As Shrum et al. (2005) suggest, '[w]hile tourists, parents and hobbyists were the target markets for manufacturers, professional observers of social life were beneficiaries'. Indeed, Secrist et al. (2002) describe how Adobe Premiere supported their studies of infant development, making it more

possible to rearrange and navigate through video datasets. However, many researchers find that the work of social scientific video analysis places specific additional demands that are not dealt with sufficiently by these sorts of program. For example, the demands of producing textual representations of video data, such as transcriptions of talk and body movement, or the work of producing and organising analytic collections for comparative purposes, or indeed the work of collaborating on the analysis of a video dataset, raise distinctive challenges (see Box 29.1).

Many Computer Aided Qualitative Analysis Software (CAQDAS) packages do provide quite sophisticated support for digital video files (see Chapter 27, this volume). However, maybe unsurprisingly, the core CAQDAS packages tend to emphasise a certain style of code-and-retrieve, segment-and-sort analysis modelled on work with textual field notes and interview materials. There are packages (e.g. Atlas.ti) that provide hyperlinking tools to support more flexible forms of analysis, but they still focus support on links *between* segments data, rather than the detailed analysis *of* the segments themselves. For many undertaking video-based research, this can be a limitation. Whilst rough categories may be used to organise video data clips, the analytic work is often driven by the detailed consideration of single cases. Indeed, it has been suggested that for qualitative researchers, there is 'a misalignment between the increasing fidelity of audiovisual data and software tools for their analysis… the more complex the phenomena and data, the finer software tools are required' (Silver and Pataschnik, 2011: 82).

However, we are starting to see a much wider array of systems designed from within the various video analysis communities in the social sciences, whether in sociology, anthropology, linguistics, psychology or, maybe most prominently, education (see Goldman et al., 2007). As a result, there are more

---

Box 29.1   Seven requirements for video analysis tools

1. PC and Mac Compatible

- To enable use of the best, low-cost video editing software currently available without the need to change platforms

2. Interoperability

- To ensure that clips and transcripts can be moved in and out of different packages

3. Database Management

- To ensure that the same clip can be 'linked to' in a number of folders or collections without taking up additional hard-disk space

4. Flexible Video Playback

- To ensure that high quality video formats (e.g. raw digital video) can be played and that multiple video clips can be viewed simultaneously

5. Transcription Tools

- To facilitate the production of transcripts by supporting a range of text symbol types, by visualizing patterns of talk (through waveform or spectogram) and by allowing small sections of video files to be replayed repeatedly whilst the analyst simultaneously types the transcript

6. LINKS TO OTHER DATA TYPES

- To enable digital connections between different types of data in order to compare and analytically link video with field notes, transcripts, images, system logs, etc.

7. OPPORTUNITIES FOR COLLABORATIVE WORKING

- To support collaboration within collocated and distributed research teams by providing tools for, and seamless movement between, asynchronous and synchronous collaboration on video datasets.

---

software packages developed by researchers that can handle audio and video materials in more diverse ways and which are sensitive to a range of analytic perspectives beyond Grounded Theory. As Lee and Fielding (1996) anticipated, CAQDAS systems may not have been imposing an orthodoxy on qualitative research practice, but rather there was a 'cultural lag' as different approaches developed suitable systems for their needs.

So, we are seeing some 'dimensions of fineness' (Silver and Pataschnik, 2011) emerging in various packages, especially concerning (1) the integration and analysis of different data sources and (2) the transcription and representation of data extracts, but, as we shall argue, the support is more limited for (3) collaborative analysis.

Analysing Multiple Data Sources

Often video-based research projects will involve the collection of multiple views on a scene: for example, capturing different perspectives on a virtual environment (Woods and Dempster, 2011) or within a complex organisational environment (Mondada, 2014). Thus, some of the more refined packages enable researchers to manage multiple video views. Transana, for instance, enables the synchronisation and simultaneous playback of up to four different video files. Meanwhile DIVER is built to enable the manipulation of panoramic views on a scene. The Digital Replay System even supports the integration of video data with associated data relevant to analytic work, such as system logs, text messages, field notes and the like.

A key issue in the management of these multiple data sources is the issue of storage. The approach adopted by Transana is important here. A single video clip may be relevant to multiple emerging analytic categories or themes, but the size of digital video files makes it prohibitive to create numerous versions of these clips to place within analytic collections. Transana is therefore designed to enable researchers to create links across and between parts of the data to maintain a more efficient use of disk space.

Transcription and Representation

Often video-based researchers need to create annotations and transcripts using symbols that are not usually available in standard word processors. Some packages facilitate multi-layered annotation tools (e.g. ANVIL), enable analysts to view a video window whilst simultaneously creating a transcript in a separate window (e.g. DIVER, Transana, inqscribe, ELAN). Some also provide various types of graphical representation of speech (whether waveform or spectogram), which allow analysts to refine their transcriptions by viewing as well as hearing talk on the video (e.g. Transana, InqScribe, ELAN). This can increase the accuracy of the measurement of gaps in talk, for example, because the gaps can be 'seen' as well as heard.

Collaborative Analysis

There are numerous systems emerging that provide various 'fine' levels of support for social scientists to manage, manipulate and analyse their video datasets. Maybe unsurprisingly, these packages are often founded on a model of the individual analyst, but there is growing recognition of the role that new technologies can have in supporting and even enhancing team-based research. For example,

consider two of the leading tools that support collaboration in video analysis:

- DIVER (Pea *et al.*, 2004; Pea and Lindgren, 2008) has, as a fundamental design principle, the goal of supporting 'guided noticing', which creates opportunities to share perspectives on video records. This is done through posting an individual DIVE (an annotated perspective on a scene) to the webDIVER server, where it can be viewed and commented on by others. In doing so, it provides persistent and searchable records of 'video pointing activities' linked to specific moments in the video data.
- Transana-MU (Dempster and Woods, 2011) includes functionality to enable researchers to share analytic annotations and collections with remote colleagues. Multiple researchers in different locations can connect to the same dataset at the same time, and can observe changes to the dataset undertaken by their colleagues in real time. Moreover, they can use the text-based chat function to discuss and share insights.

However, these are mainly mechanisms to support *asynchronous* collaboration at the database level by providing functionality for analytic annotations, memos and notes to be linked to relevant moments in a dataset. Some limited opportunities are available for interaction through text chat, but this cannot support the richness and fluidity of a data session. In spite of the importance and prevalence of data sessions for many video analysis communities, there is at present limited support for distributed, *real time* data sessions. Providing dedicated support for group-to-group(-to-group) video data sessions is not a core focus for any of these systems, and so they each provide rather limited support for data-focused conversations.

TOWARDS DISTRIBUTED DATA SESSIONS

We need a video infrastructure that is more interaction-centric – for people to communicate deeply, precisely, and cumulatively about the video content.
(Pea and Lindgren, 2008: 236)

Through our interviews we identified a number of existing practices adopted by video analysts to address problems of distributed research (Fraser *et al.*, 2006). The usual solution was to distribute the video data (via courier or electronically) in order that individuals could analyse common datasets separately, and then groups would arrange face-to-face gatherings for data sessions. Indeed, some respondents suggested that they engaged in all aspects of research and preparation of publications over the Internet except for analysing video data together.

On the relatively rare occasions when groups do arrange for distributed data sessions, they report that their conferencing tools are rather crude. Streaming video is found not to be reliable or secure enough. Similar problems around reliability and quality related to attempts to use 'screen share' programs for data sessions, and so again groups would distribute the data in advance, via hard drive, DVD or Dropbox. They would then support the meeting via telephone, Skype, FaceTime or, in some cases, via Access Grid. Copies of the data are played separately at each site. To coordinate playback, participants shout 'press play now', so that each remote site can watch the video data at roughly the same moment before then going on to talk about it. As the discussion and the analysis of video data routinely demands constant comparison of analytic observations with the video materials themselves, this is a very unsatisfactory way of working.

Although there are numerous systems to support distributed meetings, whether in business or research contexts, these tend to focus on face-to-face discussions, rather than co-working with and around data (especially video data). Indeed, the video link is simply to provide 'back channel' information. Programs like Access Grid (Childers *et al.*, 2000), and the more sophisticated work in the Memetic project (Buckingham Shum *et al.*, 2006) carry forward this approach. However, the kinds of research meeting of concern here, namely data sessions, demand

that participants can all see and discuss video source materials. They also involve other forms of mixed media, including transcripts, images and drawings.

This dominant concern with support for 'face-to-face' meetings is rather surprising, given that Sonnenwald *et al.* (2002: 19) note that mediated collaboration is particularly suited to work situations 'where people are separated across physical distances and ... where visual information needs to be shared and acted on'. Indeed, in a study of 62 scientific collaborations, Cummings and Kiesler (2005: 718) found that 'the use of communication technology (e-mail, instant messages, phone conferences and video conferences) did not give [Principal Investigators] at multiple universities an added advantage'. As a result of their study, Cummings and Kiesler (2005: 718) argue that collaboratories need more technologies to help 'sharing and learning', to 'track the trajectory of tasks' and to hold 'ongoing [research] conversations'.

There have been some attempts to repurpose the ePresence event broadcasting tool to support video data sessions (Baecker *et al.*, 2007). Although the system allows for collaborative video viewing, the authors argue that '[i]f ePresence is to serve as a collaboratory ... then its capabilities for representation, reflection and interaction need to be enhanced' (Baecker *et al.*, 2007: 471). Of particular note is the fact that support for interaction and collaboration are limited. Existing tools to support meetings provide clumsy support for people to share, discuss and gesture over and around video data and associated materials. Thus there remains limited support for distributed data sessions.

Our MiMeG project explored and developed technological solutions to this. The MiMeG software enables members of a research team located at two or more sites to simultaneously watch and discuss fragments of video data. The control of the video playback is assigned to one site, but participants can choose to formally switch control to other sites. All sites are able to annotate

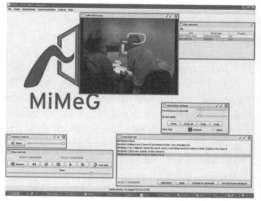

Figure 26.2 The MiMeG Interface includes video windows, playback controls, annotation controls and windows for other media (transcripts, images, etc.). The system can be used with computer screen and mouse or projection screen and pen-based input

the video stream in real time by drawing on it using mouse or pen input, and these annotations appear on all screens simultaneously. They can also be recorded for later replay, reflection and further analysis. Participants are also able to display associated images and transcripts at all sites simultaneously. Furthermore, the system runs on PC or Mac platforms and, using Skype, participants are connected via a simple audio-conferencing link. A more comprehensive introduction to the software can be found in Fraser *et al.* (2006) (see Figure 26.2).

There is no built-in video view of the other group. We did try using the Skype video conferencing tool for this, but it provides a fairly rudimentary image of others which participants find too basic to add value. The integration of more advanced video conferencing tools would raise standard problems of integrating the common workspace in meaningful ways (see Hindmarsh *et al.*, 2000). The development of the system began from an understanding that the video data is critical to the work of the session. Indeed, recent studies have shown that, especially for visually complex tasks in which the focus of attention changes frequently (such as identifying and orienting to features in video data), a shared

view of the 'task space' is essential, and can be more useful than a limited view of the 'person space' afforded by traditional video conferences (e.g. Kraut *et al.*, 2002).

The package is open source, but is now unsupported. Our experiences with this system allow us to reflect more generally on some of the challenges facing similar eResearch tools designed to exploit the affordances of video to share and distribute data between research groups and beyond.

CHALLENGES: 'ETHICS' AND MATTERS OF PERSPECTIVE

In the course of developing this software and putting it to work with existing research teams in the UK and elsewhere, we encountered a range of social, organisational and technical problems concerning the distribution, sharing and discussion of social scientific video data (see Tutt *et al.*, 2007). These include, for example, a number of thorny issues associated with institutional firewalls. On the one hand, universities are keen to support inter-institutional research, and on the other they are keen to restrict access into their own networks. As a result, we have faced persistent (although variable, depending on the institutions involved) problems in securing robust connections between institutions to support MiMeG. In addition, there are challenges relating to the 'interoperability' of video formats and indeed packages.

However, here we will focus on two more general concerns: issues of ethics and trust when sharing video data over the Internet and related technologies (see also Eynon *et al.*, this volume), and difficulties associated with distributed colleagues developing a common orientation or perspective on video data.

Ethics and Trust in Video-based Research

Retaining rich multimedia data, for instance as examples in research reports, raises forcefully ethical issues like anonymity, ownership and confidentiality (Gibbs *et al.*, 2002, 30).

Ethical issues affect video analysts to differing degrees, depending largely on the nature of their recordings. For example, those carrying out lab-based experimental research face fewer ethical concerns than those recording naturally occurring data featuring children or medical patients. However, although the use of digital video is growing significantly, there remains a relative lack of guidance on its use in the ethical statements of the major research associations. Whilst there are significant differences between digital video and other forms of social scientific data (e.g. questionnaires, interviews, field notes), there is little or no explicit mention of its use in the ethical guidelines of the American Sociological Association (ASA, 1999), the Economic and Social Research Council (ESRC, 2015) or the Social Research Association (SRA, 2003). That said, the Visual Sociology group of the British Sociological Association (BSA, 2006) has developed a revised version of the BSA's ethical guidelines that considers the use of visual materials in research. Also, rather interestingly, the General Medical

Council (2011) provides, in some ways, the most comprehensive account of the use of video materials, but of course focuses purely on the recording of medical patients.

In the legal domain, the UK Data Protection Act (1998) does potentially bear upon the use and distribution of digital video in social scientific research. Here, the security of data related to identifiable living individuals is paramount and, with regard to digital data security, the ESRC Research Ethics Framework states:

> Researchers may not appreciate the threat to data integrity and security presented by routinely-used collection and storage methods, such as computer files on hard drives and similar devices, portable computing equipment and memory, email and databases. Periodic audit of data storage arrangements at all levels is likely to be necessary to ensure compliance with both legal obligations and good research practice.
>
> (ESRC, 2015: 23)

The implications of this are that the sharing of video data across the Internet should be entirely secure and probably authorised in consent prior to collection. These challenges will be considered in a moment. However, the attitudes, opinions and existing practices of social scientists working with video materials are also significant in this regard. In work reported elsewhere (see Fraser *et al.*, 2006), we note that one interviewee suggested that 'I'm unhappy with a lot of the legalisms. I think it's more my own sense of having a responsibility to the [participants]'– a statement that reflected the sentiments of many of our interviewees. The conditions of gaining access to some organisations or other sensitive settings often rests on restrictions regarding use and distribution of video data. Furthermore, the responsibilities that the interviewee implied also extends to concerns around sharing video data when there is a possibility that other researchers might be able to form different conclusions, without first-hand experience of the setting and the participants.

Recording digital video for research purposes usually concerns participants in one of two ways. The most common fear from participants is that they might appear on the television and be depicted in a bad light. The other (lesser) worry is that they will not appear on television at all. It is difficult to guarantee appearances on a TV show. However, the more common fear demands close control on data and a good relationship with participants. For these reasons, researchers are keen not to release control over their data.

One basic issue relates to the difficulties of retaining confidentiality when faces are visible on screen. There are steps that can be taken using video editing packages to blur or otherwise obscure the faces on moving images. This can be tedious work, but it is generally not difficult. For example, it is often necessary to add an effect or image to an area of the screen in order to obscure the face – of course as the person moves, the position of the overlaid image will need to be adjusted. More intelligent software tools are increasingly available, but a more significant problem relates to constraints imposed by the analytic orientation. If the analyst needs to present the relevance of gaze or facial expression, then obscuring the face is not an appropriate solution. In these instances, the researcher should ensure that consent allows for videos to be shared with faces visible.

Attempts to distribute social scientific video data over Internet-based technologies present additional challenges. Essentially an issue of control arises where the extent to which the data can be accessed and redistributed by others is at best uncertain because the digital transmission of data is never entirely secure. Streaming video is increasingly a feature of Internet technologies, most notably through the community-building website of 'YouTube'; however, there is no way of preventing someone retaining copies of a video stream that has been delivered to their computer. Technically, efforts go simply into *making it difficult* for others to copy the files, for example by setting files to self-destruct after a period of time, or most commonly by running the video through the computer's short-term memory so that it

is not stored on the hard drive. The memory is therefore wiped every time the user closes the application or shuts down the computer. However, these techniques can be fairly easily modified by the recipient, and so they cannot guarantee security.

Similarly, the encryption of streaming videos does not prevent individuals from intercepting and copying the video file. Complex access and encryption mechanisms would still not be able to guarantee the security of data. Furthermore, if relying on these mechanisms, it would be much harder for researchers to articulate the details of the security mechanisms, complicating matters of preparing consent forms, applying to ethics committees and, most importantly, working with those being recorded.

The technology for streaming video data is readily and widely available and simple to use, but given a range of personal, ethical and technical issues it is unclear that the willingness from the research community to use it is so apparent. Indeed, this may be borne out in the slow take-up of opportunities to publish data in electronic journals. As mentioned earlier, there are technical opportunities for researchers to embed digital video data within articles in electronic journals. However, aside from a small number of exceptions (e.g. Brown, 2004; Büscher, 2005; Lomax and Casey, 1998), this opportunity has not been widely adopted by the video-analysis communities. Relatedly, despite the drive to archive data in the social scientific community, again there are very few video-based datasets available. In part, these trends can be related to the lack of control over the use of data that can be assured by those managing the journals and archives.

To try to retain security as far as possible with the MiMeG software, we began with a model of data sharing in which we retained key elements of existing practice. Essentially we assumed that data would be distributed amongst the research team, but rather than having to meet face-to-face to work on the data, MiMeG would facilitate a distributed data session. As all parties have access to the raw data, there is no need to stream the video. The only data transmitted over the Internet, therefore, is 'positional' information to ensure that the video is playing simultaneously at each site.

This solution exhibits additional system-performance benefits. There are well-known problems of 'lag' associated with streaming video between sites, and with lower-performance network links, this can mean that video data will run slowly and maybe even at different speeds at different locations. In terms of supporting communication between researchers, this could be disastrous to any attempts at successful deployment. For MiMeG, because the video does not need to be streamed, the only information that the remote sites need to share is information about the frame being viewed at each site in order that they can be aligned. This avoids many of the problems of lag associated with transmission of complex multimedia data.

With later versions of MiMeG, we decided to provide options for researchers to select for themselves how to distribute data. The basic option described earlier is still possible. Alternatively, there is an option within MiMeG to send the digital video file prior to the beginning of the data session, thus the file is distributed electronically once and then is held at each remote site. The third option is to stream the data during the data session in order that a copy of the video is not released in bulk by the main site. This will be useable only if researchers are using very high-performance networking connections. This set of options then allows the researchers to decide the level of security with which they are most comfortable for each dataset.

Sharing Perspectives

Aside from ethical and technical issues associated with the distribution of video data over the Internet, there are also practical matters of communication to be considered in the development of tools to support distributed data sessions. These are significant problems that

are common in the design and development of groupware systems more generally. Indeed, in his review of collaboratories, Finholt (2002: 93) notes that 'a challenge for collaboratory developers is producing tools and applications that compensate for the absence of shared setting' and the difficulties of sharing orientation towards objects of interest. Many scholars similarly suggest that collocation provides an ease of establishing joint reference to objects which is very difficult to attain in existing video conferencing systems (e.g. Luff *et al.* 2014; Olson and Olson 2000).

Essentially the workspace for remote collaborators is fragmented. The physical environments in which the participants are working are separated and this has a range of implications. Often the reason for co-workers to get together is to discuss common visual materials, whether documents, charts, slides, images, photographs, models, prototypes or, in the case at hand, video data. Object-focused discussions in everyday work settings can draw on the embodied resources of participants (gaze, gesture and the like) to encourage others to seamlessly shift orientation from one (feature of an) object to another. However, when the space is split over two or more remote sites, problems arise. Accounts of co-working through shared document editors or virtual reality, or even advanced video conferencing systems, routinely describe problems that participants face in achieving a common orientation to some (feature of an) object (e.g. Hindmarsh *et al.*, 2000).

This matter is further problematised when the objects of interest are dynamic, moving images. As video is not static (unless on freeze frame), the phenomena to be discussed are fleeting – they may appear on screen for only a fraction of a second. A glance, a gesture, a nod, a movement of a pen, or whatever, are difficult enough for an individual to *spot*, let alone to show to others at a remote site.

In co-present data sessions, participants have a full range of embodied resources at hand to reveal phenomena (see Figure 26.3). For example, they can point towards the

Figure 26.3   Embodied resources for indicating action on-screen: pointing, gesturing, enacting

screen, or they can gesture over it, or even 'enact' on-screen behaviours (see Tutt and Hindmarsh, 2011). In distributed data sessions, participants therefore require the tools and resources to be able to interconnect bodily conduct at the remote site with visible features on the video data that they are watching locally. A video window provided by standard desktop video conferencing systems adds little in this regard. Indeed, a much higher quality video view on the 'task space' of the other(s) (not just a typical 'head and shoulders' view) is critical to get a real sense of the action at the remote site (Kraut *et al.*, 2002). This would at least provide some sense of the gestures produced or the design of enactments of on-screen activity.

Furthermore, significant effort needs to be focused on the means for annotating the video stream and associated materials. From our studies of distributed data sessions, the design of annotations needs to be highly flexible, and so we implemented freeform annotations to enhance communicative possibilities. Moreover, it is critical that the emerging form of the annotation can be seen as it is produced, rather than after the event. This enables the recipient to see the emerging trajectory of the annotation and for the producer to reshape the annotation in the course of its production. This, however, is a non-trivial problem and demands further research and development.

THE RIGHT BRAIN STRIKES BACK... AGAIN

Collaborative research is not new to qualitative social science. There is a long and distinguished history of such work, particularly within ethnography. One needs only to consider the pioneering studies of medical socialisation (Becker *et al.*, 1961) or factory work (Roethlisberger and Dickson, 1939) or indeed the collaborations between Margaret Mead and Gregory Bateson on the collection and analysis of anthropological film in the 1930s and 1940s (Jacknis, 1988). However, the emergence of new communications technologies and the proliferation of digital video do provide enhanced opportunities for such research collaborations.

Digital video collaboratories can, in the coming years, become realistic ventures, connecting experts in formal and informal networks more readily across the globe and making coordination and collaboration in inter-institutional funded research projects more flexible. Furthermore, these tools provide the potential to make significant changes to the organisation not only of research, but also of research training. Currently, the constraints of time, space and resources restrict opportunities for international experts to contribute to graduate schools across the globe. The systems outlined here represent emerging opportunities for research students to have comments on, and contributions to, their early analytic endeavours from experts overseas.

However, there are still technical, organisational and social challenges to be met. It is clear from numerous studies in the sociology of technology that successful technical developments arise in and through changing social and organisational forms. The availability of technology does not ensure its use.

The emergence of the e-Social Science programme in the UK and the Cyber-Research initiative in the US were heralded with an emphasis on the opportunities afforded by Grid computing to interrogate larger datasets, to more efficiently and systematically find and retrieve instances in datasets, to make datasets available for others to re-analyse, and to support the building and testing of more robust models of human conduct. Although these strengths will appeal to many positivist researchers, they do not resonate well with the analytic concerns of many qualitative researchers in the social sciences. This chapter has attempted to explore some alternative benefits of emerging eResearch tools and technologies – benefits that build on a more sympathetic understanding of contemporary qualitative research practice.

In his seminal work 'The Right Brain Strikes Back', Michael Agar (1991) argued for the importance of fitting technological developments to social scientific forms of inquiry, not simply by addressing those problems that computers lend themselves to, but by identifying the real problems facing social scientists in order to make real innovations. The challenge for eResearch is to ensure that Agar's call is at the heart of its technological developments. The emphasis must be on addressing social scientists' problems and demands, rather than building systems that simply exploit what is technically feasible. The CAQDAS field has continued to mark Agar's words; eResearch must do the same. To do that we need a thorough understanding of social scientific practice, and therefore a clear sociology of social scientific knowledge.

ACKNOWLEDGEMENTS

This work has been supported by the MiMeG ESRC e-Social Science Research Node (Award No. RES-149–25-0033). The chapter draws on research undertaken by all members of the VidGrid and MiMeG research teams and as such I am deeply indebted to them, especially Mike Fraser, Katie Best, Greg Biegel, Marie Gibbs, Christian Heath, Anne Manuel, Muneeb Shaukat and Dylan Tutt. I am also grateful to my colleagues in video-based research for insights and updates, and to the editors for their constructive and supportive comments on earlier drafts.

NOTES

1 Discourse and Rhetoric Group
2 Centre for Language, Interaction, and Culture
3 University of California Los Angeles
4 Work, Interaction & Technology research centre

REFERENCES

Agar, M. (1991) 'The right brain strikes back'. In N. Fielding and R.M. Lee (eds.), *Using Computers in Qualitative Research*. London: Sage Publications, pp. 181–94.

American Sociological Association (ASA) (1999) *Code of ethics and policies and procedures of the ASA committee on professional ethics*. New York, NY: ASA.

Antaki, C., Biazzi, M., Nissen, A. and Wagner, J. (2008) 'Managing moral accountability in scholarly talk: the case of a conversation analysis data session', *Text and Talk*, 28: 1–30.

Baecker, R., Fono, D. and Wolf, P. (2007) 'Towards a video collaboratory'. In R. Goldman, R. Pea, B. Barron and S. Derry (eds.), *Video Research in the Learning Sciences*. Mahwah, NJ: Lawrence Erlbaum, pp. 461–78.

Banks, M. (2001) *Visual Methods in Social Research*. London: Sage Publications.

Becker, H.S., Geer, B., Hughes, E.C. and Strauss, A.L. (1961) *Boys in White; Student Culture in Medical School*. Chicago, IL: University of Chicago Press.

Berners-Lee, T. (1999) *Weaving the Web: Origins and Future of the World Wide Web*. London: Texere Publishing.

Bezemer, J. and Mavers, D. (2011) 'Multimodal transcription as academic practice: a social semiotic perspective', *International Journal of Social Research Methodology*, 14(3): 191–206.

British Sociological Association (BSA) Visual Sociology Group (2006) *Statement of Ethical Practice*. Durham, UK: BSA.

Brown, B. (2004) 'The order of service: the practical management of customer interaction', *Sociological Research Online*, 9(4). Available at http://www.socresonline.org.uk/9/4/brown.html (accessed 27 July, 2016).

Bryan, F. (2003) *Rouge: Pictured in its Prime*. Dearborn, MI: Ford Books.

Buckingham Shum, S., Slack, R., Daw, M., Juby, B., Rowley, A., Bachler, M., Mancini, C., Michaelides, D., Procter, R., De Roure, D., Chown, T. and Hewitt, T. (2006). 'Memetic: an infrastructure for meeting memory'. Proceedings of the 7th International Conference on the Design of Cooperative Systems, Carry-le-Rouet, France, 9–12 May.

Büscher, M. (2005) 'Social life under the microscope?', *Sociological Research Online*, 10 (1).

Available at http://www.socresonline.org.uk/10/1/buscher.html (accessed 27 July, 2016)

Childers, L., Disz, T., Olson, R., Papka, M.E., Stevens, R. and Udeshi, T. (2000) 'Access grid: immersive group-to-group collaborative visualization'. In Proceedings of the 4th International Immersive Projection Technology Workshop, Ames, Iowa, 19 June 2000.

Cummings, J.N. and Kiesler, S. (2005) 'Collaborate research across disciplinary and organizational boundaries', *Social Studies of Science*, 35 (5): 703–22.

Dempster, P.G. and Woods, D.K. (2011) 'The economic crisis through the eyes of Transana', *Forum: Qualitative Social Research*, 12 (1): Article 16.

Economic and Social Research Council (ESRC) (2015) *Framework for Research Ethics*. Swindon, UK: ESRC.

Finholt, T.A. (2002) 'Collaboratories', *Annual Review of Information Science and Technology*, 36: 73–107.

Fraser, M., Hindmarsh, J., Best, K., Heath, C., Biegel, G., Greenhalgh, C. and Reeves, S. (2006) 'Remote collaboration over video data: towards real-time e-social science', [Special issue: Collaboration in e-Research, M. Jirotka, R. Procter, T. Rodden and G. Bowker (eds.)], *Computer Supported Cooperative Work*, 15 (4): 257–79.

General Medical Council (2011) 'Making and using visual and audio recordings of patients'. Available at http://www.gmc-uk.org/guidance/ethical_guidance/making_audiovisual.asp (accessed 27 July, 2016).

Gibbs, G.R., Friese, S. and Mangabeira W.C. (2002) 'The use of new technology in qualitative research', *Forum Qualitative Sozialforschung/Forum: Qualitative Social Research*, 3 (2). Available at http://www.qualitative-research.net/index.php/fqs/article/view-Article/847 (accessed 27 July, 2016).

Goldman, R., Pea, R., Barron, B. and Derry, S. (eds.) (2007) *Video Research in the Learning Sciences*. Mahwah, NJ: Lawrence Erlbaum.

Goodwin, C. (2013) 'The co-operative, transformative organization of human action and knowledge', *Journal of Pragmatics*, 46 (1): 8–23.

Grimshaw, A. (1982) 'Sound–Image data records for research on social interaction: some questions answered', *Sociological Methods and Research*, 11 (2): 121–44.

Hafner, K. and Lyon, M. (1998) *Where Wizards Stay Up Late: The Origins of the Internet.* New York, NY: Simon and Schuster.

Heath, C. (2013) *The Dynamics of Auction: Social Interaction and the Sale of Fine Art and Antiques.* Cambridge: Cambridge University Press.

Heath, C., Hindmarsh, J. and Luff, P. (2010) *Video in Qualitative Research.* London: Sage Publications.

Heritage, J. (1984) *Garfinkel and Ethnomethodology.* Cambridge: Polity.

Hindmarsh, J., Fraser, M., Heath, C., Benford, S. and Greenhalgh, C. (2000) 'Object-focused interaction in collaborative virtual environments', *ACM Transactions on Computer–Human Interaction (ToCHI),* 7 (4): 477–509.

Jacknis, I. (1988) 'Margaret Mead and Gregory Bateson in Bali: their use of photography and film', *Cultural Anthropology,* 3 (2): 160–77.

Kraut, R., Gergle, D. and Fussel, S. (2002) 'The use of visual information in shared visual spaces: informing the development of virtual co-presence'. In Proceedings of the 2002 ACM Conference on Computer Supported Cooperative Work (CSCW 2002). New York, NY: ACM Press, pp. 31–40.

Lee, R. and Fielding, N. (1996) 'Qualitative data analysis: representations of a technology; a comment on Coffey, Holbrook and Atkinson', *Sociological Research Online,* 1 (4). Available at http://www.socresonline.org.uk/1/4/lf.html (accessed 27 July, 2016).

Lomax, H. and Casey, N. (1998) 'Recording social life: reflexivity and video methodology', *Sociological Research Online,* 3 (2). Available at http://www.socresonline.org.uk/3/2/1.html (accessed 27 July, 2016).

Luff, P., Patel, M., Kuzuoka, H. and Heath, C. (2014) 'Assembling collaboration: informing the design of interaction spaces', *Research on Language and Social Interaction,* 47 (3): 317–29.

Mondada, L. (2014) 'Instructions in the operating room: how the surgeon directs their assistant's hands', *Discourse Studies,* 16 (2): 131–61.

Olson, G. and Olson, J. (2000) 'Distance matters', *Human Computer Interaction,* 15 (2/3): 139–78.

Pea, R. and Lindgren, R. (2008) 'Video collaboratories for research and education: an analysis of collaboration design patterns', *IEEE Transactions On Learning Technologies,* 1 (4): 235–47.

Pea, R., Mills, M., Rosen, J., Dauber, K., Effelsberg, W. and Hoffert, E. (2004) 'The DIVER project: interactive digital video repurposing', *IEEE Multimedia,* 11 (1): 54–61.

Roethlisberger, F. and Dickson, W. (1939) *Management and the Worker: Technical versus Social Organization in an Industrial Plant.* Cambridge, MA: Harvard University Press.

Secrist, C., De Koeyer, I., Bell, H. and Fogel. A (2002) 'New tools for understanding infant development in qualitative research', *Forum Qualitative Sozialforschung/Forum: Qualitative Social Research,* 3 (2). Available at http://www.qualitative-research.net/index.php/fqs/article/view/847/1840 (accessed 27 July, 2016).

Shrum, W., Duque, R. and Brown, T. (2005) 'Digital video as research practice: methodology for the millennium', *Journal of Research Practice,* 1 (1): Article M4. Available at http://jrp.icaap.org/index.php/jrp/article/view/6/12 (accessed 27 July, 2016).

Silver, C. and Patashnick, J. (2011) 'Finding fidelity: advancing audiovisual analysis using software', *Forum: Qualitative Social Research,* 12 (1): Article 37.

Social Research Association (SRA) (2003) *Ethical Guidelines.* London: SRA.

Sonnenwald, D., Solomon, P., Hara, N., Bolliger, R. and Cox, T. (2002) 'Collaboration in the large-using video conferencing to facilitate large group interaction'. In A. Gunasekaran, O. Khalil and M. Syed (eds.), *Knowledge and Information Technology Management in 21st Century Organizations.* Hershey, PA: Idea Group Publishing, pp. 115–36.

Tutt, D. and Hindmarsh, J. (2011) Reenactments at work: Demonstrating conduct in data sessions', *Research on Language & Social Interaction,* 44 (3): 211–36.

Tutt, D., Hindmarsh, J., Shaukat, M. and Fraser M. (2007) 'The distributed work of local action: interaction amongst virtually collocated research teams'. In Proceedings of the European Conference on Computer-Supported Cooperative Work (ECSCW 2007). Berlin: Springer, pp. 199–218.

UK Parliament (1998) Data Protection Act 1998. London: The Stationery Office.

Woods, D.K. and Dempster, P.G. (2011) 'Tales from the bleeding edge: the qualitative analysis of complex video data using Transana', *Forum: Qualitative Social Research*, 12 (1): Article 17.

Wulf, W. (1989) 'The national collaboratory'. In J. Lederberg and K. Uncaphar (eds.), *Towards a National Collaboratory: Report of an Invitational Workshop at the Rockefeller University*. Washington, DC: National Science Foundation.

FURTHER READING

Heath *et al.* (2010) outline an ethnomethodological approach to the analysis of video-based materials. Silver and Pataschnick (2011) chart the history of CAQDAS in relation to audiovisual data. Finholt (2002) provides a review of the emergence of collaboratories in scientific research. Both Olson and Olson (2000) and Cummings and Kiesler (2005) suggest why distance matters by outlining the limits to technical support for distributed collaborative research work. Agar (1991) encourages the development of new technologies for social scientists to be driven by problems and issues in social research, rather than by what is technically possible.

List of Websites

Adobe Photoshop	http://www.adobe.com/uk/products/photoshop.html
Adobe Premiere	http://www.adobe.com/products/premiere/
ANVIL	http://www.dfki.de/~kipp/anvil/index.html
Audacity	http://sourceforge.net/projects/audacity/files/
CAQDAS	http://caqdas.soc.surrey.ac.uk/
CatDV	http://www.squarebox.com
Digital Replay System	http://thedrs.sourceforge.net/
DIVER	http://diver.stanford.edu/
Dropbox	https://www.dropbox.com/
ELAN	https://tla.mpi.nl/tools/tla-tools/elan/
Final Cut	http://www.apple.com/final-cut-pro/
iMovie	http://www.apple.com/mac/imovie/
InqScribe	http://www.inquirium.net/products/inqscribe
MiMeG	http://mimeg.sourceforge.net/
QuickTime	http://www.apple.com/quicktime/
Sound Soap	http://www.bias-inc.com/products/soundsoap/
Soundstudio	http://felttip.com/ss/
Transana	http://www.transana.org/

## 27

CAQDAS at a Crossroads: Affordances of Technology in an Online Environment

Christina Silver and Sarah L. Bulloch

THE HISTORY OF CAQDAS AND CURRENT DEVELOPMENTS

Software designed to facilitate the analysis of qualitative data, collectively known as Computer Assisted Qualitative Data AnalysiS (CAQDAS) packages, became available during the 1980s. Like other software supporting aspects of qualitative research, from document and bibliographic management, transcription, data collection, writing and visualisation (Paulus *et al.*, 2014), CAQDAS packages have since widely become seen as essential tools for researchers (Gibbs, 2014). Despite roots in the academic social sciences, their application extends far beyond to government, applied and commercial sectors.

The fact that separate groups developed CAQDAS packages at around the same time but in different countries and with different methodological impetus is significant. Tesch's (1990) seminal work relating analytic approaches to computing techniques highlighted from the outset of the CAQDAS

trajectory that a range of analytic approaches results in the need for various software solutions (Fielding and Lee, 1991). It also explains the number of packages that have emerged and the differences between them (Silver and Lewins, 2013). The 1990s saw convergence in functionality, predominantly oriented around features designed to facilitate *qualitative* approaches to *qualitative* data, including data handling, content searching, code and retrieve, metadata organisation, Boolean and proximity querying and writing tools. Although several programs came to dominate the field, no global market-leader emerged.

Academic uptake was driven by those engaging with new technologies as part of their professional development – software developers who were themselves academics and methodologists across disciplines (Fielding and Lee, 2007). Discussion concerning the implications of CAQDAS has featured from the outset with distinct 'for' and 'against' camps. Some of the resistance to CAQDAS was ill-informed and has impacted upon the pace of uptake, although recent investigations of patterns of use have shown particular growth since 2000 (White *et al.*, 2012, Woods *et al.*, 2015, Gibbs, 2014).

This chapter focuses on current developments shaping the CAQDAS trajectory, particularly in relation to online methods. We consider the increasingly impactful interaction between technical, methodological and practical developments and the questions this raises. Technical developments include data digitization, technological normalization and the growth of online tools (both CAQDAS and others). Methodological developments include trends in online methods, mixed methods, social media and visual analysis and the use of bigger data sets. Developments that pose practical challenges include citizen research, collaborative and cross-disciplinary research and commercial engagement with qualitative research.

Several changes are observable in response to these developments, which we discuss using selected examples. First is the increase in data formats acceptable to CAQDAS packages, now ranging beyond textual formats to include visual (still/moving images), bibliographic (imports from Endnote, Refworks, etc.), and database material (including mixed data such as that derived from online surveys, social media and other Internet-harvested data). Second is a move to provide multi-user, server or online versions that facilitate team-working. Third, parallel CAQDAS versions are available for different operating platforms and App versions for tablets. In addition, new software tools are emerging that challenge the position of traditional CAQDAS programs. These developments benefit users by opening up the field, fostering cross-disciplinary and cross-sector collaboration and encouraging the appropriation of new methodologies and technologies. Fourth, CAQDAS packages are increasingly providing features designed to facilitate quantitative approaches to qualitative data and mixed approaches to mixed data as well as the core qualitative tools associated with their initial

development. How these developments manifest in individual CAQDAS packages differs such that we are currently witnessing a new divergence between products.[1] Technological and analytic divergence and proliferation rather than convergence and standardisation will thus continue to frame the future of the field, raising pertinent challenges and opportunities for developers, methodologists, users and teachers.

CAQDAS AND TRENDS IN ONLINE DATA COLLECTION METHODS

Integrating multiple data forms within one study, whether textual accounts, non-textual materials, or qualitative *and* quantitative data, is a common analytic strategy. This section discusses the analytic tactics[2] required for, and made available by CAQDAS packages, for capturing, integrating and analysing such material, specifically when originally generated online.

Currently, no CAQDAS packages allow for direct[3] analysis of 'live' online materials; they must first be 'harvested'. This is true for online applications, software installed on a server and locally on a hard drive. Working with online materials is therefore divided into two phases: data collection (sampling or harvesting) and data analysis. CAQDAS packages currently fall into two groups in this respect: those that address both phases and those that address only the analysis phase.

Some CAQDAS packages have recently developed 'add-ons' or components built for the purpose of capturing online materials. For example, NCapture is a web browser extension that supports NVivo users to work with online materials; enabling capturing of webpages, online PDFs and social media data (Facebook, Twitter and YouTube). There are different options for formatting and importing, including automatic transference of metadata into classifying attributes, options for including posted YouTube comments and

Twitter Retweets and choices about the format of harvested material. Content harvested as PDF is highly functional within NVivo. For example, webpage front-end structure and the text in advertisements within the page are searchable and codeable, allowing for analysis beyond user-generated content. Images embedded within PDFs can be coded, although, as is the case in most other CAQDAS packages,[4] it only allows for the selection of rectangular areas and retrieval display is limited and somewhat distorted because the coded area is highlighted in colour. Imported material, whether in PDF or database form, retains the source active hyperlinks, allowing navigation from the harvested material back to the web to 'follow' leads and, where relevant, re-harvest altered content. Particularly useful with Twitter data is the option to 'merge matching social media databases' upon import via NCapture. This prevents cumulative harvesting resulting in duplication, thereby attending to challenges presented by working with the ever-evolving nature of online content.

Texifter, a cloud-based platform, has both the harvesting and analysis of online materials at its core. Whilst it is modular in its construction (with DiscoverText, CloudExplorer and FOIA Toolkit working off the SIFTER™ engine), its central premise is to enable processing of voluminous online materials. This includes harvesting and analysing large-scale online archives and merging data from various sources, including text files, email, open-ended answers to surveys, and online sources including Facebook, Google+, blogs, Tumblr, Disqus and Twitter. Timespans during which live web content is captured automatically can be set, as can the number of times within the timespan that capturing (termed 'fetching') takes place. It is possible to set fetches up to 12 months in advance. Additional functions include classification (machine coding), redaction and identification and clustering of duplicates. Data can be filtered by metadata, such as when and from where a tweet was posted and according to socio-demographic

information. The full suite of tools therefore allows for both the capturing and the analysis of online materials.

These two developments are examples of what may come to constitute a shift in emphasis in the CAQDAS landscape, enabling researchers to engage in the act of capturing *and* incorporating online materials directly from one product. Amongst the advantages of such single-software solutions are that researchers (1) may be less likely to face a skills deficit and more likely to save time by not having to identify, learn about and download multiple software packages, and (2) that they thus avoid compatibility issues that can occur as proprietary software constantly develops.

Packages that have not developed such tools can be used in conjunction with a range of stand-alone 'middleware' (Fernandes, 2008) in order to harvest online materials. Because CAQDAS packages do not currently allow for direct analysis of live Web material, data collection involves the rendering 'static' of sampled Web material and converting it into a format legible by the chosen software. The technical requirements of harvesting are discussed in Welser *et al.* (2008), who refer to the processes of scraping, parsing and the use of structured query language databases as activities integral to the collection of online data, the technicalities of which are foreign to the vast majority of researchers. Fernandes (2008: 8) highlights further challenges in the collection of online materials, stating that 'although it is tempting to think of the Internet as a vast cornucopia of data riches simply there to be consumed, […] existing infrastructural constraints obstruct ready and unimpeded access to those riches'. The technical and analytical skills required for both harvesting and analysing web materials may not co-exist within individuals. Human and technological challenges still abound. But what are the options for researchers using CAQDAS packages that have not integrated the capturing of online materials?

Capturing online materials begins with web browsers. Although they each work slightly differently, those most commonly used (Firefox, Chrome, Internet Explorer, Safari) interface with other software to allow harvesting in a variety of formats. Text-based and mixed material is commonly converted to PDF when harvested. This display format retains the visual structure of a webpage, including text and images, and, usually, transformed text remains machine readable. Although most CAQDAS packages can import PDF files, their nature varies depending on how and when they were created and certain limitations of the format affect the analysability of content. For example, conversion includes specific paragraph structures which usually cannot be changed. This affects the reliability with which results of text-search and coding exercises that rely on paragraph structure can be automated (see later), with often unexpected results in terms of the breadth of coding that can be applied. In addition, converting social media content into PDF sometimes limits what is displayed, such as truncating content rather than capturing its entirety. Despite these limitations, harvesting online material using a PDF converter constitutes a bridge to working within a wide variety of CAQDAS packages.

Other formats can also function as a bridge between online material and CAQDAS packages. Text-only (*.txt), Rich Text (*.rtf) and MS Word (*.doc, *.docx) files are flexible and fully functional in all CAQDAS packages, but spreadsheet formats (*.xlx, *.xlsx and *.csv) function in different ways. Data can often be imported as the full database, displaying similarly to how they do in spreadsheet or statistical software packages. This can be cumbersome from a display perspective, as well as variously functional because code retrieval sometimes returns the full content of a partially coded cell. More flexible options, provided differently by Atlas.ti, MAXQDA and QDA Miner, convert databases into a series of text documents and categories upon importation, such that qualitative fields are extracted and treated as text and quantitative fields as numeric variables

(see Fielding *et al.*, 2013, for in-depth discussion of this functionality).

Despite the emergence of bespoke CAQDAS harvesting tools and options for bridging, there is still a way to go before online material can be harvested in formats that are completely true to their web origins *and* completely functional in all CAQDAS packages.

COLLABORATIVE AND ONLINE WORKING WITH CAQDAS

Recent years have witnessed increased demand for collaborative and online rather than local working arrangements, of which developments such as Dropbox and Google+ are testimony. The operating platform has historically been an issue in the CAQDAS field, with most pioneer programs being initially developed for PCs.[5] This has changed significantly with most now offering Mac versions, some also Linux and the beginnings of a move to online solutions. For individual researchers, the ability to access materials and undertake analysis online is attractive because it heightens mobility, allowing work from any Internet-enabled location. For research teams, the comparative affordances of working online may be even greater.

Collaborative working comes with the challenge of how to bring together progress made by different team members. With ever-increasing emphasis from funding bodies on large-scale multi-disciplinary multi-national consortia, many researchers find themselves working on bigger projects in larger teams. What are the options open to teams needing to combine analysis and how is this related to online working?

Technically, there are three ways of working collaboratively using CAQDAS packages, two of which involve online activities (see Hindmarsh, this volume). First, each researcher may work separately on local copies of the project which are merged together at set time points. As this does not involve simultaneous or online working, care has to be taken in splitting and combining work. Most CAQDAS packages allow for the merging of stand-alone projects in this way (e.g. Atlas.ti, HyperRESEARCH, NVivo, MAXQDA, QDA Miner). Second, where multi-user versions exist (e.g. Transana and NVivo), projects are hosted on a networked server, which multiple researchers log into and access simultaneously. Third are online packages (e.g. Dedoose, Discovertext), which do not require local or server-based installation but are accessed by logging on via a web browser. Here we focus on server-based and online multi-user working because they are more recent developments and pertinent to our focus on online methods.

Transana-MU and NVivo for Teams are separate versions of their stand-alone equivalents. They are installed on a networked server and allow projects to be stored centrally and accessed simultaneously by multiple researchers. Their technical set-up is slightly different, as are the features provided for concurrent team-working, but both obviate the need for complex merging protocols to combine the work of individual researchers. Both include a centrally held team-work journal that can be used to detail project development across all contributing researchers. Amongst the specific benefits of Transana-MU are its cost-effectiveness; its availability for both Mac and PC users; the choice to set up one's own server or use the Transana Cloud Service; a chat window enabling real-time communication; and the local storage of media-files that significantly speeds up data transfer. For NVivo for Teams, each researcher needs a license for the stand-alone product and the server version. Central to its set-up is the NVivo for Teams Manager and Project owner(s); the latter granting users access to projects and the former managing the connections between them. At the time of writing, the server version is available for NVivo for Windows, but not NVivo for Mac. Amongst the advantages of using NVivo for

Teams are that the project size is not limited to 10GB (as it is with stand-alone projects); and that permissions can be centrally managed, enhancing security and ethics.

Packages that allow online multi-user working include Dedoose and DiscoverText. Dedoose, released in 2009, was developed specifically to enable concurrent online multi-user work, and DiscoverText, available since 2011 as an online platform, allows for synchronous, multi-user working. Dedoose stores projects on the cloud and is designed for all modern Internet browsers. The web-based interface is platform-independent, and thus works equally well for Mac and PC users, and the ability to work concurrently without complicated server installations and set-ups is beneficial. Users can access projects from any web-enabled device, rather than being limited to machines that have specific software installed. Dedoose tracks the actions of different researchers and users can be added to projects at any point. Access works by logging-in using a password. Different levels of access can be given to different users and inter-coder reliability can be measured via code application and code weighting tests.

Although online working facilitates collaboration in various ways, important considerations and challenges remain. Online working leads to dependence on Internet connectivity, which can be particularly problematic for mobile methods, participatory methods and projects undertaken in certain geographic areas. In addition, uploading data to a cloud or server hosted and maintained by a third party requires researchers to understand security protocols and to ensure they are in line with ethical requirements. In consortia where several institutions are involved, which may have different regulations, this requires planning. However, online applications obviate issues of software version and platform compatibility and the update protocols used by different team-members. Often overlooked, this issue is critical to successful, iterative team working and can cause problems for teams working with stand-alone packages.

Regardless of whether work is conducted using an online application, server version or stand-alone package, the issue of project management is pertinent. To ensure consistency across different researcher's contributions (as well as 'mergeability' where work is conducted locally), the team must develop, set-out and adhere to appropriate coding, annotating and memoing practices. When work progresses inductively, it is critical to develop standardised ways to feed additions back to colleagues. These issues must be planned for and pilot exercises are highly advisable.[6] In addition is the issue of coding consistency. Most CAQDAS packages now incorporate tools for coder-reliability testing, although these vary in their premise and results. Even when they are not included, there are ways to manually compare. The relevance of the concept of coder-reliability testing may be on the rise given the trend towards bigger data and larger analytic teams. Qualitative research may be diversifying away from a prevalence of small samples towards an inclusion of larger data. With this trend, representativeness, reliability and replicability become more pressing issues. New affordances, including mixed methods, bigger data and automation (discussed later), give rise to new challenges such as larger teams of coders and, potentially, a greater emphasis on more statistically driven assessments of inter-coder reliability.

OPENING UP QUALITATIVE ANALYSIS

The capabilities of the Internet and increasing digital literacy greatly open up possibilities for citizens to undertake research, enabling wider engagement in practices hitherto the preserve of professionals (Smith et al., this volume; Fielding, 2014). Web-based and non-bespoke tools offer accessible, open-source and cheap alternatives to professional CAQDAS, and are increasingly appropriated for research tasks. These developments are in line with broader normalisation of mobile digital technologies and their rapid developmental pace. Some CAQDAS packages are beginning to respond. Here we discuss the release of mobile app versions by two pioneer CAQDAS developers; the release of Quirkos, a program specifically developed to open-up computer-assisted analysis; and possibilities for using non-bespoke and Web 2.0 tools for analytic purposes.

Currently, app versions are available for Atlas.ti (since 2013 Atlas.ti Mobile for the iPad) and MAXQDA (since 2014 the MAXApp for iOS and Android). Providing mobile accompaniments to their corresponding full versions, initial developmental focus has been on enabling data collection, 'tagging' and note-taking tools. Apps access the image, audio and video capturing features of tablets or smart-phones, enabling recorded data to be instantly available for 'on-the-go' reflection and initial conceptualisation via touch-screen technology. They also utilise embedded location technology to 'tag' captured data with geographic co-ordinates. Importation into the full package is straightforward and streamlined (via Dropbox or iTunes) when the full range of analytic capabilities are provided. App version capabilities blur data collection and analysis, which are often seen as distinct research phases, making the apps particularly attractive for researchers adopting 'grounded' approaches where these phases are expressly iterative; for researchers undertaking ethnographic studies where many different forms of materials are gathered; and also for mobile methodologies.

Although currently in their infancy, these apps have the potential to revolutionise the way CAQDAS-conversant researchers go about their profession. Similar to the impetus of Quirkos' development (see later), CAQDAS apps offer a means to enable non-professional researchers to contribute to data collection and analysis. Although at the time of writing there are no academically published articles concerning their affordances,[7] they will no doubt develop considerably in forthcoming years and we can expect to see other CAQDAS packages following suit. There will likely always be limits to the extent to which app versions can fully support varied approaches to analysis as a result of both limited screen real-estate and technological capabilities of mobile technologies. Nevertheless, this constitutes a potential turning-point in the way CAQDAS develops.

Related is the addition in MAXQDA of Emoticodes, a development that reflects the rise of 'emojis' (electronic graphic symbols, including 'smileys' that originated in Japan) since being integrated into most mobile technologies. Designed to transcend the limits of text-based coding, MAXQDA's coding system includes more than 300 emoticons and symbols, organised into thematic groups that can be used in combination with, or to the exclusion of, customary textual code-labels. Emoticode functionality is fully integrated into MAXQDA's full- and app-version features, such that symbols appear alongside coded data segments and are visualised in output representations resulting from matrix-based queries and other visual tools. This development offers an additional means of opening up analysis, particularly in citizen, collaborative, cross-national and multilingual contexts. For example, equivalence in application and interpretation of codes is a frequent issue in collaborative projects, compounded in cross-cultural studies when analysts may not have shared understandings of concepts. Expressing concepts using words when not all analysts have the same mother-tongue has the potential for confusion for cross-cultural conceptualisation. Symbols can of course also be interpreted and used differently, but as the proliferation of emojis inevitably continues, the potential for more universally understood applications increases. Their integration into Apple technology in 2011 was likely significant to this end, and although different proprietary mobile operators have developed and defined different variants, we might expect standardisation in emoji symbols to increase over time.

It remains to be seen whether this development will have a significant impact on the way coding is undertaken within MAXQDA[8] and whether other CAQDAS developers incorporate similar functionality. However, it is timely in the context of generations of digitally-native researchers that have grown up using emojis in mobile communication, engaging with CAQDAS technologies.

App versions and Emoticodes are examples of ways in which CAQDAS programs are harnessing wider technological developments and offering ways of widening participation in research. A recent development that goes beyond this by specifically focusing on involving non-professionals in every stage of a project is the development of Quirkos. Released in 2014, Quirkos represents a potentially significant step-change in the field, with its central idea being to 'make text analysis so easy, that anyone can do it'. Quirkos includes core qualitative text analysis features characteristic of all CAQDAS packages (Silver and Bulloch, 2015) but its look and feel is rather different. For instance, its layout is designed for tablet usage, encouraging touchscreen actions, and its default settings show non-linear, mind-map-like visualization of 'quirks' (or codes). There are many examples of research participants being involved in research projects; however, most are either at the data collection phase of a project and/or the seeking of feedback as part of interpretive validation. Quirkos is the first bespoke CAQDAS package that specifically aims to bridge the divide between professional practice and lay contribution to involve both parties in all stages of analysis by developing an interface and a suite of features that are as easy to conceptually understand as to technically operate.

A study of the impact of the 2014 referendum for Scottish independence (Turner, 2015) engaged non-specialist researchers to undertake participatory coding in order to explore the ease with which they could use the program for qualitative thematic coding. That these participants found the process easy, quicker than anticipated, interesting and enjoyable (Turner, 2015), suggests that the aim of developing a bespoke CAQDAS program that can be harnessed by non-professional analysts has been achieved. As its features are developed to become more equivalent to other programs, we can expect its use to increase and for reflective publications on its affordances to appear. The extent to which it will open up access to qualitative analysis for those who do not have a background in professional academic or applied research remains to be seen. However, it is anticipated that it will be well utilised for participatory approaches to qualitative research in which research participants can actively contribute to analysis without extensive time needing to be given over to learning the package (Silver and Bulloch, 2015).

A third example of how current changes in the field are opening up qualitative analysis is the development of Web 2.0 and other non-bespoke tools. The term Web 2.0 is used to describe the focus on enabling collaboration and the sharing of information online that is the feature of the second generation of the world-wide-web. Its orientation around users generating online content and analysing their own and others' engagement with it, using tools akin to those professional researchers use in CAQDAS packages to undertake analysis, has potentially profound implications for CAQDAS (di Gregorio, 2010). Although designed for alternative purposes, tools such as blogs, wikis, video/image sharing websites and social networking provide online spaces where researchers can not only communicate their research outputs but undertake forms of analysis. Blogs, in particular, are becoming increasingly omnipresent amongst academic and applied researchers as means of raising awareness about and gathering feedback on their work whilst it is ongoing, as well as disseminating results. This is occurring within a broader context of a move towards open access publishing, which we can expect to further encourage this trend.

Many of the tools available in Web 2.0 applications are analogous to those developed within CAQDAS packages for bespoke qualitative analytic tasks, such as tagging (akin to coding) and commenting (akin to annotating). In addition are applications such as Onenote and Evernote, designed as general-purpose note-taking tools but which also include tools for generating data (for example, web-capture and clipping, Optical Character Recognition (OCR) capabilities and dictation), storing and managing data (creation of notebooks with any number of sub-levels), searching (word searching within and across notes), memoing (annotating notes with additional comments), coding (tagging of notes and paragraphs within notes), linking (hyperlinking from within notes) and collaboration (sharing of notes and chat functions). CAQDAS packages include a range of features that can be used for more sophisticated analytic purposes, but the growing availability of free, low-cost and/or open source tools that can be appropriated for analytic tasks enables researchers without access to customised CAQDAS packages to undertake analysis.

These developments bring with them challenges for CAQDAS as well as opportunities. The growing availability of a range of digital tools for social scientists (for an overview, see Paulus *et al.*, 2013) offer a plethora of options. Some CAQDAS developers have released free or 'lite' versions, opening up access to their tools to those with resource constraints. Others are increasing the number of proprietary formats that can be imported, including OneNote and Evernote as well as from a range of bibliographic tools (Endnote, RefWorks, Menderley, Zotero). We are therefore seeing a cross-fertilisation of features, with CAQDAS-like features appearing in other software programs and tools available in other applications increasingly appearing in CAQDAS packages.

MIXED METHODS, BIGGER DATA AND AUTOMATION

The term 'mixed methods' generally refers to the bringing together of some form of qualitative and quantitative data and there is much discussion about design-types for doing so (Creswell and Plano Clark, 2011; Tashakkori and Teddlie, 2010). However, in the context of CAQDAS, 'mixed methods' also relates to ways in which qualitative or quantitative *analyses* can be combined, therefore bringing into focus *how* mixing occurs as well as *what* is being mixed and *when* the mixing occurs, which has received less attention (Silver and Lewins, 2014). What affordances do CAQDAS packages have in terms of carrying out mixed analyses? Bazeley (2006) outlines that the use of software enables different approaches to be undertaken within a single analysis as well as different forms of data to be integrated during analysis in three key ways: (1) by combining text and numeric data, (2) by converting one form to another and (3) by combining and converting iteratively or in generating blended data for further analyses. Here we consider both data and approaches to analysis.

In terms of data, there are two considerations: type and amount. Most CAQDAS packages now accept a range of qualitative (text, audio, still/moving images), quantitative (numeric databases) and mixed data (combined numeric and alphanumeric databases). CAQDAS packages have long enabled the integration of quantitative information with associated qualitative records in the form of, for example, importing demographic or other numeric metadata pertaining to individuals and groups of respondents or other materials and linking them. This enables qualitative data to be interrogated according to those factors, for example comparing how individuals with certain socio-demographic characteristics report an experience or discuss an attitude. Enabling the incorporation of mixed datasets, for example survey-type data that contains both numeric information from closed-questions and textual material from open-ended questions in the same file, is a more recent development, but most CAQDAS packages now enable it. As such, type of data is usually only a key driver for choosing between CAQDAS packages in

certain circumstances, for example when working primarily with visual data.

Although most CAQDAS packages can handle thousands of files, processing speed is usually affected when working with larger datasets. Kitchin defines 'big data' as

> huge in volume, consisting of terabytes or petabytes of data; high in velocity, being created in or near real-time; diverse in variety, being structured and unstructured in nature; exhaustive in scope, striving to capture entire populations or systems (n=all); fine-grained in resolution and uniquely indexical in identification; relational in nature, containing common fields that enable the conjoining of different data sets; flexible, holding the traits of extensionality (can add new fields easily) and scaleability (can expand in size rapidly).
>
> Kitchin, 2014: 262

Of the packages discussed here, and applying this definition, only DiscoverText and Provalis Research's Prosuite (QDA Miner, WordStat and SimStat) come anywhere close to handling 'big data'. Nevertheless, moves towards analysing bigger datasets using CAQDAS packages are observable, which raises questions about approaches to analysis, and thus the tools CAQDAS packages provide to analyse volumes of data that cannot reasonably be read and analysed in-depth by humans.

The CAQDAS landscape is complex in terms of analytic approaches, with two pertinent dimensions: (1) the types of results that are required, i.e. whether qualitative, quantitative or mixed and (2) the means by which to arrive at those results, i.e. the need for assistance with or automation of coding. Just as qualitative and quantitative approaches sit on a continuum with respect to these dimensions, so do CAQDAS packages. At one end, qualitative approaches, such as grounded theory and Interpretive Phenomenological Analysis (IPA), require a true adherence to fully grounded, inductive and iterative ways of working, typically including extensive data familiarisation and pre-coding. Such approaches lend themselves to smaller datasets and prioritize the role of the human interpreter, likely considering automated processes to be anathema. On the other end, approaches such as quantitative content analysis, text mining and data analytics, may require the application of inferential statistics, formal testing of hypotheses that follow the standard requirements of normal distributions, sampling theory, representativeness, etc. Such approaches lend themselves to larger datasets and likely necessitate assistance with, or automation of, qualitative coding.

Researching the social world on, through and in the Internet involves a host of automated processes. The very act of searching the web involves a number of these, as does the fact that browsers are constantly running protocols to determine what you see on the web, where and how. Working in a partially automated environment, therefore, is second nature to the researcher conducting online research. CAQDAS packages engage with the issue of automation to differing degrees, and can be broadly categorized into three groups in terms of the types of results that can be generated and the means to arrive at them. Some have largely maintained their original qualitative roots, up to this point focusing development primarily on supporting qualitative approaches to qualitative data (e.g. Atlas.ti, Quirkos, Transana). Such packages include features for quantifying qualitative data, such as frequency information pertaining to code-application and co-occurrence, but have less-developed tools for other forms of mixed analysis and tend to include only rudimentary text-searching and auto-coding tools.

Second are packages originally developed as qualitative analysis software but have more recently added quantitative tools (e.g. HyperRESEARCH, MAXQDA, NVivo). Such packages now include a range of (rather different) ways of quantifying qualitative data and analyses of them. For example, MAXQDA's Quote Matrix generates a tabular joint display of qualitative and quantitative output, showing coded segments based on variable characteristics; its Typology

Tables visualize variable-values based on previously created qualitative typologies; its Configuration Tables show coding patterns for sets of codes; and its Statistics of sub-codes create frequency tables and editable diagrams for sub-codes. MAXQDA has also recently released MAX Analytics Pro which incorporates the ability to undertake statistical analysis within MAXQDA. In addition, some offer ways to assist with and automate coding. For example, MAXQDA's Dictionary and MAXDictio Coder functions allow users to build categories of words and phrases that are used to search for and code text, and NVivo's pattern-based coding function compares passages of text to those already coded in order to facilitate researchers in identifying whether relevant data have been missed.

Finally are the applications which were specifically developed to provide mixed methods solutions (e.g. Dedoose, QDA Miner (with WordStat and SimStat) and DiscoverText), which currently have the most sophisticated options for conducting mixed analyses, although the emphasis of each is rather different. For example, Dedoose focuses on interactive data visualisations, containing a range of pre-configured charts that represent the intersections between the results of qualitative coding and various forms of quantification that can be explored and filtered in a variety of ways. It includes tools for measuring inter-rater reliability (code application and code weighting tests), but as yet has no functions for automating coding or undertaking statistical analysis. Provalis Research's suite of tools, however, stretches the boundaries of what is possible in CAQDAS packages in terms of mixing analyses because, when used together, they outstrip what is possible in other packages in relation to quantitative, mixed and statistical analysis (Silver, 2014). QDA Miner is Provalis Research's qualitative component with features equivalent to other CAQDAS packages; WordStat is a text-mining component with tools for identifying textual material for coding through the use of user-generated dictionaries; and SimStat offers a range of statistical analysis features. Used in combination, the possibilities for conducting mixed analyses of mixed data are greatly extended because tools for visualizing coding patterns and trends, exploring relationships in coding, and using inferential statistics to test hypotheses can be used together (Silver, 2014). Discovertext has automation at its heart, enabling the mixing of human and computer training, thus enabling the development of bespoke analytic approaches by users (see Brent, this volume).

Assistance with accessing textual material in the form of word and phrase searching, with or without Key Word In Context (KWIC) functionality and resultant autocoding, has been available in most CAQDAS packages since their inception. These features have a good fit with the full range of analytic approaches in that they can serve to facilitate data familiarisation, locate passages and narratives and contribute to ensuring all relevant data are captured. As discussed earlier, assistance with and automation of coding on the basis of text patterns is a key area of current CAQDAS development and in the context of big data analytics we can expect this to continue. Assistance and automation has historically presented a concern amongst parts of the qualitative methods community for fear that such features compromise the search for and interpretation of meaning, a task often considered that humans are best equipped to undertake. Packages that 'learn' from the analyst by enabling relevant hits to be prioritized and irrelevant ones dismissed in subsequent searches, strike a balance between automation and human interpretation (see Brent, this volume). They are therefore best placed to harness technological advances in the context of the needs of big data analytics and mixed methods approaches whilst preserving the value of qualitative interpretation.

What is the role of CAQDAS in relation to carrying out mixed methods in an online environment? The volume of material potentially gatherable via online in comparison to offline methods highlights the growing potential for CAQDAS use. Larger sample sizes, even in the context of qualitative materials, are possible and therefore drawing quantitative insights that require more representative samples becomes possible. This allows for meaningful use of descriptive statistics and potentially beyond to inferential statistics. Recent developments in the mixed methods capacities mean CAQDAS packages are a realistic way of connecting quantitative and qualitative insights, not only by enabling the integration of different forms of data, but also enabling the application of different analytic methods to that data. The challenge is that there are still few CAQDAS packages offering tools catering for the extremes of qualitative and quantitative approaches, particularly the latter, requiring researchers to use other tools to undertake statistical analysis. This is an example of where the opportunities provided by online methods are still ahead of the research community. There is a general trend towards more qualitative work in the qualitative/quantitative balance (see also Smith *et al.*, this volume), but although there are differences in methodological skills across countries and disciplines, there may be comparatively few researchers sufficiently skilled in the full range of analysis methods to be able to apply advanced quantitative methods as well as truly inductive qualitative methods.

DISCUSSION: CAQDAS AT A CROSSROADS

The developments discussed here raise two pertinent issues: (1) CAQDAS's role in the increasingly technological and online context of research methods and (2) how new generations of researchers can be equipped to harness them powerfully. These issues place the field at a crossroads; the way developers and researchers respond to the former and teachers respond to the latter will impact upon the future of CAQDAS.

Trends in data usage and analytic methods are changing. Although CAQDAS packages are responding, the use of non-bespoke tools is gaining ground; raising questions about which packages are considered 'CAQDAS' and the extent to which they will continue to maintain their place. Introduced by Fielding and Lee (1991) following the first conference bringing together the fields' methodological and technical pioneers,[9] the term 'CAQDAS' emphasizes that software *assists* rather than *carries out* analysis. Nevertheless, critiques from those resistant to CAQDAS use have historically coalesced around concerns about software 'taking over' the interpretive processes involved in qualitative analysis, that, it is argued, only humans can do. Concerns involve contentions that software distances analysts from data; perceptions that the tools prioritise code-and-retrieve methods and thus homogenise analytic approaches; suggestions that their use mechanises analytic techniques and promotes quantification to the extent that the interpretivist foundations of qualitative research are undermined; criticisms about feature availability and misconceptions that CAQDAS packages only support certain types of analysis (Bazeley, 2006). CAQDAS users and teachers have countered such concerns, arguing that the analyst remains in control of the analytic process and that CAQDAS packages are tools that can be harnessed for various purposes (Silver and Lewins, 2014; Rivers and Bulloch, 2011). Coding-assistance and text-mining, however, are designed to contribute to the analytic process and their increasing inclusion in CAQDAS not only contributes to product divergence, but further blurs the parameters of what constitutes a CAQDAS package.

Given the roots of the acronym, it is logical to refer to the CADQAS Networking Project's definition, which states that CAQDAS refers to

packages which include tools designed to facilitate a qualitative approach to qualitative data. [...They] may also enable the incorporation of quantitative (numeric) data and/or include tools for taking quantitative approaches to qualitative data. However, they must directly handle at least one type of qualitative data and include some – but not necessarily all – of the following tools for handling and analysing them: Content searching tools; Linking tools; Coding tools; Query tools; Writing and annotation tools; Mapping or networking tools.[10]

This definition is broad enough to include all of the packages discussed here, and more besides.[11] However, the increasing move to include tools for integrating data types, analytic approaches and options for automation demands consideration as to whether the emphasis on qualitative data and qualitative analytic approaches remains accurate in terminological terms and desirable in analytic terms. Is it time to adjust the acronym to remove the explicit emphasis on the qualitative?

One danger is emphasizing mixed methods, and automation may further alienate purist qualitative researchers' resistance to software use. Although the software's existence neither necessitates their use nor excludes the ability or validity of working in purely qualitative ways, as rapid technological development continues the possibilities afforded by machine learning technology will inevitably be increasingly incorporated. The extent to which CAQDAS users harness the potential for increased analytic assistance or resist these developments remains to be seen. The rise of the use of bigger data, that by necessity requires automation, can only mean this issue becomes increasingly pressing.

The potential effect of concurrent development and penetration of non-bespoke analytic tools is also important. CAQDAS packages have developed significantly since their emergence and now have a firm place in professional research practice. The Internet enables bigger data-sets to be harvested, and CAQDAS enables bigger data-sets to be integrated and aspects of analysis to be automated. However, CAQDAS packages are not the only applications available in our arsenal of tools to understand the online world, and they will therefore need to keep up with the pace of technological, methodological and practical developments to remain at the cutting-edge.

So what do researchers want CAQDAS to be and do? As some packages move towards increasing diversification of tools, seemingly attempting to 'be all things to all people', others focus on specific analytic affordances, user-groups or solution-types. Do we want one package that does everything or do we prefer to utilize several applications, thus constructing our own bespoke suite of tools for particular purposes? No doubt developers and researchers have different opinions, but what about new generations of researchers?

Contemporary students have different expectations of technology than their predecessors because they have never really known a time without computers, the Internet or mobile devices (the exception being mature students). For the digitally conversant, it is obvious that technology can be used to facilitate analysis, and therefore debates must move beyond *whether* to use CAQDAS to detailed discussion about *how* to do so powerfully. Equipping students with the skills to harness technology appropriately for analytic tasks can no longer be side-stepped (Silver and Rivers, 2016). Research into how CAQDAS is taught is relatively scarce but continued demand for workshop-based learning illustrates that non-bespoke tools are not filling the gap. In addition, demand for training outside of degree programmes illustrates that learning about the technological tactics for undertaking analysis is frequently separated from learning about analytic strategies (Silver and Woolf, 2015; Carvajal, 2002; Gilbert *et al*, 2014).

Facilitating a step-change in CAQDAS teaching requires an accessible and adaptable pedagogy that transcends the specificities of products, applications and modes of instruction (Silver and Woolf, 2015). Detailed accounts of specific modules are valuable, and yet it is all too easy for lecturers to dismiss such accounts as irrelevant to their own contexts as a result of disciplinary, methodological or logistical differences. Some present a 'one-size-fits-all' method for CAQDAS use; however, this is inappropriate because of the variety in objectives, methodologies and analytic procedures. It is not surprising that researchers are resistant to using and lecturers are resistant to teaching CAQDAS when it is presented in a way that homogenizes the variety that is prized in qualitative and mixed methods research.

The rise of online methods adds a layer of complexity to the appropriate teaching and harnessing of CAQDAS packages because contemporary users seek flexible applications that support the whole research process, from problem formulation, through data collection, analysis and representation. CAQDAS packages have a huge potential in this regard, as illustrated by Schmieder's (2015) modularized curriculum for using CAQDAS packages for interview question analysis, Paulus and Bennet's (2015) discussion of integrating CAQDAS into a graduate research methods course and Silver and Woolf's (2015) exposition of Five-Level QDA as a CAQDAS pedagogy.

Although some CAQDAS packages are moving towards enabling the harvesting of online data and providing tools to facilitate a broader range of analytic approaches, the latter phases of the research process are less well supported. For example, there is a lack of flexibility in transforming the results of analytic work undertaken in CAQDAS packages into dynamic and accessible formats, in particular for generating non-linear representations, such as visual narratives, hypertexts or reportage (Silver and Patashnick, 2011). Although visualization tools are being developed in some CAQDAS packages, they are basic in comparison to what can be generated from big data analytics. In the context of online methods, these limitations are significant because those conducting research on, through or in the Internet require dynamic options for representation that reflect the multidimensionality of the Internet and data.

CONCLUSION

This chapter has provided an overview of the current state-of-the-art with regards customized CAQDAS packages in the context of online methods. It has detailed some of the significant moves towards providing effective solutions for harvesting online data, highlighting the divergence in practice with regards to software that is developing bespoke harvesting tools and that relies on researchers making use of non-CAQDAS tools for the harvesting phase.

The discussion of collaborative and online working touched on the recent advances in multi-platform working, as well as the significant opportunities and challenges posed by the proliferation in server- and online, multi-user-based working solutions across various packages.

Making the case that the field is seeing an opening up of analysis beyond the academic professions through the proliferation of web-based and non-bespoke tools that offer accessible, open-source and cheap alternatives to professional CAQDAS, the chapter also raised the question of the distinctiveness of CAQDAS packages in this fast-evolving space.

CAQDAS has responded to the mushrooming of material about the social world that is generated online by increasingly enabling the analysis of bigger data, automation, the integration of different forms of data, and also the application of different analytic methods to that data. What this means for the traditional identification of these packages with primary *qualitative* approaches remains to be seen.

These various discussions paint a picture of the field of CAQDAS at a crossroads. In order to maintain their place in professional practice and be adopted by non-professionals, software developers need to attend to the potential for CAQDAS packages to be utilized for all stages of the research process and to continue to respond to developments occurring in the sphere of online methods. This is likely to involve attending to the full triad of technical, methodological and practical concerns that researchers face today and may well result in increasing divergence in products.

NOTES

1 See the CAQDAS Networking Project website for software reviews http://www.surrey.ac.uk/sociology/research/researchcentres/caqdas/support/choosing/index.htm Accessed 1st October, 2015.

2 In referring to 'analytic strategies' and 'analytic tactics', we apply the definitions used by Woolf (2014) and Silver and Woolf (2015), in which strategies relate to *what you plan to* do in an analysis and are, in varying degrees, iterative and emergent in qualitative data analysis (QDA); and tactics relate to *how you plan to do it*, which when using CAQDAS packages comprise the use of cut-and-dried, pre-determined software tools.

3 Drawing on Silver and Lewins (2014), we distinguish between working 'directly' and 'indirectly' with source data. Analytic activities that are examples of direct working include annotating and coding parts of a data source. In contrast, activities that constitute indirect working include writing critical reflections about data sources.

4 Transana is an exception here, which has recently developed much more refined tools for coding and annotating still images (see Silver and Lewins, 2014).

5 Notable exceptions are HyperRESEARCH and Transana.

6 The CAQDAS Networking Project website provides generic and specific team-working protocols for merging separate CAQDAS projects when working with stand-alone versions (see http://www.surrey.ac.uk/sociology/research/researchcentres/caqdas/support/teamworking/index.htm) Accessed 1st October, 2015.

7 See the ATLAS.ti blog (http://blog.atlasti.com/?_ga=1.181453735.1265748858.1432378242) and the MAXQDA blog (http://www.maxqda.com/blog) for informal accounts of the use of mobile apps by researchers. Accessed 15th October 2015.

8 At the time of writing there are no published articles reporting studies that have used MAXQDA emoticodes, but developers report interest in the functionality amongst their users and discussion of their potential was a feature at the 2014 CAQD conference, which brought together MAXQDA developers, trainers and users.

9 The Surrey Research Methods conference was held at the University of Surrey, UK in 1989 and resulted in Fielding and Lee (1991) and the setting up of the CAQDAS Networking Project in 1994.

10 http://www.surrey.ac.uk/sociology/research/researchcentres/caqdas/support/choosing/caqdas_definition.htm Accessed 15th October, 2015.

11 It is also relevant to the term Qualitative Data Analysis Software (QDAS), which is sometimes used to refer to this group of software packages.

REFERENCES

Bazeley, P. (2006) 'The contribution of computer software to integrating qualitative and quantitative data and analyses', *Research in the Schools,* 13(1): 64–74.

Carvajal, D. (2002, revised 2007). The Artisan's Tools. Critical Issues When Teaching and Learning CAQDAS [47 paragraphs]. *Forum Qualitative Sozialforschung / Forum: Qualitative Social Research,* 3(2), Art. 14, http://nbn-resolving.de/urn:nbn:de:0114-fqs0202147. (Accessed 15th October 2015)

Creswell, J. W., and Plano Clark, V. L. (2011) *Designing and Conducting Mixed Methods Research.* (2nd ed). Los Angeles, CA: Sage Publications.

di Gregorio, S. (2010) 'Using Web 2.0 tools for qualitative analysis: an exploration'. Presented at the International Conference on System Sciences, 5–10 January, 2010, Hawaii.

Fernandes, A. A. A. (2008) 'Middleware for distributed data management'. In N. G. Fielding, R. M. Lee and G. Blank (eds.), *The SAGE Handbook of Online Research Methods.* London: Sage Publications, pp. 97–115.

Fielding, N. G. (2014) 'Qualitative research and our digital futures', *Qualitative Inquiry,* 20 (9): 1064–73.

Fielding, N. and Lee, R. M. (1991) *Using Computers in Qualitative Research.* London: Sage Publications.

Fielding, N. and Lee, R. M. (2007) 'Honouring the past, scoping the future'. Plenary paper presented at CAQDAS 2007: Advances in Qualitative Computing Conference, Royal Holloway, University of London, 18–20 April.

Fielding, J., Fielding, N. and Hughes, G. (2013) 'Opening up open-ended survey data using qualitative software', *Quality and Quantity,* 47(6).

Gibbs, G. (2014) 'Using software in qualitative research'. In U. Flick (ed.), *The Sage Handbook of Qualitative Data Analysis.* Los Angeles, CA: Sage Publications, pp. 277–94.

Gilbert, L. S., Jackson, K. and di Gregorio, S. (2014) 'Tools for analysing qualitative data: the history and relevance of qualitative data analysis software'. In J.M Spector *et al.* (eds.), *Handbook of Research on Educational Communications and Technology.* Springer Science and Business Media. New York. pp. 231–6

Kitchin, R. (2014) 'Big Data, new epistemologies and paradigm shifts', *Big Data and Society,* 1(1).

Paulus, T. M. and Bennett, A. M. (2015) 'I have a love–hate relationship with ATLAS.ti™': integrating qualitative data analysis software into a graduate research methods course. *International Journal of Research and Method in Education,* 1–17.

Paulus, T. M., Lester, J. and Dempster, P. (2014) *Digital Tools for Qualitative Research.* 1st edn. Thousand Oaks, CA: Sage Publications.

Rivers, C. and Bulloch, S. L. (2011) 'CAQDAS – A Contributor to Social Scientific Knowledge?' *NCRM Methods NEWS,* Spring: 2–3.

Schmieder, C. (2015) Interview question generation and qualitative data analysis software. A modularized curriculum. University of Wisconsin-Maddison. Available at http://static1.squarespace.com/static/51e93258e4b09e55a0347903/t/557a598de4b03a9a1065c4f4/1434081677506/Curriculum_Q_Generation_June2015.pdf (Accessed 15th October 2015.)

Silver, C. (2014) Software Review: QDA Miner (with WordStat and SimStat) *Journal of Mixed Methods Research,* 9(4):386–7.

Silver, C. and Bulloch, S. L. (2015) 'QUIRKOS 1: distinguishing features and functions', The CAQDAS Networking Project. Available at http://www.surrey.ac.uk/sociology/research/researchcentres/caqdas/files/Quirkos%20-%20distinguishing%20features-July2015.pdf (accessed 10th October 2015).

Silver, C. and Lewins, A. (2013) 'Computer Assisted Analysis of Qualitative Research: trends, potentials and cautions'. In P. Leavy (ed.), *The Oxford Handbook of Qualitative Research Methods.* Oxford: Oxford University Press, pp. 606–38.

Silver, C. and Lewins, A. (2014) *Using Software in Qualitative Research: A Step-By-Step Guide.* 2nd edn. London: Sage Publications.

Silver, C. and Patashnick, J. (2011) Finding Fidelity: Advancing Audiovisual Analysis Using Software [88 paragraphs]. *Forum Qualitative Sozialforschung / Forum: Qualitative Social Research,* 12(1), Art. 37, http://nbn-resolving.de/urn:nbn:de:0114-fqs1101372. Accessed 10th October 2015.

Silver, C. and Rivers, C. (2016) 'The CAQDAS Postgraduate Learning Model: An interplay between methodological awareness, analytic adeptness and technological proficiency',

International Journal of Social Research Methodology, 19(5): 593–609.

Silver, C. and Woolf, N. (2015) 'From guided-instruction to facilitation of learning: the development of Five-level QDA as a CAQDAS pedagogy that explicates the practices of expert users', *International Journal of Social Research Methodology* 8(5):527–43.

Tashakkori, A. and Teddlie, C. (eds.) (2010) *Sage Handbook of Mixed Methods in Social and Behavioral Research.* 2nd edn. Los Angeles, CA: Sage Publications.

Tesch, R. (1990) *Qualitative Research: Analysis Types and Software Tools.* New York, NY: Falmer Press.

Turner, D. (2015) *Overview of a Qualitative Study on the Impact of the 2014 Referendum for Scottish Independence in Edinburgh, and Views of the Political Process.* Edinburgh: Quirkos.

Welser, H. T. and Smith, M. and Fisher, D. and Gleave, E. (2008) 'Distilling digital traces: computational social science approaches to studying the Internet'. In N. G. Fielding, R. M. Lee and G. Blank (eds.), *The Sage Handbook of Online Research Methods.* London: Sage Publications, pp. 116–140.

White, M. J., Judd, M. D. and Poliandri, S. (2012) 'Illumination with a dim bulb? What do social scientists learn by employing qualitative data analysis software in the service of multimethod design?', *Sociological Methodology,* 42(1): 43–76.

Woods, M., Paulus, T., Atkins, D. P. and Macklin, R. (2015) 'Advancing qualitative research using Qualitative Data Analysis Software (QDAS)? Reviewing potential versus practice in published studies using ATLAS.ti and NVivo, 1994–2013', *Social Science Computer Review.*

Woolf, N. (2014) 'Analytic strategies and analytic tactics'. In S. Friese and G. Ringmayr (eds.), ATLAS.ti User Conference 2013: *Fostering Dialog on Qualitative Methods.* Berlin: University Press, Technical University Berlin, pp. 1–3.

## PART VIII

Online Secondary Analysis: Resources and Methods

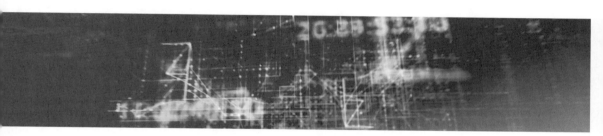

## 28

Online Access to Quantitative Data Resources

Louise Corti and Jo Wathan

INTRODUCTION

Data collected during social science and social policy research and also policy administration represent rich and unique resources that can be reworked and reanalysed, providing opportunities for new analyses. By making data available online for reuse, new potential uses are opened up, enabling researchers to access data that they would not be able to collect themselves for a range of reasons.

This chapter introduces services that have been established to facilitate access to these rich quantitative data sources. The ease with which this is achievable has much to do with the data services providing online access to many resources. We discuss the role of supporting materials and processes that are needed to make quantitative data available, understandable and useful for the longer term.

Around the world there are a number of well-established disciplinary-based data services, like the UK Data Service and the US Inter-University Consortium for Political and Social Research (ICPSR). These services have national remits bringing together expertise across a number of fields to make key national and international socio-economic datasets shareable, usable and sustainable. We describe how these two organisations have established services designed to meet the data and information needs of today's social science researchers and data analysts. Data acquisition and processing, quality assurance procedures; systematic resource discovery systems; value-added support materials; and web-based interfaces for survey and aggregate data browsing, exploration and data download are all key features of successful service delivery.

We then explore the potential of dealing with new and novel forms of data and how provenance and quality assessment of these sources presents methodological challenges for data services. First we describe key data types and how they are reused.

HOW ARE DATA REUSED?

The history of data reuse is as old as social science itself – one of the earliest classic sociological case studies famously drew on administrative records (Durkheim, 2006 first published 1897). However, the reuse of existing data for a fresh purpose, known as 'secondary analysis', came of age in the 1970s to 1980s (Hyman, 1972; Dale et al., 1988). It coincided with the naissance of survey computing and the growth in available survey data sources containing the necessary anonymous individual-level records to facilitate flexible analysis.

Large surveys and opinion polls have been collected and made available through dedicated data archives since the 1950s. Alongside holding major government surveys, data services also developed to host major academic surveys, census data sources, national and international time series, cross-national studies, qualitative and mixed method data.

Recently, attention has also turned to sources that have previously been harder to obtain, whether that is providing secure routes to more detailed data, administrative data and other 'big' data which arises from commercial and other sources (Smith et al., this volume). At the time of writing, exciting developments in all of these areas are underway, and we discuss these later in the chapter.

Secondary analysis has many benefits. It can reduce respondent burden, enable data linkage, including across methods, spawn the creation of new datasets, inform policy disputes about the interpretation of analyses, provide transparency within research as data used by others is available for interrogation, and enable methodologists to learn from each other (US National Academy of Sciences, 2005). Often the most useful data are the most expensive to collect. Indeed, a major advantage of using data that already exist is that they do not need to be collected afresh. Collecting high quality, reliable, representative data is expensive and technically demanding.

In the US, the American Housing Survey (AHS) is a continuous survey that provides data on selected housing and demographic characteristics. Sampling both occupied and vacant housing units, it is conducted biennially by the Bureau of Census and funded via the US Department of Housing and Urban Development (HUD). In 2015, a budget of US$34.1 million was requested by HUD for its support (US Department of Housing and Urban Development 2015). In the UK, the English Housing Survey, conducted annually, is the most authoritative survey on housing conditions. It is a probability survey of approximately 13,000 households composed of a household survey supplemented with a physical survey for a subsample of approximately 6,700 households. This requires both expertise that is beyond the scope of most primary researchers and costs approximately £4 million per year (Department for Communities and Local Government, 2015). By way of contrast, consider that in the year 2014/15 the UK's principal funder of social science research, the Economic and Social Research Council, provided standard grants totalling just under £24 million over a year across all disciplines (Economic and Social Research Council, 2015).

Both surveys produce statistical reports and microdata for further analysis. The latter is available via the UK Data Service while AHS public-use files can be downloaded from the US Census Bureau. Both housing surveys have been run on a regular basis for a number of decades. These repeated surveys permit comparison of groups over time, using data that was collected from representative samples at that time; something which is not readily achievable retrospectively for reasons of recall and mortality.

In order to understand individual process over time and the life-course, longitudinal studies can be used to offer greater scope for powerful re-analysis (Ruspini, 2002). Examples include the Panel Study on Income Dynamics (Institute for Social Research, 2015), which is a longitudinal study of 18,000 individuals started in the US in 1968; the Birth to Twenty (Birth to Twenty Study, 2012) which is a cohort of babies born in Johannesburg-Soweto in 1990; or Understanding Society in the UK, starting in 2009 with 50 to 60 thousand individuals which is a development of the smaller British Household Panel Study which dates back to 1993 (Institute for Social and Economic Research, 2015).

International time series are a different form of data produced by organisations such as the International Labour Organisation (ILO), World Bank, United Nations and International Energy Authority. They are statistical indicators covering economic and other indicators of countries' performance and development, which permit comparisons between countries and over time. The geographical scope would be impossible without the cooperation of a large number of nations, many of whom provide data on the basis of membership of these multinational organisations. For example, the ILO has 186 nation state members bound by statistical regulations and guidance (ILO, 2015) that enables data gathering that would be difficult to achieve without this level of authority and structured international cooperation.

WAYS OF REUSING DATA

There is no doubt that data reuse is a commonplace and important approach to research. Smith (2008) reviewed the extent of secondary data analysis and quantitative methods more widely, in selected British education, sociology and social work journals. She found that while secondary analysis was not widespread in social work papers, 42 per cent of the quantitative papers in education used secondary analysis compared with 75 per cent of the quantitative papers in sociology. In economics, secondary analysis is core to most research practice.

The following benefits are based on a typology suggested by Corti and Thompson (2012).

Providing description and context. This approach is particularly common for primary small scale studies or case studies where existing data serves to contextualise both the study and its findings. Ara *et al.* (2012), for example, used information from the UK Health Survey for England to quantify benefits of obesity interventions. Cribb and colleagues (2013) used the UK Labour Force Survey to explore changes in workforce participation of men and women following an increase in the state retirement age, the findings of which were taken up by policymakers in their Economic and Fiscal Outlook accompanying the 2013 UK Budget.

Comparative research, restudy or follow-up. Comparative research may be across time or place. Famous early classic re-studies include Hubert Llewellyn Smith's (1930–35) repeat of Charles Booth's (1891–1902) poverty survey in London. Comparison brings greater power to answer research questions, for example when data can be combined with data beyond its original sample or geographical limitations. Poortinga *et al.* (2013), for example, used studies in Japan and Britain to understand attitudes to nuclear power in the aftermath of Fukiyama. Effort needs to be made to ensure that one is comparing like with like when two or more separate studies are being used. For example, equivalence in the meaning and coding of variables cannot be assumed, such as level of education across countries. Exploration into such conceptual and practical matters must be made, the literature consulted. Recoding can be carried out to help harmonise measures and categories.

New questions and interpretations. This is the classic secondary analysis approach to data reuse – asking new questions of old data. For example, Mastrocinque (2013) combines several years of British Crime Survey data to explore the factors that influence whether or not a victim gives a victim statement in court. Walters *et al.* (2015) used the four waves of data from the US National Longitudinal Study of Adolescent to Adult Health during the period 1994 to 2008, to see how school problems and anti-social attitudes in adolescent years affected adult criminal and substance abuse in early adulthood.

Replication or validation of published work. Although scientific method is premised on replicability, most re-studies do not usually involve attempts to validate or undermine researchers' previous analyses. However, the pursuit of objective verification of results has demanded attention following some recent well-known cases of obviously fraudulent research in psychology and the crisis of hidden results and publication bias in clinical trials reporting (Enserink, 2012; Goldacre, 2015). The Reproducibility Project carried out independent replications of 100 studies in psychology, and preliminary results suggest that only 39 of the 100 key findings could be replicated (Baker, 2015). In clinical trials, concerns about the concealment of results and publication bias have escalated, with journals like the *British Medical Journal* claiming that they will only publish trials that commit to sharing data on request (Loder and Grives, 2015).

Research design and methodological advancement. Well-documented descriptions of the research methods used in a former investigation can inform the design of a new study. Sampling methods, data collection, fieldwork strategies and interview protocols are all used by study designers to follow best practice. Similarly, tried and tested question wording used in national major surveys can be reused when designing local surveys to ensure comparability with the results of major household surveys.

Analysts can also assess data quality in terms of coding approaches. Platt, Simpson and Akinwale (2005) explored the impact of the discontinuity between 1991 and 2001 UK census ethnicity classifications. In instances where the information is available, researchers can exploit survey 'paradata' (data about how a survey was administered) to explore methodological issues, like non-response or interviewer effects.

Teaching and learning. There is a need for students to engage with 'real' data to obtain results that relate to the real world, and to tackle real data handling problems (Smith, 2008). Real data is well suited to teaching substantive social science as well as facilitating the teaching of research methods and can really engage students. In the UK and US, efforts to improve statistical literacy amongst students of social science have created some useful resources to help students confront secondary data, including those created by data services (Wathan *et al.* 2011).

FINDING AND ACCESSING ONLINE DATA SOURCES

Social science data archives, known as domain repositories, are key to data access. In this section we outline the role of data archives in publishing data and supporting users of data. Although there is a 50+ year history for some of the world's oldest social science data archives, they have had to evolve and develop new access services that meet the needs of today's users (and potential) users.

We take as our case studies two of the world's oldest and best–funded social science data archives: the ICSPR based at the University of Michigan in the US and the UK Data Service, a federal service established in 2012, led by the UK Data Archive and founded at the University of Essex in the UK in 1967.

THE EVOLUTION OF ONLINE DATA SERVICES

Data archives were established in both the US and Europe in the 1960s. As collections grew and the number of archives increased, collaborations started to develop more harmonized approaches to data storage, access and documentation standards, most notably the Data Documentation Initiative (DDI) (DDI Alliance, 2015). In the late 1970s, the

Council of European Social Service Data Archives (CESSDA) and the International Federation of Data Organisations (IFDO) were founded, which both promoted networks of data services for the social sciences and fostered cooperation on key archival strategies, procedures and technologies. The fruits of this collaboration have been more consistent tools, common standards, inter-service communication and formal structures for data sharing.

Early data archives pre-dated the Internet as we know it by decades. The gradual development of online data services has meant that from the mid-1990s onwards many users interact primarily with a data service online. Online data delivery now incorporates online analysis, visualisation and web-based training.

This has been in a context of a boom in online data publishing. Data sharing policies amongst research funders have driven exponential growth in open and restricted data

repositories, hosting all kinds of research data. The international re3data.org registry lists around 1,200 data repositories, 355 of which specialise in the humanities and social sciences (re3data.org, 2015). Figure 28.1 shows the breakdown by country, with 40 per cent appearing in the US.

With more institutional data repositories holding local data comes a need for portals to enable data to be discovered. Research Data Australia is a one-stop shop portal for discovering hundreds of research data resources dispersed across Australia (Australian National Data Service (ANDS), 2013). Similarly, NARCIS in the Netherlands is a portal for the discovery of datasets and publications (NARCIS, 2013).

Some academic journals are also playing a role in ensuring data that underpin published findings are available for readers and reviewers. In the social sciences economics, political science and psychology have led the way. Journal policies do vary, either expecting

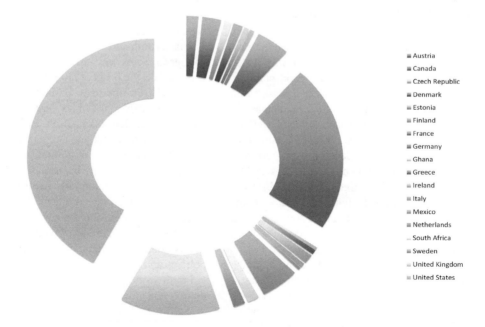

Figure 28.1   Breakdown of social science specialist data repositories by country, re3data.org, 2015

research data to be made available upon request; submitted as supplemental material; deposited in a suitable or mandated domain or public repository. For example, *Nature* journals mandate specific repositories for particular disciplines and, for social science, repositories include the UK Data Service ReShare and ICPSR openICPSR self-deposit systems (SpringerNature, 2015).

It is not enough, however, to simply publish data as is – formats may not be suited to numeric data extraction if published as a pdf, there may be little or no documentation to understand the data and the data store may not have longer-term preservation in mind. In the next section we set out the issues involved in ensuring that data access is sustainably maintained in order that data stay available for years to come. We also outline why these matters are critical to creating sustainable access to useful data for research.

HOW DATA ARE ACQUIRED AND PREPARED FOR ONLINE ACCESS

The social science data archiving community has done much to establish and promote common standards and shared good practice. Global data sharing activities that have come about over the last couple of years, such as via the global Research Data Alliance (RDA), have looked to the social science community to learn about robust data infrastructure and shared data description methods (RDA, 2015).

Processes are based around different phases in archive activity: collection planning, acquisition and processing leading to release, followed by maintenance and support.

Data services typically select and appraise potential data collections against criteria established in collection development policies designed to ensure that they are appropriate for reuse and long-term preservation. Both the UK Data Service and ICPSR have dedicated Collections Development Policies

(UK Data Service, 2015a; ICPSR, 2013). Significant factors to account for when appraising and selecting data for acquisition include significance, uniqueness, usability, volume, formats, costs and potential future use (UK Data Service, 2014).

Data acquisition, often referred to as 'deposit', is the process whereby data and related materials are transferred to a data repository. Acquisition is achieved through receiving data files and associated data documentation from data owners and ensuring that all legal permissions are in place to enable data to be shared. Formal deposit agreements are used by data services to establish that intellectual property and commercial ownership rights in the data can permit data sharing (UK Data Service, 2015b).

Data services use bespoke in-house procedures to prepare data and documentation for online access (UK Data Archive, 2014a, 2014b, 2014c). When data are acquired, the data service checks data integrity, missing values and anomalies or inconsistencies in the data. File formats are also examined to ensure they are the optimal format for long-term preservation and dissemination. Data are then assessed for disclosure risk to ensure that survey respondents who consented to data being collected on the basis of anonymity cannot be identified from the data. Examples of potentially disclosive variables are geographic location, detailed occupation and industry, household size, exact age and any other variable which alone or in combination is unique. Where this is so, it may be necessary to group values to remove potentially identifiable values. For example, age might be banded into categories and household size may be 1, 2, 3, 4, 5 and 6+. The amount of work of this type that is done will depend on the data service's policies and resources.

Finally, the quality and composition of descriptions and documentation is examined to ensure that the context of data provided is meaningful to users. Data have maximum reuse potential when sufficient documentation is made available. Questionnaires, code books, interviewer instructions, technical reports and outputs are all required to interpret survey data. Original and subsequent publications resulting from use of the data are also captured and made available to users. Valuable related non-digital materials can be digitised (all or part) and made available, or at least referenced. Without this kind of documentation, it is difficult for potential users to determine whether any data set is appropriate, or to correctly interpret results produced. Large repeated surveys tend to produce very high quality documentation, such as detailed technical reports. The Health Survey for England, for example, has exemplary documentation (NatCen Social Reseach, 2011).

The documentation files supplied by the depositor that provide the key to interpretation of data are combined into a User Guide(s), currently made available in PDF/A format. Both the UK Data Service and ICPSR endeavour to work with data creators in the early stages to ensure that good data management practices are adhered to, and that high quality documentation is produced and kept along the way (Corti *et al.*, 2014).

A structured metadata record is created that captures core descriptive attributes of the study and resulting data. The DDI metadata standard is used by many social science archives across the world. The DDI is a rich and detailed metadata standard for social, behavioural and economic sciences data used by most social science data archives in the world. A typical DDI record will contain mandatory and optional metadata elements relating to study, data file and variable description:

- *Study description* elements contain information about the context of the data collection, scope of the study (e.g. topics, geography, time, data collection methods, sampling and processing), access information, information on accompanying materials and provides a citation;
- *File description* elements indicate data format, file type, file structure, missing data, weighting variables and software used;
- *Variable-level descriptions* set out the variable labels and codes, and question text where available.

This is known as the *DDI Codebook* standard. Over the past few years, the DDI metadata standard is incorporating more aspects of the survey lifecycle to capture information from questionnaire design to output data files, known as the *DDI Lifecycle* (Vardigan, 2013).

One of the end points of the 'data ingest' process is converting the resulting package of data and documentation files to suitable user-friendly formats (typically for microdata, SPSS, Stata or delimited text formats), placing these on a preservation system and publishing them online.

The accessibility of the resulting data depends on their characteristics. At both the UK Data Service and ICPSR, data are made available on a 'spectrum of access', depending on the disclosure risk in the data. Different terminology is used in different countries. Table 28.1 summarises UK and US licensing and access.

Different versions of data collection with appropriate levels of detail could, potentially, be archived into each of the categories in Table 28.1, creating three versions made available for different kinds of users.

The reader will note the amount of human effort that goes into preparing data in established data services. As the size or volume of the data increases, manual processes involved in data cleaning and preparation become unsustainable. We shall return to how data services can deal with data assessment and treatment of big data in the last part of the chapter.

Table 28.2 summarises in-house data processing and enhancement procedures at the UK Data Service, with the activities in italics being reserved for selected high-use datasets, such as the large scale surveys.

Finally, making data available is not the end of the archive's work. Data must be maintained over time to ensure its continued usability. Data formats are updated as software changes and older formats become obsolete. Data updates may also become available as data depositors make corrections either in response to the discovery of errors, or in light of improved estimates of population characteristics. In this respect, archives

Table 28.1   Access categories for microdata: UK Data Service and ICPSR

Details	Class – UK Data Service	Class – ICPSR	UK License type	Access control
Less detail	Open data	Open data	Open licence without any registration UK Open Government Licence (OGL) for Crown Copyright data Creative Commons Attribution 4.0 International Licence for other data	Open, all uses allowed. Attribution/ citation required
Identifying variables treated, banded or aggregated	Safeguarded data	Public-use files	End user licence	Users registered and authenticated, and, where appropriate, special conditions agreed to
Detailed geographic identifier or detailed occupational codes	Controlled data	Scientific-use files	Bespoke secure access licence	Requiring user accreditation and registration through training and approval by a data access committee, and users to be authenticated

form a vital role in keeping track of changes. Indeed, there is no other central point where depositors can be certain that future users will look to discover such changes. By maintaining data, future users benefit from a growing wealth of historical data.

FINDING AND ACCESSING DATA

Data archives offer online data catalogues with links to access data, supporting documentation and guidance on how to use the data. Examples of searchable online data catalogues for social scientists include the UK Data Service, ICPSR, the Roper Center and Harvard–MIT Data Centre and various European countries' social data archives. CESSDA hosts a federated catalogue that enables users to search for national survey data across the member states that have archives (Council of European Social Science Data Archives, 2015). National member archives include GESIS in Germany, the Lithuanian Data Archive and So.Da.Net in

Table 28.2   Summary of in-house data processing and enhancement procedures at the UK Data Service

Check data files for basic inconsistencies in data
Review data for disclosive information
Carry out data enhancement to agreed standards
Add or edit variable and value labels in survey data files
Improve and harmonise file names according to data collection event
Generate data files in multiple file formats for preservation and dissemination
Collate and prepare user documentation as bookmarked PDF/A documents
Create enhanced DDI-compliant catalogue metadata
Gather citations to related publications for inclusion in the catalogue metadata
Assign a Digital Object Identifier (DataCite DOI) to the data collection
Release data via the UK Data Service download system, *Discover*
Prepare and publish key survey data and metadata to Nesstar online data exploration system

Note: Enhanced data processing procedures in *italics*

Figure 28.2   UK Data Service Discover catalogue search on the word 'unemployment'

Greece, Other national data services exist in Australia and South Africa.

'Discover' is the search tool for the UK Data Service's catalogue. Users can search and browse by various facets (UK Data Service, 2015c). An example of a catalogue search on the word 'unemployment' is shown in Figure 28.2. Catalogue records are indexed on search engines like Google, and so a Google search will also locate datasets. In our example we look for recent UK surveys relating to unemployment.

Searching on the term 'unemployment' returns 1,740 hits, which can be filtered by facets on the left of the display window. Facets include data type, subject, country and dates. To limit our study to UK surveys we restrict our search by selecting 'UK studies' in the data type facet, now yielding 1,522 results. Limiting the search further to those studies published in 2015 produces a more manageable list of six results.

To view the catalogue entry for any of the studies in the results, one simply clicks the title of the study in the results list. Figure 28.3 shows the catalogue record for the January to March 2015 Quarterly Labour Force Survey, a well-known major government survey covering key topics in employment and training.

The record includes an abstract, key information and documentation as well as download link where appropriate. The ease of access relates to where the data falls in terms of the access spectrum described in Table 28.1. The illustrated file is 'safeguarded' and can be downloaded by all those who register with the service and agree to some simple licence conditions. All access is free because the UK Data Service is funded to provide free data access services and does not seek cost recovery.

Popular studies such as this are also available to 'Explore online' in Nesstar. Nesstar is the UK Data Service's online data browsing, analysis, subsetting and download tool that enables easy access to richly documented variables. Instant tabulation and graphing can be done (UK Data Service, 2015d). Full question text, universe and routing information is

Figure 28.3   UK Data Service Discover Catalogue record for the January to March 2015 Quarterly Labour Force Survey

typically displayed alongside variable name, code values and labels, and frequencies. Using Nesstar, a user can specify subsets and download data tables in a range of formats. A frequency table is shown in Figure 28.4 from the UK Quarterly Labour Force Survey, 2015. It gives the wording and applicability of the question as well as the distribution of the variable. We can see that this dataset contains 1,225 individuals made redundant in the last three months (9.7 per cent of those who left a last job in the last three months).

The ability to browse data quickly is particularly useful when assessing whether a dataset might be appropriate for a research question. A researcher seeking to explore the characteristics of the subpopulation of those who had been made redundant in the previous three months might be concerned to be starting with such a small group as this.

If we had chosen to explore hits for time series rather than UK surveys in our Discover search we would have found the Organisation for Economic Co-operation

and Development (OECD) Main Economic Indicators Databank, 1960–2014, an aggregate data series. The data are available to 'explore online' via the UK Data Service's aggregate data browsing system, UK.stat (UK Data Service, 2015e). In this system, users can create tables and graphs of selected indicators by selecting variables, like country, years and indicator. Figure 28.5 shows a graph in UK.stat of GDP growth rate for the previous period for the UK and the US. The table can also be downloaded for a particular query in csv or Excel format.

In the US, a search on unemployment in the ICPSR catalogue brings up over 1,400 results (ICPSR, 2015a). Results can be filtered by subject, geography, data format, time period, restriction type and how recent they are, as shown in Figure 28.6.

ICPSR also has dedicated topical archives that are individually supported by government departments. Examples include the National Archive of Criminal Justice Data, Health & Medical Care Archive, and the

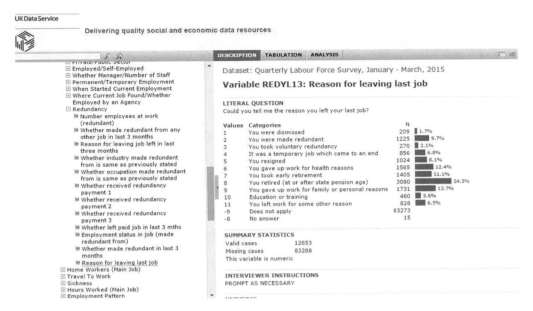

Figure 28.4   Frequency table in Nesstar from the Quarterly UK Labour Force Survey, 2015

National Addiction & HIV Data Archive Programme (ICPSR 2015b). At ICPSR, data access works in a different way to the UK cases earlier. ICPSR restricts access to its data to a paid membership in order to raise revenue necessary for its organisation. ICPSR also publishes some of its key survey data in the online data explorer tool, Survey Documentation and Analysis (SDA) (UC Berkeley, 2015). This is very similar to

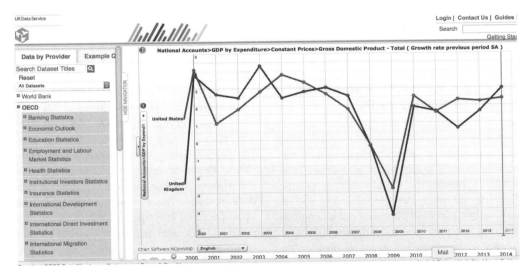

Figure 28.5   Time series chart from the OECD of GDP by expenditure for the US and UK, in UK.stat

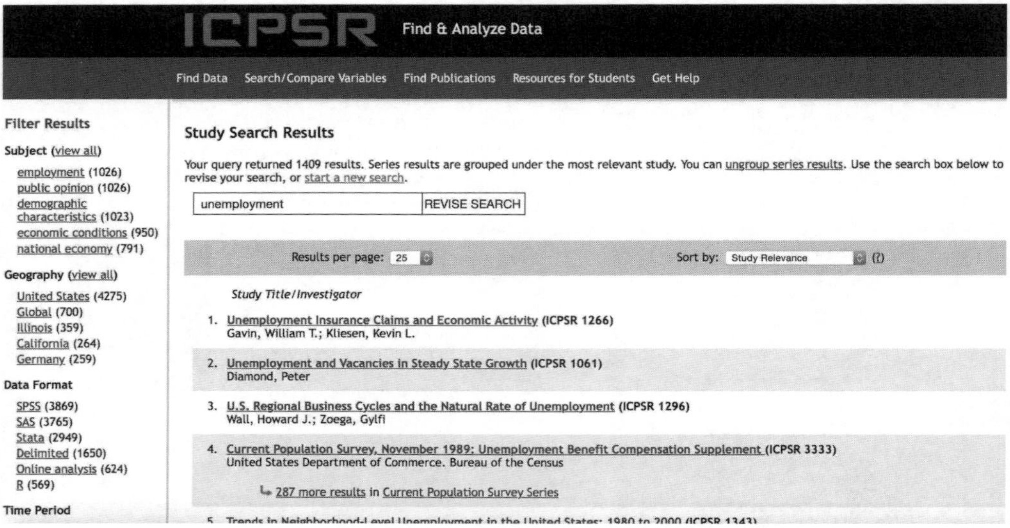

Figure 28.6   Search results for the term 'unemployment' from the ICPSR data catalogue

Nesstar, allowing the user to view frequency distributions for variables, create tabulations on the fly, select subsets and download data.

Both data services provide a host of user support and self-guided training and instructional materials, in the form of step-by-step guides, videos and short webinars. These show the reader or viewer how to confront and analyse particular data sources (UK Data Service, 2015f; ICPSR, 2015c).

ENGAGING WITH NEW AND NOVEL FORMS OF ONLINE DATA

Although data archives have played a leading role in opening up access to digital social and economic data, useful numeric data are now available online from many access points. Keeping up with the global landscape is impossible, especially because not all sources are long-lived. Accordingly, the role of social science data services needs to develop in order to signpost users to new sources and to help document their quality, validity and reliability.

Online Open Data

Governments and organizations have embraced open data in efforts to be more transparent about their activities. By opening up their information for all to access, the innovation and economic potential of public sector information can be better harnessed. By 2015, some 290 open data initiatives have been launched by governments and organizations around the world – at national, regional and international levels (CTIC, 2015).

Data.gov (2015), the US government portal launched in 2009 (Madrigal, 2009) – a mere four months after Obama launched his plans for government transparency. In the UK, the government's Open Data White Paper of 2012 set out standards for the timely release of open public sector data in standardized, machine-readable and open formats. It outlined what citizens, the public sector and businesses could expect from government and public services to harness the benefits of open data (Cabinet Office, 2012). By July 2015, the UK government data portal held 26,400 datasets and showcases how open government data have been used in apps, reports, and services (data.gov.uk, 2015).

Other public data sources are made available via real-time data feeds, such as current weather reports or stock market share prices. The ability to create 'smart cities' relies on open data. NYC Open Data is a portal of hundreds of New York City public datasets made available by city agencies and organizations in an effort to improve the transparency and accountability of the city's governance. Data of interest include parking facilities and electricity consumption by zip code (NYC Open Data, 2015).

Transactional Data

The term 'transactional' data is typically referred to when considering data created by a transactional system, primarily used for administrative purposes. Examples are information from a company payroll (e.g. wages), banking (loans or payments), loyalty programmes (supermarket cards), telephony (mobile phone call records) or security systems (swipe cards). The data tend to sit in relational databases. In most cases the proprietary nature and commercial value in these sources makes them hard to access for research purposes. For archives, this is a challenge and, at present, the main way to gain access is through bespoke contracts with data owners for very specific purposes, sometimes at cost. Historical data may be easier to negotiate access to because its market value is less, but the issue then becomes one of data confidentiality and disclosure risk. The key is to work closely with the data owner to gain trust and a mutual understanding of the benefits of letting skilled researchers analyse the data. A good example is the UK Consumer Research Data Centre (CDRC) which has brokered strong relationships with companies holding such transactional data (CDRC, 2015)

Citizen Science Research and Crowd-Sourced Data

As online data resources for research are so readily available, scientists have begun to exploit the power of new online crowd-sourcing facilities. Sources include social media and images from public interest areas like space exploration. We have seen the rise of 'citizen science' where lay members of the public gather and analyse data for the public good through enthusiasm and collaboration with experts (Citizen Science Alliance (CSA, 2015). Projects range from the classical sciences to climate science and from ecology to planetary science. Galaxy Zoo (2015) is possibly the best known, asking its citizen researchers to classify galaxies according to their shapes, generating 50 million classifications from 150,000 volunteers. Maps closer to home have also been generated from crowd sourcing. OpenStreetMap has been created this way and has proved a useful resource for reuse, particularly where other mapping sources' reusability is limited by licence or copyright (OpenStreetMap, 2015).

Interestingly, we might observe that the boundaries between formal social research methods and lay or crowd-sourced analyses are becoming blurred. Social scientists can easily harness the power of distributed lay analysts to work on research tasks that a single research team could never envisage. A powerful example is the Smithsonian project, which used crowdsourcing to digitise millions of historical documents (McKenzie, 2013).

Social Media Data

Finally, we return to social media data that contain both text and numeric variables. There has been great interest in exploiting these online sources for research. Although commercial brokers providing search and retrieve platforms are in use, various academic projects are seeking to archive bespoke chunks of data. The Library of Congress has attempted to collect Tweets, but the archive has become full rather quickly and neither suitable infrastructure nor technology are in place yet to serve data to researchers due to the large volume and rights issues (Scola, 2015). In the US, a team of digital humanities researchers at Northeastern has been developing a Boston Marathon digital archive featuring stories, photos, videos, oral histories, social media, and other materials related to the tragic Boston Marathon bombing (St Martin, 2013).

In the UK, the Collaborative Online Social Media Observatory project (COSMOS, 2015) has worked across disciplines to elucidate some of the methodological, theoretical, empirical and technical dimensions of social media data in social and policy contexts. It provides a software platform for open Twitter data, with research use cases. One exemplary project is addressing the understanding of the role of social media in the aftermath of youth suicides, funded by the Department of Health (Scourfield, 2015).

ASSESSING THE QUALITY OF OPEN DATA SOURCES

In investigating open data sources available around the world, we note a massive rise in their number. New governmental public sector portals appear on a monthly basis, researchers are sharing data on free repository systems like FigShare and DataVerse, and journals are increasingly publishing data to support results in papers (FigShare 2015; Institute for Quantitative and Social Science, 2015).

Unless funding is ongoing and sustainable DOIs are used, there is little guarantee of ongoing discoverability and availability of data sources. To this end, archives are keen to encourage good practice in these areas.

Focusing on open data, a casual browser will observe that the sources vary massively in consistency. Many open data stores offer a range of machine-readable download options and some conform to standard metadata

schemas; indeed, these have shaped the transparency agenda for some years. However, other open data are published intermittently without dedicated funding to do so and can be less well documented. Good metadata and accessibility (persistence of web links) are the main problems, with many data available only via a spreadsheet or downloadable file, which are of less benefit to programme developers, who are building web services and apps and who want to access data programmatically.

Programmers typically wish to access data via APIs (Application Programming Interfaces). A number of public sector organisations have begun to publish open data via in-house APIs to meet governments' transparency agendas and some agencies have really excelled. Organisations like the World Bank and UK Meteorological Office have invested significantly in providing programmatic access to open data via APIs (World Bank, 2015; Met Office, 2015). The Met Office provides maps, charts, forecasts in real-time as well as historical data, and runs hackathons bringing together data and data scientists in one space to develop innovative ideas, which can lead into products and services.

To address the quality of open numeric data, a number of certification systems have evolved to help establish the quality and robustness of open data systems, and offer some kudos to a published dataset by listing their own catalogues. An example of such an awarding body is the Open Data Institute (ODI) in the UK, which also has an evolving number of local branches across the world, such as in Australia (ODI, 2015). Certificates require the data publisher to provide evidence (in the form of a web page) that can demonstrate transparency for the processes and systems in place to manage and publish data. The evidence focuses on the need for detailed machine-actionable metadata as well as clarity on property legal rights and terms of use.

Social science archives do not yet routinely provide access to their open data via APIs. In summer 2015, the UK Data Service collaborated with the company AppChallenge to launch a developer contest using open data in their collection about the Quality of Life of European citizens (AppChallenge, 2015). The #EULife AppChallenge aimed to crowd source exciting new apps and ways of using the information provided from an open data-set, European Quality of Life 2007–11, which was made available via a newly constructed API (Eurofound, 2015). The data files were anonymised, 'harmonised' and fully labelled. This process ensured that question variables and response sets (e.g. single, married, etc.) matched across the two years of data collection to allow ease of comparability. Additionally, suitable weights were available in the data file so that any results displayed in resulting apps (e.g. percentages) would match published findings from the data owner's website. These aspects of 'data quality' are critical for archives when publishing open data, with a clear preoc-cupation with transparency about provenance and documentation.

For the UK Data Service, this outing was a step change, creating a new mode of data delivery (API) and the addition of more detailed metadata than it previously provided. By engaging with such experts in the open data space, data archives can move forward with embracing such new outlets and new users. Looking to the future we anticipate greater provision of data using cloud-based services, where due to the size and the power required to compute, data are no longer moved to the researcher, but instead the researcher moves to the data. This model is nothing new for astronomy or climate scientists who utilise purpose-built shared data and analysis facili-ties. Storage and archiving of the data presents new challenges as the data streams are continu-ously being added to. In this case, data are best referenced, and/or segmented by time stamps at appropriate intervals to meet the needs of researchers. An example might be deciding how to split up smart energy meter data that is collected every 5 seconds but might be better made available in 30 minute slots.

Finally, in the 'big data' era, researchers see the benefits of working with novel and more complex data sources, often across disciplinary boundaries. With this, there is potential for deficits in confidence or skills for researchers to become even greater. Good metadata and quality assurance skills are needed for retrieving, assessing, manipu-lating and analysing big data, and thinking 'algorithmically', and trainers are respond-ing to this growing demand (Cambridge Undergraduate Quantitative Methods, 2015).

RESEARCH EXAMPLES OF LINKING NUMERIC ONLINE DATA

Linking data sources can add analytic power to individual sources. For example, survey microdata can be linked to other data, espe-cially geographical contextual data, directly through common identifiers or characteristics. We will now provide some brief case studies:

Case study 1: Social and Environmental Inequalities in Rural England

Huby (2010) investigated social and environ-mental inequalities and injustice in rural England to inform policy by compiling exist-ing data sources into a single dataset of socio-economic and environmental characteristics at the level of census Super Output Areas (SOA). Data used included UK census data, the National Travel Survey, land cover map, Countryside Stewardship, Environmental Stewardship and Environmentally Sensitive Area schemes data, Land Registry house prices data, Centre for Sustainable Energy and Road Traffic Accident data.

Case study 2: Combining Ordnance Survey, Census Data and Crowd-Sourced Maps

Datashine is an online mapping platform produced as part of a wider project at

University College London to mine big open data (Cheshire and O'Brien, 2015). The maps take standard 'chloropleth' maps, which colour census output areas according to their census characteristics. This is then combined with mapping data from Ordnance Survey and OpenStreetMap, superimposing maps showing transparent buildings. The colours from the lower layer 'shine' through where there are buildings, with the result that maps are intuitive and interpretable, as shown in Figure 28.7.

Case study 3: Data.gov mashathon 2010, an Energy Mashup

The National Renewable Energy Laboratory (2010) undertook a project that sought to ask how residential energy use varied across the US, linking US public energy data available online. A 'mashup' was created at the first Data.gov 'mashathon' event to compare energy use characteristics for seven cities with populations of just over half a million people. With differing electricity rates, median income levels, energy-related incentives and types of Smart Grid programs being

introduced, cities across the country are transitioning to a new energy marketplace in unique ways. Open data from 2008 electric sales, revenue and average price data from the Energy Information Administration (EIA) were linked with data from OpenEI.org, the US Census and SmartGrid.gov. The project produced an online visualization map showing energy use statistics about each city, the local electric utility organization, rebates and financial incentive programmes and up-to-date information about local Smart Grid projects. Cities could be compared and contrasted to see how local utility rates, median income and other regional characteristics relate to average annual electricity use. The data product evolves over time as energy data are added and updated.

Case Study 4: DBPedia

An example of a published linked open dataset is DBPedia, which is a crowd-sourced effort that links structured information in Wikipedia entries to each other and beyond to other data sources (DBPedia, 2015). It publishes a number of interesting projects and use

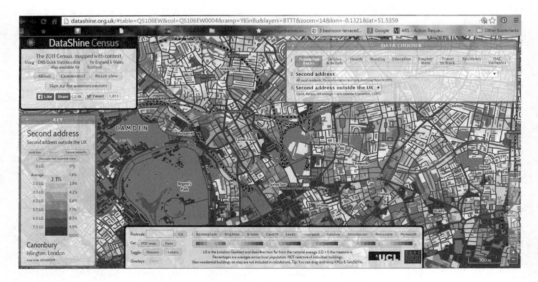

Figure 28.7   2011 UK Census mapped with context in DataShine 7

cases, including one on linking geo-located data with other geo-related data sources such as Geonames, the US Census, EuroStat and the CIA world fact book (Hellman, 2015).

CONCLUSION

Secondary analysis of data permits a range of valuable analyses to be undertaken quickly, effectively, transparently and with minimal respondent burden. Online access to data has simplified and speeded up access to numeric data. Digital formats have enabled users to easily consult full documentation, explore and analyse data online and to make linkages between appropriate resources in a context of an increasingly complex data infrastructure.

The number of online data outlets has grown significantly over the past five years, but dedicated domain specific data services, like the UK Data Service and ICPSR have a role in helping set the high standard for high quality data publishing. As new and larger data types come on stream, so data services need to adapt, providing new platforms and new tools for selecting and querying data, alongside the traditional download of smaller datasets.

Perhaps the biggest challenge for established data services is in finding ways to describe effectively the underlying methods used to create these records, providing potential users with a fuller understanding of the provenance and meaning of readily available data. Here collaboration with survey methodologists is beneficial, some of whom have already moved into this space. This community already provides best practice guidance in techniques for dealing with known bias in data such as non-response and other missing data, and can help elucidate further statistical procedures for dealing with additional uncertainty in big data.

This is a fast moving area with much to be resolved and at least as much potential for the researcher. However, we need to ensure that researchers and data services themselves are well equipped to deal with the challenges ahead, with a need for statistical, methodological and computational skills.

REFERENCES

AppChallenge (2015) EULIfe AppChallenge. Available at http://eulife.appchallenge.net (accessed 31 July 2015).

Ara, R., Blake, L., Gray, L., Hernandez, M., Crowther, M., Dunkley, A., Warren, F., Jackson, R., Rees, A., Stevenson, M., Abrams, K., Cooper, N., Davies, M., Khunti, K. and Sutton, A. (2012) 'What is the clinical effectiveness and cost-effectiveness of using drugs in treating obese patients in primary care? A systematic review,' *Health Technology Assessment* 16(5), pp. 1–202.

Australian National Data Service (ANDS) (2013) Research Data Australia. Available at http://researchdata.ands.org.au/ (accessed 31 July 2015).

Baker, M. (2015) 'First results from psychology's largest reproducibility test', *Nature News*, 30 April. Available at http://www.nature.com/news/first-results-from-psychology-s-largest-reproducibility-test-1.17433 (accessed 31 July 2015).

Birth to 20 Study (2012) *About us. Birth to 20 Study*. Faculty of Health Science. University of Witwatersrand, Johannesburg. Available at https://www.wits.ac.za/health/research-entities/birth-to-20/birth-to-twenty/ (accessed 17 July 2016).

Booth, Charles (1891–1902) *Life and Labour of the People in London*. London: Williams and Norgate, Macmillan.

Cabinet Office (2012) *Open Data White Paper: Unleashing the Potential*. UK Government Cabinet Office. Available at http://data.gov.uk/sites/default/files/Open_data_White_Paper.pdf (accessed 31 July 2015).

Cambridge Undergraduate Quantitative Methods (2015) 'Preparing social scientists for the world of big data', Research Features. University of Cambridge, 18 June 2015. Available at http://www.cam.ac.uk/research/features/preparing-social-scientists-for-the-world-of-big-data#sthash.ahGTJzKB.dpuf (accessed 31 July 2015).

Cheshire, J. and O'Brien, O. (2015) Datashine: about the project. Available at http://blog.datashine.org.uk/about/ (accessed 31 July 2015).

Citizen Science Alliance (CSA) (2012) Homepage. Available at http://www.citizensciencealliance.org/ (accessed 31 July 2015).

Collaborative Online Social Media Observatory (COSMOS) (2015) What is COSMOS: social media and data mining. Available at http://www.cs.cf.ac.uk/cosmos/ (accessed 31 July 2015).

Consumer Data Research Centre (CDRC) (2015) Homepage. Available at http://cdrc.ac.uk (accessed 31 July 2015).

Corti, L. and Thompson, P. (2012) 'Secondary Analysis of Archive Data'. In J. Goodwin (ed.). *SAGE Secondary Data Analysis*, London: Sage Publications, pp. 297–313.

Corti, L., Van den Eynden, V., Bishop, L. and Woollard, M. (2014) *Managing and sharing research data: a guide to good practice*. London: Sage Publications.

Council of European Social Science Data Archives (2015) Member Organizations. CESSDA. Available at http://cessda.net/eng/National-Data-Services/CESSDA-Members (accessed 17 July 2016).

Cribb, J., Emmerson, C. and Tetlow, G. (2013) 'Incentives, shocks or signals: labour supply effects of increasing the female state pension age in the UK', *IFS Working Paper No.* W13/03, Institute for Fiscal Studies. doi:10.1920/wp.ifs.2013.1303. Available at http://www.ifs.org.uk/wps/wp1303.pdf (accessed 31 July 2015).

CTIC (2015) Open data @CTIC. Asturias, Fundación CTIC. Available at http://datos.fundacionctic.org (accessed 31 July 2015).

Dale, A., Arber, S. and Proctor, M. (1988) *Doing Secondary Analysis*. London: Allen & Unwin.

data.gov (2015) The home of the US Government's open data. Available at http://data.gov (accessed 31 July 2015).

data.gov.uk (2015) Data.gov.uk. Opening up Government. Available at http://data.gov.uk/data/search (accessed 31 July 2015).

DDI Alliance (2015) *Why use DDI?* Available at http://www.ddialliance.org/what (accessed 31 July 2015).

Department for Communities and Local Government (2015) *Consultation on the future shape of the English Housing Survey.* Available at https://www.gov.uk/government/uploads/system/uploads/attachment_data/file/397096/Consultation_on_the_future_shape_of_the_English_Housing_Survey.pdf (accessed 31 July 2015).

DBPedia (2015) Homepage. Available at http://dbpedia.org (accessed 31 July 2015).

Durkheim, E. (2006) *On Suicide*. London: Penguin.

Economic and Social Research Council (ESRC) (2015) *Annual Report and Accounts.* Swindon, UK: ESRC.

Enserink, M. (2012) 'Diederik Stapel under investigation by Dutch prosecutors', *Science*, 2 October. American Association for the Advancement of Science. Available at http://www.sciencemag.org/news/2012/10/diederik-stapel-under-investigation-dutch-prosecutors (accessed 17 July 2016).

Eurofound (2015) European quality of life survey time series: 2007 and 2011. Open Access [computer file]. SN: 7724, July 2015. Colchester, UK: UK Data Archive. Available at http://dx.doi.org/10.5255/UKDA-SN-7724-1 (accessed 31 July 2015)

FigShare (2015) Homepage. Available at http://figshare.com (accessed 31 July 2015).

Galaxy Zoo (2015) Galaxy Zoo (Zooinverse project). Available at http://www.galaxyzoo.org/ (accessed 31 July 2015).

Goldacre, B. (2015) 'Scientists Are Hoarding Data And It's Ruining Medical Research', *BuzzFeed News*, 22 July. Available at http://www.buzzfeed.com/bengoldacre/deworming-trials (accessed 31 July 2015).

Hellman (2015) *Mobile and Geographic Applications Project.* Available at http://wiki.dbpedia.org/use-cases/mobile-and-geographic-applications-0 (accessed 31 July 2015).

Huby, M. (2010) *Social and Environmental Inequalities in Rural England, 2004–2009* [computer file]. SN: 6447, July 2010. Colchester, UK: UK Data Archive. http://dx.doi.org/10.5255/UKDA-SN-6447-1 (accessed 31 July 2015).

Hyman, H. H. (1972) *Secondary Analysis of Sample Surveys*. New York, NY: Wiley.

Institute for Quantitative and Social Science (2015) The Dataverse Project. Harvard

College. Available at http://dataverse.org (accessed 31 July 2015).

Institute for Social and Economic Research (2015) Understanding Society. University of Essex. Available at https://www.understandingsociety.ac.uk (accessed 31 July 2015).

Institute for Social Research (2015) The Panel Study of Income Dynamics (PSID). Institute for Social Research, University of Michigan. Available at http://psidonline.isr.umich.edu (accessed 31 July 2015).

International Labour Organization (ILO) (2015) Standards and guidelines on labour statistics. Available at http://www.ilo.org/global/statistics-and-databases/standards-and-guidelines/lang–en/index.htm (accessed 17 July 2016).

Inter-University Consortium for Political and Social Research (ICPSR) (2013) Collection development policy. Available at http://www.icpsr.umich.edu/icpsrweb/content/datamanagement/policies/colldev.html (accessed 31 July 2015).

Inter-University Consortium for Political and Social Research (ICPSR) (2015a) Find and analyze data. University of Michigan. Available at http://www.icpsr.umich.edu/icpsrweb/ICPSR/ (accessed 31 July 2015).

Inter-University Consortium for Political and Social Research (ICPSR) (2015b) ICPSR thematic collections. Available at http://www.icpsr.umich.edu/icpsrweb/content/membership/partners/archives.html (accessed 31 July 2015).

Inter-University Consortium for Political and Social Research (ICPSR) (2015c) Teaching and Learning with ICPSR. University of Michigan. Available at https://www.icpsr.umich.edu/icpsrweb/instructors/index.jsp (accessed 31 July 2015).

Llewellyn Smith, H. (1930–1935) *The New Survey of London Life and Labour*. London: P.S. King

Loder, E. and Grives, T. (2015) 'The BMJ requires data sharing on request for all trials', Editorial. *British Medical Journal,* 2015: 350. doi: http://dx.doi.org/10.1136/bmj.h2373 Available at http://www.bmj.com/content/350/bmj.h2373 (accessed 31 July 2015).

Madrigal, A. (2009) 'Data.gov launches to mixed reviews', *Wired*, 21 May. Available at http://www.wired.com/2009/05/datagov-launches-to-mixed-reviews/ (accessed 31 July 2015).

Mastrocinque, J.M. (2013) 'Victim personal statements: an analysis of notification and utilization', *Criminology and Criminal Justice,* 14(2): 216–34.

McKenzie, H. (2013) 'Smithsonian turns to crowdsourcing for massive digitization project', *Pando.* 8 November. Available at https://pando.com/2013/11/08/smithsonian-turns-to-crowdsourcing-for-massive-digitization-project/ (accessed 31 July 2015).

Met Office (2015) *Met Office DataPoint*. Available at http://www.metoffice.gov.uk/datapoint (accessed 31 July 2015).

NatCen Social Research (2011). *User Guide for the Health Survey for England, 2011*. UK Data Service. Website. (discover.ukdataservice.ac.uk/Catalogue/?sn=7260&type=Data catalogue#documentation)

NARCIS (2013) National Academic Research and Collaborations Information System. Royal Netherlands Academy of Arts and Sciences. Available at http://www.narcis.nl (accessed 31 July 2015).

National Renewable Energy Laboratory (2010) Data.gov Mashathon 2010: an energy mashup. Open EI. Available at http://en.openei.org/apps/mashathon2010/ (accessed 31 July 2015).

NYC Open Data (2015) Homepage. Available at https://data.cityofnewyork.us/ (accessed 31 July 2015).

Open Data Institute (ODI) (2015) The mark for quality and trust for open data. Available at https://certificates.theodi.org (accessed 31 July 2015).

OpenStreetMap (2015) Homepage. Available at openstreetmap.org (accessed 31 July 2015).

Platt L., Simpson, L. and Akinwale, B. (2005) 'Stability and change in ethnic groups in England and Wales', *Population Trends*, Autumn (121): 35–46.

Poortinga, W., Aoyagi, M. and Pidgeon, N. F. (2013) 'Public perceptions of climate change and energy futures before and after the Fukushima accident: a comparison between Britain and Japan', *Energy Policy,* 62: 1204–11. Available at http://dx.doi.org/10.1016/j.enpol.2013.08.015 (accessed 31 July 2015).

re3data.org (2015) Registry of Research Data Repositories. Available at http://www.re3data.org (accessed 31 July 2015).

Research Data Alliance (RDA) (2015) Research Data Sharing without Barriers. Available at https://rd-alliance.org (accessed 31 July 2015).

Ruspini, E. (2002) *Introduction to Longitudinal Research*. London: Routledge.

Scola, M. (2015) 'Library of Congress Twitter Archive is a huge #FAIL', *Politico*, 11 July. Available at http://www.politico.com/story/2015/07/library-of-congress-twitter-archive-119698.html#ixzz3hPhSXbQt (accessed 31 July 2015).

Scourfield, J. (2015) *Research on social media and suicide*. COSMOS, University of Cardiff. Available at http://www.cs.cf.ac.uk/cosmos/research-on-social-media-and-suicide/ (accessed 31 July 2015).

Smith, E. (2008) *Using Secondary Data in Educational and Social Research*. Oxford: Oxford University Press.

SpringerNature (2015) *Recommended data repositories*. Available at http://www.nature.com/sdata/data-policies/repositories (accessed 31 July 2015).

St Martin, G. (2013) 'Researchers developing Boston Marathon digital archive', *News@Northeastern*, 24 May. Available at http://www.northeastern.edu/news/2013/05/our-marathon-project/ (accessed 31 July 2015).

UC Berkeley (2015) *SDA: Survey Documentation and Analysis*. Available at http://sda.berkeley.edu (accessed 31 July 2015).

UK Data Archive (2014a) *Quantitative data ingest processing procedures*. University of Essex. Available at http://www.data-archive.ac.uk/media/54770/ukda081-ds-quantitativedataprocessingprocedures.pdf (accessed 31 July 2015).

UK Data Archive (2014b) *Qualitative data collection ingest processing procedures*. University of Essex. Available at http://www.data-archive.ac.uk/media/54767/ukda093-ds-qualitativeprocessingprocedures.pdf (accessed 31 July 2015).

UK Data Archive (2014c) *Documentation ingest processing procedures*. University of Essex. Available at http://www.data-archive.ac.uk/media/54785/ukda078-ds-documentationprocessingprocedures.pdf (accessed 31 July 2015).

UK Data Service (2014) *Collection development selection and appraisal criteria*. University of Essex. Available at http://ukdataservice.ac.uk/media/455175/cd234-collections-appraisal.pdf (accessed 31 July 2015).

UK Data Service (2015a) *Collection Development Policy*. University of Essex. Available at http://ukdataservice.ac.uk/media/398725/cd227-collectionsdevelopmentpolicy.pdf (accessed 31 July 2015).

UK Data Service (2015b) Licence Agreement. University of Essex. Available at http://ukdataservice.ac.uk/deposit-data/how-to/regular-depositors/deposit (accessed 31 July 2015).

UK Data Service (2015c) Discover. Data catalogue. University of Essex. Available at http://discover.ukdataservice.ac.uk/?sf=Data catalogue (accessed 31 July 2015).

UK Data Service (2015d) Nesstar catalogue. University of Essex. Available at nesstar.ukdataservice.ac.uk (accessed 31 July 2015).

UK Data Service (2015e) Guide to using UKDS. Stat. University of Essex. Available at https://stats.ukdataservice.ac.uk (accessed 31 July 2015).

UK Data Service (2015f) *User support materials*. University of Essex. Available at http://ukdataservice.ac.uk/use-data (accessed 31 July 2015).

US Department of Housing and Urban Development (2015) *Policy Development and Research, Research and Technology: 2015 Summary Statement and Initiatives*. Available at http://portal.hud.gov/hudportal/documents/huddoc?id=fy15cj_rsrch_tech.pdf (accessed 31 July 2015).

US National Academy of Sciences (2005) *Expanding Access to Research Data: Reconciling Risks and Opportunities*. Washington, DC: National Academies of Science.

Vardigan M. (2013) 'The DDI matures: 1997 to the present', *IASSIST Quarterly*, 37(1–4): 45–50. Available at http://www.iassistdata.org/sites/default/files/iq/iqvol371_4_vardigan.pdf (accessed 31 July 2015).

Walters, G. D. (2015) 'Criminal and substance involvement from adolescence to adulthood: precursors, mediators, and long-term effects', *Justice Quarterly*, 32(4): 729–47.

Wathan, J., Brown, M. and Williamson, L. (2011) 'Increasing secondary analysis in undergraduate dissertations: a pilot project'. In G. Payne and M. Williams (eds.) *Teaching Quantitative Methods*. London: Sage Publications, pp.121–141.

World Bank (2015) Developer information. Available at http://data.worldbank.org/node/9 (accessed 31 July 2015).

## 29

Secondary Qualitative Analysis using Online Resources

Patrick Carmichael

INTRODUCTION

This chapter explores the secondary analysis of qualitative data, the impact that network technologies have had on this, and the research potential for secondary analysis of data that is accessed across both the public Internet and networks of research archives. Secondary analysis allows not only the reassessment of the approaches and arguments of researchers, it also enables individuals and communities not involved in the original research to engage with data in new ways that reflect emerging perspectives or research strategies, some of which may be further supported and enabled by technological developments. Network technologies offer the potential to allow data, analyses, researchers and participants to be distributed in both space and time, but these technologies need to be carefully developed and deployed, and critically evaluated in order to avoid the creation of what have been called 'data tombs' (Fayyad and Uthurusamy, 2002: 32) in which data 'rest in peace' with little

opportunity for subsequent access, let alone secondary analysis.

Both the practices of secondary analysis and the technologies to allow them to take place in online environments (or even simply to be undertaken by researchers at a distance) have been dominated by quantitative data and the research practices that generate and consume them. There are long traditions of data sharing and reuse both in the pure and applied sciences (examples being astrophysical, epidemiological and climate data) and in the social sciences, where census data and social and economic indicator data are widely shared. Data archiving and sharing, and the secondary analysis that it might enable, are less well established in qualitative research contexts, with mixed-method and longitudinal studies therefore also often proving difficult to implement.

Since the first edition of this Handbook was published, the technological landscape against which secondary analysis might take place has changed significantly, and alongside this there have been methodological developments; new patterns of participatory and collaborative research have emerged; and there have been changes in the ways in which research is conceptualized, funded, organised and its success and impact measured. The relationships between these developments are complex: the research potential of many emerging technologies (often not designed with research in mind) has only become apparent through experimentation (a good example would be the realisation of the research potential of social media platforms, micro-blogging and 'crowd-sourcing' of data). At the same time, technology developers responding to interest in online research and 'data journalism' have developed more sophisticated search, retrieval and visualisation technologies, many of which feature in other chapters in this Handbook.

However, before considering some of these developments and a number of illustrative examples of how secondary analysis of qualitative sources might be enabled in online research, it is worth exploring some of the broader debates surrounding the reuse and reanalysis of qualitative sources in particular.

THE NATURE, PURPOSE AND CHALLENGES OF SECONDARY ANALYSIS OF QUALITATIVE DATA

Secondary analysis is conventionally defined as involving the use of data collected in prior research to pursue some new direction or answer new research questions, and is thus differentiated from meta-analysis or systematic reviews (Corti and Bishop, 2005; Heaton, 1998, 2004, 2008; Irwin and Winterton, 2011; Szabo and Strang, 1997). Heaton's (2004) review of studies involving secondary analysis of qualitative data revealed that the majority of these involved what are described as 'supplementary analysis', focusing on aspects of data that were not addressed or only partially addressed in the original

research. Less common were 'supra-analyses' (which investigated new research questions or issues) and reanalyses of original research questions, the latter involving interrogation or critique of the original researchers' analysis (Heaton, 2004: 39–46). Secondary analysis of data by the original researchers is not precluded: in fact, Heaton (2004: 37) suggests that at least some analysis which is described as 'secondary' may be primary analysis undertaken by the original researchers some time after the original research or may be inspired by a concern that primary analysis was incomplete or inadequate.

Heaton also identifies the importance of secondary analysis as an element in research approaches alongside other qualitative or quantitative data analysis (Heaton, 2004: 47–5). This may take place in the course of comparative or longitudinal studies; where quantitative data such as cohort studies are used to provide a context for qualitative data such as interviews or case studies, or where other research has suggested new lines of enquiry or conceptual frameworks. Irwin and Winterton (2012) offer an interesting reflexive account of their experiences of working with existing data sets gathered in the course of two prior projects as part of the UK Economic and Social Research Council 'Timescapes' programme (Holland, 2011). They carried out secondary analysis of research data from two prior studies ('Work and Family Lives' where data had been collected in Edinburgh in 2007–2010, and 'Men as Fathers', which collected data in East Anglia in 2000–2008) formulating research questions informed by recent empirical and theoretical work on continuity and change in gender, work and care arrangements. These extended and often multi-method approaches contribute to a blurring of the distinction between secondary analysis, meta-analysis and theory-building. This is also the case when analysis takes place in the context of action research in that 'co-interpretation' activities involving participants may involve the revisiting of previously collected data as part of an iterative research design.

Another compelling rationale for undertaking secondary analysis is that it provides access to rich data, particularly those collected in unusual research settings, or which give voice to rarely heard participants – another argument made by Irwin and Winterton (2012) in the previous example. Long-Sutehall *et al.* (2010) describe how secondary analysis of data gathered across multiple previous research projects proved useful when researching sensitive issues with an 'elusive population' (Long-Sutehall *et al.*, 2010: 336) – in this case, family members' experiences of brain-stem death related to organ and tissue donation. It was known that recruitment to the prior projects had been difficult, and so using what data had been collected was judged to be a more efficient strategy than initiating new data collection. Another example is the body of work built up by Walkerdine (1988), which provides detailed insights into the development of mathematical concepts in pre-school children in their homes, rather than in better-documented school settings. In this example, the sharing of data and its secondary analysis has enabled a rich theoretical debate: records of dialogues between parents and children have been analysed from cognitivist and social perspectives; have contributed to post-structuralist exploration of gender and class; and have informed comparisons between home- and school-based learning. Other arguments for undertaking secondary analysis include time- and cost-effectiveness (although the costs of initial preparation and archiving of data need to be taken into account); reduction of burden on participants; and allowing triangulation and generalisation from findings (Fielding and Fielding, 2000; Hammersley, 1997; Szabo and Strang, 1997).

The diversity of qualitative research and the epistemological underpinnings of different perspectives are reflected in attitudes towards, and approaches to, secondary analysis. Some of the most successful instances of sharing of qualitative data have occurred where contributors and users of data have a domain-specific shared repertoire and a common epistemological basis for their approaches: a good example

is the international CHILDES (Child Language Data Exchange System) network, which supports computer-aided conversation analysis and its associated database 'TalkBank'[1] (MacWhinney, 2000a, 2000b). At the same time, there is also a distinctive position on secondary analysis, advanced by Mauthner *et al.* (1998): that not 'having been there' to share the epistemological perspectives of the original researchers is an insurmountable barrier to secondary analysis, and that the primary role of secondary analysis is methodological exploration, rather than substantive engagement with research data. Despite technological developments (for example, video and audio data rather than simply transcripts can now be archived) and metadata schemes that allow original researchers to provide rich contextual information about the settings in which data were collected, this remains the principal objection that some qualitative researchers make to secondary analysis and work with archival data.

An alternative view of secondary analysis stresses its pragmatic and methodologically eclectic character (Heaton, 2004: 116–21), arguing that it may be thought of as 'bricolage' in that it often draws on multiple datasets, sources and methodological approaches. This perspective in general de-emphasizes the importance of personal involvement in original research and challenges the distinction between primary and secondary analysis, pointing to examples from other disciplines where reanalysis is not only the norm but also a distinctive aspect of disciplinary practice (Bishop, 2007, 2009; Fielding, 2004; Thompson, 2000). It also echoes calls for reform of practice within certain social science disciplines: Stenhouse (1978), for example, suggests that educational research might take the lead from historians and calls for a collective effort to develop a 'contemporary history' of education in which quality of analysis and methodological transparency are closely aligned. This would entail research data being explicitly structured and presented so as to encourage reanalysis, with audit trails being provided to allow for critical engagement with the interpretative frameworks and processes of the original researchers.

Although there is a temptation to dismiss 'eclectic' approaches as taking insufficient account of epistemological issues or being post-epistemological, it is important to recognise that such approaches may not simply be opportunistic. Rather, they may represent distinctive methodological and political standpoints informed by commitments to widening participation in research, or to a view of reanalysis and recontextualisation as a continuing knowledge construction activity.

There is room both in what might be described as the 'epistemologically circumscribed' and the 'epistemologically eclectic' perspectives for engagement with 'classic studies', although the identification of a study as a 'classic' makes methodologically and epistemologically neutral reassessment difficult, given the tendency for 'classic' to become 'exemplary' or even to define or circumscribe disciplinary norms (Parry and Mauthner, 2005; Savage, 2005). Savage points out that the normative nature of many texts in social science means that they focus on how researchers should conduct their research, rather than how they actually went about their research; and that even purportedly reflexive accounts are often very selective and reflect highly theorised and subjective stances. This is a strong argument for broadening of the scope of secondary analysis beyond the data collected and archived to include research instruments, fieldnotes and research minutes, which provide insights into the nature of research processes, issues, dilemmas and macro- and micro-political agendas.

Proponents of both perspectives outlined here (the continuing debate is reviewed by Irwin and Winterton (2012) and Medjedović (2011), amongst others) acknowledge that secondary analysis has a role in learning about research methodology in general, as well as about the specific practices and processes employed by researchers. Corti and Bishop (2005) describe a range of specifically pedagogical rationales for engaging students and early-career researchers in secondary analysis, including engagement with rare or exemplary studies; exemplification of enduring issues and questions in research; and allowing students to engage with the complexities of real data in a way that specially constructed datasets developed for teaching purposes do not. Amongst other arguments, Seale (2011), who writes not only about secondary analysis in general, but about his use of online sources in his own research, highlights the value of making available data to students who would not otherwise have the opportunity either to collect them or to engage in the theoretical discussions around their analysis.

Debates about the possibility, nature and purpose of secondary analysis are thrown into high relief in online contexts for a number of reasons. First, there is a set of issues about the actual practices of preparing, describing and archiving data in digital repositories – specifically, how to capture as much as possible of the original researchers' intentions and the nuances of the data collection process. Second, the concerns that critics of secondary analysis have are liable to be exacerbated when secondary analysis is carried out at a distance, by researchers who do not understand the original research context, or who use data selectively. On the other hand, well-documented and structured online resources have the potential to invite and encourage secondary analysis, support longitudinal and comparative research, and support research training and researcher development, opening up new opportunities for students of qualitative methods around the world who would otherwise have little opportunity to engage with classic studies, innovative methods and 'elusive populations'.

Case study: the Cambridge Conference Archive of Education Evaluations

The issues raised in the previous section – both with enabling reanalysis and supporting research methods training – informed the development of a digital archive of qualitative data collected during a series of influential educational evaluation studies.[2] This has been developed in association with the members of the 'Cambridge Conference on Evaluation', a network that has existed since 1972 (see MacDonald and Parlett, 1973). Most of the data in this largely qualitative archive were collected in the course of publicly funded evaluations in the UK, US, Australia, and Ireland and carried out by members of the Cambridge Conference between 1975 and 2005. The majority of these are case studies, although they vary widely in their nature and scope. The research outputs, instruments and data from the evaluations are, for the most part, in the public domain, and have been published or made available to the public in some form. However, many date from the period before widespread Internet use became commonplace (and so only a small proportion of the data were 'born digital'), and more widespread awareness and access has, for the most part, been through academic journal articles, limited print-runs of other publications by the evaluation team or commissioning bodies, and informal dissemination.

With the exception of a few examples (such as Stake's *The Art of Case Study Research* (1995), which presented substantive data collected in his case study of Harper School in the US within a highly discursive methodological account), publications have been necessarily selective in the data they have presented, alluding to the scope of the evaluations and discussing methodological issues and research processes rather than documenting them in full.

The initial design of an electronic archive representing these studies was informed by Stenhouse's (1978) vision of 'case data' being made available for secondary analysis across a wider research community, and the potential of emerging multimedia technology to address this (Walker, 2002). This process was assisted by the original participants in the projects, who provided contextual

information and guidance as to the roles and interrelationships of specific elements of the data. The evaluations were selected not simply on the grounds of being 'classics' (although some, such as Stake's Harper School study (1995) and the study of bilingual schooling in Boston in the early 1980s – published as *Bread and Dreams* (MacDonald *et al.*, 1982) – arguably have this status amongst education evaluations). Rather, the intention was to represent a broad range of educational evaluations with varied approaches, interpretational frameworks, and patterns of impact and dissemination. Although the archive as a whole can be seen as an historical collection, in that the studies document and reflect the evolution of educational policy, it also illustrates important and enduring issues, questions and dilemmas regarding the role and responsibilities of evaluators; ethical frameworks and informed consent; the purposes and conduct of evaluation; and the relationship of evaluation to the development of policy and practice. The original data are supplemented and placed in context by interpretative accounts and interviews with original participants in the evaluations, which are presented both as video excerpts and transcripts. Many of the documents in the archive illustrate the point made earlier regarding the conversion of paper archives – they are extensively edited and richly annotated, and as such it proved more appropriate to store these in the electronic archive as image files rather than to attempt optical character recognition or transcription in order to generate text documents.

The development of this particular archive represents a pragmatic response to the issue of subsequent users of the data not having participated in the original study and not having shared the epistemological standpoints of the original participants. The circumstances in which the original evaluations were carried out were frequently complex and, in many cases, innovative research approaches had been developed in order to 'do justice' to these complexities. By working with the original participants it was possible to construct collections of data, research instruments and other 'working documents' in order to represent this as fully as possible. Drafts of interpretative accounts and reports were included in the archive, along with final versions, as were terms of reference, plans and protocols, original fieldnotes, 'found' objects and documents, journals and minutes of meetings at which key decisions had been made. The attribution of significance to specific documents or data was an iterative process. On some occasions, the re-visitation of 'paper' archives of evaluations was a stimulus for the participants to provide reflexive and illuminative commentaries, while on others it was these commentaries and interviews that threw light on the reasons for specific items having been archived in the first place. This led to a shift in emphasis from a phase of archive development that was primarily descriptive (which the project team described as the 'what's in the box?' phase, in recognition of the fact that much of the archive content was in paper form and stored in boxes and box-files), to a phase that was more concerned with why things were 'in the box'.

The question of 'context' or rather, how best to document the various contexts relevant to the data, was gradually elaborated as the archive was developed. Conscious of the concern that the 'context' of data collection is confused with the original interpretative frameworks of the primary researchers (Parry and Mauthner, 2005: 340), the multiple meanings of 'context' were explored in some detail. As well as basic descriptive information, aspects of each evaluation that came to be represented included the political and policy contexts (at local, regional, national and international levels) in which the data were collected; the methodological context and interpretational frameworks; and issues such as different research approaches espoused and employed by members of teams of evaluators. Equally significant was the need to gain an understanding of the contexts in which data had been selected, organised and described as archives (paper

and electronic) and were constructed, reconstructed and repurposed. In some cases, original data had been through several phases of reorganisation, secondary analysis and incorporation into pedagogical applications, and so the selection of data and its incorporation into the new electronic archive represented merely the most recent in a sequence of such activities – the process of 'going online' was as context-laden as any other in the history of these project data.

Most of the secondary analysis opportunities for the archive have, at least initially, been predominantly 'pedagogical' and oriented towards providing students and early-career researchers and evaluators with opportunities to engage with methodological issues. This pattern highlights a final significant aspect of 'context', which we might call the 'context of reuse' and that is itself a product of increased availability of online resource alluded to at the end of the previous section.

In the course of a subsequent major research and development project, 'Ensemble: Semantic Web Technologies for the Enhancement of Case Based Learning', which ran from 2008–2012 (Carmichael, 2012; Martínez-García *et al.*, 2012) the archive was further developed using a range of web tools and approaches informed by 'Semantic Web' approaches (enhanced search facilities; the use of structured taxonomies of terms; and visualisation tools such as maps and timelines (described in detail in Carmichael, 2011). This new version of the archive was then used as the basis of a number of research capacity-building initiatives aimed at early career researchers in education. As both the archive and the semantic technologies were developing, these were seen as part of a participatory evaluation of their potential – what Boedker and Petersen (2000: 61–2) describe as 'learning-in-use … understanding and developing use … once a computer-based artefact has been taken over by users … [yielding] insight about the developmental aspects of use'. As well as providing useful 'user feedback' on the design of the digital archive itself, and confirming Corti and Bishop's (2005) assertions as to the peda-gogical opportunities offered by engaging in secondary analysis, what also emerged from interviews with participants was the increased confidence that they felt they had in using a wider range of data sources, presenting quali-tative data as elements of reports, and using what (to them) were unfamiliar and innova-tive methods. This was particularly evident in cases where they felt constrained by exist-ing reporting procedures, with one evalua-tor working on a government-funded project stating:

> We tried using the pro-forma documents … [but in our project] we wanted to tell stories and it just didn't seem to fit … the Buddy project [one of those in the Archive] … when we saw that, and it is taking on really complicated issues … but what does the work is *the story that gets told.*
> Carmichael, 2011: 333

What is evident in these accounts is the way in which appropriately designed online resources can allow researchers to engage in secondary analysis of richly contextualised qualitative data and make associations between the narra-tives of the original researchers and their own circumstances.

ELECTRONIC RESOURCES FOR SECONDARY ANALYSIS

The Cambridge Conference Archive was developed using a combination of estab-lished and emerging software, standards and network technologies. In doing so, it drew on practice and advice from a number of major data archives that have developed technolo-gies, archiving practices, ethical and access frameworks oriented towards archiving qual-itative data with the intention not only that it is preserved, but available for reuse. These include the UK Data Archive (UKDA),[3] the Council of European Social Science Data Archives (CESSDA)[4] and the Inter-university Consortium for Political and Social Research

(ICPSR).[5] Despite the valuable work carried out by these organisations, national-level infrastructures for qualitative archiving remain patchy in their coverage and in some cases are limited in their capacity. Medjedović (2011) highlights a continuing lack of national infrastructure and describes how set-ting up the 'Archive for Life Course Research' (ALLF) at the University of Bremen was in part a response to a lack of alternatives capa-ble of supporting the 'methodological and data-related conditions' required for second-ary analysis of qualitative sources.

In terms of the actual technologies required to enable secondary analysis, an enduring concern is how best to adequately describe data and represent the various elements of contextual information which may need to accompany them – and as the account of the development of the Cambridge Conference archive makes clear, this can be a complex task. This involves both provision of meta-data to describe documents or other data, participants, the circumstances of the data collection, and the broader research context in which this collection took place, and anno-tation within texts – even before any coding or memo writing takes place.

Most solutions, both proprietary and non-proprietary, make use of Extensible Markup Language (XML) as a basis for data descrip-tion and interchange, as well as a means of presenting data consistently across electronic applications and platforms. It allows the representation of the content and structure of data, while at the same time excluding formatting and styling. This makes it ideal for data exchange, and as such makes it an effective basis for both the representation of descriptive metadata and additional annota-tions within documents, as long as the latter are, themselves, structured as XML content. In the case of the Cambridge Conference archive, most of the archive's contents were scanned and digitised documents, and so the use of XML was limited to metadata records, with subsequent analysis at text level requir-ing the use of optical character recognition prior to computer-based analysis or a return to pencil-and-paper annotation.

XML is used in combination with metadata and document markup standards, which determine the structure of the documents and the vocabulary that can be used if interoperability and reuse is required. An example of a well-established and widely used XML standard with many applications is the Dublin Core Metadata Set,[6] which was originally designed to provide a straightforward means of generating human- and machine-readable bibliographical records (Heery, 1996). It can be embedded within the text of web pages and other resources, is used by publishers to disseminate details of publications and forms the basis of the metadata records used in a wide range of databases and electronic repositories. Dublin Core is often used to provide a minimum set of descriptors for documents, although these may be supplemented by descriptive elements drawn from other metadata sets and standards according to the nature of the data concerned. Even then, one of the challenges for data sharing and secondary analysis is that provision of 'lowest common denominator' descriptions can lead to a 'flattening' of complex data and loss of detail. There is a tension between ensuring that data are discoverable and can be used across systems (which tends to involve using widely used standards, vocabularies and formats) and adequate representation of the nuances of discipline-specific, theorised or local research practice.

In the context of development of data for secondary analysis, formatting text as XML does provide a way of representing not only descriptive metadata, but qualitative data itself. Textual data may be represented using minimal markup similar to that used for webpage authoring (XHTML, or Extensible Hypertext Markup Language), or can be structured using the much richer markup language developed by the Text Encoding Initiative (TEI),[7] which provides a repertoire of structural elements along with means of representing annotations, deletions and additions to

handwritten and typed texts in a consistent form. The TEI is concerned primarily with the electronic representation of written texts, other 'fine-grained' text markup systems allow the representation of variation in tone, pronunciation and conversational practices (such as interjections) and, where transcripts have been generated from video data, the intercalation of data describing movements, gestures and facial expressions.

These codings could also, of course, be related to interpretational frameworks and analytic categories, or could be used to provide extra contextual information to inform secondary analysis – that is, texts could be made available 'part-coded'. This goes much further than the well-established practice of sharing 'code books' alongside analyses, and obviously represents a significant expenditure of time and effort on the part of original researchers, as well as demanding XML-enabled Computer-Aided Qualitative Data Analysis Software (CAQDAS) applications to allow codings and annotations attached 'non-destructively' to texts.[8] Such an approach would probably be most likely to take place in the context of preparation of electronic resources with clear pedagogical purpose and audience, or of documents of wide interest and with a potentially large audience interested in secondary analysis.

For data other than texts (images, audio and video for example), a wide variety of metadata schemes allow the identification of elements or regions of images; time segments of audio; and multiple descriptive metadata 'streams' describing activity by different participants who are featured. Of these, those most appropriate as the basis of any strategy to promote secondary analysis are those that are non-destructive; the video editing, analysis and coding applications, for example, which typically store metadata separately from the original video data ('tagging' external to the data rather than 'captioning' within it) and thus allows 'cross-coding' and intercoder reliability checking; collaborative analysis; and, of course, primary and subsequent secondary analysis to proceed independently of each other.

At 'document level' the Dublin Core Metadata Element Set provides a core set of descriptive categories, although, as previously mentioned, these are often supplemented by locally developed and applied descriptors and vocabularies. Fulfilling a comparable role in describing people are metadata schemes such as FOAF or 'Friend of a Friend'.[9] FOAF allows individuals to be linked to what it describes as 'projects', but these are only loosely defined; more formal are research project description systems such as the Common European Research Interchange Format (CERIF),[10] development of which has been driven by demands for exchange of research information within and beyond the European Union. Cutting across all these levels is the Data Documentation Initiative (DDI),[11] which offers a multi-level description vocabulary including not only descriptions of the contents of documents, but also associated projects, methodologies, research instruments used to collect the data they contain and access restrictions applied to them (Blank and Rasmussen, 2004).

If XML is the basis for the representation of structured content, then Resource Definition Format (RDF) provides the means of representing the relationships between elements of that content, and as such is a key element of the emerging 'Semantic Web'. RDF offers a means of linking data (whether these be whole documents, fragments, annotations or details of authorship or attribution) in arbitrarily complex 'weblike' structures, which may be extended, revised and presented to users in a variety of different formats or viewed through different portals. RDF can, in comparison to other formats, appear verbose and complex, but this belies an underlying simplicity, which allows RDF-enabled resources to be shared, aggregated and incorporated into other resources – even if they originate from different sources.

RDF also allows the prospect of seamless integration of resources located in remote, networked repositories, on local servers, and individual users' 'client-side' data held on their own computers. Characteristically, RDF documents contain only metadata, expressed as 'triples' (for example, 'name-author-document' or 'document-published-date') allowing multiple metadata records to exist (perhaps authored by different individuals) all referring to a single online resource (such as a text) or element within it (such as a paragraph or utterance), without the need for destructive transformation of the original text. The separation of original documents from analyses, which themselves may be analysed, all within a common framework for data exchange, provides the basis for the development of collaborative annotation and analysis tools. Such frameworks would allow multiple researchers to develop parallel coding schemes or analyses of a shared online resource or set of resources. At the same time, this illustrates how the availability of online resources can contribute to blurring of the distinctions among primary analysis, secondary analysis and meta-analysis as data become 'extensible' and reusable beyond the boundaries of original cases.

Alongside these developments in data and document description has come the development of digital repositories, which allow the storage not only of data in multiple formats (texts, images, audio and video) but also the metadata records that accompany them and which may comprise large numbers of RDF statements ('triples') expressing all of the linkages between codes, annotations, memos and data fragments that might emerge in the course of qualitative analysis (which may, of course, involve multiple researchers working collaboratively). These digital repositories may also need to enact data security policies (allowing only selected individuals or groups to access confidential data) while at the same time exposing data and analyses to search engines and human users. Most work has been done in this respect by the developers of the Fedora Digital Repository[12] (Lagoze et al., 2006) and although a full description of the technical aspects of this system is beyond the scope of this chapter, some examples of how it can be configured with a view to data sharing and secondary analysis may prove useful.

The Cambridge Conference Archive described earlier was constructed using Fedora to store project data and metadata records, and was able to draw on these existing metadata records to construct a 'triple-store' – effectively, a single database of every relationship in the entire archive. This enabled the development of much more sophisticated search interfaces allowing users to ask questions of the form 'find me more examples like this' or 'what else has this person commented upon?' It was this that enabled visualisation tools to be incorporated into the archive allowing more intuitive and exploratory approaches by users. In another project, The University of Prince Edward Island's IslandArchives Project[13] stores a large collection of audio data relating to the history and cultural heritage of Prince Edward Island in Canada. In this case, the data are exposed via a virtual collaboration environment, which allows university researchers to curate and 'steward' data, build communities of enquiry and invite public participation in further projects.

Martínez-García and Corti (2012) describe another prototype Fedora-based digital archive designed to allow data collected from small-scale student and practitioner projects to be archived, curated, shared and reanalysed. A particular challenge for these types of projects is that they are difficult to aggregate or 'scale up', and it is difficult for subsequent practitioner-researchers to avoid 'reinventing the wheel' when they come to carry out their own enquiries. Martínez-García and Corti (2012: 278–279) describe how they combined a number of the technologies already described:

> Data [stored in Fedora] are described using the frameworks of the DDI, to document research instruments; Dublin Core, a popular metadata standard for bibliographical records; and QuDEx[14], a standard published by the UK Data Archive for representing complex qualitative collections (and the relationships between their associated resources) including annotated data … Finally, it uses the Exhibit Web Application Framework [a well-supported set of web visualisation tools][15] to allow searching, browsing and display of collection contents.

This allowed the construction of linked collections comprising (typically) a student report or dissertation, research instruments, multimedia content, interview transcripts, survey data and secondary sources such as policy documents on which they had drawn in their projects.

NEW DEVELOPMENTS AND DIRECTIONS

The technical frameworks, developments and examples described above have taken place against a rapidly changing technological, political and methodological backdrop. These developments have meant that secondary analysis of qualitative data now extends far beyond the idea of one researcher carefully reanalysing another's data. The ubiquity of personal technologies capable of gathering image, audio and video data means that the sheer volume of data online is increasing rapidly, and at the same time government drives towards transparency and accountability means that large-scale digitisation and data-sharing initiatives have allowed wider access to hitherto inaccessible research materials. In this concluding section, I will briefly discuss three areas of current interest: the emergence of 'linked', 'open' and 'big' data; opportunities for methodological innovation (and for some established methods to be revisited); and the implications of these developments for qualitative researchers.

LINKED, OPEN AND BIG DATA

The vision of the 'Semantic Web' that was first proposed in the early 2000s stressed seamless and, to the 'end user', invisible, interoperability, with web services and 'agents' (personalised search tools) using machine reasoning across a web of interconnected data (Berners-Lee *et al.*, 2001). This ambition has been tempered (partly in recognition of the challenges of making data available) and some Semantic Web activity has been reframed as building instead a 'Linked Web of Data' underpinned by use of common data formats, consistent metadata and permanent Internet addresses (Bizer *et al.*, 2009). For example, moves to offer 'open data' from government sources online[16] in order to extend and enhance a linked data cloud have encouraged discussion of opportunities for public engagement and new research possibilities. Although less ambitious than the broader vision of the Semantic Web, the idea of the linked web of data has lowered the bar to participation and to the realization of the benefits of a wide range of Semantic Web technologies. In research settings this has enabled a more pragmatic adoption of Semantic Web technologies with the potential to enhance existing systems and applications including some of those described in this chapter.

The terms 'linked' and 'open' data are often used interchangeably – but it is important to recognise that not all linked data are 'open' (linked data approaches may be used within access controlled data networks) and many 'open' government documents are in proprietary and sometime non-machine readable formats (precluding their easy 'linking'). For the qualitative researcher interested in secondary analysis, the latter can of course prove useful sources, but their use will involve different strategies to those possible with wholly digital data sources, and technological tools may be of limited use. Also sometimes conflated with open and linked data is the notion of 'big' data – the vast volumes of data 'born digital' through Internet-enabled communication, information exchange and surveillance, and in some cases available for public access, again typically through 'open'

government data hubs. Gurin (2014) offers an interesting analysis of the relationships between these sometimes technological, but more often rhetorical, claims to openness, linkage and scale, pointing out that much 'big data' is anything but 'open' (and in fact is a fiercely guarded commodity) and that many 'open government' initiatives are highly selective in the data that is actually released. In many cases, it is the disciplinary communities – mainly in the sciences and medicine – that (as already mentioned) have traditions of data sharing and who have made the most rapid progress in using 'big data' approaches in support of their research activities.

For the qualitative researcher, these developments may seem to be of little relevance because Government Data Hubs and other similar online sources seem dominated by large statistical datasets. The UK Data Hub's education collection, for example, seems largely comprised of government 'Statistical Releases' (of enrolments, attendance, exclusions, assessment outcomes, and social and economic indicators, and so on) from national to local level, but it is also a rich source of policy documents, reports and evaluations. Such hubs represent important elements of the 'linked web of data' and exemplify standards and expectations of formats, standards and data quality, as well as giving useful insights into the mindsets of policymakers. 'Big data' initiatives, which at first glance seem very far from the interests and concerns of qualitative researchers, provide not only a context and comparator for qualitative research, but may also provide the technological frameworks and approaches that will allow the primary and secondary analysis of extensive 'big qualitative' data – not only of texts but also of the volumes of multimedia data that are now being produced by researchers and research participants and subjects as part of 'life-streaming', digital ethnography, and oral history and community memory projects. These topics are covered in other chapters in this Handbook, but it is worth those researchers who plan to use these methods to consider the implications of their methodological choices for subsequent data management, archiving and, potentially, for subsequent secondary analysis.

METHODOLOGICAL INNOVATION

The second reason that many developments in online technologies are relevant to secondary qualitative analysis is the new patterns of collaboration and novel research relationships that digital networks, virtual collaboration environments and shared digital repositories enable. As research funders increasingly expect to see distributed, international and multidisciplinary research teams bringing together those with distinctive expertise, the likelihood of research data being collaboratively analysed across research teams, either contemporaneously or as part of a sequential research design, increases. In these kinds of research environments, the distinction between primary and secondary analysis that we have already discussed becomes even more blurred.

This means that even within the lifetime of a single research project, data may be generated, analysed, deposited in a shared online environment of some kind (usually accompanied by some descriptive metadata) and then retrieved and analysed again by other members of the research team, who may be located in another location entirely. As described by Laterza *et al.*, (2007) in a study of such research teams as part of a research and development project into virtual research environments, online technologies and the research practices that they enable are co-constituted. Research practice evolves alongside technologies, and a contested notion such as 'secondary analysis' is particularly malleable and subject to changes brought about by the emergence of new technological opportunities.

A good example of this is the resurgence of interest in Grounded Theory, a distinctive approach to qualitative enquiry that characteristically involves close engagement with data, *in vivo* coding and the careful development of codes and categories that are authentic to research participants, rather than being overlain by the researchers' preconceptions and biases. It has proved particularly effective in studies where practice and experiences are poorly understood and undertheorised, for example paramedical staff, care workers and those in emergent and inter-professional settings.

Much contemporary Grounded Theory is informed by the work of Charmaz, who has argued for the use of Grounded Theory approaches within broader research designs informed by social constructivism and reflective practice (Charmaz, 2014), and it is here that the links with archiving and secondary analysis become apparent. From its inception, there has been nothing to prevent Grounded Theory being used by groups of researchers, or for researchers to critically interrogate the conduct of others' enquiries (Corbin and Strauss, 1990: 422). Weiner (2010), drawing on Charmaz's ideas, has described how Grounded Theory can be effectively practiced within 'loose research designs' including those in which teams are separated by time and space, include visitors and where initial analysis by one team member formed the focus for discussion and reanalysis by others. Charmaz (2014) also argues that although the vast majority of Grounded Theory studies have been based on interviews and participant observation, its approaches may be applied to extant sources and literature, policy documents and the work of other researchers.

There are clearly opportunities for the technologies described here to enable distributed, secondary analysis within Grounded Theory approaches, and it is notable that the work of Long-Sutehall *et al.* (2010) on secondary analysis of 'elusive populations' as part of the 'Timescapes' programme, and which was mentioned earlier in this chapter, does indeed use a collaborative Grounded

Theory framework informed by Charmaz's approach. This kind of productive interaction and reworking of research approaches does not have to be restricted to Grounded Theory or to any particular kind of data – there are many opportunities for researchers to explore which different methodological approaches, established or emergent, can be enabled by the use of well-structured original data and metadata, and supported and mediated through well-designed digital environments.

THE CHANGING ROLE OF THE RESEARCHER

What is without doubt is that since the first edition of this Handbook, several of the technologies that were at that time emergent, have become much more widely established and the 'technology stack' available to researchers in support of secondary analysis of qualitative data is more extensive and robust. Martínez-García and Corti's (2012) example demonstrates this well when compared with projects from a decade earlier, with their model of student research projects building on underpinning 'layers': QuDEX, RDF, XML and Dublin Core metadata.

It is also clear from even a cursory glance at recent research literature that many scholars who identify themselves as qualitative researchers have been exploring the use of online methods; engaging with data management issues and data archiving; and taking advantage of the range of existing data and other resources that are now online. At the same time, there is a new expectation on the part of the funders and evaluators of research that researchers will have, if not a full range of technological competences, an awareness of how best to increase the reach and impact of their work through careful data preparation, archiving, publication and support for subsequent research – in short, not only to take part in secondary analysis of data, but to enable it

as well. In the UK, the expectation from the main research funders is that data emerging from publicly funded research will be made available as a 'public good', and although this might currently involve primarily quantitative data, the requirements do not distinguish between the methods used or the nature of the data generated (Engineering and Physical Sciences Research Council, 2011; Research Councils UK, 2015). Similar expectations are built into the European Union 'Horizon 2020' programme within which an 'Open Data Pilot' (European Commission, 2013) demands that funded research projects have a data management policy that will actively enable data sharing and reuse.

Against this background, the potential for secondary analysis of online qualitative data, supported by methodological innovation, combined with data sharing and open data initiatives and enabled by the ongoing development of digital archive technologies, is considerable. What it depends upon, however, is a continuing dialogue between technologists designing online environments, the authorities responsible for interoperability standards and researchers willing and able to articulate their practices, concerns and commitments.

ACKNOWLEDGEMENTS

The author would like to acknowledge the contributions of the members of the Cambridge Conference on Evaluation and the associated ESRC project 'Representing Context in an Archive of Educational Evaluations' and the team of the Economic and Social Research Council–Engineering and Physical Sciences Research Council research project 'Ensemble: Semantic Technologies for the Enhancement of Case Based Learning', particularly Agustina Martínez-García and Louise Corti. I am also grateful to Christina Carmichael for her insights into Grounded Theory.

NOTES

1 http://www.talkbank.org/
(Accessed 1 August 2016).
2 The archive is online and publicly accessible at http://www.evaluating-education.org.uk (Accessed 19 October 2016).
3 http://www.data-archive.ac.uk/
(Accessed 1 August 2016).
4 http://www.nsd.uib.no/cessda/
(Accessed 1 August 2016).
5 http://www.icpsr.umich.edu/
(Accessed 1 August 2016).
6 http://www.dublincore.org/
(Accessed 1 August 2016).
7 http://www.tei-c.org/ (Accessed 1 August 2016).
8 The idea of non-destructive transformation of texts is important in CAQDAS applications in which multiple codings are attached to a single text – for example, during cross-coder reliability checking. In order to compare patterns of analysis, the 'original' text must remain unchanged by coding or annotation – so the analysis remains external to the text. This contrasts with the editing paradigm of most 'wiki' applications, for example, where multiple authors can alter the text itself (see Silver and Bulloch, this volume).
9 http://www.foaf-project.org
(Accessed 1 August 2016).
10 http://www.eurocris.org/cerif/
(Accessed 1 August 2016).
11 http://www.ddialliance.org/
(Accessed 1 August 2016).
12 http://fedorarepository.org/
(Accessed 1 August 2016).
13 http://islandarchives.ca/ivoices
(Accessed 1 August 2016).
14 http://data-archive.ac.uk/create-manage/projects/qudex (Accessed 1 August 2016).
15 http://www.simile-widgets.org/
(Accessed 1 August 2016).
16 For example, the US Government data hub at http://www.data.gov and the UK data hub at http://data.gov.uk (Accessed 1 August 2016).

REFERENCES

Berners-Lee, T., Hendler, J. and Lassila, O. (2001) 'The Semantic Web', *Scientific American*, 284(5): 34–43.
Bishop, L. (2007) 'A reflexive account of reusing qualitative data: beyond primary-secondary dualism', *Sociological Research Online*, 12(3). Available at: http://www.socresonline.org.uk/12/3/2.html (Accessed 1 August 2016).
Bishop, L. (2009) 'Ethical sharing and reuse of qualitative data', *Australian Journal of Social Issues*, 44(3): 255–72.
Bizer, C., Heath, T. and Berners-Lee, T. (2009) 'Linked data – the story so far', *International Journal of Semantic Web and Information Systems*, 5(3): 1–22.
Blank, G. and Rasmussen, K. (2004) 'The Data Documentation Initiative: the value and significance of a worldwide standard', *Social Science Computer Review*, 22(3): 307–18.
Boedker, S. and Petersen, M. (2000) 'Design for learning in use', *Scandinavian Journal of Information Systems*, 12: 61–80.
Carmichael, P. (2011) 'Research capacity building in education: the role of digital archives', *British Journal of Educational Studies*, 59(3): 323–39.
Carmichael, P. (2012) *Ensemble: Semantic Technologies for the Enhancement of Case Based Learning ESRC End of Award Report RES-139-25-0403-A*. Swindon, UK: Economic and Social Research Council.
Charmaz, K. (2014) *Constructing Grounded Theory*. London: Sage Publications.
Corbin, J. and Strauss, A. (1990) 'Grounded theory research: procedures, canons and evaluative criteria', *Zeitschrift fur Soziologie*, 19(6): 418–27.
Corti, L. and Bishop, L. (2005) 'Strategies in teaching secondary analysis of qualitative data', *Forum Qualitative Sozialforschung/ Forum: Qualitative Social Research*, 6(1). Available at: http://nbn-resolving.de/urn:nbn:de:0114-fqs0501470 (Accessed 1 August 2016).
Engineering and Physical Sciences Research Council (EPRSC) (2011) EPSRC Policy framework on Research Data. Available at: http://www.epsrc.ac.uk/about/standards/researchdata/ (Accessed 1 August 2016).
European Commission (2013) *Guidelines on Data Management in Horizon 2020*. Available at: http://ec.europa.eu/research/participants/data/ref/h2020/grants_manual/hi/oa_pilot/h2020-hi-oa-data-mgt_en.pdf (Accessed 1 August 2016).
Fayyad, U. and Uthurusamy, R. (2002) 'Evolving data into mining solutions for insights', *Communications of the ACM*, 45(8): 28–31.

Fielding, N. (2004) 'Getting the most from archived qualitative data: epistemological, practical and professional obstacles', *International Journal of Social Research Methodology*, 7 (1): 97–104.

Fielding, N. and Fielding, J.L. (2000) 'Resistance and adaptation to criminal identity: using secondary analysis to evaluate classic studies of crime and deviance', *Sociology*, 34 (4): 671–89.

Gurin, J. (2014) 'Big data and open data: what's what and why does it matter?' *The Guardian,* 15 April. Available at: http://www. theguardian.com/public-leaders-network/2014/apr/15/big-data-open-data-transform-government (Accessed 1 August 2016).

Hammersley, M. (1997) 'Qualitative data archiving: some reflections on its prospects and problems', *Sociology*, 31(1): 131–42.

Heaton, J. (1998) 'Social research update 22: secondary analysis of qualitative data'. Technical report, University of Surrey Department of Sociology. Available at: http://sru.soc.surrey. ac.uk/SRU22.html (Accessed 1 August 2016).

Heaton, J. (2004) *Reworking Qualitative Data*. London: Sage Publications.

Heaton, J. (2008) 'Secondary analysis of qualitative data: an overview', *Historical Social Research/Historische Sozialforschung*, 33(3): 33–45.

Heery, R.M. (1996) 'Review of metadata formats: iafa/whois++, marc, text encoding initiative, Dublin core, uniform resource characteristics', *Program*, 30(4): 345–73.

Holland, J. (2011) 'Timescapes: living a qualitative longitudinal study', *Forum Qualitative Sozialforschung/Forum: Qualitative Social Research*, 12(3). Available at: http://nbn-resolving.de/urn:nbn:de:0114-fqs110392 (Accessed 1 August 2016).

Irwin, S. and Winterton, M. (2011) *'Debates in qualitative secondary analysis: critical reflections. A Timescapes Working Paper Series 4'*. Available at: http://www. timescapes.leeds.ac.uk/assets/files/WP4-March-2011.pdf (Accessed 1 August 2016).

Irwin, S. and Winterton, M. (2012) 'Qualitative secondary analysis and social explanation', *Sociological Research Online*, 17(2): 4. Available at: http://www.socresonline.org. uk/17/2/4.html (Accessed 1 August 2016).

Lagoze, C., Payette, S., Shin, E. and Wilper, C. (2006) Fedora: an architecture for complex objects and their relationships. *International Journal on Digital Libraries*, 6: 124–38.

Laterza, V., Carmichael, P. and Procter, R. (2007) 'The doubtful guest? A virtual research environment for education', *Technology, Pedagogy and Education*, 16(3): 249–67.

Long-Sutehall, T., Sque, M. and Addington-Hall, J. (2010) 'Secondary analysis of qualitative data: a valuable method for exploring sensitive issues with an elusive population?', *Journal of Research in Nursing*, 16(4): 335–44.

MacDonald, B. and Parlett, M. (1973) 'Rethinking evaluation: notes from the Cambridge Conference', *Cambridge Journal of Education*, 3(2): 74–82.

MacDonald, B., Adelman, C., Kushner, S. and Walker, R. (1982) *Bread and Dreams – A Case Study of Bilingual Schooling in the USA*. Norwich, UK: Centre for Applied Research in Education, University of East Anglia.

MacWhinney, B. (2000a) *The CHILDES Project: Tools for Analyzing Talk, Volume 1: Transcription Format and Programs*. 3rd edn. Mahwah, NJ: Lawrence Erlbaum.

MacWhinney, B. (2000b) *The CHILDES Project: Tools for Analyzing Talk, Volume 2: The Database*. 3rd edn. Mahwah, NJ: Lawrence Erlbaum.

Martínez-García, A. and Corti, L. (2012) 'Supporting student research with semantic technologies and digital archives', *Technology, Pedagogy and Education*, 21(2): 273–88.

Martínez-García, A., Morris, S., Tracy, F., Tscholl, M. and Carmichael, P. (2012) 'Case based learning, pedagogical innovation and semantic web technologies', *IEEE Transactions on Learning Technologies*, 5(2): 104–13.

Mauthner, N., Parry, O. and Milburn, K. (1998) 'The data are out there, or are they? Implications for archiving qualitative data', *Sociology*, 32(4): 733–45.

Medjedović, I. (2011) 'Secondary analysis of qualitative interview data: objections and experiences: results of a German feasibility study', *Forum Qualitative Sozialforschung/ Forum: Qualitative Social Research*, 12(3). Available at: http://nbn-resolving.de/ urn:nbn:de:0114-fqs1103104 (Accessed 1 August 2016).

Parry, O. and Mauthner, N. (2005) 'Back to basics: who reuses qualitative data and why?', *Sociology*, 39(2): 337–42.

Research Councils UK (RCUK) (2015) RCUK Common Principles on Data Policy. Available at: http://www.rcuk.ac.uk/research/datapolicy/ (Accessed 1 August 2016).

Savage, M. (2005) 'Revisiting classic qualitative studies', *Forum Qualitative Sozialforschung/ Forum: Qualitative Social Research*, 6(1). Available at: http://nbn-resolving.de/ urn:nbn:de:0114-fqs0501312 (Accessed 1 August 2016).

Seale, C. (2011) 'Secondary analysis of qualitative data'. In D. Silverman (ed.), *Qualitative Research*. 3rd edn. London: Sage Publications, pp. 347–64.

Stake, R. (1995) *The Art of Case Study Research*. Thousand Oaks, CA: Sage Publications.

Stenhouse, L. (1978) 'Case study and case record: towards a contemporary history of education', *British Education Research Journal*, 4(2): 21–39.

Szabo, V. and Strang, V.R. (1997) 'Secondary analysis of qualitative data', *Advances in Nursing Science*, 20(2): 66–74.

Thompson, P. (2000) 'Re-using qualitative research data: a personal account', *Forum Qualitative Sozialforschung/Forum: Qualitative Social Research*, 1(3). Available at: http://nbn-resolving.de/urn:nbn:de:0114-fqs0003277 (Accessed 1 August 2016).

Walker, R. (2002) 'Case study, case records and multimedia', *Cambridge Journal of Education*, 32(1): 109–27.

Walkerdine, V. (1988) *The Mastery of Reason: Cognitive Development and the Production of Rationality*. London: Routledge.

Weiner, C. (2010) 'Making teams work in grounded theory'. In A. Bryant and K. Charmaz (eds.), *The SAGE Handbook of Grounded Theory*. London: Sage Publications, pp. 293–310.

## 30

Finding and Investigating Geographical Data Online

David Martin, Samantha Cockings and Samuel Leung

INTRODUCTION

Geographical location is a unique and important aspect of many social phenomena, and is implicitly or explicitly recorded in much social data. The uses of geographical location in research can be essentially divided between data linkage and spatial analysis. Geographical location provides a key mechanism for social scientists to link data between sources when relationships are not explicit in the observed (or observable) data and include, for example, the association between individuals and geographical areas. Geographical locations of some type are increasingly included in routine data collection. Knowledge of an area can provide us with information on service delivery, community and neighbourhood characteristics, or explicitly geographical information such as accessibility measures. Common examples include health service catchment areas, demographic and social profiles and lengths of journey to work. This type of information can be of importance both in secondary analysis when

there is a need to link between, for example, published surveys and census information, and in primary research when the researcher's own questionnaire or interview data need to be set in the context of previously published data.

Spatial analysis encompasses a wide range of methods for the identification and interpretation of patterns and relationships in geographical data, beginning with simple mapping and extending to many sophisticated spatial analysis methods which are beyond the scope of this chapter. A key feature of geographical data is that it is mappable, and it is for this reason that it has generally been collected and displayed in cartographic form. The advent of the computer handling of geographical information, and particularly the emergence of software known as 'geographical information systems' (GIS), made much more explicit the separation between the underlying geographical data and its visual representation. The widespread use of geographical data on the Internet reflects this distinction and it is possible to obtain both geographical information, which is not explicitly mapped (for example, encyclopaedia entries with associated latitude and longitude coordinates), and maps or images, which convey spatial information graphically but without associated coordinate data. Aerial photographs, for example, convey visually recognisable geographical patterns in a landscape, but do not contain any formally structured data about features or objects such as towns or roads. The extraction of these features requires complex specialist processing. It is worth noting that GIS are very important to the professional mapping and analysis of geographical data, but are covered extensively in dedicated textbooks and cannot be treated here in depth (for guidance, see, for example, Burrough and McDonnell, 1998; DeMers, 2008; Heywood *et al.*, 2011; Longley *et al.*, 2015). In GIS software and literature an important distinction is made between coordinate-based (vector) data and pixel-based (raster) data. This has implications for the display and analysis of geographical data online and will be discussed further later.

Longley *et al.* (2005) argue that there are several grounds on which spatial data have 'special' characteristics, specifically a recognition that nearby geographical phenomena show stronger relationships than distant ones, that conditions in one location are different from those elsewhere and that different layers of geographical information tend to be highly correlated. An extensive case for the benefits brought to the social sciences through geographical approaches is presented by Goodchild and Janelle (2004). Rana and Joliveau (2009) explore the emergence of the term 'NeoGeography', referring to the widespread embedding of geographical information through a very broad range of technologies and practices. Regardless of the exact terminology used, it is clear that we are in a period of rapid expansion of geographical data online, which is being used in ever-novel ways. Most recently, we can see that geographical location is an important dimension of many emergent forms of 'Big Data' (Kitchin, 2013), such as geolocated social media posts, household energy records from smart meters and mobile

telephone records. A sound understanding of geographical referencing underpins the ability to properly conduct more advanced methodologies such as multilevel modelling (Kreft and de Leeuw, 1998), geographically weighted regression (Fotheringham *et al.*, 2002) and statistical methods for the integration of many individual and aggregate datasets (for example, Mitchell *et al.*, 1998; Williamson *et al.*, 1998). Brunsdon and Singleton (2015) and Fotheringham and Rogerson (2009) provide excellent overviews of more advanced spatial analysis methods.

Social science researchers frequently face geographical referencing challenges, from the simplest data linkage to the implementation of advanced statistical and computational models. Although more advanced methods often require the use of specialist software, finding and investigating geographical data online can make a substantial contribution to the research process and it is not necessary to be an expert in order to effectively employ the simpler forms of mapping and spatial analysis. Best practice in this area requires an understanding of the principles involved and the ability to locate and evaluate the most appropriate datasets and methods.

The remainder of this chapter is organized as follows. The next section introduces some key concepts in the geographical referencing of social science objects and analysis. We then move on to a review of the representation of these objects as geographical data. Two major sections address online sources of geographical data and online tools for geographical data analysis. The chapter concludes with general recommendations about how to proceed and some of the key developments to look out for.

GEOREFERENCING SOCIAL SCIENCE OBJECTS

The social sciences deal with many objects of study, including individuals, families, households, jobs, events, organisations, journeys and networks. It is entirely possible to meaningfully study these phenomena aspatially – for example, examining the relationships between individuals within a household, or studying unemployment rates by age group – without any regard for their geographical location. There is also a long tradition of describing geographical patterns with 'global' statistics, in the form of single statistical values which describe entire distributions in terms of metrics such as clustering, dispersion, spatial correlation, etc. However, it is important to recognize that each of these phenomena is geographically situated: it has a spatial location. If we are able to record these locations, then it becomes possible to undertake explicitly spatial analyses (for example, to explore the way in which family structure varies in different neighbourhoods), to produce 'local' statistics of geographical associations (Anselin, 1995) and to use location as a means of linking otherwise disconnected data (for example, to identify the local unemployment rate at the place of residence of each survey respondent). We refer to this addition of locational references to otherwise aspatial information as geographical referencing or georeferencing. The spatial nature of social science phenomena opens up potential avenues for research that are not possible if they are treated aspatially, but it is necessary to understand the ways in which social science objects of study may be associated with spatial locations. The social sciences differ in important ways from the physical sciences, where the spatial coordinates of the object of study, such as a coastline, can be directly surveyed. In the social sciences, phenomena such as people, neighbourhoods or flows are often more difficult to define clearly, and also tend to be mobile. This makes the provision of explicit and unambiguous spatial coordinates more challenging.

The increasing use of smart devices is gradually shifting the balance towards direct capture of locations in social data, an issue explored in greater detail later, but geographical referencing in the social sciences is still largely indirect by reference to some intermediate geography such as an address, postal code or administrative area (Martin, 2005). This is especially true in the case of official and administrative data sources. We now outline five categories of indirect geographical referencing widely used in the social sciences.

The first category relates to individual addresses. These include the residential or work addresses of survey respondents, the addresses of workplaces or other organisations and the addresses of locations at which events take place – for example, shops and hospitals where services are delivered. Postal addresses, such as '#440 Main Street, Eastville, AR 72205', are widely used in common language and it is generally possible to assign locations in the form of spatial coordinates (such as latitude and longitude or a map reference), either directly or by matching via postal/zip codes to published directories of locations.

A second major category of geographical references relates to areas. These may be areas used for administrative, electoral or statistical purposes, such as 'County of Wiltshire'. Sometimes these areas are used because no more precise location is known, but more often because data at the individual level have been deliberately aggregated in order to preserve the confidentiality of census or survey respondents. A particular challenge with areal unit names is that their use in common language may not correspond exactly with their formal definition in administrative or statistical terms. Thus 'Paris' may be used to refer to a built-up area, a collection of administrative divisions, the area within an orbital highway or an ill-defined urban area associated with particular landmarks. These may all be of interest to an urban sociologist, although some will be more meaningful than others in terms of the lives of Parisians. Geographical areas are formally defined by a descriptor (a textual name or alphanumerical code, such as 'Wisconsin' or 'E00117689') and a set of boundary locations, or some-times simply a centroid location, represent-ing a central point within the area. A special feature of area-based socio-economic data is known as the modifiable areal unit problem (Openshaw, 1984). This identifies the fact that the values of variables aggregated over geographical areas (for example, unemploy-ment rates) are dependent on both the scale and aggregation of the area boundaries. Thus, if we were to redraw the boundaries to make larger or smaller zones, or simply to recon-figure the boundaries at the same level of aggregation, we would produce differences in the observed values. Areally aggregated data are also ecological data, and relation-ships observed between variables at one level of aggregation would not necessarily hold at other levels. Although widely used, area data should therefore be interpreted with caution.

A third category of phenomena is those that are best described as linear features connect-ing two or more locations, for example roads and paths, journeys to work or migration routes. More subtle examples include flows of commodities, or communications links such as telephone calls. In common language these phenomena may be given identifiers such as 'the X7 bus route', or may be defined only by their start and end points, such as a pair of home and work addresses.

Many social science phenomena do not fit neatly into these three categories because they take place at spatial locations that are not readily described by indirect referenc-ing systems such as addresses or areas, for example a theft from a car parked beside a lake. This event may be one of a series of objects of criminological study that dis-play interesting geographical patterns, but which cannot be described except by com-plex textual description and for which it is not usually possible to identify specific grid references after the event. Other examples might include road accidents or environmen-tal quality. In the latter case, neighbourhoods will display different aesthetic characteristics potentially affecting quality of life, but these characteristics cannot easily be assigned exact spatial coordinates.

A further category of phenomena to which it can be challenging to assign appropriate spatial locations is those which have multiple (or mobile) locations or can be recognized at multiple geographical scales. For exam-ple, the identity of a major retail chain and location of its registered office will not be an appropriate spatial reference for the place of employment of its many employees who work in local branches or routinely travel between sites. In these special cases, the most appropriate spatial location to be cap-tured will depend on the specific purpose for which the researcher needs the information – the employment researcher and the business analyst may decide to treat this information in quite different ways.

THE REPRESENTATION OF GEOGRAPHICAL DATA

Geographical data are created when loca-tions are recorded alongside non-locational attributes or observations, for example when a postcode or street address is added to a survey response. In the social sciences, these have long been derived indirectly from loca-tions originally captured by the surveying activities of national mapping agencies. Relevant data may also be derived from vari-ous forms of remote sensing (Campbell and Wynne, 2011; Lillesand et al., 2015), includ-ing image-type data being captured by satel-lite observation or aerial photography and the digitisation of historical maps. Newer forms of data are being generated with locations already attached at the point of capture (sometimes termed 'geotagging') by loca-tionally aware devices such as mobile phones and cameras which variously interact with the Global Positioning System (GPS) (Spencer et al., 2003), mobile phone trans-mitters and WiFi hotspots, all of which can be used to assign geographical coordinates to digital objects such as conversations and photographs. Social media posts, such as Tweets, may be geo-located in this way by the devices on which they are created, or may be associated with references to geographical names selected by the user, such as when a Facebook user checks-in to a specific location. Whether or not these mechanisms are used is dependent on the preferences of the contributor, which has implications for data coverage and bias, discussed later in the chapter. Most social science applications rely on geographical locations which have already been recorded for other purposes, for example by relating individuals to addresses or postal codes where the address locations are derived from national mapping databases or similar sources.

All geographical data are affected by considerations of generalisation, scale, projection, accuracy and precision. Although these are most commonly associated with cartographic representation, they are equally critical to geographical information obtained or used online. There is a somewhat separate field of study which relates to the preparation and presentation of high-quality cartography for online presentation, but that is not the principal focus of this chapter. Readers wishing to pursue online cartography in more detail should consult, for example, Kraak and Brown (2001) and also Zook *et al.*, this volume. Basic cartographic considerations strongly influence the appropriateness of geographical data for specific purposes, as well as the degree of confidence which the user can have in the results. Our aim here is not to provide extensive reference information on these complex issues, which are well covered in the cartographic literature (see, for example, Robinson *et al.*, 1995; Monmonier, 1996), but rather to assist the social scientist in understanding the range of issues that they should be aware of when using online geographical data. As with all secondary data analysis, the user must pay particular attention to those aspects of data collection and structure which reflect the original creator's

conceptualisations and intentions, but which may have unintended consequences for the secondary use.

A map is a graphical representation of selected features from the 'real' world. Since most people are familiar with maps, we will discuss such cartographic issues through the use of examples based around maps before identifying some of the specific characteristics of social science data in this context. First, features that are considered of relevance to one map will be omitted from others – for example, a subway route map does not contain many (if any) above-ground features such as streets or landmarks, whereas these may be the only elements of a sketch map for finding a restaurant. This selectivity of geographical information is relevant to the use of all mappable data found online – we need to be aware that the creator of the data may have had very different inclusion criteria from ourselves and we need to consider the impact that this could have on our own use of the map or data. Further, features may be represented in different levels of detail on different maps. For example, a minor road shown in great detail on a local map may be shown as a straight line or omitted completely from a national road atlas; a further example would be the practice of showing a city as a single symbol in an atlas, but as a shaded area in a regional map. These examples might affect the calculation of distances, for example when assessing the accessibility of services, or the classification of specific places as 'urban' or 'rural'. These conventional and necessary cartographic practices of selectively including or simplifying features are broadly known as 'generalisation', closely related to the concept of 'map scale', which is perhaps of most importance when entire features have been omitted, of which the user may be unaware.

A sketch map may have a notional scale, but positions and distances may be entirely approximate. Most professionally produced maps will have a specified scale, whereby there will be a fixed and known relationship

(a) 1:25,000 (or 1/25,000)

(b) One centimetre to two hundred and fifty metres

(c) 0   5km

Figure 30.1   Alternative representations of map scale

between distances on the map and those in the real world. The scale of a map may be presented as a representative fraction, textual description or scale bar, as illustrated in Figure 30.1(a)–(c). When viewing maps via online mapping software, it is especially important to recognize that map scale must be treated with extreme caution: the apparent scale of the map will be affected by basic parameters such as the width of the user's screen. If scales such as '1:25,000' or '4 cm to 1 km' are shown on the screen, it is most important to determine whether these relate to the image being viewed or to the original source. These considerations are especially relevant when dealing with scanned (raster) map images, whereby zooming to a larger scale map on the screen may represent nothing more than redrawing the same image with no change to the detail included. It is most helpful when a scale bar, such as that shown in Figure 30.1(c), or a rectangular grid of known size (e.g. 1 km) is integral to the map because these will be rescaled in constant proportion to the map itself.

Closely related to these considerations is the issue of map projection (Iliffe, 2008). Maps of areas on the surface of the earth, whether on paper or computer screen, suffer the inconvenience that the earth's surface is curved while the map is flat. It is therefore impossible to represent the scale and relative positions of features without some distortion. These issues cannot be ignored for social science applications, even if the exact locations of topographic (physical) features are

considered to be of subsidiary importance. The way that the curved surface is projected onto the flat image is termed the 'projection', and numerous variations exist. There is unfortunately no single map projection that is suitable for mapping the entire world. The choice of projection depends on the location and shape of the mapped region, as well as on the intended purpose of the outputs. A social science user may find themselves needing to combine data referenced to different projections and coordinate systems, for example social media posts collected using GPS technology embedded in a locationally aware device and referenced to a global system in latitude and longitude, with official statistics published for administrative areas such as London Boroughs or counties in the US, mapped and referenced using a national or state grid system (Ordnance Survey, 2008). In these situations, GIS software provides functions for the re-projection of geographical data, but this type of processing facility is not usually available online. It is also important to bear in mind that no matter how sophisticated GIS may appear, data manipulation can never put back geographical details that were not part of the original data collection.

Data quality assessment is an essential prerequisite to any form of geographical linkage or analysis. Geographical data are often assessed by their accuracy and precision. Although the two concepts are quite similar and even interchangeable in common language, they have very different technical definitions and should be considered separately. Figure 30.2 illustrates the geographical referencing of an address within an area of housing. Accuracy is a measure of the truthfulness of the data in relation to reality, whereas precision is concerned with the consistency of data capture and recording. The latter is normally constrained by the resolution or level of detail of the data capture system, whereas the former is affected by the choice of tools and methods and also by human error and environmental factors. For instance, correctly describing the location of a survey

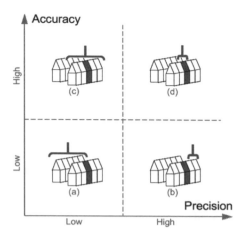

Figure 30.2   Four scenarios to illustrate the effects of accuracy and precision in address referencing. The bracket represents the geographical reference, while the shaded house is the true location of the referenced address.

respondent as being in the 'Mount Pleasant' neighbourhood is free from geographical bias and is thus an accurate spatial description (instance (c) in Figure 30.2). By contrast, describing the respondent's location as '57 Highfield Lane' is a much more precise locational description, but may be inaccurate – for example if the respondent actually lives at '55 Highfield Lane' (instance (b) in Figure 30.2). A survey response geographically coded with 'Mount Pleasant' will be correctly matched to other records for Mount Pleasant, while the '57 Highfield Lane' address may fail to match with other records relating to the same respondent. The figure also illustrates alternatives whereby the address is imprecise and inaccurate (a), or precise and accurate (d). Address matching is a well-recognized data linkage problem in the domain of censuses and surveys and can contribute significantly to under-enumeration. In order to improve or maintain data quality, geographical information users must always assess and prepare to adopt different strategies according to their intended application.

A further aspect of geographical data quality is coverage. We would expect formally surveyed data such as that provided by a national mapping agency to be complete, in the sense that (subject to the timeliness of updates) all towns, roads and buildings should be shown if they are within the scope of the survey and to conform to published quality standards. However, the mapping of a flu epidemic reported to a health service or attendance at a major sports event reported through social media are subject to numerous potential sources of undercoverage and bias. Not all patients will visit a doctor and not all crowd members will post about the event, and so we cannot be confident that any resulting map will be complete. Unlike formal sources, we do not have information about the sampling frame or data quality. Furthermore, the sources of missingness will themselves not be randomly distributed through the population or over space. Adults with influenza who are otherwise healthy are less likely to consult their doctor than those who are elderly; sports fans in different demographic groups may be more likely to use different social media platforms or mobile devices, thereby affecting their representation within the overall dataset. Coverage will also be influenced by Internet connectivity, urban/rural location and other geographically specific factors, and the physical environment may also affect GPS accuracy. Even for those included, factors such as the success with which patients' addresses or places mentioned in social media posts can be unambiguously associated with exact locations will further affect the quality of the dataset eventually received by the analyst.

When using geographical data for georeferencing purposes, it is particularly important that the user considers the scale, projection, accuracy and precision of their data. Online mapping tools offer many functions for the redrawing of maps, for example by switching geographical objects on or off, or zooming to different scales. However, unless different sets of underlying data are used at the various levels of zoom, there is a risk of inappropriately condensing or magnifying the features on the map. Particular care must be taken with map references embedded within geographical datasets, such as point locations or geographical boundary files because these cannot represent true geographical features more precisely than was possible at their original scale, whatever manipulations may subsequently have been applied to them. For example, many real estate agents' websites include mapping of properties for sale. These representations appear to provide symbols at the location of each individual property, whereas they are most often simply placed on the map at a centroid relating to the associated postal or zip code. In this case, the locational data relating to the properties for sale may be accurate, but imprecise. This can pose particular problems when linking or mapping geographical features that have been derived from differently scaled maps, for example when allocating property locations into service delivery areas such as those defined by a local government or health authority.

ONLINE SOURCES OF GEOGRAPHICAL DATA

In this section and the next we discuss some broad categories of online geographical data resources and tools. It is not our intention to commend any particular site over another, but rather to suggest examples of the resources available, summarized in Tables 30.1, 30.2 and 30.3. Since the details of individual sites can change quite rapidly, our classification is generic, providing a structure that should help the novice user to understand what to look for.

We can helpfully divide online geographical data into formally and informally published sources. By 'formal' here we are referring to the online availability of data which have been explicitly published as a data product and for which the web is one, or the principal, dissemination mechanism. There has been a substantial international shift towards Open Data. This may refer to datasets collected and maintained by public bodies such as national mapping agencies and statistical organizations which have been made freely available under permissive open licences, although the data series are still formally collected, quality assured and published. Examples include the OS OpenData series available from Great Britain's Ordnance Survey and an increasing range of government information around the world. The same organizations will often continue to produce and offer higher-specification products which are offered for fees and under more restrictive conditions governing access and reuse. Set against these formally published data sources are an enormous variety of informally published geographical data. These include datasets which have been created by members of online communities and made available for reuse by others. A prime example of this is the OpenStreetMap (OSM) project, which aims to deliver an open, community-maintained map of the world (Haklay and Weber, 2008). This latter type of user-generated content has become known as volunteered geographic information, or 'VGI' (Goodchild, 2007). We might consider the geographical locations associated with many social media posts as another type of VGI: they can offer powerful geographical insights but are not comprehensively or systematically collected and should pose many data quality questions to the researcher. In reality the distinction between formal and informal sources is not always entirely clear, but it is helpful to maintain the distinction as it often reflects important aspects of data documentation, ownership and overall quality.

Table 30.1 provides examples of a range of online geographical data sources. The first section of the table provides examples of portals that are designed specifically to help the user locate geographical datasets. These range from the European Union's INSPIRE

Table 30.1 Example sources of online geographical data

Find geographical data		
INSPIRE	INSPIRE European Geoportal	http://inspire-geoportal.ec.europa.eu/
Data.gov	US federal, state and local geographic data	http://catalog.data.gov/dataset
Data.gov.uk	UK government public data portal	http://data.gov.uk/data/search
Download geographically referenced data		
GADM	GADM database of Global Administrative Areas	http://www.gadm.org/
WorldPop	Population mapping project with freely downloadable data, especially covering Africa, Asia and South America	http://www.worldpop.org.uk/
American FactFinder	US census data	http://factfinder.census.gov/
Neighbourhood Statistics	England and Wales census data	http://www.neighbourhood.statistics.gov.uk/
UK Data Service	UK social science data service	http://www.ukdataservice.ac.uk/
Geograph	Web community-produced geographically referenced UK photography	http://www.geograph.org.uk/
Statistics South Africa	South African census data	http://www.statssa.gov.za/
Download map and imagery data		
OpenStreetMap	Open community-generated mapping of the world	http://www.openstreetmap.org/
The National Map	Downloadable United States Geological Survey (USGS) GIS data	http://nationalmap.gov/
EarthExplorer	USGS online catalogs of satellite and aerial imageries	http://geoportal.statistics.gov.uk
getmapping.com	Aerial photography and mapping products for purchase	http://www.getmapping.com/
Open Geography Portal	Open geography geoportal from Office for National Statistics (ONS) – England and Wales administrative and boundary datasets	https://geoportal.statistics.gov.uk/
OS OpenData	Open datasets from Ordnance Survey, the GB National Mapping Agency	https://www.ordnancesurvey.co.uk/opendatadownload/products.html
Digimap	Ordnance Survey (Digimap) and census and administrative boundary data (UKBorders), some limited for use at registered UK academic institutions	http://edina.ac.uk/maps/
Geoscience Australia	Geoscience Australia's catalogue of maps and spatial data	http://www.ga.gov.au/search/index.html#/

geoportal to national projects such as the UK's data.gov.uk service. These portals will tend to have more complete coverage of the formally published geographical data sources for which appropriate metadata records have been produced. The second and third sections of Table 30.1 make a distinction between sites that offer downloadable geographically referenced data and those that provide mapping data. In GIS terms, this is a distinction between the attributes that we might want to display on a map (such as administrative names, unemployment rates or crime levels) and the geographical information that defines the positions of point, line and area features (such as schools, roads and local government areas). Typical of the downloadable geographically referenced data sources are sites provided by national statistical organisations that publish census data and other official statistics, and which most often incorporate geographical codes relating to administrative or data publication areas: Table 30.1 provides illustrative examples covering a range of countries. This category is truly enormous and could be extended to cover most secondary data sources in the social sciences that include any kind of locational reference. These data may be downloaded and analysed in statistical software, or linked to appropriate geographical data and mapped or analysed spatially.

It is almost impossible to write a systematic review of this constantly changing and ever-expanding field, but online portals, statistical agency websites and data archives offer the most fruitful starting points for those searching for specific data (see Corti and Wathan, this volume). Walford (2002) provides a helpful overview of the principles involved, although any reader seeking specific contemporary data is advised to start with the (continually updated) online portals rather than published volumes.

The second section of the table comprises sites that primarily exist for the download of geographical data. WorldPop is an academically led project that publishes freely downloadable data. In this case, the population estimates are referenced to map grid squares rather than geographical boundaries. Innes *et al.* (this volume), discuss access to data from social media platforms. These provide a very different type of geographical data, whereby location is usually captured coincidentally and the data stream grows organically as thousands of individual users contribute content. In the case of most social media, geographical location is not a core data element, but some, such as the Geograph photo-sharing site (Table 30.1), are entirely built around geographically referenced content. The mapping data sites in the third section of the table focus on data designed primarily for use in GIS. These are variously free to download, available on a pay-per-use basis or offered as subscription services, but for most social science applications are likely to provide the background geographical references and locational framework.

The potential need for payment leads to very important considerations of data ownership and copyright. As with all secondary data sources, users should take particular care to ensure that they comply with the terms and conditions associated with geographical data. Maps and mapping data are protected by copyright law in just the same way as other published products, and the placement or embedding of mapping data on a website does not necessarily imply that it may be freely reproduced or reused. Indeed, geographical data are often subject to more restrictive terms and conditions than mainstream social science datasets resulting from academic studies or published by official statistical agencies. Researchers are particularly advised to read and comply with any terms and conditions associated with mapping data from online sources, especially if these are to be reproduced in published outputs or websites. There are considerable variations in this respect, with open licences (such as Creative Commons or Open Government Licences) being the most permissive.

GEOGRAPHICAL DATA ANALYSIS ONLINE

Table 30.2 provides a range of examples of online resources for mapping and spatial analysis. Again, the functionality provided by these types of resource is constantly changing, but here we have imposed a four-way classification as follows: tools which permit a degree of geographical data linkage; those which provide functions for topographic mapping (i.e. producing the kind of background map that you would expect to obtain from a road atlas or national mapping agency); those which provide thematic mapping and a degree of spatial analysis; and finally a few examples of more sophisticated tools that can be downloaded from the web and then used locally – sometimes in conjunction with online data. We shall now consider each of these categories/classes in turn.

Geographical Linkage

Geographical data linkage covers all forms of association between data items where the linkage relies on geographical location. This may include a very wide range of scenarios, but two of the most commonly encountered are linkage between points and areas (for example individual addresses and census zones) and between sets of incompatible areas (for example, administrative or census zones at different points in time).

Geographical data linkage can essentially be performed by the use of pre-prepared lookup tables or by spatial calculations undertaken using GIS software. Relatively simple calculations can be performed to convert between coordinate systems, but the allocation (for example) of a large set of geographical point locations into coordinate-based area boundaries is a significant computing task and therefore not widely available online. For this reason, most online geographical linkage resources are restricted to the use of lookup tables or simple calculations. The most common sites are those in which the user enters a single geographical reference, such as a place name or postal code, and is supplied with a range of matching locational descriptors such as latitude and longitude, administrative area names or codes. These utilities are sometimes also offered as downloadable databases or web services, which can be called interactively from other websites. The GeoNames site provides examples of all three modes of working. The GeoConvert utility, by contrast, is an example of a UK service that will process large quantities of the users' own data. Data files containing postal or area codes are uploaded to the service, which will then return files to which matching codes have been appended, or it will even perform weighted reallocation of the supplied data values to a different set of geographical objects. This example is based on the National Statistics Postcode Directory, a directory of UK postcodes and administrative area codes. The underlying information is created and maintained using GIS tools, allowing application services such as GeoConvert to provide information to users on a lookup basis. The most recent versions of the directory used by GeoConvert are now available under an open licence and may be downloaded from the ONS Geoportal (Table 30.1) and manipulated directly by the user.

In general, it is the case that more analytical flexibility is available to the user who is prepared to download the source datasets and undertake local processing. Matching by geographical location provides a means to associate geographical objects when there is no predefined relationship, for example these might be street addresses and the extent of a flood. The two geographical datasets (a set of address locations and one or more polygons representing the flood) may be obtained from separate online sources but can be readily intersected using GIS software. Most GIS tools will offer a range of overlay and intersection tools, for example counting or aggregating the value of points falling in the same polygon (how many addresses were flooded?) or alternatively adding the characteristics of the polygon to each point (was each address flooded or not?). These tools can be applied to any combination of object types, including overlay of two incompatible sets of polygons in order to calculate the values of their attributes in the intersections (Longley *et al.*, 2015).

Mapping

Basic mapping sites have grown enormously in popularity and there are very many to choose from – the entire list is far too extensive and changes too frequently to permit an exhaustive review. Essentially, these sites provide online viewers for background mapping and aerial photography that can be accessed with only a web browser. Functionality is generally limited to simple map controls, such as panning and zooming, route finding and a limited range of lookup tools for specifying the location to be mapped. Most are based on vector data, which is redrawn according to the zoom level selected, allowing additional detail at large mapping scales. It is important to understand that these sites often do not permit downloading of the underlying data – maps can be printed or saved, subject to certain terms and conditions, but mostly cannot be interrogated or manipulated in external GIS or mapping software (indeed, conditions of use will often prohibit any attempt to do so). Some of these sites additionally provide a separate access channel known as a web mapping service, which provides geographical data download on demand direct to the user's own software, either as subscription (e.g. Ordnance Survey) or open (e.g. OpenStreetMap; OS OpenData) services.

Spatial Analysis

The sites listed under the thematic mapping and spatial analysis section of Table 30.2

Table 30.2 Example mapping and spatial analysis tools online

Geographical data linkage		
MapIt: Global	Online service to map geographical points to administrative areas	http://global.mapit.mysociety.org/
GeoNames	US/world geographical names lookup	http://www.geonames.org/
Nearby	UK-oriented geocoder and conversion tool	http://www.nearby.org.uk/
GeoConvert	UK academic-use geographical conversion tool specialising in postcode and administrative geography codes	http://geoconvert.mimas.ac.uk/
Route/topographic mapping		
MapQuest	General purpose mapping and directions	http://www.mapquest.com/
ViaMichelin Maps and Routes	General purpose mapping and directions	http://www.viamichelin.com/
Google Maps	General purpose mapping and directions	http://maps.google.com/
OpenStreetMap	Open community-generated mapping of the world	http://www.openstreetmap.org/
OS Maps	Free mapping from Ordnance Survey, UK's national mapping agency for non-commercial use	http://www.ordnancesurvey.co.uk/
Thematic mapping and spatial analysis		
Thematic Mapping Engine	Online tool to visualise global statistics on Google Earth	http://thematicmapping.org/engine/
American Factfinder	US census and neighbourhood thematic mapping	http://factfinder.census.gov/
Cancer Mortality Maps	US National Cancer Institute cancer mortality maps tools	http://ratecalc.cancer.gov/
Neighbourhood Statistics	England and Wales census and neighbourhood thematic mapping	http://www.neighbourhood.statistics.gov.uk/
What's in Your Backyard?	UK Environment Agency – mapping of flood hazard, pollution, waste	http://apps.environment-agency.gov.uk/wiyby/default.aspx
Downloadable mapping and spatial analysis tools		
Google Earth	Free viewer and processing software for online geographical content	http://www.google.com/earth/
Explorer for ArcGIS, ArcGIS Explorer Desktop	Free data viewers for ESRI format GIS data	http://www.esri.com/software/arcgis/explorer
GeoDa	Free introductory spatial data analysis software released by the Arizona State University	http://geodacenter.github.io/
QGIS	Free and open source geographical information systems	http://www.qgis.org/
gvSIG	Free and open source geographical information systems	http://www.gvsig.com/

cover a variety of functions and are mostly focused on a specific application. These are not sites designed to undertake analysis of users' own data, but rather to allow online exploration and mapping of data from a particular organisation or relating to a specific theme. Many of the national statistical organisations' sites offer not just download of statistical data, but also functions to select variables from a census or national survey, to choose a geographical study area by interacting with background mapping or entering area codes, and to produce shaded area maps of the selected variables, often with associated graphs and summary tables. These are produced as onscreen graphics and can generally be printed or saved, but not directly downloaded for GIS use. Similar functionality is offered by specialist sites, such as the examples in Table 30.2 that permit interactive cancer mapping for the US and interrogation of flood risk and environmental hazards in the UK. There are many such resources available from agencies responsible for the delivery of services or monitoring of standards, and they span both formally and informally published data sources.

An interesting example of analysis undertaken using several of the online geographical data sources mentioned here is Malleson and Andresen's (2015) exploration of crime patterns in the city of Leeds using a combination of census data, reported crime published from the police.uk website and Twitter data to obtain an alternative population denominator measure. They demonstrate changes in the location of crime hotspots as different sources are used to reflect the size of the underlying population. A second example is provided by Swier *et al.* (2015) which describes an exploration by a national statistical organization of the potential use of Twitter data to augment existing population statistics. The analysis reveals the ability of these social media data to detect, for example, movement of student populations throughout the year, which is not discernible from conventional sources. Both studies demonstrate clearly the potential and

pitfalls of combining online sources of geographical data.

Downloadable Tools

The final section of Table 30.2 provides examples of the numerous tools that are available for download from the web and that offer more extensive spatial analysis and exploration options. These are rather different from all the other examples cited here in that they do not operate within a web browser but require installation on the user's own computer. Here it becomes difficult to draw a definite distinction between those tools that are truly online and those which are simply distributed by download from the web. As examples, we have specifically selected Google Earth, ArcExplorer, GeoDa, QGIS and gvSIG.

Google Earth is an example of a tool known as a 'virtual globe' and can be thought of as a specialized web browser (a 'geobrowser'), which embeds geographical functionality (Butler, 2006). The software must be downloaded and installed on the users' device but, when run, it is able to access both online and locally saved geographical data. In addition to the simple functions available from the mapping sites cited earlier, more explicitly geographical tools are provided, such as the ability to interact with the geographical representation in more sophisticated ways, to measure distances, define areas and record locations. Importantly, the user is able to create and save their own geographical datasets, which can be stored locally or shared with other users via the web. Google Earth has led to popularity of a simple geographical data format known as KML, which can also be created and read by standard GIS software, aiding the transfer of data between a wide range of users and software platforms. This is similar in concept to Wikipedia or Geograph, mentioned earlier, whereby a body of information is created piecemeal by an extensive user community, but there is no direct quality control of the content. Although the core Google Earth mapping layers will be from identifiable sources, comparable to the other online mapping sites, users should beware of the provenance, coverage and quality of all community-created content. A common feature of shared mapping resources of this type (or indeed any shared authorship project) is a tendency for duplication and errors to arise. Examples include the creation of multiple but slightly differing locations for the same object (e.g. the Eiffel Tower in Paris) or the incorrect labelling of a less well-known location. Both have the potential to mislead the unsuspecting user, accustomed to dealing with professionally compiled and validated datasets. Despite these potential risks, major VGI projects such as OpenStreetMap also benefit from the tendency for a large and active user base, including expert moderators and editors, to correct errors thereby continuously enhancing overall quality (Goodchild and Li, 2012).

The two Explorer tools for ArcGIS are downloadable specialized viewers for geographical data in a proprietary format, specifically 'shapefiles' used by ArcGIS, a leading GIS software product. This can be very useful for those wishing to publish or view GIS data but who do not have access to a full GIS system. In particular, it can be used to view many of the downloadable geographical datasets cited earlier and it offers the user much greater control over layers, scale and map display than the online mapping systems. The third example, GeoDa, is an instance of a downloadable spatial analysis software tool, which again uses shapefiles as a data-exchange format but permits the calculation of various statistical measures of spatial association. There are many downloadable tools of this type, particularly resulting from academic or open source software initiatives.

The final two entries in the table, QGIS and gvSIG are examples of fully functional free GIS software that can be downloaded and installed on the user's own device. These will read most of the downloadable data from the other sources listed in this chapter and offer an extensive range of data manipulation and analysis options. They are in many respects functionally similar to proprietary GIS software such as ArcGIS but with the important distinction that there is no warranty or support service. These free and open source software tools are themselves the product of online communities and users take on both the risks and benefits of engaging with this very different software environment.

HOW TO PROCEED

In this final section, we reiterate some key messages from the chapter, point to some areas of ongoing development and suggest useful online resources. An inherent difficulty when writing about any type of online resource is the speed at which they change. Nevertheless, we have sought in this chapter to draw out some very important principles for the social science user of online geographical data. In particular, we have drawn a distinction between geographical data and maps. Each map is just a static realisation of the underlying data that has been constructed according to a complex set of rules and conventions. The user of geographical data online, as with any secondary data source, should always attempt to understand as much as possible about the original intentions of the data creator and the processing which has already been applied. Online sources range from high-quality and well-documented official statistics to community-generated data, which may be highly variable in quality and coverage and for which documentation may be limited. In addition to data, online resources now include a range of enormously powerful tools for geographical data linkage, mapping and analysis.

Not only do individual websites undergo significant redesigns or fall into disuse, but the technologies by which online data are

Table 30.3 Further resources for online geographical data in the social sciences

Google Maps API	APIs for embedding Google maps into own websites	https://developers.google.com/maps/
The R Project	The R project free software environment for statistical computing and graphics	http://www.r-project.org/
CSISS	Centre for Spatially Integrated Social Science at the University of California Santa Barbara	http://www.csiss.org/
Geo-Refer	GEOgraphical REFERencing resources for social scientists	http://www.restore.ac.uk/geo-refer/

structured and accessed are continually evolving. Table 30.3 contains examples of two technologies that have relevance here and which may whet the keen reader's appetite to go further. The first is the Google Maps application programming interface (API). This allows a developer to embed interactive mapping from the Google Maps web resource within their own web pages, creating a page which is a combination of their own geographical information and the external mapping site. APIs are provided by various mapping and social media services of the type discussed here and increasingly facilitate the creation of 'mashups', or websites which contain data from multiple sources (see Smith *et al.*, this volume). For the reader who wants to undertake advanced statistical and spatial analysis that goes beyond that provided by the tools already discussed, there are also powerful spatial data analysis and manipulation functions available within open source software environments such as R (Brunsdon and Comber, 2015). Although the specific technologies and terminologies may change, future users of geographical data online will find an increasingly interconnected series of resources and may come to consider these tools as important dissemination media for their own results and presentations. Finally, we provide two examples of sites designed specifically to help the social scientist. The Centre for Spatially Integrated Social Science at the University of California Santa Barbara provides many useful pages covering conceptual material, resources and links. The Geo-Refer site, produced by ourselves, provides a library of learning resources targeted at social scientists

whose primary discipline is not geography, but whose research requires them to use and link geographically referenced data. The site allows the user to profile their own needs and interests and assembles customized tutorials with relevant examples (with a UK orientation). The overall message is that there is an enormous and rich collection of geographical data online – it has great potential but must be used with care!

ACKNOWLEDGEMENT

The authors gratefully acknowledge the support of Economic and Social Research Council award PTA-035–25-0029.

REFERENCES

Anselin, L. (1995) 'Local indicators of spatial association', *Geographical Analysis*, 27, 93–115.

Brunsdon, C. and Comber, L. (2015) *An Introduction to R for Spatial Analysis and Mapping*. London: Sage Publications.

Brunsdon, C. and Singleton, A. (2015) *Geocomputation: A Practical Primer*. London: Sage Publications.

Burrough, P.A. and McDonnell, R.A. (1998) *Principles of Geographical Information Systems*. Oxford: Oxford University Press.

Butler, D. (2006) 'Virtual globes: The web-wide world', *Nature*, 439, 776–8.

Campbell, J.B. and Wynne, R.H. (2011) *Introduction to Remote Sensing*. 5th edn. London: Guilford Press.

DeMers, M.N. (2008) *Fundamentals of Geographic Information Systems*. 4th edn. New York, NY: Wiley.

Fotheringham, A.S. and Rogerson, P.A. (2009) *The SAGE Handbook of Spatial Analysis*. London: Sage Publications.

Fotheringham, A.S., Brunsdon, C. and Charlton, M. (2002) *Geographically Weighted Regression: The Analysis of Spatially Varying Relationships*. Chichester, UK: Wiley.

Goodchild, M.F. (2007) 'Citizens as sensors: the world of volunteered geography', *GeoJournal*, 69, 211–21.

Goodchild, M.F. and Janelle, D.G. (2004) 'Thinking spatially in the social sciences'. In M.F. Goodchild and D.G. Janelle (eds.), *Spatially Integrated Social Science*. Oxford: Oxford University Press, pp. 3–18.

Goodchild, M.F. and Li, L. (2012) 'Assuring the quality of volunteered geographic information', *Spatial Statistics*, 1, 110–20.

Haklay, M. and Weber, P. (2008) 'OpenStreetMap: user-generated street maps', *IEEE Pervasive Computing*, 7(4), 12–18.

Heywood, I., Cornelius, S. and Carver, S. (2011) *An Introduction to Geographical Information Systems*. 4th edn. London: Pearson.

Iliffe, J.C. (2008) *Datums and Map Projections for Remote Sensing, GIS and Surveying*. 2nd edn. London: Whittle.

Kitchin, R. (2013) 'Big data and human geography: opportunities, challenges and risks', *Dialogues in Human Geography*, 3, 262–7.

Kraak, M.-J. and Brown, A. (eds.) (2001) *Web Cartography: Developments and Prospects*. London: Taylor and Francis.

Kreft, I. and de Leeuw, J. (1998) *Introducing Multilevel Modelling*. London: Sage Publications.

Lillesand, T.M., Kiefer, R.W. and Chipman, J.W. (2015) *Remote Sensing and Image Interpretation*. 7th edn. New York, NY: Wiley.

Longley, P.A., Goodchild, M.F., Maguire, D.J. and Rhind, D.W. (2005) 'Introduction'. In P. Longley, M. Goodchild, D. Maguire and D. Rhind (eds.), *Geographical Information Systems: Principles, Techniques, Management and Applications*. 2nd edn. Chichester, UK: Wiley, pp. 1–20.

Longley, P.A., Goodchild, M.F., Maguire, D.J. and Rhind, D.W. (2015) *Geographic Information Science and Systems*. 4th edn. Hoboken, NJ: Wiley.

Malleson, N. and Andresen, M. (2015) 'The impact of using social media data in crime rate calculations: shifting hot spots and changing spatial patterns', *Cartography and Geographic Information Science*, 42, 112–21.

Martin, D. (2005) 'Spatial representation: the social scientist's perspective'. In P. Longley, M. Goodchild, D. Maguire and D. Rhind (eds.), *Geographical Information Systems: Principles, Techniques, Management and Applications*. 2nd edn. Chichester, UK: Wiley, pp. 71–80.

Mitchell, R., Martin, D. and Foody, G. (1998) 'Unmixing aggregate data: estimating the social composition of enumeration districts', *Environment and Planning A*, 30, 1929–41.

Monmonier, M. (1996) *How to Lie with Maps*. 2nd edn. Chicago, IL: University of Chicago Press.

Openshaw, S. (1984) *The Modifiable Areal Unit Problem*. Concepts and Techniques in Modern Geography. No 38. Norwich, UK: Geo Books.

Ordnance Survey (2008) *A Guide to Coordinate Systems in Great Britain: An Introduction to Mapping Coordinate System and the Use of GPS Datasets with Ordnance Survey Mapping*. Southampton, UK: Ordnance Survey.

Rana, S. and Joliveau, T. (2009) 'NeoGeography: an extension of mainstream Geography made by everyone for everyone?' *Journal of Location Based Services*, 3, 75–81.

Robinson, A., Morrison, J., Muehrcke, P., Kimerling, A. and Guptill, S. (1995) *Elements of Cartography*. 6th edn. New York, NY: Wiley.

Spencer, J., Frizzelle, B., Page, P. and Vogler, J. (2003) *Global Positioning System: A Field Guide for the Social Sciences*. Oxford: Blackwell.

Swier, N., Komarniczky, B. and Clapperton, B. (2015) *Using geolocated Twitter traces to infer residence and mobility*. GSS Methodology Series No 41. Titchfield, UK: Office for National Statistics.

Walford, N. (2002) *Geographical Data: Characteristics and Sources*. Chichester, UK: Wiley.

Williamson, P., Birkin, M. and Rees, P.H. (1998) 'The estimation of population microdata by using data from small area statistics and samples of anonymised records', *Environment and Planning A*, 30, 785–816.

FURTHER READING

To date, there are no standard textbooks which bring together all the themes identified in this chapter. For readers wanting to further explore the potential of geographical data online, we recommend the following:

Goodchild, M.F. and Janelle, D.G. (eds.) (2004) *Spatially Integrated Social Science*. Oxford: Oxford University Press.
An introduction and overview of geographical thinking applied to the social sciences:
Walford, N. (2002) *Geographical Data: Characteristics and Sources*. Chichester, UK: Wiley.
An introduction to GIS, specifically from a social science perspective:
Steinberg, S. J. and Steinberg, S. L. (2006) *Geographic Information Systems for the Social Sciences: Investigating Space and Place*. Thousand Oaks, CA: Sage Publications.
Although not specifically focused on web-based information sources, this is a text that provides an extensive introduction to geographical data:
Wilson, J.P. and Fotheringham, A.S. (eds.) (2007) *The Handbook of Geographic Information Science*. Oxford: Blackwell. This book provides a research-oriented overview of the very many opportunities and challenges of working with geographically referenced data.

Websites

The website of the Centre for Spatially Integrated Social Science at the University of California Santa Barbara (http://www.csiss.org/) provides an extensive collection of readings, examples and links to other resources.

Our own website GEOgraphical REFERencing (http://www.restore.ac.uk/geo-refer/) provides resources for social scientists that allows the social science user to profile their own interests and receive customized tutorial material covering concepts, methods, data and examples.

## 31

Mapping Spaces: Cartographic Representations of Online Data

Matthew Zook, Ate Poorthuis
and Rich Donohue

INTRODUCTION

This chapter provides a broad overview of the principles of cartographic design and outlines a workflow for mapping online data containing geographic coordinates. Although this review does not go into detail about software and code – after all, the exact flavors of code are in constant flux – it does emphasize the key building blocks and logics behind map-making that remain constant. Ultimately, maps are defined by the message they communicate and the insight they provide, not the specific techniques used to create them. Maps created from code, rather than pen and ink, are a relatively recent phenomenon and researchers must continue thinking carefully about the questions, data, and design of maps (Krygier and Wood, 2011). Although the growth of geospatial information on the web has changed the production, distribution, and consumption of maps, the principles by which we think carefully about the data and how they're represented can be carried forth

through these technologized processes. In other words, every map-in-the-making (from those scrawled on a bar napkin to online spatial data exploration) should start with a question, think carefully about the data used, and explore design solutions to create a visual representation or interpretation of that data.

PRINCIPLES OF CARTOGRAPHIC DESIGN FOR THEMATIC MAPS

It is often tempting to let the end goal of visual representation drive the mapping process. After all, powerful online mapping tools make it relatively easy to load point data – geotagged tweets, Instagram photos, etc. – and make a map full of placemarks. However, unless one is careful, this often results in problematic maps that may look fantastic but misrepresent the data and/or create misleading or even pointless visualizations. Like any data analysis, mapping can be tricky. The goal of good cartographic design is to create maps that help users gain insight to questions or problems embedded in the world.

When most people envision a map, they think of what are called reference maps, used to represent the *location* of spatial phenomena such as roads, houses and rivers. But for most social science research we are primarily concerned with thematic maps (or 'data maps') used to illustrate the spatial distribution of geographic attributes or variables. From a cartographic design perspective, a good thematic map provides users two key things: (1) the overall form of the geographic distribution (the 'spatial pattern') of a phenomenon, and (2) the specific values associated with it. However, thematic maps are inherently subjective and, despite being 'data-driven', are fundamentally about emphasizing something at the expense of something else. In other words, thematic maps are best thought of as propositions about the world in which they both represent and recreate reality.

Data in Design

The first step in thematic mapping is to reflect on how the nature of the data itself shapes what can be done in a map. Data used in maps are generally classified by three different levels of measurement: (1) nominal/categorical, (2) ordinal, and (3) numerical. This is not an arbitrary distinction because it directly impacts how data are best represented visually. For example, *nominal* data might compare different types – tweets, Facebook posts and Yelp reviews – but these types are not orderable – a tweet is not inherently more than a Facebook post. But some data, such as popularity or ranking, does indicate a difference in magnitude. When this is not precise – the most popular post is more than the least popular but we aren't clear by how much – it is an *ordinal* measurement and we should use an appropriate representation on the map. The final level of measurement – *numerical* – allows the use of more exact measurements,

such as number of users, to precisely compare measurements, for example having 5,000 users is half as much as 10,000. These differences in levels of measurement directly impact a number of cartographic design choices (Slocum *et al.*, 2009; Dent *et al.*, 2008).

A second key consideration about the nature of data is classification. Classification involves taking a large number of observations and grouping them into data ranges or 'classes.' When mapped, each range, or class, can be given a distinct color (or in the case of grayscale, brightness), thus reducing the total number of colors on the map and making it more legible. Imagine for a moment that each tweet in a dataset were assigned its own color; technically possible, but functionally map users would be hard pressed to distinguish between that many colors. Classification, however, is a double-edged sword because it obscures and hides the details of the dataset and the world it measures. Classification also depends on the nature of the question asked and whether there are critical break points. In the case of online data, the question 'Which countries have a Twitter user per capita rate that is higher than the median rate?' calls for a different classification than 'Which countries have more than 500,000 Twitter users'. There are standard conventions for classifications – natural breaks, quintiles, equal intervals, etc. – and each can produce a very different looking map with the same data. One is not necessarily more appropriate than another and so it is important to be cognizant of how classification may change the look and message of a map (Slocum *et al.*, 2009).

The third data-related issue revolves around standardizing data in order to bring better clarity. There is a semi-famous XKCD comic by Randall Munroe that critiques Internet maps as primarily just showing population densities.[1] Whether the topic is subscribers to *Martha Stewart Living* or Furry Pornography, the pattern looks the same because it is primarily a function of population. The standard answer to this critique is to use per capita figures to control for population-driven phenomena, a particularly key issue when making comparisons between locations. However, it is not always appropriate to standardize data – sometime it is important to represent information as total counts – and even when standardization is useful, the selection of the denominator is based on the question. For example, for online data, an offline census of population is not necessarily the most appropriate means for normalization and it can be important to compare a subset of an online phenomenon with the totality of an online phenomenon. This is the approach that we outline in this chapter.

Generalization Across Scales

The second step in cartographic design is recognizing that maps use techniques of generalization to represent the world. Maps are *not* powerful because they represent the real world as accurately and exhaustively as possible; rather, it is quite the opposite: 'The act of generalization gives the map its raison d'etre' (Robinson *et al.* 1995: 42). Good maps reduce the amount of information shown via a number of generalization processes including:

- **Selecting:** given the rich detail of the world (both online and offline), the first step is selecting what data to map.
- **Eliminating:** closely related to selecting is removing extraneous details that often come with a base map. For example, do street names, building footprints and borders contribute to the message of the map or are they distracting?
- **Symbolizing:** not only is it not possible to draw every detail of the world, but even those selected cannot be represented with picture-perfect quality. Thus, symbolization allows one to take one thing – say a complicated building – and represent it with another thing – such as a simple star or dot.
- **Aggregating:** it is also standard cartographic practice to aggregate spatial data (multiple railroad tracks, clusters of tweets) into larger wholes in order to use a single symbol for multiple occurrences.
- **Collapsing:** another scale-related generalization is collapsing when polygon figures are transformed

into simpler features. For example, rivers obviously have width but maps often represent them with single lines.
- **Simplifying:** often the line work used to create boundaries or lines is overly detailed and simplification can create more visually. Mapshaper[2] is a free online tool for simplifying lines in maps.
- **Smoothing:** one possible drawback of simplifying is creating jagged and 'ugly' lines. To counter this, map makers often apply smoothing to line work.
- **Displacing:** another technique when map elements begin to bump up against each other is to displace one of them slightly. This is particularly useful when both elements are key and when one might cover up the other.
- **Exaggerating:** sometimes the goal of a map is to highlight something (e.g. a road or border) and it is exaggerated via line width or size.

These generalizations can be dramatic or subtle and there is not a single best approach. An awareness of these elements, however, contributes to better looking maps that more clearly convey the map maker's goals (Monmonier, 2014).

Thematic Map Types and Associated Symbology

The next step in cartographic design is selecting an appropriate map type and associated symbology for the phenomenon to be mapped. There are a number of thematic map types with a variety of representational techniques and symbology that can be used to display different kinds of data (see Figure 31.1). To summarize the map types quickly:

Choropleth maps use defined polygons, e.g. states, counties, or user-created grid cells, etc., to display values for aggregated data within each area.

Isopleth maps visualize continuous phenomena (e.g. temperature or elevation) and each area represents the same value.

Proportional symbol maps use differing sized symbology located at the site of a phenomenon to compare magnitudes (e.g. the number of tweets per state).

Choropleth

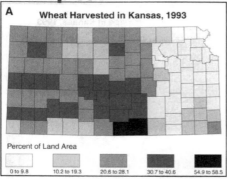

Isopleth

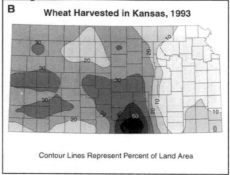

Proportional Symbol

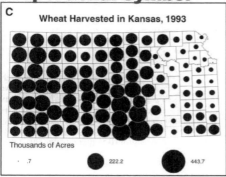

Dot Map

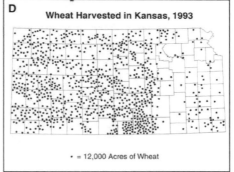

Figure 31.1 Types of thematic maps

Source: Slocum *et al.* (2009).

Dot maps show the actual location of each observation within a dataset (e.g. car crashes or tweets) when there is a one-to-one relationship and the general distribution of a phenomenon when there is a one-to-many relationship (e.g. a 'dot density' map).

In selecting a thematic map type, it is useful to classify the phenomenon along two continua in which the vertical axis represents a discrete–continuous continuum and the horizontal axis operates along an abrupt–smooth continuum (see Figure 31.2). Although the boundaries of these rules are fluid, this acts as a useful guide for selecting an appropriate map type and symbology. For example,

online phenomena can often be patchy and abrupt (especially when mapped to space) and thus isopleth or heat maps are not particularly appropriate representations despite their popularity.

Effective Graphic Variables

The fourth step in cartographic design is understanding how graphic variables – location, size, value, texture, hue, orientation, and shape – work and the ways people understand them in maps. The French cartographer Jacques Bertin outlined a grammar of visual representation of how different graphic variables are best suited

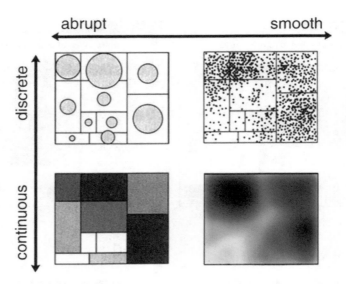

Figure 31.2   Character of the distribution of phenomena influences the map type

Source: MacEachren (1992).

for various representational tasks (Bertin, 1983). Bertin's graphic variables adhere to a similar logic because is associated with levels of measurement. For example, it makes little sense to use different shapes or colors for visually encoding ordinal or numerical data because variances in shape or color do not logically correspond to bigger or smaller. Instead, these variables are better suited for nominal data and the use of size – small, medium, and large circles – is more effective for visually encoding ordinal data. To be clear, not all graphic variables carry the same impact, and cartographers have spent a lot of time working out which ones are most effective for particular tasks.

Of all the graphic variables, color has long been a fundamental way through which one symbolically encodes information within a map. Choosing color is not merely about finding colors that we like or that look pretty; rather it is best practice to adhere to a suite of conventional and perceptual rules. Effective use of color simplifies and clarifies maps, elicits subjective or emotional reactions, and can be used to help develop figure ground contrast. There are also perceptual issues with

color that are 'hard-wired' into our eye–brain system. For example, nearly 8 percent of the male population experiences *red–green color impairment,* and so these color combinations should generally be avoided.

Working effectively with color in maps can be tricky and it is easiest for novice map makers to use standard color schemes defined around three axes of color representation – hue (levels of red, green, blue), lightness (amount of blackness) and saturation (amount of whiteness). Color schemes can be considered in three basic senses:

- **Nominal or qualitative color schemes** use *different hues* to encode qualitative, categorical, non-numeric, non-rankable information (lightness and saturation should remain consistent across the scheme).
- **Sequential color schemes** represent either orderable, rankable categories (such as low/medium/high) or numerical data and use the same *hue* with *variations in lightness.*
- **Divergent color schemes** use two sequential color schemes stitched end-to-end to encode ordinal or numerical data with a critical, meaningful mid-point.

ColorBrewer[3] is a handy online tool for selecting perceptually graded color schemes in which the distinctions between different classes perceptually appear to be equal. The tool helps users choose from a variety of nominal, sequential, and divergent color schemes and is highly recommended for novice mapmakers (Harrower and Brewer, 2003; Brewer, 2005).

Map Projections and Scale

The final step in cartographic design is the selection of an appropriate map projection, i.e. the process by which the ellipsoidal earth is distorted to project onto a two dimensional surface. Making the transition comes with a cost, i.e. the surface of the earth becomes distorted, either in terms of area, form, distance, or direction. Cartographers use different map projections to minimize or maximize these distortions in particular ways. Although there is not a single best projection – it depends on the scale, focus, and purpose of the map – the Robinson, Van der Grinten and Winkel tripel projections have been used by National Geographic in their global maps and are good choices. The decision for a projection, however, is not always in the hands of the mapmaker. Case in point, most online mapping services use the Google Mercator projection (which greatly distorts the size of areas away from the equator, e.g. Greenland) because it preserves directional angles at local scales. Thus, while cartographers universally dislike this projection, it regularly appears in online maps (Crampton, 2011).

UNDERSTANDING THE ONLINE DATA BEHIND MAPS

Given the key role that data plays in cartographic design, an important part of the mapping process is obtaining a clear understanding of the genealogy of the data in use. After all,

data do not just exist; they are always *made* by different people, by different ways of measuring, and with different intentions. Because of that, data will never tell a story by themselves. The meanings derived by a map reader are influenced, intentionally or unintentionally, by everything the data touches along the way: from how and by whom they were collected to how they were stored and then subsequently visualized. This is especially the case for online data sets derived from social media. They can be gathered at great speed and in great quantities but have decidedly different controls and intents than more officially sourced datasets. With such data and current software, one can make a gorgeous looking map within minutes, albeit without much critical reflection. But in that case, one often ends up with a map that does not really tell anything – or, worse, a map that communicates something that is pertinently false or misleading (Poorthuis *et al*, 2016). In the past few years, maps of Twitter data have become ubiquitous but often the maps are accompanied by little interrogation of how this visualization relates to the real world, offline or online. As Shelton *et al.* (2015, 198) note, 'it's important to keep in mind that offline, material social processes, such as persistent social inequalities, continue to shape the data as we interact with it, never including everyone equally or in a representative fashion' (see also Poorthuis *et al.*, 2016).

By thoroughly interrogating the dataset, we often discover that the data we have in hand – or that is easy to acquire – is not the most appropriate data for the question we are asking. Twitter data is readily available, but as Graham *et al.* (2015) demonstrate, there are many other data sources that can provide insight on information use and human activity. Significant additional analysis may be needed to make a meaningful map from that data that actually answers our starting question. That is more work, but making eloquent maps from good data is not necessarily either quick or easy.

Getting Online Data

Although retaining a critical mindset about the data, this chapter now reviews the steps to obtain it. The tried-and-trusted way for map-makers to gather data was quite hands-on – going out in the field (or hiring people to do the dirty work) to measure roads, pinpoint buildings or survey people. Even relatively recently, getting data collected by someone else, e.g. the Census, entailed sending a written request and in return getting a floppy drive, CD-ROM, or DVD (depending on the decade) with the data set. More recently, governments and public institutions started to make large parts of their data available online. This wasn't a natural or automatic thing for these entities, and pressure for increased availability of 'open data' is ongoing. Often these data can be downloaded as ready-made files directly from purposely built government sites. For example, in the US, the Census Bureau provides Factfinder,[4] and cities and other institutes host data warehouses or repositories such as New York City's Open Data platform.[5] Similar platforms exist in many nations and cities around the world.

Concurrently, a number of online services and social media sites (mostly for-profit companies) are collecting a tremendous amount of information about their users, e.g. Google saving users' browsing and searching behavior. Some of these companies make (part of) their data available to the public through an Application Programming Interface (API), which is a structured way of interacting with a specific data service. Most APIs are well documented and so just a little programming experience can provide access to a wealth of data. In practice, this means that a single line of code can be used to request data from an API to either build a database or to update a map. Although this chapter does not review the specifics of API data queries, there are many readily available tutorials for a range of datasets, including the Twitter API used in this case study.[6]

Spatial Data Formats

Because APIs are well structured one can request that data are returned in a specific format. Ever since people started collecting structured data and measurements (from the ancient Romans to the accounting books of the Dutch East Indies Company), it has been common practice to store data in tabular form with each observation recorded in a separate row and each column representing a separate variable such as the CSV (or comma separated values) format. Another common format for encoding data – especially obtained via an API – is JSON, (JavaScript Object Notation). JSON is a data-interchange format used by many programming languages. Instead of having a single header row like CSV, it repeats the names of the variables for each row. Although JSON is widely adopted in the tools and techniques used in mapping, it is not organized along the more familiar rows and columns of tabular data and thus can be a bit daunting to read.

Spatial data is somewhat special and requires some different data formats to handle the points, lines and polygons used in digital mapping. Storing this data – particularly for lines and polygons – is complicated and therefore dedicated spatial files formats such as shapefiles (developed by the GIS company ESRI in the 1990s to store spatial vector data) or GeoJSON and TopoJSON are used. Spatial data may come in all kinds of formats initially, e.g. an Excel spreadsheet of point locations, and therefore converting data to an appropriate spatial data format is a regular part of the work flow. Traditionally, people use desktop GIS software (ESRI's ArcGIS, or the open source and free QGIS) but there are also a range of online tools available for data transformation such as Mapshaper or Mr Data Converter[7] for converting data from one format to another.

It is important to note here that spatial data and the information related to the location encapsulated within cannot be taken at face value. Especially with online data, researchers need to be aware of both the *precision* as well as the *accuracy* of the spatial data. First, precision indicates how precise or exact the spatial location is. For example, if one were to locate a single tweet, this can be done on the country, city, neighborhood, or even street level with ever increasing precision. Similarly, when coordinates are provided in latitude–longitude format, an increasing number of decimal places means an increasing precision. Second, accuracy refers to how closely that location in the data actually resembles the location in the real world. For example, in cities with high buildings a GPS fix might be difficult to obtain and accidentally locate a user or tweet one block away from their actual location. With online social media the issue of precision and accuracy is further confounded by the inherent bias in social media. For example, Twitter users are never a representational sample of the entire population but rather a very specific subset of the population. Even more, Twitter users that choose to ('opt in') add a location to each of their tweets are an even more specific group of users. In sum, any research with geosocial media has to be aware of issues with bias, precision and accuracy present in each of these data sets (Crampton *et al.*, 2013, Li *et al.* 2013; Longley *et al.* 2015).

Case Study of Geotagged 'Pizza' Tweets

Online data comes in many forms – email transaction logs, networked sensors, etc. – but this chapter focuses primarily on social interaction or activity that has been associated with geographical information. These kinds of data represent a range of activities, are drawn from different media, stored in various formats and have different levels of locational precision. Far from a standard set of data, online data is a wild collection of life online. Thus, this data has both real advantages – data on topics not gathered by official sources, real-time availability, socio-spatial reach – as well as some strong disadvantages – representativeness, preformed versus natural activity, unstructured, and messy formats. Moreover, online data is often laden

with privacy and ethical issues as they include traces of daily life captured without people's conscious decision to opt in. When location information is aggregated, one can gain detailed insight on subjects' movements including home locations, which is a subject of real concern (e.g. Crampton *et al.*, 2013; Elwood and Leszczynski, 2011; Leszczynski 2012; Poorthuis *et al.*, 2016).

Given the length of this article, the actual mechanics and use of code will not be covered but there are a number of tools that we recommend. First, a desktop software package such as ArcGIS or the free open-source program QGIS provide GIS functionality from making a simple map to advanced spatial analysis. In addition, a number of online services such as CartoDB and Mapbox provide relatively easy (and free) tools for making online maps. Those with programming experience should consider using the JavaScript library Leaflet, which only requires a few lines of code to create fairly polished-looking maps, especially those that use or need a pre-designed basemap in the background. Of course, mapping technology is fast moving and so any recommendation is subject to change even after a few months. Therefore, we also recommend searching for online tutorials for the latest tools and tutorials.

Getting to Know Social Media Data

One of the fundamental rules with working with social media data is that the research process and methods used do not necessarily change. Granted online datasets tend to be much larger than traditional Census data but it is also decidedly different from survey and interview data; namely, it is an unintended contribution to research rather than the result of designed instruments and thus it is unclear what exactly is measured. The rest of this chapter details a workflow for dealing with geotagged social media data in order to begin to identify spatial patterns. To be clear, this is a preliminary phase in such an analysis and those interested in more advanced spatial analysis should explore the wealth of texts written on this topic (see Brunsdon and Comber, 2015, for a recent, accessible introduction).

A key part of using social media data is understanding its anomalies and idiosyncrasies. Even using the term social media is a catch-all and the data used here, tweets, differs in a number of crucial ways – population base, cultural practice, intended purpose – from other media and services. It is therefore important to review the available variables associated with Twitter data. In addition to the actual text (and links and graphics) of the tweet itself, tweets contain a timestamp (including the time zone of the user), the user's name and image used in the profile, the number of followers and who else is being followed as well as many other data fields (more specific reviews of Twitter data are available in Crampton *et al.* 2013; Leetaru *et al.* 2013; Graham *et al.*, 2014). In this one little piece of social media, a whole range of research trajectories – relational, temporal, spatial, textual, visual – might be pursued. Of course, the richness of the data also brings with it a number of problems, including data management and handling that can require the cooperation of computer scientists and an investment in hardware and software packages.

Rather than be side-tracked by this, we focus on how fairly conventional practices within the geographic research tradition can be applied to social media data. First, one must simply choose a research topic that is addressable with social media data, which is often easier said than done (Poorthuis and Zook, 2014). As an example, this chapter uses the term 'pizza' to ask questions about the spatial variation in tweets that contain this text string (as well as some variations). The dataset is drawn from all geotagged tweets in the US (about 2 to 3 percent of all tweets) sent from June 2012 to July 2015. The data was extracted from the Digital Online Life and You (DOLLY) archive at the University of Kentucky (FloatingSheep, 2013), but rather than using all geotagged tweets containing the term 'pizza' we used a random sample for easier processing.

The topic of pizza is useful as a case study for a number of reasons. First it highlights how social media can capture culture (and other) practices that are generally not contained in official census or even industry databases. One might reasonably develop a database of pizza restaurants in the US but this still has little relevance for consumer behavior. Second, pizza is a relatively common text string appearing in social media and thus provides enough observations that it can successfully be aggregated across a larger number of areal units or counties. Third, the term pizza itself is readily interpreted as making reference to the food item or an associated object or place, e.g. pizza pan or pizza parlor. In contrast, consider the term 'hot', which has multiple meanings ranging from temperature to beauty to popularity. Even using the term 'pizza', we are careful here to limit our interpretation of its presence as an indicator of attention rather than impose a deeper meaning. Although techniques do exist to do this, for example qualitative analysis of tweets or algorithmic sentiment analysis, this chapter focuses solely on the spatial patterning of this attention rather then engaging with its nature, cause or effects. Keeping these cautions in mind, this case study examines the geography of tweets containing the term 'pizza' within the continental US.

Finding Patterns in Space

Although it is important to have a sufficient number of observations for analysis, big numbers do not necessarily result in good research. For example, if we simply map all the data points (see Figure 31.3a) the result is essentially a distribution of population density, a type of online data mapping that unfortunately occurs far too frequently in the popular press (Field, 2014). A more specific issue tied to cartographic representation is that, at the scale of the US, many of these

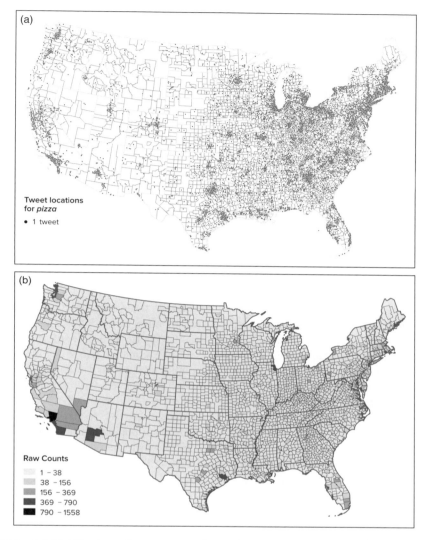

Figure 31.3   (a) Distribution of tweets containing the term pizza and (b) distribution of tweets containing the term pizza aggregated to counties

points overlap (known as over-plotting), making it difficult to understand the particular spatial pattern. This problem can be addressed by making every point slightly translucent and so locations with many points will gradually shade to a darker color. Of course, these darker areas remain large population centers – after all, people tweet where people live – and thus not much

additional understanding is obtained. Another technique would be to make the map interactive and allow a user to switch scales (zoom in and out) and thus get a better sense of clustering with a city or neighborhood. These kind of maps, however, are more technically challenging to implement, and do not work in static representations (such as those provided here).

A third approach is to create density surfaces (more commonly known as heat maps) that show the relative intensity of a phenomenon across space. Although these maps are widely used and popular, they are problematic when used for human activities. This is because the methodology for creating heat maps – the most common are called kernel density estimation or kriging – are based on an assumption of a continuous surface, e.g. temperature or weather. Because human actions (including tweets) are discrete and non-continuous events, the assumption of a continuous flow breaks down. Rich neighborhoods might abut poor areas or a tech center might be adjacent to abandoned factories and thus using heatmaps for social media data like tweets is suspect (see Longley *et al.*, 2005; Galton, 2004).

Aggregating up the individual data points into larger units (in this case counties) represent a fourth technique for studying the spatial patterns of pizza tweets. Figure 31.3b illustrates the number of tweets by county and results in a more interpretable visualization that also side-steps the over-plotting issue of Figure 31.3a. This approach, however, has the issue that county size within the US varies tremendously. This is most visible in the Southern California and Nevada region where the sheer size of some counties – particularly San Bernardino in California and Clark County in Nevada – make their concentrations stand out on the map. Although a larger area provides more space for activity, the tweets in these particular counties are largely concentrated in urban zones, which are then 'extended' to the entire footprint of the county. These counties stand in contrast to heavily populated but spatially smaller counties in the

Eastern seaboard, which contain many tweets but have less visual impact. A solution to this size problem is to create new identically sized spatial units for aggregation (see Shelton *et al.*, 2014) that can reduce the presence of large counties with urban cores. This chapter does not pursue this technique because using self-created units also means that one cannot then tie social media data to official data sources that are only available for officially defined spatial areas, a quality that many social science researchers are loath to lose. However, this 'binning' into new units is perfectly correct and can be useful in some circumstances.

Normalization and Odds Ratios

Although these steps have allowed the analysis to move beyond the simple plotting of points (Figure 31.3a), it still remains largely a visualization of where people live as the number of tweets for any phenomenon is closely correlated with population density. The most useful approach is to normalize the examined activity (e.g. pizza tweets) by a measure of population (e.g. pizza tweets per capita). With social media data, however, selecting the correct metric for population is fraught with potential problems because simply using Census reports of population assumes that the adoption and frequency of use of a particular service is the same across demographics and space. Places where a smaller/larger proportion of the population is tweeting or tweeting at a lower/higher rate than the population average will be misrepresented. Instead, a preferred approach is to normalize the examined social media activity (e.g. pizza tweets) by the overall level

(a)
$$OR = \frac{p_i/p}{r_i/r}$$

(b)
$$\ln(OR) - 1.96 * \sqrt{\frac{1}{p_i} + \frac{1}{p} + \frac{1}{r_i} + \frac{1}{r}}$$

$$OR_{lower} = e$$

Figure 31.4 (a) Odds ratio formula and (b) formula for lower bound of confidence interval of activity in social media (e.g. all tweets). This provides a pizza tweets per total number of tweets measure that more accurately reflects when a particular area stands out from the overall norm.

The downside to this approach is that the resulting metric – Clark County, NV has 11,812 pizza tweets for every 1,000,000 tweets – does not make a lot of sense intuitively. It is better, therefore, to use a metric such as the odds ratio that is commonly used in medical statistics (Bland and Altman, 2000) (see Figure 31.4a), where p_i is the number of pizza tweets in area i and p is the total number of pizza tweets in the US, r_i is the total number of tweets in area i and r is the grand total of all tweets in the US. The odds ratio is extremely useful in controlling differences related to size. To obtain a measure for all tweets in a particular area and the US, we again extracted a dataset from the DOLLY archive, more specifically a 0.01 percent random sample of all tweets sent during the time period under study. The result is a very easy to interpret metric – the odds ratio – in which places with a score of 1 have precisely the number of pizza tweets as one would expect given the overall level of Twitter activity. Locations that score < 1 have less attention to pizza than one would expect, and places with odds ratios > 1 have more tweets containing the term pizza than anticipated. The resulting spatial pattern (see Figure 31.5a) shows a relatively uniform distribution of pizza tweets across the U.S., a not unsurprising result given the popularity of this food.

Just using the odds ratio, however, does not guarantee a meaningful result because the odds ratio may be heavily influenced by only a handful of tweets in counties that just do not see high levels of tweeting activity. This chapter uses a random sample of pizza domains for easier processing but it also highlights the value of calculating confidence intervals for the odds ratio (see Figure 31.4b). When plotting only the lower bound of the confidence interval for the odds ratio, we ensure that for any counties displayed with an odds ratio > 1, we are 95 percent confident that the odds ratio is indeed *at least* that. The resulting pattern (see Figure 31.5b) is largely similar to that in Figure 31.5a, but many of the less populous counties now have much lower odds ratios. This makes sense because with lower sample sizes in those counties, the confidence interval is much wider than for counties with a higher number of tweets. In this specific case, one could, of course, alleviate part of this issue by increasing the sample size of the 'random' data set but this case study does not do so in order to emphasize the importance in controlling for noise in a dataset, something that frequently comes up when distributing a dataset to hundreds or thousands of spatial units. What at first seemed to be an adequately large number can quickly become problematic for some units.

Exploring Pizza Space and Time

This analysis now turns to the particular power of social media to explore topics for which there has historically been little to no data. Staying with the theme of pizza, this section reviews the spatial distribution of tweets referencing three pizza-related cultural markers (1) Digiornos – the number one frozen pizza sold in the US; (2) Little Caesers – a take-out pizza chain headquartered in Detroit, MI; and (3) California Pizza Kitchen (CPK) – a more upscale pizza restaurant headquartered in Los Angeles, CA. All maps use the odds ratio and confidence intervals outlined earlier.

The map of tweets referencing Digiornos is remarkably similar to the map of pizza tweets in general (Figure 31.5b) and is indicative of a mass-market consumer good that is readily available (and consumed) without a tremendous degree of spatial variation. This is consistent with other similar consumer brands such as Budweiser in the case of beer (see FloatingSheep, 2015) and as such provides a useful control and test of the validity

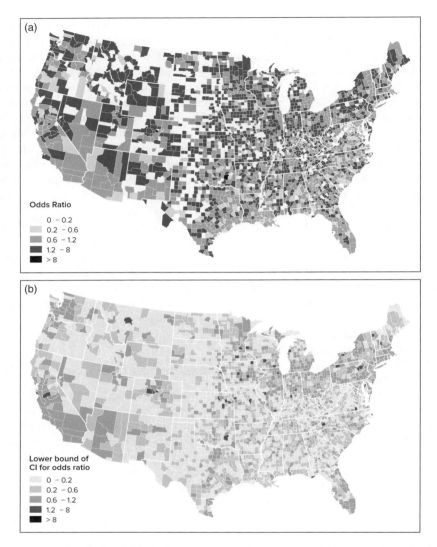

Figure 31.5   (a) Odds ratio of pizza tweets by county and (b) Lower bound of confidence interval for odds ratio of pizza tweets by county

of this approach. In contrast, the maps of tweets referencing Little Caesers and CPK show clear spatial patterning. Although Little Caesars is the third largest pizza chain in the US (as evidenced by the patterning of tweets across the country), there is also a clear concentration within Michigan. This analysis did not explore the nature of the Twitter activity behind this cluster, i.e. was it promotional

material, references to headquarters, or a higher per capita number of establishments, but it aptly demonstrates how careful spatial analysis of social media can illuminate and reflect the world. The pattern shown in Figure 31.6c for CPK stands in marked contrast to the first two, with many fewer counties in the US emerging as locations with CPK tweets. The counties that do emerge are

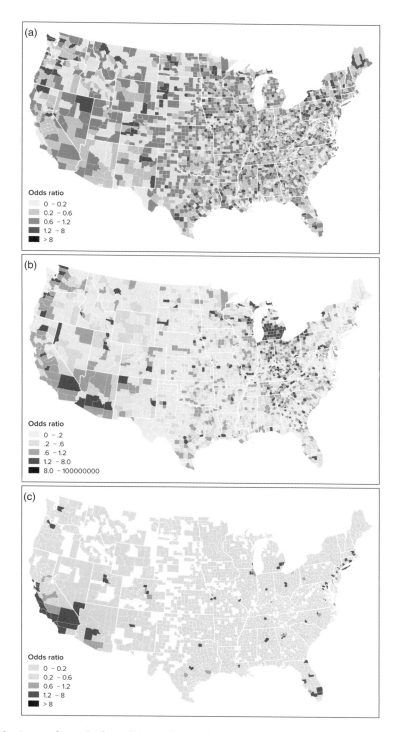

Figure 31.6   Lower bound of confidence interval for odds ratio of pizza tweets by county for (a) Digiornos, (b) Little Caesars (c) California Pizza Kitchen

almost uniformly urban and the sites for CPK franchises.

Although this kind of analysis provides an interesting look at the distribution of consumer attention to particular brands, it does not reveal much about spatial contours of cultural practice and values. This is again one of the real strengths of social media because it captures the everyday practices and utterances of large segments of the population. Although other (and arguably more socially important) analyses are possible (see Shelton *et al.*, 2014, 2015) this chapter continues with the case study of pizza by comparing two geographically constrained pizza cultures; namely, deep-dish pizza and pizza slices. Although spatially mobile, these practices are strongly associated with the urban centers of Chicago and New York, respectively, and we would expect to see this reflected within the attention of Twitter users. As Figures 31.7a and 31.7b demonstrate, there are larger regional clusters around both these cities, showing the connection between offline cultures and social media attention.

Although the clusters in Figures 31.7a and 7b are relatively easy to identify, many spatial patterns are much more difficult to discern and the selection of visual variables for a map can focus or distract attention. In addition to the visual interpretation, it is important therefore to also refer to statistical measures of clustering. In this step we expand from examining the significance for one spatial unit, e.g. the odds ratio for a single county, and compare the odds ratio for a single county to that of its neighbors. This analysis is run across the entire set of spatial units – in this case all counties in the US – to identify cases where local clustering is occurring in a statistically significant way. The standard approach to this is to calculate a Moran's I (Burt *et al.*, 2009). When we ran this analysis for deep-dish pizza we confirmed that the pattern shown around Chicago (Figure 31.7a) was statistically significant (Moran's I of 0.21). However,

cluster analysis depends upon the shape and size (as well as placement) of spatial units and so care should be taken in conducting and interpreting such analyses.

Finally, it is important to recognize that geotagged social media contains many more useful fields than just location (Crampton *et al.*, 2013). Distribution over time or networks may prove to be more important in understanding any particular phenomenon. Using the same data sets mapped in Figures 31.6a (Digiornos) and 31.7a (deep dish), we can examine the data for temporal rather than spatial variation. Aggregating the tweets into days of the week we again calculate an odds ratio, in this case comparing tweets referencing Digiornos or deep dish. The resulting odds ratio for each day measures the amount of Twitter attention on deep-dish pizza (values > 1) or Digiornos (values < 1). The temporal pattern is clear, with both Fridays and Saturdays exhibiting much more attention to deep dish versus Mondays to Thursdays when discussion of frozen pizza is much more evident (Figure 31.8). This again corresponds to known cultural practices (going out for dinner on the weekends) and the relatively longer cooking time required for this version of pizza (making it a less likely choice for the busier work week).

CONCLUSION

The goal of this chapter is to provide an overview of some of the basic tenets of mapmaking with a specific focus on using these techniques to map online data. This review is far from a comprehensive treatment of cartographic principles or GIS but it does provide those unfamiliar with mapping an initial guide on how to approach the spatial dimension of online data.

This chapter has largely treated online spatial data as ontologically secure and emphasizes issues of technique rather than considering

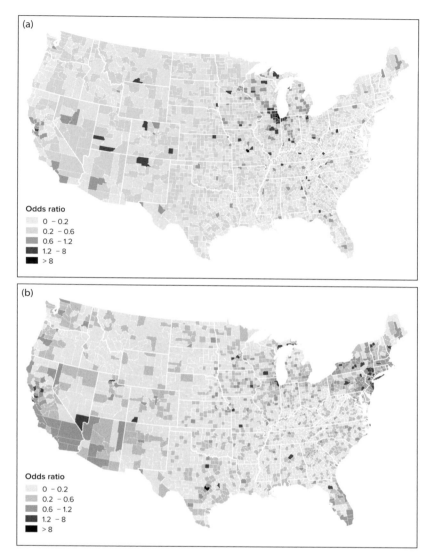

Figure 31.7   Lower bound of confidence interval for odds ratio of pizza tweets for (a) slice (b) deep dish

deeper questions about the process by which these data are created or what exactly they signify. These issues, however, are extremely relevant. For example, researchers engaged in mapping online data should regularly interrogate the data with which they work. How is a particular type of social media data created and who owns it? How are we enrolled in its use? What were the users' expectations (particularly regarding privacy) for the use of this data? How are users (both individuals and communities) disciplined by the data and the analysis that emerges from it?

Although these questions do not necessarily proscribe the use of online data in research or mapping, it is absolutely crucial

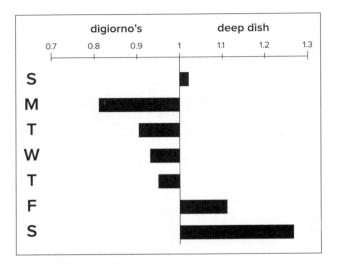

Figure 31.8   Temporal distribution of Digiornos pizza tweets versus deep-dish pizza

Source: Authors' analysis

that researchers raise them. We live in an era of 'big data' that is produced by seemingly every social and economic interaction, and unless we treat its analysis with care, the maps we create run the risk of doing unintentional harm in our efforts to better understand the world.

NOTES

1   https://xkcd.com/1138/. Accessed on August 14, 2015.

2   http://www.mapshaper.org/ Accessed on August 14, 2015.

3   http://colorbrewer.org Accessed on August 14, 2015.

4   http://factfinder2.census.gov/   Accessed   on August 14, 2015.

5   https://nycopendata.socrata.com   Accessed   on August 14, 2015.

6   https://dev.twitter.com/overview/documentation Accessed on August 14, 2015.

7   http://shancarter.github.io/mr-data-converter/ Accessed on August 14, 2015.

REFERENCES

Bertin, J. (1983). *Semiology of graphics: diagrams, networks, maps*. Redlands, CA: ESRI Press.

Bland, J. M. and Altman, D. G. (2000). 'The odds ratio'. *British Medical Journal*, 320(7247), 1468. http://doi.org/10.1136/bmj.320.7247.1468 Accessed on August 14, 2015.

Brewer, C. (2005). *Designing Better Maps: A Guide for GIS Users*. Redlands, CA: ESRI Press.

Brunsdon, C. and Comber, L. (2015). *An Introduction to R for Spatial Analysis and Mapping*. London: Sage Publications.

Burt, J.E., Barber, G.M. and Rigby, D.L. 2009. *Elementary Statistics for Geographers*. New York, NY: Guilford Press.

Crampton, J.W. (2011). *Mapping: A Critical Introduction to Cartography and GIS*. Vol. 11. New York, NY: John Wiley & Sons.

Crampton, J., Graham, M., Poorthuis, A., Shelton, T., Stephens, M., Wilson, M. and Zook, M. (2013). 'Beyond the geotag? Deconstructing "big data" and leveraging the potential of the Geoweb'. *Cartography and Geographic Information Science (CaGIS)*, 40(2), 130–9. doi:10.1080/15230406.2013. 777137 Accessed on August 14, 2015.

Dent, B., Torguson, J. and Hodler, T. (2008). *Thematic Map Design. The Plenum Series on Demographic Methods and Population Analysis*. New York: McGraw-Hill.

Elwood, S. and Leszczynski, A. (2011). 'Privacy, reconsidered: new representations, data practices, and the Geoweb'. *Geoforum*, 42(1), 6–15. http://doi.org/10.1016/j.geoforum.2010.08.003 Accessed on August 14, 2015.

Field, K. (2014). 'I'm wondering when people will realise the animated ectoplasm twitter maps don't actually show anything http://t.co/SJVYLyBn1F' [tweet]. June 17. Available from: https://twitter.com/kennethfield/status/478775510386741248 Accessed on August 14, 2015.

FloatingSheep. (2013). 'DOLLY'. Available from http://www.floatingsheep.org/p/dolly.html Accessed on August 14, 2015.

FloatingSheep. (2015). http://www.floatingsheep.org/2015/07/beerTweets.html Accessed on August 14, 2015.

Galton, A. (2004). 'Fields and objects in space, time, and space-time'. *Spatial Cognition and Computation*, 4(1), 39–68.

Graham, M., Hale, S.A. and Gaffney, D. (2014). 'Where in the world are you? Geolocation and language identification in Twitter'. *The Professional Geographer*, 66(4), 568–78. http://doi.org/10.1080/00330124.2014.907699 Accessed on August 14, 2015.

Graham, M., Sabbata, S. and Zook, M. (2015). 'Towards a study of information geographies: (im)mutable augmentations and a mapping of the geographies of information'. *Geo: Geography and Environment*. doi:10.1002/geo2.8/epdf

Krygier, J. and Wood, D. (2011). *Making maps: a visual guide to map design for GIS*. New York, NY: Guilford Press.

Harrower, M. and Brewer, C.A. (2003). 'ColorBrewer.org: an online tool for selecting colour schemes for maps'. *Cartographic Journal*, 40(1), 27–37.

Leetaru, K., Wang, S., Cao, G., Padmanabhan, A. and Shook, E. (2013). 'Mapping the global Twitter heartbeat: the geography of Twitter'. *First Monday*, 18(5), 290–307. http://doi.org/10.1287/orsc.1050.0122 Accessed on August 14, 2015.

Leszczynski, A. (2012). 'Situating the geoweb in political economy'. *Progress in Human Geography*, 36(1), 72–89. http://doi.org/10.1177/0309132511411231 Accessed on August 14, 2015.

Li, L., Goodchild, M. F. and Xu, B. (2013). 'Spatial, temporal, and socioeconomic patterns in the use of Twitter and Flickr'. *Cartography and Geographic Information Science*, 40(2), 61–77. http://doi.org/10.1080/15230406.2013.777139 Accessed on August 14, 2015.

Longley, P.A., Adnan, M. and Lansley, G. (2015). 'The geotemporal demographics of Twitter usage'. *Environment and Planning A*, 47(2), 465–84. http://doi.org/10.1068/a130122p Accessed on August 14, 2015.

Longley, P.A., Goodchild, M.F., Maguire, D.J. and Rhind, D.W. (2005). *Geographic Information Systems and Science*. 2nd edn. New York, NY: Wiley.

MacEachren, A.M. (1992). 'Visualizing uncertain information'. *Cartographic Perspectives*, 13, 10–19.

Monmonier, M. (2014). *How to Lie with Maps*. Chicago, IL: University of Chicago Press.

Poorthuis, A. and Zook. M. (2014). 'Artists and bankers and hipsters, oh my! Mapping Tweets in the New York Metropolitan Region'. *Cityscape*, 16(2), 169–73. Available from: http://www.huduser.org/portal/periodicals/cityscpe/vol16num2/ch13.pdf Accessed on August 14, 2015.

Poorthuis, P. and Zook, M. (2015). 'Small stories in Big Data: gaining insights from large spatial point pattern data sets'. *Cityscape* [special issue], 151–60.

Poorthuis, A., Zook, M., Shelton, T., Graham, M. and Stephens, M. (2016). 'Using geotagged digital social data in geographic research'. In N. Clifford, M. Cope, T. Gillespie & S. French (eds.), *Key Methods in Geography*. 3rd edn. London: Sage, pp. 248–70.

Robinson, A.H., Morrison, J.L., Muehrcke, P.C., Kimerling, A.J. and Guptill, S.C. (1995). *Elements of Cartography*. New York, NY: John Wiley & Sons.

Shelton, T., Poorthuis, A., Graham, M. and M. Zook. (2014). 'Mapping the data shadows of Hurricane Sandy: Uncovering the sociospatial dimensions of "big data"'. *Geoforum*, 52(3), 167–79. http://dx.doi.org/10.1016/j.geoforum.2014.01.006 Accessed on August 14, 2015.

Shelton, T., Poorthuis, A. and Zook, M. (2015). 'Social media and the city: rethinking urban socio-spatial inequality using user-generated geographic information'. *Landscape and Urban Planning.* Volume 142, pp. 198–211.

Slocum, T., McMaster, R., Kessler, F. and Howard, H. (2009). *Thematic Cartography and Geographic Visualization*. 3rd edn. Upper Saddle River, NJ: Pearson/Prentice Hall.

## PART IX

The Future of Online Social Research

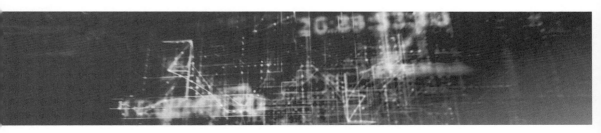

## 32

Engaging Remote Marginalized Communities using Appropriate Online Research Methods

Brian Beaton, David Perley, Chris George and Susan O'Donnell

INTRODUCTION

Many marginalized communities are left out of research initiatives due to their geographic, political, cultural, social and economic isolation and challenges. When research does happen, it often focuses on how the population is disadvantaged, portraying community members as passive and damaged subjects rather than active agents with the capacity for resurgence and self-determination. One result of ignoring these populations and environments or portraying them as helpless subjects is that the research is used to create unbalanced policies and programs that can have a further negative impact on the community members and ultimately the entire society.

Appropriate online research methods with marginalized communities involve using participatory action research (PAR) approaches. Together, online research with PAR can provide marginalized groups with an opportunity to develop their capacity to gather and share their information and stories; create

the products (reports, presentations and articles) for required programs, policies and projects; and work with researchers and partners to positively influence sustainable and healthy environments for future generations. Although in-person contact and face-to-face information sharing is critically important for establishing long-term, meaningful relationships and partnerships with marginalized communities, online tools are essential to maintaining collaborative relationships between researchers and their remote community partners.

Participatory action research involves producing knowledge jointly to create critical interpretations of the world that are accessible and understandable to everyone involved and actionable (Chatterton *et al.*, 2007). It brings together action and reflection, theory and practice aimed at both practical solutions to issues of concern to people and the flourishing of individuals and communities (Reason and Bradbury, 2001). Given that many of the challenges facing marginalized communities are structural and embedded within wider social relations, we believe that the action component of PAR with marginalized communities needs to be two-pronged, aimed both at solutions in the specific communities and at structural changes that will benefit all marginalized communities. PAR challenges researchers to work closely with communities to identify and integrate local knowledge systems and resources into the research so everyone involved is sharing, learning and benefiting from each other.

Marginalized groups are increasingly demanding that researchers working with their communities use collaborative strategies to design and conduct their research. Participatory action research that supports positive community social and economic development and changes are preferred methodologies. 'PAR was born in the soil of discontent, understanding critical inquiry to be a tool for social change' (Fine *et al.*, 2008: 160). In *Research is Ceremony: Indigenous Research Methods*, Wilson (2008: 155) writes 'participatory action research is so useful for Indigenous people because it really fits well … into our paradigm, because the idea is to improve the reality of the people you are working with'. Collaborating with communities and their organizations and focusing on each community as a unique whole is critical. Smith's (2012) *Decolonizing Methodologies* identifies the benefits of strong research partnerships with marginalized communities. Involving Indigenous people (scholars, Elders and community members) in all stages of the research process helps to ensure that the methodology is rooted in the epistemology of that particular community. In this way, ally partner scholars in the research can develop a deeper understanding of these unique worldviews and epistemologies. The desired outcome is for the research to appropriately reflect and enrich the community's knowledge base. In Canada and elsewhere in the world, academic researchers working with marginalized communities are often guided by government and institutional guidelines.[1]

PAR can challenge research that focuses on the problems rather than the strengths of marginalized communities. For example, in Canada, most of the research conducted on remote Indigenous communities highlights their poverty and health problems. The resulting discourse and hegemony of damage-centred research is now deeply rooted in many sectors of society. In contrast, Tuck (2009) advocates a desire-centred research approach with marginalized people and their communities. Other Indigenous theorists forcefully advocate for appropriate research methodologies involving participatory action research work in Indigenous communities to develop a more positive and accurate presentation (Battiste, 2013; Smith, 2012; Wilson, 2008).

Understanding the strength of individuals in marginalized communities can be challenging for researchers based in universities in far-away urban centres. In addition, doing any type of research work in remote communities is difficult for academics for many reasons. Participatory action research is even more challenging due to the time, financial and personal commitments required. Professors and most academic researchers are required to teach and be on campus for most of their time. Securing adequate funding and time release to support PAR in far-away, difficult-to-reach communities is always a challenge. PAR requires a strong partnership between everyone involved in this work. Establishing trust, transparency, accountability, constructive, beneficial activities and relationships that work for the community, its members and the research team can take a very long time (Kindon *et al.*, 2007). The pressure to publish or perish influences many academics and their choices for research fields. Interactive technologies including videoconferencing allow researchers and communities to meet together across wide distances to plan and collaborate together.

Finding ways to conduct appropriate and respectful online research with remote marginalized communities is the focus of this chapter. Our chapter includes a case study of online research with remote Indigenous communities using an online questionnaire as well as other online methods to gather and share information. Other chapters in this Handbook include an overview of online surveys (Vehovar and Lozar Manfreda, this volume), sampling and design methods (Fricker, this volume; Toepoel, this volume) and a review of different online survey software tools (Kaczmirek, this volume). Our work provides a context for using these methodologies with remote communities, highlighting the significant value of working closely with marginalized communities, adapting the methods in a culturally appropriate way.

To engage Indigenous communities, researchers must first respect their cultural practices and territories. Recognizing and honouring the unceded traditional territories of the Wolastoqey nation as the place for the creation of this chapter is an essential initial step for the authors. We thank the Wolastoqey people for sharing their lands and resources that make the production of this material possible and the Cree, Oji-Cree and Ojibway nations that partnered with us and shared a small part of their story within this chapter.

THE CANADIAN CONTEXT OF THE RESEARCH

Most Canadians live in urban centres near the southern border with the US. The Canadian north is dotted with small, remote, politically autonomous Indigenous communities. In many northern areas in Canada there are no permanent roads, and expensive flights on small planes are the only way to reach remote communities. Many of the remote communities are connected by local community networks using a variety of technologies to connect the buildings, including wireless, cable and fibre infrastructure, and to the digital backhaul to other communities and urban centres and networks (Beaton and Campbell, 2014). Communication

technologies are quickly adopted and adapted in these environments to meet local political, social, health, education and economic needs of the communities. These technologies assist to address the isolation experienced and maintain connections as families and community members relocate to other communities across the region. Social media, videoconferencing and mobile tools have become important tools to gather, protect and share information and traditional knowledge (Molyneaux *et al.*, 2014). The availability and high level of usage of these networks makes online research with these communities possible and appropriate (Gratton and O'Donnell, 2011).

It is only since England colonized the land we now call Canada that the original people have been living on small, rural and remote reserve lands with limited access to the resources needed to develop their communities. The terms of the treaties signed with the colonial entities have been upheld by the Supreme Court of Canada, but the governments of the day continue to fight their treaty obligations in court (Palmater, 2011). As a result, most Indigenous communities in Canada continue to struggle against colonial governments and corporate efforts to access the resources on their lands and remove the people from their traditional territories. Despite the relative prosperity of Canada, the majority of these marginalized communities experience high levels of unemployment and poverty.

In this challenging environment, the most successful research initiatives are committed and long-term involving researchers whom the communities trust. The case study in this chapter is an effort by an ongoing research partnership between a university in the province of New Brunswick near the Atlantic coast in Eastern Canada and an Indigenous council representing communities in northern Ontario more than 3,000 kilometres away. The collaborative study used an online questionnaire to engage community members living and surviving in five remote, fly-in communities. The communities are small, with populations ranging from several hundred to one thousand people, and a total population of about 2,400 in the five communities.

For more than a decade, the First Nations Innovation (FNI) research project based at the University of New Brunswick has been using information and communication technologies (ICT) to partner and collaborate with Indigenous organizations and their member communities. Two of this chapter's authors are Indigenous academics working with FNI and the other two FNI authors identify as long-time settler allies of Indigenous people, having worked many years with Indigenous organizations. The FNI project has used various collaborative online methods to connect with their partners remotely and to conduct research with remote communities. For example, these include an Indigenous-controlled videoconferencing network for regular monthly meetings to connect all four FNI partners across three time zones in an audio-visual public sphere (McKelvey and O'Donnell, 2009) and to conduct focus groups between remote community members and researchers located in far-away institutions (Gratton and O'Donnell, 2011). An advantage to marginalized communities and researchers alike is that the videoconference medium enables research to be two-way. These tools support the community to initiate its own enquiries and make its own spontaneous input. This is especially valuable at a time when response rates to online methods have been heavily affected by 'swipe and delete' responses to research requests, particularly when they are received on smaller screen tablet devices (Dillman, in this volume).

The focus of our collaborative research has been to document how the remote Indigenous communities are using ICT in interesting and innovative ways, including distance education, telehealth and a range of other online applications, services and activities. Our work has highlighted many community strengths but also how structural inequalities – particularly how public

funding is disbursed for telecommunications networks in rural and remote regions of the country – have a significant negative impact on community efforts to use digital networks and ICT effectively (McMahon et al., 2014). More recently, we formed the First Mile Connectivity Consortium (FMCC) to work to change the government policies shaping telecommunication network development. We consider all our activist work to be part of our PAR methodology and we use online networks extensively to make it happen.

WORKING WITH INTERMEDIARY ORGANIZATIONS THAT BRIDGE DIGITAL DISPARITIES

Building long-term relationships with remote communities requires partnerships with the intermediary organizations with which the communities work (McMahon et al., 2013). In the Canadian context, these intermediary organizations are generally membership-based and governed by an Indigenous council comprised of the leadership of the communities they serve. A prime example of intermediary organizations in Canada is the not-for-profit councils that represent a group of communities often sharing a common culture and language.

McMahon et al. (2013) describe intermediary organizations as mediators between organizations, government and institutions that operate industry-standard IT infrastructure. The leadership of these intermediary organizations is most often paid staff rather than the elected officials who lead the communities for specific terms. Around the world, groups often referred to as non-government organizations (NGOs) perform similar functions to these intermediary organizations. Building partnerships with these organizations means researchers have contact people who are often available for longer term relationships. Given that these intermediary organizations are working with and accountable to the communities they serve, they are usually located in nearby small urban centres that tend to have more stable digital infrastructure and ICT processes than the remote communities (McMahon *et al.*, 2013). For example, the intermediary organizations usually have a clear process in place and funding for digital network and ICT support, software licenses, equipment and staff training. In comparison, the ICT support and training is usually challenging for the communities to access (Beaton and Carpenter, 2014). In this way, intermediary organizations can help to bridge the gap between the researchers and the communities they collaborate with (McMahon *et al.*, 2013).

The online research methods proven to be most successful within these challenging environments are those led by the communities and their intermediary organizations working collaboratively with their academic partners (McMahon *et al.*, 2013). For example, Gratton and O'Donnell (2011) worked closely with the Keewaytinook Okimakanak council as the intermediary organization to plan and conduct their research, including arranging the focus groups, community facilities, community-owned digital networks and videoconferencing equipment, local resource people, and planning the research methodology and questions. The online questionnaire discussed in the case study in this chapter is another example of participatory action research working with intermediary organizations and meeting the research needs of the partner communities.

Indigenous languages are severely challenged by the English language that dominates online and the academic publishing world. Translating culturally appropriate guidelines and protocols into an online environment is a challenge for any researcher wanting to work with remote marginalized communities. Partnering with intermediary organizations and community researchers makes it possible to support the inclusion of Indigenous language speakers who are often the Elders in these communities and the keepers of the traditional knowledge. Integrating

a mix of communication technologies in the data collection process, for example supporting oral presentations with videoconferencing (Gratton and O'Donnell, 2011), makes it possible for everyone to participate. Employing local translators and community researchers supports the leadership's efforts to own and manage research that contributes to their community.

The researchers worked closely with intermediary organizations when forming the non-profit FMCC organization. FMCC[2] is an advocacy organization comprised primarily of intermediary organization partners. FMCC prepares and submits written and oral interventions to change national policy related to telecommunications networks. The goal is to create a more equitable telecommunications infrastructure that benefits rural and remote communities. The FMCC work is a key element of the PAR methodology.

SELF-DETERMINATION APPLIED TO RESEARCH AND DIGITAL NETWORKS

As suggested earlier, conducting research with marginalized communities requires an approach that both builds community capacity and recognizes community members as active agents of change. In the experience of the authors, critical researchers working with marginalized communities need to be guided by an approach that recognizes their potential for self-determination.

In Canada, researchers can be guided by an approach called 'OCAP' – Ownership, Control, Access and Possession – or self-determination applied to research. We believe that OCAP principles can be more widely applied to research with marginalized communities globally. The principles of OCAP were first developed by the National Aboriginal Health Organization in Canada in their attempt to protect and control research data supporting Indigenous communities across the country (Schnarch, 2004;

Assembly of First Nations, 2007). Since the OCAP principles appeared a decade ago, they have been cited and applied in other countries, including the US and Australia (Winter *et al.*, 2014). OCAP principles state that communities own information collectively; have a right to control all aspects of research and information management of a research project from inception to completion; must have access to information and data about themselves no matter where it is held; and can assert and protect ownership of data. The OCAP approach supports communities to refuse to work with researchers who do not respect their ability to do their own research. Owning, controlling, accessing and possessing all aspects of a community's existence supports a sustainable environment rich in culture, history and future opportunities.

OCAP can and has been applied to online networks (Kakekaspan *et al.*, 2014). This has two implications for online research with marginalized communities. First, the research must support building capacity in the communities to effectively manage the content, traffic and services on their local online networks. Second, researchers must recognize that marginalized communities have a right to own and control the local broadband network in their communities in order to support the flow of information and services. Positioning the communities as producers of content and innovative managers of their infrastructure and digital networks creates a constructive research environment for everyone. Putting the communities first when digital networks and resources are planned and financed means the resources are made available and managed by the communities.

OCAP applied to digital networks is also called the 'First Mile' approach, a counterstrategy to the traditional Last Mile colonial solution that government programs use to fund private telecommunications corporations to develop and deliver the digital services in marginalized communities (McMahon *et al.*, 2011). By using the First Mile approach, these communities at the end

of the road are able to identify, develop and deliver a digital strategy addressing their needs, ensuring they receive the services they require (McMahon *et al.*, 2014).

The OCAP and decolonization work being undertaken by marginalized communities demand appropriate responses from researchers and will shape the methodologies they choose to employ. Communities need access to the research data and the resources to properly present and document their stories and requirements. Researchers wanting to understand and learn from the communities must identify strategies to work closely with the communities and their partners to ensure local ownership and control of the information in order that it continues to be accessed by and within the possession of community members for future reference.

Ferreira *et al.* (2004) and Ramírez *et al.* (2003) are among the earliest authors outlining the need for participatory evaluation of ICT in their work with the remote Indigenous communities in northern Ontario. The benefits to researchers doing participatory and collaborative online research with remote and rural marginalized communities are multifold. Building and maintaining relationships with the communities through the effective use of digital networks adds value to both the research and the infrastructure. Unfortunately, some institutions still make it difficult for online community-based research by creating policy and pricing obstacles for researchers to use their facilities and equipment. Community networks depend on researchers and their institutions to provide adequate compensation for the use of community-owned networks and facilities (O'Donnell *et al.*, 2008). When researchers and communities have easy and convenient access to these online technologies, they can support long-term and cost-effective engagement and involvement in the research process. Research projects that contribute to the costs of community-owned digital networks when they are working with remote marginalized communities provide another economic benefit in the communities.

EMPLOYING CULTURALLY APPROPRIATE RESEARCH, COMMUNICATION AND DATA PROTOCOLS

The challenge most researchers working with marginalized communities experience is being able to switch from an urban institutional-centric research approach to a community-centric approach (Perley and O'Donnell, 2005). Researchers working with marginalized communities are in the unique position of conducting research in often very challenging, very expensive environments. If their research is of any value, researchers are privileged to be gathering and documenting information that can contribute to the future well-being of the community. It is important for researchers to acknowledge their own place and privilege in this process to understand and appreciate the importance of the work being undertaken. Recognizing the actual contributions of the community, their intermediary organizations and the people provides researchers with the opportunity to value and support local ownership of the information being shared.

As we suggested earlier, research is viewed suspiciously and often resented by communities when researchers arrive to get their information and then leave without being heard from again (Smith, 2012; Walmark, 2009; Wilson, 2008). Researchers interested in working with marginalized communities must be prepared to leave most of their personal academic experiences in the places where those teachings work best. Marginalized communities and their histories are often rich in oral traditions, narratives and ceremony. Learning about and celebrating these aspects of the communities requires researchers to be open to learning a new way of understanding and seeing the world around them. Wilson (2008: 15) describes recent research work as efforts to bring 'communities into the research process [with] the usefulness of the research becoming more visible and beneficial to the communities'. Communities often demand a collaborative and leadership role in any research work that involves their members, teachings or lands. Returning to the communities, providing reports in formats useful to community leaders and understanding that the research and development work is ongoing are important considerations for researchers planning participatory action research.

Once again, intermediary organizations and their trusted staff members become important partners to developing and delivering online research. Indigenous knowledge is unique simply due to the fact that the people have lived and survived on their lands for thousands of years. How their information is gathered, presented and used must be carefully considered and protected. In Canada, intermediary organizations are developing processes and data protocols for ensuring appropriate handling of the research data (McMahon et al., 2015). As marginalized groups and Indigenous academics challenge the traditional approach to doing research with their communities, new guidelines and protocols are being created by the communities and their intermediary organizations. For example, the Mi'Kmaw Ethics Watch[3] is endorsed by the Mi'Kmaq Nations to protect Mi'kmaq peoples and their knowledge when any form of research is conducted in their communities. The research requirements in all sectors, including health, environmental, social and humanities, are established by experts and endorsed by the community leadership. All researchers are required to submit their research proposals for review by Mi'Kmaq academics who ensure their standards are upheld and respected for any type of research being conducted in their communities. Online researchers must carefully respect these requirements and avoid possible conflicts before their research work is able to proceed. Other Indigenous groups also have their similar protocols to follow, including the Keewaytinook Okimakanak Research Institute (KORI)[4] highlighted in the chapter's case study. Researchers who recognize that every community has its own ethical guidelines, often available only in an oral format, respect the local knowledge and experience.

Several policies, created by the FNI research project partners, are available online for communities and other research teams.[5] The FNI team created the data governance policy to support the intermediary organizations working with their membership as they create new research partners and relationships. The data governance policy provides a clear statement highlighting that the ownership and control of the community information belongs with the community. Planning and delivering all research requires the support for the involvement of the community and their designated intermediary organization throughout the entire research process. Identifying and financing community-based engagement includes tasks such as data storage on local servers and shared online; local staffing and training; clearly defining roles, responsibilities and expectations; along with other requirements outlined in the policy. Researchers must be prepared to hand over the research data to the communities or their intermediary organizations if that is required. These considerations challenge traditional research and researchers but they also enrich the research process through the inclusion of others and making research practical and applicable to everyone.

BUILDING COMMUNITY RESEARCH CAPACITY

Including appropriate employment and training strategies for local researchers creates short- and long-term opportunities for doing research in the communities. Every position, whether it is part- or full-time in small, remote communities is another asset as people contribute to their family's and the community's existence. The contemporary mixed economy supports every family

member as they work together to provide for all the needs of everyone, from the youngest member to the Elders (Abele and Delic, 2014; Beaton et al., 2014). Researchers who invest in local community capacity, training and research employment opportunities within these environments become allies in the community's struggles for development.

The Keewaytinook Okimakanak Research Institute is one example of how a group of small, remote First Nations directs their own research work. The institute was established in 2004 with the long-term goal of having Indigenous community researchers in each First Nation (Walmark, 2009). Over the past decade, the Institute created training opportunities, partnerships with other researchers and employment projects with their partner First Nations. Transferring their power, privilege and resources to the people in the communities is the unstated goal of all the members of this research institute.

The publications policy created by the FNI research project is an example of research requirements supporting local capacity development. This document is also available online at the First Mile website.[6] The production of reports, presentations, papers and articles is an important component for every researcher but these products are equally important to marginalized communities. Recognizing the ownership of the information and providing the means for ensuring the resulting products are accurate and respectful is just as important as gathering the data. Supporting the co-authorship and co-presentation of the information is another strategy for creating capacity building opportunities in the communities. Most of this production work is completed online by email and using document sharing tools. Final products are then shared online, for example the FNI research and publications website where documents are available for download. Handing the data back to the community can present challenges for conventional ethics policies. Eynon et al. (this volume) propose creative options in addressing these ethical issues.

CASE STUDY: AN ONLINE QUESTIONNAIRE WITH REMOTE INDIGENOUS COMMUNITIES AND ACTION FOR CHANGE

This case study centres on the development and administration of an online community questionnaire with five remote Indigenous communities. The study was designed to explore the effectiveness of local and regional economic and social enterprises and services and the use of ICT in the communities. Delivering the questionnaire in the winter of 2014 using PAR methodology meant preparations had to begin more than seven months before the questionnaire went live. The PAR work leading up to the questionnaire made it possible for the communities, the intermediary organization staff and the leaders to participate in the development of the questions so that the responses would be useful to them afterwards. The information obtained from the online community questionnaire is now available for the communities and their intermediary organizations to plan and create new opportunities addressing local needs and priorities. Our PAR research is possible due to the long history of partnership development, professional exchanges, production and research work existing among all the participants.

Keewaytinook Okimakanak (KO)[7] is the intermediary organization partner in the research, working with researchers from the University of New Brunswick (UNB). KO is a second-level support organization representing six small, remote communities located in northwestern Ontario, Canada. The KO leaders established their KO Research Institute (KORI) to work with academic researchers to ensure all research being conducted in their communities properly addresses their needs. The KORI team began working with UNB on a research initiative that after ten years developed into the FNI research project. The authors of this chapter are all researchers on the FNI team. Monthly FNI videoconference meetings continue to support and strengthen the ongoing

partnership with all the members of the team. The FNI website[8] continues to evolve as it highlights the changing and dynamic work being undertaken by the partners.

KO staff and community members were involved in every step of the online community questionnaire process. Their involvement was critical in the planning, development and testing of the questions as well as the later data analysis, presentation of the findings and production of articles using the information obtained from the community questionnaire. As stated earlier, participatory action research is possible for our research due to our past work and long-term relationship with KO and the remote KO First Nations. Research planning meetings with the FNI researchers and the chiefs of the communities involved discussing our future research plans and reaffirming our working relationship between FNI and KORI. The KO community chiefs eventually formally endorsed our proposed research with a supporting resolution passed at a chiefs meeting. This formal recognition by KO makes the online survey using PAR methodology appropriate and respectful in this context.

Planning for the February 2014 start of the online community questionnaire meant beginning our preparation work in June 2013. The collaborative work involved drafting the sample community questionnaire using the online SurveyMonkey tool; preparing the FNI application to UNB's Research Ethics Board; consulting with each KO department manager (health, education, research, administration, public works, etc.) to determine the questions they wanted to include about their programs and services; and reviewing and seeking approval for the final questionnaire. In the end, the 2014 community questionnaire included 29 questions, many multiple choice with comment boxes that allowed both quantitative and qualitative information to be obtained.

To support the appropriate delivery of the questionnaire, the FNI research project provided funding to contract local community researchers. The community researchers supported local first language residents to complete the online questionnaire, providing translation and technical support as required. The research team organized online meetings to advertise for, contract and train the community researchers. Each community researcher completed the draft community questionnaire and provided feedback to ensure its acceptability in their community. Job descriptions and an employment contract were prepared.

The UNB researchers worked with the community researchers to advertise and promote the online community questionnaire in each community. We included prize draws to encourage community members to complete the online questionnaire and sent email notices to community members in advance of the launch date. Notices about the questionnaire were also posted online on each community Facebook site. The community questionnaire results were closely monitored to avoid duplicate submissions and to ensure the data being contributed was from individual community members. Weekly reports were provided for each of the community researchers to encourage more local promotion and support for community members. We distributed promotional posters and email messages throughout the eight weeks that the community questionnaire was left open. Other methods to reach community members included the posters and flyers distributed by the local researcher along with local television and radio notices on their community channels.

When the online questionnaire was closed, a total of 237 community questionnaires contained data useful for analysis. It represented the most comprehensive data gathering exercise ever with these remote communities. A preliminary summary document of the results was prepared and shared by email with the research team. The preliminary results were also presented to other academics at UNB. While the community reports were being prepared, two papers based on the results were co-authored by members of the KO team and a community member and co-presented at a major Canadian social sciences conference (Beaton and Carpenter, 2014; Beaton *et al.*, 2014). The papers are available online and are a product model for the type of collaborative work involved in conducting PAR research with communities in the margins of our society.

The researchers worked with KORI to produce a comprehensive report for KO highlighting the information obtained, including feedback by community members in their own words about the community services delivered by each of the different KO departments (health, education, public works, etc.). The UNB researchers travelled to different KO offices in the region to present and discuss the report, summarizing the findings from the community questionnaire about KO programs and services. The KO report was also made available online on the e-community websites.[9]

The researchers then worked with KORI to produce unique reports for each community based on the data collected in that community. Preparing and reviewing the research results for each KO community took considerable effort by the researchers working closely with the KORI team. The unique comprehensive reports designed for distribution online required the review and approval of the director of KORI. In addition to the unique community reports, the researchers worked with KORI to produce large posters (two feet × three feet) with questionnaire results and community photographs so some of the information could be displayed in public places in each partner community in an appealing and informative format. The reports and posters were made available online for community viewing, along with the academic papers co-authored by the UNB researcher, KO and the community members.

The FNI and KORI teams used online tools including email, videoconferencing and Facebook to organize and coordinate the research visits to the KO communities. The logistics were considerable because all the communities are remote fly-in locations and few communities have direct scheduled flights between them. Guest accommodations are often difficult to find in the communities due to a busy but short summer construction season and a general lack of housing. During the community visits, the UNB researchers took the community reports and posters into each KO community and shared the information with community leaders and members during formal and informal meetings. The visits ranged from four days to more than a week in each community. The findings from the questionnaire provide the KO organization and each of the KO communities with valuable information, which is now being used in planning efforts. Additional research data was obtained during these community visits by conducting a set of structured interviews with community members and KO staff members. This new data set is now being analysed and will be used in future papers, presentations and funding applications in partnership with the communities. Building and strengthening relationships with the communities and the KO organization is an ongoing requirement of the FNI research work.

A key finding from the online questionnaire was the desire by community members for additional training and educational opportunities supporting land-based activities and traditional lifestyles. This finding is now directing the action component of the PAR methodology: leading the development of projects involving renewable energy and local entrepreneurship in the remote communities. The projects each require training initiatives utilizing the local digital networks and resources. The work involved in each of these developments is supported by past research and future research needs.

The online environment was used throughout the research supporting the planning, the delivery and the follow up of this portion of the PAR. The various online tools were essential components of this research providing a means for sharing information, providing training and support, and distributing and archiving results. For Indigenous language speakers and community members without access or experience in using the online tools, the local community

researcher continues to be available to assist them in understanding the survey tool and for sharing the information. One constraint of the survey was its length and the amount of time it took some respondents to complete it. Delivering the survey in person continues to be the ideal strategy but costs, distance and time involved in doing in-person surveys has been a barrier in the past. Not having community data has led to a lack of information to use in community and program planning. That is the main reason why online methods are more appropriate in this context.

Moving forward with PAR involves ongoing videoconference meetings with the research partners to plan future work. Expanding on the earlier research, we will continue to use PAR methodology to examine how the remote KO communities are developing culturally appropriate and sustainable skills training, and to what extent digital technologies are used to support these activities. The team will use the online tools described throughout this chapter to engage and involve the communities in all aspects of the work. Training and local capacity developments are key components of future research. Working with the community-owned Internet high school[10] to develop training support programs and services expands local opportunities. Developing local research and training opportunities in the renewable energy sector, entrepreneurship and land-based activities provides new data sets and long-term employment opportunities in these environments. Broadly our research will use the online strategies outlined to identify the requirements and components for effective, community-based training and skills initiatives in small, remote communities in Canada.

SUMMARY AND CONCLUSIONS

Digital technology is a two-edged sword. Residents of remote communities are using online tools extensively – in particular

Facebook – to maintain social and cultural connections (Molyneaux *et al.*, 2014). Using these technologies to conduct research can support communities to find the answers to some of the many challenges they are experiencing. However, most communication online is in English and digital technologies are supporting the further erosion of fragile Indigenous languages. Digital networks can also be used as tools of settler colonialism and to further develop the extractive industries that are severely compromising Indigenous ways of life. Given these realities, researchers must find ways to conduct research with marginalized communities that will support the development and sustainability of their local research capacity.

Marginalized communities are creating their own research institutes to support and deliver research that meets their needs and priorities. The collaborative FNI research described in the case study with KORI in northern Ontario and UNB highlights how it is possible to use digital tools extensively to build partnerships with academic institutions and academics who respect local self-determination. Intermediary organizations that are owned and directed by the communities they represent are important partners in working effectively with the people in these remote regions.

Given the many challenges facing remote communities, there have been considerable efforts by research granting agencies to fund research with communities in a manner that supports community capacity-building. The mandatory guidelines for ethical research involving humans that all university researchers must abide by in Canada has an entire chapter devoted to conducting ethical research with marginalized communities (Tri-Council, 2010). Despite this support and guidance however, few researchers are conducting research with remote marginalized communities for many of the practical reasons noted in this chapter. More resources and proper support systems are required to ensure these communities are properly represented in the literature.

The challenge of using online research methods is one restraint for many researchers. A huge disparity exists between urban university-based researchers and remote community members when considering the access and availability of different digital infrastructure, connectivity, IT support, tools such as databases and software and other online resources. At the same time, marginalized communities and their regional partners do have access to many of their own online tools, for example a videoconferencing network that they use regularly to communicate with each other. Unfortunately, university-based researchers often have difficulty finding ways to access and use their university videoconferencing network to communicate with their remote partners. Building these digital bridges in order that the Indigenous networks are recognized, utilized and properly resourced is an important component for any researcher working with remote communities.

Successful research partnerships between university-based researchers and remote communities, like the FNI project based at UNB, are working closely with their partners making the video tools work for visual communication. Creating strong relationships and maintaining the trust between partners despite the vast geographical distance between them is crucial to successful research partnerships.

After more than ten years of working with marginalized communities, strategic guidelines for good practices for online research methodologies have emerged. In summary, these good practices include:

- Partnering with intermediary organizations to conduct research in their member communities.
- Establishing and supporting collaborative, long-term, respectful relationships.
- Using a wide range of online tools creatively, appropriately and effectively – including social media, videoconferencing, websites and mobile tools – to maintain partnerships and to gather, protect and share information and traditional knowledge.

- Ensuring ownership, control, access and possession of the research data and that local knowledge remains with the communities and the people.
- Integrating local worldviews and epistemologies into all aspects of the research by creating a process to meaningfully involve local scholars, knowledge keepers and community members.
- Learning and growing with the community throughout the entire sharing process with the effective use of interactive, two-way communication technologies.
- Sharing the research data with the communities in co-produced reports and presentations that are useful to them.
- Working with the communities to build local capacity to use and sustain research in the future.
- Developing and delivering research training and resources required by the community.
- Co-presenting research results including co-authoring papers and articles ensuring local ownership of the stories and knowledge.
- Working with the community to leave a lasting product that contributes to local well-being and future opportunities.
- Working with intermediary organizations on action to make structural changes through better regulations and policies benefitting all marginalized communities.

Several important resources for researchers interested in PAR are referenced in this chapter. Smith's *Decolonizing Methodologies* (2012) highlights 25 action research projects involving marginalized Indigenous communities around the world. Denzin *et al.*'s *Handbook of Critical and Indigenous Methodologies* (2008) contains many chapters describing best practices for working with marginalized communities. Kindon *et al.*'s *Participatory Action Research Approaches and Methods* (2007) takes a grounded theory approach to connecting people and research to place using action research. Reason and Bradbury's *Handbook of Action Research: Participative Inquiry and Practice* (2001) is an excellent guide for anyone considering action research. The quarterly *Journal of Action Research*[11] is now in its thirteenth year of publishing quality articles about effective and ethical PAR initiatives.

Effective online research initiatives with any marginalized community include looking to the future and building and sustaining long-term, mutually beneficial applied projects that include a shared research component. Using online research methods with marginalized communities works well when the work benefits both the communities and the researchers. The experiences and research requirements for doing this type of work in these challenging environments provide lessons that can be applied to any marginalized community in the world. The results and the experience will be beneficial for all researchers everywhere.

ACKNOWLEDGEMENTS

The authors would like to thank the reviewers of an earlier version of this chapter who provided very helpful suggestions for improvement. Our research is supported by the Social Sciences and Humanities Research Council of Canada (SSHRC). The SSHRC-funded First Nations Innovation (FNI) research project (http://fn-innovation-pn.com and http://first-mile.ca) provides employment, guidance, training, support and resources. FNI research project partners are Keewaytinook Okimakanak (KO-KNET and KORI) (www.knet.ca), the First Nations Education Council (www.cepn-fnec.com), Atlantic Canada's First Nation Help Desk/Mi'kmaw Kina'matnewey (www.firstnationhelp.com) and the University of New Brunswick department of Sociology (www.unb.ca).

NOTES

1 The Tri-Council, the three main government research funding bodies in Canada (Canadian Institutes of Health Research, Natural Sciences and Engineering Research Council of Canada, and Social Sciences and Humanities Research Council of Canada, 2010) have created the Tri-Council

Guidelines for research with Human Subjects that highlight the requirement for researchers to collaborate and work with Indigenous communities using a holistic approach. The Tri-Council guidelines are mandatory for all university researchers in Canada.

2 http://firstmile.ca (Accessed July 15, 2016).
3 http://www.cbu.ca/mrc/ethics-watch (Accessed July 15, 2016).
4 http://research.knet.ca (Accessed July 15, 2016).
5 See, for example, http://firstmile.ca/resources/sharing-resources (Accessed July 15, 2016).
6 http://firstmile.ca (Accessed July 15, 2016).
7 http://kochiefs.ca (Accessed July 15, 2016).
8 http://firstmile.ca (Accessed July 15, 2016).
9 See http://e-community.knet.ca (Accessed July 15, 2016).
10 http://kihs.knet.ca (Accessed July 15, 2016).
11 http://arj.sagepub.com (Accessed July 15, 2016).

REFERENCES

Abele, F. and Delic, S. (2014). 'Aboriginal youth employment in northern Canada'. SSHRC Knowledge Synthesis Grant report. Retrieved October 21, 2016 from http://carleton.ca/3ci/wp-content/uploads/Aboriginal-Youth-Employment-Report-March-20-2014.pdf

Assembly of First Nations. (2007). *OCAP: Ownership, Control, Access and Possession – First Nations Inherent Right to Govern First Nations Data*. Report prepared for Assembly of First Nations.

Battiste, M. (2013). *Decolonizing Education: Nourishing the Learning Spirit*. Saskatoon, SK: Purich Publishing Limited.

Beaton, B. and Campbell, P. (2014). 'Settler colonialism and First Nations e-communities in northwestern Ontario'. *Journal of Community Informatics*, 10(2).

Beaton, B. and Carpenter, P. (2014). *A Critical Understanding of Adult Learning, Education and Training Using Information and Communication Technologies (ICT) in Remote First Nations*. Canadian Association for Study of Indigenous Education, Brock University, St Catherines, ON, May.

Beaton, B., Seibel, F. and Thomas, L. (2014). *Valuing the Social Economy and Information and Communication Technologies (ICT) in Small Remote First Nations*. Association of Social Economy and Non-Profit Research, Brock University, St Catherines, ON, May.

Chatterton, P., Fuller, D. and Routledge, P. (2007). 'Relating action to activism: theoretical and methodological reflections'. In S. Kindon, R. Pain and M., Kesby (eds.), *Participatory Action Research Approaches and Methods: Connecting People, Participation and Place*. Routledge Studies in Human Geography, 22. London: Routledge, pp. 216–22.

Denzin, N., Lincoln, Y. and Smith, L. T. (2008). *Handbook of Critical and Indigenous Methodologies*. Los Angeles, CA: Sage Publications.

Ferreira, G., Ramírez, R. and Walmark, B. (2004). 'Connectivity in Canada's far north: participatory evaluation in Ontario's Aboriginal communities. Measuring the information society: what, how, for whom and what?'. Workshop, September, Brighton, UK. Available from http://knet.ca/documents/Ferreira-Ramirez-Brighton-Paper.doc (accessed July 15, 2016).

Fine, M., Tuck, E. and Zeller-Berkman, S. (2008). 'Do you believe in Geneva? Methods and ethics at the global–local nexus'. In N. Denzin, Y. Lincoln and L. T. Smith (eds.), *Handbook of Critical and Indigenous Methodologies*. Los Angeles, CA: Sage Publications, pp. 157–80.

Gratton, M.-F. and O'Donnell, S. (2011). 'Communication technologies for focus groups with remote communities: a case study of research with First Nations in Canada'. *Qualitative Research*, 11(2), 159–75.

Kakekaspan, M., O'Donnell, S., Beaton, B., Walmark, B. and Gibson, K. (2014). 'The First Mile approach to community services in Fort Severn First Nation'. *Journal of Community Informatics*, 10(2).

Kindon, S. L., Pain, R. and Kesby, M. (2007). *Participatory Action Research Approaches and Methods: Connecting People, Participation and Place*. London: Routledge.

McKelvey, F. and O'Donnell, S. (2009). 'Out from the edges: multi-site videoconferencing as a public sphere in First Nations'. *Journal of Community Informatics*, 5(2).

McMahon, R., Whiteduck, T. and Beaton, B. (2013). 'Shaping First Nations broadband policy in Canada: Indigenous community intermediary organizations in the age of austerity'. World Social Science Forum, Montreal, QC, Canada, October.

McMahon, R., LaHache, T. and Whiteduck, T. (2015). 'Digital data management as Indigenous resurgence in Kahnawà:ke'. *The International Indigenous Policy Journal*, 6(3). Available from: http://ir.lib.uwo.ca/iipj/vol6/iss3/6 (accessed July 15, 2016).

McMahon, R., O'Donnell, S., Smith, R., Walmark, B., Beaton, B. and Simmonds, J. (2011). 'Digital divides and the 'first mile': framing First Nations broadband development in Canada'. *The International Indigenous Policy Journal*, 2(2). Available from: http://ir.lib.uwo.ca/iipj/vol2/iss2/2 (accessed July 15, 2016).

McMahon, R., Gurstein, M., Beaton, B., O'Donnell, S. and Whiteduck, T. (2014). 'Making information technologies work at the end of the road'. *Journal of Information Policy*, 4, 250–69.

Molyneaux, H., O'Donnell, S., Kakekaspan, C., Walmark, B., Budka, P. and Gibson, K. (2014). 'Social media in remote First Nation communities'. *Canadian Journal of Communication*, 39(2), 275–88.

O'Donnell, S., Beaton, B. and McKelvey, F. (2008). *Videoconferencing and Sustainable Development for Remote and Rural First Nations in Canada*. National Research Council publications. Available from http://nparc.cisti-icist.nrc-cnrc.gc.ca/npsi/ctrl?action=shwart&index=an&req=5764202&lang=en (accessed July 15, 2016).

Palmater, P. (2011). 'Stretched beyond human limits: death by poverty in First Nations'. *Canadian Review of Social Policy*, 65/66, 112–27.

Perley, S. and O'Donnell, S. (2005). 'Broadband video communication research in First Nation communities'. Presented at the Canadian Communication Association Annual Conference (CCA 2006), York University, Toronto, ON, June.

Ramírez, R., Aitkin, H., Kora, G. and Richardson, D. (2003). 'Community engagement, performance measurement and sustainability: experiences from Canadian community based networks'. *Canadian Journal of Communication*, 30(2), 259–80.

Reason, P. and Bradbury, H. (2001). *Handbook of Action Research: Participative Inquiry and Practice*. London: Sage Publications.

Schnarch, B. (2004). 'Ownership, control, access, and possession (OCAP) or self-determination applied to research: a critical analysis of contemporary First Nations research and some options for First Nations communities'. *Journal of Aboriginal Health*, 1(1): 80–95.

Smith, L. T. (2012). *Decolonizing Methodologies: Research and Indigenous Peoples*. 2nd edn. London: Zed Books.

Tri-Council. (2010). *Tri-Council Policy Statement: Ethical Conduct for Research Involving Humans*. Canadian Institutes of Health Research, Natural Sciences and Engineering Research Council of Canada, and Social Sciences and Humanities Research Council of Canada.

Tuck, E. (2009). 'Suspending damage: A letter to communities'. *Harvard Educational Review*, 79(3), 408–29.

Walmark, B. (2009). 'Reclaiming First Nations research: The Keewaytinook Okimakanak Research Institute'. Paper presented at the Aboriginal Policy Research Conference, Ottawa, ON, March.

Walmark, B., O'Donnell, S. and Beaton, B. (2005). *Research on ICT with Aboriginal communities: Report from RICTA 2005*. Available at http://nparc.cisti-icist.nrc-cnrc.gc.ca/eng/view/object/?id=fe0ff91e-fc04-49cd-a83d-85799a8fbaf1 (accessed July 15, 2016).

Wilson, S. (2008). *Research is Ceremony: Indigenous Research Methods*. Black Point, NS: Fernwood Publishing.

Winter, J. S., Buente, W., Buskirk, P. A. (2014). 'Opportunities and challenges for First-mile development in rural Hawaiian communities'. *Journal of Community Informatics*, 10(2).

## 33

Web- and Phone-based Data Collection using Planned Missing Designs

William Revelle, David M. Condon,
Joshua Wilt, Jason A. French, Ashley Brown
and Lorien G. Elleman

The past few years have seen a revolution in the way that we are able to collect data. Using diaries (Bolger *et al.*, 2003; Green *et al.*, 2006) or smartphones (Mehl and Conner, 2012; Wilt *et al.*, 2011b) to measure states within subjects across multiple time periods, or the web to collect measures on thousands of subjects at a time (Gosling *et al.*, 2004; Rentfrow *et al.*, 2008; Revelle *et al.*, 2010; Wilt *et al.*, 2011a) has led to an exciting explosion in the amount of data collected. However, most of these studies ask the same questions of all of their participants.

In this chapter we review an alternative approach where we intentionally give each participant just a small subset of the items of interest but, with the power of basic psychometrics and sampling theory, are able to analyse the data as if far more items were presented. We refer to this procedure as Synthetic Aperture Personality Assessment (SAPA) (Condon and Revelle, 2014; Revelle *et al.*, 2010) to emphasize the use of synthetic covariance matrices. That is, we find the correlations between composite scales, not based upon scoring the raw items, but rather by synthetically finding the covariances between scales based upon basic covariance algebra applied to the pairwise complete item covariances. We think of these techniques as analogous to the techniques used in radio astronomy where the resolving power (aperture) of a set of radio telescopes may be greatly increased by synthesizing the signals collected by each individual telescope. Indeed, by combining the signals of radio telescopes scattered around the world, the effective aperture of these long baseline radio telescopes is the size of the entire earth. Because our covariance matrices are based upon data sets with a great deal of intentionally missing data, we also refer to our data as Massively Missing Completely at Random (MMCAR).

Our approach is not new for it was discussed by Frederic Lord (1955) and then elaborated (Lord, 1977) in the assessment of ability. A variant of the technique that uses Balanced Incomplete Blocks (BIB) or 'spiraling' has been applied in large-scale international surveys such as the Programme for International Student Assessment (PISA) (Anderson *et al.*, 2007). However, with the exception of our own work, we are not aware of the widespread use of this technique in smaller scale studies nor the complete emphasis on randomness that we have used. In this chapter we review the basic technique, discuss how to analyse the data, consider the effective sample size and resulting precision of estimates based upon scales and items, and then we give a few examples of SAPA-based results. We emphasize the application of these procedures to web-based data collection because we have not yet implemented experience sampling or ecological momentary assessments more broadly defined with SAPA technique. However, we believe the techniques are relevant to both within-subject and between-subject means of data collection.

In the spirit of open science, all the software we have developed and all the items we use are in the public domain. We use open-source software for data collection and analysis and public domain items measuring temperament, ability and interests. In addition, we periodically publish the raw data to allow other researchers to use them (e.g. Condon and Revelle, 2015a, 2015b, 2015c, 2016).

Consider the basic problem of trying to determine the relationship between two or more constructs. In the past, psychological scales would be developed for each construct, the relevant items would be given to a relatively small set of subjects and the covariances/correlations between these constructs would be found by scoring scales based upon the individual item responses. A typical procedure would include administering a number of inventories to a set of freshmen in a group-testing situation at the beginning of a school term. With the normal limitations of such a design, questionnaires could be given to a group of 100–500 students, each of whom would answer all items given, probably at the rate of about 1–6 items per minute,

depending on their difficulty. The total testing time would limit the number of items given, and in an hour only several questionnaires, each with 20–40 items, would be given. Another design, taking much longer, would be to recruit a community sample willing to take many questionnaires over the course of several years, e.g. the Eugene–Springfield Community Sample (ESCS) of Goldberg (1999). This procedure has led to a correlation matrix of several thousand items based upon approximately 800 subjects. A third technique, of course, is to use web-based data collection from volunteers, for example in studies such as the German Socio-Economic Panel Study (Wagner *et al.*, 2007); the *http:// www.outofservice.com/bigfive* website, which collects data for studies such as Rentfrow and Gosling (2003) and Rentfrow *et al.* (2008); or the site run by John Johnson *www.personal. psu.edu/faculty/j/5/j5j/IPIP/ipipneo300.htm*, which presents either a 60- or 300-item version of the International Personality Item Pool (IPIP–NEO) (Buchanan *et al.*, 2005; Johnson, 2005). In all these approaches, scales are found by combining scores on the individual items. Unfortunately, volunteers are usually unwilling to answer very many items and thus one is faced with a bandwidth versus fidelity trade-off. One can either ask a few items each for many constructs with the resulting low reliabilities, or many items for each of a few constructs with more reliability but less coverage.

COLLECTING MMCAR DATA USING SAPA

An alternative procedure (SAPA) is to ask a few items for each construct from many subjects, but to randomly sample the items from a much larger pool of items. This allows for identification of the covariances between scales based on the composite covariances of the items rather than the raw item responses. This procedure takes advantage of the fact that people want to know about themselves (perhaps following the Delphic maxim to 'know thyself') and makes up the lack of precision associated with giving few items with the abundance of traffic available on the web. Based upon the participant's responses, the SAPA Project website (sapa-project.org) offers customized and individualized personality feedback and was originally adapted from Buchanan *et al.* (2005) and Johnson (2005) but has since been greatly modified.

We do not actively advertise the site and have found that some of the traffic comes from people who have posted their feedback from us on their personal webpages, while others find it by searching the web for 'personality tests' or 'personality theory', etc. Recent evidence suggests that such self-selected participants do not differ a great deal from those who are actively recruited to participate in probability-based national panel studies (Hays *et al.*, 2015). Unfortunately, both means of data collection suffer from respondents' willingness to participate and the reasons to opt into a sample are only slightly different from the reasons to opt out (Ansolabehere and Rivers, 2013). However, it is important to realize that not everyone is willing to participate in web-based surveys (Pew Research Center, 2015). As would be expected, given that many of our participants are in college, the daily and monthly rates will vary during the year, but we have been averaging about 45,000 participants a year.

A reasonable question is how valid Internet surveys are in general, and ours in particular. We have compared our item structures and sample characteristics with those reported in the intensive study of the 800–1,000 people who were individually given many of the items we have used (the ESCS of Goldberg and Saucier, 2016). As we discuss later, in terms of ethnicity, age and education, our sample is much more diverse than the ESCS, but the factor structures are remarkably similar. Additional validity data will come from as yet unanalysed data of peer reports for a subset of our participants. Within the US, the distribution of our sample by state correlates with US Census population values of 0.95. Our sample is certainly more diverse than is normally achieved at a selective research institution, which tends to produce more White, Educated, Industrial, Rich, Developed (WEIRD) subjects (Henrich *et al.*, 2010) than in our sample. However, it is certainly not representative of even the US population because, as we show later, our sample is younger, more educated and has a higher proportion of females than the US population.

The SAPA Logic

Suppose one is interested in measuring facet level data from the 'Big 5' measures of personality (the so-called CANOE or OCEAN of personality: Conscientiousness, Agreeableness, Neuroticism, Openness and Extraversion; Digman, 1990; Goldberg, 1990) and eventually the relationship of these facets to measures of ability (Carroll, 1993; Gottfredson, 1997) and interests (Holland, 1959). Each facet might reflect 5–10 items, with 2–5 facets per broader domain, the measures of ability might include 50–100 items and the measures of interests might involve 100–400 items. That is, the desired item pool is in the order of 400–600 items. But the typical subject is not willing to answer more than 40–75 items. The SAPA solution is to sample items completely at random from the larger pool (or perhaps systematically sample randomly from each of the temperament, ability and interest domains) and then present the items in random sets of 25 at a time. At the end of each set of 25 items, subjects are asked if they want to continue and, if so, another 25 items are presented. They may stop whenever they want and feedback is presented to them based upon the items they have taken. Although the precision of measurement for each construct for each person is low, the precision of the synthetically formed covariances/correlations between scales measuring each construct is quite high.

How does this work? From the larger pool of P items, n items are then selected with probability p_i, where $n = \overline{p_i}P = \sum_{i=1}^{P}(p_i)$ i.e. the average probability of any item being chosen, p_i, multiplied by the size of the total item pool. Thus, for N subjects filling out the questionnaire, each item has roughly p_iN responses. More importantly, the average number of responses to each pair of items (i, j) is p_ip_jN. Consider the case of three months of data with $N = 10,000$, $P = 500$ and $p_i = p_j = 0.1$ or $n = 50$. Every one of the 500 items has been given roughly 1,000 ($\overline{p_i}N$) times and there are roughly 100 observations per pair of items (p_ip_jN). (These numbers are given merely for example purposes. In reality we tend to collect data for longer periods of time and build up about 500–1,000 pairwise observations.) The subscript on the item probabilities reflects our relative interest in the content of the item. Demographic variables are presented with $p_i = 1$, while more exploratory items might be given with $p_i = 0.05$. When developing new ability items with a concern for their difficulty or when presenting items that are temporally relevant (e.g. attitudes towards an election), item presentation probabilities are increased and they might be presented with $p_i = 0.5$.

Item level statistics (e.g. the mean or variance) are based upon the $\overline{p_i}N$ observations, while item inter-covariances are based upon p_ip_jN pairwise complete covariances. Structural analyses (e.g. factor analysis or principal components analysis), the internal consistencies of the individual scales (e.g. coefficients α and ω_h) and also the correlations between individual scales may be found by basic matrix operations on the total inter-item covariance matrix rather than on the raw data matrix. This is not magic, but merely a function of covariance algebra.

In addition to the randomly chosen temperament, ability and interest items, we also collect demographic information from all participants. These data include age, education, marital status, parental education, height, weight, smoking history, country and state of residence, and for those who say they are from the US, their ZIP Code. For these items, $p_i = 1$ and the precision of the resulting statistics are based upon the N participants measured.

Software used to present SAPA items

There are logically three different phases of presenting items and storing the individual responses. All three phases use open-source software with specific code developed for this project. The phases are (1) specifying the item bank, (2) presenting the items and (3) storing the results and giving feedback.

Item Bank

The item bank is stored using MySQL, an open-source relational database management system that is supported by a large user community and also has a commercial version. With the use of extensive help files from the MySQL community, programming is relatively easy. The database is structured with a list of roughly 4,400 temperament, ability and interest items; 2,413 of the temperament items are taken from the open-source International Personality Item Pool (IPIP; Goldberg, 1999).

The IPIP was developed by Lew Goldberg who adapted a short stem item format developed in the doctoral dissertation of Hendriks (1997) and items from the Five Factor Personality Inventory developed in Groningen (Hendriks et al., 1999). Goldberg (1999) used about 750 items from the English version of the Groningen inventory, and has since supplemented them with many more new items in the same format. The initial development of the IPIP was controversial because some believed that commercial developers could do a better job (Costa and McCrae, 1999). The citation count to the IPIP belies this belief. With at least 2,382 Google Scholar citations to the original publication (Goldberg, 1999) and 1,636 to the subsequent discussion (Goldberg *et al.*, 2006), it is safe to say that open-source personality measurement is a good idea. The IPIP items have been translated into at least 39 languages by at least 65 different research teams, but the SAPA site is currently using just English-based items (taken from ipip.ori.org).

We supplemented the IPIP item bank with 92 interest items taken from the Oregon Vocational Interest Scales (ORVIS; Pozzebon *et al.*, 2010), 60 from the O*Net markers of Holland's RIASEC dimensions of interests (Armstrong *et al.*, 2008; Holland, 1997; Rounds *et al.*, 2010), 60 music preference items (Liebert, 2006), 30 Right Wing Authoritarian items (Altemeyer, 2004), 78 items from the Eysenck Personality Questionnaire (Eysenck *et al.*, 1985), 30 items taken from inventories (e.g. Jackson, 2009; Smederevac *et al.*, 2014) to measure aspects of Reinforcement Sensitivity Theory (Smillie, 2008), 220 items to measure aspects of personality disorders (Krueger *et al.*, 2013), 15 items from the Santa Barbara Sense of Direction scale (Hegarty *et al.*, 2002), as well as 60 ability items developed as part of the International Cognitive Ability Resource project (ICAR; Condon and Revelle, 2014). Additional items that were taken from a number of different scales were given in prior years. The master list of the 4,300 items from the IPIP, ORVIS, O*Net and other sources that we use are available at https://sapa-project.org/MasterItemList/.

Presentation Software

Using the server-side scripting language, PHP: Hypertext Preprocessor, we query the MySQL server for items to present and then display them using HyperText Markup Language 5 (HTML5) on an APACHE-based web server. Participant responses are then pre-processed and stored back to the MySQL server. As would be expected in any software development environment, our PHP scripts have improved over the years to take advantage of changes in MySQ, PHP and to the HTML5. The site was originally hosted at the personality-project.org website and has since been migrated to the sapa-project.org website. (Both of these are hosted at Northwestern University, Evanston, IL).

From the user's perspective, they see a number of screens with 'radio button' response options or a few text box options. These screens or 'pages' include:

Welcome:

A brief description of the SAPA project, an FAQ about the test, the research behind SAPA, links to literature about current research in individual differences and the benefits that may accrue to the user.

Consent form:

A brief discussion about how long the test will take, how all responses are anonymous, that participants will receive feedback based upon our norms and a consent button to start the test.

Demographics:

One question is whether people have taken the survey before, others ask age (in a text box). Pulldown menu options ask about gender, height, weight, marital status, relationship status, frequency of exercise, smoking history, country and state/region where the person grew up, level of education, university major (if relevant), employment status, general field of work and then parental education. More recently, we have started asking about the participants postal or ZIP Code. At this point, the user is assigned (invisibly) a random identification number (RID) that will be used to check for repeated entries in the same web browser session.

First and subsequent page of questions:

Each page has 25 questions, the first 21 of which are sampled from the temperament and interest item banks, the final four are ability items sampled from our ability item bank. At the end of each of the first three pages, subjects are told that they will have more accurate feedback if they continue. At the end of the fourth page, they are given personality feedback based upon scores calculated from the items they have answered.

Optional subsequent pages:

Participants are offered the possibility of continuing on and filling out more items about such things as creative accomplishments, or of sending a message to a friend to rate them on various personality attributes.

Storage and Feedback

As the participant is filling out the survey, results are transmitted to the MySQL server at the end of every page and stored with their RID. Once the participant selects the option saying that they are finished with the entire set of (randomly administered) items to which they chose to respond, they are given scores on various personality scales. These were originally based upon the Big 5 factors but have more recently been replaced with hierarchically organized factors scores with 3, 6 and 12 factors. This scoring is done by applying a key of all possible items for each scale and finding the average response given to the items that were presented. The graphic output gives a location of each of the scores on a line along with a confidence interval for each score.

Data Security

When we first started the site, and for the subsequent eight years, the SAPA project was hosted on an Apple Macintosh desktop computer in the Personality, Motivation and Cognition laboratory at Northwestern University, Evanston, IL. We updated our security settings on APACHE, MySQL and PHP relatively frequently, but not enough to prevent a MySQL injection from taking over the system. After recovering the data (with one week's worth of data lost to the hacker), we moved the site to a more professionally managed server at the main computer cluster on campus. We mention this as a warning of the problems of maintaining web servers.

ANALYZING SAPA/MMCAR DATA

The basic logic of the SAPA procedure follows from some fundamental principles of psychometrics with respect to correlations of items and correlations of item composites. It is well known that the correlation between two scales, A and B with n and m items, respectively, is $\dfrac{Cov_{AB}}{\sqrt{V_A V_B}}$.

But since the covariance of two item composites is merely the sum of the covariances of the separate items, $Cov_{AB} = \sum\limits_{j=1}^{n}\sum\limits_{k=1}^{m}(cov_{a_i b_j})$ and, similarly, the variance of a composite is the sum of the variances and covariances of the items in that composite $Var_A = \sum\limits_{j=1}^{n}\sum\limits_{k=1}^{n}(cov_{a_i a_j})$, then

$$r_{AB} = \frac{Cov_{AB}}{\sqrt{V_A V_B}}$$

$$= \frac{\sum\limits_{j=1}^{n}\sum\limits_{k=1}^{m}(cov_{a_i b_j})}{\sqrt{\sum\limits_{j=1}^{n}\sum\limits_{k=1}^{n}(cov_{a_i a_j})\sum\limits_{j=1}^{m}\sum\limits_{k=1}^{m}(cov_{b_i b_j})}}. \quad (1)$$

More compactly, in matrix algebra, and for the general case of multiple scales, let the raw data be the matrix $\mathbf{X}$ with N observations on P items converted to deviation scores (with most rows having only n non-missing items). The item variance–covariance matrix is $\mathbf{C} = \mathbf{XX'}N^{-1}$ and scale scores, $\mathbf{S}$ are found by $\mathbf{S} = \mathbf{K'X}$. $\mathbf{K}$ is a keying matrix, with $\mathbf{K}_{ij} = 1$ if *item$_i$* is to be scored in the positive direction for scale j; 0 if it is not to be scored and −1 if it is to be scored in the negative direction. In this case, the covariance between scales, $\mathbf{C}_s$, may be found by pre- and post-multiplying the item covariance matrix with a matrix of the keys:

$$\mathbf{C}_s x = \mathbf{K'X(K'X)'}N^{-1}$$

$$= \mathbf{K'XX'K}N^{-1} \quad (2)$$

$$= \mathbf{K'CK}.$$

The scale correlations, R_s are found by pre- and post-multiplying the scale covariance matrix $\mathbf{C}_s$ by the inverse of the scale standard deviations, which are merely the square roots of the diagonal of $\mathbf{C}s$:

$$R_s = (diag(\mathbf{C}_s))^{-.5} \mathbf{C}_s (diag(\mathbf{C}_s))^{-.5} \qquad (3)$$

That is, the covariance between any set of scales can be found by multiplying the transposed keying matrix by the inter-item covariance matrix times the keying matrix. The correlations are found by dividing this product by the standard deviations.

Although the correlational structure of the *items* requires the raw data, the correlations of *scales* can be found by keying the item correlation matrix into scale correlations, not the raw data matrix. In the case of a SAPA/MMCAR design, this is very important because although the individual item correlations can be found by 'pairwise complete correlations' or 'available case correlations', it is highly unlikely that any one participant has complete data for any scale. We conduct our structural analyses at the item and scale covariance level, rather than at the raw data level. We believe that the greater resolution of item-level and scale-level covariances made possible by our technique compensates for the lack of complete subject data analysis.

In order to process our SAPA data, we have developed a number of functions included in the *psych* package (Revelle, 2015) in the open-source statistical system R (R Core Team, 2015). These functions are specifically meant to handle the massively missing data structures that we use and are referenced later. In addition, we have developed an additional package, SAPATools (French and Condon, 2015), to facilitate data extraction from the MySQL server and to do some basic data cleaning. Unless explicitly mentioned, the R functions discussed in the following pages are all from the *psych* package.

Data Cleaning

After importing the data from the MySQL server into R, either using functions in the *RMySQL* (Ooms *et al.*, 2015) package, the *SAPA-tools* package, or by just reading the file using a normal HTML browser and copying to the clipboard, the data need some preliminary data checking and cleaning. Some participants will take the questionnaire, receive their feedback and then go back to the beginning of the page to do it again. This is detected by keeping the RID permanent for the web browser session. Thus, the data are first cleaned by removing all duplicate RID numbers. (The data are, however, maintained so that we could, if we desire, go back and find out the characteristics of those who enter more than one set of questions.) Additional data cleaning procedures includes removing subjects who report ages less than 14 or more than 90 and excludes those participants who tell us they have previously participated in the survey.

Basic Item Information

Descriptive statistics (means, standard deviations, ranges, etc.) are found for all items using the `describe` function. Demographic information is available for all participants, whereas temperament, ability and interest items are given to just random subsets of participants. Pairwise counts of the frequency of particular item pairs are examined to facilitate further analysis (given the changing nature of items being administered, not all item subsets are administered together – this is particularly the case when doing exploratory studies). Correlations between ability items are found using tetrachoric correlations; correlations between temperament and interest items are found by polychoric correlations. Correlations of continuous variables (e.g. age, height, weight) with dichotomous (ability) or polytomous (temperament and interests) items are found using polyserial correlations. All of these correlations are done using the `mixedCor` function.

Scale Level Structures

The real power of the SAPA procedure is evident when we examine the correlational structure either at the item or at the scale level. Factor analyses of the item level covariances are done using the `fa` function and two-parameter item response theory statistics based upon these factor analyses (McDonald, 1999) are done using the `irt.fa` function. For instance, the tetrachoric correlation matrix of dichotomous ability items may be factored using a minimum residual factor analysis function `fa` and the resulting loadings, λ_i are transformed to item discriminations by $a = \dfrac{\lambda}{\sqrt{(1-\lambda^2)}}$. The difficulty parameter, δ, is found from the τ parameter of the tetrachoric function and the factor loadings of the factor analysis of the tetrachoric matrix: $\delta = \dfrac{\tau}{\sqrt{(1-\lambda^2)}}$. Similar analyses may be done with polytomous item responses using polychoric correlations and distinct estimates of item difficulty (location) for each item response.

Similarly, analysis of internal structure of each scale may be done based upon the correlation matrices using functions to find α (`alpha`, `scoreItems`), $\omega_{hierarchical}$ and ω_{total} (`omega`) (Revelle and Zinbarg, 2009) as well as the signal/noise ratio of each scale (`scoreItems`). The hierarchical cluster structure based upon the item correlations (Revelle, 1979) is found using the `iclust` function. When examining the correlations of nested scales, that is scales with overlapping items, because they might be subscales of other scales, we use a correction derived from Cureton (1966) and Bashaw and Anderson Jr (1967) (`scoreOverlap`).

Individual and Group Level Scores

When describing the personality characteristics of certain subgroups (e.g. college majors, occupations, ZIP Codes), it is necessary to use scores based upon the raw data. To do this, we use IRT-based estimates from the available items for each subject using `irt.fa` and `score.irt`. This procedure, although highly correlated with just adding the item responses, allows slightly more precision in that it takes into account item discriminations and item endorsement frequencies (difficulties).

It is important to realize that the correlations between scales using the synthetic procedures may differ from those based upon the simple sum or IRT-based scores. This is because of the missingness in the data. The individual level scores for a particular measure might be based upon 2–4 items, and the subsequent correlation with another similar scale will be attenuated by the missingness in the data. However, the structural correlations, based upon the covariance of all of the items in the scale (as many as 20–50) will be much less attenuated.

Because of the sample size, it is also possible to find the correlational structure of the mean scores for groups organized by college major or occupation, for example. These correlations are *between-group* correlations and will not necessarily be the same, and indeed usually are not the same, as the correlations pooled *within-group* or the *overall* correlations. Although some dismiss these correlations of aggregates as showing 'the ecological fallacy' (Robinson, 1950) or the Yule–Simpson 'paradox' (Kievit et al., 2013; Simpson, 1951; Yule, 1903), we find that they tell us meaningful information about how individuals aggregate into groups (Revelle and Condon, 2015).

PRECISION OF SAPA/MMCAR DATA

The standard error of the correlation between two particular items will be the classical standard error $\sigma_r = \dfrac{\sqrt{1-r^2}}{\sqrt{N-2}}$. For complete data, this is the same formula for the correlation of composite scales. But what about the standard errors of SAPA-based composite scales? What is the appropriate sample size? Is it the number of participants who take any individual pair of items ($p_i p_j N$) or is it somehow closer to N? To answer this question, we rely on simulation. The following is based partly on the work of Brown (2014) who has done a much more thorough simulation than is reported here.

For a population covariance matrix of 0 between two sets of items that correlate 0.3 within and 0 between, we took 1,000 random samples of 10,000 cases for complete data, and for data with a probability of observing a particular item of 0.1, 0.125, 0.25, 0.5 and 1. That is, for the 0.1 condition, the probability of any pair of items having data was 0.01.

In addition, we simulated scales with 1, 2, 4, 8 or 16 items. Each of the 1,000 random samples governed by a particular combination of scale size and proportion of observed items produced a sample correlation calculated in one of two different ways: either as pairwise complete, or using the full information maximum likelihood (FIML) method. Each sample scale correlation was also corrected for alpha reliability, and minres oblimin factor analyses sought a two-factor solution whenever scale size was 16. Four sets of statistics (uncorrected and corrected correlations, factor loadings and intercorrelations) and their standard errors were computed by taking the mean and standard deviation, respectively, of the appropriate set of 1,000 sample statistics.

Results indicated that uncorrected correlations, which were derived using the SAPA method, approach their latent values as scale size increases; that is, as one aggregates over more items. This suggests that analysts who do not correct for reliability would do well to aggregate over items as SAPA does. In addition, both uncorrected and corrected correlations' standard errors decrease as scale size increases; this effect seems to be more pronounced with larger quantities of missing data. In essence, aggregating over items increases effective sample size more than might be expected based solely on the number of cases and the probability of observing a given item (Figure 33.1). Effective sample size, N_e is merely a function of the standard error, σ_r, of the correlation, r, which is $\sigma_r = \sqrt{\dfrac{1-r^2}{N-2}}$. Thus $N_e = \dfrac{1-r^2}{\sigma_r^2} + 2$.

We find the standard error by simulation to estimate the effective sample size. Finally, and as expected, more missing data tends to produce slightly more biased, less precise results among corrected correlations and factor intercorrelations. Factor loadings were less precise when more data were missing, but the effect of missing data on bias was, in this case, relatively small.

Also of interest here is the fact that the FIML method did not greatly improve upon the quality of the relevant statistics. Both statistical bias and data patterns, as described earlier, were the same regardless of analytic method. FIML produced slightly more precise solutions than the standard SAPA method, but it is much more computationally intense and time-consuming and, moreover, it is better suited to the analysis of data that possesses only a few distinct patterns of missingness, as in the commonly used balanced incomplete block design. Based upon our simulations (Brown, 2014), we propose that our method represents a simple and economical way for survey researchers with sample sizes of at least 200 to increase breadth of coverage without sacrificing statistical rigor. Obviously, for smaller sample sizes, the sampling probability for each item needs to be larger than we are using for our larger samples.

EXAMPLES OF SAPA RESULTS

The following are short summaries of some of the major projects conducted using SAPA. These include analysis of the correlates of items differing in their saturation of affective, behavioural, cognitive and desire content (Wilt, 2014), and examinations of alternative

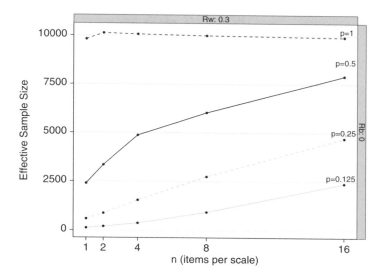

Figure 33.1   The effective sample size is a function of the observed standard error of the correlation and is Ne = $(1-r^2)/\sigma_r^2$ + 2. For this particular simulation, the average within scale correlation was set to .3 and the average between set correlation to 0. Means shown are from 1,000 replications. What is important to observe is when using the MMCAR composite scales, that effective sample size increases dramatically as the number of items per scale is increased

structures of items administered in several different personality inventories (Condon, 2014). We have already reported the development of an open-source ability test used in the SAPA project (Condon and Revelle, 2014) and are now using SAPA procedures to validate other item types. In addition, one of the powers of the technique is that side studies can be conducted by introducing items with relatively low probabilities of being included and then just waiting a long time, or alternatively give some items with a high probability of being administered and then run them for just a few weeks.

Demographics of the SAPA Participants

The demographics in this section are based on a sample of 207,002 participants, whose self-report data were collected between August 2010 and December 2015. Participants

from this sample are 63 per cent female. Participants grew up in 215 countries, with the US accounting for 73 per cent of the sample. Twenty-two countries besides the US have 500 or more participants, with the top three being Canada (8,895), the UK (5,577) and Australia (4,024). Participants from the US identify as 67 per cent white, 10 per cent African American, 9 per cent Hispanic, 5 per cent Asian American, 1 per cent Native Alaskan/Hawaiian/American, 6 per cent multiracial and 1 per cent 'other'. The mean age of participants is 26 (sd = 11; $median$ = 22). The age distribution is highly skewed for both males and females (Figure 33.2). The modal participant is between 19 and 22 and is currently in college or university (Table 33.1). This distribution is roughly the same for males and females (Figure 33.3).

These results highlight both a strength and weakness of voluntary web-based data collection. In terms of age and gender it is clearly the case that our data are not representative of

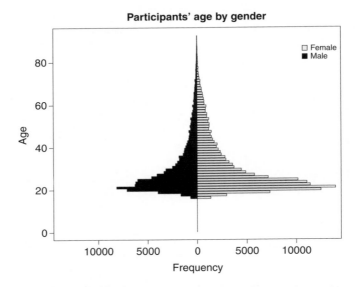

Figure 33.2   Although there are roughly twice as many females as males, the age distributions are roughly the same

the population. However, it is also the case that our data represent much greater diversity of subject characteristics than found in the typical university-based sample or even community-based samples such as the ESS.

Personality Questionnaires and the ABCDs

Personality traits have been conceptualized as individual differences in patterns of affect (A), behaviour (B), cognition (C) and desire

(D) over time and space (Allport, 1937; Johnson, 1997; Revelle, 2008; Winter *et al.*, 1998), and yet the most common assessments of the Big 5 traits (Costa and McCrae, 1992b; Goldberg, 1992) do not explicitly refer to these ABCD components (Pytlik Zillig *et al.*, 2002). We therefore conducted a content analysis in order to identify items for each Big 5 trait that reflected primarily one A, B, C or D content (Wilt, 2014; Wilt and Revelle, 2015). We identified items from each ABCD domain for each trait and created facet scales from these items: for example, the ABCD

Table 33.1   Highest education attained, by age

Education level	Age					
	14–18	*19–22*	*23–29*	*30–39*	*40–49*	*50–90*
< 12 years	25,319	463	325	236		165
High school graduate	7,363	2,477	1,715	1,152	715	624
Currently in university	13,263	44,210	16,747	9,016	4,279	1,870
Some college	164	2,166	3,202	2,547	1,538	1,205
College degree	152	3,086	9,810	6,599	3,683	2,571
In graduate or professional school	164	1,089	4,860	2,031	887	386
Graduate or professional degree	42	271	3,570	5,019	3,322	3,009

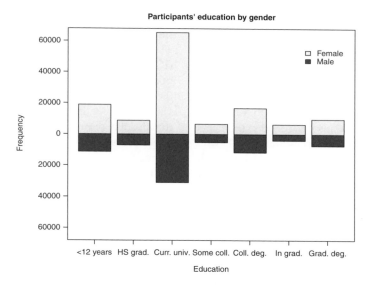

Figure 33.3   The female-to-male ratio of participants is highest for college students

facet scales of agreeableness were labelled as sympathetic *affect*, considerate *behaviour*, trusting *cognition* and *desire*. Using the *psych* package (Revelle, 2015) in R (R Core Team, 2015), we employed the SAPA technique to generate a synthetic correlation matrix containing the ABCD items assessing the Big 5. From this correlation matrix, we determined that (1) a Big 5 structure emerged from factor analysis of the items; (2) even when correcting for item overlap, using the scoreOverlap function, Big 5 trait domain scales correlated highly with their respective ABCD facet scales, (3) ABCD scales within each trait were positively correlated with each other and (4) items had strong correlations with their respective ABCD facet scale.

The Factor Structure of Personality Inventories

A primary goal of the SAPA-project for the past several years has been to examine the structural properties of a number of personality inventories that share overlapping items in the IPIP. Although there are 1,034 items

contained in eight different inventories: 100 in the Big 5 marker scales (Goldberg, 1999), 100 in the Big 5 aspect scales (DeYoung *et al.*, 2007), 240 in the IPIP–HEXACO (Ashton *et al.*, 2007), 300 in the IPIP–NEO (Goldberg, 1999), 127 in the IPIP–Multidimensional Personality Questionnaire (Tellegen and Waller, 2008), 48 items in the Questionnaire Big 6 scales (Thalmayer *et al.*, 2011), and 79 in the Eysenck Personality Questionnaire (Eysenck *et al.*, 1985); there are only 696 unique items. For instance, some of the 100 items in the Big 5 factor markers (Goldberg, 1999) are the same as the ones used in the Big 5 Aspects Scales (DeYoung *et al.*, 2007). This set of 696 items includes all the items from at least 255 of the personality scales listed at the IPIP website, including IPIP items designed to match these inventories as well as the Hogan Personality Inventory, for example (Hogan and Hogan, 1995).

Based upon the correlation matrix of nearly 24,000 participants, we tested for the number of factors that would best represent the structure. Unfortunately, the exploratory factor structure of these 696 items did not yield any clean solution for the number of factors, but the most interpretable solutions represented 3, 5 or 15 factors (Condon, 2014). Most importantly, these solutions were not nested in the standard hierarchical representation reported by many, but were best described as forming a heterarchy. With careful item analysis, a set of 150 items was found to represent all levels of this heterarchy quite well, with scales that could reliably distinguish these 3, 4 or 15 dimensions. The data for the 23,681 participants and the 696 items are available for others to use through *DataVerse*, an open-source data repository (Condon and Revelle, 2015b, 2015c).

Work is underway to examine how these dimensions relate to differences in interests and desires across college majors and across occupational groups as these appetites are reflected in the interest dimensions known as the Realistic, Investigative, Analytic, Social, Enterprising, Conventional (RIASEC) (Holland, 1997).

The International Cognitive Ability Resource

Cognitive ability assessment differs from many other measures of individual differences because it requires tools that evaluate maximal performance levels rather than levels of typical behaviour. In other words, cognitive ability items are objectively scored as correct or incorrect. This important difference makes it more challenging to measure cognitive ability than other constructs; more test security is required to maintain fairness and validity. Still, researchers and clinicians are strongly motivated to employ cognitive ability measures that can provide quick, reliable and cost-efficient assessment by virtue of the fact that the many aspects of cognitive ability are highly predictive of a wide range of outcomes (Deary, 2009).

Several brief electronic measures of cognitive ability are available, but few (if any) are both widely validated and available for use in non-proctored environments (i.e. over the Internet). None exist in the public domain. The International Cognitive Ability Resource (ICAR; Condon and Revelle, 2014) was developed in order to fill this absence. Following the initial creation of four item types that were validated using the SAPA-Project, an international collaboration of German, British and American universities has since been formed to encourage the development of a range of cognitive ability measures (see icar-project.com for more information).

A prior report of the preliminary results was based upon the first 65,000 subjects (Revelle *et al.*, 2010) and a subsequent report discussed the validation of the expanded inventory with another 24,000 participants (Condon and Revelle, 2014). The data from this latter article are available in an open-source repository (Condon and Revelle, 2015a, 2016). Sample data from this project are also available as the `ability` data set in the *psych* package.

EXAMPLES OF SCALE DEVELOPMENT AND VALIDATION ACROSS BROAD DOMAINS

The breadth of constructs that can be simultaneously assessed using the the SAPA methodology allows for evaluation of the relative contribution of factors across broad domains of individual differences. By domains, we allude to the affective, cognitive and conative domains which have long been recognized in the social sciences (McDougall, 1923; Condon, 2014; Holland, 1959, 1997; Carroll, 1993; McGrew, 2009; Costa and McCrae, 1992a; Digman, 1990; Goldberg, 1990). If not for the use of the SAPA technique, cross-sectional evaluation of the contribution of these broad domains of individual differences to achievement would be impractical because thorough evaluation of cognitive abilities, vocational interests and temperament in addition to achievement outcomes would require several hours of participants' time and attention. We have previously reported SAPA studies on music preferences (Liebert, 2006; Revelle *et al.*, 2010) and trust (Evans and Revelle, 2008) and have since extended these to studies of psychopathy (Wright, 2014) and creative achievements.

SUMMARY AND CONCLUSIONS

Telemetric methods have revolutionized the ways in which we can collect data. However, there is a natural tendency to continue our traditional reluctance to have missing observations even as we collect orders of magnitude more data. We believe that this is a mistake and have outlined the power of using a Massively Missing Completely At Random (MMCAR) item administration technique. We have shown the power of introducing such missingness into our designs. We have also emphasized the methodology and results from our web-based project (SAPA), but believe that similar techniques would be useful with modern smart phone apps.

FUNDING

Partially supported by a grant from the National Science Foundation: SMA-1419324 to William Revelle.

REFERENCES

Allport, G. W. (1937). *Personality; a psychological interpretation*. New York, NY: H. Holt and Company.

Altemeyer, B. (2004). Highly dominating, highly authoritarian personalities. *Journal of Social Psychology*, *144*(4), 421–47. doi:10.3200/SOCP.144.4.421–448.

Anderson, J., Lin, H., Treagust, D., Ross, S. and Yore, L. (2007). Using large-scale assessment datasets for research in science and mathematics education: programme for International Student Assessment (PISA). *International Journal of Science and Mathematics Education*, *5*(4), 591–614. doi:10.1007/s10763-007-9090-y.

Ansolabehere, S. and Rivers, D. (2013). Cooperative survey research. *Annual Review of Political Science*, *16*(1), 307–29. doi:10.1146/annurev-polisci-022811-160625.

Armstrong, P. I., Allison, W. and Rounds, J. (2008). Development and initial validation of brief public domain RIASEC marker scales. *Journal of Vocational Behavior*, *73*(2), 287–99. doi:10.1016/j.jvb.2008.06.003.

Ashton, M. C., Lee, K. and Goldberg, L. R. (2007). The IPIP–HEXACO scales: an alternative, public-domain measure of the personality constructs in the HEXACO model. *Personality and Individual Differences*, *42*(8), 1515–26. doi:10.1016/j.paid.2006.10.027.

Bashaw, W. and Anderson Jr, H. E. (1967). A correction for replicated error in correlation coefficients. *Psychometrika*, *32*(4), 435–41. doi:10.1007/BF02289657.

Bolger, N., Davis, A. and Rafaeli, E. (2003). Diary methods: capturing life as it is lived. *Annual Review of Psychology*, *54*, 579–616. doi:10.1146/annurev.psych.54.101601.145030.

Brown, A. D. (2014). Simulating the MMCAR method: An examination of precision and bias in synthetic correlations when data are 'massively missing completely at random'. Unpublished master's thesis, Northwestern University, Evanston, IL.

Buchanan, T., Johnson, J. A. and Goldberg, L. R. (2005). Implementing a five-factor personality inventory for use on the internet. *European Journal of Psychological Assessment*, *21*(2), 115–27. doi:10.1027/1015-5759.21.2.115.

Carroll, J. B. (1993). *Human cognitive abilities: a survey of factor-analytic studies*. New York, NY: Cambridge University Press. doi:10.1017/CBO9780511571312.

Condon, D. M. (2014). An organizational framework for the psychological individual differences: integrating the affective, cognitive, and conative domains. Unpublished doctoral dissertation, Northwestern University, Evanston, IL.

Condon, D. M. and Revelle, W. (2014). The International Cognitive Ability Resource: Development and initial validation of a public-domain measure. *Intelligence*, *43*, 52–64. doi:10.1016/j.intell.2014.01.004.

Condon, D. M. and Revelle, W. (2015a). Selected ICAR data from the SAPA-Project: Development and initial validation of a public-domain measure. *Harvard Dataverse*. doi:10.7910/DVN/AD9RVY.

Condon, D. M. and Revelle, W. (2015b). Selected personality data from the SAPA-Project: 08dec2013 to 26jul2014. *Harvard Dataverse*. doi:10.7910/DVN/SD7SVE.

Condon, D. M. and Revelle, W. (2015c). Selected personality data from the SAPA-Project: on the structure of phrased self-report items. *Journal of Open Psychology Data*, *3*(1). doi:10.5334/jopd.al.

Condon, D. M. and Revelle, W. (2016). Selected ICAR data from the SAPA-Project: development and initial validation of a public-domain measure. *Journal of Open Psychology Data*. doi:10.5334/jopd.25.

Costa, P. T. and McCrae, R. R. (1992a). Four ways five factors are basic. *Personality and Individual Differences*, *13*(6), 653–65. doi:10.1016/0191-8869(92)90236-I.

Costa, P. T. and McCrae, R. R. (1992b). *NEO PI-R professional manual*. Odessa, FL: Psychological Assessment Resources.

Costa, P. T. and McCrae, R. R. (1999). Reply to Goldberg. In I. Mervielde, I. Deary, F. De Fruyt and F. Ostendorf (eds.), *Personality psychology in Europe*. Vol. 7. Tilburg, The Netherlands: Tilburg University Press, pp. 29–31.

Cureton, E. (1966). Corrected item-test correlations. *Psychometrika*, *31*(1), 93–6. doi:10.1007/BF02289461.

Deary, I. J. (2009). Introduction to the special issue on cognitive epidemiology. *Intelligence*, *37*, 517–19. doi:10.1016/j.intell.2009.05.001.

DeYoung, C. G., Quilty, L. C. and Peterson, J. B. (2007). Between facets and domains: 10 aspects of the big five. *Journal of Personality and Social Psychology*, *93*(5), 880–96. doi:10.1037/0022-3514.93.5.880.

Digman, J. M. (1990). Personality structure: emergence of the five-factor model. *Annual Review of Psychology*, *41*, 417–40. doi:10.1146/annurev.ps.41.020190.002221.

Evans, A. M. and Revelle, W. (2008). Survey and behavioral measurements of interpersonal trust. *Journal of Research in Personality*, *42*(6), 1585–93. doi:10.1016/j.jrp.2008.07.011.

Eysenck, S. B., Eysenck, H. J. and Barrett, P. (1985). A revised version of the Psychoticism scale. *Personality and Individual Differences*, *6*(1), 21–9. doi:10.1016/0191-8869(85)90026-1.

French, J. A. and Condon, D. M. (2015). *SAPA Tools: Tools to analyze the SAPA Project*. (R package version 0.1.)

Goldberg, L. R. (1990). An alternative 'description of personality': the big-five factor structure. *Journal of Personality and Social Psychology*, *59*(6), 1216–29. doi:10.1037/0022-3514.59.6.1216.

Goldberg, L. R. (1992). The development of markers for the big-five factor structure. *Psychological Assessment*, *4*(1), 26–42. doi:10.1037/1040-3590.4.1.26.

Goldberg, L. R. (1999). A broad-bandwidth, public domain, personality inventory measuring the lower-level facets of several five-factor models. In I. Mervielde, I. Deary, F. De Fruyt and F. Ostendorf (eds.), *Personality psychology in Europe*. Vol. 7. Tilburg, The Netherlands: Tilburg University Press. pp. 7–28.

Goldberg, L. R. and Saucier, G. (2016, January). *The Eugene-Springfield Community Sample: Information Available from the Research Participants* (Tech. Rep. No. 56–1). Eugene, OR: Oregon Research Institute.

Goldberg, L. R., Johnson, J. A., Eber, H. W., Hogan, R., Ashton, M. C., Cloninger, C. R. and Gough, H. G. (2006). The International Personality Item Pool and the future of public-domain personality measures. *Journal of Research in Personality*, *40*(1), 84–96. doi:10.1016/j.jrp.2005.08.007.

Gosling, S. D., Vazire, S., Srivastava, S. and John, O. P. (2004). Should we trust web-based studies? A comparative analysis of six preconceptions about internet questionnaires. *American Psychologist*, *59*(2), 93–104. doi:10.1037/0003-066X.59.2.93.

Gottfredson, L. S. (1997). Why g matters: the complexity of everyday life. *Intelligence*, *24*(1), 79–132. doi:10.1016/S0160-2896(97)90014-3.

Green, A. S., Rafaeli, E., Bolger, N., Shrout, P. E. and Reis, H. T. (2006). Paper or plastic? Data equivalence in paper and electronic diaries. *Psychological Methods*, *11*(1), 87–105. doi:10.1037/1082-989X.11.1.87.

Hays, R. D., Liu, H. and Kapteyn, A. (2015). Use of internet panels to conduct surveys.

Behavior Research Methods, *47*(3), 685–90. doi:10.3758/s13428-015-0617-9.

Hegarty, M., Richardson, A. E., Montello, D. R., Lovelace, K. and Subbiah, I. (2002). Development of a self-report measure of environmental spatial ability. *Intelligence*, *30*(5), 425–47. doi:10.1016/S0160-2896(02)00116-2.

Hendriks, A. A. J. (1997). The construction of the five-factor personality inventory (FFPI). Unpublished doctoral dissertation, Rijksunivsiteit Groningen, Groningen, The Netherlands.

Hendriks, A. A. J., Hofstee, W. K. and De Raad, B. (1999). The five-factor personality inventory (FFPI). *Personality and Individual Differences*, *27*(2), 307–25. doi:10.1016/S0191-8869(98)00245-1.

Henrich, J., Heine, S. J. and Norenzayan, A. (2010). The weirdest people in the world? *Behavioral and Brain Sciences*, *33*, 61–83. doi:10.1017/S0140525X0999152X.

Hogan, R. and Hogan, J. (1995). *The Hogan Personality Inventory manual*. 2nd. edn. Tulsa, OK: Hogan Assessment Systems.

Holland, J. L. (1959). A theory of vocational choice. *Journal of Counseling Psychology*, *6*(1), 35–45. doi:10.1037/h0040767.

Holland, J. L. (1997). *Making vocational choices: A theory of vocational personalities and work environments*. Lutz, FL: Psychological Assessment Resources.

Jackson, C. J. (2009). Jackson-5 scales of revised reinforcement sensitivity theory (r-rst) and their application to dysfunctional real world outcomes. *Journal of Research in Personality*, *43*(4), 556–69. doi:10.1016/j.jrp.2009.02.007.

Johnson, J. A. (1997). Units of analysis for the description and explanation of personality. In R. Hogan, J. A. Johnson and S. R. Briggs (eds.), *Handbook of personality psychology*. San Diego, CA: Academic Press, pp. 73–93.

Johnson, J. A. (2005). Ascertaining the validity of individual protocols from web-based personality inventories. *Journal of Research in Personality*, *39*(1), 103–29. doi:10.1016/j.jrp.2004.09.009.

Kievit, R. A., Frankenhuis, W. E., Waldorp, L. J. and Borsboom, D. (2013). Simpson's paradox in psychological science: a practical guide. *Frontiers in Psychology*, *4*(513), 1–14. doi:10.3389/fpsyg.2013.00513.

Krueger, R., Derringer, J., Markon, K., Watson, D. and Skodol, A. (2013). *The personality inventory for DSM-5 (PID-5)*. Washington, DC: American Psychological Association.

Liebert, M. (2006, May). A public-domain assessment of music preferences as a function of personality and general intelligence. Honors Thesis. Department of Psychology, Northwestern University, Evanston, IL.

Lord, F. M. (1955). Sampling fluctuations resulting from the sampling of test items. *Psychometrika*, *20*(1), 1–22. doi:10.1007/BF02288956.

Lord, F. M. (1977). Some item analysis and test theory for a system of computer-assisted test construction for individualized instruction. *Applied Psychological Measurement*, *1*(3), 447–55. doi:10.1177/014662167700100313.

McDonald, R. P. (1999). *Test theory: a unified treatment*. Mahwah, NJ: Lawrence Erlbaum Associates.

McDougall, W. (1923). *Outline of psychology*. Oxford: Scribners.

McGrew, K. (2009). CHC theory and the human cognitive abilities project: Standing on the shoulders of the giants of psychometric intelligence research. *Intelligence*, *37*(1), 1–10. doi:10.1037/h0040767.

Mehl, M. R. and Conner, T. S. (2012). *Handbook of research methods for studying daily life*. New York, NY: Guilford Press.

Ooms, J., James, D., DebRoy, S., Wickham, H. and Horner, J. (2015). RMySQL: Database Interface and MySQL Driver for R [Computer software manual]. Retrieved from http://CRAN.R-project.org/package=RMySQL (R package version 0.10.3).

Pew Research Center. (2015, September). *Coverage error in internet surveys*. Retrieved from www.pewresearch.org/files/2015/09/2015-09-22_coverage-error-in-internet-surveys.pdf

Pozzebon, J. A., Visser, B. A., Ashton, M. C., Lee, K. and Goldberg, L. R. (2010). Psychometric characteristics of a public-domain self-report measure of vocational interests: the Oregon Vocational Interest Scales. *Journal of Personality Assessment*, *92*(2), 168–74. doi:10.1080/00223890903510431.

Pytlik Zillig, L. M., Hemenover, S. H. and Dienstbier, R. A. (2002). What do we assess when we assess a big 5 trait? A content analysis of the affective, behavioral and cognitive processes represented in the big 5 personality inventories. *Personality and Social Psychology Bulletin*, *28*(6), 847–58. doi:10.1177/0146167202289013.

R Core Team. (2015). R: A language and environment for statistical R Foundation for Statistical Computing, Vienna, Austria. https://www.R-project.org/

Rentfrow, P. J. and Gosling, S. D. (2003). The do re mi's of everyday life: the structure and personality correlates of music preferences. *Journal of Personality and Social Psychology*, *84*(6), 1236–56. doi:10.1037/0022-3514.84.6.1236.

Rentfrow, P. J., Gosling, S. D. and Potter, J. (2008). A theory of the emergence, persistence, and expression of geographic variation in psychological characteristics. *Perspectives on Psychological Science*, *3*(5), 339–69. doi:10.1111/j.1745-6924.2008.00084.x.

Revelle, W. (1979). Hierarchical cluster-analysis and the internal structure of tests. *Multivariate Behavioral Research*, *14*(1), 57–74. doi:10.1207/s15327906mbr1401_4.

Revelle, W. (2008). The contribution of reinforcement sensitivity theory to personality theory. In P. J. Corr (ed.), *The reinforcement sensitivity theory of personality*. Cambridge: Cambridge University Press, pp. 508–27.

Revelle, W. (2015). *psych*: procedures for personality and psychological research [Computer software manual]. http://cran.r-project.org/web/packages/psych/ (R package version 1.5.8).

Revelle, W. and Condon, D. M. (2015). A model for personality at three levels. *Journal of Research in Personality*, *56*, 70–81. doi:10.1016/j.jrp.2014.12.006.

Revelle, W. and Zinbarg, R. E. (2009). Coefficients alpha, beta, omega and the glb: comments on Sijtsma. *Psychometrika*, *74*(1), 145–54. doi:10.1007/s11336-008-9102-z.

Revelle, W., Wilt, J. and Rosenthal, A. (2010). Individual differences in cognition: new methods for examining the personality-cognition link. In A. Gruszka, G. Matthews and B. Szymura (eds.), *Handbook of individual differences in cognition: attention, memory and executive control*. New York, NY: Springer, pp. 27–49.

Robinson, W. S. (1950). Ecological correlations and the behavior of individuals. *American Sociological Review*, *15*(3), 351–7.

Rounds, J., Su, R., Lewis, P. and Rivkin, D. (2010). *O* NET[textregistered] interest profiler short form psychometric characteristics: Summary*. Raleigh, NC: National Center for O* NET Development.

Simpson, E. H. (1951). The interpretation of interaction in contingency tables. *Journal of the Royal Statistical Society. Series B (Methodological)*, *13*(2), 238–41.

Smederevac, S., Mitrovič, D., Čolovič, P. and Nikolašević, Ž. (2014). Validation of the measure of revised reinforcement sensitivity theory constructs. *Journal of Individual Differences*, *35*(1), 12–21. doi:10.1027/1614-0001/a000121.

Smillie, L. D. (2008). What is reinforcement sensitivity? Neuroscience paradigms for approach–avoidance process theories of personality. *European Journal of Personality*, *22*(5), 359–84. doi:10.1002/per.674.

Tellegen, A. and Waller, N. G. (2008). Exploring personality through test construction: Development of the multidimensional personality questionnaire. In G. J. Boyle, G. Matthews and D. H. Saklofske (eds.), *The SAGE handbook of personality theory and assessment*. London: Sage Publications, pp. 261–92.

Thalmayer, A. G., Saucier, G. and Eigenhuis, A. (2011). Comparative validity of brief to medium-length Big Five and Big Six personality questionnaires. *Psychological Assessment*, *23*(4), 995–1009. doi:10.1037/a0024165.

Wagner, G. G., Frick, J. R. and Schupp, J. (2007). *The German Socio-Economic Panel Study (SOEP) – evolution, scope and enhancements* (Tech. Rep.) The German Socio-Economic Panel Study DIW Berlin 10108 Berlin, Germany: SOEP Paper No. 1. doi:10.2139/ssrn.1028709.

Wilt, J. (2014). A new form and function for personality. Unpublished doctoral dissertation, Northwestern University, Evanston, IL.

Wilt, J. and Revelle, W. (2015). Affect, behavior, cognition and desire in the Big 5: an analysis of item content and structure. *European Journal of Personality*, *29*(4), 478–97. doi:10.1002/per.2002.

Wilt, J., Condon, D. and Revelle, W. (2011a). Telemetrics and online data collection: Collecting data at a distance. In B. Laursen, T. D. Little and N. Card (eds.), *Handbook of developmental research methods*. New York, NY: Guilford Press, pp. 163–80.

Wilt, J., Funkhouser, K. and Revelle, W. (2011b). The dynamic relationships of affective synchrony to perceptions of situations. *Journal of Research in Personality*, 45, 309–21. doi:10.1016/j.jrp.2011.03.005.

Winter, D. G., John, O. P., Stewart, A. J., Klohnen, E. C. and Duncan, L. E. (1998). Traits and motives: toward an integration of two traditions in personality research. *Psychological Review*, *105*(2), 230–250. doi:10.1037/0033-295X.105.2.230.

Wright, Z. E. (2014, May). Creating a self-report measure of psychopathy using items from the Personality Inventory for the DSM-5. Honors Thesis. Department of Psychology, Northwestern University, Evanston, IL.

Yule, G. U. (1903). Notes on the theory of association of attributes in statistics. *Biometrika*, *2*(2), 121–34.

## 34

Social Cartography and 'Knowing Capitalism': Critical Reflections on Social Research and the Geo-Spatial Web

Harrison Smith, Michael Hardey[†],
Mariann Hardey and Roger Burrows[1]

INTRODUCTION

This chapter explores how what Thrift (2005) has termed *knowing capitalism,* is increasingly invested in developing new techniques, methodological frameworks, and cultural discourses that exploit the potential of social cartography to realize new forms of economic value and analytical power. Social cartography is defined here as an analytical concept that encompasses new cartographic information practices specifically derived from non-expert epistemologies and everyday users of new interactive mapping technologies, platforms and software. Although there are many sites, case studies and applications for this new social cartography, of specific interest to us here is exploration of the development of the geo-spatial Web 2.0 (the Geoweb) that combines interactive mapmaking with crowdsourced, volunteered and open data practices. This chapter therefore explores the emergence of the Geoweb by examining its genealogical connections with

knowing capitalism through a critical examination of its rhetorical, cultural and politico-economic approaches to social cartography. The rationale of the chapter is to stimulate future research into how these new geo-spatial tools can offer social scientists new methodological approaches to doing research, while also scrutinizing the underlying political economies of knowing capitalism that consider how the diffusion of cartographic literacies and data is embedded in a neo-liberalization of empirical research.

Geographic Information Systems (GIS) typically require years of training in software such as ArcGIS or QGIS, as well as access to expensive data sets licensed by the private sector. By contrast, the Geoweb is perceived to signal a social diffusion of cartographic knowledge production in everyday life that leverages vernacular information practices and non-expert information literacies. This diffusion echoes larger structural changes in the social relations of new media information practices that coalesce around the value of crowdsourcing and social production, for example, geotagged social media in the wake of natural disasters such as the 2012 'superstorm' Hurricane Sandy, or Crampton *et al.*'s (2013) analysis of the geography of Tweets that used the specific hashtag #LexingtonPoliceScanner. The rationales for producing new forms of civic participation and community engagement,[2] crisis management and other critical epistemologies of social stratification stress the value of non-expert knowledge. However, this is not to suggest an oversimplification; that the Geoweb represents some kind of antithesis to knowing capitalism – far from it. An overview of its political economy shows how the Geoweb emerged in tandem with knowing capitalism, specifically through its shared social history with the neoliberalization of geo-spatial infrastructures. The Geoweb is embedded in larger political economies of what has been termed 'commercial sociology' (Burrows and Gane, 2006) that commodify specific kinds of geo-spatial data into social knowledge that has market potential and, thus, exacerbates the institutional distinctions and distributions of intellectual and economic capital necessary for conducting research. New questions and discourses around methodological reliability and validity therefore begin to surface and position the Geoweb as a boundary object between, on the one hand, grassroots community praxis through vernacular epistemologies and, on the other, the processes of capital accumulation realized from the commercialization of empirical sociological and geo-spatial research.

This chapter responds to the observation of a growing 'crisis' in empirical sociology caused by the emergence of commercial sociology and consumer analytics through big data infrastructures. It is divided into three sections. First, it examines the 'spatial turn' in sociology to trace the theoretical discussions around knowing capitalism and the crisis of empirical sociology since the publication of the first edition of this volume. In doing so, we focus specifically on the tensions between epistemological conventions of validity with ethical dilemmas of pragmatic research, and how these are causing irreversible shifts to spatial perceptions.

The second section examines the epistemological and cultural frameworks that define the Geoweb as social cartography and as a new set of practices for extracting value in knowing capitalism. This analysis is also characteristic of neoliberal methodological frameworks that configure geo-spatial research within a performative logic of social media interactivity and information exchange. This kind of research, in other words, necessitates a methodological principle that clearly articulates explicit social, political, economic or cultural objectives. Interactivity with geo-spatial media therefore becomes embedded within a neoliberal individualization of social research, and in much the same way that characterizes much of the rationale of social media.

Finally, the chapter will introduce some basic Geoweb tools and applications used in contemporary geo-spatial research. The purpose here is to identify tools that may be relevant for social scientists interested in learning about the potential of the Geoweb for stimulating new research, civic participation, governance and praxis. Two tools in particular will be explored in order to contrast the potential of the Geoweb for research and praxis: Ushahidi, a crowdsourced platform for disaster response and crisis management mapping, and Carto, a commercial Software as a Service (SaaS) platform that exploits big data infrastructures through economies of scale. In so doing, we hope to demonstrate how knowing capitalism has become multi-faceted in scope, method and discourse. The particular nature of power, in other words, cannot simply be reduced to a linear analysis that exclusively privileges institutions of capital – new ways of producing social knowledge through geo-spatial tools may actually work concurrently and in contradistinction to the grand narratives of neoliberal capitalism.

PART 1: A CRISIS OF KNOWING?

The first edition of this volume critiqued the methodological distinctions of sociological research between academic and commercial institutions by framing new spatial tools for doing social research within a larger political economy of 'knowing capitalism' (Thrift, 2005) and the supposed 'coming crisis of empirical sociology' (Savage and Burrows, 2007, 2009). It was argued that the production of empirical knowledge by sociologists employed by academic institutions was being superseded by commercial organizations that exploit sociological methods for the generation of economic value. The work of academic sociologists therefore increasingly became less important when compared to the analytical powers of knowing capitalism. At stake was a political concern for authority and legitimacy over a set of empirical methods that academics once perceived to claim jurisdiction over. This methodological privilege assumed largely altruistic beliefs around the value of sociological knowledge for realizing beliefs of social change and empowerment by marginalized communities and social forces. Correspondingly, the real danger was the displacement of empirical research (particularly quantitative research) into the hands of commercial sociologists interested almost exclusively in leveraging social research for economic ends. Here, inequalities are effectively re-inscribed through hierarchical forces that govern the distribution of social resources and privilege, and became manifest through methodological discourses of epistemological jurisdiction and authority over the production of social knowledge. In Thriftian terms, various commercial objectives for targeting and influence become the imperative of knowing capitalism.

This controlled commercialization of research methods was evidenced most notably in the development of Internet Based Neighbourhood Information Systems (IBNIS): geo-spatial tools and GIS that classify populations through a complex of multivariate data sets into discrete geodemographic clusters (Burrows and Gane, 2006; see also Harris et al., 2005). Using postal codes as a spatial grid for visualizing socio-economic distributions, geodemographics can exploit public census and private sector data to typify and classify populations into discrete market segments primarily to influence beliefs and behaviours, and in turn creating new socio-economic distinctions of social stratification and class conflict that reflect institutional objectives. In Canada and the US, the PRIZM segmentation system uses postal and ZIP codes to divide the population into 66 discrete segments. The UK uses a similar system, MOSAIC, developed by Experian, that divides the population into 67 segments. Geodemographics are in effect deeply symbolic practices of material and cultural distinction that stratify populations into spatial clusters based on their propensities, lifestyles and tastes (Bourdieu, 1984). In doing so, geodemographics function to reproduce social, economic and cultural distinctions through spatial segmentation and clustering. In Bourdeusian terms, geodemographics enact hierarchies of symbolic violence and market worth that structures the distribution of social and economic resources. Geodemographics work precisely because they are designed to accomplish pragmatic goals, all under the cultural and normative axiom: 'you are where you live'.

Geodemographics align with a performative logic of knowing capitalism by enacting markets into coherent segments of clearly definable ideal types. This allows for increasingly sophisticated techniques of population management and strategies of resource distribution by typifying people into discrete clusters of worth. Uprichard et al. (2009) argue that the epistemological and methodological aspects of geodemographic classifications are directly related to a performative logic of capital. They work because they are designed to work for the purposes assigned by the classifiers developing these systems of knowing. Epistemological conventions of reliability and validity, in effect, take an ancillary role in favour of key performance indicators that assess their capacity for goal-rational performance and efficiency. This means that geodemographics are largely determined by the specific data points chosen, as well as the underlying rationales that form the discourse of coding space into a form of analytical power.

However, this discourse of coding space is not necessarily exclusive to institutional agents of capital. Of particular importance here is to understand how new technologies and software exist alongside a larger popularization of cartographic literacies and interactive geo-spatial media by non-experts. The first edition of this chapter noted how the particular way of producing social knowledge through maps is not necessarily exclusive to Web 2.0 interfacing. Abrams and Hall (2006) argue that 'new cartographies' were already emerging that diffused cartographic understandings and sense making onto everyday life that had come to represent a new cartographic turn in the social sciences. They connected this to a longer theoretical argument developed in Fredrick Jameson's (1984) cognitive aesthetics based on the supposed incapacity for individuals to intuitively comprehend the de-centred nature of subjectivity within larger global socio-economic and cultural contexts (Toscano and Kinkle, 2015). A more recent application is in the data visualization of coders to mashup data and showing these as interactive spatial content, for example the mapping of data by the Energy Information Administration from the US Clean Power Plan to visualize the most common sources of fuel (Muyskens et al., 2015).

The necessity to develop new aesthetical knowledges of spatial subjectivity highlights the role maps play in everyday information practices and sense making (for a more in-depth discussion on research around everyday information practices, see Savolainen, 2008). Out of the speculation that empirical sociology might be in a state of crisis of distinction and authority, numerous discussions have surfaced that either acknowledge or critique this claim. Crompton (2008), for example, published an editorial response for the British Sociological Association arguing the real crisis stems from a lack of expertise and formal training in quantitative research methods. As sociology attempts to position itself as an authority, and thereby influence the power structures of social relations, the primary issue is a lack of skilled quantitative sociologists. These concerns were also expressed in an earlier issue of *Sociology* in Williams et al. (2008) survey of sociological methods that showed how the vast majority of sociological research is dominated by qualitative studies. However, Platt (2014) notes that there are significant conceptual and operational challenges in comparing the extent to which certain journals or countries tend to emphasize certain methods over others. Moreover, it is not always clear what kinds of conclusions can be drawn from such observations in that the character of papers published does not necessarily correlate to judgments concerning the methodological skills, knowledges and literacies of a field.

The perceived decline of quantitative empirical research in academic sociology[3] is therefore in many respects made worse by the proliferation of commercial sociology that often (but not always) relies on sophisticated multivariate analysis (as in the case of geodemographics) by highly skilled researchers equipped with large quantities of statistical data or now, increasingly, access to 'big data' infrastructures (Savage and Burrows, 2009; Burrows and Savage, 2014; Mosco, 2014). Such commercial sociology is also not bound by the same ethical oversight that pertains in much of the academy that routinely scrutinizes research proposals through a centralized bureaucracy and normative philosophy of risk management. It is possible that commercial sociology is able to produce new forms of knowledge through ethical de-regulation. As big data analytics continues to gain momentum, it is therefore worth considering how the crisis of empirical sociology might become further amplified as the distinction between methodological validity and economic performance becomes increasingly blurred, or worse, dismissed as irrelevant.

A compelling example of these kinds of tensions came to a boiling point in both public and intellectual discourse with the publication of a study on 'emotional contagion' by researchers employed by Facebook and Cornell University. The study explored how the emotional responses of Facebook users could be discreetly manipulated over time, causing audiences to internalize and even reproduce the emotional nature of social media content (Kramer *et al.*, 2014).

The 'experiment' leveraged an extremely large sample (N = 689,003) over a week, and manipulated exposure to 'negative' emotional expressions in user newsfeeds and measured the extent of similar emotional reproduction. Results showed that consistent exposure to negative emotional content could cause users to post content with a similar emotional nature. The same results were found when users were exposed to 'positive' emotional content, as well as content with no perceived emotional connotations. The significance of this study remains contested, but suggests that affective states can be reproduced by other users through controlled information exposure. Public response to this study was mixed, but focused on the ethical implications for social media companies like Facebook (guided of course by imperatives of marketing acquisition and conversion) to influence the patterns of information production and sense making to realize particular economic objectives. Beyond the Huxleyan potential for audience inculcation, many were also quick to address the practical potential for extracting economic value by discreetly influencing consumer behaviours and attitudes. As one journalist from *Forbes* observed:

> What harm might flow from manipulating user timelines to create emotions? Well, consider the controversial study published last year (not by Facebook researchers) that said companies should

tailor their marketing to women based on how they felt about their appearance. That marketing study began by examining the days and times when women felt the worst about themselves, finding that women felt most vulnerable on Mondays and felt the best about themselves on Thursdays.
>
> McNeal, 2014

The reporter continues by speculating on the extent to which social media might enhance such abilities for audience targeting and conversion based on the temporal nature of social media interactivity, speculating that this will ultimately become a routine practice of social media:

> The Facebook study, combined with last year's marketing study suggests that marketers may not need to wait until Mondays or Thursdays to have an emotional impact, instead social media companies may be able to manipulate timelines and news feeds to create emotionally fueled marketing opportunities.
>
> McNeal, 2014

For sociologists, the challenge is to address how their particular expertise can likewise engender processes of social change that do not exclusively serve the institutions of capital accumulation or audience exploitation. The 'real' crisis of empirical sociology is therefore not simply a methodological distinction of jurisdictional authority and expertise, but concerns about how research can accomplish specific objectives of exploitation and profit by those privy to new forms of data collection and analytical power, as well as the simultaneous political economy of information access and literacy wherein academics are increasingly seen as data illiterate and politically fragmented. Quantitative methods, typically grouped into descriptive and inferential studies, may now require that we acknowledge a new set of methodological objectives based on how the analytical powers of knowing capitalism enact subjective aesthetics and performances. For academics, the question is about how these new tools can be leveraged for social alterity and praxis that do not necessarily reproduce institutional hierarchies of distribution and privilege. At the same time, such a question continues to stress the discursive nature of power/knowledge whereby academic epistemologies stress the theoretical importance of their discipline, but in turn may risk reifying conventions of intellectual privilege over the field of social life itself.

PART II: THE GEOWEB AS SOCIAL CARTOGRAPHY

The questions and dilemmas we have posed are clearly beyond the scope of one chapter, but it is worth further considering the extent to which new geo-spatial infrastructures can realize alternate objectives and rationales for producing knowledge. One possible answer is the emergence of geo-spatial tools that utilize principles of crowdsourcing, open data, mashups and Web 2.0, although it is of course necessary to highlight that this is not being framed through technological determinism. These new geo-spatial interfaces do not require years of intensive training in formal GIS such as ArcGIS or QGIS. Collectively, this is referred to as the geospatial Web 2.0 and denotes the emergence of new mapping technologies, as well as new cartographic literacies used routinely by everyday populations for a variety of innovative applications for creating and sharing personalized maps. These include community activism, civic participation, municipal governance, disaster and emergency crisis mapping, as well as using geo-spatial media to understand local environmental issues – all of which define the particular nature of social problems embedded in larger structures and forces of globalization. The Geoweb effectively represents a new form of social cartography that capitalizes on vernacular understandings of space through interactive, mobile and ubiquitous cartographic media. Collectively, this may offer the potential to realize new social truths about complex socio-geographical issues and power struggles, and include a new agile

software approach to better respond to evolving revisions for user requirements.

However, such beliefs are complicated by political economy, whereby the beliefs and values of digital humanitarianism and social justice are contrasted by issues of audience labour, information access and ownership, as well as with the potential for realizing highly intrusive forms of surveillance and social sorting (Lyon, 2003). Here, the Geoweb represents an extension of knowing capitalism, particularly as it intersects with processes of commodification and ownership (Smith, 2014). In this light, efforts to address data literacies by vernacular epistemes of bottom–up social cartography must be considered within overarching market forces of economic and cultural production. Social cartography is actually antecedent to the Geoweb (Paulston, 1996), but what has changed, and makes the Geoweb unique, is the intersection of political and cultural economy that frame the beliefs and practices of geo-spatial knowledge production to accomplish political objectives of knowing capitalism. In our view, this requires a new resurgence of critical discourse and research to properly understand the capacity of interactive maps for new forms of social research, education and praxis.

This second part will set out the Geoweb as an emerging form of social cartography by exploring its epistemological and cultural frameworks of knowledge production. Next, it will provide a brief overview of the political economy of the Geoweb to understand the structural forces and social relations of production. The contention of this section is that the power afforded by the neoliberalization of geo-spatial infrastructure and knowing capitalism is contingent on the power relations that structure its production. The Geoweb is politically, economically and culturally heterogeneous. It is impossible to reduce the Geoweb as exclusively an instrument of knowing capitalism or of grassroots praxis; ultimately, it depends on the social relations of information production, access, literacy and ownership.

CULTURAL EPISTEMOLOGIES

The Geoweb mobilizes a different rhetoric concerning the social authority of maps that is not based on the traditional discourse of scientific realism, or the regulatory institutions based in sovereign powers of the state (see Crampton, 2003). The Geoweb is socially constructed around mobilizing locally situated knowledges and volunteered or crowdsourced epistemologies of place (Elwood 2008; Elwood, et al., 2012; Brabham, 2013). This is significant because although many key aspects of knowing capitalism revolve around harvesting transactional data from government and commercial databases, entirely different sets of data produced through cultures of 'prosumption' may undermine or possibly enhance the analytical power realized from such transactional knowledge (Beer, 2009; Beer and Burrows, 2013; Ritzer and Jurgenson, 2010). In turn, it poses important questions on the agential and subjective rhetorics of Geoweb data production.

Goodchild (2007) proposes the term 'Volunteered Geographic Information' (VGI), to denote the production of geographic information by private citizens with little to no expertise in GIS or cartography. Goodchild focuses on websites and social media platforms that leverage interactive maps to allow individuals to label, name or describe specific places, such as Wikimapia.[4] Instrumental to this new 'democratization' of GIS is the development of new protocols and tools for georeferencing, such as the emergence of Global Positioning Systems (GPS) that are now routinely embedded in many everyday new media devices, such as smartphones and cameras, as well as new methods for 'geocoding' and 'geotagging' the Earth's surface that leverage vernacular 'folksonomies'. For Goodchild, one of the most significant contributions VGI can make is its emphasis on producing knowledge about local places and activities that may go unnoticed by institutional authorities, such as the state or the media. For Elwood et al. (2012), the epistemological foundations of

VGI derive their value from principles similar to user-generated crowdsourced principles of collective intelligence in that the knowledge is often asserted rather than authoritative. That is, the knowledge produced through volunteered practices contains no inherent guarantee of validity or reliability, but instead is valued for its underlying principles of social production that stress the authenticity of perception and experience by local populations whom volunteer their phenomenological knowledge for collective action. The specific nature of volunteerism has been the cause of some disagreement in Geoweb scholarship. Tulloch (2008) argues that VGI contain inherent similarities to earlier forms of social cartography such as Public Participatory GIS (PPGIS). In this respect, such cartography is not necessarily new, but instead has been an ongoing concern within various discussions of GIScience and critical epistemologies of GIS since the mid 1990s (see Sieber, 2006; Elwood, 2008).

The social cartography of Geoweb data is valued for its capacity to critique the hierarchical privileges of scientific and state authority derived from traditional cartography by offering more democratic forms of information literacy. For some, this means that the Geoweb is imbricated with the rise of the 'citizen sensor' whereby users of geospatial tools are embedded in vernacular regimes of geo-coding. This could include the routine disclosure of mobility patterns through mobile geo-locative media, such as geo-referenced hashtags that offer new possibilities for vernacular knowledge and interactivity (Goodchild, 2007; Wilson, 2012; de Souza e Silva, 2006). Thus, new forms of the cartographic data are premised on creating new geocoded subjects and notions of selfhood informed by interpretive socio-spatial frameworks. The Geoweb requires a reconfiguration of spatial perception and awareness guided by instrumentalized rationales of spatial experience. Wilson (2011), for example, examined volunteer geocoding programs in urban slums that recruited volunteers to assess and itemize various kinds of deviance, such as graffiti, overturned shopping carts, litter and damaged public infrastructure. This effectively amounts to developing new perceptions of urban space to manage deviance by identifying specific sites of abnormal behaviour to guide future biopolitical policies.

Although such research is in its nascency, future work could be done to ascertain the extent to which everyday analytical frameworks of spatial perception are increasingly geocoded to specific institutional norms of neoliberal urbanization. This would suggest that the Geoweb might in effect reinforce the normalizing gaze of surveillance for biopolitical governance. Rather than producing new forms of spatial knowledge that empowers local groups, it could also be deployed to sanitize space from aesthetic differences inscribed by socio-economic neoliberalization. This theory has been developed extensively by critical urban geographers who have studied the reconfigured 'splintering' of urban infrastructures (Graham and Marvin, 2001; Graham and Wood, 2003; Graham, 2004).

What is important, is to consider the underlying social relations of data production. The Geoweb is significant because it can leverage open data sources and non-expert forms of social production. This suggests that public institutions no longer represent primary producers of spatial data. Curry (1998: 88) argues that 'we no longer own our own location' to highlight the replacement of institutional cartographic expertise by privatized epistemologies. This shifts norms of ownership, particularly by 'leasing' out data and analytical power to government (sometimes, ironically, by purchasing public data at a discount), enabling scalable forms of neoliberal privatization of geo-spatial tools and data by the private sector that was once the domain of the state (Zook and Graham, 2007). This places severe challenges for levelling socio-economic inequalities, particularly as institutions of property become part of the fabric of cyberspace (see also Zittrain, 2008).

At the same time, governments and municipal bodies have invested in open data portals to allow easy and free access to various data streams, usually to optimize government services (Johnson and Sieber, 2011; Sieber and Johnson, 2015).[5] Longo (2011) argues that open data portals for government offer a three-pronged benefit for developing new forms of governance and civic participation, including the development of third-party citizen services; the expansion of policy networks for knowledge creation; and the potential for open data to increase the transparency and accountability of government. However, others argue that open data will not absolutely lend itself to such objectives because it is still possible that existing digital divides and socio-economic conflicts might curtail some of the idealist principles of open data. This effectively raises concerns that those most pre-dispositioned to exploit open data are in fact highly trained experts in GIS and the private sector. It may eventually become necessary to expand some of the underlying conventions of social production in open data and the Geoweb to address more substantial matters of data literacy. Gurstein (2011), for example, argues for developing 'effective data use' policies to ensure a myriad of political and social objectives.

POLITICAL ECONOMIES

We may have good reason to believe that the cultural aspects of social cartography and the underlying epistemological frameworks of the Geoweb will enable a diverse set of stakeholders to develop new spatial epistemologies. A complete history of this is well beyond our scope here. What is worth highlighting is that there have been very few studies that have sought to embed the Geoweb within larger frameworks of political economy and critical theory (Elwood and Leszczynski, 2011; Elwood, 2008; Smith, 2014). Leszczynski (2012) argues that the Geoweb is historically contingent upon larger shifts towards the neoliberalization of the state and spatial infrastructures. For Leszczysnki, the Geoweb did not simply emerge out of Web 2.0 trends, but follows a genealogy of market liberalization away from a strictly state-controlled domain towards the creation of geo-spatial media as a new mass market for the private sector. Despite the creation of open and free tools such as openstreetmap.org, the vernacular aspects of the Geoweb are dominated by commercial companies and are ripe for commercial exploitation. Another example is upmystreet.com, now owned by the property company Zoopla in the UK. We pay attention to intellectual property regimes and ownership, and especially companies like Google whom exert significant pressure on the social relations of geo-spatial knowledge production through strategic acquisitions to maintain market control (Smith, 2014).

The Geoweb emerged from a historical trend towards spatial data liberalization in the 1990s, and from the development of technical and organizational data standards by key geographic agencies of the US government. The Geoweb can be traced back by analysing the creation of the National Spatial Data Infrastructure (NSDI) by the Federal Geographic Data Committee (FGDC) in the US. The FGDC and the NSDI sought to instil laissez-faire free market principles onto domains once exclusive to government, including geo-spatial infrastructure. In the 1970s, the US government recognized the trend towards digitizing cartographic data, but also found evidence of overlap and redundancy. The Federal Interagency Coordinating Committee on Digital Cartography (FICCDC), which included representatives from the Departments of Agriculture, Commerce, Defence, Energy, Housing and Urban Development, State, Transportation, Federal Emergency Management Agency, and National Aeronautics and Space Administration, was charged with developing an organizational framework for digitalizing cartographic information. By the 1990s, the FICCDC was transformed into the FGDC and

called for the development of a 'resource' to maximize the efficient production, distribution and use of geo-spatial data. This resource was to become known as the NSDI.

In 1994, President Clinton launched the NSDI through Executive Order #12906, which was later amended by President Bush in 2003 by Executive Order #13286 to include the Department of Homeland Security. According to President Clinton, the NSDI is part of a larger program to 'reinvent government', especially in a time where visions of the information 'superhighway' were abounding all levels of government. Executive Order #12906 sets forth the development of a publicly accessible geographic data clearinghouse in an effort to harmonize data standards and reduce governmental waste. The NSDI explicitly acknowledges the role of networked computers and communication in producing and consuming cartographic maps. The NSDI's primary purpose is the social and technical framework for organizing the use of geo-spatial data amongst a variety of sectors, and specifically addresses the need for non-governmental actors to play a key role in the future production of geo-spatial data. The NSDI Cooperative Agreements Program (CAP) in particular sought to leverage the private sector and other non-federal governmental agencies through a merit-based granting system. The CAP has issued over 700 grants since 1994 to maximize digitization of geo-spatial data by leveraging the private sector. Since May 2007, in Europe, there has been a legal framework in place to mandate the creation of a European SDI at national levels.[6]

Understanding governance structures has historically been a key technique for analysing the power relations that structure the production of particular media content. Although new technologies are rapidly emerging, the generic components underpinning the Geoweb are relatively constant: framework data, metadata, interoperability, praxis, access, user-groups, imagery and scale. Key differences are in the approach, institutional and/or commercial scope and ambition. The standards for data infrastructure are also very similar (see Craglia, 2007). The Open Geospatial Consortium (OGC), for example, is a powerful standards setting organization that seeks to develop the potential of geo-spatial content for both industry and government. Without the OGC's role in standards setting, it is questionable whether something like the Geoweb could ever really exist. The OGC's governance structure is an excellent example for understanding the inter-relationship between industry and government in the production of information standards and infrastructures, or put another way, for understanding the political economy of geo-spatial media.

The OGC is a private sector-based standards organization that emerged out of military divestment. The vast majority of members are from the private sector, and indeed if OGC members are ranked in terms of influence and power, we find a handful of powerful American corporations at the top tier, including private defence contractors and large tech companies. Although the standards themselves are open in that they are free to use or modify for any purpose, the actual capacity of determining standards is much more complex and demonstrates an emphasis on allowing the private sector, as well as key US government agencies, to have a substantial role in determining the overall direction and scope of Geoweb standards. This can largely be explained by once again taking into consideration the long-term historical direction of geo-spatial development, particularly the NSDI's role in stimulating the private sector in establishing a market for geo-spatial media.

The political economy of the Geoweb is important because it draws attention to how the Geoweb is embedded in the rise of commercial sociology and simultaneously the decline or withdrawal of state resources in cartographic knowledge production. This neoliberalization of geo-spatial infrastructure operates on numerous levels, including the diffusion of expertise towards 'non-expert' vernacular understandings of space and place; the creation of crowdsourced epistemologies whereby Geoweb users contribute or labour in various forms of social production; and finally in the politics of geo-spatial infrastructure. Significantly, the changing institutional governing bodies of spatial data standards such as the OGC are governed by an assemblage of public and private entities typically based in the US.

PART III: APPLICATIONS

It is important to realize that map making has typically been employed to address issues of population management, and therefore directly intersects with sociological knowledge production. A classic example is the epidemiological maps of cholera outbreaks in London that were juxtaposed by the locations of public water pumps by John Snow. Another example is the London poverty maps created by Charles Booth that drew strong correlations between poverty and health. Such rationales for mapping eventually went on to influence the development of the Chicago School of Sociology, which in turn became a key pillar in the foundation of geodemographics and then, ultimately of relevance here, towards the use of GIS for knowing capitalism.[7]

Elwood and Leszczynski (2013) argue that the significance of the Geoweb is the underlying knowledge politics and epistemological strategies of validity and authority enacted by new mapping practices. They view the Geoweb as offering the ability to re-situate geovisual epistemologies around an exploratory engagement with content, rather than simply being used for cartographic abstraction and representation. Underlying these epistemological strategies are entirely different sets of criteria necessary for engendering claims of reliability and validity – criteria that are not necessarily grounded in methodological claims of normal positivist science, but instead around transparency, peer-verification and 'witnessing'. The Geoweb's capacity for creating new tools and methodologies for social science research is, in this sense, seen as embedded within larger cultural epistemologies of praxis whereby interfaces of social cartography are equated with democratic and civic change. However, we should not assume that the Geoweb (and its ancillary institutions of open data and crowdsourcing) is developed exclusively by marginalized communities. The interactive properties of Geoweb mapping are situated in heterogeneity of political or social goals. In some cases, this is not exclusively accomplished by one specific user, but could be crowdsourced by a multitude of networked users guided by more or less coherent objectives of social change.

Ushahidi, for example, is a free and open-source non-profit crisis mapping company that leverages principles of the Geoweb and crowdsourcing to create activist mapping for social justice issues worldwide. Ushahidi (the Swahili name for testimony) was created in the aftermath of the 2007 Presidential elections in Kenya and created a Google map of eyewitness reports of violence collected from email and mobile SMS reports from on-the-ground testimony. Since then, Ushahidi's mission statement has been to 'change the way information flows in the world, and empower people to make an impact with open-source technologies, cross-sector partnerships, and ground-breaking ventures,' and has been used in numerous humanitarian missions wrought through political conflict, war or natural disasters such as the 2010 Haiti earthquakes (Ushahidi, 2015). Ushahidi also offers a suite of other products for crisis mapping and disaster response, including Ping,[8] a check-in tool for emergencies; CrisisNET, a consolidated source of crisis data;[9] and it even manufactures hardware for rugged conditions such as BRCK, a self-powered mobile Wi-Fi router.[10]

For Roche (2013), the Geoweb has now become an indispensable part of crisis management because it offers the capacity to centralize the dissemination of information from both authoritative and non-authoritative sources. These affordances for crisis management, however, have begun to stimulate new discussions around the role of 'victim' epistemologies and how such information may enhance or sometimes complicate the institutional processes of crisis management by authorities but, more importantly, might also risk placing new burdens on victims of these crises to stay connected to various data sources in real time in order to seek assistance or relief. Thus, although crisis mapping tools may create new affordances that enhance the efficiencies of aid and rescue, it may also place new responsibilities on individual victims of these events to self-manage crisis, effectively re-inscribing neoliberal individualizations of risk management (Beck, 1999; Bauman, 2001).

A further application of the Geoweb that may be of value for realizing new avenues for social science research is from SaaS platforms developed by the private sector that offer easy to use geo-spatial tools and interfaces for web browsers by exploiting cloud computing storage (for a discussion on the political economy of cloud computing, see Mosco, 2014). Carto[11] serves as an excellent case in point primarily because it operates under a 'Freemium' business model so that anyone can begin to use the platform but may eventually need to pay licensing fees to take fuller advantage of more powerful analytical tools. Of particular interest is the ability to integrate datasets from commercial providers, including social media platforms such as Instagram (now owned by Facebook), marketing datasets from SalesForce, or data from traditional GIS tools such as ArcGIS. The functionality and user interface of Carto is in many respects remarkable because it could allow anyone to produce sophisticated analytical maps, such as choropleth and animated torque maps, with very little difficulty. It also offers more advanced users tools such as Cascading Style Sheets (CSS) and Structured Query Language (SQL) editing panels for a greater degree of precision, control and finesse over created maps. A social scientist with little-to-no training in GIS could, in theory, download a dataset from any open data portal, import their data into a Carto map and manipulate the data through various data 'wizard' tools within minutes to test their hypotheses.

Carto serves a multitude of markets and applications, including banking and finance, education and research, journalism and media, as well as non-profit sectors. Carto is scalable to its clientele, offering numerous pricing models from 'free' to enterprise solutions from USD$9,000 per year. This is significant because it underscores the underlying neoliberal political economies of the Geoweb with regards to its profound connections to commercial empirical sociology, but it may also offer grassroots community organizations the potential to use these tools for minimal to no cost. In other words, the pricing models and scalability of Geoweb infrastructures, such as Carto (which is connected to external datasets and the cloud), reflect and potentially reinforce socio-economic differences and conflicts. It also demonstrates how the Geoweb is not simply a cultural epistemology of social production that exclusively serves an idealization of networked publics – it is highly commodifiable and scalable to meet a heterogeneity of agendas and interests. The promise of accessibility, interactivity and ease becomes dependent on access to capital and labour necessary for leveraging more complex tools, data sets and analytical power.

DISCUSSION

The Geoweb in its most idealized form presents social scientists with the capacity to engage with geo-spatial interfaces and datasets in ways never before imagined, and without possessing certain data literacies of GIS. It can, and probably will, become integrated into the repertoire of 'normal' social science methods. This represents a significant benefit that provides new tools to visualize complex socio-demographic phenomena, and can perhaps allow social scientists a realization of new kinds of analytical knowledge.

At the same time, the political economy of the Geoweb suggests that market imperatives of commercial sociology will exact a strong influence on the overall scope of cartographic production. Here, access to capital – both economic and intellectual – will in all probability reinforce distinctions of authority and expertise despite the ideological assumptions of the Geoweb with respect to democratization, accessibility and empowerment. In this respect, the capacity to create and interact with geo-spatial data through these new interfaces cannot be framed exclusively as a grassroots method for crowdsourced forms of social production and praxis because the private sector arguably remains the primary consumer in this market. Moreover, data licensing, standards and the increasing move towards cloud-based SaaS indicates that the Geoweb's connections with social praxis may indeed be a legacy that is eventually being replaced by the imperatives of the market – a history not unfamiliar to new media as a whole. Commodification, commercialization and control over the social relations of data production and the underlying technological modes for retention and analytics are therefore perceived to become a necessary priority for future research in the Geoweb.

This chapter has sought to re-evaluate some of the key arguments forwarded in the first edition concerning the status of empirical sociology and the jurisdictional questions engendered by knowing capitalism. The Geoweb was identified as a key development in social cartography and was analysed by comparing its cultural epistemologies and its embeddedness in neoliberal political economies of geo-spatial infrastructure. It then offered a brief comparison between two Geoweb platforms that arguably exemplify its cultural and commercial potential. It is worth considering how digital maps might begin to become part of the routine set of methods that sociologists could mobilize for conducting empirical research, as the declining necessity for expertise in GIS might offer sociologists new avenues for engaging with empirical and quantitative data. This may in effect permit a greater degree of interdisciplinary discussion between, for example, sociology and geography. At the same time, the Geoweb does not absolve the crisis of empirical sociology, nor is it entirely clear the extent to which jurisdictional challenges posed by knowing capitalism are being sufficiently addressed. Issues around data literacy and expertise remain at the foreground of intellectual labour, but the Geoweb, as this chapter hoped to argue, shows how the flow of power is not unidirectional or necessarily detrimental to the future of empirical sociology.

NOTES

1 This chapter is dedicated to the memory of Mike Hardey, who died on 27 March 2012. In the first edition, this chapter was titled 'Cartographies of knowing capitalism and the changing jurisdiction of empirical sociology' and was co-authored by Mike and Roger Burrows. For this new edition we have invited Harrison Smith to substantially update the chapter, and also Mariann Hardey – Mike's daughter and a social media scholar – to provide additional input. We hope the resulting chapter remains true to the ethos, interests and concerns that Mike had throughout his career. Both Mariann and Roger sorely miss him.

2 What some have recently termed 'digital civics', see http://digitalcivics.org.uk/ (accessed August 5, 2016).

3 In a UK and Australian context for certain, but perhaps also now in Scandinavia and Canada as well? Mainstream sociological research practice has always been more quantifiably inclined in the US and Japan, but even here there is some evidence that the balance between qualitative, quantitative and supposed 'mixed-methods' research design is shifting.

4 See http://wikimapia.org/ (accessed August 5, 2016).

5 See data.gov for an example of a large-scale open data repository from the United States Government. Similar open data portals are found at all levels of government throughout the world, but particularly in developed nations.

6 This legal framework is called Infrastructure for Spatial Information in Europe (INSPIRE) (www.ecgis.org/inspire) (accessed August 5, 2016).

7 For a more detailed history of maps, see Pickles (2004); Wood (1992, 2010); Curry (1998); Crampton (2009).

8 See http://www.ushahidi.com/product/ping/ (accessed August 5, 2016).

9 See http://www.ushahidi.com/product/crisisnet/ (accessed August 5, 2016).

10 See http://www.ushahidi.com/product/brck/ (accessed August 5, 2016).

11 See http://carto.com (accessed August 6, 2016)

REFERENCES

Abrams, H. and Hall, P. (2006). 'Whereabouts'. In H. Abrams and P. Hall (eds.) *Else/Where: Mapping New Cartographies of Networks and Territories*. Minneapolis, MN: University of Minnesota Press, 12–24

Bauman, Z. (2001). *The Individualized Society*. Cambridge: Polity Press.

Beck, U. (1999). *World Risk Society*. Cambridge: Polity Press.

Beer, D. (2009). 'Power through the algorithm? Participatory web cultures and the technological unconscious'. *New Media & Society*, 11(6), 985–1002. doi:10.1177/1461444809336551.

Beer, D. and Burrows, R. (2013). 'Popular culture, digital archives and the new social life of data'. *Theory, Culture & Society*, 30(4), 47–71. doi:10.1177/0263276413476542.

Bourdieu, P. (1984). *Distinction: A Social Critique of the Judgement of Taste* (Trans. by Richard Nice). London: Routledge.

Brabham, D. C. (2013). *Crowdsourcing*. Cambridge, MA: MIT Press.

Burrows, R. and Gane, N. (2006). 'Geodemographics, software and class'. *Sociology*, 40(5), 793–812. doi:10.1177/0038038506067507.

Burrows, R. and Savage, M. (2014). 'After the crisis? Big Data and the methodological challenges of empirical sociology'. *Big Data & Society*, 1(1), 1–6. doi:10.1177/2053951714540280.

Craglia, M. (2007). 'Volunteered Geographic Information and Spatial Data Infrastructures: when do parallel lines converge'. In Position Paper for the Specialist Meeting on

Volunteered Geographic Information, Santa Barbara, CA, December 13–14.

Crampton, J. W. (2003). 'Cartographic rationality and the Politics of geosurveillance and security'. *Cartography and Geographic Information Science*, 30(2), 135–148.

Crampton, J. W. (2009). 'Cartography: Maps 2.0'. *Progress in Human Geography*, 33(1), 91.

Crampton, J. W., Graham, M., Poorthuis, A., Shelton, T., Stephens, M., Wilson, M. W. and Zook, M. A. (2013). 'Beyond the geotag: situating "big data" and leveraging the potential of the Geoweb'. *Cartography and Geographic Information Science*, 40(2), 130–9. doi:10.1080/15230406.2013.777137.

Crompton, R. (2008). 'Forty years of sociology: some comments'. *Sociology*, 42(6), 1218–27. doi:10.1177/0038038508096942.

Curry, M. R. (1998). *Digital Places: Living with Geographic Information Technologies*. London: Routledge.

de Souza e Silva, A. (2006). 'From cyber to hybrid: mobile technologies as interfaces of hybrid spaces'. *Space and Culture*, 9(3), 261–78. doi:10.1177/1206331206289022.

Elwood, S. (2008). 'Volunteered geographic information: future research directions motivated by critical, participatory, and feminist GIS'. *GeoJournal*, 72(3–4), 173–83. doi:10.1007/s10708-008-9186-0.

Elwood, S., Goodchild, M. F. and Sui, D. Z. (2012). 'Researching volunteered geographic information: spatial data, geographic research, and new social practice'. *Annals of the Association of American Geographers*, 102(3), 571–90. doi:10.1080/00045608.201 1.595657.

Elwood, S. & Leszczynski, A. (2011). 'Privacy, reconsidered: New representations, data practices, and the geoweb'. *Geoforum*, 42(1), 6–15. doi:10.1016/j.geoforum.2010.08.003.

Elwood, S. & Leszczynski, A. (2013). 'New spatial media, new knowledge politics'. *Transactions of the Institute of British Geographers*, *38*(4), 544–59. doi:10.1111/j.1475-5661.2012.00543.x.

Federal Geographic Data Committee (FGDC). (2004). *The Federal Geographic Data Committee: Historical Reflections – Future Directions*. Available at http://www.fgdc.gov/resources/whitepapers-reports/white-papers/fgdc-history (accessed 5 Aug 2016).

Goodchild, M. F. (2007). 'Citizens as sensors: the world of volunteered geography'. *GeoJournal*, 69(4), 211–21. doi:10.1007/s10708-007-9111-y.

Graham, S. (ed.) (2004). 'The software sorted city: rethinking the "digital divide"'. In S. Graham (ed.), *The Cybercities Reader*. London: Routledge, pp. 324–31.

Graham, S. and Marvin, S. (2001). *Splintering Urbanism: Networked Infrastructures, Technological Mobilities and the Urban Condition*. London: Routledge.

Graham, S. and Wood, D. (2003). 'Digitizing surveillance: categorization, space, inequality'. *Critical Social Policy*, 23(2), 227–48.

Gurstein, M. (2011). 'Open data: empowering the empowered or effective data use for everyone?' *First Monday*, 16(2).

Harris, R., Sleight, P. and Webber, R. (2005). *Geodemographics, GIS, and Neighbourhood Targeting*. Hoboken, NJ: Wiley.

Jameson, F. (1984) 'Postmodernism, or the cultural logic of late capitalism', *New Left Review*, 146, July–August 1984, 53-92.

Johnson, P. A. and Sieber, R. E. (2011). 'Motivations driving government adoption of the Geoweb'. *GeoJournal*, 77(5), 667–80. doi:10.1007/s10708-011-9416-8.

Kramer, A. D. I., Guillory, J. E. and Hancock, J. T. (2014). 'Experimental evidence of massive-scale emotional contagion through social networks'. *Proceedings of the National Academy of Sciences of the United States of America,* 111(24), 8788–90.

Leszczynski, A. (2012). 'Situating the Geoweb in political economy'. *Progress in Human Geography*, 36(1), 72–89. doi:10.1177/0309132511411231.

Leszczynski, A. (2014). 'On the neo in neogeography'. *Annals of the Association of American Geographers*, 104(1), 60–79. doi:10.1080/00045608.2013.846159.

Longo, J. (2011). '#Opendata: digital-era governance thoroughbred or new public management Trojan Horse?'. *Public Policy & Governance Review*, 2(2), 38.

Lyon, D. (ed.). (2003). *Surveillance as Social Sorting: Privacy, Risk, and Automated Discrimination*. London: Routledge.

McNeal, G. S. (2014). 'Facebook manipulated user news feeds to create emotional responses'. *Forbes*. Available at http://www.

forbes.com/sites/gregorymcneal/2014/06/28/ facebook-manipulated-user-news-feeds-to-create-emotional-contagion/ (accessed 5 August 2016).

Mosco, V. (2014). *To the Cloud: Big Data in a Turbulent World*. Boulder, CO: Paradigm.

Muyskens, J., Keating, D. and Granados, S., (2015). 'Mapping how the United States generates it electricity'. *The Washington Post,* analysis of Energy Information Administration. Available at https://www.washingtonpost.com/graphics/national/power-plants/ (accessed 3 August 2015).

Paulston, R. G. (ed.) (1996) *Social Cartography: Mapping Ways of Seeing Social and Educational Change*. New York, NY: Garland.

Pickles, J. (2004). *A History of Spaces: Cartographic Reason, Mapping and the Geo-coded World*. London: Routledge.

Platt, J. (2014) 'Using journal articles to measure the level of quantification in national sociologies', *International Journal of Social Research Methodology*, doi:10.1080/13645 579.2014.947644.

Ritzer, G. and Jurgenson, N. (2010). 'Production, consumption, prosumption: the nature of capitalism in the age of the digital "prosumer"'. *Journal of Consumer Culture*, 10(1), 13–36. doi:10.1177/1469540509354673.

Roche, S., Propeck-Zimmermann, E. & Mericskay, B. (2013). 'GeoWeb and crisis management: Issues and perspectives of volunteered geographic information'. *GeoJournal*, 78(1), 21–40. doi:10.1007/s10708-011-9423-9

Savage, M. and Burrows, R. (2007). 'The coming crisis of empirical sociology'. *Sociology*, 41(5), 885–99. doi:10.1177/0038038507080443.

Savage, M. & Burrows, R. (2009). 'Some further reflections on the coming crisis of empirical sociology'. *Sociology*, 43(4), 762–72. doi:10.1177/0038038509105420

Savolainen, R. (2008). *Everyday Information Practices: A Social Phenomenological Perspective*. Lanham, MD: The Scarecrow Press.

Sieber, R. E. (2006). 'Public participation geographic information systems: a literature review and framework'. *Annals of the Association of American Geographers*, 96(3), 491–507.

Sieber, R. E. and Johnson, P. A. (2015). 'Civic open data at a crossroads: dominant models and current challenges'. *Government Information Quarterly*. doi:10.1016/j.giq.2015.05.003.

Smith, H. (2014). *Open and Free? The Political Economy of the Geospatial Web 2.0. Geothink White Paper Series*. Available at http://geothink.ca/wp-content/uploads/2014/06/Geothink-Working-Paper-001-Shade-Smith1.pdf (accessed 5 August 2016).

Thrift, N. (2005). *Knowing Capitalism*. London: Routledge.

Toscano, A. and Kinkle, J. (2015) *Cartographies of the Absolute*. London: Zero Books.

Tulloch, D. L. (2008). 'Is VGI participation? From vernal pools to video games'. *GeoJournal*, 72(3–4), 161–71. doi:10.1007/s10708-008-9185-1.

Uprichard, E., Burrows, R. and Parker, S. (2009). 'Geodemographic code and the production of space'. *Environment and Planning A*, 41(12), 2823–35. doi:10.1068/a41116.

Ushahidi. (2015). Mission Statement. Available at http://www.ushahidi.com/mission/ (accessed 5 August 2016).

Williams, M., Payne, G., Hodgkinson, L. and Poade, D. (2008) 'Does British sociology count? Sociology students' attitudes toward quantitative methods'. *Sociology*, 42(5): 1003–21.

Wilson, M. W. (2011). '"Training the eye": formation of the geocoding subject'. *Social & Cultural Geography*, 12(4), 357–376. doi: 10.1080/14649365.2010.521856.

Wilson, M. W. (2012). 'Location-based services, conspicuous mobility, and the location-aware future'. *Geoforum*, 43(6), 1266–75. doi:10.1016/j.geoforum.2012.03.014.

Wood, D. (1992). *The Power of Maps*. New York, NY: Guilford Press.

Wood, D. (2010). *Rethinking the Power of Maps*. New York, NY: Guilford Press.

Zittrain, J. L. (2008). *The Future of the Internet and How to Stop it*. New Haven, CT: Yale University Press.

Zook, M. A. and Graham, M. (2007). 'The creative reconstruction of the Internet: Google and the privatization of cyberspace and digiplace'. *Geoforum,* 38(6), 1322–43. doi:10.1016/j.geoforum.2007.05.004.

35

Online Environments and the Future of Social Science Research

Michael Fischer, Stephen Lyon
and David Zeitlyn

INTRODUCTION

History doesn't repeat itself, but it sure rhymes.
Attributed to Mark Twain

New generations of social scientists face a different range of possibilities and prospects in their careers than many academics currently in post. The Internet and related communications technologies (IRCT) are playing a major role in these differences. The Internet has greatly impacted social scientists' practice, as well as advancing the scale of activities rendered feasible, resulting in significant changes in the kinds of research carried out and, importantly, the kinds of subject deemed 'researchable'. More important, IRCT are social infrastructures that people use to create new social phenomena, which become objects of study for social scientists.

People are using IRCT to change the world around us, creating circumstances that change quickly over such large areas that apparently continual adaptation – technological, social and cultural – is necessary. This trend will expand apace. The opportunities for social scientists will be driven by changes in societies and advances in our research methods, and we will perform some things better, or at least on a larger scale. We will be able to carry out hitherto unimagined activities relating to data collection, analysis and dissemination. Concurrently, many of the social and cultural forms that emerge create situations we are ill equipped to understand. We require new capabilities to enable social scientists to operationalise some well-established conceptual and terminological descriptions and understandings. We must also develop new theoretical concepts and vocabularies.

How will we deal with new kinds of social relationships? What do we do with the vast amounts of data that become available from technologically enhanced observation and participation? How will the formidable ethical issues be addressed? How do we study social and cultural phenomena that may exist for a few years, months or only weeks?

How do we adapt to a dependence on 'smart' technological assistants in our research? How will we be able to disseminate our results, not just in static form but in formats that directly interact with potential users? What further technological change can we expect? Perhaps the best way to predict the short-term future (3–7 years) of the impact of IRCT on social science research is simply to look at what a minority of computer and network-savvy individuals are able to do now. Dow (1992) accurately predicted much of the development of computing in mainstream anthropology, simply by looking at what the minority were doing at the time. The contributions to this volume will serve as a model for the short-term development of IRCT-related research.

Predicting the longer term future (8–20 years) is more problematic. Today, visions and trends are evident which, if continued, will lead to identifiable future practices. However, any number of factors can interfere with current trends and derail the best-laid futurology. One can, nevertheless, still differentiate between probable, possible, improbable and (probably) impossible applications of IRCT over the coming 20 years. Although our grasp of future history might be weak, by focusing on the development of capabilities we can get a handle on what tools and resources people (and researchers) have available to build our future.

This chapter discusses how new or expanded capabilities emergent from IRCT may contribute to changing social science research, particularly how research topics, methods and capabilities might change with increasing integration of IRCT into the daily social lives of most people in developed and developing societies. We have not limited ourselves to online research because we believe that firm distinctions between online and offline research are a present phenomenon, and that online research will rapidly become one of the many different contexts within which research is carried out – not the odd one out. However, we expect all social science research to change, for the very reasons

that online research will become accepted and ordinary when online social phenomena become integrated into wider social and cultural life.

There are two broad themes: new social formations, phenomena and conditions that arise because of access to IRCT technologies; and new methods that become available to carry out social research using IRCT technologies. These two themes will, of course, co-occur and will quickly converge.

We can relate only to capabilities that may underlie research methods, not specific future methods. We discuss some of the major new capabilities which are likely and offer some examples. Similarly, we do not make specific predictions of wider social change, but rather new social capabilities. We discuss so-called virtual groups, but for the most part we shall leave predictions about specific future social and cultural development to our, and the reader's, science fiction avatars.

CHANGE AND CHANGES TO IRCT TECHNOLOGIES

Although there is a tendency to focus on technology as a material process, technology is also a process of social and cultural instantiations of ideational innovation (Fischer, 2004, 2006a), the adaptive transformation of ideas into practice. We view technology as anything people use to extend or expand their capabilities, directly or indirectly (following Hall, 1976).

In this context, what are recognised as technologies result from ideas whose instantiation have social and cultural histories (these were successful), which in turn creates a sense of inevitability for their future. The development of material futures is never linear. Technological development and human extensions (Hall, 1976) are formed by adaptive processes. As human culture transforms the material world (Fischer, 2006a), new possibilities emerge for instantiation of our prior symbolic constructions. Core cultural ideas will also change over time, but much more slowly than how people instantiate these into the world.

Many of the visions instantiated using the Internet considerably preceded the Internet itself (see, for example, Bush, 1945). Much of the current development of IRCT instantiates broad visions (fantasies?) from the mid-twentieth century, inspired by figures such as Arthur C. Clarke, who in his fiction described global networks, networked libraries with search engines, personal videoconferencing and cell phones, and J. C. R. Licklider, whose anticipatory visions directly contributed to bringing the ARPANET (Advanced Research Projects Agency Network) to reality. However, the material forms that manifest these visions, the social and cultural formations and uses people make of the productions and interactions of these visions go well beyond what was envisaged. From a given starting point we can extrapolate *what* future capabilities there may be, but not necessarily the *forms* these will take, nor the outcomes of their manifestation and uses.

Much of what we discuss will not sound very futuristic. There is a very good reason for that because we are only looking over the next 20 years. Although people often perceive that technologies arrive and rapidly change the world around us, our experience so far is that it takes at least 15–20 years (aka the 'Fischer fifteen-year rule') for new capabilities to become pervasive following their first entry as a deliverable technology. Researchers are a bit more precocious than this, and for specialists with technical skills the period is more like 3–7 years, and specialists without technical skills up to 10 years. But for a capability to become pervasive in the research community as a whole, the period is very similar to the general public's. Much of what we discuss is partially achievable now, but is often still dependent on current and future research for continued development – so that covers the next 20 years quite well.

Although it is possible that currently unknown *fundamental* 'new technologies' may emerge over this period, it is unlikely

that those would have a great impact for at least 10 or 20 years afterwards. For example, microcomputer technology was first delivered by Intel as a commercial technology in 1968, and gained mass acceptance in the form of microcomputers in the period between 1983 and 1985. Email was first introduced on the ARPANET around 1972–3, but did not achieve mass acceptance in universities until around 1988. Telnet (for interactive sessions between networked computers) was also introduced in 1972–3 and FTP (File Transfer Protocol, for file transfers between networked computers) in 1973. The 'web' was introduced in 1991 between a few institutions, expanded slowly during 1993–4, and began to become a phenomenon from mid-1994 (after the release of Windows 95) – nearly 22 years after FTP (whose functionality it incorporates) and 18 years after the first public online information services (Leiner *et al.* 2012 [2003]).

Any increase in IRCT-mediated ('online') social relations will result in social change by definition. A principal topic of this volume is just how we, as social scientists, should go about the study of these relationships. For instance, some researchers have been attracted to online research because of the appearance of new online communities. Others have been attracted to the use of online panels and surveys to study more traditional social institutions and formations, and many researchers are simply grappling with the impact of IRCT on what they would consider to be more conventional research settings.

The use of technology in social science research is hardly new (or uncontested). But IRCT supports many new opportunities and capabilities for data collection and documentation, theory and analysis. Aspects of the research process that IRCT can most greatly impact are:

- Communication – the capacity to gather, disseminate and exchange information. This includes data collection, whether through direct contact with people or by sensors (cameras, global

positioning systems (GPS), heart-rate monitors and environmental sensors), collaboration with researched colleagues or research colleagues and dissemination of the outcomes of research.
- Representation – the capacity to describe, model and visualise information: how information is aggregated, visualised, described, modelled, transcribed, presented, transformed, reduced, expanded and interrelated.
- Storage – the capacity to retain and retrieve information: the form, medium and availability of retained information (most often representations).

IRCT greatly enhances the scope and integration of each of these processes in research; communications is no longer an end-point after the fact, but an integral part of the computational environment. Code, processes and data can be distributed across the network, greatly expanding not only the capacity of researchers to exchange and share resources, but also transforming how research is done, its replicability and the production of sustainable outcomes.

COMMUNICATIONS

Communicating complex symbolic messages did not, of course, begin with the Internet. Generative language development and then writing, respectively, made new kinds of social organisation possible, although the strongest forms of this claim have been questioned (see Goody and Watt 1963). Eisenstein (1979) posited similar radical changes following the printing press (see also Zeitlyn, 2001).

The advent of telegraphy, telephony, radio, photography, film and television each had profound impacts on how people were able to record, transmit and use information that cannot be subsumed within the capabilities originating with language, writing and printing. Each technological development enables new means for forming and maintaining social relationships, while rendering some types of social relationship less critical or obsolete. Internet communication via email, conferencing and collaborative web applications transforms the ways in which social scientists can exchange information and develop friendships and collaborations. The gamut of FTP and resulting services enables sharing immensely large distributed datasets of disparate data types with relatively low cost and effort.

The current rise of mobile Internet platforms, such as phones and tablets (see Silver and Bulloch, this volume), has radically transformed the concept of locale. As video-based communications has spread to phones and tablets, most researchers have participated in a video conference at some stage of their research. Although there is still a vague scepticism about the ability of such formats to genuinely replace more conventional forms of meetings, this scepticism is rapidly receding. Replacing meetings was the original trajectory for video- conferencing, but improvements in video presence technologies in conjunction with mobile devices have increased the frequency of communications, irrespective of the impact on physical meetings.

One of the obvious growth areas in Internet communications is transmission of this real time 'presence' data, including audio, video, live camera feeds, physiological measurements such as heart rate, and geographical location. The main trend of developing capabilities over the next two decades in research communication will be increasing pervasiveness in exchanging expanded indices of presence. Presence is what we individually bring to a situation and context. Communicating presence brings more of ourselves and the others we interact with into a common context. The telephone was a great stride in presence, and found its way into the research process, sometimes controversially (at least where sampling was an issue). Increasingly 'presence' will refer to our ability to exert influence or be influenced, physically or otherwise, over a communications link.

Improvements in sensors and actuators will enable transmission not only of sound and image but also of heat, odour, taste and surface texture. Transmissions will be not just as digital representations but increasing with the capacity to materially reproduce these at all networked locations. We will meet in simulated environments for demonstrations, meetings, data collection or processing using simulated representations of ourselves and others in simulated space transposed over a shared composite locale. Interactions will not be limited to the simulated space; we will link actions that we and others take in our local locale to reactions in the composite locale. The effective transmission of material objects over communications channels will be commonplace because instructions will be sent to devices that manufacture objects (perhaps like an elaborate 3D printer or using 'smart' materials that reassemble themselves into requested forms).

What is likely to transform the way social scientists carry out their work is the pervasiveness and the complexity of the presence-focused communication. Current mobile communication devices have substantial capacity for complex communication including file transfer, video and audio in synchronous and asynchronous modes. Moreover, much of the communication does not happen between two people directly, but with some form of software agent acting as mediator, directly engaging in the communication. At the moment we can see this in electronic calendars, Amazon-style user-focused pages recommending further purchases based on previous browsing history, or social computing sites such as Facebook, Twitter or Reddit where software agents create personalised resources or viewpoints. Software will continue this trend in simulating people to the extent that routine conversations may well be with (or between) software agents that brief their 'operator' later. The only way humans may be able to differentiate some communication between software agents or people is the inefficiency and delayed response time of the person.

With respect to research practices, we anticipate three relevant types of change: Changes to the profile of potential collaborative partners; Changes in the ways certain kinds of 'field' research may be conducted;

Changes in the ways in which the mundane aspects of being a member of an institution are acted out.

Network services already make possible geographically distributed teams of researchers who coordinate their efforts and effectively create something akin to research centres without a physical location. In 1995, Zeitlyn created a Virtual Institute of Mambila Studies (VIMS), which brings together resources relevant to the international pool of Mambila specialists. More recently, many projects in the Social Sciences, such as Kinsources[1] and Complex Social Science Gateway,[2] have emerged, involving many individuals and organisations distributed globally to construct, use and collaborate in specialised research areas, not only with shared data, but also shared resources and tools for analysis that leverage shared data. Organisations such as the Human Relations Area Files (HRAF)[3] are refactoring their current web application into a suite of software services researchers use to greatly customise access to HRAF data, the procedures applied to data and the creation of sharable documents containing outcomes of searches or analyses, all of which utilise network communications to reference a common set of data on the Internet.

Changes to siting the 'field' are underway. Webcams constitute a legitimate area of study for the social sciences.[4] The capacity for streaming 'presence' data changes how primary field data can be collected, disseminated and made available for secondary research. Social media will result in more and more 'traces' of people's presence. Short-term field research combined with judicious use of networked presence data in partnership with local academics and informants is potentially a means for collecting ethnographic data and increasing the reliability of those data.

To summarise, much of the 'future' of pervasive communication is in fact the present! Little new technology is required to achieve the ubiquitous disparate communications context we believe is emerging.

However, new technological developments will enhance many aspects of this communication and widen the range of people using it. We can predict some outcomes:

1   Collaboration will rely on pervasive multi-format interactions, all of which are possible today, but which will be simpler, more integrated and more robust.
2   As such communication becomes more pervasive; the objections about impersonality or partiality will recede. In other words, people will develop new ways of inferring closeness, intimacy and trust through online interaction.
3   Individuals will change their assumptions about privacy and trust, as currently suggested by subdued reactions to increasingly regular cases of personal data being lost, stolen or leaked from financial organizations, insurers and government, which are regarded more as inconveniences than major scandals.
4   Pervasive online communication, like simple email and multimedia presentation software before it, will become part of the baseline set of software tools that all social scientists will be assumed to have mastered.

REPRESENTATION

When collecting data and documenting human practices, institutions, languages, societies and cultures, social science researchers directly incorporate new technologies of representation in a primary sense, and also data derived from what people create using the technologies (new and old) at their disposal. Data is derived from and is represented by fieldnotes, sketches, transcription, photography, telephones, radio, audio recording, film and video, and – increasingly common these days – interactive media distributed over the Internet (Macfarlane, 1987; Farnell, 1995; Biella, 1997; Fischer and Zeitlyn, 1999).

Researchers are familiar with recording aural and visual data as part of data collection. These recordings can be used reflexively in the field to elicit detailed descriptions, to interpret and to disseminate knowledge. The advent of hypertext expands the capability to interrelate components of both data sources and data representations, with the addition of links between segments of different media, allowing researchers to record knowledge about the interoperation of the people, processes and objects depicted by the media, both their own and knowledge elicited from their local research collaborators on the ground (Biella, 2004; Ruby, 2005). This capability has, however, been little used by mainstream researchers.

Computer representations have generally been considered by most people as virtual objects – abstract representations of real things. Increasingly, computer representations are achieving first-class object status, where people can manipulate and exchange these as they would 'real' objects. Initially for video game players, and more recently for users of mobile technology such as the iPhone, configurable objects are increasingly common in people's lives, mediating interactions between people, and thus becoming as much objects of social research as any other human artefact. Inexpensive hand-held 3D scanners are becoming available on phones or tablets, producing hybrid images that integrate a 3D mesh representation of an object rendered on the surface with photographic data. These are objects that can be further manipulated with computer-based tools, imported into new scenes and material copies reproduced on a 3D printer. In conjunction with development in 3D capture and display technologies, such 3D objects will increasingly replace 2D digital photography and video for research. Rather than simple recordings of light, a recorded event will have discrete objects interacting with each other, objects with persistence in the recording that can be associated with further data and identified in other recordings.

The development of mobile computing platforms and improvements in authoring complex interactive media creates the capability for recording physical interaction with embedded media objects available in the field (Zeitlyn and Fischer, 1999; Bagg *et al.*, 2006). Phones and tablets already have software for single platform capture, editing and display of media, and mobile platforms will replace conventional cameras, computers and displays for most researchers, as well as the general population. Developments in projective and perceptual displays will make mobile platforms more mobile, in the form of watches, rings, pendants and badges. Widespread subcutaneous cyborg modifications beyond medical applications, where hardware is embedded directly within the body, is likely to remain mostly a minority activity over the next two decades, although we can anticipate governments and corporations to promote 'ID chipping' of people and parents chipping their children.

The availability of embedded computers and computer sensors will greatly extend capability. In 2016, tiny computers with speed and storage roughly comparable to desktop computers of just a few years ago are commodities. These are miniaturised to a size somewhat smaller than a fingernail, very inexpensive and able to operate for substantial periods on small power cells. These will use similarly miniaturised sensors that can measure and record many details of a person's interaction with their environment and with other people, including proximity, motion, acceleration, rotation, skin temperature, brain and nerve activity, blood chemistry and anything else that can be measured.

For example, presently researchers, tourists, and nearly anyone with a phone are using GPS technology in conjunction with digital photography and video to add spatial and temporal location to the mix of relationships that are recorded with the image (Fischer, 2003; also Happel, 2005). The research day, week or season can be played back temporally and spatially (say on a map), evoking recorded media, notes and other time-stamped data that is associated with the researcher's presence (Fischer, 2006b).

Similarly, social networking is beginning to draw on sensor readings, for example GPS functionality in photo tags can invoke Google Maps to display where the photo was taken, and Nike+ offers a running shoe that logs information regarding the run to an iPod Nano and then uploads data to the Nike+ website[5] where runners can compare runs. Social apps such as foresquare.com alert users when they are in the proximity of friends or other users meeting a certain profile.

In other words, the trend is to increase our capacity to record much more of the research context and process, and this greatly expands the kinds of data we have accessible to us, including sensor data recorded by potential research subjects on their own initiative. Multi-megapixel photography and HD Video, combined with new, cheap 360×180-degree lenses, already make it possible to visually record a complete scene, not just an aperture of a few degrees.

All this will, of course, create new issues for how to represent and use this staggering array of data. Conventional methods, such as statistical summarisation of particular views of the data, will of course continue to be used. But we will be increasingly driven to disaggregated designs, where we build layers of abstraction and aggregation over the dataset while retaining links to the underlying data. Some data will be real-time streams, constantly generated by the activity of potential research subjects. If not 'on-line', data will increasingly be 'on-tap'. Research design will generally transcend towards disaggregation and data reuse.

Embedded systems can control actuators that translate data into effects in the world. Common actuators currently mostly produce movement, sound, light and heat, but texture mapping and odour synthesis have been demonstrated, and in principle any sense can be reproduced individually. The opportunities for aggregating these into research data representations are, as the 1970s microcomputer sales slogan stated, only limited by our imagination. Certainly a range of new research based on controlled experiences is likely, as well as the production of 'identikit' data instruments where people create experiences for the benefit of the researcher as data.

There will be a very strong technological push over the next two decades outside the social science community for development of multi-sense sensors and actuators, driven by a major industry theme often referred to as the Internet of Things (Madakam *et al.*, 2015) or IoT. The broad conception is literally to put everything in the world directly online, by either observing it, or attaching sensors and actuators to it, all interfaced to the Internet. These will range from household appliances that report and track their contents to the deployment of billions of small sensors into public and private environments, creating smart environments that track any interaction and make this data available on the Internet, as well as perhaps being able to display personal public service information (or personally focused advertisements) on the lawn of a public park. Social scientists have a range of opportunities and responsibilities over this period, if nothing else to help ensure that this does not result in a surveillance and control system that far exceeds the worst nightmares of George Orwell. But these plans almost guarantee that, even if the dream (or nightmare) of the IoT fails for some technical or social reason, there will be an unprecedented amount of data regarding people and their interactions with each other and the environment around them.

There are two basic issues that emerge in relating these capabilities to research methods. The ethical dimensions of research on this scale, which depends on near or real-time information relating directly to individuals, are vast. But at present this level of detail is largely irrelevant to our research questions and research methods, and in many ways, beyond our present conceptual capacity.

There are, however, connections with existing research methodologies. Ethnographic studies, although usually on a smaller scale, have encompassed much larger communities by using a combination of immersive observation in sub-groups, whilst evaluating the results of immersive observation through sampling the larger population (Moody and White, 2003; also Fischer, 2006c). Mass observation studies have made sense of the records of thousands of people's self-observation. Larson and Csikszentmihalyi (1983; Csikszentmihalyi, 1991) – introduced 'beeper' technology to ground and contextualise the interactions of large research populations, with participants reporting activities under way when the beeper sounded. Each of these techniques seeks to impart meaning to the behaviours that can be observed.

At first blush it appears that all we get from the capability to access large sets of detailed data is a lot of behavioural data, with no meanings associated with that data. But because it is all disaggregated data, there are opportunities to do a great deal more. In the early days of research using satellite imagery a similar situation prevailed. There were many measurements of different aspects of an area, but researchers could not assess much more than what the measurements themselves entailed: how much light of different frequencies was reflected. To use this data for environmental research, research was done to examine the areas the images represented, producing baseline data on physical topography, plant cover, buildings, crops, fields, bodies of water, vehicles and other objects, which were then related to the imagery.

The outcome of this process made it possible to identify similar 'ground-truth' areas in new locations.

What will be needed is the development of 'proofing' subsets of the behavioural data, in order that findings from the 'proofed' data can be extended to the larger set of observations. Methods for this purpose are under development and are included broadly within the relatively new research activity of data mining (see Baram-Tsabari *et al.*, this volume). Data mining depends on relating patterns in disaggregated data streams to knowledge (and sometimes guesses) about the processes that produce that data. Rather than a return to pure behaviourism for all social scientists, we can therefore use the behavioural outcomes of ideationally driven processes as indices for identifying the likely presence of similar processes elsewhere. Thus, data mining can, in limited circumstances, replicate emic-driven processing by people.

This methodology is related to many present social science research perspectives. Some of us carry out small-scale ethnographic studies, or focus groups, or do sample surveys of some fragment of a population. We attempt to identify the social processes at work in these studies. We then attempt to generalise the results, based on ethnic or cultural group, social group, educational group, language group, etc. The principal difference here is that we are directly relating the patterns we observe and have 'proofed' to the larger population, not just through a few well-studied proxies.

New methods and means of representation and visualisation developed to support e-Science (Fielding, 2003; Fielding and Macintyre, 2006), multi-agent based simulation, shared network tools, and the Internet of Things (Madakam et al., 2015) will increase our capacity to work with multiple views of the disaggregated data (Bainbridge, 2007), enabling multiple research designs to be instantiated during, or even after, the data collection, the use of hybrid designs such as interactive dynamic statistical sampling, and composite representations that are 'layered' so that the original data is always available regardless of the level of abstraction (Fischer, 1998).

If considerable ethical issues can be resolved, with sufficient resources it becomes possible to track the movements and interactions, visual and aural context and the 'presence' data of an entire population.

STORAGE

Recent developments in 'intelligent' machine data storage have produced conceptual tools that are certain to have an impact on the kinds of research social scientists are not only able to imagine, but indeed will be required to conduct. The present model of storage has been to associate particular bits of information with particular places. The advent of Internet search engines demonstrates that this model has seen its day. There is simply too much information in too many places to organise using a simple set of addresses or locations.

One possibility is to access information based on its content (semantically) rather than its location. The idea of semantic or associative storage has a long history, in fact it goes back to the visionary paper by Bush (1945). It was founded in one of the earliest programming languages, Lisp in 1958 (see McCarthy, 1979), and has appeared more recently in the Semantic Web (Fensel et al., 2002). The semantic storage concept goes beyond matching content, as with keywords or classifiers, but rather depends on a model of 'understanding' the content and entailments of the content in different contexts.

Semantic storage systems enable software to infer meaning from data and relationships between data. There have been a number of increasingly sophisticated partial solutions to the problems, working around the fact that machines do not think as humans do; that is to say, that although a human with a reasonable search engine is capable of identifying related information across a range of websites, a machine is greatly handicapped by the ways in which such data is currently stored, largely because as yet we have not been able to model how we understand the content. Another approach, which underlies much of what makes search engines such as Google work well for some applications, is effectively based on data mining – the choices that people make after they do a search (what they clicked on) is recorded. Future searches are ranked on how close these are to past searches, and tend to 'promote' popular choices from those searches. Over time, each search is augmented by earlier searchers' choices.

Most current solutions involve adding different kinds of metadata (what machines use to infer relationships) to the content, and this has made it possible to produce prototypical versions of a Semantic Web, in which a range of inferences may be generated automatically. At present there are limitations imposed by the absence of such metadata in most web repositories, as well as scalability problems (Owens, 2005). The scalability issue is sure to be resolved, but the absence of pervasive metadata on the web is not as easily addressed. Data formats such as RDF (Resource Description Framework) and OWL (Ontology Web Language) are based on describing data relationships using terms and relationships in subject 'ontologies' in order that the researcher draws 'semantic' inferences from data sets stored in this format based on models defined by a researcher or standardised models supported by the research community. These are simply not, at present, designed with most social scientists (or many other categories of people for that matter) in mind. Part of the problem is the amount of specialist labour required to classify each online resource to fit the classification scheme that permits inference to take place (Brent, this volume, highlights this issue). This will change in part through better integration of social science knowledge of how people organise complex data. Kinship terminologies, for example, offer a very simple, but yet very robust algebraic mechanism for ordering relationships of extremely large numbers of individual people (Read, Fischer and Lehmann 2014). Other sorts of indigenous systems used to order the natural world share similar properties of simplicity, with impressive scalability, which are, at present, arguably limited by aspects of human cognition other than the inference systems themselves. Greater inclusion of natural or evolved human systems of inferring relationships, we expect, will enhance the capacity of human users to make ever greater use of the vast array of complex data available.

Indeed, we see evidence that such mechanisms for ordering relationships are already being successfully implemented in social networking sites in two ways. First, the sites ask users to classify friends according to a set of criteria, which will then enable relationships between friends of friends to emerge; second, friends in common automatically get highlighted, which enables a certain measure of the coherence of a given set of networks (see Hogan, this volume). Similarly, sites such as Flickr and Digg serve as an online folksonomy, where users create their own labels or 'tags' for images and web resources.

Folksonomy sites, where people are increasingly tagging most of what they create themselves in their own terms, combined with our own research on how people organise and use knowledge, should provide rich data for social science research *and* have applications to creating the Semantic Web. At the end of this process we can look to having intelligent 'assistants' to help us identify and analyse data, rather than simple workstations on our desks.

All of these content-based approaches highlight a serious upcoming dilemma for social scientists. All of these depend on making judgements regarding content, effectively aggregating the data based on particular biases or goals. The extent to which researchers are isolated from the criteria underlying these judgements represents the extent to which they are isolated from the fully disaggregated data. However, there will be too much data with too much complexity for most researchers to work with it directly. We will have to wait to see precisely how research evolves to resolve, or at least limit, the impact of this approach. Solutions will probably depend on various kinds of triangulation, development of researcher controls over the process, and new understandings of broader more holistic data environments within which many of these problems may simply be rendered irrelevant.

SOCIAL CHANGE

The immediate basis for discussing possible future social change is change in the period from 1990 to 2015, much of which is discussed in this collection. We have argued that the major driver of social change from IRCT is a trend towards pervasive, and even ubiquitous, communication. Since 1990 email has developed from a niche mode of communication for academics to a mainstream medium worldwide. This trend is not confined to the Internet. Seemingly, regardless of economic circumstances, mobile phones, once mainly a source of irritation in restaurants and trains, are a possession of the majority of people in most nations. Access to the Internet has changed from episodic connections using simple modems to pervasive connections via mobile or landline broadband, and increasingly using high-speed fibre-based or high-speed mobile connections, with a strong trend towards 'always-on' mobile connections and applications.

In the developed world we already have the capacity for pervasive communication. We can phone, email, instant message (IM) or text most of our social partners at any time, as can they. We interact often on social Internet sites. Our ways of interacting with each other are adapting rapidly, particularly among the young, whose opportunities for physical contact are becoming increasingly restricted. There are imbalances based on relative income, but surprisingly this absolute gap, at least in terms of being connected at all, has diminished rather than enlarged. This is true for nations with emerging economies as well, where some of the poorest nations on Earth have 70 per cent or more individual connectivity at some level for mobile networks.

Currently, communication is dominated by written and spoken language and, to a more limited extent, images, still or animated. Although the episodic period is very much reduced, there remains a socially imposed periodicity on communication. While the generations born prior to 1975 tend to regard privacy as an important element of their lives, those born since 1985 are much more apt to regard any aspect of their lives as public, though in their control. The rise of social sites in the period following 2002 has resulted in vast amounts of information about day-to-day private life being published on the Internet. In 1999, Scott McNealy, then CEO of Sun Microsystems, commented, 'You have zero privacy anyway. Get over it' (from Sprenger, 1999). If the ethos of the 1960s was reflected in Andy Warhol's suggestion that everyone could have 'fifteen minutes of fame', by 2030 it will likely be radical to offer people 'fifteen minutes of anonymity.'

Since the appearance of the first webcam in 1993, hundreds of people have published their lives on the Internet, and hundreds of millions regularly provide day-to-day details, photographs and videos. Increasingly, individuals will use pervasive wireless networks to broadcast their day in progress, at least to what they perceive to be their social network. Conventions of management of image will evolve with both transmission and access to this information. It will not be a 'raw' transparent record, but another tool in presentation of self and of group, perhaps even designed to 'edit' the public record available otherwise.

The use of CCTV has expanded greatly in the period up to 2015, and is likely to continue. Countries like the UK have vast numbers of cameras covering city centres, shopping outlets, and – increasingly – residential streets. Plans to 'chip' vehicles, together with sensors in the roads, will track movements. Mobile phones can be tracked using either triangulation to transmitters or, increasingly, embedded GPS. Individuals are placing GPS trackers in their vehicles (and on their children) that can 'phone home' coordinates when the car starts, leaves a specified zone, or operates at high speed, and can be phoned to covertly listen in.

It is likely that over the next two decades more and more use of cameras, 'smart'

ID cards, chipped pets, chipped children, environmental sensors in smart environments and the Internet of things, together with peoples' own choices and interactions, will be accessible online, probably to a large extent publicly, so that 'privacy' groups may force public access as the only solution to protecting people from specialist government and commercial surveillance, transforming a threat to a resource that will modify social relations. With respect to online research and social science research in general, more and more information will be available to us, and our potential research subjects will themselves be using this information as a part of forming their own lives, and thus of the meanings that they manage. Increasingly these relationships will be conducted and managed online.

VIRTUAL COMMUNITIES

One outcome that will emerge from this increasing capacity to 'know' people from their online presence is a great realignment of how people manage social relationships. Robin Dunbar argues that individual people can efficiently manage social relationships based on personal knowledge in relatively small numbers, about 150–200 in total (Dunbar, 1993). Although we might want to quibble on the actual quantity, numbers of at most a few hundreds are consistent with most studies of personal networks and ethnographic accounts (de Ruiter *et al.*, 2011). People faced with this much information, on so many people, could be expected to either substitute 'virtual' relationships for locally situated relationships, or to develop culturally acceptable technological aids to managing more relationships, as has been the long-standing practice of sales folk, account managers and ethnographers.

Castells (1996, 2001) refers to real virtuality, as opposed to virtual reality; by that he means the virtual space which becomes as real and integral to people's lives as more traditionally recognisable realities. Cyber communities are cropping up and creating ways to fill in the gaps of online sociality and render it increasingly 'real', with increasingly ambitious achievements in the 'real' world. Initially this was largely of interest to social scientists interested in studying themed groups or marginalised groups that for one reason or another found it difficult or impossible to be more open in their community activities, but the techniques for people to overcome the impersonal nature of socialising on social computing sites are emerging and easier to implement and interpret.

Online sociality has developed over the past 40 years from technically apt special purpose groups, such as those underlying the forums of HumanNets on the ARPANET, to whole new forms of sociality; the groups within Open Source, who have redefined concepts for intellectual property, groups that have contributed to political change such as MoveOn.org and the movements that emerged in the Arab Spring. Groups have formed around prior social relations, such as Facebook or LinkedIn, as well as groups that spread information, such as Twitter or Huffpost, and countless groups that organise around themes (such as space travel, boating or writing) who communicate largely through contributions to building a joint resource with limited person to person communication (Applin, 2014).

Developments such as these support the view that most of the present focus on 'virtual relationships' should, following Castell's lead, be seen as a variation of 'actual' social relationships. These relationships are not virtual, but simply based on new forms of reciprocation or exchange, and indeed it is likely that such social relationships in the future will be based on more 'real' information than at present. In any case the boot-strapping processes for children and young people transforming the 'virtual community' into 'community' are already well established.

TEMPORARY COMMUNITIES

Temporary communities offer a number of opportunities for social scientists. When people come together for a common cause, motivated by interests which have, to some extent, built-in expiry dates, it becomes possible to observe conscious community-building techniques. Many of these will fail because the people involved have never seriously tried to understand what makes communities remain cohesive through differences of opinion, disagreements about resource allocation and the host of other incidents that arise and cause people to decide they would be better off either with another group or on their own. Primate and hunter-gatherer populations demonstrate the propensity of small groups to have very fluid group composition and to break up and rejoin frequently. With sedentarisation comes the need for more complex mechanisms for conflict resolution and negotiation. Interestingly, the kinds of special-interest community made possible by IRCT may need far simpler and less robust conflict-resolution mechanisms because the scope of interaction is highly restricted. Moveon.org had effectively developed an online movement more or less in opposition to George Bush and the War on Terror. It is almost inconceivable that all the members of Moveon.org would cooperate well in face-to-face settings, and even less likely that they would agree on all the major issues in foreign policy confronting the US.

Nevertheless, in a sense such a movement is evidence of IRCT's ability to foster temporary communities around restricted sets of issues. The communities need not be tested in the way residential neighbourhoods might be because one will never be confronted with the reality that one's community fellows in fact are selfish, or xenophobic on some issues, or sexist or racist in some ways. To some extent, the members may imbue other members with agreeable characteristics, using the logic that if someone was against the War on Terror, or did not care for George Bush as President of the US, then he or she must also agree with me on X, Y or Z. Using such logic, it becomes possible to create very powerful online communities with limited capacity for longevity. When over time conditions underlying the original formation of the group are resolved, then many such movements will disappear as well. Much as the war protests against Vietnam created odd bedfellows in the US, so too can opposition to global events create unusual coalitions of individuals. What makes these interesting, and possibly the result of a kind of IRCT revolution, is their pervasively distributed locality. Apart from the fact that the most widespread of such temporary communities, for the moment, use English as their language of communication, they bring together the IRCT-savvy individuals from literally around the world. We expect that such temporary communities will rise and fall with increasing rapidity, and that one of the areas of social science investigation will be when and where such communities arise and why. Clearly not all the actions of global capitalism have provoked successful temporary resistance communities, despite the fact that some individuals will almost certainly try, and so it will be the task of social scientists to identify possible causes for success or failure of such groups.

CHANGE IN ETHICAL STANDARDS

Social scientists' awareness of ethical standards greatly increased over the latter half of the twentieth century, and over the next decade or so it is likely that ethical attitudes, and thus ethical standards, will change substantially. Eynon *et al.* (this volume) discuss many relevant ethical and legal issues that can be extrapolated into the future.

It is already clear that social scientists' attitudes towards privacy are lagging well behind public standards, while the societies around us are tolerating, if not promoting, ever-escalating, hair-raising contexts as entertainment. It is also clear that informed consent cannot be obtained for most web-cam streams or satellite imagery. Streams of 'presence' data from 'smart environments' in the future will likely be similar. Is it ethical to do research based on such public resources? If we decide it is, is it still so if we commission the camera or smart environment?

As attitudes in our culture and society shift and privacy is redefined, we can expect our own ethical attitudes to change, and with these ethical standards of research. We are each, in our respective research communities, going to have to arrive at decisions about what we can and cannot use ethically in our research.

COMPLEXITY

It is clear that those social scientists who take up the challenge of dipping into this vast vortex of data will require methods that are different from the norm today. The foundation for appropriate methods is already being developed by social scientists, including the contributors to this volume, and others who are adapting research methods from the physical sciences trading under the 'Complex Systems' label (for example, Human Complex Systems, UCLA; Santa Fe Institute, Complex Social Science Gateway, UC Irvine). Basically the complex systems approach represents a union between small-group or individual studies producing disaggregated research, and large aggregated studies that have typically depended on mathematical summarisation. The basic idea underlying research involving complex systems is that most social phenomena 'emerge' from the interaction of individuals and their contexts, which are ever-changing because of the actions of individuals and the emergent nature of social phenomena.

The complex systems approach crosses most of the traditional divides that have

developed in the social sciences: it is both reductionist and non-reductionist, aggregated and disaggregated, symbolic and material, macro and micro, formal and informal. The area is also fiercely interdisciplinary and multi-disciplinary. Research methods depend on collecting data and representing explicitly and individually all the agents in a process, usually heterogeneous agents who all have their individual properties as well as their discrete representation. Agents may be represented by a few heterogeneous features or variables, or with a great deal of fidelity. Examples of this approach in social science have included studies of crowd behaviour, drug addiction (Agar, 2005), pastoral nomads (Kuznar and Sedlmeyer, 2005; White and Johansen, 2004), agricultural change (Fischer, 2002), and social change in institutions (Fischer, 2006c). Even where there are small numbers of heterogeneous agents, the complexity of creating models where the phenomena under study can emerge generally requires computing support. Larger models challenge the capacity of high performance computing, requiring facilities similar to those required by astronomers who model galaxies and physicists who model entire atmospheres, molecule by molecule.

Although the study of Human Complex Systems under the complexity/emergence paradigm is still in its early days, this would appear to be an appropriate way to utilise the greater volume of data we anticipate within the socially more complex formations we expect to form. However, the techniques being developed, the cyber-infrastructure that will be developed to accommodate this research and the issues that will emerge from this research should supplement, not replace, existing approaches to research. Nevertheless, even 'conventional' research methods must be adapted to the scope of data used, matching small case results to large-scale databases, incorporating advances in theory that emerge, and determining how to adaptively use new techniques such as agent-based modelling and data mining, which also represent viable approaches to working with large amounts of continuous data (see Elsenbroich, this volume).

CONCLUSION

On the one hand, much of what we have 'predicted' is in fact already possible and already being done – but only in small numbers and by a relatively computer-savvy elite/minority. But software tools will become easier to use and will no longer be the exclusive domain of a technological elite. The network society is an increasingly pervasive reality that social scientists will not be able (or want) to ignore. The information society is either around the corner, or we are already in the middle of it. Perhaps we will know which in 10 years' time; but we can be certain that whether it is here now or just imminent, the world has changed from 20 years ago. In 1970, Alvin Toffler's *Future Shock* (1970) articulated what life-as-normal was to be for all of us from now on. It is no longer just the baby-boomers who are lost in the world they have found as adults – it would appear that every generation is doomed to look back on their childhood world and wonder where it went. The flow of information and capital has introduced a greater demand for resilience and flexibility and a willingness, or at least an ability, to re-form oneself and one's community attachments based on a shifting set of contingencies. Although the likes of Manuel Castells (1996) and Frank Webster (1995) perceptively recognised the broad strokes of such a transformation in the 1990s (and even, to a lesser extent Daniel Bell in his post-industrial society formulation of the early 1970s), it remains the task of social scientists to put the empirical flesh on the bones of such grand social theory and to identify specific mechanisms for coping with such a shifting and uncertain dynamism at the level of real individuals and real communities, either virtually real or really real.

NOTES

1 http://kinsources.net/ (accessed 16 August 2016)
2 http://socscicompute.ss.uci.edu/ (accessed 16 August 2016)
3 http://hraf.yale.edu/ (accessed 16 August 2016)
4 For examples see http://www.webcam-index.com/ and http://www.earthcam.com/ (accessed 16 August 2016)
5 https://www.nike.com/gb/en_gb/p/activity (accessed 16 August 2016)

REFERENCES

Agar, Michael (2005) 'Agents in living color: towards emic agent-based models', *Journal of Artificial Societies and Social Simulations*, 8 (1). Available at http://jasss.soc.surrey.ac.uk/8/1/4.html (accessed 15 November 2015).

Bagg, Janet, Fischer, Michael and Zeitlyn, David (2006) 'ImageInterviewer'. In Michael Fischer and David Zeitlyn (eds.), *AnthroMethods*. Canterbury, UK: CSAC Monographs.

Bainbridge, William Sims (2007) 'The scientific research potential of virtual worlds'. *Science*, 317 (5837): 472–6.

Biella, Peter (1997) *Yanomamo Interactive: Understanding the Ax Fight on CD-ROM* (Case Studies in Cultural Anthropology Multimedia). Belmont, CA: Wadsworth Publishing.

Biella, Peter (2004) *Maasai Interactive* (CDROM). Belmont, CA: Wadsworth Publishing.

Bush, Vannevar (1945) 'As we may think'. *Atlantic Monthly*, July 1945, 101–8. Available at http://www.theatlantic.com/magazine/archive/1945/07/as-we-may-think/303881/

Castells, Manuel (1996) *The Rise of the Network Society*. Oxford: Blackwell.

Castells, Manuel (2001) *The Internet Galaxy: Reflections on the Internet, Business, and Society*. Oxford: Oxford University Press.

Csikszentmihalyi, Mihaly (1991) *Flow: The Psychology of Optimal Experience*. New York, NY: Harper Collins.

de Ruiter, Jan, Weston, Gavin and Lyon, Stephen M. (2011) 'Dunbar's number: group size and brain physiology in humans re-examined', *American Anthropologist*, 113(4): 557–68.

Dow, James (1992) 'New direction for computer applications for anthropologists'. In Margaret, S. Boone and John J. Wood (eds.), *Computing Applications for Anthropologists*. Belmont, CA: Wadsworth, pp. 267–82.

Dunbar, Robin I.M. (1993) 'Co-evolution of neocortical size, group size and language in humans', *Behavioral and Brain Sciences*, 16 (4): 681–735.

Eisenstein, Elizabeth L. (1979/1997) *The Printing Press as an Agent of Change: Communications and Cultural Transformations in Early-Modern Europe*. Cambridge: Cambridge University Press.

Farnell, Brenda (1995) *Wiyuta: Assiniboine Storytelling with Signs* (CD-ROM). Austin: University of Texas Press.

Fensel, Dieter, Wahlster, Wolfgang, Lieberman, Henry and Hendler, James (2002) *Spinning the Semantic Web: Bringing the World Wide Web to Its Full Potential*. Cambridge, MA: MIT Press.

Fielding, Nigel (2003) 'Qualitative research and e-social science: appraising the potential', Swindon, UK: Economic and Social Research Council.

Fielding, Nigel and Macintyre, Maria (2006) 'Access grid nodes in field research', *Sociological Research Online*, 11 (2). Available at http://www.socresonline.org.uk/11/2/fielding.html (accessed 15 November 2015).

Fischer, Michael (1998) 'Counting things and interpreting ideas: anthropological conventions in the use of "hard" versus "soft" models'. In M. Fisher (ed.), *Postmodern Applications to Natural Resources Development*. Canterbury, UK: CSAC Monographs, pp. 43–77. Available at http://lucy.ukc.ac.uk/PostModern/ (accessed 15 November 2015).

Fischer, Michael (2002). 'Indigenous knowledge and expert knowledge in development'. In Paul Silatoe and Alan Bicker (eds.), *The Contribution of Indigenous Knowledge to Economic Development*. London: Harwood.

Fischer, Michael (2003) 'Research note on linking GPS co-ordinates and visual media'. In Michael Fischer and David Zeitlyn (eds.), *AnthroMethods*. Canterbury, UK: CSAC Monographs.

Fischer, Michael (2004) 'Integrating anthropological approaches to the study of culture: the "hard" and the "soft"', *Cybernetics and Systems*, 35 (2/3): 147–62.

Fischer, Michael (2006a) 'Cultural agents: a community of minds'. In Oguz Dikenelli, Marie-Pierre Gleizes and Alessandro Ricci (eds.), *Engineering Societies in the Agents World VI. Lecture Notes in Computing Science*. Berlin: SpringerVerlag, pp. 259–74.

Fischer, Michael (2006b) 'Configuring anthropology', *Social Science Computing Review*, 24 (1): 3–14.

Fischer, Michael (2006c) 'The ideation and instantiation of arranging marriage within an urban community in Pakistan, 1982–2000', *Contemporary South Asia*, 15 (3): 325–39.

Fischer, Michael D. and Zeityn, David (1999) *ERA resource guide and sampler CD for teachers and students*. Canterbury, UK: CSAC, University of Kent at Canterbury.

Goody, Jack and Watt, Ian (1963/1968) 'The consequences of literacy'. In Jack Goody (ed.), *Literacy in Traditional Societies*. Cambridge: Cambridge University Press.

Hall, Edward T. (1976) *Beyond Culture*. New York, NY: Basic Books.

Happel, Ruth (2005) 'The importance of place – GPS and photography'. Available at https://web.archive.org/web/20080409021622/http://www.microsoft.com/windowsxp/using/digitalphotography/prophoto/gps.mspx (accessed 16 August 2016).

Kuznar, Lawrence A. and Sedlmeyer, Robert (2005). 'Collective violence in Darfur: an agent-based model of pastoral nomad/sedentary peasant interaction', *Mathematical Anthropology and Cultural Theory* 1(4). Available at http://escholarship.org/uc/item/67x4t8ts (accessed 16 August 2016).

Larson, R. and Csikszentmihalyi, M. (1983) 'The experience sampling method', *New Directions for Methodology of Social and Behavioral Science*, 15: 41–56.

Leiner, Barry M., Cerf, Vinton G., Clark, David D., Kahn, Robert E., Kleinrock, Leonard, Lynch, Daniel C., Postel, Jon, Roberts, Lawrence G. and Wolff, Stephen, (2012 [2003]) 'A brief history of the Internet'. In *Histories of the Internet*. The Internet Society. Available at http://www.internetsociety.org/sites/default/files/Brief_History_of_the_Internet.pdf (accessed 16 August 2016).

Macfarlane, Alan (1987) 'The Cambridge experimental videodisc project', *Bulletin of Information on Computing and Anthropology, Kent University,* Issue 5.

Madakam, Somayya, Ramaswamy, R. and Tripathi, Siddharth (2015) 'Internet of Things (IoT): a literature review', *Journal of Computer and Communications*, 2015(3): 164–73. Available at http://dx.doi.org/10.4236/jcc.2015.35021 (accessed 28 August 2015).

McCarthy, John (1979/1996) 'The history of Lisp'. Available at http://www-formal.stanford.edu/jmc/history/lisp/lisp.html (accessed 8 August 2007).

Moody, James and White, Douglas (2003) 'Structural cohesion and embeddness: a hierarchical concept of social groups', *American Sociological Review*, 68 (1): 103–27.

Owens, A. (2005) 'Semantic storage: overview and assessment'. Technical Report IRP Report 2005, Electronics and Computer Science, University of Southampton. Available at http://eprints.ecs.soton.ac.uk/11985/ (accessed 10 August 2007).

Read, Dwight, Fischer, Michael and Lehman, F. K. (Chit Hlaing) (2014). 'The cultural grounding of kinship: a paradigm shift', *L'Homme* n. 210, pp. 63–90.

Ruby, Jay (2005) *Oak Park Stories* (CD-ROM series). Watertown, MA: Documentary Educational Resources.

Sprenger, Polly (1999) 'Sun on Privacy: "Get Over It"'. *Wired*, 26 January. Available at http://archive.wired.com/politics/law/news/1999/01/17538 (accessed 15 November 2015).

Toffler, Alan (1970). *Future Shock*. New York: Random House.

Webster, Frank (1995) *Theories of the Information Society*. London: Routledge.

White, Douglas R. and Johansen, Ulla C. (2004). *Network Analysis and Ethnographic Problems: Process Models of a Turkish Nomad Clan*. Oxford and Lanham: Lexington Books.

Zeitlyn, David (2001) *Reading in the Modern World. Writing and the Virtual World: Anthropological Perspectives on Computers and the Internet*. Canterbury: CSAC Monographs. Available at http://csac.anthropology.ac.uk/CSACMonog/RRRweb./ (accessed 16 August 2016).

Zeitlyn, David and Fischer, Michael (1999) 'Africa divination: Mambila and others'. In M. Fischer and D. Zeitlyn (eds.), *Experience Rich Anthropology*. Canterbury: CSAC Monographs Available at http://era.anthropology.ac.uk/Era_Resources/Era/Divination/index.html (accessed 16 August 2016).

FURTHER READING

'A brief history of the Internet' by those who made the history, including Barry M. Leiner, Vinton G. Cerf, David D. Clark, Robert E. Kahn, Leonard Kleinrock, Daniel C. Lynch, Jon Postel, Lawrence G. Roberts, Stephen Wolff. In *Histories of the Internet*, The Internet Society. http://www.internetsociety.org/sites/default/files/Brief_History_of_the_Internet.pdf (accessed 16 August 2016).

Leiner et. al. present a brief history organised around four aspects: technological evolution; operations and management; social aspect; commercialisation aspect.

## 36

Online Research Methods and Social Theory

Grant Blank

The enormous growth in online activities has created new opportunities for research. These opportunities are theoretical as well as methodological. The theoretical opportunities have been present in prior chapters but never emphasized; this chapter brings theory into focus without losing sight of methods. Specifically, the chapter discusses the explanatory power of theory based on online methodologies to address important social issues. Using this goal, it describes two themes common in the preceding chapters: big data and the qualitative data revolution. Each theme presents problems as well as opportunities and the goal of this chapter is to explore how methods and theory work together to define and mitigate the problems as well as exploit the opportunities.

The link between methods and theory has a history almost as long as modern science itself. It begins at the dawn of empirical science, over 350 years ago. One of the earliest scientific communities was formed around Robert Boyle, leading a group of experimentalists who were exploring the relationships between pressure,

temperature, and volume. Their primary technology was a vacuum pump that they called an 'air pump'. Their findings were codified into what we now know as 'Boyle's Laws'. (Much of the following discussion is drawn from Shapin and Shaffer, 1985 and Zaret, 1989).

These early scientists are interesting, not just because they developed some of the earliest experimental research methods using the advanced technology of the day and not just for their exploration of the relations between pressure, temperature, and volume, but also because their work is intimately linked to social theory. The mid-1600s in England was a period of political turmoil: there was the English Civil War, the Regicide (1649), the creation of the Republic (1649–53), Oliver Cromwell's Protectorate (1653–58), and the Restoration of the Stuart monarchy in 1660. As they attempted to understand this period of bitter political, social, and religious conflict, many Englishmen came to the conclusion that the fundamental source of social conflict was differing views of religious truth. The implication of this assumption was that if everyone believed in the same religion then these extraordinary conflicts would end.

The Restoration of the Monarchy in 1660 had restored a central political authority, but it did not dampen religious strife. As a result, the 1660s were marked by a new crisis of civil authority. The issue was the role of religious belief, particularly the Protestant and Puritan emphasis on an individual's personal religious beliefs. This created a problem that became a major source of tension and conflict.

The problem was that it is very difficult to settle disputes when everyone relies on their own personal vision of truth. Under such circumstances, how can anyone determine whose personal vision is fairer? More just? Or, in any sense, better? In fact, when people believe that their highly individual versions of truth are the only correct version then political compromise and accommodation becomes very difficult. Thoughtful Englishmen saw society and politics splitting into a large number of semi-hostile groups, each suspiciously defending its personal vision of the truth. This was not attractive, for it looked like the jealous incompatibility of these visions might make a cohesive society with normal politics impossible.

In this social environment, the experimental scientists offered an alternative vision of community. This community claimed to have created an understanding of conflict and social unity that stood in stark contrast to the disorder plaguing English society. Their signal achievement was that they were able to settle disputes and achieve consensus without resorting to violence and without powerful individuals imposing their beliefs on others.

Facts were uncovered by experiments, attested to by competent observers. When there was a disagreement it could be settled by appeal to facts made experimentally manifest and confirmed by competent witnesses from within the community. Stable agreement was won because experimentalists organized themselves into a defined and bounded society that excluded those who did not accept

the fundamentals of good order. Consensus agreement on facts was an accomplishment of that community. It was not imposed by an external authority. In this sense, facts were social; they were made when the community freely assented.

This did not imply consensus was always easily reached. Indeed, Hooke's vehement disagreements with Newton and others anticipated a long line of hostile quarrels among scientists. This is another respect in which the early experimentalists formed something that looks like science.

Despite their internal disagreements and despite the inevitable tensions of ego and competition for status, in the context of strife-ridden post-Civil War society the model of a community committed to joint discovery of facts was an attractive alternative. It contributed to the political support required to set up the early institutions that supported and fostered the development of science: the Royal Society and its journal.

The point is that a fundamental link between social theory and research methods was embedded in the culture of science from the very beginning. Neither methods nor theory existed independently of each other. This chapter investigates how theory and methods influence each other in online work. This chapter does not develop new theory; instead, it suggests two possibilities. First, online developments are creating new opportunities for substantive theory just as they are creating new data and new methodology. The new theoretical opportunities come in part from the new social forms and new communities being created by online technologies. They also come from the fact that online research can offer a novel perspective that casts new light on older, pre-existing social forms. Second, certain online methods have an affinity for certain kinds of theoretical explanations. This is an interesting limitation because it means that some theories cannot be developed with certain online methods.

A volume on methods leads naturally to a particular *kind* of theory. This is not the 'grand theory' of Marx, Weber, and Durkheim; instead, it is the middle-range theory or substantive theory that is commonly used in conjunction with standard methodological tools like statistical hypothesis testing. This sort of theory has several relationships to methods. Theoretical concepts are operationalized in scales or indices; in survey questions; by counting or describing attributes of people, organizations, or websites; or by coding qualitative data into appropriate categories. Relations between concepts are described by hypotheses, which may form the basis for inferential tests. Related hypotheses can be collected into theories that may be modeled with statistical, computational, or mathematical methods. The theory and all its components remain fairly concretely tied to empirical data and to measurement. The payoff from the use of this kind of theory is often a clearer understanding of contemporary social problems or issues. Thus this chapter discusses the explanatory power of theory based on online methodologies to address important social issues.

In the course of this task I draw together many common methodological themes from prior chapters. This is a personal reading of these chapters and no one should infer that my opinions are shared by the authors themselves or by other editors. I found that the papers in this volume each attempt to deal with new opportunities offered by gathering data online while suggesting ways to cope with special problems posed by online research. I generally draw on online examples with some comparison to offline work. I found two common themes. Each theme reflects attempts to deal with new problems or opportunities in online work. They are:

1　Big data
2　The qualitative data revolution

BIG DATA

Since the first edition of this Handbook, the term 'big data' has become a popular way to describe one of the distinctive characteristics of online research. Online data come not only in large quantities, but also very quickly and in immense variety, and so big data are often seen as consisting of the 'three Vs': volume, velocity and variety (Laney, 2001). The sources of big data are many. Any electronic transaction leaves a digital trace. In cashless financial transactions, communication via email, text messages, mobile telephone call records, wikis, games, photo or video sharing sites, or online interactions with official government agencies, many formerly ephemeral aspects of people's lives are digitally captured and stored. For anyone familiar with the painful cost of collecting data offline, the extent and easy availability of ready-made digital data is breathtaking. Adding to the available data are a number of 'open data' or 'open government' initiatives that seek to make digital data collected by government available to anyone who wants to download it (Longo, 2011; Sieber and Johnson, 2015). The declining cost of storage and ease of accessibility are driving rapid increases in digital record gathering and storage, reinforcing these trends. These developments are likely to continue and they will encourage much more use of online data in future research.

Most of this is unobtrusive, as Dietmar Janetzko's chapter on nonreactive data collection says, in the sense that people are recorded as they go about their ordinary lives. They create data that can be used for research, although it is not generated as research data. Any digitally stored data can be used for research.

Digital records accumulate, leaving minutely detailed records of social interaction. Welser *et al*. (2007b: 117) comment that such records 'present social scientists with an opportunity to study in unprecedented scale and scope the dynamics, structure and results of social interaction'. There are many research possibilities here and they are widely recognized, including in five chapters in this volume: Baram-Tsabari *et al*.'s chapter on data mining *and* big data; Bright's chapter on big data; Innes *et al.*'s chapter on social media; Hookway and Snee's chapter on the blogosphere; and Thelwall's chapter on sentiment analysis (see also Lazer *et al.*, 2009).

Some have argued big data has little relation to theory and that it signals the end of theory (Anderson, 2008; Cukier and Mayer-Schönberger, 2013). Anderson argues the case: 'Petabytes allow us to say: "Correlation is enough". We can stop looking for models. We can analyze the data without hypotheses about what it might show'. We can see why this is implausible by looking at the best book ever written about big data, *Moneyball* (Lewis, 2003). Michael Lewis tells the story of how undervalued athletes at one of the poorest teams in professional baseball, the Oakland Athletics, won so many games. Big data are at the center of this story. Big data have a track record in baseball. Detailed baseball statistics go back over a century. You can reasonably wonder, with decades' worth of detailed data available to people who spend their entire professional lives in the game, can anything possibly remain novel or undiscovered? Under general manager Billy Beane, the Athletics discovered that baseball professionals had been looking at the wrong data for decades. For example, batting averages, thought to measure ability to get on base, were not the same as the on-base percent, a more accurate measure of potential runs. Time-honored tactics like bunting and base stealing were ineffective and did not contribute to runs scored. The core of the problem was bad theory. In baseball, as in social science, theory is key because theory tells you what data to look at. If you don't have a good theory, you will look at the wrong data and you will be misled, as baseball professionals were for decades.

It is notable that the people who argue against theory are not themselves experienced data analysts. Perhaps they do not give enough weight to the fact that the initial form of the data is rarely the form that yields the most useful information. Data have to be merged, pooled, scaled, reorganized and transformed in order to make them useful. The on-base percent, for example, is a combination of several statistics. Administrative data is organized and stored using data structures that meet administrative reporting needs, not those that facilitate social science data analysis. Good theory tells you how to convert your data into meaningful numbers. Data critically depend on theory in the sense that theory tells you how to (re-)construct your data so that they become meaningful. Correlations are no better than the data they are based on. There is no such thing as data without theory. Big data without theory is nonsense.

Although big data does not diminish the value of theory, it has a number of subtle, often serious problems. Some are worth describing here because their solutions have theoretical implications. To begin with, many of these data are not available because they are proprietary. Corporations collect them for their economic purposes. Private companies are usually unwilling to supply datasets to researchers because of privacy and competitive fears. Once they give data to a researcher, it is out of their control. The data could be mined for important competitive information if it fell into their competitors' hands; therefore, giving proprietary data to a researcher requires a major leap of faith and trust, with no likely business benefit. It isn't likely to happen easily or often. An example of proprietary data used for research is Marc Sanford's (2007) retail scanner data. After 14 months of persuasion, requiring what Sanford describes as 'countless hours on the phone' and signing several legal agreements designed to limit the use of the data, and ensure security and confidentiality, Sanford was given over 750 million records. An example of public email is the Enron data (see Klimpt and Yang, 2004; Culotta *et al.*, 2004), discussed in chapters in this Handbook by Janetzko and also Eynon *et al.* It consists of about 200,000 emails exchanged between 151 top executives. The emails were released as part of the court cases that followed the Enron accounting fraud. These are exceptions that prove the rule.

In addition to having access to proprietary data, corporations have another advantage when it comes to use of big data. They can treat anyone as a potential customer, and this vastly simplifies how they use big data. Take Amazon as an example. Whenever I visit Amazon.com, it can treat me as a buyer. It doesn't care that my real motive for looking at a book is because I want the ISBN or because I need to find the correct spelling of the third author's name for a list of references. Amazon's theory that explains my visit is simple and straightforward: I intend to buy. Outside of business schools and marketing, social science theories are usually more complex. For social scientists, both meaning and motives matter. Many actions can have multiple meanings and so it becomes much harder to account for people's actions. The theory required to explain action becomes much more complex. Online big data is often transactional data, and so all researchers know are the things people did. They have no access to attitudes, emotions, motives or meaning. This means big data are much less useful for any theory where meaning plays an important role (but see later for suggestions for extracting meaning from textual data). Furthermore, Amazon loses nothing if its theory is wrong; it can treat me as a potential buyer with no consequences. This isn't true in social sciences. A wrong theory weakens scientists' professional reputations and it diminishes their ability to predict or understand.

Even when something like an Open Government initiative (Smith *et al.*, this volume) solves the proprietary data problem and makes big data available for research, there are three serious problems. First, during the 1980s and 1990s many social sciences went through a methodological debate about the relative value of quantitative and qualitative data. There is no space here to describe the ontological, epistemological, and political issues revealed in the debate (see Sale *et al.*, 2002); my point is that the debate led to a

much clearer sense of the relative strengths and weaknesses of each. Quantitative data are best able to generalize to populations using reliable measures. Qualitative data often have greater nuance, a clearer understanding of the importance of context and are better at establishing the mechanisms that generate behavior. Big data are another form of quantitative data and they suffer from exactly the same weaknesses as other quantitative data. They lack nuance, context and are generally unable to capture the subtle context of people's lives (for more detailed discussion of this debate, see Bryman, 1984; Fine and Elsbach, 2000; Lieberman, 2010).

Second, other forms of quantitative data have notable strengths not shared by big data. Big data researchers tend to emphasize correlations between factors because that is something that big data can do really, really well. However, establishing causality requires that data be collected according to research designs that isolate the effects of individual variables. This is critical in certain contexts; many theories make causal claims, and public policy needs specific research designs to establish causal links between policy interventions and relevant outcomes. Big data may be more useful to monitor existing programs as part of an ongoing established policy. Except for cases where natural or designed experiments are possible, establishing causality is not a strength.

One solution to the first and second problems is the use of mixed methods. Combining qualitative and big data methods can be done in several ways. One, called *complementarity*, uses the strengths of one to offset the weaknesses of the other. A second, called *confirmation* or *triangulation*, attempts to confirm the findings from one methodology by the other method. Both advantages are very strong and they have contributed to widespread use of mixed methods throughout the social sciences. (Methodologists will recognize that I am oversimplifying, see Small, 2011, for a more complex summary of the use and value of mixed methods).

The third problem is that most digital traces are collected and stored for administrative purposes and their content reflects the needs and convenience of bureaucrats or accountants, not the requirements of good research design or social theory. They typically do not contain fundamental variables that social scientists incorporate into their theories. Education and occupation, for example, are often not included in financial records. Marital status, religion, and ethnicity are rarely available. Everywhere attitudes are missing. When data are voluntarily deposited on social media, websites, blogs, listservs, Usenet, and online games, they only contain the information that users think important, which is inconsistent from person to person. It is usually impossible to get income, education, marital status, gender, or age. While there are interesting attempts to infer race and gender based on names, these have large errors and they remain in the proof of concept stage (Mislove *et al.*, 2011; Sloan *et al.*, 2013). Big data is not a substitute for reliable measures of variables that make a big difference in people's lives. With many theoretically important variables unavailable, people are, at best, thinly described. How much can researchers know about a social setting when they know so little about the people? Big data may be a mile wide, but it is an inch deep. Big data is thin data.

Geography is one solution to this third problem. Some kinds of big data have a geographic basis – they are, for example, coded with postcode or zip code information – and they can be merged with other geographically coded data like census data or police crime statistics. The unit of analysis becomes a spatial unit, like American census tracts, British census Output Areas, London Boroughs, or Chicago neighborhoods. The variables are something like the proportion of each gender or the proportion of each marital status in each borough. This can add race, ethnicity, education, income, crime rates, house prices, or whatever substantive variables are missing. This is how Sanford (2007) added theoretically important variables to his retail scanner data. The availability of key substantive variables for geographical units is leading to a surge in spatially based social analysis and theory (see chapters by Zook *et al.*, Martin *et al.* and Smith *et al.*, this volume). We may be entering the golden age of geography.

In almost all cases, big data require time-consuming, highly skilled work to put datasets into a condition where interesting substantive problems can be addressed. They are usually stored in a format designed for efficient administrative storage and reporting. This is almost never the form needed for statistical analysis or network analysis. Appropriate data have to be extracted from the existing tables and merged, disaggregated or aggregated to theoretically meaningful levels and into a format that software used for statistical analysis or network analysis will accept. Such tasks are time-consuming even for skilled people and they require serious data management skills, which are usually not taught as part of graduate training and are, in fact, rare among social scientists. There will be social science uses for some of this new data, but they depend on creative, imaginative thought to make them workable. A notable example is Marc Smith's NetScan work collecting Usenet mail headers (see Welser *et al.*, 2007a; Welser *et al.*, 2007b). This example is in many respects typical of other attempts to create useful social data and theory from electronic traces. The dataset is a collection of every possible Usenet message header, 1.2 billion of them. This is the social science version of collecting the entire haystack of data.

An alternative strategy complements the 'collect everything' approach of NetScan. It involves the use of sampling using a mobile phone application. Mihaly Csikszentmihalyi's experience sampling method (ESM) stands in sharp contrast to both qualitative and quantitative 'collect everything' research strategies. The ESM is a data gathering technique that exploits mobile technology; subjects are given a mobile phone app (originally a beeper). They are sent a short set of questions at random times during the day. The questions ask what they are doing and how they feel. This gives a continuous stream of data about individuals' moods, opinions, activities, and interactions with other people. Hektner *et al.* (2007) has details and summarizes the entire research stream. This method too has weaknesses, but they are different weaknesses. They are mostly the well-known problems of questionnaire research: response rates, sampling bias, reliability, validity, and others.

The use of the ESM has a variety of advantages. The questionnaires give more direct access to internal states; to attitudes, emotions and meanings. Questionnaires can be designed to ask about theoretically grounded empirical categories. Finally, the data are based on a random sample of times of the day. The point is, instead of spending the time and money to collect everything, and having to spend more time deciding what you really want, and then throwing away all the data you collected that you decided that you don't need, you can simply collect what you wanted to begin with. Samples are really valuable; they are much faster and easier to collect and to analyze. You lose very little by employing a sample. I think it is a reasonable methodological question: under what circumstances is there value in collecting more than a random sample? Why not collect only the data you need in the first place?

I was born in Missouri, which is called the 'show-me' state. This nickname supposedly comes from Missourians habit of asking people to 'show me' the evidence. There is something to be said for this; in the context of online methodology, show me the theoretical payoff. It is hard to find a concept as striking or as influential as Csikszentmihalyi's (1991) idea of flow, developed out of his studies using the ESM.

In addition to administrative or government-collected data, big data has a second form: online researchers who can collect their own data have it easy. Internet and online surveys are cheap and fast compared to the offline alternatives. Responses can be automatically checked for consistency and stored directly in a dataset, ready for analysis; indeed, simple analyses, such as descriptive statistics, frequencies and standard cross-tabulations, can be automatically produced. This can largely eliminate the time-consuming, difficult, and costly steps of data cleaning and data input. Five chapters in this Handbook discuss this: Vehovar and Manfreda's overview of online surveys; Fricker's sampling methods for online surveys; Toepoel's Internet survey instrument design; Kaczmirek's Internet survey software tools; and Dillman *et al.*'s mixed mode surveys. The special problem of online survey research is that there is no way to construct a sampling frame. There is no online equivalent to random digit dialing or postal address files; therefore, it is not generally possible to select online respondents according to some randomized process. Even if Internet usage reached saturation levels, for most populations the sampling frame problem would remain intractable. There are exceptions, as Fricker points out in his chapter, for example a survey of an organization where the organization has a complete list of its members and everyone has an email address. But this is unusual. A more general solution to this problem, discussed by both Fricker and Dillman *et al.*, is to use mixed mode research. Sometimes online and offline data collection can be combined to overcome the lack of a random sample in online research while still retaining most of the advantages of low cost and easy administration.

Without a sampling frame, almost all Internet surveys rely on self-selected respondents collected into large, pre-constituted panels. This yields cheap, speedy results, but the problems are serious. Respondents are often recruited from advertisements on web pages and they are paid for participation. This produces a pool of respondents guaranteed to be biased. Surveys usually attempt to correct their selection bias by using quota sampling of the panel and using post-stratification weights. These attempts are only partially successful. The core problem is that this process is almost guaranteed to produce biased data. The Pew Research Center (Keeter *et al.*, 2015) compared an unusually high quality online sample with a randomly selected offline sample. It found that there were significant differences, particularly in responses to Internet-related variables. Some of these problems became embarrassingly public in the polling errors predicting the 2015 British general election outcome (Curtice, 2016; Sturgis *et al.*, 2016). The accuracy of Internet polls may be sufficient for marketing purposes, but scholarly use remains problematic.

For other online data, like clicks, Tweets, and email messages, sample sizes can be, at least potentially, extremely large. Website click-through data can have sample sizes of over 100 million cases (remember, that is the sample!). As the Hindmarsh chapter on real-time video analysis points out, cheap cameras and inexpensive disk storage increase the feasibility of video recordings. The resulting data can contain records of individuals, almost unprecedented in their details.

The low cost of online data collection and the possibility for using video have been widely noticed. Less widely recognized is the fact that the low cost and easy access to subjects also applies to ethnographic research. Six chapters describe the implications of online research for various forms of qualitative data collection: Hine's chapter on virtual ethnography; O'Connor and Madge's chapter on online interviewing; Hookway and Snee's chapter on blogs; Abrams and Gaiser's chapter on virtual focus groups; the Hindmarsh chapter on real-time video; and the Silver and Bulloch chapter on new affordances of CAQDAS. Enormous amounts of qualitative data can be collected very quickly. For blogs, listservs, social media, or email the digital form is the only form in which the data exist. These data do not need to be converted to digital form by transcription and this eliminates major

costs, time delays, and sources of error. The new wealth of data opens a real opportunity for all kinds of innovative research.

There is no free lunch in online data collection. One price of simple, low-cost access to subjects is a set of complicated, difficult ethical questions. Ethics are discussed in several chapters, but they are comprehensively addressed in the Eynon *et al.* chapter on ethics and ethical governance. There are two primary protections for social science research subjects, anonymity and informed consent, and under online conditions both are more difficult to achieve. The same easy access to online data and the ease of matching individual respondents to other datasets that makes online data collection so much simpler also makes it much easier for someone to break anonymity and discover the identity of individual respondents. Files in all their versions are often preserved on backups, which are often automatically created and not always under control of the researcher. Someone could obtain an early version of a file with identifiers still in place, possibly without the researcher even knowing. An obvious situation where this could occur is when a government agency is interested in a research project that collected data on illegal actions, such as criminal behavior, drug use, illegal immigration, or terrorism.

What will we do with all these Data?

The signal characteristic that distinguishes online from offline data collection is the enormous amount of data available online. As we think about our newfound wealth of data, I want to raise two skeptical questions, one for qualitative data and the second for quantitative data.

The sources of massive amounts of qualitative data that are being and could be collected include automated security cameras, social media content, as well as purposefully collected data like video and audio tapes. These data promise a remarkably fine-grained, detailed picture of people in all kinds of social situations. Given this fact, here is the place to raise the key question: so what? What is the payoff? Does the availability of this enormous volume of data promise soon-to-come advances in our understanding of society, politics, and culture, along with much better theory? My best-guess answer to this question is 'probably not'.

To see why, it is necessary to realize that detailed qualitative data is not new. Ecological psychologists (e.g. Barker and Wright, 1951, 1954) collected it over 60 years ago. Barker and his students created and published minute-by-minute records of the activities of children from morning to night. We can reasonably ask, if there is going to be a major payoff from data-intensive studies of social life, why haven't we heard more about the ecological psychologists? Why aren't they more important? Why didn't people pay attention?

One answer is that the theory Barker developed was exceptionally closely tied to concrete social settings and situations. Barker studied under Kurt Lewin and he was influenced by Lewin's theories of the importance of the environment in predicting behavior. Barker himself argued that behavior was radically situated, meaning that accurate predictions about behavior require detailed knowledge of the situation or environment in which people find themselves. His work often consisted of recording how expected behavior is situational: people act differently in different behavioral settings, for example in their roles as students or teachers in school or as customers in a store. In his theory of behavior settings, Barker is fairly explicit that he believes broad, 'grand' theories cannot usefully predict behavior. Since Barker focuses so tightly on behavior in a very local setting, his research doesn't generalize very well to other settings. This is an implication built into the idea of behavioral settings and it is intentional. Ecological psychology has sustained its intellectual ground as a school, but its results turn out to be fairly limited in

their applications. This is a disadvantage. Other researchers, looking for theories that help them in their research, will not find rich sources of insightful ideas that they can use. Since few other researchers found the ecological psychologists' work useful, it was not widely adopted.

The ecological psychologists actually observed people, and observers can gain insight into emotions because they are often visually inescapable. Transaction data may be voluminous but transactions provide no realistic way to infer internal emotional states. This is a serious limitation because much human action depends on meaning. The same actions can have multiple meanings and, for different people, they can have completely different meanings. Without the ability to gain access to meanings it is very hard to develop or test any theory based on meaning, emotions, or any mental states.

Of course, no researcher has complete access to internal states like emotions or meaning. To a greater or lesser extent, meanings, motives, or other mental states always have to be inferred. It is a matter of the degree to which meaning can be inferred from particular kinds of data. The point here is that many forms of big data supply much less direct access to internal states than some other kinds of data.

The problems of fine-grained data raise a key question: under what circumstances are detailed, fine-grained data about social life useful? Most answers to this question describe the use of case studies in data-intensive research. Burawoy (1991) developed the 'extended case method' as a way to use detailed case studies to identify weaknesses in existing theory, and to extend and refine theory, for example by describing subtypes of a phenomenon. Ragin (1987) links case studies to the study of commonalities where comparable cases are studied to construct a single composite portrait of the phenomenon. Case studies are holistic and they emphasize causal complexity and conjunctural causation. This use of cases is similar to that used by anthropological ethnography, where holistic understanding is a central goal. What can we learn from these two examples? Both emphasize the importance of case selection.

If you can only study a few cases, then how you select those cases is key. Flyvbjerg (2006) summarizes four case selection strategies to maximize the researcher's ability to understand the phenomenon (see also Ragin, 1992). Average or ordinary cases are not rich sources of information; instead, extreme or deviant cases may reveal more about the relevant actors and mechanisms. These cases are chosen to emphasize a central aspect of a phenomenon. Often a theoretical sampling strategy is used: choose cases as different as possible. If this 'maximum difference' strategy is followed, then any commonalities discovered are much more likely to be fundamental to the phenomenon rather than artifacts of a biased selection of cases. Third, critical cases have special characteristics or properties that make them unusually relevant to the problem. For example, a case can be chosen because it seems most likely to *dis*confirm the hypothesis of interest. If the hypothesis is *confirmed* for this case, then the researcher can argue that it is likely to be true in all less critical cases. The researcher argues 'This case had the best chance of falsifying my argument and it failed; hence, my argument must be true'. Finally, cases can be selected because they form an exemplar. These cases form the basis for exemplary research that shows how a particular paradigm (Kuhn, 1970) can be applied in a concrete research setting. An example is Geertz's (1973) study of the 'deep play' of the Balinese cockfight. The importance of case selection underlines that there is no substitute for good research design. For fine-grained data to be useful, it must be carefully chosen to illuminate issues of broader interest.

Research design is usually driven by a theoretical understanding of what to investigate. Theory is important because it gives direction and focus to research. It identifies important issues and categories. It suggests the kinds of research settings and data that could speak to those issues. It suggests relevant related concepts to investigate. This can be overstated and many theories are also vague and incomplete. In practice there are limits to the ability of theory to guide empirical research. But within these limits, theories play a major role in research design.

There are some research settings where individual cases are of great interest: the French Revolution is one example. But under most circumstances, cases are more interesting as examples of a more general phenomenon. Here theory plays a key role: theory connects cases. It is broader than individual cases and so it tells us which cases are examples of the same event or situation and which cases are different. Powerful theories can link disparate settings that seem to have little in common, and show how they are actually examples of the same phenomenon. For researchers, the categories and links between categories that make up a theory supply conceptual tools to help them think about their research, their research site(s), and their data. Theories are good to think with. As noted earlier in the discussion of ecological psychology, one of the most valuable payoffs from theory is that theories developed in one setting may serve as sources of creative ideas for researchers working in other settings.

THE QUALITATIVE DATA REVOLUTION

Although our ability to record social transactions has increased dramatically, our ability to analyze the recorded data has not expanded nearly so fast. On one hand, certain types of analysis are much easier today. All types of quantitative analysis, for example, have benefited. One effect of the additional computational power is that many more models can be examined and model diagnostics are easier. Statistics have always been a way to summarize data. In general, the ideas of central tendency, spread, and other statistical concepts can summarize a large dataset about as effectively as a small one. As datasets become larger, the nature of the statistical summaries does not change. Networks and data archives give researchers convenient access to statistics and data that they could never use before (see Corti and Wathan's chapter on archives and secondary analysis, and Carmichael's chapter on secondary analysis of qualitative data). The use of games for research purposes has blossomed (see Verhagen *et al.*'s chapter) and simulations of social settings have become much easier (see Elsenbroich's chapter).

In general, computer power makes possible much more thorough explorations of data using statistical, computational, and graphical techniques. Graphical analysis and visualization has blossomed remarkably with the increase in computing power. Computers draw all kinds of diagrams and plots so much faster than they can be drawn by hand. The advances in online research methods have been almost wholly positive for quantitative researchers.

Qualitative research is different. Collection of qualitative data has always been extremely slow and difficult. No longer. Vast quantities of text are now available in digital form. Silver and Bulloch's chapter on new affordances of CAQDAS highlights the collection of new forms of data: web pages, online role playing games, emails, blogs, video, still images, etc. Carmichael's chapter on secondary qualitative analysis describes developments in secondary analysis that further increase the availability of data. There have also been advances in qualitative, non-statistical analysis. Brent's chapter on artificial intelligence and Hindmarsh's chapter on video analysis point to some of those advances. The process has been improved by the use of qualitative analysis software like NVivo, Atlas.ti, Qualrus, or QDA Miner. The software adds reliability and speed, as well as new capabilities like Boolean retrievals and semi-automated coding of text. There is a lot of potential here. Qualitative analysis of text has always been a particularly strong method to gain access to attitudes, motives, and meaning.

Qualitative analysts have mostly reacted to their newfound wealth of data by ignoring it. They have used their new computerized analysis possibilities to do more detailed analysis of the same (relatively small) amount of data. In spite of the deluge of textual data and the advances in artificial intelligence and in software, qualitative analysis has not changed much. Most current forms of qualitative analysis are too slow and require too much hand work. They don't scale well and so they cannot be used to analyze the volumes of readily available text. Qualitative analysis was once a theory-rich, data-poor field. Now the biggest bottleneck for qualitative work has shifted. It used to be data collection but that is no longer true. Qualitative analysis is no longer limited by the difficulty of getting text; it is now data-rich but methodology has not kept up. In a nutshell, the need is for a way to summarize large amounts of text in a theoretically meaningful way. The enormous amount of text requires an automated summary process.

Considerable work has been done on the automated processing of text. I am aware of projects working with web pages, email, blogs, and online versions of newspapers. The most sophisticated work is proprietary, owned by corporations or governments. Major statistical software companies have produced text mining software, for example SAS Institute's Text Miner, SPSS's LexiQuest products, and Stata's link to QDA Miner. These are designed to analyze unstructured text with machine learning, natural language processing, and visualization tools. Popping's chapter (this volume) on analysis of text covers these approaches and more. The academic work is based on qualitative analysis software, such as NVivo, MAXQDA, or Qualrus. There is also software specifically developed to support mixed mode research, like QDA Miner. Looking at these products, it is clear that any sort of truly automated processing of text is in the future, except in some highly restricted domains where controlled vocabularies can be used.

We need a procedure that is (1) automated; (2) scalable to large amounts of text; and (3) sensitive to meaning. Meaning can only be derived from the context. Determining context and meaning is not something that computers do well. This has been a crippling limit on the use of automated categorizing of text or other qualitative data (see Thelwall's chapter). One technique promises a scalable way to summarize text that also handles context. The contextual possibility is crude by the standards of qualitative research, but it is an approach to meaning. By this, I do not mean that computers can determine meaning – that is still a problem for the analyst – but there are techniques that are context-sensitive and that is a crucial first step. Topic models are a promising class of text analysis methods. They provide a (relatively) automated procedure to code the content of a body of text into a (relatively) small set of substantively meaningful categories called 'topics'.

A 'topic' is understood as a group of words that appear together frequently. Topics can be thought of as a single theme or a coding category. The model of authorship for topic models is that authors have a bag of words that they use to write about a topic. As they write they reach into their bag and choose the most appropriate words. Different topics generally have different bags of words, although some words may be used in multiple topics. Topic models attempt to reconstruct the bags of words that authors use for each topic. The primary output is the list of words associated with each topic. The lists of words are believed to reflect the hidden structure of topics in the text.

The task of the analyst is to work backwards from the words to identify the original topic. This is an inductive process. Topics are not labeled by the program. There is no sense in which any topic modeling algorithm 'understands' the words. The analysis must determine the meaning of the text. The goal of the analyst is to find topics that are substantively meaningful and theoretically interpretable. For examples of social science use of topic models, see Mohr and Bogdanov (2013) and their references.

Topic models are a class of procedures that try to group things together. They are classification algorithms. Many possible algorithms are available, from well-known procedures like principal components and cluster analysis to recently developed procedures like latent Dirichlet allocation. Relatively little research has been done to investigate how or whether different algorithms produce different results on real data. Topic model algorithms are beginning to be integrated into qualitative analysis software. SAS Institute's Text Miner and Provalis' QDA Miner both have topic modeling available. There is a serious need for qualitative methods that scale to large amounts of text and are sensitive to context and meaning. These are tools that can complement traditional qualitative methods. I look forward to a productive convergence of computer science and social science to advance social theory.

The Irony of Big Data

Big data holds great promise, but we are just beginning to understand what it is useful for. There is great irony in the current situation. The tools to handle numerical forms of data are well-developed and widely available, but they have little ability to help us research meaning. On the other hand, textual big data gives us much better access to meaning, but the methodologies for handling text are weak and underdeveloped. Their potential is mostly unrealized. For big data to really fulfill its promise, we really need to do both. Lewis (2003) has shown how baseball was transformed when big data was combined with imaginative new theories. Can the same be done in the social sciences?

REFERENCES

Anderson, C. (2008) 'The end of theory: the data deluge makes the scientific method obsolete'. *Wired*, June 23. http://www.wired.com/2008/06/pb-theory/ (accessed on December 15, 2015)

Barker, R. G. and Wright, H, F. (1951) *One boy's day: a specimen record of behavior*. New York, NY: Harper.

Barker, R. G. and Wright, H. F. (1954) *The Midwest and its children: a psychological ecology of an American town*. Evanston IL: Row, Peterson.

Bryman, A. (1984) 'The debate about quantitative and qualitative research: a question of method or epistemology?', *British Journal of Sociology*, 35 (1): 75–92.

Burawoy, M. (1991) 'The extended case method'. In M. Burawoy (ed.), *Ethnography unbound: power and resistance in the modern metropolis*. Berkeley, CA: University of California Press, pp. 271–89.

Csikszentmihalyi, M. (1991) *Flow: the psychology of optimal experience*. New York, NY: HarperCollins.

Cukier, K. and Mayer-Schönberger, V. (2013) *Big data: a revolution that will transform how we live, work and think*. New York, NY: Houghton-Mifflin.

Culotta, A., Bekkerman, R. and McCallum, A. (2004) 'Extracting social networks and contact information from email and the Web'. *Proceedings of the First Conference on Email and AntiSpam* (CEAS) July 30–31, Mountain View, CA. Available at http://scholarworks.umass.edu/cgi/viewcontent.cgi?article=1035&context=cs_faculty_pubs (accessed July 28, 2016).

Curtice, J. (2016) *British Social Attitudes. The benefits of random sampling: lessons from the 2015 UK general election*. London: NatCen. Available at http://www.bsa.natcen.ac.uk/media/39018/random-sampling.pdf (accessed February 25, 2016).

Fine, G. A. and Elsbach, K. D. (2000) 'Ethnography and experiment in social psychological theory building: tactics for integrating qualitative field data with quantitative lab data', *Journal of Experimental Social Psychology*, 36: 51–76.

Flyvbjerg, B. (2006) 'Five misunderstandings about case-study research', *Qualitative Inquiry*, 12 (2): 219–45.

Geertz, C. (1973) 'Deep play: notes on the Balinese cockfight'. In C. Geertz (ed.), *The interpretation of cultures*. New York, NY: Basic Books, pp. 412–54.

Hektner, J. M., Schmidt, J. A. and Csikszentmihalyi, M. (2007) *Experience sampling method: measuring the quality of everyday life*. Thousand Oaks, CA: Sage Publications.

Keeter, S., McGeeney, K. and Weisel, R. (2015) *Coverage error in Internet surveys: who web-only surveys miss and how that affects the results*. Washington DC: Pew Research Center. Available at http://www.pewresearch.org/files/2015/09/22_coverage-error-in-internet-surveys.pdf (accessed July 28, 2016).

Klimt, B. and Yang, Y. (2004) 'Introducing the Enron corpus'. *Proceedings of the First Conference on Email and Anti-Spam* (CEAS) July 30–31, Mountain View, CA. Available at http://nl.ijs.si/janes/wp-content/uploads/2014/09/klimtyang04a.pdf (accessed July 28, 2016).

Kuhn, T. S. (1970 [1962]) *The structure of scientific revolutions*. 2nd edn. Chicago, IL: University of Chicago Press.

Laney, D. (2001) *3D data management: controlling data volume, velocity, and variety*. META Group, February 6. Available at https://blogs.gartner.com/doug-laney/files/2012/01/ad949–3D-Data-Management-Controlling-Data-Volume-Velocity-and-Variety.pdf (accessed July 29, 2016).

Lazer, D., Pentland, A. S., Adamic, L., Aral, S., Barabasi, A.-L., Brewer, D., Christakis, N., Contractor, N., Fowler, J. and Gutmann, M. (2009). 'Life in the network: the coming age of computational social science', *Science*, 323 (5915): 721.

Lewis, M. (2003) *Moneyball: the art of wining an unfair game*. New York, NY: W.W. Norton.

Lieberman, E. S. (2010) 'Bridging qualitative-quantitative divide: best practices in the development of historically oriented replication databases', *Annual Review of Political Science*, 13: 17–59.

Longo, J. (2011) '#Opendata: digital-era governance thoroughbred or new public management Trojan Horse?', *Public Policy & Governance Review*, 2 (2): 38.

Mislove A., Lehmann S., Ahn Y., Onnela J. and Rosenquist J. (2011). 'Understanding the demographics of Twitter users'. *Proceedings of the Fifth International AAAI Conference on Weblogs and Social Media*, July 17–21, Barcelona, pp. 554–57.

Mohr, J. and Bogdanov, P. (2013) 'Introduction – topic models: what they are and why they matter', *Poetics*. 41: 545–69. doi:10.4135/9780857020055.n7.

Ragin, C. C. (1987) *The comparative method: moving beyond qualitative and quantitative strategies*. Berkeley, CA: University of California.

Ragin, C. C. (1992) '"Casing" and the process of social inquiry'. In C. C. Ragin and H. S. Becker (eds.), *What is a case? Exploring the foundations of social inquiry*. Cambridge: Cambridge University Press, pp. 217–26.

Sale, J. E. M., Hohfeld, L. H. and Brazil, K. (2002) 'Revisiting the quantitative-qualitative debate: implications for mixed-methods research', *Quality & Quantity*, 36: 43–53.

Sanford, M. (2007) Consumption and the urban milieux: using consumption as a measure of similarity for defining urban neighborhoods. PhD dissertation, unpublished, University of Chicago.

Shapin, S. and Schaffer, S. (1985) *Leviathan and the air-pump: Hobbes, Boyle, and the experimental life*. Princeton, NJ: Princeton University Press.

Sieber, R. E. and Johnson, P. A. (2015) 'Civic open data at a crossroads: dominant models and current challenges', *Government Information Quarterly*. doi:10.1016/j.giq.2015.05.003.

Sloan, L., Morgan, J., Housley, W., Williams, M., Edwards, A., Burnap, P. and Rana, O. (2013) 'Knowing the Tweeters: deriving sociologically relevant demographics from Twitter', *Sociological Research Online*, 18 (3): 7. Available at http://www.socresonline.org.uk/18/3/7.html (accessed July 29, 2016). doi:10.5153/sro.3001.

Small, M. L. (2011) 'How to conduct a mixed methods study: recent trends in a rapidly growing literature', *Annual Review of Sociology*, 37: 57–86. doi:10.1146/annurev.soc.012809.102657.

Sturgis, P., Baker, N., Callegaro, M., Fisher, S., Green, J., Jennings, W., Kuha, J., Lauderdale, B. and Smith, P. (2016) *Report of the Inquiry into the 2015 British general election opinion polls*. London: Market Research Society and British Polling Council. Available from http://eprints.ncrm.ac.uk/3789/1/Report_final_revised.pdf (accessed July 29, 2016).

Welser, T. Gleave, E., Fisher, D. and Smith, M. (2007a) 'Visualizing the signatures of social roles in online discussion groups', *Journal of Social Structure*, 8 (2). Available at https://www.cmu.edu/joss/content/articles/volume8/Welser/ (accessed December 15, 2015).

Welser, T., Smith, M., Fischer, D. and Gleave, E. (2007b) 'Distilling digital traces: computational social science approaches to studying the Internet'. In N. Fielding, R. Lee and G. Blank (eds.), *Handbook of online research methods*. London: Sage Publications, pp. 116–41. doi:10.4135/9780857020055.n7.

Zaret, D. (1989) 'Religion and the rise of liberal democratic ideology in seventeenth-century England', *American Sociological Review*, 54 (April): 163–79.

Name Index

Subject Index